Marriages & Families

Changes, Choices, and Constraints

EIGHTH EDITION

Nijole V. Benokraitis

University of Baltimore

Pearson

Boston   Columbus   Indianapolis   New York   San Francisco   Upper Saddle River
Amsterdam   Cape Town   Dubai   London   Madrid   Milan   Munich   Paris   Montreal   Toronto
Delhi   Mexico City   São Paulo   Sydney   Hong Kong   Seoul   Singapore   Taipei   Tokyo

Editor-in-Chief: Dickson Musslewhite
Publisher: Charlyce Jones-Owen
Program Manager: Seanna Breen
Editorial Assistant: Maureen Diana
Development Editor: Carol Alper
Director of Marketing: Brandy Dawson
Senior Marketing Manager: Maureen Prado Roberts
Marketing Assistant: Karen Tanico
Project Manager: Manuel Echevarria
Procurement Manager: Mary Fischer
Procurement Specialist: Diane Peirano
Director of Design: Blair Brown

Art Director and Cover Design: Anne Nieglos
Design Interior: Irene Ehrmann
Cover Art: Claire Fraser/ImageZoo/Corbis
Director of Media & Assessment: Brian Hyland
Media Production Manager: Peggy Bliss
Media Project Manager: Claudine Bellanton
Full-Service Project Management: Bruce Hobart
Printer/Binder: Manufactured in the United States by RR Donnelley
Cover Printer: Phoenix Color/Hagerstown
Text Font: Sabon

Credits and acknowledgments borrowed from other sources and reproduced, with permission, in this textbook appear on appropriate page within text or on page 541.

Microsoft® and Windows® are registered trademarks of the Microsoft Corporation in the U.S.A. and other countries. Screen shots and icons reprinted with permission from the Microsoft Corporation. This book is not sponsored or endorsed by or affiliated with the Microsoft Corporation.

Library of Congress Cataloging-in-Publication Data
Benokraitis, Nijole V. (Nijole Vaicaitis)
  Marriages & families : changes, choices, and constraints / Nijole V. Benokraitis, University of Baltimore. — Eighth edition.
     pages cm
  Includes bibliographical references and index.
  ISBN 978-0-205-91819-5
  1. Families—United States.   2. Marriage—United States.   I. Title. II. Title:
  Marriages and families.
  HQ536.B45 2015
  306.850973--dc23

                                                                            2013040815

10 9 8 7 6 5 4 3
V011

Student Edition: ISBN-10: 0-205-91819-0
ISBN-13: 978-0-205-91819-5
Instructor Review Copy: ISBN-10: 0-205-91820-4
ISBN-13: 978-0-205-91820-1
A la Carte: ISBN-10: 0-205-91835-2
ISBN-13: 978-0-205-91835-5

www.pearsonhighered.com

To my husband, Vitalius.

Brief Contents

Appendices   These documents are available at www.mysoclab.com.

APPENDIX A   Sexual Anatomy

APPENDIX B   Sexual Problems, Dysfunctions, and Treatment

APPENDIX C   Conception, Pregnancy, and Childbirth

APPENDIX D   Birth Control and Disease Prevention Techniques

APPENDIX E   HIV, AIDS, and Other Sexually Transmitted Infections

APPENDIX F   Premarital and Nonmarital Agreements

Contents

Features

Ask Yourself

Applying What You've Learned

Changes

Choices

Constraints

Cross-Cultural and Multicultural Families

Preface

Welcome to the eighth edition of *Marriages & Families: Changes, Choices, and Constraints*! As in the past, a basic premise of this text is that information about family life can help us better understand the families in which we were raised and are forming ourselves. The significance of families extends beyond personal experience, however. Our marriages and families affect and are affected by larger social structures such as the economy, politics, education, religion, health care systems, and military organizations.

Scholarly Work, Comprehensiveness, and Readability

This new edition incorporates information from almost 1,600 new books, scholarly articles, and reports. Providing students with the most up-to-date material and emerging issues on family behavior enhances their "pool of knowledge" (as one of my undergraduate sociology professors used to say) and helps them make better decisions in their everyday lives.

Marriages & Families offers students a comprehensive introduction to many issues facing families in the twenty-first century. Although written from a sociological perspective, the book incorporates material from other disciplines: history, economics, social work, psychology, law, biology, medicine, and anthropology. The material also encompasses family studies, women's studies, and gay and lesbian studies, as well as both quantitative and qualitative studies. Nationally representative and longitudinal data are supplemented by insights from clinical, case, and observational studies.

Readability continues to be one of this textbook's most attractive features. A major reason for this book's success is that it discusses theories and recent studies in ways that students find interesting. As one of my students once said, "This is the first textbook I've had where I don't count how many more pages I have to read while I'm still on the first page."

In addition, faculty reviewers have consistently described the writing as "very clear" and "excellent." According to one reviewer, for example, "The interesting anecdotes and quotes help to maintain the student's interest while also providing realistic examples of the topic under discussion."

Continuity of Major Themes on the Contemporary Family

Marriages & Families continues to be distinguished from other textbooks in several important ways. It offers comprehensive coverage of the field, allowing instructors to select chapters that best suit their needs. It balances theoretical and empirical discussions with practical examples and applications.

The text highlights important contemporary *changes* in society and the family. It explores the *choices* that are available to family members and the *constraints* that often limit their choices. It also examines the diversity of U.S. families, using *cross-cultural* and *multicultural* material to encourage students to think about the many critical issues that confront the family of the twenty-first century.

More Changes

Changes that affect the structure and functioning of today's families inform the pages of every chapter. In addition, several chapters focus on some major transformations in American society. Chapter 4, for example, examines the growing cultural diversity of the United States, focusing on African American, American Indian, Latino, Asian American, Middle Eastern, and interracial marriages and families. And Chapter 16 discusses how the rapid graying of America has affected adult children, grandchildren, and even great-grandchildren; family members' roles as caregivers; family relations in general; and the distribution of resources between the young and the old.

More Choices

On the individual level, family members have many more choices today than ever before. People feel freer to postpone marriage, to cohabit, or to raise children as single parents. As a result, household forms vary greatly, ranging from commuter marriages to those in which several generations live together under the same roof.

As reproductive technology becomes increasingly sophisticated, many infertile couples and even menopausal women can now have children. With the growing acceptance of civil unions and same-sex marriages, many agencies, colleges, businesses, and state governments now offer same-sex couples more health, retirement, and other benefits than ever before.

Technological advances—such as the Internet, smartphones, and texting—have decreased our privacy, but they've also brought many family members together. People can contact one another quickly and relatively inexpensively, as well as gather information about their genealogy from many sources. In addition, sometimes people find a mate through online dating services.

More Constraints

Family members' choices are more varied today than in the past, but we also face greater macro-level constraints. Government policies and legal institutions have a major impact on most families through tax laws, welfare reform, and even in defining what a family is. Because laws, public policies, and religious groups affect our everyday lives, I have framed many discussions of individual choices within the larger picture of the institutional constraints that limit our choices.

Cross-Cultural and Multicultural Diversity in the United States

Contemporary American marriages and families vary greatly in structure, dynamics, and cultural heritage. Thus, discussions of gender roles, social class, race, ethnicity, age, and sexual orientation are integrated throughout this book. To further strengthen students' understanding of the growing diversity among today's families, I have also included a series of features that focus on families from many cultures as well as racial and ethnic groups within the United States. This material will encourage students to think about the many forms families may take and the different ways that family members interact.

What's New in the Eighth Edition?

As past users know, a top priority of each new edition of this textbook is to thoroughly update national data and to provide the results of groundbreaking research that addresses the diversity of marriages and families. Because my major goal is to make each edition better than the previous one, I have revised all the chapters to reflect the latest theory and research, and I have updated examples throughout *Marriages & Families*. Specifically, new, updated, and expanded coverage includes the following:

Chapter 1: The Changing Family

- Updates the demographic changes that characterize U.S. families, how technology affects families, the impact of popular culture, myths about the family, and growing ethnic diversity
- Offers new material on polygyny in other societies

Chapter 2: Studying the Family

- Updates material on online surveys, evaluation research, and scientific dishonesty
- Presents a new discussion on content analysis, 2010 census strengths and limitations, social desirability bias, and introduces the concepts *probability* and *nonprobability samples*

Chapter 3: The Family in Historical Perspective

- Expands and updates the section on "The Family Since the 1960s"

Chapter 4: Racial and Ethnic Families: Strengths and Stresses

- Updates the material on immigration, social class, health and economic well-being, and the model minority
- Offers new data on the foreign-born population, Arab Americans, the prevalence of interracial/interethnic marriages, and introduces the concept of *colorism*
- A **new feature** ("The Changing Face of the Midwest") examines how recent immigrants are revitalizing many small towns

Chapter 5: Socialization and Gender Roles

- Includes new material on gender stereotypes, and science, technology, engineering, and mathematics (STEM) majors
- Updates the analysis of global male violence, gender inequality across cultures, socialization, and gender roles at home and in the workplace, politics, education, and religion
- Introduces three new concepts: *gender ideology, gender script*, and *role model*
- **Two new features** are presented: "Should Children's Toys Be Gender Neutral?" and "Male Violence: The World's Worst Countries to Be a Woman"

Chapter 6: Love and Loving Relationships

- Updates the material on biological perspective of love, exchange theory of love, jealousy, love in long-term relationships, and love in other cultures
- Includes new material on Facebook friends, narcissism, stalking, and cyberstalking

Chapter 7: Sexuality and Sexual Expression throughout Life

- Updates the discussion of sexual scripts, girls' hypersexualization, female genital mutilation/cutting, casual sex, societal reactions to lesbians, gay men, bisexuals, and transgender people (LGBTs), sex throughout life, sexual infidelity, and socially transmitted diseases (STDs)
- Provides new data on Kinsey's sexuality continuum, the "sexy babes" trend, early puberty and sex, Supreme Court decision on violent video games, LGBT prevalence, sex during the middle and later years, and why many parents don't talk about sex
- A **new feature** is provided: "What Are Some of the Myths about Sex and Sexual Response?"

Chapter 8: Choosing Others: Dating and Mate Selection

- Provides recent data on traditional dating, hooking up, mail-order brides, online dating, speed dating, mate selection across cultures, arranged marriages, and breaking up
- Has new discussions of stayovers, attitudes about romance and interracial marriage, changes in black–white dating behavior, demographic characteristics of dating violence, how technology facilitates date violence, and interfaith, interracial, and interethnic marriages

Chapter 9: Singlehood, Cohabitation, Civil Unions, and Other Options

- Updates the discussion of civil unions, states where same-sex marriages are legal, gives insights into why more Americans are living alone and why young people are postponing marriage
- Updates the material on who cohabits, why, and the benefits and costs of cohabitation

Chapter 10: Marriage and Communication in Intimate Relationships

- Provides a current discussion of why marriage rates are falling, prenuptial agreements, same-sex marriages, how marriage affects health, what couples fight about, and the U.S. Supreme Court decision on same-sex marriage
- Offers new data on marriage by race and ethnicity, what purchases spouses hide, and the negative effects of communication problems
- Introduces the concept *validation*
- A **new feature** is presented: "Are Diamond Engagement Rings Losing Their Shine?"

Chapter 11: To Be or Not to Be a Parent: More Choices, More Constraints

- Updates the material on what it costs to raise a child, U.S. and global birthrates, nonmarital childbearing, why birth rates have decreased, reasons for infertility, why people are postponing parenthood, domestic/international/transracial adoption, medical and high-tech solutions to infertility, abortion rates, and decreasing abortion services
- Introduces the concept *egg freezing*
- Offers new data on fathers and postpartum depression, why many teens don't use contraception, adoption by same-sex partners, and unintended pregnancy

Chapter 12: Raising Children: Promises and Pitfalls

- Updates the material on ideal versus realistic parenting, whether spanking works, social class and parenting, parenting in same-sex families and over the life course, boomerang children, child care, and foster care
- Offers new data on how same-sex and opposite-sex parenting differ, bed-sharing, and the impact of electronic media on children's well-being
- Introduces two new concepts: *maternal gatekeeping* and *medicalization*

Chapter 13: The Economy and Family Life

- Revises and updates discussions of globalization, offshoring, unions, how the economy affects families, women's labor force rates, two-income families, and inequality in the workplace
- Introduces the concept of *glass escalator*
- A **new feature** is included: "Some Perks and Perils of Telecommuting"

Chapter 14: Domestic Violence and Other Family Health Issues

- Updates material on intimate partner violence (prevalence, severity, variations by age, gender, race/ethnicity, and social class), child maltreatment effects, elder mistreatment, substance abuse, obesity, depression, suicide, and other family health problems
- New data and discussion of women who abuse men, violence among same-sex partners, and smoking as a major health problem
- Introduces the concept *polyvictimization*

Chapter 15: Separation, Divorce, Remarriage, and Stepfamilies

Faculty who have used previous editions of *Marriages & Families* will notice that I have merged Chapters 15 and 16. I did so because the four topics—separation, divorce, remarriage, and stepfamilies—are interrelated, and I wanted to avoid repetition as well as decrease the number of chapters in the textbook.

- Offers new data on divorce among racial-ethnic groups, same-sex couples, and how and why remarriage rates vary among racial ethnic groups
- Updates the material on divorce, remarriage rates, the effects of social class and the economy on divorce, how divorce affects adults and children, who pays and gets child support, the cumulative effect of divorce, and the diversity and demographic characteristics of stepfamilies

Chapter 16: Families in Later Life

- Updates life expectancy rates in the United States compared with other countries, old-age-dependency ratio, dementia and Alzheimer's, why many people are postponing retirement, the rise of custodial grandparents and multigenerational households, physician-assisted suicide, widowhood, caregivers, and recipients
- Introduces a new concept: *durable power of attorney for health care*
- Provides new data and discussions of aging diversity by race and ethnicity, why disability rates have increased, and the rising competition for scarce resources between the young and the old

Features in the Eighth Edition

I have maintained several popular features such as the Data Digest and the "author's files" quotations based on my students' comments and class discussions.

Data Digest

I introduced the Data Digest in the second edition because "all those numbers" from the Census Bureau, empirical studies, and demographic trends often overwhelmed students (both mine and others). Because this has been a popular feature, I've updated the U.S. statistics and have included information about other countries. The Data Digest that introduces each chapter provides students with a thought-provoking overview of current statistics and trends and makes "all those numbers" more interesting and digestible.

The first question from my students is usually "Will this material be on the exam?" Not in my classes. I always saw the Data Digest as piquing student curiosity about the chapter rather than providing a lot of numbers to memorize. Some instructors tell me that their students have used the Data Digest to develop class presentations or course papers.

DATA DIGEST

- The **"traditional" family** (in which the husband is the breadwinner and the wife is a full-time homemaker) declined from 40 percent of all U.S. households in 1970 to 20 percent in 2010.

- More than 14 million American **singles ages 30 to 44 have never been married**, representing 24 percent of all people in that age group.

- The U.S. **median age at first marriage** is the highest ever recorded: 28.7 years for men and 26.5 years for women.

- On average, **first marriages that end in divorce** last about eight years.

- The percentage of **children under age 18 living with two married parents** fell from 77 percent in 1980 to 64 percent in 2012.

- **Children make up 24 percent of the population,** down from a peak of 36 percent in 1964.

Sources: Kreider and Elliott, 2009; Kreider and Ellis, 2011; Tavernise, 2011; Federal Interagency Forum on Child and Family Statistics, 2012; U.S. Census Bureau, 2012; U.S. Census Bureau, Current Population Survey, 2012; Annual Social and Economic Supplement, 2012; U.S. Census Bureau News, 2012.

Material from Author's Files

Faculty who reviewed previous editions of *Marriages & Families*, and many students as well, liked the anecdotes and personal experiences that illustrate sometimes abstract theories and concepts. In this new edition, I weave more of this material into the text. Thus, I include many examples from discussions in my own classes (cited as "author's files") to enliven theoretical perspectives and abstract concepts.

Pedagogical Features

The pedagogical features in *Marriages & Families*—ranging from the "Since You Asked" items to features in each chapter—have been designed to capture students' attention and to help them understand and recall the material. Each has been carefully crafted to ensure that it ties in clearly to the text material, enhancing its meaning and applicability.

Learning Objectives

Learning objectives are new to this edition of *Marriages & Families*. Each chapter begins with learning objectives that indicate what students should know after reading the material. The learning objectives are reinforced with specific questions at the end of each chapter that unite the topics, help students gauge their comprehension, and signal what topics they might have to reread.

LEARNING OBJECTIVES
After you read and study this chapter you will be able to:

Compare the manifest and latent functions of dating.	8.1
Outline the characteristics, benefits, and costs of traditional and contemporary dating patterns.	8.2
Describe five strategies for meeting dating partners.	8.3
Compare three mate-selection theories.	8.4
Describe some of the mate-selection differences across cultures.	8.5
Describe the prevalence of dating violence, and explain why it occurs and its consequences.	8.6

Encouraging Students to Think More Critically

All editions of this textbook have prodded students to think about themselves and their families in the "Ask Yourself" features. Because of their popularity, especially in sparking lively class discussions, I've expanded two features ("Making Connections" and "Stop and Think") that were introduced in the sixth edition:

Making Connections

At several points in each chapter, these items ask students to link the material to their own lives by relating it to a personal experience, by integrating it with studies discussed in the chapter, or by "connecting" with classmates who might be sitting next to them in class.

Stop and Think

These critical thinking questions are at the end of features throughout the textbook. The purpose of these items is to encourage students to reflect about current topics, both personally and compared with other cultures.

Since You Asked

Each chapter has between eight and ten questions that introduce an important idea or concept or preview a controversial issue about families and marriages. Many of these questions are similar to those that my students have raised in class or online discussions.

Applying What You've Learned

This series of features emphasizes the connection between research findings and students' own attitudes and experiences. The material, both new and revised, asks students to apply what they're reading to their own personal situations and to consider how to improve their decision making and current relationships.

Applying What You've Learned — **Am I Prejudiced?**

All of us, whether we realize it or not, sometimes have strong positive or negative feelings about other racial-ethnic groups. Answer the questions in this quiz as honestly as possible. After you finish, look at the key.

Usually True	Usually False		Usually True	Usually False	
☐	☐	1. Latino men have a more macho attitude toward women than do other men.	☐	☐	6. The majority of Asian Americans tend to be shy and quiet.
☐	☐	2. African Americans, both women and men, are more likely to commit crimes than are members of other racial-ethnic groups, including whites.	☐	☐	7. Most Asian Americans aren't as sociable as other people.
☐	☐	3. Don't trust Arab Americans. Some are decent, but most want to spread Islam and aren't loyal to the United States.	☐	☐	8. Most whites are simply more capable than other groups—especially African Americans and Latinos—in doing their jobs.
☐	☐	4. Asian American business owners are greedier than other business owners.			
☐	☐	5. There are some exceptions, but most Latinos don't succeed because they're lazy.			

KEY TO "AM I PREJUDICED?"

Of these eight items, the higher your score for "usually true," the more likely that you're prejudiced and stereotype racial-ethnic groups. The purpose of this quiz is to encourage you to think how you feel about people outside your immediate circle.

Sources: Based on material in Godfrey et al., 2000; Lin et al., 2005; and Esposito and Mogahed, 2007.

Informative and Engaging Illustration Program

Most chapters contain figures that, in bold and original artistic designs, demonstrate concepts such as the exchange theory of dating, romantic versus lasting love, and theories of mating, as well as presenting descriptive statistics in innovative and visually appealing ways.

Figures and Tables

Many students tend to skip over figures and tables because they're afraid of numbers, they don't trust statistics (see Chapter 2), or the material seems boring or complicated. Regardless of which textbooks I used and in *all* the courses I taught, I routinely highlighted some of the figures in class. As I tell my students, a good figure or table may be more memorable than an author's explanation. To encourage students to look at data, I have streamlined many figures.

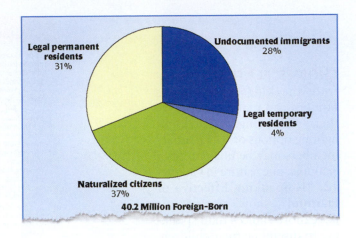

FIGURE 4.2 **Legal Status of the U.S. Foreign-Born Population, 2010**
Source: Based on Passel and Cohn, 2011.

Key Terms and Glossary

Important terms and concepts appearing in boldface type within the text are defined in the margins where they first appear. All key terms and their definitions are repeated in the Glossary at the end of the book.

hormones Chemical substances secreted into the bloodstream by endocrine glands

Thought-Provoking Features

Reflecting and reinforcing the book's primary themes, three groups of features focus on the changes, choices, and constraints that confront today's families. A fourth group of features illustrates racial-ethnic families in the United States and cross-cultural variations in other countries. The other two series of features help students assess their own knowledge and gain insights about family life.

CHANGES FEATURES show how marriages and families have been changing or are expected to change in the future. Some of them are historical, some are anecdotal, and some are empirically based. For example, a feature in **Chapter 9, "Why Do Americans Favor or Oppose Same-Sex Marriages?"** examines some of the beliefs and attitudes that fuel continuing debates on same-sex marriage.

Changes **Why Do Americans Favor or Oppose Same-Sex Marriages?**

Homosexuality and especially same-sex marriages are among the most controversial issues in America, dividing friends, families, and religious communities. Here are some of the beliefs and attitudes that fuel the debates.

Same-sex marriage should be legal because . . .

- Attitudes and laws change. Until 1967, for example, interracial marriages were prohibited.

- Gay marriages would strengthen families and long-term unions that already exist. Children would be better off with parents who are legally married.

- It would be easier for same-sex couples to adopt children, especially children with emotional and physical disabilities.

- There are no scientific studies showing that children raised by gay and lesbian parents are worse off than those raised by heterosexual parents.

- Every person should be able to marry someone that she or he loves.

- Same-sex marriages would benefit religious organizations both spiritually and emotionally and bolster membership.

- Gay marriages are good for the economy because they boost businesses such as restaurants, bakeries, hotels, airlines, and florists.

Same-sex marriage should not be legal because . . .

- Interracial marriages are between women and men, but gay marriages violate many people's notions about male–female unions.

- Children need a mom and a dad, not a gay/lesbian couple.

- All adopted children—those with and without disabilities—are better off with parents who can provide heterosexual gender role models.

- There are no scientific studies showing that children raised by gay and lesbian parents are better off than those raised by heterosexual parents.

- People can love each other without getting married.

- Same-sex marriages would polarize church members who are opposed to gay unions and decrease the size of congregations.

- What's good for the economy isn't necessarily good for society, especially its moral values and religious beliefs.

Sources: LaFraniere and Goodstein, 2007; Masci, 2008a; Pew Forum on Religion & Public Life, 2008a; Semuels, 2008a; Bennett and Ellison, 2010; Olson, 2010; Sprigg, 2011.

STOP AND THINK . . .
- Many states have passed laws that limit marriage to a man and a woman. Do you agree or not? Why?
- What other reasons can you add for each side of the debate?

CHOICES FEATURES illustrate the kinds of decisions families can make to improve their well-being, often highlighting options of which family members may be unaware. For example, one feature in **Chapter 12, "Is Spanking Effective or Harmful?"** shows that parents have more choices than spanking to discipline their children.

CONSTRAINTS FEATURES point out some of the obstacles that limit our choices. These features highlight the fact that although most of us are raised to believe that we can do whatever we want, we are often constrained by macro-level socioeconomic, demographic, and cultural factors. For example, a feature in **Chapter 13, "Some Reasons for the Rising U.S. Inequality,"** shows that many Americans are struggling to survive economically not because they have low educational levels and lack motivation, but because of other economic factors such as corporate welfare, a surge of low-paying jobs, and offshoring.

CROSS-CULTURAL AND MULTICULTURAL FAMILIES FEATURES illustrate the diversity of family structures and dynamics, both in the United States and in other countries. For example, a feature in **Chapter 6, "Modern Arranged Marriages in India,"** contrasts the American open style of dating with arranged courtship and marriage in India.

APPLYING WHAT YOU'VE LEARNED FEATURES ask students to think critically about research findings on a personal level. Such reflections should stimulate students to challenge common misconceptions about family life and to improve their own decision making and relationships. For example, a feature in **Chapter 14, "Some Warning Signs of Intimate Partner Abuse,"** asks students to consider whether they or other family members recognize some of the signs of abuse before it actually occurs.

ASK YOURSELF FEATURES are self-assessment exercises that encourage students to think about and evaluate their knowledge about marriage and the family. They help students develop guidelines for action, either their own or on another's behalf. For example, the feature in **Chapter 6, "If This Is Love, Why Do I Feel So Bad?"** helps students evaluate their current situations and make the decision to leave an abusive relationship.

Supplements

The supplement package for this textbook is exceptional. Each component has been meticulously crafted to amplify and illuminate materials in the text.

INSTRUCTOR'S RESOURCE MANUAL WITH TESTS   Revised by Henry Borne of Holy Cross College in Indiana and Ann Marie Kinnell at the University of Southern Mississippi, each chapter in the manual includes the following resources: chapter learning objectives, chapter overview, lecture suggestions and classroom discussions, activities, and multimedia resources. Designed to make your lectures more effective and to save preparation time, this extensive resource gathers together the most effective activities and strategies for teaching your Marriage and Family course.

Also included in this manual is a test bank of approximately 2,000 multiple-choice, true/false, short-answer, and essay questions. Additionally, each chapter of the test bank includes a ready-made 10-item quiz with an answer key for immediate use in class.

The Instructor's Resource Manual with Tests is available to adopters at www.pearsonhighered.com and through the MySocLab website for *Marriages & Families, 8e.*

MYTEST   This computerized software allows instructors to create their own personalized exams, to edit any or all of the existing test questions, and to add new questions. Other special features of this program include random generation of test questions, creation of alternate versions of the same test, scrambling question sequence, and test preview before printing. For easy access, this software is available within the instructor section of the MySocLab website for *Marriages & Families, 8e,* or at www.pearsonhighered.com.

POWERPOINT PRESENTATIONS   You have the option in every chapter of choosing from Lecture and/or Line Art presentations. The Lecture PowerPoint slides follow the chapter outline and feature images from the textbook integrated with the text. The Line Art PowerPoint features all the art, organized by chapter, available in a PowerPoint-ready format. They are available to adopters at www.pearsonhighered.com and through the MySocLab website for *Marriages & Families, 8e.*

MySocLab™

MySocLab is an easy-to-use online resource that allows instructors to assess student progress and adapt course material to meet the specific needs of the class. This resource enables students to diagnose their progress by completing an online self-assessment test. Based on the results of this test, each student is provided with a customized study plan, including a variety of tools to help him or her fully master the material. MySocLab then reports the self-assessment results to the instructor as individual student grades as well as an aggregate report of class progress. Based on these reports, the instructor can adapt course material to suit the needs of individual students or the class as a whole.

MySocLab includes several exciting new features. *Social Explorer* provides easy access to census data from 1790 to the present. You can explore the data visually through interactive data maps. *MySocLibrary* contains numerous original source readings with discussion questions and assessment exercises.

Contact your local Pearson Education representative for ordering information, or visit www.myfamilylab.com.

Acknowledgments

First and foremost, I'm grateful to the Pearson editorial, development, and production team for making this book possible. I have greatly profited from the team's dedication and impressive skills.

Colleagues always play a critical role in revisions. For this edition, I received valuable input from:

Wanda Clark, South Plains College

Stephen Kandeh, University of Science and Arts of Oklahoma

Dan Muhwezi, Butler Community College

Sara Winslow, Clemson University

Meifang Zhang, Midlands Technical College.

Also, Dr. Constance T. Gager, Associate Professor, Department of Family and Child Studies, Montclair State University, and her graduate assistant, Jessica Szweada, updated parts of Chapter 9.

I thank my family for their unfaltering patience and sense of humor throughout life's little stresses, especially my research and writing. They've been high-tech consultants when my hard drive crashed, and always supportive in helping me meet deadlines.

Last, but not least, I have benefited greatly from the suggestions of faculty and students who have contacted me during the past few years. I have incorporated many of their reactions in the eighth edition and look forward to future comments.

Thank you, one and all.

About the Author

Nijole V. Benokraitis, professor emerita of sociology at the University of Baltimore, taught the Marriage and Family course for almost 25 years. Professor Benokraitis received a B.A. in sociology and English from Emmanuel College in Boston, an M.A. in sociology from the University of Illinois at Urbana-Champaign, and a Ph.D. in sociology from the University of Texas at Austin.

Being a strong proponent of applied sociology, Professor Benokraitis required her students to enhance their knowledge through interviews, direct observation, and other hands-on learning methods. She also enlisted her students in community service activities such as tutoring and mentoring inner-city high school students, writing to government officials and other decision makers about specific social problems, and volunteering research services to nonprofit organizations. See www.allmysoc.com to find out more about Dr. Benokraitis's background, and selected publications and professional activities. Professor Benokraitis and her husband, Dr. Vitalius Benokraitis, have two adult children, Gema and Andrius.

The author looks forward (and always responds) to comments on the 8th edition of *Marriages & Families: Changes, Choices, and Constraints*. She can be reached at nbenokraitis@ubalt.edu.

The Changing Family

((• **Listen** to Chapter 1 on **MySocLab**

- The **"traditional" family** (in which the husband is the breadwinner and the wife is a full-time homemaker) declined from 40 percent of all U.S. households in 1970 to 20 percent in 2010.

- More than 14 million American **singles ages 30 to 44 have never been married,** representing 24 percent of all people in that age group.

- The U.S. **median age at first marriage** is the highest ever recorded: 28.7 years for men and 26.5 years for women.

- On average, **first marriages that end in divorce** last about eight years.

- The percentage of **children under age 18 living with two married parents** fell from 77 percent in 1980 to 64 percent in 2012.

- **Children make up 24 percent of the population,** down from a peak of 36 percent in 1964.

Sources: Kreider and Elliott, 2009; Kreider and Ellis, 2011; Tavernise, 2011; Federal Interagency Forum on Child and Family Statistics, 2012; U.S. Census Bureau, 2012, U.S. Census Bureau, Current Population Survey, 2012; Annual Social and Economic Supplement, 2012; U.S. Census Bureau News, 2012.

Compared with a few generations ago, a family tree today is beginning to look more like a tangled forest. For example, Rob, a 61-year-old magazine editor, has six children ranging in ages from 12 to 33: two children with a woman who was his longtime unmarried partner, two children born to a lesbian couple with his donated sperm, and two stepdaughters with his current wife (Holson, 2011: A1). Rob's family tree will become even more "tangled" if he remarries, or if any of his children marry, divorce, remarry, and have biological or adopted children.

As this example shows, contemporary family arrangements are changing. You'll see in this chapter and others that individual choices have altered some family structures, but many of these changes are due to larger societal transformations. Before continuing, test your knowledge about U.S. families by taking the "Ask Yourself" quiz.

ASK YOURSELF

How Much Do You Know about Contemporary American Families?

True False

☐ ☐ 1. Teenage nonmarital births have increased over the past 20 years.

☐ ☐ 2. Cohabitation (living together) increases the chance of having a happy and lasting marriage.

☐ ☐ 3. Singles have better sex lives than married people.

☐ ☐ 4. The more educated a woman is, the less likely she is to marry.

☐ ☐ 5. People get married because they love each other.

True False

☐ ☐ 6. Divorce rates have increased during the past few decades.

☐ ☐ 7. Having children increases marital satisfaction.

☐ ☐ 8. Married couples have healthier babies than unmarried couples.

☐ ☐ 9. Generally, children are better off in two-parent stepfamilies than in single-parent families.

☐ ☐ 10. Family relationships that span several generations are less common now than in the past.

(The answers to these questions are on page 4.)

What Is a Family?

It may not seem necessary to define a familiar term such as *family*, but its meaning differs from one group of people to another and may change over time. The definitions also have important political and economic consequences, often determining family members' rights and obligations.

Under Social Security laws, for example, only a worker's spouse, dependent parents, and children can claim benefits. Many employers' health care benefits cover a spouse and legal children but not adult partners, either heterosexual or homosexual, who are unmarried but have long-term committed relationships, or children born out of wedlock. A child isn't legally a member of an adopting family until social service agencies and the courts have approved the adoption. And, some of the most contentious arguments about what is a family involve disputes about who inherits property when a relative dies. Thus, definitions of the word *family* affect people's lives by expanding or limiting their options.

Some Traditional Definitions of the Family

Traditionally, *family* has been defined as a unit made up of two or more people who are related by blood, marriage, or adoption; live together; form an economic unit; and bear and raise children. The U.S. Census Bureau, for instance, defines the family as two or more people living together who are related by birth, marriage, or adoption (see Lofquist et al., 2012).

Many social scientists have challenged such traditional definitions because they exclude a number of diverse groups that also consider themselves families. Social scientists have asked: Are child-free couples families? What about cohabiting couples? Foster parents and their charges? Elderly siblings who live together? Gay and lesbian couples, with or without children? Grandparents raising grandchildren? What about a woman or man and her or his dog?

Some Current Definitions of the Family

For our purposes, a **family** is an intimate group of two or more people who (1) live together in a committed relationship, (2) care for one another and any children, and (3) share activities and close emotional ties. Some people may disagree with this definition because it doesn't explicitly include marriage, procreation, or child rearing, but it's more inclusive of a wide variety of family forms than traditional views.

Definitions of the family are becoming even more complicated and controversial. As reproductive technology advances, a baby can have several "parents": an egg donor, a sperm donor, a woman who carries the baby during a pregnancy, and the couple intending to raise the child. If that's not confusing enough, the biological father or mother might be dead by the time the child is actually conceived because sperm and eggs can be frozen and stored (see Chapter 11).

A definition of the family could also include **fictive kin**, nonrelatives who are accepted as part of the family because they have strong bonds with biological family members and provide important services and care. These emotional ties may be stronger and more lasting than those established by blood or marriage (Dilworth-Anderson et al., 1993). James, an African American in his forties and one of my former students, still fondly recalls Mike, a boarder in his home, who is a good example of fictive kinship:

> *Mike was an older gentleman who lived with us from my childhood to my teenage years. He was like a grandfather to me. He taught me how to*

 1.1 Explain how traditional and contemporary definitions of family differ.

Since you asked . . .
- Does it *really* matter how we define *family*?

Since you asked . . .
- Are couples who don't have children a family?

 Read on **MySocLab**

Document: Beyond the Nuclear Family: The Increasing Importance of Multigenerational Bonds

family An intimate group of two or more people who (1) live together in a committed relationship, (2) care for one another and any children, and (3) share activities and close emotional ties.

Watch on **MySocLab**

Video: How a Family Is Defined

fictive kin A family in which nonrelatives are accepted as part of a family.

Modern Family, a popular television show, includes a nuclear family, a remarried aging family patriarch with his Colombian trophy wife and her son, and a gay couple and their adopted Vietnamese daughter. Do you think that this show represents contemporary American families?

MAKING CONNECTIONS

- Ask three of your friends to define *family*. Are their definitions the same as yours?

- According to one of my students, "I don't view my biological family as 'my family' because my parents were abusive and didn't love me." Should we be able to choose whomever we want as family members because of emotional rather than biological ties?

- In a recent survey (Powell et al., 2010), 30 percent of the respondents considered pets, but not gay couples, as family. Do you agree? Or not?

ride a bike, took me fishing, and always told me stories. He was very close to me and my family until he died. When the family gets together, we still talk about old Mike because he was just like family and we still miss him dearly. (Author's files)

A recent variation of fictive kin includes single mothers—many of whom are unmarried college-educated women—who turn to one another for companionship and help in child care. For example, they take turns watching one another's kids (including taking them to Saturday-morning gymnastics classes and on short summer vacations), help during crises (such as a death in the family), and call each other when they need advice about anything from a child who is talking late to suggestions on presenting a paper at a professional conference (Bazelon, 2009).

1.2 Describe five family functions and two marriage rules that are similar worldwide.

How Are Families Similar?

The family institution exists in some form in all societies. Worldwide, families are similar in fulfilling some functions, such as encouraging marriage, and trying to ensure that children select the "right" mate.

Family Functions

Since you asked . . .

- Do we *really* need families?

norm A culturally defined rule for behavior.

Families vary considerably in the United States and globally but must accomplish at least five important functions to ensure a society's survival (Parsons and Bales, 1955). As you read this section, think about how your own family fulfills these functions.

SEXUAL ACTIVITY Every society has **norms**, or culturally defined rules for behavior, regarding who may engage in sexual relations, with whom, and under what circumstances. The United States has laws against sexual activity with minors, but some other societies around the world permit marriage with girls as young as age 8.

ANSWERS TO "How Much Do You Know about Contemporary American Families?"

All the answers are *false*.

1. Teenage nonmarital births have decreased over the past 20 years, especially since the early 2000s (see Chapters 10 and 11).

2. Couples who are living together and plan to marry *soon* have a good chance of staying together after a marriage. In most cases, however, "shacking up" decreases the likelihood of marriage (see Chapter 9).

3. Compared with singles, married people have more and better sex and enjoy it more, both physically and emotionally (see Chapter 7).

4. College-educated women tend to postpone marriage but are more likely to marry, over a lifetime, than their non–college-educated counterparts (see Chapters 9 and 10).

5. Love is not the major or even the only reason for getting married. Other reasons include societal expectations, economic insecurity, and fear of loneliness (see Chapters 6, 10, and 16).

6. Divorce rates have been dropping since the early 1980s (see Chapter 15).

7. The arrival of a first baby typically pushes mothers and fathers apart. Generally, child rearing lowers marital satisfaction for both partners (see Chapters 11 and 12).

8. Social class is a more important factor than marital status in a baby's health. Low-income mothers are less likely than high-income mothers to have healthy babies, whether or not they're married (see Chapters 11 through 14).

9. Income levels are usually higher in stepfamilies than in single-parent families, but stepfamilies have their own problems, including interpersonal conflicts with new parent figures (see Chapter 15).

10. Family relationships across several generations are more common and more important now than they were in the past. People live longer and get to know their kin, aging parents and grandparents often provide financial support and child care, and many relatives maintain ties with one another after a divorce or remarriage (see Chapters 3, 4, 12, 15, and 16).

Throughout history, one of the oldest rules regulating sexual behavior is the **incest taboo**—cultural norms and laws that forbid sexual intercourse between close blood relatives, such as brother and sister, father and daughter, uncle and niece, or grandparent and grandchild. Sexual relations between close relatives can increase the incidence of inherited genetic diseases and abnormalities by about 3 percent (Bennett et al., 2002). Incest taboos are based primarily on social constructs, however, that probably arose to preserve the family in several ways (Ellis, 1963):

- They minimized jealousy and destructive sexual competition that might have undermined a family's survival and smooth functioning. If family members who were sexual partners lost interest in each other, for example, they might have avoided mating.
- Because incest taboos ensured that mating would take place outside the family, a wider circle of people could band together in cooperative efforts (such as hunting), in the face of danger, or in war.
- By controlling the mother's sexuality, incest taboos prevented doubts about the legitimacy of her offspring and the children's property rights, titles, or inheritance.

Most social scientists believe that incest taboos are universal, but there have been exceptions. The rulers of the Incan empire, Hawaii, ancient Persia, and the Ptolemaic dynasty in Egypt practiced incest, which was forbidden to commoners. Some anthropologists speculate that wealthy Egyptian families practiced sibling marriage to prevent losing or fragmenting their land. If a sister married her brother, the property would remain in the family in the event of divorce or death (Parker, 1996).

PROCREATION AND SOCIALIZATION Procreation is an essential family function because it replenishes a country's population. Some married couples choose to remain child free, while others go to great lengths to conceive children through reproductive technologies (see Chapter 11). Once a couple becomes parents, the family embarks on socialization, another critical function.

Through **socialization**, children acquire language; absorb the accumulated knowledge, attitudes, beliefs, and values of their culture; and learn the social and interpersonal skills they need to function effectively in society. Some socialization is unconscious and may be unintentional (see Chapter 5), but much socialization is both conscious and deliberate, such as raising children in a particular religion.

We are socialized through **roles**, the obligations and expectations attached to a particular status or position in society. Families are important role-teaching agents because they delineate relationships between mothers and fathers, siblings, parents and children, and other relatives and nonfamily members. Some of the rights and responsibilities associated with our roles are not always clear because family structures shift and change. When parents experience divorce or remarriage, for example, some of the new role expectations may be fuzzy or even contradictory (see Chapter 15).

ECONOMIC SECURITY The family is also an important economic unit that provides financial security and stability. Families supply food, shelter, clothing, and other material resources that ensure the family's physical survival. Especially during the economic downturn that began in late 2007, many families have relied on their kin for loans to pay off credit debts or rent; help in caring for children while searching for a job after being laid off; and a place to live, such as with parents or grandparents, after a home foreclosure (see Chapters 12, 13, and 16).

The labor force participation of mothers with children under 6 years old surged from 39 percent in 1975 to 64 percent in 2011 (*Women in the Labor*

incest taboo Cultural norms and laws that forbid sexual intercourse between close blood relatives, such as brother and sister, father and daughter, or mother and son.

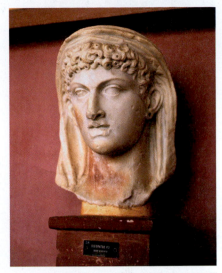

Cleopatra, the last pharaoh of ancient Egypt, is said to have been the issue of at least 11 generations of incest. She, in turn, married her younger brother.

socialization The process of acquiring the language, accumulated knowledge, attitudes, beliefs, and values of one's society and culture and learning the social and interpersonal skills needed to function effectively in society.

role The obligations and expectations attached to a particular status or position in society.

CHAPTER 1 The Changing Family **5**

Families provide the love, comfort, and emotional support that children need to develop into happy, healthy, and secure adults.

primary group A small group of people who are characterized by close, long-lasting, intimate, and face-to-face interaction.

secondary group A temporary collection of people who are characterized by formal, impersonal, and short-term relationships and work together to achieve common tasks or activities.

social class A group of people who have a similar standing or rank based on wealth, education, power, prestige, and other valued resources.

 Watch on MySocLab

Video: Family Values

Force. . ., 2013). The traditional family, in which Mom stays home to raise the kids, is a luxury that most families today simply can't afford. Because of high unemployment rates, depressed wages and salaries, and job insecurity, many mothers must work outside the home whether or not they want to (see Chapters 5 and 13).

EMOTIONAL SUPPORT   A fourth function of the family is to give its members emotional support. American sociologist Charles Horton Cooley (1909/1983) proposed the concept of **primary group**, a small group of people who are characterized by close, long-lasting, intimate, and face-to-face interaction. The family is a critical primary group because it provides the nurturance, love, and emotional sustenance that its members need to be happy, healthy, and secure. Our close friends are usually members of our primary groups, but they may come and go. In contrast, our family is usually our steadfast and enduring emotional anchor throughout life.

Sociologists later introduced the concept of **secondary group**, a temporary collection of people who are characterized by formal, impersonal, and short-term relationships and work together to achieve common tasks or activities. Members of secondary groups, such as co-workers, have few emotional ties to one another, and they typically leave the group after attaining a specific goal. While you're taking this course, for example, you, most of your classmates, and your instructor make up a secondary group. You've all come together for an academic term to study marriage and the family. Once the course is over, most of you may never see one another again.

You might discuss this course with people in other secondary groups, such as co-workers. They will probably listen politely, but usually don't really care how you feel about a class or a professor. Primary groups such as your family and close friends, in contrast, usually sympathize, drive you to class or your job when your car breaks down, offer to do your laundry during exams, and console you if you don't get that much-deserved "A" in a course or a promotion at work.

I use a simple exercise to distinguish between my primary and secondary groups: I don't hesitate to call a primary group member at 3:00 A.M. to pick me up at the airport because I know he or she will be happy (or at least willing) to do so. In contrast, I'd never call someone from a secondary group, such as another faculty member with whom I have no emotional ties.

SOCIAL CLASS PLACEMENT   A **social class** is a group of people who have a similar standing or rank in society based on their wealth, education, power, prestige, and other valued resources. People in the same social class tend to have similar attitudes, values, and leisure interests. We inherit a social position based on our parents' social class, but we can move up or down the social hierarchy in adulthood depending on our own motivation, hard work, connections, or even luck by being at the right place at the right time (see Chapters 12 and 13).

Social class affects many aspects of family life. There are class variations in when people marry, how many children they have, how parents socialize their children, and even how partners and spouses relate to each other. Middle-class couples are more likely than their working-class counterparts to share housework and child rearing, for example. And as you'll see in later chapters, families on the lower rungs of the socioeconomic ladder face greater risks than their middle-class counterparts of adolescent nonmarital child bearing, dropping out of high school, committing street crimes, neglecting their children, and being arrested for domestic violence (see Chapters 10, 12, and 14).

Marriage

Marriage, a socially approved mating relationship that people expect to be stable and enduring, is also universal. Countries vary in their specific norms and laws dictating who can marry whom and at what age, but marriage everywhere is an important rite of passage that marks adulthood and its related responsibilities, especially providing for a family. U.S. marriages are legally defined as either ceremonial or nonceremonial. A *ceremonial* marriage is one in which the couple must follow procedures specified by the state or other jurisdiction, such as buying a license, waiting a certain amount of time after applying for the license, and being married by an authorized official.

Some religious groups are endogamous because they require couples to marry within their own faith.

Some states also recognize **common-law marriage**, a *nonceremonial* relationship that people establish by living together. Generally, there are three requirements for a common-law marriage: (1) living together for a period of time (not defined in any state); (2) presenting oneself as part of a married couple (such as using the same last name, referring to the other as "my husband" or "my wife," and filing a joint tax return); and (3) being legally able to marry. Common-law marriages are legal in 10 states and the District of Columbia. Another 7 states recognize common-law marriage only under certain conditions, such as those formed before a certain date (National Conference of State Legislatures, 2013).

In both kinds of marriages, the partners must meet minimum age requirements, and they can't engage in **bigamy**, marrying a second person while a first marriage is still legal. When common-law marriages break up, numerous legal problems can arise, such as a child's inheritance rights and a parent's responsibility to pay child support. In addition, the rights and benefits of common-law marriages are usually recognized only in the state that has legalized them. Ceremonial marriage usually provides more advantages such as social approval and health insurance benefits for spouses.

Since you asked . . .
- Does living together mean that someone is in a common-law marriage?

marriage A socially approved mating relationship.

common-law marriage A nonceremonial relationship that people establish by living together.

bigamy Marrying a second person while a first marriage is still legal.

Endogamy and Exogamy

All societies have rules, formal or informal, about the "right" marriage partner. **Endogamy** (often used interchangeably with *homogamy*) is a cultural practice that requires marrying within one's group. The groups might include those that are similar in religion (such as Catholics marrying Catholics), race or ethnicity (such as Latinos marrying Latinos), social class (such as the rich marrying the rich), or age (such as young people marrying young people). In many societies, marrying cousins is not only commonplace but desirable (see "Why Does Cousin Marriage Matter in Iraq?").

Exogamy (often used interchangeably with *heterogamy*) is a cultural practice that requires marrying outside one's group, such as not marrying one's relatives. In the United States, for example, 25 states prohibit marriage between first cousins (National Conference of State Legislatures, 2013), but violations are rarely prosecuted. Even when there are no such laws, cultural traditions and practices, as well as social pressure, usually govern our choice of marital partners.

endogamy A cultural practice that requires marrying within one's group (often used interchangeably with *homogamy*).

exogamy A cultural practice that requires marrying outside one's group (often used interchangeably with *heterogamy*).

How Do Families Differ Worldwide?

There are also considerable worldwide family variations. Let's begin with family structure.

1.3 Describe five ways families differ worldwide.

Cross-Cultural and Multicultural Families — Why Does Cousin Marriage Matter in Iraq?

According to some of my students, "It's disgusting to even think about marrying a cousin." Why, then, are such endogamous marriages prevalent in parts of the Middle East, Africa, and Asia? For example, half of all marriages in Iraq, Pakistan, and Nigeria are between first or second cousins.

This form of marriage is both legal and preferred in societies in which families are organized around clans with blood relationships. Each clan is a "government in miniature" that provides the services and social aid that Americans routinely receive from their national, state, and local governments.

The largest and most unified clans have the greatest amount of power and resources. They, in turn, socialize family members not to trust the government, which is often corrupt, but to be attached to kin, clan, or tribe.

Cousin marriages in Iraq (as in many other countries) create intense internal cohesiveness and loyalty that strengthen the clan. If, for example, a man or woman married into another clan, he or she would deplete the original group's resources, especially property, and threaten its unity. In addition, cousins who marry are bound tightly to their clans because their in-laws aren't

strangers but aunts and uncles who know them best and have a strong interest in supporting the marriage.

Sources: Bobroff-Hajal, 2006, and Michels, 2008.

STOP AND THINK . . .

- What are the functions of endogamy and cousin marriages in Iraq?
- Canada and Europe allow marriages between first cousins. Should the United States do the same?

Family Structure

family of orientation The family into which a person is born or adopted.

family of procreation The family a person forms by marrying and having or adopting children.

kinship system A network of people who are related by marriage, blood, or adoption.

Most people are born into a biological family, or *family of origin*. If a person is adopted or raised in this family, it's her or his **family of orientation**. By leaving this family to marry or cohabit, the individual becomes part of a **family of procreation**, the family a person forms by marrying and having or adopting children. This term may be somewhat dated, however, because in several types of households—such as child-free or gay and lesbian families—procreation isn't a key function. Each type of family is part of a larger **kinship system**, a network of people who are related by blood, marriage, or adoption.

For nearly a century, the nation's family structure was stable. Between 1880 and 1970, for example, about 85 percent of all children lived in two-parent households. Then, in the next three decades, the numbers of divorces and single-parent families skyrocketed. By 2012, almost one in four children was living in a mother-only home (see *Figure 1.1*).

Nuclear and Extended Families

nuclear family A family made up of a wife, a husband, and their biological or adopted children.

extended family A family that consists of parents and children as well as other kin, such as uncles and aunts, nieces and nephews, cousins, and grandparents.

Western societies tend to have a **nuclear family** structure that is made up of married parents and their biological or adopted children. In much of the world, however, the most common family form is the **extended family**, which consists of parents and children as well as other kin, such as uncles and aunts, nieces and nephews, cousins, and grandparents.

As the number of single-parent families increases in industrialized countries, extended families are becoming more common. By helping out with household tasks and child rearing, extended families make it easier for a single parent to work outside the home. Many Americans assume that the nuclear family is the most common arrangement, but such families have declined (see Data Digest).

Residence Patterns

patrilocal residence pattern Newly married couples live with the husband's family.

matrilocal residence pattern Newly married couples live with the wife's family.

neolocal residence pattern Newly married couples set up their own residence.

Families also differ in where they live. In a **patrilocal residence pattern**, newly married couples live with the husband's family. In a **matrilocal residence pattern**, they live with the wife's family. And in a **neolocal residence pattern**, the couple sets up its own residence.

Around the world, the most common pattern is patrilocal. In industrialized societies such as the United States, married couples are typically neolocal. Since the early 1990s, however, the tendency for young married adults to live with the parents of either the wife or husband—or sometimes with the grandparents of one of the partners—has increased. At least half of all young couples can't afford a medium-priced house, whereas others have low-income jobs, are supporting children after a divorce, or just appreciate the benefits of a multigenerational household (see Chapters 12 and 16).

Authority and Power

Residence patterns often reflect who has authority in the family. In a **matriarchal family system**, the oldest females (usually grandmothers and mothers) control cultural, political, and economic resources and, consequently, have power over males. Some American Indian tribes have a matriarchal tradition and in some African countries, the oldest females have considerable authority and influence. For the most part, however, matriarchal societies are rare.

Worldwide, a more typical pattern is a **patriarchal family system**, in which the oldest males (grandfathers, fathers, and uncles) control cultural, political, and economic resources and, consequently, have power over females. In some patriarchal societies, women have few rights within or outside the family; they may not be permitted to work outside the home or attend college. In other patriarchal societies, women may have considerable decision-making power in the home but few legal rights, such as getting a divorce or running for political office (see Chapter 5).

In **egalitarian family systems**, both partners share power and authority about equally. Many Americans think they have egalitarian families, but U.S. families tend to be patriarchal. Employed women, for example, shoulder almost twice as much housework and child care as men, and are more likely than men to care for aging family members (see Chapters 10 and 16).

Monogamy and Polygamy

In **monogamy**, one person is married exclusively to another person. When divorce and remarriage rates are high, as in the United States, people engage in **serial monogamy**. That is, they marry several people, but one at a time—they marry, divorce, remarry, redivorce, and so on.

Polygamy, in which a man or woman has two or more spouses, is subdivided into *polygyny*—one man married to two or more women—and *polyandry*—one woman with two or more husbands. Nearly 1,000 cultures around the world allow some form of polygamy, either officially or unofficially (Epstein, 2008).

Although rare, polyandry exists. Among the Pimbwe people in western Tanzania, Africa, for example, some women have several husbands because of a shortage of women and the difficulty of one man to provide for a family (Borgerhoff Mulder, 2009). Polyandry has never been common in India, but there are pockets in some isolated and remote areas where polyandry is practiced. In these communities, a woman has several husbands, who are usually brothers. This ancient practice served several important functions: The family was more likely to survive in harsh environments if there was more than one husband to provide food; if one husband died, the others cared for the widow; and polyandry was a form of birth control. A woman has a limited number of childbearing years, whereas a man can produce dozens of children (Polgreen, 2010).

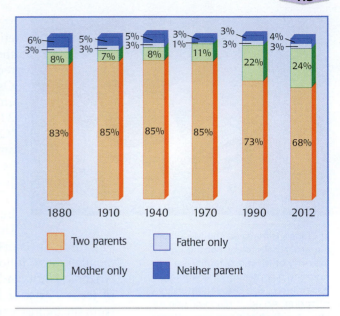

FIGURE 1.1 **Where U.S. Children Live, Selected Years, 1880–2012**
Note: Some of the columns may not sum to 100 percent due to rounding. *Sources:* Based on Fields, 2001, Figure 7; U.S. Census Bureau, Current Population Survey, 2012 Annual Social and Economic Supplement, 2012, Table C3; U.S. Census Bureau, 2012.

matriarchal family system The oldest females control cultural, political, and economic resources.

patriarchal family system The oldest males control cultural, political, and economic resources.

egalitarian family system Both partners share power and authority about equally.

monogamy One person is married exclusively to another person.

serial monogamy Individuals marry several people, but one at a time.

polygamy A woman or man has two or more spouses.

Listen on MySocLab

Audio: NPR: Defending and Attacking Polygamy in Saudi Arabia

Since you asked . . .
• Is serial monogamy a modern version of polygamy?

In China's Himalayas, the Mosuo are a matriarchal society. For the majority of Mosuo, a family is a household consisting of a woman, her children, and the daughters' offspring. An adult man will join a lover for the night and then return to his mother's or grandmother's house in the morning. Any children resulting from these unions belong to the female, and it is she and her relatives who raise them (Barnes, 2006).

MAKING CONNECTIONS

You may not even remember some of the television shows that came and went during the 1990s. Some, such as *Married . . . with Children, Home Improvement, Frasier*, and *The Bill Cosby Show*, are now syndicated. Others, such as *Two and a Half Men, The New Adventures of Old Christine*, and *Modern Family*, show a wide variety of family structures.

- How many of the TV programs—in the past or now—are representative of most U.S. families? Or of your own family?

- Why do you think that "reality" TV shows about polygyny, such as *Big Love* and *Sister Wives*, are so popular?

In contrast to polyandry, polygyny is common in many societies, especially in some regions of Africa, South America, and the Middle East. According to the Quran, a Muslim is permitted up to four wives at one time. In Saudi Arabia, for example, Osama bin Laden—who orchestrated the 9/11 terrorist attacks and was killed by U.S. Navy Seals in 2013—had 4 wives and 21 children. His father had 11 wives and 54 children (Coll, 2008; McGirk, 2011). No one knows the rate of polygamy worldwide, but polygyny has increased in countries such as Libya, South Africa, and Saudi Arabia (Brulliard, 2009; Al-Jassem, 2011; Nossiter, 2011).

Western and other industrialized societies forbid polygamy, but there are pockets of isolated polygynous groups in the United States, Canada, and Europe. The Church of Jesus Christ of Latter-day Saints (Mormons) banned polygamy in 1890 and excommunicates members who follow such beliefs. Still, an estimated 300,000 families in Texas, Arizona, Utah, and Canada are headed by males of the Fundamentalist Church of Jesus Christ of Latter Day Saints (FLDS), a polygamous sect that broke off from the mainstream Mormon Church more than a century ago. Wives who have escaped from these groups have reported forced marriage between men in their sixties, and girls as young as 10 years old have experienced sexual abuse and incest (Janofsky, 2003; Madigan, 2003).

In 2011, Warren Jeffs, leader of the FLDS sect in Texas, was sentenced to life in prison for sexually assaulting two girls, ages 12 and 15, that he said were his "brides." At the time, Jeffs had 78 wives, 24 of them under age 17. He claimed that polygyny is a means to gain divine acceptance, but prosecutors showed jurors a page from one of Jeffs's personal journal in which he wrote: "If the world knew what I was doing, they would hang me from the highest tree." Seven other FLDS men, also convicted of sexual assault and bigamy, received sentences of between 6 and 75 years (Forsyth, 2011).

Some Americans are concerned that the nuclear family is becoming less common. Many social scientists contend, however, that viewing the nuclear family as the only normal or natural type of family ignores many other household forms. One researcher, for example, identified 23 types of family structures, some of which included only friends or group-home members (Wu, 1996). Family structures have varied not only across cultures and time but also within a particular culture or historical period (see Chapter 3).

In India, Ziona Chana has the world's largest polygynous family—39 wives, 94 children, and 33 grandchildren (so far). They all live together in a 100-room mansion (*Daily Mail Reporter*, 2011).

Some Myths about the Family

Families in the United States and around the world are diverse, but we sometimes get bogged down by idealized images of what a "good" family looks like. Some myths are more harmful than others, but let's first look at five common fictions about the family.

Myths about the Past

We often hear that in the good old days there were fewer problems, people were happier, and families were stronger. Because of the widespread influence of movies and television, many of us cherish romantic notions of life in earlier times.

These highly unrealistic images of the family were presented in television shows such as *Father Knows Best* and *Leave It to Beaver* in the 1950s and early 1960s; *The Partridge Family*, *The Brady Bunch*, and the strong, poor, but loving rural families such as *The Waltons* and *Little House on the Prairie* in the 1970s; and *Dr. Quinn, Medicine Woman* in the late 1990s. Other popular television shows such as *The Bill Cosby Show* and *Everybody Loves Raymond* were probably appealing because they humorously evoked images of happy families whose members solved all of their conflicts and problems and lived happily.

Many historians maintain that such golden days never existed. We romanticize them only because we know so little about the past. Even in the 1800s, many families experienced out of wedlock births, domestic violence, and desertion by a parent or spouse (Demos, 1986; Coontz, 1992).

As the "Diary of a Pioneer Daughter" illustrates, family life in the good old days was filled with deprivation, loneliness, and danger. Families worked very hard and often were crushed by accidents, illness, and disease. Until the mid-1940s, a much shorter life expectancy meant that parental death often led to children's placement in extended families, foster care, or orphanages (Walsh, 1993). Thus, the chances of not growing up in a nuclear family were greater in the past than they are now.

1.4 Describe five myths about families and distinguish between functional and dysfunctional myths.

Read on **MySocLab**

Document: The Way We Weren't: The Myth and Reality of the "Traditional" Family

During the 1950s and early 1960s, a number of television programs, such as *Leave It to Beaver*, portrayed the "perfect family" as traditional, white, suburban, middle class, and always harmonious.

Constraints   Diary of a Pioneer Daughter

Many scholars point out that frontier life was anything but romantic. Malaria and cholera were widespread. Because of their darkness, humidity, and warmth, as well as the gaping windows and doors, pioneers' cabins were ideal environments for mosquitoes. Women and children have been described as doing household tasks with "their hands and arms flailing the air" against hordes of attacking mosquitoes (Faragher, 1986: 90).

Rebecca Bryan Boone, wife of the legendary pioneer Daniel Boone, endured months and sometimes even years of solitude when Boone hunted in the woods or went on trading trips. Besides doing household chores, she chopped wood, cultivated the fields, harvested the crops, and hunted for small game in the woods near her cabin. Rebecca was a strong and resourceful woman, but she told a traveling preacher that she felt "frequent distress and fear in her heart" (Peavy and Smith, 1994: xi).

Historian Joanna Stratton (1981) examined the letters, diaries, and other documents of pioneer women living on the Kansas prairie between 1854 and 1890. A 15-year-old girl's diary describes, vividly, an incident after a neighbor, Mr. Johnson, built a sod house but, after 2 years, went to the closest town to find work. Mrs. Johnson was homesick for her family in the east, worried about being alone, and got very sick: "At night she was frightened because the wolves would scratch on the door, on the sod, and on the windows, so my mother and I started to sit up nights with her." Shortly after Mrs. Johnson died, the wolves grew bolder: "One got his head in between the door casing, and as he was trying to wriggle through, mother struck him in the head with an ax and killed him. I shot one coming through the window. . . . We fought these wolves five nights in succession. . . ." After the funeral, Mr. Johnson sold the house, badly torn down by wolves, and moved away (p. 81).

STOP AND THINK . . .

- Do historical descriptions of pioneer life differ from those that we've seen on television shows such as *The Waltons* and *Little House on the Prairie*?
- If we had time machines, would you want to be transported to the good old days of pioneers?

In the so-called good old days, many families in the midwest, such as these Nebraska homesteaders, lived in dugouts made from sod cut out from the prairie.

People who have the nostalgia bug aren't aware of several facts. For example, teenage pregnancy rates were higher in the 1950s than they are today, even though a higher proportion of teen mothers were married (many because of "shotgun marriages"). Until the 1970s, few people ever talked or wrote about child abuse, incest, domestic violence, marital unhappiness, sexual harassment, or divorce. Many families lived in silent misery and quiet desperation because these issues were largely invisible. In addition, parents spend more time with their children today than they did in the good old days (see Chapter 12).

Myths about What Is Natural

Many people have strong opinions about what is natural or unnatural in families. Remaining single is more acceptable today than it was in the past, but there is still a lingering suspicion that there's something wrong with a person who never marries (see Chapter 9). And we sometimes have misgivings about child-free marriages or unmarried committed relationships. We often hear, for instance, "It's only natural to want to get married and have children" or "Gays are violating human nature." Other beliefs, also surviving from so-called simpler times, claim that family life is natural and that women are natural mothers (see Chapter 5).

The problem with such thinking is that if motherhood is natural, why do many women choose not to have children or abuse their children? If homosexuality is unnatural, how do we explain its existence since time immemorial? If getting married and creating a family are natural, why do millions of men abandon their children or their pregnant partners?

Myths about the Self-Sufficient Family

Among our most cherished values are individual achievement, self-reliance, and self-sufficiency. The numerous best-selling self-help books on topics such as parenting, successfully combining work and marriage, and having great sex also reflect our belief that we should improve ourselves, that we can pull ourselves up by our bootstraps.

We have many choices in our personal lives, but few families—past or present—have been entirely self-sufficient. Most of us need some kind of help at

one time or another. Because of unemployment, economic downturns, and recessions, the poverty rate has increased since 1970, and many of the working poor are two-parent families (DeNavas-Walt et al., 2012). From time to time, these families need assistance to survive.

The middle class isn't self-sufficient, either. In the 1950s and 1960s, for example, many middle-class families prospered not because of family savings or individual enterprise, but as a result of federal housing loans, greater access to public higher education, and publicly financed roads linking homes in the suburbs to jobs in the cities (Coontz, 1992).

Currently, people who have reached retirement age, whether poor or rich, are eligible for Medicare and Social Security, and the government provides numerous tax cuts for middle-income and affluent families (see Chapters 13 and 16). Even if you're in the middle class, you or other family members have probably collected unemployment payments after being laid off. State merit scholarships are more likely to subsidize the college costs of students from middle class and rich families than those from poor families (Baum and Payea, 2011; Kantrowitz, 2011). And regardless of one's social class, the federal government spends billions every year on K–12 public education, public broadcasting, local beaches and recreation centers, farm subsidies, clean drinking water, highways, and many other projects and programs that make many people's lives more comfortable (Grunwald, 2012).

The Myth of the Family as a Loving Refuge

One sociologist has described the family as a "haven in a heartless world" (Lasch, 1977: 8). That is, families provide love, nurturance, and emotional support. The home can also be one of the most physically and psychologically brutal settings in society. An alarming number of children suffer from physical and sexual abuse by family members, and intimate partner violence is widespread (see Chapter 14).

Many parents experience stress while balancing the demands of work and family responsibilities. In addition, the U.S. unemployment rate swelled from 4 percent in 2006 to almost 10 percent in 2012 (see Chapter 13). The anxiety underlying an unemployed person's ability to provide for his or her family is bound to negatively affect the family's dynamics and to challenge the assumption that the family is always a loving refuge.

Also, family members are often unrealistic about the daily strains they encounter. For example, if people expect family interactions to always be cheery and pleasant, tension may surge even when routine problems arise. And especially for families with health or economic problems, the home may be loving, but not always a haven in a heartless world.

Myths about the Perfect Marriage, the Perfect Family

People often experience a clash between marital expectations and reality. For example, one woman compared marriage to taking an airplane to Florida for a relaxing vacation, but landing in the Swiss Alps. Instead of swimming and sunshine, there's snow and cold: "It's one hell of a surprise when you get off that marital airplane and find that everything is far different from what one had assumed" (Lederer and Jackson, 1968: 39).

This observation, made in 1968, is still relevant today (see Chapter 10). Even if partners live together and believe that they know each other well, many may find themselves in the Swiss Alps instead of Florida after tying the knot.

Explore on MySocLab

Activity: Domestic Life: A Battle of the Sexes?

Watch on MySocLab

Video: Idealized Family

Numerous marriages dissolve because the partners cling to myths about conjugal life. After the perfect wedding, the perfect couple must be everything to each other: good providers, fantastic sexual partners, best friends, sympathetic confidantes, stimulating companions, and spiritual soul mates (Rubin, 1985). Are such expectations realistic?

Myths about the perfect family are just as pervasive as those about the perfect marriage. According to historian John Gillis (1996, 2004), we all have two families: one that we live *with* (the way families really are) and another that we live *by* (the way we would like families to be). Gillis maintains that people have been imagining and reimagining the family since at least the late Middle Ages because the families we are born and marry into seldom satisfy most people's need for a sense of continuity, belonging, unity, and rootedness.

These and other myths can spark dissatisfaction and conflict. Instead of enjoying our families as they are, we may waste a lot of time and energy searching for family relationships that exist only in fairy tales and TV sitcoms. Most myths about the family are dysfunctional, but some can be functional.

Why Myths Are Dysfunctional

Myths are *dysfunctional* when they have negative (though often unintended) consequences that disrupt a family. The myth of the perfect family can make us miserable. We may feel that there is something wrong with *us* if we don't live up to some idealized image. Instead of accepting our current families, we might pressure our children to become what *we* want them to be or spend a lifetime waiting for our parents or in-laws to accept us. We may also become critical of family members or withdraw emotionally because they don't fit into a mythical mold.

Myths can also divert our attention from widespread social problems that lead to family crises. If people blame themselves for the gap they perceive between image and reality, they may not recognize the external forces, such as social policies, that create difficulties on the individual level. For example, if we believe that only bad, sick, or maladjusted people beat their children, we will search for solutions at the individual level, such as counseling, support groups, and therapy. You'll see in later chapters, however, that numerous family crises come from large-scale problems such as racism, greedy corporate executives, economic downturns, and unemployment.

Why Myths Can Be Functional

Not all myths are harmful. Some are *functional* because they bring people together and promote social solidarity (Guest, 1988). If myths give us hope that we can improve marriage and family life, for example, we won't give up at the first sign of problems. In this sense, myths can help us maintain emotional balance during crises. Myths can also free us from guilt or shame. For instance, "We fell out of love" is a more face-saving explanation for getting a divorce than "I made a stupid mistake" or "I married an alcoholic."

The same myth can be both functional and dysfunctional. Belief in the decline of the family has been functional in generating social policies (such as child-support legislation) that try to keep children of divorced families from sinking into poverty. But this same myth is dysfunctional if people become unrealistically preoccupied with finding self-fulfillment and happiness.

Since you asked . . .

- Do myths affect me and my family?

MAKING CONNECTIONS

- Do media images of the family affect your perceptions? When you watch some TV shows, for example, do you feel disappointed in or better about your own family?

- Do you believe any (or all) of the myths about marriage and the family that you've just read? If so, how are these beliefs functional or dysfunctional in your life?

1.5

1.5 Describe three perspectives on why families are changing.

Three Perspectives on the Changing Family

We've defined the family, examined how families are similar and different, and then considered some of the current myths about family life. Let's now look at three views on how the American family is changing.

Several national surveys show that Americans place a high value on family. For example,

- Among high school seniors, 80 percent of girls and 72 percent of boys say that having a good marriage and family life is "extremely important" to them (Wilcox and Marquandt, 2011).

- Almost 74 percent of first-year college students (both women and men) say that raising a family is "very important" in their lives (Pryor et al., 2010).

- Almost 7 in 10 Americans are optimistic about the future of marriage and the family (Morin, 2011).

Despite such upbeat findings, many Americans believe that the family is falling apart. Some journalists and scholars refer to the "vanishing" family, "troubled" marriages, and "appalling" divorce statistics as sure signs that the family is disintegrating. Others contend that such hand-wringing is unwarranted.

Who's right? There are three schools of thought. One group contends that the family is declining; a second group argues that the family is changing but not declining; and a third, smaller group maintains that the family is more resilient than ever (see Benokraitis, 2000, for a discussion of these perspectives).

The Family Is Declining

More than 100 years ago, the *Boston Quarterly Review* issued a dire warning: "The family, in its old sense, is disappearing from our land, and not only are our institutions threatened, but the very existence of our society is endangered" (cited in Rosen, 1982: 299). In the late 1920s, E. R. Groves (1928), a well-known social scientist, warned that marriages were in a state of "extreme collapse." Some of his explanations for what he called the "marriage crisis" and high divorce rates have a surprisingly modern ring: self-indulgence, a concern for oneself rather than others, financial strain, and incompatible personalities. Those who believe that the family is in trouble echo Groves, citing reasons such as individual irresponsibility, minimal commitment to the family, and just plain selfishness.

Many conservative politicians and influential academics argue that the family is deteriorating because most people put their own needs above family duties. This school of thought claims that many adults are unwilling to invest their psychological and financial resources in their children or that they give up on their marriages too quickly when they encounter problems (Popenoe, 1996; Wilson, 2002).

Some adherents of the "family decline" school of thought believe that marriage should exist for the sake of children and not just adults. Simply telling children we love them is not enough. Instead of wasting our money on a divorce industry that includes lawyers, therapists, and expert witnesses, the argument goes, we should be investing in children by maintaining a stable marriage (Whitehead, 1996).

People who endorse the "family is declining" perspective point to a number of indicators. Much of the recent data show, for example, that fewer adults are married, more are divorced or remaining single, more are living together outside of marriage or alone, more children are born out of wedlock, the number of single-parent homes has surged, married women have fewer children, and many parents are spending less time with their children now than during the 1960s (Pew Research Center, 2010; Wilcox and Marquardt, 2011; Jacobsen et al., 2012).

Watch on MySocLab

Video: Population Growth and Decline

Since you asked . . .
- Many of the families we know seem to be loving and close knit. So why do many people think that the family is in trouble?

Some cities and towns have refused to give unmarried partners a "permit of occupancy" because they and their children aren't viewed as a family. City officials say that the laws prevent overcrowding. Others argue that such laws are legislating morality by defining the family as a married, heterosexual couple and their children.

The Family Is Changing, Not Declining

Others argue that the changes we are experiencing reflect long-term trends. For example, more women have entered the labor force since 1970, but the mother who works outside the home is not a new phenomenon. Mothers sold dairy products and woven goods during colonial times, took in boarders around the turn of the twentieth century, and held industrial jobs during World War II (see Chapter 3).

Many analysts also contend that family problems have *always* existed. Family studies published in the 1930s, for example, included issues such as divorce, desertion, and family crises resulting from discord, delinquency, and depression (Broderick, 1988).

Similarly, there have always been single-parent families. The percentage of single-parent households has doubled since 1980, but that percentage tripled between 1900 and 1950 (Stannard, 1979). Divorce, also, isn't a recent phenomenon; it became more common in the eighteenth century. Among other changes at that time, parents had less control over their adult married children because there was little land or other property to inherit and the importance of romantic love increased (Cott, 1976).

How do Americans feel about the sweeping changes in the structure of U.S. families that have unfolded over the past half century? The reactions are mixed: 31 percent believe that the changes are generally good for society; 32 percent believe that the changes are generally bad for society; and 37 percent are tolerant, but skeptical, particularly about more mothers of young children working outside the home and more gay and lesbian couples raising children (Morin, 2011).

Many researchers maintain that there is little empirical evidence that family change is synonymous with family decline. Instead, data support both perspectives—the belief that the family is in trouble as well as the notion that most families are resilient despite ongoing changes in gender roles, divorce rates, and alternatives to marriage such as living together (Amato, 2004).

The Family Is More Resilient than Ever

According to a third school of thought, families are more resilient, loving, and stronger than in the past. Consider the treatment of women and children in colonial days: If they disobeyed strict male authority, they were often severely punished. And, in contrast to some of our sentimental notions about the good old days, only a small number of white, middle-class families enjoyed a life that was both gentle and genteel:

> For every nineteenth-century middle-class family that protected its wife and child within the family circle . . . there was an Irish or a German girl scrubbing floors in that middle-class home, a Welsh boy mining coal to keep the home-baked goodies warm, a black girl doing the family laundry, a black mother and child picking cotton to be made into clothes for the family, and a Jewish or an Italian daughter in a sweatshop making "ladies" dresses or artificial flowers for the family to purchase (Coontz, 1992 : 11–12).

Those who espouse the "family is more resilient" perspective contend that changes in family life have strengthened family relationships, including marriages. In the past, many people stayed in unhappy marriages because of strong social norms and legal divorce obstacles. Today, in contrast, adults can more easily get a divorce, establish a new relationship, and raise children in a happier home (Hull et al., 2010).

As you'll see in later chapters, the happiest families are those in which adults (married or unmarried, and with and without children) share domestic and work

responsibilities. Especially among employed mothers, a greater equality of sharing housework and child care increases both the husbands' and wives' marital satisfaction.

Some social scientists also argue that despite myriad problems, families are happier today than in the past because of the increase in multigenerational relationships. Many people have grandparents, feel close to them, and often receive both emotional and economic support from these family members. The recent growth of the older segment of the population has produced four-generation families. More adults in their 60s may be stressed out because they are caring for 80- to 100-year-old parents. On the other hand, more children and grandchildren grow up knowing and enjoying their older relatives (see Chapter 16).

Each of the three schools of thought provides evidence for its position. Which perspective, then, can we believe? Is the family weak, or is it strong? The answer depends largely on how we define, measure, and interpret family weakness and strengths, issues we address in Chapter 2. For better or worse, the family continues to change.

MAKING CONNECTIONS

- Which of the three perspectives on the family is closest to your own views? Why?
- Do you think that marriages are becoming obsolete? Why or why not?

How Are U.S. Families Changing?

Each chapter shows how the family is changing. Demographic transitions, shifts in the racial and ethnic composition of families, and economic transformations all play a role in these changes.

1.6 Explain how U.S. families have been changing in terms of demographic characteristics and racial-ethnic diversity.

Demographic Changes

Two demographic changes have had especially far-reaching effects on families. First, U.S. birthrates have declined. Since the end of the eighteenth century, most American women have been bearing fewer children, having them closer together, and finishing child rearing at an earlier age. Second, the average age of the population rose from 17 in the mid-1800s to nearly 37 in 2011 (U.S. Census Bureau, 2012).

Both of these shifts mean that a large proportion of Americans now experiences the empty-nest syndrome—the departure of adult children from the home—at an earlier age, as well as earlier grandparenthood and prolonged widowhood. In addition, as Americans live longer, many adults must care for both children and elderly parents (see Chapters 11, 12, and 16). Other changes include more nonmarital births, more people living alone, more working mothers, and more older people (see *Figure 1.2*). We'll take a brief look at these changes now and examine them more closely in later chapters.

CHANGES IN FAMILY AND NONFAMILY HOUSEHOLDS The U.S. Census Bureau divides households into family and nonfamily. A *family household* consists of two or more people living together who are related through marriage, birth, or adoption. *Nonfamily households* include people who live alone or with nonrelatives (roommates, boarders, or cohabiting couples). In 2010, 34 percent of all households were nonfamily households, a substantial increase from 19 percent in 1970 (Fields, 2004; Lofquist et al., 2012).

The number of married-couple households with children under age 18 declined from 40 percent in 1970 to 20 percent in 2010. The percentage of children under age 18 living in one-parent families more than doubled during this same period (Lofquist et al., 2012). A major reason for the increase in one-parent families is due to the surge of births to unmarried women (see *Figure 1.2a*).

SINGLES AND COHABITING COUPLES Singles make up one of the fastest-growing groups for three reasons. First, many young adults are postponing marriage. Second, and at the other end of the age continuum, because people live

Explore on MySocLab

Activity: Families: Growth, Change, and the Census

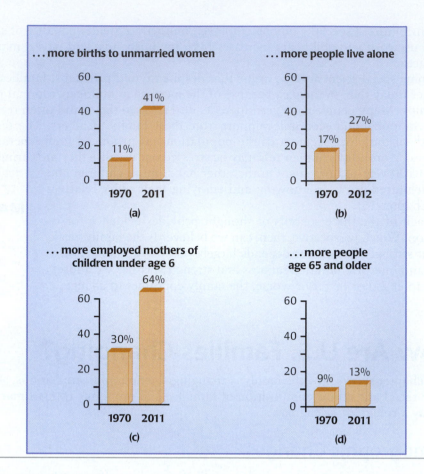

FIGURE 1.2 American Families—Then and Now

Sources: Based on data in Fields, 2004; Purcell and Whitman, 2006; Hamilton et al., 2012; "Unmarried and single . . ." 2012; "Older Americans . . ." 2013.

longer, they are more likely than in the past to outlive a partner. Third, older women who are divorced or widowed remarry at much lower rates than do older men, which increases the number of singles in their later years (see Chapters 15 and 16). Also, singles are now more likely than in the past to live alone (see *Figure 1.2b*) because they have the income to do so and enjoy their privacy (see Chapters 9 and 16). The percentage of cohabiting couples has also climbed since 1970. This number will probably continue to grow because there is greater societal acceptance of unmarried couples living together (see Chapters 8 and 9).

DIVORCE AND REMARRIAGE   Divorce rates have *decreased* since the late 1980s, but almost one out of every two first marriages is expected to end in divorce. Teen marriages and marriages entered into because the woman became pregnant are especially likely to unravel (see Chapter 15). Stepfamilies are also more common than in the past. About 12 percent of Americans are currently in their second, third, or fourth marriage. One of three Americans is now a stepparent, a stepchild, a stepsibling, or some other member of a stepfamily. We'll examine marriage, divorce, and remarriage in Chapters 10 and 15.

ONE-PARENT FAMILIES   As more adults remain single into their thirties and because divorce rates are high, the number of children living with one parent has increased (see Data Digest). Of all one-parent households, 87 percent are mother-child families (U.S. Census Bureau, 2012). We'll look at one-parent families more closely in several later chapters.

EMPLOYED MOTHERS   The high participation of mothers in the labor force since the 1980s has been one of the most striking changes in U.S. families. The percentage of two-earner married couples with children under age 18 surged from 31 percent in 1976 to 54 percent in 2010 (U.S. Census Bureau, 2002, 2012).

Explore on MySocLab

Activity: Single Parent Households

More than 6 out of every 10 married women with children under age 6 are in the labor force (see *Figure 1.2c*). This means that many couples are now coping with domestic and employment responsibilities while raising young children. We'll examine the characteristics and constraints of working mothers and two-earner couples in Chapter 13.

OLDER PEOPLE   Americans are living longer than ever before. The 4 percent increase of people age 65 and older since 1970 may seem small (see *Figure 1.2d*), but this population rose from 19 million in 1970 to nearly 41 million in 2011 ("Older Americans Month: May 2013," 2013). Many children enjoy having grandparents well into their own adulthood, but our aging population is also placing significant strains on family caregiving and national health care costs (see Chapter 16).

Racial and Ethnic Diversity

What do you call a person who speaks three languages? Multilingual.

What do you call a person who speaks two languages? Bilingual.

What do you call a person who speaks one language? American.

As this joke suggests, many people stereotype (and ridicule) the United States as a single-language and single-culture society. In reality, it's the most multicultural country in the world: Diversity is booming, ethnic groups speak many languages, and foreign-born families live in all the states.

ETHNIC DIVERSITY IS BOOMING   The nation's foreign-born, nearly 40 million people, account for almost 13 percent of the total U.S. population, up from 8 percent in 1990. America's multicultural umbrella includes about 150 distinct ethnic or racial groups among more than 309 million inhabitants. By 2025, only 58 percent of the U.S. population is projected to be white—down from 86 percent in 1950 (see *Figure 1.3*). By 2050—little more than a generation away—whites may make up only half of the total population because Latino and Asian populations are expected to triple in size (Grieco et al., 2012).

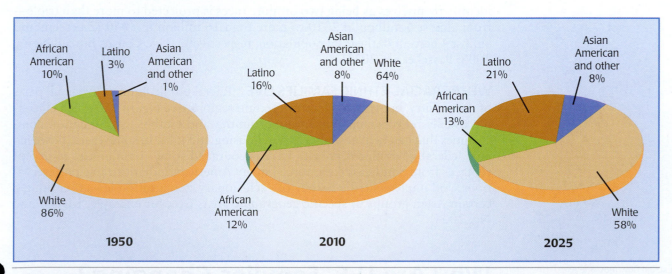

FIGURE 1.3 Racial and Ethnic Composition of the U.S. Population, 1950–2025
Note: "Asian American and other" includes American/Indian/Alaskan Native, Native Hawaiians and Pacific Islanders, some other race, and those who identify themselves with two or more races.
Sources: Based on U.S. Census Bureau, 2008; Passel et al., 2011.

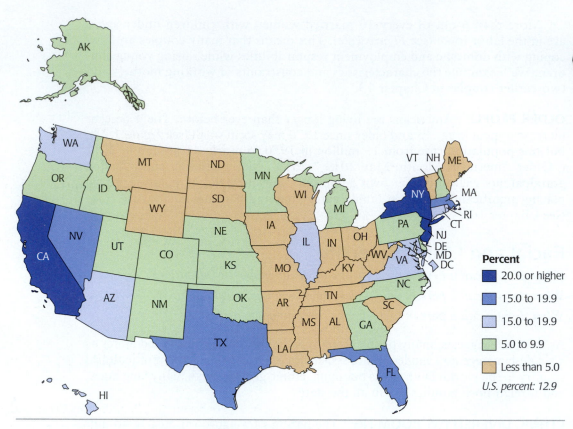

FIGURE 1.4 **Percent Foreign-Born in the United States, 2010**
Source: Grieco et al., 2012, Figure 1.

Despite the earlier joke about Americans speaking only one language, U.S. residents speak approximately 336 languages. About 85 percent of the foreign-born population speaks a language other than English at home compared with about 10 percent of the native population (Grieco et al., 2012; U.S. Census Bureau, 2012).

The multiracial population is also increasing. The number of Americans who identify themselves as being two or more races is projected to more than triple—from almost 6 million in 2010 to more than 16 million in 2050 (2 percent and almost 4 percent of the total population, respectively) (U.S. Census Bureau News, 2008; Passel et al., 2011).

WHERE RACIAL-ETHNIC FAMILIES LIVE   Racial-ethnic families live in all parts of the country, but tend to cluster in certain regions (see *Figure 1.4*). Such clustering usually reflects employment opportunities and established immigrant communities that can help newcomers find housing and jobs. In some cases, however, past federal government policies have encouraged some communities to accept refugees from Southeast Asia, forced many American Indians to live on reservations, and implemented a variety of exclusionary immigration laws that limited certain Asian groups to specific geographic areas (see, for example, Kivisto and Ng, 2004).

1.7 Explain how macro-level constraints affect families' micro-level choices.

Why Are U.S. Families Changing?

Family changes reflect both the choices people make (such as deciding to marry later or to have children) and the constraints that limit those choices (such as unemployment or family policies). To understand people's choices, social scientists

often rely on a **micro-level perspective**, focusing on people's social interaction patterns in specific settings. To understand the constraints that limit people's options, they use a **macro-level perspective**, focusing on large-scale patterns and processes that characterize society as a whole. Both perspectives, and the ways in which they are interrelated, are crucial in understanding the family.

micro-level perspective A social science perspective that focuses on people's social interaction patterns in specific settings.

macro-level perspective A social science perspective that focuses on large-scale patterns and processes that characterize society as a whole.

Micro-Level Influences on the Family

Consider the following scenario: Two students meet in college, fall in love, and marry after graduation. They find well-paying jobs, live in a luxury condominium, drive a BMW, and vacation in Hawaii. Then they have an unplanned child. The wife quits her job to take care of the baby, the husband loses his job, and the wife goes to work part time. She has difficulty balancing her multiple roles of mother, wife, and employee, while he becomes depressed and frustrated with his efforts to find work. The stress and arguments between the partners increase, and the marriage ends.

When I ask my students what went wrong, most take a micro-viewpoint and criticize the couple: "They should have saved some money," "They didn't need a BMW," "Haven't they heard about contraceptives?" and so on. Almost all of the students blame the divorce on the two people involved because they were unrealistic, immature, or made bad decisions.

There's much to be said for micro-level explanations because we make personal choices, but they should be kept in perspective. Many marriage and family textbooks and pop psychology books emphasize the importance of individual choices but ignore macro-level variables. Micro-analyses are limited because they can't explain some of the things over which families have very little control. For these broader analyses, we must turn to macro explanations.

Macro-Level Influences on the Family

The couple who got a divorce made some unwise personal decisions, such as not saving their money and perhaps not using contraceptives effectively or at all. However, the relationship deteriorated, in the end, because of macro-level factors such as unemployment and the unavailability of inexpensive high-quality day care services. Constraints such as economic forces, technology, popular culture, social movements, and family policies limit our choices and require macro-level explanations.

THE ECONOMY The Industrial Revolution and urbanization sparked widespread changes that had major impacts on the family (see Chapter 3). By the late eighteenth century, factories replaced the local industries that employed large numbers of women and children. As families became less self-sufficient and their members increasingly worked outside the home, parents' control over their children diminished.

In the 1980s and 1990s, many U.S. corporations began to move their operations to developing countries. Over time, these moves resulted in layoffs of millions of American workers. As the U.S. economy changed, low-paying service jobs replaced higher-paying manufacturing jobs. At the other end of the continuum, the higher-paying jobs require at least a college degree, so many people seeking these jobs tend to postpone marriage and parenthood (see Chapters 9 and 11). The financial crisis that began in late 2007 resulted in high unemployment rates, reduced work hours, a loss of health benefits, and financial distress, all of which have a disruptive effect on family life in the United States and around the world (see Chapter 13).

TECHNOLOGY Advances in medical and other health-related technologies have led to a decline in infant death rates and to longer life spans. On the other hand, because many Americans now live into their eighties and beyond, they risk falling into poverty; they require expensive medical services that may not be covered by

Since you asked . . .
- Has technology strengthened or weakened our family
  relationships?

Medicare or private insurance plans; or they simply outlive their retirement savings. The middle-aged—sometimes called the *sandwich generation*—must cope both with the demands of raising their own children and helping their aging parents (see Chapters 12 and 16).

Among recent technological innovations, the Internet and online interaction have had a widespread influence on many families. One example is *social media*—websites that don't just give information but also promote social interaction. These include social networking sites (e.g., Facebook, LinkedIn, and Twitter), gaming sites (e.g., *Second Life*), video sites (e.g., YouTube), and blogs (websites providing commentary, diary entries, or informational essays in a series of posts).

Some people believe that e-mail, texting, and social networking sites are intrusive because they replace close personal relationships with superficial but time-consuming online interactions. The critics maintain that these technologies allow us to filter and minimize human contact (Turkle, 2011). According to one technology consultant, "Social relationships cannot improve when people spend less and less time in face-to-face encounters." Says another, "With the advent of . . . Facebook, YouTube, etc., we allow all aspects of our lives to be shared with selected friends and family without actually having to reach out and tell them what we're up to" (Anderson and Rainie, 2010: 11, 16).

Since you asked . . .
- Do you text to avoid phone calls from family members, especially parents?

Others contend that digital technology is cutting into family time. For example, some children complain that they rarely receive their parents' full attention because a parent is often immersed in e-mail, texting, or being online even when pushing a swing, driving, or eating dinner (Young, 2011). In effect, some parents are paying more attention to their technology than to their children.

Some commentators predicted that technology would pull families apart. However, 64 percent of adults say that twenty-first–century communication technology has made their families closer than when they were growing up because they can stay in touch with adult children who have moved out (Smith, 2011). Cell phones have increased the frequency of interaction between parents, especially if both are employed, to coordinate schedules and to stay in touch with each other and their children throughout the day. Also, many parents report spending more time with their children by playing home video games with them. In the case of young adults who are away at college, parents say that family members interact more often than in the past through email and texting (Kennedy et al., 2008).

popular culture Beliefs, practices, activities, and products that are widely shared among a population in everyday life.

Among other benefits, e-mail and the Internet have encouraged long-distance conversations between parents, children, and relatives that might otherwise not occur because of busy schedules. Family members who are scattered coast to coast can become more connected by exchanging photos on the Web, organizing family reunions, tracking down distant relatives, tracing their ancestral roots, and getting online health information for family members (Hampton et al., 2011; Fox and Brenner, 2012; Gibbs, 2012).

Also, people in their eighties and nineties say that using e-mail and the Internet makes them more "wellderly" instead of elderly. One grandparent exclaimed, "Oh my gosh, I've never felt so young. I'm sitting around all these young people—they're on the Web and I'm on the Web. I'm talking to my granddaughter and she's off in Europe!" (White, 2008: 10B).

POPULAR CULTURE **Popular culture** refers to beliefs, practices, activities, and products that are widely shared among a population in everyday life. Popular culture includes television, the Internet, pop music, magazines, radio, advertising, sports, hobbies, fads, fashions, and movies—it is one of our major sources of information *and* misinformation about family life. Television is especially influential in transmitting both fact and fiction

"But, sweety, why don't you just read my blog, like everyone else?"

because, in a 65-year lifetime, the average American spends nine years in front of a TV set (Statistic Brain, 2012).

People don't always believe everything they read or see on television or online, but popular culture shapes our attitudes and behavior. For example, many of my students who claim that they "never pay any attention to ads" come to class wearing branded apparel such as Budweiser caps, Nike footwear, and Old Navy t-shirts.

SOCIAL MOVEMENTS   Over the years, a number of social movements have changed family life. The *civil rights movement* of the 1960s had a major impact on most U.S. families. Because of affirmative action legislation, members of many minority groups were able to take advantage of educational and economic opportunities that improved their families' socioeconomic status. Minority applicants were able to receive small business loans, and minority employees in corporations were considered for promotion to higher-level positions (see Chapters 4 and 13).

In 2006, 2010, 2012, and 2013, hundreds of thousands of Latinos and their supporters participated in demonstrations and rallies in Washington, DC, and other cities, calling on Congress to offer citizenship to undocumented (illegal) immigrants and their families.

The *women's movements*—in the late 1800s and especially in the 1970s—transformed many women's roles and, consequently, family life. As women gained more rights in law, education, and employment, many became less financially dependent on men and started questioning traditional assumptions about gender roles.

The *gay rights movement* that began in the 1970s challenged discriminatory laws in areas such as housing, adoption, and employment. Many companies now provide benefits to their employees' gay or lesbian partners; a number of adoption agencies assist lesbians and gays who want to become parents; numerous municipalities and states recognize civil unions; and some states have legalized same-sex marriages (see Chapters 8–12).

People who are alarmed by high divorce rates and the increase in cohabitation are joining a burgeoning *marriage movement*. Among other things, the marriage movement seeks to repeal no-fault divorce laws and wants to reduce federal and state benefits for children born to unmarried low-income mothers. It also promotes abstinence among young people, lobbies for funding programs that promote marriage, and embraces women's homemaker roles. In addition, the marriage movement encourages proponents to lobby lawmakers to pass state laws that require couples to take premarital counseling classes and marital skills programs (Wood et al., 2012). As "Should Uncle Sam Be a Matchmaker?" shows, however, not everyone is enthusiastic about such proposals.

FAMILY POLICIES   **Family policy** refers to the measures that governments take to improve the well-being of families. Some policies directly address family formations and processes (e.g., adoption, marriage, divorce, domestic violence, and welfare reform). Others have an indirect impact on family life (e.g., health care, housing, poverty, and substance abuse) (Bogenschneider and Corbett, 2010).

family policy The measures that governments take to improve the well-being of families.

Families don't just passively accept policy changes. Instead, parents and family members have played critical roles in major social policy changes such as those dealing with the education of children with disabilities, child pornography, joint custody of children after divorce, the right of older people to die with dignity, and better nursing care facilities (see Chapters 7, 12, 15, and 16).

ASK YOURSELF

Should Uncle Sam Be a Matchmaker?

In 2003, Congress passed a bill that allotted $1.5 billion over five years to promote marriage as part of welfare reform. The money was used for a variety of pro-marriage initiatives, including the following:

- Encouraging caseworkers to counsel pregnant women to marry the father of the child
- Reducing the rate of out-of-wedlock births
- Teaching about the value of marriage in high schools
- Providing divorce counseling for the poor
- Sponsoring programs that might produce more marriages (Brotherson and Duncan, 2004)

A very vocal marriage movement enthusiastically endorses such initiatives. Some of the movement's members justify marriage initiatives by pointing to the economic costs—from welfare to child support enforcement—that states incur because of high divorce rates and teens' nonmarital births. Others, such as conservative religious groups, maintain that the government should pass policies to support and strengthen marriage because "marriage and family are institutions ordained by God" (Wilcox, 2002).

Most recently, President Obama's administration has funded a $5 million national media campaign that extols the virtues of marriage for 18- to 30-year-olds. The campaign includes ads on Facebook and MySpace, videos on YouTube, spots on radio talk shows, ads in magazines and public transit, and a new Website, TwoOfUs.org (Jayson, 2009).

There are critics of such pro-marriage initiatives. Some scholars point out that many men's incomes are too low to lift a family out of poverty (Ooms et al., 2004). Others charge that promoting marriage for low-income women stigmatizes them (but not high-income unmarried mothers) and compels them to stay in abusive or unhappy relationships. Some also maintain that these programs blame individuals and try to change their attitudes and behavior instead of addressing macro-level problems such as unemployment, low wages, and low-quality K–12 public schools (Randles, 2009). Moreover, most pro-marriage programs don't work: They have minimal or no effect on couples' relationship quality, marriage rates, and preventing out-of-wedlock births (Wood et al., 2012).

Some directors of fatherhood programs are also opposed to promarriage legislation. They believe that marriage isn't a "quick fix" because many poor men have a lot of problems. As Robert Brady of the Young Fathers Program in Denver observed, "I wonder if these conservatives would be so dedicated to marriage promotion if it was their daughters they were trying to marry these guys off to" (Starr, 2001: 68).

STOP AND THINK . . .

- Is the government meddling in people's private affairs by using tax dollars to promote marriage? Or doing what's good for us?
- Do you think that many people are poor because they're not married? That they're not married because they're poor? Or other reasons?

1.8 Explain why multicultural, cross-cultural, and global perspectives are important in understanding families.

A Multicultural, Cross-Cultural, and Global Perspective on the Family

Why does this textbook include material on subcultures within the United States (American Indians, African Americans, Asian Americans, Middle Eastern Americans, and Latinos) and cultures in other countries? First, unless your family tree is 100 percent American Indian, your ancestors were slaves or immigrants to this country. Their cultural beliefs and practices shaped current families. The U.S. population today is a mosaic of many cultural, religious, ethnic, racial, and socioeconomic groups. Thus, a traditional white, middle-class model isn't adequate for understanding our marriages and families.

A second reason for our multicultural and cross-cultural approach is that the world today is an "international place" where "the changes facing families are not only national but are also global, encompassing social forces that transcend national and even regional or continental borders" (Karraker, 2008: 2, 5).

The Internet has changed our communication processes significantly, effectively shrinking the modern world and linking people across continents. As members of the global community, we need to be familiar with family practices and customs in other cultures.

A study of students at Northern Arizona University found that those who had participated in international study programs described their experiences as eye-opening in understanding other cultures. Consider, for example, a third-year college student who went to Italy for a year of studies:

> When she sat down for dinner with her host family on her very first night, she asked for some water with her meal, a common request in the United States. Yet, the response she got from a 75-year-old Italian was not what she had expected: "Wine is for drinking, water is for washing," he said. With this, she was welcomed to the world of living and studying abroad. (Van Hoof and Verbeeten, 2005: 42)

A third reason for this text's cross-cultural emphasis is that U.S. businesses recognize the importance of understanding other societies. Since the late 1980s, more companies have been requiring their employees to take courses about other cultures before going abroad and want employees who are proficient in more languages than just English (Berdan, 2012). For example, one of my students, who got a job with a *Fortune* 500 company, believed that she had an edge over some very tough competitors because she had learned Portuguese and had some knowledge of Portuguese and Brazilian culture.

Fourth, understanding the customs of other countries challenges our notion that U.S. families are the norm. According to sociologist Mark Hutter (1998: 12),

> Americans have been notorious for their lack of understanding and ignorance of other cultures. This is compounded by their gullible ethnocentric belief in the superiority of all things American and not only has made them unaware of how others live and think but also has given them a distorted picture of their own life.

Hutter's perspective—and that of this text—is that understanding other cultures helps us understand ourselves.

Finally, families are changing around the world. Instead of clinging to stereotypes about other countries, cross-cultural knowledge and information "may result in understanding instead of conflict" (Adams, 2004: 1076).

CONCLUSION

There have been *changes* in family structures, but families of all kinds seek caring, supportive, comforting, and enduring relationships. There is nothing inherently better about one type of family form than another. Instead, people create families that meet their needs for love and security.

The greatly expanded *choices* in family structure means that the traditional definition of family no longer reflects the interests of any one particular group. Such fluidity also generates new questions. Who, for example, will provide adequate child care when both parents are employed? And is it possible to pursue personal happiness without sacrificing obligations to other family members?

Our choices often are limited by *constraints*, especially at the macro-level, such as the economy and government policies. To deal with changes, choices, and constraints, we need as much information as possible about the family. In the next chapter, we'll see how social scientists conduct research on families, gathering data that make it possible for us to track the trends described in this and other chapters, and to make informed decisions about our choices.

On MySocLab

REVIEW QUESTIONS

1.1. Explain how traditional and contemporary definitions of family differ.

1. Why have traditional definitions of *family* been challenged in recent decades?

2. How do traditional and more recent definitions of family differ?

3. What are fictive kin? What purposes do they serve?

1.2. Describe five family functions and two marriage rules that are similar worldwide.

4. Why are the five family functions necessary for a society's survival?

5. How do endogamy and exogamy differ?

1.3. Describe five ways that families differ worldwide.

6. Worldwide, what family characteristics are more common than others?

7. Which family characteristics have been changing in U.S. families?

1.4. Describe five myths about families and distinguish between functional and dysfunctional myths.

8. Why do the five myths persist? What purposes do they serve?

9. How and why are myths both functional and dysfunctional?

1.5. Describe three perspectives on why families are changing.

10. How, in general, do these three perspectives differ?

11. What kinds of evidence, specifically, do the three perspectives use to support their positions?

1.6. Explain how U.S. families have been changing in terms of demographic characteristics and racial-ethnic diversity.

12. How, specifically, have U.S. families changed demographically since 1970?

13. How is the United States becoming more racially and ethnically diverse?

1.7. Explain how macro-level constraints affect families' micro-level choices.

14. What's the difference, if any, between micro-level and macro-level perspectives?

15. What macro-level changes have affected U.S. families? How?

1.8. Explain why multicultural, cross-cultural, and global perspectives are important in understanding families.

16. What are three reasons for adopting a cross-cultural perspective in understanding the family?

Studying the Family

Listen to Chapter 2 on MySocLab

LEARNING OBJECTIVES

After you read and study this chapter you will be able to:

Describe three ways that theory and research can help people make better decisions about their families.	**2.1**
Describe eight major family theoretical perspectives, identify whether each is macro- and/or micro-level, and summarize the strengths and limitations of each perspective.	**2.2**
Describe seven data-collection methods that researchers use to study families, and identify each of the method's strengths and limitations.	**2.3**
Describe the ethical standards that researchers must follow, and explain the political, religious, and community constraints that researchers encounter.	**2.4**

DATA DIGEST

- **The return rate for mailed census questionnaires** was 78 percent in 1970, 75 percent in 1980, 65 percent in 1990, and 74 percent in 2000 and 2010.

- A national public opinion **poll costs between $30 and $50 per respondent**—or about $30,000 to $50,000 for a telephone survey of 1,000 people.

- **The response rate of a typical telephone survey** decreased from 36 percent in 1997 to 9 percent in 2012.

- Among U.S. adults, **59 percent have searched online** for information about health.

- DNA tests, which trace our genetic origins, have found that **at least 4 percent of Americans don't know that their father isn't their biological parent**.

- Almost **half of Americans (most of them women) purchase at least one self-help book in their lifetimes**. As a result, this genre rose from $581 million in sales in 1998 to almost $9 billion in 2003. The sales are expected to be about $12 billion by 2012.

Sources: Edmonston, 1999; Marketdata Enterprises, 2004; Carpenter, 2008; Zarembo, 2009; "2010 Census Mail Participation Rate Map," 2010; Fox, 2011; Pew Research Center for the People & the Press, 2012; Tulumello, 2012.

When my mother died, the funeral director called *twice* to confirm the information before submitting it to Maryland's Division of Vital Statistics. Even though I provided the same accurate data both times, the death certificate had three errors: My mother died at age 87, *not* 88; she completed ten years of education, *not* eight; and tobacco *didn't* contribute to her death because no one in our family smoked.

When I see such mistakes, I wince. Here's a good example, I think, of why many people—including students—often distrust statistics. "Statistics mean never having to say you're certain," some quip. Others firmly believe the well-known quote, "There are three kinds of lies: lies, damned lies, and statistics."

Data collection isn't perfect. Even so, it's a far better source of information about families and other topics than personal opinions, experiential anecdotes, or other nonscientific ways of understanding our world. This chapter will help you evaluate the enormous amount of information we encounter on a daily basis. Let's begin with the issue of why a basic understanding of family theory and research is important.

2.1 Describe three ways that theory and research can help people make better decisions about their families.

 Watch on MySocLab

Video: Importance of Sociological Theory

Why Theories and Research Are Important in Our Everyday Lives

The words *theory* and *research* are often intimidating. Many of us may distrust statistics when they're different from our beliefs. For example, many Americans believe the conventional wisdom that children turn out better if they grow up in a home where the family gathers around the dinner table each night. Recent research shows, however, that eating dinner together doesn't affect a child's academic or behavioral outcomes (Miller et al., 2012).

There are practical reasons why theory and research are important: (1) What we don't know can hurt us, (2) theories and research help us understand

ourselves and our families, and (3) they improve our ability to think more critically and make informed decisions in our own families.

What We Don't Know Can Hurt Us

Many Americans, especially women, rely on talk shows for information on a number of topics. During 2009 alone, Oprah Winfrey featured and applauded guests who maintained, among other things, that children contract autism from the measles, mumps, and rubella (MMR) vaccinations they receive as babies; that fortune cards can help people diagnose their illnesses; and that people can wish away cancer (Kosova and Wingert, 2009)—*all of which are false.*

Such misinformation can be dangerous. Because of the "MMR vaccinations can cause autism" scare, about 30 percent of U.S. parents are hesitant to vaccinate their children (Kennedy et al., 2011). Partly because of such fears, by mid-2011, the United States was experiencing the largest increase in measles cases since 1996. For every 1,000 children who get measles, one or two die (McCauley and Chenowith, 2011; see also Gibson, 2012, for other recent examples of "celebrity bogus science").

Many websites are maintained by people who know little about family issues. Some of these sites charge consumers up to $5,000 to become "certified stepfamily counselors," even though there's no such certification requirement in the United States. Another site charges $500 for eight hours of audiotapes on how to lead marriage workshops (Siwolop, 2002). Needless to say, no one can become knowledgeable about leading such workshops after listening to only a few hours of audiotapes.

In other cases, we may simply be wasting our money on pills that have little effect on our health and longevity. For example, the medical world long ago noted that societies where diets are high in fatty fish such as salmon and sardines have lower rates of heart disease. The sale of fish oil supplements soared in the United States from $100 million in 2001 to $1.1 billion in 2011 (Weise, 2012). Recently, however, medical researchers reviewed 20 well-designed clinical studies and concluded that taking fish oil supplements doesn't reduce deaths, cardiac-related deaths, heart attacks, or strokes (Rizos et al., 2012). Eating healthy foods, not taking pills, helps prevent heart disease.

Many children are obese because, at a young age, they develop an appetite for food that's high in sugar and fat content.

Since you asked . . .
- Can I trust talk shows and websites on family issues?

Theories and Research Help Us Understand Ourselves and Our Families

Theories and research illuminate many aspects of our family life. For example, does spanking correct a child's misbehavior? Suppose a 2-year-old throws a temper tantrum at a family barbecue. One adult comments, "What that kid needs is a good smack on the behind." Another person immediately disagrees: "All kids go through this stage. Just ignore it." Who's right? In fact, empirical studies show that neither ignoring a problem nor inflicting physical punishment stops bad behavior (see Chapter 12).

Consider another example. Many Americans, especially nutritionists and parents, have blamed the food industry for children's obesity because of school vending machines that sell food and drinks that are high in sugar and fat (Layton and Eggen, 2011). However, several recent national studies have found that children's weight gains weren't due to buying soft drinks, candy, and other junk food at school. Instead, parents establish children's eating habits and food preferences at home, and years before youngsters start going to school (An and Sturm; 2012; Van Hook and Altman, 2012).

Theories and Research Help Us Make Informed Decisions

We rarely read a newspaper, newsmagazine, or online article without coming across statistics that affect some aspect of our lives. We listen numbly to the probabilities of dying earlier than expected because of our genetic inheritance, lifestyle, or environment. We are inundated with information on the importance of exercising, losing weight, lowering cholesterol levels, and not smoking.

Some of the information is sound, but much is biased, inaccurate, or generated by unlicensed, self-proclaimed "experts." They whip up anxieties and then sell solutions that include their own books and consulting services. As "Self-Help Books: Let the Reader Beware" shows, one of the best ways to protect yourself against false and misleading information is to be informed.

Students in family courses sometimes feel that they and their instructor are on different planets. At the beginning of a semester, for example, I've heard my students grumble, "I took this course to find out how to avoid a divorce after I get married. Who cares about divorce statistics!"

Choices | Self-Help Books: Let the Reader Beware

Just before he died at age 94, Dr. Benjamin Spock agreed with his long-estranged sons that he had been too career driven to spend much time with his family (Maier, 1998). Yet Spock was one of the most respected family experts in America; his books on child rearing were best-sellers for more than 50 years. For centuries, people have turned to self-help material to solve their personal problems.

Self-improvement can enhance our coping skills, reduce stress, and make life more enjoyable, but what's the quality of the advice? For example, a recent study evaluated 63 top-selling stepfamily self-help books that practitioners recommend to their clients. The researchers found that only 13 were of high quality and based on empirical evidence rather than opinion. Even fewer addressed critical topics such as stepfamily legal issues and protecting children from stepparents' and parents' conflict (Coleman and Nickleberry, 2009).

Many self-help books and articles in popular magazines are based on personal opinion and anecdotes rather than scholarly research. As a result, these materials can create five problems:

1. *They can threaten relationships.* Numerous self-help books encourage the reader to make new demands on a spouse or children. Such one-sided advice can increase conflict that the family may not be able to handle.

2. *They can make people feel worse.* Much of the positive thinking advice ("I can succeed") sets up unrealistic expectations, and self-congratulatory positive thinking ("I'm a lovable person") frees people from facing their shortcomings (Ehrenreich, 2009; Wood et al., 2009).

3. *They often reinforce gender stereotypes.* Many of the best-selling self-help books on heterosexual relationships tend to exaggerate the differences between women and men, leading to conclusions that are contrary to research findings (Kratchick et al., 2005; Signorella and Cooper, 2011).

4. *They oversimplify complex problems.* Many popular writers gloss over complicated family relationships. Some "experts" claim that reduced frequency of sexual intercourse can lead to depression. In fact, many factors may trigger depression, and sex isn't at the top of the list (see Chapters 7 and 10).

5. *They generalize limited findings.* One author interviewed 150 aging celebrity women and then offered advice to all older women. A reviewer noted, correctly, that the experiences were those of a select group of people who "have the luxury and the time to wallow in midlife crises" and to indulge in plastic surgery. Even if aging women wanted to do so, most can't afford plastic surgery or other expensive treatments (such as Botox injections or chemical peels) that require repeated treatments (Reynolds, 2007).

STOP AND THINK . . .

As you read self-help articles and books, ask yourself the following questions:

- Does the writer cite research or only anecdotal material? If the writer cites himself or herself, are the references scholarly or only personal stories? According to one researcher, "If modern science has learned anything in the past century, it is to distrust anecdotal evidence" (Park, 2003: B20).

- Does the author describe only a few families (especially those with problems) but generalizes the "findings" to all families?

- Does the writer make it sound as though life is exceedingly simple, such as following seven steps for family happiness? Family interaction and behavior are much more complex than throwing a few ingredients into the pot and stirring.

In fact, by learning something about research, you will be able to make more informed decisions about finding a suitable mate and, quite possibly, avoiding a divorce. In addition, knowing something about *how* social scientists study families will enhance your ability to think critically before making a decision. For example, we often hear that grief counseling is essential after losing a loved one. However, four in ten Americans are better off *without* such counseling. Grief is normal and people can often work through their losses on their own, whereas counseling sometimes prolongs the feelings of depression and anxiety (Stroebe et al., 2000).

This chapter won't transform you into a theorist or researcher, but it will help you ask some of the right questions when you are deluged with popular nonsense. Let's begin with the most influential marriage and the family theories that guide social science research.

Theoretical Perspectives on Families

Someone once observed, "I used to have six theories about parenting and no children. Now I have six children and no theories." This quip suggests that there's no relationship between theory and practice. As you saw in Chapter 1, however, theories about families are often translated into policies and laws that affect all of us.

Ideas have consequences. For instance, people who theorize that the family is disintegrating might propose micro-level solutions such as cutting off public assistance to unmarried mothers. In contrast, those who theorize that the family is changing might propose macro-level remedies such as providing girls and young women with better access to schooling and jobs, both of which decrease the likelihood of early sexual involvement and pregnancy (see Chapter 11).

As people struggle to understand families, they develop theories. A **theory** is a set of statements that explains why a phenomenon occurs. Theories drive research, help us analyze our findings, and, ideally, offer solutions for family problems.

One family sociologist compares theories to the fable of the six blind men who felt different parts of an elephant and arrived at different explanations of what elephants were like. The man who felt the side of the elephant compared it to a massive, immovable wall. The man who felt the trunk thought the elephant was like a rope that could move large objects. Similarly, different theories explain different aspects of the elephant—in this case, families (Burr, 1995).

There are about a dozen or so influential family theories. Let's consider eight that are the best known: two macro-level theories, three theories that are both micro- and macro-level, and three micro-level theories that focus on face-to-face interaction and personal dynamics (see *Figure 2.1*).

Family researchers typically use more than one theoretical framework because each perspective answers particular questions. Because reality is complex, the "coexisting theories concentrate on a different aspect of real life" (Winton, 1995: 2). For greater clarity, let's look at each perspective separately. (Many social scientists use the terms *theories*, *theoretical perspectives*, and *theoretical frameworks* interchangeably.)

The Structural Functional Perspective

Structural functional theory (often shortened to *functionalism*) examines how a society's interdependent parts work together to ensure its survival. When functionalists study families, they look at how families contribute to a society's stability (through procreation and socialization, for example), and the relationships between family members and between families and other institutions such as education and religion. For example, according to functionalists, adult

---

2.2 Describe eight major family theoretical perspectives, identify whether each is macro- and/or micro-level, and summarize the strengths and limitations of each perspective.

Explore on MySocLab

Activity: Family: Theories and Questions

theory A set of statements that explains why a particular phenomenon occurs.

Since you asked . . .
- Why isn't there one nice, simple theory about the family?

structural functional theory Examines how a society's interdependent parts work together to ensure its survival (often shortened to *functionalism*).

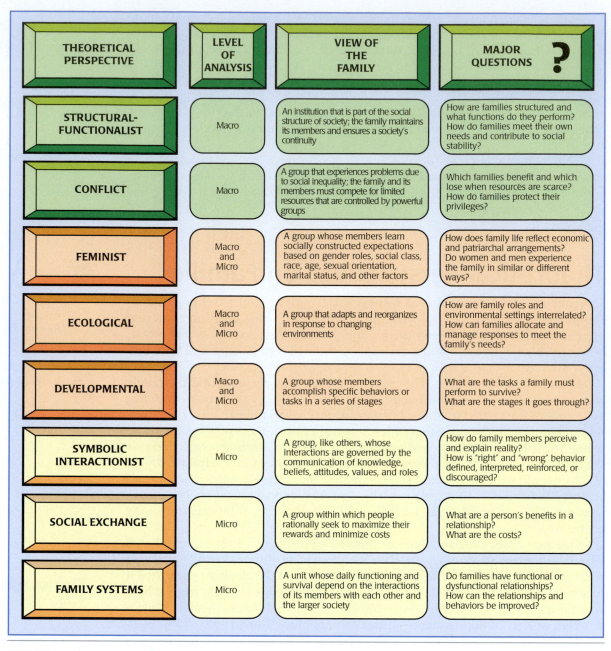

THEORETICAL PERSPECTIVE	LEVEL OF ANALYSIS	VIEW OF THE FAMILY	MAJOR QUESTIONS ?
STRUCTURAL-FUNCTIONALIST	Macro	An institution that is part of the social structure of society; the family maintains its members and ensures a society's continuity	How are families structured and what functions do they perform? How do families meet their own needs and contribute to social stability?
CONFLICT	Macro	A group that experiences problems due to social inequality; the family and its members must compete for limited resources that are controlled by powerful groups	Which families benefit and which lose when resources are scarce? How do families protect their privileges?
FEMINIST	Macro and Micro	A group whose members learn socially constructed expectations based on gender roles, social class, race, age, sexual orientation, marital status, and other factors	How does family life reflect economic and patriarchal arrangements? Do women and men experience the family in similar or different ways?
ECOLOGICAL	Macro and Micro	A group that adapts and reorganizes in response to changing environments	How are family roles and environmental settings interrelated? How can families allocate and manage responses to meet the family's needs?
DEVELOPMENTAL	Macro and Micro	A group whose members accomplish specific behaviors or tasks in a series of stages	What are the tasks a family must perform to survive? What are the stages it goes through?
SYMBOLIC INTERACTIONIST	Micro	A group, like others, whose interactions are governed by the communication of knowledge, beliefs, attitudes, values, and roles	How do family members perceive and explain reality? How is "right" and "wrong" behavior defined, interpreted, reinforced, or discouraged?
SOCIAL EXCHANGE	Micro	A group within which people rationally seek to maximize their rewards and minimize costs	What are a person's benefits in a relationship? What are the costs?
FAMILY SYSTEMS	Micro	A unit whose daily functioning and survival depend on the interactions of its members with each other and the larger society	Do families have functional or dysfunctional relationships? How can the relationships and behaviors be improved?

FIGURE 2.1 **Major Theoretical Perspectives on the Family.**

family tasks are best accomplished when spouses carry out two distinct and specialized types of roles—*instrumental* and *expressive* (Parsons and Bales, 1955).

FAMILY ROLES The husband or father, the "breadwinner," performs **instrumental roles**: providing food and shelter for the family and being hardworking, tough, and competitive. The wife or mother plays the **expressive roles** of the "homemaker": providing the emotional support and nurturing that sustain the family unit. These family roles characterize what social scientists call the *traditional family*, a family form that many conservative groups would like to preserve (see Chapter 1).

These and other family roles are *functional* because they create and preserve order, stability, and harmony. They also provide the physical shelter and emotional support that ensure a family's health and survival. Anything that interferes with these tasks is seen as *dysfunctional* because it jeopardizes the family's smooth functioning. For example, abuse of a family member is

instrumental role The breadwinner role of the father or husband who provides food and shelter for the family.

expressive role The supportive and nurturing role of the wife or mother who sustains the family unit.

dysfunctional because the negative physical and emotional consequences threaten the family's continuity.

FAMILY FUNCTIONS   There are two general kinds of functions in families and other institutions. **Manifest functions** are purposes and activities that are intended and recognized; they are clearly evident. **Latent functions** are purposes and activities that are unintended and unrecognized; they aren't immediately obvious. Consider weddings. The primary manifest function of the marriage ceremony is to publicize the formation of a new family unit and to legitimize sexual intercourse (see Chapter 1). Its latent functions include communicating a hands-off message to past or prospective lovers, outfitting the couple with household goods through wedding gifts, and redefining family boundaries to include in-laws or stepfamily members.

In a traditional family, the father is the breadwinner and the mother is the homemaker.

manifest functions Purposes and activities that are intended, recognized, and clearly evident.

latent functions Purposes and activities that are unintended, unrecognized, and not immediately obvious.

INSTITUTIONAL CONNECTIONS   Functionalists also note that the family affects, is affected by, and is interrelated to other institutions such as law, politics, and the economy. For example, politicians (many of whom are lawyers and businesspeople) play a major role in setting policies that determine, among other things, whether a marriage is legal, who can adopt a child, and which family members can claim Social Security payments (see Chapter 1).

CRITICAL EVALUATION   Structural functionalism was a dominant perspective in the 1950s and 1960s, but later came under attack for being so conservative in its emphasis on order and stability that it ignored social change. For example, this perspective still sees divorce as dysfunctional and as signaling the disintegration of the family rather than as indicating positive change (as when individuals end an unhappy relationship).

Some critics also maintain that functionalists shouldn't assume that just because some aspects of the family are functional, they should be maintained (Ingoldsby et al., 2004). For instance, expecting males to be instrumental and females to be expressive places a burden on both sexes—including fathers who are laid off and mothers who work outside the home.

Functionalism is useful in understanding families on a macro level, but it doesn't show how families interact on a daily basis. It also doesn't take into account that disagreements aren't necessarily dysfunctional but a normal part of family life. Also, feminist scholars, especially, have criticized structural functionalism for viewing the family narrowly through a white, male, middle-class lens.

The Conflict Perspective

Another macro-level theory, the conflict perspective, has a long history (see Adams and Sydie, 2001). It became popular in the United States in the late 1960s, when African Americans and feminists started to challenge functionalism as the dominant explanation of families and marriages.

Conflict theory examines how groups disagree, struggle for power, and compete for scarce resources such as wealth and power. In contrast to functionalists, conflict theorists see conflict and the resulting changes in traditional roles as natural, inevitable, and even desirable because many of the changes improve people's lives. Specifically, conflict theories have been useful in identifying some of the inequities within and across families, and promoting structures and values that are less oppressive.

conflict theory Examines how groups disagree, struggle for power, and compete for scarce resources such as wealth and power.

SOCIAL CLASS AND POWER   For conflict theorists, families perpetuate social stratification. Those in high-income brackets have the greatest share of capital, including wealth, that they can pass down to the next generation. Such

inheritances reduce the likelihood that all families have equal opportunities or equal power to compete for resources such as education, decent housing, and health care.

Unlike functionalists, conflict theorists see society not as cooperative and stable but as a system of widespread inequality. There is continuous tension between the haves and the have-nots: The latter are mainly children, women, minorities, and the poor. Much research based on conflict theory focuses on how those in power—typically white, middle-aged, wealthy males—dominate political and economic decision making in U.S. society.

FAMILY PROBLEMS   Conflict theorists view many family difficulties as resulting from widespread societal problems rather than individual shortcomings. For example, shifts in the U.S. economy have led to a decline in manufacturing and the loss of many well-paying blue-collar jobs. This has had a profound influence on many families, sending some into a spiral of downward mobility. Unemployment rates doubled between 2005 and 2010, and taxpayers are still paying for the mismanagement and greed of corporations that the U.S. government has bailed out (see Chapter 13). Racial discrimination also has a negative impact on many families, often blocking their access to health services, education, and employment.

CRITICAL EVALUATION   Some social scientists criticize conflict theory for stressing clashes and coercion at the expense of order and stability. According to critics, conflict theory presents a negative view of human nature as selfish while neglecting the importance of love and self-sacrifice, which characterize many family relationships. Some critics also believe that the conflict perspective is less useful than other approaches because it emphasizes institutional constraints rather than personal choices in everyday family life.

Another criticism is that conflict theorists don't propose how families can improve. Some family theories focus on solutions. In contrast, conflict theories often address primarily competition, power, control, and similar problems (Ingoldsby et al., 2004).

Feminist Perspectives

feminist theories Examine social, economic, and political inequality between women and men in society.

Feminist theories examine the social, economic, and political inequality between women and men in society. There are many types of feminism, each with a different emphasis (see, for example, Lindsey, 2005; Lorber, 2005; and Andersen and Witham, 2011). Despite the variations, feminist family theories generally address gender inequality, family diversity, and social change using both micro and macro approaches.

GENDER INEQUALITY   According to Rebecca West, an English journalist and novelist who died in 1983, "I myself have never been able to find out precisely what feminism is; I only know that people call me a feminist whenever I express sentiments that differentiate me from a doormat." *Any* person—male or female, straight or gay, young or old—who believes that *both* sexes should have equal political, educational, economic, and other rights is a feminist, even if he or she refuses to identify with this label.

A core issue for feminist family scholars (both women and men) is gender inequality, both at home and in the workplace, and how gender inequality intersects with race, ethnicity, and social class. For example, the poorest older adults are most likely to be minority women, and caregivers of the old—who are predominantly women—must often leave their jobs or work only part time to accommodate caregiving (see Chapter 16).

FAMILY DIVERSITY   Feminist family scholars, more than any other group, have been instrumental in broadening our view of families. For these scholars,

Since you asked . . .
• Can men be feminists?

limiting families to the traditional nuclear definition excludes many other family forms such as long-term cohabiting couples, single parents and their children, multigenerational families living together, same-sex families, stepfamilies, and fictive kin (see Chapter 1).

EMPHASIS ON SOCIAL CHANGE   Since the early 1980s, feminist scholars have contributed to family theory and social change in several ways:

- They have initiated legislation to address family violence and to impose stiffer penalties for men who assault children and women.

- They have endorsed greater equality between husbands and wives as well as unmarried partners, and have pushed for legislation that provides employed women and men with parental leave rights (see Chapters 5 and 13).

- They have refocused much of the research to include fathers as involved, responsible, and nurturing family members who have a profound effect on children and the family (see Chapters 4 and 12).

CRITICAL EVALUATION   One criticism is that feminist scholars focus primarily on issues that affect women, and not men, and don't pay enough attention to other forms of oppression such as age, disability, and religious intolerance (Ingoldsby et al., 2004). In terms of ethnicity, there is still considerably more contemporary feminist scholarship on white and African American families than on others, especially American Indian and Middle Eastern families (see Chapter 4).

A second criticism is that feminists, by emphasizing diversity, overlook commonalities that make families more similar than different (Baca Zinn, 2000). A related issue is that some feminist scholars have a tendency to view full-time homemakers as victims rather than as individuals who choose the role. Thus, some maintain, feminist scholars are "in danger of refusing to listen to a multiplicity of women's voices" (Johnson and Lloyd, 2004: 160).

Some critics, including some feminists, also question whether feminist scholars have lost their bearings. For example, some maintain that instead of focusing on personal issues such as greater sexual freedom, feminist scholarship should emphasize broader social issues, particularly wage inequality (Rowe-Finkbeiner, 2004; Chesler, 2006).

The Ecological Perspective

Ecological theory examines how a family influences and is influenced by its environment. Urie Bronfenbrenner (1979, 1986), a major advocate of ecological theory, proposed that four interlocking systems shape our development and behavior.

INTERLOCKING SYSTEMS   These systems range from the most immediate settings, such as the family and peer group, to more remote contexts in which a child is not involved directly, such as technological changes and ideological beliefs (see *Figure 2.2*). The four systems are the following:

1. The *microsystem* is made up of the interconnected behaviors, roles, and relationships that influence a child's daily life (such as parents' toilet-training their child).

2. The *mesosystem* is composed of the relationships among different settings (for example, the home, a day care center, and schools). Parents interact with teachers and religious groups; children interact with peers; and health care providers interact with both children and parents.

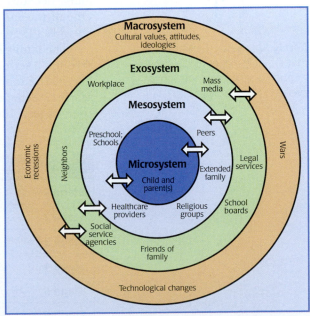

Explore on MySocLab

Activity: Family Diversity: Who Takes Care of Whom?

ecological theory Examines how a family influences and is influenced by its environment.

FIGURE 2.2 An Ecological Model of Family Development
Source: Based on Bronfenbrenner, 1979.

3. The *exosystem* consists of settings or events that a person doesn't experience directly but that can affect her or his development (such as parents' employment).

4. The *macrosystem* is the wider society and culture that encompasses all the other systems.

All four of these embedded systems, or environments, can help or hinder a child's development and a family's functioning. Researchers have used the ecological perspective in understanding family-related issues such as adolescent and marital well-being, successful community drug-prevention programs, and the stresses of the early years of parenthood (see Bogenschneider, 1996; Marin and Brown, 2008; Cox et al., 2011; Helms et al., 2011).

CRITICAL EVALUATION   Ecological theory is useful in explaining family dynamics and proposing programs to deal with issues such as youth violence, but critics note several limitations. Ecological theories try to explain growth as resulting from changes in the environment, but explanations of disintegration (such as aging) are notably absent. It's also not always apparent exactly how and when environments produce changes in individuals and families. Finally, it's unclear how the interactions among the four systems affect nontraditional families such as stepfamilies, gay and lesbian households, and intergenerational families living under one roof. Because the ecological perspective describes primarily nuclear, heterosexual, and white families, some critics have wondered how nontraditional families fit in (White and Klein, 2002; Telleen et al., 2003; Schweiger and O'Brien, 2005).

The Family Development Perspective

family development theory
Examines the changes that families experience over the lifespan.

Family development theory examines the changes that families experience over their lifespans. This is the only theoretical perspective that emerged out of a specific interest in families and still focuses exclusively on the family (rather than the relationships between dating couples, for example).

THE CLASSIC FAMILY LIFE CYCLE   Family development theory evolved over many decades (see White and Klein, 2002, for a description of this evolution). One of the earliest variations, still popular among some practitioners, is Evelyn Duvall's (1957) model of the family life cycle.

family life cycle The transitions that a family makes as it moves through a series of stages or events.

The **family life cycle** consists of the transitions that a family makes as it moves through a series of stages and events. According to this classic model and others like it, the family life cycle begins with marriage and continues through child rearing, seeing the children leave home, retirement, and the death of one or both spouses (see *Table 2.1*).

TABLE 2.1	The Classic Portrayal of the Family Life Cycle
Stage 1	Couple without children
Stage 2	Oldest child younger than age 30 months
Stage 3	Oldest child between ages 2-1/2 and 6
Stage 4	Oldest child between ages 6 and 13
Stage 5	Oldest child between ages 13 and 20
Stage 6	Period ending when the youngest child leaves the family unit
Stage 7	Empty nest to retirement
Stage 8	Retirement to death of one or both spouses

DEVELOPMENTAL TASKS CHANGE OVER TIME As people progress through various stages of the family life cycle, they accomplish **developmental tasks**. That is, they learn to fulfill various role expectations and responsibilities, such as showing affection and support for family members and socializing with people outside the family.

Depending on our developmental stage, we learn to interact and handle different challenges as we grow older. For example, young children must deal with teasing, children ages 6 to 10 must cope with getting bad grades and bullying at school, older children face pressure to use drugs, and 16- to 22-year-olds report that their greatest difficulties are trouble at work and school. For adults, the greatest source of stress is family conflict. For many of the elderly, the biggest problems include a decline in physical mobility, dependence on caregivers, and paying for prescriptions and other living expenses (Ellis et al., 2001).

DEVELOPMENTAL TASKS ARE MULTIFACETED Developmental stages and tasks vary in different kinds of families, such as single-parent families, childless couples, stepfamilies, and grandparent–grandchild families. The complex situations and problems that confront families in an aging society are multigenerational. If a couple divorces, for instance, the ex-spouses aren't the only ones who must learn new developmental tasks in relating to their children and each other. Grandparents may also have to forge different ties with their

developmental tasks Specific role expectations and responsibilities that must be fulfilled as people move through the family life cycle.

Choices
Kinscripts: Ensuring Family Survival during Tough Times

Family life cycle patterns differ markedly in terms of needs, resources, gender roles, race and ethnicity, and social class. In a study of low-income African American families that has become a classic, sociologists Linda Burton and Carol Stack (1993) proposed the concept of *kinscript* to explain the life courses of many multigenerational families. Kinscript roles arise in response to both extreme economic need and intense commitment by family members to ensure the survival of future generations, and require kin-work, kin-time, and kin-scription.

"Kin-work" is the collective labor that families share to endure over time. It includes providing help during childbirth, intergenerational care of children or dependents, and support for other relatives.

"Kin-time" is the shared understanding among family members of when and in what sequence family members should provide caregiving during transitions such as marriage, childbearing, and grandparenthood. For example, an employed single mother may rely on siblings, parents, and grandparents to pick kids up from school or provide after-school care.

"Kin-scription" is the process by which kin-work is assigned to specific family members, usually women. Women often find it difficult to refuse the demands of kin because they, and not men, are expected to keep families together because of the general belief that women are more nurturing than men.

Rebecca Anderson, 54 years old and battling lupus, became a mother again when she took in five nieces and nephews, whose three sets of parents could not care for them. Anderson's husband, Alton, who does not live with Rebecca, helps with the children occasionally, but provides no financial support.

STOP AND THINK . . .

- How do kinscripts challenge the popular notion that poor families are looking for handouts rather than relying on themselves to ensure a family's survival?
- Do kinscripts describe your family? Why or why not?

grandchildren, an ex–son-in-law or ex–daughter-in-law, and step-grandchildren if either of the parents remarries (see Chapters 15 and 16).

Also, the family life course may differ greatly for poor and middle-class families. As "Kinscripts: Ensuring Family Survival during Tough Times" shows, poor families must be especially creative and resilient to keep their members together throughout the life course.

CRITICAL EVALUATION   Most of the family development studies are micro level, but some examine family patterns cross-culturally and historically (see Thornton, 2001). This perspective is especially useful for therapists and practitioners who counsel families that are experiencing problems such as constant arguments or sexual infidelity.

Critics point out several limitations. First, some believe that the family life cycle stages are artificial because "the processes of life are not always so neatly and cleanly segmented" (Winton, 1995: 39). Second, despite the recent work on kinscripts and extended families, most developmental theories are limited to examining nuclear, heterosexual, and traditional families. For example, gay and lesbian households are generally excluded from family life course analyses (Laird, 1993).

A third criticism is that family development theory is largely descriptive rather than explanatory (Ingoldsby et al., 2004). For example, this perspective explores *how* developmental tasks change over time, but not *why* some family members are more successful than others in learning the necessary developmental skills across a life course or why white, nuclear, middle-class families can vary quite a bit in parenting styles (see Chapter 12).

Fourth, some critics question why developmental theories often gloss over sibling relationships, which are among the most important emotional resources we have throughout life and especially after the last parent dies (McGoldrick et al., 1993). Thus, some have concluded, family development theory still "deals with a fairly small part of the elephant" (Burr, 1995: 81).

The Symbolic Interaction Perspective

symbolic interaction theory
Examines the everyday behavior of individuals.

Symbolic interaction theory (sometimes called *interactionism*) is a micro-level perspective that examines individuals' everyday behavior (see Goffman, 1959). Symbolic interactionists examine how our ideas, beliefs, and attitudes shape our daily lives, including those of our families. For a symbolic interactionist, a father's batting practice with his daughter isn't simply batting practice. It's a behavior that conveys messages such as "I enjoy spending time with you" or "Girls can be good baseball players."

The Japanese tea ceremony is an ancient ritual that involves more than just preparing and serving tea. It also requires learning the rules on proper gestures, language, clothing, utensils, and behavior.

SYMBOLS   The symbolic interaction perspective looks at subjective, interpersonal meanings and how we communicate them using *symbols:* words, gestures, or pictures that stand for something. If we are to interact effectively, our symbols must have *shared meanings*, or agreed-upon definitions. Such shared meanings include wearing engagement and wedding rings, following time-honored family traditions, and celebrating important events such as birthdays and anniversaries.

SIGNIFICANT OTHERS   One of the most important shared meanings is the *definition of the situation*, or the way we perceive reality and react to it. Relationships often break up, for example, because partners have different perceptions of the meanings of dating, love, communication, and sex. As one of my students observed, "We broke up because Dave wanted sex. I wanted intimacy and conversation." We typically learn our definitions of the situation

through interaction with **significant others**, people in our primary groups—such as parents, close friends, relatives, and teachers—who play an important role in our socialization (see Chapters 1 and 5).

FAMILY ROLES According to symbolic interaction theory, each family member plays more than one role. A man, for example, may be a husband, father, grandfather, brother, son, uncle, and so on. Roles are *relational*, or complementary, because they're connected to other roles—mothers have children, husbands have wives, and aunts have nieces and nephews. Roles also carry *reciprocal* rights and responsibilities. For instance, parents must take care of their children and expect obedience. Children have the right to be safe and fed, but are also expected to be courteous and perform assigned tasks.

Roles require different behaviors both within and outside the family, and people modify and adjust their roles as they interact with other role players. For example, you probably interact differently with Mom, Grandma, and Uncle Ned than you do with your brothers and sisters. And you probably interact still differently when you're talking to someone else's parent, a professor, or an employer.

CRITICAL EVALUATION One of the most common criticisms of symbolic interaction theory is that it ignores macro-level factors that affect family relationships. For instance, families living in poverty, and especially single mothers, are likely to be stigmatized and must often raise their children in unsafe neighborhoods. Such constraints increase stress, feelings of helplessness, and family conflict—all of which can derail positive everyday interactions (Dodson and Luttrell, 2011).

A related criticism is that interactionists sometimes have an optimistic and unrealistic view of people's everyday choices. Most of us enjoy little flexibility in our daily lives because deeply embedded social arrangements and practices benefit those in power. For example, people are usually powerless when corporations transfer jobs overseas or cut the pension funds of retired employees.

A third criticism is that interactionists often overlook the irrational and unconscious aspects of behavior (LaRossa and Reitzes, 1993). That is, people don't always behave as reflectively as symbolic interactionists assume. We often act impulsively or make hurtful comments, for instance, without thinking about the consequences of our actions or words.

The Social Exchange Perspective

The fundamental premise of **social exchange theory** is that people seek through their interactions with others to maximize their rewards and to minimize their costs (see Homans, 1974; Blau, 1986). As a result, most people will continue in a relationship as long as there are more benefits than losses or both are about equal.

WHAT DO WE EXCHANGE? We bring to our relationships a variety of resources—some tangible, some intangible—such as energy, money, material goods, status, intelligence, control, good looks, youth, power, talent, fame, or affection. People "trade" these resources for more, better, or different assets that another person has. And as long as the costs are equal to or lower than the benefits, the exchanges will seem fair or balanced (see Chapters 8, 10, and 14).

From a social exchange perspective, when the costs of a marriage outweigh the rewards, the couple may separate or divorce. On the other hand, many people stay in unhappy marriages or relationships because the rewards seem equal to the costs: "It's better than being alone," "I don't want to hurt the kids," or "It could be worse."

ARE OUR EXCHANGES CONSCIOUS? Cost–reward decisions may or may not be conscious. Some of the research on stepfamilies shows, for example, that even though they're unhappy, partners sometimes stay together because it seems easier

significant others People in our primary groups who play an important role in our socialization.

 Watch on MySocLab

Video: Symbolic Interactionism

 Read on MySocLab

Document: The Nature of Symbolic Interactionism

social exchange theory Proposes that people seek through their interactions to maximize their rewards and minimize their costs.

Since you asked . . .
- Why don't people just leave romantic relationships or marriages when they feel unloved?

to do so compared with the problems of going through a (or another) divorce. As a result, family members may adapt to the existing situation rather than consciously seek a more beneficial or rewarding relationship (see Chapter 15).

CRITICAL EVALUATION   Some critics contend that exchange theorists put too much weight on rational behavior. People don't always calculate the potential costs and rewards of every decision. In other cases, some of our behavior is impulsive, some people are more self-aware than others, and we rarely have the personal power, skills, resources, or social status to make the decisions we want (see, for example, Miller, 2005, and Zafirovski, 2005).

Exchange theory is also limited to explaining behavior that is motivated by immediate costs or rewards. In many ethnic groups, family duties take precedence over individual rights. Traditional Asian cultures stress filial responsibility, which requires children, especially sons, to make sacrifices for the well-being of their parents and siblings (Hurh, 1998; Do, 1999). Similarly, many Middle Eastern families teach children to value family harmony rather than "me first" benefits (see Chapter 4).

The Family Systems Perspective

family systems theory Views the family as a functioning unit that solves problems, makes decisions, and achieves collective goals.

Family systems theory views the family as a functioning unit that solves problems, makes decisions, and achieves collective goals. The emphasis is not on individual family members but on how the members interact within the family system, how they communicate, how family patterns evolve, and how individual personalities affect family members (Rosenblatt, 1994; Day, 1995).

WHAT HOLDS FAMILIES TOGETHER?   Family systems analysts are interested in the implicit or explicit rules that hold families together. A key concept is *equilibrium*. That is, a change in one part of the family or the external environment sets in motion an adjustment process to restore the family to the way it was in the past—to regain equilibrium. Thus, during stressful times such as illness, unemployment, or the death of a loved one, family members must make changes and adapt so that the family can keep going (Broderick, 1993).

According to the family systems perspective, family members must work together to make decisions and solve problems.

CRITICAL EVALUATION   Some critics maintain that family systems theory has generated a lot of terminology but little insight into how the family really functions. Also, because the perspective originated in the study of dysfunctional families in clinical settings, some question whether the theory can be applied to healthy families. Finally, because much of research is based on case studies, the results are limited because they can't be generalized to larger groups (Holman and Burr, 1980; Nye and Berardo, 1981; Day, 1995).

MAKING CONNECTIONS

- Return to *Table 2.1* (p. 36) for a moment. Does this model illustrate your family of orientation? What about your family of procreation? If not, how have the stages you've experienced been different?

- Why does your family behave the way it does? Which theory or theories seem to be the most useful to you in answering this question? Why?

Combining Theories

We've looked at eight of the major family theories separately, but researchers and practitioners often use several perspectives to interpret data or choose intervention strategies. For example, a counselor might draw on social exchange, symbolic interaction, development, and systems theories to shed light on the problems in a couple's relationship.

Counselors who work with children with attention deficit hyperactivity disorders (ADHD) typically combine ecological and family systems perspectives in conducting assessments and

developing interventions (Bernier and Siegel, 1994). Instead of simply focusing on the child or the family, clinicians usually observe the child in his or her natural environment, involve the child's teacher, and educate grandparents about ADHD. Thus, both researchers and practitioners often rely on several theories to explain or respond to family-related issues.

Family Research Methods

Why are we attracted to some people and not to others? Why are many young adults postponing marriage? To answer these and other questions about the family, social scientists typically use seven major research methods: surveys, clinical research, field research, secondary analysis, content analysis, experiments, and evaluation research. (See *Table 2.2* for a summary of these data-collection methods.)

Family researchers also rely on qualitative and quantitative approaches. In **qualitative research**, social scientists examine and interpret nonnumerical material that they then interpret. Examples of qualitative data include verbal or written narratives, letters, diaries, photographs, and other images such as online ads (see Gilgun, 2012, for a history of qualitative family research). In **quantitative research**, researchers focus on a numerical analysis of people's responses or specific characteristics. Examples include collecting or examining data on race and ethnicity, family size, and age at first marriage. Census Bureau data are probably the most comprehensive sources of quantitative information about family-related characteristics.

2.3 Describe seven data-collection methods that researchers use to study families, and identify each of the method's strengths and limitations.

 Watch on MySocLab

Video: Research Methodology

qualitative research A data-collection process that examines and interprets nonnumerical material.

quantitative research A data-collection process that focuses on a numerical analysis of people's responses or specific characteristics.

TABLE 2.2	Seven Common Data Collection Methods in Family Research	
Method	**Strengths**	**Limitations**
Surveys	Fairly inexpensive and simple to administer; interviews have high response rates; findings often can be generalized to the whole population.	Mailed questionnaires may have low response rates; respondents may be self-selected; interviews usually are expensive.
Clinical research	Helps people who are experiencing family problems; offers insights for theory development.	Usually time consuming and expensive; findings can't be generalized.
Field research	Flexible; offers deeper understanding of family behavior; can be expensive or inexpensive depending on the project's scope and location.	Difficult to quantify and to maintain observer-participant boundaries; the observer may be biased or judgmental; findings can't be generalized.
Secondary analysis of existing data	Usually accessible, convenient, and inexpensive; often longitudinal and historical.	Information may be incomplete; some documents may be inaccessible; some data can't be collected over time.
Content analysis	Usually inexpensive; can recode errors; unobtrusive; permits comparisons over time.	Can be labor intensive; coding is often subjective (and may be distorted); may reflect social class bias.
Experiment	Attempts to demonstrate cause and effect; usually inexpensive; many available participants; can be replicated.	Subjects aren't representative of larger populations; artificial laboratory setting; findings can't be generalized.
Evaluation research	Usually inexpensive and versatile; valuable in real-life applications.	The quality of research varies; the social context may affect the researchers and the results.

Watch on MySocLab

Video: Qualitative Methods in Research

Since you asked . . .

- Because they've never contacted me, my family, or my friends, how can pollsters draw conclusions about our behavior or attitudes?

surveys Data-collection methods that systematically collect information from respondents through questionnaires or interviews.

population Any well-defined group of people (or things) that researchers want to know something about.

sample A group of people (or things) that are representative of the population that researchers want to study.

probability sample Each person (or thing) has an equal chance of being chosen because the selection is random.

nonprobability sample There is little or no attempt to get a representative cross-section of a population.

Neither method is inherently better or worse than the other; the choice depends on the researcher's purpose. For instance, if you wanted in-depth information on grandparents who are raising their grandchildren, you'd use qualitative methods. If, on the other hand, you wanted to find out whether the number of grandparents who are raising their grandchildren has increased over the years, you'd use quantitative methods. Or, if you were interested in both questions, you'd use both methods.

Surveys

Researchers use **surveys** to systematically collect data from respondents through questionnaires or interviews. Before the data collection begins, researchers must first decide on the population and sample.

POPULATIONS AND SAMPLES A **population** is any well-defined group of people (or things) that researchers want to know something about. Obtaining information about and from populations is problematic, however. The population may be so large that it would be too expensive and time consuming to conduct the research. In other cases—such as adolescents who use drugs—it's impossible even to identify the population we would like to study.

As a result, researchers typically select a **sample**, a group of people (or things) that are representative of the population they want to study. In a **probability sample**, each person (or thing) has an equal chance of being chosen because the selection is random. *Random-digit dialing* involves selecting area codes and exchanges followed by four random digits. In a procedure called *computer-assisted telephone interviewing (CATI)*, the interviewer uses a computer to select random telephone numbers, reads the questions to the respondent from a computer screen, and then keys the replies into pre-coded spaces. Because the selection is random, the findings can be generalized to the population from which the sample was drawn.

In a **nonprobability sample**, there is little or no attempt to get a representative cross-section of a population. Instead, researchers use other criteria, such as convenience or the availability of participants. The findings can't be generalized to *any* group because the people (or things) have not been selected randomly; that is, they have not had an equal chance of being selected for the study.

Millions of viewers choose a winner by voting for their favorite *American Idol* singer. Does the voting represent all of the show's fans?

Television stations, newsmagazines, and entertainment shows often provide a toll-free number or an Internet site and encourage viewers to "vote" on an issue or a person (as is done on the popular TV contest *American Idol*). According to one observer, such Internet polls are "good for a few laughs" but are little more than "the latest in a long series of junk masquerading as indicators of public opinion because the participants aren't representative of everyone's opinion" (Witt, 1998: 23).

But what if a million people cast a vote? Don't such large numbers reflect how most people think? No. Because the respondents are self-selected, the pollster simply has "junk" from a very large number of people. Since the mid-1990s, the number of online surveys, including polls, has boomed. Are the results valid? "How Good Are Online Surveys?" examines some of the benefits and costs of this data-collection method.

QUESTIONNAIRES AND INTERVIEWS Researchers collect survey data using questionnaires, face-to-face or telephone interviews, or a combination of these tools. Questionnaires can be mailed, used during an interview, or self-administered to large groups of respondents. Student course evaluations are good examples of self-administered questionnaires. The telephone is popular because it's an inexpensive way to collect data. Computer-assisted telephone interviewing, for example, generates a probability sample and provides interviewers with a consistent set of questions.

STRENGTHS Surveys—whether by phone or a self-administered questionnaire—offer many advantages. They're usually inexpensive, easy to administer, and have a fast turnaround rate. When assured that their answers will remain anonymous or confidential, respondents are generally willing to answer questions on sensitive topics such as income, sexual behavior, and drug use.

Changes | How Good Are Online Surveys?

Two types of electronic surveys are becoming increasingly popular. The first type is a survey sent via e-mail, either as text in the body of the message or as an attachment. The second type is the more familiar survey that is posted on a website. How scientific are these online surveys? And can researchers draw accurate conclusions from the results?

Online surveys offer many benefits. Most important, they are cost effective and can represent a broad spectrum of the general population. Second, because respondents can choose when to take the survey and how much time to devote to each question, they are more likely to provide thoughtful answers. Third, Web surveys provide respondents with visual material, including videos, to look at and respond to (Helm, 2008; Keeter 2009, 2010).

Online surveys also have limitations. A major problem is that if respondents, though large in number, haven't been chosen randomly and don't represent a population, the results can't be generalized. A related drawback is that research firms often reward participants with gifts, certificates, or cash, which means that the incentives generate self-selected groups.

Third, Internet usage varies greatly by factors such as social class and age. For example, the higher a family's income and a person's education level, the greater the likelihood of being an Internet user. And, of those age 65 or older, only 52 percent use the Internet (Zickuhr and Madden, 2012). This means that the findings will be distorted because they don't include older people or those from lower socioeconomic levels.

The fourth limitation of online surveys is that marketing research can be especially deceptive. For example, a survey's "terms of use" might tell respondents that if they accept a $10 coupon toward a future purchase, the company has the right to sell any of the person's information (including credit/debit card numbers) to another company or to automatically enroll them in a membership that can cost at least $15 a month. Often, however, respondents don't read the fine print authorizing marketers to do so (Dang, 2008).

STOP AND THINK . . .
- Have you ever participated in an online survey? Why or why not?
- So far, there are no established federal guidelines for online surveys. Should there be such guidelines? Or should respondents be responsible for reading the fine print and deciding whether or not to participate?

With the innovation of "robo-polls," the entire interview is conducted by a programmed recording that interprets the respondent's spoken answers, records them, and determines how to continue the interview. This method is cost effective because it cuts out the cost of hiring people, but respondents may be more reluctant to answer sensitive questions (Babbie, 2013).

Face-to-face interviews have high response rates (up to 99 percent). Interviewers can also record the respondent's body language, facial expressions, and intonations, which are often useful in interpreting verbal responses. If a respondent doesn't understand a question or is reluctant to answer, the interviewer can clarify, probe, or keep the respondent from digressing. An astute interviewer can also gather information on variables such as social class by observing the respondent's home and neighborhood.

In some isolated locations, census workers must often travel to places that are inaccessible by road or without conventional postal addresses. In the 2000 and 2010 censuses, they relied on snowshoes, all-terrain vehicles, airplanes, cross-country skis, lobster boats, horses, and even dog sleds to reach remote dwellings (Associated Press, 2010).

LIMITATIONS   One of the major limitations of surveys that use mailed questionnaires is a low response rate, often only about 10 percent (Gray et al., 2007). If the questions are unclear, complicated, or seen as offensive, respondents may simply throw the questionnaire away or offer opinions on subjects they know nothing about (Babbie, 2013). During the 2010 census, the Census Bureau used only a short form and slogans such as "10 Questions, 10 Minutes" to encourage people to mail back the forms.

Telephone surveys also have response problems. Because many people have become oversaturated with marketing research, they use caller ID or voicemail to avoid accepting calls from strangers. Telephone surveys have become especially problematic because of the increased use of cell phones (Thee, 2007). Because cell users are more likely than the general population to be young, it's difficult to draw a probability sample. In addition, people who use their cell phones in public places, and many do, may be unwilling to answer questions about sensitive topics (Christian et al., 2010).

Surveys might also be problematic because people may skip or lie about questions that they consider intrusive. As a result, the research results will be invalid or incomplete because the researcher may have to scrap a key variable such as income.

Another concern is a *social desirability bias*—the tendency of respondents to give the answer that they think they "should" give or that will cast them in a favorable light (Cooperman, 2010). For example, the proportion of Americans who say they voted in a given election is always much higher than the actual number of votes cast. Respondents also underreport behaviors perceived negatively (such as using alcohol or illicit drugs or having multiple sexual partners), but exaggerate attendance at religious services, watching the evening news, and washing their hands after using a restroom (Prior, 2009; Radwin, 2009; Zezima, 2010).

There's also a problem of a survey's sponsorship. For example, the highly respected Harris poll reported, several weeks before Valentine's Day in 2005, that 37 percent of Americans said that a lobster dinner is the most romantic meal. It turned out that the poll had been sponsored by the Red Lobster restaurant chain (Moore, 2005).

Unlike questionnaires and telephone surveys, face-to-face interviews can be very expensive. They can also be dangerous. During the 2010 census, for example, a number of Americans, frustrated with the economy and government, took their anger out on census takers. Hundreds of census workers were shot at with pellet guns; hit by baseball bats; spat at; and confronted with shotguns, packs of snarling pit bulls, pickaxes, crossbows, and hammers (Morello, 2010).

Because the survey is the research approach you will encounter most often, it's important to be an informed consumer. As "Can I Trust This Survey?" shows, you can't simply assume that the survey is accurate or representative of a larger population.

Clinical Research

Clinical research studies individuals or small groups of people who seek help from mental health professionals and other social scientists. Many clinical researchers focus on family conflict and intervene in traumatic situations such as marital rape and incest. They also try to change negative interactions such as hostile communication patterns and family environments that lead to eating disorders, drug use, and other problems.

Clinical research often relies on the *case study method*, a traditional approach used by social workers, psychologists, clinical sociologists, and marriage counselors. A case study provides in-depth information and detailed and vivid descriptions of family life (see LaRossa, 1984, for good examples of case studies across the life course). Clinical practitioners work with families or individuals on a one-to-one basis, but they also use other research methods such as experiments and direct observation (that we'll examine shortly).

STRENGTHS   Case studies are typically linked with long-term counseling, which can be beneficial for individuals and families. Useful intervention strategies can be disseminated fairly quickly to thousands of other practitioners. Clinicians may also offer insights about family dynamics that can enrich theories such as symbolic interaction or family systems perspectives. Researchers can then incorporate these insights into larger or more representative studies that use surveys or other data-collection methods.

LIMITATIONS   Clinical research and case studies are usually time consuming and expensive. Clinicians typically see only people with severe problems or those who are willing and financially able to seek help. Therefore, the results aren't representative of average or even of troubled families.

Another problem is that clinical studies are subjective and rarely ask, "Where's the evidence?" If a client complains that he has a terrible mother, for example, clinicians may try to help the patient cope better instead of meeting the mother or talking to other family members. As a result, some critics contend, subjective clinical opinions are often contrary to empirical evidence (see Begley, 2009, and Wright, 2009). It is *not* true, for instance, that low self-esteem causes aggression, drug use, and low achievement. How parents treat a child in the first years of life does *not* determine a child's later intellectual and emotional success. Nor do abused children inevitably become abusive parents, causing a cycle of abuse (see Chapters 12 and 14).

clinical research The study of individuals or small groups of people who seek help from mental health professionals or other social scientists.

Field Research

In **field research**, researchers collect data by systematically observing people in their natural surroundings. Field research usually is highly structured and typically involves carefully designed projects in which data are recorded,

field research Data are collected by systematically observing people in their natural surroundings.

described, and sometimes converted into quantitative summaries. The studies examine complex communication patterns, measure the frequency of specific acts (such as the number of nods or domineering statements), and note the duration of a particular behavior (such as length of eye contact) (Stillars, 1991). Thus, field research is much more complex and sophisticated than it appears to be to the general public or to an inexperienced researcher.

TWO KINDS OF OBSERVATIONS   Field research includes several types of observation. In *participant observation*, researchers interact naturally with the people they are studying but don't reveal their identities as researchers (see "Is My Classmate an Undercover Professor?").

In *nonparticipant observation*, researchers study phenomena without being part of the situation. For example, child psychologists, clinicians, and sociologists often study young children in classrooms through one-way mirrors.

Some field research studies are short term (such as observing whether and how parents discipline their unruly children in grocery stores during a few weeks or months). Others, called *ethnologies*, require a considerable amount of time in the field. For example, Sudhir Venkatesh (2008), while a graduate student at the University of Chicago, spent more than 6 years studying the culture and members of the Black Kings, a crack-selling gang in Chicago's inner city. Researchers sometimes combine both participant and nonparticipant observation (see Anderson, 1999).

STRENGTHS   Field research is more flexible than some other methods. For instance, the researcher can decide to interview (rather than just observe) key people after beginning to collect data. Most important, because field research rarely disrupts a natural setting, the people being studied aren't influenced by the researcher's presence. For example, sociologist Phillip Davis (1996) and some of his research assistants have observed adults' verbal aggression and corporal punishment of children in public settings such as indoor shopping malls, zoos, amusement parks, flea markets, city streets, rapid transit stations, bus depots, and toy stores.

LIMITATIONS   Observation can be expensive if a researcher needs elaborate recording equipment, must travel far or often, or lives in a different society or community for an extended period. Researchers who study other cultures must often learn a new language, which is a time-consuming task.

ASK YOURSELF

Is My Classmate an Undercover Professor?

For one academic year, Cathy Small, an anthropology professor at Northern Arizona University, posed as a full-time undergraduate student and enrolled in the university where she teaches. After the university approved the project, Small paid her tuition, registered for five courses each semester, and moved into a dorm. She didn't tell her classmates that she was a professor and revealed her identity only to a few students with whom she developed close friendships.

Small found that many undergraduates valued future careers more than their coursework; that students read only the material they thought would be on an exam; that cheating was common; and that many of the dorm students spent more time socializing, drinking, and partying than preparing for classes. She concluded, however, that being a student in the twenty-first century is more stressful than she had imagined.

Small's book, published under the pseudonym Rebekah Nathan (2005), received positive comments primarily from parents and college administrators who got an inside view of student life, especially the numerous pressures of a student culture that emphasizes both fun and achievement. Others, especially faculty and researchers, criticized Small's undercover research as dishonest and unethical (Farrell and Hoover, 2005).

STOP AND THINK . . .

- Field researchers often go undercover to observe their subjects. Why, then, did some people criticize Small's participant observer role as dishonest and unethical?

- Do you think that pretending to be a student for a year is similar to being a student over a number of years?

A field researcher may encounter other barriers in collecting the data. Homeless and battered women's shelters, for example, are usually—and understandably—wary of researchers' intruding on their residents' privacy. Even if the researcher has access to such a group, it's often difficult to maintain objectivity while collecting and interpreting the data because the topic can evoke strong emotional reactions such as anxiety, anger against perpetrators, and sympathy for subjects.

Another problem is the researchers' ability (or lack of it) to recognize and address their own biases. Because observation is personal and subjective, it can be difficult to maintain one's objectivity while collecting and interpreting the data (see Venkatesh, 2008).

Secondary Analysis of Existing Data

Family researchers also rely heavily on **secondary analysis**, an examination of data that have been collected by someone else. The data may be historical materials (such as court proceedings), personal documents (such as letters and diaries), public records (such as state archives on births, marriages, and deaths), and official statistics (such as those generated by the Census Bureau in *Figure 2.3*).

secondary analysis An examination of data that have been collected by someone else.

The availability and usage of large-scale data sets have grown dramatically in the past two decades. The *Journal of Marriage and Family*, a major periodical in the field of family studies, reflects the growing reliance on secondary data sources. In 2003, 75 percent of the studies published in this journal used secondary data analysis, compared with only 33 percent in 1983 (Hofferth, 2005).

Many of the statistics in this textbook come from secondary analysis. The sources include the U.S. Census Bureau and other government agencies, reputable nonprofit organizations, and university research centers (see Greenstein, 2006, for a summary of the major sources of secondary analysis in family research).

STRENGTHS Secondary analysis is usually accessible, convenient, and inexpensive. Census Bureau information on topics such as employment, household income, and medical insurance is readily available at public and college libraries and on the Internet.

Because secondary data often are *longitudinal* (collected at two or more points in time) rather than *cross-sectional* (collected at one point in time), they offer the added advantage of allowing the researcher to examine trends (such as age at first marriage) over time. Increasingly, both longitudinal and cross-sectional publications provide the reader with colorful pie charts and other figures that are easy to read and understand; the publications also incorporate PowerPoint® presentations.

Another advantage of secondary analysis is the high quality of the data. Nationally known survey organizations have large budgets and well-trained staff equipped to address any data-collection problems. Because the samples are representative of national populations, researchers can be more confident about generalizing the findings.

→ NOTE: Please answer BOTH Question 5 about Hispanic origin and Question 6 about race. For this census, Hispanic origin are not races.

5. **Is this person of Hispanic, Latino, or Spanish origin?**
   - ☐ **No,** not of Hispanic, Latino or Spanish orgin
   - ☐ Yes, Mexican, Mexican Am., Chicano
   - ☐ Yes, Puerto Rican
   - ☐ Yes, Cuban
   - ☐ Yes, another Hispanic, Latino, or Spanish origin—*Print orgin, for example, Argentinean, Colombian, Dominican, Nicaraguan Salvadoran, Spaniard, and so on.* ↘

6. **What is this person's race?** *Mark one ⊠ or more boxes.*
   - ☐ White
   - ☐ Balck, African Am., or Negro
   - ☐ American Indian or Alaska Native—*Print name of entrolled or principal tribe.* ↘

☐ Asian Indian	☐ Japanese	☐ Native Hawaiian
☐ Chinese	☐ Korean	☐ Guamanian or Chamorro
☐ Filipino	☐ Vietnamese	☐ Samoan
☐ Other Asian—*Print race, for example, Hmong, Laotian, Thai, Pakistani, Cambodian, and so on.* ↘		☐ Other Pacific Islander—*Print race, for example, Fijian, Tongan, and so on.* ↘

   - ☐ Some other race—*Print race.* ↘

FIGURE 2.3 Reproduction of the Questions on Hispanic Origin and Race from the 2010 Census
Source: U.S. Bureau, 2010 Census Questionnaire.

LIMITATIONS   Secondary analysis has several drawbacks. First, the data may not provide the information needed. In 2000, for example, the Census Bureau changed how it counted race and ethnicity to include the growing numbers of recent immigrants and mixed-race Americans. Doing so increased the accuracy of gauging racial and ethnic diversity, but created 63 categories of possible racial-ethnic combinations. As a result, today's numbers are different from those before 2000, making comparisons across time on race and ethnicity problematic (Saulny, 2011).

Second, accessing historical materials may be difficult because the documents may be fragile, housed in only a few libraries in the country, or part of private collections. Determining the accuracy and authenticity of historical materials can also be problematic.

Third, the data may not include specific information the researcher is looking for. If you wanted to examine some of the characteristics of couples who are separated but not divorced, for example, you'd find little national data. Consequently, you'd have to rely on studies with small and nonrepresentative samples or collect such data yourself.

Content Analysis

content analysis A data-collection method that systematically examines some form of communication.

Content analysis is a data-collection method that systematically examines some form of communication. This is an unobtrusive approach that a researcher can apply to almost any form of written or oral communication: speeches, TV programs, newspaper articles, advertisements, office e-mails, songs, diaries, advice columns, poems, or Facebook chatter, to mention just a few.

The researcher develops categories for coding the material, sorts and analyzes the content of the data in terms of frequency, intensity, or other characteristics, and draws conclusions about the results. One year the students in my family courses did a content analysis of online birth announcements. (They found, among other things, that the images routinely portrayed the girls as passive and the boys as active.)

Family researchers and other social scientists have used content analysis to examine a number of topics. A few examples are images of women and men in video games and music videos, changes in child-rearing advice in popular parenting magazines, and gender and ethnic differences in yearbook photographs (Martins et al., 2009; Rutherford 2009; Clarke, 2010; Downs and Smith, 2010; Zhang et al., 2010; Wallis 2011; Wondergem and Friedlmeier, 2012).

STRENGTHS   A major advantage of content analysis is that it is usually inexpensive and often less time consuming than other data-collection methods, especially field research. For instance, if you wanted to examine the content of television commercials that target older people, you wouldn't need fancy equipment, a travel budget, or a research staff.

Also, researchers can correct coding errors fairly easily by redoing the work. This is not the case with surveys. If you mail a questionnaire with poorly constructed items, it's too late to change anything.

A third advantage is that content analysis is unobtrusive. Because researchers aren't dealing with human subjects, they don't need permission to do the research and don't have to worry about influencing the respondents' attitudes or behavior.

Finally, researchers can obtain specific data over time. In one study, the researchers analyzed gender portrayals in the 101 top-grossing G-rated films in the United States and Canada between 1990 and 2005 (Smith et al., 2010). It would be very difficult, using most other data-collection methods, to analyze such material over a 15-year period.

LIMITATIONS   Content analysis can be very labor intensive, especially if a project is ambitious. In the research on the top-grossing films, for instance, it took several years to code the major characters' words and behavior. A related disadvantage is that the coding may be subjective. Having several researchers on a

project can increase coding objectivity, but many content analyses are performed by only one researcher.

Finally, content analysis often reflects social class bias. Because most books, articles, speeches, films, and so forth are produced by people in upper socio-economic levels, content analysis rarely captures the behavior or attitudes of working-class and poor people. Even when documents created by lower-class individuals or groups are available, it's difficult to determine whether the coding reflects a researcher's social class prejudices.

Experiments

Unlike surveys, field research, secondary analysis, and content analysis, an **experiment** is a carefully controlled artificial situation that allows researchers to manipulate variables and measure the effects. A researcher tests a prediction, or *hypothesis*, stating that one specified variable affects another ("Watching a film on racial discrimination reduces prejudice"). The *independent variable* (watching a film on racial discrimination) predicts that there will be an effect on the *dependent variable* (reducing prejudice).

In the *experimental group*, the subjects are exposed to the independent variable (watching the film). In the *control* group, they are not. Before the experiment, the researcher measures the dependent variable (prejudice) in both groups using a *pretest*. After the experimental group is exposed to the independent variable (the film on racial discrimination), the researcher measures both groups again using a *posttest*. If the researcher finds a difference in the scores on the dependent variable, she or he assumes that the independent variable has a causal effect on the dependent variable.

Family research that uses experiments is rare because "children or adults cannot be assigned at random to different family types, to different partners, to different income groups" (Hofferth, 2005: 903–904). In contrast, medical researchers routinely search for cause-effect relationships between many variables, such as diet and blood pressure or stress and physical illness. Still, experimental designs are useful in studying family-related issues such as the effectiveness of anger management workshops, interaction skills between partners, and the usefulness of support groups in coping with the death of a child or divorce (see, for example, Ebling and Levenson, 2003, and Fetsch et al., 2008).

STRENGTHS   A major advantage of the controlled (laboratory) experiment is its isolation of the causal variable. For example, if students who get information in sex education classes show changes in their attitude toward casual sex, a school might decide to provide sex education for all of its students.

A second strength of experimental designs is their low cost. Usually, there's no need to purchase special equipment and most participants expect little or no compensation. Also, experiments often are less time consuming than data-collection methods such as field research.

A third advantage is that experiments can be replicated many times and with different participants. Such replication strengthens the researchers' confidence in the *validity*, or accuracy, and *reliability*, or consistency, of the research findings.

LIMITATIONS   One disadvantage of laboratory experiments is their reliance on student volunteers or paid respondents. Students often feel obligated to participate as part of their grade, or they may fear antagonizing an instructor who's conducting a study. Participants might also give the answers that they think the researcher expects. In the case of paid subjects, those who are the busiest, don't need the extra cash, move, or become ill may not participate fully or may drop out of the study.

A second and related disadvantage is that the results of experimental studies can't be generalized to a larger population because they come from small or self-selected samples. For example, college students who participate in

experiment   A carefully controlled artificial situation that allows researchers to manipulate variables and measure the effects.

 Watch on MySocLab
Video: Experiments

Researchers often study interaction by observing people in natural settings. What are the advantages and disadvantages of experimental designs such as this one?

experiments aren't necessarily representative of other college students, much less of people who aren't in college.

Another limitation is that experiments, especially those conducted in laboratories, are artificial. People *know* that they're being observed and may behave very differently than they would in a natural setting.

Finally, even if a researcher finds that there's an association between variables (such as watching a film and reducing prejudice), it doesn't mean that the former "causes" the latter. For example, the control group's responses in the posttest may have been influenced by other factors, such as the participants giving socially desirable responses or being in a racial-ethnic course that changes some of their prejudices.

Evaluation Research

evaluation research The process of determining whether a social intervention has produced the intended result (also known as *program evaluation*).

Evaluation research (also known as *program evaluation*) is the process of determining whether a social intervention has produced the intended result (Babbie, 2013). In family studies, social interventions are typically programs and strategies that seek to prevent or change negative outcomes such as teenage pregnancy, delinquency, substance abuse, interpersonal violence, and unemployment. Evaluation research isn't a specific method but relies on all the standard data-collection methods described previously.

Like clinical research, evaluation research is *applied*. It assesses a social program for an agency or organization and compares a program's achievements with its goals (Weiss, 1998). Administrators can use the findings to improve a program or to initiate a new service such as an after-school program.

STRENGTHS Evaluation research is valuable for several reasons. First, because local and state governments have been cutting their budgets since the early 1980s, social service agencies often rely on evaluation research to streamline their programs, and to achieve the best results at the lowest possible cost because they have to do more with less (Kettner et al., 1999).

Second, evaluation research is versatile because it includes qualitative and quantitative approaches. It can address almost any topic such as the effectiveness of driver education programs, "Just Say No" abstinence programs in schools, job training programs, and premarital counseling, to name just a few. The research costs can also be low if, for example, researchers can use secondary analysis rather than collect new data.

Third, evaluation research addresses real-life problems that confront many families and communities. Because state and local resources are shrinking and there are hundreds of intervention strategies, evaluation research can be invaluable to program directors or agency heads in deciding which programs to keep, improve, or cut (Peterson et al., 1994).

LIMITATIONS A number of research evaluations are flawed or inadequate because they're poorly designed. Many evaluations address only one or a few of the many factors in intervention strategies and outcomes that affect behavior. For example, adolescent usage of illicit drugs is not only due to individual high-risk decisions but also to multiple interrelated ecological contexts such as peers, school policies, and cultural values (see *Figure 2.2* on p. 35 and the related discussion). Other weaknesses include using nonprobability samples but generalizing the results; not including important variables, such as a person's sex, because some interventions work better for women than men; and not measuring long-term effects (Jakubowski et al., 2004; Bandy, 2012; Bell et al., 2012).

The social context also affects evaluation research because of politics, vested interests, and a conflict of interests. Agency heads may ignore the results if the study shows that the program isn't tapping the neediest groups, the administrators are wasting money, or caseworkers are making serious mistakes. Groups that fund the evaluation may pressure researchers to present only positive findings. Also, the results aren't well received if they contradict deeply held beliefs, challenge politicians' pet projects, or conflict with official points of view (Reardon-Anderson et al., 2005; Olson, 2010; Babbie, 2013).

Consider the DARE (Drug Abuse Resistance Education) program, introduced in 1983. DARE relied on trained volunteers from local police departments to address elementary school children on the dangers of drug use. When social scientists evaluated DARE in 1994, 1998, and 1999, however, they concluded that there was no significant difference in the drug use of students who had completed the DARE curriculum and those who had not. When DARE funding was threatened, its promoters dismissed the evaluation research results as "voodoo science" (Miller, 2001). Since then, academic researchers have worked with DARE programs to revise the curriculum, but there have been no evaluations so far.

Researchers have to weigh the benefits and limitations of each research approach in designing their studies, and often use a combination of strategies to achieve their research objectives. Despite the researcher's commitment to objectivity, ethical debates and politically charged disagreements can influence much family research.

DARE programs have been popular with schools, police departments, parents, and politicians across the country. However, evaluation research has found that the curriculum doesn't reduce the incidence of drug use among students.

MAKING CONNECTIONS

- If you get information from the Internet, how do you determine whether the material is accurate?

- Suppose the dean of your college asked you to evaluate your courses. What variables would you examine, and why? Do you think that your social context might affect the findings you report or omit? Why or why not?

Ethics, Politics, and Family Research

Researchers today operate under much stricter guidelines than they did in the past. In conducting their research, what ethical and political dilemmas do family researchers (and other social scientists) encounter?

Ethical Research

Because so much research relies on human subjects, the federal government, university institutional review boards (IRBs), and many professional organizations have formulated ethics codes to protect research participants. Among other

2.4 Describe the ethical standards that researchers must follow, and explain the political, religious, and community constraints that researchers encounter.

Since you asked . . .

- If I participate in a research study, how can I be sure that any information about me will be confidential?

professional organizations, the National Council on Family Relations and the American Sociological Association have published codes of ethics to guide researchers. *Table 2.3* summarizes the key elements of these codes. Regardless of the discipline or the research methods used, all ethical standards have at least three golden rules:

- First, *do no harm* by causing participants physical, psychological, or emotional pain.

- Second, the researcher must get the participants' *informed consent* to be in a study. This includes the participants, knowing what the study is about and how the results will be used. Sociologists can use deception (such as not revealing that they are researchers) if doing so doesn't harm the participants, if the research has been approved by an IRB, and if the researcher explains the purpose of the study to participants at the end of the research (American Sociological Association, 1999: 14).

- Third, researchers must always protect a participant's *confidentiality*, even if the participant has broken a law that she or he tells the researcher about.

TABLE 2.3 Some Basic Principles of Ethical Family Research
• Obtain all participants' consent to participate and their permission to quote their responses, particularly if the research concerns sensitive issues.
• Do not exploit participants or research assistants involved in the research for personal gain.
• Never harm, humiliate, abuse, or coerce participants, either physically or psychologically. This includes the withholding of medications or other services or programs that might benefit participants.
• Honor all guarantees to participants of privacy, anonymity, and confidentiality.
• Use the highest methodological standards and be as accurate as possible.
• Describe the limitations and shortcomings of the research in published and unpublished reports.
• Identify the sponsors who funded the research.

Since you asked. . .

- How do ethics violations affect us?

SCIENTIFIC DISHONESTY For the most part, ethical violations are unintentional because they result from ignorance of statistical procedures, simple arithmetic mistakes, or inadequate supervision. However, some disciplines are more susceptible to scientific dishonesty than others. Medical researchers, especially, have been accused of considerable scientific misconduct. Some of the alleged violations have included the following: changing research results to please the corporation (usually tobacco or pharmaceutical companies) that sponsored the research; being paid by companies to deliver speeches to health practitioners that endorse specific drugs, even if the medications don't reduce health problems; allowing drug manufacturers to ghostwrite their articles (and even draft textbooks) that are published in prestigious medical journals; and falsifying data (Blumenstyk, 2009; Johnson, 2010; Basken, 2011; Ornstein and Weber, 2011; Project on Government Oversight, 2010; Shamoo and Bricker, 2011).

In the social sciences, including family studies, some data-collection methods are more prone to ethical violations than others. Surveys, secondary analysis, and content analysis are less vulnerable because the researchers typically don't interact directly with subjects, affect their behavior, or become personally involved with the respondents. In contrast, experiments and field research can raise ethical questions (see "Is My Classmate an Undercover Professor?" on p. 46).

Scholars also face emerging ethical questions when they do research using social networks and other online environments. Institutional review boards lack

experience with Web research and sometimes unintentionally approve social science research that might violate ethics guidelines.

Ethics violations affect all families. For example, the National Alliance for the Mentally Ill, despite its numerous contributions, embraces claims on the prevalence of mental disorders—based on methodologically flawed studies—that contend that half of Americans suffer from a mental disorder, especially depression, at some point in their lives. In fact, scientific studies show that about 75 percent of depressive symptoms are normal and temporary (such as worrying about an upcoming exam or grieving the death of a family member or friend). If mental-health organizations can convince politicians that mental illness is widespread, however, they can get more funding for mental-health services, including normal and temporary depression. And pharmaceutical companies are eager to sell costly antidepressant drugs. As a result, many groups benefit by labeling even normal depression as an "overwhelming problem" (Horwitz and Wakefield, 2006: 23; see also Chapter 12).

www.benitaepstein.com

© Benita Epstein 1996

"I already wrote the paper. That's why it's so hard to get the right data."

Political, Religious, and Community Pressures

The late Senator William Proxmire became famous (or infamous, some believe) for his "Golden Fleece" awards to social research projects that he ridiculed as a waste of taxpayers' money. Some of his examples included studies of stress and why people fall in love. The legitimacy of social science research becomes especially suspect in the eyes of political, religious, and some community groups when the studies focus on sensitive social, moral, or political issues.

One of the most controversial research topics is human sexuality. Alfred Kinsey and his colleagues carried out the first widely publicized research on sexuality in the late 1940s and early 1950s. The studies had some methodological flaws, such as using only volunteers, but many social scientists have hailed Kinsey's research as a major springboard that launched scientific studies of human sexuality in subsequent decades (see Chapter 7).

Research on teenage sexual behavior is valuable because it provides information that public health agencies and schools can circulate about sexually transmitted diseases (such as HIV) and contraception. Nonetheless, many local jurisdictions have refused to let social scientists study adolescent sexual behavior. Some parents believe that such research violates student privacy and might make a school district look bad (if a study reports a high incidence of drug use or sexual activity, for example). Some religious groups, school administrators, and politicians have also opposed studies on teen sexuality because they believe that the research undermines traditional family values or makes deviant behavior seem normal (Carey, 2004; Kempner et al., 2005).

In some extreme cases, doing research on topics that politicians don't approve of may jeopardize a scholar's current or future employment. For example, a tenured professor at a large research university came close to being fired by a governor who disapproved of his research on abstinence education (Bailey et al., 2002). More recently, several legislators grilled and threatened to fire sociology and education faculty members at a major state university who taught sexuality courses and listed topics such as oral sex and male prostitution as their research interests (Stombler, 2009).

MAKING CONNECTIONS

- Some researchers violate ethical guidelines to bring in more money for their institutions. Is this acceptable, especially if the grants provide funds that can be used to reduce class sizes, pay for much-needed computer labs, and increase library staff and student services?

- On a number of sites (such as www.ratemy professors.com), students can say anything they want about faculty. Should students identify themselves instead of submitting the evaluations anonymously? Are the comments representative of all the students in a course? Should faculty set up similar public sites and evaluate students by name?

CONCLUSION

Like the family itself, the study of marriage and the family reflects *changes* in the evolution of theories and *constraints* resulting from the limitations of research designs. There has been much progress in family research, and researchers have more *choices* in the methods available to them. At the same time, "there is plenty of reason for marriage and family scholars to be modest about what they know and humble about what they do not" (Miller, 1986: 110). One of the things we should know more about is how historical processes have shaped the contemporary family, the topic of the next chapter.

On MySocLab

 Study and **Review** on MySocLab

REVIEW QUESTIONS

2.1. Describe three ways that theory and research can help people make better decisions about their families.

1. How and why can misinformation about family issues be dangerous?

2. What is the relationship between theory and research, particularly regarding families?

2.2. Describe eight major family theoretical perspectives, identify whether each is macro- and/or micro-level, and summarize the strengths and limitations of each perspective.

3. How, specifically, do the eight theories differ in understanding and explaining families?

4. What is the difference between a macro-level and micro-level perspective? Is one more useful than the other in understanding families?

5. What are the strengths and weaknesses of each theoretical perspective?

6. Why do researchers and practitioners use several theoretical perspectives to interpret data or choose intervention strategies?

2.3. Describe seven data-collection methods that researchers use to study families and identify each of the method's strengths and limitations.

7. How does qualitative and quantitative research differ? Is one approach better than the other?

8. How, specifically, do the seven data-collection methods differ?

9. State two strengths and two limitations of each data-collection method.

10. How do researchers know which data-collection methods to use?

2.4. Describe the ethical standards that researchers must follow, and explain the political, religious, and community constraints that researchers encounter.

11. Why is it important to follow ethical research codes?

12. Why are researchers in some disciplines more likely to violate ethical rules?

13. What family-related topics spark the greatest resistance by some religious groups, parents, school administrators, and politicians? Why?

The Family in Historical Perspective

Listen to Chapter 3 on MySocLab

LEARNING OBJECTIVES	
After you read and study this chapter you will be able to:	
Compare families today and those in Colonial America.	**3.1**
Compare the family experiences of early American Indians, African Americans, and Mexican Americans.	**3.2**
Describe the impacts of industrialization, urbanization, and immigration on the American family.	**3.3**
Describe three important factors that shaped the modern family.	**3.4**
Explain two important trends that changed the family during the "golden fifties."	**3.5**
Describe three ways that families in the United States have changed since the 1960s.	**3.6**

DATA DIGEST

- Between **20 and 33 percent of women in Colonial America were pregnant at the time of marriage**.

- During the **Great Depression**, one of four Americans was unemployed and farm income fell by 50 percent.

- **Average household size declined** from 4.6 in 1900 to 2.6 in 2000, or by 44 percent.

- Of the almost 7 million **women who were employed** during World War II, 75 percent were married.

- In 1890, **the median age at first marriage** was 26 for men and 22 for women. By 1940, the age declined to 24 for men, but remained the same for women. Between 1950 and 1970, the median age at first marriage was 23 for men, and 21 for women.

- **Divorce rates** per 1,000 couples increased from 3 in 1890 to 8 in 1920, 9 in 1940, and 18 in 1946. The rate declined to 9 in 1958, and then reached 11 in 1967.

Sources: Demos, 1970; Chafe, 1972; Plateris, 1973; Tuttle, 1993; Hobbs and Stoops, 2002; Fields, 2004.

n 1890, Joel Coleman, a recent Jewish immigrant to New York City who was living in a crowded and dilapidated tenement house, wrote home:

> *Dear Father . . . Right now, during the winter, work is very slow. It happens every winter; therefore, we see to it that we have put something aside for those winter months. On the whole my life here is not bad and I cannot complain about America, except for one thing—my health was better at home, in Poland, where the air was better. Here I often get sick, but I prefer not to write about it (Wtulich, 1986: 218).*

Other immigrants' letters, like Coleman's, often spoke of loneliness, low wages, hard and intermittent work, language barriers, poverty, and numerous hardships. Life was difficult and unpredictable in the "land of plenty."

Historians have raised some interesting questions about the past: Were the American colonists as virtuous as they have been portrayed, especially in K–12 textbooks? Did people really pull together to help each other during the Great Depression? Were the 1950s as happy as many people insist they were? This chapter addresses these and similar questions.

3.1 Compare families today and those in colonial America.

Listen on MySocLab

Audio: NPR: History of U.S. Marriage

The Colonial Family

Colonial families differed from modern ones in social class, religious practices, and geographic dispersion, but family roles and family structure were similar. The diversity that characterizes modern families also existed in colonial times.

Family Structure

The nuclear family was the most prevalent family form both in England and in the first English-speaking settlements in the United States. An elderly grandparent or an apprentice sometimes lived with or near his or her family, but few households were made up of extended families for long periods (Goode, 1963; Laslett, 1971). Families typically started out with six or seven children, but high infant death rates resulted in small households, with large age differences between the children.

The Puritans who migrated to New England and founded Plymouth colony in Massachusetts in 1620 were Protestants who adhered to strict moral and religious values. They believed that the community had a right to intervene in families that did not perform their duties properly. In the 1670s, for example, the Massachusetts General Court directed towns to appoint parish officers to ensure that marital relations were harmonious and that parents disciplined unruly children (Mintz and Kellogg, 1988).

Few people survived outside families during the colonial period. Most settlements were small (fewer than 100 families), and each family was considered a "little commonwealth" that performed a variety of functions. The family was a

- Self-sufficient *business*, in which all family members worked together to produce and exchange goods
- *School* that taught children to read
- *Vocational institute* that instructed children and prepared them for jobs through apprenticeships
- Miniature *church* that guided its members in daily prayers, personal meditation, and formal worship in the community
- *House of correction* to which the courts sentenced idle people and nonviolent offenders to be servants
- *Welfare institution* that gave its members medical and other care and provided a home for relatives who were orphaned, aging, sick, or homeless (Demos, 1970)

As you'll see later in this chapter, all these functions changed considerably with the onset of industrialization.

Sexual Relations

Colonial Americans tried to prevent premarital intercourse in several ways. One was *bundling*, a courting custom in which a fully dressed young man and woman spent the night in a bed together, separated by a wooden board. The custom was adopted because it was difficult for the young suitor, who had to travel many miles (either by foot or horseback), to return home the same night, especially during harsh winters. Because the rest of the family shared the room, it was considered quite proper for the bundled young man and woman to continue their conversation after the fire was out (McPharlin, 1946).

Despite safeguards such as bundling, premarital sex was common because a large number of colonial women were pregnant at the time of marriage (see the Data Digest). Keep in mind, however, that sexual activity was generally confined to engaged and married couples. The idea of a casual meeting that included sexual intercourse would have been utterly foreign to the Puritans.

Nonmarital births were also fairly common among young women who immigrated to the southern colonies as indentured (contracted) servants. They typically came to the United States alone because they were from poor families that could not afford to migrate together. Because these very young (under age 15) women were alone and vastly outnumbered by men, they were vulnerable to sexual attacks, especially by employers (Harari and Vinovskis, 1993).

Puritans condemned adultery and illegitimacy because they threatened family stability. Sometimes local newspapers denounced a straying spouse publicly:

Catherine Treen, the wife of the subscriber, behaved in the most disgraceful manner, by leaving her own place of abode, and living in a

In the early colonies, courting couples were usually, but not always, chaperoned by parents and other adults. As a result, large numbers of young women were pregnant when they married (see text).

criminal state with a certain William Collins, a plaisterer, under whose bed she was last night, discovered, endeavoring to conceal herself. Her much injured husband thinks it absolutely necessary to forewarn all persons from trusting after such flagrant proof of her prostitution (cited in Lantz, 1976: 14).

Few records, however, documented men's extramarital affairs. Although frowned upon, a husband's infidelity was considered normal. And because the courts did not enforce a father's economic obligation, it was women who paid the costs of bearing and raising out-of-wedlock children (Ryan, 1983). As you can see, the double standard (which we discuss later) isn't a modern invention.

Husbands and Wives

Husbands and wives worked together to make sure the family survived. As in modern society, colonists expected spouses to have strong relationships. Inequalities, however, were very much a part of early American family life.

PERSONAL RELATIONSHIPS In general, women were subordinate to men; the wife's chief duty was to obey her husband. New England clergymen often referred to male authority as a "government" that women must accept as "law." In the southern colonies, husbands often denounced assertive wives as "impertinent" (Ryan, 1983). A woman's social status and her power and prestige in the community came from the patriarchal head of the household, usually her husband or father, but other patriarchal heads included a brother or other male relative, such as an uncle (see Chapter 1).

The "well-ordered" family was based on a number of mutual responsibilities. Husbands and wives were expected to show each other "a very great affection." They should be faithful to each other and were instructed to be patient and to help each other: "If the one is sick, pained, troubled, distressed, the other should manifest care, tenderness, pity, compassion, and afford all possible relief and succour" (Scott and Wishy, 1982: 86).

In the Plymouth colony, women had the right to transfer property. In 1646, for example, when a man wanted to sell his family's land, the court called in his wife to make sure that she approved of the sale. The courts also granted liquor and other business licenses to women. And they sometimes offered a woman protection from a violent husband. For example, the Plymouth court ordered a whipping for a man who kicked his wife off a stool and into a blazing fireplace (Demos, 1970; Mintz and Kellogg, 1988). Such protections weren't typical in other colonies, however.

In a few cases, the local courts permitted divorce. The acceptable grounds were limited to desertion, adultery, bigamy, and impotence. Incompatibility was recognized as a problem but not serious enough to warrant divorce. It wasn't until about 1765, when romantic love emerged as a basis for marriage, that "loss of affection" was mentioned as a reason for divorce (Cott and Pleck, 1979).

WORK AND THE ECONOMY Men were expected to be industrious, hardworking, and ambitious, and they were responsible for the family's economic survival. Husbands and wives often worked side by side. Men, women, and children all produced, cultivated, and processed goods for the family's consumption. When necessary, men cared for and disciplined the children while women worked in the fields.

Much of women's work was directed toward meeting the needs of others. In his 1793 *Female Guide*, a New Hampshire pastor defined women's role as "piety to God—reverence to parents—love and obedience to their husbands—tenderness and watchfulness over their children—justice and humanity to their dependents" (quoted in Cott, 1977: 22–23).

Both sexes were praised for being wealthy and industrious, but men were expected to initiate economic activity and women were expected to support them and to be frugal. In 1692, the influential minister and author Cotton Mather described women's economic role as being only "to spend (or save) what others get" (Cott, 1977).

In some cases, unmarried women, widows, and those who had been deserted by their husbands turned their homemaking activities into self-supporting businesses. Some used their homes as inns, restaurants, or schools and sold homemade foods. Others made a living by washing, mending, nursing, serving as midwives, or producing cure-all and beauty potions.

Some widows continued their husbands' businesses in masculine areas such as chocolate and mustard production, soap making, cutlery, coach making, rope making, publishing, printing, horseshoeing, net making, and whaling and running grocery stores, bookstores, drugstores, and hardware stores. And some of these businesswomen advertised regularly in the local newspapers (Matthaei, 1982).

In general, however, the economic roles of women, especially wives, were severely constrained. Women had little access to credit, couldn't sue to collect debts, weren't allowed to own property, and were rarely chosen as executors of wills (Ryan, 1983).

Children's Lives

Poor sanitation, crude housing, limited hygiene, and dangerous physical environments characterized Colonial America. Between 10 and 30 percent of all children died before their first birthday, and fewer than two out of three children lived to see their tenth birthday. Cotton Mather (1663–1728) fathered 14 children, but only one outlived his father: Seven died shortly after birth, one died at age 2, and five died in their early twenties (Stannard, 1979).

In the New England colonies, children's lives were dominated by the concepts of repression, religion, and respect (Adams, 1980). Puritans believed that children were born with original sin and were inherently stubborn, willful, selfish, and corrupt. The entire community—parents, school, church, and neighbors—worked together to keep children in their place.

Compared with contemporary children, Puritan children were expected to be extraordinarily well behaved, obedient, and docile (see *Figure 3.1*). Within

Since you asked . . .
- Why did colonial women have so many children?

OF CHILDREN'S BEHAVIOR WHEN AT HOME

1. Make a Bow always when you come Home, and be immediately uncovered [take off your hat].

2. If thou art going to speak to thy Parents, and see them engaged in discourse with Company, draw back until afterwards; but if thou must speak, be sure to whisper.

3. Never speak to thy Parents without some Title of Respect, as Sir & Madam.

4. Dispute not, nor delay to Obey thy Parents' Commands.

5. Go not out of Doors without thy Parents leave, and return within the Time by them limited.

6. Quarrel not nor contend with thy Brethren or sisters, but live in love, peace, & unity.

7. Grumble not nor be discontented at anything thy Parents appoint, speak, or do.

8. Bear with Meekness and Patience, and without Murmuring or Sullenness thy Parents' Reproofs or Corrections: Even tho' it should so happen that they be causeless or undeserved.

FIGURE 3.1 Rules for Colonial Children
Source: Adapted from Wadsworth, 1712, in Scott and Wishy, 1982. For George Washington's rules of civil behavior for adults, see Haslett (2004).

40 years of their arrival in Plymouth, however, many colonists worried that their families were disintegrating, that parents were becoming less responsible, and that children were becoming less respectful of authority. Ministers repeatedly warned parents that their children were frequenting taverns, keeping "vicious company," and "tending to dissoluteness (unrestrained and immoral behavior)" (Mintz and Kellogg, 1988: 17). These concerns sound pretty modern, don't they?

Wealthy southern families were more indulgent of their children than were well-to-do families in the northern colonies, but in less affluent families, child labor was nearly universal. Even very young children worked hard, either in their own homes as indentured servants or as slaves. For example, several shiploads of "friendless boys and girls" were kidnapped in England and sent to the Virginia colony to provide cheap and submissive labor for American planters (Queen et al., 1985).

Because girls were expected to be homemakers, they received little formal education. The New England colonies educated boys, but girls were generally barred from schooling. They were commonly admitted to public schools only during the hours and seasons when boys were occupied with other affairs or were needed in the fields. As one farmer stated, "In winter it's too far for girls to walk; in summer they ought to stay at home to help in the kitchen" (quoted in Earle, 1899: 96). Women who succeeded in getting an education were often ridiculed:

> John Winthrop—the first governor of the Massachusetts Bay Colony— maintained that such intellectual exertion [as education and writing books] could rot the female mind. He attributed the madness of Ann Hopkins, wife of the Connecticut governor, to her intellectual curiosity: "If she had attended her household affairs . . . and not gone out of her way to meddle in the affairs of men whose minds are stronger, she'd have kept her wits and might have improved them usefully" (Ryan, 1983: 57).

Social Class and Regional Differences

The experiences of colonial families differed because of a number of regional and social class variations. In a study of Salem, Massachusetts, families between 1790 and 1810, sociologist Bernard Farber (1972) identified three social classes with very different socialization patterns that supported the economic structure:

- In the *merchant class*, or upper class, the patriarchs typically were shipping and commercial entrepreneurs. Family businesses were inherited, and partnerships were expanded through first-cousin marriages.

- Highly skilled occupations, apprenticeship systems, and cooperation among relatives characterized the *artisan class*, or middle class. Children were encouraged to be upwardly mobile and to find secure jobs.

- The *laboring class*, or working class, was made up mainly of migrants to the community. These people, who had no voting privileges and little education, provided much of the unskilled labor needed by the merchant class.

Colonial families also differed from one region to another. In the northern colonies, people settled in villages; in the southern colonies, they settled on isolated plantations and farms. There was an especially rigid stratification system among wealthy families, poor whites, indentured servants, and black slaves in the southern colonies.

Applying What You've Learned

How Colonial Is Your Family?

Answer the following questions based on the family you grew up in.

Yes No

☐ ☐ **1.** The main focus of my family was making ends meet.

☐ ☐ **2.** The children in our family began to do chores as early as possible.

☐ ☐ **3.** Discipline was harsh at times.

☐ ☐ **4.** The needs of the family were more important than individual needs.

☐ ☐ **5.** Our family was the center of our everyday lives.

☐ ☐ **6.** Religion was a main theme in our family.

☐ ☐ **7.** Father's rule was most important in our family.

☐ ☐ **8.** We learned basic reading, writing, and arithmetic at home.

☐ ☐ **9.** We had to get along with one another.

☐ ☐ **10.** My parents often ignored my feelings.

☐ ☐ **11.** My parents had a big say in who I dated.

☐ ☐ **12.** For my parents, romance was not as important as hard work in a potential mate.

☐ ☐ **13.** One of my parents was subordinate to the other most of the time.

☐ ☐ **14.** My parents still have strong control over my life.

Source: Based on Hammond and Bearnson, 2003: 24.

Key to "How Colonial Is Your Family?"

Add up all the "yes" answers. A score of 15 represents high colonial family traits. A score of 0 signifies no traits. If you received a high score, does this surprise you? Do high scores suggest that many modern families have traces of the colonial family? Or not?

After reading this section, some of my students dismiss the colonial family as a relic of the past. Others believe that their families have many similar characteristics. Take the quiz "How Colonial Is Your Family?" to decide for yourself.

Early American Indian, African American, and Mexican American Families

> **3.2** Compare the family experiences of early American Indians, African Americans, and Mexican Americans.

European explorers and settlers who invaded North America in the sixteenth and seventeenth centuries pushed the original inhabitants, American Indians and Mexicans, out of their territories. Except for adults who arrived in the colonies as servants—and in general they chose to indenture themselves—African Americans are the only people who did not come to America voluntarily.

The experiences of these three groups were quite different. Some families and tribes fared better than others, and there was considerable diversity within each group.

American Indians

Scholars believe that American Indians migrated to North America from Asia over a period of 30,000 years. By the time European settlers arrived, there were almost 18 million Indians living in North America who spoke approximately

300 languages. Tribes today speak 150 native languages, but many are vanishing quickly (Greenberg and Ruhlen, 1992; Ashburn, 2007; Reich et al., 2012). American Indians were diverse racially, culturally, and linguistically. This variation was reflected in kinship and family systems as well as in interpersonal relations.

FAMILY STRUCTURE Family structures and customs varied from one Indian society to another. For example, polygyny was common in more than 20 percent of marriages among Indians of the Great Plains and the northwest coast. In contrast, monogamy was the norm among the Hopi, Iroquois, and Huron nations. Some groups, such as the Creek, allowed polygyny, but few men took more than one wife because only the best hunters could support more than one wife and all of the children (Price, 1981; Braund, 1990).

matrilineal Children trace their family descent through their mother's line, and property is passed on to female heirs.

patrilineal Children trace their family descent through their father's line, and property is passed on to male heirs.

Approximately 25 percent of North American Indian tribes were **matrilineal**, which means that children traced their family descent through their mother's line rather than through that of the father (**patrilineal**). The women owned the houses, the household furnishings, the fields and gardens, the work tools, and the livestock, and all this property was passed on to their female heirs (Mathes, 1981).

Historians say that Indian women were often better off than their white counterparts. In contrast to filmmakers' stereotypes of the docile "squaw," Indian women wielded considerable power and commanded respect in many bands and tribes. "American Indian Women: Chiefs, Physicians, Politicians, and Warriors" describes some of the roles of Indian women.

Cross-Cultural and Multicultural Families

American Indian Women: Chiefs, Physicians, Politicians, and Warriors

European Christian missionaries and U.S. federal government agents saw Indian women as too powerful and independent. Nonetheless, many American Indian women and men had equal relationships. Besides being wives and mothers, they were also chiefs, physicians, politicians, and warriors.

Chiefs: Some women became chiefs because of their achievements in battle. Others replaced husbands who died. Like their male counterparts, female chiefs could declare war, resolve disputes in the community, and punish offenders.

Physicians: Women could be medicine women, or shamans, the Indian equivalent of doctors. In many Indian cultures, women also played crucial roles as spiritual leaders.

Politicians: Because a number of tribes were matrilineal and matrilocal, many women had political power. Among the Lakota, for example, a man owned only his clothing, a horse for hunting, weapons, and spiritual items. Homes, furnishings, and other property belonged to women. In many tribes, women were influential decision makers.

Warriors: Among the Apache, some women warriors were as courageous as the men, and Cheyenne women distinguished themselves in war. Lakota women maintained warrior societies, and among the Cherokee, one of the fiercest warriors was a woman who also headed a women's military society.

Women could stop war parties by refusing to supply the food needed for the journey. An Iroquois woman could initiate a war party by demanding that a captive be obtained to replace a murdered member of her clan. Creek women often were responsible for raising "war fervor" against enemies (Mathes, 1981; Braund, 1990; Stockel, 1991; Jaimes and Halsey, 1992).

Lozen, an Apache Indian, was a brave warrior and fought alongside Geronimo in the late 1800s. She was also a midwife and a healer.

STOP AND THINK . . .
- How did the roles of many white female colonists differ from those of their American Indian counterparts?
- Does this description of the varied roles of American Indian women reflect the images of them that you've seen in Hollywood movies or television shows?

MARRIAGE AND DIVORCE American Indian women typically married between ages 12 and 15, after reaching puberty. Men married at slightly older ages, between 15 and 20, usually after they had proven their ability to hunt and to provide for a family. Some parents arranged their children's marriages; others allowed young men and women to choose their own spouses.

Family structures and customs also varied. Among the Shoshone, there were no formal marriage ceremonies; the families simply exchanged gifts. Also, there were no formal rules of residence. The newly married couple could live with the family of either the groom or the bride or establish its own independent home.

Among the Zuñi of the Southwest, marriages were arranged casually, and the groom moved into the bride's household. Divorce was easy among the Zuñi and other tribes. If a wife was fed up with a demanding husband, she would simply put his belongings outside their home, and they were no longer married. The man accepted the dismissal and returned to his mother's household. If a husband wanted a divorce, he would tell his wife he was going hunting and then not return home (Stockel, 1991).

In the Great Plains, most Teton parents arranged marriages, but some unions were based on romantic love. Marriages were often lifetime associations, but divorce was easy and fairly common. A man could divorce a wife for adultery, laziness, or even excessive nagging. Both parties usually agreed to divorce, but a man could humiliate a wife by casting her off publicly at a dance or other ceremony.

CHILDREN Most Indian families were small because of high infant and child death rates. In addition, mothers nursed their children for several years, often abstaining from sexual relations until the child was weaned.

Among most American Indian nations, childhood was a happy time and parents were generally kind and loving. Mohave and Zuñi parents, for example, were indulgent; children were carefree, and discipline was rare and mild. Children were taught to be polite and gentle. Unruly children were frightened into conformity by stories of religious bogeymen rather than by physical punishment. Grandparents on both sides of the family played an active role in educating children and telling stories that reinforced the tribe's values.

PUBERTY In most Indian societies, puberty rites were more elaborate for girls than for boys. Among the Alaskan Nabesna, for example, a newly menstruating girl was secluded, forbidden to touch her body (lest sores break out) or to travel with the tribe, and had to observe strict food taboos. In contrast, among the Mohave, the observance of a girl's puberty was a private family matter that didn't include any community rituals.

Among the Teton, a boy's puberty was marked by a series of events, such as his first successful bison hunt, his first war party, his first capture of enemy horses, and other brave deeds, all of which his father commemorated with feasts and gifts to other members of the tribe.

Some tribes also emphasized the *vision quest*, a supernatural experience. After fasting and taking ritual purifying baths in a small, dome-shaped sweat lodge, a young boy left the camp and found an isolated place, often the top of a butte or other elevated spot. He then waited for a vision in which a supernatural being instructed him on his responsibilities as an adult (Spencer and Jennings, 1977).

THE IMPACT OF EUROPEAN CULTURES The French, Spanish, Portuguese, and British played a major role in destroying much of American Indian culture. Europeans exploited the abundant North American resources of gold, hardwood forests, fertile land, and fur. Missionaries, determined to convert the "savages" to Christianity, were responsible for some of the cultural destruction.

Since you asked . . .

- Is it true that American Indian men dominated the women?

" They like our turkey dinner tradition, but they're not so sure about the **wife-swapping.** "

Disregarding important cultural values and beliefs, missionaries tried to eliminate religious ceremonies and practices such as polygyny and matrilineal inheritance (Price, 1981).

Indian tribes coped with military slaughter, enslavement, forced labor, land confiscation, coerced mass migration, and involuntary religious conversions (Collier, 1947). By the end of the seventeenth century, staggering numbers of American Indians in the East had died from diseases for which they had no immunity, such as influenza, measles, smallpox, and typhus. The Plymouth colony was located in a deserted Indian village whose inhabitants had been devastated by epidemics carried by European settlers.

By the 1670s, only 10 percent of the original American Indian population of New England survived. At least 50 tribes became extinct as a result of disease and massacre. In the eighteenth and nineteenth centuries, the diversity of American Indian family practices was reduced even further through ongoing missionary activities, intrusive federal land policies, and intermarriage with outside groups (John, 1988).

African Americans

One colonist wrote in his journal that on August 20, 1619, at the Jamestown settlement in Virginia, "there came . . . a Dutch man-of-warre that sold us 20 negars." These first African Americans were brought over as indentured servants. After their terms of service, they were free to buy land, marry, and hire their own labor.

These rights were short lived, however. By the mid-1660s, the southern colonies had passed laws prohibiting blacks from testifying in court, owning property, making contracts, legally marrying, traveling without permission, and congregating in public places. The slave trade grew in both the northern and southern colonies over several decades.

Some early statesmen, such as President Thomas Jefferson, publicly denounced slavery but supported it privately. In 1809, for example, Jefferson maintained that "the Negro slave in America must be removed beyond the reach of mixture" for the preservation of the "dignity" and "beauty" of the white race. At the same time, Jefferson had a slave mistress, Sally Hemmings, and fathered children with her. Inconsistent to the end, he freed five of his slaves in his will but left the other 182 slaves to his heirs (Bergman, 1969).

FAMILY STRUCTURE   Until the 1970s, sociologists and historians maintained that slavery had emasculated black fathers, forced black mothers to become the matriarchs of their families, and destroyed the African American family. Historian Herbert Gutman (1983) dispelled many of these beliefs with his study of 21 urban and rural communities in the South between 1855 and 1880. Gutman found that 70 to 90 percent of African American households were made up of a husband and wife (although they couldn't marry legally) or a single parent and her or his children.

Among black women who were heads of households, most held that position not because they had never married but because their husbands had died or were sold to another owner. Women usually had only one or two children. Thus, according to Gutman, in the nineteenth century, black families were stable, intact, and resilient.

3.2

Since you asked . . .
• Did slavery destroy the black family?

MARRIAGE Throughout the colonies, it was difficult for a slave to find a spouse. In northern cities, most slaves lived with their masters and weren't allowed to associate with other slaves. In the southern colonies, most slaves lived on plantations that had fewer than 10 slaves. Because the plantations were far apart, it was difficult for slave men and women to find a mate of roughly the same age. In addition, overwork and high death rates due to disease meant that marriages didn't last very long (Mintz and Kellogg, 1988).

To ensure that slaves would remain on the plantations and bear future slaves, many owners encouraged them to marry (even though the marriages were not recognized legally) and to have large families. Yet marriages were fragile. As "A Slave Auction" shows, owners often separated family members. Studies of slave families in Mississippi, Tennessee, and Louisiana show that such auctions ended 35 to 40 percent of marriages (Gutman, 1976; Matthaei, 1982).

Constraints A Slave Auction

Alex Haley was a journalist who had taught himself to read and write, and had a 20-year career in the U.S. Coast Guard. He was catapulted to fame when his book, *Roots: The Saga of an American Family* (1976), became a best-seller and was made into one of the first mini-series on television. In the book, Haley traced six generations of his ancestors, the first of whom was abducted at age 16 from Gambia, West Africa, in 1767. The following excerpt is a powerful description of how African families were destroyed by slavery:

During the day a number of sales were made. David and Caroline were purchased together by a Natchez planter. They left us, grinning broadly, and in a most happy state of mind, caused by the fact of their not being separated. Sethe was sold to a planter of Baton Rouge, her eyes flashing with anger as she was led away.

The same man also purchased Randall. The little fellow was made to jump, and run across the floor, and perform many other feats, exhibiting his activity and condition. All the time the trade was going on, Eliza was

crying aloud and wringing her hands. She besought the man not to buy him, unless he also bought herself and Emily. She promised, in that case, to be the most faithful slave that ever lived.

The man answered that he could not afford it, and then Eliza burst into a paroxysm of grief, weeping plaintively. Freeman turned round to her, savagely, with his whip in his uplifted hand, ordering her to stop her noise, or he would flog her. Unless she ceased that minute, he would take her to the yard and give her a hundred lashes. . . . Eliza shrunk before him and tried to wipe away her tears, but it was all in vain. She wanted to be with her children, she said, the little time she had to live.

All the frowns and threats of Freeman could not wholly silence the afflicted mother. She kept on begging and beseeching them, most piteously, not to separate the three. Over and over again she told them how she loved her boy. A great many times she repeated her former promises—how very faithful and obedient she would be, how hard she would labor day and night, to the

last moment of her life, if he would only buy them all together.

But it was of no avail; the man could not afford it. The bargain was agreed upon, and Randall must go alone. Then Eliza ran to him, embraced him passionately, kissed him again and again, and told him to remember her—all the while her tears falling in the boy's face like rain.

Freeman damned her, calling her a blubbering, bawling wench, and ordered her to go to her place, and behave herself, and be somebody. . . . He would soon give her something to cry about, if she was not mighty careful, and that she might depend on.

The planter from Baton Rouge, with his new purchase, was ready to depart. "Don't cry, mama. I will be a good boy. Don't cry," said Randall, looking back, as they passed out of the door.

What has become of the lad, God knows. It was a mournful scene indeed. I would have cried myself if I had dared.

Source: Adapted from Solomon Northrup, cited in Meltzer (1964: 87–89).

HUSBANDS AND FATHERS   Several black scholars have noted that white, male, middle-class historians and sociologists have misrepresented the slave family (McAdoo, 1986; Staples, 1988). One example is the portrayal of husbands and fathers. In contrast to popular conceptions of the African American male as powerless, adult male slaves provided important role models for boys:

> *Trapping wild turkeys required considerable skill; not everyone could construct a "rabbit gum" equal to the guile of the rabbits; and running down the quick, battling raccoon took pluck. For a boy growing up, the moment when his father thought him ready to join in the hunting and to learn to trap was a much-sought recognition of his own manhood (Genovese, 1981: 239–40).*

These activities increased families' nutritional intake and supplemented monotonous and inadequate diets.

African male slaves also often served as surrogate fathers to many children, both blood relatives and others. Black preachers, whose eloquence and morality commanded the respect of the entire community, were also influential role models. Men made shoes, wove baskets, constructed furniture, and cultivated the tiny garden plots allotted to their families by the master (Jones, 1985).

WIVES AND MOTHERS   Many historians describe African American women as survivors who resisted the slave system. Mothers raised their children, cooked, made clothes for their families, maintained the slave cabin, and toiled in the fields. Because the African American woman was often both a mammy to the plantation owner's children and a mother to her own, she experienced the exhausting *double day*—a full day of domestic chores plus a full day of work outside the home—at least a century before middle-class white women coined the term and later substituted *second shift* for *double day* (see Chapters 5 and 13).

Black women got little recognition for such grueling schedules and were often subjected to physical punishment. Pregnant slaves were sometimes forced to lie face down in a specially dug depression in the ground, which protected the fetus while the mother was beaten, and some nursing mothers were whipped until "blood and milk flew mingled from their breasts" (Jones, 1985: 20).

In the South, children as young as age 2 or 3 were put to work. They fetched things or carried the train of a mistress's dress. Masters often gave slave children to their own offspring as gifts (Schwartz, 2000).

Only a few female slaves worked in the master's home, known as "the big house." Most females over age 10 worked in the fields, sunup to sundown, six days a week. As a result, mothers had to struggle to maintain a semblance of family life:

> *Occasionally, women were permitted to leave the fields early on Saturday to perform some chores around the slave quarters. Their homes were small cabins of one or two rooms, which they usually shared with their mate and their children, and perhaps another family secluded behind a crude partition (Ryan, 1983: 159).*

Popular films such as *Gone with the Wind* often portray house slaves as doing little more than adjusting Miss Scarlett's petticoats and announcing male suitors. In reality, domestic work was as hard as fieldwork. Fetching wood and water, preparing three meals a day over a smoky fireplace, and washing and pressing clothes for an entire family was backbreaking labor.

Female servants sometimes had to sleep on the floor at the foot of the mistress's bed. They were often forced into sexual relations with the master.

The kitchens that slaves worked in were so hot, especially in summer, there was often a separate building to prevent fires and keep the temperature down in the main house.

Injuries were common: Minor infractions met with swift and severe punishment, and servants suffered abuse ranging from jabs with pins to beatings that left them disfigured for life (Jones, 1985).

ECONOMIC SURVIVAL *Ethnic Notions*, a memorable documentary, shows that many Hollywood movies, books, and newspapers have portrayed slaves as helpless, passive, and dependent people who couldn't care for themselves. Recent evidence has challenged such stereotypes. For example, an archaeological team that excavated Virginia plantations found evidence that some enslaved Africans were entrepreneurs: They traded fish and game for children's toys, dishes, and other household items (Wheeler, 1998).

Also, many slaves hid important personal possessions and items stolen from plantation owners in underground storage areas. Thus, slaves were hardly meek or submissive. Instead, they used effective tactics such as negotiating with their masters over assigned tasks and breaking tools to slow the pace of their work (Berlin, 1998; Morgan, 1998).

AFTER EMANCIPATION After slavery was abolished in 1863, many mothers set out to find children from whom they had been separated many years earlier. Numerous slaves formalized their marriages, even though the $1 fee for the marriage license equaled about two weeks' pay for most. A legal marriage was an important status symbol, and a wedding was a festive event (Degler, 1981; Staples, 1988; King, 1996).

Some writers have claimed that the African American family, already disrupted by slavery, was further weakened by migration to cities in the North in the late 1800s (Frazier, 1939; Moynihan, 1970). However, many black migrants tried to maintain contact with their families in the South. When black men migrated alone, "a constant flow of letters containing cash and advice between North and South facilitated the gradual migration of whole clans and even villages" (Jones, 1985: 159). Others returned home frequently to join in community celebrations or to help with planting and harvesting on the family farm. Thus, many African American families remained resilient despite difficult conditions.

Mexican Americans

After 30 years of war and conflict, in 1848 the United States annexed territory in the West and Southwest that was originally part of Mexico. Despite the provisions of the Treaty of Guadalupe Hidalgo, which guaranteed security of their property, the federal government confiscated the land of most Mexican families. Land speculators defrauded countless other landowners. Most of the Mexicans and their descendants became laborers. The loss of land, an important economic base, had long-term negative effects on Mexican American families (see Chapter 4).

WORK AND GENDER Whether they were born and grew up in the United States or migrated from Mexico, Mexican laborers were essential to the prosperity of southwestern businesses. Employers purposely avoided hiring Mexicans for skilled jobs because "they are available in such [great] numbers and . . . they [would] do the most disagreeable work at the lowest wages" (Feldman, 1931: 115).

During the 1800s, men typically worked on the railroads or in mining, agriculture, ranching, or low-level urban occupations (such as dishwashing). Women worked as domestics, cooks, live-in house servants, or laundresses; in canning and packing houses; and in agriculture (Camarillo, 1979).

By the 1930s, Mexican women made up a major portion of the workers in the garment-manufacturing sweatshops in the Southwest. American labor codes stipulated a pay rate of $15 a week, but Mexican women were paid less than $5, and some earned as little as 50 cents a week. If the women protested, they lost

3.2

Mexican women made up a large number of the sweatshop workers in the Southwest.

familism A cultural belief that family relationships take precedence over the concerns of individual family members.

Since you asked . . .

• Why were many Mexican families tightly knit?

machismo A concept of masculinity that stresses attributes such as dominance, assertiveness, pride, and sexual prowess.

their jobs. Illegal migrants were especially vulnerable because they were intimidated by threats of deportation (Acuna, 1988). Despite the economic exploitation they faced, many Mexican families preserved traditional family structures, family roles, and child-rearing practices.

FAMILY STRUCTURE   Mexican society was characterized by **familism**; that is, family relationships took precedence over individual well-being. (You'll see in Chapter 4 that familism still characterizes much of contemporary Latino culture, including Mexican Americans.) The nuclear family often embraced an extended family of several generations, including cousins, in which kin provided emotional and financial support.

A key factor in conserving Mexican culture was the practice of *compadrazgo*, in which parents, children, and the children's godparents maintained close relationships. The *compadres*, or co-parents, were godparents who enlarged family ties, similar to the fictive kin described in Chapter 1. Godparents were close family friends who had strong ties with their godchildren throughout life and participated in rites of passage such as baptism, confirmation, first communion, and marriage.

The godparents in the *compadrazgo* network provided both discipline and support. They expected obedience, respect, and love from their godchildren. They were also warm and affectionate and helped the children financially whenever possible. For girls, who led cloistered and protected lives, visiting their godparents' families was a major source of recreation (Williams, 1990).

FAMILY ROLES   Women were the guardians of family traditions, even though many mothers worked outside the home because of economic necessity. Despite the disruptions caused by migratory work, women nurtured Mexican culture through folklore, songs, baptisms, weddings, and celebrations of birthdays and saints' days (Garcia, 1980). In the traditional family, women defined their roles primarily as homemakers and mothers, whereas the male head of the family had all the authority. Masculinity was expressed in the concept of **machismo**, which stresses male attributes such as dominance, assertiveness, pride, and sexual prowess (see Chapter 4 for recent controversies about the *machismo* concept).

This notion of male preeminence carried with it the clear implication of a double standard. Men could engage in premarital and extramarital sex, for example, but women were expected to remain virgins until marriage; to be faithful to their husbands; and to limit their social relationships, even after marriage, to family and female friends (Mirande, 1985; Moore and Pachon, 1985).

CHILDREN   The diaries, letters, and other writings available today suggest that, at least in middle- and upper-class families, children were socialized according to gender. Boys did some of the same domestic chores as their sisters, but they had much more freedom than girls did. Young girls were severely restricted in their social relationships outside the home. A girl was expected to learn how to be a good mother and wife—a virtuous example for her children and the "soul of society" (del Castillo, 1984: 81).

According to the diary of a teenage girl who lived on the outskirts of San Antonio, Texas, from 1889 to 1892, her brother was responsible for helping with tasks such as laundry and chopping wood. He was allowed to go into town on errands and to travel around the countryside on his horse. In contrast, she wasn't allowed to go into town with her father and brother or to attend chaperoned dances. She couldn't visit neighbors, and she attended only one social event in

a six-month period, when her family traveled into town to visit her aunt during Christmas (del Castillo, 1984).

THE EUROPEAN INFLUENCE Although they suffered less physical and cultural destruction than American Indians did, Mexican Americans endured a great deal at the hands of European frontiersmen, land speculators, and politicians. By the mid-1800s, when most Mexican Americans were beginning to experience widespread exploitation, newly arrived European immigrant families were also harnessed under the yoke of industrialization.

MAKING CONNECTIONS

- Look at *Figure 3.1* on p. 59 again. Some of my students think that such rules for colonial children were ridiculous. Others think that we should resurrect some of these practices because many parents are too permissive. What do you think?

- Regardless of your cultural heritage, did your ancestors' experiences affect your family's values and behavior?

Industrialization, Urbanization, and European Immigration: 1820 to 1930

3.3 Describe the impacts of industrialization, urbanization, and immigration on the American family.

The lives of many U.S. families changed dramatically from about 1820 to 1930 as a result of two massive immigration waves from Europe. More than 10 million immigrants—mostly English, Irish, Scandinavian, and German—arrived during the first wave, from 1830 to 1882. During the second wave, from 1882 to 1930, immigrants were predominantly Russian, Greek, Polish, Italian, Austrian, Hungarian, and Slavic.

The Industrial Revolution led to extensive mechanization, which shifted home manufacturing to large-scale factory production. As the economic structure changed, a small group of white, Anglo-Saxon, Protestant (often referred to as WASP), upper-class families prospered from the backbreaking labor of Mexicans, Asians, European immigrants, and many American-born whites. European immigrants endured some of the most severe pressures on family life.

Family Life and Social Class

Immigrants, poor single women and mothers, and low-income family members had to work outside the home to earn enough to purchase goods and services. By the late eighteenth century, the family lost its function as an economic unit in higher-income classes. The growth of new industries, businesses, and professions helped create a new middle class and a new ideology among upper- and middle-class white families about the home, work, and the ideal of womanhood later termed the *cult of domesticity* (Welter, 1966).

THE DEBUT OF THE "CULT OF DOMESTICITY" The **cult of domesticity** glorified women's domestic role. This ideology defined the world of work as male, and the world of the home as female. Women were viewed as less vigorous and forceful than men and therefore less suited to public life, including the rough world of work that exposed people to temptations, violence, danger, corruption, and selfishness.

cult of domesticity An ideology that glorified women's domestic roles.

Such attitudes encouraged separate spheres of activity: By the early 1800s, most middle- and upper-class men's work was totally separated from the household, and family life revolved around the man's struggle to make a living (and be the "breadwinner"). The good wife turned the home into a comfortable retreat from the pressures that the man faced in the workplace and stayed home to raise and nurture their children (and be the "housewife").

Since you asked . . .
- Why did the role of housewife emerge?

Between 1820 and 1860, women's magazines, ministers' sermons, and physicians in popular health books defined and applauded the attributes of "true

Changes | Characteristics of "True Womanhood"

One author describes nineteenth-century working-class women as "without corsets, matrons with their breasts unrestrained, their armpits damp with sweat, with their hair all over the place, blouses dirty or torn, and stained skirts" (Barret-Ducrocq, 1991: 11). Expectations for upper-class women (whom middle-class women tried to emulate) were quite different because the cult of domesticity required every good and proper young woman to develop and adhere to four cardinal virtues: piety, purity, submission, and domesticity.

Piety True women were believed to be more religious and spiritual than men. Motherhood was a religious obligation, and a lack of religion in females was considered "the most revolting human characteristic." If a woman had to read, she should choose spiritually uplifting books from a list of "morally acceptable authors," preferably religious biographies.

Purity True women were pure in heart, mind, and body, and the loss of virginity before marriage was worse than death. In *The Young Lady's Friend*

(1837), Mrs. John Farrar gave practical advice about staying out of trouble: "Sit not with another in a place that is too narrow; read not out of the same book; let not your eagerness to see anything induce you to place your head close to another person's." Without sexual purity, a woman was a lower form of being, a "fallen woman," unworthy of a man's love and unfit for any company.

Submission Men were the movers and doers, whereas good women were passive bystanders. True women were expected to be gentle, passive, obedient, childlike, weak, dependent, and protected. Unlike men, they should work silently, unseen, and only for affection, not for money or ambition. A woman should stifle her own talents and devote herself "to sustain her husband's genius and aid him in his arduous career."

Domesticity Domesticity was a woman's most prized virtue. Woman's place was in the home, which was supposed to be a cheerful place, so that brothers, husbands, and sons would not go elsewhere to have a

good time. Women should keep busy at morally uplifting tasks, one of which was housework. For example, the repetitiveness of routine tasks (such as making beds) inculcated patience and perseverance, and proper management of the home was considered a complex art: "There is more to be learned about pouring out tea and coffee than most young ladies are willing to believe."

Sources: Welter, 1966: 151–174; Ryan, 1983.

STOP AND THINK . . .

- How do you think the characteristics of true womanhood affected attitudes toward poor, employed, minority, and immigrant women?
- How did the cult of domesticity shape many women's and men's roles in terms of their choices and constraints? Do you think that any of the four virtues still reflect our attitudes toward women today?

---

womanhood." Women were judged as "good" if they displayed four cardinal virtues (see "Characteristics of 'True Womanhood' ").

New attitudes about the true woman became paramount in redefining the role of the wife as nurturer and caregiver rather than as workmate. Many lower socio-economic women weren't seen as true women because, like men, they worked outside the home. In these social classes, many children often dropped out of school to work and to help support their families. In addition, most spouses in these families had little time to show love and affection to their children or to each other.

As romantic love became the basis for marriage, couples had more freedom in choosing their partners based on compatibility and personal attraction. As households became more private, ties with the larger community became more fragile, and spouses turned to each other for affection and happiness much more than in the past (Skolnick, 1991).

CHILDREN AND ADOLESCENTS Fathers' control over their children began to erode. By the end of the seventeenth century, fathers had less land to divide among their sons. This meant that they had less authority over their children's sexual behavior and choice of a marriage partner. The percentage of women who were pregnant at the time of their marriage shot up to more than 40 percent by the mid-eighteenth century, suggesting that parents had become less effective in preventing premarital intercourse (Mintz and Kellogg, 1988).

Because a marriage was less likely to involve a distribution of the family's land and property, children were less dependent on their fathers for economic

support. Also, new opportunities for nonagricultural work, along with labor shortages in cities, prompted many children to leave home and thus escape from the authority of strict fathers. Perhaps the biggest change was that, largely in the middle class, adults started to view and treat children as more than "miniature adults." Children began to spend more time playing than working, and adolescence became a stage of life that didn't involve adult responsibilities.

Another sign of change was that people published more books for and about children. Adults began to recognize children's individuality by giving them names that were different from their father's or mother's. They also began, for the first time, to celebrate birthdays, especially those of children. There was also a decline in physical punishment, and physicians and others began to recognize the early onset of sexual feelings in children (Ariès, 1962; Degler, 1981; Demos, 1986).

Among the working classes and the poor, however, child labor was widespread, and children were a critical resource in their family's survival. In a survey of Massachusetts working-class families in 1875, for example, children under age 15 contributed nearly 20 percent of their family's income (Mintz and Kellogg, 1988).

The Impact of Immigration and Urbanization

Immigration played a key role in the Industrial Revolution in the United States. Immigrants provided a large pool of unskilled and semi-skilled labor that fueled emerging industries and gave investors huge profits.

In the first large immigration waves during the 1800s, paid middlemen arranged for the shipment of immigrants to waiting industries. For example, Asians were channeled into the western railroads, Italians were funneled into public works projects and used as strikebreakers, and Hungarians were directed toward the Pennsylvania coal mines. Later immigrants followed these established paths into industrial America (Bodnar, 1985).

Very few immigrant families escaped dire poverty. Because men's wages were low, most married women were also in the labor force. Some worked at home making artificial flowers, threading wires through tags, or crocheting over curtain rings. Some were cleaning women or seamstresses, did laundry, or sold cakes. Others took in boarders and lodgers, especially after their children left home (Hareven, 1984; Weatherford, 1986).

Like the men, women of different ethnic groups tended to move into specific jobs. For example, Italian women were more likely than Polish or Greek women to reject domestic labor, which would take them out of the Italian community and into other people's homes. Instead, they were more likely to work as seasonal laborers for fruit- and vegetable-processing companies and to do seamstress work at home (Squier and Quadagno, 1988). By the turn of the nineteenth century, a woman's occupation was usually tied to her race and ethnicity. That is, Asian, African American, and immigrant women worked in laundering, food processing, tobacco production, and textile factories, whereas white women— especially those with some schooling—were stenographers and teachers.

Family Life and Work

By 1890, all but 9 of the 369 industries listed by the U.S. Census Bureau employed women. Many of these industries were especially eager to hire "greenhorns" and women "just off the boat" who would work for low wages. Greenhorns

These Pennsylvania miners and "breaker boys"—youngsters who sorted the mined coal into categories—worked as many as 14 hours a day for very low pay. Like most miners of this period, they were immigrants who performed backbreaking labor during the U.S. Industrial Revolution.

Since you asked . . .
• Are employed mothers a
  modern phenomenon?

were often underpaid or not paid at all. In some cases, employers delayed wage payments for several months and then closed their shops, disappearing overnight (Manning, 1970).

By the late 1800s, Irish girls as young as age 11 were leaving home to work as servants; 75 percent of all Irish teenage girls were domestic servants. Even though they were hired only for housekeeping, many had to care for children, were sexually assaulted by their male employers, and were not paid their full wages (Ryan, 1983).

Most manufacturing jobs were segregated by sex. In the tobacco industry, for example, even though cigar rolling traditionally had been a woman's task in Slavic countries, men obtained these well-paying jobs. Immigrant women were relegated to damp and smelly basements, where they stripped the tobacco, which was then rolled by men who worked "upstairs" under better conditions and for much higher wages (Ryan, 1983).

HOUSING   One of the biggest problems for immigrant families was the lack of decent housing in densely populated cities. One Philadelphia tenement house, for instance, housed 30 families in 34 rooms. A Lithuanian couple and their five children lived in a tiny closet of a home that contained only slightly more air space than the law required for one adult. The buildings were jammed together so tightly that the immigrant population of one block in New York City was equal to that of an entire town. Women increased their kitchen wall space by reaching out the window and hanging utensils on the outside wall of the house next door (Weatherford, 1986).

HEALTH   Epidemics and disease were rampant among immigrant families. A cholera epidemic that barely touched the rest of New York City's population killed nearly 20 percent of the residents of a crowded immigrant neighborhood. Because a third of tenement rooms had no windows or ventilation, many immigrants contracted tuberculosis, which, at the time, was incurable.

In Lawrence, Massachusetts, where 90 percent of the population consisted of immigrants, a third of the spinners in the textile mills died of respiratory diseases, such as pneumonia and tuberculosis, before they had worked there for 10 years. These diseases were triggered by the lint, dust, and machine fumes of the unventilated mills. Moreover, the excruciating noise of the mills often resulted in deafness, and many workers were injured by faulty machines (Weatherford, 1986).

FAMILY CONFLICT   Epidemics and dilapidated housing weren't the only problems the immigrant families faced. Most suffered many of the ills that come with poverty and isolation in a strange and often hostile new environment: crime, delinquency, a breakdown of marital and family relations, and general demoralization. Living quarters shared with relatives put additional pressures on already strained marital ties (Thomas and Znaniecki, 1927).

PREJUDICE AND DISCRIMINATION   Like American Indians, Mexicans, and African Americans, most European immigrants met with enormous prejudice, discrimination, and economic exploitation. Much inequality was created and reinforced by high-ranking, highly respected, and influential people who had been educated in the most prestigious colleges and universities in the United States (see "Stereotypes about European Immigrants").

Despite the prejudice and discrimination they encountered, most immigrant families overcame tremendous obstacles. Rarely complaining, they worked at low-status jobs with low wages and encouraged their children to achieve and move up the social class ladder.

Cross-Cultural and Multicultural Families — Stereotypes about European Immigrants

On October 28, 1886, President Grover Cleveland dedicated the Statue of Liberty in New York Harbor, on whose pedestal are inscribed Emma Lazarus's famous welcoming words: "Give me your tired, your poor, your huddled masses yearning to breathe free." As the following examples show, however, Lazarus's poem didn't reflect reality:

1886: The U.S. consul in Budapest advised that Hungarian immigrants were not "a desirable acquisition" because, he claimed, they lacked ambition and would work as cheaply as the Chinese, which would interfere "with a civilized laborer's earning a 'white' laborer's wages."

1891: Congressman Henry Cabot Lodge called for restrictions on immigration because (referring especially to Jewish and Polish immigrants) the immigrants represented the "lowest and most illiterate classes," which were "alien to the body of the American people."

1910: Members of the eugenics movement contended that through intermarriage, immigration would contaminate the "old stock" of white Anglo-Saxon Americans with feeblemindedness, criminality, and pauperism. Many eugenicists, such as Robert DeCoucy Ward of Harvard, were faculty members at prestigious eastern universities.

1914: Edward A. Ross, a prominent sociologist at the University of Wisconsin and a self-proclaimed immigration watchdog, wrote: "That the Mediterranean people are morally below the races of northern Europe is as certain as any social fact."

1922: Kenneth L. Roberts, a Cornell graduate, served as a correspondent for the *Saturday Evening Post* on immigration questions. He warned that "if a few more million members of the Alpine, Mediterranean, and Semitic races are poured among us, the result must inevitably be a hybrid race of people as worthless and futile as the good-for-nothing mongrels of Central America and Southeastern Europe."

1946: After World War II, the immigration of displaced persons revived old fears. Several influential senators argued that political immigrants should not be permitted to enter the United States because of their "alien philosophies" and "biological incompatibility with Americans' parent stocks."

Source: Carlson and Colburn, 1972: 311–350.

STOP AND THINK . . .

- Did your ancestors experience prejudice and discrimination? Did such experiences shape how they raised their children?
- If you're a recent immigrant, what kinds of prejudice and discrimination have you and your family encountered?

The Modern Family Emerges

The Great Depression of the 1930s, World War II, the baby boom of the 1950s, and the increasing economic and political unrest of the decades since the 1960s have all influenced the American family—sometimes for better, sometimes for worse. Some social scientists maintain that the modern family emerged around 1830: Courtship became more open, marriages were often based on affection rather than financial considerations, and parents centered more of their attention on children. Others believe that the modern family emerged at the beginning of the twentieth century, especially with the rise of the "companionate family" (Burgess et al., 1963; Degler, 1983).

3.4 Describe three important factors that shaped the modern family.

The Rise of the Companionate Family (1900–1930)

At the turn of the twentieth century, married couples, particularly in the white middle class, morphed into what sociologists Ernest Burgess and Harvey Locke (1945) called the **companionate family**. These were families that were built on mutual affection, sexual attraction, compatibility, and personal happiness between husbands and wives. Thus, unlike the past, husbands and wives weren't just economic units, but depended on each other for company and a sense of togetherness. The companionate family also included a couple's children: The affection between parents and children was more intimate and more open, and adolescents enjoyed greater freedom from parental supervision.

companionate family A type of family built on mutual affection, sexual attraction, compatibility, and personal happiness between husband and wife.

This new independence generated criticism, however. Many popular magazines, such as *The Atlantic Monthly, The Ladies' Home Journal*, and the *New Republic*, contained articles with concerns about "young people's rejection of genteel manners, their defiant clothing and hairstyles, their slang-filled language, and their 'lewd' pastimes . . . (such as smoking, attending petting parties, and going out on school nights). Public condemnation and moral outrage were widespread" (Mintz and Kellogg, 1988: 119). Do any of these complaints about young people sound familiar?

The Great Depression (1929–1939)

On October 29, l929, the U.S. stock market crashed and the Great Depression of the 1930s began. By 1932, massive layoffs put millions out of work. Banks failed, wiping out many families' savings. Hunger became common and long breadlines formed at charities distributing food. Still, families had a wide range of experiences, resulting from factors such as residence, social class, gender, race, and ethnicity.

URBAN AND RURAL RESIDENCE Many people who farmed land owned by others could not pay their rent either in cash or in a share of the crops. Husbands sometimes left their families to search for jobs. Some women who couldn't cope with such desertion took drastic steps to end their misery. In 1938, for example, in Nebraska, a mother of 13 children committed suicide by walking into the side of a train because "she had had enough" (Fink, 1992: 172).

Even when husbands remained at home, some families lost their land and personal possessions. Parents made enormous sacrifices to feed their children. As one jobless father stated, "We do not dare to use even a little soap when it will pay for an extra egg or a few more carrots for our children" (McElvaine, 1993: 172).

To help support their families, many young men and women who had been raised on farms moved to cities seeking jobs. Young women were more likely to find jobs because there was a demand for low-paid domestic help. The money they sent home from their wages of $10 or so a week helped their families buy clothes and other necessities.

SOCIAL CLASS The most devastating impact of the Great Depression was felt by working-class and poor families. More than half of all married women—especially those in poor southern states such as South Carolina, Mississippi,

During the Great Depression, millions of families experienced dire poverty. Many families lived on farms, such as in Alabama (left). In urban centers, such as New York City (right), the unemployed waited in long breadlines to receive free food from the government.

Louisiana, Georgia, and Alabama—were employed in low-paying domestic service or factory jobs (Cavan and Ranck, 1938; Chafe, 1972).

When working-class mothers found jobs, older children, especially girls, looked after their younger brothers and sisters and often had to drop out of school to do so (McElvaine, 1993). Boys were expected to work after school or drop out of school to supplement their family's meager income. In contrast to middle-class children, those from working-class families did not enjoy a carefree adolescence.

Some working-class children became part of the "transient army" that drifted from town to town looking for work. Most slept in lice-ridden and rat-infested housing when they could afford to pay 10 or 15 cents for a urine-stained mattress on the floor. Others slept on park benches, under shrubbery and bridges, in doorways, in packing crates, or in abandoned automobiles (Watkins, 1993).

As blue-collar employment in the male-dominated industrial sectors decreased, white-collar clerical and government jobs increased. Women took many of these jobs. The wages of white, middle-class women enabled their families, even during the Great Depression, to maintain the standard of living and consumer habits that they had enjoyed during the affluent 1920s.

Upper-middle-class families fared even better. Affluent families made only minor sacrifices. Some cut back on entertainment, did not renew country club memberships, and decreased services such as domestic help. Few reported cutbacks in their food budgets, however, and many of these families continued to take summer vacations and buy new cars (Morgan, 1939).

Since you asked . . .

- Did the Great Depression have a devastating impact on *all* Americans?

RACE The Great Depression was an economic disaster for many white people, but African Americans suffered even more. Unemployment was much higher among blacks than among whites. As layoffs began in 1929 and accelerated in the following years, blacks were often the first to be fired. By 1932, black unemployment had reached approximately 50 percent, twice as high as the national average. As the economic situation deteriorated, many whites successfully demanded that employers replace blacks with whites in unskilled occupations such as garbage collector, elevator operator, waiter, bellhop, and street cleaner.

In some government jobs, employers set an unofficial quota of 10 percent black, on the theory that this represented, roughly, the percentage of African Americans in the general population. In fact, the percentage of government employees who were black was only about 6 percent. Even those who were able to keep their jobs faced great hardship. A study conducted in Harlem in 1935 found that the wages of skilled black workers who could find work dropped nearly 50 percent during the Great Depression (McElvaine, 1993; Watkins, 1993).

GENDER ROLES In many families, unemployment wreaked havoc on gender roles. The authority of the husband and father was based on his occupation and his role as provider. If he lost his job, he often suffered a decline in status within the family. Understandably, men were despondent: "Sometimes the father did not go to bed but moved from chair to chair all night long" (Cavan and Ranck, cited in Griswold, 1993: 148).

Men who couldn't provide for their families often became depressed, preoccupied, and abusive; drank more; or spent much of their time searching for jobs. As fathers became physically and emotionally distant, their power in the family and their children's respect for them often decreased, and adolescents became more independent and rebellious (Griswold, 1993).

In 1932, an executive order decreed that only one spouse could work for the federal government. The widespread unemployment of men therefore put pressure on women, especially married women, to resign from some occupations. In addition, school boards fired married female teachers, and some companies dismissed married women. More than 77 percent of the

school districts in the United States would not hire married women, and 50 percent had a policy of firing women who got married (Milkman, 1976; McElvaine, 1993).

When women did work, the federal government endorsed lower pay rates for women. For example, the federal Works Progress Administration (WPA) paid men $5 per day, compared with only $3 for women (Milkman, 1976).

World War II (1939–1945)

World War II triggered even greater changes in work roles and family life. Families began to experience these changes after the United States entered the war in 1941.

WORK ROLES   Workers were scarce, especially in the defense and manufacturing industries, because many able-bodied men had been drafted. Initially, employers were unwilling to recruit women for traditionally male jobs. And many women, especially white middle-class women, were reluctant to violate traditional gender roles.

In 1942, however, prompted by both the Women's Bureau of the U.S. Department of Labor and organized women's groups, employers began to fill many jobs, especially those in nontraditional positions, with women. The government, supported by the mass media, was enormously successful in convincing both men and women that a woman's place was in the workplace and not the home:

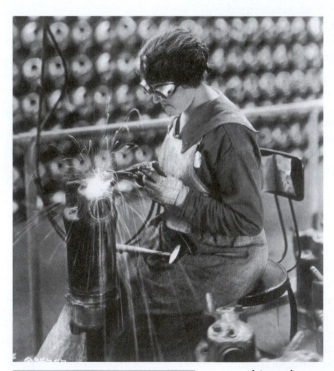

Millions of women worked in American factories, steel mills, and shipyards during World War II. Many found it hard to give up their new-found jobs and financial independence, but most were replaced by men who returned from the war in 1945.

In all the media, women at work were pictured and praised, and the woman who did not at least work as a volunteer for the Red Cross was made to feel guilty. . . . Even the movies joined in. The wife or sweetheart who stayed behind and went to work became as familiar a figure as the valiant soldier-lover for whom she waited (Banner, 1984: 219).

Millions of women, including mothers and even grandmothers, worked in shipyards, steel mills, and ammunition factories (see the Data Digest). They welded, dug ditches, and operated forklifts. For the first time, black women were recruited into high-paying jobs, making some of the greatest economic gains of all women during that period.

Hundreds of thousands of domestic servants and farm workers left their jobs for much better-paying positions in the defense and other industries. In the superb documentary film, *The Life and Times of Rosie the Riveter*, black women describe the pride and exhilaration they felt at having well-paying jobs that they genuinely enjoyed.

Because of the labor shortage, this was the only time when even working-class women were praised for working outside the home. Two of the best-selling magazines during that time, the *Saturday Evening Post* and *True Story*, supported the government's propaganda by portraying working-class women in very positive roles:

Stories and advertisements glorified factory work as psychologically rewarding, as emotionally exciting, and as leading to success in love. Both magazines combated class prejudice against factory work by portraying working-class men and women as diligent, patriotic, wholesome people. . . . Working-class women were resourceful, respectable, warmhearted, and resilient (Honey, 1984: 186–187).

FAMILY LIFE Divorce rates had been increasing slowly since the turn of the century, but they reached a new high a year after the end of World War II. In 1940, one marriage in six had ended in divorce compared with one in four in 1946 (Mintz and Kellogg, 1988).

Some wives and mothers who had worked during the war enjoyed their newfound economic independence and decided to end unhappy marriages. In other cases, families disintegrated because of the strains of living with a man who returned partially or completely incapacitated. Alcoholism, which was rampant among veterans, was believed to be the major cause of the increase in divorces after the war (Tuttle, 1993).

For some people, the war postponed rather than caused divorce. Some couples, caught up in war hysteria, courted briefly and married impulsively. In many cases, both the bride and the young soldier matured during the husband's prolonged absence and had little in common when they were reunited (Mowrer, 1972).

Perhaps one of the greatest difficulties that many families faced was their children's reaction to fathers whom they barely knew or had never even seen. As "Daddy's Coming Home!" shows, despite widespread rejoicing over the end of the war, a father's return was unsettling for many children.

Changes   Daddy's Coming Home!

Soldiers returning from World War II encountered numerous problems, including unemployment and high divorce rates. Historian William M. Tuttle Jr. (1993) solicited 2,500 letters from men and women, then in their fifties and sixties, who had been children during World War II. What most of these people had in common were the difficulties they and their families experienced in adjusting to the return of their fathers from military service.

Some children feared that their fathers wouldn't stay and therefore avoided becoming too attached. Others were bitter that their fathers had left in the first place. One "war baby" was 18 months old when her father returned from the war. When her mother told her to hug her Daddy, she ran to a large framed photo of him and took it in her arms.

Some children, especially those who were preschoolers at the time, were frightened of the strange men who suddenly moved into their homes. One woman remembered watching "the stranger with the big white teeth" come toward her. As he did, the 4-year-old ran upstairs in terror and hid under a bed. Some recalled feeling angry because

The G.I. Bill enabled many World War II veterans to go to school and improve their job opportunities. But for many vets with families, such as William Oskay Jr. and his wife and daughter, daily life required many sacrifices and hardships.

their fathers' return disrupted their lives. Grandparents had often pampered children whom they helped to raise. In contrast, the returning father, fresh from military experience, was often a strict disciplinarian and saw the child as a brat.

If the children had been very close to their mothers, they became resentful of their fathers for displacing them in the mother's affections. Others were disappointed when the idealized image they had constructed of Daddy didn't match reality or when a father who had been described as kind, sensitive, and gentle returned from the war troubled or violent.

Readjustment was difficult for both children and fathers. Some households adjusted to the changes, but in many families the returning fathers and their children never developed a close relationship.

STOP AND THINK . . .

- Do you think that the relationship between children and fathers helps explain the spike in divorce rates in 1946? Why or why not?
- In 1973, at the end of the Vietnam War, Congress replaced the draft with an all-volunteer military force. Based on your personal experiences or readings, do you think that the volunteer soldiers who have returned from the wars in Iraq and Afghanistan have experienced fewer family difficulties than World War II soldiers?

Watch on MySocLab

Video: A Society of Consumers

The Golden Fifties

After World War II, propaganda about family roles changed almost overnight because returning veterans needed jobs. Women were no longer welcome in the workplace. Ads now depicted happy housewives engrossed in using household appliances and the latest consumer products. The women portrayed in short stories and in articles in women's magazines were no longer nurses saving soldiers' lives on the battlefield, but mothers cooking, caring for their children, and pleasing their husbands. In the 1950s, middle-class people, especially, became absorbed in their families.

Gender Roles

Movies and television shows created and reinforced two stereotypical portrayals of women: innocent virgins such as Doris Day and Debbie Reynolds or sexy bombshells such as Marilyn Monroe and Jayne Mansfield. Television applauded domesticity on popular shows such as *I Love Lucy*, *Ozzie and Harriet*, *Leave It to Beaver*, and *Father Knows Best*.

Once again, and reminiscent of the cult of domesticity that arose during the 1800s, popular culture encouraged women to devote their lives to being good wives and nurturing mothers. For example, marriage manuals and child care experts such as Dr. Benjamin Spock advised women to please their husbands and to be full-time homemakers. By the mid-1950s, 60 percent of female undergraduates dropped out of college to marry (Banner, 1984).

baby boomers People born between 1946 and 1964.

The post–World War II period produced a generation of **baby boomers**, people born between 1946 and 1964, when birth rates surged. Family plans that had been disrupted by the war were renewed. Women continued to enter the job market, but many middle-class families, spurred by the mass media, sought a traditional family life in which the husband worked and the wife devoted herself to the home and the children.

The editor of *Mademoiselle* echoed a widespread belief that women in their teens and 20s should avoid careers and instead raise as many children as the "good Lord gave them." And many magazine and newspaper articles encouraged families to participate in "creative" activities such as outdoor barbecues and cross-country camping trips (Chafe, 1972).

Moving to the Suburbs

In the 1950s, suburbs mushroomed, attracting nearly two-thirds of those who had lived in cities. The interest in moving to the suburbs reflected a number of structural and attitudinal changes in American society.

The federal government, fearful of a return to an economic depression, underwrote the construction of homes in the suburbs (Rothman, 1978). The general public obtained low-interest mortgages, and veterans were offered the added incentive of purchasing a home with a $1 down payment. There was a huge demand for housing; from 1945 to 1960, 15 million housing units were built. By 1960, 60 percent of Americans owned their own homes (Buhle et al., 2008).

Homeownership rates climbed steadily over the years, reaching 69 percent in 2004. In mid-2009, however,

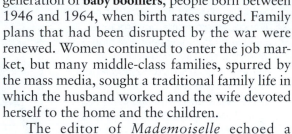

When suburbs mushroomed during the 1950s, many critics mocked the small, detached, single-family homes as "cookie cutters" (above). Are houses practically stacked on top of one another in some recently developed suburbs—such as the one south of Denver, Colorado (below)—more original and not cookie cutters?

Mad Men, a popular television show that began in 2007, suggests how gender roles began to change at the end of the 1950s. For example, some middle-class suburban house-wives started to feel lonely and ignored as their successful husbands worked long hours. Some wives turned to alcohol and extramarital affairs to counteract their feelings of alienation.

Since you asked . . .
- How did suburban living change family life?

because of unemployment, home foreclosures, and the financial crisis, American homeownership dropped to 67 percent (Callis and Cavanaugh, 2009). Home sales are rising as this book goes to press.

Massive highway construction programs and automobile ownership enabled people to commute from the suburbs to the city. Families wanted more room and an escape from city noise, dirt, and crowding. One woman still recollects moving to the suburbs as "the ideal life": "We knew little about the outside world of poverty, culture, crime, and ethnic variety" (Coontz, 2005: 240).

The greater space offered more privacy for both children and parents: "The spacious master bedroom, generally set apart from the rooms of the children, was well-suited to a highly sexual relationship. And wives anticipated spending many evenings alone with their husbands, not with family or friends" (Rothman, 1978: 225–226).

The suburban way of life added a new dimension to the traditional role of women:

> *The duties of child-rearing underwent expansion. Suburban mothers volunteered for library work in the school, took part in PTA activities, and chauffeured their children from music lessons to scout meetings. Perhaps most important, the suburban wife was expected to make the home an oasis of comfort and serenity for her harried husband (Chafe, 1972: 217–218).*

An Idyllic Decade?

Were the fifties as idyllic as earlier generations fondly recall? Some writers argue that many of these nostalgic memories are myths. "Contrary to popular opinion," notes historian Stephanie Coontz (1992: 29) "*Leave It to Beaver* was not a documentary." In fact, the golden fifties were riddled with many family problems, and people had fewer choices than they do today. For example,

- *Consumerism* was limited primarily to middle- and upper-class families. In 1950, a supermarket stocked an average of 3,750 items; in the 1990s, most markets carried more than 17,000 items.

- Black and other ethnic families faced *severe discrimination* in employment, education, housing, and access to recreational activities.

- *Domestic violence and child abuse*, although widespread, were invisible (see Chapter 14).

- Many young people were forced into *"shotgun" marriages* because of premarital pregnancy; young women—especially if they were white—were pressured to give up their babies for adoption.
  - About 20 percent of mothers had *paying jobs*. Child care services are still inadequate today, but they were practically nonexistent in the 1950s.
  - *Open homosexuality was taboo* because only heterosexuality was considered normal. As a result, practically all lesbians and gay men kept their sexual orientation a secret and married people of the opposite sex.
  - Many people, including housewives, tried to escape from their unhappy lives through *alcohol or drugs*. The consumption of tranquilizers, largely unheard of in 1955, soared to almost 1.2 million pounds in 1959 (Coontz, 1992; Crispell, 1992; Reid, 1993).

MAKING CONNECTIONS

- Based on your observations or experiences, have suburbs changed since the 1950s?
- *Many* Americans—even those born long after the decade was over—view the 1950s as the good old days when, presumably, families were happy and closely knit. Do you wish that you could've been raised during the 1950s? Why or why not?

3.6 Describe three ways that families in the United States have changed since the 1960s.

 Read on MySocLab

Document: How History and Sociology Can Help Today's Families

 Explore on MySocLab

Activity: A Lot Can Change in 10 Years: 21st Century Families

The Family Since the 1960s

When I was in graduate school during the early 1970s, our textbooks on marriage and family typically covered three major topics—courtship, marriage, and having children—and in that order. The authors sometimes devoted a chapter to premarital sex and perhaps one chapter to black families, but they often described divorce, interfaith marriage, premarital pregnancy, and homosexuality as deviant or problems (see, for example, Reiss, 1971). We never read (or heard) about family violence and almost nothing about singlehood, cohabitation, stepfamilies, or one-parent families.

American families have experienced numerous changes since the 1960s and 1970s. As you saw in Chapter 1, technological innovations have transformed everyday communication, young people have greater access to and are more influenced by popular culture than ever before, social movements challenged traditional attitudes about family life, and social scientists became more interested in examining families in other societies. Since the l970s, three of the major shifts have occurred in family structure, gender roles, and economic concerns.

Family Structure

In the 1970s, families had lower birth rates and higher divorce rates compared with the 1950s and 1960s, and larger numbers of women entered colleges and graduate schools. In the 1980s, more people over age 25 postponed marriage, and many who were already married delayed having children (see Chapters 9 and 11).

Out-of-wedlock births, especially among teenage girls, declined in the late 1990s, began to climb in 2006, and the number of one-parent households increased dramatically (see Chapters 7 and 9). The number of two-income families burgeoned, along with the number of adult children who continued to live at home with their parents because of financial difficulties (see Chapter 12).

Gender Roles

In her influential book, *The Feminine Mystique* (1963), Betty Friedan (1921–2006) criticized the push toward domesticity and documented the dissatisfaction of many college-educated women who felt unfulfilled in their full-time roles as wives and mothers. Friedan's book didn't change gender roles overnight. In 1975, for example, and even though I worked full time as a college professor, I couldn't take out a credit card in my own name and needed my husband's signed permission to get a credit card even in his name. Nonetheless, *The Feminine Mystique* had a significant impact in sparking the women's movement in the

late 1960s and challenging traditional roles throughout the 1970s and 1980s. We'll cover these topics in later chapters, but by the early 1980s, women's employment was becoming central to a family's economic advancement, and two-income families faced the stressful task of juggling work and family life. Perhaps most important, men experienced less pressure to be the sole breadwinner.

Economic Concerns

The twenty-first century began with numerous problems that affected families. When the stock market plunged in the "dot-com bubble" of 2001, many older people had to go back to work because their retirement portfolios shrank by at least 50 percent. Many young adults were laid off from promising high-tech jobs and scurried to find *any* employment that paid more than a minimum wage (see Chapters 13 and 16).

After the terrorist attacks on September 11, 2001, federal and state governments funneled billions of dollars into homeland security and the war in Iraq. Health care costs skyrocketed. In mid-2008, the U.S. economy spiraled downward into another, even more severe stock market crash, and, by early 2013, the U.S. wars in Iraq and Afghanistan had cost taxpayers at least $3.7 *trillion* (Watson Institute for International Studies, 2013). As a result, agencies gutted many family programs and services, especially for poor and working-class families.

In the late 1960s, feminists protested women's exclusion from high paying jobs. One result was more women in managerial jobs during the 1980s.

CONCLUSION

If we examine the family in a historical context, we see that *change*, rather than stability, has been the norm. Moreover, families differed by region and social class even during colonial times. The experiences and *choices* open to American Indians, African Americans, Mexican Americans and many European immigrants were very different from those available to white middle-class Americans, whose lives were romanticized by many television programs during the 1950s.

Macro-level *constraints* such as wars and shifting demographic characteristics have also affected families. Many survived despite enormous hardships, but are still coping with macro-level constraints such as an unpredictable economy. The next chapter examines some of the ongoing changes, choices, and constraints across contemporary racial and ethnic families.

On MySocLab

 **Study** and **Review** on MySocLab

REVIEW QUESTIONS

3.1. **Compare families today and those in Colonial America.**

1. What are the differences, if any, between colonial and contemporary U.S. families in terms of family structure, sexual attitudes and behavior, husband-wife relationships, and children's lives?

2. How and why did the experiences of colonial families differ across social classes and regions?

3.2. **Compare the family experiences of early American Indians, African Americans, and Mexican Americans.**

3. How did American Indian, African American, and Mexican families differ in terms of family structure, family roles, and children's socialization?

4. How did Europeans affect American Indian, African American, and Mexican families?

3.3. Describe the impacts of industrialization, urbanization, and immigration on the American family.

5. How did industrialization and urbanization affect native-born white families, immigrants, and minorities?

6. What were the major obstacles that immigrants experienced?

3.4. Describe three important factors that shaped the modern family.

7. How did companionate families differ from their predecessors?

8. Did the Great Depression have a devastating impact on all families?

9. How did World War II affect family life and women's labor force participation?

3.5. Explain two important trends that changed the family during the "golden fifties."

10. How and why did gender roles change during the 1950s?

11. Why did suburbs mushroom during the 1950s? And how did suburbanization change family life?

3.6. Describe three ways that families in the United States have changed since the 1960s.

12. How and why have family structure and gender roles changed since the 1960s?

13. How and why have families' economic problems increased since the turn of the twenty-first century?

Racial and Ethnic Families: Strengths and Stresses

((•)) **Listen** to Chapter 4 on **MySocLab**

LEARNING OBJECTIVES

After you read and study this chapter you will be able to:

Describe how and explain why racial-ethnic diversity is changing the U.S. population.	**4.1**
Explain why race and ethnicity are important in understanding marriages and families.	**4.2**
Describe the characteristics of and variations among African American families.	**4.3**
Describe the characteristics of and variations among American Indian families.	**4.4**
Describe the characteristics of and variations among Latino families.	**4.5**
Describe the characteristics of and variations among Asian American families.	**4.6**
Describe the characteristics of and variations among Middle Eastern American families.	**4.7**
Describe how and explain why interracial and interethnic relationships are changing American marriages and families.	**4.8**

DATA DIGEST

- Canada and the United States **represent only about 5 percent of the world's population but receive more than half of the world's immigrants**.

- **Four states and the District of Columbia are "majority-minority,"** meaning that whites make up less than half of the population. Hawaii leads the nation with 77 percent minority, followed by the District of Columbia (65 percent), New Mexico and California (60 percent each), and Texas (55 percent).

- More than half of the **growth in the total U.S. population between 2000 and 2011** was due to the increase in the Latino population but, since 2010, Asians have been **the fastest-growing race or ethnic group**.

- In 2011, **more than half of the U.S. population younger than age 1 were minorities**; more than 7 percent of the babies were two or more races, up from barely 5 percent in 2000.

- The U.S. population that self-identified as **having an Arabic ancestry** increased by 76 percent between 2000 and 2010.

- In 2010, almost 9.1 million Americans **self-identified as two or more races**, a 32 percent increase since 2000.

Sources: Passel et al., 2011; Jones and Bullock, 2012; Taylor et al., 2012; U.S. Census Bureau, 2012; U.S. Census Bureau Newsroom, 2012; Asi and Beaulieu, 2013; "Asians fastest-growing. . . ," 2013.

Regardless of our ancestry, race and ethnicity are important parts of our lives. Chapter 3 provided a brief historical summary of racial-ethnic families. This chapter focuses on contemporary African American, American Indian, Latino, Asian American, and Middle Eastern families. We'll also look at interracial and interethnic dating and marriages. Let's begin with an overview of the growing diversity of U.S. families.

4.1 Describe how and explain why racial-ethnic diversity is changing the U.S. population.

Since you asked . . .

- How has U.S. immigration changed?

 Explore on MySocLab

Activity: Diversity on Maui, Hawaii

 Explore on MySocLab

Activity: Diversity in American Society

The Increasing Diversity of U.S. Families

Much of the racial and ethnic diversity in U.S. households is because the United States is a magnet that draws people from hundreds of nations.

Our Changing Immigration Mosaic

The current proportion of foreign-born U.S. residents is smaller than in the past. In 1900, about 15 percent of the total U.S. population was foreign born, compared with about 13 percent in 2010 (Grieco and Trevelyan, 2010).

The United States has more foreign-born residents than any country in the world—1 in 8 people. There has also been a significant shift in many immigrants' country of origin. In 1900, almost 85 percent of immigrants came from Europe. By 2010, in contrast, Europeans made up only 12 percent of all new immigrants. Today, immigrants come primarily from Asia (mainly China and the Philippines) and Latin America (mainly Mexico) (see *Figure 4.1*; see also Grieco and Trevelyan, 2010).

The Foreign-Born Population

The United States admits more than 1 million immigrants every year—more than any other nation. A major change has been the rise of *undocumented* (also called *unauthorized* and *illegal*) immigrants—from 180,000 in the early 1980s to 11.1 million in 2011. Undocumented immigrants make up 28 percent of all foreign-born U.S. residents (see *Figure 4.2*), 4 percent of the nation's population, and 5 percent of its labor force (Passel and Cohn, 2011; Pew Hispanic Center, 2013).

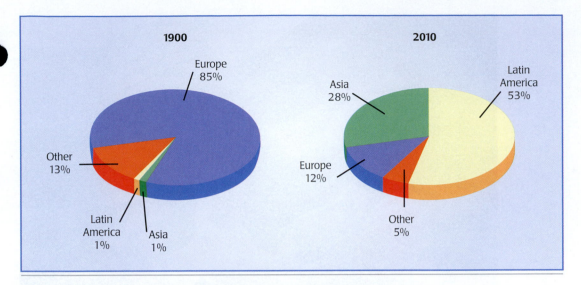

FIGURE 4.1 Origins of U.S. Immigrants: 1900 and 2010
Note: Latin America includes the Caribbean, Central America (including Mexico), and South America.
Sources: Based on data in U.S. Department of Commerce, 1993, and U.S. Census Bureau, 2013.

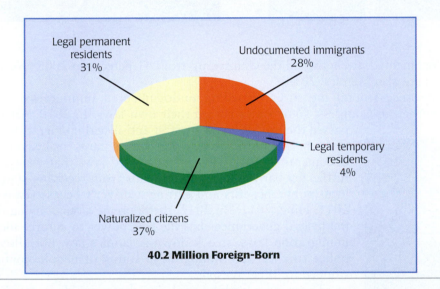

FIGURE 4.2 Legal Status of the U.S. Foreign-Born Population, 2010
Source: Based on Passel and Cohn, 2011.

About 62 percent of undocumented immigrants are from Mexico, 17 percent are from Central and Latin America, 7 percent are from Asia, and 14 percent are from other countries, including Canada and Europe (Hoefer et al., 2011).

Most immigrants—legal and undocumented—come to the United States for economic opportunities; less than 10 percent arrive as refugees who are fleeing political, religious, or other oppression in their own countries (Martin and Midgley, 2010). The unauthorized immigrant population peaked at 12 million in 2007, but has decreased since then because of a doubling of deportations, more border apprehensions, a rapid decline in job opportunities due to the Great Recession, passage of state laws targeted at undocumented immigrants, and, to a lesser extent, conversion to legal status (Passel and Cohn, 2011; Llana, 2012; Portes, 2012).

REACTIONS TO UNDOCUMENTED IMMIGRANTS In mid-2013, almost 78 percent of Americans favored giving undocumented immigrants a chance to become U.S. citizens if they met certain requirements such as having jobs, paying fines and back taxes, and passing background checks. The survey also found that 54 percent of Americans believed that immigrants, whether legal or

Since you asked

• Are illegal immigrants stealing U.S. jobs?

Every year, millions of immigrants become U.S. citizens. At Fenway Park in Boston, more than 3,000 people took the oath of citizenship in one huge ceremony.

After millions of undocumented immigrants fled to other states from Arizona, Alabama, and Georgia because of harsh laws, many employers complained that their produce was rotting in the fields because native-born Americans were unwilling to work for low wages. Other employers couldn't find enough construction and landscaping laborers to clean up and rebuild communities in the aftermath of devastating tornados. Many farmers believe that 80 percent of their workers are undocumented immigrants (Shepherd, 2011; Richardson, 2012; Jordan and Peters, 2013).

undocumented, strengthened the country, up from 41 percent in 2005 (Nelson, 2013; see also Mendes, 2013).

Because federal measures regarding undocumented immigration have languished in Congress, some states passed their own laws. In 2010, Arizona passed the broadest and strictest anti-illegal immigration law in recent U.S. history that required immigrants to always carry documents. In 2011, five states passed laws that went even further by barring illegal immigrants from receiving state or local public benefits and getting a driver's license (Fausset, 2011; Hing, 2011). In 2012, the Supreme Court, saying that the federal government has the sole power to enforce illegal immigration laws, struck down Arizona's law, but allowed police to check the immigration status of people lawfully stopped for other reasons.

Those who endorse policies that provide a "path to citizenship" maintain that undocumented immigrants provide numerous economic benefits for their host countries. They clean homes and offices, toil as nannies and busboys, serve as nurses' aides, and pick fruit—all at low wages and in jobs that most U.S.-born workers don't want. Undocumented immigrants are also more likely than U.S.-born people to work in dangerous jobs (such as mining, logging, and construction) that have high fatality rates due to accidents. Shortly after Arizona cracked down on undocumented immigrants, the state lost revenue of at least $141 million in the tourist industry alone because native-born workers in this sector depended on undocumented immigrants to work in the lowest-paying jobs. In 2012, farmers in Washington state let a quarter of their apples rot in the fields because they didn't have enough immigrant pickers, and native-born Americans didn't want such low-paying and difficult jobs (Orrenius and Zavodny, 2009; Zuehlke, 2009; Wolgin and Kelley, 2011; Millman, 2012a).

Many scholars argue that, in the long run, easing illegal immigrants' path to citizenship would bring more benefits than costs. For example, undocumented immigrants constitute an untapped source of revenue to support Social Security and Medicare payments for older (and primarily white) Americans. Naturalized citizens, on the other hand, earn higher wages, which decreases the likelihood

of family poverty; pay billions in state and federal taxes; and contribute to U.S. culture (Pastor et al., 2010; Shierholz, 2010).

Race and Ethnicity Still Matter

Social scientists routinely describe Latino, African American, Asian American, Middle Eastern, and American Indian families as minority groups. A **minority group** is a group of people who may be treated differently from the dominant group because of their physical or cultural characteristics, such as gender, sexual orientation, religion, or skin color. A **dominant group** is any physically or culturally distinctive group that has the most economic and political power, the greatest privileges, and the highest social status.

Minority groups may outnumber whites in a country or state (see Data Digest), but they typically have less power, privilege, and social status. Most whites, in contrast, are privileged because of their skin color. Feminist educator Peggy McIntosh (1995: 76–77) describes white privilege as "an invisible package of unearned assets that I can count on cashing in each day." "Am I Privileged?" provides some examples of "cashing in" if you're white.

Some Patterns of Dominant-Minority Group Relations

Throughout our nation's history, dominant-minority relations have varied. As you saw in Chapter 3, European colonists engaged in *expulsion* by forcing American Indians out of their tribal lands. Also, the dominant group controlled African Americans, even after slavery was abolished, through *segregation*, the physical

Since you asked . . .

• Why would many whites reject the argument that they're privileged?

4.2 Explain why race and ethnicity are important in understanding marriages and families.

minority group People who may be treated differently or unequally because of their physical or cultural characteristics, such as gender, sexual orientation, religion, or skin color.

dominant group Physically or culturally distinctive group that has the most economic and political power, the greatest privileges, and the highest social status.

Read on MySocLab

Document: Talking Past Each Other: The Black and White Language of Race

ASK YOURSELF

Am I Privileged?

Do we live in a color-blind society? No, according to most social scientists. White people are rarely conscious of the advantages and disadvantages associated with skin color because they enjoy a variety of everyday benefits that they take for granted. Here are a few of the 46 privileges that McIntosh (1995: 79–81) lists:

1. I can go shopping and feel fairly assured that I will not be followed or harassed by store detectives.

2. I can turn on the television or open to the front page of the paper and see people of my race widely and positively represented.

3. I can be sure that my children will be given curricular materials that reflect their race.

4. Whether I use checks, credit cards, or cash, I can count on my skin color to send the message that I am financially reliable.

5. If a traffic cop pulls me over, I can be sure that I haven't been singled out because of my race.

6. I can be late to a meeting without having the lateness reflect on my race.

7. I can easily buy posters, postcards, greeting cards, toys, and children's magazines featuring people of my race.

8. I can do well in a difficult situation without being called a credit to my race.

Some of those who are white don't feel privileged because being white *and* wealthy *and* male brings more privileges than simply having white skin (Rothenberg, 2008). For example, low-income white females don't see any benefits in being white because their skin color doesn't seem to bring them any privileges.

STOP AND THINK . . .

• Would you add other benefits to this list of white privileges?

• In 2013, Jon Stewart, the host of *The Daily Show*, quipped that Americans have solved the "race issue" because they elected a black president twice. Stewart was being sarcastic, but is any discussion of white privilege now being outdated because many minority group members have achieved considerable political power?

assimilation Conformity of ethnic group members to the dominant group's culture.

pluralism Maintaining aspects of immigrants' original cultures while living peacefully with the host culture.

acculturation Adapting to the language, values, beliefs, roles, and other characteristics of the host culture.

racial group People who share physical characteristics, such as skin color, that members of a society consider socially important.

ethnic group People who identify with a common national origin or cultural heritage.

racial-ethnic group People with distinctive racial and cultural characteristics.

There's much variation in skin color across and within groups. People of African descent have at least 35 different hues or shades of skin tone (Taylor, 2003). Because our skin contains different amounts of melanin (a pigment that affects skin, eye, and hair color), brown skin can vary considerably even within the same family.

separation of groups in residence, education, workplaces, use of public facilities, and social functions.

In contemporary U.S. society, the ways we relate to one another have become more complex. To understand some of this complexity, think of a continuum. At one end of the continuum is **assimilation**, or conformity of ethnic group members to the culture of the dominant group, including intermarriage. At the other end of the continuum is **pluralism**, maintaining many aspects of one's original culture—including using one's own language and marrying within one's own ethnic group—while living peacefully with the host culture.

Still others—those in the middle of the continuum—blend into U.S. society through **acculturation**, the process of adopting the language, values, beliefs, roles, and other characteristics of a host culture (such as attaining high educational levels and securing good jobs). Like pluralism, acculturation doesn't include intermarriage, but the newcomers merge into the host culture in most other ways.

What kinds of physical and cultural characteristics differentiate minority groups from a dominant group? Two of the most important are race and ethnicity.

Race

A **racial group** refers to people who share visible physical characteristics, such as skin color and facial features, that members of a society consider socially important. Contrary to the popular belief that race is determined biologically, race is a *social construction*, a societal invention that labels people based on physical appearance. As few as 6 of the body's estimated 35,000 genes determine the color of a person's skin. Because all human beings carry 99.9 percent of the same genetic material (DNA), the "racial" genes that make us look different are miniscule compared with the genes that make us similar (Graves, 2001; Pittz, 2005).

For social scientists, physical characteristics such as skin color and eye shape are easily observed and mark particular groups for unequal treatment: "Each of us is born with a particular collection of physical attributes, but it is society that teaches us which ones to value and which ones to reject" (Rothenberg, 2008: 3). As you'll see in this and other chapters, as long as we sort ourselves into racial categories and act on the basis of these characteristics, our life experiences will differ in terms of access to jobs and other resources, how we treat people, and how they treat us (Duster, 2005).

Ethnicity

An **ethnic group** (from the Greek word *ethnos*, meaning "nation") refers to people who identify with a particular national origin or cultural heritage. Cultural heritage includes language, geographic roots, customs, food, traditions, and religion. Ethnic groups in the United States include Puerto Ricans, Chinese, blacks, and white ethnic groups such as Italians, Swedes, Hungarians, Jews, and many others.

Like race, ethnicity—an individual or group's cultural or national identity—can be a basis for unequal treatment. As you saw in Chapter 3, many white European immigrants experienced discrimination because of their ethnic roots.

Racial-Ethnic Group

Sociologists refer to people who have distinctive physical and cultural characteristics as a **racial-ethnic group**. Some people use the terms *race* and *ethnicity* interchangeably, but remember that *race* is a social concept that refers to physical characteristics, whereas *ethnicity* describes cultural characteristics. The term *racial-ethnic* incorporates both physical and cultural traits.

Describing racial-ethnic groups has become more complex because the U.S. government allows people to identify themselves in terms of both race and ethnicity. In the 2000 and 2010 U.S. Censuses, for example, Latinos could check off "Black" or "White" for race and "Cuban" for ethnic origin. Such choices generate dozens of racial-ethnic categories. People tend to prefer some "labels" to others, but they vary.

The Naming Issue

In 1976, the U.S. government instructed federal agencies to use the word *Hispanic* or *Latino* to categorize Americans who trace their roots to Spanish-speaking countries, but the labeling doesn't fit easily with these Americans' own sense of identity. About 51 percent identify themselves most often by the family's country or place of origin and use terms such as *Mexican, Cuban, Salvadoran,* and so on. Another 24 percent identify themselves as *Hispanic* or *Latino,* but 21 percent use *American* to describe themselves, and this share rises to 40 percent among those who were born in the United States (Taylor et al., 2012). The Pew Hispanic Center, among other research organizations, uses *Hispanic* and *Latino* interchangeably, but *Hispanic* is preferred in the Northeast and Florida, whereas *Latino* is more popular in the West and Southwest.

Labels for blacks have changed over time, from hurtful racial epithets to *colored, Negro,* and *Afro-American* (Kennedy, 2002). Currently, most people, including African American scholars, use *black* and *African American* interchangeably. I find the same results when I poll my black students informally. Some are vehement about using *African American* to emphasize their African ancestry; others prefer *black* (with or without a capital *B*).

We see similar variations in the usage of *Native American* and *American Indian.* Although these groups prefer their tribal identities (such as Cherokee, Apache, and Lumbi) to being lumped together with a single term, American Indians often dispute whether someone is full blooded or mixed blood, and belongs to a tribe (Snipp, 2002).

Racism, Prejudice, and Discrimination

Racism, prejudice, and discrimination harm everyone, but have the most negative impact on racial-ethnic groups.

RACISM **Racism** is a set of beliefs that one's own racial group is inherently superior to others. Using this definition, anyone can be racist if she or he believes that another group is inferior. It's a way of thinking about racial and ethnic differences that justifies and preserves the social, economic, and political interests of dominant groups (Essed and Goldberg, 2002).

Whereas blacks see racism as a continuing problem, many whites view it as pretty much "solved." After all, we have an African American president and a Latina Supreme Court justice, many law firms advertise summer positions that are limited to minority candidates, and minorities now own a large proportion of small businesses. One outcome of such changes is that many whites now believe that anti-white bias is a bigger social problem than anti-black bias (Bernstein, 2011; Norton and Sommers, 2011). Such beliefs aren't supported by data, but they fuel prejudice and discrimination.

PREJUDICE **Prejudice** is an *attitude* that prejudges people, usually in a negative way, who are different from "us" in race, ethnicity, religion, or some other characteristic. If an employer assumes, for example, that white workers will be more productive than those from minority groups, she or he is prejudiced. All of us can be prejudiced, but minorities, rather than whites, are

racism Beliefs that one's own racial group is inherently superior to others.

> **Since you asked . . .**
> • Can minorities be racist?

 Watch on MySocLab

Video: White Privilege in the U.S.

prejudice An *attitude* that prejudges people, usually in a negative way.

Applying What You've Learned — Am I Prejudiced?

All of us, whether we realize it or not, sometimes have strong positive or negative feelings about other racial-ethnic groups. Answer the questions in this quiz as honestly as possible. After you finish, look at the key.

Usually True	Usually False	
☐	☐	**1.** Latino men have a more macho attitude toward women than do other men.
☐	☐	**2.** African Americans, both women and men, are more likely to commit crimes than are members of other racial-ethnic groups, including whites.
☐	☐	**3.** Don't trust Arab Americans. Some are decent, but most want to spread Islam and aren't loyal to the United States.
☐	☐	**4.** Asian American business owners are greedier than other business owners.
☐	☐	**5.** There are some exceptions, but most Latinos don't succeed because they're lazy.

Usually True	Usually False	
☐	☐	**6.** The majority of Asian Americans tend to be shy and quiet.
☐	☐	**7.** Most Asian Americans aren't as sociable as other people.
☐	☐	**8.** Most whites are simply more capable than other groups—especially African Americans and Latinos—in doing their jobs.

KEY TO "AM I PREJUDICED?"

Of these eight items, the higher your score for "usually true," the more likely that you're prejudiced and stereotype racial-ethnic groups. The purpose of this quiz is to encourage you to think how you feel about people outside your immediate circle.

Sources: Based on material in Godfrey et al., 2000; Lin et al., 2005; and Esposito and Mogahed, 2007.

---

typically the targets. Before you read any further, take the short "Am I Prejudiced?" quiz and think about some of your feelings about racial-ethnic groups.

Prejudice is less harmful than discrimination because it's an attitude rather than a behavior. Nevertheless, prejudice may lead to discrimination.

discrimination An *act* that treats people unequally or unfairly.

Watch on MySocLab

Video: Racial Stereotypes and Discrimination

Watch on MySocLab

Video: Discrimination at Swim Club

DISCRIMINATION **Discrimination** is *behavior* that treats people unequally or unfairly because of their group membership. It encompasses all sorts of actions, ranging from social slights (such as not inviting minority co-workers to lunch) to rejection of job applicants and racially motivated hate crimes (see Lucas, 2008).

Individual discrimination is harmful action on a one-to-one basis by a member of a dominant group against a member of a minority group. In a recent national survey, for example, 74 percent of blacks, compared with only 31 percent of whites, said that they were personally discriminated against because of their race (Romano and Samuels, 2012).

In *institutional discrimination* (also called *systemic discrimination* and *structural discrimination*), minority group members experience unequal treatment and opportunities as a result of the everyday operations of a society's laws, rules, policies, practices, and customs. Institutional discrimination is widespread. Recently, for instance, Wells Fargo Home Mortgage, one of the largest and most powerful banks in the United States, settled a $175 million lawsuit which alleged that minorities, particularly blacks and Latinos, experienced thousands of home foreclosures because of discriminatory lending practices (Broadwater, 2012).

Discrimination, both individual and institutional, also occurs *within* racial-ethnic groups. For example, immigrants from both Mexico and Central

American countries, such as El Salvador, speak the same language (Spanish) and migrate to Los Angeles, California, in large numbers. El Salvadorans, however, believe that many Mexican American business owners discriminate against Central and South Americans, even those in low-paying jobs (Bermudez, 2008).

The most useful analyses would involve a comparison of racial-ethnic families across the same variables, such as gender roles or parent–child relationships. With a few exceptions, however, most studies vary considerably in sampling, research design, over time, and focusing on only one or two racial-ethnic families at a time. Let's begin with African American families.

MAKING CONNECTIONS

- What do you think would be the costs and benefits of increasing or decreasing current immigration rates? Should the United States continue to deport illegal immigrants? Or give them a chance at citizenship?

- Provide some examples of situations in which you (or someone else) who is prejudiced might not discriminate and in which you (or someone else) who discriminates might not necessarily be prejudiced.

African American Families

In 2011, African Americans were the second largest minority group but are expected to increase less than other groups by 2050 (see *Table 4.1*). Of the 44 million blacks, more than 3 million were from Africa, the Caribbean, and Central or South America (U.S. Census Bureau, 2012, July 6). They speak different languages and vary widely in their customs, cuisines, and religious practices.

Because of such diversity, there is no such thing as *the* African American family. Like other U.S. families, black families vary in kinship structure, gender roles, parent–child relationships, and health. You'll notice, however, as your read the rest of this chapter, that social class has an important impact on black and other families.

4.3 Describe the characteristics of and variations among African American families.

 Read on MySocLab

Document: African American Families: A Legacy of Vulnerability and Resistance

Family Structure

Until 1980, married-couple families among African Americans were the norm because most of the children grew up in households with married parents. Since then, black children have been more likely than children in other racial-ethnic groups to grow up with only one parent, usually a mother (see *Figure 4.3*). This shift reflects a number of social and economic developments: postponement of marriage, high divorce and separation rates, low remarriage rates, male unemployment, and out-of-wedlock births (topics we'll examine in later chapters).

TABLE 4.1	U.S. Population by Race and Ethnicity, 2011 and 2050 (projected)	
In percentages		
	2011	**2050**
White	63	49
Latino	17	25
Black	13	15
Asian	5	9
American Indian/Alaska Native	1.6	2
Native Hawaiian/Other Pacific Islander	.3	.5

Note: The percentages include people who identified themselves with one race or ethnicity, or more than one.

Sources: Based on author's calculations of U.S. Census Bureau, 2013, May, Table 3; and U.S. Census Bureau, 2012, December, Table 4.

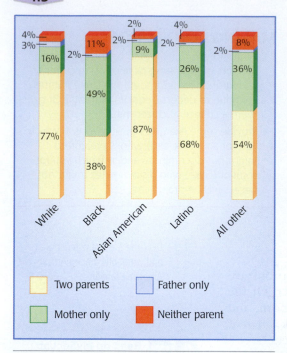

FIGURE 4.3 Where U.S. Children Live, by Race and Ethnicity, 2012
Notes: The "all other" includes American Indian and Alaska Native children, but there are no current data on their percentage. For all groups, most of the children living with neither parent live with one or more grandparents. "Two parents" includes children living with parents who are and aren't married to each other.
Sources: Based on U.S. Census Bureau, Current Population Survey, 2012. 2012, November, Table C3.

Since you asked . . .

- What are some of the problems that many African American parents face in raising their children?

---

racial socialization Parents teach their children to negotiate race-related barriers and experiences in a racially stratified society and to take pride in their ancestry.

Some black fathers leave girlfriends who become pregnant because the men don't want a long-term commitment or don't have the money to support a child. Others die young, are in jail, or are involved in crime and drugs. Some out-of-wedlock fathers visit their children, play with them, and care for them while the mothers are working. The number of such fathers is increasing, but it's still low (see Chapters 9 and 12).

Female-headed households have been and can be stable over time, giving children the love and discipline they need, and are an accepted (although not necessarily the preferred) type of family structure among African Americans. In addition, black adult males (such as sons, brothers, uncles, and grandfathers) often provide critical emotional and financial support to their female kin who head households (Sudarkasa, 2007).

Gender Roles

African American families are often stereotyped as matriarchal (see Chapter 1), but an egalitarian family pattern, in which both men and women share equal authority, is a more common arrangement. For example, black husbands are more likely than their white counterparts to share household chores (John and Shelton, 1997; Xu et al., 1997). The more equal sharing of housework and child care probably reflects black husbands' willingness to pitch in because their wives are employed. Also, many grew up in families in which the mother worked outside the home and black men participated in raising children and doing housework (see Chapters 5 and 13).

The division of domestic work isn't equal, however. Black married women are still more likely than men to do most of the traditional chores, such as cooking, cleaning, and laundry, and to be overworked. Some of the instability in black marriages, as in white marriages, is a result of conflicts that occur when wives expect men to do more of the traditionally female domestic tasks (Livingston and McAdoo, 2007).

Parents and Children

Most African American parents play important roles in their children's development. Many black fathers make a conscious effort to be involved in their children's lives because their own fathers were absent. Others are simply devoted to their kids:

> [My older son and I] do everything together. I learned to roller-skate so that I could teach him and then go skating together. I'm the one who picks him up from school. I'm one of his Sunday school teachers, so he spends Sundays with me at church while my wife stays at home with our two-month-old son (Penha-Lopes, 1995: 187–188).

In 2004, Bill Cosby, an African American actor and author, sparked an uproar when he criticized poor black parents for raising irresponsible children (see "Is Bill Cosby Right about Black Families?"). The comments stirred up considerable debate that still continues.

Because blacks, more than any other group, experience racism on an everyday basis, many African American parents, regardless of social class, engage in **racial socialization**, a process in which parents teach their children to overcome race-related barriers and experiences and to take pride in their ancestry. Because race awareness occurs at about 2 to 3 years of age, most black parents discuss race with their children, especially about overcoming discrimination and succeeding in a racially stratified society (Van Ausdale and Feagin, 2001; Burton et al., 2010).

Another important issue that many black parents face is *colorism*, receiving more privileges or disadvantages, even within the same racial or ethnic group, because of the lightness or darkness of one's skin. Skin color varies across all groups,

Choices   Is Bill Cosby Right about Black Families?

On several occasions, Bill Cosby has scolded low-income black parents and their kids for foolish behavior and decisions:

"It is not all right for your 15-year-old daughter to have a child," he told 2,400 fans in a high school in Milwaukee. He lambasted young men in Baltimore for knocking up "five, six girls." He tongue-lashed single mothers in Atlanta for having sex within their children's hearing "and then four days later, you bring another man into the house" (Cose, 2005: 66).

According to Cosby, many poor black parents waste what little money they have buying their kids $500 sneakers instead of "Hooked on Phonics." He also said that he was fed up with

"knuckleheads" who don't speak proper English and with women who have eight children with eight different men (American Rhetoric Online Speech Bank, 2004).

Many people, regardless of race or ethnicity, agree with Cosby. Others think that he is picking on poor kids and their parents and that low-income youth usually make good purchasing decisions. Those who disagree with Cosby also believe that upper-middle-income blacks who benefited from the civil rights movement are too quick to criticize poor blacks who aren't achieving the same level of financial success (Chin, 2001; Dyson, 2005; Coates, 2008).

Despite criticism, especially from African Americans, Cosby repeated

and elaborated on his controversial views later in a book that blamed parents for relinquishing their family responsibilities in increasing numbers, not providing proper role models, and waiting for handouts instead of taking control of their lives (see Cosby and Poussaint, 2007).

STOP AND THINK . . .

- Are low-income parents and their children making bad choices? Or are they adapting to problems beyond their control?
- Is Cosby right? Or is he holding poor black families to a higher standard that most other Americans don't meet?

including white people, but blacks, as you learned earlier, are more likely than other groups to have many skin tones. Researchers have documented the prejudice and discrimination related to colorism (see, for example, Bonilla-Silva, 2009, and Burton et al., 2010). The only remedy, if any, is to make people more aware of some of the negative effects of colorism both within and across racial-ethnic groups.

Health and Economic Well-Being

According to one of my students, hard-working African American fathers often ignore their health:

I know many black fathers who died before reaching the age of 60. My dad was one of those men. He was a hard worker and stable provider for his family, but he died at the age of 53 due to diabetes and high blood pressure. In general, I think that black men's health often goes unnoticed (Author's files).

Social class has a strong effect on health. Across all groups, the higher one's socioeconomic status (SES, measured by income, education, and occupation), the more likely a person is to afford health insurance and high-quality medical care, and to engage in lifestyles, such as not smoking and healthier eating, that prolong life (National Center for Health Statistics, 2013).

A primary reason for lower-quality health care is economic, and African Americans are among the poorest Americans. Nearly 34 percent of black families have annual incomes of $50,000 or more (De-Navas Walt et al., 2012). Still, the median family income of African Americans is the lowest of all racial-ethnic groups (see *Figure 4.4*).

Across all social classes, there are health gaps between blacks and other groups. For example, the number of people diagnosed with asthma grew by

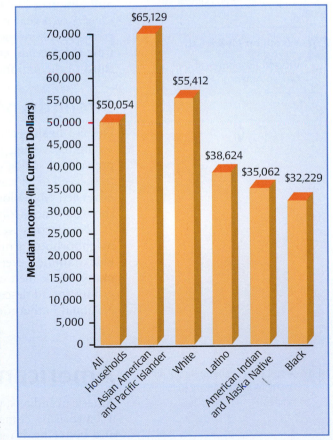

FIGURE 4.4 U.S. Median Household Income by Race and Ethnicity, 2011
Sources: Based on "American Indian and Alaska Native . . .," DeNavas-Walt et al., 2012, Table A-1.

African Americans often pitch in during times of need. Morgan State University's men's basketball coach Todd Bozeman (center) adopted his nephew Okoye (right) when the boy's father, Bozeman's older brother, died in 2007 from a pulmonary embolism. Okoye's mother had died of bone cancer three years earlier. Also pictured are Bozeman's wife (front) and biological children (Klingaman, 2008).

 Watch on MySocLab

Video: Economics of the African American Family

more than 4 million from 2001 to 2009. Scientists don't know why asthma rates are rising, but they increased the most (almost 50 percent) among black children ("Asthma in the U.S.," 2011).

Among racial-ethnic groups, white women are the most likely to get breast cancer, but black women are the most likely to die from this disease. It could be that black women are diagnosed at later stages of the disease or that doctors aren't as aggressive in screening and treating black women with cancer, but no one knows for sure (Williams, 2011; Whitman et al., 2012).

Despite the existence of low-cost, highly effective preventive treatment, black men and women are much more likely to die of heart disease and stroke than their white counterparts. Infants born to black women are 1.5 to 3 times more likely to die than infants born to women of other races and ethnicities, and black women have higher maternal death rates than any other group (Frieden, 2011; Johnson, 2011; see also Chapter 11). As Congress continues to cut health services for the poor, black families—especially those headed by women—will be the ones most likely to experience health problems. Kin provide important emotional and financial support during hard times, but they may feel overburdened when economic difficulties are chronic (Lincoln et al., 2005).

More than two-thirds of African Americans (compared with less than one-third of whites) have no financial assets such as stocks and bonds (Oliver and Shapiro, 2001). Black families inherit less wealth than do white families. Over a two-year period, for example, black families receive $5,013 less in large gifts and inheritances than white families, adding up to substantial amounts over time (McKernan et al., 2012). In addition, discrimination accounts for about a third of the national black–white wage gap (Fryer et al., 2011).

Strengths of the African American Family

Despite health, economic, and other problems, black families have numerous strengths: strong kinship bonds, an ability to adapt family roles to outside pressures, a strong work ethic despite recessions and unemployment, determination to succeed in education, and an unwavering spirituality that helps them cope with adversity. Many low-income black families, especially those headed by mothers, show enormous fortitude and coping skills (Edin and Lein, 1997; McAdoo, 2002).

Numerous self-help institutions (churches, voluntary associations, neighborhood groups, and extended family networks) enhance the resilience of black families, even in the poorest communities. In the past decade, for example, many black men across the country have organized mentoring and self-help groups for adolescents and young fathers through national programs such as the National Fatherhood Initiative and the Center for Urban Families.

4.4 Describe the characteristics of and variations among American Indian families.

American Indian Families

American Indians, who used to be called the "vanishing Americans," have staged a "surprising comeback" because of higher birth rates, longer life expectancy, and better health services (Snipp, 1996: 4). The 5.1 million American Indians and Alaska Natives (AIANs) make up only 1.6 percent of the U.S. population, but are expected to increase to almost 9 million by 2050 ("American Indian and Alaska Native . . .," 2012).

American Indian and Alaska Native families are heterogeneous. Of the 565 federally recognized tribes, 8 have more than 100,000 members. The

Cherokee, with almost 820,000 members, is the largest, followed by the Navajo and Choctaw (Norris et al., 2012). Tribes speak 150 native languages (although many are quickly vanishing) and vary widely in their religious beliefs and cultural practices. Thus, a Comanche-Kiowa educator cautions, "Lumping all Indians together is a mistake. Tribes . . . are sovereign nations and are as different from another tribe as Italians are from Swedes" (Pewewardy, 1998: 71; Ashburn, 2007).

Family Structure

In 2011, there were almost 558,000 AIAN family households: 57 percent were married couples, 32 percent were mother-only, and 11 percent were father-only families ("American Indian and Alaska Native . . .," 2012). Families have a variety of living arrangements that include large extended households, nuclear families, divorced parents, and single-parent families, on and off the reservation. Living in an extended family provides many resources, such as assistance with child care, money, transportation, and emotional and moral support. However, living in such households can increase stress, especially when elders in the home criticize their own children about the way they parent or because they are not making enough money (Cheshire, 2006).

In many American Indian languages, there is no distinction between blood relatives and relatives by marriage. Among some groups, aunts and uncles are considered intimate family members. Sometimes the father's brothers are called "father," uncles and aunts refer to nieces and nephews as "son" or "daughter," and a great-uncle may be referred to as "grandfather" (Sutton and Broken Nose, 1996).

There are two remaining speakers of Kiksht, a language spoken for centuries by the Wasco tribe along Oregon's Columbia River, and neither remembers all the words. Radine Johnson and her grandmother, who is one of the last Kiksht speakers, are working together to record and teach the language to tribal children (Clark, 2008). Pictured here, Radine is teaching Kiksht at a tribal preschool.

Gender Roles

Research on contemporary American Indian families, husbands and wives, and gender roles is virtually nonexistent (Kawamoto and Cheshire, 2004). One exception is a study of 28 off-reservation Navajo families. Here, the researcher found that mothers spent significantly more time than did fathers in cleaning, food-related work, and child care responsibilities. Compared with fathers in other cultural groups, however, the Navajo fathers' involvement in household labor and child-related tasks was high—between 2 and 3 hours per day. The wives reported higher levels of commitment (always pitching in), cohesion (making sacrifices for others), and communication (expressing concerns and feelings). Both husbands and wives, however, felt equally competent in solving family problems and coping with everyday issues (Hossain, 2001).

Parents and Children

Children are important members of American Indian families. Parents spend considerable time and effort in making items for children to play with or use in activities and ceremonies (such as costumes for special dances, looms for weaving, and tools for gardening, hunting, and fishing). Many tribes teach spiritual values and emphasize special rituals and ceremonies (Yellowbird and Snipp, 2002).

Adults teach children to show respect for authority figures by listening and not interrupting. As one tribal leader noted, "You have two ears and one mouth for a reason." Mothers, especially, strive to transmit their cultural heritage to their children. They emphasize the importance of listening to and observing adults to learn about their identity (Gose, 1994; Dalla and Gamble, 1997; Cheshire, 2001).

Some American Indian parents believe that they are losing control over their children's behavior, especially hanging around with friends and drinking. Some researchers see a relationship between American Indian adolescents' risk-taking behavior (such as using drugs and dropping out of school) and fragile family connections. For instance, migration off reservations has weakened the extended family, a principal mechanism for transmitting values and teaching accountability (Machamer and Gruber, 1998).

Elders and Grandparents

Elders are important to a child's care, upbringing, and development, and they contribute to a family's cohesiveness and stability. Children are taught to respect their elders because old age is viewed as a badge of honor—a sign that one has done the right things and has pleased the creator. As a result, elders have traditionally played a central role in a family's decision making. They serve as mentors and advisors and reinforce cultural norms, values, and roles. Despite such contributions, elders are also dealing with an increasing number of issues ranging from poverty to poor health and minimal access to services in both urban and reservation areas (Kawamoto and Cheshire, 2004).

Health and Economic Well-Being

Deaths due to motor vehicle crashes are up to three times higher for men than women, and twice as high among American Indians and Alaska Natives as other groups (West and Naumann, 2011). Among AIANs ages 15 to 34, suicide is the second leading cause of death (behind auto accidents), and is almost twice as high as the national average for that age group ("Suicide," 2010). Auto crashes and suicides are often related to excessive alcohol use among both youth and adults (see "American Indians and Alcohol Use: Facts and Fictions").

Many tribal leaders believe that one of the reasons for the high alcoholism and suicide rates, especially among youth, is the gradual erosion of American Indian culture. Children who live in urban neighborhoods have a particularly hard time maintaining their cultural identity and often feel like outsiders in both the American Indian and white cultures. In response, hundreds of programs nationwide are fighting addiction by reinforcing American Indian cultural practices and values (Sanchez-Way and Johnson, 2000; Sagiri, 2001).

Many AIANs are better off today than they were a decade ago, but long-term institutional discrimination has been difficult to shake. For example, 30 percent live below the poverty line compared with 16 percent of the general population. The median household income of AIANs is slightly higher than that of African American households, but lower than that of other racial-ethnic groups (see *Figure 4.4* on p. 93). This group's educational levels have increased, but only 13 percent of AIANs have a bachelor's degree or higher, compared with 29 percent of the general population ("American Indian and Alaska Native . . .,").

In 2011, one of four civilian-employed American Indians worked in a management or professional occupation, but 16 percent of AIANs were unemployed compared with 9 percent of the general population ("American Indian and Alaska Native . . .,"). American Indian tribes now own 37 percent of the U.S. gambling industry. Few tribes benefit, however, because many casinos

In many states, American Indians hold powwows, gatherings that include dancing, singing, and celebrating the family. The purposes of powwows are to honor American Indian culture and to bring people together to express a sense of community with one another and with the universe.

Since you asked . . .
- Why is alcohol abuse a serious problem among many American Indians?

Constraints

American Indians and Alcohol Use: Facts and Fictions

Alcohol consumption is a serious health problem in many AIAN communities. More than half of the alcohol consumption by U.S. adults is in the form of *binge drinking*, consuming four or more alcoholic drinks on one or more occasions for women and five or more for men. American Indians and Alaska Natives report more binge drinking episodes per month and higher alcohol consumption per episode than any other racial-ethnic group (Kanny et al., 2011; CDC *Vital Signs . . .*, 2012).

Alcohol-related deaths among AIANs account for 12 percent of all deaths compared with 3 percent in the general population. Half of all deaths every year among AIANs in motor vehicle traffic crashes and from liver disease are due to alcohol. Alcohol use is often involved in suicides, and 62 percent of crimes among AIANs—compared with 42 percent for the general population—involve drinking by the offender (Perry, 2004; Naimi et al., 2008; "Congressional Hearing . . . ," 2009).

Alcohol abuse is a problem, but there are many stereotypes and myths about the "drunken Indian." In reality,

- A wide variation in the prevalence of drinking exists from one tribal group to another.

- About 75 percent of alcohol-related deaths are due to sporadic binge drinking rather than chronic alcoholism.

- Serious injuries (such as car accidents) due to alcohol often result in death because many Indians live in rural, remote environments where medical care is far away or unavailable.

- There are considerable variations in alcohol-related deaths across regions. The highest death rates are in the Northern Plains (the Dakotas, Iowa, Minnesota, and Nebraska), and the lowest are in Alaska and the Southern Plains (Arkansas, Kansas, Oklahoma, and Texas) (May, 1999; Naimi et al., 2008).

According to many tribal leaders, several major beer companies have targeted American Indians with their marketing strategies. The poorest reservations often accept sponsorship from brewing companies for annual tribal fairs and rodeos.

STOP AND THINK . . .

- American Indian and Alaskan Natives die at higher rates than other Americans from tuberculosis (600 percent higher), alcoholism (510 percent higher), and diabetes (189 percent higher) (Indian Health Service, 2006). Why do we often hear about high AIAN alcoholism rates but not about the high rates of diseases such as tuberculosis and diabetes?

- Alcohol commercials dominate most television sports programs. Should the commercials be banned in the Northern Plains? Or would such restrictions jeopardize free enterprise and freedom of speech?

Mohegan Sun in southern Connecticut (left) is one of the largest casinos in the United States. It has spent some of its profits on college tuitions, a $15 million senior center, other social programs, and health insurance for tribal members. In contrast, some of the poorest tribes, such as the Navajo and Hopi, who have rejected gambling for religious reasons, often live in poverty (right).

are in remote areas that don't attract tourists. In other cases, powerful tribes have cast out some clans to increase their own share of the profits (Dadigan, 2011; Dao, 2011; Millman, 2012b). Outside of gaming, the number of AIAN-owned businesses grew from fewer than 5 in 1969 to nearly 237,000 in 2007, most of them in construction, retail trade, and health care ("American Indian and Alaska Native . . . ," 2012).

MAKING CONNECTIONS

- Many American Indian languages are becoming extinct. Is this a normal part of a group's acculturation into a host society? Or should the languages be preserved at all costs?

- According to many tribal leaders, American Indian youth have high alcoholism and suicide rates because they often feel alienated from both their own and white cultures. Why do you think that youth from other minority groups—especially Latinos and Asian Americans, who are also straddling two cultures—have lower alcoholism and suicide rates?

Strengths of the American Indian Family

Despite numerous obstacles, American Indians have made considerable economic progress by insisting on self-determination and the rights of tribes to run their own affairs. For example, in 1996, a Blackfeet tribal member filed a class action lawsuit claiming that federal government officials stole or squandered billions of dollars in land royalties meant for American Indians in exchange for oil, gas, grazing, and other leases over a century. The case went through hundreds of motions, seven trials, and dozens of rulings and appeals. In 2012, a U.S. Court of Appeals upheld the $3.4 billion settlement (Volz, 2012).

Strengths of the American Indian family include *relational bonding*, a core behavior that is built on widely shared values such as respect, generosity, and sharing across the tribe, band, clan, and kin group. Another strength is a spirituality that sustains the family's identity and place in the world (Cross, 1998; Cheshire, 2006).

4.5 Describe the characteristics of and variations among Latino families.

Read on MySocLab

Document: Mexican Americans and Immigrant Incorporation

Latino Families

About one in three Americans is a member of a racial or ethnic minority group, but Latinos are the largest racial-ethnic group (see *Table 4.1* on p. 91). Some Latinos trace their roots to the Spanish and Mexican settlers who founded cities in the Southwest before the arrival of the first English settlers on the East Coast (see Chapter 3). Others are recent immigrants or children of the immigrants who arrived in large numbers at the beginning of the twentieth century.

Of the Latinos living in the United States, most are from Mexico (see *Figure 4.5*). Spanish-speaking people from many different countries vary widely in their customs, cuisines, and cultural practices, but we focus here primarily on characteristics that Latino families share, noting variations among different groups when possible.

Family Structure

The growth of the Latino population this century is due mainly to births in the United States, not recent immigration. By age 44, on average, Mexican American women have more children (2.5) than other Latinas (1.9), black women (2.0), and white and Asian/Pacific Islander women (1.8 each) (Taylor and Lopez, 2011).

About 68 percent of Latino children live in two-parent families, down from 78 percent in 1970 (see *Figure 4.3* on p. 92 and Lugaila, 1998). Shifting social norms, economic changes, and immigration patterns have altered the structure of many Latino families. Latino couples born in the United States are more likely to divorce, and there are more out-of-wedlock births, particularly among adolescents. Some young Latino children may also be more likely to live with relatives than only with parents because new immigrants depend on family sponsors until they can become self-sufficient (Garcia, 2002; see also Chapters 11 and 15).

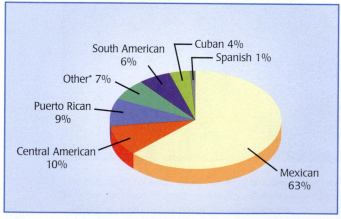

* Includes people who didn't specify a country of origin in the 2010 Census.

FIGURE 4.5 U.S. Latinos by Origin, 2010
Note: Central American includes countries such as El Salvador, Honduras, and Guatemala; South American includes countries such as Argentina, Bolivia, and Venezuela. *Source:* Based on Ennis et al., 2011, Table 1.

Gender Roles

Gender and parenting roles vary depending on how long a family has lived in the United States, whether the wife or mother works outside the home, and the extent of the family's acculturation into U.S. society. Gender roles may also

change in response to job opportunities and new family policies, and as people approach retirement. Latino men often suffer from the *machismo* stereotype, a concept of masculinity that emphasizes dominance, aggression, and womanizing (see Chapter 3).

The mainstream press often ignores such positive elements of *machismo* as courage, honor, *respeto* (a respect for authority, tradition, and family); *dignidad* (avoiding loss of dignity in front of others); and close ties with the extended family. Men who have been raised in a culture with traditional conceptions of masculinity often feel honor and pride in being breadwinners and family protectors. When it's difficult to meet these gender role expectations, they may be at a greater risk than their acculturated counterparts for problems such as depression, substance abuse, violence, and reluctance to seek psychological assistance (Ojeda et al., 2008).

Some scholars contend that *machismo* is a ludicrous stereotype because many Latino men participate in domestic work and child rearing. Among Dominican immigrants, for example, many husbands share some housework and consult their wives about expensive purchases (Pessar, 1995; González, 1996).

Other researchers report that there are elements of *machismo* even in families that have nontraditional gender roles. For example, studies of Puerto Rican and Central American families found that working mothers were primarily responsible for the care of the home and the children. Men in working-class households balked at sharing household responsibilities and child care even when their wives worked full time outside the home (Repak, 1995; Toro-Morn, 1998). Among Mexican American families, husbands tend to be more controlling if both spouses hold traditional attitudes about gender roles, if women don't work outside the home, and if the couples espouse Mexican (rather than European American) culture (Wheeler et al., 2010).

The female counterpart of *machismo* is *marianismo*. *Marianismo*, associated with the Virgin Mary in Catholicism, expects women to remain virgins until marriage and to be self-sacrificing and unassuming (De La Cancela, 1994; Mayo, 1997). Girls are still much more likely than boys to be supervised and monitored, but *marianismo* may be an ideal rather than a reality as evidenced by the high nonmarital pregnancy rates of Latina adolescents (see Chapters 5, 7, and 9).

Since you asked . . .
- Is *machismo* a stereotype or a reality?

Parenting

Even when they're in the labor force, many Latinas devote much of their lives to having and raising children (DeBiaggi, 2002). Fathers don't do nearly as much parenting as do mothers, but compared with white fathers, Latino fathers are more likely to supervise and restrict their children's TV viewing, regulate the types of programs they watch, and require them to finish their homework before going outside to play (Toth and Xu, 2002; see also Chapter 12).

Among Mexican American families, and regardless of social class, mothers are the primary socialization agents in teaching their children cultural values (such as showing respect for adults and embracing their ethnic identity) (Knight et al., 2011). You'll see shortly that Asian American and Middle Eastern parents try to do the same.

Among recent immigrants, especially, acculturation has both benefits and costs. During the acculturation process, first and later generations often acquire the necessary English language skills, competitive values, and education that increase the likelihood of moving up the economic ladder. Mexican immigrant mothers of young children who take adult education courses increased their involvement in their children's education and speeded their acculturation. For example, the mothers saw how the U.S. education system works, interacted more frequently and more confidently with teachers and school personnel, and ultimately enhanced their children's academic progress (Crosnoe and Kalil, 2010).

On the other hand, acculturation, particularly in low-income neighborhoods, may result in Latino adolescents' higher rates of delinquency and crimes (Gibson and Miller, 2010). Like their white counterparts, middle-class Latinos who have acculturated to U.S. society tend to be more permissive in raising their children (Harwood et al., 2002). As you'll see in Chapter 12, permissive parenting—regardless of race, ethnicity, or social class—often produces children who are rebellious and self-centered.

Familism and Extended Families

For many Latino households, familism and the extended family have traditionally provided emotional and economic support. In a national survey, for example, 94 percent of Latinos who were primarily Spanish speakers and 88 percent of those who were bilingual, compared with 67 percent of the general U.S. population, said that relatives are more important than friends (Pew Hispanic Center, 2004).

FAMILISM *Familism*, you recall, refers to family relationships in which sharing and cooperation take precedence over one's personal needs and desires (see Chapter 3). Many Mexican American families, for example, survive primarily because they have the emotional and economic support of kin who arrived in the United States earlier. In other cases, especially during economic downturns and family illness or death, familism helps families pull together and decreases the likelihood of stressed parents treating their children in more negative ways, such as being excessively punitive, verbally and physically abusive, or unpredictable (Kochhar, 2005; Behnke et al., 2008).

Is *familism* still thriving? It depends on the family's origin. For example, *familism* is more common among families of Mexican or Cuban origin than those who have their roots in Puerto Rico or the Caribbean, and is most characteristic of recent immigrants (Cherlin, 2010; Knight et al., 2011).

And are the results of *familism* always positive? *Familism* helps new immigrants, especially, to cope with the everyday stresses of discrimination, unemployment, and learning to survive in a different culture. A recent study of two-parent Mexican-origin families found that familistic values reduced parental conflict and increased nurturing parenting that, in turn, increased the likelihood of children doing well in school (Taylor, Lopez et al., 2012). On the other hand, a study of Mexican American adolescents, ages 12 to 17, found that these children, usually girls, who were expected to care for their teenage sisters' infants, often experienced stress, depression, and lower grades due to their increased absence from school (East and Weisner, 2009).

EXTENDED FAMILIES Extended family members (relatives, godparents, and even close friends) exchange a wide range of goods and services, including elderly and child care, temporary housing, personal advice, and emotional support. Some Mexican Americans practice "chain migration," in which those already in the United States find employment and housing for other kin who are leaving Mexico (López, 1999; Sarmiento, 2002).

The importance of extended families varies by place of residence and social class, but there's a complex relationship between these variables. For example, Mexican Americans in higher socioeconomic classes who live with or near their relatives are more able and likely to provide money or goods. On the other hand, those with higher income and education levels experience greater geographic mobility because of career opportunities, decreasing the likelihood of contact and financial help (Sarkisian et al., 2007).

Since you asked. . .
• Is *familism* as strong today as in the past?

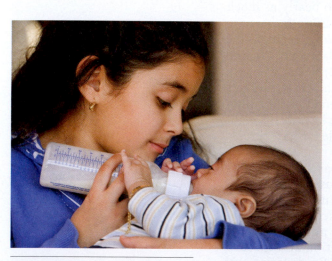

Mexican American adolescents, especially girls, are often expected to provide care for their teenage sisters' babies.

Health and Economic Well-Being

Latinos are less likely than other racial-ethnic groups to have health insurance coverage (see *Figure 4.6*). They often can't afford private insurance, work in jobs that offer no health benefits, or may not be eligible for government health programs (DeNavas-Walt et al., 2012). Nevertheless, Latinos as a group have higher life expectancy rates than whites, blacks, and American Indians; are less likely than other groups, including whites, to experience hypertension (high blood pressure), which increases the risk for heart disease and strokes; and are less likely to engage in binge drinking and to die from illicit drugs and prescription abuse (Kanny et al., 2011; Keenan and Rosendorf, 2011; Miniño, 2011; Paulozzi, 2011).

Latinos' generally better health is changing. Acculturation has increased many Latinos' adopting unhealthy behaviors (e.g., smoking, excessive alcohol consumption, high-calorie diets) that, in turn, have increased their cancer and heart disease rates and deaths (Siegel et al., 2012; see also Tavernise, 2013).

The median household income of Latinos is 59 percent that of Asian Americans, but higher than that of American Indians and African Americans (see *Figure 4.4* on p. 93). Almost 38 percent of Latino families earn $50,000 a year or more (see *Figure 4.7*), up considerably from only 7 percent in 1972, but there's a great deal of variation across Latino subgroups. Almost 49 percent of Cuban families earn this much, compared with 42 percent of Puerto Rican families, 44 percent of those from Central South America, and 37 percent of Mexican American families (U.S. Census Bureau, 2012). And for the first time in U.S. history, more Latino children are living in poverty—25 percent in 2011—than children of any other racial or ethnic group, including whites (Lopez and Velasco, 2011; Gonzalez-Barrera and Lopez, 2013).

As with other groups, the socioeconomic status of Latinos reflects a number of interrelated factors, especially education level, English language proficiency, recency of immigration, and occupation. Many Latinos who were professionals in their native land find only low-paying jobs. Often they don't have time to both work and learn English well enough to pass accreditation exams to practice as doctors, lawyers, and accountants. In Miami, for example, many Cuban physicians have learned English and obtained licenses to practice medicine. But, says one Cuban American doctor, "I know neurosurgeons who are working in warehouses or factories or as gas attendants" (Ojito 2009: D1).

Despite their generally lower economic and educational attainment, many Latinos are successful. They own 2.3 million businesses, up 44 percent from 2002. Between 1995 and 2005, many foreign-born Latino immigrants earned better hourly wages than their predecessors because they tended to be older, better educated, and more likely to be employed in construction than in agriculture (Kochhar, 2007; "Hispanic Heritage . . .," 2012). Among their many contributions, Latinos have breathed life into a number of small midwestern towns (see "The Changing Face of the Midwest").

Strengths of the Latino Family

Despite their economic vulnerability and considerable discrimination, many Latino families are resilient and adaptive. About 75 percent, compared with 58 percent of the general population, believe that most people can get ahead if they work hard, and almost 70 percent of new immigrants, compared with

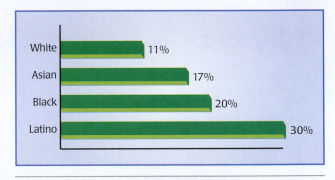

FIGURE 4.6 **Percentage of Americans without Health Insurance, by Race and Ethnicity, 2011**
Source: Based on DeNavas-Walt et al., 2012, Table 7.

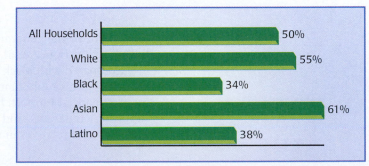

FIGURE 4.7 **Percentage of Households with Annual Incomes of $50,000 or More, by Race and Ethnicity, 2011**
Source: Based on DeNavas-Walt et al., 2012, Table A-1.

Changes

The Changing Face of the Midwest

The West and South are home to most Latinos, but by 2010, Latino growth was most rapid in the South and Midwest (Passel et al., 2011). Mexican farmworkers, primarily migrants, have worked in the Midwest since the 1930s. The new residents now also include Puerto Ricans, Central Americans, and South Americans (Martinez, 2011).

The population of many rural towns and small cities has been dropping for several generations, resulting in closed businesses and churches, shrinking classrooms, and vacant houses. Because of plunging native-born school enrollments, one small town closed the high school and sold the building on eBay (Sulzberger, 2011).

Latinos are now breathing new life into small rural towns and cities that have been "staggering toward the grave." In western Kansas, for example, Latinos have reopened shuttered storefronts with bakeries, restaurants, clothing stores, and computer repair shops; filled the schools with children; opened new churches; and bought vacant houses. Many others have difficult jobs in meatpacking plants and on farms, feedlots, and oil fields (Sulzberger, 2011: A1).

Ottumwa, a small town in Iowa, lost thousands of jobs as the railroads closed many routes, a large meatpacking plant shut down, and every public school experienced plummeting enrollments and severe budget cuts. Latinos—primarily of Mexican,

Salvadoran, and Guatemalan descent—increased Ottumwa's population. The population growth attracted a Menards home-improvement store, a Wal-Mart supercenter, a new $4 million development anchored by a Kohl's store, doubled the value of taxable property, and rejuvenated the public schools (Jordan, 2012).

The new residents want the opportunity to live quiet lives in communities that are similar to those in which they were raised. Some communities have welcomed the newcomers, but others are unhappy. Some lifelong residents complain, for example, that "the dining options are Mexican, Mexican, or Mexican"; the crime rates have increased; many of

the Latinos aren't learning English; and "they feel like strangers in their hometown" (Sulzberger, 2011: A1).

STOP AND THINK . . .

- Are rural towns and cities too small to support multiculturalism? What are the alternatives?

- Some lifelong residents complain that many of the newcomers aren't learning English. How might they respond if reminded that it was only the children and grandchildren of their ancestors (such as the French, Germans, and Norwegians) who learned English?

58 percent of the general population, say that religion is very important in their lives (Taylor, Lopez et al., 2012).

Compared with black and white families, Latinos are much less likely to get large monetary gifts or inheritances. In fact, Latino families are more likely to give than to receive financial support. For example, they're five times as likely as white families to support their parents, and many immigrants send large amounts of income to family members and relatives in their home country (McKernan et al., 2012).

4.6 Describe the characteristics of and variations among Asian American families.

Asian American Families

The more than 18 million Asian Americans comprise almost 6 percent of the U.S. population and encompass a broad swath of cultural groups. They come from at least 26 countries in East and Southeast Asia (including China, Taiwan,

Korea, Japan, Vietnam, Cambodia, and the Philippines) and South Asia (especially India, Pakistan, and Sri Lanka), and there are at least 19 Asian languages spoken in the United States ("Asian/Pacific American heritage . . .," 2013). A majority (62 percent) identify themselves by their country of origin (e.g., Vietnamese, Chinese) (Taylor et al., 2012).

These diverse origins mean that there are vast differences in languages and dialects (and even alphabets), religions, cuisines, and customs. Asian Americans also include Native Hawaiian and other Pacific Islanders from Guam and Samoa. Chinese are the largest Asian American group, followed by Filipinos and Asian Indians (see *Figure 4.8*). Combined, these three groups account for 55 percent of all Asian Americans.

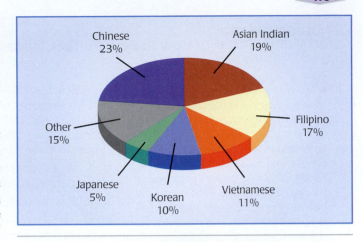

FIGURE 4.8 **Asian Americans by Origin, 2010**
Note: "Other" includes people from at least 13 countries, including Laos, Cambodia, and Sri Lanka, and Native Hawaiian/Pacific Islander.
Sources: Based on Hoeffel et al., 2012, Figure 7.

Family Structure

Asian American family structures vary widely depending on the country of origin, time of arrival, past and current immigration policies, whether the families are immigrants or refugees, and the parents' original socioeconomic status. Average household size varies across groups—from a high of 5 for Hmong to a low of 2.4 for Japanese families (Taylor et al., 2012).

Most Asian American children grow up in two-parent homes (see *Figure 4.3* on p. 92). They're also more likely than the general population to live in multigenerational family households that include parents, children, unmarried siblings, and grandparents. Female-headed homes, whether because of divorce or nonmarital births, are much less common among Asian Americans than other groups. For example, Asian American women have the lowest number of nonmarital births, and about two-thirds of the unmarried mothers are U.S.-born rather than recent immigrants (Taylor et al., 2012).

Read on MySocLab

Document: Intimacy at a Distance, Korean American Style: Invited Korean Elderly and Their Married Children

Marriage and Gender Roles

Asian Americans stand out for their strong emphasis on family. They have the highest marriage rates and the lowest divorce rates (see Chapter 15). Compared with 34 percent of all U.S. adults, 54 percent say that having a successful marriage is one of the most important things in life (Taylor et al., 2012).

Gender roles tend to be traditional in many Asian American families, but vary by social class, country of origin, and length of residence in the United States. For example, both Korean and Vietnamese immigrant women have almost always worked outside the home, but those in later generations have created a more gender-balanced family environment, such as men's greater participation in housework, instead of following traditional gender roles where all housework is the woman's responsibility (Kawamoto and Viramontez Anguiano, 2006). Because Filipino culture historically has had a less patriarchal gender role structure than other groups, husbands and wives tend to have egalitarian relationships (Espiritu, 1995).

Parents and Children

In many Asian American families, the strongest family ties are between parent and child rather than between spouses. Indeed, 67 percent of Asian American adults, compared with only 50 percent of all U.S. adults, say that being a good parent is one of the most important things in life (Taylor et al., 2012).

Parents sacrifice their personal needs in the interests of their children. In return, they expect *filial piety:* respect and obedience toward one's parents (Chan, 1997).

Cross-Cultural and Multicultural Families

How to Be a Perfect Taiwanese Kid

Many immigrant parents—Latino, Middle Eastern, and African—emphasize education as the route to upward mobility and success. The value of education is embodied in the Chinese proverb, "If you are planning for a year, sow rice; if you are planning for a decade, plant trees; if you are planning for a lifetime, educate people." For many Asian American parents, securing a good education for their children is a top priority (Ishii-Kuntz, 2004).

By excelling in school, the child brings honor to the family. Educational and occupational successes further enhance the family's social status and ensure its economic well-being as well as that of the next generation (Chan, 1999). The following tongue-in-cheek observations about how to be the perfect Taiwanese kid (Ng, 1998: 42) from the parents' perspective would apply to many other Asian American families as well:

1. A perfect score on the SAT [Scholastic Aptitude Test].
2. Play the violin or piano at the level of a concert performer.
3. Apply to and be accepted by 27 colleges.
4. Have three hobbies: studying, studying, and studying.
5. Go to a prestigious Ivy League university and win a scholarship to pay for it.
6. Love classical music and detest talking on the phone.
7. Become a Westinghouse, Presidential, and eventually a Rhodes Scholar.
8. Aspire to be a brain surgeon.
9. Marry a Taiwanese American doctor and have perfect, successful children (grandkids for *ahma* and *ahba*).
10. Love to hear stories about your parents' childhood, especially the one about walking 7 miles to school without shoes.

According to a recent national survey, 66 percent of Asian Americans said that parents should have a lot or some influence on their children's choice of profession; 61 percent said the same about their children's choice of spouse (Taylor et al., 2012).

Asian American parents tend to exercise more control over their children's lives than do non–Asian American parents. They often use guilt and shame rather than physical punishment to keep their children in line and to reinforce the children's strong obligations to the family. In Chinese American families, for example, *guan* ("to govern") has a positive connotation. *Guan* also means "to care for" or "to love." Therefore, "parental care, concern, and involvement are synonymous with a firm control and governance of the child" (Chao and Tseng, 2002: 75; Fong, 2002).

Whether it's a myth or a reality, Asian American parents have a reputation as strict and demanding. Overall, 62 percent of Asian Americans believe that most American parents don't put enough pressure on their children to succeed in school. Their views of their own parenting approaches are quite different. Very few Asian Americans (9 percent) say that parents from their country of origin put too little pressure on their children to excel in school. Instead, they believe that parents from their country of origin put about the right amount of pressure (49 percent). About 39 percent of Asian Americans say that parents from their country of origin's subgroup put too much pressure on their children to excel in school. Just 9 percent say the same about all American parents (Taylor et al., 2012). "How to Be a Perfect Taiwanese Kid" illustrates the emphasis on academic achievement.

Health and Economic Well Being

Overall, Asian Americans are healthier than other racial-ethnic groups and whites. They're more likely than blacks or Latinos to have health insurance (see *Figure 4.6* on p. 101). They also have the highest life expectancy rates—81 years for males and 87 years for females (National Institutes of Health, 2006).

Many Asian Americans' longer lifespans may be due to a number of interrelated factors. For example, this group has the lowest (or one of the lowest) rates of obesity, heart disease and stroke deaths, vehicle-related deaths, suicides

and homicides, drug-induced deaths, and deaths due to AIDS (Crosby et al., 2011; Keenan and Rosendorf, 2011; Logan et al., 2011; Paulozzi, 2011; West and Naumann, 2011).

A major reason for many Asian Americans' better health is their high socio-economic status (Beckles and Truman, 2011). They have the highest median household income (see *Figure 4.4* on p. 93). They also have the highest education levels. Almost 21 percent, compared with 11 percent of the general population, have a graduate or professional degree. Because of their high education levels, Asian Americans are more likely than other racial-ethnic groups or whites to be concentrated in highly skilled and high-paying occupations such as information technology, science, engineering, and medicine (Batalova, 2011; Kim, 2011; "Asian/Pacific American Heritage . . .," 2013).

The most successful are Asian Indians: 70 percent have at least a college degree, and they have the highest annual median household income (almost $93,000 in 2011) compared with about $43,000 for Bangladeshi ("Asian/Pacific American Heritage . . .," 2013).

Because of their educational and economic success, Asian Americans are often hailed as a "model minority." Such labels are misleading, however, because there is considerable variation across subgroups. For example, among Asian Americans age 25 and older, more than 63 percent of Hmong, Laotians, and Cambodians and 50 percent of Native Hawaiians and Vietnamese haven't attended college, compared with only about 23 percent of Filipinos and Asian Indians (Teranishi, 2011).

Why are some Asian American groups more successful than others? There are five major reasons. First, the U.S. Immigration and Naturalization Service screens immigrants, granting entry primarily to those who are the "cream of the crop." For example, nearly 66 percent of Filipino immigrants are professionals, usually nurses and other medical personnel, and more than two-thirds of all Asian Americans from India are professionals with advanced degrees beyond college (Adler, 2003; "Asian/Pacific American Heritage . . .," 2013).

Second, the Buddhist and Confucian values and traditions of many Asian immigrants resemble the traditional middle-class prerequisites for success in America. All three ideologies emphasize hard work, education, achievement, self-reliance, sacrifice, steadfast purpose, and long-term goals (see, for example, Yoon, 1997).

The third reason that some Asian American groups are more successful than others is that many of their households are larger than average and include more workers. Especially in two-income families, particularly professionals, common among many Asian Americans, an employed wife can almost double a family's income (see Chapter 13).

Fourth, the most successful Asian Americans are those who speak English relatively well *and* have high education levels. The subgroups with both characteristics are Asian Indians and Filipinos. In contrast, Vietnamese Americans have among the lowest education levels and the least likely to say that they speak English well enough to carry on a conversation (Taylor et al., 2012).

A final reason for many Asian American families' success is fairly straightforward: They usually work harder than their non-Asian counterparts. For example, Asian American students are more likely than other racial-ethnic groups, and often white students, to finish high school, enroll in and graduate from college, and achieve graduate degrees (Carey, 2005; Pryor et al., 2007). About 69 percent of Asian Americans, compared with 58 percent of all Americans, believe that they can get ahead if they work hard. About 93 percent of Asian Americans describe themselves as "very hard working;" just 57 percent say the same about Americans as a whole (Taylor et al., 2012).

In 2007, Asian Americans owned 1.5 million businesses, an increase of 40 percent from 2002 ("Asian/Pacific American Heritage . . .," 2013). Asian Indians own about 43 percent of the 47,000 hotels and motels in the United States. In many cases, the owners bought run-down lodgings and converted them to upscale Sheraton and

Asian American youths, such as Sukanya Roy, an Asian Indian from Pennsylvania, often win spelling bees and science contests. In 2011, Roy, an eighth-grader, won the Scripps National Spelling Bee with the correct spelling of *cymotrichous*. (I, too, had to look it up.)

Since You Asked . . .
- What is a "model minority"?

Hilton hotels (Yu, 2007). Asian Americans have also been more successful than other minority groups in penetrating corporate suites. In 1995, for example, all of the *Fortune 500* CEOs were white. By 2008, four were black men, five were Latino men, and seven were Asian Americans, two of them women (DiversityInc, 2008).

Strengths of the Asian American Family

Asian American families vary significantly in their country of origin, time of immigration, ability to speak English, and other factors. Generally, however, the strengths of Asian American families include stable households in which parents encourage their children to remain in school, and offer personal support that reduces the stress produced by discrimination and leads to better emotional health (Barringer et al., 1993; Leonard, 1997).

Asian American families are changing. Still, more than half (compared with 34 percent of the general population) believe that having a successful marriage is very important (Taylor et al., 2012).

4.7 Describe the characteristics of and variations among Middle Eastern American families.

Middle Eastern Families

The term *Middle East* refers to "one of the most diverse and complex combinations of geographic, historical, religious, linguistic, and even racial places on Earth" (Sharifzadeh, 1997: 442). The Middle East encompasses about 30 countries that include Turkey, Israel, Iran, Afghanistan, Pakistan, and a number of Arab nations (such as Algeria, Egypt, Iraq, Jordan, Kuwait, Lebanon, Palestine, Saudi Arabia, Syria, and the United Arab Emirates).

Of the 57 million people in the United States who speak a language other than English at home, more than 3 percent speak Middle Eastern languages such as Armenian, Arabic, Hebrew, Persian, or Urdu (U.S. Census Bureau, 2012). Most Middle Eastern Americans are of Arab ancestry. According to the Census Bureau, there are more than 1.5 million Americans of Arab descent, accounting for less than 0.5 percent of the total population (Asi and Beaulieu, 2013). Those who identify themselves as Arab Americans come from many different countries (see *Figure 4.9*). As in the case of Asian American families, Middle Eastern families make up a heterogeneous population that is a "multicultural, multiracial, and multiethnic mosaic" (Abudabbeh, 1996: 333).

Family Structure

Among Arab American families, the average household size varies, from a high of 4.3 among Yemeni to a low of 2.7 among Lebanese—about the size of the average U.S. household (Asi and Beaulieu, 2013). Arab American women born in the United States have low fertility rates: just under two children per lifetime (which is lower than the average among all U.S. women). Many women postpone childbearing and have fewer children because they pursue college and professional degrees and have high employment rates (Kulczycki and Lobo, 2001).

Most Middle Eastern children (84 percent) live with both parents, compared with 69 percent of all American children. Middle Eastern families frown on divorce. Iranians, for example, view divorce as a calamity (*bala*) and equate it with an "unfortunate fate" that should be avoided at all costs. Divorce rates for U.S.-born Middle Eastern families are increasing, but the percentages are much lower than the national average (almost half of all marriages). Unless a parent

Steve Jobs—the late co-founder, chairman, and chief executive of Apple Inc.—was adopted. His birth parents were two unmarried university students. His birth father was a Syrian-born Muslim, and his birth mother was a U.S.-born Catholic of Swiss descent. The father put the baby up for adoption because his girlfriend's family wouldn't allow her to marry an Arab ("Steve Jobs . . . ," 2011).

is a widow or a widower, single parenthood is seen as abnormal (Aswad, 1997; Hojat et al., 2000).

Nuclear families are the norm, but extended family ties are important. "The typical Lebanese," for example, "views family as an extension of him or herself" (Richardson-Bouie, 2003: 528). Households composed of parents and children maintain close contact with relatives. These relationships provide financial, social, and emotional support.

Marriage and Gender Roles

For most Middle Easterners, and unlike many Western families, the family is the center of life. Shame against the family should be avoided at all costs, age and wisdom (instead of youth and beauty) are honored, and friends are treated courteously but are not seen as important as family members (Office of the Deputy Chief . . . , 2006). Many Middle Eastern families value close and reciprocal ties between husbands and wives. Marriage is often a "family affair," and gender role expectations are usually clearly delineated.

MARRIAGE   Marriage is endogamous (see Chapter 1), favoring unions between cousins in some groups and people from the same national group. Marriage is a sacred ceremony and is regarded as central to the family unit. Generally, it's a contract between two families and is rarely based on the Western concept of romantic love. Marriages are often arranged or semi-arranged but children can turn down their parents' choices of a suitable mate (see Chapters 8 and 10).

GENDER ROLES   Middle Eastern culture mandates distinct gender role expectations. Men have been socialized to be the family's providers and to protect their wives, children, and female kin. A "good" husband, then, supports his family and makes decisions that promote the family's well-being. In most cases, the husband is the highest authority in the family and has the final decision on family issues (Aswad, 1999; Joseph, 1999).

Women anchor the family's identity. A "good" wife takes care of the home and children, obeys her husband, and gets along with her in-laws. She doesn't challenge her husband, particularly in public, and doesn't work outside the home, especially when the children are young. Men have many privileges, but women have considerable influence and status at home and in child rearing (Simon, 1996).

A wife should always act honorably and do nothing that humiliates her husband and relatives. Premarital sex and extramarital affairs are out of the question because they bring shame to the family and kin. According to some young women, such gender role expectations are comforting rather than restrictive because they protect women from assaults and competition for dates (Shakir, 1997).

Gender roles are changing, however. Many Middle Eastern women work out of economic necessity. The women who are most likely to be employed, however, at least among Arab Americans, are those without children at home. In effect, then, patriarchal systems dictate that Middle Eastern women in some groups can be in the labor force only when they don't have traditional responsibilities such as raising children (Read, 2004).

Parents and Children

According to an Arabic saying, "To satisfy God is to satisfy parents." Satisfying parents means following the family's customs and traditions, respecting one's cultural identity, and living up to gender role expectations.

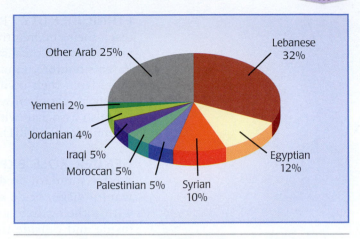

FIGURE 4.9 **Arab Americans by Origin, 2010**
Note: "Other Arab" includes those from the Middle East and North Africa.
Source: Based on Asi and Beaulieu, 2013, Table 1.

Since you asked . . .
- How has acculturation changed Middle Eastern families?

 Read on MySocLab

Document: Growing Old in an Arab American Family

ETHNIC IDENTITY   Parents and children usually have strong bonds. Parents also teach their children to feel a lifelong responsibility to their siblings and parents and to respect their aunts, uncles, cousins, and grandparents (Ajrouch, 1999). Parents reinforce ethnic identity by encouraging their children to associate with peers from their own culture. Many Armenian children, for example, attend language school on weekends. These adolescents not only learn their language but also associate with Armenian classmates who have similar cultural values (Phinney et al., 2001).

GENDER ROLE EXPECTATIONS   Many Middle Eastern parents have a double standard on dating and curfews. Girls are guarded because husbands want a virgin bride and not "damaged goods." Boys are expected to marry within their ethnic group, but they have much more freedom to date, both inside and outside their group. According to a Lebanese mother, "We just feel the boy can take care of himself. If a boy goes out with a girl, nobody's going to point a finger at him." In contrast, a girl who dates or dresses "the wrong way" will ruin her reputation and dishonor the family's name (Simon, 1996; Ajrouch, 1999).

Girls are expected to perform traditional domestic chores and serve men. Some girls accept these roles, but others complain. According to a young Lebanese woman,

> So many times I would be asked to fix my brother's bed. I was told, "He is a boy." And I would say, "He has arms and legs." Or sometimes he would be sitting, and he would say, "Go get me a glass of water." I would say, "Never! Get your own." My family would say to me, "Your head is so strong, it cannot be broken with a hammer" (Shakir, 1997: 166).

The double standard often creates conflict between daughters and their parents. Middle Eastern teenage girls who spend much time with their American friends, especially, balk at the restrictions on dating. These and other disagreements can strain intergenerational relationships.

Economic Well-Being

Middle Eastern Americans tend to be better educated and wealthier than other Americans. For example, 45 percent of Arab Americans have a college degree or higher compared with only 28 percent of the general population; 18 percent have a postgraduate degree, which is nearly twice the U.S. average of 10 percent. Because of their generally higher educational levels, the proportion of U.S. Arabs working in management jobs is higher than the U.S. average, 42 percent and 34 percent, respectively (Office of the Deputy Chief . . . , 2006; Arab American Institute Foundation, 2012b).

In 2010, the median income of Arab American households was almost $57,000 compared with about $52,000 for all U.S. households. As in other groups, however, there are wide variations. For example, Lebanese had higher median family incomes ($67,300) than Iraqis ($32,000) (Asi and Beaulieu, 2013).

Not all Middle Eastern Americans are successful, of course. In 2008, the proportion of U.S. Arabs living in poverty (14 percent) was lower than that of the general population (19 percent), but increased to 28 percent for single mothers. Lebanese and Syrians have the lowest poverty rates, 11 percent, compared with more than 26 percent for those from Iraq and many other Middle East countries (Brittingham and de la Cruz, 2005; Arab American Institute Foundation, 2012b).

"We smelled middle-eastern cooking."

Strengths of the Middle Eastern Family

Middle Eastern Americans cope with prejudice and discrimination because they have a strong ethnic identity, close family ties, and religious beliefs that secure children to their communities. Most important, perhaps, many Middle East families have extended kin networks and relatives on whom they can count during hard times (Ajrouch, 1999; Hayani, 1999).

MAKING CONNECTIONS

- If you're a member of a racial-ethnic family, what do you see as its major strengths? What about its weaknesses?
- What are some of the benefits and costs of maintaining one's ethnic-racial identity instead of acculturating?

Interracial and Interethnic Relationships and Marriages

4.8 Describe how and explain why interracial and interethnic relationships are changing American marriages and families.

When President Obama filled out the 2010 Census form, he checked the "Black, African American, or Negro" box. The son of a black father from Kenya and a white mother from Kansas, the president could have checked off both black and white or "other" (Yemma, 2010). The president is just one of the growing number of Americans who are biracial or multiracial.

Growing Multiracial Diversity

As you saw earlier in this chapter, the 2000 U.S. Census allowed people to mark more than one race and ethnicity for the first time, which generated about 126 categories and combinations. In 2010, 97 percent of Americans reported being only one race, but almost 3 percent (9 million people) self-identified as being of two or more races, up from 2.4 percent in 2000. Every state saw its multiple-race population jump by at least 8 percent, but Native Hawaiians/Pacific Islanders were the most likely to identify themselves as belonging to two or more races (see *Figure 4.10*). Almost a third of those reporting two or more races were Latinos (Jones and Bullock, 2012).

Read on MySocLab

Document: Breaking the Last Taboo: Interracial Marriage in America

Interracial and Interethnic Dating and Marriage

Interracial and interethnic marriages reflect *exogamy*, or marrying outside of one's particular group (see Chapters 1 and 8). Laws against **miscegenation**, marriage or sexual relations between a man and a woman of different races, existed in the United States as early as 1661. It wasn't until 1967, in the U.S. Supreme Court's *Loving v. Virginia* decision, that antimiscegenation laws were overturned nationally, but not everyone is happy about interracial relationships. In 2012, for example, a Baptist congregation in Kentucky voted to ban interracial couples from becoming members or participating in worship activities (Adams, 2012).

In 1958, only 4 percent of Americans approved of black–white marriages, compared with 87 percent in 2013 (Newport 2013). A large majority (63 percent) of Americans say that they'd be fine with a family member's marriage to someone of a different racial or ethnic group (Wang, 2012). Attitudes about interracial marriages are changing, but what about behavior?

miscegenation Marriage or sexual relations between a man and a woman of different races.

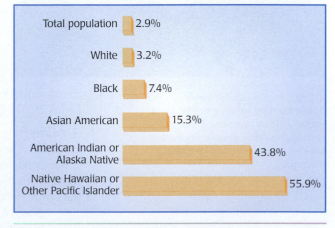

FIGURE 4.10 **Percentage of Americans Who Identify Themselves as Being More than One Race, 2010**
Note: Of the almost 309 million U.S. population in 2010, only 0.3 percent said they were three or more races. *Source:* Based on Jones and Bullock, 2012, Figure 10.

PREVALENCE OF RACIAL-ETHNIC INTERMARRIAGES Racial-ethnic intermarriages have increased slowly—from only 0.7 percent of all marriages in 1970 to almost 9 percent in 2010. In 2010, also, 18 percent of heterosexual unmarried couples were of different races and 21 percent of same-sex couples were interracial. A record 15 percent (1 in 7) of new U.S. marriages were between people of different races or ethnicities, more than double the share in 1980

(7 percent). Asian Americans were more likely than any other major racial or ethnic group to intermarry. Among all newlyweds in 2010, 9 percent of whites, 17 percent of blacks, 26 percent of Latinos, and 28 percent of Asians married outside their racial-ethnic group (Fields and Casper, 2001; Lofquist et al., 2012; Wang, 2012).

There are also notable differences by sex. In 2010, Asian women were twice as likely as Asian men to "marry out" (36 percent and 17 percent, respectively). Among blacks, the gender pattern ran the other way: 24 percent of all males married outside their race, compared with just 9 percent of women. Intermarriage rates among whites and Latinos didn't vary by sex (Wang, 2012).

SOME REASONS FOR INTERMARRIAGE VARIATIONS The increase of and racial-ethnic variations in intermarriage rates are due to a number of interrelated factors, both micro level and macro level. Let's begin with proximity.

1. *Proximity.* We tend to date and marry people we see on a regular basis. For example, one of the reasons why recent Asian American newlyweds have high intermarriage rates is due to Asian Americans now being much more likely (81 percent) than blacks (59 percent), Latinos (57 percent), and whites (10 percent) to live in a racially mixed neighborhood (Taylor et al., 2012). Doing so increases the chances of meeting and socializing with other racial-ethnic people.

2. *Socioeconomic status.* You'll see in Chapter 8 that intermarriage can improve one's social standing, as when some minority women marry white men who have lower educational levels than the women. For the most part, however, the higher one's social class, the greater the likelihood of intermarriage. Educated minority group members often attend integrated colleges, and their workplaces are more integrated than in the past. College-educated people, especially young adults, are also more likely than those with lower educational levels to see intermarriage in a positive light (Passel et al., 2010; Chen and Takeuchi, 2011; Wang, 2012).

In 1992, rock musician David Bowie married Iman, a model from Somalia. They have one child. Do such high-profile people encourage greater acceptance of interracial marriage?

3. *Availability of potential spouses.* People often marry outside their racial-ethnic groups because of a scarcity of eligible mates within their own group. Because the Arab American population is so small, for example, 80 percent of U.S.-born Arabs have non-Arab spouses. In contrast, and despite the recent spike among newlyweds, intermarriage rates for Latinos and Asian Americans have decreased since 1990—for both women and men—because the influx of new immigrants has provided a larger pool of eligible mates (Kulczycki and Lobo 2002; Qian and Lichter 2011).

4. *Acculturation.* Acculturation affects intermarriage rates, but is also related to the availability of potential spouses and attitudes. Among Asian Americans, for example, Japanese Americans have the highest intermarriage rates, both historically and currently, because many families have been in the country for four or five generations, have acculturated, have a small pool of eligible Japanese mates, and are generally more accepting of intermarriage than are more recent immigrants. In addition, the number of Japanese Americans is small compared with that of many other Asian American groups. This decreases the opportunities for Japanese Americans to find a desirable mate within their own group (Hwang et al., 1994; Rosenfeld, 2002).

MAKING CONNECTIONS

• How do you feel about interethnic and interracial dating and marriage? Do your views differ from those of your parents or grandparents?

• Are racial-ethnic intermarriages desirable because they reflect an acceptance of other groups? Or do they dilute cultural heritages?

The number of Asian Indians is larger than that of Japanese Americans (see *Figure 4.8* on p. 103), but in 2010, half of the Japanese newlyweds married non-Asians compared with only 13 percent of Asian Indians. These differences may be due to many Asian Indians

being less acculturated, having a large pool of college-educated women within their own group, and holding traditional views such as believing that parents should influence their children's choice of a profession and spouse (see Taylor et al., 2012).

CONCLUSION

The racial and ethnic composition of American families is *changing* primarily because of an influx of recent immigrants from many non-European countries. There are also many variations both between and within racial-ethnic groups in family structure, extended kinship networks, and parenting styles. This means that families have more *choices* outside the traditional, white, middle-class family model. Choices often are steeped in *constraints*, however, because as you'll see in the next chapter, gender roles also play an important role in every family's daily life.

On MySocLab

✓ **Study** and **Review** on MySocLab

REVIEW QUESTIONS

4.1. Describe how and explain why racial-ethnic diversity is changing the U.S. population.

1. How and why has the U.S. foreign-born population changed since 1900?

2. How and why have Americans' attitudes toward undocumented immigrants been changing?

4.2. Explain why race and ethnicity are important in understanding marriages and families.

3. Because whites make up less than half of the population in some states, aren't they a minority group?

4. What are the differences, if any, among racism, prejudice, and discrimination?

4.3. Describe the characteristics of and variations among African American families.

5. How do black families vary in kinship structure, values, and gender roles?

6. How, specifically, does social class affect black families' health and economic well-being?

4.4. Describe the characteristics of and variations among American Indian families.

7. How do American Indian families vary in family structure, gender roles, and parenting?

8. Why do many American Indians experience economic problems, especially since they own much of the gambling industry?

4.5. Describe the characteristics of and variations among Latino families.

9. How do Latino families vary in terms of structure, gender roles, parenting, and living in extended families?

10. How and why do Latino families differ regarding where they came from, social class, and acculturation?

4.6. Describe the characteristics of and variations among Asian American families.

11. How do Asian American families differ from their country of origin in terms of family structure, gender roles, and when they arrived in the United States?

12. Why are Asian Americans often described as a "model minority"? Is the description appropriate or a stereotype?

4.7. Describe the characteristics of and variations among Middle Eastern American families.

13. How and why are many Middle Eastern families similar?

14. What are some of the major differences across subgroups?

4.8. Describe how and explain why interracial and interethnic relationships are changing American marriages and families.

15. Why have interracial and interethnic marriages increased since 1967? Are some racial-ethnic groups more likely to intermarry than others?

16. What are the micro- and macro-level factors that affect intermarriage rates?

CHAPTER

5

Socialization and Gender Roles

((• **Listen** to Chapter 5 on **MySocLab**

LEARNING OBJECTIVES

After reading and studying this chapter you will be able to:

5.1 Define and illustrate the following concepts: sex, gender, gender identity, gender roles, and gender stereotypes.

5.2 Describe the nature–nurture debate and the evidence for each perspective.

5.3 Compare five theoretical perspectives that explain why gender roles differ.

5.4 Describe and illustrate five sources of learning gender roles.

5.5 Explain how gender ideologies affect traditional and nontraditional gender roles.

5.6 Describe and illustrate how gender roles vary in adulthood.

5.7 Compare gender inequality across cultures.

- Nearly 794 million people in the world (11 percent of the world's population) are illiterate; **two-thirds of them are women**.

- Among 135 countries, the United States **ranks only 55th in the number of women at the highest-ranking political positions**, and well below developing countries such as Nicaragua (#5), Bangladesh (#8), Philippines (#14), and Cuba (#19).

- Men comprise less than **50 percent of the U.S. population age 18 and older**, but they account for 96 percent of Fortune 500 and Fortune 1000 CEOs, 93 percent of Hollywood directors, 87 percent of Wikipedia contributors, 86 percent of Rock and Roll Hall of Fame inductees, 85 percent (each) of authors of op-ed articles in influential national newspapers and senior executives at Fortune 100 firms, 84 percent of partners at the country's largest law firms, 82 percent of the U.S. Congress, 74 percent of college presidents, 73 percent of the country's state and federal judges, and 67 percent of the U.S. Supreme Court justices.

- If they had a choice, 49 percent of American women compared with 24 percent of men **would rather be stay-at-home moms and stay-at-home dads** than have a job.

- Among U.S. adults, 25 percent believe that **the most satisfying marriage** is one where the man is the sole breadwinner, 71 percent believe that the most satisfying marriage is one where both spouses have jobs, and 4 percent aren't sure.

Sources: Kohut et al., 2010; Carmon, 2011; Cohen, 2011; *CIA World Factbook*, 2012; Cook and Kim, 2012; Hausmann et al., 2012; Refki et al., 2012; Saad, 2012; U.S. Census Bureau, 2012; Catalyst, 2013; Center for American Women and Politics, 2013.

D o you know what would have happened if there had been Three Wise Women instead of Three Wise Men? They would have asked for directions, arrived on time, helped deliver baby Jesus, cleaned the stable, made a casserole, brought practical gifts, and there would be peace on Earth. Does this joke stereotype women and men? Or do you think that it contains a kernel of truth?

You saw in Chapter 1 that *socialization*, a major function of the family, establishes our social identity, teaches us role taking, and shapes our behavior. In this chapter, we examine gender roles in the context of socialization: how we learn gender roles and how they affect our everyday lives and family relations. First, however, take the "Ask Yourself" quiz to see how much you know about women and men.

ASK YOURSELF

How Much Do You Know about U.S. Women and Men?

True False

- **1.** Women are the weaker sex.
- **2.** The percentage of married women who keep their maiden name has increased since the mid-1990s.
- **3.** Americans would prefer to work for a male boss than a female boss.
- **4.** Women talk more than men.
- **5.** Women suffer more from depression than men.
- **6.** Women are more likely than men to divulge personal information.

True False

- **7.** Men smile more often than women.
- **8.** Women and men don't care whether a baby is a boy or a girl ("just as long as it's healthy").
- **9.** Most women are confident about managing their financial affairs.
- **10.** A heart attack is more likely to be fatal for a man than for a woman.

(The answers to this quiz are on p. 120.)

113

5.1

5.1 Define and illustrate the following concepts: sex, gender, gender identity, gender roles, and gender stereotypes.

Watch on **MySocLab**

Video: Similarities and Differences Between Men and Women

sex The biological characteristics with which we are born and that determine whether we are male or female.

Watch on **MySocLab**

Video: Sexual Orientation and Gender

gender The learned attitudes and behaviors that characterize women and men.

gender identity An individual's perception of himself or herself as masculine or feminine.

How Women and Men Are Similar and Different

Many Americans, primarily because of the mass media and self-help writers (see Chapter 2), believe that men and women are very different. You'll see later in this chapter that both sexes often describe men as aggressive, courageous, and ambitious. In contrast, they see women as emotional, talkative, patient, and affectionate.

Do these traits characterize you, your family members, and friends? Probably not. Your mom may be aggressive and ambitious and your dad emotional and talkative. Or both may be aggressive, emotional, or talkative, depending on the situation. And either or both parents may change over the years.

Is There a Difference between Sex and Gender?

Many people use the terms *sex* and *gender* interchangeably, but they have distinct meanings. *Sex* is a biological designation, whereas *gender* is a cultural creation that teaches us to play male or female roles (Muehlenhard and Peterson, 2011).

SEX **Sex** refers to the biological characteristics with which we are born—our chromosomal, anatomical, hormonal, and other physical and physiological attributes. Such biological characteristics determine whether we have male or female genitalia, whether we will menstruate, how much body hair we will have and where it will grow, whether we're able to bear children, and so on. Sex *influences* our behavior (such as shaving beards and wearing bras), but it does *not determine* how we think, feel, and act. We learn to be feminine or masculine through our gender, a more complex concept than sex.

GENDER **Gender** refers to learned attitudes and behaviors that characterize women and men. Gender is based on social and cultural expectations rather than physical traits. Thus, most people are *born* either female or male, but we *learn* to associate conventional behavior patterns with each sex. For example, a significant gender difference in smiling emerges around age 11, intensifies during adolescence, and continues through midlife. Girls and women smile more than boys and men, more expansively, more frequently, and across more situations. Such gender differences, at least in U.S. culture, suggest that we learn early in life that even facial expressions, such as smiling, are considered more appropriate, and even desirable, for females than males (Wondergem and Friedlmeier, 2012).

GENDER IDENTITY People develop a **gender identity**, a perception of themselves as masculine or feminine, early in life. Many Mexican baby girls but not boys have pierced ears, for example, and hairstyles and clothing for American toddlers differ by sex. Gender identity, which typically corresponds to a person's biological sex, is learned in early childhood and usually remains relatively fixed throughout life.

Gender identities arise because most people internalize many of the cultural meanings associated with their biological sex, and regulate their behavior to conform to a culture's expectations of femaleness and maleness. Our gender identity becomes part of our self-concept, but people differ in the extent to which a gender identity is important to them (Witt and Wood, 2010). For example, men who regard themselves as masculine may be passive, and women who see themselves as feminine may be aggressive.

Regardless of sex, gender, and gender identity, both sexes *experience* emotions such as anger, happiness, and sadness just as deeply. What differs is how women

Many people view female athletes as "unfeminine," "butch," or "less powerful" than men. Do such stereotypes characterize most female athletes, such as Serena Williams, pictured here?

and men *express* their emotions. For example, men are more likely to suffer in silence, whereas women tend to show their emotions more openly (Simon and Nath, 2004). Such differences are largely due to gender roles.

GENDER ROLES   One of the functions of the family is to teach its members appropriate **gender roles**, the characteristics, attitudes, feelings, and behaviors that society expects of males and females. As a result, we learn to become male or female through interactions with family members and the larger society.

Social scientists often describe our roles as *gendered*, treating and evaluating males and females differently because of their sex:

> *To the extent that women and men dress, talk, or act differently because of societal expectations, their behavior is gendered. To the extent that an organization assigns some jobs to women and others to men on the basis of their assumed abilities, that organization is gendered. And to the extent that professors treat a student differently because that student is a man or a woman, their interaction is gendered (Howard and Hollander, 1997: 11).*

Because gender roles are learned and not innate, we can change them. Many women now pursue graduate degrees and contribute to the family's finances, and many men participate in raising children and do more housework than in the past.

GENDER STEREOTYPES   For the most part, U.S. society still has fairly rigid gender roles and widespread **gender stereotypes**, expectations about how people will look, act, think, and feel based on their sex. We tend to associate stereotypically female characteristics with weakness and stereotypically male characteristics with strength. Consider, for example, how often we describe the same behavior differently for women and men:

- He's firm; she's stubborn.
- He's careful about details; she's picky.
- He's honest; she's opinionated.
- He's raising good points; she's "bitching."
- He's a man of the world; she's "been around."

Stereotypes may seem harmless, but they can have negative consequences. A study of 624 letters of recommendation for college faculty jobs found that women

gender roles The characteristics, attitudes, feelings, and behaviors that society expects of males and females.

gender stereotype Expectations about how people will look, act, think, and feel based on their sex.

and men, regardless of qualifications, were often described differently. Female candidates were often characterized as "agreeable," "warm," and "kind." Male candidates were often described as "assertive," "confident," and "ambitious." Being agreeable and assertive are important traits for most jobs, but female-typed characteristics—for both men and women—decreased the candidates' chance of being hired (Madera et al., 2009).

The Nature–Nurture Debate

Most biologists maintain that the differences in women's and men's behavior are due to innate biological characteristics. In contrast, many social scientists, including sociologists, underscore the importance of socialization and culture in understanding human development. This difference of opinion is called the *nature–nurture debate* (see *Table 5.1*).

How Important Is Nature?

Those who argue that nature (biology) shapes behavior point to three kinds of evidence: developmental and health differences between males and females, the effects of sex hormones, and some cases of unsuccessful sex reassignment.

DEVELOPMENTAL AND HEALTH DIFFERENCES   Boys mature more slowly, get sick more often, and are less likely to have mastered the self-control and fine-motor skills necessary for a successful start in school. Boys are also at greater risk than girls for most of the major learning and developmental disorders—as much as four times more likely to suffer from autism, attention deficit disorder, and dyslexia. Girls, however, are at least twice as likely as boys to suffer from depression, anxiety, and eating disorders (Eliot, 2012).

Among adults, the senses of smell and taste are more acute in women than in men, and hearing is better and lasts longer in women than in men. Women, however, have a higher risk of developing diabetes. Some conditions (such as migraine headaches and breast cancer) are more common in women, whereas others (such as hemophilia and skin cancer) are more common in men (McDonald, 1999; Kreeger, 2002a, 2002b).

EFFECTS OF SEX HORMONES   Scientists don't know why there are such health differences between women and men, but they believe that hormones provide part of the answer. All males and females share three sex **hormones**, chemical substances secreted into the bloodstream by endocrine glands: *estrogen* (dominant in females and produced by the ovaries), *progesterone* (present in high levels during pregnancy and also secreted by the ovaries), and *testosterone* (dominant

Since you asked . . .

- Are people automatically masculine or feminine because they were born male or female?

hormones Chemical substances secreted into the bloodstream by endocrine glands.

TABLE 5.1	The Nature–Nurture Debate
Nature	**Nurture**
Human development is . . .	**Human development is . . .**
Innate	Learned
Biological, physiological	Psychological, social, cultural
Due largely to heredity	Due largely to environment
Fairly fixed	Very changeable

On the left: A photo of Dr. Ben Barres as a bridesmaid in 1988 before he underwent sex surgery. On the right, Dr. Barres, a neurobiologist at Stanford University's Medical Center, says, "By far, the main difference I have noticed is that people who don't know I am transgendered treat me with much more respect" than when he was a woman. "I can even complete a whole sentence without being interrupted by a man."

in males and produced by the testes). All of these hormones are present in minute quantities in both sexes before puberty.

After puberty, varying levels of these hormones in males and females produce different physiological changes. For example, testosterone, the dominant male sex hormone, strengthens muscles but threatens the heart. It triggers the production of low-density lipoprotein, which clogs blood vessels. Therefore, men are at twice the risk of coronary heart disease as are (premenopausal) women. The dominant female sex hormones, especially estrogen, make blood vessels more elastic and strengthen the immune system, making females more resistant to infection. Having too much or too little estrogen in the body, however, can have negative effects such as increased chances of heart disease and breast cancer (Wizemann and Pardue, 2001).

UNSUCCESSFUL SEX REASSIGNMENT   Some scientists point to unsuccessful attempts at sex reassignment as another example favoring the nature-over-nurture argument. Beginning in the 1960s, John Money, a highly respected psychologist, published numerous articles and books in which he maintained that gender identity is not firm at birth but is determined as much by culture and nurture as by hormones (see, for example, Money and Ehrhardt, 1972).

Several scientists have challenged such conclusions. As "The Case of Brenda/David" shows, Money's most famous sex reassignment experiment doesn't support his contention that infants born as biological males can be successfully raised as females.

How Important Is Nurture?

Most social scientists maintain that nurture is more significant than nature because socialization and culture shape human behavior. They often point to three types of data to support their argument: global variations in gender roles, international differences in male violence rates, and successful sex reassignment cases.

CROSS-CULTURAL VARIATIONS IN GENDER ROLES   In a classic study, anthropologist Margaret Mead (1935) observed three tribes that lived within short distances of one another in New Guinea and found three combinations

Choices

The Case of Brenda/David

In 1963, twin boys were being circumcised. The penis of one of the infants, David, was accidentally burned off. Encouraged by John Money, the parents agreed to reassign and raise David as "Brenda." Brenda's testicles were removed and later surgery would construct a vagina. Money reported that the twins were growing into happy, well-adjusted children, setting a precedent for sex reassignment as the standard treatment for 15,000 newborns with similarly injured genitals (Colapinto, 1997, 2001).

In the mid-1990s, a biologist and a psychiatrist followed up on Brenda's progress and concluded that the sex reassignment had not been successful. Almost from the beginning, Brenda refused to be treated like a girl. When her mother dressed her in frilly clothes as a toddler, Brenda tried to rip them off. She preferred to play with boys and stereotypical boys' toys such as machine guns. People in the community said that she "looks like a boy, talks like a boy."

Brenda had no friends, and no one would play with her: "Every day I was picked on, every day I was teased, every day I was threatened" (Diamond and Sigmundson, 1997: 300).

When she was 14, Brenda rebelled and stopped living as a girl: She refused to wear dresses, urinated standing up, refused to undergo vaginal surgery, and decided that she would either commit suicide or live as a male. When her father finally told her the true story of her birth and sex change, David recalls that "all of a sudden everything clicked. For the first time things made sense and I understood who and what I was" (Diamond and Sigmundson, 1997: 300).

Brenda had a mastectomy (breast removal surgery) at the age of 14 and underwent several operations to reconstruct a penis. Now called David, at age 25, he married and adopted his wife's three children. He committed suicide in 2004 at the age of 38, an act that some researchers attributed to the physical and mental torments he

suffered in childhood that "haunted him the rest of his life" (Colapinto, 2004).

Several Johns Hopkins scientists followed 14 boys who had been surgically altered as infants and raised as girls. The infants had a rare disorder, occurring once in every 400,000 births, in which the penis was small or nonexistent, despite the presence of testicles. Five of the boys were happily living as girls. The others were living as males or had reassigned themselves, taking on boys' names and dressing in masculine clothes (Reiner and Gearhart, 2004).

STOP AND THINK...

- What would you do if you had to make a decision about a child's sex reassignment?
- Because some boys who had been surgically altered happily lived as girls, can scientists conclude that nurture is more important than nature in shaping gender identity?

of gender roles. Among the Arapesh, both men and women nurtured their children. The men were cooperative, sensitive, and rarely engaged in warfare. The Mundugumors were just the opposite. Both men and women were competitive and aggressive. Neither parent showed much tenderness, and both often used physical punishment to discipline the children. The Tchambuli demonstrated the reverse of Western gender roles. The women were the economic providers. The men took care of children, sat around gossiping, and spent a lot of time decorating themselves for tribal festivities. Mead concluded that attributes long considered either masculine (such as aggression) or feminine (such as nurturance) were culturally—rather than biologically—determined.

CROSS-CULTURAL VARIATIONS IN MALE VIOLENCE   If men were innately aggressive, they would be equally violent across all societies. This isn't the case. The proportion of women who have ever suffered physical violence by a male partner varies considerably: 90 percent in Pakistan, 61 percent in Peru, 36 percent in the United States, and 13 percent in Japan (Chelala, 2002; World Health Organization, 2005; Black et al., 2011; TrustLaw, 2011). All mass murderers (those who have killed a large number of people during one incident) have been men, but most of the mass murders, usually committed by white males, have occurred in the United States (Christakis, 2012; Farhi, 2012). Such variations reflect cultural laws and practices and other environmental factors (nurture) rather than biology or genetics (nature) (Chesney-Lind and Pasko, 2004).

Cross-Cultural and Multicultural Families | **Male Violence: The World's Worst Countries to Be a Woman**

Women make up half the world's population, do two-thirds of the world's work, earn one-tenth of the world's income, and own one-hundredth of the world's property. In some of the most patriarchal countries around the world, women have few legal rights, their movements are severely restricted, and violence is a common occurrence.

- **Afghanistan:** If male family members and relatives can't pay a debt, young girls are given away or kidnapped, ending up as sexual slaves or in forced marriages; 87 percent of women have experienced physical, psychological, or sexual abuse or forced marriages; and 92 percent of Afghan women believe that a husband is justified in beating his wife if, for example, she argues with him, refuses sex, or burns the food.

- **Democratic Republic of Congo:** More than 1,150 women are raped every day, at least 420,000 each year (60 percent by husbands and partners and 40 percent by government or insurgent soldiers); 35 percent of women have experienced intimate partner sexual violence.

- **Pakistan:** About 91 percent of women experience domestic violence in their lifetimes; over 1,000 girls are victims of "honor killings" every year. An *honor killing* is the murder of a family member, usually a female by a male, who is believed to have shamed the family by behavior such as engaging in premarital and extramarital sex, and wearing inappropriate clothes.

- **India:** More than 100 million girls and women are victims of sex trafficking; 50 million girls are "missing" since 2000 because of female infanticide (killing female infants) and feticide (sex-selective abortion). As many as 100,000 women a year are killed over dowry disputes (the money or goods that a wife brings to her husband at marriage).

- **Somalia:** Militant groups and government soldiers have raped and gang-raped thousands of girls and women; 98 percent of girls, mostly between ages 4 and 11, must endure genital mutilation (see Chapter 7).

- **Egypt:** About 23 percent of women have experienced physical punishment or violence by a parent after age 18; 33 percent of women have experienced domestic violence; 80 percent of women have been sexually harassed; and 96 percent of girls have been genitally mutilated.

Sources: Martin, 2010; Yount and Li, 2010; Clark, 2011; Clifton, 2012; Gettleman, 2011; Peterman et al., 2011; TrustLaw, 2011; Central Statistics Organization and UNICEF, 2012; Peter, 2012; Rubin, 2012; Harris, 2013.

Some societies exercise much more control than others over women's behavior. In some Middle Eastern countries, for example, women (but not men) are killed if they dishonor the family by engaging in premarital or extramarital sex (see Chapters 7 and 14). As "Male Violence: The World's Worst Countries to Be a Woman" shows, men can control women using violence because cultural and religious values, customs, and laws relegate females to second-class citizenship.

This doesn't mean that *all* men are aggressive and *all* women are nonviolent. In the United States, for example, women make up 18 percent of all those arrested for violent crimes, including homicide (Federal Bureau of Investigation, 2011).

SUCCESSFUL SEX ASSIGNMENT You saw earlier that some scientists cite the Brenda/David case as evidence of the imprint of biology on gender roles and identity. Others maintain that successful sex assignments of intersexuals demonstrate the powerful effects of culture.

Intersexuals (called *hermaphrodites* in the past) are people born with both male and female sex organs (internal and/or external). Parents of intersexual infants usually choose a sex for the child and pursue surgical and hormonal treatments to change the ambiguous genital organs. The parents raise the child in the selected gender role: the name is male or female, the clothes are masculine or feminine, and the child is taught to behave in gender-appropriate ways. Such sex assignments, most of which are successful, suggest that socialization may be more important than biology in shaping a child's gender identity. In addition,

thousands of American transsexuals who have undergone sex surgery report living happily and not regretting the surgery (Vitello, 2006).

What Can We Conclude about the Nature–Nurture Debate?

A growing number of sociologists—who are calling for a "genetically informed sociology"—maintain that the nature *or* nurture debate is becoming outdated in understanding socialization processes and outcomes (Ledger, 2009). Ignoring the impact of genetics, they argue, leads to an incomplete understanding of behavior because genes shape our lives and could help explain why there is so much variation across families and other groups.

People have at least 52 characteristics—such as aggression, leadership traits, and cognitive ability—that are partially inherited (Freese, 2008). Our social environment can enhance or dampen these genetic characteristics. For example, children who are genetically predisposed to obesity don't always become overweight if parents discourage overeating and encourage physical activity (Martin, 2008).

Do obese parents affect their children's weight and health?

Social scientists, including sociologists, who study the relationship between genetics (nature) and the environment (nurture) maintain that research that combines both aspects enhances our understanding of how social factors affect genetic predispositions (see Schnittker, 2008; D'Onofrio and Lahey, 2010; Shanahan et al., 2010). Research reviews on the differences between the sexes have concluded that females and males are much more alike than different on a number of characteristics, including cognitive abilities, verbal and nonverbal communication, leadership traits, and self-esteem (Hyde, 2005, 2006). Why, then, do gender roles differ?

ANSWERS TO "A Gender Quiz: How Much Do You Know about U.S. Women and Men?"

1. **False.** Infant mortality rates vary by race and ethnicity, but the death rate for male infants is 18 percent higher than for female infants. And, on average, American women live about 5 years longer than men.

2. **False.** The number of married women who kept their maiden names increased from 2 percent in 1975 to 20 percent by the mid-1990s. Currently, only about 6 percent of women keep their maiden names after marriage.

3. **True.** About 46 percent have no preference, but of the rest, more (32 percent) say they would prefer to work for a male boss than a female (22 percent) boss. These preferences have been similar since 1941.

4. **False.** In most situations, men tend to talk more and longer than women.

5. **True.** Women are two to three times more likely than men to suffer from depression. Women's societal roles affect their happiness, which, in turn, can affect brain functions. In addition, women's brains produce less of the feel-good chemical serotonin.

6. **False.** Both sexes self-disclose by divulging personal information but are more comfortable doing so with women than with men.

7. **False.** Women smile more than men probably because they're expected to do "emotion work." Smiling is one way to restore harmony and reduce tension when people disagree.

8. **False.** In a recent Gallup poll, 40 percent of men compared with 28 percent of women said that if they could have only one child, they would prefer a boy.

9. **True.** Women and men spend at similar levels, have about the same credit debt, and are equally knowledgeable about their finances. Women often make savvier decisions about stock than men because they're less willing to make risky investments. However, 58 percent of men, compared with 44 percent of women, say that they feel confident about their money and finances.

10. **False.** A heart attack is more likely to be fatal for a woman than for a man. Women with heart disease are less likely than men to be diagnosed correctly, treated promptly, and less likely to receive cardiac rehabilitation.

Sources: Sugg, 2000; Vaccarino et al., 2002; Vakili et al., 2002; LaFrance et al., 2003; Goldin and Shim, 2004; Gooding and Kreider, 2010; Seligson, 2010; National Center for Health Statistics, 2011; Newport, 2011; Wood, 2011; Kenrick, 2013.

Why Do Gender Roles Differ?

A common misconception is that our gender roles are carved in stone by about age 4. In fact, gender roles change throughout the life course. There are many explanations for these changes, but let's consider five of the most common theories: (1) sociobiology, (2) social learning, (3) cognitive development, (4) symbolic interaction, and (5) feminist theories (*Table 5.2* summarizes these theories).

5.3 Compare five theoretical perspectives that explain why gender roles differ.

Read on MySocLab

Document: Sex and Temperament in Three Tribes

Sociobiology

Sociobiology is the study of how biology affects social behavior. Sociobiologists argue, for example, that evolution and genetic factors (nature) can explain why men are generally more aggressive than women. To ensure the propagation of their genes, males must prevail over their rivals. The competition includes aggression, violence, weapons, and plain nastiness: "In the animal world, human and nonhuman, competition is often intense. Males typically threaten, bluff, and if necessary fight one another in their efforts to obtain access to females" (Barash, 2002: B8).

Sociobiological explanations are controversial because practically every behavior is influenced by the environment, socialization, and culture. As you saw earlier, male aggression and violence vary considerably across societies. And, when cultural groups are invaded or attacked by enemies, women warriors can be as fierce as their male counterparts (see Chapter 3 on American Indian women during colonial times).

sociobiology The study of how biology affects social behavior.

Social Learning Theory

Social learning theory posits that people learn attitudes, beliefs, and behaviors through social interaction. The learning is a result of reinforcement, imitation, and modeling (Bandura and Walters, 1963; Lynn, 1969).

Reinforcement occurs when we receive direct or indirect rewards or punishments for particular gender role behaviors. For example, a little girl who puts on her mother's makeup may be told that she is cute, but her brother will be scolded ("boys don't wear makeup"). Children also learn gender roles through indirect reinforcement. For example, if a little boy's male friends are punished for crying, he will learn that "boys don't cry."

Another way children learn to behave as boys or girls is through *observation* and *imitation*. Even when children are not directly rewarded or punished for "behaving like boys" or "behaving like girls," they learn about gender by watching who does what in their families. A father who is rarely at home because he's always working sends the message that men are supposed to earn money.

social learning theory Posits that people learn attitudes, beliefs, and behaviors through social interaction.

Since you asked . . .
- Are mothers responsible for their daughters' obsession with beauty and appearance?

TABLE 5.2	Theoretical Explanations of Gender Roles
Perspective	**View of Gender Roles**
Sociobiology	Evolution and genetic factors (nature) determine gender roles
Social Learning	Gender role socialization can be direct (rewarding or punishing behavior and role modeling) and indirect (imitation and modeling)
Cognitive Development	Children learn appropriate gender attitudes and behavior as they pass through a series of developmental steps
Symbolic Interaction	Gender roles are social constructions that emerge through day-to-day interaction and vary across situations because of other people's expectations
Feminism	Gender roles differ due to socialization, patriarchy, and gender scripts

role model A person we admire and whose behavior we imitate.

A mother who is always complaining about being overweight or old sends the message that women are supposed to be thin and young.

Because parents are emotionally important to their children, they are typically a child's most powerful **role models**, people we admire and whose behavior we imitate. Other role models, as you'll see shortly, include siblings, teachers, friends, and even celebrities. Social learning theories help us understand why we behave as we do, but much of the emphasis is on early socialization rather than on what occurs throughout life. Thus, these theories don't explain why gender roles can change in adulthood or later life. Social learning theories also don't explain why reinforcement and modeling work for some children but not others, especially those in the same family, and even identical twins.

Cognitive Development Theory

cognitive development theory Posits that children acquire female or male values on their own by thinking, reasoning, and interpreting information in their environment.

In contrast to social learning theories, **cognitive development theory** posits that children acquire female or male values on their own by thinking, reasoning, and interpreting information in their environment. According to this perspective, children pass through a series of developmental stages in learning gender-appropriate attitudes and behavior.

By age 3 or 4, a girl knows that she is a girl and prefers "girl things" to "boy things" simply because she likes what is familiar or similar to her. By age 5, most children anticipate disapproval from their peers for playing with opposite-sex toys, and they avoid those toys as a result. After acquiring masculine or feminine values, children tend to identify with people of the same sex as themselves (Kohlberg, 1969; Maccoby, 1990; Bussey and Bandura, 1992).

Children use cues to evaluate the behavior of others as either gender appropriate ("good") or gender inappropriate ("bad") to fit into their social worlds. Such sex typing becomes more rigid during adolescence, when young people want to conform to their peers' gender stereotypes, but more flexible during adulthood because peers become less influential. Generally, however, people who have internalized sex-typed standards tend to expect stereotypical behavior from others (Hudak, 1993; Renn and Calvert, 1993).

Cognitive development theories offer useful insights on the relationship between maturation and learning gender roles, but say little about individual differences among children (why one daughter is a tomboy, for example, whereas another is very feminine). (We'll examine an influential cognitive development theory in depth in Chapter 12.) Another limitation is that developmental theories exaggerate gender learning as something that children do themselves. Instead, according to symbolic interactionists, learning gender roles is shaped by our cultural context.

Symbolic Interaction Theories

For symbolic interactionists (also known simply as *interactionists*), gender roles are *socially constructed categories* that emerge in social situations (see Chapter 2). We "do gender," consciously and unconsciously, by accommodating our behavior to other people's gender role expectations. Among co-workers, for example, both sexes are more likely to interrupt women than men because men are generally viewed as more authoritative than women (Robey et al., 1998; Wood, 2011).

In a process that sociologist Erving Goffman (1959, 1969) called *impression management*, we provide information and cues to others to present ourselves in a favorable light while downplaying or concealing our less appealing qualities. According to Goffman, all of us engage in impression management almost every day by controlling the image we project.

This child's mother is preparing her for a beauty pageant. How would social learning theories explain the mother's and child's behavior?

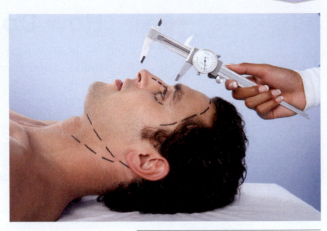

Men, like women, have surgical procedures, an example of impression management.

Consider our obsession with our physical appearance. In 2012, there were over 10.1 million cosmetic procedures in the United States, a 250 percent increase since 1997. The top surgical procedure for women was breast augmentation; more than 2 percent of the patients were females age 18 and younger and age 65 and older. Men comprised only 10 percent of the cosmetic procedures, but the number has increased more than 106 percent since 1997. The top two surgical procedures for men were liposuction and nose surgery, and 64 percent of all procedures were for men between the ages of 35 and 64 (American Society for Aesthetic Plastic Surgery, 2012; Morgan, 2012). Men color their hair, get hair transplants and facelifts, and, like women, use anti-aging products hoping to appear younger than they are.

Symbolic interaction theories are valuable in explaining how gender and gender roles shape our everyday lives. One limitation is that interactionists credit people with more free will than they have. For both sexes, for example, impression management is more difficult for lower socioeconomic groups and older people because both groups have fewer resources to purchase goods and services to enhance the image they project (Powers, 2004). In addition, interactionists tend to downplay or ignore macro-level and structural factors that affect our gender roles. For example, when millions of Americans are fired because of a plunging economy, gender roles become unpredictable and stressful, especially if one or both partners can no longer provide for a family.

Feminist Theories

Many feminist scholars, like interactionists, view gender as a socially constructed role that is taught carefully and repeatedly. Consequently, one's **gender script—**how society says you're supposed to act because of your sex—becomes "so natural as to be seen as an integral part of oneself" (Fox and Murry, 2001: 382).

Gender scripts result, over time, in valuing men more than women. Even in Women's Studies courses, many of the female college students want to focus on male experiences and perspectives, are concerned that men in the class may feel uncomfortable, and sometimes even express a preference for male faculty in these courses (Sharp et al., 2008).

For most feminist theorists, the much lower number of women in powerful positions (see Data Digest) is due to **sexism**, an attitude or behavior that discriminates against one sex, usually females, based on the assumed superiority of the other sex. If people changed their individual attitudes about traditional roles, according to feminist scholars, behavior would change across a society. Besides addressing gender scripts and sexism, feminist scholars have shown that gender roles have a powerful impact on families and are interlinked with other institutions. For example, family gender roles are often unequal because the economy and the government, including ours, don't have paid parental leave and pay women less than men in similar jobs (Ferree, 2010; see also Chapter 13).

Feminist perspectives provide insightful analyses of gender roles but have been criticized for being too narrow. For example, women in upper classes have more status and privileges than do men in lower classes, and are less confined to playing traditional gender roles because they can hire low-income women as maids, cooks, and nannies. Some men have also accused feminist scholars of not addressing issues such as how gender roles harm men ("A real man is always stoic and emotionless"), and sexist stereotypes ("All men are slobs" or "Men always want sex") (Frantz and Brand, 2012). One might also question whether gender scripts are as rigid, especially over time, as many feminists claim.

gender script How society says someone is supposed to act because of her or his sex.

sexism An attitude or behavior that discriminates against one sex, usually females, based on the assumed superiority of the other sex.

MAKING CONNECTIONS

- Drawing on your own experiences, do you think that women and men are similar? Or different? Why?
- Think about how you were raised. Who played a major role in teaching you to behave like a male or female? What happened, if anything, when you broke the rules?

5.4 Describe and illustrate five sources of learning gender roles.

Read on MySocLab

Document: Night to His Day: The Social Construction of Gender

Watch on MySocLab

Video: Gender Socialization

Since you asked . . .

• Why are parents important in shaping our gender roles?

How Do We Learn Gender Roles?

We learn gender roles from a variety of sources. Some of the most important socialization agents are parents, siblings, peers, teachers, and popular culture.

Parents

Siblings, aunts, uncles, grandparents, and other family members are important role models in our socialization (see Chapters 7, 12, and 16). Parents, however, are usually a child's first and most influential socialization agents, often treating male and female infants differently from birth. They hold girls more gently and cuddle them more. Fathers, especially, are more likely to jostle and play in a rough-and-tumble manner with boys (Parke, 1996). Parents also shape their children's gender roles through differential treatment in several important ways, including talking, setting expectations, and providing opportunities for various activities.

TALKING Parents often communicate differently with boys than with girls, starting at a very early age. Even when babies are as young as 6 to 14 months, mothers often talk more to their daughters than to their sons and comfort and hug their daughters more often. Mothers also give boys more room to explore their environment on their own, which teaches and reinforces a sense of independence. Thus, even babies receive gendered messages about their expected behavior months before they start to speak (Clearfield and Nelson, 2006).

In the case of toddlers, how parents talk to their children often depends on the social context. When parents are engaged in physical care giving, they tend to be assertive ("Eat your peas"). When playing, fathers are more likely than mothers to give polite commands ("Please don't bang on that!") rather than requests ("Can you stop banging on that?"), and to ignore their children's demands ("Want toast, not truck"). Such parental differences send the message that men are more authoritative than women, and that women are less demanding and more compliant than men (Lindsey et al., 2010). By the time they start school, many boys use threatening, commanding, and dominating language ("If you do that one more time, I'll punch you"). In contrast, many girls seek agreement and cooperation ("Can I play, too?") (Shapiro, 1990).

Parents are important socialization agents. This 3-year-old may be inspired to follow in his father's occupational footsteps.

Watch on **MySocLab**

Video: Women's Changing Family Role

SETTING EXPECTATIONS Parents' expectations are also often gender typed. People accept crying as a normal emotion of young children, but these reactions change as children grow older. Well before children are age 13, parents disapprove when boys cry. Parents encourage boys to control their emotions for several reasons, such as to avoid being teased and appearing unmanly, particularly outside the home. In contrast, when girls cry, they are comforted, resulting in girls' and women's crying more often than their male counterparts, and across most societies (Jellesma and Vingerhoets, 2012).

Nationally, 10- to 17-year-old boys spend about 30 percent less time than girls doing household chores and more than twice as much time playing. In addition, boys are up to 15 percent more likely than girls of the same age to get an allowance for doing household chores (Swanbrow, 2007). Parents typically assign child care and cleaning to daughters and home main-tenance work to sons. Girls are also given duties much earlier in childhood and adolescence than are boys (Leaper, 2002). These gender-stereotyped responsibilities, as you'll see shortly, lay the foundation for role differences in adulthood.

Mothers sometimes start criticizing their children's—espe-cially their daughters'—weight and physical appearance in elementary school. And throughout adolescence, fathers make more comments about appearance to their daughters than to their sons (Schwartz et al., 1999; Smolak et al., 1999). Such gender-typed expectations may result in girls' negative body images and eating disorders (see Chapter 14).

Gender-biased expectations can also affect academic per-formance. By as early as the fourth grade, for example, and regardless of report card grades, many mothers and fathers believe that boys have more natural ability than girls do in math, believe that math is more important for boys than for girls, expect boys to get high grades in math, and encourage sons to pursue careers that require math skills. Such gender stereotypes influence children's self-perceptions that, in turn, affect their subsequent math achievement and career choices (Gunderson et al., 2012).

© Vahan Shirvanian/www.CartoonStock.com

PROVIDING OPPORTUNITIES Here's what one of my students said when we were discussing this chapter:

> Some parents live their dreams through their sons by forcing them to be in sports. I disagree with this but want my [9-year-old] son to be "all boy." He's the worst player on the basketball team at school and wanted to take dance lessons, including ballet. I assured him that this was not going to happen. I'm going to enroll him in soccer and see if he does better (Author's files).

Is this mother suppressing her son's natural talent in dancing? We'll never know because she, like many parents, expects her son to enact gender roles that meet with society's approval.

During childhood and adolescence, parents provide children with activities and opportunities that a culture defines as gender appropriate. Parents may want their sons and daughters to be successful, but gender-typed socialization—whether con-scious or unconscious—can derail many parents' good intentions.

Play and Peer Groups

Play is important in children's development because it provides pleasure; forms friendships; and builds communication, emotional, and social skills. Peer groups are also important in our socialization. A **peer group** consists of people who are similar in age, social status, and interests. All of us are members of peer groups,

peer group People who are similar in age, social status, and interests.

but peers are especially influential until about our mid-twenties. After that, co-workers, spouses, children, and a few close friends are usually more central than peers in our everyday lives. Play and peer groups are important sources of socialization, but they can also encourage gender-stereotypical attitudes and behavior.

PLAY   From an early age, play is generally gender typed. Among preschoolers, when playing alone, girls prefer feminine activities (such as playing with dolls) whereas boys are more likely to play with balls and transportation toys. However, when girls and boys are in mixed-sex play groups, they are as likely to play with "masculine" as with "feminine" toys. Thus, gender-typed play breaks down and promotes a greater range of activities (Goble et al., 2012).

In 2010 and 2011, the top-selling toys for girls were dolls, animal toys (e.g., Zhu Zhu pets), and cooking sets. The top-selling toys for boys were video games, ride-on toys (e.g., pedal cars), "blaster" guns, Lego, and Transformers (Rattray, 2010; Rowland, 2011). Girls' sections of catalogs and toy stores are swamped with cosmetics, dolls and accessories, arts and crafts kits, and housekeeping and cookware. In contrast, boys' sections feature sports equipment, building sets, workbenches, construction equipment, and toy guns. Some family scholars propose that children's toys should be more gender neutral to encourage play for boys and girls that promotes less gender stereotyping (see "Should Children's Toys Be Gender Neutral?").

Barbie was the top-selling toy in the twentieth century (Towner, 2009), and is still a favorite among young girls. According to many critics, the problem with Barbie dolls is that they idealize unrealistic body characteristics such as large breasts, a tiny waist, and small hips (see *Table 5.3*). One of the results is that many girls and women try to achieve these fictional expectations through diets (that may lead to eating disorders) and cosmetic surgery (see Chapter 14).

Male dolls (but they're called "action figures") have grown increasingly muscular over the years. GI Joes, for example, have biceps that are twice as large as those of a typical man and larger than those of any known bodybuilder. These action figures (and comic strip heroes) put boys at risk of developing the

Choices   Should Children's Toys Be Gender Neutral?

Hamleys, London's version of F.A.O. Schwarz in the United States, recently dismantled its pink "girls" and blue "boys" sections. It now has gender neutral red-and-white signs. Rather than floors dedicated to Barbie dolls and action figures, merchandise is now organized by types (Soft Toys) and interests (Outdoor), for example (Orenstein, 2011).

In Sweden, Top-Toy Group, a licensee of the Toys "R" Us brand, published a "gender-blind" catalogue for the 2012 Christmas season. For example, "On some pages, girls brandish toy guns and boys wield blow-dryers and cuddle dolls" (Molin, 2012: D12).

The United States is going in the opposite direction. A study of the (English language) U.S. Disney Store website analyzed 527 toys and concluded that the toys were highly gendered in several ways. First, of the

61 percent of "Boys' Toys," nearly all were action toys, small vehicles, weapons, and building toys; nearly all of the 22 percent of "Girls' Toys" were dolls or related to beauty, cosmetics, jewelry, and domestic work. Only 17 percent of the toys (such as stuffed animals and musical instruments) were gender neutral. Second, the color palettes were strikingly different. The boys' toys were typically bold colors (red, black, brown); the girls' toys were usually pink or lavender. The researchers noted that if children played with a greater variety of toys, both sexes would "develop a wider repertoire of skills" (Auster and Mansbach, 2012: 386).

In 2011, 91 percent of Lego sets were purchased for boys. In 2012, Lego unveiled its "Friends" collection, building toys for even the "girliest of girls." The site (friends.lego.com) features 9 dolls that encourage little

girls to use Lego play sets to construct, among other things, a beauty shop, outdoor bakery, speedboat, stables, and a bunny house. All of the play sets are in pastel colors, usually pink, lavender, and light green. Statistics aren't available, but according to a company executive, three times more girls were building with Lego bricks after Lego Friends was launched (LEGO Friends, 2012; Kapp, 2013).

STOP AND THINK...

- Do you believe that toys should be gender neutral?
- Do you think that toys have any effect on children's future adult roles as parents, employers, and workers?

TABLE 5.3	Real Women and Barbie	
	Average Woman	**Barbie**
Height	5'4"	6'
Weight	145 lbs	101 lbs
Dress size	11–14	4
Bust	36–37" *	39"
Waist	29–31"	19"
Hips	40–42"	33"

* Without breast implants. Also, the average woman has a B cup compared with Barbie's FF cup.
Source: Data cited in Anorexia Nervosa and Related Eating Disorders, Inc., 2006.

"Barbie syndrome"—unrealistic expectations for their bodies. As a result, some researchers maintain, increasing numbers of men are becoming preoccupied with working out and taking dangerous drugs such as anabolic steroids (Field et al., 2005).

SIBLINGS AND PEERS Older siblings can be positive role models when they encourage their younger brothers and sisters to do well in school and stay away from friends who get in trouble. On the other hand, older siblings may transmit beliefs that having sex at an early age, smoking, drinking, and marijuana use aren't "a big deal" (Altonji et al., 2010; McHale et al., 2012).

Peer influence usually increases as children get older. Especially during the early teen years, friends often reinforce desirable behavior or skills in ways that enhance a child's self-image ("Wow, you're really good in math!"). Because peers can be positive role models, children acquire a wide array of information and knowledge by observing their peers. Even during the first days of school, children learn to imitate their peers at standing in line, raising their hands in class, and being quiet while the teacher is speaking. Among teens and young adults who are lesbian, gay, or bisexual, heterosexual friends can be especially supportive in accepting one's homosexuality and disclosing it to family (Shilo and Savaya, 2011).

Not all peer influence is positive, however. Among seventh- to twelfth-graders, having a best friend who engages in sexual intercourse, is truant, and uses tobacco and marijuana increases the probability of imitating such behavior (Card and Giuliano, 2011). Among adolescents and college students, poor physical fitness and obesity among friends increases the likelihood of adopting or maintaining an unhealthy diet and developing health problems (Carrell et al., 2010; Salvy et al., 2012).

In U.S. society, many adolescents want to be popular. Feeling unpopular can be especially harmful for teenage girls. Among girls ages 12 to 19, for instance, those who see themselves as unpopular gain more weight every year than do those who see themselves as popular (McNeeley and Crosnoe, 2008). The reasons for the weight gain aren't clear, but teenage girls' and boys' self-assessments often differ from those of their peers. For example, among middle school students, about 75 percent of those who perceive themselves as unpopular are viewed as popular by their peers (McElhaney et al., 2008). From a symbolic interaction perspective, many preteens and teens experience unnecessary anguish because there's a disconnect between how they see themselves and how their peers see them.

Teachers and Schools

Gender strongly shapes both students' and teachers' experiences. However unintentionally, teachers and schools often transmit and reinforce gendered attitudes and practices that follow boys and girls from preschool to college.

PRIMARY AND SECONDARY EDUCATION   By the time children are 4 or 5 years old, school fills an increasingly large portion of their lives. Because many parents are employed, schools have had to devote more time and resources to topics—such as sex education and drug abuse prevention—that were once the sole responsibility of families (see Chapter 7). In many ways, then, schools play an increasingly important role in socialization. Teachers are among the most important socialization agents. From kindergarten through high school, teachers play numerous roles in the classroom—instructor, role model, evaluator, moral guide, and disciplinarian, to name just a few.

When children enter kindergarten, they perform similarly on both reading and mathematics tests. By the third grade, however, boys, on average, score higher than girls in math and science assessment tests and lower than girls in reading tests. These gaps increase throughout high school (Dee, 2006).

Teachers' attitudes toward the subject matter influence their instructional techniques, how they teach the content, and, eventually, their students' attitudes toward a subject. Of the almost 3 million U.S. teachers at elementary and middle schools, only 18 percent are men, increasing to 42 percent in high school (*Women in the Labor Force*, 2013). Compared with teachers in Europe and elsewhere, many U.S. teachers have neither certification nor a college degree in the subject they teach. For example, only 8 percent of fourth-grade math teachers in the United States majored or minored in math, compared with 48 percent in Singapore (Crowe, 2010).

Negative stereotypes about girls' abilities in math and science can also significantly lower girls' test scores and lower their aspirations. When teachers tell girls and boys in elementary and middle schools that both are equally capable in math and science, "the difference in performance essentially disappears" (Hill et al., 2010: 2). Thus, believing in gender differences can actually *produce* differences.

HIGHER EDUCATION   Since 1981, there have been more females than males enrolled in college, and women—across all racial/ethnic groups—now earn a larger percentage of associate, bachelor's, and master's degrees than men (Aud et al., 2012). A major gender gap is the underrepresentation of women in the high-paying fields of science, technology, engineering, and mathematics (STEM). In elementary, middle, and high school, girls and boys take math and science courses in roughly equal numbers and about the same numbers leave high school planning to pursue STEM majors in college. After a few years, however, men outnumber women in nearly every STEM field, and in some—such as physics, engineering, and computer science—women earn only 20 percent of the bachelor's degrees. Their numbers decline further at the graduate level and yet again in the workplace (Hill et al., 2010; Beede et al., 2011).

Why is there a gradual attrition? In college, female students are initially as persistent as men in a STEM major and get higher grades, but they are less satisfied than men with the core courses and more likely to doubt their ability to succeed in a male-dominated discipline. As a result, women's professional self-confidence falters and they change majors (Cech et al., 2011; Shapiro and Williams, 2012). The exit from a STEM major is also associated with having few female faculty role models, and many female and male science professors' beliefs that female students will benefit less from mentoring because they're less competent than men (Hunt, 2010; Moss-Racusin et al., 2012; Williams and Ceci, 2012).

Can more female role models in schools reduce the gender gap in STEM fields?

Popular Culture and the Media

Media myths and unrealistic images assault our gender identity on a daily basis. A few examples from advertising, newspapers and magazines, television, and music videos illustrate how the media reinforce sex stereotyping from childhood to adulthood.

ADVERTISING   In the print media, young people see 45 percent more beer ads and 27 percent more ads for hard liquor in teen magazines than adults do in their magazines (Strasburger et al., 2006; see also Jernigan, 2010). Girls ages 11 to 14 are subjected to about 500 advertisements a day on the Internet, billboards, and magazines in which the majority of models are "nipped, tucked, and airbrushed to perfection" (Bennett, 2009: 43). Many girls and young women believe that they have to be gorgeous, thin, and almost perfect to be loved by their parents and boyfriends (Schwyzer, 2011).

What effect do such ads have on girls' and women's self-image? About 43 percent of 6- to 9-year-old girls use lipstick or lip gloss, 38 percent use hairstyling products, and 12 percent use other cosmetics. Girls from 8 to 12 years old spend more than $40 million a month on beauty products, 80 percent of 10-year-old girls have been on a diet, and 80 percent of girls ages 13 to 18 list shopping as their favorite pastime (Bennett, 2009; Hanes, 2011; Seltzer, 2012).

Many women, especially white women, are unhappy with their bodies. An analysis of 77 recent studies of women's media images concluded that there is a strong association between exposure to media depicting ultrathin actresses and models, many women's dissatisfaction with their bodies, and their likelihood of engaging in unhealthy eating behaviors such as excessive dieting (Grabe et al., 2008).

Men's health and fitness magazine ads routinely feature models who have undergone several months of extreme regimens, including starvation and dehydration, to tighten their skin and make their muscles "pop." The magazines also use camera and lighting tricks and Photoshop to project an idealized image of hypermasculinity that, in reality, is impossible to attain (Christina, 2011; see also Ricciardelli et al., 2010).

ELECTRONIC MEDIA   Because of iPads, smartphones, YouTube, and social networking sites such as Facebook, young people are rarely out of the reach of the electronic media. How does such technology affect socialization and gender roles?

The American Academy of Pediatrics (2001: 424) advises parents to avoid television entirely for children younger than age 2. The Academy also counsels parents to limit the viewing time of elementary school children to no more than 2 hours a day to encourage more interactive activities "that will promote proper brain development, such as talking, playing, singing, and reading together." Still, 68 percent of children under age 2 view 2 to 3 hours of television daily; 20 percent have a television in their bedroom, as do one-third of 3- to 6-year-olds; and the average U.S. child, especially in black families, is exposed to 4 hours of background TV daily that reduces the quality of parent–child interactions and children's cognitive ability such as concentrating on homework (Garrison and Christakis, 2005; Vandewater et al., 2007; Lapierre et al., 2012).

Concerned that ultrathin images of models promote girls' and young women's eating disorders, Spain, Israel, and Italy now require models to have a healthy body mass index (BMI). France passed a law that makes it a crime to promote "excessive thinness" or extreme dieting (Rubin, 2013). Should the United States pass similar laws?

The Princess and the Frog, an animated film, generated much less in global ticket sales than Disney executives expected. Believing that boys don't want to see movies with "princess" in the title, Disney studios' *Tangled*, pictured here, features a swashbuckling male lead (Chmielewski and Eller, 2010).

TABLE 5.4	How Do Electronic Media Affect Children?		
Among All 8- to 18-Year-Olds, Percentage Who Said That They . . .			
	Heavy Users (more than 16 hours/day)	Moderate Users (3 to 16 hours/day)	Light Users (less than 3 hours/day)
Get good grades (A's and B's)	51	65	66
Get fair/poor grades (C's or lower)	47	31	23
Have been happy at school this year	72	81	82
Are often bored	60	53	48
Get into trouble a lot	33	21	16
Are often sad or unhappy	32	23	22

Source: Based on Rideout et al., 2010: 4.

The average young American now spends practically every waking minute—except for the time in school—using a smartphone, computer, television, or other electronic device. In 2009, those ages 8 to 18 spent 7.5 hours a day with some type of electronic media, which is more time than most adults spend in a full-time job. Generally, youths who spend more time with media have lower grades and lower levels of personal contentment (see *Table 5.4*). These findings are similar for girls and boys across all categories of age, race/ethnicity, parents' social class, and single- and two-parent households (Rideout et al., 2010).

There is also a growing consensus that violent video games make violence seem normal. Playing violent video games such as *Grand Theft Auto IV*, *School Shooter*, and *God of War 4* can increase a person's aggressive thoughts, feelings, and behavior both in laboratory settings and in real life. Violent video games also encourage male-to-female aggression because much of the violence is directed at women (Anderson et al., 2003; Carnagey and Anderson, 2005). Still, it's not clear why violent video games affect people differently. Many young males enjoy playing such video games, for example, but aren't any more aggressive, vicious, or destructive than those who aren't video game enthusiasts (Kutner and Olson, 2008).

MAKING CONNECTIONS

- How much did parents, teachers, and peers influence your gender role?
- To decrease advertisers' influence on children, many European countries have banned TV ads on children's television programs. Should the United States do the same?

5.5 Explain how gender ideologies affect traditional and nontraditional gender roles.

Since you asked . . .
- Should the man be the boss in the family?

gender ideology Attitudes regarding the appropriate roles, rights, and responsibilities of women and men in society.

Gender Ideologies and Traditional Gender Roles

According to one of my male students, "When a woman attempts to assume the head position in the family, it will lead to a loss of order and stability in the family." This remark sparked a lively class discussion, but such traditional views of gender roles are fairly common.

Gender ideology (also called *gender role ideology*) refers to attitudes regarding the appropriate roles, rights, and responsibilities of women and men in society. *Egalitarian gender ideologies* endorse women's and men's shared breadwinning and nurturing family roles. In contrast, *traditional gender role ideologies* emphasize distinct instrumental and expressive family roles for men and women.

Instrumental and Expressive Roles

Explore on **MySocLab**

Activity: The Laboring Family: Negotiating Gender Roles

You'll recall that functionalists developed a family model in which the male fulfilled an instrumental role and the female fulfilled an expressive role. Some critics view these descriptions of traditional gender roles as outdated (see Chapter 2), but they're a reality in many U.S. homes and worldwide.

INSTRUMENTAL ROLES   Traditionally, *instrumental role players* (husbands and fathers) must be "real men." A "real man" is a procreator, a protector, and a breadwinner. Producing children proves his virility, and having boys is especially important to carry on his family name. The protector ensures his family's physical safety, and the breadwinner's primary job is to provide financial security.

EXPRESSIVE ROLES   Traditionally, *expressive role players* (wives and mothers) provide the emotional support and nurturing that sustain the family unit and support the husband/father. They should be warm, sensitive, and sympathetic. For example, the expressive role player encourages her son to try out for Little League, and is always ready to comfort a husband who has had a bad day at work.

One of women's expressive roles is that of kin-keeper, a role that is often passed down from mother to daughter. Kin-keepers spend much time maintaining contact with relatives, e-mailing friends and families, organizing family reunions, or holding gatherings during the holidays or for special events such as birthdays and anniversaries (Chesley and Fox, 2012).

Some Benefits and Costs of Traditional Gender Roles

Traditional gender roles have both benefits and costs (see *Table 5.5*). They may be chosen consciously or a result of habit, custom, or socialization. Remember, too, that traditional relationships vary regarding gender ideology and actual behavior. For example, men with a traditional gender ideology ("A woman's place is in the home") are likely to have employed wives if the men have no college degree and low-paying jobs (Glauber and Gozjolko, 2011).

BENEFITS   Traditional gender roles provide stability, continuity, and predictability. Because each person knows what is expected, rights and responsibilities are clear. Husbands and wives don't have to argue over who does what: If the house is clean,

TABLE 5.5	Some Benefits and Costs of Traditional Gender Roles			
For Men . . .			**For Women . . .**	
Benefits	**Costs**	**Benefits**	**Costs**	
A positive self-image in being the provider	Loss of identity in the case of unemployment	Not having to juggle employment and domestic tasks	Loss of financial security if there's a separation or divorce	
Little marital stress in climbing a career ladder because the wife takes care of the kids and the home	Little time with wife or children	Time to focus on the husband–wife relationship	Is often alone because the husband is working long hours or makes numerous out-of-town trips	
Doesn't have to do much, if any, housework or child care	Wife may feel unappreciated or overburdened	Lots of time with children	Feeling useless when children leave home	
Has a sexual partner who isn't stressed out by having a job and caring for the family	Wife may feel taken for granted because she should always be available for sexual intercourse	Nurturing a husband and children and enjoying their accomplishments	Feeling like a failure if the children aren't successful, or feeling isolated and helpless if the husband is abusive	

she's a "good wife"; if the bills are paid, he's a "good husband." As long as both people live up to their role expectations, they're safe in assuming that they'll meet the other's needs financially, emotionally, and sexually.

Some women stay in traditional relationships because they don't have to work outside the home or be responsible for economic decisions. An accommodating wife can enjoy both power and prestige through her husband's accomplishments. A good mother not only controls her children but can also be proud of guiding and enriching their lives (Harris, 1994).

When a traditional husband complained about his traditional wife's spending too much money, she composed and gave her husband a "help wanted" ad. In the ad, the wife specified the necessary qualifications that included the following:

> *Working full time, being on call 24 hours a day and seven days a week, shopping, cooking, cleaning, doing the laundry, caring for the children, feeding and cleaning up after the dog, mowing the lawn, shoveling snow, paying the bills, and running all the errands. The new hire would also pinch pennies, be a constant friend and companion, always patient, and never complain* ("Want Ad Proves . . .," 1997).

This ad is a good example of how men benefit from traditional marriages, especially because wives don't nag their husbands about sharing domestic chores. The wives benefit because they don't have the tension of being pulled in many directions—such as juggling jobs and housework. Such clearly designated duties can decrease both partners' stress.

COSTS Traditional gender roles have their drawbacks. Even when traditional families try to scale down their standard of living, a sole breadwinner is under a lot of pressure: "When mothers quit work to care for babies, fathers must shoulder unbearable stress to provide for more dependents" (Alton, 2001: 20).

Sometimes the seemingly distant man is quiet because he's continuously worried about the family's economic well-being. Because many men derive their self-esteem from work and the breadwinner role, losing a job can send some men into severe depression, seeking solace in alcohol, frustrated rages that end in violence, and even suicide (Scelfo, 2007; Dokoupil, 2009).

In the most dangerous male-dominated jobs (from lumberjacks to firefighters to soldiers), men are likely to be injured on the job and suffer 92 percent of fatal occupational injuries. Men also have a lower life expectancy than women. There are many reasons for men's lower longevity, but one possibility is that traditional men "tough out" pain and not see a doctor unless absolutely necessary (Frantz and Brand, 2012).

Among women, a traditional wife can expect little relief from never-ending tasks that may be exhausting and monotonous. Such difficulties may be one reason why stay-at-home mothers are more likely than employed mothers or other employed women to report experiencing negative emotions such as sadness, anger, and depression (see *Table 5.6*). The stay-at-home mothers with the lowest emotional well-being are those with annual household incomes of less than $36,000 (Mendes et al., 2012). This suggests that social class is associated with women's traditional roles and emotional well-being.

And what are her options if a stay-at-home mom is unhappy? Traditional values such as being nurturing, dependent, and submissive can discourage some women from leaving abusive relationships. If she's been out of the workforce for a number of years, she might be worse off after a divorce. Or a woman who has left all the money matters to her husband may find after his death that he did little estate planning and that their finances are in disarray (see Chapters 14 and 16).

Men in traditional marriages whose wives aren't employed can also have a negative impact on women's jobs. In several recent studies, for example, the

TABLE 5.6 **Women's Negative Emotions, by Motherhood and Employment Status**

	Stay-at-home moms	Employed moms	Employed women (No child at home)
Worry	41%	34%	31%
Sadness	26%	16%	16%
Stress	50%	48%	45%
Anger	19%	14%	12%
Depression	28%	17%	17%

Note: This national study was based on women between the ages of 18 and 64. In this table, "employed moms" and "employed women" worked either full or part time. The last three columns represent the percentage of all women in the study, not all of whom are included here. Thus, 41 percent in column 2 should be interpreted as "41% of all women who experienced worry were stay-at-home moms."
Source: Based on Mendes et al., 2012.

researchers found that men in traditional marriages, compared with those in egalitarian marriages, disliked women's presence in the workplace, distrusted women leaders, had negative views of workplaces with many women, and often denied qualified women promotions. The men believed that women should concentrate on helping their husband's career rather than focusing on their own (Desai et al., 2012).

WHY DO TRADITIONAL GENDER ROLES PERSIST? First, for some families, traditional gender roles are rewarding, especially when a couple works out mutually satisfying arrangements to share breadwinning and family care responsibilities. Whether the reasons are based on religious beliefs, cultural values, or socialization, traditional gender roles can provide a sense of accomplishment in meeting a family's needs.

Second, traditional gender roles are profitable for business. The unpaid work that women do at home (such as housework, child rearing, and emotional support) means that companies don't have to pay for child care services or counseling for stressed-out male employees. Many men work extra hours without additional pay to keep their jobs (see Chapter 13). Thus, companies increase their profits.

Third, traditional roles maintain male privilege and power. If women are perceived as not having leadership qualities, men can dominate political and legal institutions. They can shape laws and policies to maintain their vested interests without being challenged by women who are unhappy with the status quo.

Gender Roles in Adulthood

According to the mainstream media, women are dominating society as never before, men are in a "state of crisis," and some even predict the "end of men" (see Rosin, 2010). These writers worry that women are outpacing men in education, becoming the family breadwinners, and doing less housework and child care than men (Mukhopadhyay, 2011; Schwyzer, 2011).

Others argue that there is still widespread **gender stratification**—people's unequal access to wealth, power, status, opportunity, and other valued

5.6 Describe and illustrate how gender roles vary in adulthood.

 Read on MySocLab

Document: Religion and the Domestication of Man

Army Pfc. Lori Piestewa was the first female American soldier killed in combat in Iraq and the first American Indian woman killed while fighting for the U.S. military. Here, Piestewa's older daughter, age 4, attends a memorial service for her mom with her grandparents, who are raising the girls.

Since you asked . . .

* If you had a choice, would you rather be employed or stay at home and take care of the house and family?

 Watch on **MySocLab**

Video: The Changing Role of Men

Since you asked. . .

* Is a man in an apron sexy?

 Watch on **MySocLab**

Video: Work and Family

resources because of their sex. We'll examine some of this stratification in greater depth in later chapters. For now, let's look briefly at gender inequality in the family, workplace, politics, education, religion, and everyday interactions.

Gender and Family Life

If they were free to do either, 51 percent of American women and 76 percent of American men would prefer to have a job outside the home rather than stay at home and take care of the house and family (Saad, 2012). Few adults have this choice, however, and employment rarely lightens women's domestic workload.

CHILD CARE AND HOUSEWORK Women sometimes complain that men's domestic participation is minimal:

I'm always amused when my husband says that he'll "help" me make our bed. I guess he "helps" because he feels making the bed is my responsibility, not his, even though we both sleep in it. When I mow the lawn, it's no big deal. But when he occasionally helps make the bed or does the dishes, he expects a litany of thank-you's and hugs (Author's files).

Employed women, especially mothers, often grumble that they have to do *everything*—work outside the home, raise children, and do all the housework. Are they right?

In 2012, men reported doing 2 hours of housework on an average day compared with 2.6 hours for women. On an average day, women spent 1.1 hours on child care for children under age 6 compared with men's 26 minutes a day. Since 2003, both mothers and fathers have been spending less time on child care and domestic tasks, and there is greater sharing of the household labor. Nonetheless, women spend from 33 to 55 percent more time than men do on child care and household tasks (U.S. Bureau of Labor Statistics News 2005; U.S. Bureau of Labor Statistics, American Time Use Survey, 2013).

Women are still doing more of the housework and child care, but there's been a shift since 1965. As *Figure 5.1* shows, fathers with children under age 18 in the home have increased the number of hours they spend on child care and housework, but less time in paid work. Mothers' housework has decreased since 1965, but their paid work and child care hours have increased (Parker and Wang, 2013).

Employed wives and husbands who share some of the housework report more frequent sex (Gager and Yabiku, 2010). Men's greater participation in housework reduces women's stress and promotes friendship, satisfaction, and intimacy. According to one husband, for example, if he wants to be sure of a romantic evening, he goes for the vacuum cleaner rather than buying his wife flowers (Shellenbarger, 2009).

In a recent national survey, 57 percent of women said they want help more often from their partner or spouse. However, 42 percent said that they don't trust their partner or spouse to meet their standards of clean (Byron, 2012). Thus, many women may be increasing their domestic chores because they judge their husbands and partners too harshly on housework.

FAMILY-WORK CONFLICTS Among working parents with children under age 18, 56 percent of mothers and 50 percent of fathers say it's difficult to juggle work and family responsibilities; 40 percent of mothers and 34 percent of fathers

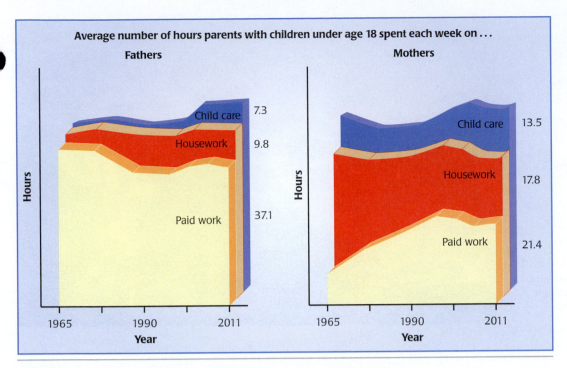

Average number of hours parents with children under age 18 spent each week on . . .

Fathers

Child care — 7.3
Housework — 9.8
Paid work — 37.1

Mothers

Child care — 13.5
Housework — 17.8
Paid work — 21.4

FIGURE 5.1 **How Mothers' and Fathers' Roles Have Changed, 1965 to 2011**
Source: DeSilver, 2013.

"always" feel rushed. Fathers (46 percent) are much more likely than mothers (23 percent) to worry about not spending enough time with their children. Fathers' concerns aren't surprising because they devote an average of 7 hours per week to child care, compared with 14 hours a week for mothers (Parker and Wang, 2013; see also Aumann et al., 2011).

Gender and the Workplace

There has been greater workplace equality, but we still have a long way to go. In the United States (unlike many European countries), the average male employee still doesn't have options for flexible schedules, paternity leaves, or extended absences for household matters, and women often have to postpone or forgo having children if they want to pursue a career. We'll examine family and work roles at some length in Chapter 13. Here, let's briefly consider sex-segregated jobs and sexual harassment.

SEX-SEGREGATED WORK A number of U.S. occupations are filled almost entirely by either women or men. For example, between 92 and 98 percent of all registered nurses, child care workers, secretaries, dental hygienists, and preschool and kindergarten teachers are women. From 96 to 99 percent of all pilots, mechanics, plumbers, and loading machine operators are men. Women have made progress in the higher-paying professional occupations that require at least a college degree, but 76 percent of architects, 78 percent of dentists, and 92 percent of electrical engineers are men (*Women in the Labor Force*, 2013). The issue isn't women and men working in different spaces or locations, but that male-dominated occupations usually pay higher wages (see Chapter 13).

SEXUAL HARASSMENT **Sexual harassment** is any unwanted sexual advance, request for sexual favors, or other conduct of a sexual nature that makes a person uncomfortable and interferes with her or his work. It includes *verbal*

Watch on MySocLab

Video: Working Women

sexual harassment Any unwanted sexual advance, request for sexual favors, or other conduct of a sexual nature that makes a person uncomfortable and interferes with her or his work.

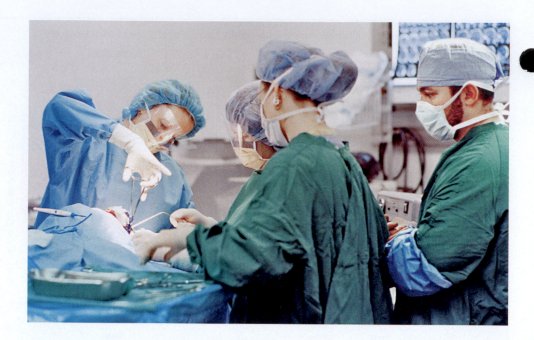

Increasing numbers of men are pursuing traditionally female occupations such as nursing, whereas more women are becoming physicians, including brain surgeons, a traditionally male-dominated occupation.

behavior (such as pressure for dates or demands for sexual favors in return for hiring, promotion, or tenure, as well as the threat of rape), *nonverbal behavior* (such as indecent gestures or the display of posters, photos, or drawings of a sexual nature), and *physical contact* (such as pinching, touching, or rape).

Between 1997 and 2011, the Equal Employment Opportunity Commission (EEOC) received almost 206,000 formal sexual harassment complaints, 84 percent of them from female employees (U.S. Equal Employment Opportunity Commission, 2011b). Lawyers say the statistics would be much higher, but many companies now require new employees to agree to arbitrate complaints, including sexual harassment, as a condition of being hired (Green, 2011).

Nearly two-thirds of Americans say that sexual harassment is a serious problem in this country. About 25 percent of women have been sexually harassed at work. Only 40 percent of them reported the incident, however, because they believed that doing so wouldn't do any good or they feared being fired or demoted (Clement, 2011).

Gender and Politics

In 1872, Victoria Chaflin Woodhull of the Equal Rights Party was the first female presidential candidate. Since then, 36 women have sought the nation's highest office, but none has broken the glass ceiling of a male-dominated U.S. presidency.

Unlike a number of other countries (including Great Britain, Germany, India, Israel, Pakistan, Argentina, Chile, and Philippines), the United States has never had a woman serving as president or even vice president. In the U.S. Congress, 82 percent of the members are men. In several other important elective offices (such as governor, mayor, or state legislator), only a handful of the decision makers are women (see *Table 5.7*), and this number hasn't changed much since the early 1990s (Center for American Women and Politics, 2013).

Women's voting rates in the United States have been higher than men's since 1984 (U.S. Census Bureau, 2012). Why, in contrast, are there so few women in political office? First, it may be that women, socialized to be nurturers and volunteers, see themselves as supporters rather than doers. As a result, they may

TABLE 5.7	U.S. Women in Elective Offices, 2013	
Political Office	**Total Number of Office Holders**	**Percentage Who Are Women**
Senate	100	20
House of Representatives	435	18
Governor	50	5
State Legislator	7,383	24
Attorney General	50	16
Secretary of State	50	24
State Treasurer	50	16
State Comptroller	50	8
Mayor (100 largest cities)	100	12

Source: Based on material at the Center for American Women and Politics, 2013.

spend many hours organizing support for a candidate rather than running for political office themselves.

Second, women are less likely than men to receive encouragement to run for office (such as from a political party or its leaders). As a result, even successful women are twice as likely as men to rate themselves as not qualified to run for office. In contrast, men are two-thirds more likely than women with similar credentials to consider themselves qualified or very qualified to run for office (Lawless and Fox, 2005).

Third, there is a lingering sexism, among both men and women, that "from the pulpit to the presidency" men are better leaders (Tucker, 2007: A9). The pervasive sexism in media coverage of political candidates was especially evident during the 2008 presidential campaign. Compared with men, women received considerably less media coverage of their political campaigns, or the coverage was more disparaging (Zurbriggen and Sherman, 2010).

For feminist scholars, women's lower participation in decision-making bodies results in men controlling many aspects of women's health, including reproductive rights. In both 1970 and 2012, Congress convened all-male panels before making decisions about passing legislation on women's contraception. Recently, Republican presidential candidates have championed states' rights to criminalize birth control, governors have signed laws that define life as beginning before conception, and funding for abortions for poor and uninsured women has dwindled (Bolton, 2012; see also Chapter 7 for an in-depth discussion of these and other sex-related issues).

Gender and Education

In public K–12 schools, as rank and pay increase, the number of women decreases. Among all full-time teachers, 85 percent of the teachers at the elementary level are women; the number drops to 58 percent in high school. Among principals, the number of women drops from 59 percent at elementary schools to 29 percent in high schools (Aud et al., 2012).

In 2012, an influential congressional committee held hearings on women's contraception coverage. Pictured here is the first panel of witnesses. Where are the women?

Because women across all racial and ethnic groups are more likely than men to finish college, some observers have described this phenomenon as "the feminization of higher education" (McCormack, 2011; Pollard, 2011). As *Figure 5.2* shows, almost equal numbers of girls and boys are high school graduates. Women have sailed past men in earning associate's, bachelor's, and master's degrees, but their percentage of professional and doctoral degrees drops considerably. Such data contradict the description of higher education as feminized.

You saw earlier that there are large sex differences by academic major because many women avoid or drop out of STEM fields. Even when women earn doctoral degrees in these male-dominated fields, they're less likely than men to be hired (see Milan, 2012). Also, once hired, women faculty members are less likely than their male counterparts to be promoted. Since 1982, one-third of all recipients of Ph.D. degrees have been women, but as the academic rank increases, the number of female faculty members decreases (see *Table 5.8*). There's also a gender gap in higher education administration. For example, the percentage of female college and university presidents rose from 2006 to 2011, but women still comprise only 26 percent of this group (Cook and Kim, 2012).

Gender and Religion

Religion shapes gender and family roles in many ways. The Ten Commandments teach children to honor their parents and teach married couples to be faithful to each other. Across all age and faith groups in 145 countries, women tend to be more religious than men in believing in God, praying, attending services, and saying that religion is very important in their lives (Pew Forum on Religion & Public Life, 2008; Deaton, 2009; Kosmin and Keysar, 2009; Taylor et al., 2009). It may be that women are expected to be more pious and spiritual because, especially as nurturers, they transmit religious values to their children. Another reason may be men's greater involvement in public life (e.g., employment, politics) that demands more of their time and energy.

Women are more likely than men to be religious, but they're often shut out of leadership positions. Women earned 33 percent of theology degrees in 2009, a dramatic increase from only 2 percent in 1970. Still, women make up only

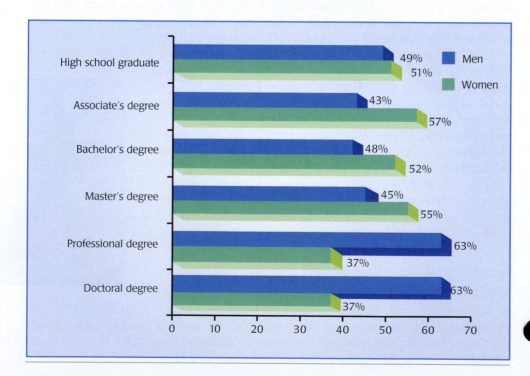

FIGURE 5.2 **U.S. Educational Attainment, 25 Years and Older, by Sex, 2012**
Source: Based on data in U.S. Census Bureau, Current Population Survey, 2012 Annual Social and Economic Supplement, 2012 Table 2, http://www.census.gov/hhes/socdemo/education/data/cps/2012/tables.html (accessed July 1, 2013).

TABLE 5.8	As Rank Increases, the Number of Female Faculty Members Decreases
Rank	**Percentage of Female Faculty Members**
Professor	28
Associate Professor	41
Assistant Professor	48
Instructor	55

Note: Of the almost 729,000 full-time faculty members in 2009, 43 percent were women.
Source: Based on Snyder and Dillow, 2012, Table 264.

about 13 percent of the nation's clergy, and only 3 percent of female clergy lead large congregations (those with more than 350 people) (Winseman, 2004; U.S. Census Bureau, 2012). Even in liberal Protestant congregations, female clergy tend to be relegated to specialized ministries with responsibilities for music, youth, or Bible studies (Banerjee, 2006; Bartlett, 2007).

Gender and Language

Women and men are more similar than different in their interactions. A study that recorded conversations of college students in the United States and Mexico found that women and men spoke the same number of words daily—about 16,000. An analysis of studies published since the 1960s concluded that men are generally more talkative than women, but their talkativeness depends on the situation. During decision-making tasks, men are more talkative than women, but when talking about themselves or interacting with children, women are generally more talkative than men (Leaper and Ayres, 2007; Mehl et al., 2007).

Other studies support the findings that our cultural norms and gender role expectations shape the sexes' communication patterns. Generally, women are socialized to be more comfortable talking about their feelings, whereas men are socialized to be dominant and take charge, especially in the workplace. Because women tend to use communication to develop and maintain relationships, *talk is often an end in itself*—a way to foster closeness and understanding. Women often ask questions that *probe for a greater understanding* of feelings and perceptions ("Do you think it was deliberate?" or "Were you glad it happened?"). Women are also much more likely than men to do *conversational "maintenance work,"* such as asking questions that encourage conversation ("Tell me what happened at the meeting") (Lakoff, 1990; Robey et al., 1998).

Compared with women, men's speech often reflects *conversational dominance*, such as speaking more frequently and for longer periods of time. Men also show dominance by interrupting others, reinterpreting the speaker's meaning, or rerouting the conversation. They tend to express themselves in assertive, often absolutist, ways ("That approach won't work"). Compared with women, men's language is typically more forceful, direct, and authoritative rather than tentative (Tannen, 1990; Mulac, 1998; see also Chapter 10).

Only 18 percent of U.S. teachers in elementary and middle schools are males. The salaries are low, compared with other occupations, but gender stereotypes also discourage men's participation. Especially in the lower grades, men who are nurturing or affectionate may be accused of being gay or a pedophile (James, 2013).

MAKING CONNECTIONS

- Some people maintain that instrumental and expressive roles no longer exist. Others argue that both roles are flourishing. Think about your parents, your spouse or intimate partner, or your friends. Does their behavior reflect instrumental and expressive roles? What about your behavior?

- Think about your home, workplace, or classes. Have you noticed any differences in the ways that women and men interact?

Since you asked . . .

- Are there any countries where women are better off than men?

Gender Inequality across Cultures

According to the World Economic Forum (an independent, nonprofit international organization), "No country in the world has achieved gender equality" (Hausmann et al., 2012: 33), but there's considerable variation worldwide. Such cross-cultural differences show that gender roles are learned rather than innate.

In a study of 22 countries in different regions of the world, at least 90 percent of the respondents in 13 countries said that women and men should have equal rights (Kohut et al., 2010). Attitudes and behavior are very different, however, according to the Global Gender Gap Index.

The Global Gender Gap Index

There's no easy way to compare gender equality around the world. Still, the Global Gender Gap Index (GGGI) measures women's status and quality of life in 135 countries, representing more than 90 percent of the world's population. The GGGI is based on key indicators in four fundamental categories: economic opportunity and participation, educational attainment, political empowerment (women and men in the highest political positions), and health and survival (Hausmann et al., 2012).

The GGGI isn't an overall measure of a country's development or wealth; rather, it gauges the relative equality between men and women on an indicator. For example, Saudi Arabia, one of the wealthiest countries in the world, and which has some of the most educated women in the world (including STEM college and advanced degrees), ranks near or at the bottom in terms of women's economic and political participation (Charles, 2011; Hausmann et al., 2012; Rashad, 2012).

Overall Gender Inequality Worldwide

Of the 135 countries examined using the GGGI in 2012, Iceland, Norway, Finland, Sweden, and New Zealand had the greatest gender equality in economic opportunity and participation, educational attainment, health and survival, and political empowerment. The United States ranked only 22nd, and behind some poor countries such as Cuba, Lesotho, Nicaragua, and the Philippines. The biggest gender gaps were in the Middle East, North Africa, and sub-Saharan Africa. In 2012, the five bottom countries in gender equality were Chad, Pakistan, Saudi Arabia, Syria, and Yemen. In all countries and regions, the areas of greatest gender inequality were in economic opportunity and participation and political leadership (Hausmann et al., 2012). *Table 5.9* shows the countries with the highest and lowest GGGI scores in both of these areas.

Economic Opportunity and Participation

Women's economic opportunities and participation depend on a culture's attitudes, values, customs, and laws. Regarding attitudes, the biggest gender gaps on whether women and men should have the same rights, including economic participation, are in Egypt, Nigeria, Kenya, Indonesia, Jordan, and Pakistan. In Nigeria, for example, only 35 percent of men, compared with 56 percent of women, believe that women should have the same economic opportunities and participation as men. In Egypt, 45 percent of men, compared with 76 percent of women, believe that both sexes should have equal rights (Kohut et al., 2010). Such data show that not all women endorse equal rights. Even if they do, they follow laws, passed by men, that restrict women's behavior to the home.

Across 131 countries, 33 percent of men, compared with 18 percent of women, have "good jobs"—those that are full-time, provide health insurance, and ensure labor rights. Of those in the workforce, 23 percent of women, compared

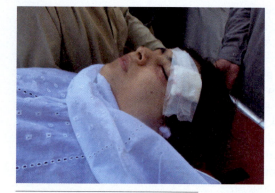

In 2012, a Pakistani gunman shot Malala Yousufzai, a 14-year-old girl—once in the head and once in the neck—when she was going home from school because she advocated girls' education. The Taliban is an Islamic fundamentalist militant group that operates in many Middle East and African countries. It denounces girls' education because the education endorses "obscene" pro-West attitudes. Yousufzai, pictured here, has been recovering, but the Taliban promised to kill her and her family if they continue to promote girls' schooling ("Pakistan Taliban Shoot Girl Activist," 2012).

TABLE 5.9 Countries with the Highest and Lowest Gender Equality in Economic Opportunity and Participation and Political Empowerment, 2012

GGGI Scores on Economic Opportunity and Participation		GGGI Scores on Political Empowerment	
Countries with the Highest Scores	Countries with the Lowest Scores	Countries with the Highest Scores	Countries with the Lowest Scores*
Mongolia, Bahamas .84	Iran .41	Iceland .73	Botswana, Fiji .04
Burundi, Norway .83	Algeria .38	Finland .56	Egypt, Iran, Mongolia .03
Malawi, Lesotho .82	Saudi Arabia, Yemen .34	Norway .56	Oman, Yemen .02
Luxembourg, United States .81	Pakistan .31	Nicaragua, Sweden .50	Kuwait .01
Mozambique .80	Syria .27	Ireland .41	Belize, Brunei Darussalam, Lebanon, Qatar, Saudi Arabia .00

*With a score of .16, the United States ranks only 55th in the world in women's political empowerment.

Note: In the GGGI, a score of 1 means gender equality. Thus, in the first cell, Mongolia's score of .84 means that there are 84 women for every 100 men who have economic opportunity and participation. Another way to interpret the .84 is that the gender gap is 16 percent in favor of men.

Source: Based on Hausmann et al., 2012, Table 5.

with 16 percent of men, are *underemployed*—working part-time when they want a full-time job and working below their level of education, skill, and experience. Women's underemployment rates are highest in sub-Saharan Africa and Latin America, and lowest in East Asia and the countries that broke away from the Soviet Union (Marlar, 2011).

Globally, female-owned firms account for 40 percent of all privately held businesses and generate $1.9 trillion in annual sales ("The X Factor," 2011). However, only 4 percent of the CEOs of Fortune 500 companies and 16 percent of all U.S. corporate board members are women—about the same as in 1998. In contrast, Finland, Sweden, Norway, and seven other European countries have laws requiring 40 percent of all board members to be women (Kowitt and Arora, 2011; McGregor, 2011). Some CEOs endorse similar quotas for the United States because gender-diverse groups have higher levels of cooperation and a wider pool of skills. Others maintain that mandatory quotas can result in less experienced boards (Green, 2012; Huppke, 2012; Chu and Ramstad, 2012).

Since you asked . . .
- Should the U.S. government require its corporations to impose gender quotas to increase women's presence in boardrooms?

Political Empowerment

As indicated in *Table 5.9*, gender equality worldwide in political empowerment is much lower, even in the countries with the highest scores, than economic opportunity and participation. Worldwide, 19 percent of those holding seats in national legislatures are women. Rwanda has 56 percent, followed by seven countries in which women comprise 40 to 46 percent of those in high-level

Women in Kenya, Africa, acquired the right to vote only in 1963 but now constitute 54 percent of the country's voting population. In both tribal villages and urban centers, women line up to vote for important issues such as the right to inherit money and property.

political positions. In contrast, only 18 percent of the U.S. Congress is comprised of women (Clifton and Frost, 2011; Center for American Women and Politics, 2013).

Of the 197 world leaders who are presidents or prime ministers, only 11 percent are women (Institute for Women's Leadership, 2011). A study of 188 countries worldwide found that women occupied only 20 percent of the positions in decision-making bodies that are comparable with our Congress. The United States ranks 71st in women's political leadership, well below many African, European, and Asian countries, and even below most of the Arab countries that many Westerners view as repressing women (Inter-Parliamentary Union, 2011).

At the other end of the continuum, Saudi Arabia, with a score of 0, is the lowest-ranking country in the world on women's political empowerment (Hausmann et al., 2012). In 2011, King Abdullah announced that, beginning in 2015, women will be able to run as candidates in municipal elections, serve on the king's advisory board (which doesn't have power to enact any legislation), and, with a male family member's approval, "will even have the right to vote" ("Saudi Arabia and Its Women," 2011; "Saudi King Announces New Rights for Women," 2011; Ignatius, 2013).

Why do women in many countries have few political rights and little political clout? Only half of all national governments have legal requirements to include women in political positions. Even then, women make up only 30 percent of the governing bodies in Argentina, Cuba, Finland, India, Sweden, Rwanda, and other countries (Inter-Parliamentary Union, 2011).

CONCLUSION

The past 25 years have seen the beginning of dramatic *changes* in some aspects of gender roles. More people today say that they believe in gender equality, and unprecedented numbers of women have earned college degrees and entered the labor force.

Do most people really have more *choices?* Men now do more of the household chores and participate in child care, but the domestic division of labor is still far from equal. Many men are still expected to spend many hours at work because they're breadwinners, and women are still expected to shoulder most of the housework and child care.

Changes in gender roles also bring *constraints* for both sexes at every level: personal, group, and institutional. In the next chapter, we examine how changes in gender roles affect love and intimate relationships.

On MySocLab

✓ **Study** and **Review** on MySocLab

REVIEW QUESTIONS

5.1. Define and illustrate the following concepts: sex, gender, gender identity, gender roles, and gender stereotypes.

1. Are sex and gender interchangeable terms? Why or why not?

2. What's the difference between gender identity and gender roles? Provide an example of each concept.

3. What are some of the most common gender stereotypes? Are they harmless?

5.2. Describe the nature–nurture debate and the evidence for each perspective.

4. What, briefly, is the nature–nurture debate?

5. What kind of evidence does each side use to support its argument of the importance of nature or nurture in explaining the differences between women and men?

6. Why do some sociologists argue that the nature–nurture debate is becoming outdated?

5.3. Compare five theoretical perspectives that explain why gender roles differ.

7. How do the five theoretical perspectives on gender roles differ?

8. What is a strength and weakness of each of the five theoretical perspectives?

5.4. Describe and illustrate five sources of learning gender roles.

9. How, specifically, do we learn gender roles from parents, siblings and peers, teachers, and the popular culture?

10. How does our gender role socialization affect our everyday behavior?

5.5. Explain how gender ideologies affect traditional and nontraditional gender roles.

11. How do traditional and egalitarian gender ideologies differ?

12. What are some of the benefits and costs of traditional gender roles for both women and men?

5.6. Describe and illustrate how gender roles vary in adulthood.

13. How, specifically, do adult gender roles differ at home, the workplace, politics, education, and religion?

14. How do men and women tend to communicate differently? Why?

5.7. Compare gender inequality across cultures.

15. What is the GGGI?

16. How do countries vary in gender equality?

17. How does the United States compare with other countries, especially in women's economic participation and political empowerment?

6

Love and Loving Relationships

((• **Listen** to Chapter 6 on **MySocLab**

LEARNING OBJECTIVES

After you read and study this chapter you will be able to:

6.1 Compare self-love, friendship, and love.

6.2 Explain the concept of love.

6.3 Explain why caring, intimacy, and commitment are important components of love.

6.4 Compare the six theoretical perspectives that explain love.

6.5 Describe four functions of love.

6.6 Explain how people experience love and some of love's obstacles.

6.7 Explain why love goes wrong.

6.8 Compare romantic and long-term love.

6.9 Explain how and why love varies across cultures.

- **Love is great for business.** In 2013, Americans spent almost $19 billion, the highest amount in history, on Valentine's Day gifts. The average man spent twice as much ($176) as the average woman ($89); 20 percent bought Valentine's Day presents for their pets.

- About 28 percent of Americans believe that **there is only one true love** for each person.

- Among Facebook users, **the average number of "friends"** is 319 for those ages 18 to 34, 198 for those ages 35 to 46, 156 for those ages 47 to 56, and 42 for those age 75 and older.

- **Should women propose to men?** Yes, according to 77 percent of men and 63 percent of women.

- Among those ages 65 and older, **47 percent report being passionately in love**, but 83 percent say that "true love can exist without a radiant sex life."

- Nearly half of all single people in 24 countries believe that **finding a sweetheart would bring them the greatest happiness in life**.

Sources: Armstrong, 2004b; Schwartz, 2010; Allen, 2012; Goo, 2012; Cohn, 2013; National Retail Federation, 2013.

Love means different things to different people. As "On Love and Loving" shows, love has been a source of inspiration, witticisms, and even political action for centuries. In this chapter, we explore the meaning of romance and love, why people love each other, the positive and negative aspects of love, and how love changes over time. We also look at some cross-cultural variations in people's attitudes about love. Let's begin with some of the differences between liking and loving.

Changes — On Love and Loving

Throughout the centuries many writers have commented on the varieties, purposes, pleasures, and pain of love. Here are some examples:

- **I Corinthians 13:4–7:** "Love is patient and kind; love is not jealous or boastful; it is not arrogant or rude. . . . Love bears all things, believes all things, hopes all things, endures all things."

- **William Shakespeare (1564–1616):** "To say the truth, reason and love keep little company together nowadays."

- **Hindustani proverb:** "Life is no longer one's own when the heart is fixed on another."

- **Abraham Cowley (1618–1667):** "I love you, not only for what you are, but for what I am when I am with you."

- **Ninon de Lenclos (1620–1705):** "Much more genius is needed to make love than to command armies."

- **Irish saying:** "If you live in my heart, you live rent free."

- **Elizabeth Barrett Browning (1806–1861):** "How do I love thee? Let me count the ways. I love thee to the depth and breadth and height my soul can reach."

- **Japanese saying:** "Who travels for love finds a thousand miles only one mile."

- **William Thackeray (1811–1863):** "It is best to love wisely, no doubt; but to love foolishly is better than not to be able to love at all."

- **Robert Browning (1812–1889):** "Take away love and our earth is a tomb."

- **Marlene Dietrich (1901–1992):** "Grumbling is the death of love."

- **Turkish proverb:** "When two hearts are one, even the king cannot separate them."

- **Anonymous:** "Nobody is perfect until you fall in love with them."

- **Che Guevara (1928–1967):** "The true revolutionary is guided by a great feeling of love."

- **John Lennon (1940–1980):** "All you need is love."

- **Katherine Hepburn (1907–2003):** "Sometimes I wonder if men and women really suit each other. Perhaps they should live next door and just visit now and then."

- **Cher (1946–):** "The trouble with some women is that they get all excited about nothing—and then marry him."

- **Oprah Winfrey (1954–):** "Lots of people want to ride with you in the limo, but what you want is someone who will take the bus with you when the limo breaks down."

- **Jay Leno (1950–):** "Today is Valentine's Day—or, as men like to call it, Extortion Day!"

Liking and Loving

Love—as both an emotion and a behavior—is essential for human survival. The family is usually our earliest and most important source of love and emotional support (see Chapter 1). It is in families that we learn to love ourselves and, consequently, to love others.

Self-Love

Actress Mae West once said, "I never loved another person the way I loved myself." Such a statement may seem self-centered, but it's insightful. Social philosopher Erich Fromm (1956) saw self-love, or love for oneself, as essential for our social and emotional development and as a prerequisite for loving others.

For social scientists, self-love is an important basis for self-esteem. People who like themselves are more open to criticism and less demanding of others. Those who don't like themselves may not be able to reciprocate friendship. Instead, they constantly seek relationships that will bolster their poor self-image (Casler, 1974).

Friendship

A *friend* is someone you care about, can count on for companionship and assistance, and with whom you enjoy interacting. A number of studies have found, consistently, that friends have a big effect on our physical, social, and psychological health, and sometimes an even bigger impact than our family members. For example, people ages 70 and older who have social networks—especially those including friends and not just family members—live longer; people with friends are generally happier than their isolated counterparts; and those with strong friendships experience less stress because friends offer physical assistance (such as running errands) and emotional support (Giles et al., 2005; Christakis and Fowler, 2007; Parker-Pope, 2009).

Our friends often differ. For example, we can discuss politics with some friends but not others. Some can offer us sound financial advice, and yet we have other friends we may turn to for highly personal or spiritual issues. Despite such benefits, most Americans' number of *close friends* has shrunk from three to two since the late 1980s, and 25 percent of the population ages 18 and over report having no close friends at all (McPherson et al., 2008).

Recent national surveys in the United States, Canada, and Europe have consistently found that the larger the number of real-life friends, and the more frequently people see them, the happier they are. In contrast, the number of online friends doesn't increase happiness or satisfaction with life (Helliwell and Huang, 2013).

In 2012, Facebook subscribers in the United States reported having an average of 229 friends (Goo, 2012; see also Data Digest). A woman complained that Facebook's 5,000 limit was too low for her vast number of friends (Daum, 2009). Is everyone on your Facebook page or in your Twitter circle *really* a friend? How many of them really care, for example, about your cat or favorite music, or are interested in viewing photos of your last vacation (Deresiewicz, 2009)? Nonetheless, 40 percent of Facebook users say that they have one or two close friends with whom they discuss important matters online (Hampton et al., 2011).

A family's love binds people emotionally and lightens their disappointments.

Such research findings suggest that many of us have few, if any, close friends over our lifetime, but we often hear self-help books proclaim that only friends

become lovers or intimate partners. Is this true? Or does friendship and love differ?

Friendship and Love

Do you like people whom you don't love? Sure. Do you love people whom you don't like? No—at least not in a healthy relationship. In his classic research on "the near and dear," sociologist Keith Davis (1985) identified eight qualities of friendship:

Friends are accepting, understanding, and supportive.

- **Enjoyment.** Friends enjoy being with each other most of time. They feel at ease despite occasional disagreements.
- **Acceptance.** Friends accept each other the way they are. They tolerate faults and shortcomings instead of trying to change each other.
- **Trust.** Friends trust and look out for each other. They lean on each other during difficult times.
- **Respect.** Friends respect each other's judgment. They may not agree with the choices the other person makes, but they honor his or her decisions.
- **Mutual support.** Friends help and support each other without expecting something in return.
- **Confiding.** Friends share experiences and feelings. They don't gossip about each other or backstab.
- **Understanding.** Friends are sympathetic about each other's feelings and thoughts. They can often "read" each other without saying very much.
- **Honesty.** Friends are open and honest. They feel free to be themselves and say what they think.

Since you asked . . .
- Is it possible to love someone you don't like?

Love includes all these qualities and three more—sexual desire, priority over other relationships, and caring to the point of great self-sacrifice. A relationship can start off with friendship and develop into love. It's unlikely, however, that we can "really" love someone who isn't a friend. And love, like friendship, develops over time. But just what is love? What attracts people to each other? And are lust and love similar? Before you read any further, take the "How Much Do You Know about Love?" quiz.

ASK YOURSELF

How Much Do You Know about Love?

The following statements are based on the material in this chapter.

Fact	Myth	
☐	☐	**1.** There is an ideal mate for every person; just keep looking.
☐	☐	**2.** Women are more romantic than men.
☐	☐	**3.** Love conquers all.
☐	☐	**4.** Men's and women's love needs are different.
☐	☐	**5.** Real love lasts forever.
☐	☐	**6.** Everybody falls in love sooner or later.
☐	☐	**7.** Love brings happiness and security.
☐	☐	**8.** Love endures and overcomes all problems.
☐	☐	**9.** Men are more interested in sex than in love.
☐	☐	**10.** I can change the person I love.

(The answers are on page 149.)

6.2

6.2 Explain the concept of love.

What Is Love?

When asked what love is, a 9-year-old boy said, "Love is like an avalanche where you have to run for your life." And according to a 6-year-old girl, "Love is when mommy sees daddy on the toilet and she doesn't think it's gross."

During the war in Iraq, a U.S. soldier wrote his 15-month-old daughter a letter that said, in part, "You are the meaning of my life. You make my heart pound with joy and pride. No matter what happens to me or where we go, you will always know that I love you." The letter was found on the soldier's body when he died in the crash of a Black Hawk helicopter shot down by insurgents (Zoroya, 2005).

We have all experienced love and believe that we know what it is. Love, however, is an elusive concept: There's no universally agreed on definition of love, affectionate feelings can change, acceptable expressions of love vary across time and cultures, and, as you'll see shortly, there are different types of love.

What Are Some Characteristics of Love?

As the fallen soldier's letter illustrates, parental love is strong and deep. Among many adolescents and adults, romantic love is usually short-lived. In contrast, many married couples and gay/lesbian partners experience long-term love. All types of love, nonetheless, are multifaceted, based on respect, and often demanding.

LOVE IS MULTIFACETED Love has many dimensions. It can be romantic, exciting, obsessive, and irrational. It can also be platonic, calming, altruistic, and practical. Love defies a single definition because it varies in degree and intensity and in different social contexts. At the very least, and as you'll see shortly, love includes caring, intimacy, and commitment.

LOVE IS BASED ON RESPECT Love may involve passionate yearning, but respect is more important. If respect is missing, the relationship isn't based on love. Instead, it's an unhealthy or possessive feeling or behavior that limits people's social, emotional, and intellectual growth (Peele and Brodsky, 1976).

LOVE IS OFTEN DEMANDING Long-term love, especially, has nothing in common with the images of infatuation or frenzied sex that we get from movies, television, and romance novels. These misconceptions often lead to unrealistic expectations, stereotypes, and disillusionment.

Long-term love is closer to what one writer calls "stirring-the-oatmeal" love (R. Johnson, 1985). This type of love is neither exciting nor thrilling; rather, it is usually mundane and unromantic. It means paying bills, scrubbing toilet bowls, being up all night with a sick baby, and performing myriad other tasks that aren't very sexy.

Some partners take turns stirring the oatmeal. Others break up or get a divorce. Whether we decide to tie the knot or not, why are we attracted to some people and not others?

What Attracts People to Each Other?

Some Americans believe that everyone has "only one true love" (see Data Digest). Such beliefs are romantic but unfounded. Cultural norms and values, not fate, bring people together. We'll never meet hundreds of potential lovers because they're filtered out by formal or informal rules based on factors such as age, race, social class, religion, sexual orientation, health, or physical appearance (see Chapter 8).

Open communication can enhance a loving relationship.

Beginning in childhood, parents indirectly encourage or limit future romances by living in certain neighborhoods and selecting certain schools. During the preteen years, peer practices and expectations shape romantic experiences. For example, even seventh-graders have rules, such as not going out with someone their friends don't like, or telling parents as little as possible because "parents nose around, get into people's business, and talk to other parents" (Perlstein, 2005: 33).

Romance may cross cultural or ethnic borders, but criticism and approval teach us what is acceptable and with whom. All societies—including the United States—have rules about *homogamy* (dating and marrying within one's group) and *heterogamy* (dating and marrying someone outside an acceptable group) (see Chapters 1 and 8). Even if we "fall in lust" with someone, our sexual yearnings won't necessarily lead to falling in love if there are strong cultural taboos against it. These taboos explain, in part, why we don't always marry our sexual partners.

Do Lust and Love Differ?

Lust and love differ quite a bit. Psychologists Pamela Regan and Ellen Berscheid (1999) differentiate among sexual arousal (lust), sexual desire, and romantic love. They describe *sexual arousal* as a physiological rather than an emotional response, one that occurs either consciously or unconsciously (see Chapter 7). *Sexual desire*, in contrast, is a psychological state in which a person wants "to obtain a sexual object that one does not now have or to engage in a sexual activity in which one is not now engaging" (p. 17).

Sexual desire may or may not lead to *romantic love*, an intense feeling that can provide happiness when fulfilled or deep suffering when the feeling isn't reciprocated. Once desire evaporates, disillusioned and disappointed lovers will wonder where the spark in their relationship has gone and may reminisce longingly about "the good old days."

This doesn't mean that sexual desire *always* culminates in sexual intercourse or that romantic love and long-term love are synonymous. Married couples may love each other even though they rarely, or never, engage in sexual intercourse for health and other reasons. Regardless of the nature of love, healthy loving relationships reflect a balance of caring, intimacy, and commitment.

ANSWERS TO "How Much Do You Know about Love?"

All ten statements are myths. Eight or more correct answers indicate that you know a myth when you hear one.

1. We can love many people, and we can love many times. This may be one reason why people marry more than once.

2. Men fall in love more quickly, are more romantic, and suffer more intensely when their love isn't returned.

3. Because almost one out of two U.S. marriages ends in divorce, love isn't enough to overcome all problems and obstacles. Differences in race, ethnicity, religion, economic status, education, and age can often stifle romantic interest.

4. As in friendship, both men and women want trust, honesty, understanding, and respect from those they love.

5. Love can be genuine but not last forever. People today live much longer, the world is more complex, and even marital partners change as they mature and grow older.

6. Some people have deep emotional scars that make them suspicious and unloving; others are too self-centered to give love.

7. Love guarantees neither happiness nor security, and it doesn't "fix" people who are generally insecure or anxious about themselves or their relationships.

8. People who love each other make sacrifices, but emotional or physical abuse shouldn't be tolerated. Eventually, even "martyrs" become unhappy, angry, depressed, and resentful.

9. During the romantic stage, both women and men may be more interested in sex than in love. As love matures, both partners value attributes such as faithfulness and patience and making the other person feel wanted.

10. You can only change yourself. Trying to change someone usually results in anger, resentment, frustration, and unhappiness.

Caring, Intimacy, and Commitment

You'll see shortly that people fall in love for many reasons: They are physically attracted to each other, have shared interests, seek companionship, or simply want to have fun. In any type of love, however, caring about the other person is essential.

Caring

Love includes *caring*, or wanting to help the other person by providing aid and emotional support (Cutrona, 1996). We often use metaphors for love such as "I'm crazy about you" or "I can't live without you," but such terms of endearment may not be translated into ongoing, everyday behavior such as valuing your partner's welfare as much as your own.

Caring means responding to the other person's needs. If a person sees no evidence of warmth or support over time, there will be serious doubts that a partner *really* loves her or him. This doesn't mean that a partner should be submissive or docile. Instead, people who care about each other bolster each other's self-confidence and offer encouragement when there are problems. When a person is sensitive to a partner's needs, the relationship will become more intimate and will flourish.

Intimacy

Definitions of intimacy vary, but all of them emphasize feelings of closeness. For example, an analysis of couples (Brown, 1995) found that people experience intimacy when they

- Share a mutual emotional interest in each other
- Have some sort of history together
- Have a distinct sense of identity as a couple
- Hold a reciprocal commitment to a continued relationship
- Share hopes and dreams for a common future

Still other writers distinguish among three kinds of intimacy—*physical* (sex, hugging, and touching), *affective* (feeling close), and *verbal* (self-disclosure). They also point out that physical intimacy is usually the least important of the three (see, for example, Piorkowski, 1994).

Self-disclosure refers to communication in which one person reveals his or her honest thoughts and feelings to another person with the expectation that truly open communication will follow. In intimate relationships, partners feel free to expose their weaknesses, idiosyncrasies, hopes, and insecurities without fear of ridicule or rejection (Brown, 1995).

Lovers will reveal their innermost thoughts, and spouses feel comfortable in venting their frustrations because their partners are considered trustworthy, respectful, and their best friends or confidantes. Self-disclosure does *not* include nagging, which decreases intimacy. If you pick at your partner, you're saying "I'm better than you. Shape up." Most people resent nagging because it implies superiority by the person who's nagging.

Intimacy includes more than the relationship between two adults. It's also a bond between children and parents, adult children and their parents, children and stepparents, children and grandparents, and so on. Much research has emphasized the role of the mother in intimate ties with children, but a father's love is just as important. If a father is close to his children, he can play a crucial role in their development of self-esteem, emotional stability, and willingness to avoid drugs and other risky behavior (Rohner and Veneziano, 2001; see also Chapter 12).

In adult love relationships, intimacy increases as people let down their defenses, learn to relax in each other's company, and are mutually supportive

Since you asked . . .
- Can there be intimacy without sex?

self-disclosure Open communication in which one person offers his or her honest thoughts and feelings to another person in the hope that truly open communication will follow.

during good and bad times (Josselson, 1992). Caring and intimacy, in turn, foster commitment.

Commitment

Many of my students, particularly women, complain that their partners are afraid of "the big C"—commitment. The ultimate commitment is marriage, but as our high divorce rates show, marriage and commitment don't always go hand in hand (see Chapter 15).

Commitment is a person's intention to remain in a relationship and work through problems. Mutual commitment can arise out of (1) a sense of loyalty and fidelity to one's partner; (2) a religious, legal, or moral belief in the sanctity of marriage; (3) continued optimism about future rewards—emotional, financial, sexual, or others; and (4) strong emotional attachments. Many people end their relationships, even if they still love each other, if they feel that mutual commitment isn't increasing (Brown, 1995; Fehr, 1999; Sprecher, 1999).

In a healthy relationship, commitment has many positive aspects, such as affection, companionship, and trust. Each partner is available to the other not just during times of stress but day in and day out. Even when we're tempted to be unfaithful if our partners don't pay as much attention to us as we'd like or if we feel overwhelmed with daily responsibilities, committed partners will persevere during rough times (Molinari, 2010).

Commitment in a secure relationship isn't a matter of hearts and flowers. Especially on Valentine's Day, businesses profit by convincing men that they should buy their sweethearts and wives chocolates, roses, jewelry, clothes, and other "stuff" to show their love (Payne, 2012). Instead, commitment demonstrates—repeatedly and in a variety of situations—that "I'm here, I will be here, I'm interested in what you do and what you think and feel, I will actively support your independent actions, I trust you, and you can trust me to be here if you need me" (Crowell and Waters, 1994: 32).

Successful couples are able to work through their problems and remain committed to each other.

MAKING CONNECTIONS

- How are your friendships similar to and different from your love relationships? Can you be in love with several people at the same time?
- How do you define love? Is your definition the same as that of your friends?
- How many times have you been in love? Were your feelings similar in all cases? Did they change as you grew older?

Some Theories about Love and Loving

6.4 Compare the six theoretical perspectives that explain love.

Why and how do we love? Biological explanations tend to focus on why we love. Psychological, sociological, and anthropological theories try to explain how as well as why.

The Biochemistry of Love

Biological perspectives maintain that love is grounded in evolution, biology, and chemistry. Biologists and some psychologists see romance as serving an evolutionary purpose by drawing men and women into long-term partnerships that are essential for child rearing. On often dangerous grasslands, for example, one parent cared for offspring while the other foraged for food.

Researchers using magnetic resonance imaging (MRI) to study brain activity have found an interplay between hormones, chemicals, and neurotransmitters (chemical messengers in the brain) in creating the state we call love. When lovers claim that they feel "high," it's probably because they are. For example, dopamine is released when people do something highly pleasurable, whether it's falling in love or taking drugs. Norepinephrine, another stimulant, can produce sleeplessness, elation, and euphoria. And, during the early stages of emotional attachment, oxytocin promotes trust and other positive feelings (Fisher et al., 2010; Schneiderman et al., 2012; Fredrickson, 2013).

Since you asked . . .
- Is love due to physical biochemical changes?

As infatuation wanes and attachment grows, another group of chemicals called endorphins takes over. Unlike stimulants, endorphins calm the mind, eliminate pain, and reduce anxiety. This, biologists say, explains why people in long-lasting relationships report feeling comfortable and secure (Walsh, 1991; Fisher, 2004; Brizendine, 2006).

The loss of a loved one may be linked to physical problems. According to brain images and blood tests, traumatic breakups can release stress hormones that travel to cells in one part of the brain. The resulting stress can bring on chest pain and even heart attacks ("a broken heart") (Najib et al., 2004; Wittstein et al., 2005).

Critics see three problems with biological perspectives. First, they typically rely on tiny samples of volunteers (9 to 17 people, in some cases), and usually only women. Second, chemicals (such as dopamine) that apparently trigger intense romantic love are also found in gamblers, cocaine users, and even people playing computer games (Young, 2009). Thus, it's not clear how chemicals and neurotransmitters "cause" love. Third, biological theories don't explain why there are cultural variations in how people experience and express love (Perrin et al., 2011).

Sociological perspectives—and some psychological theories—claim that culture, not chemicals, plays Cupid. The best known social science theories that help us understand the components and processes of love include attachment theory, Reiss's wheel theory of love, Sternberg's triangular theory of love, Lee's research on the styles of loving, and exchange theories.

Attachment Theory

Attachment theory proposes that infants need to develop a relationship with at least one primary caregiver, usually the mother, for normal social and emotional development. British psychiatrist John Bowlby (1969, 1984) asserted that attachment is an integral part of human behavior from the cradle to the grave. Adults and children benefit by having someone look out for them—someone who cares about their welfare, provides for their basic emotional and physical needs, and is available when needed.

American psychologist Mary Ainsworth (Ainsworth et al., 1978), one of Bowlby's students, assessed infant–mother attachment in her classic "strange situation" studies. In both natural and laboratory settings, Ainsworth created mild stress for an infant by having the mother temporarily leave the baby with a friendly stranger in an unfamiliar room. When the mother returned, Ainsworth observed the infant's and the mother's reactions to each other.

Ainsworth identified three infant–mother attachment styles. About 60 percent of the infants with sensitive and responsive mothers were *secure* in their attachment. The babies showed some distress when left with a stranger, but when the mother returned, they clung to her for just a short time and then went back to exploring and playing.

About 19 percent of the infants displayed *anxious/ ambivalent* attachment styles when their mothers were inconsistent—sometimes affectionate, sometimes aloof. The infants showed distress at separation but rejected their mothers when they returned. The remaining 21 percent of the infants, most of whom had been reared by caregivers who ignored their physical and emotional needs, displayed *avoidant* behavior by ignoring the mothers after they returned.

Some of the infant attachment research has been criticized for usually relying on laboratory settings instead of natural ones, and for not addressing cross-cultural differences in child-rearing practices (see Feeney and Noller, 1996). Despite such criticisms, many researchers propose that adult

attachment theory Proposes that infants need to develop a relationship with at least one primary caregiver, usually the mother, for normal social and emotional development.

Watch on MySocLab

Video: Attachment in Infants

Early attachment to primary caregivers helps children develop successful relationships in adulthood.

intimate relationships often reflect these three attachment styles (see Mikulincer and Shaver, 2012, for an overview of some of this research).

Using a "love quiz" based on Ainsworth's three attachment styles, psychologist Cindy Hazan and her associates interviewed 108 college students and 620 adults who said they were in love (Hazan and Shaver, 1987; Shaver et al., 1988). The respondents were asked to describe themselves in their "most important romance" using three measures:

- **Secure style:** I find it easy to get close to others and am comfortable depending on them and having them depend on me. I don't often worry about being abandoned or about someone getting too close to me.

- **Avoidant style:** I am somewhat uncomfortable being close to others; I find it difficult to trust them completely and to depend on them. I am nervous when anyone gets too close and when lovers want me to be more intimate than I feel comfortable being.

- **Anxious/ambivalent style:** Others are reluctant to get as close as I would like. I often worry that my partner doesn't really love me or won't want to stay with me. I want to merge completely with another person, and this desire sometimes scares people away.

The researchers also asked the respondents whether their childhood relationships with their parents had been warm or cold and rejecting. *Secure adults* (about 56 percent of the sample), who generally described their parents as having been warm and supportive, were more trusting and confident of their romantic partner's love.

Anxious/ambivalent adults (about 20 percent) tended to fall in love easily and wanted a commitment almost immediately. *Avoidant adults* (24 percent of the sample) had little trust for others, had the most cynical beliefs about love, and couldn't handle intimacy or commitment.

Several studies have tracked attachment styles from toddlerhood to adulthood and have found that attachment styles can change over the life course regardless of a person's early childhood experiences. If, for example, we experience disturbing events such as parental divorce, the breakup of a relationship, being dumped a few times in succession, or our own divorce, we may slip from a secure to an avoidant style. Alternatively, positive experiences, including romantic love, can change a person from an avoidant to a secure attachment style (Hollist and Miller, 2005; Simpson et al., 2007; McCarthy and Casey, 2008).

Therefore, "the view that children's experiences set attachment styles in concrete is a myth" (Fletcher, 2002: 158). Instead, critics point out, events such as divorce, disease, and financial problems are far more important in shaping a child's well-being by age 18 than any early bonding with his or her mother (Lewis, 1997; Hays, 1998; Birns, 1999). Some feminist scholars also maintain that attachment theory and research often ignore fathers' bonding with their children, and neglect questions such as how social class and differences between men's and women's power influence attachment (Knudson-Martin, 2012).

Reiss's Wheel Theory of Love

Sociologist Ira Reiss and his associates proposed a *"wheel theory of love"* (see *Figure 6.1*) that generated much research for several decades. Reiss described four stages of love: rapport, self-revelation, mutual dependency, and personality need fulfillment (Reiss, 1960; Reiss and Lee, 1988).

In the first stage, partners establish *rapport* based on culturally similar upbringing, social class, religion, and educational level (see Chapter 1 on endogamy). Without rapport, according to Reiss, would-be lovers don't have enough in common to establish an initial interest.

FIGURE 6.1 The Wheel Theory of Love Reiss compared his four stages of love to the spokes of a wheel. A love relationship begins with rapport. In a lasting relationship, rapport continues to build as the wheel turns, deepening the partners' need fulfillment, mutual dependence, and increasing the honesty of their self-revelation. *Source:* Based on Reiss, 1960: 139–145.

In the second stage, *self-revelation* brings the couple closer together. Because each person feels more at ease in the relationship, she or he is more likely to disclose intimate and personal feelings, and to engage in sexual activities.

In the third stage, as the couple becomes more intimate, the partners' *mutual dependency* increases: They share ideas, jokes, hopes, and fears. In the fourth and final stage, the couple experiences *personality need fulfillment*. The partners confide in each other, make mutual decisions, support each other's ambitions, and bolster each other's self-confidence.

Like spokes on a wheel, these stages can turn many times—that is, they can be repeated. For example, partners build some rapport, then reveal bits of themselves, then build more rapport, then begin to exchange ideas, and so on.

The spokes may keep turning to produce a deep and lasting relationship. Or, during a fleeting romance, the wheel may stop after a few turns. The romantic wheel may "unwind"—even in a single evening—if the relationship droops because of arguments, lack of self-disclosure, or conflicting interests.

Sociologist Dolores Borland (1975) modified the wheel theory, proposing that love relationships can be viewed as "clock springs," such as those in a watch. Relationships can wind up and unwind several times as love swells or ebbs. Tensions, caused by pregnancy and the birth of a child, for example, may wind the spring tightly. If the partners communicate and work toward a common goal, such tensions may solidify rather than sap the relationship. On the other hand, relationships can end abruptly if they are so tightly wound that the partners cannot grow or if one partner feels threatened by increasing or unwanted intimacy.

Some critics have noted that both the wheel theory and the clock-spring theory ignore the variations in intensity between stages of a relationship. People may love each other, but the intensity of their feelings may be high on one dimension and low on another. For example, a couple may have rapport because of similar backgrounds but may experience little personality need fulfillment because one partner is controlling or unwilling to confide in the other (Albas and Albas, 1987; Warner, 2005).

Sternberg's Triangular Theory of Love

Watch on MySocLab

Video: Triangular Theory of Love: Robert Sternberg

Instead of focusing on stages of love, psychologist Robert Sternberg and his associates (1986, 1988) posited that love has three important components: intimacy, passion, and decision/commitment:

- *Intimacy* encompasses feelings of closeness, connectedness, and bonding.
- *Passion* leads to romance, physical attraction, and sexual consummation.
- *Decision/commitment* has a short- and a long-term dimension. In the short term, partners make a decision to love each other; in the long term, they make a commitment to maintain that love over time.

According to Sternberg, the mix of intimacy, passion, and commitment can vary from one relationship to another. Relationships thus range from *nonlove*, in which all three components are absent, to *consummate love*, in which all the elements are present.

Even when all three components are present, they may vary in intensity and over time for each partner. Sternberg envisioned the three components as forming a triangle (see *Figure 6.2*). In general, the greater the mismatching of dimensions, the greater the dissatisfaction in a relationship.

Let's use Jack and Jill to illustrate this model. If Jack and Jill are "perfectly matched" (*Figure 6.2A*), they will be equally passionate, intimate, and committed, and their love will be "perfect." Even if the degree to which each of them wants intimacy and commitment varies a little, they may still be "closely matched" (*Figure 6.2B*).

If both are about equally passionate, but Jack wants more intimacy than Jill does, and Jill is unwilling to make the long-term commitment that Jack wants,

they will be "moderately mismatched" (*Figure 6.2C*). And if they want to marry (make a commitment), but Jill is neither as intimate nor as passionate as Jack, they will be "severely mismatched" (*Figure 6.2D*).

Some find this theory useful in counseling. If, for instance, people recognized that love encompasses more than just passion—which is actually a fleeting component of love—there would be fewer unfulfilled expectations and less disappointment. A decline of passion is normal and inevitable if a relationship moves on to commitment, which creates a more stable union than just "being in love" (García, 1998).

Like the other perspectives, the triangular theory of love has limitations. "Perfectly matched" exists only in Disney movies. Also, love varies depending on one's marital status. Intimacy and passion may be much stronger in casual dating, for example, than in marriage. Commitment, on the other hand, is much higher among married couples than among dating or engaged couples (Lemieux and Hale, 2002).

Lee's Styles of Loving

Canadian sociologist John Lee (1973, 1974) developed one of the most widely cited and studied theories of love. According to Lee, there are six basic styles of loving: eros, mania, ludus, storge, agape, and pragma, all of which overlap and may vary in intensity (see *Table 6.1*).

EROS Eros (the root of the word *erotic*) means love of beauty. Because it is also characterized by powerful physical attraction, eros epitomizes "love at first sight." This is the kind of love, often described in romance novels, in which the lovers experience palpitations, light-headedness, and intense emotional desire.

Erotic lovers want to know everything about each other—what she or he dreamed about last night and what happened on the way to work. They often like to wear matching T-shirts and matching colors, to order the same foods when dining out, and to be identified with each other as totally as possible (Lasswell and Lasswell, 1976).

MANIA Characterized by obsessiveness, jealousy, possessiveness, and intense dependency, **mania** may be expressed as anxiety, sleeplessness, loss of appetite, headaches, and even suicide because of real or imagined rejection by the desired

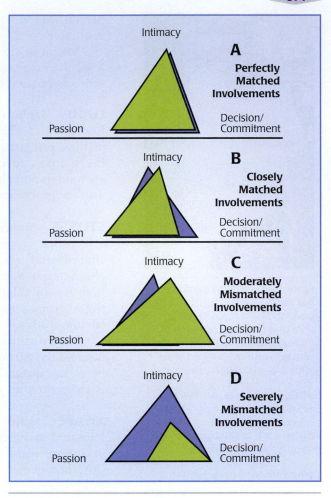

FIGURE 6.2 The Triangular Theory of Love
This theory of love suggests how people can be very close on some dimensions but far apart on others. *Source:* Adapted from Sternberg, 1988.

eros Love based on beauty and physical attractiveness.

mania Love that is obsessive, jealous, and possessive.

TABLE 6.1	Lee's Six Styles of Love	
	Meaning	**Major Characteristics**
Eros	Love of beauty	Powerful physical attraction
Mania	Obsessive love	Jealousy, possessiveness, and intense dependency
Ludus	Playful love	Carefree quality, casualness, fun-and-games approach
Storge	Companionate love	Peaceful and affectionate love based on mutual trust and respect
Agape	Altruistic love	Self-sacrificing, kind, and patient
Pragma	Practical love	Sensible, realistic

Source: Adapted from Lee, 1973, 1974.

Erotic love is initially passionate but usually short-lived. It can also develop into a companionate love that includes commitment, intimacy, and a sharing of common interests and activities with a long-term partner.

ludus Love that is carefree and casual, "fun and games."

storge Love that is slow-burning, peaceful, and affectionate.

companionate love Love that is characterized by feelings of togetherness, tenderness, deep affection, and supporting each other over time.

agape Love that is altruistic and self-sacrificing and is directed toward all humankind.

pragma Love that is rational and based on practical considerations, such as compatibility and perceived benefits.

person. Manic lovers are consumed by thoughts of their beloved and have an insatiable need for attention and signs of affection.

Mania is often associated with low self-esteem and a poor self-concept. As a result, manic people typically aren't attractive to those who have a strong self-concept and high self-esteem (Lasswell and Lasswell, 1976).

LUDUS **Ludus** is carefree and casual love that is considered "fun and games." Ludic lovers often have several partners at one time and aren't possessive or jealous, primarily because they don't want their lovers to become dependent on them. Ludic lovers have sex for fun, not emotional rapport. In their sexual encounters, they're typically self-centered and may be exploitative because they don't want commitment, which they consider "scary."

STORGE **Storge** (pronounced "STOR-gay") is a slow-burning, peaceful, and affectionate love that comes with the passage of time and the enjoyment of shared activities. Storgic relationships lack the ecstatic highs and lows that characterize some other styles of loving. For many social scientists, storgic love is equivalent to **companionate love** that is characterized by feelings of togetherness, tenderness, deep affection, and supporting each other over time (Brink, 2007).

In companionate love, sex occurs later than in erotic, manic, and ludic love because the partners' goals are usually marriage, home, and children. Even if they break up, storgic lovers are likely to remain friends, and passion may be replaced with spirituality, respect, and contentment (Murstein, 1974).

AGAPE **Agape** (pronounced "AH-gah-pay") is an altruistic, self-sacrificing love that is directed toward all humankind. Agape is always kind and patient and never jealous or demanding, and it doesn't seek reciprocity. Lee pointed out, however, that he didn't find a single instance of agape during his interviews.

Intense agape can border on masochism. For example, an agapic person might wait indefinitely for a lover to be released from prison, might tolerate an alcoholic or drug-addicted spouse, or might be willing to live with a partner who engages in illegal activities or infidelity (Lasswell and Lasswell, 1976).

PRAGMA **Pragma** is rational love based on practical considerations. Indeed, it can be described as "love with a shopping list." A pragmatic person seeks compatibility on characteristics such as background, education, religious views, occupational interests, and recreational pursuits. If one person doesn't work out, the pragmatist moves on to search for someone else.

Pragmatic lovers look out for their partners by encouraging them, for example, to ask for a promotion or finish college. They are also practical when it comes to divorce. For example, a couple might stay together until the youngest child finishes high school or until both partners find better jobs (Lasswell and Lasswell, 1976).

Researchers have developed dozens of scales to measure Lee's concepts of love (see Tzeng, 1993). Use "What Do *You* Expect from Love?" to reflect on some of your attitudes about love.

Exchange Theory

Social scientists often describe love as a *social exchange process* (see Chapter 2). Romantic and long-term love relationships involve social exchanges in the sense that they provide rewards and costs for each partner. If the initial interactions are reciprocal and mutually satisfying, a relationship will continue. If, however, our needs are mismatched (see *Figure 6.2*) or change over time, our love interests may wane or shift between adolescence and later life.

Use this scale to examine your own and your partner's attitudes about love. If you've never been in love or don't have a partner now, answer in terms of what you think your responses might be in the future. There are no wrong answers because these items were designed simply to increase your understanding of the different types of love. For each item, mark **1** for "strongly agree," **2** for "moderately agree," **3** for "neutral," **4** for "moderately disagree," and **5** for "strongly disagree."

Eros

1. My partner and I were attracted to each other immediately after we first met.
2. Our lovemaking is very intense and satisfying.

3. My partner fits my standards of physical beauty and good looks.

Ludus

4. What my partner doesn't know about me won't hurt him or her.
5. I sometimes have to keep my partner from finding out about other partners.
6. I could get over my partner pretty easily and quickly.

Pragma

7. In choosing my partner, I believed it was best to love someone with a similar background.
8. An important factor in choosing my partner was whether or not he or she would be a good parent.
9. One consideration in choosing my partner was how she or he would affect my career.

Agape

10. I would rather suffer myself than let my partner suffer.
11. My partner can use whatever I own as she or he chooses.
12. I would endure all things for the sake of my partner.

Storge

13. I expect to always be friends with the people I date.
14. The best kind of love grows out of a long friendship.
15. Love is a deep friendship, not a mysterious, passionate emotion.

Sources: Based on Lasswell and Lasswell, 1976, pp. 211–124; Hendrick and Hendrick, 1992a, 1992b; Levesque, 1993, pp. 219–150.

LOVE DURING ADOLESCENCE Exchange theory is especially helpful in explaining why romantic love is short-lived among adolescents. Adolescent love is usually intense but also self-centered. Because adolescents are still "finding themselves," they often form relationships with peers who offer many benefits and few costs ("I can call him whenever I'm lonely" or "I'm hookin' up with a knockout cheerleader this weekend").

LOVE DURING ADULTHOOD As we mature, our perceptions of rewards and costs usually change. We might decide, for example, that nurturing a relationship with someone who's patient and confident outweighs the benefits of being with someone who's "a good catch" or "a knockout" but is controlling and self-centered. In a recent survey, 67 percent of unmarried people said that they don't want to date someone who's deep in debt (Ambrose, 2010).

LOVE DURING LATER LIFE We also weigh the costs and benefits of love later in life. As you'll see in Chapters 8 and 16, men age 60 and over prefer much younger women who are attractive, interested in sex, and could become the men's caregivers in case of health problems. In contrast, older women are more likely than their male counterparts to be interested in financial stability.

MAKING CONNECTIONS

- Return to *Figure 6.2* and think about your current love relationship. (If you're currently not involved with someone, reflect on a past relationship.) Are you and your partner matched in intimacy, passion, and commitment? Or is any one of these characteristics not important in your relationship?

- Think about Lee's styles of loving (*Table 6.1*). Do you and your partner have similar or different attitudes about love? If your styles of loving differ, does this create problems, or does it make the relationship more interesting? Did your past relationships break up because your partner's style of loving was different from yours?

Functions of Love and Loving

6.5 Describe four functions of love.

One historian argues that love is dysfunctional because it creates high divorce rates. That is, because many Americans are in love with love, their unrealistic expectations result in unhappiness and the dissolution of marriages (Coontz, 2005).

In contrast, a number of researchers and family practitioners believe that love is at the core of healthy and well-functioning relationships and families. One

psychologist goes even further by maintaining that "love is as critical for your mind and body as oxygen" (McGrath, 2002). Whether or not you agree with such an assertion, love fulfills many purposes that range from ensuring human survival to having fun.

Love Ensures Human Survival

Since you asked . . .

• How important is love for our survival?

Love keeps our species going. Because children can be conceived without love, there is no guarantee that people who engage in sex will feel an obligation to care for their offspring. Unlike sex, love implies a commitment. By promoting an interest in caring for helpless infants, love ensures the survival of the human species.

Suicide is perhaps the most dramatic example of the effects of the lack of love. People who commit suicide often feel socially isolated, rejected, unloved, or unworthy of love. According to some military leaders, for example, about 60 percent of U.S. Army suicides are due to failed relationships, especially intimate ones (Schindler, 2009; see also Chapter 14).

Love doesn't guarantee that we'll live to be 100, of course. Instead, researchers suggest, there is a link between loving relationships and enjoying better health.

Love Enhances Our Physical and Emotional Health

Numerous studies show a connection between our emotions and our physical and emotional well-being. Babies and children who are deprived of love may develop a wide variety of problems—depression, headaches, physiological impairments, and psychosomatic difficulties—that sometimes last a lifetime. In contrast, infants who are loved and cuddled typically gain more weight, cry less, and smile more. By age 5, they have higher IQs and score higher on language tests (Hetherington et al., 2006; see also Chapter 12).

A national study of recent high school graduates found that being in a love relationship enhances one's health. Individuals not involved in any kind of romantic relationship (dating, cohabitation, marriage) were at the greatest risk of using, continuing to use, or escalating their use of marijuana, smoking cigarettes, and heavy drinking, even when using all three substances was low in high school.

Over the years, many U.S. soldiers deployed to Iraq and Afghanistan have found strength by thinking of their loved ones at home (see Platt, 2006). Here, an American soldier shows photographs of his children to young Iraqis in Beijia, a village south of Baghdad.

In contrast, the more serious and enjoyable the relationships—particularly when a partner wasn't substantially involved in substance use—the lower the likelihood of beginning, continuing, or escalating substance use (Fleming et al., 2010).

In adulthood, chronic stress, whether due to a demanding job or an unloving home life, elevates blood pressure. Arguing or just thinking about a fight also raises blood pressure. People in unhappy marriages may be less healthy because stress can change the levels of certain hormones in the blood and weaken the immune system. As a result, people who are stressed face a higher risk of heart disease and other illnesses (Kiecolt-Glaser and Newton, 2001; Cacioppo et al., 2002; Glynn et al., 2002).

According to a highly respected heart physician, love is good medicine. People who are lonely are more likely to engage in self-destructive behavior and to suffer from cardiovascular disease than people who have a strong network of caring people in their lives. "I'm not aware of any other factor in medicine—not diet, not smoking, not exercise, not genetics, not drugs, not surgery—that has a greater impact on our quality of life, incidence of illness, and premature death" (Ornish, 2005: 56).

In effect, friends, family, and loving relationships over a lifetime can help counteract the normal wear and tear of life as we age. People in their seventies who have had a lot of supportive friends, good relationships with their parents and spouses, and little criticism from their spouses and children suffer from fewer risk factors for diseases and death, including high blood pressure, high cholesterol levels, and abnormal blood sugar metabolism than those who have not enjoyed good relationships (Seeman et al., 2002).

Love Is Fun

Without love, life is "a burden and a bore" (Safilios-Rothschild, 1977: 9). Love can be painful, but it's also enjoyable and often exciting. For example, it's both comforting and fun to plan to see a loved one; to travel together; to write and receive e-mail and text messages; to exchange presents; to share activities; to have someone care for you when you're sick or grumpy; and to know that you can always depend on someone for comfort, support, and advice.

One of the biggest myths in our popular culture is that love "just happens." Numerous movies, especially those targeted at women (sometimes called "chick flicks"), appeal to female viewers who long for romance and a dashing guy who will sweep them off their feet and solve all their love problems. Some examples include *Gone With the Wind* (1939), *An Officer and a Gentleman* (1982), *How Stella Got Her Groove Back* (1998), and *The Notebook* (2004). In reality, love doesn't appear out of nowhere. It takes time and effort to get and keep love.

Experiencing Love

For most people, caring, trust, respect, and honesty are central to love. There are some differences, however, in the ways that people express and experience love.

Are Women or Men More Romantic?

In 2011, romance fiction generated $1.4 billion in sales, giving it the largest share of the overall trade book market, and is now the fastest-growing segment of the e-book market. Besides good writing, the only other requirement of this genre is a happy ending. Most of the readers are women (91 percent), between the ages of 30 and 54, and more than half live with a spouse or intimate partner (Romance Writers of America, 2012).

6.6 Explain how people experience love and some of love's obstacles.

Since you asked . . .
- Are women more romantic than men?

Such data might suggest that women are more romantic than men. However, the readers (ranging from sales clerks to college professors) say that the books are entertaining, well-written, and have interesting plots. Romance fiction is similar to other mysteries or historical novels, but the leading character or heroine is a female who decides when and with whom to have sex (Bosman, 2010).

During a recent online discussion, Emily, one of my students, wrote the following:

> It's important to distinguish the truly romantic men from the "What-do-I-need-to-do-to-get-her-in-bed" romantic men. Truly romantic men do things for you that take a substantial amount of time and energy and involve some sacrifice on their part. For example, for Valentine's Day my boyfriend spent hours making me an absolutely beautiful Valentine's Day card. That meant more to me than dinner at a fancy restaurant (Author's files).

Many of the female students in class thought that Emily's boyfriend was an exception. However, several studies have found that men seem to fall in love faster than do women, are more likely than women to say that they're in love, to initiate romantic e-mail exchanges, and to be almost as likely as women to prefer romance to sex (Alvear, 2003; Saad, 2004; Thompson and O'Sullivan, 2012).

Adolescent boys are at least as romantic as adolescent girls, but they're more reluctant to talk about their emotions: They want to avoid ridicule by male peers, and they have lower self-confidence levels in navigating romantic relationships. Boys from homes with parental divorces, remarriages, and cohabitations are more likely than their female counterparts to have romantic relationships and more partners in grades 7 through 12. The reasons for these gender differences are unclear, but may be due to boys' feeling more comfortable in discussing family problems in romantic relationships than in same-sex friendships (Giordano et al., 2006; Cavanagh et al., 2008).

One of women's biggest complaints is that the men who profess to love them are reluctant to marry them. Women sometimes belittle men for being "commitment dodgers," "commitment phobics," "paranoid about commitment," and "afraid of the M word" (Crittenden, 1999; Millner and Chiles, 1999). Romance and commitment are different, however. Men can be very romantic but not see love as necessarily leading to marriage (see Chapter 9).

Are Women or Men More Intimate?

When women complain about a lack of intimacy, they usually mean that the man doesn't communicate his thoughts or feelings. Many men believe that such criticisms are unfair because they show intimacy through sex. Whereas many women want to feel close emotionally before being sexual, many men assume that sex is the same as emotional closeness (Piorkowski, 1994; Cloke, 2012). For women, intimacy may mean talking things over. For men, as "Do I Love You? I Changed Your Oil, Didn't I?" shows, it may mean *doing* things (such as taking care of the family cars).

Men and women may show affection differently, but there are more similarities than differences in their attitudes toward love. In a study based on Lee's typology (see *Table 6.1*), the researchers analyzed the attitudes of people ages 17 to 70. They found that *both* women and men valued passion (eros), friendship and companionship (storge), and self-sacrifice (agape). As a result, the researchers criticized the shallowness of popular books, such as Gray's *Men Are from Mars, Women Are from Venus*, that trumpet "the radical differences in men's and women's approach to partnering relationships" (Montgomery and Sorell, 1997: 60).

Since you asked . . .
- Do men have more trouble with intimacy than women?

Choices

"Do I Love You? I Changed Your Oil, Didn't I?"

Are men less loving than women because they equate love with sex and rarely talk about their feelings? Not according to sociologist Francesca Cancian (1990: 171). She maintains that the fault lies not in men but in women's definitions of loving, which ignore masculine styles of showing affection:

We identify love with emotional expression and talking about feelings, aspects of love that women prefer and in which women tend to be more skilled than men. At the same time we often ignore the instrumental and physical aspects of love that men prefer, such as providing help, sharing activities, and sex.

Cancian calls excluding men's ways of showing affection the "feminization of love." Because of this bias, men rarely get credit for the kinds of loving actions that are more typical of them. According to Carol Tavris (1992: 255),

What about all the men . . . who reliably support their families, who put the wishes of other family members ahead of their own preferences, or who act in a considerate way when conflicts arise? Such individuals are surely being mature and loving, even if they are not articulate or do not value "communication."

Many social scientists contend that a man who is a good provider, changes the oil in his wife's car, or fixes his child's bike is showing just as much love as a wife who tells her husband she loves him and shares her innermost thoughts and feelings with him. One might even argue that actions are more important than words in showing love.

According to Cancian, the feminization of love intensifies conflicts over intimacy. As the woman demands more verbal contact, the man feels increased pressure and withdraws. The woman may then increase her efforts to get closer. This leads to a vicious cycle in which neither partner gets what she or he wants. As the definition of love becomes more feminized, men and women move further apart (Tucker, 1992). One way to break this cycle is to give both men and women credit for the things they do to show their love for each other and for their families.

STOP AND THINK . . .

- Do you agree or disagree with Cancian that women have feminized love? Why?
- Consider your parents', your friends', and your own relationships. Do you think women and men express their love differently? If so, how do they differ?

What Are Some Obstacles to Experiencing Love?

A number of obstacles can derail our search for love. Some are *macro level*—for example, the impersonality of mass society, demographic variables, and our culture's emphasis on individualism. Others are *micro level*—such as personality and family characteristics.

MASS SOCIETY AND DEMOGRAPHIC FACTORS Our society's booming technologies—such as texting and e-mail—decrease opportunities for face-to-face interaction and tend to dehumanize interpersonal communication. In response, a love industry has mushroomed. Computerized matchmaking, Internet chat rooms, singles bars, and dozens of books promise singles that they can find love and counteract the isolation and impersonality of our society. You'll see in Chapter 8, however, that the majority of singles are most likely to meet a future love through introductions by family members and friends.

Economic issues also constrain our romantic lives. Chronic job insecurity, unemployment, and underemployment (when your job is below your education or skill level) are transforming many intimate relationships. Believing that their manhood is measured by the size of their income, men with low-paying jobs don't have the money to spend on dates, are unwilling to make a long-term commitment, or experience conflict with current intimate partners who have to support the men financially. A partner's high debt can crush an engagement, and men with traditional gender ideologies tend to report a low quality of a romantic relationship if the woman has higher earnings (Lieber, 2010; Coughlin and Wade, 2012; Parramore, 2012).

Demographic variables such as age, income, and occupation also shape our love experiences. Because older men tend to marry younger women, older women

typically face a shortage of eligible partners. If women, regardless of age, are financially independent, they're less likely to plunge into a relationship, including marriage, because they're unwilling to take on additional housework (see Chapters 9 and 16).

"ME-FIRST" INDIVIDUALISM   Our cultural values encourage individualism and competition rather than a sense of community and cooperation. This emphasis on the individual leads to a preoccupation with self (Bellah et al., 1985; Kass, 1997). We still hear statements such as "Look out for number one" and "If it feels good, do it." Measuring love solely in terms of feeling good leaves us unequipped to handle its difficult or demanding aspects, such as supporting a partner during unemployment or caring for a loved one who has a long-term illness.

Some writers maintain that we have been steeped in narcissistic messages that encourage self-improvement and self-serving behavior, often at the expense of the couple or the family (Wilson, 2002; Twenge and Campbell, 2009). As a result, these writers argue, our culture, especially the popular media, focuses on fleeting sexual liaisons rather than long-term commitments.

PERSONALITY AND FAMILY CHARACTERISTICS   Sometimes personality traits or family history get in the way of love. Biochemistry may initially attract people to each other, but similar personalities, feelings, and interests strengthen a romantic relationship and keep it going. If, for example, one partner is usually pessimistic or withdrawn while the other is typically optimistic and outgoing, romantic attraction and commitment will diminish. Romances also tend to fizzle if a person's family members or close friends disapprove of the relationship and discourage his or her investing large amounts of time, resources, or emotions in a budding romance (Gonzaga et al., 2007; Lehmiller and Agnew, 2007).

Many young adults, particularly females, whose parents have undergone hostile divorces, report that they are cynical about love or afraid to fall in love. Or a child who was molested by a family member or relative may be distrustful of future intimate relationships (Rodberg, 1999; see also Chapter 14).

Despite such difficulties, some social scientists believe that couples can overcome past problems and forge healthy adult love relationships, especially if they are determined to do so, and regardless of social class and race or ethnicity (Busby et al., 2005; Hill, 2005). Still, many of our love connections go awry.

6.7   Explain why love goes wrong.

When Love Goes Wrong

You saw, at the beginning of the chapter, that some philosophers believe that self-love promotes love for others. However, self-love can also lead to narcissism, which thwarts romantic relationships. Jealousy and other controlling forms of behavior also hinder our ability to love and be loved.

Narcissism: Playing with Love

Narcissists are people who have a grandiose self-concept and a sense of superiority and entitlement; they admire themselves and tend to manipulate and exploit others. From elementary school through adulthood, males are more narcissistic than females, and male narcissism increases between ages 14 and 18 (Carlson and Gjerde, 2009; Zhou et al., 2012).

Narcissists believe that they are unique, smarter, and more attractive than others, and they constantly seek attention. Narcissists can be enjoyable dating partners because they can be charming and flattering to get what they want. Compared with non-narcissists, they tend to have fancier clothes, friendlier face expressions, and more self-assured body language. However, don't expect them

to be interested in a long-term committed relationship because they're more interested in themselves than others (Twenge and Campbell, 2009; Back et al., 2010).

To maintain their dominance in romantic relationships, many narcissists resort to game-playing (ludic) love. They see themselves as superior to their partners and seek status—a spotlight on themselves—rather than meeting their partners' needs. As a result, they may be unfaithful, break confidences, and keep their partners guessing about the extent of their commitment.

If a partner gets fed up with their "me, me, me" self-focus, narcissists aren't troubled by breakups. Because they may have already been cheating, they can link up right way with another romance waiting in the wings. In some cases, narcissists can be dangerous. If they feel rejected—even outside of dating relationships—they can become angry, aggressive, and even violent (Twenge and Campbell, 2003; Bushman et al., 2009).

Why are males more narcissistic than females?

Jealousy: Trying to Control Love

A 78-year-old great-grandmother killed her 85-year-old ex-boyfriend, shooting him in the head four times as he read a newspaper at a senior citizens' home. She was angry that their year-long romance was ending because the man had found another companion. "I did it, and I'd do it again!" she shouted to the police (Bluestein, 2005).

Regardless of age, people experience *jealousy* when they believe that a rival is competing for a lover's affection. The jealous person feels threatened and is suspicious, obsessive, angry, and resentful. Some people are even jealous when their partner spends time with family members or relatives, or pursues hobbies (Brehm, 1992; Hanna, 2003).

WHY ARE LOVERS JEALOUS?   Love flourishes when it's based on trust and respect. In contrast, jealousy is usually an unhealthy manifestation of insecurity, low self-confidence, and possessiveness (Douglas and Atwell, 1988; Farrell, 1997). Jealous people tend to depend heavily on their partners for their own self-esteem, consider themselves inadequate as mates, and believe that they're more deeply involved in their relationship than their partner is. All of us have some of these traits, so why are some of us more jealous than others?

Children who grow up in homes where parents mistrust the opposite sex, where there is continuous parental conflict, or with rejecting or overprotective parents are more likely than others to report jealousy and fears of abandonment in their love relationships (Hayashi and Strickland, 1998; Nomaguchi et al., 2011). In some cases, people who are jealous distrust a partner because of their own cheating. In other cases, jealousy is triggered by a real or imagined rivalry. Jealous lovers often insist that their jealousy proves their love. In reality, jealousy is hostile and destructive.

ARE WOMEN OR MEN MORE JEALOUS?   There is ongoing debate about this question. According to evolutionary psychologists, jealousy evolved a million or so years ago. Men worried about sexual infidelity because they might unknowingly end up raising someone else's child rather than passing on their own genes. In contrast, women were more concerned about their partners' emotional rather than sexual entanglements. If a man became emotionally attached to other women, who would bring home food to ensure the family's survival? Thus, according to evolutionary psychologists, twice as many men as women report jealousy over a mate's sexual infidelity (Buss et al., 1996; Buss, 2000).

 Read on MySocLab

Document: Sexual Infidelity among Married and Cohabiting Americans

Since you asked . . .
- Is intense jealousy proof of one's love?

Filmed in 1987, *Fatal Attraction* has become a "modern classic" in dramatizing some of the deadly effects of stalking.

Some researchers have criticized evolutionary perspectives for relying on samples of college students, whose responses aren't representative of the larger population. Others contend that evolutionary studies are flawed because they ask only hypothetical questions ("How would you feel *if* your partner were unfaithful?") (DeSteno et al., 2002; Varga et al., 2011).

When researchers asked adults (other than college students) about their *actual* experiences, they found that both men and women—whether heterosexual or gay—were more jealous of emotional than sexual infidelity. Greater jealousy of a partner's emotional affairs may be due to two reasons. First, they blame themselves ("Maybe I don't satisfy her or him sexually"). Second, they see an emotional affair as more threatening because it could develop into a long-term relationship that may produce offspring who compete for the father's affection and resources (Harris, 2003; Varga et al., 2011).

JEALOUSY AND STALKING *Stalking* involves a pattern of harassing or threatening tactics used by a perpetrator that is both unwanted and a cause of fear or emotional distress in the victim. By the mid-1990s, all 50 states, the District of Columbia, and U.S. territories had passed anti-stalking laws. State laws vary, but typically include unwanted phone calls, letters, or e-mail; following, watching, or spying on a victim by using listening devices, cameras, or a global positioning system (GPS); and approaching or showing up in places such as victim's home, workplace, or school when it's unwanted (Black et al., 2011; Catalano, 2012). Among all U.S. victims,

- Of the 6.6 million stalking cases in 2010, almost 79 percent of the victims were women.

- During their lifetime, 16 percent of women and 5 percent of men experienced stalking in which they feared that they or someone close to them would be harmed or killed.

- About 66 percent of female victims (compared with 41 percent of men) have been stalked by a current or former intimate partner (Black et al., 2011).

Cyberstalking, a more specific type of stalking, is threatening behavior or unwanted advances using e-mail, texting, social networking sites such as Facebook, and other electronic communications devices. About 60 percent of cyberstalking victims are women. Many chat rooms may evolve into offline stalking, including abusive or harassing phone calls, vandalism, threatening or obscene mail, trespassing, and physical assault (Baum et al., 2009; Ginty, 2011).

IS JEALOUSY UNIVERSAL? Although it's widespread, jealousy is *not* universal. Surveying two centuries of anthropological reports, Hupka (1991) found two types of cultures: In one, jealousy was rare (for example, the Todas of southern India); in the other, jealousy was common (for example, the Apache Indians of North America).

Toda culture discouraged possessiveness of material objects or people. It placed few restrictions on sexual gratification, within or outside of marriage. In contrast, Apache society prized virginity, paternity, and fidelity. While a man was away from home, for example, he had a close relative keep secret watch over his wife and report on her behavior when he returned.

Based on the variations he found in different cultures, Hupka concluded that jealousy is neither universal nor innate. Instead, jealousy is more common in societies in which women are regarded as property and expressing jealousy is culturally acceptable.

Other Controlling Behavior

Extreme jealousy isn't the only type of unhealthy behavior in intimate relationships. Threatening to withdraw love or causing guilt feelings can be distressing. Inflicting severe emotional and physical abuse can be especially devastating.

"IF YOU LOVED ME . . ."   Controlling people want power over others. For example, one of the most common ways of pressuring people to have sex (used especially by men) is to accuse a partner of not loving them: "If you *really* loved me, you'd show it" (see Chapter 7).

People threaten to withdraw love to manipulate other kinds of behavior as well. Many students choose majors they hate because they don't want to upset parents who insist that they become a doctor, a lawyer, an accountant, and so on. I've seen women drop out of college because their husbands or boyfriends blamed them for always studying instead of demonstrating their love by taking care of the house, preparing dinner on time, and being free on weekends. Using pressure and ultimatums, controllers force their partners or family members to give up their own interests to please the controller.

Controllers aren't all alike: "A wealthy executive may use money and influence, while an attractive person may use physical allure and sex" to manipulate others (A. Jones and Schechter, 1992: 11). In many cases, manipulators know the harm they're doing, but do so to gratify their own needs and wishes (Schnarch, 2011). As "If This Is Love, Why Do I Feel So Bad?" shows, controllers use a variety of strategies to dominate and control a relationship. They may also switch strategies from time to time to keep the controlled person off balance.

ASK YOURSELF

If This Is Love, Why Do I Feel So Bad?

If you often feel bad about your relationship, what you're experiencing may be control, not love. Controllers use whatever tactics are necessary to maintain power over another person: nagging, cajoling, coaxing, flattery, charm, threats, self-pity, blame, insults, or humiliation.

In the worst cases, controllers may physically injure and even murder people who refuse to be controlled. As you read this list, check any items that you've experienced. Individually, the items may seem unimportant, but if you check off more than two or three, you may be dealing with a controller instead of forging your own choices in life.

☐ My partner calls me names: "dummy," "jackass," "whore," "creep," "bitch," "moron."

☐ My partner always criticizes me and makes even a compliment sound like a criticism: "This is the first good dinner you've cooked in months."

☐ Always right, my partner continually corrects things I say or do.

☐ My partner withdraws into silence, and I have to figure out what I've done wrong and apologize for it.

☐ My partner is jealous when I talk to new people.

☐ My partner often phones or unexpectedly comes by the place where I work to see if I'm "okay."

☐ My partner acts very cruelly and then says I'm too sensitive and can't take a joke.

☐ When I express my opinion about something, my partner doesn't respond, walks away, or makes fun of me.

☐ My partner says that if I ever leave, he or she will commit suicide and I'll be responsible.

☐ When my partner has a temper tantrum, he or she says it's my fault or the children's.

☐ My partner makes fun of my weight, clothes, or appearance.

☐ Whether my partner is with me or not, she or he is jealous of every minute I spend with my family or other relatives or friends.

☐ My partner throws things at me or hits, shoves, or pushes me.

Source: Based on Jones and Schechter, 1992: 16–22.

GUILT TRIPS   People often use guilt to justify behavior that has nothing to do with love. Some parents rely on strategies such as love withdrawal and guilt to control children's behavior. *Behavioral control* is usually direct ("I have to ask my mom's permission to go out with friends"). *Psychological control* is more covert and manipulative ("My mom refuses to talk to me when she's mad at me"). Behavioral control sometimes has positive effects such as higher academic achievement and staying out of trouble. In contrast, some of the negative consequences of psychological control include adolescents who sacrifice their interests to preserve the parent–child relationship. Doing so may result in developing depressive symptoms such as sadness or low self-esteem (Mandara and Pikes, 2008; see also Chapter 12 on parenting styles).

Guilt trips continue when children become adults. Older parents and relatives sometimes use guilt to manipulate middle-aged children. One of the most disabling guilt trips is the "affection myth," in which children are taught that love is synonymous with care giving. Children and grandchildren may be taught that, regardless of their own circumstances, they must care for elderly family members, including moving them into their own homes. As a result, younger family members sometimes endure enormous stress, even though their relatives would get much better medical care at a good-quality nursing facility (see Chapter 16).

In other situations, married couples or those who are living together try to induce guilt through a sense of obligation: "If you really loved me, you'd take care of me. Can't you see how much I care about you?" (Harvey and Weber, 2002: 90). Such recriminations demonstrate emotional blackmail, not love.

EMOTIONAL AND PHYSICAL ABUSE   People sometimes use love to justify severe emotional or physical neglect and abuse. A partner who is sarcastic or controlling or a parent who severely spanks or verbally humiliates a child isn't expressing love for the child's own good, as they often insist. They are simply being angry and brutal; violence is *never* a manifestation of love (see Chapter 14).

"The most insidious aspect of family violence" is that children grow up unable to distinguish between love and violence and believe "that it is acceptable to hit the people you love" (Gelles and Cornell, 1990: 20). The film *What's Love Got to Do with It?*, based on singer Tina Turner's biography, portrays Turner as enduring many years of violence because she believed that doing so proved her love and commitment to her husband, Ike.

OTHER PERVERSE REASONS FOR LOVE   Some people are in love for "dubious and downright perverse reasons" (Solomon, 2002: 1). In many cases, we profess love for someone because we're really afraid of being alone or coping with changes (such as meeting new people after breaking up). Or we might stay in a bad relationship because we want to avoid a partner's hostility after breaking up.

In other cases, we don't want to hurt someone's feelings by admitting we don't love her or him. If we promise to "love, honor, and obey" (although many couples have substituted "cherish" for "obey" in their marital vows), we may feel obligated to stay with a spouse even though the love has dwindled over the years (or we never really loved him or her to begin with). In addition, is it realistic to promise to love someone for the next 50 to 60 years—especially if her or his behavior becomes abusive?

Pop/rock singer Tina Turner, born in 1939, abruptly left her husband, Ike, after an especially vicious beating. She fled in 1976 after 14 years of a marriage that became increasingly controlling and abusive. Tina reportedly had nothing more than 36 cents and a gas station credit card. Hiding from Ike, she stayed with various friends, relied on food stamps to survive, and slowly rebuilt her singing career. Turner remarried in 2013.

Unrequited Love

In unrequited love, one doesn't reciprocate another's romantic feelings. Why not? First, someone who's average in appearance may fall in love with someone who's gorgeous. Because people tend to choose partners who are similar

to themselves in dating and marriage (see Chapter 8), loving someone who's much better looking is likely to be one-sided.

A rebuff is especially painful if the person senses that physical appearance is the major reason for being cast aside (Baumeister and Wotman, 1992). We often hear both women and men complain that the object of their affections "never took the time to get to know me." These accusations imply that other characteristics such as personality, intelligence, and common interests should be more important than looks.

Second, love may be unrequited when only one of the partners wants to progress from hooking up or casual dating to a serious romance. It can be very upsetting, even traumatic, to realize that the person one is dating, and perhaps having sexual relations with, is in the relationship just for the fun of it (as with ludic lovers, including narcissists) and doesn't want to become more serious or exclusive.

Some people wait, sometimes for years, for someone to return their love. They assume that the situation is bound to get better (Duck, 1998). It's emotionally healthier to let go of an unrequited love and develop relationships with people who care about you.

MAKING CONNECTIONS

- Have you ever gone out with a narcissist? If so, how long did the relationship last? Did you enjoy the experience in some ways?

- Have you ever dumped someone? If so, how did you cut the strings? Or, if you were the one who was dumped, how did you deal with the situation?

How Couples Change: Romantic and Long-Term Love

6.8 Compare romantic and long-term love.

 Watch on MySocLab

Video: Leroy and Geneva

In the words of writer William Somerset Maugham (1874–1965), "We are not the same person this year as last; nor are those we love. It is a happy chance if we, changing, continue to love a changed person."

Romantic love was less common in the United States in the 1800s than it is today for several reasons: Life expectancy was shorter, living in isolated towns and homes made it difficult to meet a variety of lovers, and most people didn't live long enough to fall in love more than once. Today, with increased life spans, greater geographic mobility, and high divorce rates, we may fall in love with many people during our lifetime.

Romantic love can be both exhilarating and disappointing. In contrast, long-term love provides security and constancy. Let's begin with some of the characteristics of romantic love.

Since you asked . . .

- If you don't feel romantic about your partner, can you still love him or her?

Some Characteristics of Romantic Love

Romantic love is usually a passionate and dizzying experience:

- Lovers find it impossible to work, study, or do anything but think about the beloved.
- Their moods fluctuate wildly; they are ecstatic when they hope they might be loved, despairing when they feel that they're not.
- They find it impossible to believe that they could ever love again.
- They fantasize about how their partner will declare his or her love.
- They care so desperately about the other person that nothing else matters; they are willing to sacrifice anything for love.
- Their love is "blind," and they idealize each other (Tennov, cited in Hatfield, 1983: 114).

Romantic love is intense, emotional, ardent, and sometimes melodramatic ("I can't live without you!"). It can also be self-absorbed and self-serving. As you saw earlier, for example, narcissists enhance their own self-esteem rather than being interested in their partner ("What else do you like about *me*?" versus "How are *you* doing?"). Romantic love thrives on two beliefs—love at first sight and fate.

LOVE AT FIRST SIGHT Some Americans believe in love at first sight because we're engulfed by novels, songs, films, and television shows that depict strangers falling in love the moment they see each other. Online dating sites, particularly eHarmony, tout commercials that practically promise subscribers that they'll experience "chemistry" with someone. Self-help books such as *The Soulmate Secret* (2011) by Arielle Ford, who ran her own public relations firm, rely on the love-at-first-sight concept to sell millions of copies every year.

FATE Many people believe fate and destiny are important components of romantic love. Songs tell us that "you were meant for me" and "that old black magic has me in its spell." In reality, fate has little to do with love. Romantic love is typically ignited not by fate but by factors such as a similar social class, physical attractiveness, and a need for intimacy (Shea and Adams, 1984; Benassi, 1985; see also Chapter 8).

Love in Long-Term Relationships

Many people equate romance with love, but romance is only a stepping-stone. Romance draws people together and may jump-start love, but it often fizzles as the first few months (or years) of passion evaporate (Brander, 2004; Brink, 2007). Some characteristics of romantic and long-term love overlap. Both reflect attributes such as trust, understanding, and honesty (see *Figure 6.3*). There are also some striking differences.

First, romantic love is fairly effortless compared with lasting love, which is more demanding. It takes much less work to plan a romantic evening than to be patient with a partner day after day, year after year. Thus, it's easier to fall in love than to stay in love.

Second, romantic love is often self-centered, whereas long-term love is altruistic. Romantic lovers are usually swept away by their own fantasies and obsessions, but lasting love requires putting the partner before oneself and making him or her feel cherished. Love that isn't obsessive also characterizes long-term relationships (Acevedo and Aron, 2009; Bernstein, 2013).

Third, romance is typically short-lived because love changes over time. Flaws that seemed cute during a whirlwind courtship may become unbearable a year after the wedding. For example, his dumpy furniture may have seemed quaint

FIGURE 6.3 Romantic Love and Long-Term Love: How Do They Differ? If you are currently (or have been) in a relationship with someone, is (was) your relationship one of romantic love? Or long-term love? *Source:* Based on Fehr, 1993, pp. 87–120.

Unique to Romantic Love	Common to Both	Unique to Long-Term Love
• Romantic Walks • Obsession • Longing • Candlelit Trysts • Going Out for Dinner • Picnics and Sunsets • Playfulness • Fantasy • Physical Attraction • Loss of Sleep • Ecstasy	• Trust • Caring • Communication • Honesty • Friendship • Respect • Understanding • Having Fun Together • Passion (but More Intense in Romantic Love)	• Patience • Independence • Putting Other before Self • Possibility of Marriage • Making Other Feel Wanted

until she realized that he refuses to spend any money on home furnishings. And values, especially religious beliefs, become increasingly important after the birth of the first child (Trotter, 1986).

Fourth, gestures usually differ. Romantic love gestures are typically outward expressions of affection such as flowers and other gifts, constant intimate touching, texting little love notes, and candlelit dinners. Gestures in long-term love are less tangible and materialistic. Examples include honesty, listening even though you'd rather be watching TV, and making sacrifices. According to Mae, age 92, who's been married for 70 years, gifts are "very sweet and nice when you're 20 or 25, but we are so safe and secure in our love for each other, there's no need for that kind of thing" (Lieber, 2011: B1).

Fifth, long-term love grows and develops, whereas romantic love is typically short-lived and self-centered. Romantic lovers often feel insecure about themselves or the relationship. As a result, one of the partners may demand constant attention, a continuous display of affection, and daily "I love you" reassurances (Dilman, 1998). Most of us appreciate tokens of love, verbal or behavioral. However, never-ending and self-absorbed commands such as "prove to me that you love me" can become tedious and annoying.

Sixth, companionate (storgic) love is more characteristic of long-term relationships compared with passion and game playing in romantic love. Those who are the happiest describe their love as companionate and committed. Committed partners, ruled by the head as much as the heart, are faithful to each other and plan their future together (Dush et al., 2005; Bowe, 2010).

Finally, demographic variables play a role in sustaining love. For example, two national polls found an association between socioeconomic status and long-term relationships: "Having enough income to be out of poverty may alleviate financial problems enough to reduce stress and thereby facilitate feelings of love"

What REAL love looks like...

DAVE GRANLUND © www.davegranlund.com

Choices   Helping Love Flourish

Several family practitioners (Hendrix, 1988; Osherson, 1992) have some suggestions for creating a loving environment. The suggestions don't guarantee everlasting love, but are worth considering:

- Good relationships don't just happen; we create them through conscious effort and work.
- One partner should be pleased, rather than threatened, by the other partner's successes or triumphs.
- Love may be one of life's greatest experiences, but it's not life itself.
- People who feel loved, accepted, and valued are more likely to treat others in a similar manner.
- It's not what you say but what you do that maintains love.
- Stable relationships are always changing. We must learn to deal with both our own changes as individuals and the changes we see in our mates.
- Love is poisoned by infidelity. If a loved one is deceived, it may be impossible to reestablish trust and respect.
- Blame is irresponsible. It discourages communication, makes people feel angry, and damages self-esteem.
- It may be difficult to forget occasional cruel words or acts, but forgiveness is essential in continuing a healthy relationship.
- Even though partners are very close, they must respect the other person's independence and his or her right to develop personal interests and other friendships.

(Smith, 1994: 34). Money may not buy love, but its absence can douse love's flames.

What does long-term love look like? Here's one description:

Happy couples have similar values, attitudes, interests, and to some degree, personality traits. They also share a philosophy of life, religion, vision, or passion that keeps them marching together in spite of minor differences. . . . They are autonomous, fair-minded, emotionally responsive individuals who trust one another. . . . Because they are separate selves, they also enjoy spending time apart to solidify their own individuality without feeling threatened by potential loss or abandonment (Piorkowski, 1994: 286).

"Helping Love Flourish" on the previous page offers some practical advice on achieving a satisfying and lasting relationship.

6.9 Explain how and why love varies across cultures.

Love across Cultures

The meaning and expression of love vary from one culture to another. In Western societies that emphasize individualism and free choice, love is a legitimate reason for dating, living together, getting married, or getting a divorce ("the spark is gone"). In cultures that stress the group and the community, arrangements between families are more important than romantic love.

Romantic Love

The early colonists believed that marriage was far too important to be based on love; politics and economics, not romance, were the key factors in selecting a partner. It was only in the early twentieth century that people came to expect marriage to be based on love, sexual attraction, and personal fulfillment (Coontz, 2005; see also Chapter 3).

Because romantic love exists in at least 89 percent of societies, it's a nearly universal phenomenon. A number of studies in China, Hong Kong, Taiwan, and Hawaii have found that many people, especially the young, believe in passionate love (Jankowiak and Fischer 1992; Doherty et al., 1994; Cho and Cross, 1995; Goodwin and Findlay, 1997).

Romance is least important in societies where kin ties take precedence over individual relationships. In Burma, India, and Mexico, college students said that storgic, agapic, and pragmatic love are more desirable than manic, erotic, and ludic love styles. In much of China, similarly, love is tempered by recognition that a match needs parental approval. In Saudi Arabia and some other Middle Eastern countries, public embracing between men and women is taboo, the sexes can't mix in public, and a woman who is caught with an unrelated man can be flogged, arrested, or killed (Moore, 1998; Slackman, 2008).

As you saw in Chapter 1, the Indian government endorses marriage across castes, but not everyone supports such policies. Also, some radical groups have denounced celebrating Valentine's Day—especially popular among young, middle-class urbanites—as offensive to Indian culture and have tried to disrupt

Since you asked . . .
• Are Americans too romantic about love?

Many marriages in India are still arranged, but "Bollywood" movies feature romantic love, passion, infatuation, and even obsession. Why do you think that the films are so popular?

businesses that sell Valentine's Day gifts and cards (Wax, 2008; Magnier and Ramaswamy, 2009).

In Japan, which has one of the highest divorce rates in the world, expressing love and affection is uncommon, especially among men, who rarely see their wives and children; many companies pressure men to put their job first and to demonstrate their loyalty by working long hours. To increase husbands' appreciation of their wives, a man founded a Devoted Husband Organization and declared January 31 as "Beloved Wives Day," during which a husband is supposed to tell his wife that he loves her for all that she does every day for him and their family. Beloved Wives Day hasn't become a national holiday, but more men are joining the organization to show respect and affection for their wives and to avoid divorce (Kambayashi, 2008; DeLong, 2011).

Arranged Love

In the United States and other Western countries, people often become engaged and then inform family and friends. Worldwide, a more typical pattern is **arranged marriage**, in which parents or relatives choose the children's partners. It's expected that the partners' love for each other will grow over time.

In many countries, arranged marriages are the norm because respect for parents' wishes, family traditions, the kin group, and the well-being of the community are more important than the individual's feelings. In fact, people in many societies find American beliefs about dating and romance at least as strange as some Americans find the concept of arranged marriages (see "Modern Arranged Marriages in India").

arranged marriage Parents or relatives choose the children's partners.

 Read on MySocLab

Document: Sometimes the Perfect Mate Is Someone You Hardly Know

---

Cross-Cultural and Multicultural Families — Modern Arranged Marriages in India

In India, the majority of marriages are arranged by parents or elders: "There has never been any room for romantic marriage in Indian society on the line of Western societies" (Singh, 2005: 143). Arranged marriages help maintain social and religious traditions, preserve group solidarity, and can augment a family's reputation and financial assets (Nesteruk and Gramescu, 2012).

There are variations in different regions and social classes, however. Educated, upper-middle-class women are allowed to marry whomever they want, but many opt for arranged marriages. One young woman explained: "Love is important, but it's not sufficient." She's reportedly happily married to a man whom she had met just three times before their engagement. In most cases, children can reject undesirable candidates (Lakshmanan, 1997; Epstein, 2010).

A young Indian American has convinced her parents to let her date instead of having an arranged marriage. She says, however, "In college, I just could not understand why anyone would marry someone without falling in love first. But as I've seen [my parents'] love grow over the years, I have had a deeper appreciation for their arranged marriage" (Luhar, 2013).

Why do arranged marriages persist in much of India? Shy people can end up with a good partner because parents and relatives seem to do a good job in choosing mates. Also, arranged marriages offer stability because the couple's families stand behind them: "If the relationship between the couples is about to go haywire . . . parents of both spouses make concerted efforts to resolve the crisis" (Singh, 2005: 144).

Arranged marriages also persist because of family ties. Even financially independent couples usually live with the husband's parents. As a result,

similar backgrounds and compatibility with in-laws are more important in India than in the West. The advantage is considerable family support if a marriage runs into trouble. These may be some of the reasons why India has one of the lowest divorce rates in the world (Epstein, 2010).

STOP AND THINK . . .

- Why are arranged marriages less fragile than marriages based on love?
- In arranged marriages, factors such as social class and religion are more important than romantic love or physical attraction. If Americans endorsed arranged love, do you think that our divorce rates would decrease? Why or why not?

In arranged marriages in Sri Lanka, men and women who fall in love usually tell their parents about their choices. In Turkey, about 52 percent of women live in arranged marriages, but there is a trend toward love marriages among younger, better-educated, and urban women. In Canada, some second-generation Muslim Pakistani women are rebelling against arranged marriages. Others participate willingly because they can't find a suitable partner on their own or believe that their parents know best (de Munck, 1998; Zaidi and Shuraydi, 2002; Nauck and Klaus, 2005).

Studies of arranged marriages in India and Bangladesh show that, in most cases, love gradually increases and becomes stronger (Epstein, 2010) but that's not always the case. As you saw in Chapter 5, if the husband is abusive in an arranged marriage, women can't escape. In some countries such as Afghanistan, Iran, and Iraq, women who defy arranged marriages are stoned, burned to death, hanged, or shot, often by male family members or men in the community (Fleishman, 2010; Healy, 2011; see also Chapter 5).

MAKING CONNECTIONS

- Have you ever experienced love at first sight? If so, how long did the relationship last? Do you believe that you're destined to meet that "special someone"?

- Some of my students—including those in their thirties and forties—believe that long-term relationships are pretty boring because the romance wanes. Do you agree?

CONCLUSION

When love is healthy, it *changes* how we feel about ourselves and others. Love can inspire and motivate us to care for family members, friends, and lovers. Love also creates *choices* in the ways that we may find happiness during dating, marriage, and old age. There are *constraints*, however, because we sometimes confuse love with jealousy or controlling behavior. Love is essential to human growth and development, but it's often shrouded in myths and hampered by obstacles. Do love and sex go together? Not always, as the next chapter shows.

On MySocLab

✓ **Study** and **Review** on MySocLab

REVIEW QUESTIONS

6.1. Compare self-love, friendship, and love.

1. Why is love a complex phenomenon? What characteristics are minimally necessary for a loving relationship?

2. How are self-love, friendship, and love similar? How do they differ?

6.2. Explain the concept of love.

3. What are three characteristics of love?

4. What attracts people to each other? How do lust and love differ?

6.3. Explain why caring, intimacy, and commitment are important components of love.

5. How do caring and intimacy differ?

6. Is commitment a feeling rather than a behavior? Explain.

6.4. Compare the six theoretical perspectives that explain love.

7. How do the following differ: biochemistry perspectives, attachment theory, the wheel theory of love, the triangular theory of love, Lee's styles of loving, and exchange theory? What is a weakness of each perspective?

6.5. Describe four functions of love.

8. What purposes does love serve?

9. What are some of the negative effects when people are deprived of love?

6.6. Explain how people experience love and some of love's obstacles.

10. Are women more romantic than men? What are the similarities and differences in the way that men and women express intimacy?

11. What are the macro-level and micro-level obstacles to love?

6.7. Explain why love goes wrong.

12. Is jealousy healthy? Is it universal?

13. What kinds of harmful and controlling behavior kill love?

14. Why is love unrequited?

6.8. Compare romantic and long-term love.

15. What are some of the characteristics of romantic love? How do beliefs about love at first sight and fate influence romance?

16. How are romantic love and long-term love similar? How do they differ? And why?

6.9. Explain how and why love varies across cultures.

17. In which societies is romantic love least important? Why?

18. How do free choice and arranged marriages differ? Why do the latter characterize many societies?

CHAPTER

7

Sexuality and Sexual Expression throughout Life

((• **Listen** to Chapter 7 on **MySocLab**

LEARNING OBJECTIVES

After you read and study this chapter you will be able to:

7.1 Explain how sexuality is a product of our sexual identity, sexual orientation, and sexual scripts.

7.2 Explain why we have first-time sex, casual sex, and sex in committed relationships.

7.3 Describe five primary sources that influence our sexual behavior.

7.4 Describe at least four types of sexual behaviors.

7.5 Describe the prevalence, sexual behaviors, and societal reactions to lesbian, gay, bisexual, and transgender sex.

7.6 Explain how sexual behavior changes over the life course.

7.7 Define sexual infidelity, describe its prevalence, explain why it occurs, and discuss its consequences.

7.8 Describe the prevalence of sexually transmitted diseases, their causes, effects, risks, and increasing rates.

- Nearly half of all high school students (49 percent of males and 46 percent of females) have had sexual intercourse, but **40 percent didn't use a condom during the last time**. The first sexual intercourse is at about age 17.

- By age 44, **the median number of opposite-sex partners** is 3.4 for women and 6.4 for men.

- Among those ages 15 to 44, 5 percent of men and 13 percent of women **have had sexual contact with a same-sex partner** at least once.

- Among Americans **age 60 and older**, 31 percent of women and 45 percent of men reported having had vaginal intercourse from a few times per month to every week.

- Globally, 38 percent of couples say that the best thing about their relationship is the sex. **Nearly 60 percent of Brazilians,** compared with only 15 percent of Japanese, rank their sex lives above all else in making them happy.

- Worldwide, **34 million people are living with HIV/AIDS**. In 2010, almost 2 million people died of AIDS-related diseases. The largest number of deaths (1.2 million) was in Africa.

Sources: Reece et al., 2010; Schick et al., 2010; Chandra et al., 2011; Allen, 2012; Eaton et al., 2012; World Health Organization, 2012.

I n the movie *Annie Hall*, a therapist asks two lovers how often they have sex. The male rolls his eyes, and complains, "Hardly ever, maybe three times a week." The female exclaims, "Constantly, three times a week!" As this anecdote illustrates, sex is more important for some people than others. Besides physical contact, sex engages our brain and emotions. Culture shapes our sexual development, attitudes, and actions. As a result, there are significant differences from one society to another in defining what is normal or abnormal. In addition, sexual behavior changes throughout life. Before you read any further, take the "How Much Do You Know about Sex?" quiz.

ASK YOURSELF

How Much Do You Know about Sex?

1. Birth control pills offer protection against sexually transmitted diseases (STDs). ☐ True ☐ False

2. Among married American men, how many would you estimate have ever had an extramarital affair?
   - **a.** Fewer than 10 percent
   - **b.** About 10 percent
   - **c.** About 20 percent
   - **d.** About 30 percent
   - **e.** About 40 percent
   - **f.** About 50 percent
   - **g.** More than 50 percent

3. If your partner is truly meant for you, sex is easy and wonderful. ☐ True ☐ False

4. Petroleum jelly, skin lotion, and baby oil are good lubricants to use with a condom or diaphragm. ☐ True ☐ False

5. About 10 percent of the U.S. population is exclusively homosexual. ☐ True ☐ False

6. A female can get pregnant during her menstrual flow (her period). ☐ True ☐ False

7. A female can't get pregnant if the man withdraws his penis before he ejaculates. ☐ True ☐ False

8. Oral contact with a partner's genitals isn't "really" sex. ☐ True ☐ False

9. The length of the average man's erect penis is about
   - **a.** 2–4 inches
   - **b.** 5–7 inches
   - **c.** 8–9 inches
   - **d.** 10–11 inches
   - **e.** 12 inches or longer

10. In the United States, syphilis is one of the two most common STDs. ☐ True ☐ False

(Answers are on page 178.)

Sexuality and Human Development

Sexuality isn't just a physical activity. Among other things, it's the product of our sexual identity, sexual orientation, and sexual scripts.

Sexual Identity

sexual identity Awareness of ourselves as male or female and the ways that we express sexual values, attitudes, feelings, and beliefs.

Sexual identity is an awareness of ourselves as male or female and the ways that we express our sexual values, attitudes, feelings, and beliefs. It involves placing ourselves in a category created by society (such as female and heterosexual) and learning, both consciously and unconsciously, how to act in that category.

Sexuality is a multidimensional concept that incorporates psychological, biological, and sociological components such as sexual desire, sexual response, and gender roles (Bernhard, 1995). *Sexual desire* is the sexual drive that makes us receptive to sexual activity. *Sexual response* encompasses the biological aspects of sexuality, which include experiencing pleasure or orgasm. *Gender roles* are the behaviors that women and men enact according to culturally prescribed expectations (see Chapter 5).

In a typical situation, a man may be aroused by a woman's cleavage because our society considers breasts sexy (sexual desire), may experience an erection (sexual response), and may then take the initiative in having sexual intercourse with a woman whom he finds attractive (gender roles). But what if the man is aroused by other men rather than by women?

Since you asked . . .

- Am I gay if I'm attracted to someone of my own sex?

Sexual Orientation

sexual orientation A preference for sexual partners of the same sex, the opposite sex, both sexes, or neither sex.

homosexual A person who is sexually attracted to people of the same sex.

heterosexual A person who is sexually attracted to people of the opposite sex.

bisexual A person who is sexually attracted to people of both sexes.

asexual Lacking any interest in or desire for sex.

Sexual identity incorporates **sexual orientation**, a preference for sexual partners of the same sex, the opposite sex, both sexes, or neither sex:

- **Homosexuals** (from the Greek root *homo*, meaning "same") are sexually attracted to people of the same sex. *Gay* is often used for men and women, while *lesbian* refers to homosexual women. *Coming out* is a person's public acknowledgment that she or he is gay.

- **Heterosexuals**, often called *straight*, are attracted to people of the opposite sex.

- **Bisexuals**, sometimes called *bis*, are attracted to people of both sexes.

- **Asexuals** lack any interest in or desire for sex.

Sexual orientation isn't as clear-cut as most people believe. Alfred Kinsey (1948) and his associates' classic study found that most people weren't exclusively heterosexual or homosexual. Instead, they fell somewhere along a continuum in terms of sexual desire, attractions, feelings, fantasies, and experiences. More recently, *sexologists*, people who study the sexual behavior of human beings, have added those who identify themselves as asexual (see *Figure 7.1*).

A person's sexual orientation and behavior aren't always consistent. Asexuality may be a permanent or temporary condition because of choice or the effects of medications. Bisexuals may be attracted to people of both sexes but engage in sexual behavior primarily with women or with men. Heterosexuals might fantasize about having same-sex experiences. And homosexuals who haven't come out may have sexual intercourse only with heterosexual partners because they fear being labeled "gay" (Kinsey et al., 1948; Rieger et al., 2005).

Heterosexuality is the predominant sexual orientation worldwide, but, as you'll see later in this chapter, homosexuality and bisexuality exist in all societies. Many gays and lesbians deny or try to suppress their sexual orientation because our society is still

0 Exclusively heterosexual	4 Usually homosexual
1 Predominantly heterosexual	5 Predominantly homosexual
2 Usually heterosexual	6 Exclusively homosexual
3 Bisexual	7 Asexual

FIGURE 7.1 Sexuality Continuum
Sources: Based on Kinsey et al., 1948, p. 638; and Kinsey Institute, 2011.

characterized by **heterosexism**, the belief that heterosexuality is superior to and more natural than homosexuality. **Homophobia**, the fear and hatred of homosexuality, is less overt today than in the past but is still widespread.

Despite considerable prejudice and discrimination, some people believe that their biological sex, their gender identity, and a perception of themselves as either masculine or feminine conflict. These individuals have a transgender sexual orientation.

Our cultural expectations dictate that we are female or male, but a number of people are "living on the boundaries of both sexes" (Lorber and Moore, 2007: 141). **Transgender people** encompass several groups whose behavior doesn't conform to the sex to which they were assigned at birth (American Psychological Association, 2011):

- **Transsexuals:** people who are born with one biological sex but choose to live their life as another sex—either by consistently cross-dressing or by surgically altering their sex (see Chapter 5).

- **Intersexuals:** people whose medical classification at birth isn't clearly male or female (this term has replaced *hermaphrodites*).

- **Transvestites:** people who cross-dress at times but don't necessarily consider themselves a member of the opposite sex.

The acronym LGBT refers, collectively, to lesbians, gay men, bisexuals, and transgender people, and men and women who don't identify themselves with any specific sexual orientation. Today, LGBTs are becoming increasingly more visible but, as you'll see shortly, their acceptance is mixed.

WHAT DETERMINES OUR SEXUAL ORIENTATION? No one knows why we're straight, gay, bisexual, or asexual. *Biological theories* maintain that sexual orientation may be strongly molded by biological factors, particularly the early influence of sex hormones after conception and around childbirth.

A growing body of research also shows that there are clusters of childhood traits and behaviors that are related to adult sexual orientation. For example, pre-gay boys and pre-lesbian girls are gender-nonconforming at an early age compared with their heterosexual counterparts in terms of play and choice of clothes (see LeVay, 2011, for a comprehensive summary of these and other studies). Others contend that sexual orientation must have biological roots because, across cultures, the proportion of the population that is homosexual is roughly the same (Barash, 2012).

Social constructionist theories hold that sexual behavior is largely the result of social pressure, and that culture, not biology, plays a large role in forming our sexual identity. For example, and despite their homosexual inclinations, many straight men who have sex with other men refuse to accept the possibility that they're gay or bisexual. In effect, then, and because of societal pressure to be straight, many gay men and lesbians are living heterosexual lives (Golombok and Tasker, 1996; Patterson, 2002).

One example of social constructionist theories is the case of *hijras*. An estimated 50,000 to 5 million live in India and are considered members of a "third sex"—neither male nor female. Most are born male, and some are intersexuals, but all dress as women and act in feminine ways. The word *hijra* is sometimes used in a derogatory way, but *hijras* often perform religious ceremonies that are supposed to bring good luck and fertility, and some have been elected to high political positions (Ilkkaracan and Jolly, 2007).

So far, no study has shown conclusively that either genes or the environment "causes" sexual orientation. Consequently, researchers speculate that a combination of genetic and cultural factors influence our sexual orientation (see Slater, 2013).

After a sex-change operation in 2009, Chastity Bono—the daughter of Sonny and Cher—became Chaz, a male. His debut on *Dancing with the Stars*, a popular television program, was controversial because many people objected to including a transsexual contestant.

heterosexism The belief that heterosexuality is superior to and more natural than homosexuality.

homophobia A fear and hatred of homosexuality.

transgender people A term that encompasses transsexuals, intersexuals, and transvestites.

Since you asked . . .
- What is a "transgender"?

transsexuals People who are born with one biological sex but choose to live their life as another sex.

intersexuals People whose medical classification at birth isn't clearly male or female.

transvestites People who cross-dress at times but don't necessarily consider themselves a member of the opposite sex.

Since you asked . . .
- Do we inherit our sexual orientation?

SEXUAL ORIENTATION AND GENDER   Some scholars assert that gender is a more powerful factor than sexual orientation in shaping a person's behavior. That is, there are more similarities between straight and gay men and between straight women and lesbians than there are between lesbians and gays. For example,

- Lesbians and heterosexual women usually have monogamous relationships; gays and heterosexual men are more likely to have more than one lover at a time.

- For lesbians and heterosexual women, love and sex usually go hand in hand; many gays and heterosexual men often separate emotional intimacy from sex.

- Compared with gay and heterosexual men, lesbians and heterosexual women aren't interested in having sex with strangers (or in public places). Both groups of men, but not women, are likely to "cruise" for sexual partners.

- Heterosexual and homosexual men—not women—are the mainstay of some industries, including prostitution, pornography, topless or gay bars, and escort services (Caldwell and Peplau, 1990; Goode, 1990; Fryar et al., 2007).

Such findings may seem like male bashing, but the researchers are simply pointing out that gender roles may be more important than sexual orientation in shaping our sexual scripts.

Sexual Scripts

sexual script Specifies the formal or informal norms for acceptable or unacceptable sexual activity.

We like to think that our sexual behavior is spontaneous, but all of us have internalized sexual scripts. A **sexual script** specifies the formal or informal norms for acceptable or unacceptable sexual activity, including which individuals are eligible sexual partners, and the boundaries of sexual behavior. Sexual scripts can change over time and across groups, but are highly gendered in two ways—women's increasing hypersexualization and a persistent sexual double standard. Gender also shapes our sexual scripts.

GENDER AND SEXUAL SCRIPTS   As you saw in Chapter 5, boys are typically expected to be masculine and girls are supposed to be feminine. Two of the negative effects of male sexual scripts are the expectation that males should be sexually aggressive, and that their sexual urge is uncontrollable. Many sexually healthy men in their twenties, thirties, and forties now use impotence drugs—such as Viagra and Levitra—because they believe the myth that a "real man" is always ready to be a sexual superman. Some companies sell men's briefs that have a penis sling, making the "bulge in the pants" larger than it is. Women, too, try to live up to unrealistic sexual scripts by undergoing breast augmentation surgery—despite the chance of infection or even death—because in our culture large breasts "are part of the ideal female body" (Roan, 2005: F1; White, 2011).

In virtually every media form—including television, music videos, magazines, video games, the Internet, and advertising—girls and women are sexualized (e.g., dressed in revealing clothes) and physical beauty is emphasized. Such sexualization can result in females being dissatisfied with their bodies, experiencing low self-esteem, tolerating sexual harassment and sexual violence, and a greater likelihood of having sex at an early age (Zurbriggen et al., 2007).

ANSWERS TO "How Much Do You Know about Sex?"

Scoring the test:
Each question is worth 1 point. A score of 10 is an "A," 8 or 9 a "B," 7 a "C," 6 a "D," and below 6 an "F."

Correct answers:
1. false, 2. c, 3. false, 4. false, 5. false, 6. true, 7. false, 8. false, 9. b, 10. false.

SEXUAL SCRIPTS AND THE "SEXY BABES" TREND   Sexualized messages are reaching ever-younger audiences and teach or reinforce the idea that girls and women should be valued for their "sexiness" rather than their personalities and abilities. For example, there are "bikini onesies" for infant girls, sexy lingerie for girls 3 months and older, padded bras for 7- and 8-year olds (that's right, for 7- and 8-year-olds!), and 80 percent of girls ages 13 to 18 list shopping as their favorite activity (Hanes, 2012).

Are baby bikinis cute? Or offensive? On the right is a an ad for perfumes, but where are the clothes? How do such images reinforce women's sexual scripts?

Many girls are obsessed about their looks, and from an early age, for a variety of reasons, including their mothers' role modeling. By age 9, for example, girls start imitating the clothes, makeup, and behavior of mothers who dress and act in highly sexualized ways (Starr and Ferguson, 2012).

Media images also play a large role in girls' hypersexualization. Girls and boys see cheerleaders (with increasingly sexualized routines) on TV far more than they see female basketball players or other athletes. And, a study of the 100 top-grossing films in 2008 found that 13- to 20-year-old females were far more likely than their male counterparts to be depicted in revealing clothes (40 percent vs. 7 percent), partially naked (30 percent vs. 10 percent), and physically attractive (29 percent vs. 11 percent). In television shows, women are now represented in more diverse roles—such as doctors, lawyers, and criminal investigators—but they're often sexy ("hot"). Also, top female athletes regularly pose naked or semi-naked for men's magazines (Hanes, 2011; Smith and Choueiti, 2011).

Who benefits from girls' and women's hypersexualization? Marketers who convince girls (and their parents) that being popular and "sexy" requires the right clothes, makeup, hair style, and accessories, create a young generation of shoppers and consumers who will increase business profits more than ever before (Levin and Kilbourne, 2009).

SEXUAL SCRIPTS AND THE DOUBLE STANDARD   You'll recall that the double standard emerged during the nineteenth century (see Chapter 3). Some believe that the *sexual double standard*—a code that permits greater sexual freedom for men than women—has eroded. Others argue that women are still expected to confine their sexual behavior to committed relationships, whereas men are allowed (even encouraged) to have as many sexual partners as they want (see Ronen, 2010).

There are numerous examples of the sexual double standard. Among U.S. adolescents, the higher the number of sexual partners, the greater the boy's popularity. In contrast, girls who have more than eight partners are far less popular than their less-experienced female peers (Kreager and Staff, 2009). About 30,000 American women undergo vaginal surgery (hymenoplasty) every year to repair the hymen. This "revirgination" is especially popular among women whose lovers want to experience intercourse with a virgin even though the men themselves aren't virgins ("Like a virgin?" 2006). Another indicator of the persistence of the double standard is the high rate of rape and other sexual assaults on women because much sexual violence is still dismissed as masculine misbehavior rather than as a crime (see Chapters 8 and 14).

The sexual double standard isn't limited to the United States. Female genital mutilation/cutting, still practiced extensively in many parts of the world, reflects a double standard that allows men to mutilate women under the guise of making them more marriageable. Men have no comparable constraints. In 1979, the World Health Organization denounced the practice as indefensible on medical and humane grounds. As "Tradition or Torture? . . . " shows, however, millions of girls are still subjected to these procedures.

Cross-Cultural and Multicultural Families

Tradition or Torture? Female Genital Mutilation/Cutting

This 4-year-old in Kurdistan, Iraq, screams in pain during her circumcision. In another case in the same region, a 7-year-old girl prepared happily for a party that her mother promised. Instead, she was circumcised. As the operator sliced off part of the little girl's genitals, she "let out a high-pitched wail heard throughout the neighborhood" (Paley, 2008: A9).

Most of the 140 million girls and women who have undergone female genital mutilation/cutting (FGM/C) live in 29 African countries, Indonesia, and some Middle Eastern countries. The FGM/C custom is also increasing in Europe, Australia, Canada, and the United States because some recent immigrants maintain the practice. Each year, an estimated 3 million girls undergo FGM/C.

There are several types of FGM/C. In *excision*, part or all of the clitoris and the labia minora are removed. (Appendix A provides information on sexual anatomy.) This operation often results in the growth of scar tissue that blocks the vaginal opening.

Infibulation combines removal of the clitoris and labia minora with excision of the inner layers of the labia majora. The raw edges of these inner layers are then sewn together with cat gut or acacia thorn. A sliver of wood or straw is inserted into the tiny opening that remains, allowing the slow, often painful passage of urine and menstrual flow.

When the woman marries, her husband uses his penis, razors, knives, or other instruments to penetrate the vagina during intercourse. The opening must be further enlarged for childbirth.

The age at which a girl undergoes FGM/C varies from one country to another. The girl may be only a few days old, but most are between 3 and 12 years old. The operator, typically an elderly village woman who may have poor eyesight, cuts off the clitoris and then scrapes the labial flesh even though the little girl howls and writhes in pain. The procedure can have a number of immediate and long-term complications:

- The girl could hemorrhage and die.
- A rupture of the internal division between the vagina and the bladder or rectum could cause continual dribbling of urine or feces for the rest of the woman's life.
- The woman could feel severe pain during intercourse or become sterile because of infections in her reproductive organs.
- During childbirth, even if the birth canal opening is enlarged, the woman could experience perineal tears or even die because the baby can't emerge through the mutilated vulva.

Cultures that practice FGM/C justify it on the grounds that it controls a girl's sexual desires and therefore preserves her morality, chastity, and fidelity. Because female virginity is a prerequisite for marriage, FGM/C ensures a girl's marriageability and the family's honor. If mothers refuse to participate, their daughters would be ostracized, remain unmarried, and become financially destitute. Female genital mutilation/ cutting has been banned in some African countries, and many African and Egyptian women have protested FGM/C, but the practice continues.

Sources: Paley, 2008; Mullen, 2009; Clifton and Feldman-Jacobs, 2011; Kristof, 2011; United Nations Children's Fund, 2011.

STOP AND THINK . . .

- Female genital mutilation/cutting is an accepted ritual in many countries. Should the United States and other nations intervene if they don't agree with these customs?
- Even though breast implants and liposuction are voluntary, are they more civilized than FGM/C in making women's bodies more acceptable to men?

7.2 Explain why we have first-time sex, casual sex, and sex in committed relationships.

Why We Have Sex

Sex, including the first penile-vaginal intercourse experience, doesn't "just happen." It typically progresses through a series of stages such as approaching, flirting, touching, or asking directly for sex. Although it may be passionate,

first-time sex typically, even among adolescents, occurs after some planning and thought (Sprecher and McKinney, 1993; Gillmore et al., 2002).

People have sex for pleasure and for procreation, but also to get rid of a headache, to celebrate a special occasion, to get a promotion, and to feel closer to God. After asking almost 2,000 college students why they have (or would have) sex, the researchers came up with 237 reasons that they grouped into four categories (see *Table 7.1*), and found that many of the reasons were gendered. For example, men were more likely to use sex to gain status or enhance their reputation, whereas women were more likely to say that they wanted to express their love for someone.

First-Time Sex

There are a variety of reasons for having sex the first time. They range from developmental to structural factors.

DEVELOPMENTAL REASONS   On average, U.S. children are beginning puberty at much younger ages, including breast development for girls at age 8, and genital enlargement for boys at age 9 (Biro et al., 2010; Herman-Giddens et al., 2012). The earlier onset of puberty results in a gap between physical sexual maturity, brain development, and social maturity. This gap, warns a medical researcher, could be a recipe for early sexual behavior. Developing early is associated with psychological and social pressures that young girls may not be equipped to handle, including sexual advances from older boys and men. Girls may look older than their age, but mentally, they're much the same as other 7- and 8-year-old girls (Goodwin, 2010; Beck, 2012).

Overweight teen females (but not males) are likely to have their first sexual experience later than normal-weight teens, in part because they encounter social exclusion from peer groups (Cheng and Landale, 2010). Teens with emotional problems such as antisocial behavior are more likely than their counterparts to have first-time sex before turning 15 (McLeod and Knight, 2010).

INTERPERSONAL REASONS   The majority of first sexual relationships are with a romantic partner. In a national study of those ages 12 to 21, the 45 percent who had had sexual intercourse were romantically involved and progressed from activities such as holding hands and kissing to exchanging presents and touching a partner's genitals (O'Sullivan et al., 2007).

A person may feel obligated to have sex for fear of hurting the other's feelings or losing his or her interest (Abrahams and Ahlbrand, 2002). Others experience physical arousal and follow their impulses or are simply curious about sex.

Since you asked . . .

• Is our sexual behavior different in casual and committed relationships?

 Watch on MySocLab

Video: From an Objective Point of View: The Decision to Have Sex

 Watch on MySocLab

Video: Just Like You Imagined: A Look at the Lives of Young People's Relationships

TABLE 7.1	Why People Have Sex	
Category	**Reasons**	**Examples**
Physical	Stress reduction, pleasure, physical desirability, and experience seeking	"The person had beautiful eyes" or "a desirable body," or "was a good kisser" or "too physically attractive to resist." Or "I wanted to achieve an orgasm."
Goal Attainment	Obtaining resources, social status, and revenge	"I wanted to even the score with a cheating partner" or "break up a rival's relationship" or "make money" or "be popular." Or "because of a bet."
Emotional	Love, commitment, and expression of feelings	"I wanted to communicate at a deeper level" or "lift my partner's spirits" or "say 'Thank you.'" Or just because "the person was intelligent."
Insecurity	Boosting one's self-esteem, duty, pressure, and guarding a mate from competitors	"I felt like it was my duty," "I wanted to boost my self-esteem," or "It was the only way my partner would spend time with me."

Source: Based on Meston and Buss, 2007.

SITUATIONAL REASONS At least 10 percent of girls who first have sex before age 15 describe it as unwanted. Among adolescents ages 15 to 17, 36 percent of males and 29 percent of females say that they were pressured to have sex—usually by male friends or boyfriends (Albert et al., 2003; Holt et al., 2003). Such early sexual victimization increases the chances, after age 18, of having multiple sexual partners, exchanging sex for drugs, and being diagnosed with a sexually transmitted disease (STD) (Smith and Ford, 2010).

A teenage boy might have sex the first time to stop being teased and harassed about being a virgin or to quash rumors that he's gay (Pascoe, 2007). Among high school students, binge drinking raises the likelihood of having first-time sex, sex with multiple partners, and not using contraceptives (DeSimone, 2010b).

STRUCTURAL FACTORS Structural factors also affect first-time sex. Teenagers are more likely to engage in sex at an early age if they experience family turbulence that includes parental conflict before or during a divorce, remarriage, and redivorce; if they live with single parents who are sexually active; or if they live in neighborhoods in which adults who are role models don't have steady jobs and bear children out of wedlock. In such situations, adolescents may disengage from their parents, looking to peers for emotional support, and thereby hasten their entry into sexual activity (Moore and Chase-Lansdale, 2001; Wu and Thomson, 2001; Upchurch et al., 2001). As you'll see shortly, other social institutions, such as religion, have mixed effects in accelerating or delaying first-time and subsequent sex among never-married adolescents.

Casual Sex

Especially during young adulthood, casual sex serves several functions—experimenting, experiencing pleasure without unwanted commitment, building self-confidence by choosing partners, and enjoying closeness and intimacy, however fleeting (Christina, 2011). Casual sex is typically ludic because the partners "just want to have fun" (see Chapter 6). As in the case of first-time sex, binge drinking leads to frequent casual sex, with many partners, and risky behavior such as not using condoms (DeSimone, 2010a). Casual lovers may become friends, never see each other again, or develop long-term relationships.

Sex in Committed Relationships

In short-term relationships, sex can be an expression of love and affection. It can increase intimacy and a feeling of closeness that is emotional (expressing feelings), social (retaining friends), intellectual (sharing ideas), and recreational (sharing interests and hobbies). Sex can encourage self-disclosure, telling a partner about one's hopes and insecurities. It also involves an exchange of resources such as trading sex for status or attention (see Chapters 2, 6, and 10 on exchange theories).

All of these characteristics, plus several others, are present in long-term relationships. When a close bond continues over time, sexual and other physical expressions of intimacy maintain the relationship and foster interdependence because the partners rely on each other for sexual satisfaction. In addition, many people in long-term relationships have sex because they want children and plan to raise them together.

Whether you're sexually active or not, how did you do on the quiz, on page 175? According to some instructors, their students—like mine—usually get a C (if they're honest in reporting their scores). But even if you got a C, you probably know more about sex than most of your peers or even the average American adult.

A sociologist has observed that "when the subject is sexuality, facts have a pretty poor reputation in America" (Klein, 2012). He might be right. For example,

The reasons for having sex often differ in casual and committed relationships.

31 percent of teen mothers aged 15 to 19 with unintended pregnancies didn't use contraceptives because they assumed they wouldn't get pregnant (though it's not clear why) (Harrison et al., 2012). Among teens aged 18 to 19, 41 percent said that they know little or nothing about condoms, and 75 percent said the same about the contraceptive pill (Guttmacher Institute, 2012). Among sexually active U.S. young adults between the ages of 18 and 29, only 34 percent, including those who used rhythm methods (see Appendix D), knew that a woman's fertile period is halfway between two menstrual periods. In the same age group, a "startling" 40 percent believed that birth control pills and condoms don't prevent pregnancy (Berger et al., 2012; Frost et al., 2012).

You'll see later in this chapter that many older people also lack knowledge about core sexual issues and their impact on health. Why are many of us so misinformed about sex?

MAKING CONNECTIONS

- How would you describe your sexual scripts? Have they remained constant or changed over time? Do your sexual scripts—or those of your friends, partners, and children—reflect a sexual double standard?

- Think about yourself, your friends, or your children. Why do people have sexual intercourse the first time? Or casual sex?

Who Influences Our Sexual Behavior?

7.3 Describe five primary sources that influence our sexual behavior.

We learn sexual attitudes and behaviors in a cultural context. The primary sources of sexual socialization are parents, peers, siblings, religion, the media and popular culture, and sex education programs in schools.

Parents

When reporters asked Charles Barkley, the former National Basketball Association star, how he'd handle his 12-year-old daughter's future boyfriends, he said, "I figure if I kill the first one, the word will get out." Although humorous, Barkley's statement reflects a fairly typical—but unrealistic—parental stance: "I'll make sure my kid won't have sex until she/he is . . . 18, 21, or married."

WHY ARE PARENTS IMPORTANT? As with other development, parents play an important role in their children's sexual socialization. Ideally, parents (or guardians) should be the first and best sex educators because they're experienced and have their children's interests at heart. When parents are effective sex educators, there are a number of positive adolescent outcomes. Sexual knowledge, in particular, delays first-time sexual intercourse, lowers sexually risky behavior (e.g., not using contraceptives), decreases the number of unwanted pregnancies, and increases control over one's sexual behavior (Albert et al., 2003; Longmore et al., 2009; Guilamo-Ramos et al., 2011; Killoren et al., 2011; Madkour et al., 2012).

More specifically, a combination of key parental factors has the greatest success in delaying adolescents' first-time sex. Some of these factors include daily contact and interaction (e.g., regular meals together); honest and open communication about sex, risky sex, and the effect of substance use; a good parent–child relationship; sharing activities (e.g., sports or hobbies); and parental monitoring (e.g., setting curfews, knowing the child's friends and whereabouts) (VanCampen and Romero, 2012).

Parents face distinct challenges, however, as teens get older, spend more time with their friends, and begin to date. Knowing that dating provides opportunities for having sex, parents often try to control their adolescents by increasing monitoring and limiting a teen's dating choices. Disagreements on both issues may increase parent–child conflict and the debut of first-time sex. Demographic and personal characteristics also affect early sexual initiation. For example, teens are more likely to engage in first-time sex if they have low grades, use alcohol, and are raised in single-parent homes and poor neighborhoods (Longmore et al., 2009).

Fathers who discuss sex with their young sons tend to delay their adolescents' sexual intercourse.

DO PARENTS TALK ABOUT SEX?   There's one consistent finding across racial/ethnic families, in different regions of the country, with diverse family structures, and across social classes: Parents are nearly unanimous in feeling responsible for their children's sex education and wanting their children to have a family with a loving and committed partner (Akers et al., 2010; Wilson et al., 2010a, 2010b; Byers and Sears, 2012). Are most parents talking to their children about sex? Not as much as they should, according to researchers, adolescents, and parents themselves, and the discussions are often gendered.

By age 18, almost 97 percent of U.S. teenagers have received some formal sex education, but usually not from parents (Martinez et al., 2010). As *Figure 7.2* shows, female and male teenagers (although the percentages are low) are almost equally likely to have talked to their parents about STDs and how to prevent HIV/AIDS. However, parents are more likely to talk to their daughters than sons about abstinence ("How to say no to sex"), birth control methods, and where to get birth control. Only 38 percent of teen boys have talked to their parents about how to use a condom. We'll address the reasons for the gender differences shortly, but such data suggest that females, not males, are responsible for preventing pregnancy.

Many parents' sexuality education, even early in childhood, is gendered. A survey of U.S. mothers of 3- to 6-year-old children found that mothers were more likely to tell their daughters than sons that sex and having babies should be confined to marriage, thereby teaching girls a stricter "moral standard" (Martin and Luke, 2010). When children are preteenagers (aged 10 to 12), parents become more concerned about external threats to their children's healthy sexual development. They worry about the ready accessibility of pornography on the Internet and cable TV, negative role models on TV, sexting, sexual predators, the explicit sexual content of music, video games, and advertising. Many parents also worry about peer pressure to engage in sexual behavior at increasingly younger ages. Black parents, in particular, are concerned that their daughters, who are reaching puberty at a young age, as you saw earlier, are attracting inappropriate attention from older boys and men (Wilson et al., 2010a).

To counter the negative effects of the media and peer pressure, parents often rely on several strategies in talking to their preteens about sex. Some of the most common techniques include creating opportunities to talk about sex (as when watching TV), maintaining a good relationship with their children, talking about

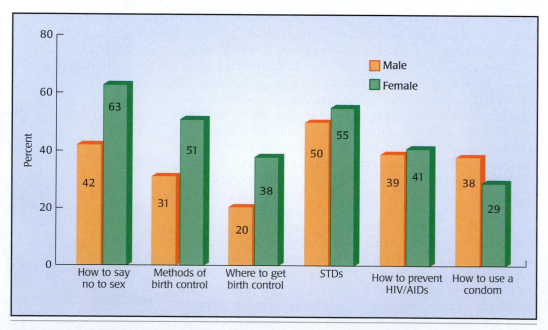

FIGURE 7.2 **U.S. Teenagers Who Talked with a Parent about Sex, by Topic and Sex, 2006–2008**
Source: Martinez et al., 2010, Figure 4.

what is happening in sex education classes, and using resources such as books and religious teachings that they read and discuss (Wilson et al., 2010a).

Generally, many parents believe that teens, but *not* theirs, are sexually active. Thus, it's not necessary to talk about sex. Parents also encounter teen resistance because the adolescents believe they know what they're doing, are embarrassed about sex discussions, and/or don't want parents to interfere in their lives (Elliot, 2012). Specifically, however, and as *Table 7.2* shows, many parents don't talk about sex because of their, and not their children's, attitudes and expectations.

Peers and Siblings

Except for Asian youth, peers are among the most common sources of information about sex, and females are more likely than males to discuss sexual issues, especially contraception, with their close girlfriends (Holt et al., 2003; Jones and Biddlecom, 2011b). Because friends are often misinformed about sex, however, the instruction may be similar to the blind leading the blind. As you saw earlier, many adolescents know little about topics such as women's fertile periods and the proper usage of contraceptives.

Adolescents who have problematic relationships with their parents tend to compensate by seeking out supportive friends. If the friends engage in deviant behavior, such as getting drunk or high, adolescents are likely to do the same, increasing their likelihood of risky sexual behavior (Killoren et al., 2011).

Even though they aren't the best sources of information, peers can be helpful. Often they are more open than parents about discussing sex,

TABLE 7.2	Why Many Parents Don't Talk to Their Children about Sex
Reasons	**Examples**
Belief that children aren't ready to hear about sex	"I don't want to plant ideas in my child's head if she or he isn't thinking about sex," "I don't want to destroy my child's innocence"
Not knowing how to talk about sex	"I don't know how to start conversations about sex," "I might not be able to answer questions about things like STDs"
Parents' lack of time or energy	"I'm a single parent who works all day, and don't have the time to talk to my kids about sex," "My wife and I work, and spend most of our time on family chores"
Children's not wanting to discuss sex	"Our kids don't want to talk about sex," "Our kids already think they know it all and their parents are old-fashioned and out of touch with what's going on"
Parents' embarrassment or discomfort	"My parents never talked to me when I was a kid, so I find it difficult to talk about sex with my children," "If my kids ask, I don't want to tell them about my 'wild days' as a teenager when I used drugs and/or had many sexual partners," "I don't feel comfortable in discussing topics such as masturbation"
Parents haven't thought about needing to discuss sex	"I've just never thought about discussing sex with my kids because they have sex education classes in school"
Dysfunction in some families	"I'm not around much of the time because I do drugs," "My partner is in jail and the kids are in foster homes"
Language and cultural barriers between parents and children	"I have a hard time talking to my kids because I speak little English, and they speak little Spanish," "My kids want to be independent instead of following my country's traditions of parents being an authority"
Parents' fears that talking about sexuality might send mixed messages	"I don't want my daughter to have sex or get pregnant, but if I teach her about contraceptives, she might think that sex is OK," "If I discuss using condoms with my son, he might assume that having sex is OK"
Parents' lack of knowledge about some topics	"I've told my son to use condoms, but I don't know what birth control my daughter can use besides the pill," "I don't know too much about STDs"

Sources: Based on Eisenberg et al., 2004; Akers et al., 2010; Wilson et al., 2010a, 2010b; Byers and Sears, 2012.

including telling their less sexually experienced friends to use condoms. College students who feel distant with their parents cite friends as important sources of support and learning when they've regretted their sexual decision making, such as having unprotected sex or having sex with people they barely know (Allen et al., 2008; Jones and Biddlecom, 2011c).

Adolescents are least likely to learn about sex from their brothers and sisters, but older siblings can play an important role in their younger siblings' sexuality. Older siblings may not tell their younger brothers and sisters to "just say no" to sex, but can play a beneficial role in advising their younger siblings, especially boys, to use condoms (Holt et al., 2003; Kowal and Blinn-Pike, 2004).

Religion

When sociologists and other social scientists study people's religious behavior, they measure *religiosity*, the way people demonstrate their religious beliefs. The measures include how often people attend religious services, how involved they are in religious activities, and whether they think their religion actually influences their everyday decisions.

Religious parents who monitor their children's activities and have strong parent–child relationships tend to delay their children's sexual activity. However, parents with similar characteristics who aren't religious have the same effects (Manlove et al., 2008; Longmore et al., 2009).

Except for a very small minority of evangelical college students who attend religious institutions, most college students keep religion and sex separate. Others redefine sex. For example, evangelical students who have had oral or anal sex still consider themselves virgins because they view such behaviors as not "real sex" (Freitas, 2008).

A national study of American teenagers concluded that there is little association between religiosity and sexual behavior. For example, 80 percent of teenagers who identified themselves as evangelical or born-again Christians said that sex should be saved for marriage. However, they were more likely than their mainline Protestant, Jewish, or Catholic counterparts to lose their virginity, and at a younger age (Regnerus, 2007).

Nationally, evangelicals agree that premarital sex is a sin, but among those who have never been married, 42 percent of adolescents and almost 80 percent of those aged 20 to 24 have had sex. Of those who accidentally get pregnant, 30 percent get an abortion (The National Campaign . . . , 2010; Jones and Dreweke, 2011). Often, then, religion seems to affect attitudes more than behavior.

The Media and Popular Culture

Media are among the most powerful forces in young Americans' lives today. Among all 8- to 18-year-olds, the average amount of time spent using media increased from less than 6½ hours a day in 1999 to more than 8½ hours a day in 2009 (Rideout et al., 2010). Almost 9 hours a day is longer than most adults spend at work each day. Television, movies, music, magazines, video games, songs, and websites offer a constant stream of messages about a number of topics, including sex. Let's look at a few of these sources.

Since you asked . . .

- Does sex-saturated media content affect young people's behavior?

MOVIES   Rating systems aren't strictly enforced (few moviegoers are stopped from seeing R-rated films, for example), and X-rated videos are accessible to people in most age groups. Also, film ratings have become more lenient. Since 1992, many films that were rated PG-13 ("Parents strongly cautioned") are now rated PG ("Parental guidance suggested"). This "ratings creep" has increased the

likelihood that adolescents and even young children see sexual images in movies (Thompson and Yokota, 2004).

You learned earlier that, among the top-grossing films, young females are far more likely than their male counterparts to be sexualized. Much sexual content may not register with some young adolescents, but it shapes sexual decision making by reinforcing permissive sexual norms. For example, the emphasis on casual sex sends the message that there is no connection between sex and commitment (Brown et al., 2002; Regnerus and Uecker, 2011).

TELEVISION AND VIDEO GAMES Sex is a staple on most television shows. Some form of sexual content, including sexual intercourse, appears in 70 percent of all television shows, up from 56 percent in 1998. Adolescents' exposure to sexual imagery is even more common in music videos (Kunkel et al., 2005; Roberts et al., 2009).

In 2011, the Supreme Court ruled (7–2 in *Brown v. Entertainment Merchants Association*) that video games, even ultraviolent ones, that are sold to minors are protected by the First Amendment's guarantee of free speech. The majority of the justices said that none of the scientific studies *prove* that violent games *cause* minors to act aggressively, and that parents, not the government, should decide what is appropriate for their children (Schiesel, 2011; Walls, 2011).

The video game industry was jubilant over the decision. Many parents and lawmakers, on the other hand, agreed with one of the dissenting justices that it makes no sense to forbid selling a 13-year-old boy a magazine with an image of a nude woman, but not an interactive video game in which the same boy "actively . . . binds and gags the woman, then tortures and kills her" (Barnes, 2011: A1; see also Chapter 5).

THE INTERNET You'll see in the next section that comprehensive school-based sex education has declined. As a result, many adolescents have turned to the Internet for sexual health information. The bad news is that of 177 sexual health websites that teens turn to, 46 percent of those addressing contraception and 35 percent of those discussing abortion contain inaccurate information (Buhi et al., 2010).

The good news is that many adolescents are becoming more savvy in evaluating websites. A qualitative study of 58 high school juniors and seniors found that only 5 of the interviewees believed that the Internet is an accurate source of information about sex. Teens were wary of online sites because "anyone can make up a website," including Wikipedia, and believed, correctly, that "sex sells stuff." Some of the strategies that the teens used included focusing on .org, .edu, and .gov sites, and those associated with health or medical sources (e.g., WebMD or public health departments) (Jones and Biddlecom, 2011b).

School-Based Sex Education

You've seen that many parents don't talk to their children about sex, and that the media and popular culture deluge us with unrealistic portrayals of sexuality. Consequently, many schools and community groups have assumed responsibility for teaching children and adolescents about sex.

About 90 percent of parents approve of schools' providing a *comprehensive sexuality education* (CSE). These programs start in kindergarten and continue through twelfth grade. They include age-appropriate, medically accurate information on a broad number of topics, including anatomy, relationships, abstinence, contraception, and disease prevention.

Even though only 10 percent of parents want an abstinence-only curriculum in public schools, 26 states require schools to emphasize abstinence. Especially in the South, most school districts have chosen abstinence-only curricula (Boonstra, 2009; Landry et al., 2011; Guttmacher Institute, 2012).

In 2001, the Bush administration established a federal program to fund abstinence-only curricula, which has cost more than $1 billion so far. President Obama promised to shift abstinence-only programs to teen pregnancy prevention programs, but this

Two of MTV's most popular reality shows have been *16 and Pregnant* and *Teen Mom*. The producers say that the goal of both programs is to decrease teen pregnancy by showing the harmful effects of not using protection or birth control and the resulting struggles in raising a baby. Critics argue that the shows glamorize teen pregnancy and motherhood, make the teen moms instant celebrities, and ignore the long-term negative impact on the mothers' and children's healthy social development (Thompson, 2010). What do *you* think?

Since you asked . . .
- Should parents or schools be responsible for sex education?

 Watch on MySocLab

Video: Sexuality Education Debate

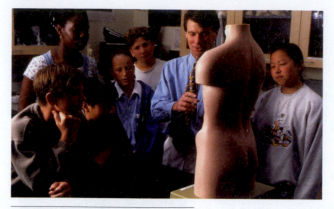

This teacher is talking to ninth-graders about sexually transmitted diseases and contraception. Should teachers provide this information? Or should parents be responsible for educating their children about sexuality?

MAKING CONNECTIONS

- Did your home life influence your sexual behavior or sexual decision making?
- What kind of sex education classes, if any, did you have in elementary, middle, and high school? Did the classes affect your sexual behavior?
- Do you think it's realistic to expect people to remain virgins if they marry in their twenties or thirties?

 Watch on MySocLab

Video: Flirting

hasn't happened. In 2012, Congress approved $180 million for CSE curricula and $55 million for abstinence-only programs. The latter allocation is modest compared with the past, but its proponents believe that "it could open the door to greater amounts in the future" (Boonstra, 2012: 6).

Abstinence-only advocates argue that "Just say no" programs to delay sex until marriage work. However, a number of recent and nationally representative studies show that this isn't the case. For example,

- Among adolescents who took virginity pledges, between 82 percent and 88 percent who were sexually active a year later denied having taken the pledge (Rosenbaum, 2009; Thomas, 2009).

- Among 15- to 19-years-olds, abstinence-only education didn't reduce the likelihood of having premarital sex; those who received a CSE program had a lower risk of unintended pregnancies and STDs (Kohler et al., 2008; Guttmacher Institute, 2012; Hall et al., 2012).

- A review of 56 studies that evaluated abstinence-only and CSE programs found that most abstinence-only programs didn't delay initiation of sex; two-thirds of the CSE programs both delayed young people's initiation of sex and increased condom and contraceptive use (Kirby, 2008; see also Trenholm et al., 2008).

- In states with predominantly abstinence-only programs—almost all are in the South—unintended teen pregnancy rates are almost twice as high as those of states with a CSE curriculum (SIECUS, 2011; Beadle, 2012; Conklin, 2012).

Which sex education programs are most effective? Those that are comprehensive, provide accurate information on reproduction, emphasize abstinence but also discuss condoms and other birth control methods, begin in elementary school before adolescents engage in sexual intercourse, and target high-risk groups of youth who live in poor neighborhoods (Mueller et al., 2008; Sullivan, 2009).

7.4 Describe at least four types of sexual behaviors.

Sexual Behaviors

Americans—young, old, and in-between—engage in sexual behaviors that include 41 different combinations of sex acts (Herbenick et al., 2010a). Besides intercourse, sex encompasses many other behaviors, including flirting, kissing, autoeroticism, and oral and anal sex.

Flirting

Flirting, or acting amorously without serious intentions, is usually one of the first steps to capture another person's interest. Whether flirting is nonverbal (such as sustained eye contact) or verbal (such as "I love talking to you"), it signals sexual interest. One of the dangers of flirting is that the intentions may be misinterpreted. Men are more likely than women to mistake being friendly as being seductive, which sometimes results in men sexually harassing women (Farris et al., 2008; Rutter and Schwartz, 2012).

Kissing

Many countries in the Middle East forbid public physical contact, including kissing, between women and men. In some parts of India, public kissing brings a $12 fine. Kissing is considered a "highly erotic act" that couples shouldn't

experience until they're married. Government officials believe that public kissing encourages permissive Western cultural norms regarding sexual behavior. A city mayor in central Mexico had to retract an edict, after numerous protests, that violators of a public-kissing ban would be punished (Sappenfield, 2007; Ellingwood, 2009).

In the United States, public kissing is acceptable (or at least tolerated) in public spaces such as stores, restaurants, or on the street. Thus, unlike some other societies, Americans see kissing in public as perhaps in bad taste but normal in expressing one's sexuality.

Autoeroticism

Autoeroticism refers to arousal of sexual feeling without an external stimulus. Two of the most common forms of autoeroticism are sexual fantasies and masturbation.

autoeroticism Arousal of sexual feeling without an external stimulus.

SEXUAL FANTASIES   Most of us, but men more than women, have *sexual fantasies*—mental images of sexual activities. Sexual fantasies often mirror gender roles (see Chapter 5). Women's fantasies, for example, are typically romantic, passive, and submissive. Men are more likely to fantasize about a large number of partners and casual sexual encounters (Battan, 1992; Geer and Manguno-Mire, 1996).

Sexual fantasies are emotionally and psychologically healthy. They can provide a safety valve for pent-up feelings or a harmless escape from boring, everyday routines, such as "having sex on the 50-yard line at a sold-out football game" (Patterson and Kim, 1991: 79). Fantasies can also boost our self-image because we don't have to worry about penis or breast size, physical attractiveness, height, or weight. Because we have total control in producing and directing a fantasy, we can change or stop it whenever we want (Masters et al., 1992).

MASTURBATION   When asked what sex would be like in the future, comedian Robin Williams replied, "It's going to be you—and you." **Masturbation** is sexual self-pleasuring that involves some form of direct physical stimulation. It may or may not result in orgasm, but it typically includes rubbing, stroking, fondling, squeezing, or otherwise stimulating the genitals. It can also involve self-stimulation of other body parts, such as the breasts, the inner thighs, or the anus. Most masturbation is solo, but can also include a partner (mutual masturbation).

Masturbation often begins in childhood and continues throughout life. Prepubertal children may stimulate themselves without realizing that what they're doing is sexual. For example, one girl learned when she was 8 years old that she could produce an "absolutely terrific feeling" by squeezing her thighs together (Nass et al., 1981). Thus, many children discover masturbation accidentally.

Although often stigmatized, masturbation is the most common of all sex acts. Across almost all age groups, masturbation is more common among men than women (see *Table 7.3*). There may be several reasons for the gender differences: Men are more likely than women to consume pornography and to masturbate while doing so; men are freed from the emotional connections that many women seek; men often masturbate to supplement their sexual lives, whereas women do so to substitute for sex; and social norms still include the idea that "nice girls don't touch themselves" (see Rutter and Schwartz, 2012).

Like sexual fantasies, masturbation fulfills several needs: It can relieve sexual tension, provide a safe means of sexual experimentation (avoiding disease and unwanted pregnancy), and ultimately transfer learning about one's sexuality to two-person lovemaking. Masturbation can be as sexually satisfying as intercourse, and doesn't hinder the development of social relationships during young adulthood or create problems in a marriage (Leitenberg et al., 1993; Kelly, 1994).

masturbation Sexual self-pleasuring that involves some form of direct physical stimulation.

Since you asked . . .
• Is masturbation abnormal?

TABLE 7.3	How Often Single and Married Americans Masturbate, by Age and Sex				
Percentage who report masturbating "A few times per month to weekly"					
	Males			**Females**	
Age Groups	Single	Married	Single	Married
18–24	23%	30%	24%	28%
25–29	31	23	20	16
30–39	32	25	23	20
40–49	29	25	22	14
50–59	28	17	15	10
60–69	20	20	13	6
70 and older	23	11	5	1

Sources: Based on Herbenick et al., 2010c, Table 6, and Reece et al., 2010, Table 6.

Heterosexual Oral, Anal, and Vaginal Sex

In a study of college students, a large majority said that penile-vaginal intercourse and penile-anal intercourse (98 percent and 78 percent, respectively) constituted sex, but only 20 percent believed the same was true of oral-genital contact (Hans et al., 2010). Many people assume that sexual intercourse refers to heterosexual, vaginal-penile penetration, but the term applies to any sort of sexual coupling, including oral and anal, and between opposite-sex and same-sex partners. *Coitus* specifically means penile-vaginal intercourse and is therefore a heterosexual behavior. Most cultures around the world commonly refer to coitus as *sexual intercourse*, a more general term for vaginal intercourse.

fellatio Oral stimulation of a man's penis.

cunnilingus Oral stimulation of a woman's genitals.

There are two types of *oral sex*. **Fellatio** (from the Latin word for "suck") is oral stimulation of a man's penis. **Cunnilingus** (from the Latin words for "vulva" and "tongue") is oral stimulation of a woman's genitals. Fellatio and cunnilingus can be performed singly or simultaneously. Simultaneous oral sex is sometimes called "69," indicating the physical positions of the partners. *Anal sex* is the manual stimulation of the rectum that involves inserting a penis, finger, dildo (penis-shaped object), or vibrator.

VARIATIONS BY GENDER AND AGE By the eighth grade, 9 percent of U.S. middle-schoolers under age 15 have had vaginal intercourse, and 8 percent have had oral sex (De Rosa et al., 2010). Among those ages 15 to 19, almost half have had oral sex and about 13 percent have had anal sex (see *Figure 7.3*). Such data show that many teens are engaging in a range of sexual activities rather than substituting one for another (Kaiser Family Foundation, 2008; Lindberg et al., 2008).

The number of teens who have had oral but no vaginal sex has increased since 2002 (Chandra et al., 2011). Adolescents who have oral sex prior to first-time vaginal intercourse may be doing so because they view oral sex as "not really sex." Rather, they view it as a way to delay vaginal intercourse, to maintain one's virginity (especially among those who are religious), and to avoid the risk of pregnancy and STDs (Regnerus and Uecker, 2011; Copen et al., 2012).

By age 24, larger numbers of women and men have had anal sex, but vaginal intercourse and oral sex rates are the most common. By age 44, males are more likely than females to have had anal sex, but vaginal intercourse is the most common type of sexual activity (see *Figure 7.3*). Such data show that there are

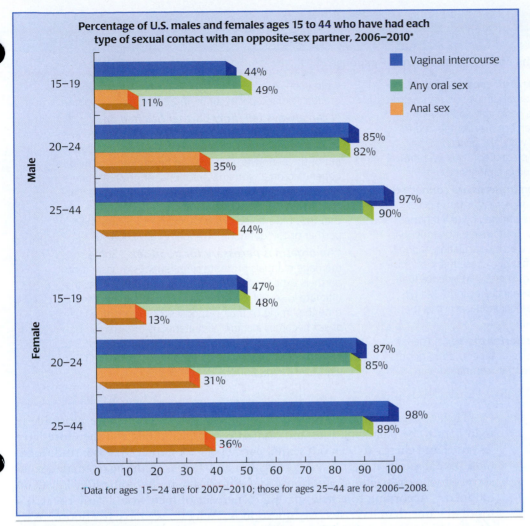

Percentage of U.S. males and females ages 15 to 44 who have had each type of sexual contact with an opposite-sex partner, 2006–2010*

Legend:
- Vaginal intercourse
- Any oral sex
- Anal sex

Male:
- 15–19: 44%, 49%, 11%
- 20–24: 85%, 82%, 35%
- 25–44: 97%, 90%, 44%

Female:
- 15–19: 47%, 48%, 13%
- 20–24: 87%, 85%, 31%
- 25–44: 98%, 89%, 36%

*Data for ages 15–24 are for 2007–2010; those for ages 25–44 are for 2006–2008.

FIGURE 7.3 Types of Sexual Contact
Sources: Based on Chandra et al., 2011, Tables 5 and 6; Copen et al., 2012, Table 1.

few gender differences across sexual experiences and that both men and women engage in diverse sexual behaviors throughout adulthood.

Some people find oral and anal sex pleasurable, whereas others find it revolting. According to a female college student, for example, oral sex is like "blowing your nose in my mouth" (Wade and Cirese, 1991: 334). Even when people are disgusted, they provide or receive oral or anal sex for many reasons such as being drunk, direct and constant pressure from or wanting to please a partner, a fear that a partner will end a relationship if his or her requests are rejected, and avoiding conflict or tension that saying no might generate (Regnerus and Uecker, 2011).

Oral and anal sex, like other sexual behaviors, depend on personal preference. Many people don't realize, however, as you'll see later in this chapter, that sexual diseases can be transmitted orally and anally, resulting in syphilis, gonorrhea, and herpes, as well as the papilloma virus, which can cause cervical cancer.

SEX AND THE GENDER GAP There isn't a large gender gap in terms of engaging in oral, anal, and vaginal intercourse for people aged 15 to 44 (see *Figure 7.3*), but is there a gap for the number of sexual partners? A recent national study found that, by age 44, and on average, men (6 percent) reported having had twice as many sexual relationships with opposite-sex partners as women (3 percent). Also, by age 44, many more men (21 percent) than women (8 percent) reported at least 15 sex partners (Chandra et al., 2011).

ASK YOURSELF

What Are Some of the Myths about Sex and Sexual Response?

- **"Withdrawal is an effective birth control method."** In males, the first responses to sexual stimulation are swelling and erection of the penis. The penis may emit several drops of fluid that aren't semen but may contain sperm cells. If this fluid is discharged while the penis is in the vagina, the woman can be impregnated. Thus, withdrawal before ejaculation can still result in a pregnancy.

- **"Erections, ejaculations, and orgasms are connected."** Penile erections, ejaculations, and orgasms don't occur simultaneously because they're affected by different neurological and vascular systems. Thus, men who argue that a penile erection must be followed by ejaculation during sexual intercourse lest they suffer dire consequences ("blue balls") are, quite simply, wrong. There's no evidence that any man has ever died of a "terminal erection." Many partners are fully satisfied by tender sexual activities that don't necessarily include orgasm.

- **"The bigger the penis, the better the sex."** There's no association between the size of a penis and "good sex." There's also no evidence that, compared with white men, African American men have larger penises, greater sexual capacity, or an insatiable sexual appetite.

- **"I can always tell if my partner has had an orgasm."** Except in the movies, women's orgasms are rarely accompanied by asthmatic breathing and clutching of the bedposts. Orgasm can be explosive or mild, depending on a woman's emotional or physical state, stress, alcohol consumption, and a variety of other factors. Nearly half of women and 11 percent of men say that they have faked orgasms, mainly to please their partner or to "get done" (Langer et al., 2004).

- **"An orgasm is necessary for good sex."** Some marriage manuals promote simultaneous orgasm (both partners experiencing orgasm at the same time) as the ultimate in sexual pleasure. Many people try to fine-tune the timing of their responses, but working so hard at sex becomes a chore. Simultaneous orgasm can be satisfying, but so are independent orgasms. About 5 to 10 percent of women never experience an orgasm but enjoy sex (Lloyd, 2005).

These differences are largely due to gender roles. Women are more likely than men to be balancing jobs and domestic responsibilities and therefore have less time and energy to seek out sexual partners (see Chapter 5). Also, traditional male sexual scripts focus on sex as recreational, whereas traditional female sexual scripts focus on feelings, emotions, and commitment. As comedian Jay Leno quipped, "According to a new survey, 76 percent of men would rather watch a football game than have sex. My question is, 'Why do we have to choose? Why do you think they invented halftime?'"

SOME MYTHS ABOUT SEX AND SEXUAL RESPONSE   Fantasies, sounds, smells, touch, images, and a variety of other stimuli can arouse our sexual feelings. **Sexual response** is our physiological reaction to sexual stimulation. Sexual response can vary greatly by age, gender, and health. Despite these variations, there are a number of myths about sex and sexual response that many people believe (see "What Are Some of the Myths about Sex and Sexual Response?").

sexual response A physiological reaction to sexual stimulation.

7.5 Describe the prevalence, sexual behaviors, and societal reactions to lesbian, gay, bisexual, and transgender sex.

 Watch on MySocLab

Video: Being Gay in the U.S.

Lesbian, Gay, Bisexual, and Transgender Sex

Human sexuality ranges along a continuum (see *Figure 7.1* earlier in the chapter). There's also considerable variation within the LGBT community in terms of sexual identity, sexual attraction, sexual behavior, and public reactions.

Prevalence

How many LGBT people are there in the United States? No one knows for sure because, among other reasons, researchers define and measure sexual orientation differently, respondents may not be willing to disclose this information, and people who engage in same-sex behavior often identify themselves as straight (Gates, 2011a, 2011b). Americans estimate that 25 percent of the population

is gay or lesbian (Morales, 2011; Taylor et al., 2013). In contrast, a recent national study found that only about 3.5 percent of Americans identified themselves as LGBT (Gates and Newport, 2012). This population is split nearly evenly between lesbians/gays and bisexuals, women are more likely than men to be bisexual, and 0.3 percent is transgender (see *Figure 7.4*).

Sexual Behaviors

Fewer than 4 percent of Americans identify themselves as LGBT, but 15 percent of American women and 5 percent of men have been sexually attracted to the same sex. Twice as many females (12 percent) as males (6 percent) have had same-sex physical contact. And, among those aged 15 to 21 who identify themselves as straight, 11 percent of females and 4 percent of males have had same-sex sexual contact (Chandra et al., 2011; McCabe et al., 2011). Thus, as noted earlier, sexual identity, attraction, and behavior overlap.

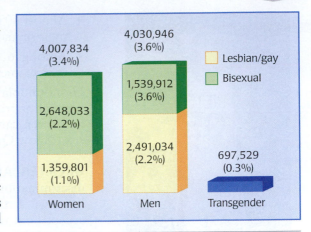

FIGURE 7.4 Estimated Percent and Number of U.S. Adults Who Identify As LGBT
Source: Gates, 2011a, Figure 5.

Societal Reactions to Homosexuality

Australian passports now designate "M" for male, "F" for female, and "X" for transgender ("Australian Passports . . . ," 2011). In India, the 2011 national census for the first time offered three options: male, female, or a "third sex" that includes LGBTs (Cohn, 2011). And in Thailand, which has the world's biggest transsexual population, an airline has recently recruited "third sex" flight attendants (Mutzabaugh, 2011).

These examples show that some attitudes are changing, but many countries in Asia, Africa, and the Middle East don't tolerate LGBTs (Samuels, 2008; Williams and Maher, 2009; Kuai, 2011; IDAHO Committee, 2012). Homosexuals, particularly gay men, may be legally tortured, stoned, imprisoned, or killed. In Africa, four nations impose a death penalty on gay men, and 20 countries may imprison gay men and lesbians from a month to a lifetime (Baldauf, 2010). In the United States, societal reactions range from homophobia to growing acceptance of gays and lesbians.

HOMOPHOBIA According to one scholar, what makes gay people different from others is that "we are discriminated against, mistreated, [and] regarded as sick or perverted" (Halperin, 2012: B17). Homophobia often takes the form of *gay bashing*: threats, assaults, or acts of violence directed at homosexuals. Of the more than 6,200 hate crimes reported to U.S. law enforcement agencies in 2011, almost 21 percent of the victims were LGBT, but much gay bashing isn't reported (Federal Bureau of Investigation, 2012).

There are many other manifestations of homophobia in the United States. According to national surveys, for example,

- Some parents have blocked health curricula that discuss homosexuality in public schools; others have demanded kindergarten teachers to stop using books that contain pictures of same-sex parents (Simon, 2005; Doyle, 2012).

- Gay and lesbian teens in grades 7 through 12 were 40 percent more likely than their straight peers to be punished by schools, police, and the courts for similar misbehavior such as truancy, drinking, shoplifting, burglary, selling drugs, and physical violence (Himmelstein and Brückner, 2011).

- Lesbian, gay, bisexual, and transgender sex students ages 13 to 17 were twice as likely as their straight peers to be assaulted, harassed, shoved, or kicked at school (Human Rights Campaign, 2012).

Since you asked . . .
- Are Americans homophobic?

In mid-2013, the Washington Wizards' Jason Collins appeared on the cover of *Sports Illustrated*. "I'm a 34-year-old NBA center, I'm black, and I'm gay," he wrote (Collins and Lidz, 2013: 34). Why do you think his coming out received national coverage?

- Almost 60 percent of LGBT adults have been subjected to slurs or jokes about their sexual orientation (Taylor et al., 2013).
- Among 6,500 transgender people, 90 percent experienced harassment, mistreatment, or discrimination on the job (Grant et al., 2011).

Homophobia is widespread, but are many of us hypocrites? For example, a number of prominent anti-gay conservative preachers, ministers, and lawmakers have been caught in gay sex scandals that included paying male prostitutes for sex ("How Queer Is That?" 2010).

GREATER ACCEPTANCE About 63 percent of Americans believe that discrimination against gays and lesbians is a problem (Jones, 2012). In 2013, however, a record number of Americans, 59 percent, said that society should accept homosexuality (up from 46 percent in 1994); and 81 percent of those younger than age 30 felt this way (Cohen, 2013; Newport and Himelfarb, 2013). Numerous municipal jurisdictions, corporations, and smaller companies now extend more health care and other benefits to gay and lesbian employees and their partners than to unmarried heterosexuals who live together. More states and the U.S. Supreme Court have legalized same-sex marriages (a topic we'll discuss in Chapter 10), and large numbers of Americans support policies that give lesbians and gays equal rights in the workplace and elsewhere (see *Figure 7.5*).

There are many other indicators of greater LGBT acceptance. In 2012, a year after the military dropped its "don't ask, don't tell" policy for gay service members, the Army promoted the first openly gay female officer to brigadier general. In 2013, the Pentagon added benefits for same-sex partners, including use of numerous family-oriented facilities and services on U.S. military bases and pay if one is taken prisoner or missing in action (Wald, 2012; Cloud, 2013). More than 50 college campuses have gender-neutral housing that also accommodates transgender students (Tilsley, 2010). More than 3,000 colleges and universities have LGBT student clubs, and many actively recruit gay students (Lipka, 2011). And, since the mid-1990s, a multitude of LGBT characters have appeared in leading and supporting roles on prime-time TV in popular programs such as *The Simpsons*, *Grey's Anatomy*, *Desperate Housewives*, *The Office*, *The Good Wife*, *Glee*, *Modern Family*, *Smash*, and *American Dad* (Gay and Lesbian Alliance Against Defamation, 2012).

MAKING CONNECTIONS

- How would you feel if your best friend told you she or he was gay? What if one of your parents did so? Your brother or sister? Your adolescent daughter or son? Or, if you're gay and have come out, how did your family and friends react?

- Are television programs with LGBT characters a sign of progress? Or offensive?

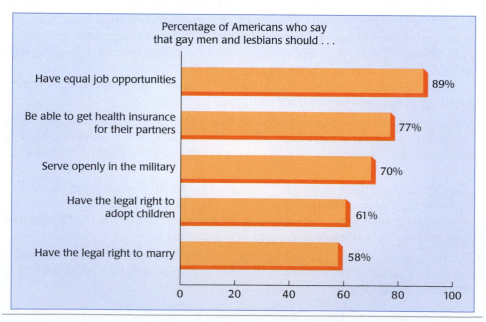

Percentage of Americans who say that gay men and lesbians should . . .

Have equal job opportunities	89%
Be able to get health insurance for their partners	77%
Serve openly in the military	70%
Have the legal right to adopt children	61%
Have the legal right to marry	58%

FIGURE 7.5 Attitudes about Gay and Lesbian Rights
Sources: Based on "Gay and Lesbian Rights," 2012; Cohen, 2013.

Sexuality throughout Life

We may love dozens of people over our lifetime, but we usually have sex with very few of them. We might also have sex with people we don't love. There is also another option: abstinence.

Virginity and Abstinence

A *virgin* is someone who has never experienced sexual intercourse. About 58 percent of never-married adolescents aged 15 to 19 report never having had sexual intercourse, an increase from 46 percent in 1991 (Eaton et al., 2008; Martinez et al., 2011). There are many factors associated with early sexual intercourse among adolescents (see *Table 7.4*). But why are some teens with similar characteristics more likely to abstain than others? And why do adults go without sex?

WHY TEENS ABSTAIN FROM SEXUAL INTERCOURSE There are several possible explanations for the decline of teen sexual intercourse since the early 1990s. First, values and practical considerations affect decisions about sex. Among teenagers ages 15 to 19, the most important reason (for 41 percent of females and 31 percent of males) is that sexual intercourse is "against my religion or morals." The next two reasons for females, and in order of priority, are "don't want to get pregnant" and "haven't found the right person yet." For males, the second most common reason was not having found the right person yet, followed by not wanting to get a female pregnant (Martinez et al., 2011).

Second, almost half of adolescents believe that a wide range of other sexual behaviors—including genital touching and oral and anal sex—aren't "really sex." Many say they're virgins and don't see themselves as violating their morals or religious views about abstaining from sex until marriage (Bersamin et al., 2007; Masters et al., 2008). Furthermore, some teenagers define themselves as virgins because they haven't had sexual intercourse *recently* (Jones and Biddlecom, 2011c). In effect, then, many adolescents are having sex, but not sexual intercourse.

Third, family dynamics—such as child–parent connectedness and good communication—may delay sexual initiation. As you saw earlier, regardless of religiosity, parents who monitor their children's activities and have

During a purity ball, girls as young as age 4 promise their dads to remain virgins and fathers vow to protect their daughters' chastity until marriage. Proponents maintain that the balls are held in 48 states every year, but there are no accurate numbers (Oppenheimer, 2012). Why aren't there purity balls or similar events for boys?

TABLE 7.4	Factors Associated with Adolescents' Early Sexual Intercourse

- Alcohol or other drug use
- Delinquent behavior
- Dating before age 16 or involvement in a committed relationship
- Having a low grade-point average or dropping out of school
- Living with one parent
- Mother had a first child before age 20
- Mother isn't a college graduate
- Parental divorce during adolescence
- Poverty
- Physical or sexual abuse at home or by relatives
- Minimal parental monitoring of teens' activities and friends
- Permissive parental values toward sex, including a parent who cohabits or sleeps with overnight guests
- Lack of neighborhood monitoring of adolescents, especially teens

Source: Based on author's compilation of studies cited in this chapter.

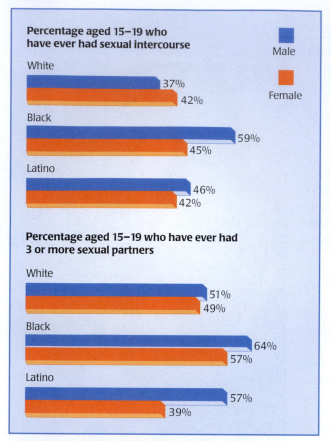

Percentage aged 15–19 who have ever had sexual intercourse

White
- Male 37%
- Female 42%

Black
- Male 59%
- Female 45%

Latino
- Male 46%
- Female 42%

Percentage aged 15–19 who have ever had 3 or more sexual partners

White
- Male 51%
- Female 49%

Black
- Male 64%
- Female 57%

Latino
- Male 57%
- Female 39%

Male (blue) / Female (orange)

FIGURE 7.6 **U.S. Sexually Experienced Teens, 2010**
Note: The data are for never-married teenagers. For males, the median number of female partners was 1.8; for females, the median number of male partners was 1.4.
Source: Based on Martinez et al., 2011, Tables I, VII, and VIII.

Watch on MySocLab

Video: Adolescent Sexuality

strong parent–child relationships can delay their children's first sexual intercourse.

WHY ADULTS ABSTAIN FROM SEXUAL INTERCOURSE

Data on lifetime adult abstinence is limited, but by age 44, only 0.4 percent of women and 1.3 percent of men haven't had sexual intercourse with an opposite-sex partner (Chandra et al., 2011). Major reasons for adult abstinence include not having a partner, chronic illness, mental-health problems, sexual dysfunctions, and a partner's infidelity. From a social exchange perspective, partners remain in celibate relationships because companionship, love, and friendship are more important than sexual activity (Donnelly and Burgess, 2008). Unlike food, sleep, and shelter, sex isn't necessary for physical survival. Sexual relationships can be satisfying, but neither virginity nor abstinence is fatal.

Sex and Adolescents

Millions of teens are delaying sexual intercourse, but much larger numbers are sexually active. By age 19, about 43 percent have had sexual intercourse, and the rates are higher for females than males (see *Figure 7.6*). However, white, black, and Latino males are more likely than their female counterparts to have had three or more sexual partners (Martinez et al., 2011).

RELATIONSHIP CHARACTERISTICS

The majority of teenagers ages 15 to 19 have their first sexual intercourse with someone that they describe as "going steady," but the percentage is higher for females (70 percent) than males (56 percent). In the same age group, males (28 percent) are more likely than females (16 percent) to have had first-time sex with someone they had just met or who was just a friend (Martinez et al., 2011). Moreover, sexually active males are more likely than females to have had 3 or more partners (see *Figure 7.6*). Such data suggest that young males are more casual about sex and may go steady to get sex.

UNWANTED AND AMBIVALENT SEXUAL INTERCOURSE

Nationwide, 5 percent of males and 11 percent of females report having had unwanted first-time sex before age 20; most were African Americans. Another 48 percent of females and 33 percent of males said that they had mixed feelings about first-time sex. Black females (57 percent) and black males (40 percent) were the most likely to be ambivalent about first-time sex (Martinez et al., 2011). Unwanted sex, particularly among black youth, is due largely to some of the factors listed in *Table 7.4*. It's not clear, however, whether the ambivalence about first-time sex among teenagers is due to peer pressure, parental factors, environmental variables, cultural values, or a combination of these reasons.

Sex and Singles

Singles constitute diverse groups of people—those who have never married, are widowed and divorced, and who cohabit. There are more singles, more years of being single, and more opportunities to engage in a wide range of sexual relationships that have become acceptable (as you'll see in Chapters 9 and 10). As a result, a common belief is that singles have "swinging" sex lives and an unlimited number of eager partners. Is this true? Or a stereotype?

FREQUENCY OF SEX   Outside of masturbation, how much sex singles have depends on a variety of factors such as gender, age, health, appearance, grooming, and being in a partnered relationship. For example,

Since You Asked . . .
• Do singles have great sex lives?

- Single fat women (those who are defined as "obese" in terms of body mass) are more likely than their male counterparts to date less and have less sex (Gailey, 2012).

- Single men have more sex than women because they are more likely (17 percent) than women (5 percent) to have several sexual partners at the same time (Paik, 2010).

- Among those ages 18 to 94, women and men who live together have sex more frequently than those who are dating (Herbenick et al., 2010c; Reece et al., 2010).

- Among singles ages 18 to 94, those who report better health have a greater interest in sex and are able to have more sex (Herbenick et al., 2010c; Reece et al., 2010).

NUMBER OF SEXUAL PARTNERS   Across all types of relationships, by age 44, men have had more sexual partners than women. As *Table 7.5* shows, and perhaps surprisingly, females and males who are unattached (never married and not cohabiting) are the least likely to have had 15 or more sexual partners (7 percent of women and 15 percent of men). In contrast, those who are divorced but not living with someone have had the highest number of sexual partners.

Among the unmarried, why have never married singles had fewer sexual partners than those who were formerly married? Age is an important factor. Because most Americans have been postponing marriage, divorced people are older and have had more sexual opportunities. The widowed, particularly women, have had fewer sexual partners because they usually become single in their fifties or later and have a small pool of eligible sexual partners. Also, people who live together tend to become partnered at a young age, which results in having fewer sexual partners over a lifetime (see Chapters 9, 15, and 16).

But why the large gender differences across all types of relationships? Because sexual double standards persist, many women may limit the number of sexual partners because they're wary of being seen as "loose" and "sexually easy." For women more so than for men, higher educational attainment is also associated with fewer sexual partners. For example, 12 percent of women with lower education levels have had 15 or more partners compared with 7 percent of college-educated women (Chandra et al., 2011). Many young women who pursue a college degree have less time for sex and "might hold off on sex because they're thinking through potential consequences such as unwanted pregnancies" (Friedman, 2011: 42).

TABLE 7.5	Some Singles Have More Sexual Partners Than Others	
Percentage aged 15–44 who have had 15 or more opposite-sex sexual partners		
	Females	**Males**
Currently married	6% (2.5)*	22% (4.9)
Never married, not cohabiting	7% (3.2)	15% (4.1)
Currently cohabiting	14% (4.6)	32% (7.3)
Formerly married, not cohabiting	19% (5.3)	47% (11.9)

* The figures in parentheses indicate the median number of sexual partners.
Source: Based on Chandra et al., 2011, Tables 3 and 4.

"Over all, I liked it, but I have a couple of notes."

Exchange theory also helps explain gender differences in the number of sexual partners. Among the formerly married who aren't cohabiting, 19 percent of women compared with 47 percent of men have had 15 or more partners (see *Table 7.5*). You'll see in later chapters that women in comparable jobs earn less than men, often leave the workplace to have and raise children, and get custody of children after a divorce but have low child support payments. Low income, family responsibilities, and becoming less physically attractive means that formerly married women have fewer resources to attract sexual partners.

Marital Sex

Generally, higher sexual satisfaction is associated with marital stability (Veroff et al., 1995; Yeh et al., 2006). Married couples may enjoy sex but, over time, may not desire it as much because the sexual context of their relationships changes.

FREQUENCY OF SEX "I got married," says one guy to another, "so that I could have sex three or four times a week." That's funny," says his buddy. "That's why I got divorced." In fact, several national studies show that married couples tend to have sex more frequently than singles and cohabitors. Sexual frequency tends to decrease as people age regardless of marital status, but less so for married couples than others (Herbenick et al., 2010c; Reece et al., 2010). When marital sex decreases in frequency, it's usually because the social context changes.

THE SEXUAL CONTEXT OF MARRIAGE Marital sexual frequency and satisfaction can decrease if people experience nonsexual problems (such as alcoholism and poor communication) in their relationship. As a marriage matures, concerns about earning a living, making a home, and raising a family become more pressing than the desire for lovemaking. About 53 percent of adults say that everyday fatigue saps their sex lives because they're overworked, anxious about the economy, and devote much of their time to raising kids (Consumer-Reports .org, 2009; Yabiku and Gager, 2009).

Sex is especially satisfying if both spouses believe—in terms of social exchange theory—that their rewards and costs are similar (Lawrance and Byers, 1995; Waite and Joyner, 2001). For example, marital commitment, love, and security (rewards) often outweigh fatigue and low sexual frequency (costs). Also, in terms of exchange theory, because sexuality occupies a less prominent role among married couples than singles and cohabitors, lower sexual frequency is less problematic. Marriage involves a broad range of activities that include having and raising children, sharing financial assets, and developing relationships with in-laws (Yabigu and Gager, 2009). Some of these activities may be stressful, but the benefits are equal to or higher than the costs.

Sex during the Middle and Later Years

Since you asked . . .

- How does sexual behavior change as people get older?

A majority of adults ages 45 and older agree that a satisfying sexual relationship is important, but it's not their top priority. Good health, close ties with friends and family, financial security, spiritual well-being, and a good relationship with a partner are more gratifying than a sexual connection (Jacoby, 2005).

SEXUAL ACTIVITY Because married people stay together longer than singles or cohabitants, researchers typically collect data on married couples to examine how sexuality changes over time. Both qualitative and quantitative studies (see Chapter 2) show that as people age, they experience lower levels of sexual desire and some sexual activities, but fairly slowly.

A national study of married Americans ages 57 to 85 found that 29 percent were sexually inactive for 1 year or more. The individuals tended to be wives, people age 63 or older, married a long time (35 years, on average), and college educated; also, the husbands were 11 or more years older than their wives, and one or both partners had physical or mental-health problems (Karraker and Delamater, 2013).

About a third of married couples age 70 and older have vaginal intercourse, and among 75- to 85-year-olds, nearly 23 percent have sex four or more times a month (Lindau et al., 2007; Herbenick et al., 2010c; Reece et al., 2010). In other cases, couples in their seventies and eighties emphasize the importance of emotional intimacy and companionship, and are satisfied with kissing, cuddling, and caressing (Heiman et al., 2011; Lodge and Umberson, 2012).

These and other studies show that sexual activity among older couples declines but doesn't disappear. In long-term marriages, many mid- and later-life couples say that their relationship is closer and more satisfying. According to a husband and wife in their sixties, for example, as they grew older, their marriage changed from being lovers to companions: "You have someone to go through your later years with and share things with . . . sex is a real small part of the relationship" (Lodge and Umberson, 2012: 437–438).

Fred Thompson—a politician, actor, and attorney—married a second wife who was 24 years younger than he was. In this marriage, he fathered a second child at age 64. Why, in contrast, are most men unlikely to marry women twice their age? And how do many people feel about a woman who marries a man half her age?

 Watch on **MySocLab**

Video: Sex and Sexual Dysfunction

HEALTH AND SEXUALITY Poor health affects sexuality throughout the life course. It's not until about age 70, however, that frequency of sexual activity, in both men and women, begins to decline significantly. Lifelong habits (e.g., smoking, alcoholism) can hasten the onset of heart disease and vascular problems. Some illnesses, such as diabetes, as well as some medications for high blood pressure can also decrease sexual interest for both sexes and cause impotence in older men (Lindau et al., 2007).

Despite such difficulties, many older men and women engage in sex and enjoy it. A reporter asked a 90-year-old woman who married an 18-year-old man, "Aren't you afraid of what could happen on the honeymoon? Vigorous lovemaking might bring on injury or even a fatal heart attack!" She smiled and replied, "If he dies, he dies!"

SEXUAL DOUBLE STANDARDS Older men aren't under the same pressure as women to remain young, trim, and attractive. When comparing her own public image with that of her actor husband, the late Paul Newman, actress Joanne Woodward once remarked, "He gets prettier; I get older."

The aging process may enhance a man's desirability because he has more resources and power. In contrast, an older woman may be regarded as an asexual grandmother: "Because attractiveness is associated with feelings of well-being, a perceived decline in appearance can be particularly devastating for women" (Levy, 1994: 295–296).

You learned earlier that midlife women worried about their sex appeal, whereas midlife men felt less masculine because of erectile dysfunctions. Such anxieties decrease for married couples in their seventies and eighties. As lovers become companions, sexual scripts become less important, and sexual double standards diminish or disappear (Lodge and Umberson, 2012).

As people age, the biggest impediment to sex, especially for widows or divorcees, is a partner gap. Because our culture frowns on liaisons and marriages between older women and younger men but approves of matches between older men and younger women, single older women have a small pool of eligible sexual partners (see Chapters 6, 9, and 16).

MAKING CONNECTIONS

- What advice would you give younger people who are pressured by their friends, girlfriends, or boyfriends to have sex?
- What kind of sex do you enjoy most? Least? Why? If you haven't had sexual intercourse yet, do you fantasize about it?
- How would you feel if your widowed 80-year-old parent, grandparent, or great-grandparent had an unmarried sexual partner?

Explore on MySocLab

Activity: Behind Closed Doors: Adultery, Attitudes, and Behaviors

Watch on MySocLab

Video: Infidelity

Sexual Infidelity

About 94 percent of Americans believe that having an extramarital affair is morally wrong, up from only 70 percent in 1970. Most of the remaining 6 percent tend to be men, those with a graduate degree, people who are divorced or separated, and those who admit having cheated on their spouses (Newport, 2009; Carr 2010; Newport and Himelfarb, 2013). People might also be defining sexual infidelity differently.

What Is Sexual Infidelity?

Some people use the terms *affair, infidelity, adultery, unfaithful*, and *extramarital sex* interchangeably. Others define infidelity more broadly as "a breach of trust" and "a betrayal of a relationship" in *any* committed relationship—married or not (Pittman, 1990: 20). For many, extramarital sex is more damaging than infidelity among people who are dating or live together because a married partner breaks a civil contract that's legally binding. Extramarital sex also violates a religious promise to be faithful.

EMOTIONAL INFIDELITY Emotional infidelity can be devastating to both married and unmarried couples. Almost one out of four American women believes that a sexual act isn't necessary for a person to be unfaithful; lust is enough to qualify (Covel, 2003).

Many family therapists agree that affairs don't have to include sexual intercourse because emotional infidelity also violates expectations of trust in a committed relationship. Emotional infidelity includes secrecy (meeting someone without telling your spouse or partner), emotional intimacy (confiding things you haven't told your spouse or partner), and even being mutually attracted to someone else (Glass, 2002).

ONLINE INFIDELITY People who engage in online relationships see them as harmless distractions from boredom. Some family practitioners, however, believe that Internet romances are betrayals because they involve emotional infidelity: People share personal information (including comments about marital dissatisfaction), become more secretive, and may spend more time with a cyber-lover than with a spouse or partner (Young, 2001). Because online infidelity violates a trust, it can elicit hurt, anger, depression, and insecurity.

There are numerous sites specifically devoted to helping married people cheat online. The people involved may never meet, but about a third do so. Cyber-affairs may eventually break up a marriage or a relationship (Komando, 2012).

How Common Is Sexual Infidelity?

An ongoing problem for researchers—even those who use meticulous sampling procedures—is collecting accurate data on sexual infidelity. Most respondents don't want to admit cheating, and the results may vary somewhat because of different time frames, age groups, and how the questions are phrased. Nonetheless, the most highly respected national surveys have produced similar results.

If you believe talk shows, about half of married Americans have been unfaithful. In fact, in any given year, about 4 percent of married people (4 percent of men and 3 percent of women) have sex outside of their marriage. Over a lifetime, about 17 percent have had extramarital sex (19 percent of men and 14 percent of women). This rate has fluctuated only slightly since 1991 (Taylor et al., 2006; Drexler, 2012). In committed relationships, married and unmarried, 16 percent of the partners have cheated (21 percent of men and 11 percent of women) (Langer et al., 2004).

Since you asked . . .
• Isn't online sex just harmless entertainment?

The marital infidelity gender gap has been declining since the early 1990s, particularly among those under age 45, but male rates have decreased whereas female rates have increased. Still, women are more likely than men to say that extramarital sex is always wrong (Carr, 2010; Marano, 2012).

Despite the data, year after year my students refuse to believe that most married people are faithful. They point to talk shows and their own personal experiences. For example,

"I work as a bartender part time and hang out in bars on the weekends. I watch people leave my bar all the time and all I can think of is his poor wife waiting at home."

"I find it hard to believe that only 17 percent of married people have cheated. Most are lying."

"A lot of men, single or married, think with their penis. You'll never convince me that only about 21 percent of men have cheated on their wives." (Author's files)

Their suspicions are partly warranted because researchers agree that sexual infidelity is underreported. However, until national surveys use similar sampling strategies, age subgroups, and questions, the available data show that marital sexual infidelity isn't as rampant as most Americans believe.

Why Are People Unfaithful?

Why is there such a difference between what we say we should do (94 percent of Americans who say that marital infidelity is wrong) and what we do (17 percent who have affairs)? The reasons for adultery include both macro and micro factors.

MACRO REASONS   Among the many macro explanations for extramarital sex, some are especially important:

1. *Economic problems* such as unemployment, underemployment, and home foreclosures strain relationships and increase the incidence of sexual infidelity.

2. *The purpose of marriage* has changed for many people. Procreation is still important, but many couples marry primarily for companionship and intimacy (see Chapter 1). When these needs aren't met, outside relationships may develop.

3. *The anonymity of urban life* encourages infidelity: "Not only is there exposure to large numbers of potential partners, there's more opportunity to escape detection" (Marano, 2012: 65).

4. Because today people *live longer*, marriages can last as long as 60 years, increasing the chances for conflict, dissatisfaction, and infidelity.

5. There is *greater opportunity for sexual infidelity*. More travel, more late nights on the job, and more interaction with co-workers who have similar interests increase the temptation to have an affair (Drexler, 2012).

6. Changing *gender roles* also increase infidelity. As women become more economically independent, and especially if they earn more than their spouses, they feel freer to make their own decisions, including having an affair (Paul, 2010).

7. The *mass media*, especially television shows and movies, often portray sexual infidelity as normal and acceptable: "Scan the plots on television any given week in television, and there seems to be more extramarital sex than marital sex" (Drexler, 2012: 63).

8. *Technological advances* have increased the likelihood of sexual infidelity. Social networks, such as Facebook, have expanded opportunities for

Desperate Housewives, a television show that aired between 2004 and 2012, often focused on extramarital sex. Why do you think it was so popular?

developing romantic relationships, and numerous sites provide "married dating services for discreet encounters" (Yancey, 2011).

9. There are *few negative legal and marital consequences* for extramarital sex. In 24 states and U.S. territories, laws define marital infidelity as a criminal act that can be prosecuted, but the laws are rarely used in divorce and child custody cases, prosecuted, or enforced (Bronner, 2012). Also, only 50 to 60 percent of Americans say that adultery would be an "automatic deal breaker for their marriage" (Hanes, 2010: 27).

MICRO REASONS   There are also a number of micro explanations for sexual infidelity:

1. *The need for emotional or sexual satisfaction* may propel people into extramarital sex. Women who are unfaithful often feel that their husbands don't communicate with them, have no time for them except in bed, and feel lonely. Men, in contrast, often want more sex than they're getting (Weaver, 2007).

2. Both sexes, but twice as many men as women, have extramarital sex because it's *exciting*. As a 38-year-old man in a committed relationship said, "I like variety and a more wild sex life." Women, in contrast, are more likely to be unfaithful if they seek emotional attention or fall in love with someone else (Weaver, 2007).

3. Sexual infidelity *enhances egos*. As people grow older, they may try to prove to themselves that they're still physically and socially desirable and attractive. Men with low self-esteem are more likely than women with low self-esteem to engage in infidelity to bolster their egos (Whisman et al., 2007).

4. Sex, including infidelity, involves a *social exchange*. Aging men get sex from attractive young women if the men have status, power, prestige, or wealth (Baumeister and Vohs, 2004).

5. People are unfaithful because they think that they *can get away with it*. As what one journalist dubbed "alpha males," many politicians assume that they "can get away with stuff" because they're rich or powerful (Page, 2008: 15A). Many popular self-help books advise couples to "heal," rather than leave, an adulterer (see, for example, Glass and Staeheli, 2004; MacDonald, 2010). Thus, discovery of infidelity doesn't necessarily end a marriage or a relationship (see Confer and Cloud, 2011).

6. Extramarital sex can be a form of *revenge or retaliation* against a spouse for involvement in a similar activity, real or imagined (Kinsey et al., 1953).

7. An extramarital relationship may provide a *way out of marriage*. Some people might deliberately initiate an affair as an excuse to dissolve an unhappy marriage (Walsh, 1991).

Macro and micro reasons often overlap in explaining sexual infidelity. For example, a weak economy (a macro-level variable) can worsen personal dissatisfaction (a micro-level variable) and increase the likelihood of having extramarital sex.

What Are Some of the Consequences of Sexual Infidelity?

Some partners are forgiving, but infidelity is one of the most common reasons for divorce (see Chapter 15). The injured spouse typically feels deceived, betrayed, and depressed. The aggrieved person may also experience doubts about his or her own desirability, adequacy, or worth. After finding out about Tiger Woods' serial

adultery, his wife divorced him. She described herself as having gone through hell, betrayed, and feeling stupid and embarrassed for never suspecting anything (Boren, 2010).

Marriage counselors point out that most extramarital affairs devastate the entire family. They can have an especially negative impact on children, who often feel insecure and confused, particularly if the marriage collapses because of the affair. Because very young children are self-centered, they may feel that they're somehow to blame for what has happened (see Chapter 15).

The effects of infidelity among public figures are mixed. President Bill Clinton's oral sex scandal with intern Monica Lewinsky didn't affect his reputation, reelection, or political prominence. On the other hand, after extramarital activities and an out-of-wedlock son were uncovered, 2008 presidential candidate John Edwards withdrew from national politics and was divorced by his wife. David Petraeus, a highly respected and decorated four-star Army general, resigned as director of the Central Intelligence Agency, after admitting an affair with his female biographer. The wives and families suffer, but many of the mistresses are paid well to pose on the covers of *Playboy* and celebrity magazines.

Extramarital sex also has broad structural implications for society as a whole. Group solidarity is necessary for a society's survival. Because family members depend on one another for emotional support, their unity and cohesiveness can be threatened by sexual intruders.

MAKING CONNECTIONS

- Do you think that emotional infidelity, including cyber-sex, is a form of sexual infidelity? Or just a harmless romantic game (the ludic love discussed in Chapter 6)?

- Would you tell a co-worker, friend, relative, or family member that his or her partner or spouse is unfaithful? Would *you* want to be told?

- Is infidelity justified if it helps people endure a difficult situation, such as caring for a spouse or partner with a long-term physical or mental illness? Or being married to someone who's emotionally and sexually distant?

Sexually Transmitted Diseases

Sexuality is part of everyday life, but it's not always smooth and carefree. Appendix B provides information about sexual problems and their treatment. Here we'll briefly examine sexually transmitted diseases, infections, and illnesses that are transmitted almost entirely through sexual contact.

Sexually transmitted infections (STIs) are illnesses transmitted through sexual activity (vaginal, oral, and anal). As a result of the infection, and once there are observable symptoms, the STI becomes a **sexually transmitted disease** (STD). Even when there are no symptoms, STIs can be passed from one person to another.

One of the most serious (and still fatal, in many cases) STDs is the **human immunodeficiency virus (HIV)**, the virus that causes AIDS. **Acquired immunodeficiency syndrome (AIDS)** is a degenerative disease that attacks the body's immune system and makes it unable to fight a number of diseases, including some forms of pneumonia and cancer.

How Widespread Are STDs?

There are nearly 19 million new STD cases in the United States every year. Sexually transmitted diseases affect females and males across all ages and economic levels, but nearly half of all STDs occur in people under age 25, and minorities are the most likely to be infected. (Unless noted otherwise, much of the data in this section are based on Centers for Disease Control and Prevention, 2012a, 2012b.)

There are at least 50 types of STDs (see Appendix E for information about some of these diseases, their symptoms, and treatment). Today, *syphilis* is the least common STD, but it has increased since 2005, particularly among blacks ages 15 to 19. Many of the infected are young men having sex with men (MSM) who, in turn, infect heterosexual women.

The most common STD is *chlamydia*, a bacterial infection, followed by *gonorrhea*. New incidence rates of HIV and AIDS are small by comparison (see *Figure 7.7*), but those infected can be treated, not cured. Without early screening and treatment, 10

7.8 Describe the prevalence of sexually transmitted diseases, their causes, effects, risks, and increasing rates.

Since you asked . . .
- What's the difference between STIs and STDs?

sexually transmitted infections (STIs) Illnesses transmitted through sexual activity.

sexually transmitted diseases (STDs) Observable symptoms that occur after a sexually transmitted infection.

human immunodeficiency virus (HIV) The virus that causes AIDS.

acquired immunodeficiency syndrome (AIDS) A degenerative disease that attacks the body's immune system and makes it unable to fight a number of diseases.

 Watch on MySocLab

Video: He Said, She Said: Safe Sex

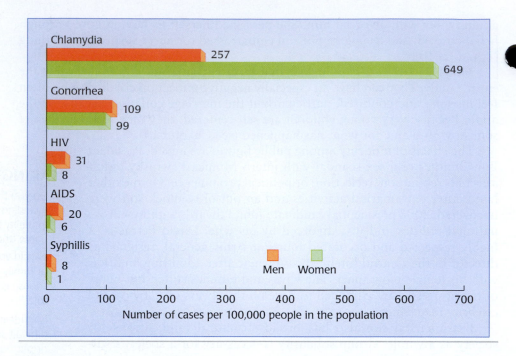

FIGURE 7.7 **Cases of Selected STDs in the United States, by Sex, 2010–2011** **These figures are conservative because many people don't realize that they're infected and don't seek medical care. The actual rates may be four to five times higher.** *Sources:* Based on Centers for Disease Control and Prevention, 2010, 2012b.

to 40 percent of women with gonorrhea develop *pelvic inflammatory disease (PID)* that can have life-threatening complications. About 20 million Americans (67 percent of them women), have *human papilloma virus (HPV)* that can infect women's and men's genital areas. Almost 4 million Americans also have an STD called *trichomoniasis*, caused by a parasite passed from an infected person during sex.

First reported on June 5, 1981, AIDS had taken the lives of almost 620,000 Americans by the end of 2009. About 1.2 million Americans are living with AIDS, and there were more than 48,000 new HIV infections in 2010. Death rates for AIDS have been decreasing, but some groups are especially vulnerable. As *Figure 7.8* shows, the incidence of diagnosed HIV is highest among men, African Americans, and men having sex with men. Of those diagnosed with HIV in 2010, only 12 percent of males, compared with 86 percent of females, became infected during heterosexual contact.

How Do People Spread STDs?

Childbirth and breast milk can pass on HIV, but the most common infections are through sexual activity:

- **Oral and anal sex.** The viruses or bacteria that cause STDs can enter the body through bleeding gums, tiny cuts in the mouth and anus, or sores in the mouth or throat.

- **Vaginal sex.** Contact with infected body fluids (blood, vaginal secretions, semen) spreads STDs.

- **Drug use.** Using any kind of drug, including alcohol and marijuana, can impair one's judgment, reduce the likelihood of using condoms, and increase the likelihood of having sex with multiple partners.

- **Sharing needles.** Sharing needles or syringes for drug use, ear piercing, and tattooing exposes people to infected body fluids or skin.

- **Multiple partners.** Any sexual contact with many different partners increases the risk of becoming infected with whatever STDs they have. Bisexual men are especially vulnerable because they tend to have more partners than heterosexual and gay men (Jeffries, 2011).

Some myths about HIV transmission still linger, but none of the following transmit HIV: insect bites, sweat, tears, sneezing, coughing, food preparation, toilet seats, blood donations, or a swimming pool that uses chlorine.

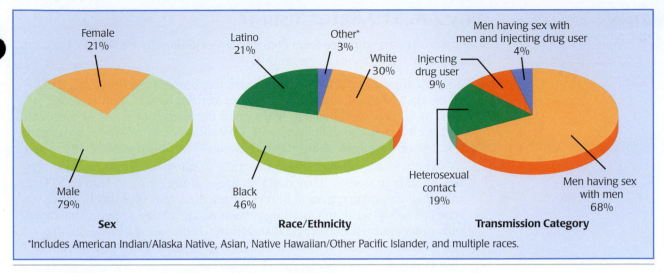

FIGURE 7.8 **Diagnoses of HIV Infection among U.S. Adults and Adolescents, 2010**
Source: Based on Centers for Disease Control and Prevention, 2010, Tables 1a and 1b.

What Are Some Effects of STDS?

Much of the time, STDs have no symptoms, particularly in women. However, a person who is infected can pass the diseases on to a partner. Sexually transmitted diseases can cause cancer, birth defects, miscarriages, and in some cases, death. Untreated chlamydia can cause permanent damage to the reproductive organs, often resulting in infertility in women and sterility in men. Gonorrhea can result in infertility in men. A baby born to an infected mother may become blind.

Without early screening and treatment, 10 to 40 percent of women with gonorrhea develop *pelvic inflammatory disease*. This condition can result in infertility in women and life-threatening ectopic pregnancy when the fertilized egg implants itself in the fallopian tube rather than the uterus. The tube can rupture and, without surgical intervention, cause death. Certain types of HPV can result in genital warts and cancers in the cervix, vulva, penis, anus, and head and neck. There is treatment for HPV, but no cure for herpes or genital warts (CDC National Prevention Information Network, 2012).

Are STDs More Dangerous to Women Than Men?

Both men and women get STDs, but women have more serious and more frequent complications for several reasons. First, as you saw earlier, men are more likely than women to have sex at an early age and with more partners over a lifetime. This means that women have a greater risk of getting all of the STDs that a man's past and present partners have had. Second, the lining of the vagina is thinner and more delicate than the skin on a penis, so it's easier for bacteria and viruses to penetrate. Third, compared with men, women are less likely to have symptoms of some common STDs, such as chlamydia and gonorrhea. Fourth, women may not see symptoms as easily as men. For example, genital ulcers, as from herpes or syphilis, can occur in the vagina and may not be easily visible, whereas men are more likely to notice sores on their penis. Fifth, HPV, the most common STD infection in women, is the main cause of cervical cancer; HPV is also common in men, but most don't develop any serious health problems. Finally, untreated STDs have disproportionally negative long-term consequences for women because they can permanently affect women's reproductive plans such as causing infertility, and passing STDs to their babies with negative results such as stillbirths, brain damage, blindness, and deafness (CDC Fact Sheet, 2011, 2013).

Since you asked . . .
• Can people prevent STIs and
  STDs?

Why Are STD Rates Rising?

Both macro-level and micro-level factors help explain why STD rates are rising. In terms of macro reasons, for example,

1. *Societal stigma and a lack of information promote infections.* In 2010, those ages 13 to 24 accounted for 26 percent of new HIV infections. Almost 60 percent didn't know they had the virus, but many of those who had been tested and diagnosed with HIV didn't enter or stay in treatment because of the stigma that HIV still carries (Whitmore et al., 2012).

   Many young people believe that they're safe from STDs because "I'm having only oral sex." They don't realize that oral sex can lead to STDs, including chlamydia, genital herpes, gonorrhea, and syphilis. Fellatio tends to be riskier than cunnilingus because ejaculated sperm carry more infectious material than vaginal secretions. Both forms of oral sex are risky, however, because vaginal liquids carry bacteria that can affect the skin (Clark-Flory, 2012; Copen et al., 2012).

   The number of people over age 50 who have STDs, including HIV, has been rising sharply. Many are sexually active, but older women, especially, aren't concerned about becoming pregnant, don't think they're at risk for STDs, assume that their partners are "safe," and, consequently, discontinue or don't insist that men wear condoms (Sanders et al., 2010; Schick et al., 2010).

2. *Assimilation increases risky behavior.* As immigrants become more Americanized, they lose the "healthy immigrant effect," which includes avoiding drugs that increase the likelihood of risky sexual behavior and having unprotected heterosexual and MSM sex (Flores and Brotanek, 2005; Killoren et al., 2012).

   Among young Latinos aged 16 to 22, current U.S. sexual values may displace traditional cultural values, especially for Latinas. Young men who follow traditional *machismo* sexual scripts (see Chapters 4 and 5), emphasize satisfying sexual needs with one or more partners, have sex at an early age, and use condoms inconsistently or not at all. Young Latinas may believe that virginity is important, but during the assimilation process, they are likely to have sex and not use condoms (or contraceptives) because they love their partners and believe that the males are sexually faithful (Deardoff et al., 2010).

3. *Poverty spreads infections.* African Americans are six times more likely to be infected with chlamydia than are whites, and half of all HIV-infected people are African Americans. Minority women in poor neighborhoods, where there is often a scarcity of eligible men, usually select sexual partners from the same high-risk neighborhood (Adimora and Schoenbach, 2005).

   Low-income women, especially among blacks, engage in risky sexual behavior because of a combination of structural and situational reasons. The women may not insist on condom usage, even when they suspect that the men have STDs, including HIV, because they're homeless, fear violence or a loss of financial support for themselves and their children, are using drugs, or exchange sex for money or drugs (Ober et al., 2011; Miles et al., 2013).

4. *Family environment increases risky behavior.* An unstable home life where there is substance use, violence, and child abuse may increase a teen's engaging in risky sexual behavior such as having many sexual partners, not using condoms, and drinking alcohol or using drugs during sexual intercourse (Eaton et al., 2012; Secor-Turner et al., 2013).

At the micro level, individual characteristics and choices spike infection rates. For example,

1. *Males, especially, are ambivalent about an unplanned pregnancy.* Nationally, among never-married teenagers ages 15 to 19 who don't use condoms, 19 percent of males and 13 percent of females said that they would be "a little pleased" or "very pleased" if the female had an unintended pregnancy. Among those ages 18 to 29, 53 percent of the men and 36 percent of the women felt the same way (Martinez et al., 2011; Higgins et al., 2012).

2. *Drug use increases risky sexual behavior.* People age 25 and younger are more likely than those aged 26 to 44 to engage in risky sexual behavior while high on alcohol or drugs, have more sexual partners, or exchange sex for drugs or money (van Gelder et al., 2011).

3. *People don't always believe test results.* Among those aged 18 to 26 who engaged in risky sexual behavior, only 28 percent who tested positive for a STD believed the results because they hadn't experienced any symptoms, such as painful sores or blisters, or genital warts (Wildsmith et al., 2010).

4. *People aren't aware of a partner's sexual activities.* Many adults don't use condoms because they don't know that a partner is also having sex with other people, has injected drugs, or has recently tested positive for a STD, including HIV (Witte et al., 2010).

5. *The benefits outweigh the costs.* Even when females (both adolescents and young adults) are aware of their partners' risky sexual behavior, they do what they're told if the males threaten physical violence or ending a relationship. Aware of women's anxiety about jeopardizing a relationship and women's desire to show their trust, love, and commitment, men can insist that women have unwanted anal sex, and not use a condom during vaginal intercourse (Carter et al., 2010; Silverman et al., 2011; Akers et al., 2012).

HIV has become a manageable disease, but at what cost? Young adults who were infected with HIV at birth say, for example, that medications impair their short-term memory making school and job prospects difficult, or have negative side effects such as high cholesterol levels. Some have developmental and behavioral problems; many grapple with hostility toward parents who infected them and grieve for parents who have died. The mortality for young people with HIV is 30 times higher than for similarly aged people in the general population (Belluck, 2010).

The number of AIDS-related deaths in Africa has fallen by 32 percent since 2005, but the continent still has the highest rates, worldwide, of adults and children who die of AIDS (Moore, 2013). Here, an HIV/AIDS educator addresses youth in Uganda.

CONCLUSION

One of the biggest *changes* since the turn of the century is that we're better informed about our sexuality. We have more *choices* in our sexual expression, and most people recognize that sexuality involves more than just the sex act. There are also a number of *constraints*. We are often unable or unwilling to give young people the information they need to make intelligent decisions about sex. Gay men and lesbians still face discrimination and harassment, and our health and the lives of our children are threatened by the rising incidence of STDS. These changes, choices, and constraints have significant effects on peoples' search for suitable marriage partners and other long-term relationships. We'll examine these issues in the next several chapters.

On MySocLab

 **Study and Review on MySocLab**

REVIEW QUESTIONS

7.1. Explain how sexuality is a product of our sexual identity, sexual orientation, and sexual scripts.

1. Why is sex more important for some people than for others?

2. What are the components of human sexuality? And how do biological and social constructionist theories differ in explaining sexual behavior?

3. How do sexual scripts affect our sexual activities, attitudes, and relationships?

7.2. Explain why we have first-time sex, casual sex, and sex in committed relationships.

4. How do adolescent girls and boys differ in their sexual activities?

5. What are some of the reasons for early premarital sex?

6. What function does sex serve in a long-term relationship?

7.3. Describe five primary sources that influence our sexual behavior.

7. How useful is the information about sex that we receive from parents, peers, and siblings?

8. How do religion, the media, popular culture, and school-based sex education affect our sexual behavior?

7.4. Describe at least four types of sexual behaviors.

9. What kinds of behaviors involve sexual activity?

10. How does sexual behavior vary by gender and age?

7.5. Describe the prevalence, sexual behaviors, and societal reactions to lesbian, gay, bisexual, and transgender sex.

11. How many LGBT people are there in the United States? How many Americans have had same-sex sexual contact?

12. Are Americans becoming more or less accepting of lesbians and gay men?

7.6. Explain how sexual behavior changes over the life course.

13. Why do some teens and adults abstain from sexual intercourse?

14. Do single women or men have more sex? How does the sexual behavior of single and married people differ?

15. What factors affect the sexual activities of people in their sixties and older?

7.7. Define sexual infidelity, describe its prevalence, explain why it occurs, and discuss its consequences.

16. How common is sexual infidelity?

17. What are some of the macro- and micro-level reasons for unfaithfulness?

7.8. Describe the prevalence of sexually transmitted diseases, their causes, effects, risks, and increasing rates.

18. Which groups are the most likely to be infected with HIV? Why?

19. Are all STDs curable?

20. What are the macro- and micro-level variables that help explain the rise of STDs?

Choosing Others: Dating and Mate Selection

((• **Listen** to Chapter 8 on **MySocLab**

LEARNING OBJECTIVES

After you read and study this chapter you will be able to:

Compare the manifest and latent functions of dating.	8.1
Outline the characteristics, benefits, and costs of traditional and contemporary dating patterns.	8.2
Describe five strategies for meeting dating partners.	8.3
Compare three mate-selection theories.	8.4
Describe some of the mate-selection differences across cultures.	8.5
Describe the prevalence of dating violence, and explain why it occurs and its consequences.	8.6
Describe breaking up, and explain why it occurs and its consequences.	8.7

DATA DIGEST

- Among high school seniors, **those who said that they never date** increased from 15 percent in 1976 to 30 percent in 2010.

- Of all U.S. adults who have dated online, 53 percent have dated **more than one person simultaneously**.

- Among U.S. single adults age 50 and older, **63 percent of men want to** date a much younger woman compared with 22 percent of women who want to date a much younger man.

- About 66 percent of Americans **wouldn't consider dating someone who didn't like their dog**.

- Almost half of U.S. online daters say that **the most important factor is physical characteristics**.

- In 2011, the **annual revenue for the online dating industry worldwide** was almost $1.1 billion, and is expected to increase to $2.3 billion by 2016.

Sources: American Kennel Club, 2006; Miller, 2011; Child Trends Data Bank, 2012; Statistic Brain, 2012; PR Newswire, 2013.

Someone once joked that dating is the process of spending a lot of time and money to meet people you probably won't like. Being single has its advantages (see Chapter 9), but most of us want a lifelong partner. Regardless of which words we use—*dating, going out, hooking up, having a thing*, or *seeing someone*—mate selection is a process that, many people hope, will result in finding an intimate partner or marriage mate.

Traditional college students (those who live on campus and are under age 25) may dismiss **dating**—the process of meeting people socially for possible mate selection—as old fashioned because "there's no time, no money, and no need" (Wolcott, 2004: 11). Dating may be dead on many college campuses, but not elsewhere. For example, 24 percent of high school seniors say that they date frequently, and dating is common among Latino undergraduates (Child Trends Data Bank, 2012; Eaton and Rose, 2012). How we meet people has changed, as you'll see shortly, but dating is still popular.

dating The process of meeting people socially for possible mate selection.

8.1 Compare the manifest and latent functions of dating.

marriage market A process in which prospective spouses compare the assets and liabilities of eligible partners and choose the best available mate.

Why Do We Date?

The reasons for dating seem self-evident, but dating is more complex than just getting together. Sociologists describe the dating process as a **marriage market** where people compare the assets and liabilities of eligible partners and choose the best available mate.

Everyone has a "market value," and whom a person "trades" with depends on one's resources. Like most other choices we make, dating involves taking risks with the resources we invest. The more valuable the catch, the more likely we are to devote time and money to looking attractive, accommodating the partner's personality or interests, or getting along with her or his family and friends. In contrast, one-night stands entail few risks (if the partners don't contract STDs and the woman doesn't get pregnant) and little investment of resources.

Also, people use their resources differently if the relationship is new. As one of my students observed, people may invest more time than money in a partner if they're no longer in the marriage market:

It's very expensive to date. When two people are in a comfortable relationship, there is less need to impress that person with fancy dinners and costly dates (Author's files).

Dating fulfills a number of functions. They can be *manifest*—the purposes are visible, recognized, and intended—or *latent*—the purposes are unintended or not immediately recognized (see Chapter 2). Keep in mind that the functions often overlap.

Changes | Courting throughout U.S. History

Young people in colonial America often had premarital sex. As a young woman wrote passionately to her lover,

> O! I do really want to kiss you. How I should like to be in that old parlor with you. I hope there will be a carpet on the floor for it seems you intend to act worse than you ever did before by your letter. But I shall humbly submit to my fate and willingly, too. . . (Rothman, 1983: 401).

There were also practical considerations. An engaged woman's parents conducted economic negotiations with her fiancé's family, and most young men couldn't even think about courtship until they owned land. They were advised to select women who were industrious, hardworking, and sensible. Affection was expected to blossom into love after marriage. A New York woman wrote, "If a man is healthy and does not drink and has a good little handful of stock and a good temper and is a good Christian, what difference can it make . . . which man she takes?" (Ryan, 1983: 40–41).

Before the Industrial Revolution, most courtships took place within the hustle and bustle of community life. Young people could meet after church services, during picnics, or at gatherings such as barn raisings and dances. Buggy rides were especially popular: There was no room in the buggy for a chaperone, and "the horse might run away or lose a shoe so that one could be stranded on a lonely country road" (McPharlin, 1946: 10).

At the turn of the twentieth century, especially among the middle classes, gentlemen "called" on women. A woman or her mother invited a suitor to visit at the woman's home, and other family members were present. If the relationship proceeded toward engagement, the couple enjoyed some privacy in the parlor (Bailey, 1988).

With the advent of bicycles and telephones, parlor sofas and porch swings were quickly abandoned. People began to use the term *dating*, which referred to couples setting a specific date, time, and place to meet. When the automobile came into widespread use in the early 1920s, dating took a giant step forward. "The car provided more privacy . . . than either the dance hall or the movie theater, and the result was the spread of petting" (Rothman, 1984: 295). Young people now had the mobility to meet more frequently, informally, and casually.

Until the early 1970s, dating reflected a strict and gendered code of etiquette. Men initiated dates and paid all the expenses. Women waited to be asked out and provided companionship (and sometimes sex) during a date.

STOP AND THINK . . .

- Did the colonists have the right idea in being practical about courtship? Or should courtship always involve love?
- Talk to your parents, grandparents, or other relatives about dating in the 1950s and 1960s. What were some of the advantages and disadvantages of the dating rituals?

As "Courting throughout U.S. History" shows, dating is a recent invention. It emerged in the United States in the twentieth century and became a well-established rite of passage in the 1950s. How we date has changed, but why and whom we date and why we break up have been fairly constant over time.

Manifest Functions of Dating

Dating fulfills several important manifest functions:

- *Maturation:* Dating sends the message that an adolescent is reaching puberty. She or he becomes capable of engaging in developmental tasks such as emotional intimacy outside the family and, often, sexual expression (see Chapter 7).

- *Fun and recreation:* Going out with people we like relieves boredom, stress, and loneliness. Online dating sites report that their membership spikes during stressful economic times, probably because people seek relationships to lessen their anxiety (Carpenter, 2008). And, as more people postpone marriage (see Chapter 9), dating becomes an important recreational activity.

- *Companionship:* Regardless of one's age, dating can be a valuable source of companionship. It can also ease the heartbreak of being widowed. One of my students described her 72-year-old mother as being very depressed after the death of her husband, to whom she had been married for 50 years, until she "met a wonderful man and they started socializing."

- *Love and affection:* Dating is a socially accepted way to enjoy intimacy. Both women and men say that they initiated a date because they were in love or wanted a caring and serious relationship (Clark et al., 1999). If the relationship fizzles, the marriage market offers other opportunities for finding love.

Since you asked . . .
- Why are my parents and friends so critical of the people I date?

- *Mate selection:* In a cartoon, a woman, hand on the doorknob of her apartment, turns to her date and says: "I had a nice time, Steve. Would you like to come in, settle down, and raise a family?" Whether or not people admit it, dating is usually a search for a marital partner. Adolescents often become angry if their parents criticize their dates with remarks such as "We don't want you to marry this guy" or "She's not good enough for you." The teenager's impatient rebuttal is usually "I'm not going to marry him (her). We're just going out!"

Parents are often judgmental because they know that dating can lead to marriage. In contrast, as you'll see later in this chapter, there's little need for dating in cultures where parents arrange their children's marriages.

The Wodabe, a nomadic West African tribe, value and honor male beauty. The males perform a dance, showing off the whiteness of their teeth and eyes, at an annual competition at which women select the most beautiful man.

Latent Functions of Dating

Dating also fulfills several important latent functions:

- *Socialization:* Through dating, people learn about expected gender roles; family structures that differ from their own; and different attitudes, beliefs, and values. This kind of learning is especially valuable for adolescents, who can test and hone their communication skills in one-on-one settings (Berk, 1993).

- *Social status:* Going out with an attractive or successful person enhances one's status and prestige. Being popular or going out with someone who's popular can also increase one's standing in a social group.

- *Fulfillment of ego needs:* Being asked out on a date or having one's invitation accepted boosts a person's self-esteem and self-image. Self-confidence rises if the date goes well or if the partner is flattering and attentive.

- *Sexual experimentation and intimacy:* Many teenagers learn about sex during dating. Females, especially, report that their first sexual intercourse occurred in a steady or serious dating relationship. As dating becomes more committed or frequent, young people are more likely to want and have sex (see Chapter 7).

- *Big business:* Dating provides a significant economic market for products and services such as clothing, grooming, food, and entertainment. A huge industry of self-help dating books, always targeted to women, has convinced them that there's something wrong with them if they're not dating or haven't found their "true love" (Mukhopadhyay, 2011). By 2011, the number of people using dating apps (applications) grew faster than the number using all apps (Newark-French, 2011).

Manifest and latent dating functions often change over time. As people mature, status may become less relevant and companionship more important, especially if the dating partners plan to marry.

The Dating Spectrum

8.2 Outline the characteristics, benefits, and costs of traditional and contemporary dating patterns.

Unlike a few generations ago, dating today is distinct from courtship and may or may not end in marriage. Traditional dating is still common, but there are a number of newer forms of getting together, as well as some combinations of traditional and contemporary dating.

Traditional Dating

The *traditional date*, which prevailed until the 1970s, is still a way to meet potential spouses. In traditional dating, males and females follow clear, culturally defined gender role scripts, at least among the middle classes. Both women and men expect the man to take control, including initiating the date, deciding where to go, picking up the woman, paying for the date, and taking her home. The expectation is unstated, but members of both sexes often assume that the woman will show her gratitude in some way—usually through a goodnight kiss, making out, or intercourse (Eaton and Rose, 2011).

The popularity of traditional dating is particularly evident in formal events such as *coming-out parties* or debutante balls, at which young women, usually from the upper classes, are introduced to society (Kendall, 2002). Other cultural rites of passage include the *bat mitzvah* for girls and the *bar mitzvah* for boys in Jewish communities. These rituals mark the end of childhood and readiness for adult responsibilities and rights, including dating.

In many Latino communities, the *quinceañera* (pronounced kin-say-ah-NYAIR-ah) is a coming-of-age rite that celebrates a girl's entrance into adulthood on her fifteenth birthday. *Quince* (pronounced KEEN-say) means 15 in Spanish. The *quinceañera* is an elaborate and dignified religious and social affair sponsored by the girl's parents. It typically begins with a Catholic Mass and is followed by a reception at which 14 couples (each couple representing one year in the girl's life before the *quince*) serve as her attendants. The girl may be allowed to date boys after her *quinceañera*. There is no comparable rite of passage for Latino boys.

Quinceañeras are a multimillion-dollar industry. Many large retail and bridal stores carry a large selection of gowns and accessories, and travel agencies offer *quinceañera* celebrations to numerous destinations that are often booked solid into the next year. In 2001, Mattel came out with a *Quinceañera Barbie* that is available in toy stores throughout the nation.

Contemporary Dating

In contrast to traditional dates, much of contemporary dating is usually casual and includes hanging out, getting together, and "hooking up." There are also traditional-contemporary combinations that can lead to engagement and marriage.

HANGING OUT Parents and adolescents in many American homes engage in a familiar dialogue:

Parent: Where are you going?
Teenager: Out.

The *quinceañera* has many rituals. After a traditional waltz in which the young woman dances with her father, she tosses a bouquet to the boys to determine who will win the first dance with her.

Parent: What will you do?
Teenager: Just hang out.
Parent: Who will be there?
Teenager: I don't know yet.
Parent: When will you be back?
Teenager: I'm not sure.

Whether hanging out occurs on a neighborhood street corner, at a fast-food place, or in a mall, it's a time-honored adolescent pastime. A customary meeting place may be set, with people coming and going at different times. Or, once a group gets together, the members decide what they want to do and the information is quickly spread by text messages. Hanging out is possible both because many parents respect their teenagers' privacy and independence and because many 16- and 17-year-olds have access to cars.

Since you asked . . .

• What are the benefits and costs of casual dating?

GETTING TOGETHER   *Getting together* is more intimate and structured than hanging out. A group of friends meets at someone's house or a party. Either males or females can organize the initial effort, and the group often pools its resources, especially if alcohol or other drugs are part of the activities.

Typically, getting together involves "floating." The group may meet at someone's house for a few hours, decide to go to a party later, spend a few hours at a mall, and wind up at another party. Adolescents see getting together as normal and rational—"You get to meet a lot of people" or "We can go someplace else if the party is dead"—but many parents worry that the gatherings can become unpredictable or dangerous because of drug use.

Getting together is popular for several reasons. Because the activities are spontaneous, there's little anxiety about preparing for a formal date or initiating or rejecting sexual advances. The experience is less threatening emotionally because the participants don't have to worry about finding a date or getting stuck with someone (such as a blind date) for the entire evening.

It also relieves females of sexual pressure because they may help organize the get-together, share in the expenses, and come alone or with friends (rather than as part of a couple). People may pair off, but there's less pressure to have a date as a sign of popularity.

Finally, getting together decreases parental control over the choice of friends. Parents usually don't know many of the adolescents in the group and are less likely to disapprove of friendships or compare notes with other parents.

HOOKING UP   *Hooking up* is a casual sexual encounter, no strings attached. It's a vague term that can mean anything from kissing and genital fondling to oral sex and sexual intercourse. After an initial hookup, partners may hook up again or, in some cases, start dating and become exclusive couples (Bogle, 2008).

At many high schools, hooking up is more common than dating. At some college campuses, 76 percent of the students have hooked up five times, on average, and 28 percent have had 10 or more such encounters (England et al., 2007). It seems, then, that hooking up isn't a passing fad but is becoming the norm, especially among young people.

Commonly, but not always, hooking up takes place when both people are drinking or using other drugs. They might also hook up with casual friends or a former girlfriend or boyfriend. In the case of "friends with benefits" (FWB), a variation of hooking up, friends have sex with each other as a form of recreation that involves everything from kissing to sexual intercourse (Denizet-Lewis, 2004; Bisson and Levine, 2009).

Hooking up is a short-lived casual sexual experience that has both benefits and costs.

Hooking up has its advantages. For both sexes, there's little or no expectation of a future commitment. Many men prefer hookups because they're inexpensive

compared with dating. For many college women, hookups offer sex without becoming involved in time-consuming relationships that compete with schoolwork, dealing with boyfriends who become demanding or controlling, and experiencing breakups. Hookups also remove the stigma of not being able to get dates but being able to experience sexual pleasure, and making people feel sexy and desirable (Bogle, 2008; Armstrong et al., 2010; Bradshaw et al., 2010; Rosin, 2012).

Hooking up also has disadvantages, especially for women. Among college students, for example, men are more likely than women to initiate sex; more than twice as many men as women experience an orgasm because the men aren't attentive to what pleases women sexually and show no affection; and women who hook up generally get a reputation as "sluts" (England and Thomas, 2009; Armstrong et al., 2010, 2012). In effect, then, and despite the advantages of hooking up, the sexual double standard persists (see Chapter 7).

Regarding "friends with benefits," FWB encounters provide a relatively safe and convenient environment for recreational sex because both people feel comfortable and trust each other. The disadvantages include complications such as wanting an unreciprocated romantic commitment, which can end a friendship, and creating conflict among a close circle of friends whose relationships don't include sex (Bisson and Levine, 2009).

Traditional-Contemporary Combinations

Several dating patterns incorporate both traditional customs and contemporary trends. For example, even though it's now more acceptable for members of either sex to initiate a date or to invite someone to a prom or dinner date, many gender scripts remain remarkably traditional.

PROMS AND HOMECOMING PARTIES *Proms* and *homecoming parties* are still among the most popular traditional dating events. As in the past, they're formal or semiformal. Women receive corsages; men are typically responsible for transportation and other expenses; and both men and women, but especially women, invest quite a bit of time and money in preparing for these events.

Contemporary changes include prom "turn-about" invitations (those extended to men by women) and dining out beforehand with a large group of couples. Couples might prolong the event by holding a group sleepover (presumably but rarely chaperoned by parents), staying out all night and returning after breakfast, or continuing the festivities into the weekend at a nearby beach or other recreational area.

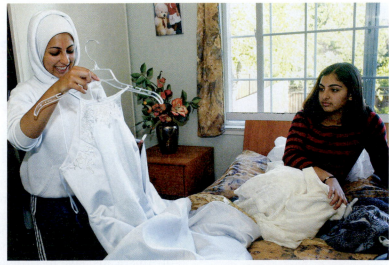

DINNER DATES One of the most traditional forms of dating, the *dinner date* is "the cornerstone of romance" (Scott, 2011). Dinner dates, like first dates of any kind, are still highly scripted. The man typically initiates the date, opens doors, and starts sexual interaction (such as kissing the woman goodnight or making out). The woman spends a good deal of time on her appearance, depends on the man to make the plans, and often responds to a sexual overture rather than making the first move. Thus, making a good impression early in the dating relationship is still largely synonymous with playing traditional gender roles (Rose and Frieze, 1993; Regan, 2003).

The rise of the women's movement in the 1970s led to the custom of *going Dutch*, or splitting the costs of a date. Sharing dating expenses frees women to initiate dates and relieves them from feeling that they should "pay off" with sex.

Some U.S. Muslim girls have organized all-girl high school proms that include gowns and dancing. It's a response to Muslim religious and cultural beliefs in which dating, dancing with or touching boys, or appearing without wearing a *hijab* (a head scarf or a veil that covers the face) isn't permitted (Brown, 2012).

STAYOVERS An emerging dating trend is "stayovers" in which couples spend three or more nights together but maintain separate homes. It's a middle ground between casual dating and more formal commitments such as moving in together or getting married. The benefits include maintaining control over the pace of the relationship and possessions if there's a breakup. According to some critics, however, stayovers promote an "obsession with independence" and playing house instead of making a commitment (Jamison and Ganong, 2011; Taylor, 2011).

Dating in Later Life

Among single U.S. adults age 50 and older, 45 percent are actively dating. In the same age group, 17 percent of the never-married want to date and marry, and 46 percent of divorced singles and 29 percent of widowed are interested in dating but not marrying again (PR Newswire, 2013).

Dating after divorce or being widowed can be both therapeutic and intimidating. It can enhance one's self-esteem, decrease loneliness, and involve reassessing one's strengths and weaknesses as one forges new relationships. Dating can also provide companionship while a person is still grieving a spouse's death.

Dating can also be daunting. A recently divorced person may be bitter toward the opposite sex, or a parent may worry about a child's reactions to her or his dating. Widowed people may be nervous about reentering the marriage market, feel guilty about their romantic yearnings, and experience anxiety about their physical appearance or sex appeal.

Despite their initial uneasiness, many divorced and widowed people establish new and satisfying relationships through dating (see Chapters 15 and 16). Some seek out their teen heartthrobs online, rekindle the old flame, and marry. Not all such reunions have a happy ending, however. People change over the years, and memories of first loves are usually highly romanticized. For example, the class Don Juan is still attentive, but now he's also bald and fat, has bad breath, and cheats on his wife (Russo, 2002).

MAKING CONNECTIONS

- Many people believe that hooking up decreases the artificiality and pressure of dating. Some maintain, however, that such recreational sex means less romance, less passion, and less intimacy because many women are giving out "free samples" (Mansfield, 2004). What do *you* think?

- How does one refer to a romantic partner, especially in social situations? "Significant other" can mean a parent, sibling, or close friend; "partner" or "companion" doesn't sound quite right; "lover" isn't acceptable in most social circles; and "the person I'm seeing" might prompt unwanted questions about your relationship. Which term(s) do you, your family members, and friends use? Why?

8.3 Describe five strategies for meeting dating partners.

Meeting Others

About 62 percent of Americans met their current spouses at work or school or through friends and family members (Chadwick Martin Bailey, 2013). People have also relied on other strategies that range from personal classified ads to online dating sites.

Personal Classified Advertisements

Personal classified advertisements for dating and matrimony have existed for centuries. They first appeared in newspapers in the early 1700s and later in magazines. Advertisers typically described her or his qualities and those sought in an ideal partner. The ads became more prevalent during the 1960s and 1970s, but never became a widely socially acceptable way to find a mate. Only 1 percent of Americans have met romantic partners through personal ads. There are still some personal printed ads in newspapers and magazines, but many are now online (e.g., Craigslist and most newspaper sites) (Finkel et al., 2012).

Mail-Order Brides

American men seeking wives can access one or more of 200 international services that publish photographs and descriptions of women, usually from economically disadvantaged regions such as the Philippines, Russia, Ukraine, and other Eastern European and South Asian countries.

Most of the men are white, college educated, middle-aged, and anywhere from 20 to 50 years older than the young brides they seek. Complaining that American women are too independent, too demanding, and too critical, the men typically want women with relatively little education who are raised in cultures in which a married woman is expected to be a docile and obedient homemaker. Many U.S. brokers adorn their sites with photos of bikini-clad women and market the women as quiet, submissive, and easily controlled (Weir, 2002; Terzieff, 2006).

The mail-order bride industry is booming. The number of mail-order marriages in the United States more than doubled between 1999 and 2007, when more than 16,500 such unions occurred (Wayne, 2011). Because the mail-order bride business is largely unregulated, there's no way of knowing how many of these marriages are successful. Often, the American Prince Charming turns out to be an abuser. Some have murdered their wives; some have beaten, choked, and raped their brides; and others control their spouses by denying them any contact with their families at home or with their current American neighbors (Hanes, 2004).

Beginning in 2006, the International Marriage Broker Regulation Act required U.S. men seeking a visa for a prospective bride to disclose any criminal convictions for domestic violence, sexual assault, or child abuse. Broker agencies were angry about the law, but there's little enforcement. Most of the women stay in abusive relationships and don't report assaults because they speak little English; have no money and no friends in the United States; don't know that they can leave abusive husbands without being deported; and fear that their families will blame them, and not their husbands, for a breakup (Milbourn, 2006; Terzieff, 2006).

In other cases, the women advertising through matchmaking websites are more interested in entering the United States than finding a lifelong husband. Sometimes, for example, an Internet bride leaves the marriage immediately after obtaining legal permanent resident status (Robinson, 2008).

A selling point on many U.S. mail-order websites is a woman's submissiveness. One company founder boasted that the females are "unspoiled by feminism" and a good investment: "You take a beautiful woman from the Czech Republic, you bring her into your home, and she does all your cooking and cleaning and ironing. At the end of the day, the service is free" (Wayne, 2011: 71).

Professional Matchmakers

The first professional matchmaker was probably Henry Robinson, a London businessman, who provided "marriage brokerage" services in 1650. Using his directory of addresses to determine who was single and marriageable and where she or he lived and worked, Robinson set people up to go on dates. His service cost sixpence (six cents) but was free to people who were poor (Writer's Almanac, 2010).

In the United States, online dating is booming, but some find the process too time consuming, are disappointed with the results, or want more privacy. As a result, professional matchmaking services are thriving.

Some matchmakers charge little for their service—$50 per introduction, plus a $50 one-time registration fee—but many fees are considerably higher. For example, Serious Matchmaking Incorporated charges fees beginning at $20,000 for an initiation fee, plus $1,000 for a one-year membership that includes 12 dates. The services consist of an "image consultant" who suggests wardrobe changes (for both women and men) and a trip to a bridal shop so that a woman can visualize herself getting married. Many of the consultants themselves are single. After spending thousands of dollars with a consultant, one woman said that she met her husband through an online dating service at a cost of $160 (Marder, 2002; Thernstrom, 2005).

Professional matchmakers, such as the one on the right, arrange dates between singles who are hoping to find a mate.

How successful are matchmakers in finding mates? They may be better at getting rich than they are at marrying people off. For example, Daniel Dolan, a Harvard-trained corporate lawyer, became a multimillionaire after creating and franchising his "It's Just Lunch" (IJL) matchmaking service. The purpose of IJL is to set up busy professionals with meetings over lunch. The brochures and online advertising claim that "dating experts" thoughtfully pair up people based on personality, appearance, and goals (Fass, 2004).

Many IJL participants, however, have complained about numerous problems. Nationally, for example, both women and men said that they wasted $1,200 to $1,500 for a year's membership fees because they had only one or two dates (that were disastrous); IJL never met their basic dating criteria (such as age, weight, interests, health, not smoking, and not having children); members didn't receive refunds when dates didn't show up; and IJL sales representatives didn't return calls involving complaints or they pressured people to accept dates that they didn't want because "your criteria are unrealistic" ("It's Just Lunch," 2006).

Speed Dating

Speed dating is a dating approach, developed in the late 1990s, in which singles attend an event, such as at a local restaurant, where they engage in a series of brief face-to-face interactions with 14 or more potential romantic partners. The participants go from one table to another, spending about 10 minutes chatting with each person. At the end of an hour or two, they "grade" one another and decide whether they'd be willing to get together with each of them in the future.

Since 1999, speed dating has spawned a number of companies that serve heterosexuals, gays, and a variety of ethnic and age groups. Because U.S. Muslims are prohibited from dating at all before marriage, speed dating (known as *halal* dating) offers the opportunity for women and men to meet each other while being

chaperoned. A young sheikh, or religious leader, usually leads a group discussion about the importance of marriage before the participants break up into speed dating groups (Al-Jadda, 2006).

Speed dating has several benefits. It's inexpensive (about $30 per function), takes little time, guards against stalking because the participants use only their first names, usually draws people from the same region, and avoids the awkwardness of blind dates. Some people initially feel embarrassed or uncomfortable about attending ("What if someone I know is there?"). According to the events' organizers, however, more than half of the participants meet someone with whom there's mutual interest in another date (Morris, 2003).

Speed dating also has several disadvantages. Because the participants engage in only a few minutes of conversation, they often rate potential daters on very superficial criteria such as appearance rather than more substantive traits such as values and lifestyle. Also, the larger the number of participants, the more likely they are to experience a "choice overload," resulting in saying "no" to a large number of potential dating partners (Finkel et al., 2012).

During this speed-dating event, dozens of singles spend five to ten minutes with each person. Event organizers send contact information if the participants choose each other.

Since you asked . . .

- Is online dating better than offline dating in finding a mate?

Online Dating

Millions of people are turning to the Internet to find romance. They can meet hundreds of potential partners online, and discuss anything from radishes to romance. There are more than 1,500 online dating sites, and new ones keep popping up. Some of the largest—such as Match.com, plentyoffish.com, and zoosk.com—have from 3 million to 7 million profiles in their databases (Ganeva, 2012; Jayson, 2012).

Numerous dating sites—and many are free—now exist for almost every imaginable group. A few examples include Jdate.com (for Jewish singles), GothicMatch

.com (for avid vampire enthusiasts), BeautifulPeople.com (for narcissists), WeWaited.com (for virgins), OnlyFarmers .com, Gay.com, ChristianSingles.com, Catholic-Singles.com, and BlackPlanet.com. Sites such as MuslimMatch.com help hundreds of thousands of Muslims worldwide find partners with similar Islamic views and religious commitment levels (Armario, 2005; Gagnon, 2011; McCann, 2013).

A major advantage of many online dating sites is their convenience and low cost. Many dating sites and apps are free, and geography-based technology allows people to arrange spur-of-the-moment dates. Subscribers can sift candidates based on height, age, mutual interests, and dozens of other traits. Skype, an Internet phone service, lets singles connect all over the world for free. Webcams and microphones allow people to see and hear each other and to decide whether to pursue a relationship offline (Semuels, 2006, 2008; Jayakumar, 2012). Another advantage is that subscribers can use code names and remain anonymous as long as they wish.

Online dating is especially useful for singles who have difficulty meeting potential romantic partners. People age 45 and older are the fastest-growing group of online dating service users, and those ages 55 and older are visiting online dating sites more than any other age group (Rosenbloom, 2011). One reason is that the youngest baby boomers turned 65 in 2011, have high divorce rates, and are now looking for new mates. The Internet can be especially helpful to older women: Many don't have the same dating opportunities as men or find that men their age in their own community are looking for younger women (see Chapter 16).

A comprehensive review of the scientific literature on online dating concluded that, outside of increasing the pool of eligible dating partners, online dating services haven't improved romantic outcomes compared with offline conventional dating. First, dating sites fail to collect a lot of crucial information—such as communication patterns, problem-solving abilities, and sexual compatibility—that lead to failed relationships. Second, dating sites don't take into account the real-life environment surrounding the relationship. When couples encounter stress because of job loss, financial strain, long-term illness, or infertility, the risk for breaking up increases. Third, many sites (including Match.com, eHarmony.com, and Chemistry.com) use "mathematical matching algorithms" that promise to find "your perfect partner." Matching people based on similar personality traits, however, doesn't accurately predict the success of a relationship. Only face-to-face meetings and time give people a realistic picture of their compatibility, particularly coping with unpleasant events (Finkel et al., 2012).

Online dating has other downsides. People may be dishonest or have an unrealistically high opinion of themselves. Women tend to lie about their age and weight ("Her photo must have been taken 10 years and 40 pounds ago"). Men tend to lie about their weight, height, income, and occupation. Moreover, about 20 percent of online male daters are married (Fernandez, 2005; McCarthy, 2009).

Some women who believe that they've encountered lying and cheating men online are fighting back. Websites such as DontDateHimGirl.com are dedicated to outing men who are married, having sex with other men, or who lie about their personal characteristics (such as age, educational attainment, and weight). Some men have been outraged by such public accusations, but few have contested the charges (Alvarez, 2006).

Other online daters are turning to "online date detectives" and apps that run background checks. For example, MyMatchChecker .com, founded by a retired detective and police chief, can run basic background searches on any person someone has met on a dating site. DateCheck, an iPhone app, encourages users to "look up before you hook up" (Rosenbloom, 2010).

Dating services report that some service members are finding romance with someone in the United States while serving in Iraq or Afghanistan. Some of these long-distance courtships have led to marriage.

Watch on MySocLab
Video: Online Dating

Watch on MySocLab
Video: The Downside of Internet Dating

MAKING CONNECTIONS

- How do *you* meet other eligible singles? Or are you waiting for Cupid to come to you?
- Millions of people have paid up to $350 for a two-day weekend workshop on how to get a date (Stout, 2005). Is successful dating teachable? Or can most people land good dates through a trial-and-error process?
- Have you or your friends ever tried online dating? If so, were you happy with the results? If you've never cyber-dated, why not?

Since you asked . . .
- Can you date and marry anyone you want?

filter theory Posits that people sift eligible mates according to specific criteria and thus reduce the pool of potential partners to a small number of candidates.

homogamy Dating or marrying someone with similar social characteristics (sometimes called *endogamy*).

propinquity Geographic closeness.

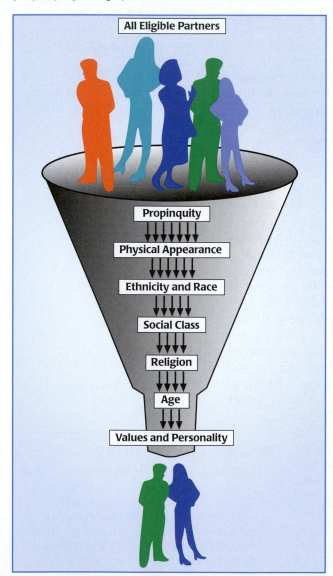

All Eligible Partners

Propinquity
Physical Appearance
Ethnicity and Race
Social Class
Religion
Age
Values and Personality

FIGURE 8.1 The Filter Theory of Mate Selection

Why We Choose Each Other: Some Mate-Selection Theories

Sociologists have offered several explanations of mate-selection processes (see Cate and Lloyd, 1992, for a summary of some of these theoretical perspectives). Some of the most influential theories include filter theory, social exchange theory, and equity theory. Let's begin with filter theory.

Filter Theory: Homogamy and Narrowing the Marriage Market

Theoretically, we have a vast pool of eligible dating partners. In reality, our marriage market is limited by our culture and social structure. According to **filter theory**, we sift eligible people according to specific criteria and thus reduce the pool of potential partners to a small number of candidates (Kerckhoff and Davis, 1962). In effect, then, most of us select dating partners and marry people who are similar to ourselves because filtering processes shape and limit our choices. *Figure 8.1* depicts the filter theory of mate selection.

The major filtering mechanism is homogamy. Often used interchangeably with the term *endogamy* (see Chapters 1 and 4), **homogamy** refers to dating or marrying someone with similar social characteristics, such as ethnicity and age. Some of the most important filtering variables are propinquity, physical appearance, race and ethnicity, religion, age, social class, values, and personality.

PROPINQUITY Geographic closeness, or **propinquity**, one of the first filters, limits whom we meet, get to know, interact with, and subsequently date and marry. Most people who are currently in serious long-term relationships or are married met through family and friends or in a work or school setting. For example, 39 percent of U.S. workers have dated a coworker. Also, a growing number of cities have densely populated gay neighborhoods in which men and women easily meet potential partners at the grocery store, recreational facilities, or church (Sullivan, 2006; Chadwick Martin Bailey, 2013; Suddath, 2013).

PHYSICAL APPEARANCE Once propinquity brings us together, looks matter. A number of studies show that men and women choose partners whose physical attractiveness is similar to their own (Berscheid et al., 1982; Feingold, 1988; McNulty et al., 2008).

Physically attractive people benefit from a "halo effect": They're *assumed* to possess other desirable social characteristics such as warmth, sexual responsiveness, kindness, poise, sociability, and good character. They're also seen as having more prestige, happier marriages, greater social and professional success, and more fulfilling lives. In reality, life satisfaction is much the same for both attractive and less attractive people (Brehm et al., 2002; Olson and Marshuetz, 2005).

Throughout the world, men (regardless of their looks) are more likely than women to want an attractive mate (Buss and Schmitt, 1993). In the United States and many other Western countries, and particularly for women, attractiveness is synonymous with slimness, youth, and big breasts.

You saw in Chapters 5 and 7 that the pressure for U.S. girls to be thin and attractive begins as early as elementary school and continues into old age. Businesses are delighted by women's obsession with their looks. Says one marketing analyst, "Anything with the words 'age defying' sells" (Mayer, 1999: A1). As a result, we can be seduced into believing that we've halted or slowed the aging process by using a variety of products, and most of those products target women. Among them are age-defying toothpaste, hosiery, creams, and makeup.

Online makeover businesses are also flourishing. The services—which can cost up to $2,000—rewrite personal profiles, start initial e-mail conversations, airbrush photos, or hire professionals to take the most flattering pictures (Alsever, 2007).

ETHNICITY AND RACE Worldwide, people tend to date and marry those within their own ethnic and racial group. About 91 percent of Americans did so in 2010 (see Chapter 4). According to a recent national survey, however, large numbers of blacks and whites, particularly men, said that being in a good romantic relationship was very important, and that they'd marry someone of another race (see *Table 8.1*).

These are attitudes. What about behavior, such as dating, a precursor to marriage? Except for white women, black–white interracial dating increased between 2006 and 2011 (see *Figure 8.2*). The rates are much lower, for both women and men, than for those who say they would be willing to marry someone of another race. For example, comparing the data in *Table 8.1* and *Figure 8.2*, a whopping 82 percent of white men said they would marry someone of a different race, but only 51 percent dated interracially in 2011.

You saw in Chapters 4 through 6 that many immigrant parents strongly prefer homogamous marriages for their children in terms of ethnicity, race, and religion. As children become more assimilated into U.S. culture, however, their dating preferences and behavior become more heterogamous. Among online daters, for example, both Latinas and Latinos are more likely than blacks and whites to prefer dating outside their own racial/ethnic group. However, endogamy is strongest among Latino Internet daters who live in cities (such as Los Angeles) with a high percentage of Latinos, speak little English, have less than a college degree, and feel strongly about preserving a Latino identity (Feliciano et al., 2011).

SOCIAL CLASS Most of us face strong pressures to date and marry people of similar (or preferably higher) social standing. Despite the popularity of films such as *Pretty Woman*, in which a powerful business mogul marries a prostitute, very few of the rich and powerful marry outside their social group (Kendall, 2002). Most Americans are unlikely to date and marry those from very different backgrounds—primarily because people from the same social class have similar attitudes, values, and lifestyles (Kalmijn, 1998; Charles et al., 2011).

The top row shows photographs of online daters before they used the services of makeover coaches. The bottom row shows their "after" photos.

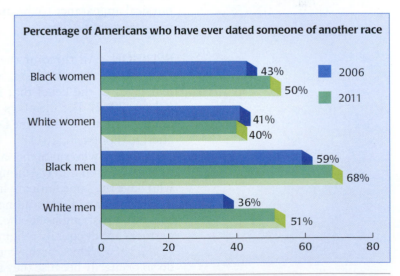

Percentage of Americans who have ever dated someone of another race

	2006	2011
Black women	43%	50%
White women	41%	40%
Black men	59%	68%
White men	36%	51%

FIGURE 8.2 Changes in Black–White Dating Behavior, 2006 and 2011 Overall, the percentage of Americans who have ever dated someone of another race has increased. *Source:* Based on data in *Washington Post*, 2012.

TABLE 8.1	U.S. Attitudes about Romance and Interracial Marriage among Blacks and Whites, 2011	
Percentage who said that . . .		
	. . . it's very important for them to be in a good romantic relationship	. . . they would be willing to marry someone of another race
Black women	44	67
White women	52	62
Black men	63	80
White men	60	82

Source: Based on data in *Washington Post,* 2012.

Parents may not have to exert much pressure on their children to date someone of their own kind because communities are typically organized by social class. Schools, churches, and recreational facilities reflect the socioeconomic status of neighborhoods. Thus, it's highly improbable that children living in upper-class neighborhoods will ever meet children from middle-class, much less working-class, families.

One researcher described colleges and universities as "matrimonial agencies" that are arranged hierarchically because students at Ivy League, private, public, and community colleges have few chances to meet one another. Because they influence their children by helping them choose a college, many parents narrow their children's dating choices in terms of social class (Eckland, 1968).

Social class also interacts with other variables to promote homogamy. Blue-collar and white-collar workers rarely meet each other in the workplace because they occupy different physical spaces and have different schedules. At colleges and universities, for example, staff and maintenance workers are usually housed in different buildings or floors and rarely interact. If we add religion, age, and physical appearance to the mix, homogamy reduces the number of eligible dating partners even further.

RELIGION All three of the major religions practiced in the United States—Catholicism, Protestantism, and Judaism—have traditionally opposed interfaith marriages in the belief that they weaken individuals' commitment to the faith (Glenn, 2002). For members of the Church of Jesus Christ of Latter-Day Saints, finding a spouse of the same faith is central to being a Mormon and having a happy afterlife (Boorstein, 2011).

Couples who share the same religious beliefs and practices tend to be happier than those who don't. Among whites, blacks, and Latinos, for example, couples who have the same faith are likely to engage in regular in-home worship activities (e.g., prayer and Bible readings) and to say that they have a good marital relationship and satisfying home life. However, there can be considerable conflict when partners aren't equally religious, such as not attending religious services (Ellison et al., 2010). Thus, perhaps the couples who "pray together and stay together" do so primarily because they share other activities, such as shopping and cooking together, and have similar personality traits that override religious differences.

AGE In some African and Middle East countries, girls under age 13 are often married off to men who may be 30 or 40 years older. Americans are age-endogamous because they tend to date and marry within the same age group.

Typically, the man is only a few years older than the woman. Among people who are dating, a large majority (68 percent) say that they wouldn't marry a man who is 10 or more years younger than they are; 65 percent of men say that they wouldn't marry a woman who is 10 or more years older than they are (2006 Dating Trends Survey, 2006; see also, Chapter 10).

Men often seek younger women because they want to have families. In some cases, however, a woman may find that a much older man may be unwilling to have children, especially if he has a family from a previous marriage or is expected to share in the child-rearing responsibilities. Large age differences may also lead to generation gaps in lifestyles, such as music preferences, recreation, and family activities. Successful women who have their own resources sometimes seek younger, attractive men with few assets but who can be "molded" (K. A. Moore et al., 2006). There's little evidence, however, that such unions are widespread.

VALUES AND PERSONALITY   In the 1950s and 1960s, some theories were based on the belief that people are drawn to each other because of *complementary needs;* in other words, opposites attract (Winch, 1958). This and similar perspectives have fallen out of scientific favor because the vast majority of research shows that people tend to select mates with similar demographic characteristics, values, attitudes, and interests (that is, "birds of a feather flock together") (Regan, 2003; Rick et al., 2011).

Some men looking for love flaunt flashy accessories such as sports cars and expensive watches and clothes. Such luxury spending may attract dates and sexual flings, but not marriage partners. Many women aren't impressed with such *conspicuous consumption* (attaining costly items to impress others with one's wealth or status). They often, and correctly, interpret pricey displays as signaling interest in a short-term sexual tryst rather than a long-term relationship that involves financial planning for the future (Sundie et al., 2011).

A 31-year-old flight attendant was stunned when, during her first date with a handsome man, he asked her "What's your credit score?" He dropped her after a few dates, even though he said that she was perfect for him because "[my] low credit score was his deal-breaker" (Silver-Greenberg, 2012: A1). It's difficult to know how many daters factor credit scores into their romantic calculations, but doing so is realistic because businesses use credit scores to determine people's ability to qualify for mortgages, car loans, apartment leases, and credit cards—all of which are important in long-term relationships.

According to many financial advisors, "tightwads" shouldn't marry "spendthrifts." Dating or marrying someone with very different views about finances is a major source of conflict because "Couples don't fight over love; they fight over money" (Opdyke, 2010). You'll see in Chapter 15 that financial problems are a foremost reason for divorce.

Political preferences also matter. People may not be concerned about politics at the beginning of a relationship, but at some point in the dating process, they filter out people who don't share similar political views. Because spouses don't tend to adapt to one another's political beliefs over time, incompatible political ideologies, like financial behavior, can be a major source of arguments. In contrast, similar social and political views tend to promote marital stability and long-term relationships (Alford et al., 2011; Klofstad et al., 2012).

Similar personalities are also important in dating and, eventually, marital satisfaction. Couples who are similar on characteristics such as self-reliance

Men are more likely than women to seek a physically attractive partner, but members of both sexes tend to choose partners whose physical appearance is similar to their own.

Since you asked . . .
• Do opposites attract?

and optimism are generally happier because personality differences can spark anger and resentment. Also, people who are similar in personality tend to have similar emotional responses (such as amusement, anger, or sadness) that enhance a relationship (Gaunt, 2006; Gonzaga et al., 2007; Humbad et al., 2010).

Filter theory explains how we narrow our pool of eligible partners. Increasing numbers of people, however, are expanding their marriage markets through heterogamy.

Heterogamy: Expanding the Marriage Market

heterogamy Dating or marrying someone with social characteristics that differ from your own (sometimes called *exogamy*).

Often used interchangeably with the term *exogamy* (see Chapter 1), **heterogamy** refers to dating or marrying someone with social characteristics that differ from your own. The differences include social class, race, ethnicity, religion, and age. In India, for example, heterogamy rules forbid marriage between individuals of similarly named clans, even though the families have never met (Singh, 2005).

Worldwide, mate selection is still limited by homogamy. Increasingly, however, many people have more choices in dating people of the same sex (see Chapters 9 and 10) and across social classes, religions, and racial and ethnic boundaries.

hypergamy Marrying up to a higher social class.

SOCIAL CLASS   Most of us marry within our social class, but not always. **Hypergamy** refers to marrying up to a higher social class. Initially, many Britons frowned on Prince William's engagement to Kate Middleton because she's a "commoner." Her parents are "fabulously rich," but not of "noble birth" (Faiola, 2010).

hypogamy Marrying down in social class.

Hypogamy, in contrast, refers to marrying down in social class. In a much-publicized dating advice book, journalist Lori Gottlieb (2010) claims that single, successful women have gotten too picky. Instead, they should marry down by grabbing "Mr. Good Enough." The problem with such advice, according to feminist writers, is that "Settling, which is essentially lowering your standards and expectations for yourself . . . is what women have done for generations . . . [and] leads to high divorce rates, sexless marriages, cheating, and generally unhappy lives" (Mukhopadhyay, 2011: 128; see also Rivers, 2010).

Since you asked . . .
- Why do some African Americans disapprove of interracial dating?

INTERFAITH RELATIONSHIPS   Historically, religion has been an important factor in dating and mate selection in the United States and many other countries. Now, U.S. interfaith dating and marriages are more common. For example, 37 percent of married Americans are in religiously mixed marriages (Pew Forum on Religion & Public Life, 2008).

Religiosity is important for people who have traditional values about gender roles (such as the belief that men should be breadwinners and women should be full-time homemakers). However, religious beliefs are less important for couples who have egalitarian attitudes about family roles and who seek partners with similar personalities (Gaunt, 2006). Race and ethnicity, in contrast, still play a major role in who we date and marry.

Is Kate Middleton's marriage to Prince William an example of hypergamy, hypogamy, or both?

INTERRACIAL AND INTERETHNIC RELATIONSHIPS   U.S. interracial and interethnic marriage rates have risen (see *Figure 8.3*). In 8 percent of all marriages and 15 percent of all new marriages, the bride and groom are of a different race or ethnicity. In 2010, Asian American newlyweds had the highest interracial

and interethnic rates (28 percent), followed by Latinos (26 percent) (Wang, 2012).

However, and especially among blacks and Asian Americans, there are significant gender differences in marrying outside of one's racial or ethnic group. As *Figure 8.4* shows, black women and Asian men are the least likely to intermarry. Black men are almost three times more likely than black women to marry someone outside of their race (24 percent and 9 percent, respectively). More than any other group, African American women face what one black journalist calls a "marriage crunch": "The better educated we are, the less likely we are to meet brothers who can match our credentials. The more successful we are, the less likely we are to meet brothers who can match our pocketbooks" (Chambers, 2003: 136).

One in nine black men ages 20 to 34 are in prison or jail, decreasing the pool of eligible partners. Since 1976, nearly twice as many black women as black men have earned bachelor's, doctoral, and professional degrees (in fields such as medicine, law, and theology). Thus, many well-educated and successful black women find that they have a small number of eligible mates who match their education and income levels (Pew Center on the States, 2009; Snyder and Dillow, 2012).

Because of the shortage of eligible mates, many black women are *interdating*, going out with a member of another racial or ethnic group. Some black female writers, especially, encourage African American women to expand their horizons by dating and marrying interracially instead of waiting for that one "good" black man to come along and sweep them off their feet (Folan, 2010).

Not everyone embraces such advice. In 2009, for example, a justice of the peace in Louisiana refused to grant a marriage license to an interracial couple: "I'm not a racist. I just don't believe in mixing the races that way" (Time, 2009: 8). And as "Why I Never Dated a White Girl" shows, a number of African Americans also disapprove of interracial dating.

Asian men (see *Figure 8.4*) also have much lower intermarriage rates (17 percent) than Asian women (36 percent). The reasons reflect both choices and constraints. A study of heterosexual online dating profiles found that 21 percent of Asian men compared with only 6 percent of Asian women specified wanting to date only Asians (Robnett and Feliciano, 2011). This suggests that many Asian men are more endogamous than Asian women.

The same study found that 40 percent of Asian women but only 10 percent of Asian men excluded Asians from their preferences. Moreover, more than 90 percent of Latinas, black, and white women excluded Asian men from their dating choices. The reasons for the exclusion aren't clear (perhaps many women see Asian men as more foreign), but women's choices limit Asian men's dating pool. Conversely, Asian men may have lower intermarriage rates than Latino and white men because the recent influx of Asian immigrants has expanded Asian men's pool of eligible mates (see Wang, 2012).

Filter theory proposes that social structure limits our opportunities to meet people who are different from us. What influences our decision to stay in a

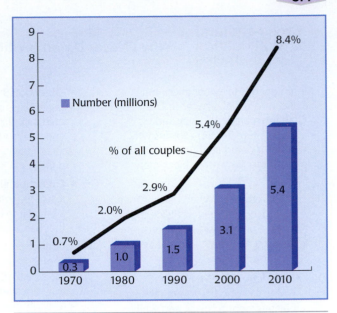

FIGURE 8.3 Interracial Marriages Have Increased in the United States
Sources: Based on Lee and Edmonston, 2005, Figure 1; and Wang, 2012.

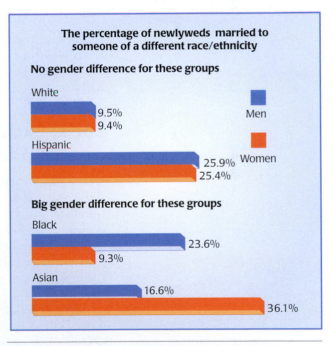

FIGURE 8.4 Intermarriage Rates of Newlyweds, by Sex, Race, and Ethnicity, 2010
Source: Wang, 2012: 9.

Cross-Cultural and Multicultural Families | Why I Never Dated a White Girl

Interdating is fairly common, but still controversial. Lawrence Otis Graham, a black attorney and author (1996: 36–56) explains why he's never dated a white woman and, presumably, why other black men shouldn't either:

- **Objection 1:** When black leaders or advocates marry outside their race, such decisions demonstrate less commitment to black people and our causes.

- **Objection 2:** We fear that intermarrying blacks are making a statement to black and white America that black spouses are less desirable partners and are therefore inferior.

- **Objection 3:** Interracial marriage undermines our ability to introduce our black children to black mentors and role models who accept their racial identity with confidence and pride.

- **Objection 4:** Because it diffuses our resources, interracial marriage makes it difficult to build a black America that has wealth, prestige, and power.

- **Objection 5:** We worry that confused biracial children will turn their backs on the black race once they discover that it's easier to live as a white person.

- **Objection 6:** Today's interracial relationships are a painful reminder of a 250-year period in black

American history when white people exploited our sexuality.

STOP AND THINK . . .

- Do you agree with Graham's reasons for not dating and marrying outside the African American community? Or do you think that his objections are outdated?

- Graham says why he believes that interracial dating and marriage are dysfunctional. Think back to the discussion of manifest and latent functions of dating at the beginning of the chapter. How is interdating functional?

relationship or to move on? Exchange theory and equity theory maintain that satisfaction is a key factor in weighing our mate selection investments and liabilities.

Social Exchange Theory: Dating as Give and Take

Social exchange theory posits that people will begin (and remain in) a relationship if the rewards are higher than the costs. *Rewards* may be intrinsic characteristics (intelligence, a sense of humor), behaviors (sex, companionship), or access to desired resources (money, power). *Costs*, the price paid, may be unpleasant or destructive behavior (insults, violence) or losses (a lower social class, time invested in a relationship). "Am I Seeing the Wrong Person?" offers advice from practitioners in recognizing some of the costs of staying in an unhealthy relationship.

What, specifically, are some of the resources that people exchange in dating? One is money. When there's a scarcity of eligible single women, both sexes expect men to spend more on dinners, Valentine's Day gifts, and engagement rings, even if doing so increases men's credit card debt (Griskevicius et al., 2012).

About 62 percent of American men and 44 percent of American women have done something special for someone (saying "I love you," preparing a special meal, buying an expensive present) because they hoped it would lead to sex. People who are physically attractive trade this attribute for a partner's higher education and income level. Among midlife adults (ages 40 to 69), men, never-married singles, and those who are sexually permissive are more willing to date people of a different race or religion or with much less money (Orr and Stout, 2007; Carmalt et al., 2008; Fitzpatrick et al., 2009). Thus, people weigh their rewards and costs in choosing dating partners.

ASK YOURSELF

Am I Seeing the Wrong Person?

Because often "love is blind," many people overlook serious flaws and marry Mr. or Ms. Wrong. Here are some red flags that should alert you to possible problems.

- **Don Juans and other sexual predators.** Men admit using a variety of "lines" to persuade women to have sex. These Don Juans will *declare their love for you* ("I don't want to have sex with you—I want to make love to you"), *flatter you* ("You're one of the most beautiful women I've ever seen"), *make meaningless promises* ("I swear I'll get a divorce"), *threaten you with rejection* ("If you loved me, you would"), *put you down* if you refuse ("You're really old-fashioned"), or *challenge you* to prove that you're "normal" ("Are you gay?").

- **Incompatibility of basic values.** Initially, it may be exciting to be with someone who's very different. In the long run, however, serious differences in values may jeopardize a relationship.

- **Rigid sex roles.** If your partner wants you to be a full-time homemaker and parent but you want a career, there may be conflict.

- **Emotional baggage.** If your partner often talks about an ex-partner—comparing you with her "saintly" dead husband or his past lovers—she or he is living in the past instead of getting to know you.

- **Extreme jealousy and violent tendencies.** Stay away from someone who's possessive, jealous, or violent. Characteristics such as a bad temper, frequent angry outbursts, constant criticism, and sudden mood swings won't decrease in the future.

- **Substance abuse.** Someone who is addicted to alcohol or other drugs is the wrong choice for a mate. Watch for slowed responses, slurred speech, glassy eyes, extreme mood swings, or failure to keep dates.

- **Excessive time spent with others.** Does your partner spend several nights a week with others while you spend time alone? If your partner is always on the phone, or if family "emergencies" often come before your needs, there will probably be similar conflicts in the future.

- **Mr. Flirt and Ms. Tease.** If your partner is flirtatious or a sexual tease, watch out. Flirting may be entertaining at first, but not over the long run.

- **Lack of communication.** Good communication is essential for a good relationship. Feelings of boredom, evidence of your partner's disinterest, or finding that you have little to talk about may signal serious communication problems that will decrease intimacy.

- **Control freaks.** Does your partner always try to change or control you or the relationship? Do you constantly feel criticized, judged, scrutinized, and corrected, especially in public?

- **Blaming others for problems.** It's always someone else's fault if something goes wrong ("My boss didn't appreciate me" instead of "I was fired because I always came in late").

Sources: Powell, 1991; Collison, 1993; Kenrick et al., 1993.

Equity Theory: Dating as a Search for Egalitarian Relationships

According to **equity theory**, an extension of social exchange theory, an intimate relationship is satisfying and stable if both partners see it as equitable and mutually beneficial (Walster et al., 1973). Equity theory advances several basic propositions:

- The greater the perceived equity, the happier the relationship.

- When people find themselves in an inequitable relationship, they become distressed. The greater the inequity, the greater the distress.

- People in an inequitable relationship will attempt to eliminate their distress by restoring equity.

Equity theory reflects the American sense of fair play, the notion that one has a right to expect a reasonable balance between costs and benefits in life. If we give more than we receive, we usually become angry. If we receive more than our fair share of benefits, we may feel guilty. In each case, we experience dissatisfaction with the relationship. We try to decrease the distress and restore equity by changing our behavior, persuading a partner to change his or her behavior, or by convincing ourselves that the inequity doesn't exist (Miell and Croghan, 1996).

Consider Mike and Michelle, who were initially happy with their dating relationship. Among other exchanges, she helped him with his calculus and he

equity theory Proposes that an intimate relationship is satisfying and stable if both partners see it as equitable and mutually beneficial.

 Read on MySocLab

Document: Egalitarian Daters/Traditionalist Dates

MAKING CONNECTIONS

- Think about the people you've dated or the person you've married. Did filter theory influence your behavior? If so, which variables were the most important?

- Have you weighed rewards and costs in deciding whom to date (or marry) or break up?

- Some people maintain that interracial dating and interracial marriage are healthy because they'll will break down our society's racial-ethnic barriers. Others argue that interracial relationships dilute one's cultural heritage. What do *you* think?

helped her write a paper for a sociology class. By the end of the semester, Michelle was still helping Mike with his calculus assignments, but Mike was no longer helping Michelle with her sociology paper because he had joined the swim team. According to equity theory, Mike might feel guilty and increase his help, Mike and Michelle could renegotiate their contributions, or one or both could break up the relationship.

Judgments about equity vary depending on the stage of the relationship. As two people get acquainted, severe inequity usually ends further involvement. Once a relationship becomes a long-term commitment, people tolerate inequity—especially if they plan to marry—because they're optimistic about the future. In most long-term relationships, however, and especially as people make transitions (such as parenthood), perceived inequities can increase stress and dissatisfaction (Sprecher, 2001).

8.5 Describe some of the mate-selection differences across cultures.

A Multicultural View of Mate Selection

Societies around the world vary considerably in their mate-selection methods. Some of these variations involve differences between modern and traditional approaches, heterogamy and homogamy, and arranged marriages.

Traditional and Modern Societies

Most countries don't have the open courtship systems that are common in Western nations. Instead, factors such as wealth and the practice of child marriages reinforce traditional mate-selection arrangements.

Read on MySocLab

Document: Mate Selection and Marriage around the World

dowry The money, goods, or property a woman brings to a marriage.

WEALTH In some Mediterranean, Middle Eastern, and Asian societies, a **dowry**—the money, goods, or property that a woman brings to a marriage—is an important factor in mate selection and marriage. Women with large dowries can attract the best suitors. If the bride's family fails to meet dowry expectations, their newlywed daughter may face crushing responsibilities in her new household, violence, and even death (see Chapters 5 and 6).

Even though the Indian government has outlawed the dowry system, it still flourishes. Many women who disapprove of dowries in principle regard them as necessary, in practice, to attract the most desirable men and as a way for young couples to obtain household goods (Srinivasan and Lee, 2004).

bride price The required payment by the groom's family to the bride's family.

Whereas a dowry is a payment by the family of the bride, a **bride price** is the required payment by the groom's family. The payment varies from a few cattle to thousands of dollars. In South Sudan, the bride price has risen 44 percent since 2005. An educated wife costs 50 cows, 60 goats, and about $12,000 in cash. At that price, many bachelors have gone into debt or have joined cattle-raiding gangs, which set off a cycle of reprisals and tribal violence (Richmond and Krause-Jackson, 2011).

Some have criticized the bride price for treating women as property and for discouraging marriage among poor men. Many defend the custom, however. For example, many rural Africans argue that paying for a bride bonds families and decreases the likelihood of wife abuse. In Afghanistan, a bride price ensures a man's getting a virgin (sometimes as young as 8 years old) who will till fields, tend livestock, and bear children. In return, the bride's family delivers the girl from hunger and pays off some debts (Bearak, 2006; Calvert, 2006).

In Libya, Egypt, and other developing parts of the Arab world, young men are putting off marriage because they can't provide brides with a home and a sizeable bride price, as custom demands. In Egypt, the poorest grooms and their fathers must save their total income for about eight years to afford a wedding.

In some communities, charities pay for mass weddings—such as this one in Idku, Egypt—to help couples, many in their late thirties and forties, who can't afford to marry.

To encourage marriage in the poorest communities, the government and charities help finance mass weddings (Knickmeyer, 2007; Slackman, 2008).

CHILD BRIDES The minimum age at which people may marry varies widely from one country to another. In industrialized societies, the minimum age at marriage may be 16 or 18. In traditional countries in Africa, parents can betroth a baby girl to a friend's 4-year-old son, before the girl is 10 years old, or to a man who may be 20 or 30 years older than the girl (Wilson et al., 2003; Modo, 2005).

More than 25,000 girls a day are forcibly married before the age of 18, many as young as 9 years old. The countries with the highest percentage of child brides are those in parts of Africa, Bangladesh (in South Asia), and the Middle East. Child brides often suffer from sexual abuse, domestic violence, and becoming mothers at a young age before their bodies are fully developed. Doing so puts the girls at high risk of maternal and infant death, and premature birth of infants with lifelong cognitive problems (Hervish and Feldman-Jacobs, 2011; Schnall, 2012).

Child marriage violates international laws on women's rights, but the practice is increasing in some countries. In Iran, for example, the number of girls who were wed before the age of 10 doubled between 2009 and 2010. Conservative leaders defend child marriage as complying with Islamic Sharia law; critics argue that child brides are exploited by their fathers who must pay off debts to older men (Tait, 2012).

Heterogamy and Homogamy

Worldwide, mate selection varies according to heterogamy and homogamy norms. Heterogamy, you recall, involves marrying outside one's social group, whereas homogamy refers to marrying someone within one's social group.

In a number of developing societies, the younger the bride, the higher the price she fetches. A father uses the bride price to ward off poverty, buy farm animals, and pay off debts. Pictured here, this 11-year-old in Afghanistan was married off to a 40-year-old man. She had hoped to be a teacher but was forced to quit school when she got married.

HETEROGAMY Heterogamy is thriving in many countries because people don't have prospective marriage mates in their own social group. Often, heterogamous marriages are based on economic decisions. For example, the number of women from mainland China who married foreigners rose from 26,000 in 1991 to 68,000 in 2006. The rates plunged in 2008, however, when the global economic crisis began: "Many Chinese women married their husbands [in Germany]

These men from South Korea are meeting potential brides during a marriage tour in Vietnam.

for their success and now [the men] are losing their jobs and cars. Many of them can't even pay their mortgages" (Ford, 2009: 5).

To escape poverty, many Vietnamese women in their early twenties are marrying foreigners, mostly from Taiwan and South Korea, who are in their forties or older. The wedding usually occurs shortly after the men spend a few days on a marriage tour to select their brides. In social exchange terms, the men—especially those from rural areas where women have moved to cities to work—find young wives who are eager to please. The women meet their obligation of saving their parents from destitution in old age, which many Vietnamese consider a child's greatest duty. The men promise to send the parents a monthly stipend and sometimes help the bride's father pay off some debts. Some of the women endure ongoing abuse after the wedding, but others are happy and have no regrets (Onishi, 2007; Santana, 2008; Kay, 2011).

To protect women from abuse, the Cambodian government recently ruled that foreign men older than age 50 or who make less than $2,500 per month can no longer marry Cambodian women. The regulations, according to female lawmakers, hope to prevent "fake marriages," in which elderly men, particularly from South Korean, "use marriage to obtain a free maid" (Masis, 2011: 6).

HOMOGAMY In many traditional societies, mate selection is strictly homogamous. In Afghanistan, for example, there is an old saying that "a marriage between cousins is the most righteous because the engagement was made in heaven." Across the Arab world, an average of 45 percent of married partners are related (Kershaw, 2003; Aizenman, 2005).

Homogamy has its advantages. In India—where 70 percent marry within their own caste—homogamous mate selection ensures that people marry within their social class and can pass down their wealth to a kin group. In both India and Turkey, homogamy ensures strong and continuing family ties (Nauck and Klaus, 2005; Banerjee et al., 2009).

Homogamy also has costs. In Cuba—despite the government's formal policy of racial heterogeneity—racist beliefs about black inferiority and racial purity discourage people from seeking partners with lighter or darker skin colors. In Sri Lanka, classified ads for marriage partners ask respondents to indicate their caste because educated people don't want to mate with people from lower socioeconomic groups (Roschelle et al., 2005; Magnier, 2006).

Homogamy can also increase the chances of passing down diseases. In some parts of Saudi Arabia, for example, in which blood relatives range from 55 to 70 percent of married couples, such inbreeding produces genetic disorders, including thalassemia (a potentially fatal blood disease), sickle cell anemia, spinal muscular atrophy, diabetes, deafness, and muteness. Educated Saudis have begun to pull away from the practice, but the tradition of marrying first cousins is still deeply embedded in Saudi culture. In Afghanistan, where first-cousin marriages are common because women are prohibited from mingling with unrelated men, doctors are finding that children have a higher chance of being born with birth defects and diseases, such as brain disorders and mental retardation, that might be inherited (Kershaw, 2003; Aizenman, 2005).

Arranged Marriages

In many cultures, the most important obligation of parents is to help their children find a suitable spouse, settle down, and have a family. As a result, matchmakers (who are usually parents and female relatives) wield enormous power in arranging marriages (Janmohamed, 2010).

In arranged marriages, the family or community is more important than the individual. Such marriages increase solidarity between families, kinship groups,

Since you asked . . .
• Are arranged marriages vanishing?

clans, and tribes. Arranged marriages are disappearing in some developing countries but are a mainstay in many others. In India, for example, as many as 90 percent of marriages are arranged, and 71 percent of the people believe that such unions are more successful than "love marriages" (Cullen and Masters, 2008). Pakistan legalized marriage without the consent of a woman's guardian in 2003, but some form of arranged marriage is the most common way for Pakistanis to find spouses (Ladly, 2012).

Arranged marriages often involve marrying a first cousin as the top choice. In 2008 alone, 4,000 Pakistani girls born in Great Britain were coerced into marrying first cousins or other men during visits to Pakistan. Islam doesn't allow forced arranged marriages, but such cultural practices are common in societies where men dominate and can force girls and women to marry against their will "to preserve culture and lineage" (Tohid, 2003: 7; Grose, 2008; James, 2012).

In some societies, the penalties for dishonoring a family by refusing an arranged marriage are severe. In Afghanistan, couples who have eloped have been stoned. In India, around 900 people are killed each year by parents and male relatives for marrying someone against a parent's wishes. In Pakistan, similarly, women who enter what are called "freewill marriages" may be killed (Nordland, 2010; "Death Penalty for 10 . . .," 2011; Ladly, 2012; see also Chapter 5).

How Mate-Selection Methods Are Changing

Some countries in Asia and the Middle East are changing in how people meet and choose mates. Arranged marriages are widespread in rural areas and small towns, but people who live in cities often meet their mates in the same kinds of settings as Westerners—on college campuses, at parties, in public places, and increasingly via online dating sites.

China and India are experiencing a glut of single men and a scarcity of single women. In both countries, a preference for sons, available technology to determine the sex of the fetus, and easy access to abortion have resulted in a surplus of men. In China, for example, there are 40 million males who, in 2020, will be unable to find and marry young Chinese women their age (Hesketh et al., 2011; Poston et al., 2011; Larmer, 2013).

CHINA   China has responded to the preponderance of males by implementing some Western-style mate-selection methods, including newspaper and magazine ads and online dating sites (Jiang, 2011). In Beijing, on any of four days each week, hundreds of parents go to one of the city's three parks to play matchmaker. Anxious that their mid-twenties children are still unmarried because they're in fast-track jobs and don't have time to date, the parents are determined to find mates for them. They come prepared with photos and computer printouts describing the adult child and his or her desired mate—for example, "Male, 28 years old, 1.72 meters tall [about 5' 6"], a junior college graduate from an upper-middle-class family, seeking a shorter woman between 16 and 23 years of age, with a high school degree, a stable income, and a Beijing residence permit" (Epstein, 2005: 1A).

Parents aren't the only ones trying to fix up their children. In 2011, singles themselves swamped matchmaking events held in Beijing during the Chinese New Year holidays, with an estimated 50,000 at a weeklong event in the capital's Ditan Park (Duncan, 2011). Also, many manufacturing companies sponsor matchmaking events such as speed dating to attract and retain young workers (Chu, 2013).

Because of the surplus of men, college-educated Chinese women are becoming pickier. According to the founder of Jiayuan.com, China's largest online dating agency, female customers list owning a house and a good salary as the main criteria. "Now, if you don't find someone suitable, you just don't settle" (*Bloomberg News*, 2012: 14). A recent Beijing-based survey found that 75 percent of women consider a man's ability to purchase a home before agreeing to marry him ("Are High House Prices . . .," 2013). Despite the gender imbalance, Chinese

Explore on MySocLab

Activity: Fishing for a Mate? Eligibility Characteristics in Alaska

Every Sunday, parents gather at a park in Nanjing, China, to find mates for their unmarried children. Parental matchmaking has become more aggressive because many urban Chinese youth, often in their mid- to late-twenties, are busy with careers and are postponing marriage.

women face intense pressure to marry before age 28 to avoid being rejected and stigmatized as "leftover women" (Larmer, 2013: BU1).

INDIA   Besides relying on paid matchmakers, India has scores of matrimonial websites that are similar to dating sites. Parents and others post "biodata" that include information on recreational interests, education, height and weight, complexion color, personality, monthly pay, drinking and smoking habits, and especially family history (including caste and sometimes blood type) (Abdulrahim, 2008; Narayan, 2013).

Because many young people living in India and overseas who meet on a matrimonial website marry within a few weeks, increasing numbers of parents are hiring "wedding detectives" who investigate a prospective groom's background. As India's middle and upper classes grow, so do dowries, which often invite fraud, especially by men living abroad. With an estimated 30,000 brides who are abandoned every year by suitors who disappear after collecting a dowry, detective agencies are a thriving new industry (Wax, 2008).

Traditional dating sites, such as Match.com, haven't been very popular because matrimonial websites, professional matchmakers, and parents do a better job of finding prospective mates. However, sites that provide a combination of dating, social networking, and offline "friending" are becoming popular (Seligson, 2011).

JAPAN AND SOUTH KOREA   In Japan and South Korea, the mating game has also changed, in part because more women are acquiring a college education, finding jobs, postponing marriage, or preferring to remain single. To retain the loyalty of unmarried employees in the under-40 age bracket, several companies in Japan have engaged matrimony brokerage firms to act as matchmakers for those seeking a spouse. In South Korea, leading companies such as Samsung ask agencies to organize group blind dates as a benefit for single employees, and major banks vie for rich private customers by offering free matchmaking for their children (Sang-Hun, 2007; Ito and Yui, 2010).

OTHER COUNTRIES   In some parts of Spain, the Dominican Republic, Ecuador, and Colombia, women are scarce because they've left home to work in cities. To help men find mates, some enterprising farmers have organized "Cupid crusades." Women who are disenchanted with city life board a bus and spend a day with a group of bachelors: "Lonely hearts mingle over roasted lamb and a halting *pasodoble*, or two-step." An event usually lasts eight hours, and some of the encounters result in marriage (Fuchs, 2003).

Iranian lawmakers are considering legalizing matchmaking websites because of a "marriage crisis." Young people, particularly those in urban areas, are postponing marriage because of unemployment, traditional lavish wedding parties and dowries that many parents can't afford, women enrolling at universities in larger numbers than men, and pursuing careers. "Young single people are a headache for authorities trying to maintain a religious state; authorities fear that the longer young adults are single, the more likely they are to indulge in premarital sex or other perceived vices" (Mostaghim and Alpert, 2012: 22).

Harmful Dating Relationships: Power, Control, and Violence

So far we've focused on the positive side of dating: how people meet and what qualities they look for in marital partners. Dating also has a dark side that includes power, control, and violence.

Power and Control in Dating Relationships

Sociologist Willard Waller's (1937) *principle of least interest* states that the partner who is less interested in the relationship has more power, and, as a result, more control. Conversely, the person who is very interested in continuing the relationship is more dependent, has less power, and, as a result, can be manipulated or exploited (Lloyd, 1991; Sarch, 1993).

Men often maintain power and control during a dating relationship through direct strategies such as threats and aggression; women more often use indirect strategies such as hinting, withdrawing, or attempting to manipulate a partner's

8.6 Describe the prevalence of dating violence, and explain why it occurs and its consequences.

 Watch on MySocLab

Video: Different Types of Partner Violence

Constraints | How Abusers Control Dating Relationships

Both men and women try to control relationships. The following categories describe the experiences of female victims, but men are also subject to abusive dating relationships.

- **Jealousy and blaming:** Blaming is often based on jealousy; almost anything the partner does is considered provocative. For example, a man may criticize his partner for not being home when he calls or for talking to another man. He may say he loves her so much that he can't stand for her to be with others, including male friends.

- **Coercion, intimidation, and threats:** Abusers may coerce compliance by threatening their partners. An abuser says things such as "I'll break your neck" or "I'll kill you" and then dismisses such comments with "Everybody talks like that." Abusers also threaten to commit suicide or to attack a partner's family.

- **Isolation:** Typically, abusers spend a lot of time and energy watching their victims. They accuse family and friends of "causing trouble." Abusers may deprive victims of a phone or a car, or even try to prevent them from holding a job. If these isolating techniques work, they break the partner's ties with other friends and increase dependence on the abuser.

- **Physical abuse:** Violent acts range from slaps and shoves to beatings, rape, and attacks with weapons. Many abusers manage to convince a partner, on each violent occasion, that "I really love you" and "This will never happen again," but it does. And in some cases the last time the abuser strikes, he or she kills.

- **Emotional and verbal abuse:** Emotional abuse is very powerful. Insults, which attack a person's feelings of independence and self-worth, are generally intended to

get the partner to succumb to the abuser's demands ("Don't wear your skirt so short—it makes you look like a hooker"). The abuser often says or implies that the victim had better do what the partner wants or be left without anyone.

- **Sexual abuse:** Conflicts about sex can lead to violence. Often a male abuser decides whether to have sex, which sex acts are acceptable, and whether the couple will use condoms or other contraceptive devices.

Sources: Gamache, 1990; Rosen and Stith, 1993; Shackelford et al., 2005.

STOP AND THINK . . .
- Have you, your friends, or relatives experienced any of these forms of abuse? How did you react?
- Do you think that we can really love someone we're afraid of?

---

emotions (Christopher and Kisler, 2004; Garbarino, 2006). "How Abusers Control Dating Relationships" examines some coercive tactics in more detail.

Prevalence of Dating Violence

Since you asked . . .
- Are men or women guiltier of dating violence?

Control often increases as a relationship progresses from casual to more serious dating. Men are much more likely than women to use physical force and sexual aggression, but women can also be physically and emotionally abusive (Christopher and Kisler, 2004; Prothrow-Stith and Spivak, 2005; see also Chapter 14).

DATING VIOLENCE   Dating violence is widespread. Consider the following statistics:

- Among 13- to 14-year olds, 20 percent knew friends and peers who had been kicked, hit, slapped, or punched by a boyfriend or girlfriend (Liz Claiborne Inc., 2008; for similar findings among those ages 12 to 17, see Mulford and Giordano, 2008).

- Almost 10 percent of U.S. high school students said that they had been hit, slapped, or physically hurt on purpose by a girlfriend or boyfriend (Eaton and Rose, 2012).

- Among young adults ages 20 to 24, 26 percent experienced violence with a romantic partner, either as a victim or a perpetrator (Scott et al., 2011).

- Among couples ages 18 to 28, 36 percent reported experiencing violence; 20 percent were mutually abusive (Berger et al., 2012).

- About 27 percent of college women have been raped or have suffered attempted rape (Lauerman, 2013).

Dating violence is rarely a one-time event. Many women misinterpret the violence as evidence of love. According to a domestic violence counselor, "With so little real-life experience, girls tend to take jealousy and possessiveness to mean 'he loves me' " (L. Harris, 1996: 5). A ninth-grade Latina echoed these sentiments on why her friends tolerate abuse: "She's going to be like, 'Well, it's because he cares about me and doesn't want me to do it again and he loves me' " (Ocampo et al., 2007: 184).

ACQUAINTANCE AND DATE RAPE   In 2012, the FBI revised its 85-year-old legal definition of *rape*. The new definition includes men as victims; oral, anal, and vaginal penetration; and penetration by any body part or object.

Most dating violence and date rape occur in situations that seem safe and familiar. This is why these behaviors often come as a shock to the victim, who can't believe what is happening. Women are especially vulnerable to acquaintance and date rape. **Acquaintance rape** is unwanted and forced sexual intercourse of a person who knows or is familiar with the rapist. Acquaintance rapists may include neighbors, friends of the family, co-workers, or someone whom the victim meets at a party or get-together.

Date rape is unwanted, forced sexual intercourse in a dating situation; the victim and the perpetrator may be on a first date or in a steady relationship. Nationally, women are more likely to be raped by a date or an acquaintance than by a spouse or ex-spouse, a stranger, or a live-in partner (see *Figure 8.5*). One of the reasons date rape is so common and traumatic is that, typically, the rapist seems to be "a nice guy"—polite, clean-cut, and even a leader in the community or on campus.

acquaintance rape Unwanted and forced sexual intercourse of a person who knows or is familiar with the rapist.

date rape Unwanted, forced sexual intercourse in a dating situation.

Factors Contributing to Date Violence and Date Rape

There are many reasons for date violence and date rape. Let's begin with parenting styles and family violence.

Watch on MySocLab

Video: Sexual Violence Billboards

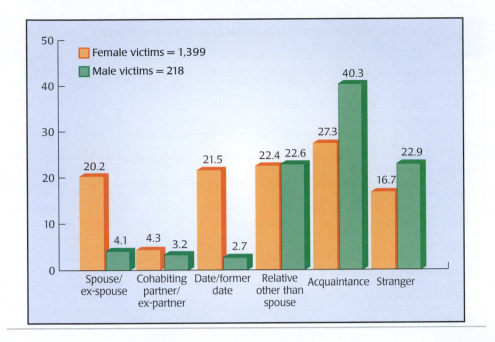

FIGURE 8.5 **Rape Victims and Victim–Offender Relationships**
Note: Percentages by sex exceed 100 because same victims were raped by more than one person.
Source: Tjaden and Thoennes, 2006, Exhibit 13.

PARENTING STYLES AND FAMILY VIOLENCE Dating violence is most common among youth who have experienced harsh and minimal parenting, had poor relationships with their parents, and abused a sibling. Such problems are compounded by growing up in a family in which children see adult violence or experience parent-to-child violence. Seeing the aggression increases the likelihood of being both an assailant and a victim during teen and adult dating (Baker and Stith, 2008; Espelage, 2011; Centers for Disease Control and Prevention, 2012).

GENDER ROLES Adopting traditional attitudes about gender roles increases the likelihood of date violence during both adolescence and adulthood. According to traditional sexual scripts (see Chapter 7), men can exert and maintain power by using verbal pressure and physical coercion to persuade a woman to have unwanted sex. Women with traditional views of gender roles may resent, but not resist, such aggression (Wright et al., 2010; Espelage, 2011; Hall and Canterberry, 2011).

Generally, men who commit date rape also hold traditional views of gender roles, seeing themselves as in charge and women as submissive. Some men who commit date rape and acquaintance rape also have stereotypical views of women's sexual behavior. They believe that women initially resist sexual advances to preserve their reputation and, consequently, prefer to be overcome sexually. In addition, some men believe that if a woman is "a tease," "loose," or "dresses like a slut," she's asking for sex (Christopher, 2001; Sampson, 2002; Topping, 2011).

DEMOGRAPHIC CHARACTERISTICS Date violence is more common in casual (25 percent) than exclusive (19 percent) relationships. Physical aggression in dating relationships is highest among adolescents, and tends to decrease in adulthood. Among young adults aged 20 to 24, white partners are less likely (23 percent) than their black (33 percent) and Latino (32 percent) counterparts to report having experienced relationship violence (Scott et al., 2011).

Among dating couples aged 18 to 28, violence is more common when both partners have only a high school diploma, have been dating longer than four years, there are children in the household, and both partners are from different racial/ethnic groups (see *Table 8.2*). We'll examine the reasons for these and other variations in Chapter 14.

In 2009, singer/songwriter Chris Brown, age 19, pleaded guilty to beating his girlfriend, pop singer Rihanna, age 21. He served five years of probation and did 180 days of community service. The couple got engaged in 2012 but broke up a year later. Despite the breakup (that may or may not last), does the engagement tell us anything about some women's accepting men's violence?

TABLE 8.2	Some Demographic Characteristics of Dating Violence among Young Adults
Percentage aged 18 to 28 who have experienced violence in their current dating relationship	
Education	
Some college or more	32%
A high school diploma	54%
Length of relationship	
Less than four years	30%
Longer than four years	60%
Children	
No children in the household	31%
Children in one or both households	63%
Partner's race-ethnicity	
Same race-ethnicity	35%
Different race-ethnicity	43%

Source: Based on Berger et al., 2012, text and Figures 4–7.

PEER PRESSURE AND SECRECY   In adolescence, there may be considerable conflict among daters over how much time they spend with each other versus with friends, jealousies because a partner seems to spend too much time with a friend of the opposite sex, and new romantic possibilities. Because many teens are inexperienced in communicating with a romantic partner and don't have constructive coping skills in dealing with frustration, they often use aggression to control a partner (Mulford and Giordano, 2008).

Peer pressure is one of the major reasons why some partners are violent and why many stay in abusive dating relationships. Secrecy protects abusers. Most teenagers are silent about abusive relationships because they don't want their friends to put pressure on them to break up. They rarely tell their parents about the abuse because they don't feel close to them, are afraid of losing their freedom, don't want their parents to think they have poor judgment, or fear that their friends will criticize them if the parents report the abuse to the police (Ocampo et al., 2007).

Peer pressure is even greater in college. In some cases, fraternity members and male athletes cover up incidents of sexual abuse, especially when it occurs during and/or after a party that includes alcohol and other drugs. And, on many college campuses, sorority leaders acknowledge that talking about relationship violence is not "socially acceptable," nor do they know how to help members who are experiencing date abuse (Larimer et al., 1999; Danis and Anderson, 2008: 337).

USE OF ALCOHOL AND OTHER DRUGS   Although they aren't the cause, alcohol and drugs play a large role in sexual assaults, including dating. Since the mid-1990s, college women have reported being raped after their drink was spiked with Rohypnol (also known as "roofies," "rope," and a variety of other street terms). When slipped into a beverage, Rohypnol's sedating effects begin within 20 minutes of ingestion and usually last more than 12 hours. Rohypnol has been called the "date-rape drug" and the "forget me pill" because many women who have been given roofies blacked out and were raped, but couldn't remember

what happened. When mixed with alcohol or narcotics, Rohypnol can be fatal (National Institute on Drug Abuse, 2011).

A more recent rape drug is GHB, or gamma hydroxybutyrate, a liquid or powder made of lye or drain cleaner that's mixed with GBL, gamma butyrolactone, an industrial solvent often used to strip floors. GHB is an odorless, colorless drug that knocks the victim out within 30 minutes. The coma-like effects of GHB last from three to six hours (National Institute on Drug Abuse, 2011).

TECHNOLOGY   Technology has facilitated dating aggression. In a recent survey, nearly 25 percent of those ages 14 to 24, usually women, said that their dating partners checked in many times a day to see where they were and with whom. Ex-boyfriends, especially, are likely to engage in "textual harassment" when they send the females hundreds of menacing text messages such as "You don't need nobody else but me" or threatening to kill their ex-girlfriends (St. George, 2010: B2).

FEW NEGATIVE SANCTIONS   Another factor that contributes to date violence is the lack of sanctions. Very few women and men report dating violence because they grew up in violent homes, endorse traditional gender roles, see dating aggression as normal, or blame themselves if they or their partners were high on alcohol or other drugs. On many college campuses, women don't report date rape because they assume, often correctly, that the school won't do anything about a complaint (Sweet, 2012; Smiler and Plante, 2013).

Some Consequences of Dating Violence and Date Rape

Adolescents who are victims of dating violence experience adverse health outcomes in young adulthood. They're more likely to be depressed and do poorly in school. They may engage in unhealthy behaviors, such as using drugs and alcohol, and are more likely to have eating disorders. Some teens think about or attempt suicide. Teens who are victims in high school are at higher risk for dating violence and date rape in adulthood (Centers for Disease Control and Prevention, 2012; Exner-Cortens et al., 2013).

Violence and rape violate both body and spirit; they can affect every aspect of the victim's life. *Even though they're not responsible for the attack*, women often feel ashamed and blame themselves for the rape. Fear of men, of going out alone, and of being home alone becomes part of their lives, as do anger, depression, and sometimes inability to relate to a caring sexual partner. *Table 8.3* lists other consequences of date violence and date rape.

TABLE 8.3   Emotional and Behavioral Problems Experienced by Victims of Date Violence or Date Rape
• General depression: Symptoms include changes in eating and sleeping patterns and unexplained aches and pains. Depressive symptoms may prevent women from attending classes, completing courses, or functioning effectively on the job. • The victim will experience feelings of powerlessness, helplessness, vulnerability, shame, and sadness. • Loss of self-confidence and self-esteem may increase the likelihood of future sexual assaults. • There will be changes in the victim's behavior in an intimate relationship and attitudes toward sexual relationships in general. • The victim will feel irritable toward family, friends, or co-workers. • Feelings of generalized anger, fear, anxiety, or suicidal thoughts and attempts will be prevalent. • The victim will be unable to concentrate, even on routine tasks. • Dependence on alcohol or drugs is likely to develop. • Unwanted pregnancy may occur.

Sources: Benokraitis and Feagin, 1995; Larimer et al., 1999; Silverman et al., 2001; Olshen et al., 2007; Exner-Cortens et al., 2013.

Since you asked . . .
- Should we break up more often than we do?

Breaking Up

A study of students at one university found that 93 percent of both sexes had been spurned by someone they passionately loved, and 95 percent had rejected someone who was deeply in love with them (cited in Fisher, 2008). And, according to several online surveys, about 35 percent have been dumped via text message (Friedman, 2011; Lab42, 2011). A classic song tells us that "breaking up is hard to do." Why, then, do so many couples break up?

Why Do We Break Up?

There are numerous reasons for breaking up dating and other intimate relationships that include both micro- and macro-level factors:

- *Individual (micro) reasons* include communication problems, different interests, emotional and physical abuse, obsessive love and controlling behavior, stalking, mismatched love and sexual needs, self-disclosure that reveals repulsive attitudes, disillusionment, dwindling affectionate behavior, infidelity, and not making a commitment (Forward, 2002; Harley, 2002; Regan, 2003).

- *Structural (macro) reasons* include moving away; economic recessions that trigger unemployment and arguments about finances; and societal reactions that disapprove of relationships between young partners, young men and older women, couples from different racial or ethnic and religious backgrounds, and same-sex partners (Martin, 1993; Regan, 2003).

How Do We React?

Breakups are usually very painful, but people react differently. As you might expect, for example, people who have fewer resources to exchange in the marriage market are more upset by dating breakups than those who have many options because they're self-confident, successful, or attractive (Schmitt and Buss, 2001).

Confusion and anger are two of the most common reactions to breakups: We feel spurned or betrayed, fear that we're unlovable, or don't know why we were rejected. Some practitioners advise avoiding a point-by-point dissection of why things fell apart because doing so can lead to physical abuse. Honesty is the best approach, such as "I'm not in love with you anymore" rather than clichés such as "It's not you, it's me" (Svoboda, 2011).

Rejection hurts, but the effect of dumping or being dumped tends to be interpreted differently. Men may be more wary of dating a woman when they learn that she dumped her last boyfriend, perhaps fearing they'll be next. Women's interest increases when they learn that a man had done the dumping, perhaps seeing it as the man being selective (Stanik et al., 2010).

Men seem to get over breakups more quickly than women. Shortly after a breakup, for example, 42 percent of men and 31 percent of women start dating someone else (Fetto, 2003). Among young adults ages 18 to 23, women are more likely than men to be depressed after a breakup because many women's self-worth is still tied to having a boyfriend, even one who's not emotionally involved in the relationship (Simon and Barrett, 2010).

Is Breaking Up Healthy?

Absolutely. A study of seventh-, ninth-, and eleventh-graders found that "churners" (those involved in on/off relationships) were twice as likely to experience mutual physical violence as their counterparts who were in a stable relationship or had broken up permanently. Churners, compared with nonchurners, were less able to prevent and manage conflict escalation due to factors such as growing up in a violent home, low self-esteem, poor communication skills, and little ability in handling stress (Halpern-Meekin et al., 2013).

In adulthood, disagreements and conflict are part and parcel of any close relationship, including marriage. However, breaking up a dating or cohabiting relationship is much less complicated than breaking up a marriage (see Chapter 15).

People who are good at monitoring their behavior ("impression management," in Goffman's terms, as you saw in Chapter 5) have skills in picking up on social cues and are unlikely to say things that upset others. The downside is that because they usually mask their true feelings to avoid conflict, they don't engage in intimate communication. As a result, they may not be able to achieve long-term happiness in their romantic relationships. People with fewer self-monitoring skills who don't avoid disagreements or hide their true feelings and opinions may initially seem unappealing. Ultimately, however, they're more genuine, honest, loyal, and capable of making a long-term commitment (Wright et al., 2007).

One of the important functions of dating and courtship is to filter out unsuitable prospective mates. Thus, breaking up is a normal process. It can also be a great relief to end a bad relationship (see Chapter 6). Whether you break up with someone, or someone breaks up with you, complaining to your family and friends about your ex is healthy. Doing so decreases the likelihood of feeling depressed and enables people to move on to the next relationship (Fagundes, 2011).

If anything, breaking up should probably occur more often than it does because most people don't circulate enough before getting married (Glenn, 2002). Ending a dating relationship provides opportunities to find a mate who may be more suitable for marriage or a long-term relationship. In addition, breaking up opens up a larger pool of eligible and interesting partners as we mature, change, and become more self-confident.

MAKING CONNECTIONS

- Some women stay in violent dating relationships because they have a "caretaker identity": They feel responsible for the man's behavior or want to rescue him from his problems (Few and Rosen, 2005). Have you known women who fit this description? Why do you think men are less likely to take on such caretaking roles?

- Some people believe that breaking up on e-mail, Facebook, or text messages is tacky. Others argue that these are quick and painless ways to end a relationship (Noguchi, 2005). What do *you* think?

CONCLUSION

We have more *choices* in mate selection than ever before. A broad dating spectrum includes both traditional and contemporary ways to meet other people. *Constraints*, however, limit many of our choices. Factors that determine who selects whom for a partner come into play long before a couple marries and despite the romantic notion that "I can date anyone I want." Some partners must also deal with aggression and violence. One response to our mate selection choices and constraints is to postpone marriage. In fact, a significant *change* today is the decision of many people to stay single longer, the subject of the next chapter.

On MySocLab

 Study and **Review** on MySocLab

REVIEW QUESTIONS

8.1. Compare the manifest and latent functions of dating.

1. Why do sociologists describe the dating process as a marriage market?

2. What, specifically, are the manifest and latent functions of dating? How do they differ?

8.2. Outline the characteristics, benefits, and costs of traditional and contemporary dating patterns.

3. How has dating changed over the years?

4. How does dating differ across age groups?

5. What are some of the benefits and costs of hanging out, getting together, hooking up, dinner dates, stayovers, and dating in later life?

8.3. Describe five strategies for meeting dating partners.

6. Are personal classified ads and professional matchmakers a modern invention?

7. What are the advantages and disadvantages of mate-selection methods such as mail-order brides, professional matchmakers, speed dating, and online dating?

8.4. Compare three mate-selection theories.

8. What's the difference between homogamy and heterogamy? How does each affect our dating and mate selection?

9. How do filter theory, social exchange theory, and equity theory differ in explaining mate selection?

10. What are some of the key variables of filter theory?

11. Which racial-ethnic groups have the highest intermarriage rates? Why?

8.5. Describe some of the mate-selection differences across cultures.

12. What factors and practices reinforce traditional mate-selection arrangements?

13. How do heterogamy and homogamy affect mate selection in many countries?

14. How and why are mate-selection methods changing in traditional and modern societies?

8.6. Describe the prevalence of dating violence, and explain why it occurs and its consequences.

15. Is dating violence most common among teenagers?

16. What factors help explain date violence and date rape?

8.7. Describe breaking up, explain why it occurs, and discuss its consequences.

17. Why do people break up?

18. Is breaking up healthy or unhealthy? Why?

Singlehood, Cohabitation, Civil Unions, and Other Options

((• Listen to Chapter 9 on MySocLab

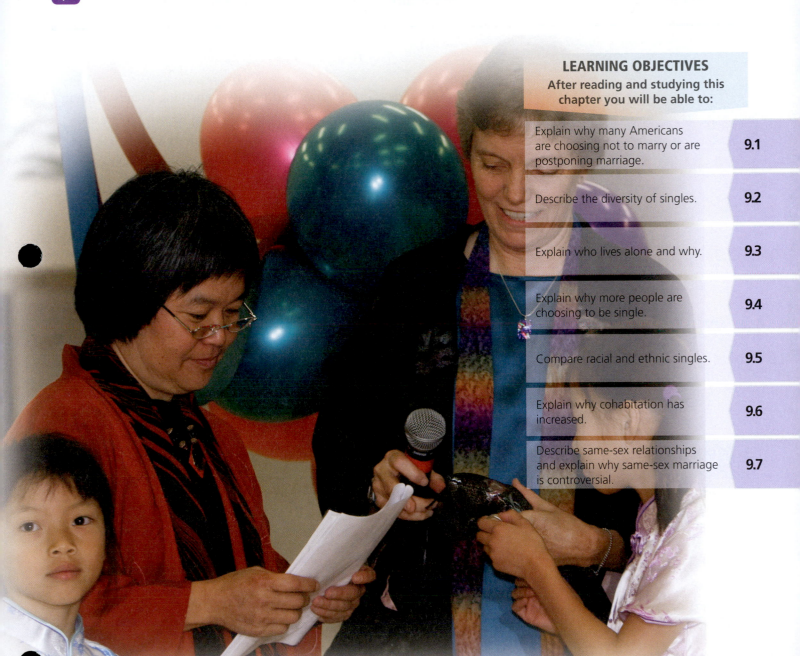

LEARNING OBJECTIVES	
After reading and studying this chapter you will be able to:	
Explain why many Americans are choosing not to marry or are postponing marriage.	**9.1**
Describe the diversity of singles.	**9.2**
Explain who lives alone and why.	**9.3**
Explain why more people are choosing to be single.	**9.4**
Compare racial and ethnic singles.	**9.5**
Explain why cohabitation has increased.	**9.6**
Describe same-sex relationships and explain why same-sex marriage is controversial.	**9.7**

- The number of **single people** (never married, separated, divorced, and widowed) increased from 37.5 million in 1970 to nearly 122 million in 2012, comprising 44 percent of all Americans age 18 and older.

- The **proportion of adults who have never been married rose** from 15 percent in 1972 to 31 percent in 2012.

- Among the never married, **78 percent would like to get married someday**.

- The proportion of households consisting of **one person living alone** increased from 17 percent in 1970 to 27 percent in 2012, comprising more than 33 million people.

- **Unmarried opposite-sex couples living together** (almost 8 million in 2010) increased by 40 percent since 2000.

- **Same-sex partners** comprise about 10 percent of all unmarried couple households.

Sources: Fields, 2004; U.S. Census Bureau, 2008; "America's families and living arrangements," 2012; Lofquist et al., 2012; Gallup Historical Trends, 2013; "Unmarried and single . . .," 2013.

The hit HBO series *Girls* follows four twenty-something friends living in Brooklyn. The main character is an unpaid intern whose parents are cutting off her financial support. Another woman is unemployed, unmarried, and accidentally pregnant. The third one wants to break up with her long-term college boyfriend. And the fourth character is desperately trying to lose her virginity. None expect to marry any time soon. This twenty-something lifestyle is realistically portrayed, but most people in "real life" eventually marry. Until then—or if the relationship fizzles—there's more freedom than ever before to pursue other alternatives. This chapter examines three nontraditional living arrangements: singlehood, cohabitation, and gay households. We'll look at other nonmarital households such as single parents and widowed people in later chapters. Before reading further, take "A Quiz about Singles." It asks how much you know about single people and provides a preview of the chapter.

ASK YOURSELF

A Quiz about Singles

True False

1. Men are more likely than women to live alone.

2. The age group with the largest number of people who live alone is between ages 25 and 34.

3. Living together is replacing marriage.

4. People who are living alone are lonely and live in small cities and suburbs.

5. The percentage of never-married people is higher for whites than for Latinos.

6. Most singles are happier than most married people.

True False

7. About the same percentage of people live in unmarried-couple households as in married-couple households.

8. Civil unions offer the same benefits as same-sex marriage, including access to federal benefits.

9. Domestic violence rates are lower among gay couples than among straight couples.

10. Most elderly singles worry about growing old and dying alone.

The answers to this quiz are on p. 245.

The Single Option

You'll recall that many people are anxious about the state of the American family (see Chapter 1). They fear that marriage is disappearing, especially because of the increase in single people (see Data Digest). Are such concerns justified?

9.1

9.1 Explain why many Americans are choosing not to marry or are postponing marriage.

Are Americans Opting Out of Marriage?

More people today than in the past are choosing not to marry, are living together, or are raising children alone. As a result, according to some social scientists, there is "a marriage problem" in the United States (Wilson, 2002). After reading this chapter, you can decide for yourself whether we have a marriage problem. It's true, however, that more people than ever believe that being single is an attractive option. This doesn't mean that singles will never marry, however. Instead, many young adults are simply choosing to marry at later ages.

Watch on MySocLab
Video: Never Married

Many Singles Are Postponing Marriage

Many young people are pursuing a college education, preparing for a job or career, and spending more time in recreational or other activities before marrying. As a result, many of us are marrying later than our parents or grandparents did.

In 1950, the median age at first marriage was 20 for women and almost 23 for men. By 2012, it had risen to almost 27 years old for women and nearly 29 years old for men. These are the oldest ages at first marriage ever recorded by the U.S. Census Bureau (see *Figure 9.1*). Remember that the *median* is the midpoint of cases. Thus, in 2012, half of all men were 29 or older and half of all women were almost 27 or older when they first married.

From a historical perspective, the present tendency to delay marriage is the norm, especially for men. Men's median age at first marriage was only slightly lower in 1890 than in 2012 (ages 27 and 29, respectively). The median for women has increased more noticeably, however, especially since 1960 (see *Figure 9.1*).

For both sexes, the younger age at first marriage in the 1950s and 1960s was a historical exception rather than the rule. As you saw in Chapter 3, World War II delayed many marriages. When the soldiers came back to the United States, there was a surge of weddings. Throughout the 1950s, the country tried to regain normalcy by encouraging both women and men in their late teens or early twenties to marry and have babies. Young couples themselves wanted to marry and form families after men returned from the war.

In the late 1960s, feminists, especially, began to question women's traditional roles both inside and outside the family. Over the past few generations, both women and men have thought more consciously and deliberately about when and whom to marry.

Is there an ideal age for first marriage? In a 1946 Gallup poll, most Americans said that the ideal age was 25 for men and 21 for women. Sixty years later, the ideal age had increased to 27 for men and 25 for women (Jones, 2006). You'll see shortly, however, that there's a growing debate, especially among some researchers and self-help writers, over whether waiting to marry is a good idea.

Even though being single has become much more acceptable, many young people still feel pressure to marry. Some of my students complain that "if you're not married by the time you're 30, people think there's something wrong with you. My family and friends are constantly telling me to get married." Unmarried women, especially, often dread family get-togethers because they're asked over and over again whether they're dating "someone special." Parents drop

Since you asked . . .
- Is there an ideal age to get married?

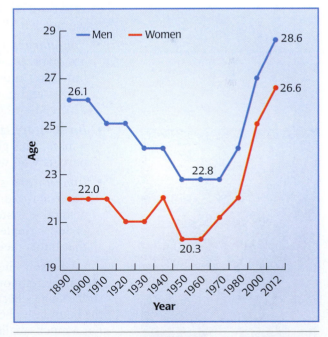

FIGURE 9.1 Many Americans Are Marrying Later
Source: Based on data from U.S. Census Bureau, Current Population Survey, 2012, Table MS-2, Estimated median age at first marriage, by sex, 1890 to the present, http://www.census.gov/hhes/families/data/marital.html (accessed July 27, 2013).

not-so-subtle hints about having grandkids, invitations to friends' weddings pile up, and "bridesmaid dresses stare back at single women when they open their closet doors" (Hartill, 2001: 15).

The older singles are, the more often friends and relatives badger them about their marriage plans. Others complain of feeling invisible and not being invited to social or family activities with married couples unless it's to be fixed up with one of the couple's single friends (DePaulo, 2006). Despite such pressure, more people are single than ever before in U.S. history.

The never married are only one cluster of a very diverse group of singles. In fact, many unmarried Americans don't identify with the word *single* because they're parents, have long-term romantic partners, or are widowed.

9.2 Describe the diversity of singles.

Singles Are Diverse

There are several kinds of singles: those who are delaying marriage; the small percentage who will never marry; the currently unmarried who are divorced or widowed but may be looking for new partners; and lesbians and gay men, who are still legally barred from marrying in 37 states. In addition, people's living arrangements may vary greatly, from living alone or cohabiting during part of one's adult life to singlehood in later life.

Single Adults in General

Singlehood reflects more characteristics than simply not being married. It can be either freely chosen or unintentional, as well as either enduring or temporary (Stein, 1981):

- *Voluntary temporary singles* are open to marriage but place a lower priority on searching for mates than on other activities, such as education, career, an active social life, and self-development. This group also includes men and women who live with each other but aren't married.

- *Voluntary stable singles* have never married and are satisfied with that choice; are divorced or widowed but don't want to remarry; are living with someone but don't intend to marry; and whose religion forbids marriage, such as priests and nuns. Also included are single parents—both never married and divorced—who are not seeking mates.

- *Involuntary temporary singles* would like to marry and are actively seeking a mate. This group includes people who are widowed or divorced and single parents who would like to get married.

- *Involuntary stable singles* are primarily older divorced, widowed, and never-married people who would like to marry or remarry but haven't found a suitable mate and accept their single status as permanent. This group also includes singles who suffer from some physical or psychological impairment that limits their success in the marriage market.

A person's inclusion in these categories can change over time. For example, voluntary temporary singles may marry, divorce, and then become involuntary stable singles because they're unable to find another suitable mate. In this sense, the boundaries between being single and being married are fluid for many people. For a much smaller number, singlehood is constant, either because it's a choice or because some people have little to trade on the marriage market (see Chapter 8).

Single Adults in Later Life

As one grows older, there's a tendency to become choosier about selecting a mate, especially because the pool of available people has decreased. And for older singles who date and want to marry or remarry, the double standard still favors men, decreasing the likelihood of their marrying older women.

At age 66, rock singer Rod Stewart fathered his eighth child. He was age 34 when he married the first time. Stewart's third wife is almost 26 years younger than he is.

AGING AND THE DOUBLE STANDARD   In mate selection, aging women are typically seen as "over the hill," whereas aging men are often described as "mature" and "distinguished." Older women are also more likely than older men to remain single after divorcing or being widowed because they're caring for relatives, primarily aging parents or/and grandchildren (see Chapter 16).

There's little research on older people who have never married, probably because only 5 percent of men and women age 65 and over fall into this category (Federal Interagency Forum on Aging-Related Statistics, 2012). Some are isolated and others have many friends; some wish they were married; and others are happy to remain single.

SOME ADVANTAGES AND DISADVANTAGES OF BEING SINGLE IN LATER LIFE   Some see older single people—whether divorced, widowed, or never-married—as lonely and unhappy. Such perceptions are accurate about older singles who are living in poverty, experience poor health, don't have caregivers to help them, or have been forsaken by their family members and friends (see Chapter 16).

Marriage may be satisfying, but it also limits one's freedom. On the positive side, never-marrieds don't have to deal with the trauma of widowhood or divorce. Many develop extensive networks of friends and relatives. They work, date, and engage in a variety of hobbies, volunteer work, and religious activities and often have lasting relationships with friends and siblings.

Some singles live with others, some alone. Let's look briefly at who lives alone and why.

Since you asked . . .
• Are most older single people lonely and unhappy?

Home Alone

Over the past few decades, for an increasing number of twenty- and thirty-somethings, living alone has become a key stage in what is now described as a "transition to adulthood." As Molly, a 39-year-old Web designer, states, "Living alone is just something I like so much. If I were living in a different time, when you went from your father's house to your husbands' house, I wonder if I would have learned as much about myself" (Klinenberg, 2012: 69).

Because more than 90 percent of all Americans marry at least once, marriage is still the norm. Household size has been shrinking, however. In 1900, nearly half of the U.S. population lived in households of six or more people (Hobbs and Stoops, 2002). A century later, more than one in four Americans lives alone, comprising 28 percent of all households (see *Figure 9.2*). Two reasons for the rapid growth in one-person households have been marriage postponement among people in their twenties and thirties, but especially the large share of people age 65 and older who prefer to live alone rather than with relatives (Jacobsen et al., 2012; Klinenberg, 2012).

9.3 Explain who lives alone and why.

Who Is Living Alone?

Singlehood is common, and singles are a diverse population. Nevertheless, there are some patterns in terms of gender, age, race and ethnicity, and geographic location.

GENDER AND AGE   More women (18.4 million) than men (14.8 million) live alone. Of all age groups, Americans age 65 and older are the most likely to live alone—44 percent compared with only 18 percent of those ages 25 to 44, and 27 percent of those ages 45 to 64 (Jacobsen et al., 2012).

ANSWERS TO "A Quiz about Singles"

All the answers to the quiz on p. 242 are false. The answers are based on material in this and later chapters.

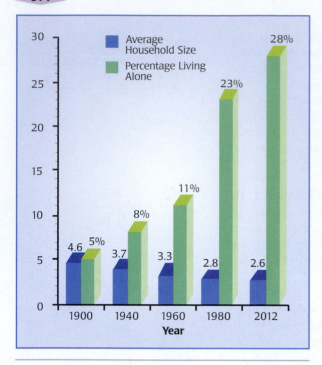

FIGURE 9.2 The American Household Is Shrinking
Both the decline in the average number of people per household and the rapidly rising numbers of people living alone have contributed to a smaller contemporary household.
Sources: Based on Hobbs and Stoops, 2002, and U.S. Census Bureau, 2012, "Families and Living Arrangements," Tables AVG1 and H1, www.census.gov/hhes/families/data/cps2012.html (accessed July 30, 2013).

Since you asked . . .
- Do people live alone because of choices or constraints?

MAKING CONNECTIONS
- Are you single? Why? For example, are you single voluntarily or involuntarily?
- Do you think there's an ideal age for marriage? If married, do you think you were too young or too old when you wed?
- Do you or your friends live alone? Why? What are some of the benefits and costs of not living with other people?

9.4 Explain why more people are choosing to be single.

There are several reasons for these gender differences. For example, on average, women live about six years longer than men, they are less likely than men to remarry after a divorce or widowhood, and, if they enjoy good health and have enough income, they can care for themselves into their eighties and even their nineties (Federal Interagency Forum on Aging-Related Statistics, 2012; see also Chapter 16).

RACE AND ETHNICITY Of all people who live alone, almost 80 percent are white ("America's families and living arrangements," 2012). Members of other racial-ethnic groups such as Latinos, Asian Americans, and American Indians are more likely to live in extended-family households because of values that emphasize caring for family members and pooling financial resources to avoid poverty (see Chapter 4).

REGIONAL LOCATION "Singleton" households—those containing only one person—tend to cluster in urban areas. In the past, singles were concentrated in large rural western states; today, living alone is most common in big cities. For example, in San Francisco, Seattle, Denver, Philadelphia, Chicago, and Washington, DC, 35 to 45 percent of the households have just one person (Klinenberg, 2012).

Why Do People Live Alone?

Rachel, one of my graduate students, recently bought a townhouse in a nice neighborhood. Rachel is 32, has a good job as a bank manager, has no children, and hopes to marry. But, she says, "I'm not going to put off making this investment until Mr. Right comes along."

Rachel's reasons for living alone echo those of other singles her age. Many Americans choose to live alone because *they can afford it*. In fact, single women now buy twice as many homes as do single men. Some of the reasons include having higher educational levels and better-paying jobs, wanting a home rather than just a place to live (such as an apartment), postponing marriage, and not depending on a man to buy a house after marriage (Knox, 2006; Coleman, 2007).

A second and related reason for living alone is that *our values emphasize individualism*. Most single Americans of all ages are highly involved in their families but prefer to live alone because doing so offers more privacy, freedom, and control over their living space than does living with parents or others.

A third reason is that Americans are *living longer and healthier lives*, making it possible for them to live independently after retirement. Even before retirement, being healthy means that people can live by themselves instead of moving in with others.

Finally, and perhaps most important, many people are living alone because they are postponing marriage or deciding not to marry. That is, they have *more options, including singlehood*. They don't want to put their lives on hold until "Mr./Ms. Right" comes along.

Why More People Are Single

Many Americans say that they're single because they're not in love and are still waiting for the right person. For social scientists, being single—especially postponing marriage—reflects an interplay of macro-level factors that affect

demographic variables, which, in turn, influence individual (micro-level) behavior (see *Figure 9.3*). Let's begin with some of the macro-level factors that delay marriage.

Macro-Level Factors

A number of macro-level variables—over which we have little or no control—affect our decisions about matrimony. A few examples include war, technology, social movements, the economy, and gender roles.

WAR, TECHNOLOGY, AND SOCIAL MOVEMENTS

Marriage rates tend to drop during a war. In Afghanistan, for example, decades of war killed, handicapped, or psychologically traumatized many men, leading to a shortage of potential Afghan husbands. After the U.S. invasion of Iraq in 2003, many couples—especially in Baghdad, the capital—postponed weddings because people died every day, making life unpredictable (Roug, 2005). Although the exact numbers of Iraqi casualties is debatable, between 111,000 and 122,000 civilians had been killed by 2013 (Carpenter et al., 2013; Iraq Body Count, 2013). Thus, besides devastating a country's population of young men, many of the married become involuntary singles through widowhood.

Technological advances in contraception, especially the birth control pill, have decreased the rates of unplanned pregnancies and so-called shotgun marriages. Women, especially, have greater control over childbearing, can avoid unwanted nonmarital births, and aren't pressured to marry the child's father. Just as important, women in their forties and even fifties can become pregnant by means of reproductive technologies. As a result, many women postpone marriage because they believe that they're no longer bound by the biological clock that has traditionally limited their ability to have children (see Chapters 7 and 11).

Several social movements have also resulted in delayed marriage or shaped our definitions of acceptable relationships. The women's movement opened up new educational and occupational opportunities for women, giving them career options rather than only marriage. The gay rights movement encouraged homosexuals to be more open about their sexual orientation and relieved the pressure to marry heterosexuals. And, most recently, there has been a surge of new books in the mass media with titles such as *Going Solo* and *Better Single Than Sorry* that promote singlehood (see, for example, DePaulo, 2006; Dubberley, 2007; Schefft, 2007; Talbot, 2007; and Klinenberg, 2012).

ECONOMIC FACTORS
Economic realities also play an important role in delaying or promoting marriage. Economic depressions, recessions, and unemployment tend to postpone marriage, especially for men. The well-paid, blue-collar jobs that once enabled high school graduates to support families are mostly gone. The job prospects for some college-educated men are also worsening rather than improving. In contrast, economic opportunities, as well as the belief that a person has access to those opportunities, encourage men to marry (Landale and Tolnay, 1991).

Economic slumps can also reduce the marriage market for singles. When incomes plummet and people are insecure about their jobs—as Americans

Macro-Level Factors

- War
- Technology
- Social Movements
- Economy
- Gender Roles

Demographic Variables

- Sex Ratios
- Marriage Squeeze
- Social Class
- Residence
- Nonmarital Childbearing

Individual Reasons

- Waiting for a Soul Mate
- Being Independent
- Enjoying Close Relationships
- Not Wanting to Make a Commitment
- Having Children
- Fearing Divorce
- Being Healthy and Physically Attractive

Postponement of Marriage

FIGURE 9.3 **Some Reasons for Postponing Marriage**

Especially for men, employment increases the likelihood of getting married.

experienced between 2008 and 2011—unhappy married couples tend to stay together because they can't afford to divorce and risk the possibility of not being able to maintain separate households (Cherlin, 2009; see, also, Chapters 10 and 15). One result is that such involuntary marriages decrease the pool of voluntary singles.

Economic factors that affect women's tendency to marry are mixed. Employment increases a woman's chances of meeting eligible men and may enhance her attractiveness as a potential contributor to a household's finances. On the other hand, women with high salaries and education levels are often unwilling to settle down with men who earn less than they do (Hacker, 2003; see also Chapters 8 and 10).

GENDER ROLES As gender roles change, so do attitudes about marriage and self-sufficiency. With the advent of washing machines, cleaning services, frozen foods, wrinkle-resistant fabrics, and 24-hour one-stop shopping, for example, men no longer depend on women's housekeeping (Coontz, 2005).

Women aren't rushing into marriage, either. Many want to get a college degree and/or start their career before settling down because it's difficult to juggle a career and a family. Also, because the stigma once attached to remaining single well into your twenties has largely vanished, many women choose to cohabit and have babies outside of marriage.

Demographic Influences

Macro-level factors delay marriage. Demographic shifts (such as changes in the sex ratio and the marriage squeeze), social class, and nonmarital childbearing also help explain the large number of singles.

sex ratio The proportion of men to women in a country or group.

THE SEX RATIO The **sex ratio**, expressed as a whole number, is the proportion of men to women in a country or group. A ratio of 100 means that there are equal numbers of men and women; a ratio of 110 means that there are 110 men for every 100 women (more males than females).

Worldwide, about 107 boys are born for every 100 girls. In the United States, the sex ratio is 105 at birth. In the 65 and over age group, the ratio is 77 because women tend to live longer than men (there are many more females than males) (Central Intelligence Agency, 2012; see also Chapter 16).

In some countries, the sex ratio is highly skewed from birth. For example, the sex ratio is 114 in Armenia, 113 in Georgia, 112 in India, and 120 in China. Because of the sex ratio imbalances, 163 million women have been deemed "missing" in the Asian region, attributed to **female infanticide**, the intentional killing of baby girls because of a preference for sons (Guilmoto, 2007; Gilles and Feldman-Jacobs, 2012; United Nations Population Fund, 2012).

female infanticide The intentional killing of baby girls because of a preference for sons.

Some researchers find that sex ratios are especially skewed within different parts of a country. For example, hoping to reduce female infanticide, the Chinese government relaxed its one-child policy by allowing inhabitants in rural areas to have a second child if their first was a girl. What's happened, however, is that many couples are now aborting or killing a second or third female infant to have a son. Thus, some provinces have sex ratios of 160 for second births, contributing to an excess of 32 million males under the age of 20 in China (Zhu and Hesketh, 2009). That's roughly the size of Canada's population.

The reasons for female infanticide and, consequently, skewed sex ratios are cultural. In many Asian countries, including China and India, there's a preference for boys because they'll carry on the family name, care for elderly parents, inherit property, and play a central role in family rituals. As a result, hundreds of thousands of female infants die every year because of neglect, abandonment, infanticide, and starvation. Others are aborted after ultrasound scanners reveal

the sex of the child (see Chapters 11 and 12). By 2020, China is expected to have 24 million more men than women, leaving the countryside filled with aging bachelors, the consequence of a gender imbalance caused by sex-selective abortions (Pulitzer Center, 2012).

In adulthood, sex ratios vary due to several factors. In Africa, for example, there are more women than men because of civil wars and AIDS deaths. In Central America, there are more men than women because women often migrate to other countries—such as the United States—for jobs.

THE MARRIAGE SQUEEZE A **marriage squeeze** is a sex imbalance in the ratio of available unmarried women and men. Because of this imbalance, members of one sex can be squeezed out of the marriage market because of differences in wealth, power, status, education, age, or other factors that diminish the pool of eligible partners.

Is there a marriage squeeze in the United States? Yes. There are large numbers of never-married people, especially adult men, across all ages (see *Table 9.1*). If we add to the pool of more than the 32 million people who were unmarried because of divorce, separation, or widowhood in 2011, the marriage market appears to be very large (U.S. Census Bureau, 2011). However, homogamy—the tendency to marry someone similar to you—narrows the pool of eligible mates. In addition, millions of women in their middle and later years experience a marriage squeeze because men their age are looking for much younger women (see Chapter 8).

Many countries are experiencing a much more severe marriage squeeze. For example, men in China, India, Korea, Taiwan, the Middle East, and other regions face a scarcity of young, single women because of skewed sex ratios (Park, 2011).

Rural regions with an oversupply of bachelors have experienced wedding scams and "runaway brides." Village customs dictate that the groom's family pay the bride's family a bride price (see Chapter 8) known as *cai li*, and the bride furnishes a dowry of mostly simple household items. Because of the scarcity of women, and the shame of men who aren't married by age 25, some families have saved or borrowed up to five years' worth of farming income to pay the *cai li* for

South Korea reduced its sex ratio from 112 in the late 1990s to 100 in 2013. The recent sex ratio balance has been attributed to a change in a centuries-old preference for baby boys that, in turn, decreased the number of female abortions. Also, the government dismantled laws that guaranteed men their family's inheritance, promoted the education of women, and endorsed equal rights for women and men in the workplace (Sang-Hun, 2007b; *CIA World Factbook*, 2013). Pictured here, girls attend the same athletic classes as boys.

marriage squeeze A sex imbalance in the ratio of available unmarried women and men.

TABLE 9.1	Who Has Never Married? By Age and Sex, 2012	
Age	**Males (%)**	**Females (%)**
Total 15+	34	28
20–24 years	89	81
25–29 years	64	51
30–34 years	39	30
35–39 years	24	20
40–44 years	20	15
45–49 years	18	13
50–54 years	12	11
55–64 years	9	9
65–74 years	5	5
75 years and older	9	8

Source: Based on data in U.S. Census Bureau, 2012, "Families and Living Arrangements," Table A1, www.census.gov/hhes/families/data/cps2012.html (accessed July 30, 2013).

Explore on MySocLab

Activity: Never Married: Trends and Patterns

brides from other provinces. A few days after the wedding, many of the brides and their families vanish (Fong, 2009).

SOCIAL CLASS Most low-income couples expect to marry, especially after the birth of a child, but they often retreat from marriage. A major reason is economic: They believe that they should first achieve a certain level of financial stability, save enough money to attain long-term goals (especially buying a house), and accumulate enough savings to host a "respectable" wedding. Their living costs might be lower if they married, but many unmarried couples postpone marriage because they feel that financial worries will increase tension, arguing, and the chances of divorce (Gibson-Davis et al., 2005).

The likelihood of marriage increases with educational attainment. For example, 60 percent of women with a college degree or higher are married compared with 28 percent of those with less than a high school diploma (Cruz, 2013). More education means more income, and more income reduces financial barriers to marriage.

NONMARITAL CHILDBEARING Nonmarital births are now common. Many never-married mothers are likely to remain single because they can't find a good husband. The marriage market is especially tight for economically disadvantaged unwed mothers because prospective partners may be unwilling to make the long-term financial and emotional commitment to raise nonbiological children. Surveys show that poor women want to marry as much as other women, but they place a greater premium on a mate who offers financial security, a prerequisite for marriage (Pew Research Center, 2010). Because of the small pool of desirable marriage mates, many of these women cohabit rather than marry (Qian et al., 2005).

Individual Reasons

Marriage offers many benefits, but there are also incentives for being single (see *Table 9.2*). A majority of adults now believe that being married or being single makes little difference in social status (64 percent), finding happiness (62 percent), or getting ahead in a career (57 percent) (Pew Research Center, 2010). Let's begin with waiting to find an ideal partner, a soul mate, that one true love.

WAITING FOR A SOUL MATE Singles sometimes delay marriage because they're waiting to meet their "ideal mate" or "one true love." A national survey found that 31 percent of men and 26 percent of women believed that there was only one true love (Cohn, 2013).

Some people believe that waiting for an ideal mate is unrealistic because a marriage involves more than emotional intimacy. If a person decides that a

Read on MySocLab

Document: What Is Marriage For?

Since you asked . . .

- Do you think that there's a soul mate out there for every person?

TABLE 9.2	Some Benefits of Marriage and Singlehood	
Benefits of Getting Married	**Benefits of Being Single**
Companionship	Privacy, few constraints, independence
Faithful sexual partner	Varied sexual experiences; cohabitation
Dependability; love	Exciting, changing lifestyle
Sharing mutual interests	Meeting new friends with different interests
Pooling economic resources	Economic autonomy
Social approval for settling down and producing children	Freedom from responsibility to care for spouse or children
Becoming a part of something larger than self	A need for independence

Sources: Based on Stein, 1981; Carter and Sokol, 1993; Klinenberg, 2012.

partner is no longer a soul mate, for example, she or he will become disillusioned and bail out. Some self-help authors advise women, especially, to settle for Mr. Not-Quite-Right instead of ending up alone (see Lipka, 2008). Also, the longer one waits to marry, the smaller the pool of eligible partners, especially among the never married (see Chapter 8).

Others contend that waiting for a soul mate isn't necessarily starry-eyed: "Perhaps more than ever before, young people have an opportunity to choose a partner on the basis of personal qualities and shared dreams, not economics or 'gender straitjackets'" (Rivers, 2001).

BEING INDEPENDENT   One of the biggest benefits of single-hood is independence and autonomy because single people can do pretty much what they please. According to a 39-year-old female magazine employee, "Work is very social and I like the peace of coming home and not having to interact with anyone" (Klinenberg, 2012: 113). And as one of my 29-year-old female students once said, "I don't plan to marry until my feet have touched six of the seven continents."

Singles with resources, such as high education levels and high-income jobs, are especially likely to be choosy about marriage partners. If they don't find someone with the traits they seek, both sexes are saying "no thanks" to marriage rather than giving up their freedom.

ENJOYING CLOSE RELATIONSHIPS AND ACTIVITIES   A common reason for getting married is companionship (see *Table 9.2*). Singles who are delaying marriage rely on peers rather than a spouse for support and companionship. Especially in large cities, singles have close friends (sometimes called "urban tribes") with whom they socialize. They may meet weekly for dinner at a neighborhood restaurant, sometimes travel together, help move one another's furniture, or join athletic leagues (Watters, 2003). The growth of urban clusters crowded with coffee shops, gyms, bars, restaurants, and shopping encourage single people to comingle rather than isolate themselves at home. Singles are also involved in many community activities. For example, a friend's single, 50-something nephew coaches Little League and volunteers at a local dog shelter in Brooklyn.

Being unmarried isn't synonymous with isolation. Many singles are involved in family life, some live with their parents or close friends, and others spend much time with nieces, nephews, and grandchildren. Women, especially, devote much of their time and resources to supporting and caring for other family members (see Chapter 12).

MAKING A COMMITMENT   There are more never-married men than women in almost all age groups (see *Table 9.1* on p. 249). Why, then, do so many women complain that "there's nothing out there"?

One reason is that many men simply don't want to get married. For example, a 25-year-old complained to an advice columnist that she had made it clear to her live-in boyfriend that she was ready to become engaged and to get married a year later, after both of them had finished law school. Instead, for Christmas he gave her a promise ring. She was hurt and insulted because "Where I come from, promise rings are for teenagers." It sounded as though the boyfriend was unwilling to make a commitment, but Amy scolded "Anxiously Awaiting" for being immature and advised her to appreciate the boyfriend's "sweet gift" instead of pressuring him to marry (Ask Amy, 2008: 6C).

Single professionals often work long hours at their jobs; sometimes this is because they want to advance their careers. Often, however, they are perceived as being less burdened with home and family responsibilities and have nothing better to do.

"We still have a few minor issues to work out: I want a huge wedding and he wants to be single."

There's an old joke about single guys: "My girlfriend told me I should be more affectionate. So I got two girlfriends!" Some family practitioners believe that men are the foot draggers—especially when there's an abundance of potential girlfriends—because there's little incentive for them to marry. Many men put off marriage because of stagnant wages and job losses, and they see marriage as a major economic responsibility that they don't want to undertake (Kreider, 2010; Mather and Lavery, 2010).

Because of the greater acceptance of premarital sex, most men can have sex and intimate relationships without getting married. Men aren't the only ones questioning marriage. A recent survey found that only 12 percent of Americans didn't want to marry, but more men than women said that marriage isn't for them (Cohn, 2013). In one study, 70 percent of low-income fathers-to-be under age 25 planned to marry their pregnant girlfriends but had more *social capital*—such as providing the mother with emotional support and participating in doctors' visits—than *financial capital*—such as jobs, money, and housing (Fagan et al., 2007). Because, however, and as you saw earlier, there's a strong association between higher social class and getting married, financial capital is more important than social capital and good intentions in many people's decisions to marry.

HAVING CHILDREN   Only 44 percent of unmarried Americans believe that having children is a very important reason to marry (Pew Research Center, 2012). Because cohabitation and parenting outside marriage are widely accepted, singles of all ages feel less pressure to get married. The percentage of births to unmarried women rose from 18 percent in 1980 to 41 percent in 2011 (Federal Interagency Forum on Child and Family Statistics, 2013).

Some researchers call middle-class, professional, unmarried women who intentionally bear children "single mothers of choice" (Mattes, 1994; Hertz, 2006; see, also, Chapter 11). Most of these women's *first* choice is to marry and *then* have children. However, as one 35-year-old mother said, "You can wait to have a partner and hope you can still have a baby. Or you can choose to let that go and have a baby on your own" (Orenstein, 2000: 149). Even if a woman finds a soul mate, he may not want to participate in child care and other domestic activities that many women now expect men to share.

FEARING DIVORCE   Divorce or prolonged years of conflict between parents can have a negative effect on young adults' perceptions of marriage. Many stay single as long as possible because they worry about divorce. If children have grown up in homes where parents divorced one or more times, they're wary of repeating the same mistake. As one 21-year-old woman said, "My father left my mother when I was 6. I don't believe in divorce" (Herrmann, 2003).

Divorce benefits children who are growing up in high-conflict homes. Children whose parents fought a lot and consequently divorced have less conflict in their own adult relationships than those whose high-conflict parents remained married. As you'll see in Chapter 15, however, divorces don't occur overnight, and their financial and emotional effects can be devastating for children.

Many singles are postponing marriage because they see it as a lifelong commitment that they might not be able to honor. According to a 24-year-old short-order cook who lives with his girlfriend, for instance, "Marriage is a big step. . . . I don't want to be one of those couples that gets married and three years later gets a divorce" (Gibson-Davis et al., 2005: 1309). Thus, many singles are hesitant to marry not because they don't believe in marriage but because they fear divorce.

Singles in large cities often go to nightclubs to meet people. Despite the racial and ethnic diversity and the large pool of eligible partners, many still can't find a mate. Why not?

BEING HEALTHY AND PHYSICALLY ATTRACTIVE   Emotional and physical health and physical appeal also affect singlehood. In the marriage market, most men are initially drawn only to good-looking women. On a scale of 1 to 10,

men who are a 2 or a 3 often go after attractive women who have many options among handsome suitors. In mismatches, "men pursue prizes beyond their grasp, when they could be perfectly content with someone who isn't viewed as a great catch. So these men lose, not only by failing to get what they covet but also in a chance for a happy ending" (Hacker, 2003: 191). People with severe physical or emotional problems are also more likely to remain single longer or not marry at all (Wilson, 2002).

Some Myths and Realities about Being Single

Marriage has its advantages, but some of the benefits have been exaggerated or romanticized. Here are some of the most popular myths and misconceptions about singlehood:

Since you asked . . .
- Are there more benefits or costs in being single?

1. *Singles are selfish and self-centered.* In reality, married people—even those without children—are less involved than singles with their parents and siblings and less likely to visit, call, or write these and other relatives. Marriage tends to reduce community ties because married people are more immersed than singles in meeting their own needs (Gerstel and Sarkisian, 2006; Cobb, 2012).

2. *Singles are well-off financially.* A number of single professionals and young college graduates in high-tech jobs are affluent, but more singles than marrieds live at or below the poverty level. In general, married couples are better off financially if both partners have paid jobs (see Chapter 13).

3. *Singles are usually lonely and miserable and want to marry.* Especially women—freed from heavy marital domestic responsibilities—are happy to "spread their wings as autonomous individuals": "Not much housework, not much shopping—just for the things I like—and being able to stay out without having to let someone at home know where I am" (Kaufmann, 2008: 87). Singles who are successful and happy—whether never married, divorced, or widowed—are rarely lonely or miserable because they have other single friends who enjoy mutual recreational activities such as traveling (DePaulo, 2012).

4. *Singles are promiscuous or don't get any sex.* As you saw in Chapter 7, most singles don't fall into either group—promiscuous or abstinent. Men, regardless of marital status, have more sex partners over a lifetime than do women, but married people report being happier with their sex lives than do singles and have sex more frequently. Unlike those who are married, however, singles have more sexual freedom without getting entangled emotionally or making a commitment (Kaufmann, 2008).

5. *Singles' children are doomed to a life of poverty as well as emotional and behavioral problems.* Single parents have their limitations, just like married parents. How children fare, however, and as you'll see in later chapters, depends largely on a parent's resources (especially income), the quality of parenting, and alcohol or other drug use.

6. *Singles worry about growing old and dying alone.* Because singles are more likely than married couples to be involved in family and community activities, they rarely worry about growing old and dying alone. For example, among single women age 45 and older, 81 percent said they weren't concerned about the prospect of being alone in their later years because they had friends they could depend on in times of crises (Kalata, 2006). And as you'll see in Chapter 16, older men—whether divorced, widowed, or never married—often have caregivers, especially adult daughters and female relatives, who provide companionship and help with health-related issues.

7. ***There's something wrong with people who don't marry.*** There's nothing wrong with being or staying single. Many singles simply believe that the disadvantages of marriage outweigh the benefits.

In general, many singles are happy, despite the widespread stereotypes that we see in movies and on television or hear about. There are many variations, of course, but much depends on factors such as income; health; personality; and involvement with family, friends, and community service. Cohabitation is another powerful force in the lives of many single people.

9.5   Compare racial and ethnic singles.

Since you asked . . .
- Why are so many African Americans single?

Racial and Ethnic Singles

Among some racial and ethnic groups, the unmarried population has increased significantly during the past few generations. Why? Many structural factors as well as attitudes and values explain some of the changes. Let's look at some of these singles more closely, beginning with African Americans.

African Americans

Compared with other groups, blacks are the most likely to be single, especially never married (see *Figure 9.4*). Many African Americans are postponing marriage, but an even higher proportion may never marry.

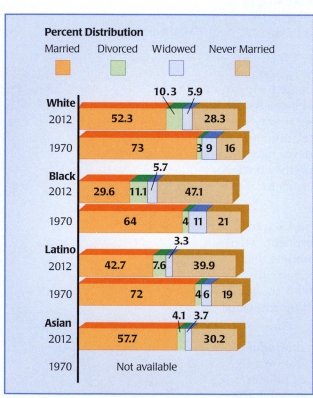

FIGURE 9.4 Changes in Marital Status, by Race and Ethnicity, 1970 and 2012
The percentage of people who are married has decreased, whereas the percentage of divorced and never-married people has increased, especially among African Americans.
Sources: Based on Saluter, 1994: vi, and U.S. Census Bureau, "Families and living arrangements," 2012, Table A1, http://www.census.gov/hhes/families/data/cps2012.html (accessed July 30, 2013).

STRUCTURAL FACTORS A major reason for the high percentage of never-married black women is a shortage of marriageable African American men. This shortage reflects many structural factors. Deteriorating employment conditions, especially in urban areas, often discourage young African American men from getting married. Occupational hazards in dangerous jobs have claimed the lives of many black men. National data from the FBI also show that disproportionately large numbers of urban black men in their twenties and early thirties are in prison or jail or are victims of homicide (McWhirter and Fields, 2012). U.S. homicide rates have been declining overall, but increased by 10 percent for black men from 2000 to 2010. The vast majority of incarcerations and homicides occur when men are ages 19 to 39—the age range when people marry.

As a group, black men earn more than black women in every occupation (see Chapter 13). Many middle-class black men are already married, however, and most college-educated black women are reluctant to marry down. In a memorable scene in the movie *Waiting to Exhale*, the black women lament the marriage squeeze (though not in those words) and consider the merits and problems of marrying hard-working black men in lower socioeconomic levels.

VALUES AND ATTITUDES Homogamy generally limits the pool of eligible mates across social classes, regardless of race (see Chapter 8). Some of my black, 30-something female students have stated emphatically, "I'm making a lot of sacrifices to be in college while working full time. I don't think a man will appreciate what I've accomplished unless he's gone through the same [expletive deleted]!" African American women are more likely to attend and graduate from college than their male peers. About 46 percent of black women complete college within six years compared with 35 percent of black men (American Council on Education, 2010).

On the other end of the spectrum, recent research finds that poor, single, black women recognize their own deficiencies that may make them a poor

marriage partner. These include low economic status, mental/physical health issues, substance use, and having children with more than one partner (Manning et al., 2011). In addition, many lower-class African American women don't see marital commitment as necessary because they're easily wooed by young black men's promise to raise a nonmarital baby (Edin and Kefalas, 2005).

Latinos

Latinas are generally less likely than black women to experience a shortage of marriageable partners, but singlehood is also increasing among Latinos (see *Figure 9.4*). There are variations among subgroups, but structural factors and attitudes explain some of the overall increases in the number of Latino singles.

STRUCTURAL FACTORS On average, the Latino population is much younger than the non-Latino population. As a result, a higher percentage of Latinos have not yet reached marriageable age. Large numbers of Mexicans who are migrating to the United States for economic reasons are postponing marriage until they can support a family. If people are undocumented (illegal) or are migrant workers, it's more difficult for them to meet eligible partners. In addition, low-paying jobs and high unemployment rates can delay marriage, especially following a recession. For example, the marriage rate for Latinos declined by over three percent between 2010 and 2012 (Baca Zinn and Pok, 2002; U.S. Census Bureau, 2012).

VALUES AND ATTITUDES Familism, as you saw in previous chapters, encourages marriage and having children. In the Cuban community, for example, because of the emphasis on the importance of marriage and children, marriage rates are high and divorce rates are low. The latter have been increasing, however, as second and third generations have assimilated American values and behaviors (Pérez, 2002).

Many Puerto Rican women and men have moved away from familistic values because the relationships between families in Puerto Rico and the United States have weakened. Even though some familistic values have changed, a number of Puerto Rican women still have extensive kinship networks both in the United States and in Puerto Rico. As a result, single Puerto Rican mothers may remain unmarried because family members are helping them raise and financially support out-of-wedlock children (Toro-Morn, 1998; Carrasquillo, 2002).

Asian Americans

Asian Americans and Pacific Islanders have some of the lowest singlehood rates. At ages 40 to 44, for example, only 13 percent of the men have never married, compared with 18 percent of white men, 20 percent of Latino men, and 34 percent of black men (U.S. Census Bureau, Current Population Survey, 2009).

As with any racial and ethnic subgroups, it's important not to lump all Asian Americans into one group because doing so obscures important cultural differences among subgroups. There are little recent national data on all of the subgroups, but the available research suggests that Asian Americans, especially those who are first generation, share some values—such as a strong belief in the importance of marriage and family—that help explain the low number of singles (see Chapter 4).

Changing attitudes toward interracial marriage have increased the pool of potential mates for many singles.

STRUCTURAL FACTORS Intermarriage decreases singlehood rates, especially among Asian American women (see Chapter 4). Marrying outside of one's own group reflects several structural factors, such as group size, sex

ratios, and acculturation. For example, 55 percent of second-generation Asian Americans are married to partners outside their ethnicity, and Japanese Americans have the highest rate of intermarriage (69 percent) (Min and Kim, 2009). The high rates suggest that Japanese Americans are less likely to be single because they decrease their marriage squeeze by choosing partners from a large pool.

Acculturation can also increase the number of singles. Despite the emphasis on family and marriage, many Asian Americans are experiencing higher divorce rates. Korean Americans born in the United States, for example, have a higher divorce rate than their immigrant counterparts. American-born Korean women, in particular, are more ready to accept divorce as an alternative to an unhappy marriage (Min, 2002). One of the results of acculturation, then, is a larger number of women and men who are single.

VALUES AND ATTITUDES Interracial marriages reflect a variety of individual factors. For example, college-educated Asian American women can maximize their social status by marrying the most advantaged men, regardless of race or ethnicity (Tsai et al., 2002).

Cultural values can also decrease the number of singles. As you saw in Chapter 4, many Asian American households see the family as the core of society. Among Chinese Americans, for example, divorce rates are much lower than in the general population. Divorced women find it difficult to survive economically and are not readily accepted in the community (Glenn and Yap, 2002). As a result, many Chinese women avoid divorcing and becoming single again at almost all costs.

MAKING CONNECTIONS

- Why are you, your classmates, and friends single rather than married? Or married rather than single?

- What would you add to the discussion of the myths and realities of being single, based on your personal experiences or observations?

9.6 Explain why cohabitation has increased.

cohabitation A living arrangement in which two unrelated people are unmarried but live together and are in a sexual relationship.

 Watch on MySocLab

Video: Marriage vs. Cohabitation

Cohabitation

Cohabitation is a living arrangement in which two unrelated people, who aren't married, live together and are in a sexual relationship. Unmarried couples also include same-sex partners, a topic we'll cover shortly.

Cohabitation Trends

Cohabiting has skyrocketed, increasing from about 430,000 couples in 1960 to over 7.8 million in 2012 (see *Figure 9.5*). This number rises by at least another 515,000 if we include same-sex unmarried partner households in the United States ("Census Bureau Releases Estimates. . .," 2011).

Cohabitation rates have risen, but there are several reasons why these figures are probably too low. First, the Census Bureau doesn't tabulate all unmarried couples in a home but only the person who rents or owns the residence and her or his unmarried partner. Second, unmarried couples—both gay and straight—may be reluctant to disclose that they're living together. Instead, they may describe themselves as roommates or friends. Third, those who believe that they're in a common-law marriage usually don't describe or view themselves as "unmarried partners" (Gates and Ost, 2004; Manning and Smock, 2005).

Cohabitation has become a common feature of American life and, for many couples, a pathway to marriage. For example, about two-thirds of first marriages are preceded by cohabitation compared with almost none during the 1950s (Brown and Manning, 2011). Keep in mind, however, that only about 7 to 9 percent of the population is cohabiting at any particular time, as in 2012. In contrast, almost half of all households are married-couple families (U.S. Census Bureau, 2012).

Types of Cohabitation

Many Americans see living together as a prelude to marriage, but cohabitation serves many purposes and varies at different stages of the life course. The most common types are dating cohabitation, premarital cohabitation, a trial marriage, or a substitute for a legal marriage.

DATING COHABITATION   Some people drift gradually into **dating cohabitation**, a living arrangement in which a couple who spends a great deal of time together eventually decides to move in together. Dating cohabitation is essentially an alternative to singlehood because the decision may be based on a combination of reasons, such as convenience, finances, companionship, and sexual accessibility. Such couples are unsure of the quality of their relationship, and there is no long-term commitment (Manning and Smock, 2005).

In this type of cohabitation, and especially among young adults, there is considerable **serial cohabitation**, living with different sexual partners over time. The partners might terminate one relationship and then move in with someone else. Even if there's an unplanned pregnancy, the man, especially, may decide to move on to another cohabiting arrangement (Wartik, 2005).

PREMARITAL COHABITATION   For many people, premarital cohabitation is a step between dating and marriage. In **premarital cohabitation**, the couple tests its relationship before getting married. They may or may not be engaged but plan to marry.

TRIAL MARRIAGE   In a **trial marriage**, the partners live together to find out what marriage might be like. This type of living together is similar to premarital cohabitation, but the partners are less certain about their relationship. Such "almost-married" cohabitation may be especially attractive to partners who wonder if they can deal successfully with problems that arise from differences in personalities, interests, finances, ethnicity, religion, or other issues.

SUBSTITUTE MARRIAGE   A **substitute marriage** is a long-term commitment between two people who don't plan to marry. For many, it's an alternative to marriage, but the motives vary widely. For example, one or both partners may be separated but still legally married to someone else or may be divorced and reluctant to remarry. In some cases, one person may be highly dependent or insecure and therefore prefers any kind of relationship to being alone. In other cases, the partners believe that a legal ceremony is irrelevant to their commitment to each other and may view their nonmarital cohabitation as equivalent to a common-law marriage (see Chapter 1).

Cohabitation is more complex than these four classifications suggest. Especially when children are involved, cohabitation can include two biological parents, one biological parent, or an adoptive parent. In addition, one or both partners may be never married, divorced, or remarried. These variations can create very different relationship dynamics—a topic that researchers are just beginning to study.

Is Cohabitation Replacing Marriage?

Some people maintain that cohabitation is replacing marriage, but there's little evidence to support such claims. For example, a large majority of never-married Americans plan to marry (see Data Digest). Many young people don't believe in

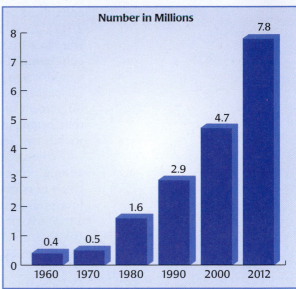

Number in Millions

1960	1970	1980	1990	2000	2012
0.4	0.5	1.6	2.9	4.7	7.8

FIGURE 9.5 Cohabitating Couples in the United States, 1960–2012
Note: These figures are for opposite-sex unmarried partners. *Sources:* Based on U.S. Census Bureau, Current Population Survey, March and Annual Social and Economic Supplements, 2005 and earlier, Table UC-1, 2006, www.census.gov/population/socdemo/hh-fam/uc1.pdf (accessed September 17, 2006); and Table UC3, 2012, www.census.gov/population/socdemo/hh-fam/cps20128.html (accessed July 20, 2013).

dating cohabitation A living arrangement in which a couple who spends a great deal of time together eventually decides to move in together.

serial cohabitation Living with different sexual partners over time.

premarital cohabitation A living arrangement in which a couple tests its relationship before getting married.

trial marriage An arrangement in which people live together to find out what marriage might be like.

substitute marriage A long-term commitment between two people who don't plan to marry.

cohabiting or don't view cohabiting as a substitute for marriage (Manning et al., 2011). In 2010, for example, among those ages 25 to 44, almost 58 percent were in a first marriage or remarriage compared with only 11 percent who were cohabiting (Copen et al., 2012).

Moreover, most cohabiting relationships are usually short lived. About 78 percent of marriages last five years or more, compared with less than 30 percent of cohabiting unions. Half of women's first premarital cohabitations that began in 1997–2001 became marriages and another one-third dissolved within five years (Copen et al., 2013).

Whether a cohabiting relationship ends in marriage or a breakup depends, among other things, on *why* people are living together. Those with the lowest levels of commitment (dating cohabitation) are more likely to split up than those in a premarital cohabitation, and serial cohabitation is much more likely than a trial marriage to end rather than lead to marriage (Lichter and Qian, 2008).

Who Cohabits?

Cohabitants are a diverse group. Many of their characteristics overlap, but there are some general patterns in terms of age, gender, race and ethnicity, social class, and religion.

AGE Unmarried couples span the life course. About 34 percent of cohabitants are 18 to 29 years old, and another 35 percent are 30 to 44 years old. Approximately 26 percent of unmarried partners are 45 to 64 years old, and nearly 5 percent are 65 and older (Lofquist, 2012).

Among cohabitants who are in their forties, one or both partners may be divorced or widowed and want close relationships, but aren't interested in remarrying because they "don't want to blend their families or complex portfolios of assets" (Haq, 2011: 21). Compared with their younger counterparts, older cohabitants (those age 50 and older) report significantly higher relationship quality and stability but view their relationship as an alternative to marriage or remarriage rather than as a prelude to them. Older cohabitants are typically not having or raising children, an important reason for marriage among younger couples (King and Scott, 2005; Brown et al., 2012).

In many cases, seniors cohabit because remarriage may mean giving up a former spouse's pension, alimony, Social Security, and medical insurance. A 72-year-old woman who lives with her 78-year-old partner, for example, has no intention of getting married because she'd lose her late husband's pension: "My income would be cut by $500 a month if I got married, and we can't afford that" (Silverman, 2003: D1).

In other cases, older couples avoid remarriage because of unpleasant divorces in the past or because their adult children fear that they will be displaced in their parents' affection—especially in their wills. Moreover, widows fear a long period of caregiving for a new husband, possibly another painful loss, or want to hang on to their new sense of freedom (Greider, 2004; Levaro, 2009).

GENDER By age 30, 74 percent of all U.S. women have cohabited, compared with 70 percent in 2002 and 62 percent in 1995 (Copen et al., 2013). When it comes to living with a man, daughters often follow their mother's lead: Young adult women whose mothers cohabited are 57 percent more likely than other women to cohabit. Also, women whose mothers have a college degree or more are significantly less likely to cohabit than are women whose mothers have less than a high school education. In this sense, attitudes about cohabitation—especially among women—may be transmitted from one generation to another (Mellott et al., 2005).

People live together rather than marry for a variety of reasons. Do you think that women or men benefit more from cohabitation? Why?

Because of the shortage of marriageable men, many low-income, cohabiting black women don't want to marry because they believe that their live-in partners will be unemployed, unfaithful, or not responsible in caring for children. Low-income white and Puerto Rican single mothers don't marry their partner, similarly, if they see the man as a poor provider or immature even though "he is the love of my life" (Jayakody and Cabrera, 2002; Edin and Kefalas, 2005).

RACE AND ETHNICITY In 2010, the highest cohabitation rates were for Latinas (57 percent), followed by white women (43 percent), and black women (39 percent). Asian women had the lowest rates (22 percent). Foreign-born Latinas had higher cohabitation rates than U.S.-born Latinas (33 percent and 25 percent, respectively) (Copen et al., 2013).

Asian women have low cohabitation rates because marriage is the norm and premarital sex and cohabitation are stigmatized (see Chapters 4 and 7). In contrast, many Latinos come from countries in Latin and Central America that have much higher cohabitation rates than those in the United States (Oropesa and Landale, 2004). Social class also helps explain the racial-ethnic cohabitation variations.

Across all ethnic groups, three out of four people who cohabit say that they're delaying marriage because "Everything's there except money." Even a modest wedding may pose a serious obstacle to marriage for working- and middle-class young adults: "Ben, a 30-year-old railroad conductor, said he did not know how he would come up with $5,000 for a wedding, exclaiming, 'Weddings are expensive!'" Some also distinguish between a "real" wedding that takes place in a religious institution instead of a "downtown" ceremony with a justice of the peace (Smock et al, 2005: 688).

SOCIAL CLASS Race, ethnicity, and gender intersect with social class in explaining cohabitation. However, cohabitation is more common among people at lower education and income levels. As *Figure 9.6* shows, women's likelihood of cohabitation decreases as their educational levels increase.

For both women and men, cohabitation is more likely at lower socioeconomic classes because those with high income and education levels have little to gain from cohabitation. Unlike people in lower socioeconomic groups, those in the middle class and higher are more likely to have jobs, to afford their own housing, and, consequently, to have more options in getting married or living independently even though they're involved romantically (Fry and Cohn, 2011; Sassler and Miller, 2011).

A number of studies show that dire economic circumstances reduce the odds of getting married. A large number of low-income men may want to marry but believe that they can't support a family. Many African American women, as you saw earlier, are unwilling to marry men with erratic employment records and low earnings. Women in low-income groups yearn for respectability and upward mobility (including home ownership and financial security). They don't marry their current boyfriend, however, if they believe that the man won't achieve economic stability (Ooms, 2002; Lichter et al., 2003; Xie et al., 2003; Carlson et al., 2004).

RELIGION Religious values also affect cohabitation rates. The most religious Americans—those who attend church weekly—are less than half as likely to cohabit as those who seldom or never attend church because they believe that premarital cohabitation is immoral and increases the odds of divorce. Thus, teenage girls who

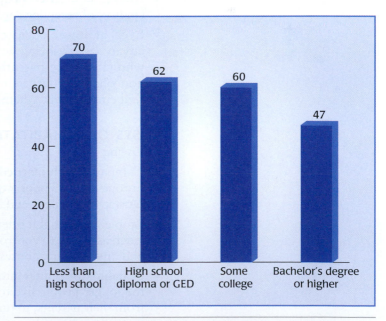

FIGURE 9.6 Women with Higher Education Levels Are Less Likely to Cohabit

Note: These data are based on a national sample of women aged 22–44 between 2006 and 2010.
Source: Based on Copen et al., 2013, Figure 2.

attend religious schools and religious services at least once a week are less likely to cohabit than those without such experiences (Houseknecht and Lewis, 2005).

However, about half of religious teenagers approve of cohabitation. Such acceptance suggests that because so many teens have grown up with a cohabiting parent or have experienced the divorce of their parents, wedding vows may no longer mean as much, even when youth or their parents are religious (Lyons, 2004; Cunningham and Thornton, 2005).

Some Benefits and Costs of Cohabitation

Cohabitation is usually one of the most controversial subjects in my classes. Some students believe that living together is immoral; others argue that it's a normal part of life. As in any other relationship (including dating and marriage), cohabitation has both benefits and costs.

BENEFITS OF COHABITATION   Some of the benefits of cohabitation include the following:

- Couples can pool their economic resources instead of paying for separate housing, furniture, utilities, and so on. Cohabiting couples can also have the emotional security of an intimate relationship but maintain their independence by having their own friends and visiting family members alone (McRae, 1999; Fry and Cohn, 2011).

- Partners can dissolve the relationship without legal problems, and they can leave an abusive relationship more easily (DeMaris, 2001).

- Couples who postpone marriage have a lower likelihood of divorce because being older is one of the best predictors of a stable marriage (see Chapter 15).

- Cohabitation can help people find out how much they really care about each other when they have to cope with unpleasant realities such as a partner who doesn't pay bills or has poor hygiene habits.

- Among unmarried people age 65 and older, cohabitation may increase the chances of receiving care that is usually provided by spouses (see Chapter 16).

- Even at lower socioeconomic levels, children can reap some economic advantages by living with two adult earners instead of a single mother. Men who experience parenthood during cohabitation are more likely than single noncohabiting fathers to become more committed to the relationship and to find employment whether the mother works or not (see Chapter 15).

COSTS OF COHABITATION   Cohabitation also has costs, including the following:

- Compared with married couples, cohabitants—both in the United States and Europe—have a poorer quality of relationship and lower levels of happiness and satisfaction (Wilcox and Marquardt, 2011; Sassler et al., 2012; Wiik et al., 2012).

- People who cohabit often demonstrate more negative behaviors after marriage (such as trying to control the partner's thoughts or feelings, verbal aggression, and anger) than spouses who didn't cohabit (Cohan and Kleinbaum, 2002).

- Cohabitation dilutes intergenerational ties. Compared with their married peers, the longer people live together, the less likely they are to give or receive help from their parents, to turn to their parents in an emergency, and to be involved in extended family activities. Also, parents might sometimes avoid contact because they're unsure of their roles when their children cohabit (Eggebeen, 2005).

- Laws in the United States don't specify a cohabitant's responsibilities and rights. For example, in many states it's usually more difficult to collect child custody payments from a cohabiting parent than from one who is separated or divorced (see Chapter 15).

Applying What You've Learned

Should We Live Together?

Most people live together because they're unwilling to make a long-term commitment or are uncertain about whether they want to marry. Such doubts are normal and should probably arise more often than they do (see Chapter 8, especially, on breaking up).

A few social scientists are adamantly opposed to the practice of living together. According to Popenoe and Whitehead (2002):

- *You shouldn't live together at all before marriage.* There's no evidence that cohabitation leads to better or stronger marriages. People shouldn't live together unless they've already set a wedding date.

- *Don't make a habit of cohabiting.* Multiple experiences of living together decrease the chances of marrying and establishing a lifelong partnership.

- *Limit cohabitation to the shortest possible period of time.* The longer you live together with a partner, the more likely it is that you, your partner, or both will break up and never marry.

- *Don't consider cohabitation if children are involved.* Children need parents over the long term. In addition, children are more likely to be abused by cohabitants than by biological parents.

On the other hand, people who live together give rational reasons for doing so (Olson and Olson-Sigg, 2002; Solot and Miller, 2002; Sassler, 2004):

- *Economic advantages:* "We can save money by sharing living expenses."

- *Companionship:* "We are able to spend more time together."

- *Increased intimacy:* "We can share sexual and emotional intimacy without getting married."

- *Easy breakups:* "If the relationship doesn't work out, there's no messy divorce."

- *Compatibility:* "Living together is a good way to find out about each other's habits and character."

- *Trial marriage:* "We're living together because we'll be getting married soon."

So where does this leave you? You might use exchange theory (see Chapters 2 and 6) in making a decision. List the costs and benefits and then decide what you want to do.

STOP AND THINK . . .

- If you live with someone (or have done so in the past), why? What would you advise other people to do?

- Look at Appendix F ("Premarital and Nonmarital Agreements"). Have you discussed any of these topics with someone you've lived with in the past or now?

- Compared with married couples, those cohabiting are more likely to break up if sexual frequency is low (Yabiku and Gager, 2009).

- Compared with married couples, most cohabitants can't receive a partner's Social Security funds, pensions, estates, and financial aid for children in college (Ambrose, 2010).

Often, after reading this section, students raise an important question: Should my girlfriend or boyfriend and I live together? Speaking sociologically, there's no simple answer to this question. Some of the research, however, suggests issues that you should think about before or during cohabitation (see "Should We Live Together?").

Cohabitation has costs, but many cohabitants are convinced that it leads to better marriages. Is this true? Or wishful thinking?

Does Cohabitation Lead to Better Marriages?

There is much debate about this question. Previous research found that couples who lived together before marriage had higher divorce rates than those who didn't live together before marriage (Bramlett and Mosher, 2002; Phillips and Sweeney, 2005; Stanley and Rhoades, 2009). Recent studies show that women who cohabit are no more likely to divorce than those who didn't cohabit *if* there's a marital commitment (engagement or definite plans to marry) prior to cohabitation (Reinhold, 2010; Stanley et al., 2010; Manning and Cohen, 2012).

Because divorce rates vary, why are some premarital cohabitants more likely than others to experience divorce? There's no single answer, but a *cohabitation*

effect and an *inertia effect* help explain why living together may have negative marital outcomes.

THE COHABITATION EFFECT   The cohabitation effect may lead to marital instability. Through cohabitation, people may come to accept the temporary nature of relationships and to view cohabitation as an alternative to marriage. Cohabitants who are independent and used to having their own way, for example, may be quick to leave a marriage (DeMaris and MacDonald, 1993). Thus, cohabitation itself can increase the likelihood of divorce, especially among dating cohabitants.

Serial cohabitation may be especially harmful to marital stability because people who engage in multiple cohabitations tend to be women with low income and education levels. Generally, for those who cohabit two or more times, the odds of divorce are 141 percent higher than for women who cohabited only with the person they married. It's not clear, however, whether the divorce rates for serial cohabitants are high because these individuals choose partners with poor communication skills or chronic mental health problems or because of a cohabitation effect (such as marriage creating new dissatisfactions that people don't want to tolerate) (Lichter and Qian, 2008; see also Tach and Halpern-Meekin, 2009).

THE INERTIA EFFECT   Some cohabitants drift into marriage because of an inertia effect. After moving in together, a couple often makes numerous decisions that make it more difficult to break up—splitting the finances, buying furniture, getting a pet, sharing possessions, spending less time with friends, and even having a child. Instead of making a conscious decision and commitment, then, the couple may slide into marriage because of inertia ("We might as well get married because there's no reason not to") (Stanley and Smalley, 2005; Stanley and Rhoades, 2009).

Some research suggests that women who limit their cohabitation to a future husband don't experience a higher risk of divorce than women who don't cohabit before marriage. For the most part, however, there's little evidence that those who cohabit before marriage have stronger marriages than those who do not (Teachman, 2003; Popenoe and Whitehead, 2006).

How Does Cohabitation Affect Children?

Since 1960, there has been an increase of more than 900 percent in the number of cohabiting couples who live with children. In fact, 20 percent of children are born to opposite-sex cohabiting couples and 40 percent will live in a cohabiting family by age 12 (Kreider and Ellis, 2011a).

For the most part, children who grow up with cohabiting couples—even when both are the biological parents—tend to have worse life outcomes than those who grow up with married couples. For example, children living in cohabiting households

• Experience more domestic violence because of the cohabiting men's lower investment in the relationship and because many women tolerate the assaults (Cunningham and Antill, 1995).

• Are more likely to be poor: When unmarried couples break up, men's household income drops by 10 percent, whereas women lose 33 percent; the percentage of women living in poverty increases from 20 to 30 percent, whereas men's poverty level remains relatively unchanged at about 20 percent (Avellar and Smock, 2005).

• Are in households in which the partners spend more on adult goods—such as alcohol and tobacco—and less on children, such as their health and education, than do married parents (DeLeire and Kalil, 2005).

Many cohabiting couples are raising children from previous relationships as well as having their own children.

• Are more likely than children from married households to experience a parent's breakup with a partner within three years of the child's birth (Rackin and Gibson-Davis, 2012).

- Tend to have poorer health than children from married households. Cohabiting fathers are less committed than married fathers in ensuring a child's well-being. Also, cohabiting parents' more stressful environments and relationships decrease children's health (McClain, 2011; Schmeer, 2011).

- Have more academic, emotional, and behavioral problems because of poverty or because one or both adults experience more parenting problems than do married couples (S. L. Brown, 2004; Seltzer, 2004; Fomby and Estacion, 2011).

Besides these difficulties, children often suffer the consequences of serial cohabitation or a parent's breakup with a partner. Nationally, children born to cohabiting versus married parents have more than five times the risk of experiencing their parents' separation. About 75 percent of children born to cohabiting parents see their parents split up before they reach age 16, compared with 33 percent of children born to married parents. The breakups increase already existing problems such as poverty for women and their children. Because cohabiting relationships are so unstable, they often aggravate personal and social difficulties for children, including behavior problems and poor academic performance (Raley and Wildsmith, 2004; Osborne et al., 2007).

Most cohabitation is short lived. Thus, many family practitioners and attorneys advise people who live together to draw up premarital and nonmarital agreements that will safeguard each person's financial assets.

Cohabitation and the Law

A few years ago, a sheriff in North Carolina fired a dispatcher because she wouldn't marry her live-in boyfriend. Four states (Florida, Michigan, Mississippi, and North Dakota) still have laws on the books that prohibit cohabitation. Most of the laws are at least 200 years old and rarely enforced. In this case, however, the sheriff believed that the dispatcher's live-in arrangement was immoral and decided to enforce the law.

Even though states rarely prosecute cohabitants who violate the laws, unmarried couples and their children have very little legal protection. An estimated 1.9 million children live in households of cohabiting couples but they have few of the automatic rights and privileges enjoyed by children of married parents ("America's families and living arrangements," 2012; see also Chapter 15).

According to many legal experts, cohabitants' best protection in financial matters is to maintain separate ownership of possessions. Cohabiting partners shouldn't have joint bank accounts or credit cards. Shared leases should also be negotiated before the partners move in together. If partners buy real estate together, they should spell out carefully, in writing, each person's share of any profit. Cars shouldn't be registered in a woman's name just to escape the high insurance premiums commonly charged to men under age 25; if there's an accident, the woman will be liable even if the man was driving.

Health insurance plans that cover a spouse rarely include an unmarried partner and her or his children. And if a partner dies and leaves no will, relatives—no matter how distant—can claim all of his or her possessions. If a couple has children, both partners must acknowledge biological parenthood in writing to protect the children's future claims to financial support and inheritance (Mahoney, 2002).

Discussing legal matters may not seem very romantic when people love each other. But when a cohabiting relationship ends, the legal problems can be overwhelming. Many attorneys recommend that cohabitants draw up a contract similar to a premarital document. Appendix F describes some of the complex issues that cohabitants are likely to encounter.

MAKING CONNECTIONS

- Have you ever cohabited? If yes, would you recommend living together to your family members or friends? If no, why not? If you haven't lived with someone, do you plan to do so in the future?

- A few years ago, the prestigious American Law Institute (2002) created a stir when it proposed that cohabitation be legalized. Unmarried couples would have the same rights and responsibilities as married couples regarding inheritance, child custody, debts, alimony, and health insurance, for example. Do you agree with this proposal?

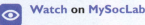

Watch on MySocLab

Video: Reaction to Gay Marriage Ban

Gay and Lesbian Couples

Regardless of our sexual orientation, most of us seek an intimate relationship with one special person. Because only the District of Columbia and 13 states, so far, have legalized same-sex marriage, most gay and lesbian couples must turn to cohabitation.

Gay and Lesbian Relationships

Gay and lesbian couples come in "different sizes, shapes, ethnicities, races, religions, resources, and quirks, and even engage in diverse sexual practices" (Stacey, 2003: 145). Of the 6.7 million unmarried-couple households, 605,000 are same-sex households ("Unmarried and single. . .," 2013).

Like heterosexuals, homosexual cohabitants must work out issues of communication, power, and household responsibilities. If there are children from previous marriages, gay and lesbian parents, like heterosexual parents, must deal with custody and child-rearing issues (see Chapters 12 and 15). Relationships can be as complicated for gay and lesbian couples as for different-sex cohabitants.

LOVE, SEXUALITY, AND COMMITMENT Most lesbians and gay men want an enduring relationship. A recent study comparing lesbian, gay, and heterosexual couples found no differences in the likelihood of long-term relationships, or the level of secure attachments and relationship satisfaction by sexual orientation. However, lesbian women reported the lowest sexual frequency whereas gay men reported the highest (Farr et al., 2010).

Gender, however, seems to shape a couple's values and practices more powerfully than does sexual orientation. Lesbian and heterosexual women, for example, are less competitive and more relationship oriented than gay or heterosexual men. In addition, both lesbian and straight women are more likely than either gay or straight men to value their relationships more than their jobs (Stacey, 2003).

POWER AND DIVISION OF LABOR A majority of gay and lesbian couples report having equal power in their relationship. When power is unequal, however, and as social exchange theory predicts, the older, higher-earner, and better-educated partner usually has more power (Sutphin, 2010).

Gay life isn't divided into "butch" and "femme" roles. One partner may perform many of the traditionally female gender roles, such as cooking, whereas the other may carry out many of the traditionally male gender roles, such as car repair. The specialization typically is based on individual characteristics, such as skills or interests, rather than on traditional husband-wife or masculine-feminine gender roles (Peplau et al., 1996; Kurdek, 2006, 2007).

PROBLEMS AND CONFLICT Like heterosexual cohabitants, gay and lesbian couples experience conflicts in four areas. In terms of *power*, all couples are equally likely to argue about finances, inequality in the relationship, and possessiveness. They are also just as likely to complain about *personal flaws* such as smoking or drinking, driving style, and personal hygiene. Couples are similar in being unhappy with some aspects of *intimacy*, especially sex and showing affection. Both groups are also equally likely to criticize partners who are *physically absent*, usually because of job or education commitments. Suspicion of lingering romantic feelings may be more common among gay and lesbian cohabitants, however, because their previous lovers are likely to remain in their social network of friends, increasing the possibility of jealousy and resentment (Kurdek, 1994, 1998). (See Chapter 7 for current statistics, research, and theoretical explanations of same-sex-violence among cohabitants.)

RACIAL-ETHNIC VARIATIONS Gay and lesbian couples often get less social support from family members than do heterosexual couples. The greatest rejection may come from racial-ethnic families, whose traditional values about marriage

and the family are often reinforced by religious beliefs because, in some faiths, homosexual behavior is considered aberrant or a sin (Hill, 2005).

Some research argues that anti-gay policies such as constitutional amendments banning gay marriage pose a greater threat to black and Latino same-sex couple families than to white same-sex couples. This is because black and Latino same-sex couples are twice as likely as white same-sex couples to be raising children and to earn less. African American same-sex cohabiting partners are more likely than their white counterparts to have jobs in the public sector, particularly government. Many of these jobs offer benefits, such as health insurance, to opposite-sex partners but not to same-sex couples due to state bans, although this is slowly changing. Many anti-gay marriage amendments and state laws block government employers from offering such benefits to their gay and lesbian employees (Cahill et al, 2007).

Lesbian and gay couples might encounter additional problems because the partner comes from a different religion or racial-ethnic group, or from a lower social class. Even if both partners have come out to their family and relatives, the family might exclude a partner in subtle ways, such as inviting the heterosexual son-in-law of two years, but not the lesbian partner of 15 years, to be in a family photo (Clunis and Green, 2000).

As this book goes to press, 14 states and Washington, DC, have legalized same-sex marriage. Do you favor or oppose gay marriage? Why?

The War over Same-Sex Unions

For the first time, a majority of Americans (53 percent) support same-sex marriage. About 46 percent oppose gay marriage, down from 68 percent in 1997 (Jones, 2013). In the past, African Americans were consistently far less supportive of legalizing gay marriage than whites. Blacks are now divided more evenly on this issue than in the past, with 44 percent in favor of and 39 percent opposed to legalizing gay marriage. Latinos support legalizing gay marriage by a wider margin: 52 percent approve and 34 percent disapprove (Pew Research Center, 2012).

Opposition to both civil unions and same-sex marriage is considerably higher among those who regularly attend religious services, live in the South, are age 65 and older, and have conservative views on family issues (Masci, 2008b; Saad, 2008). Until 2001, same-sex couples were prohibited from marrying everywhere in the world, but as you'll see in the next chapter, this situation is slowly changing in the United States and some other countries.

Since you asked . . .
- Why is same-sex marriage so controversial?

CIVIL UNIONS/DOMESTIC PARTNERSHIPS Same-sex couples have gained greater acceptance in six states with marriage alternatives such as *civil unions*, that grant all state-level spousal rights to same-sex couples, or *domestic partnerships*, that provide only some state-level benefits to both same-sex and opposite-sex couples. Civil unions provide legal recognition and all or most of the legal rights enjoyed by married heterosexual couples, including tax breaks, health benefits, approval of organ donations, and inheritance without a will.

In some states, domestic partnerships are available to both same sex and opposite-sex couples (National Conference of State Legislatures, 2013). Employers in states that allow domestic partnerships may or may not offer domestic partner health care or inheritance benefits. For example, if a husband dies, his wife automatically receives his Social Security and pensions. The same automatic transfers may not apply for domestic partners. Many domestic partners must take exhaustive and expensive legal steps to protect themselves and their families. Thus, most can still face serious financial, legal, and social challenges,

especially as they age, retire, purchase property, raise children, and seek medical treatment (Equality Maine, 2013).

In about 22 countries or some of their regions, civil unions and domestic partnerships offer varying marriage benefits ranging from joint property rights to shared parenting. Same-sex couples first walked down the aisle in the Netherlands in 2001. Since then, nearly a dozen countries have passed laws that allow same-sex marriages and domestic partnerships. Nearly 20 other countries offer some rights to same-sex couples but prohibit marriage. Many same-sex couples argue, however, that civil union legislation isn't enough because they're denied federal benefits, and being unable to marry results in their being treated as second-class citizens.

Being unable to marry also helps explain why, among cohabitants, the breakup rate for same-sex couples is twice as high as for different-sex couples.

Changes | Why Do Americans Favor or Oppose Same-Sex Marriages?

Homosexuality and especially same-sex marriages are among the most controversial issues in America, dividing friends, families, and religious communities. Here are some of the beliefs and attitudes that fuel the debates.

Same-sex marriage should be legal because . . .

- Attitudes and laws change. Until 1967, for example, interracial marriages were prohibited.

- Gay marriages would strengthen families and long-term unions that already exist. Children would be better off with parents who are legally married.

- It would be easier for same-sex couples to adopt children, especially children with emotional and physical disabilities.

- There are no scientific studies showing that children raised by gay and lesbian parents are worse off than those raised by heterosexual parents.

- Every person should be able to marry someone that she or he loves.

- Same-sex marriages would benefit religious organizations both spiritually and emotionally and bolster membership.

- Gay marriages are good for the economy because they boost businesses such as restaurants, bakeries, hotels, airlines, and florists.

Same-sex marriage should not be legal because . . .

- Interracial marriages are between women and men, but gay marriages violate many people's notions about male–female unions.

- Children need a mom and a dad, not a gay/lesbian couple.

- All adopted children—those with and without disabilities—are better off with parents who can provide heterosexual gender role models.

- There are no scientific studies showing that children raised by gay and lesbian parents are better off than those raised by heterosexual parents.

- People can love each other without getting married.

- Same-sex marriages would polarize church members who are opposed to gay unions and decrease the size of congregations.

- What's good for the economy isn't necessarily good for society, especially its moral values and religious beliefs.

Sources: LaFraniere and Goodstein, 2007; Masci, 2008a; Pew Forum on Religion & Public Life, 2008a; Semuels, 2008a; Bennett and Ellison, 2010; Olson, 2010; Sprigg, 2011.

STOP AND THINK . . .

- Many states have passed laws that limit marriage to a man and a woman. Do you agree or not? Why?

- What other reasons can you add for each side of the debate?

Because marriage isn't an option in most states, same-sex couples have fewer legal barriers in dissolving a relationship (Lau, 2012).

SAME-SEX MARRIAGE Of the couples who live in states that allow same-sex marriages, 41 percent report being married compared with only 21 percent of those living in states that haven't legalized same-sex marriage (Lofquist, 2012). Marriage comes with many benefits such as access to spouses' health insurance and pensions as well as adoption rights.

Same-sex marriage is controversial. In the United States, those who favor same-sex marriage argue that all people should have the same legal rights regardless of sexual orientation and that marriage may increase the stability of same-sex couples and lead to better physical and mental health for gays and lesbians. Those who oppose same-sex marriage contend that such unions are immoral, weaken our traditional notions of marriage, or are contrary to religious beliefs (Sullivan, 1997; King and Bartlett, 2006). "Why Do Americans Favor or Oppose Same-Sex Marriages?" provides a summary of some of the major pro and con arguments in this debate.

CONCLUSION

There have been a number of *changes* in relationships outside, before, and after marriage. Some of our *choices* include staying single longer, cohabiting, forming same-sex households, and not marrying at all. Thus, larger numbers of people are single for a greater portion of their lives. Remember, however, that our choices aren't without *constraints*. For example, many U.S. laws don't encourage or protect most nonmarital relationships.

Despite the growing numbers of unmarried people, marriage isn't going out of style; it's merely occupying less of the average adult's lifetime. There's less pressure to marry, but most of us will do so at least once in our lives. In the next chapter, we examine the institution of marriage and communication in intimate relationships within and outside of marriage.

On MySocLab   **Study** and **Review** on MySocLab

REVIEW QUESTIONS

9.1. Explain why many Americans are choosing not to marry or are postponing marriage.

1. Will most single people never marry?

2. Is postponing marriage a recent development?

9.2. Describe the diversity of singles.

3. What are the different types of singles?

4. How do single adults in general and those in later life differ?

9.3. Explain who lives alone and why.

5. Why has the average household size been shrinking since the 1940s?

6. Who, specifically, is likely to live alone? Why?

9.4. Explain why more people are choosing to be single.

7. What are some of the reasons (macro, demographic, and individual) why the number of singles has increased since the 1970s?

8. What reasons help explain why people like to live alone?

9.5. Compare racial and ethnic singles.

9. Across racial-ethnic groups, which women are the most likely to experience a shortage of marriageable partners? Why?

10. What racial-ethnic group has the lowest rates of singlehood? Why?

9.6. Explain why cohabitation has increased.

11. What are some of the benefits and costs of cohabitation?

12. Among cohabitants who marry, why do some have higher divorce rates than others?

13. How has an acceptance of cohabitation and having nonmarital children affected the age at first marriage?

9.7. Describe same-sex relationships and explain why same-sex marriage is controversial.

14. Describe two issues that gay couples face.

15. Why, specifically, do Americans favor or oppose same-sex marriage?

Marriage and Communication in Intimate Relationships

((• **Listen** to Chapter 10 on **MySocLab**

LEARNING OBJECTIVES

After you read and study this chapter you will be able to:

Explain how and why U.S. marriage rates have changed.	**10.1**
Identify the manifest and latent reasons for getting married and describe some pre-marriage and marriage rituals.	**10.2**
Compare heterosexual and same-sex marriages and discuss some cross-cultural variations.	**10.3**
Explain how marital happiness, marital success, and health are interrelated.	**10.4**
Describe how couples establish, negotiate, and learn marital roles.	**10.5**
Describe how marriages change throughout the life course.	**10.6**
Explain how communication, power, and conflict affect a relationship.	**10.7**
Describe the most common issues that couples fight about and how they deal with conflict.	**10.8**
Identify productive communication patterns that strengthen relationships.	**10.9**

- About 77 percent of men, compared with 63 percent of women, say **it's acceptable for women to propose to men**.

- Among married couples, 33 percent of women and 18 percent of men say that their pets, particularly dogs, **are better listeners than their spouses**.

- In 1980, **a typical American wedding** cost $4,000. In 2012, it cost almost $27,000, excluding the honeymoon.

- About 61 percent of couples **omit the word** obey **from their vows**, but 83 percent of brides take their husband's name.

- By age 35, **62 percent of U.S. adults are married**.

- In 2010, **41 percent of same-sex couples who lived in states that** have legalized same-sex marriage were married.

- About 63 percent of Americans say that **their marriages are "very happy**."

Sources: Armstrong, 2004b; "For Richer or Poorer," 2005; Petside, 2010; Wilcox and Marquardt, 2010; Fry, 2012; Lofquist, 2012; Wedding Report, 2013.

Dana Jackson celebrated her 100th birthday by marrying her 87-year-old boyfriend, a fellow resident she had met at a Kentucky health care center. The bride had tied the knot once before at the age of 15 (AARP, 2012). You saw in Chapter 9 that many people are postponing marriage. Others, like Jackson, marry regardless of their age.

The first part of this chapter addresses a number of marriage-related topics such as the state of marriage, marital expectations, health, and changes over the life course. The second part examines communication processes that can strengthen or undermine intimate relationships within and outside of marriage. First, however, take the marriage quiz to find out how much you know about U.S. marriages.

ASK YOURSELF

A Marriage Quiz

True False

☐ ☐ **1.** Infidelity is the top issue that couples fight about.

☐ ☐ **2.** Men and women are equally likely to say that they're happily married.

☐ ☐ **3.** The best single predictor of marital satisfaction is the quality of the couple's sex life.

☐ ☐ **4.** Married women generally are healthier than married men.

☐ ☐ **5.** Romance is the key to a long-term marriage.

☐ ☐ **6.** Latinos have higher marriage rates than either blacks or whites.

True False

☐ ☐ **7.** Having children typically brings a couple closer together and increases marital happiness.

☐ ☐ **8.** People with college degrees are less likely to marry than those with less education.

☐ ☐ **9.** If a wife is employed full time, the husband usually shares equally in housekeeping tasks.

☐ ☐ **10.** About 15 percent of Americans will never marry.

The answers to this quiz are on page 274.

Is Marriage Disappearing?

Is marriage becoming obsolete? Among never-married Americans, 61 percent want to marry, but marriage rates have decreased since the 1960s (Cohn, 2013). Why the discrepancy between people's attitudes and behavior?

10.1

10.1 Explain how and why U.S. marriage rates have changed.

Since You Asked . . .

• Why do many people say they want to marry but don't do so?

Marriage Rates Have Been Declining

At age 55 and older, almost 94 percent of Americans had been married at least once or are currently married (Kreider and Ellis, 2011b). Marriage rates have declined, however. In 1960, 72 percent of all U.S. adults age 18 and older were married. The rates decreased slowly during the next five decades. By 2011, barely half (51 percent) were married—a historic low (see *Figure 10.1*). Marriage rates are expected to decrease further because the number of newlyweds has been falling since 1980 (Cohn et al., 2011; Fry, 2012).

Some researchers have described marriage as "disappearing" because marriage rates have plunged among some groups (Wilcox and Marquandt, 2010). The marriage rates of blacks have been lower than those of whites, Latinos, and Asians since 1970, and now diverge even more. As *Figure 10.2* shows, the percentage of married African Americans is low and getting lower over time: only 31 percent compared with 61 percent in 1960.

Marriage rates also vary by educational level. People with college degrees have higher marriage rates than those with less education. During the 1960s and 1970s, most middle- and working-class Americans got married. After 1980, the marriage rates of these groups decreased. In 2010, for example, almost 64 percent of Americans with college degrees were married, compared with 47 percent of those with a high school diploma or less. In effect, there's a growing "marriage divide" between those with and without college degrees (Wilcox and Marquandt, 2010; Cohn et al., 2011; Fry, 2012).

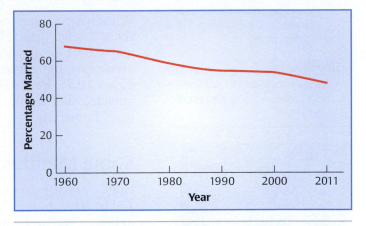

FIGURE 10.1 **U.S. Marriage Rates, 1960–2011**
Note: Based on adults ages 18 and older. "Married" includes persons whose spouse is present or absent but not separated.
Sources: Based on Cohn et al., 2011, and Fry, 2012.

 Explore on MySocLab

Activity: Decades in Review: Marital Status Change in Columbus, Ohio

Why U.S. Marriage Rates Are Falling

Attitudes about marriage are changing. In 2010, 39 percent of Americans said that marriage is becoming obsolete, up from 28 percent in 1978. Blacks (44 percent) and Latinos (42 percent) were more likely to hold this view than whites (36 percent). This belief is more common among younger generations than those age 50 and older, those with less than a college degree, those who have never married and are single parents, and those who are cohabiting parents (Cohn et al., 2011; Fry, 2012).

The question, according to one sociologist, is not why fewer people marry, but why so many are still getting married (Cherlin, 2009). In many cases, single people get more tax breaks than married couples. Because of tough economic times, 20 percent of 18- to 34-year-olds have postponed marriage. Economic downturns have a more negative impact on less-educated Americans who, consequently, are more likely to cohabit than to marry. Cohabitation and nonmarital births are now socially acceptable. Women who are self-supporting don't have to depend on marriage to ensure their financial security. Many black women can't find an eligible mate (see Chapter 8), but also say that a college or professional degree and career success are more important to them than marriage (Bennett and Ellison, 2010;

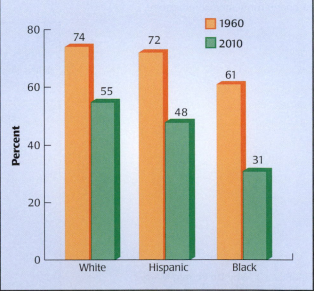

FIGURE 10.2 **Percentage Married by Race and Ethnicity, 1960 and 2010**
Note: Based on U.S. adults age 18 and older. Whites and blacks include only non-Latinos. Latinos are of any race.
Source: Cohn et al., 2011.

Isen and Stevenson, 2010; Chambers and Kravitz, 2011; Taylor et al., 2012; Trail and Karney, 2012; *Washington Post*, 2012). All of these reasons help explain why marriage rates are falling, but marriage is far from obsolete.

Why and How We Marry

When someone announces, "I'm getting married!" we respond with "Congratulations!" rather than "How come?" Those in Western societies assume that people marry because they love each other. In fact, the principal reasons for marriage aren't love but cultural values and norms that it's the right thing to do (see *Figure 10.3*). We marry for a variety of other reasons. Manifest reasons are open, intended, and visible. Latent reasons are unstated and not immediately obvious (see Chapter 2).

Some Manifest Reasons for Getting Married

Family practitioners tend to view the manifest reasons for marriage as "right" and latent reasons as "wrong." Both, however, can be dysfunctional if they result in misery and/or divorce.

LOVE AND COMPANIONSHIP   The single greatest attraction of marriage is a continuous and intimate companionship with a loved one. Among U.S. adults, 93 percent of married people and 84 percent of those unmarried say that love is a "very important" reason to marry (Cohn, 2013).

CHILDREN   A traditional reason for getting married is to have children, but it's not the main one. Compared with the responses about love and marriage, only 59 percent of married and 44 percent of unmarried Americans say that having children is a very important reason to marry (Cohn, 2013). Because marriage is a social institution (unlike singlehood and cohabitation), most societies have laws and customs that protect children within marriage but not necessarily outside of

10.2 Identify the manifest and latent reasons for getting married and describe some pre-marriage and marriage rituals.

Since you asked . . .

- Because it's easier to just live with someone, why do people marry?

Successful marriages are based on mutual respect, love, companionship, and commitment.

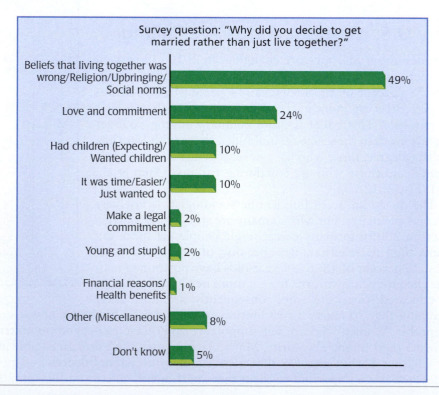

Survey question: "Why did you decide to get married rather than just live together?"

Reason	Percent
Beliefs that living together was wrong/Religion/Upbringing/Social norms	49%
Love and commitment	24%
Had children (Expecting)/Wanted children	10%
It was time/Easier/Just wanted to	10%
Make a legal commitment	2%
Young and stupid	2%
Financial reasons/Health benefits	1%
Other (Miscellaneous)	8%
Don't know	5%

FIGURE 10.3 Why Do People Marry?
Note: These data are from a national sample of American adults age 18 and older who have ever married. Responses total to more than 100 percent because respondents could offer more than one answer to this open-ended question.
Source: Based on Taylor et al., 2007: 31.

it. In many industrialized countries, however, greater acceptance of nonmarital children means that parenthood, rather than marriage, is often the first step into adulthood (Cherlin, 2009).

ADULT IDENTITY Developmental theory asserts that family members progress through various stages during the life course (see Chapter 2). Finding a job and being self-sufficient mark adulthood; so does marriage. Getting married says "I am an adult" to the community. A man who married at age 28 stated, for example, that marriage indicates that "you've finally grown up" and have "a definite position in the world" (Paul, 2002: 80).

COMMITMENT AND PERSONAL FULFILLMENT A large number of married (87 percent) and unmarried (74 percent) Americans believe that marriage should be a lifelong commitment (Cohn, 2013). Commitment includes sexual fidelity, trust, respect, and helping a partner attain her or his life goals. The happiest couples report that they help each other, spend time together, and feel emotionally close. Moreover, those who believe that the quality of a marriage depends on determination and hard work are more likely to report having good marriages than couples who believe that relationships depend on fate, luck, or chance (Olson and Olson, 2000; Hamburg and Hill, 2012).

Some Latent Reasons for Getting Married

Marrying for the "wrong" reasons usually derails a relationship. The wrong reasons may fulfill a specific purpose, such as not feeling left out because everyone else you know is getting married. Usually, however, marrying for the wrong reasons results in a short-term marriage.

SOCIAL LEGITIMACY Getting married to legitimate a nonmarital baby is one of the worst reasons for marrying (even though some religious groups might disagree). Often, the partners are young, one or both may not want to marry, and the couple may have only sex in common.

SOCIAL PRESSURE Often, well-meaning married couples tell their single friends that marriage will bring happiness (see Chapter 8). Relatives can be relentless in nagging singles to get married. Even if parents are divorced, they often encourage their children to marry. According to a 26-year-old media consultant, for example,

> My mother was in her sixties and single. Even after her own two divorces, she was by no means turned off by the idea of marriage. . . . Even though she didn't say it outright, she worried that I would become one of "those" women—thirty-five, lonely, careerist, with a cat and a studio apartment (Paul, 2002: 58).

ECONOMIC SECURITY When I was in graduate school, one of my friends, Beth, married a successful businessman. He was wealthy and she was tired of struggling to pay for tuition and bills. Within a few months, Beth was staying at the library longer and longer because she dreaded going home ("He's a great guy, but we have little in common"). Their marriage lasted two years.

Marrying someone just for her or his money won't sustain a marriage. Among other things, a partner may be stingy and watch every penny after the wedding. One or both partners may be laid off and use up their savings very quickly. Or, even if you marry someone who's rich and then get a divorce, in most states you'll have a difficult time getting any of the money if you've been married less than 10 years (see Chapter 15).

If a couple marries because of social pressure, the union is likely to be short-lived.

In 2010, I-Fairy, a robot, wed a Tokyo couple. Among other things, the robot instructed the groom to "Please lift the bride's veil," and waved its arms as the newlyweds kissed. If you want your wedding to be "really different," you can buy I-Fairy for about $68,000 ("I-Fairy Robot Weds . . .," 2010).

Since you asked . . .

• Why are wedding rituals important?

engagement The formalization of a couple's decision to marry.

REBELLION   Young people sometimes marry to get away from their parents. They flee their families for a variety of reasons: physical, verbal, or sexual abuse; conflict between the parents or with a stepparent; or a yearning for independence. Even when the reasons for getting away from one's family are valid, rebellion is an immature reason for marriage.

PRACTICAL SOLUTIONS TO PROBLEMS   People sometimes marry because they're seeking practical solutions to a problem. Dating can be disappointing (see Chapter 8), and some people hope that marriage will give them an escape hatch from their problems. It won't—because marriage is more complicated and more demanding than singlehood or cohabitation.

Most of us have heard stories about people who marry because they want a helpmate—someone to put them through medical or law school, share expenses in a new business, help care for kids after divorce or widowhood, and so on. Such marriages typically are short lived because they create more problems than they solve.

Wedding and Pre-Wedding Rituals

Marriage is a critical rite of passage in almost every culture. In the United States, the major events that mark the beginning of a marriage are engagement, showers, and bachelor or bachelorette parties, then the wedding itself. Regardless of the reasons for tying the knot, many wedding rituals reinforce the promise to make a lifelong commitment. Some people are more guarded, however, and prepare prenuptial agreements. Let's begin by looking at some of the wedding rituals that presumably cement a marriage.

ENGAGEMENT   Traditionally, an **engagement** formalizes a couple's decision to marry. According to the *Guinness Book of Records*, the longest engagement was between Octavio Guillen and Adriana Martinez of Mexico, who took 67 years to make sure they were right for each other. Most engagements are at least 65 years shorter. An engagement serves several functions:

• It sends a hands-off message to other interested sexual partners.

• It gives both partners a chance to become better acquainted with their future in-laws and to strengthen their identity as a couple.

• It provides an opportunity for secular or religious pre-marital counseling, especially if the partners are of different religions or racial and ethnic backgrounds.

• It signals the intent to make the union legal if the couple has been living together or has had a child out of wedlock.

An engagement ring symbolizes eternity. The origins of a diamond engagement ring are unclear, but some scholars believe that the tradition began with medieval Italians who believed that diamonds were created from the flames of love (Kern, 1992; Ackerman, 1994). Increasingly, however, some critics are questioning the wisdom of continuing this ritual (see "Are Diamond Engagement Rings Losing Their Shine?").

ANSWERS FOR "A Marriage Quiz"

All the items are false. The more "true" responses you checked off, the more misconceptions you have about marriage. The quiz is based on material in this chapter.

Changes | Are Diamond Engagement Rings Losing Their Shine?

A diamond engagement ring (or a wedding ring) isn't what keeps people together after a marriage. Thus, according to some critics, there are five reasons why couples should rethink or change this tradition.

1. **It's just marketing.** About 70 years ago, the De Beers mining family coined the slogan "A diamond is forever" to tie a diamond to an ultimate symbol of love.

2. **Although diamonds are abundant, they're expensive.** Related to #1, for generations, the De Beers company has stockpiled most of the world's diamond supply, monopolized the diamond industry, and squeezed out competitors who sold diamonds at much lower prices.

3. **There are many other options.** Moissanite, another mineral, looks just like a diamond, shines more brilliantly, and is made by machines. A 1-carat moissanite costs under $1,000 compared with $8,000 to $10,000 for a 1-carat diamond, depending on its cut and clarity.

4. **Spend your money more wisely.** The average American couple spends over $3,000 on a diamond engagement ring. The cost would pay for several years of babysitting, housecleaning and laundry services, furnishing a home, or investing in one's current or future children's college fund.

5. **Ethical issues.** Terrorist groups in Africa, where almost 75 percent of the world's diamonds are mined, often use diamonds (called "blood diamonds") to finance their activities and civil wars. In many cases, young children are kidnapped or sold by their parents to pay off a debt, and become slave labor in the diamond mining industry.

Sources: Based on Truong, 2010; Vanderkam, 2010; Nolan, 2011; Chriqui, 2013.

STOP AND THINK . . .

- Do you agree or disagree with those who contend that, for practical and ethical reasons, we shouldn't buy engagement rings? Why?

- Does a diamond engagement ring symbolize everlasting love? Or is it just an expensive piece of jewelry that women don't need?

BRIDAL SHOWERS AND OTHER PRE-MARRIAGE FESTIVITIES At a *bridal shower*, female friends and relatives "shower" a bride with both personal and household gifts. At a *bachelor party*, the groom's friends typically lament his imminent loss of freedom and have one "last fling." Some women also have *bachelorette parties* that include anything from dinner with female friends to a male strip show. Some of the bachelor and bachelorette parties are no longer a one-evening local event but a weekend of fun in Las Vegas, Mexico, the Bahamas, or similar locations (Internicola, 2010).

Many men now participate in the preparations for their wedding. About 80 percent attend bridal shows, give their opinions about flowers, choose products for online bridal registries, produce original wedding invitations on their computers, and make menu choices. According to one wedding planner, "I've had grooms call me five or six times a day about small details months before their weddings" (Caplan, 2005: 67).

Many brides are swept off their feet by merchandising and spend at least a year planning a perfect and often extravagant wedding ceremony (see Data Digest). Increasingly, however, attorneys are advising both women and men to invest some of their time in creating prenuptial agreements just in case the marriage fizzles after a few years.

Many of India's high-income families have expensive weddings that include up to 1,000 guests and last about a week. The super-rich families in India's rapidly growing economy entertain as many as 30,000 guests ("India Explores Ways . . . ," 2011). Most weddings are less lavish, but families usually follow century-long nuptial traditions.

PRENUPTIAL AGREEMENTS Prenuptial agreements ("prenups") are common among the very wealthy. However, a recent survey of lawyers found that there's been a marked increase of prenups among middle classes and women (Revell, 2011).

As Appendix F shows, prenuptial agreements cover numerous topics—from adultery to wills. The contracts also include agreements about disposing of premarital and marital property, whether the couple will have children (and how many), the children's religious upbringing, who gets the dog, protection of retirement accounts, and whether there will be combined or his and her savings and checking accounts.

Applying What You've Learned · Before You Say "I Do"

The best way to decrease divorce rates is to be more selective in choosing one's marital partners (Glenn, 2002). In doing so, we should spend more time planning a marriage than a wedding. Here are some questions that people who are planning to wed should ask:

- What will you contribute to the marriage?
- How often do you like to have time to yourself?
- Which holidays will we spend with which family?
- Do you or your family have a history of any health problems, both physical and mental?
- What are your career goals?
- Do you get along with co-workers?
- How much free time spent away from one another is acceptable?
- What makes you angry?
- What do you consider cheating or infidelity?
- Is religion important to you?
- Are you in debt?
- What would you do with an extra $10,000?

- Do you have to make any child support or alimony payments?
- How often do you plan to cook and clean?
- Do you want to have children? If so, how many, and who will take care of them?
- What does my family do that annoys you?
- Are there some things that you don't plan to give up after marriage?

Source: Based on Outcalt, 1998: 14–138.

STOP AND THINK . . .

- What other questions would you add?
- Instead of using such self-help lists, should couples seek premarital counseling? Or are the lists sufficient?

When a marriage crosses cultural lines, the couple sometimes incorporates some of the traditions—such as the bride's wedding attire—from both cultures.

MAKING CONNECTIONS

- If you're single, do you want to get married? If so, why? If you're married, did you marry for the "right" reasons, the "wrong" reasons, or a combination?
- Do you think that prenuptial agreements are a good idea or not? Read Appendix F before deciding.

Prenuptial agreements are controversial. Proponents contend that if there are children from a first marriage, or if one partner has considerable assets, the contract makes divorce less complicated. Because women usually are the ones who suffer financially after a divorce, a contract gives them some legal protection (Berger, 2008; Palmer, 2008). According to a financial advisor, "In the end, a prenup may not be the most romantic relationship move you'll ever make, but it could be the most valuable" (Revell, 2011: 42).

Opponents maintain that such documents set a pessimistic tone for the marriage. Also, if the contract is executed in a state other than the one in which it was drawn up, the couple will have legal problems enforcing a prenup. And, because people change over time, the contract may not reflect their future attitudes and behavior.

Regardless of how people feel about prenups, scholars and family practitioners agree that most of us don't know very much about the people we marry (see Chapter 8). "Before You Say 'I Do'" suggests some questions that couples should discuss before tying the knot, including whether or not to draw up a legal premarital contract.

THE WEDDING The wedding ceremony reinforces the idea that the marriage is a permanent bond. The presence of family, friends, and witnesses affirms the acceptance and legitimacy of the union. Even if the partners are very young, a wedding marks the end of childhood and the acceptance of adult responsibilities.

Does a marriage last longer if the wedding ceremony is traditional and religious rather than nontraditional (such as having a secular "officiant" who performs the ceremony) or a simple civil ceremony? There are no national data, but family practitioners emphasize that the wedding is far less important than the marriage. If couples and their parents go into debt to pay for an elaborate wedding, both groups may experience strained relationships. Also, snubbing future in-laws before, during, and after a wedding can have harmful outcomes. In-laws can be very supportive—emotionally and financially—when the couple runs into problems (Kiefer, 2005; Silverman, 2006).

Contemporary Marriages

When someone asked a happily married couple to what they owed their marriage of 40 years, the husband replied, "We dine out twice a week—candlelight, violins, champagne, the works! Her night is Tuesday; mine is Friday." As this anecdote suggests, married couples' relationships can vary considerably both in the United States and in other countries.

Heterosexual Marriages

On the basis of a pioneering and now classic study of 400 upper-middle-class marriages (the partners ranged in age from 35 to 55), Cuber and Haroff (1965) identified five types of marriages. Some were happy and some weren't, but all endured.

In a **conflict-habituated marriage**, the partners fight, both verbally and physically, but don't believe that fighting is a good reason for divorce. They believe that feuding is an acceptable way to try to solve problems, and they thrive on their incompatibility. Usually the reason for the conflict is minor and the partners seldom resolve their disputes.

In a **devitalized marriage**, the partners were deeply in love when they married. As the years go by, they spend time together—raising the children, entertaining, and meeting community responsibilities—but begin to do so out of obligation rather than love. They get along and, as a result, don't want a divorce. One or both partners may be unhappy, but they're both committed to staying married.

In a **passive-congenial marriage**, the partners have a low emotional investment in the marriage and few expectations of each other. Fairly independent, they achieve satisfaction from other relationships, such as those with their children, friends, and co-workers. They often maintain separate activities and interests. Passive-congenial couples emphasize the practicality of the marriage over emotional intensity.

In a **vital marriage**, the partners' lives are closely intertwined. They spend a great deal of time together, resolve conflicts through compromise, and often make sacrifices for each other. When a disagreement occurs, it is over a specific issue and is quickly resolved.

In a **total marriage**, which is similar to a vital marriage, the partners participate in each other's lives at all levels and have few areas of tension or unresolved hostility. Spouses share many facets of their lives; they may work together or have the same friends and outside interests. This type of marriage is more encompassing than a vital marriage.

Finding that approximately 80 percent of the marriages they studied fell into the first three categories, Cuber and Haroff characterized these as *utilitarian marriages* because they appeared to be based on convenience. The researchers called the last two types *intrinsic marriages* because the relationships seemed to be inherently rewarding. In their study, vital marriages accounted for 15 percent of the population and total marriages for only 5 percent.

Several later studies found that marriages are more complex and varied (see, for example, Olson and Olson, 2000). The Cuber-Haroff typology is still useful in showing that there are many types of marriages and marital relationships. None of the findings can be generalized, however, because the research was based on middle- and upper-middle-class couples or those in therapy, none of which are representative of the general U.S. married population.

Same-Sex Marriages

Same-sex marriage (also called *gay marriage*) is a legally recognized marriage between two people of the same biological sex. In the United States, and as of late 2013, same-sex marriage is legal in 14 states and the District of Columbia. However, 35 states have passed laws limiting marriage to a man and a woman, or

conflict-habituated marriage The partners fight both verbally and physically but don't believe that fighting is a good reason for divorce.

devitalized marriage The partners were initially in love; one or both may now be unhappy but are committed to staying married.

passive-congenial marriage The partners have little emotional investment in the marriage and few expectations of each other.

vital marriage The partners have a close relationship, resolve conflicts quickly through compromise, and often make sacrifices for each other.

total marriage The partners participate in each other's lives at all levels and have little tension or unresolved hostility.

Since you asked . . .
- If a couple is fighting all the time, should they get a divorce?

same-sex marriage A legally recognized marriage between two people of the same biological sex (also called *gay marriage*).

Benjamin Franklin and his wife, Deborah, presumably had a closed marriage. During 18 of their 44 years of marriage, however, they lived apart because Franklin was often abroad for extended periods, including being an ambassador to France. According to some historians, Franklin enjoyed his LAT marriage (see text) because he was typically surrounded by adoring women. His wife, loyal to the end, tolerated Franklin's sexual infidelity.

have amended their constitutions to explicitly prohibit gay marriage (National Conference of State Legislatures, 2013). Worldwide, since 2001, 16 countries, mostly in Europe, have legalized same-sex marriage so far (Masci et al., 2013).

The Defense of Marriage Act of 1996, known as DOMA, defined marriage as a "legal union between one man and one woman." In 2013, the U.S. Supreme Court struck down part of DOMA as unconstitutional. The high court didn't rule on the question of whether the Constitution guarantees a right to same-sex marriage, but said that same-sex couples in states that recognize their marriages will have equal access to more than 1,100 federal benefits that apply to other married couples (Bravin, 2013; Kendall and Favole, 2013).

Nationally, lesbians (62 percent) are more likely than gay men (38 percent) to marry. Newly married same-sex couples tend to be older than their different-sex counterparts, presumably because they've had to wait longer to enter a legal marriage (Badgett and Herman, 2011).

The number of legal same-sex marriages has grown rapidly, but empirical studies on how lesbians and gay men experience marriage and how it impacts their lives are rare. One exception is a recent study that interviewed 32 married gay men in Iowa. Some of the men said that getting legally married had a positive impact on their relationships with the families they grew up in, such as being included in family gatherings and family e-mail. Half the men had negative or mixed experiences, such as family members not attending the wedding, openly disapproving of the marriage, and withdrawing emotional support (Ocobock, 2013).

Some Cross-Cultural Variations

Worldwide, arranged or semi-arranged marriages are the norm. Marriage forms vary across cultures in other ways, too. Some couples have "living apart together" (LAT) relationships because of economic or personal reasons. In China, for instance, growing numbers of rural husbands are going to urban areas to look for jobs. The men work temporarily in nearby cities to increase their income while their wives take care of the farm, including plowing the field (Sheng, 2005).

In certain Scandinavian countries, some LAT couples remain married but have moved apart to save the relationship. They live in separate homes because "too many quarrels and too much irritation would have made the relationship deteriorate." Some maintain these arrangements indefinitely. For others, the LAT separation "might turn out to be the first step toward a calm divorce" (Trost and Levin, 2005: 358).

There are also LAT marriages in the United States. Some couples live in adjacent apartments or nearby condos, whereas others have separate houses. According to a woman who's been married for 25 years, for example, "the kids are long gone, we're now both retired, and still in our respective homes!" (Dickinson, 2011: 7). Living apart together marriages aren't the same as the "commuter marriages" (you'll meet in Chapter 13) in which couples work in different cities and see each other primarily on weekends.

10.4 Explain how marital happiness, marital success, and health are interrelated.

Marital Happiness, Success, and Health

Researchers usually measure marital success in terms of marital stability and marital satisfaction. *Marital stability* refers to whether a marriage is intact and whether the spouses have ever suggested divorce to each other (Noller and Fitzpatrick, 1993; Holman et al., 1994). *Marital satisfaction* refers to whether

each partner sees the marriage as a good one. To determine satisfaction, researchers have used concepts such as *marital conflict, contentment, commitment*, and *happiness* (Glenn, 1991; Stanley, 2007).

Measuring marital satisfaction is important for two reasons. First, longitudinal studies show that marital unhappiness is a good predictor of divorce. Second, marital unhappiness is linked to a variety of problematic outcomes, including inadequate parenting, psychological distress, and poor physical health—especially among wives (Amato et al., 2007).

Marital Happiness

The percentage of people saying that their marriages are "very happy" has fluctuated, but decreased, since the 1970s (see *Figure 10.4*). Consistently, women report being less happily married than men, a gender difference we'll examine shortly. Because happiness is a self-reported and highly subjective measure, it's impossible to know how respondents define the concept. Do they mean a passive-congenial marriage, for instance? Better than being alone? Or something else?

The measures are subjective, but many of the findings have been fairly consistent. For example, both marital stability and marital satisfaction tend to be higher for those with a college education or higher, those with similar religious practices, and those who married after age 20 instead of during their teens, but much depends on economic stress. Marital happiness decreases when couples experience poverty, job loss, and financial problems. All these events are more likely for couples at lower socioeconomic levels (Glenn, 2005; Amato et al., 2007; E. Brown et al., 2008; Day and Acock, 2013; Wickrama et al., 2013).

Generally, married people are happier than unmarried people because marriage *improves* an already happy life rather than creates one. People who are satisfied with life and have a rich social network of family members, friends, and co-workers have little to gain from marriage. On the other hand, people who are lonely and dissatisfied can sometimes find companionship by marrying (Lucas et al., 2003). Higher socioeconomic status contributes to marital well-being, but it doesn't guarantee either stability or success.

Since you asked . . .
- Why are some couples happier than others?

Marital Success

Is there a recipe for an enduring and happy marriage? Researchers have been trying to answer this question for decades. Despite what self-help books say, there are no 5, 10, or 15 steps for living happily ever after. However, social scientists have found an association between several variables and marital success.

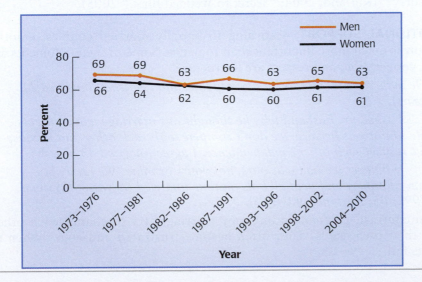

FIGURE 10.4 Percentage of Married Americans Age 18 and Older Who Said Their Marriages Are "Very Happy," by Period
Source: Marquardt et al., 2012, Figure 4.

COMPATIBILITY   Initially, people are attracted to each other because of physical appearance, but similar attitudes, values, and beliefs sustain the relationship. Similar social backgrounds (such as ethnicity, religion, and education) decrease major interpersonal differences that can lead to conflict and disagreements (see Chapter 8).

After marriage, personality may become increasingly important in maintaining a relationship. Couples are happier when they share similar personalities and emotional wavelengths. Unlike dating, marriage requires regular interaction and extensive coordination in dealing with the tasks, issues, and problems of daily living (Whyte, 1990; Luo and Klohnen, 2005; Humbad et al., 2010).

Despite popular opinion, couples who play together don't necessarily stay together. Those who participate in leisure activities together (such as watching television or playing golf) that only one spouse likes become dissatisfied and unhappy with their marriage over time (Crawford et al., 2002; Gager and Sanchez, 2003).

FLEXIBILITY   Relationships are never 100 percent compatible. Russian writer Leo Tolstoy once wrote, "What counts in making a happy marriage is not so much how compatible you are, but how you deal with incompatibility." One spouse may be better organized or more outgoing than the other, for example. Happily married couples, however, are more likely than their unhappy counterparts to discuss how to handle and adjust to such differences. They're more flexible and willing to compromise rather than try to control their spouses or insisting on doing everything their own way (Schwartz, 2006; Szuchman and Anderson, 2012).

POSITIVE ATTITUDES   Spouses who like each other as people and are good friends have happier marriages. Couples whose marriages begin in romantic bliss are especially prone to divorce because it's difficult to maintain such intensity. Those who marry after a whirlwind courtship are quickly disillusioned because they're saddled with fantasies and unrealistic expectations about married life (Pittman, 1999; Ted Huston, cited in Patz, 2000).

COMMUNICATION AND CONFLICT RESOLUTION   Compared with unhappy couples, happy couples recognize and work at resolving problems and disagreements. Sometimes conflict resolution means backing off because one or both partners are hurt or angry. My uncle, 88, once remarked that his 62-year marriage has been relatively peaceful. When he and my aunt start to argue, he simply says "You may be right," and the argument stops.

Couples who have been happily married 50 years or longer say that resolving conflict is a key ingredient for marital success. For example, "Talk out problems, work out mutual solutions, and compromise," and "You must never be afraid to say 'sorry'" (Kurland, 2004; "Secret to Wedded Bliss," 2005).

EMOTIONAL SUPPORT   According to happily married couples, emotional support is much more important than romance. Some of their comments about trust, cooperation, and respect are instructive:

He makes me feel smart, pretty, capable, and cherished (married 21 years).

I asked my husband why he thought our marriage was a success. He said it was because we don't compete with each other and because we respect each other's independence. I agree (married 33 years).

Whatever we had was ours, not yours or mine. We rarely borrowed money and paid all bills on time (married 60 years) (Mathias, 1992: B5; Kurland, 2004: 65).

In contrast, partners in unhappy marriages try to change each other to meet their own needs. They often become frustrated and angry when their efforts fail.

Marriage and Health

Overall, married people are healthier than their unmarried counterparts. They have lower rates of heart disease, cancer, stroke, pneumonia, tuberculosis, cirrhosis of the liver, and syphilis. They attempt suicide less frequently and have fewer automobile accidents than do singles. Married people are also less likely to suffer from depression, anxiety, and other forms of psychological distress (Horwitz et al., 1996; Wickrama et al., 1997; Schoenborn, 2004; Williams et al., 2010).

Why is there a positive association between marriage and physical and psychological well-being? Two major sociological explanations have focused on selection and protection effects.

THE SELECTION EFFECT Some sociologists posit that married people are healthier than their unmarried counterparts because of a "selection effect." That is, healthy people are attracted to others who are like themselves. Healthy people also tend to be happier and more sociable before marriage and don't depend on marriage to make them happy. Such characteristics increase their desirability as marriage partners among those with similar traits. They're unlikely to be attracted to people who have serious physical and psychological problems and lifestyles that include drug dependence (Wilson, 2002; Stutzer and Frey, 2006).

THE PROTECTION EFFECT Other sociologists maintain that it's not mate selection but marriage itself that makes people healthier because of a "protection effect," sometimes called a "marriage advantage." Receiving emotional, physical, and financial support from a spouse improves one's general health and longevity by reducing anxiety, preventing or lessening depression, and increasing psychological well-being (Frech and Williams, 2007).

Marriage also decreases risky activities and encourages healthy behaviors. Married people (especially men) are more likely than singles to quit smoking and less likely to drink heavily, get into fights, or drive too fast—risks that increase the likelihood of accidents and injuries (J. E. Murray, 2000; Kiecolt-Glaser and Newton, 2001). When a spouse improves her or his behavior, the other spouse is likely to do so as well. For example, smokers are five times more likely to quit smoking if their spouse quits, or reduce their alcohol consumption if their partner doesn't drink (Falba and Sindelar, 2008).

A COMBINATION OF EFFECTS Some recent data show that marriage may have both selective and protective effects. A longitudinal study followed 289 pairs of fraternal and identical male twins from ages 17 to 29, measuring their anti-social behavior (e.g., repeated illegal acts, aggression, lying, etc.). All of the men started out unmarried; by age 29, 59 percent were married. Men who were married by age 29 were less likely to have committed anti-social acts in their younger years. This finding is consistent with the selection effect (nicer men are more likely to get married). But even the more aggressive men who married reduced their anti-social behavior by 30 percent. This finding illustrates the protective effects of marriage (matrimony decreases male anti-social behavior) (Burt et al., 2010).

Varying Health Benefits of Marriage

Marriage itself isn't a magic potion that makes us healthier and happier. Instead, the health benefits vary by factors such as marital status, gender, and the quality of a marriage.

MARITAL STATUS AND HEALTH According to a recent Gallup survey, married people report the highest well-being, especially compared with those who are divorced or separated (see *Table 10.1*). Gallup has found such

Since you asked . . .
• Does marriage make people healthier, or are healthy people more likely than unhealthy people to get married?

 Watch on MySocLab
Video: Is Marriage Good for Your Health?

TABLE 10.1 Married Americans Report the Highest Well-Being

Marital Status	Well-Being Index Score*
Married	68.8
Single	65.0
Widowed	63.5
Cohabiting	63.3
Divorced	59.7
Separated	55.9
All Adults	66.2

* The well-being index is an average of scores that measured life evaluation, emotional health, work environment, physical health, healthy behaviors, and access to basic necessities. The index is calculated on a scale of 0 to 100, where a score of 100 would represent ideal well-being.
Source: Based on Brown and Jones, 2012.

consistent differences each year since it began tracking this issue in 2008 (Brown and Jones, 2012).

Note, however, that single people aren't far behind those who are married (index scores of 65 and almost 69, respectively). In the past, single men were less healthy than single women (possibly because many single women are more conscious of their physical appearance and try to control their weight), and less healthy than married men. By 2003, however, never-married men, particularly, became almost as healthy as their married counterparts because of better diets; regular exercise; and satisfying relationships, such as cohabitation outside of marriage (Liu and Umberson, 2008).

Separated Americans may have the lowest well-being scores, and lower than those divorced, because they're still struggling with the transition from marriage. In contrast, many of the divorced have already adjusted to lower economic benefits, the loss of companionship, and dealing with being single parents (see Chapter 15).

Widowed Americans have higher well-being scores than those who are divorced or separated. The differences may be due to age. The widowed tend to be older, and health problems increase as we age. You'll see in Chapter 16, however, that widowed women, more than widowers, often have a social network of family members and friends that increases their well-being.

Cohabitants have lower well-being rates than those who are widowed, divorced, or separated. Married people tend to fare better because of health insurance, for example. However, cohabitants report being happier because their relationships are more flexible, and they don't have the "structured expectations and obligations" that marriage brings (Musick and Bumpass, 2012: 13).

GENDER, MARRIAGE, AND HEALTH Overall, married women are less healthy than married men. On average, women live longer than men, but, unlike husbands, many wives experience depression and other health problems.

Many married men enjoy "emotional capital" because wives provide nurturing and companionship. Men often report that their greatest (and sometimes only) confidantes are their wives, whereas married women often talk to close friends and relatives. Thus, husbands can depend on their wives for

Since you asked. . .

• Are married men or women healthier?

caring and emotional support, but wives tend to look outside the marriage for close personal relationships (Steil, 1997; Maushart, 2002).

Wives tend to encourage behaviors that prolong life, such as regular medical checkups. Marriage also often introduces lifestyle changes that reduce some of men's bad habits such as smoking, drinking with male friends at bars, and illicit drug use, especially as part of the "singles scene" (Bachman et al., 1997). A review of almost 35 years of research found that a stable marriage is only one of seven factors that affect men's longevity. The other factors include alcohol and drug abuse, smoking, not exercising, not coping with stress, and depression (Cole and Dendukuri, 2003). Thus, marriage alone doesn't extend married men's lives.

Women typically are more attuned than men to the emotional quality of marriages. They work harder if the marriage is distressed; have many domestic responsibilities even if they work outside the home; have little time to unwind; and neglect their own health while caring for family members, including their husbands (Kiecolt-Glaser and Newton, 2001). Employed wives—especially those with children—are at especially high risk for depression because they often feel overwhelmed by the chronic strain of meeting the needs of their husband and children while also working full time (Shatzkin, 2005; Bryant et al., 2010; see also Chapter 13).

Some researchers posit that men benefit from marriage because women typically have less status and power compared with their husbands. Such inequality results in women's experiencing more physical and emotional problems, especially when there's marital discord (Wanic and Kulik, 2011). Others question such explanations because even wives who have more status and power than their husbands, and when there's little marital conflict, have more health problems. In addition, it's not clear whether and how much external factors (such as women's dissatisfaction with friends and co-workers) affect women's health (Monin and Clark, 2011).

MARITAL QUALITY AND HEALTH The quality of marriages is much more important than simply getting or being married. Couples in troubled marriages are more susceptible to illness than happier couples. Among other things, marital conflict may increase stress levels that, over the years, can contribute to higher blood pressure, which, in turn, leads to heart disease, and even increase the time needed to recuperate after an illness or surgery. Emotional stress can also accelerate psychological and physical problems that increase depressive symptoms and affect the spouses' work and family roles. A wife might medicate herself with pills and a husband might turn to alcohol to decrease the stress (Barnett et al., 2005; Kiecolt-Glaser et al., 2005; Fincham and Beach, 2010; South and Krueger, 2013). People in unhappy marriages may also experience marital burnout.

Marital Burnout

Marital burnout is the gradual deterioration of love and ultimate loss of an emotional attachment between partners. The process can go on for many years. In marital burnout, even if the spouses share housework and child care, one spouse may not give the other emotional support or complain that a wife or husband doesn't want to confide his or her innermost feelings or discuss problems (Erickson, 1993).

Marital burnout can develop so slowly and quietly that the couple isn't aware of it. Sometimes one partner hides dissatisfaction for many years. At other times both partners may ignore the warning signs (see "Am I Heading toward Marital Burnout?"). Applying social exchange theory, when the costs in the relationship become much greater than the benefits, marital satisfaction can plunge.

marital burnout The gradual deterioration of love and ultimate loss of an emotional attachment between partners.

Constraints | Am I Heading toward Marital Burnout?

All marriages have ups and downs. Checking off even as many as six of the following items doesn't necessarily mean that your marriage is in trouble, but might be an indicator of marital burnout. The earlier you recognize some of these symptoms, according to some family and health practitioners, the better your chances of improving your marriage.

- You feel bored with each other and seem to have little in common.
- There's a lack of communication; neither of you listens to the other.
- Deep down, you want a divorce, but you are staying in the relationship because it's easier than being on your own.
- There's a lack of flexibility: You can no longer compromise with each other.
- Minor irritations become major issues; one or both of you is irritable and sarcastic.

- You no longer try to deal honestly with important issues.
- You find yourself making family decisions alone.
- Your relationships with other people are closer than your relationship with your spouse.
- One of you controls the other through tantrums, violence, or threats of suicide or violence.
- You are both putting your own individual interests before the good of the marriage.
- You can't talk about money, politics, religion, sex, or other touchy subjects.
- You avoid each other.
- One or both of you subjects the other to public humiliation.
- You have increasing health problems, such as headaches, back pain, sleeplessness, high

blood pressure, recurring colds, or emotional ups and downs.
- One or both of you is abusing alcohol or other drugs.
- Shared activities and attendance at family functions have decreased.

Sources: Based on Stinnett and DeFrain, 1985; Kayser, 1993; Tsapelas et al., 2009.

STOP AND THINK . . .

- Are you experiencing marital burnout? If so, what, if anything, do you plan to do about it?
- Why do you think that many married couples—especially those who have been married at least 50 years—are less likely to undergo marital burnout?

10.5 Describe how couples establish, negotiate, and learn marital roles.

marital roles The specific ways that married people define their behavior and structure their time.

Read on MySocLab

Document: The Two Marriages

identity bargaining The process of partners negotiating adjustments to their new married roles.

Since you asked . . .

- Are marital roles instinctive?

Marital Roles

Marital roles are the specific ways that married couples define their behavior and structure their time. Even if the partners have lived together before marriage, they experience changes when they marry. From the wedding day and throughout the life course, married couples must establish marital roles and boundaries and adapt to changes.

Establishing and Negotiating Marital Roles

Many people develop idealized and unrealistic images of marriage long before they meet their mates. Especially during the first year, newly married partners must modify their idealized expectations and learn to deal with the realities of everyday married life. In **identity bargaining**, partners negotiate adjustments to their new married roles (Blumstein, 1975).

The process of learning marital roles and identity bargaining usually involves three steps. First, people have to *identify with the roles* they're performing. Doing so isn't as easy as it sounds because sometimes spouses place a higher priority on their roles as sons, daughters, brothers, sisters, and friends.

Second, people must learn to *treat their partner as a spouse*. Again, this isn't as simple as it seems because transitioning from being single to being married requires a major shift in a person's attitudes and behavior. For example, both spouses may have to curtail some of their leisure activities with their friends, and have to make mutual decisions about issues such as finances.

Third, the two people must *negotiate changes in their new roles*. If, for example, neither likes doing housework, grocery shopping, paying bills, or

maintaining cars, who will perform such tasks? Failure to agree on who does what can lead to resentment and conflict.

Initially, learning and negotiating marital roles may be difficult and confusing. Over time, however, defining marital roles helps spouses fulfill their expectations of each other and forges a strong relationship as a couple.

Establishing Boundaries and Learning More Roles

When people marry, many still have strong ties to their parents, siblings, and other kin. An important marital role is to shift one's primary loyalty from these family members to one's spouse, and to establish boundaries that preserve the spousal bond. If both partners are employed, for example, they may feel strain in living up to extended family members' expectations to visit or spend time together, thereby raising the possibility of role and marital conflict (see Chapter 5).

You'll see shortly that the better one's relationship with in-laws, the more likely the marriage will be happy and the lower the likelihood of divorce. If married couples don't establish boundaries, family bonds can become chains. In the case of one of my friends, for example, the wife's father assumed that his new son-in-law was glad to spend Saturdays on the father-in-law's home improvement tasks, and the daughter agreed with her father. The son-in-law resented the intrusion on his weekend activities, and felt that he couldn't refuse, but this was one of the reasons for the son-in-law's decision to get a divorce six years later.

Married couples also add more and new roles if they associate with one (or both) of the partner's friends, attend her or his religious services, or join new community organizations. Some women must take on the most demanding role of all—that of mother—if they're pregnant when they marry. A man must also cope with the multiple roles of husband and father.

Adapting to Changes in Marital Roles over Time

Besides learning new and more roles, married couples must also adjust to changes throughout the life course. You saw in Chapter 5 that some marital gender roles are traditional, some are egalitarian, and many are somewhere in the middle. The gender gap in housework among employed spouses has decreased, in part, because husbands with traditional views of marital roles have become more supportive and do more household chores if their wives have to work to supplement the family income (Lam et al., 2012).

Nonetheless, work–family conflict is still a critical and unresolved issue. For example, and especially among working- and middle-class families, child care remains the primary responsibility of employed mothers; nonstandard work hours (such as working evenings, on weekends, or on rotating shifts) may increase the time that a parent spends with children during the day, but it also increases maternal stress and interferes with routine family activities (such as having dinner together); and two-income couples may experience marital stress that lowers the quality of a marital relationship (Bianchi and Milkie, 2010; see also Chapters 12 and 13).

Another important change in marital roles is caring for aging parents and relatives. Many married people can't retire when they expected because they must keep working to support older relatives who don't have the resources to hire nurses and home health care assistants, or refuse help from "outsiders" because "I don't trust them." Adult children also maintain their aging parents' homes, run errands, and take time off from work to drive their parents to medical appointments. Most adult children adapt to such pressures, but doing so may decrease their own marital satisfaction (see Chapter 16).

 Watch on MySocLab

Video: Changing Gender Roles at Home

Men's contributions to housework and child care have increased since the 1970s. The longer a wife is employed, the more housework her husband often does.

MAKING CONNECTIONS

- The characteristics of a successful marriage seem like common sense. Why, then, is there so much marital conflict?
- Do you think that learning marital roles comes more easily if couples first live together? Why or why not?

How Marriages Change throughout the Life Course

From a developmental perspective, people perform different roles and learn new tasks as a marriage develops its own structure and identity. Throughout the life course, we must adjust, adjust, adjust—to agreeing on specific goals, solving marital problems, and coping with unexpected crises. The adjustments begin with the first year of marriage and continue until we die.

The Early Years of Marriage

Because most couples don't know each other as well as they should and don't attend premarital classes, they're not ready for what happens after the romantic wedding ceremonies are over.

SETTLING IN The first year of marriage involves basic adjustments. After the wedding, the couple takes on the new and unfamiliar married roles. It takes some women up to a year to feel comfortable with their new married name and the new identity of being a wife (Nissinen, 2000).

A second adjustment involves putting the marital relationship above others. While doing so, couples must also strike a balance between their relationships with their in-laws and their spouses. Parents (especially mothers) who fear losing contact with their married children sometimes create conflict by calling and visiting frequently and meddling in the couple's life (Greider, 2000; Viorst, 2003).

If both partners grew up in families in which parents were responsive to each other's emotional needs, they had good role models. Especially as newlyweds, they're more successful in weathering marital stress (Sabatelli and Bartle-Haring, 2003; Umberson et al., 2005).

MARITAL SATISFACTION After five years, approximately 10 percent of first marriages end in divorce, and 25 percent do so by the tenth year of marriage (Kreider and Ellis, 2011b). Who are the high-risk newlyweds? A study that tracked 464 newlyweds over four years found that those with the lowest marital satisfaction and highest divorce rates had three characteristics: (1) they had personality traits that they brought to the marriage such as being moody, a worrier, easily angered, and physically and/or verbally abusive, and having low self-esteem; (2) they experienced chronic stresses such as poor relationships with family, in-laws, and friends; negative experiences at school and work; financial problems; and concerns about their own or their spouse's health; and (3) they were angry and contemptuous rather than having a sense of humor, showing affection, and being interested in discussing problems with their spouses (Lavner and Bradbury, 2012). Thus, some of the reasons for early marital dissatisfaction are evident from the very beginning, probably even before people get engaged.

Two-paycheck newlyweds—especially those who marry after a long period of independence—must make the transition from "my" money to "our" money. Adjusting to a joint bank account isn't always easy because most people aren't used to pooling their money. The couple will also have to reach a consensus about paying off college loans, credit card debt, mortgage payments (if one partner just bought a house, for example), and saving for the future. And what if one's a spender and the other's a saver? Will both agree to make the necessary sacrifices?

Early in the marriage, assuming more debt decreases marital satisfaction. Newlyweds may be initially optimistic about their relationship and dealing with financial issues. As their credit card debt mounts, however, couples argue more

Beginning early in marriage, a major source of conflict is the inability to pay debts on a timely basis. Credit card debt is especially problematic because finance charges accumulate quickly, sometimes costing more than the product or service a couple buys.

about their finances, spend less time together, and think that their marriage is unfair because there are more costs than benefits (Dew, 2008).

Why do divorce rates increase after the first five years of marriage? Perhaps because some newlyweds stop wearing their rose-colored glasses. A study that tracked 222 childless couples in first marriages through their first three years found that those who were the most satisfied clung to their views of their spouses as ideal mates instead of facing reality (e.g., the spouse is self-assured rather than opinionated). Thus, the marriage continued, at least for the first three years, because one or both of the spouses, despite their disappointments, protected the marriage by convincing themselves that they had married their ideal mate (Murray et al., 2011).

Marriage and Children

One of the important functions of the family is to socialize children to become responsible and contributing members of society (see Chapter 1). In some countries, teens marry at an early age, have children, and are considered adults. In Western societies, including the United States, adolescents are dependent on their parents until their late teens and even into their mid- or late twenties. Despite postponing marriage, most couples spend much of their married life raising their offspring (see Chapter 12).

YOUNG CHILDREN Socializing children takes enormous time and patience. As a result, marital satisfaction tends to decrease after a couple has children. Most parents experience more frequent conflicts and disagreements after having children than do childless spouses. On the other hand, many couples who marry before their nonmarital child is born enjoy being married. Compared with their unmarried counterparts, after the first year of marriage they report greater financial security, a stable home life, and optimism about being good parents (Timmer and Orbuch, 2001; Whiteman et al., 2007; Kamp Dush et al., 2008).

ADOLESCENTS Raising adolescents is often even more difficult. Besides all the usual developmental tasks associated with the physical changes of puberty and emotional maturation, contemporary adolescents face more complicated lives than ever before. Both parents and children may have to cope with divorce, parental unemployment, and violence and drugs in their schools and neighborhoods (Cotten, 1999). We'll return to the adolescent years in Chapter 12.

The potential for family stress often increases as adolescents begin to press for autonomy and independence. Conflict sometimes occurs not necessarily because of the children but as a result of a dip in the parents' happiness because of marital burnout or communication problems. Sometimes changes occur suddenly because of geographic moves. Depending on the breadwinner's (usually the father's) occupation and career stage, family members may have to adjust to a new community and form new friendships.

Marriage and the Midlife Years

Like their younger counterparts, couples in their midlife years (between ages 45 and 65) must continually adapt to new conditions. The most common adjustments involve intergenerational ties, relationships with in-laws, the empty nest syndrome, and the boomerang generation.

The stresses of raising young children increase marital conflict.

INTERGENERATIONAL TIES Intergenerational ties are often positive and supportive, but irritation and ambivalence are common. A study of black and white adult children ages 22 to 49 found that parents reported more intense tension than children did, particularly regarding

the children's jobs, finances, and housekeeping habits. Both parents experienced more conflict with their daughters than their sons, possibly because daughters generally have closer relationships and more contact with their parents, both of which increase opportunities for disagreements. Also, both sons and daughters felt more stress with their mothers than with their fathers, particularly because mothers were more likely to be critical and offer unsolicited advice (Birditt et al., 2009).

RELATIONSHIPS WITH IN-LAWS In India, a bride, even in a prosperous family, often lives with an extended family in which the mother-in-law is obeyed, honored, and rules over her daughter-in-law and grandchildren (Stanley, 2012). In the United States, in contrast, there are numerous jokes about mothers-in-law ("Hey guys, looking for a great gift for your mother-in-law on Mother's Day? Why not send her back her daughter!"). We rarely, if ever, hear father-in-law jokes.

After a couple marries, most of the conflict is usually between married women and female in-laws (Apter, 2009). Why? First, women play a central role in family relationships. When a new marriage is formed and another woman enters the family circle, a mother may believe, correctly, that she's less central in her son's life and may be ambivalent about giving up the close ties with him that she enjoyed in the past. When the wife is close to her in-laws, she many find it difficult to set boundaries and, over time, will begin to see their advice or criticism as meddling (Orbuch et al., 2013).

Second, American culture doesn't have clearly delineated roles for in-laws—such as showing deference to older women as in many Asian and Middle East countries. Instead, we often hear statements such as "I'm marrying Andy, not his mother and father." This is a misconception because in-laws, like it or not, are an important part of a couple's relationship and can account for up to 43 percent of a couple's marital satisfaction (Morr Serewicz, 2008).

Third, tension is compounded because of generational differences, particularly after the birth of a grandchild. Conflict arises when the daughter-in-law and the more experienced mother-in-law wrestle over child care. Grandmothers feel excluded when their daughters-in-law ignore their presumably sage (although unsolicited) advice on proper child rearing. The younger generation, wanting control over their parenting, often rejects the advice as old-fashioned, disapproving, and intrusive (Apter, 2009).

First Lady Michelle Obama's mother, Marian Robinson, who has played an important role in her granddaughters' lives, represents the growing number of multigenerational families that include in-laws. When asked how she felt about relocating from Chicago to Washington, DC, after President Obama's election in 2008, Robinson said, "If somebody's going to be with these kids other than their parents, it better be me" (Toppo, 2008).

THE EMPTY NEST SYNDROME   Social scientists used to characterize middle-aged parents as experiencing the *empty-nest syndrome*—depression and a lessened sense of well-being, particularly among women—when children leave home. Some parents, especially mothers who have devoted their lives to bringing up children, may feel empty and useless when their kids fly from the nest.

In fact, the children's departure gives many married couples a chance to relax, enjoy each other's company, see friends, travel, and pursue their own interests. Often, both parents experience a sense of freedom and easing of responsibility that enhances their relationship (Antonucci et al., 2001; see also Chapter 12).

Some sad and lonely parents might sit at home waiting for their children to call or visit, but that's not usually the case. For example, a study that tracked the marital satisfaction of more than 100 women over an 18-year period found that their marriages improved after the kids left. Marital satisfaction increased mainly because of the quality, and not just the quantity, of time that spouses spent together after the children moved out (Gorchoff et al., 2008).

THE BOOMERANG GENERATION   Children who leave the nest sometimes fly back. This recent phenomenon is known as the **boomerang generation**—young adults who move back into their parents' home after living independently for a while. In the case of a weak economy, low income, divorce, or the high cost of housing, many young adults move back into their parents' home or never leave it in the first place. Parents try to launch their children into the adult world, but, like boomerangs, some keep coming back (see Chapter 12).

Boomerang kids can have a positive or a negative impact on their parents' marital life. Co-residence has a more negative influence on remarried parents than on parents in their first marriage largely because of conflict between children and stepparents (Mitchell and Gee, 1996). We'll examine this issue in Chapter 15).

Marital satisfaction also diminishes if a child returns home several times. The multiple returns prevent some parents from enjoying the greater intimacy, privacy, and freedom to pursue new interests that they expected when their children left home. Marital satisfaction increases, however, if the children have a good relationship with their parents during co-residence. The children can provide physical and home maintenance assistance, emotional support, advice, and companionship, all of which can improve the overall quality of family relationships (Willis and Reid, 1999).

> **boomerang generation**   Young adults who move back into their parents' homes after living independently for a while.

Since you asked . . .
- How do parents feel about their boomerangers?

Marriage and Later Life

Many older couples describe their marriage as the best years of their lives. They've developed trust and intimacy over the years, enjoy each other's company, and are happier than their younger counterparts. Couples continue to make adjustments in later life, however, as evidenced by retirement and health issues.

RETIREMENT   Older couples often report an upturn in marital happiness. They have few unresolved issues, settle conflicts more effectively than their younger and middle-aged counterparts, and savor the rewards of a long-term friendship.

Retirement typically brings more time to enjoy each other's company, but gender roles usually don't change very much. Men continue to do most of the traditional male chores, and may take on large-scale projects such as remodeling. Men might do more shopping, but women still invest much of their time in traditionally female tasks such as food preparation, laundry, and housework, and provide care for grandchildren whose parents work (Charles and Carstensen,

In 2012, Maryland was one of the three states that legalized same-sex marriage. James Scales, age 68, was married to William Tasker, age 60, shortly after midnight January 1, 2013. They had been together for 35 years.

2002; see also Chapters 12 and 16). The biggest change in later life for both sexes is physical decline.

HEALTH AND WELL-BEING   The marital quality of older couples, whether one or both are retired, depends quite a bit on the partners' health. A decline in health almost always impairs marital quality.

A recent study, and the first of its kind, tracked the emotional and physical histories of more than 1,700 older couples over a 15-year period. The participants ranged in age from 76 to 90 and many had been married for more than 40 years. The researchers found a strong relationship between "depressive symptoms" (unhappiness, loneliness, and restlessness) and "functional limitations"—the physical inability to perform such basic tasks as climbing stairs, picking up objects, cooking, and grocery shopping. The spouses' depressive symptoms waxed and waned closely with those of their partners. Functional limitations in one spouse were not only associated with her or his own depressive symptoms but also with depressive symptoms in the other spouse. Increases in depressive symptoms in one spouse were also associated with greater functional limitations in both spouses (Hoppmann et al., 2011). Thus, for better or for worse, long-term couples can become interdependent emotionally and physically.

If a spouse needs long-term care, whether at home or in a nursing facility, the caregiver undergoes tremendous stress. And if a spouse is widowed, she or he may have to forge new relationships (see Chapter 16).

Power and communication issues affect marital quality throughout the life course. Most of these issues are similar whether people are married or single.

Communication: A Key to Successful Relationships

People who have been married a long time usually give very similar reasons for their success: "We never yelled at each other," "We maintained a sense of humor," "We treated each other with respect," and "We tried to be patient."

Why Effective Communication Is Important

According to German philosopher Friedrich Nietzsche (1844–1900), "When marrying, ask yourself this question: Do you believe that you will be able to converse well with this person into your old age? Everything else in marriage is transitory." The same might be said of all intimate relationships. Trouble communicating can lead to many serious problems and a gradual deterioration of a relationship.

A study followed 136 couples for 10 years, starting within six months of their marriage. All of the couples reported high levels of satisfaction at the beginning and four years later. By the end of the tenth year, 15 percent of the couples had divorced. None of the couples had risk factors identified in previous studies of relationship dissolution, such as wavering commitment, negative personality traits, or high levels of stress. The only variables that identified those who eventually divorced were negative interaction patterns—particularly anger, contempt, nonsupportive reactions, blaming, and verbal aggression—during discussions of relationship difficulties. Eventually, the negative interaction wore people down and resulted in divorce (Lavner and Bradbury, 2012).

Negative communication patterns don't always end a marriage or other intimate relationship. Instead, hostile interaction (anger, criticism, rejection) can produce or increase depression, unhappiness, and self-doubt (Proulx et al., 2009). *Figure 10.5* provides a visual summary of some of the other negative effects of communication problems in relationships.

10.7 Explain how communication, power, and conflict affect a relationship.

Watch on MySocLab

Video: The Monster: Relationships and Communication

Since you asked. . .

• Why is effective verbal and nonverbal communication essential in any committed relationship?

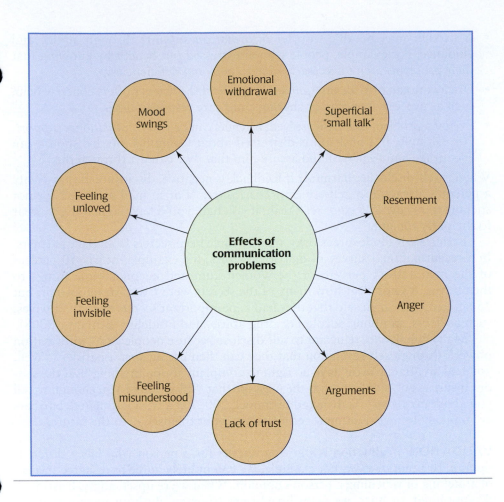

FIGURE 10.5 Some Negative Effects of Communication Problems in Relationships
Source: Author's compilation based on 23 studies published between 1990 and 2013.

Effective Communication

Our most intimate relationships are within the family, but being able to listen well and express thoughts and feelings are critical components of all close relationships. Effective communication involves establishing goals and processes such as self-disclosure and validation.

COMMUNICATION GOALS A major goal of effective communication is developing ways of interacting that are clear, nonjudgmental, and nonpunitive. A second important goal is resolving conflicts through problem solving rather than coercion or manipulation. Very little can be gained "if someone tells us how we are *supposed* to feel, how we are *supposed* to behave, or what we are *supposed* to do with our lives" (Aronson, 1995: 404).

Effective communication conveys *what* we and others feel. It also establishes an atmosphere of trust and honesty in resolving—or at least decreasing—conflict. An important first step in successful communication is self-disclosure.

SELF-DISCLOSURE *Self-disclosure* is telling another person about oneself and one's thoughts and feelings with the expectation that truly open communication will follow (see Chapter 6). In exchange theory, *reciprocal* self-disclosure increases partners' liking and trusting each other, eliminates a lot of guesswork in the relationship, and helps balance costs and benefits.

Self-disclosure is beneficial under four conditions (Derlega et al., 1993):

- *Esteem support* can reduce a person's anxiety about troubling events. If the listener is attentive, sympathetic, and uncritical, disclosure can motivate people to change significant aspects of their lives.

- A listener may be able to offer *information support* through advice and guidance. For example, people who are stressed out benefit by knowing that their problems aren't necessarily due to personal deficiencies.

- Disclosure can provide *instrumental support* if the listener offers concrete help, such as grocery shopping or sharing child care responsibilities.

- Even if a problem isn't easily solved, listeners can provide *motivational support*. For example, if a husband is distressed about losing his job, his spouse can encourage him to persist and assure him that "we can get through this."

When is self-disclosure harmful? If feedback is negative, disclosure may intensify a person's already low self-esteem. (*Disclosure:* "I'm so mad at myself for not sticking to my diet." *Response:* "Yeah; if you had, you'd have something to wear to the party tonight.")

Because self-disclosure is risky, many people keep secrets from their partners. In a recent national survey of married couples, for example, nearly 50 percent of the men and 41 percent of the women admitted keeping some things to themselves. It's not clear how many of the secrets were trivial or important, but 25 percent of the men said that they had kept important secrets from their wives, such as debts, gambling, alcohol or drug abuse, and infidelity (Bennetts, 2008).

Many couples are reluctant to self-disclose because people gain "information power" through self-revelation that they can then use against a partner ("Well, you had an affair, so you have no right to complain about anything"). If the self-disclosure is one-sided, it sends the message that "I don't trust you enough to tell you about my flaws" (Galvin and Brommel, 2000). If a trust is violated, partners are unlikely to reveal intimate information about themselves in the future.

validation Showing respect for a person who has a different opinion or point of view.

VALIDATION **Validation** is showing respect for a person who has a different opinion or point of view. For example, we can politely agree to disagree instead of attacking or ridiculing a person's opinion. When we're upset, angry, frustrated, disappointed, or hurt, we want loved ones to listen, without interrupting, to sympathize, and to validate our venting ("I understand why you're upset").

Those who care about us become personally distressed by our anguish. As a result, they're likely, and with good intentions, to try to minimize our emotional pain by giving advice ("Just let it go," "Don't let them get to you," or "Here's what you should do . . . "). Such responses, however, may seem dismissive rather than helpful because all we want is someone who listens to us, understands why we're upset, and is supportive (Winch, 2011).

Communication Problems

Despite our best intentions, many of us don't communicate effectively. Because communication involves *both* partners, we can't control or change our partner's interaction, but we can recognize and do something about our own communication style. Common communication problems include a variety of issues, ranging from not listening to using the silent treatment.

Nonverbal communication can be just as powerful as words in enhancing or reducing interaction. How does this couple's body language illustrate communication problems?

NOT LISTENING Both partners may be so intent on making their point that they are simply waiting for their turn to speak rather than listening to the other person. Consider a nondiscussion I had with my husband while I was revising this textbook:

Me: "I'm really behind on the writing deadlines."
Husband: "I think you should get a new laptop. What about a Mac this time?"
Me: "I'll probably be writing Christmas cards in February."
Husband: "I think I'll order you a few more printer cartridges."
Me: "I'll never finish these revisions on time. What I need is a clone."
Husband: "If you make a list, I'll do the grocery shopping tomorrow."

This everyday exchange illustrates the common pattern of partners talking but not communicating. One of the most important components of communication is *really* listening to the other person instead of rehearsing what we plan to say when he or she pauses for a breath. Listening and responding are especially critical when partners discuss relationship problems.

NOT RESPONDING TO THE ISSUE AT HAND If partners aren't listening to each other, they won't address an issue or problem. There are three common miscommunication patterns. With *cross-complaining*, partners present their own complaints without addressing the other person's point:

Spouse 1: "I'm tired of spending all my time on the housework. You're not doing your share."

Spouse 2: "If you used your time efficiently, you wouldn't be tired" (Gottman, 1982: 111).

With *counterproposals*, a spouse ignores or rejects a partner's suggestions and presents his or her own ideas ("Negotiating is ridiculous because they'll never fix the windows. I want to take them to court"). In the case of *stonewalling*, which is more common among men than women, one of the partners may "Hmmmm" or "Uh-huh," but he or she really neither hears nor responds; it's as though the partner has turned into a stone wall (Krokoff, 1987; Gottman, 1994; Wood, 2011). If a partner is addicted to alcohol or drugs, for example, she or he might refuse to talk about the problem:

> *Whenever someone brings up the [alcohol] issue, he proclaims that they are making a big deal about nothing, are out to get him, or are just plain wrong. No matter how obvious it is to an outsider that the addict's life may be falling apart, he stubbornly refuses to discuss it. If that doesn't work, he may just get up and walk out (Nowinski, 1993: 137).*

BLAMING, CRITICIZING, AND NAGGING Instead of being listened to and understood, partners may feel neglected or unappreciated. They believe that their spouse or partner magnifies their faults, belittles them, accuses them unjustly, and makes them feel worthless and stupid. The criticism may escalate from specific complaints ("The bank called today and I was embarrassed that your check bounced") to more global and judgmental derision ("Don't you know anything about managing money?!").

The blamer is a faultfinder who criticizes relentlessly and generalizes: "You never do anything right," "You're just like your mother/father." In blaming and criticizing, a partner may use sophisticated communication skills to manipulate a more vulnerable partner (Gordon, 1993; Burleson and Denton, 1997). If I'm an effective blamer, for example, I can probably convince you that our budget problems are due to *your* overspending rather than *my* low salary.

SCAPEGOATING Scapegoating is another way of avoiding honest communication about a problem. By blaming others, we imply that our partners, not we, should change. We may be uncomfortable about being expressive because we grew up in cool and aloof families. Or we might be suspicious about trusting people because a good friend or intimate partner took advantage of us. Regardless of the reasons, blaming parents, teachers, relatives, siblings, friends, and past or current partners for our problems is debilitating and counterproductive (Noller, 1984).

AGGRESSION Communication breaks down if one or both partners don't control their temper. Verbal aggression (e.g., insulting, threatening, saying something spiteful) creates stress and anger (Lavner and Bradbury, 2012; Webber, 2012).

REPRESSION   In an attempt to prevent a fight, sometimes couples don't disclose their wants and needs and don't address what's bothering them. They assume the problem will go away. Instead, undisclosed dissatisfaction can balloon and end a relationship (Gadoua, 2008).

DENIAL   To preserve a relationship, people often brush aside problems by trying to spin them into something positive: "She nags me every day, but I admire her honesty." Denying or rationalizing a problem doesn't make it go away. Eventually, the dissatisfaction intensifies, reaches a breaking point, and someone snaps (Diduch, 2012: 14).

COERCION OR CONTEMPT   Partners may be punitive and force their point of view on others. If this works, coercive behavior, which is related to scapegoating, can continue. Contempt can be devastating. The most visible signs of contempt are insults and name calling, sarcasm, hostile humor, mockery, and body language such as rolling your eyes or sneering (Gottman, 1994).

As you saw in "Am I Heading toward Marital Burnout?" on page 284, some of the red flags of coercion and contempt include controlling a partner through tantrums, violence, threats of violence, or threats of suicide. Also, one partner may subject the other to public humiliation ("Will you stop interrupting me all the time?!").

THE SILENT TREATMENT   People communicate even when they're silent. Silence in various contexts, and at particular points in a conversation, means different things to different people. Sometimes silence saves us from foot-in-mouth problems. Not talking to your spouse or partner, however, builds up anger and hostility. Initially, the "offender" may work very hard to make the silent partner feel loved and to talk about a problem. Eventually, however, the partner who is getting the silent treatment may get fed up, give up, or look for someone else (Rosenberg, 1993).

Power and Conflict in Relationships

Power and conflict are normal and inevitable in close relationships. Both shape communication patterns and decision making. The person who has the power to make decisions often influences many of the dynamics in marriage and other intimate relationships.

Sociologists define **power** as the ability to impose one's will on others. Whether it's a dating relationship, a family, or a nation, some individuals and groups have more power than others.

power The ability to impose one's will on others.

SOURCES OF POWER   Power isn't limited to tangible things such as money. Love, for example, is an important source of power. As you saw in Chapter 8, the *principle of least interest* explains why, in a dating relationship, the person who is less interested is more powerful than the committed partner. In marriage, similarly, if you're more committed to your marriage than your spouse is, you have less power. As a result, you may defer to your partner's wishes, do things you don't want to do, or not express negative feelings (Olen and Blakeley, 2009).

Other nonmaterial sources of power include access to information or particular abilities or talents. For example, husbands often have more decision-making power about how to spend money on expensive items, such as houses or cars, because they're typically more knowledgeable about financial matters, investments, and negotiating contracts. In traditional households, the wife may have more power than the husband in furnishing a home or raising children because she usually devotes more time to reading informational material; shopping; or becoming familiar with neighborhood professionals, such as pediatricians and dentists, who provide important services.

CONFLICT AND COMMUNICATION *Conflict* refers to discrete, isolated disagreements as well as chronic relationship problems. All partners and families, no matter how supportive and caring they are, experience conflict. A study of married couples found that the majority of participants reported an average of one or two "unpleasant disagreements" per month (McGonagle et al., 1993).

The late comedian Phyllis Diller's quip, "Don't go to bed mad. Stay up and fight!" is actually insightful. Conflict isn't bad in itself. If partners recognize and actively attempt to resolve it, conflict can strengthen a relationship. Before examining coping techniques, let's look at some of the issues that couples usually fight about.

What Couples Fight about and How They Deal with Conflict

10.8 Describe the most common issues that couples fight about and how they deal with conflict.

When asked to rate their top relationship irritants, men complain that women give them the silent treatment, bring up things the men have done in the remote past, are too critical, and are stubborn in never giving in during disagreements. Women complain that men forget important dates (such as birthdays and anniversaries), don't work hard enough at their jobs, noisily burp or pass gas, and stare at other women (Dixit, 2009).

Some of these irritants are more annoying than others, but what are the most serious disagreements about? Money is at the top of the list. Other common issues are housework, fidelity, children, and most recently, social media (see also Chapter 15 on divorce).

Money

Nationally, 51 percent of Americans don't talk about money before marriage. It's not surprising, then, that 70 percent of newlyweds say that money issues are a serious source of disagreements as early as the first year of marriage (Ordoñez, 2007; Coplan, 2008).

In another national survey, 31 percent of spouses and partners who have combined their finances have hidden money and bills and have lied about purchases, bank accounts, amount of debt owned, and/or their income (National Endowment for Financial Education, 2011). Among married couples, 80 percent spend money their spouse doesn't know about (see *Table 10.2*), and 19 percent

Since you asked. . .
- What's the harm in hiding some of my purchases from my spouse or partner?

Listen on **MySocLab**

Audio: NPR: Keeping a Marriage Solid When Money Is Tight

TABLE 10.2	What Purchases Spouses Hide
35%	Clothing and accessories
24%	Food/Dining
20%	Beauty/Personal care items
17%	Gifts
13%	Alcohol
10%	Music/CD/MP3
9%	Entertainment
9%	Child care/Items for children

Note: The numbers total to more than 100 percent because respondents gave multiple responses.
Source: Based on CESI Debt Solutions, 2010.

have credit cards their spouses don't know about. Also, 38 percent of married couples are concerned that a spouse's discovery of their "financial infidelity" would lead to a separation or divorce (CESI Debt Solutions, 2010). Some financial advisors maintain, in fact, that people should find a "financial soul mate" and not a romantic one because marriage, at its core, is (or should be) a sound monetary union (Bernard, 2008).

Even when money isn't the main reason for conflict, arguments about money are pervasive, problematic, and recurrent. Compared with other conflicts (such as those over habits, relatives, child rearing, leisure activities, and communication), fights over money last longer and are more likely to lead to depressive behavior (such as withdrawal and sadness) and physical aggression (such as shouting, shoving, and slapping) (Papp et al., 2009).

Most money fights start with finger-pointing—"How could you spend $300 on a new sweater/Blu-ray player?"—but people are really arguing about a clash of values (Dunleavey, 2010: 48). Examples of clashing financial values include saving for the future or treating oneself now, entertaining lavishly or modestly, or purchasing designer rather than unknown brands.

If you're not sure if your spending is deceptive, ask yourself: If my partner found out about my shopping expenses, would it damage the trust in our relationship? Are my buying habits hindering progress toward attaining our common goals? Other red flags include hiding bills, receipts, and purchases; having an account your mate doesn't know about; and involving the kids in your dishonesty ("Don't tell Mom/Dad") (Dunleavey, 2010).

Housework

There's considerable contention over housework, including disagreements about whether it's even a problem. For example, 24 percent of husbands but 31 percent of wives say that household chores are a major source of friction (Bennetts, 2008). In another national survey, 62 percent of couples (up from 47 percent in 1990) said that sharing household tasks was very important for a successful marriage (Taylor et al., 2007). If couples can't agree on who should do what around the house, especially when both partners are employed, tension may rise and quarrels become more frequent.

Fidelity and Sex

In almost every national survey, sexual infidelity is typically at the top of the list of what couples fight about, just behind money in second or third place, and always higher on the list than the frequency of sex. Another common pattern is that women see infidelity as a more serious problem than do men, probably because men are more likely to be unfaithful, and men are more likely than women to complain that they don't get enough sex (Taylor et al., 2007; Bennetts, 2008).

For unmarried couples, the most common violations include having sexual intercourse outside the relationship, wanting to date others, and deceiving the partner. As you saw in Chapter 7, many people, especially women, view extramarital affairs and cybersex as the most serious types of betrayal. Married and unmarried couples also argue about other violations of trust and commitment, such as lying, betraying confidences, and gossiping about each other or relatives (Jones and Burdette, 1994; Metts, 1994).

Children

Children can strengthen a relationship, but they also create strain, tension, and conflict. In addition to feeling stress because of the demands children make, partners may have different philosophies about issues such as discipline, the

importance of teaching young children self-control, and the kinds of responsibilities a child should have. As more spouses and partners collaborate in child rearing, there are more opportunities for clashes. For example, a wife may expect her husband to take on more child care tasks, but she may also resent his making decisions about the child's playmates, bedtimes, or curfews. Children are especially likely to be a source of conflict in remarriages (see Chapter 15).

Social Media

A new and increasing source of conflict among couples is the rise of social media. For example,

> Dear Amy:
>
> My husband and I have been married for 24 years. . . . He's home Sundays and two or three evenings each week. When home, he sits in front of our computer for hours responding to hundreds of e-mails and reading Facebook sites. I feel incredibly lonely when I see the great relationships he maintains with people, whereas all I get is a tired, stressed and distant husband. . . . I wonder why I stay with him. . . . I've told him how I feel—and we've done counseling twice—but he says I should leave if I don't like it. . . . [signed]Lonely

Poor communication is a key factor in unhappy relationships.

Not surprisingly, Amy told Lonely that "managing your loneliness is your responsibility," to become more engaged in friendships and community events, and to seek individual counseling to "deal with [your] painful reality" (Dickinson, 2010: 5).

Whether or not you agree with Amy's advice, communication problems due to social media usage are increasing. "If one half of a couple is not interested in broadcasting the details of a botched dinner or romantic evening . . . [and something as seemingly innocent as a house repair], Facebook postings or tweets can create irritation, embarrassment, miscommunication and bruised egos" (Holson, 2012: E1). One solution is for partners to ask for approval before posting comments and photographs that include them, but doing so might also lead to conflict ("Are you telling me what to do?!").

How Couples Deal with Conflict

It bears repeating that conflict is a normal part of life. What isn't normal or healthy is *how* couples deal with conflict.

Since you asked . . .
- Is leaving the room the best solution to an argument?

COMMON CONFLICT RESOLUTION STRATEGIES Intimate couples typically use four techniques to end—though not necessarily resolve—conflict: accommodation, compromise, standoff, and withdrawal (Vuchinich, 1987; Wilmot and Hocker, 2007).

- *Accommodation.* One person submits to another; the conflict ends when one person agrees with or goes along with the other.
- *Compromise.* Partners find a middle ground between their opposing positions; each must give in a little to accept a compromise. The compromise can be suggested either by a partner or by a third party.
- *Standoff.* The disputants drop the argument without resolving it; they agree to disagree and move on to other activities. No one wins or loses, and the conflict ends in a draw.
- *Withdrawal.* When a disputant withdraws, he or she refuses to continue the argument, either by clamming up or by leaving the room. Among the four coping techniques, withdrawal is the least effective because there's no resolution of the conflict.

Of these four approaches, compromise is the most effective way to resolve conflict.

EFFECTIVE WAYS OF HANDLING CONFLICT   One of the biggest myths about interpersonal relationships is that it's okay to "say what's on your mind" and "let it all hang out." Some partners unleash "emotional napalm" to "blow off some steam" (Noller and Fitzpatrick, 1993: 178).

In some cases, couples should probably talk less, not more, because too much talking can lead to relentless nagging, criticism, and hammering the same issues over and over. However well intentioned, constant efforts to communicate are especially futile and frustrating if partners try to change each other's personality (Dixit, 2009). For example, someone who's quiet or reserved can't suddenly become outgoing at parties to please a partner.

Displaced rage, unbridled attacks, and physical aggression aren't normal ways of handling conflict, and denying the existence of conflict can destroy a relationship. Couples who confront their problems may be unhappy in the short term but will have a better relationship in the long run. Otherwise, the anger and bitterness will fester.

Both researchers and family practitioners have suggested effective ways of dealing with anger and strife (see "Ground Rules for Fair Fighting"). Such rules don't ensure a resolution. Because they're based on negotiation and compromise, however, they offer partners a better chance of developing more constructive ways of dealing with conflict.

Choices | Ground Rules for Fair Fighting

Therapists, counselors, and researchers maintain that discussing disagreements is healthier than suffering in silence. Clinicians who work with unhappy couples offer the following advice for changing some of our most destructive interaction patterns (Crosby, 1991a; Rosenzweig, 1992):

1. Don't attack your partner. He or she will only become defensive and will be too busy preparing a good rebuttal to hear what you have to say.

2. Avoid ultimatums; no one likes to be backed into a corner.

3. Say what you really mean and don't apologize for it. Lies are harmful, and apologetic people are rarely taken seriously.

4. Avoid accusations and attacks; don't belittle or threaten.

5. Start with your own feelings. "I feel" is better than "You said." Focus on the problem, not on the other person.

6. State your wishes and requests clearly and directly; don't be manipulative, defensive, or sexually seductive.

7. Limit what you say to the present. Avoid long lists of complaints from the past.

8. Refuse to fight dirty:
   - No *gunnysacking*, or keeping one's complaints secret and tossing them into an imaginary gunnysack that gets heavier and heavier over time.
   - No *passive-aggressive behavior*, or expressing anger indirectly in the form of criticism, sarcasm, nagging, or nitpicking.
   - No *silent treatment;* keep the lines of communication open.
   - No name calling.

9. Use humor and comic relief. Laugh at yourself and the situation but not at your partner. Learning to take ourselves less

seriously and to recognize our flaws without becoming so self-critical that we wallow in shame or self-pity can decrease conflict.

10. Strive for closure as soon as possible after a misunderstanding or disagreement by resolving the issue. This prevents dirty fighting and, more important, it holds the partners to their commitment to negotiate until the issue has been resolved or defused.

STOP AND THINK

- "A good fight is essential in building a good relationship." Do you agree? Or does keeping silent and sidestepping conflict increase affection and respect?

- Have you ever used similar rules for fair fighting in your own relationships? If so, what were the results?

Productive Communication Patterns

10.9

10.9 Identify productive communication patterns that strengthen relationships.

Over time, communication problems can erode intimate relationships. It takes time to forge good communication techniques.

Psychologist John Gottman interviewed and studied more than 200 couples over a 20-year period. He found that the difference between lasting marriages and those that split up was a "magic ratio" of five to one—that is, five positive interactions between partners for every negative one:

> As long as there was five times as much positive feeling and interaction between husband and wife as there is negative, the marriage was likely to be stable over time. In contrast, those couples who were heading for divorce were doing far too little on the positive side to compensate for the growing negativity between them (Gottman, 1994: 41).

 Watch on MySocLab
Video: The Role of Humor

Improving Your Communication Style

Yelling is one of the most damaging ways of interacting. We rarely scream at guests, employers, students, or professors. Yet we do so quite often with partners, spouses, and family members, with whom we have our most important and longest-lasting relationships. "Hollering is just part of my personality" is no excuse for obnoxious and abusive behavior. Ordinary etiquette, day in and day out, can work wonders in preventing and decreasing relationship conflict.

According to researchers and practitioners, couples can increase positive communication and decrease negative interaction patterns in the following ways:

- *Ask for information.* If your partner has a complaint ("I never get a chance to talk to you because you're always busy"), address the issue. Don't be defensive ("Well, if you were around more often, we could talk"); find out why your partner is upset.

- *Don't generalize.* Accusations such as "You always do X" increase anger and tension.

- *Stay focused on the issue.* Don't bring up past events and old grudges. If you're discussing spending habits, focus on the items that were purchased recently.

- *Be specific.* A specific complaint is easier to deal with than a general criticism. "You never talk to me" is less effective than "I wish we could have 30 minutes each evening without television or the kids."

- *Keep it honest.* Honesty not only means not lying; it also means not manipulating others. Don't resort to bullying, outwitting, blaming, dominating, or controlling. Don't become a long-suffering martyr. Truthfulness and sincerity reinforce mutual trust and respect.

- *Make it kind.* Some people use "brutal honesty" as an excuse for cruelty. Temper honesty with positive statements about your partner.

- *Express appreciation.* Thanking your partner for something he or she has done will enhance both the discussion and the relationship.

- *Use nonverbal communication.* Nonverbal acts, such as hugging your partner, smiling, and holding his or her hand, can often be more supportive than anything you might say.

- *Above all, just listen.* Sharpen your emotional communication skills by being really interested in what your partner is saying rather than always focusing on yourself (Knapp and Hall, 1992; Gottman and DeClaire, 2001).

Since you asked
- Doesn't nagging show that you love and care about a person?

"She says I'm indecisive, but I don't know."

© Anthony Kelly/www.CartoonStock.com

MAKING CONNECTIONS

- Think about the conflicts you've experienced with a partner or spouse during the past year or so. What were most of the disagreements about—important or petty issues?
- When you and your partner argue, how do you react? How does your partner respond? Do you resolve the conflict? Or does it smolder until the next eruption?

CONCLUSION

Committed relationships and marriages *change* throughout the life course. Different *choices* have different consequences. Deciding to have a more egalitarian division of housework and child-rearing responsibilities, for example, can diminish some of the *constraints* that couples encounter as they juggle multiple roles. Also, deciding to interact more honestly can result in more effective communication and greater interpersonal satisfaction. Despite the constraints, marriage is an important rite of passage. Another is parenthood, our focus in the next two chapters.

On MySocLab

 Study and Review on MySocLab

REVIEW QUESTIONS

10.1. Explain how and why U.S. marriage rates have changed.

1. How have U.S. marriage rates changed since 1960, especially for racial-ethnic groups?

2. Why have U.S. marriage rates been decreasing?

10.2. Identify the manifest and latent reasons for getting married and describe some pre-marriage and marriage rituals.

3. What are some of the "right" and "wrong" reasons for getting married?

4. What is the purpose of wedding and pre-wedding rituals?

5. What are some of the benefits and costs of prenuptial agreements?

10.3. Compare heterosexual and same-sex marriages and discuss some cross-cultural variations.

6. What is the Cuber-Haroff typology? What are its strengths and limitations?

7. How do same-sex marriages differ from opposite-sex marriages?

8. How do marriages vary in the United States and other countries?

10.4. Explain how marital happiness, marital success, and health are interrelated.

9. What are the most important characteristics of a successful marriage?

10. Why, overall, are married people healthier than their unmarried counterparts?

11. How does marriage affect people's physical and mental health? What are some of the variations in terms of gender and marital quality?

10.5. Describe how couples establish, negotiate, and learn marital roles.

12. What is the process of learning marital roles?

13. Why is it important to establish marital boundaries and adapt to changes over time?

10.6. Describe how marriages change throughout the life course.

14. What adjustments must couples make during the early years of marriage?

15. How do marriages differ during the midlife years and later in life?

10.7. Explain how communication, power, and conflict affect a relationship.

16. Why is communication crucial in intimate relationships?

17. How do self-disclosure and validation affect communication?

18. What are the most common communication problems?

19. How does power affect conflict and communication?

10.8. Describe the most common issues that couples fight about and how they deal with conflict.

20. What do couples usually fight about? Why?

21. What are the least and most effective ways to resolve conflict?

10.9. Identify productive communication patterns that strengthen relationships.

22. How, specifically, can couples improve their communication styles?

To Be or Not to Be a Parent: More Choices, More Constraints

((• **Listen** to Chapter 11 on **MySocLab**

LEARNING OBJECTIVES

After you read and study this chapter you will be able to:

Describe the benefits, costs, and effects of parenthood.	**11.1**
Explain how and why birthrates are changing in the United States and globally.	**11.2**
Describe the effects of unintended and intended pregnancies and contraception usage.	**11.3**
Explain why many people are postponing parenthood and discuss the effects of such postponement.	**11.4**
Identify the reasons for infertility, people's reactions, and the available medical treatments.	**11.5**
Compare open and closed adoptions and describe transracial, same-sex, and international adoptions.	**11.6**
Describe the incidence of abortion, discuss the characteristics of and the reasons given by the women who abort, and explain why abortion rates have decreased.	**11.7**
Explain why some people are choosing to be child free.	**11.8**

DATA DIGEST

- The **number of births** in the United States decreased from 4.2 million in 1990 to 3.9 million in 2012.

- The percentage of **births to unmarried American women** rose from 18 percent in 1980 to 33 percent in 1994 and to 41 percent in 2011; among teenagers, 86 percent of all births are nonmarital.

- The number of U.S. **adoptions from other countries plunged** from an all-time high of almost 23,000 in 2005 to 8,668 in 2012.

- Of **all U.S. pregnancies, 19 percent are unwanted**, up from 9 percent in 1995.

- In 2009, U.S. **women ages 20 to 29 years accounted for 57 percent of all abortions**, compared with 13 percent for women ages 15 to 19, and 21 percent for those ages 30 to 39.

- The **number of voluntarily childless women** who are 40 to 44 years old has more than doubled—from 10 percent in 1976 to 22 percent in 2010.

Sources: Chandra et al., 2005; Guttmacher Institute, 2012; Hamilton et al., 2012; Martinez et al., 2012; Pazol et al., 2012; U.S. Department of State, 2012; Federal Interagency Forum on Child and Family Statistics, 2013; Shattuck and Kreider, 2013.

A successful physician in his fifties took his 80-year-old mother to a performance at the Civic Opera House in Chicago. They were making their way out the lobby doors to the physician's Mercedes when his mother turned to him and asked, "Do you have to go to the bathroom, dear?"

As this anecdote suggests, parenting never ends. We may change colleges, buy and sell houses and cars, switch careers, and marry more than once, but parenthood is a lifelong commitment. Today we are freer to decide whether to have children, when, and how many. Many people can also become parents despite conception problems, or we can decide to remain child free.

Parenthood is a process. *Having* children—through childbirth or adoption— is not the same as *raising* children. This chapter focuses primarily on the biological, economic, and social aspects of *becoming* a parent (or not). The next chapter examines the child-rearing roles, activities, and responsibilities of being a parent. Let's begin by looking at the early stages of becoming a parent.

11.1 Describe the benefits, costs, and effects of parenthood.

Explore on **MySocLab**

Activity: Becoming Parents (or Not)

Becoming a Parent

Across all types of U.S. families (e.g., married, never married, divorced), 60 percent have one or more children. In 2011, 74 percent of the 18- to 29-year olds who were childless and unmarried planned to have children in the future (Wang and Taylor, 2011; U.S. Census Bureau Public Information Office, 2012). Whether planned or not, a couple's first pregnancy is an important milestone. The reactions of both partners can vary, however (Cowan and Cowan, 2000: 33–45):

- *Planners* actively discuss the issue, having jointly decided to conceive a child. They're typically jubilant about becoming pregnant. As one woman said, "When I found out that I was pregnant, I was so excited I wanted to run out in the street and tell everybody I met."

- *Acceptance-of-fate couples* are pleasantly surprised and quietly welcoming of a child, even though they had not planned the pregnancy. Often, they have unconsciously or intentionally made an unspoken agreement to become pregnant by using contraceptive methods only sporadically or not at all.

- *Ambivalent couples* have mixed feelings before and after conception and even well into the pregnancy. As one woman noted, "I felt confused, a mixture of up

and down, stunned, in a daze." These couples decide to have the baby because one partner feels strongly about having a child and the other complies. Or the pregnancy might be unintended, but one or both partners don't believe in abortion.

- In *yes–no couples*, one partner may not want children, even late in the pregnancy. Typically, the woman decides to go ahead with the pregnancy regardless of what the father thinks, which sometimes causes a separation or divorce. Or, in the case of unmarried couples, the father may simply stop seeing the woman after she becomes pregnant.

Regardless of the reactions, parenthood involves both benefits and costs.

Some Benefits and Costs of Having Children

Some people weigh the pros and cons of having a baby. Many don't because it's often an emotional decision. Both emotionally and practically, what are some of the benefits and costs of becoming a parent?

BENEFITS   Our thirty-something neighbors recently had their first baby. When I asked Matt how they were doing, he exclaimed, "There's nothing like it! She's the most gorgeous baby in the world!" Matt's reaction is fairly typical. For example, 96 percent of first-time parents in a national survey said that they were "in love" with their baby, and 91 percent reported being "happier than ever before" ("Bringing up Baby," 1999).

Many people believe that their lives would be incomplete without children. Parents often say that children bring love and affection; it's a pleasure to watch them grow; and children bring fulfillment and a sense of satisfaction (Gallup and Newport, 1990). Even new parents who are struggling with a colicky infant (whose abdominal distress causes frequent crying) delight in the baby's social and physical growth.

COSTS   Parenthood isn't paradise. To begin with, having and raising children is expensive. *Figure 11.1* shows a typical year's expenses for a child 1 or 2 years old in married-couple middle-income families. These families, who have an average income of $81,600 a year, spend almost 16 percent of their earnings on a child during the first two years. By the time a child is age 17, they'll spend $242,000 (Lino, 2013).

Child-rearing costs increase when a couple has more children; when children get older; when children live in an urban area, particularly in the Northeast and West; and if a child is disabled, chronically ill, or needs specialized care that medical or welfare benefits don't cover. If one or both parents are laid off, they usually lose any medical benefits for themselves and their children (Lukemeyer et al., 2000; Lino, 2013).

Becoming a parent has other economic and social costs. Many women pay a "mommy tax": Their unpaid work at home doesn't count toward Social Security pensions, they often forgo educational opportunities, and they're more likely than men or childless women to be poor after a divorce or in old age (see Chapters 13 and 16).

Some Joys and Tribulations of Pregnancy

Pregnancy can be exciting and happy, particularly when it's planned and welcomed. For both prospective parents, it can deepen love and intimacy and draw them closer as they plan for their family's future. At the same time, pregnancy—especially the first or unplanned pregnancy—can arouse anxiety about caring for the baby properly and providing for the growing child economically.

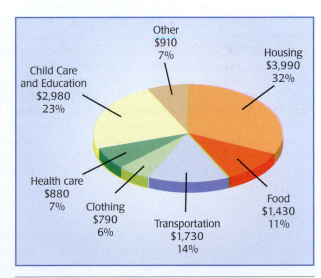

FIGURE 11.1 Yearly Cost of Raising a Child under Age 2, 2012
In 2012, middle-income married couples—those with before-tax income between $60,640 and $105,000—spent $12,710 per year for a child under age 2. This amount doesn't include the costs of prenatal care or delivery.
*Includes personal care items, entertainment, and reading materials.
Source: Based on Lino, 2013, Table 1.

The expectant mother usually experiences numerous discomforts. In the first trimester (three-month period), she may have frequent nausea, heartburn, insomnia, shortness of breath, painful swelling of the breasts, and fatigue. She may also be constantly concerned about the health of the *fetus* (the unborn child from eight weeks until birth), especially if she or the baby's father has engaged in any high-risk behaviors (see "Having Healthier Babies").

The second trimester can be thrilling because the mother begins to feel movements, or *quickening*, as the fetus becomes more active. *Sonograms* (diagnostic imaging produced by high-frequency sound waves) can reveal an image of the baby and its sex. On the downside, backaches may become a problem, and fatigue sets in more quickly.

In her third trimester, a woman may start losing interest in sex because of tiredness and the awkwardness of an ever-larger abdomen. She begins to retain water and may feel physically unattractive and clumsy. Once-simple, automatic tasks, such as tying shoelaces or picking up something on the floor, become daunting.

Vaginal births may happen quickly or be long and exhausting. Sometimes they're not possible and a woman has a *cesarean section* (surgical removal of the

fetal alcohol spectrum disorders (FASD) A range of permanent birth defects caused by a mother's use of alcohol during pregnancy.

Applying What You've Learned

Having Healthier Babies

Most babies are healthy, but if people engage in high-risk behaviors, their children may develop a variety of problems. Many are due to the parents' lifestyle rather than to genetic diseases or other disorders. Here are a few examples.

Smoking

Smoking cuts off the oxygen supply to the baby's brain; impairs the baby's growth; and is linked to spontaneous abortion, preterm (premature) birth, low birth weight, and childhood illnesses. Fetuses of women who smoke are three times more likely to have genetic abnormalities than those of nonsmokers. By age 2, these children are more likely than those of nonsmoking mothers to show problem behaviors such as defiance, aggression, and poor social skills. The children of women whose mothers and maternal grandmothers smoked during pregnancy are almost three times more likely to develop asthma by age 5. The offspring often become smokers in adolescence (Li et al., 2005; Wakschlag et al., 2006; Weden and Miles, 2012; Weinhold, 2012).

Alcohol

Infants experience a brain growth spurt that starts in the sixth month of the pregnancy and continues until age 2. Birth defects associated with prenatal alcohol exposure can occur in the first three to eight weeks of pregnancy, before a woman even knows that she's pregnant (Denny et al., 2009).

Up to 30 percent of women report drinking alcohol during pregnancy. A developing fetus's liver can't process alcohol; the fetus absorbs all of the alcohol and has the same blood alcohol content as the mother (National Organization on Fetal Alcohol Syndrome, 2012; Warren, 2012).

Alcohol use during pregnancy can result in **fetal alcohol spectrum disorders (FASD)**, a range of permanent birth defects caused by a mother drinking alcohol during pregnancy. In the United States, 40,000 children are born with

FASD-related disorders each year; 1 in 100 babies has FASD—nearly the same rate as autism. Fetal alcohol spectrum disorder disabilities, which can persist throughout life, include intellectual infirmities, speech and language delays, poor social skills, mental retardation, and physical abnormalities such as congenital heart defects and defective joints, and they cost the nation $6 billion in annual medical expenses (National Organization on Fetal Alcohol Syndrome, 2012; Warren, 2012).

Other Drugs

Almost 5 percent of pregnant women ages 15 to 44 use illicit drugs (e.g., heroin, cocaine, morphine, and opium). The mothers are likely to have infants who are addicted. The baby may experience problems such as prenatal strokes, brain damage, seizures, preterm birth, retarded fetal growth, and physical malformations (Substance Abuse and Mental Health Services Administration, 2006).

Almost 14,000 U.S. infants a year, or one born every hour, are addicted to mothers' pain pills and other opiates. Newborns in withdrawal (known as *neonatal abstinence syndrome*) are often small and at a higher risk of death than other infants.

Obesity and Eating Disorders

Women who are obese, overweight, or excessively thin before becoming pregnant are at a much higher risk than normal-weight women of having infants with birth defects such as spina bifida (an abnormal opening along the spine), heart abnormalities, and other problems. Obese women often suffer from nutrition problems—due to poor eating habits—that result in diabetes and health-related problems for infants. Pregnant women with poor diets can hurt their baby's bone growth because the fetus isn't getting enough calcium (Watkins et al., 2003; Partington et al., 2009).

baby from the womb through the abdominal wall), which afterwards is more painful for the mother and requires a longer recovery period. Both vaginal births and cesarean sections often involve bloody discharge for several weeks. Infections and fevers are also common.

Some Effects of Parenthood

You'll see in Chapter 12 that marital satisfaction normally decreases over time. For 70 to 90 percent of couples, marital bliss dips within a year after the birth of their first child. The negative effects of parenthood tend to be greater for partners with a history of parental divorce or conflict, those who have a baby shortly after marrying, and couples that fight a lot before a child's birth, argue about child care responsibilities after a baby's birth, and have low incomes (Doss et al., 2009).

As women and men take on the role of "parent," other roles such as "lover" necessarily take a back seat. Having a baby typically puts a sudden strain on a relationship if parenthood is steeped in romantic misconceptions: "For couples who thought that having a baby was going to bring them closer together, this is especially confusing and disappointing" (Cowan and Cowan, 2000: 18).

Do such findings imply that couples would be better off by not having children? No. Some couples shouldn't have children because they neglect and abuse them, but 50 percent of Americans say that adding children to the family increases their happiness (Ali, 2008).

MOTHERS AND THEIR NEWBORNS There's a widespread myth that there's instant bonding between a mother and her newborn baby (see Chapter 6). In reality, historically and across cultures, bonding may or may not occur. Many adults, not just mothers, happily nurture their infants. Because responsibility for a baby's care tends to fall heavily on new mothers, however, they often feel stressed out and are more likely than fathers to experience marital dissatisfaction (Umberson et al., 2010).

Up to 80 percent of women experience minor sadness—the so-called baby blues—after giving birth. The blues involve feeling moody, teary, and overwhelmed as well as being happy about the baby. The baby blues are due to chemical imbalances resulting from the sudden drop in estrogen and progesterone levels as the concentrations of these hormones in the placenta are expelled with other afterbirth tissue (Munk-Olsen et al., 2006; Friedman, 2009).

Between 10 percent and 30 percent of mothers plummet into **postpartum depression (PPD)**, a serious illness that can occur up to a year after childbirth and requires medical treatment. Women who experience PPD feel sad, anxious, hopeless, worthless, and have trouble caring for the baby. The causes of PPD are unknown, but they probably involve chemical imbalances as well as risk factors such as low infant birth weight, tobacco or alcohol usage, physical abuse, and emotional and financial stress before and during the pregnancy (Brett et al., 2008; Paulson and Bazemore, 2010).

Fathers, too, can experience postpartum depression. Several analyses—based on 26,000 parents, the medical records of nearly 87,000 couples, and 43 empirical studies—found that between 4 and 10 percent of fathers had PPD symptoms in the first year of their children's birth. Parents at highest risk for PPD were those with a history of depression, from low-income households, young, and men whose partners were depressed (Ramchandani et al., 2005; Davé et al., 2010; Paulson and Bazemore, 2010). In effect, then, not all fathers can fill in for a depressed mother.

Despite physical pain, the blues, and wondering whether they'll ever get two hours of uninterrupted sleep again, most mothers are elated with their infants. Many new mothers (and sometimes fathers) can spend hours describing the

Read on MySocLab

Document: Thinking About the Baby: Gender and Divisions of Infant Care

Since You Asked . . .
• Do mothers and fathers experience a child's birth differently?

postpartum depression (PPD)
A serious illness that can occur up to a year after childbirth.

Postpartum depression is most common among mothers, but also occurs among fathers.

baby's eating schedule, every yawn and facial expression, and even the bowel movements of "the cutest and most intelligent baby you've ever seen."

FATHERS AND THEIR NEWBORNS Our society tends to emphasize the importance of mothers over fathers, especially in caring for infants, but fathers are also important for infants' development. Fathers are just as effective at soothing crying babies, for example, and playing with them (Diener et al., 2002).

Like mothers, many fathers worry about being a good parent. Even when they feel anxious, many men believe that they should always be calm, strong, and reassuring—a gender stereotype. Their tendency to keep their worries to themselves may increase the tension and distance between the partners (see Chapters 5 and 10).

Fatherhood often enhances maturity: "Being a father can change the ways that men think about themselves. Fathering often helps men to clarify their values and to set priorities" (Parke, 1996: 15). New fathers express loving and affectionate emotions that are good for them and for their babies. Many fathers also forge stronger links with their own parents, who are often supportive grandparents (Johnson and Huston, 1998).

From a developmental perspective, fatherhood is an important transition in a man's life, but some men's shift to fatherhood is problematic. They may become abusive because of increased financial responsibilities, the emotional demands of new family roles, and the loss of independence that parenthood brings (Schecter and Ganely, 1995; see also Chapter 14).

Becoming a parent seems to be an individual decision, but that's not entirely the case. Most people have a choice about conception, but childbearing patterns also reflect macro-level changes.

Fathers are just as important as mothers in nurturing babies and ensuring their healthy development.

11.2 Explain how and why birthrates are changing in the United States and globally.

total fertility rate (TFR) The average number of children born to a woman during her lifetime.

fertility rate The number of live children born per year per 1,000 women ages 15 to 44.

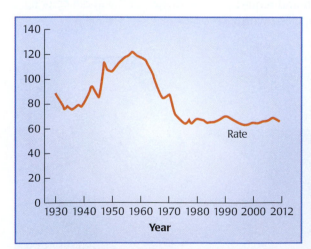

FIGURE 11.2 U.S. Fertility Rates, 1930–2012
Births per 1,000 women ages 15 to 44.
Sources: Based on Hamilton et al., 2009, 2012, Figure 1.

Birthrates in the United States and Globally

Societies must produce enough children to keep going, but 97 percent of the world's population now lives in countries where birthrates are falling (Last, 2013). Let's begin by looking at how much birthrates have changed.

How Birthrates Are Changing

Some developing countries have high birthrates, but birthrates have been plunging worldwide. What, specifically, is a birthrate?

MEASURING BIRTHRATES Demographers use several measures of birthrates depending on the level of specificity needed. The **total fertility rate (TFR)** is the average number of children born to a woman during her lifetime. In the early 1900s, U.S. women had an average TFR of 3.5, compared with 1.9 in 2012. Worldwide, Latvia and Taiwan have the lowest TFR rate (1.1); Afghanistan and nine African countries have the highest (from 6.0 to 7.1) (Kent and Mather, 2002; Haub and Kaneda, 2012).

A more specific birthrate measure is the **fertility rate**, the number of live children born every year per 1,000 women ages 15 to 44. Except for the baby boom blip of the 1950s, the U.S. fertility rate declined steadily since 1930, plateaued from the 1970s to the 1990s, and declined again to an all-time low of 63.0 in 2012 (see *Figure 11.2*).

WHY IT'S IMPORTANT TO UNDERSTAND FERTILITY RATES To maintain a stable population, a woman must have an average of two children (a TFR of about 2.1), which is considered the *replacement fertility rate* for herself and her partner.

Total fertility rates above two children indicate that a country is growing in size and the population's median age is getting younger. Rates below two children mean that a country's population is decreasing in size and growing older (*CIA World Factbook*, 2013).

The older a country's population, the more difficult it is to support people who are living into their eighties and longer who often require expensive medical services that are supported by taxes (see Chapter 16). To boost its low TFR of 1.2, South Korea's health ministry is turning off the lights in its offices once a month so staff have more time to devote to "childbirth and upbringing." The ministry also offers other incentives, including cash gifts, for staff who produce more than two babies ("S. Korea Orders . . .," 2010). Russia's president has "called on the country's women to have at least three children each" (Varadarajan, 2012: 9). In some Latin American countries, similarly, the government is becoming increasingly concerned about reversing the plummeting fertility and replacement fertility rates (Forero, 2011).

Since 2007, U.S. birthrates have decreased for many female groups—teens and adults, all racial/ethnic subgroups, in 42 states, and native-born and immigrant women. There are two exceptions: Birthrates have increased for women age 40 and older and for unmarried women (Ikramullah et al., 2011; Sutton et al., 2011; Livingston and Cohn, 2012). You'll see shortly that the birthrates of older women (most of whom are married) have increased largely because of assisted reproductive technologies and multiple births.

NONMARITAL CHILDBEARING In 1950, only 3 percent of all U.S. births were to unmarried women. In 2011, there were more than 1.6 million such births, accounting for almost 41 percent of all U.S. births. Thus, more than 4 in 10 American babies are now born outside of marriage—a new record (Hamilton and Ventura, 2012; Martin et al., 2013).

Births to unmarried women vary widely across racial-ethnic groups. White women have more nonmarital babies than do other groups. Proportionately, however, nonmarital birthrates are highest for black women and lowest for Asian American women (see *Figure 11.3*).

Teenagers account for 15 percent of all nonmarital births, compared with 74 percent for women ages 20 to 34. Thus, the number of births to unmarried women ages 20 to 34 is almost five times greater than for teenagers. Still, 86 percent of teenage births are nonmarital, compared with 60 percent for women in their twenties, and 14 percent for those ages 30 to 34 (Shattuck and Kreider, 2013).

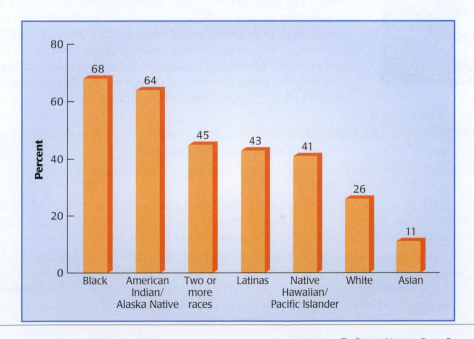

FIGURE 11.3 **Percent of Births to Unmarried Women, by Race and Ethnicity, 2011**
Source: Based on Shattuck and Kreider, 2013, Table 2.

Why Birthrates Are Changing

Except for the 1950s, why have U.S. fertility rates fallen during most of the twentieth century? Much of the decrease is due to a combination of macro-level societal factors and micro-level individual practices.

MACRO-LEVEL FACTORS The reasons for variations in birthrates are diverse, complex, and interrelated. Some of the key factors for lower fertility rates include the following:

- Economic recessions tend to decrease birthrates because of unemployment, home foreclosures, and related income problems. Birthrates dropped, for example, during the Great Depression (1930s), the energy crisis (1970s), and the Great Recession that began in 2007 (Livingston, 2011; Jordan, 2012; Mather, 2012).

- Immigrant women, both legal and undocumented, tend to have higher birthrates than the general population. Minority births in the United States, especially among young Latinas, now outnumber white births, but the birthrate of foreign-born women has recently plunged because of the economic downturn, high unemployment rates, and, consequently, decreasing immigration from Mexico (Bahrampour, 2012; "Double Bind," 2012; Livingston and Cohn, 2012; Passel et al., 2012).

- Access to health care reduces fertility rates when women get emergency contraception (EC). Sometimes called "morning-after" birth control, EC prevents implantation of the fertilized ovum in the uterine wall. Emergency contraception is most effective when taken right after sexual intercourse, but prevents pregnancy up to three days after intercourse (Chandra et al., 2005; Office on Women's Health, 2011). (Emergency contraception shouldn't be confused with the "abortion pill," as you'll learn about shortly, which stops an existing pregnancy.)

- Publicly funded family planning services that provide counseling and contraceptives, particularly for teenagers and young adults, reduce unintended pregnancies and birthrates (Kavanaugh et al., 2013).

- Social class and women's participation in the labor force have decreased birthrates. For example, postponing having children reduces the number of years to become pregnant; employed women are more likely to have a child if their partner has a good-paying job; men whose job pays well are more likely to have a child; and Americans in households earning $75,000 or more per year tend to have fewer children than adults in lower-income households, perhaps because the former are more realistic about the costs of raising a child (Macunovich, 2002; Saad, 2011; Kaufman and Bernhardt, 2012).

China, which has the world's largest population (almost 1.4 billion people in 2012), also has one of the world's lowest total fertility rates—1.6—due to a one-child policy that began in 1979 to decrease the country's surging population growth. Many rural provinces allow more than one child, but about two-thirds of Chinese people can be fined a year's salary for a second child. The rich easily circumvent the one-child policy by paying fines or traveling to other countries, which is allowed, to give birth (Murphy, 2011; Roberts, 2012; Jian, 2013).

MICRO-LEVEL FACTORS Macro-level factors alone don't explain the changing birthrates. We also make individual choices. For example,

- As you'll see later in this chapter, the number of couples who have chosen to be child free has increased.

- About 58 percent of U.S. adults say that having no more than two children is the ideal number. This is a dramatic change from 1965, when 70 percent said that three or more children was the ideal family size (Saad, 2011).

- Social contexts affect birthrates. For example, the odds of adolescent childbearing is two to three times higher among teens whose parents have less than a high school education, who live with only one parent, and whose mother had given birth as a teen (Manlove et al., 2013).

- Postponing marriage decreases birthrates. Getting married at age 25 and older, especially among college-educated women, decreases their fertility rates because of fewer childbearing years (Maitra, 2004; Mather, 2012).
- *Birth spacing*, or how often women have babies, also affects birthrates. In 2010, 20 percent of U.S. teenagers ages 15 to 19 had a repeat birth: 86 percent had a second child, and 15 percent had 3 to 6 children (Gavin et al., 2013). Women who get prenatal care after the first trimester, or get no care at all, are more likely to have a second child within 18 months than those who get prenatal care early in pregnancy. The later women get prenatal care, the more likely they are to have repeat births, increasing the number of children they have (Teitler et al., 2012).

MACRO- AND MICRO-LEVEL FACTORS OFTEN INTERSECT Macro- and micro-level variables often intersect. One example is a country's **infant mortality rate**, which is the number of babies under age 1 who die per 1,000 live births in a given year. The United States is the richest country in the world, but of 223 countries in 2012, the United States—with an infant mortality rate of 6.0—ranked only 173rd, well below other industrialized countries such as Japan (2.3) and Sweden (2.1). The U.S. infant mortality rate was also higher than some developing countries such as Slovenia (3.0) and Cuba (4.5) (*CIA World Factbook*, 2012; Haub and Kaneda, 2012).

In a *pre-term birth*, the baby is less than 37 weeks compared with 39 to 41 weeks for a full-term birth. The U.S. pre-term birthrate (1 in 8 births) is one of the highest in the industrialized world. Pre-term birth complications cause 35 percent of all U.S. newborn deaths (Save the Children, 2013). Nationally, infants born to black women are more than twice as likely to die before age 1 than are infants born to Latinas and women who are white and Asian (Hoyert and Xu, 2012; National Center for Health Statistics, 2013). The United States spends more on health care than any other nation in the world (Kaiser Family Foundation, 2011). Why, then, are our infant mortality rates, especially for African American newborns, so high?

In terms of macro-level variables, low-income families, many of whom are African Americans (see Chapter 4), don't realize the importance of or have inadequate access to prenatal care, and don't have regular checkups during pregnancy (Friedman, 2012; Hoyert and Xu, 2012). In terms of micro-level variables, even when women are aware of the risks of having unhealthy babies (see "Having Healthier Babies" on page 304), they may make unhealthy choices, such as smoking and using drugs, that result in pregnancy complications and even a newborn's death.

We've looked at some of the macro and micro reasons for falling birthrates in the United States and some other countries. A key issue is preventing pregnancy if people aren't ready for parenthood.

infant mortality rate The number of babies under age 1 who die per 1,000 live births in a given year.

Since You Asked . . .
- Why does the United States have a higher infant mortality rate than other industrialized nations?

MAKING CONNECTIONS
- If you don't have children, do you plan to have them in the future? If no, why not? If yes, at what age? And how many?
- If you're a parent, what have been the benefits and costs of having children?

Preventing Pregnancy

You saw at the beginning of this chapter that not all couples welcome parenthood. Many births are unintended, pregnancy intentions vary, and many people don't use contraceptives.

Unintended Pregnancy

Each year, almost half of all U.S. pregnancies are unintended. An **unintended pregnancy** is one that is either *mistimed* (occurs sooner than desired) or unwanted. Mistimed pregnancies are more common than unwanted ones (see *Figure 11.4*). Among unmarried women ages 20 to 29, almost 70 percent of the pregnancies

11.3 Describe the effects of unintended and intended pregnancies and contraception usage.

unintended pregnancy A pregnancy that is either *mistimed* (occurs sooner than desired) or unwanted.

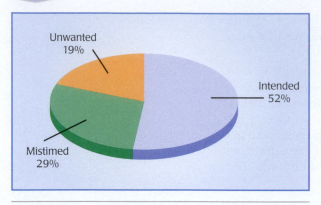

FIGURE 11.4 Almost Half of U.S. Pregnancies Are Unintended
Source: Based on Guttmacher Institute, 2012.

Since You Asked . . .

• What are the costs of having unintended pregnancies?

are unintended (Zolna and Lindberg, 2012; see also Finer and Kost, 2011, for state variations).

Repeated unintended childbearing has increased, especially among black women. For example, among women ages 33 to 37, 15 percent of white mothers have had two or more unintended births, compared with 22 percent of Latinas and 40 percent of black mothers. Some of the contributing factors include young black women's lower rates of contraceptive use and, in low-income populations, viewing unintended children as "a natural by-product of being in a serious relationship" (Wildsmith et al., 2010: 20).

Unintended pregnancies incur emotional costs, such as raising unwanted children or a man walking out on his pregnant girlfriend. One national study found that unintended births increased fathers' depressive symptoms (feeling sad, fearful, and lonely) and decreased mothers' happiness. The men experienced financial stress in providing for the unintended baby; the women felt ill-equipped to raise the child while balancing work and parenthood (Su, 2012). The fathers of unwanted and mistimed pregnancies tend to be disengaged from their toddlers, the children lag in cognitive and language development, and there's strain between the parents. Because the fathers are unprepared for parenthood, the couples' and children's well-being suffer (Bronte-Tinkew et al., 2009).

There are also macro-level costs. Raising children is expensive (see *Figure 11.1* on page 303 and the related material). About 67 percent of unintended births are publicly funded, and the proportion is 80 percent in some states. In low-income families, unintended pregnancies cost U.S. taxpayers about $11 billion a year just for the medical services to women and first-year infant care—money that could be used to finance pre-school programs in poor neighborhoods (Monea and Thomas, 2011; Sonfield et al., 2011).

Pregnancy Intentions

Why are there so many unintended pregnancies? First, and as you saw in Chapter 7, many teens, young adults, and parents don't know as much about sex as they think they do, and many schools don't have comprehensive sex education programs.

Second, not all teenagers want to avoid a pregnancy. Among never married teens ages 15 to 19, 22 percent of the mothers said that they didn't mind having an unintended pregnancy. In another national study of never married teenagers, 13 percent of females and 19 percent of males said that they would be "a little pleased" or "very pleased" if they became pregnant or got a female pregnant (Martinez et al., 2011; see Abma et al., 2010, for similar findings).

Third, many young adults are ambivalent about having an unintended pregnancy. Among unmarried women and men ages 18 to 29, for example, 33 percent believed that avoiding an unintended pregnancy wasn't very important (Hayford and Guzzo, 2013). Among those in sexual relationships, 53 percent of men and 36 percent of women were ambivalent about having an unintended birth (Higgins et al., 2012). Ambivalence and minimal motivation to avoid an unintended pregnancy can lead to low or haphazard contraceptive use.

Contraception Usage

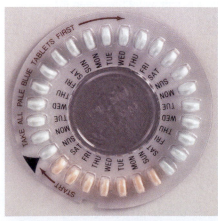

Despite widespread access to the "pill" and other forms of birth control, many Americans don't use contraception.

Teen pregnancy rates in the United States have declined, but the incidence is still the highest in the developed world. Nearly 80 percent of teen pregnancies are unintended, and young adults between the ages of 20 and 24 have the highest rate of unintended pregnancy (Finer and Zolna, 2011; American Academy of Pediatrics, 2012). **Contraception** is the prevention of pregnancy by behavioral,

mechanical, or chemical means (see *Appendix D* online). When contraception is used correctly and consistently, unintended pregnancies drop to 5 percent (Guttmacher Institute, 2012).

contraception The prevention of pregnancy by behavioral, mechanical, or chemical means.

CONTRACEPTION USE VARIES   Among females ages 15 to 44 who have ever had sex, 99 percent have used at least one contraceptive (usually condoms or the pill), and nearly 30 percent have used five or more methods. Additionally, in 2010, 11 percent of women in this age group used emergency contraception at least once, up from only 1 percent in 1995 (Daniels et al., 2013a, 2013b).

Almost all Americans have used contraception at one time or another, but there's variation by gender, age at first sex, race-ethnicity, social class, and other factors. For example,

- Girls who start having sex at age 14 or younger are the least likely to use contraception and the most likely to postpone using any birth control methods (Finer and Philbin, 2013).

- Among unmarried teens ages 15 to 19, 21 percent of females and 13 percent of males didn't use contraceptives at the first sexual experience (Welti et al., 2011).

- For never-married females and males ages 15 to 19, 39 percent of females and 21 percent of males didn't use a contraceptive at the last sexual intercourse, and the rates were highest among Latinos (Martinez et al., 2011).

- Among women ages 15 to 44 at risk of unintended pregnancy, 9 percent of Latinas, white, and Asian women don't use contraception compared with 16 percent of black women (Scommegna, 2012).

- Across all ages and racial-ethnic groups, low-income women are the least likely to use effective contraceptive methods (Guttmacher Institute, 2012).

OBSTACLES TO USING CONTRACEPTIVES   Up to 30 percent of females ages 15 to 44 stop using one or more contraceptive methods because they believe the methods aren't always effective or because a partner doesn't like using condoms (Daniels et al., 2013a). In other cases, the usage—especially for condoms and pills—is often erratic or incorrect. Females also stop using long-lasting methods, such as intrauterine devices (IUDs), because they're too expensive (Scott et al., 2011; Warren et al., 2011; Finer et al., 2012; Marcell et al., 2013).

Almost 31 percent of teenage women ages 15 to 19 believe they won't get pregnant. Among unmarried people ages 18 to 29, 19 percent of females and 14 percent of males don't use contraception because they believe that they're infertile (but only 6 percent may be) (Kaye et al., 2009; Harrison et al., 2012; Polis and Zabin, 2012).

In a study that interviewed 71 women ages 18 to 49 with a history of intimate partner violence, 53 of the women reported having experienced some type of reproductive control. Their partners prevented them from obtaining or using contraception, or purposely got the women pregnant (Moore et al., 2010).

The greater women's skepticism of contraceptive safety, the lower the usage. Also, women ages 15 to 24 decrease their use of birth control if they believe that childbearing has benefits. According to some of the women, having a baby "means somebody will love me" and/or "it could help me keep the baby's father around" (Rocca and Harper, 2012; Rocca et al., 2013: 29).

Postponing Parenthood

In 2013, actor/comedian Steve Martin, age 67, and his second wife, age 41, became first-time parents. Most men have children well before they're 67 years old, but many Americans are delaying childbearing. In the early 1970s, only 4 percent of women having their first babies were age 30 or older compared with

11.4 Explain why many people are postponing parenthood and discuss the effects of such postponement.

40 percent in 2011, and almost 7,700 were age 45 and older (Ventura et al., 2000; Hamilton et al., 2012).

Why Are Many People Postponing Parenthood?

People have more choices than in the past in deciding whether and when to have children. Both micro- and macro-level factors affect their decisions to delay childbearing.

MICRO-LEVEL FACTORS   Being single, you recall, has many attractions, including independence, the opportunity to develop a career, and more time for fun (see Chapter 9). There are similar micro-level reasons for postponing parenthood. For example,

- Daunting jobs and careers make it more difficult to meet prospective mates (see Chapter 8).

- Many single women don't want to conceive or adopt a child on their own. According to a 43-year-old woman whose mother raised her and her siblings, "The hardest thing you can be is a single, working mom" (Peterson, 2002: 2D).

- As you learned earlier, attitudes about the "ideal" family size have changed, resulting in less pressure to have more than two children.

- Women who enjoy their jobs and need money to boost their household income are often reluctant to take on balancing child rearing and paid work (see Chapter 13).

MACRO-LEVEL FACTORS   Macro-level economic and reproductive factors also play a big role in postponing parenthood. For example,

- Many young adults are delaying marriage and having children because they have high college and credit card debts, and, since the Great Recession (2007–2010) have had problems finding jobs that can support a family (Goodale, 2013).

- Disturbed by our high divorce rate, some young couples delay parenthood until they feel confident that their marriage will work (see Chapters 9 and 15).

- Advances in reproductive technology, as you'll see shortly, have reduced many women's concerns about their biological clock and finding a mate.

- Women and men are delaying childbearing because the United States—especially compared with many European countries—has abysmal family leave policies, no national child care programs, and rigid work schedules (see Chapter 13).

- A number of national studies show that the higher a woman's education level, the more likely she is to delay childbearing (Isen and Stevenson, 2010; Livingston and Cohn, 2010; Martin et al., 2012; U.S. Census Bureau Public Information Office, 2013). In 2011, for example, almost all women with less than a high school education had a first birth before age 25 compared with only 3 percent of women with a college degree or higher (Livingston and Cohn, 2013).

Some Characteristics of Older Parents

"My parents had me in their mid-forties. They were always too tired to attend many of the school functions or to take me to baseball games."

"My mother had me when she was 45 and that was in 1973. I'm living proof that older moms are good parents."

These comments by two of my students show that many of us have strong opinions about the ideal age for having children. Being an older parent has both advantages and disadvantages.

"So, have you two been doing anything reproductive?"

Watch on **MySocLab**

Video: Parenting

Since You Asked . . .

- Are there any advantages to waiting until age 40 to have children?

ADVANTAGES   Women who give birth for the first time between ages 22 and 34 have healthier babies than those who have babies during their teenage years or after age 40. The latter may experience more problems in conceiving a child. However, mothers in their teens are more likely than their older counterparts to have babies with birth defects and to experience infant deaths: Teen mothers often have poor nutrition, don't obtain adequate prenatal care, or engage in unhealthy lifestyles that include smoking and using alcohol and other drugs (Mirowsky, 2005).

Older mothers are more likely to be married and highly educated. Compared with their married counterparts, unmarried mothers are, on average, younger, have less education, have a lower income, and their children are more likely to have poor developmental outcomes such as lower language skills and more behavior problems (Livingston and Cohn, 2013; Shattuck and Kreider, 2013).

From 1980 to 2009, new-dad rates in the United States rose 47 percent in the 35 to 39 age group, 61 percent in the 40 to 44 age group, and even 18 percent among men 50 to 54 years old (Kluger, 2013). Compared with many older mothers, men who postpone parenthood earn higher salaries, have better health benefits (see Chapter 13), and don't encounter sex discrimination in the workplace. Thus, they're less likely to worry about not having the resources to raise children later in life. According to one of my students, for example, having an older dad "made life wonderful for me":

> I was only 7 years old when my dad retired. He spent a lot of time with me. He invested well and made financial decisions that were beneficial for the entire family. I think his age played a big part in having the means to make his family comfortable and raising his children without any financial burdens (Author's files).

Because their careers are better established, older fathers may have more flexibility to spend their nonwork hours and weekends with their families. They're often more relaxed, especially if they're financially secure, and forge strong emotional bonds with their offspring (Carnoy and Carnoy, 1997; Kluger, 2013).

DISADVANTAGES   The vast majority of children born to men of all ages are healthy, but scientists are finding that children of older fathers may face greater health risks, including autism and schizophrenia (Callaway, 2012). Sperm age better than eggs, but such research suggests that biological clocks may be ticking for men as well as women.

Older parents may be more patient, mature, and financially secure, but there are drawbacks to delaying parenthood. Pregnant women in their forties are at greater risk of having a baby with Down syndrome than are women in their twenties and thirties. Beyond health risks, there are some practical liabilities in becoming a father at a later age. For example, as the father turns 55, his child starts kindergarten. At age 60, dad is coaching soccer, and buried under college tuition bills at age 70. And if the child, like the father, delays marriage and family, "you might be paying for a wedding when you're 80 and babysitting for your grandchildren at 90" (Wright, 1997: E5).

Some women who have waited to have children find that it's too late to have as many as they wanted. At one point or another, many midlife parents are mistaken for grandparents. Some laugh it off, but others bristle at such errors. Adolescents and young adults whose older fathers are dead often lose out on

Many older parents who have postponed parenthood to establish their careers have the resources to provide their children with educational and other opportunities. A disadvantage is that they may not live long enough to see their grandchildren.

financial support for college, buying homes, and generous trips and gifts for their children (Crandell, 2005; Kluger, 2013). Finally, postponing parenthood may mean that parents will never get to see their grandchildren.

There are many reasons for postponing childbearing. However, millions of Americans have fewer choices because they're infertile.

11.5 Identify the reasons for infertility, people's reactions, and the available medical treatments.

infertility The inability to conceive a baby.

Infertility

Infertility is the inability to conceive a baby. It's a condition that often goes undiagnosed until a couple has had at least one year of unprotected intercourse or until a woman has had multiple miscarriages.

Infertility affects about 15 percent of all couples of reproductive age. Infertility rates have been fairly stable since the mid-1960s, but rates increase as people age. For example, the infertility rate for couples between ages 30 and 34 is more than 50 percent greater than for those between ages 25 and 29 (Mosher and Pratt, 1991; Chandra et al., 2005).

Reasons for Infertility

Infertility is due about equally to problems in males and females; each sex independently accounts for about 60 percent of cases, and a combination of male and female factors account for about 15 percent of cases. Approximately 25 percent of infertile couples are diagnosed as having *idiopathic infertility* (Expert Group on Commissioning . . ., 2009; see also Kridel, 2012), meaning that doctors don't know what's wrong. Women's reproductive organs age faster than other parts of their body, but men also have fertility problems.

Since You Asked . . .
• What causes infertility?

FEMALE INFERTILITY The two major reasons for female infertility are failure to ovulate and blockage of the fallopian tubes. A woman's failure to *ovulate*, or to produce a viable egg each month, may have a number of causes, among them poor nutrition, chronic illness, and drug abuse. Occasionally, lack of ovulation may be attributed to psychological stress (Masters et al., 1992).

Fallopian tubes carry the egg—whether or not it has been fertilized—from the ovaries to the uterus. The tubes may be blocked by scarring due to **pelvic inflammatory disease (PID)**, an infection of the uterus that spreads to the tubes, ovaries, and surrounding tissues. In turn, PID is often caused by sexually transmitted diseases such as chlamydia.

pelvic inflammatory disease (PID) An infection of the uterus that spreads to the fallopian tubes, ovaries, and surrounding tissues.

chlamydia A sexually transmitted bacterial infection.

Chlamydia, a sexually transmitted bacterial infection, is often called "the silent epidemic" because it shows no symptoms in women and men. Chlamydia is a rapidly rising cause of PID but, once diagnosed, it can be cured with antibiotics (see Chapter 7 and *Appendix E* for more information about sexually transmitted diseases).

Another reason for women's infertility is **endometriosis**, a condition in which the tissue that forms in the endometrium (the lining of the uterus) spreads outside the womb and attaches itself to other pelvic organs, such as the ovaries or the fallopian tubes. The cause of endometriosis is unknown, but some researchers believe that, in 6 to 10 percent of the cases, endometriosis may be genetic (Painter et al., 2011; see also Nyholt et al., 2012).

endometriosis A condition in which tissue spreads outside the womb and attaches itself to other pelvic organs.

MALE INFERTILITY Male infertility often results from sluggish sperm or a low sperm count. Chemical pollutants might play a significant role because men are more likely than women to work in environments where they come in contact with toxic chemicals (Kenen, 1993; Li et al., 2011).

Other possible causes of low sperm counts include injury to the testicles or scrotum; infections such as mumps in adulthood; testicular varicose veins that impede sperm development; endocrine disorders; and excessive consumption of

alcohol, narcotic drugs, or even some prescription medications. Maternal smoking during pregnancy and a male's current marijuana usage are also linked to lower sperm counts (Wang, 2013).

Prolonged and frequent use of saunas, hot tubs, and steam baths may also have a negative effect because sperm production is sensitive to temperature. In the case of obese men, excess fat in the genital area could raise the temperature of the testicles, reducing the quality and quantity of sperm. Sperm quality and the speed at which sperm travel toward an egg also decline in men older than age 50, decreasing their fertility (Bhattacharya, 2003; Marcus, 2003; Wang, 2013).

Women, especially, are heartbroken by infertility. Why do you think that they're generally unhappier than men by the couple's inability to conceive a baby? Or do you think that men are more likely to hide their feelings?

Reactions to Infertility

People respond to infertility differently, but couples are usually devastated. For many women, infertility becomes "an acute and unanticipated life crisis" that involves stigma, psychological distress, grief, guilt, and a sense of violation. As one woman said, "I feel like I'm isolated in a prison . . . no one understands how horrible this is" (Whiteford and Gonzalez, 1995: 29; see also McQuillan et al., 2003).

Though well intentioned, potential grandparents' expectations exert pressure to carry on the family line ("Do you think that I will have a grandchild before I die?"). That generational continuity will come to an end may reinforce a woman's feelings of being a failure when she doesn't conceive: "My mother-in-law has been pushing for a grandchild since the day we got married [10 years ago]" (Whiteford and Gonzalez, 1995: 34).

Many women, concerned that people will see them in a new and damaging light, engage in "information management" (Goffman, 1963). For example, they may avoid the topic whenever possible, or they may attribute the problem to a disease such as diabetes or kidney trouble, taking the focus off specific reproductive disorders. Because male infertility may be viewed as a defect in masculinity, women may accept responsibility for infertility themselves:

> When I tell them we can't have children, I generally try to leave the impression that it's me. I may mutter "tubes you know" or "faulty plumbing" (Miall, 1986: 36).

Marital satisfaction can suffer if women blame themselves or bury their feelings, especially if a partner isn't emotionally supportive. Coping with infertility is especially difficult if men distance themselves by making light of the situation or acting as if nothing is wrong (Peterson et al., 2006). Fewer than half of women with fertility problems seek medical help. For those who do, male partners become more involved after treatments begin (Johnson and Johnson, 2009).

Common Medical Treatments for Infertility

The most common medical treatments are *artificial insemination* and *fertility drugs*. Artificial insemination is the most common treatment for men with low sperm counts. Fertility drugs improve the chance of conception in infertile women.

ARTIFICIAL INSEMINATION **Artificial insemination (AI)**, sometimes called *donor insemination (DI)*, is a medical procedure in which semen is introduced artificially into the vagina or uterus during ovulation. The semen, taken from the woman's husband or another donor, may be fresh or frozen. Generally not covered by health insurance, AI usually costs between $2,000 and $3,000 ("Kan. Case Highlights . . .," 2013). According to California Cryobank, one of the nation's largest sperm banks, about 33 percent of its clients in 2009 were lesbian couples, up from 7 percent a decade earlier (Holson, 2011).

artificial insemination (AI) A medical procedure in which semen is introduced artificially into the vagina or uterus during ovulation (sometimes called *donor insemination*, or DI).

Prospective parents can browse a catalog and choose a sperm donor by eye and hair color, nationality, blood type, height, and profession. A man with a Ph.D. can make as much as $500 per ejaculation; college students can earn as much as $12,000 a year for twice-weekly donations (Dokoupil, 2011; Newton-Small, 2012).

According to a man in southern California who donated sperm to help cover living expenses while in medical school, "I could fill a banquet hall with 'my' children" (Romano, 2006: A2). A man in Britain, who donated sperm for over 30 years, has fathered more than 1,000 children. Because donors are typically anonymous, half siblings might meet and mate, not knowing that they have the same biological father and may share the same genetic problems (Newton-Small, 2012).

fertility drugs Medications that stimulate the ovaries to produce eggs.

FERTILITY DRUGS If a woman is having difficulty becoming pregnant, her physician often uses **fertility drugs**, medications that stimulate the ovaries to produce eggs. In 1997, a couple from Carlisle, Iowa, became the parents of the first septuplets ever born alive. The mother had been taking a fertility drug. For religious reasons, the couple refused to undergo a process known as *selective reduction*, aborting some of the fetuses to give the others a better chance to develop fully.

Fertility drugs have a high success rate—50 to 70 percent. A primary concern, however, is that multiple births increase the chance of babies being born pre-term and with a low birth weight. The babies who survive may suffer major health problems and lifelong learning disabilities, including cerebral palsy, developmental delays, and birth defects. Also, children whose mothers took fertility drugs are almost twice as likely as other children to have autism (H. W. Jones, 2007; Goodwin, 2010).

assisted reproductive technology (ART) A general term that includes all treatments and procedures that involve handling eggs and sperm to establish a pregnancy.

in vitro fertilization (IVF) The surgical removal of eggs from a woman's ovaries, fertilizing them in a petri dish with sperm from her husband or another donor, and transferring the embryos into the woman's uterus.

High-Tech Treatments for Infertility

Assisted reproductive technology (ART) is a general term that includes all treatments and procedures that involve handling eggs and sperm to establish a pregnancy. This technology accounts for more than 1 percent of all U.S. births every year (Sunderman et al., 2009).

Since the introduction of ART in 1981, live ART birthrates have been modest—about 30 percent overall—and decline significantly with multiple births and if the mother is age 40 or older. Still, the number of live-birth deliveries using ART has increased steadily from about 14,500 in 1996 to more than 47,000 in 2010 (Centers for Disease Control and Prevention, American Society for Reproductive Medicine . . ., 2012). The most common ART technique is in vitro fertilization.

IN VITRO FERTILIZATION In vitro fertilization (IVF) involves surgically removing eggs from a woman's ovaries, fertilizing them in a petri dish (a specially shaped glass container) with sperm from her husband or another donor, and then transferring the embryos into the woman's uterus. (An *embryo* is the developing organism up to the eighth week of pregnancy.) The IVF procedure is done on an outpatient basis and is conducted at 474 clinics in the United States alone. More than 4 million children worldwide owe their birth to this method of fertilization (Centers for Disease Control and Prevention, American Society for Reproductive Medicine . . ., 2012).

In 2010, British biologist Robert Edwards was awarded the Nobel prize in medicine. Edwards and a gynecologist developed controversial in vitro fertilization techniques that led to the birth of the first "test tube baby," Louise Brown, in 1978 (pictured here with her son).

Most IVF babies are healthy, but the procedure has drawbacks. Because more than one egg is usually implanted to increase the chances of success, nearly half of all women using IVF have multiple births. Multiple-birth babies are ten times more likely than single babies to be born pre-term, with a low birth weight,

Choices   Motherhood after Menopause

A woman's ovaries stop producing eggs after menopause, but her other reproductive organs remain viable. In later life, women can become pregnant using a younger woman's donated eggs that have been fertilized with sperm from the older woman's husband or another donor.

Since 1994, there have been 12 documented cases of women over age 60 having babies, including a 62-year-old woman in California who had 11 other children. In 2007, a 67-year-old woman from Spain gave birth to twin boys. A recipient of donor eggs and sperm at a Los Angeles fertility clinic, she lied to doctors about her age because the cutoff was age 55. She was diagnosed with cancer shortly after giving birth and died in 2009 (Pool and Bousada, 2007; Daum, 2009).

The world's oldest mom may be a woman in India who was believed to be 70 years old (her exact age is unknown) when she gave birth to boy-and-girl twins in 2008. She already had two adult daughters and five grandchildren, but she and her husband hoped to have a son. Her 77-year-old husband—who was proud and happy to finally have a son who would be an heir and work the land—had spent his life savings, mortgaged his land, sold his buffaloes, and took out a loan to pay for the IVF treatments (Daum, 2009).

Several countries, including France and Italy, have passed laws barring postmenopausal women from artificial impregnation because they view such practices as immoral and dangerous to women's health.

STOP AND THINK . . .

- Should there be age limits for IVF treatments? Why or why not?
- If countries bar women in their fifties from getting pregnant, should they also require vasectomies of men who father children in their fifties, sixties, and later?

and/or with poorly developed organs. As with fertility drug use, a low birth weight subjects infants to health risks such as lung disease, brain damage, an increased risk of developing cancer by age 19, and infant death (Mitchell, 2002; Wood et al., 2003; Källén et al., 2010).

In vitro fertilization is expensive (costing up to $25,000 per attempt), time consuming, painful, and can be emotionally exhausting. Despite the difficulties and expense, egg donation is a growing industry that allows even women who have gone through menopause to become pregnant (see "Motherhood after Menopause").

SURROGACY   **Surrogacy** is an arrangement in which a woman carries and delivers a child for another person or couple. The surrogate can be artificially inseminated with the sperm of the infertile woman's husband, the infertile couple's egg and sperm are brought together in vitro and the resulting embryo is implanted in a surrogate, or, in the case of lesbian and gay couples, the eggs or sperm are donated. In 2011, almost 1,600 U.S. babies were born through surrogacy, up from only 738 in 2004. The success rate is about 31 percent (Carney, 2010; Cohen, 2013).

A growing number of infertile couples, including some Americans, have made India a top destination for surrogacy. India's clinics charge about $20,000 for the process. In the handful of American states that allow paid surrogacy, bringing a child to term costs between $50,000 and $120,000 for brokers, legal and medical expenses, and surrogate fees (Saul, 2009; Carney, 2010).

Why do women become surrogates? A major reason is money, especially in India. A successful surrogate makes between $5,000 and $6,000. Most of the women, who are poor and come from rural areas, use the money to lift their families out of poverty and to pay for their children's education (Carney, 2010).

Some criticize India's surrogacy as "reproductive tourism" that exploits poor women by "renting their wombs, cheap" and risks their lives because of the possible complications of pregnancy and childbirth. Others argue that surrogacy improves the family's standard of living (the average income is about $500 a year), and that the doctors provide high-quality care (Chu, 2006: A1).

surrogacy An arrangement in which a woman carries and delivers a child for another person or couple.

Rock singer/songwriter Elton John, age 65, and his husband, age 50, have two sons by the same surrogate. They used the same egg donor and, both times, chose not to know which of them was the sons' biological father (Laudadio, 2013).

egg freezing A procedure that allows women to store their eggs for future use.

Watch on MySocLab

Video: Embryo Mix-Up

preimplantation genetic diagnosis (PGD) A procedure that enables physicians to identify genetic diseases in the embryo before implantation.

genetic engineering A set of technologies that can change the makeup of cells by manipulating genetic material to make an organism better in some way.

Since You Asked . . .
• Has genetic engineering gone too far? Or not far enough?

amniocentesis A procedure in which fluid is withdrawn from a woman's abdomen and analyzed for abnormalities in the fetus.

chorionic villi sampling (CVS) A prenatal test to determine abnormalities in the fetus.

EGG FREEZING   **Egg freezing** is a relatively new but increasingly popular technique that allows women to store their unfertilized eggs for future use. The procedure, usually not covered by insurance, costs between $8,000 and $18,000. Only a few thousand babies in the world have been born from frozen eggs, but thousands of U.S. women have frozen their eggs because they're delaying parenthood (Gootman, 2012; Richards, 2012).

Successful pregnancy rates are about the same using fresh or frozen eggs. Babies conceived from frozen eggs face no increased risk of birth defects or developmental problems, but fertility doctors don't know if this assisted reproductive technology will have long-term health complications for the children (Walker, 2012). Despite such unanswered questions, some potential grandparents are eager to pay for the procedure. According to a 36-year-old unmarried woman, "My mom said to me, 'Do you think we'd rather have this money sitting in an account or have a grandchild someday?'" (Gootman, 2012: A1).

PRENATAL TESTING   **Preimplantation genetic diagnosis (PGD)** is a recent but widely used ART procedure that enables physicians to identify genetic diseases, such as cystic fibrosis or Down syndrome, in the embryo before implantation. This technology allows a couple to choose only healthy embryos for transfer into a woman's uterus.

Some critics fear that PGD will increase abortion rates because of imperfect embryos and open the door to a "new eugenics" as parents customize their babies for anything "from tissue type to eye color, broad shoulders, to extreme intelligence" (Healy, 2003: F1). On the other hand, many researchers believe that PGD will eventually produce embryos that are free of fatal diseases (M. Jones, 2003).

Genetic Engineering: Its Benefits and Costs

Genetic engineering is a set of technologies that can change the makeup of cells by manipulating genetic material to make an organism better in some way. Examples include the medical and high-tech treatments for infertility you've just read about. Some people worry that genetic engineering, because it meddles with nature, is unethical and detrimental to society. Others maintain that the benefits outweigh the costs.

THE BENEFITS OF GENETIC ENGINEERING   Couples who want children but can't conceive may choose to use genetic engineering to produce children who are usually as healthy as children conceived naturally. Also, because some women experience infertility due to cancer treatments, they can freeze their eggs before chemotherapy and doctors can later reimplant the eggs to produce healthy babies (Hobson, 2004; Shevell et al., 2005).

Besides helping people conceive, genetic engineering has been valuable in detecting prenatal genetic disorders and abnormalities. Two diagnostic procedures that have become fairly common are amniocentesis and chorionic villus sampling. In **amniocentesis**, which is performed in the twentieth week of pregnancy, a needle is inserted through the abdomen into the amniotic sac, and the fluid withdrawn is analyzed for abnormalities in the fetus such as Down syndrome and spina bifida.

The same information can be produced at the tenth week by **chorionic villus sampling (CVS)**, a prenatal test to determine abnormalities in the fetus. A catheter inserted through the vagina removes some of the *villi* (fingerlike protrusions) from the *chorion* (the outer membrane that surrounds the amniotic sac). The major advantage of detecting abnormalities at these stages is that parents can decide on an abortion early in the pregnancy. Both amniocentesis and CVS have risks of spontaneous abortions and possible deformities, although such risks are quite low (about 1 to 2 percent of all cases) (Boodman, 1992).

THE COSTS OF GENETIC ENGINEERING   Assisted reproductive technology techniques increase the risk of birth defects, especially in the case of twins or multiple births (Reefhuis et al., 2009). Medical treatments for infertility are expensive and rarely covered by insurance programs. For example, repeated IVF attempts can easily cost more than $100,000 (Saul, 2009). Because only the rich can afford genetic engineering, the technology doesn't benefit all social classes.

There's also concern about issues such as parents' and scientists' right to create "designer babies" by choosing genes for a child's hair color and height ("Designer Babies," 2012); parents' right to reject imperfect fetuses; and the rights of both parents and embryos. Suppose that both parents of a fertilized egg that has been frozen die. Who's responsible for the frozen embryo? Should it be destroyed because the parents are dead? Put up for adoption? Turned over to doctors for medical research?

In 2010, there were more than 5,500 births of triplets, quadruplets, and higher-order births primarily because of IVF (Martin et al., 2012). Children of multiple births are 12 times more likely than other babies to die within a year. Many suffer from lifelong respiratory and digestive problems. They're also prone to a range of neurological disorders, including blindness, cerebral palsy, and mental retardation (Rochman, 2009).

Sperm banks, although regulated by the Food and Drug Administration, carry risks. Sperm with serious genetic diseases and disorders have been sold to hundreds of women. One Texas couple, for example, is suing a sperm bank after their child turned out to have cystic fibrosis, a potentially fatal disease (Dokoubil, 2011; Newton-Small, 2012).

Finally, how many parents can a baby have? If lesbian moms split up, for example, who has parental rights: the sperm donor, the egg donor, the mother who bears the child, or all three? And who are the parents of a child who has a sperm donor, an egg donor, a surrogate mother, and a stepparent who adopts the child?

Infertile couples sometimes enjoy vicarious parenthood through contact with children of relatives and friends. Others become increasingly involved in work-related activities and even begin to regard their childlessness as an advantage. Some couples accept infertility as a fact of life and remain childless, but many turn to adoption.

MAKING CONNECTIONS

- Should people postpone parenthood into their late thirties, early forties, and later?
- In some European countries—including Great Britain, Sweden, Norway, and the Netherlands—it's illegal to sell anonymous donor sperm. Should the United States pass similar laws, even if doing so would reduce the number of donors?
- Women who are coping with infertility often use Facebook's "hide" feature to avoid reading pregnancy and birth announcements (Shapira, 2010). Do you think that they'd post their own gleeful news if they became pregnant or had a baby? Or not do so to avoid hurting infertile couples?

Adoption: The Traditional Solution to Infertility

Adoption is taking a child into one's family through legal means and raising her or him as one's own. In the 1950s, 80 percent of U.S. nonmarital babies were given up for adoption. This rate has dropped to about 1 percent because today most nonmarital mothers keep their babies. Among all adopted children, including those adopted by relatives, only 6 percent are under age 3 (Vandivere et al., 2009; Smock and Greenland, 2010). Thus, many adoptive parents haven't been the children's primary socialization agents (see Chapter 5).

Adopted children comprise only 2 percent of the U.S. child population, but their absolute numbers are large—nearly 1.8 million. Of all domestic adoptions, half are adopted from private sources and half are adopted from foster care. Children adopted from foster care have previously been involved with the child protective services system. The children's biological parents may be dead, missing, or unable or unwilling to provide appropriate care (Child Welfare Information Gateway, 2009; Vandivere et al., 2009).

11.6 Compare open and closed adoptions and describe transracial, same-sex, and international adoptions.

adoption Taking a child into one's family through legal means and raising her or him as one's own.

Whether we arrive by birth or adoption, none of us chooses our family. We'll consider the benefits and costs of adoption, but let's first look at several types of adoption.

Open and Closed Adoption

open adoption The practice of sharing information and maintaining contact between biological and adoptive parents throughout the child's life.

Open adoption is the practice of sharing information and maintaining contact between biological and adoptive parents throughout the child's life. According to the most recent available data, in 2006, 23 states provided open access to adoption records (National Adoption Information Clearinghouse, 2006). A longitudinal study of adults who were adopted as infants found that most were glad that their open adoptions gave them an opportunity to meet their biological parents and siblings, even when some of the contacts were negative or uncomfortable (Siegel, 2012).

closed adoption The records of the adoption are kept sealed, the birth parent is not involved in the adoptee's life, and the child has no contact with the biological parents or little, if any, information about them.

In a **closed adoption**, the records of the adoption are kept sealed, the birth parent isn't involved in the adoptee's life, and the child has no contact with the biological parents and little, if any, information about them. Because of social media networks, especially Facebook, adopted children have found and contacted their birth mothers. Some birth mothers don't mind, but others resent the violation of their right to privacy, especially if the birth resulted from a rape or violent relationship. Being contacted by a biological child can renew past traumas that the mothers may have struggled to overcome. Adopted children argue, however, that they have a right to meet their biological parents and learn about genetic health histories that may affect their own children (Collins, 2005; Luscombe, 2010).

semi-open adoption There is communication between the adoptive parents, birth parents, and adopted children, but through a third party (sometimes called *mediated adoption*).

In a third option, **semi-open adoption**, sometimes called *mediated adoption*, there is communication between the adoptee and the adoptive and biological parents, but it takes place only through a third party such as a caseworker or attorney. *Table 11.1* provides some of the pros and cons of each of these adoption methods.

TABLE 11.1	The Pros and Cons of Adoption Types		
	Closed Adoptions	**Semi-Open Adoptions**	**Open Adoptions**
Pros	*Birth parents* have a sense of closure and can move on with their lives.	*Birth parents* can maintain privacy while providing some information.	*Birth parents* can develop a relationship with the child as she or he grows.
	Adoptive parents are safe from the interference or co-parenting by birth parents.	*Adoptive parents* have a greater sense of control than in open adoptions.	*Adoptive parents* have a better understanding of the child's history.
	Adopted children are safe from unstable or emotionally disturbed birth parents.	*Adopted children* don't fantasize about birth parents.	*Adopted children* are less likely to feel abandoned (they can know why they were placed for adoption) and can increase their circle of supportive adults.
Cons	*Birth parents* may experience more distress because they lack information about their child's well-being.	*Birth parents* may experience more distress about the decision because they're in contact with the adoptive family.	*Birth parents* may be disappointed if the adoptive family fails to meet all their expectations.
	Adoptive parents don't have access to much medical information about the birth family.	*Adoptive parents* may have to deal with troubling communications (letters, e-mail) between birth parents and an adopted child.	*Adoptive parents* may have difficulties dealing with emotionally disturbed birth parents.
	Adopted children may experience identity confusion because their physical traits differ from those of their adoptive parents.	*Adopted children* may want more information than third parties are willing to divulge.	*Adopted children* may feel rejected if contact with birth parents ceases or they may play their birth and adoptive families against each other.

Sources: Based on Grotevant, 2001; National Adoption Information Clearinghouse, 2002; Crea and Barth, 2009.

Transracial Adoption

Overall, 40 percent of adopted children are of a different race, ethnicity, or culture than their adoptive parent/parents (Vandivere et al., 2009). The federal Multiethnic Placement Act (MEPA) of 1994 forbids public child welfare agencies from delaying or denying a child's foster care or adoption on the basis of race, color, or national origin. The MEPA supports transracial adoption, but this policy has been controversial.

Advocates of transracial adoption maintain that many black and biracial children, especially those with emotional problems or physical disabilities, would remain in foster homes until age 18 if white parents didn't adopt them. Moreover, foster homes are costly and don't provide the permanence and stability that adoption offers (Altstein, 2006; Hansen and Pollack, 2007).

Several qualitative studies have found that transracial adopted children benefit if their parents engage in racial socialization. That is, adoptive parents can decrease the negative effects of racial discrimination by developing the children's pride in their racial or ethnic group and by teaching them strategies for managing bias and prejudice (Leslie et al., 2013; Rollins and Hunter, 2013; see, also, Chapter 4 for a discussion of racial socialization in African American families).

The National Association of Black Social Workers and the Child Welfare League, among others, oppose transracial adoptions. A major objection is that the children "are alienated from their culture of origin" and "dislodged from the ethnic community" (Kissman and Allen, 1993: 93).

Some child advocates also question the wisdom of placing African American children with white parents who may not provide the children with the strategies they need to deal with everyday racism, prejudice, and discrimination (Herring, 2007; Evan B. Donaldson Adoption Institute, 2008). Even when white parents adopt black or biracial children as infants, in adulthood some of the adoptees report struggling with rejection by extended family members, being stigmatized by black peers for being raised by white people, and not fully fitting in with either black or white friends (Samuels, 2009).

Opponents of transracial adoption maintain that white parents can't teach their African American children how to cope with being "different," to develop a positive racial-ethnic identity, and to deal with discrimination. Do you agree?

Since You Asked . . .
- Why are transracial adoptions controversial?

Adoption by Same-Sex Couples

The American Academy of Pediatrics supports lesbians and gay men who want to foster or adopt children: "A growing body of scientific literature demonstrates that children who grow up with 1 or 2 gay and/or lesbian parents fare as well in emotional, cognitive, social, and sexual functioning as do children whose parents are heterosexual" (Perrin, 2002: 341). About 52 percent of Americans favor adoption by gays and lesbians, up from 38 percent in 1999 ("Two-thirds of Democrats . . .," 2012).

Among U.S. couples with children under age 18, 2 percent of same-sex couples, compared with only 0.3 percent of opposite-sex couples, are raising a foster child. Between 2000 and 2010, the percentage of same-sex couples with adopted children increased from 9 to 20 percent. Many of these families have lesbian mothers, but gay men make up a growing share of adoptive same-sex parents, accounting for nearly 33 percent of these couples in 2010, up from 20 percent in 2000. Gay and lesbian couples are also more willing than heterosexual couples to foster and adopt children with special needs, who are among the most difficult to place (Gates, 2011; Movement Advancement Project et al., 2012; Swarns, 2012).

Same-sex adoptive parents tend to be disproportionately white and with high income and education levels, but their reasons for pursuing parenthood echo those of heterosexuals. For example, gay couples adopt children because they

love kids, believe that raising children is an important part of life, and want to improve a child's life by providing a good home, and/or because a partner has a strong desire to be a parent (Goldberg et al., 2012).

International Adoption

Because the waiting period for adopting a child from overseas is only 1 or 2 years, compared with 7 to 10 years in the United States, many Americans have turned to international adoptions (also called *intercountry adoptions*). Between 1999 and 2012, Americans adopted almost 243,000 children from at least 20 countries (U.S. Department of State, 2013).

International adoptions increased steadily until 2004 but then started dropping (see *Figure 11.5*). The decrease wasn't due to Americans' loss of interest, but to some host countries' curtailing international adoptions for cultural, political, and economic reasons. For example,

- In China, as prosperity increased, the number of abandoned children decreased. Girls still make up 95 percent of children at orphanages, but China has tightened its foreign-adoption rules, which now require adoptive parents to be younger than age 55, married, heterosexual, high-income, not obese, and not on antidepressants (Wingert, 2008; Webley, 2013).

- Russia has more than 600,000 orphans. However, President Vladimir Putin has banned adoptions by American families to strike back against a new U.S. law that will punish Russian citizens accused of violating human rights (Loiko, 2012; Khazan, 2012).

- South Korea has sharply reduced international adoptions. The reasons include encouraging domestic adoptions and thus ensuring a larger force of young workers who will support the elderly (see Chapter 16), and the government's embarrassment by the large number of international adoptions because of South Korea's successful economy (Kirk, 2013).

- Guatemala, where adoption processes averaged only six months, has tightened laws because of "widespread instances of forged paperwork, women paid to give up their newborns, babies kidnapped from hospitals and snatched from

There are more than 600,000 orphans in Russia, but only 18,000 Russians are waiting to adopt. Pictured here, children play at an orphanage in Rostov-on-Don, Russia.

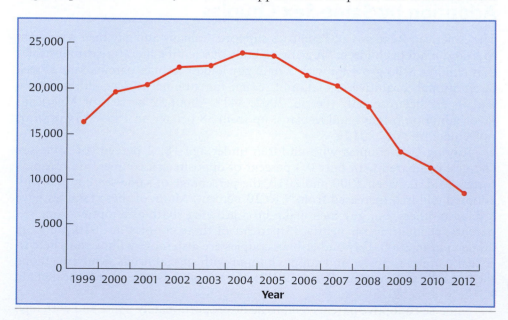

FIGURE 11.5 **International Adoptions in the United States, 1998–2012**
Source: U.S. Department of State, 2013.

their parents' arms," and some lawyers' engaging in illegal, profitable adoption practices (Llana, 2007; Webley, 2013: 37).

Some Rewards and Costs of Adoption

You learned earlier that having a biological child has both rewards and costs. The same is true of adoptions.

SOME REWARDS OF ADOPTION   The most obvious benefit of adoption is that adoptive parents and abandoned children find people to love. Most single parents are women, who tend to adopt girls or older, minority, or mentally disabled children. Without adoption, many of these children would grow up in foster homes rather than in a stable environment. Some well-known Americans who have been adopted include

- Playwrights and authors (James Michener and Edgar Allen Poe)
- Past U.S. presidents and first ladies (Gerald Ford, Herbert Hoover, and Nancy Reagan)
- Civil rights leaders and politicians (Jesse Jackson and Newt Gingrich)
- Entrepreneurs (Steve Jobs, co-founder of Apple Computer; Tom Monaghan, founder of Domino's Pizza; and Dave Thomas, founder of Wendy's)

The majority of adopted children are more likely than children in the general population to have enriching family experiences. Young children, for example, are more likely to be read to, sung to, and told stories every day, and school-age children are more likely to participate in extracurricular activities (Vandivere et al., 2009). As in nonadoptive families, adoptive parents who are warm and supportive and who encourage conversation and self-control develop closeness between siblings and other family members (Samek and Rueter, 2011).

SOME COSTS OF ADOPTIONS   Adoption also has disadvantages. An international adoption, including fees and travel, can cost up to $50,000. In contrast, it costs between $5,000 and $30,000 for a domestic adoption and almost nothing to adopt a foster child (Dagher, 2013; Webley, 2013).

Historically, many of the children, particularly from Russia, have had serious medical and emotional problems. The difficulties have required expensive specialized treatment that hasn't always resulted in positive outcomes (Pickert, 2010; Ruggierro, 2010).

Parental aggravation is more common among adoptive parents than those in the general population (11 percent compared with 6 percent). Many adopted children fare well, but they're more likely than children in the general population to be diagnosed with depression, attention deficit disorder (ADD), and attention deficit hyperactivity disorder (ADHD), especially if they're adopted at age 2 or older (Vandivere et al., 2009).

A study of more than 1,800 parents who adopted children 6 through 18 years of age found that learning disorders themselves didn't decrease parents' adoption satisfaction. However, learning disorders increased the likelihood of externalizing behavior such as breaking rules, running away, fighting, and threatening behavior that sometimes resulted in dissolving the adoption (Nalavany et al., 2009). About 3 to 8 percent of adoptions are severed because the parents can't cope with the child's severe externalizing behavior (Festinger, 2002).

The number of nonmarital births has surged since 1990 (see Data Digest), but they'd be much higher if women didn't have access to abortion. Some people see abortion as sinful; others believe that it's a responsible way to avoid parenthood, both inside and outside marriage.

MAKING CONNECTIONS

- Do you think that adoptions should be open, semi-open, or closed? Why?
- Celebrities such as Angelina Jolie and Madonna have received a lot of publicity by adopting children from, respectively, Vietnam and Africa. Do you think that they should have adopted one of the thousands of U.S.-born children who are languishing in foster homes?
- Should parents be allowed to change their minds after an adoption has been finalized?

abortion The expulsion of an embryo or fetus from the uterus.

Abortion

Abortion is the expulsion of an embryo or fetus from the uterus. It can occur naturally—as in *spontaneous abortion* or *miscarriage*—or induced medically.

Practiced by people in all societies and for centuries, abortion wasn't forbidden by the Catholic Church until 1869. The United States outlawed abortion in the 1800s when the practice became widespread among white, married, Protestant, American-born women in the middle and upper classes. Upper–middle-class white men became concerned that the country would be overpopulated by members of "inferior" new ethnic groups with higher fertility rates (Mohr, 1981). Abortion has been legal since the U.S. Supreme Court's *Roe v. Wade* ruling in 1973.

Incidence and Prevalence of Abortion

You learned earlier that only 52 percent of all U.S. pregnancies are intended. Every year, about 40 percent of the unintended pregnancies end in abortion. Over a lifetime, 33 percent of women have an abortion by age 45 (Finer and Zolna, 2011; Jones and Kavanaugh, 2011).

The number of U.S. abortions declined from 1.6 million in 1990 (the all-time high) to 1.2 million in 2008 (the most recent available data), when 2 percent of all American women had an abortion (Jones and Kooistra, 2011). The *abortion rate*, or the number of abortions per 1,000 women ages 15 to 44, increased during the 1970s, and then decreased (see *Figure 11.6*).

Who Has Abortions and Why?

Deciding to have an abortion is neither random nor impulsive. Women who have an abortion have similar demographic characteristics and reasons.

SOME DEMOGRAPHIC CHARACTERISTICS Abortion is most common among women who are young (in their twenties), white, and never married (see *Figure 11.7*). Proportionately, however, 37 percent of abortions are obtained by black women; 34 percent by white women; 22 percent by Latinas; and 7 percent by women who are Asians, Pacific Islanders, American Indians, and those of mixed races (Cohen, 2008; Guttmacher Institute, 2008).

Of all women who get abortions, 60 percent already have one or more children, 69 percent have incomes below or near the poverty level, 88 percent have the abortion in the first 12 weeks of pregnancy, and 73 percent have a

FIGURE 11.6 **U.S. Abortion Rates Have Decreased**
Source: Based on Guttmacher Institute, 2008, and Pazol et al., 2012, Figure 1.

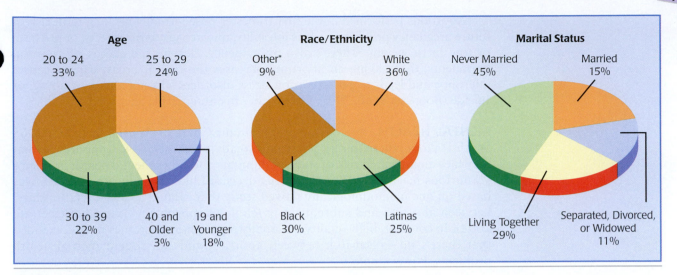

FIGURE 11.7 **Who Has Abortions?**
*Other refers to Asian/Pacific Islanders, American Indians, and Alaska Natives.
Source: Based on Guttmacher Institute, 2013.

religious affiliation (Guttmacher Institute, 2013). Among those with a religious affiliation, 28 percent of women getting abortions identify as Catholic (Jones et al., 2010). The percentages of Catholic women may be higher, but they may be reluctant to claim a religious affiliation because they're forbidden to get abortions.

SOME REASONS FOR ABORTION   Since 1987, the major reason for abortion (74 percent of all cases) has been a financial inability to support the baby. Many low-income women, especially those who already have children, believe that having an unwanted baby would plunge them deeper into poverty and create even more parenting problems. Some women consider adoption, but regard giving up a child too emotionally distressing (Finer et al., 2005; Jones et al., 2008).

More than half of women who had an abortion in 2008 experienced at least one disruptive life event a year before the abortion. For example, a higher proportion of poor women (63 percent) than those well above the poverty level (49 percent) reported events such as unemployment, which led to a loss of health insurance and, in turn, limited access to hormonal contraceptives; separation from a partner; falling behind on rent or mortgage; moving multiple times; and having had a baby the previous year. Low-income women were also much more likely than higher-income women to experience intimate partner violence that included being impregnated against their will (Jones et al., 2013).

Abortion opponents often claim that abortion availability should be reduced because most women aren't aware of the nature of abortion and don't make informed decisions. Such assumptions are false. A study of 5,100 women who had abortions found that nearly all the women were sure of their decision, even before counseling, because abortion was a better choice than having an unplanned or unwanted baby (Foster et al., 2012).

Abortion Safety

Anti-abortion groups contend that abortion endangers a woman's physical and emotional health. Are such claims accurate?

PHYSICAL HEALTH   On a physical level, a legal abortion in the first trimester (up to 12 weeks) is safer than driving a car, playing football, motorcycling, getting a penicillin shot, or continuing a pregnancy. Fewer than 0.3 percent of abortion patients experience a complication that requires hospitalization (Guttmacher Institute, 2005, 2011; Deprez, 2013b).

Since You Asked . . .
• How dangerous is abortion?

Abortions performed in the first trimester pose virtually no long-term risk of future pregnancy problems such as infertility, miscarriage, birth defects, or pre-term or low birth weight. There's also no evidence, despite the claims of abortion opponents, that having an abortion increases the risk of breast cancer, causes infertility, and leads to post-abortion stress disorders, alcohol and drug abuse, or suicide (Boonstra et al., 2006; Guttmacher Institute, 2011; Sheppard, 2013b).

MENTAL HEALTH In 2012, the 8th Circuit Court of Appeals upheld a 2005 South Dakota law requiring physicians to advise women seeking abortions that they face an increased risk of suicidal thoughts and other mental health problems ("Spurious Science . . .," 2012). This decision, like those in other states, was based on one methodologically flawed study that "found a causal relationship" between abortion and subsequent psychological problems (see Charles et al., 2008). In contrast, high-quality nationally representative studies have concluded that there's no causal link between abortion and subsequent mental health problems. For example,

- Teen and adult women who have abortions are no more likely to experience depression, low self-esteem, or mental health problems than females whose pregnancies don't end in abortion (Major et al., 2008; Warren et al., 2010).

- A history of mental health problems, not abortion, is the strongest predictor of post-abortion mental health problems (Academy of Medical Royal Colleges, 2011; Steinberg and Finer, 2011).

- A review of low- and high-quality empirical studies conducted in the United States, Great Britain, and other countries concluded that an unwanted pregnancy, not abortion, increased the risk of mental health problems (Academy of Medical Royal Colleges, 2011).

- A study of more than 86,000 Danish women who had first-time first-trimester abortions between 1995 and 2007 found no causal link between abortion and subsequent mental health problems. This study was exceptionally strong methodologically because the data were based on complete patient medical records rather than retrospective self-reports (Munk-Olsen et al., 2011).

When women experience sadness, grief, and depression after an abortion, such feelings are usually due to co-occurring factors. The factors include poverty (because low-income mothers worry about providing for a baby), a history of emotional problems and drug or alcohol abuse, or keeping the abortion secret from family and friends who stigmatize abortions (Major et al., 2008).

The overwhelming majority (82 percent) of U.S. women who don't experience intimate partner violence report that the men by whom they got pregnant knew about and supported the abortion. The support greatly improved the women's post-abortion sense of well-being (Jones et al., 2011). Social support before and after an abortion—by the male partner, family members, and friends—is important for women's emotional state, but so is the women's autonomy in deciding whether or not to have an abortion. For example, women who feel that the final decision is up to them fare better emotionally after an abortion than those who feel that the decision was made by the male partner, family, or friends (Kimport et al., 2011).

Why Abortion Rates Have Decreased

More women are having unwanted babies (see Data Digest). Why, then, have abortion rates decreased? There are several reasons, ranging from personal attitudes to structural factors such as politics and laws.

CHANGING ATTITUDES ABOUT ABORTION Seven in ten Americans oppose overturning *Roe v. Wade* (Radnofsky and Jones, 2013), but abortion is a fiercely divisive issue. Anti-abortion proponents believe that the embryo or fetus isn't

just a mass of cells but a human being from the time of conception and therefore has a right to live. In contrast, abortion rights advocates contend that the organism at the moment of conception lacks a brain and other specifically and uniquely human attributes, such as consciousness and reasoning. Abortion rights proponents also believe that a pregnant woman, not the government or religious groups, should make her own decisions.

Since 1995, the gap between Americans who identify themselves as "pro-choice" (for abortion) or "pro-life" (against abortion) has narrowed considerably (see *Figure 11.8*). More than half of Americans say that abortion "is not that important" compared with other issues, but only 28 percent believe that abortion should be legal under all circumstances ("*Roe v. Wade* at 40 . . .," 2013; Saad, 2013).

Half of Americans who attend religious services at least weekly want to overturn the *Roe v. Wade* decision, and those with a religious affiliation describe themselves as "pro-life." As income and educational attainment rise, however, the importance of religion decreases, the acceptance of abortion increases, and people are more likely to describe themselves as "pro-choice" ("Abortion Views by Religious Affiliation," 2009; "*Roe v. Wade* at 40 . . .," 2013; Saad, 2013). Thus, social class is an important variable in many Americans' abortion views.

EFFECTIVE USE OF CONTRACEPTIVES   A major reason for the overall decrease in U.S. pregnancies and abortions is a more effective usage of contraceptives (Pazol et al., 2012; Ventura et al., 2012). Women use contraception because it allows them to better care for themselves and their families, get a college degree, and achieve economic security (Frost and Lindberg, 2013). When female adolescents and young adult women understand all the birth control methods and are given the contraceptive method of their choice for free, abortion rates, repeat abortions, and teenage birthrates drop significantly and are six times lower than the national average (Peipert et al., 2012).

As much as 43 percent of the decrease in abortions since 1994 can be attributed to emergency contraception (Guttmacher Institute, 2005). In 2011, the Federal Drug Administration (FDA) allowed selling emergency contraceptives, without a prescription, to those age 15 and older, lowering the previous age 17 restriction. The Obama administration overruled the FDA decision. In 2013, a federal judge ordered the FDA to make EC available, over the counter, for anyone, and with no age restrictions. Several months later, the government said it would comply with the court ruling, ending a battle that "lasted more than a decade and spanned two White House Administrations" (Dooren, 2013; Morin and Mohan, 2013; "Plan B Contraceptive . . .," 2013).

Whereas EC prevents pregnancy, the *abortion pill* (formerly known as *RU-486*, now also known as mifepristone, *medical abortion*, and *medication*

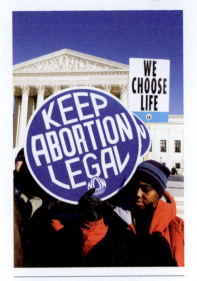

Abortion opponents and abortion-rights activists are equally passionate in their beliefs. Both sides of this highly controversial issue often stage public protests, especially in Washington, DC, to influence policy makers.

Watch on **MySocLab**

Video: Anti-Abortion March

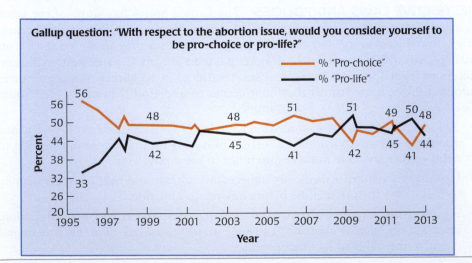

Gallup question: "With respect to the abortion issue, would you consider yourself to be pro-choice or pro-life?"

— % "Pro-choice"
— % "Pro-life"

FIGURE 11.8 U.S. Adults' Position on Abortion
Source: Saad, 2013.

abortion) stops the development of a pregnancy. Mifepristone can be used for early abortion up to 63 days—9 weeks—after the start of the last menstrual period (Planned Parenthood Federation of America Inc., 2013).

FEWER ABORTION SERVICES   Abortion rates have also decreased because there are fewer providers. One study found that 42 percent of certified nurse-midwives and 24 percent of physician assistants want training in abortion. Because of domestic terrorism by anti-abortion activists, however, few doctors perform abortions. For example, the number of abortion providers has shrunk by 38 percent since 1982; 87 percent of U.S. counties have no abortion facilities; and four states have only one abortion clinic. If a woman doesn't have the resources to travel to another state, she has little choice except to bear an unwanted or unplanned baby (Hwang et al., 2005; Jones and Kooistra, 2011; Pickert, 2013; Sheppard, 2013a).

Abortion foes have been vocal and sometimes violent in closing down abortion clinics. Since 1993, "pro-life" advocates have murdered eight abortion providers and staff members. There have been 17 attempted murders, 153 assaults, 3 kidnappings, 41 bombings, 173 arsons, 91 attempted bombings, and countless threats and incidents of vandalism and trespassing (Burkhart, 2011). In mid-2009, an anti-abortion activist shot and killed Dr. George Tiller, an abortion provider in Wichita, Kansas, while he was attending church services. After the murder, the family closed the clinic (Slevin, 2009; see also Sulzberger, 2011).

As of 2013, there were about 1,800 abortion clinics compared with 2,500 *crisis pregnancy centers (CPCs)*, that counsel pregnant women against having an abortion (Belluck, 2013). Staff at these centers—usually volunteers with no professional training—try to discourage girls and women from having abortions by "playing gruesome videos depicting bloody fetuses, withholding pregnancy test results, and even pressuring them to sign adoption papers" (Kashef, 2003: 18; see also Gibbs, 2007).

Most of the CPCs advertise themselves as "women's centers" and "clinics." When women arrive expecting a full range of services, the "staff" tell the women that having an abortion increases the risk of breast cancer, causes sterility, and leads to suicide and post-abortion stress disorders—all of which are false (National Abortion Federation, 2006; U.S. House of Representatives, 2006).

In several states, religious employees at pharmacies and medical facilities can refuse to dispense contraception and the EC pill, neither of which terminates pregnancy. The employees and pharmacists can also refuse to administer any drug that they "think" may terminate a pregnancy (Marty, 2012; Seltzer, 2012).

RESTRICTIVE LAWS AND POLICIES   The United States has some of the most restrictive abortion policies in the world, especially among industrialized countries, that force women to continue pregnancies that they don't want (Barot, 2012). During 2011 and 2012, 30 states passed a record 135 new restrictions on access to legal abortion. In the first six months of 2013 alone, state legislatures adopted 43 new provisions that limit access to abortion (Masci, 2013; "State-Level Assault . . .," 2013). For example,

- Ten states have banned women's telemedicine consultations with physicians about getting an abortion or abortion pills; this means that many women in rural areas may have to drive 300 miles to see a physician.

- Eight states require a medically unnecessary ultrasound that compels women to make two trips to a clinic before having an abortion.

- Eighteen states require that women seeking an abortion be given misleading information, such as abortion "causing" an increased risk of breast cancer and negative mental health consequences.

- Twenty states restrict abortion coverage available through state health insurance programs ("Laws Affecting . . .," 2012; Daniel and McCann, 2013; Deprez, 2013a, 2013b).

Since 2010, when Republicans won control of 25 state legislatures, there's been a gradual erosion of women's access to abortion, reduction in the number of clinics, and less funding and insurance coverage for abortion. As a result, 55 percent of all reproductive-age American women now live in states that are "hostile to abortion rights" (Gold and Nash, 2012).

MAKING CONNECTIONS

- Why are you for or against abortion?
- Are parents irresponsible if they don't abort a child who they know will be severely disabled, who will always depend on others for care, or who will probably die at an early age? Or do all fetuses have the right to be born?

Child Free by Choice

11.8 Explain why some people are choosing to be child free.

Not everyone wants to have children. For example, the percentage of women ages 40 to 44 who haven't had children has increased since 1976 (see Data Digest). Also, only 59 percent of married and 44 percent of unmarried Americans say that having children is an important reason to marry (Cohn, 2013).

"Childless" versus "Child Free"

Women are *temporarily childless* if they plan to have children in the future, *involuntarily childless* because of fertility or other biological problems, or *voluntarily childless* because they and/or their partner decided not to have children. This section is about voluntarily childless women who, in 2010, comprised almost 22 percent of all U.S. childless women ages 40 to 44 (Martinez et al., 2012). People who aren't infertile and have chosen not to have children prefer to call themselves *child free* rather than *childless*. *Childless* implies a lack or a loss, whereas *child free* connotes a choice (Paul, 2001). Often, however, researchers use both terms interchangeably (see Allen and Wiles, 2013).

Why People Choose to Be Child Free

American author Edgar Watson Howe once said that families with babies and families without babies feel sorry for each other. He may be right, but demographic variables and individual choices help explain why many people are child free.

DEMOGRAPHIC VARIABLES   Child-free women tend to be those who have never married and aren't cohabiting, have a bachelor's degree or higher, grew up with both biological parents, and are white (Martinez et al., 2012). Between 1992 and 2008, among all women ages 40 to 44, white women were the most likely to be child free, but the rates have risen for black, Hispanic, and Asian women (Livingston and Cohn, 2010).

Women with a college education and careers are more likely than their male counterparts to be child free. This gender gap probably reflects women's awareness of the challenges of balancing employment and parenthood, particularly because women still have more responsibility than men for housework and child care (Koropeckyj-Cox and Pendell, 2007; see also Chapters 5, 10, and 13).

INDIVIDUAL CHOICES   Some people decide not to have children because their family has a history of diseases such as breast and other cancers, early Alzheimer's, and muscular dystrophy. One young married woman decided "not to roll the biological dice" after testing showed that she had a 67 percent chance of passing on leukemia, the cause of her sister's death at age 8 (Handler, 2009:11).

Since You Asked . . .
- Are child-free people happy?

Because social pressure to bear children has diminished, both women and men feel freer to focus on their own goals and interests, value their independence, and do whatever they want without worrying about raising children (Valenti, 2012; Lick, 2013). However, women who don't have children experience the same social status—nonmother—differently, depending on whether the childlessness is voluntary or not. For example, women who have chosen not to have children *and* haven't internalized the belief that motherhood is an important part of a woman's social identity are happier than those who are involuntarily childless but view motherhood as an important social role (McQuillan et al., 2012).

Many people believe that marriage should come before parenthood. Others marry later in life and decide not to have children. As one husband said, "I didn't want to be 65 with a teenager in the house" (Fost, 1996: 16). A study of people ages 63 to 93 concluded that children aren't necessary for satisfaction in later life. Some of the study participants chose to be child free because they had grown up in violent homes and didn't want to repeat the same patterns; others had a network of close friends and co-workers and never wanted to have children (Allen and Wiles, 2013).

Some child-free people are teachers or other professionals who work with children but like to "come home to peace and quiet and a relaxing night with my husband" (May, 1995: 205). Others don't want to structure their lives around children's activities and school vacations and to worry about how a child will turn out, especially when they can experience parenthood vicariously through nieces, nephews, and friends' children (Rosenberg, 2011).

Some social scientists see "a social retreat from children" because the meaning and purpose of marriage has changed: "Legally, socially, and culturally, marriage is now defined primarily as a couple relationship dedicated to the fulfillment of each individual's innermost needs and drives." This emphasis on companionship has resulted in a "devaluation of child rearing" that requires sacrifice, stability, dependability, and maturity—values that no longer dominate American society (Whitehead and Popenoe, 2008: 7, 35–36).

Whether there's a social retreat from having children is debatable—there are millions of families with three or more children, there is growth in the assistive reproduction technology industry, and there are heated arguments about which parent gets custody of the children after a breakup or divorce (see Chapter 15). Moreover, among those born between 1977 and 1992, 52 percent say that being a good parent is "one of the most important things" in life. Just 30 percent say the same about having a successful marriage (Wang and Taylor, 2011).

However, numerous journalists have noted that many Americans now dress their pets better than themselves, spend more per year on veterinary than pediatrician bills, treat their pets more lovingly than their children, and often have pets (their "babies") instead of children (see, for example, Brady and Palmeri, 2007; Lynch, 2007; and Piore, 2007).

About 41 percent of Americans, down from 61 percent in 1988, believe that child-free people don't "lead empty lives." Still, 38 percent say that not having children is "bad for society" (Livingston and Cohn, 2010). Child-free couples are sometimes seen as self-indulgent, selfish, self-absorbed, workaholics, less well-adjusted emotionally, and less sensitive and loving than those with children (Sandler, 2013). As you'll see in the next chapter, raising children is a difficult task, and parents often feel unappreciated. Thus, a child-free life can be very attractive.

Mid-life couples who have decided to be child-free have more leisure time.

CONCLUSION

Attitudes about becoming a parent have *changed*. There are more *choices* today than in the past, including postponing parenthood, becoming pregnant despite infertility, and having children outside of marriage. These choices are bounded by *constraints*, however, and many expectations about parenthood are contradictory. For example, the nation develops reproductive technologies that help infertile couples become pregnant, but does little to eliminate hazardous work environments that increase people's chances of becoming infertile or having babies with lifelong physical and mental disabilities. Despite such contradictions, most people look forward to raising children, our focus in the next chapter.

On MySocLab

 Study and **Review** on MySocLab

REVIEW QUESTIONS

11.1. Describe the benefits, costs, and effects of parenthood.

1. Are people always happy about having a baby?

2. What, specifically, are the benefits and costs of having children?

3. How does parenthood change women and men?

11.2. Explain how and why birthrates are changing in the United States and globally.

4. How do social scientists measure birthrates? What do fertility rates tell us?

5. How have U.S. birthrates changed since the early 1900s? What are the macro- and micro-level factors that help explain the changes?

11.3. Describe the effects of unintended and intended pregnancies and contraception usage.

6. Why are there so many unintended pregnancies?

7. Why don't many people use contraception?

11.4. Explain why many people are postponing parenthood and discuss the effects of such postponement.

8. What are the micro and macro reasons for postponing parenthood?

9. What are the benefits and costs of postponing parenthood?

11.5. Identify the reasons for infertility, people's reactions, and the available medical treatments.

10. How many Americans are infertile? Why are women and men infertile?

11. What are the medical and high-tech treatments for infertility? What, specifically, are the benefits and risks of the treatments?

12. Why is genetic engineering controversial?

11.6. Compare open and closed adoptions and describe transracial, same-sex, and international adoptions.

13. How do open, closed, and semi-open adoptions differ? What are the pros and cons of each?

14. Why are transracial adoptions controversial? How do same-sex and opposite-sex adoptive couples differ?

15. Why have international adoptions to the United States decreased? What are the benefits and costs of adoption?

11.7. Describe the incidence of abortion, discuss the characteristics of and the reasons given by the women who abort, and explain why abortion rates have decreased.

16. Who has abortions? And why?

17. Is abortion safe?

18. Why have U.S. abortion rates decreased?

11.8. Explain why some people are choosing to be child free.

19. Why has the number of child-free people increased?

20. How do many Americans feel about people who decide not to have children?

Listen to Chapter 12 on **MySocLab**

DATA DIGEST

- Fully **69 percent of Americans say that having a father in the home is essential to a child's happiness**; only a slightly higher share (74 percent) say the same about having a mother in the home.

- Among parents with children under age 18, **64 percent of fathers and 73 percent of mothers say that they're doing an "excellent" or "very good" job as parents**.

Employed mothers (78 percent) are more likely than stay-at-home moms (66 percent) to say so.

- Among U.S. adults ages 18 to 65, 75 percent of men and 64 percent of women say that **a child sometimes needs a "good, hard spanking."**

- In 2012, 36 percent of young adults ages 18 to 31 **were living in their parents' home**, up from 31 percent in 1981.

- More than 111,000 **same-sex couples are raising** an estimated 170,000 biological, step-, or adopted children.

- Among 35 of the world's richest developed nations, **the United States ranks second highest in child poverty**.

Sources: Livingston and Parker, 2011; Adamson, 2012; Child Trends Data Bank, 2012; Fry, 2013; Gates, 2013; Parker and Wang, 2013.

According to a Swahili proverb, a child is both a precious stone and a heavy burden. Child rearing is both exhilarating and exhausting, a task that takes patience, sacrifice, and continuous adjustment. There are many rewards, but no guarantees. This chapter examines some of the most influential child development theories, diverse parenting styles, parents' impact on their children's development, and how children are doing. Let's begin by looking at contemporary parenting roles.

Contemporary Parenting Roles

Becoming a parent is a major life change. Months before the baby is born, the pregnant mother may forgo Big Macs, increase her intake of calcium-rich dairy and fresh vegetables, and eliminate cigarettes, alcohol, and other drugs. Many prospective parents shop for baby clothes and nursery furniture, and child-rearing manuals pile up on their nightstands.

A Parent Is Born

Infants waste no time in teaching adults to meet their needs. Babies aren't merely passive recipients but active participants in their own development:

> The infant modulates, regulates, and refines the caretaker's activities. . . . By fretting, sounds of impatience or satisfaction, by facial expressions of pleasure, contentment, or alertness he . . . "tells" the parents when he wants to eat, when he will sleep, when he wants to be played with, picked up, or have his position changed. . . . The caretakers, then, adapt to him . . . (Rheingold, 1969: 785–786).

Rather than simply performing parental roles, people *internalize* them in the sense that becoming a mother or father becomes part of a person's self-identity. As they transition to parenthood, the partners help each other learn the role of parent and deal with the ambiguity of what constitutes a good parent.

Parenting does *not* come naturally. It is neither instinctive nor innate. Especially with a first child, most of us muddle through by trial and error. Advice on the physical care of a baby can be valuable, but there's no template that ensures a parent's smooth passage to parenthood.

12.1 Describe parenthood's rewards and difficulties and compare idealized and realistic parenting roles.

Since you asked . . .
- Does parenting come naturally?

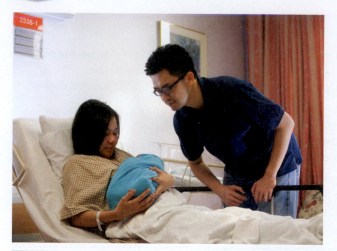

Children can be a source of great joy in many parents' lives.

role overload Feeling overwhelmed by multiple commitments.

role conflict The frustrations and uncertainties a person experiences when the expectations of two or more roles are incompatible.

role strain Conflicts that someone feels *within* a role.

Some Rewards and Difficulties of Parenting

Just as there are benefits and costs in having children, the same is true in raising them: "Parenting varies, being enormously satisfying and seemingly easy at times as well as confounding, difficult, and burdensome at other times" (Arendell, 1997: 22). Media accounts often emphasize its difficulties, but parenthood also brings happiness.

CHILDREN BRING JOY AND SATISFACTION Parenting and happiness don't always go hand in hand, but many parents report that having children has enhanced their sense of well-being (White and Dolan, 2009; Keizer et al., 2010). Parents, compared with nonparents, are generally more positive about their lives. They're also happier when taking care of their children than during 15 other common daily activities such as watching TV, cooking, working, and socializing with friends (Nelson et al., 2013).

ROLE OVERLOAD, ROLE CONFLICT, AND ROLE STRAIN A *role*, you recall, is a set of expected behavior patterns, obligations, and privileges (see Chapter 1). Employed parents often experience **role overload**, feeling overwhelmed by multiple commitments. Especially when both parents have full-time jobs, there's little time for family roles.

Role overload is closely related to **role conflict**, the frustrations and uncertainties a person experiences when the expectations of two or more roles are incompatible. Parents undergo role conflict, for example, when they're not able to attend school activities or parent–teacher meetings because of job obligations.

Role strain involves conflicts that someone feels *within* a role. A parent may experience role strain, for example, when she or he must meet the needs of both a younger and older child who have different schedules and interests. Four factors contribute to parents' role strain:

1. **Unrealistic Role Expectations.** Just as students accept the fact that some professors are better than others, most of us accept occasional mistakes by lawyers, nurses, and other professionals. Parents, however, expect and are expected to succeed with every child and may feel guilty if they "fail": "In fact, the way children turn out seems to be the only measure our culture uses to assess whether men and women are 'good' parents" (Simon, 2008: 44).

2. **Decreased Authority.** Many parents believe that they have less authority in raising kids than did parents in the past. For example, parents often feel helpless in dealing with a school bureaucracy that isn't preparing their children for the future, and countering an Internet culture that teaches their children "bad" values (Taffel, 2012).

3. **Increased Responsibility.** If parents raise several children and one runs away from home, relatives and friends would probably think that the parents had one "bad apple." In contrast, many professionals (such as psychiatrists and social workers) often automatically assume that children don't run away from good homes and might conclude that something is wrong with the parents. Such judgments increase parents' anxiety and role strain.

   A growing number of states are passing laws increasing parental liability for teenage drinking in their homes, whether or not the parent is aware that there is underage drinking. If the intoxication contributes to driving accidents, especially those that result in car crash deaths, the parents can be

sued in civil court for millions of dollars (Schwartz, 2007). Thus, parents—rather than their children—are often held accountable for a child's misbehavior that ranges from graffiti to a car crash.

4. **High Parenting Standards.**   We receive more training to get a driver's license than we do to become parents. In contrast to previous generations, parents are now expected to live up to high standards such as being informed about the latest medical technologies, watching their children closely for early signs of physical or mental abnormalities, and consulting specialists immediately if they detect learning problems.

Parents sometimes rail against accusations that they don't take charge of their children (Nelson, 2011). The frustration increases because parents' expectations often clash with reality.

Motherhood: Ideal versus Realistic Roles

First-time mothers, especially, often face enormous pressures. The myth that mothering comes naturally creates three problems. First, it assumes that a good mother will be perfect if she simply follows her instincts. Second, it implies that there's something wrong with a mother who doesn't devote 100 percent of her time to child rearing. Third, it discourages the involvement of other adults, especially fathers.

Magazine covers routinely feature celebrity moms (such as Angelina Jolie and Halle Berry) who have chic maternity clothes, perfect hairdos and makeup, expensive baby products, and, of course, nannies. The reality is very different for the typical mother: "Real mothers are worn out by broken sleep, worries about how to split their time between paying work and child-rearing, and what to do about child care" (Fisher, 2005).

Bestselling author Elisabeth Badinter (2012: 14) claims that the realities of motherhood are often obscured by a "halo of illusions." She states, "The future mother tends to fantasize about love and happiness and overlooks the other aspects of child rearing: the exhaustion, frustration, loneliness, and even depression, with its attendant sense of guilt." Unrealistic expectations of maternal perfection and "excessive child-centeredness," according to Badinter, are sending women back to the 1950s. In many circles, babies are expected to be strapped to their mothers' bosoms for the first six months of life, continuously breast-fed, and fed organic, homemade baby food, all of which tether women to the home and prevent them from going—or going back—to work (Kolhatkar, 2012). Not all mothers are chained to their babies, however. On average, for example, stay-at-home moms with children under age 6 spend only 25 hours a week on child care (Konigsberg, 2011).

The transition to motherhood is linked to a decline in marital satisfaction, primarily because women, contrary to their expectations before childbirth, believe that the child care and increased housework is unequal and unfair (Dew and Wilcox, 2011; Perry-Jenkins and Claxton, 2011). Among all employed mothers, 62 percent of wives have a child under 6 years old (U.S. Census Bureau, Current Population Survey . . ., 2012). In this group, mothers with full-time jobs spend 15 hours a week on child care compared with less than 10 hours for fathers. Employed mothers are especially likely to experience dissatisfaction and stress if they think that their partners aren't doing their share of child care (Konigsberg, 2011).

Some researchers have attributed women's higher child care hours to **maternal gatekeeping**, mothers' behaviors that encourage or discourage a father's involvement in family matters, especially parenting infants and young children. Maternal gatekeeping can be deliberate or unconscious, but scholars usually equate the concept with negative behaviors (Allen and Hawkins, 1999; Fagan and Barnett, 2003; Biehle and Mickelson, 2012). Examples include the mother's redoing dad's diaper change because it isn't up to her standards and criticizing the father's parenting.

Are American mothers too chained to their babies?

maternal gatekeeping A mother's behavior that encourages or discourages a father's involvement in family matters.

Fred Taylor, a successful former National Football League player, said that he used to think that "his career could not be complete without at least one Pro Bowl appearance," but that was before he had four children and has enjoyed fathering them (Crouse, 2007: 1). Pictured here, Taylor is coloring with two of his children.

Read on MySocLab

Document: Fathering: Paradoxes, Contradictions, and Dilemmas

MAKING CONNECTIONS

- Who did most of the child rearing when you were growing up? If you have children now, who does most of the parenting?

- A mother wrote an essay for a newspaper about her children "boring me to death." She said, among other things, that motherhood is tedious because she hates changing diapers, reading bedtime stories, and driving her children to numerous activities every day (Soriano, 2006). Should this mom never have had children? Or should parents be more open and honest about some of the negative aspects of raising children?

When mothers are negative gatekeepers, they dampen co-parenting and, consequently, fathers start doing less housework and child care. However, fathers sometimes invite maternal gatekeeping "through hesitation and apparent incompetence, sometimes due to an honest lack of experience but other times . . . to escape child care responsibilities" (Schoppe-Sullivan, 2010: F26).

Fatherhood: Ideal versus Realistic Roles

Fathers, like mothers, experience role overload, role conflict, and role strain. Many fathers who want to participate in child care find that becoming a dad isn't as easy as they had expected. For example, a 31-year-old producer in the Public Broadcasting System says that he experienced "male postpartum depression" shortly after their son was born: "My life was gone. Movies, sleeping, long showers—all gone. We became slaves to this tiny new thing living in our home, and there was no going back." Because helping care for the infant was exhausting, "I [mourned] the loss of my life as I knew it" (Schwartzberg, 2009: 17).

Such negative emotional reactions are normal—regardless of how much fathers love their infants and children—but we rarely hear about them. Instead, like women, men often have a romanticized view of parenthood sparked by media images of fathers holding a peaceful and happy baby. In the former TV program *Guys with Kids*, the three dads often hung out at a bar. The babies never cried, fussed, or demanded attention. Viewers may realize that such shows aren't realistic, but they popularize a misconception that fatherhood requires little effort.

Generally, the greater the father's involvement in child care, the better his adjustment to his new role and the relationship between the parents. A longitudinal study followed married and cohabiting couples from pregnancy until the child was 14 months. Whether the couples had traditional or egalitarian gender role attitudes, both partners were generally happier and adjusted to their first-time parental roles more successfully if the fathers played an active role in the infants' routine care (e.g., diapered or bathed the baby) *and* developed an emotional relationship with the infant (e.g., played with the baby). Doing so decreased the mothers' stress and resulted in less conflict between the partners (Riina and Feinberg, 2012).

Problems arise not when first-time fathers devote less time to child care but when they don't live up to their partners' expectations about the division of child care. In a study of married and cohabiting couples, both partners agreed that they'd share child care tasks equally. After the baby's birth, however, mothers did more child care than they had expected. When the child care expectations were violated more than once or twice, mothers became angry, depressed, and unhappy with the fathers (Biehle and Mickelson, 2012).

The quality of the partners' relationship also affects parenting. When the relationship between parents is strong, fathers are more likely to be involved in caring for their children—behavior that benefits children, mothers, and fathers themselves (Cowan et al., 2009).

How do parents affect their children's development over time? Theorists have offered various answers to this question.

12.2 Compare three important child development theories.

Child Development Theories

Social scientists have proposed a number of theories to explain child development. Three perspectives have been especially influential. George Herbert Mead (1934, 1938, 1964) focused on social interaction as the core of the developing human

being. Jean Piaget (1932, 1954, 1960) was interested in the child's cognitive development: The ability to think, reason, analyze, and apply information (see Chapter 5). Erik Erikson (1963) combined elements of psychological and sociological perspectives to create a theory that encompassed adulthood as well as childhood. Refer to *Table 12.1* as we look briefly at these major theories.

Since you asked . . .
- What helps a child develop into a mature and productive adult?

TABLE 12.1 Some Theories of Development and Socialization

Theory of the Social Self (George Herbert Mead)	Cognitive Development Theory (Jean Piaget)	Psychosocial Theory of Human Development (Erik Erikson)
Stage 1: Imitation (roughly birth to 2) The infant does not distinguish between self and others. She or he learns behavior by mimicking significant others (primarily parents, but also siblings, teachers, and peers).	**Sensorimotor stage (birth to 2)** The child develops a physical understanding of her or his environment through touching, seeing, hearing, and moving around. The child learns the concept of object permanence (e.g., a toy exists even when it is out of sight).	**I. Trust vs. mistrust (birth to 1)** *Task:* To develop basic trust in oneself and others. *Risk:* A sense of abandonment may lead to mistrust and lack of self-confidence.
Stage 2: Play (roughly 2 to 6) As children begin to use language and continue to interact with significant others, they distinguish between "self" and "other." The child learns social norms, especially that she or he is expected to behave in certain ways. The child also begins to understand other roles in "let's pretend" and other kinds of play.	**Preoperational stage (2 to 7)** Children learn to use symbols. For example, they learn to represent a car with a block, moving the block around. They learn to use language to express increasingly complex ideas. However, they still have difficulty seeing things from another person's viewpoint.	**II. Autonomy vs. shame, doubt (2 to 3)** *Task:* To learn self-control and independence. *Risk:* Parental shaming to control the child may lead to self-doubt. **III. Initiative vs. guilt (4 to 5)** *Task:* To learn new tasks and pursue goals aggressively. *Risk:* Feeling guilty for having attempted forbidden activities or been too aggressive.
Stage 3: Games (roughly 6 and older) As children grow older and interact with a wider range of people, they learn to respond to and fulfill social roles. They learn to play multiple roles and to participate in organized activities (the "generalized other").	**Concrete operational stage (8 to 12)** Children learn to discern cause and effect: They can anticipate possible consequences of an action without having to try it out. They begin to understand the views of others. They also understand that quantities remain the same even when their shape or form changes (e.g., a fixed amount of liquid poured into a tall, thin glass and into a short, wide one is the same, even though it looks different in differently shaped containers).	**IV. Industry vs. inferiority (6 to 12)** *Task:* To develop an interest in productive work rather than just play. *Risk:* Failure or fear of failure may result in feelings of inferiority. **V. Identity vs. identity confusion (13 to 19)** *Task:* To achieve a sense of individuality and of having a place in society. *Risk:* Making important decisions may lead to confusion over who and what one wants to become. **VI. Intimacy vs. isolation (20 to 30)** *Task:* To achieve close ties with others and fulfill commitments. *Risk:* Inability to take chances by sharing intimacy may result in avoiding others or in isolation.
	Formal operational stage (13 and older) Children can reason using abstract concepts. They can understand future consequences and evaluate the probable outcomes of several alternatives. They can evaluate their own thoughts and consider major philosophical issues, such as why pain and suffering exist.	**VII. Generativity vs. self-absorption (31 to 64)** *Task:* To establish and guide the next generation—especially one's children—to create ideas and products. *Risk:* Inability to bear children or create ideas or products may lead to stagnation. **VIII. Integrity vs. despair (65 and older)** *Task:* To feel a sense of satisfaction and dignity in what one has achieved. *Risk:* Disappointments and unrealized goals may lead to feelings of alienation or despair.

Mead's Theory of the Social Self

George Herbert Mead (1863–1931), a symbolic interactionist, saw the *self* as the basis of humanity that develops not out of biological urges but from social interaction. For Mead, the newborn infant is a *tabula rasa* (the Latin phrase for a "blank slate"), with no inborn predisposition to behave in any particular way. It is only as the infant interacts with other people, Mead said, that she or he begins to develop the necessary attitudes, beliefs, and behaviors to fit into society.

The child learns first by imitating the words and behavior of significant others, the people who are important in one's life, such as parents or other primary caregivers and siblings. As the child matures, he or she understands the role of the **generalized other**, people who don't have close ties to a child but who influence the child's internalization of society's norms and roles (e.g., "Let's pretend that you're the daddy and I'm the mommy"). When the child has learned the significance of roles, according to Mead, she or he has learned to respond to the expectations of society (see Chapter 5).

generalized other People who don't have close ties to a child but who influence the child's internalization of society's norms and values.

Piaget's Cognitive Development Theory

Jean Piaget (1896–1980) was interested in the growing child's efforts to understand his or her world, to learn how to adapt to that world, and to develop an independent identity. In his four major developmental stages, Piaget traced the acquisition of abilities such as differentiating oneself from the external world; learning to use language and symbols; understanding the perspective of another person; and learning to think and reason in abstract terms about the past, the present, and the future.

Piaget believed that children play an active role in learning, processing information, and seeking knowledge. He emphasized that although some children learn faster than others, they must pass through the same four stages, at similar ages, and in the same order (see *Table 12.1*). Once children have mastered the tasks of one stage, they move on to the next, which is more difficult.

Erikson's Psychosocial Theory of Development

Erik Erikson (1902–1994) is one of the few theorists whose explanation of human development encompassed the entire life span rather than just childhood and adolescence. In each of Erikson's eight stages, the developing person faces a specific challenge, or crisis, that presents both tasks and risks.

The outcome of each crisis determines whether the individual will move on successfully to the next stage. For example, a person may leave the first stage having learned to trust other people, such as parents or caregivers, or unable to count on anyone. For Erikson, resolving each of these crises is the responsibility of the individual, but successful development also reflects the person's social relationships with family members, peers, and others.

The important point in all three of these theories is that children grow and mature by learning to deal with new expectations and changes. A child who feels loved and secure has a good chance of developing into a reasonably happy and productive member of society, one of the family's major socialization functions (see Chapter 1).

These and other theories give us some insight into children's development but say little about effective parenting styles and discipline. What works and doesn't?

This 4-year-old girl seems as engrossed in her fire engine as she might be in dressing a doll. If parents and other caretakers don't steer children toward sex-stereotypical activities, both girls and boys enjoy a variety of games and toys as they're growing up.

Parenting Styles and Discipline

Someone once said that children may not remember exactly what you did or what you said, but they'll always remember how you made them feel. How do parenting styles and discipline affect children and how they feel about themselves? Let's look at some general parenting styles and then specific beliefs about discipline.

Parenting Styles

Parenting styles make a big difference in how a child turns out. A **parenting style** is a general approach to interacting with and disciplining children. Psychologist Diana Baumrind (1968, 1989, 1991) has identified four parenting styles: authoritarian, permissive, authoritative, and uninvolved.

These four styles vary on two dimensions: support and control (see *Table 12.2*). *Support*, sometimes called responsiveness, refers to the amount of affection, acceptance, warmth, and caring that a parent provides to a child. *Control*, which Baumrind also described as demandingness, is the degree of flexibility a parent shows in guiding a child's behavior. Control can range from offering suggestions to physical abuse.

AUTHORITARIAN PARENTING   Parents who use an **authoritarian style** are often demanding, rigid, and punitive. They expect absolute obedience from their children and often use forceful measures to control their behavior. Verbal give-and-take is rare because the child is expected to accept parental authority without question ("You'll do it because I said so").

Authoritarian parents typically show their children little warmth and support. The parents may be experiencing stress due to low income, parental conflict, or substance abuse. In addition, psychological factors such as depression increase the likelihood of punitive parenting styles. Children from these homes are often irritable, belligerent, and hyperactive (Bluestone and Tamis-LeMonda, 1999; Gaertner et al., 2007; Meteyer and Perry-Jenkins, 2009).

PERMISSIVE PARENTING   In the **permissive style**, parents are usually warm and responsive but not demanding. They place few requirements on their children for orderly behavior or doing household tasks. According to one observer, permissive kids (and their parents) are "downright annoying": "I never expected prissy public behavior at a clothing store for toddlers, but an astounding number of preschool-age children were pulling clothes off hangers and onto the floor while their mothers smiled absently at them" (Klein, 2006: B11).

12.3 Compare four parenting styles and describe the most effective discipline strategies.

Read on MySocLab

Document: Parents' Socialization of Children

parenting style A general approach to interacting with and disciplining children.

Since you asked . . .
- How do parenting styles affect children's development?

authoritarian style Parenting that is demanding, controlling, rigid, and punitive.

permissive style Parenting that is usually warm, responsive, and indulgent, but not demanding.

TABLE 12.2	Four Common Parenting Styles		
	Parental Support Is . . .	Parental Control Is . . .	Example
Authoritarian	Low	High	"You can't have the car on Saturday because I said so."
Permissive	High	Low	"Sure; borrow the car whenever you want."
Authoritative	High	High	"You can borrow the car after you've picked your sister up from soccer practice."
Uninvolved	Low	Low	"I don't care what you do; don't bother me."

Instead of setting boundaries, permissive parents are indulgent. They don't bully or tyrannize their children, but adolescents raised in lenient households are often less mature, less responsible, and less able to assume leadership positions in adulthood. They're also more likely to be rebellious, impulsive, and to have behavior problems such as fighting and losing their temper (Wolfradt et al., 2003; Aunola and Nurmi, 2005).

authoritative style Parenting that is demanding but also supportive and responsive.

AUTHORITATIVE PARENTING   Parents who rely on an **authoritative style** are demanding. They impose rules and standards of behavior, but they're also responsive and supportive. These parents encourage autonomy and self-reliance and tend to use positive reinforcement rather than harsh punishment. Unlike authoritarian parents, authoritative parents encourage verbal give-and-take and believe that the child has rights. They expect obedience, but are open to discussing and changing rules in particular situations when the need arises.

One of the most consistent research findings is that authoritative parenting styles produce children who are self-reliant, achievement oriented, and more successful in school. Authoritative fathers, especially, help adolescents resist peer pressure to use drugs (Eisenberg et al., 2005; Hillaker et al., 2008).

uninvolved style Parenting that is neither supportive nor demanding because parents are indifferent.

UNINVOLVED PARENTING   In the **uninvolved style**, parents are neither supportive nor demanding because they're indifferent. They spend little time interacting with their children and know little about their whereabouts or interests. Uninvolved parents can also be rejecting: They typically ignore a child as long as she or he doesn't interfere with the parents' activities. The most extreme examples include neglectful parents who lock their children in their bedrooms for hours while the parents visit friends or go to parties (Meyer and Oberman, 2001).

Children from these homes are often immature, withdrawn, or underachieving. They may also have a variety of psychological and behavioral problems, such as drug use and bullying. Because these children are used to doing what they want, they may become rebellious when confronted with demanding teachers or other authority figures (Pellerin, 2005).

WHICH PARENTING STYLE IS THE MOST EFFECTIVE?   Healthy child development is most likely in authoritative families, in which the parents are consistent in combining warmth, monitoring, and discipline. Compared with adolescents whose parents are permissive, authoritarian, or uninvolved, children from authoritative households have better psychosocial development, higher school grades, and are less likely to be swayed by harmful peer pressure (to use drugs and alcohol, for example) (Gray and Steinberg, 1999; Barnes et al., 2000; National Center on Addiction and Substance Abuse, 2008).

Authoritarian, permissive, and authoritative parenting styles can overlap. Immigrant Chinese mothers, for example, use a combination of parenting roles. They might seem authoritarian because they have high expectations about academic success, but they're also warm, nurturing, and supportive (Cheah et al., 2009; Chua, 2011).

Parenting styles also reflect cultural values. Among many recent Latino and Asian immigrants, for example, authoritarian parenting produces positive outcomes, such as better grades. This parenting style is also more effective in safeguarding children who are growing up in communities with high levels of crime and drug peddling (Brody et al., 2002; Pong et al., 2005).

Most American studies emphasize the participation of both parents in raising well-adjusted and emotionally healthy children. In some cultures, however, fathers often play a limited role in child rearing (see "Father Involvement in Japanese Families").

Cross-Cultural and **Multicultural** Families — Father Involvement in Japanese Families

In Japan, strong societal gender stereotypes encourage the husband to be the breadwinner and the wife to be the homemaker.

If only active father–child interaction is counted (such as helping children with homework), the typical Japanese father spends only between 17 to 30 minutes with his children every day. In contrast, stay-at-home Japanese mothers spend almost seven hours with their children every weekday, one of the highest rates among industrialized and some developing countries.

Some view Japanese families as fatherless because the provider role dominates a father's life. These fathers are often called "7–11 husbands" because they leave at 7:00 A.M. and return home at 11:00 P.M.

Many Japanese fathers would like to be more involved in child rearing, but they face structural, cultural, and social barriers. A major obstacle is a corporate culture that requires long working hours, socializing with colleagues after work, and accepting job transfers that expect the father to leave his wife and children behind.

To encourage greater father involvement in child rearing, in 1995 the Japanese government passed a law that guarantees up to one year of parental leave after the arrival of a child, a subsidy equivalent to about 50 percent of the employee's regular wages, and sometimes being exempt from working overtime. Fewer than 1 percent of fathers have taken this leave or plan to do so, however. They believe that doing so would burden their co-workers,

other men at the office aren't taking the leave, employers aren't supportive, and the men fear losing their jobs.

Sources: Retherford and Ogawa, 2006; Christiansen, 2009; Porter and Sano, 2009; Shatil, 2010.

STOP AND THINK . . .

- Despite men's limited parenting, Japanese children say that they respect their fathers and appreciate their hard-working provider roles. Why, then, are many families described as fatherless?
- Do you think that Japanese fathers would take paternity leave if they received 100 percent of their regular wages or salaries?

Discipline

Children must learn discipline because self-control is *not* innate. Many parents believe that both verbal and corporal punishments are appropriate forms of discipline. Are they correct?

VERBAL PUNISHMENT A national study found that most parents, in all socioeconomic groups, used verbal and psychological aggression to control or change their children's behavior (Straus and Field, 2003):

- Fully 50 percent yelled, screamed, and shouted at their infants and 1-year-old children, and 90 percent did the same with children ages 4 to 17.

- About 33 percent swore at their children, and 17 percent admitted calling them names (such as "dumb" or "lazy").

- About 20 percent threatened, at least once, to kick the child out of the house.

These percentages are probably low because many parents don't want to admit to researchers that they abuse their children verbally. Also, because the incidents are so common, parents don't remember all of them.

CORPORAL PUNISHMENT In 2007, 94 percent of American parents hit their preschool children to correct misbehavior, which is about the same percentage as in 1975, and the hitting continued, on average, for 12 years. About 35 percent disciplined their infants by slapping a hand or leg; pinching; shaking; hitting the buttocks with a hand, belt, or paddle; or slapping the infant's face. More than 50 percent of parents hit their children at age 12, 33 percent at age 14, and 13 percent at age 17. Parents who hit their teenagers did so an average of about six times a year (Straus and Stewart, 1999; Straus, 2008).

As with verbal punishment, corporal punishment rates are probably higher. However, parents don't want to admit, especially regarding very young children,

Since you asked . . .
- Does spanking improve children's behavior?

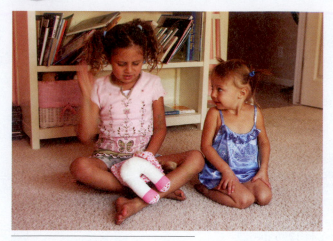

Even very young children imitate the behavior that they see or experience.

that they're more likely to spank their toddlers than to use other disciplinary methods such as time-outs (see Barkin et al., 2007).

Physical punishment of infants and children tends to be more common among low-income parents; those with less than a high school education; parents in the South; boys (particularly first-borns); mothers who have experienced physical abuse as children; and unmarried mothers, especially those under age 33. The mothers have less time and fewer money resources to engage their children in activities that relieve boredom. Mothers who move in with their romantic partners are more likely to spank their children than those who live only with their children. The residential change may raise mothers' stress that, in turn, increases the likelihood of corporal punishment (Guzzo and Lee, 2008; Chung et al., 2009; Holden, 2011).

DOES CORPORAL PUNISHMENT WORK? Physical punishment stops misbehavior in the short term, but usually has serious long-term negative outcomes. Researchers who examined 20 years of research concluded that, regardless of the country or methodology, "Virtually without exception, these studies found that physical punishment was associated with higher levels of aggression against parents, siblings, peers, and spouses" (Durrant and Ensom, 2012: 1373).

Much of the recent research on the physical punishment of infants and children has drawn the same conclusions as earlier studies: Corporal punishment increases externalizing behavior (e.g., arguing, fighting, lying, cheating, stealing, lashing out physically against people and animals, having temper tantrums, and being defiant). Externalizing behavior becomes more severe between ages 1 and

Choices   Is Spanking Effective or Harmful?

So far, 31 nations have passed laws that prohibit the corporal punishment of children (Durrant and Ensom, 2012). The United States isn't one of them. In fact, a large majority of Americans support spanking (see Data Digest).

A study that examined 14 European nations found that the countries that prohibit children's physical punishment have a much lower number of child maltreatment deaths than the countries that don't have such laws. Initially, many Swedes opposed anti-spanking laws, predicting that the children would run wild. Instead, youth crime rates, drug use, and suicide rates decreased (Straus, 2007; Gracia and Herrero, 2008).

In the United States, some spanking advocates maintain that spanking is effective, prepares children for life's hardships, and prevents misbehavior. They contend that spanking is acceptable if it's age appropriate, doesn't injure the child physically, and is used selectively to teach and correct behavior rather than as an expression of rage (Trumbull and Ravenel, 1999; Larzelere and Baumrind, 2010). In contrast,

researchers have offered a number of reasons for not spanking or hitting children:

- *Physical punishment sends the message that it's okay to hurt someone you love or someone who is smaller and less powerful.* A parent who spanks often says, "I'm doing this because I love you." Thus, children learn that violence and love can go hand in hand and that hitting is an appropriate way to express one's feelings (Hunt, 1991).

- *No human being feels loving toward someone who hits her or him.* A strong relationship is based on kindness. Hitting produces only temporary and superficially good behavior based on fear (Marshall, 2002).

- *Physical punishment is often due to a parent's substance abuse rather than a child's misbehavior.* Parents who abuse drugs are often ineffective caregivers because intoxication impairs their decision-making abilities. They're also likely to spend their time getting

and using drugs instead of caring for their children (Straus, 2007, 2008).

- *Spanking can be physically damaging.* Spanking can injure the spinal column and nerves and even cause paralysis. Some children have died after mild paddlings because of undiagnosed medical problems such as a weak lower spinal column that can't withstand a blow (American Academy of Pediatrics, 1998).

- *Physical punishment deprives the child of opportunities to learn effective problem solving.* Physical punishment teaches a child nothing about how to handle conflict or disagreements (Straus, 2010).

STOP AND THINK

- When you were a child, did your parents spank you? Did the spanking change your behavior?
- Should the United States ban spanking? Or would such laws interfere with parenting decisions?

5; consequently, spanking often becomes harsher by the time children are 6 years old, thus creating a vicious cycle. When children who were punished physically at an early age enter preschool, they have more behavior problems (such as talking back to teachers and fighting with classmates) than their nonspanked counterparts (Spieker et al., 1999; Gershoff, 2002; Slade and Wissow, 2004; Taylor et al., 2010; Gromoske and Maguire-Jack, 2012; Lansford et al., 2012).

The negative effects of corporal punishment continue into adolescence and adulthood. Adolescents who grow up in authoritarian homes (in which parents rely on spanking as a form of discipline) are more likely than children raised in authoritative homes to experience depressive symptoms such as sadness and anxiety, as well as mood swings and feeling worthless. They're more likely than their nonspanked counterparts to hit their parents and other children and to physically abuse their dating and marital partners and their own children later in life. Moreover, 2 to 7 percent of mental disorders in adulthood are linked to childhood physical punishment (Christie-Mizell et al., 2008; Straus, 2010; Afifi et al., 2012).

Because of such empirical findings, many, but not all, researchers and pediatricians believe that physical punishment is a futile disciplinary method (see "Is Spanking Effective or Harmful?"). Instead, they recommend nonphysical forms of punishment, such as removing temptations to misbehave, making rules simple, being consistent, setting a good example, and disciplining with love and patience instead of anger.

WHAT'S A PARENT TO DO? Most self-help books and self-proclaimed child experts instruct parents to always praise their kids to get them to behave. Such advice is misguided because it's not supported by research. For example, a recent study reviewed 41 studies of discipline strategies targeted at children ranging from 18 months to 11 years old. The researchers found that reprimands and negative nonverbal parental behaviors (e.g., stern looks, time-outs, taking away privileges) were more effective in improving children's behavior than constant praise or nonverbal responses (e.g., hugs and rewards such as ice cream). In the long run, consistent and well-deserved (not constant) praise strengthens the parent–child relationship (Owen et al., 2012; Petersen, 2012).

Effective discipline involves more than rewards and punishments. Children need three types of inner resources if they're to become responsible adults: positive feelings about themselves and others, an understanding of right and wrong, and alternatives for solving problems. "Some Building Blocks of Effective Discipline" describes 10 building blocks that parents can use to develop their children's inner resources.

MAKING CONNECTIONS
- Many adults who were raised in authoritarian and permissive homes are successful, happy, and confident. Why, then, do researchers maintain that authoritative parenting is the most effective?
- According to one of my students, "Spank while they're little so the law doesn't later." Do you agree?

Applying What You've Learned — Some Building Blocks of Effective Discipline

As you read these suggestions, think about what worked for you when you were growing up. If you're a parent, which of this advice do you think is most effective? And what would you add to this list?

- **Show your love.** You can express your love not only through a warm facial expression, a kind tone, and a hug but also by doing things with your children, such as working on a project together, letting them help with grocery shopping, and reading their favorite books. When children feel loved, they want to please their parents and are less likely to engage in undesirable behaviors.
- **Be consistent.** Predictable parents are just as important as routines and schedules. A child who is allowed to

do something one day and not the next can become confused and start testing the rules.

- **Communicate clearly.** Ask children about their interests and feelings. Whenever possible, encourage them. Constant nagging, reminding, criticizing, threatening, lecturing, questioning, and demanding make a child feel dumb or inadequate.
- **Understand problem behavior.** Observe a problem behavior and look for a pattern that may explain why; for example, a child becomes unusually cranky when tired or hungry. Children may also have behavioral problems because their parents are experiencing a stressful event, such as losing a job or divorce.

(continued)

- **Be positive and patient.** Sometimes children act up because they want attention. Patience and approval of good conduct encourage children to repeat the positive behavior.

- **Set up a safe environment.** Children are curious and eager to learn (see *Table 12.1* on page 337). Removing hazards shortens the list of "no's," and changing play locations relieves boredom and prevents destructive behavior.

- **Make realistic rules.** Set few rules, state them simply, and supervise closely. Don't expect more than your child can handle; for instance, don't expect a toddler to sit quietly during long religious services.

- **Defuse explosions.** Try to avert temper tantrums and highly charged confrontations (for example, distract feuding preschoolers by involving them in other activities).

- **Teach problem-solving skills.** Children younger than 4 years old need very specific guidance in solving a problem and positive reinforcement for following suggestions.

- **Give children reasonable choices.** Don't force them to do things that even you wouldn't want to do (such as eating a vegetable they hate). Removing children from the play area when they misbehave, and giving them a choice of other activities, is often more effective than scolding, yelling, or punishing.

Sources: Goddard, 1994; Rosemond, 2000.

12.4 Compare parenting variations by race, ethnicity, and social class.

Parenting Variations by Race, Ethnicity, and Social Class

There's no recipe for good parenting. Instead, much depends on variables such as whether there are one or two adults in the home, whether the parents are married or cohabiting, the number of children that demand parental time, and the degree and quality of parent–child interaction (see Dye and Johnson, 2007). Race, ethnicity, and social class intersect in shaping family life.

Parenting across Racial-Ethnic Families

We looked at socialization practices across racial-ethnic families in Chapter 4. A specific child-rearing task is spending time with children, but child outcomes are also linked to the quality of the parent–child relationship.

Read on MySocLab

Document: Our Mothers' Grief: Racial-Ethnic Women and the Maintenance of Families

SPENDING TIME WITH CHILDREN   An important factor in a child's well-being is the type and amount of interaction between children and parents. Interaction includes reading to children and taking them on outings.

Reading is an important activity: It stimulates a child's cognitive and intellectual abilities, it's a way for parents to spend time with their youngsters, and it prepares children for kindergarten. In 2007, only 26 percent of Latino children ages 3 to 5—compared with at least 44 percent of white, black, and Asian American children—had skills such as recognizing the alphabet, counting to 20 or higher, and reading storybooks (U.S. Census Bureau, Current Population Survey . . ., 2012).

Latino parents are less likely to read to their young children than are African American, Asian American, and white parents (see *Table 12.3*). However, Latino parents (51 percent) are as likely as black parents (51 percent), almost as likely as white parents (56 percent), and more likely than Asian American parents (48 percent) to want their children to graduate from college ("Half of Young Children . . .," 2011). Many Latino parents have high educational aspirations for their offspring, but don't always have the time, English language skills, or energy to engage in daily reading activities that lay a foundation for high educational attainment.

Another way to spend time with children is to take them on outings such as to a park, playground, or zoo, or to visit friends or relatives. Such trips provide opportunities for parents to talk to their children, get to know them, and enrich the children's knowledge. Among children age 11 and younger, 69 percent of white children have 15 or more outings with their parents per month compared with 55 percent of Asian American children, 47 percent of Latino children, and 43 percent of black children ("Half of Young Children . . .," 2011).

TABLE 12.3 How Often Do Parents Read to Their Kids?		
Percentage of Children Read to 7 or More Times a Week		
Race or Ethnicity of Child	Children 1 to 2 Years Old	Children 3 to 5 Years Old
White	64	56
Asian	54	51
Black	42	42
Latino	36	38

Source: Based on data in "Half of Young Children . . .," 2011, Table D9.

There may be several explanations for these racial and ethnic variations in parental reading and outings. One is marital status. African American children are the most likely to live with only one parent, usually the mother (see Chapter 4). Many single parents who work have less time and energy to interact with their children. In multigenerational homes—which tend to be black, Asian American, and Latino—mothers may be caring for older family members and depend on their children, sometimes as young as age 8, for help (see Chapter 16). Moreover, recent immigrants who don't speak English well may be uncomfortable with or unaware of recreational opportunities outside the home that are free to the public.

Many schools encourage minority dads, grandfathers, and uncles to visit schools and become more involved in their children's education.

QUALITY OF PARENTAL RELATIONSHIP A national study of adults whose children were between the ages of 6 to 17 examined the association between the quality of the parents' relationship and children's outcomes. The researchers found that, almost without exception, parents who described their relationship as happy reported that their children had few behavior problems, got along well with peers and teachers, cared about doing well in school, and discussed problems with their parents. The association between the quality of the parents' relationship and children's positive outcomes held across all racial-ethnic families and whether the parents were married or cohabiting (Moore et al., 2011). Such findings don't mean that the quality of the parents' relationship *causes* better-adjusted kids because social class is an important variable that has long-term effects on children.

Parenting and Social Class

Social scientists typically measure social class using **socioeconomic status (SES)**, an overall ranking of a person's position in society based on income, education, and occupation. Sociologists have delineated as many as nine social classes in the United States (see the classic study by Warner and Lunt, 1941).

For our purposes, *low-SES families* are those at the bottom of the economic ladder because the parents have little education and few occupational skills, work in minimum wage jobs, or are often unemployed. Most of the low-SES families are poor, but many are headed by a married couple with at least one full-time, full-year worker (see Chapter 13).

In *middle-SES* families, the parents have a high school diploma and work in blue-collar or white-collar jobs. Middle-SES families also include parents who usually have college degrees and work in semi-professional occupations such as nursing, social work, and teaching.

In *high-SES* families, the parents' occupations—mainly professional and managerial—usually require a Ph.D. or advanced degree in business, law, or medicine.

socioeconomic status (SES) An overall ranking of a person's position in society based on income, education, and occupation.

 Explore on MySocLab

Activity: Parenting in the Twin Cities

This group also includes super-rich families that have inherited their wealth (such as the Kennedy family in Massachusetts), and those who have earned rather than inherited their wealth (such as Oprah Winfrey and Mark Zuckerberg, the cofounder and CEO of Facebook).

Since you asked . . .
• How does social class affect parenting?

LOW-SES FAMILIES Most low-SES parents, especially recent immigrants, must grapple with numerous obstacles. Macro-level problems such as poverty, unemployment, and racism often create interpersonal conflict. Besides living in high-crime neighborhoods, children have little physical space at home and usually attend schools that are overcrowded, underfunded, and offer few extracurricular activities (Fuligni and Yoshikawa, 2003; Votruba-Drzal, 2003; Hernandez, 2011).

Depression is higher among economically disadvantaged mothers than among higher income mothers because of the stresses of poverty and unhappy relationships. Because depressed mothers are more likely to use harsh discipline strategies or no strategies at all, their children are more likely to act out and get into trouble at school and in the community as early as the third grade (Moore et al., 2006).

The most vulnerable low-SES families are those formed by adolescents. Often, teenage parents don't have the skills to maintain a relationship, don't have a strong parenting alliance in raising children (especially if they're no longer romantically involved), and have few resources to ensure their children's healthy development. Such problems may appear or worsen when young fathers experience employment problems because of low educational levels or if one or both partners have additional nonmarital children (Futris and Schoppe-Sullivan, 2007; Chrisler and Moore, 2012).

Especially in disadvantaged single-mother families, children are likely to experience *adultification*, a developmental process in which, although prematurely and often inappropriately, a child assumes extensive adult family roles and responsibilities (see Chapter 16). Preteen children, for example, may have to raise younger siblings when a parent is chronically ill, has mental health problems, or abuses drugs. Adultification often leads to dropping out of school, poor academic performance, feeling anxious or depressed, and even forgoing marriage. For instance, here are the thoughts of a 68-year-old African American man:

> I've been taking care of my family members since I was five and my mother told me that's what I should do. I go from one house to the other, taking care of newborn babies and sick relatives. I go where I am needed. . . . There was never any time to marry (Burton, 2007: 342).

MIDDLE-SES FAMILIES Middle-SES parents have more resources (money, time, education) to enhance their children's emotional, social, and cognitive development. Middle-SES mothers talk to their infants more, and in more sophisticated ways, than do low-SES mothers. Such interaction encourages children's self-expression and builds a vocabulary. Middle-SES parents are also more likely than lower-SES parents to seek professional advice about a child's healthy development (Bornstein, 2002; Goodman et al., 2008; Rowe and Goldin-Meadow, 2009).

Having books in the home can make a big difference in children's schooling. A study was conducted over 20 years, in 27 countries, and surveyed more than 70,000 people. The researchers found that, whether the parents went to college or had blue-collar jobs, a child whose family had only 25 books completed two more years of school than a child whose family had no books. The more books in the home, the greater the educational benefit: When parents read stories at bedtime, children learn more words and hone their reading skills (Evans et al., 2010). Public library books are free, but middle-SES parents are more likely than their low-SES counterparts to give their children books as presents and to read them together.

Children who are exposed to books and reading at a young age do better in school than those who come from homes without books.

HIGH-SES FAMILIES The more money parents have, the more they can spend on education, health care, books, and other goods and services that enhance their children's life chances and occupational success. As *Table 12.4* shows,

TABLE 12.4 Child-Rearing Expenditures from Birth to Age 17, by Social Class, 2012		
	Average Annual Family Income	Total Expenditure per Child
Low-SES families	$38,790	$173,490
Middle-SES families	$81,600	$241,080
High-SES families	$183,770	$399,780

Source: Based on Lino, 2013, Table 1.

from birth to age 17, a high-income family spends more than twice as much as a low-income family on a child. As a result, a child in a high-income family enjoys considerably more material resources than does a child in a middle- or low-income family.

You saw earlier that a majority of racial-ethnic parents *want* their children to get a college degree. However, only half of parents with annual incomes of less than $25,000, compared with 88 percent of parents with incomes over $75,000, *expect* their child to attain a four-year-college degree. At the lower end of the education continuum, low-income parents are more than eight times as likely as wealthier parents to expect their child to do no more than finish high school (19 percent and 2 percent, respectively). Because higher-income parents expect, rather than hope, that their children will graduate from college, they talk about what's going on in the classroom, provide out-of-school learning opportunities, foster positive attitudes toward school, and applaud academic achievement. As a result, the children internalize personal goals that include earning a college degree (Child Trends Data Bank, 2012).

Parenting in Lesbian and Gay Families

Of the nearly 650,000 same-sex couples who live in the United States, an estimated 19 percent of same-sex households include children under age 18. Of these households, 27 percent of the parents are lesbians and nearly 11 percent are gay men (Gates, 2013). Thus, large numbers of same-sex couples are raising children.

How Same-Sex and Opposite-Sex Parenting Is Similar

A study that examined more than 100 scientific publications over 30 years concluded that children's well-being is affected much more by their relationships with their parents, parental competence and stability, and the parents' social and economic support than by the parents' gender or sexual orientation (Perrin and Siegel, 2013). In most respects, lesbian and gay families are like heterosexual families: Parents must make a living and juggle work and domestic responsibilities, family members may disagree about the use of space or money, and both children and parents must develop problem-solving skills (Goldberg and Sayer, 2006).

A longitudinal study that began in 1987 followed lesbian mothers and their 78 children (by donor insemination) from birth to age 17. The researchers found that the children grew up to be healthy, happy, and well-adjusted teenagers. There were no differences in psychological adjustment, gender identity, and gender scripts between adolescents raised by the lesbian mothers and heterosexual parents. The teens got good grades, enjoyed close friendships, and gave their mothers

12.5 Compare parenting in same-sex and opposite-sex couples.

Since you asked . . .
- Are children raised by same-sex parents different from those raised by opposite-sex parents?

 Watch on MySocLab

Video: Same Sex Marriages and Families

Employed mothers, regardless of sexual orientation, have to struggle to be able to spend quality time with their children.

high marks as role models. Also, almost 3 percent of the teens (all of them boys) identified themselves as predominantly to exclusively homosexual compared with almost 4 percent of their counterparts in the general population (Bos et al., 2012; Gartrell et al., 2012; van Gelderen et al., 2012a).

Lesbian and gay parents tend to co-parent more equally than heterosexual parents, but the division of labor isn't "genderless." One parent tends to do more of the child care and housework, and the partner who provides a larger portion of the household income usually has more power in making financial decisions. Also, as in the case of opposite-sex parent households, lesbian and gay parents are more accepting when daughters, but not sons, violate gender stereotypes (e.g., it's all right for girls to play baseball but not for boys to play with Barbie dolls) (Biblarz and Savci, 2010).

How Same-Sex and Opposite-Sex Parenting Differ

Young children, especially, often think that having same-sex parents is "no big deal." According to one 8-year-old, for example, "I just say I have two moms— 'Mom' and 'Mamma Sheri.' They're no different from other parents except that they're two girls" (Gilgoff, 2004: 42). Nationally, however, 35 percent of Americans, although down from 50 percent in 2007, say that gay and lesbian couples raising children is "a bad thing for society" (Kohut et al., 2011).

Because of such negative views, gay and lesbian parents face the burden of raising children who often experience prejudice and discrimination because of their parents' sexual orientation. Adolescents are most likely to be stigmatized by their classmates, but also encounter negative reactions from teachers, extended family members, friends' parents, employers, and sometimes even strangers. The stigmatization includes teasing, ridicule, disapproval, being asked annoying question about their parents, stereotyped as being "different," and excluded from social and family activities (van Gelderen et al., 2012a, 2012b).

Lesbian and gay parents must deal not only with such interpersonal stigmas but also with legal exclusion in the many states that prohibit same-sex marriages (see Chapter 10). Some adolescents and young adults with lesbian, gay, and bisexual parents don't believe that same-sex marriages should be legalized because of potential disadvantages such as divorce. They recognize, however, that they and their parents don't benefit from a range of legal protections that would make their lives easier (Goldberg and Kuvalanka, 2012).

Most of us associate child rearing with raising children and adolescents, but parenting spans a lifetime. Because people live much longer than in the past, they also create multigenerational families.

12.6 Describe parenting across the life course.

Parenting over the Life Course

Raising children from infancy to adulthood requires numerous adjustments over time. Because constructive or harmful parenting practices can be passed down to the next generation, understanding the changes that take place over the life course can improve family relationships (Chen and Kaplan, 2001).

Parenting Infants and Babies

Infancy, the period of life between birth and about 18 months, encompasses only a small fraction of the average person's life span but is a period of both extreme helplessness and enormous physical and cognitive growth. Myths create unnecessary anxiety and guilt for many parents because they have false expectations or unrealistic goals.

SOME MYTHS ABOUT BABIES Some of the ideas parents have about child development, especially from self-help books and talk shows, reflect common misperceptions about a baby's early years. Here are some of the most widespread myths about babies:

1. *Myth 1:* *You can tell in infancy how bright a child is likely to be later on.* A baby's early achievements—such as reaching, sitting, crawling, or talking—are rarely good indicators of intelligence. For example, early agility in building with blocks or imitating words has almost no relationship to later performance in school (Segal, 1989).

2. *Myth 2:* *The more stimulation a baby gets, the better.* Babies can be overstimulated, agitated, or even frightened into withdrawal by constant assaults on their senses by an intrusive rattle, toy, or talking face. Millions of parents buy enrichment products such as flash cards and educational software for children as young as 6 months ("Your baby will learn the numbers 1–20!" according to some ads). Baby DVDs may be doing more harm than good because infants 8 to 16 months old who watch them learn fewer words than those whose parents talk to them, tell them stories, and expose them to a rich vocabulary (Zimmerman et al., 2007).

3. *Myth 3:* *Parents who pick up crying babies will spoil them.* It's impossible to spoil a child who is younger than 1 year old. Crying is the only way a baby can tell parents that he or she is hungry, wet, soiled, or sick. Parents should pick up their baby as much as they want and not worry about discipline at such a young age (Bornstein, 2002).

4. *Myth 4:* *Special talents surface early or not at all.* Many gifted children don't recognize or develop their skills until adolescence or later. For example, jazz musician Louis Armstrong was a neglected and abandoned child. It was only years later, when he was living in the New Orleans Colored Waifs Home for Boys, that he was taught to play a trumpet, and his talent was ignited.

5. *Myth 5:* *Parental conflicts don't affect babies.* Babies as young as 1 year old understand the facial expressions and voice tones of people around them and react accordingly. Thus, parental yelling or arguing affects a baby (Mumme and Fernald, 2003).

Children typically learn more by interacting with a parent than by playing with educational toys.

BED SHARING *Bed sharing,* an infant's or child's sleeping in the same bed as a parent, common throughout much of the world, is a recent and controversial trend in the United States. Some groups and pediatricians advocate bed sharing. They contend that bed sharing promotes parent–infant bonding, makes nighttime breast-feeding easier, and gives everyone a good night's sleep. The mother may "instinctively" awaken if the baby's breathing changes. Proponents also say that when mothers work outside the home, bed sharing gives them more opportunities to touch and be close to the infant, both of which are beneficial to the baby's development (Sears et al., 2005).

A study of bed-sharing mothers differentiated between "intentional bed sharers," parents who endorse the ideology of bed sharing, and "reactive bed sharers," parents who reluctantly bed share because of an infant's nighttime problems. The researchers found that marital satisfaction declined and stress rose for the reactive but not intentional bed sharers (Messmer et al., 2012). Thus, bed sharing benefits some parents more than others.

Since you asked . . .
- Is sharing a bed with a baby healthy or risky?

These preschoolers are attentive to their teacher's instructions on how to use a computer. If they're loved and supported by their parents and families, children are more likely to meet this and other challenges successfully.

The American Academy of Pediatrics and many health providers discourage bed sharing with infants: It can lead to accidental deaths if the infant falls out of bed or becomes wedged between a wall and a mattress or under a pillow, or when a parent rolls on top of the baby. Infants are especially vulnerable if a parent is obese or using alcohol or other drugs. The risk of *sudden infant death syndrome* (SIDS) increases anywhere from two- to tenfold when parents bed share, but medical researchers don't know why (Ogilvie, 2012).

Another problem is that children who sleep with parents at an early age often continue to do so until they're even 11 years old because they have nightmares, are afraid of severe weather, or just want more attention. Some parents are paying "sleep consultants" up to $400 an hour to learn how to dislodge their children from their beds (P. Green, 2007: D1).

Parenting Children

The quality of relationships with adults and other caregivers has a profound effect on a child's development. Some wonder, however, whether American parents have become too involved in their children's lives.

DAILY INTERACTION   Engaging infants in talk increases their vocabulary. By age 2, toddlers who know more words have better language skills that, in turn, help them control their behavior at age 3 and later. Instead of getting frustrated and having tantrums, children who have better language skills can voice their thoughts and are better at taking charge of a situation (Vallotton and Ayoub, 2011).

A majority of children interact with their parents quite a bit. About 72 percent have dinner with one or both parents every day, 57 percent receive parental praise three or more times a day, and the same percentage talks or plays together with a parent three of more times in a typical day ("Half of Young Children . . .," 2011). And, as you saw earlier, father's child-rearing participation has increased.

PARENTS' AND CHILDREN'S INPUTS   Parents shape a child's environment, but each baby has its own genes, physical appearance, temperament, and personality. Some children are easier to satisfy and soothe and have a happy demeanor. Others are more cautious and shy. Still others are difficult to please and seem constantly dissatisfied (Ambert, 2001).

There can be considerable differences between children's personality and behavior in the same family, and even between identical twins. One of my colleagues tells the story of his twin girls, who received exactly the same dolls when they were 3 years old. When the parents asked the girls what they would name the dolls, one twin chattered that the doll's name was Lori, that she loved Lori, and she would take good care of her. The second twin muttered, "Her name is Stupid," and flung the doll into a corner. By adolescence, identical twins can be very different emotionally even though they're the same age, gender, ethnicity, and social class; live in the same community; attend the same school; and share the same genetically based traits (Crosnoe and Elder, 2002; Lytton and Gallagher, 2002).

IS CHILDHOOD TOO MEDICALIZED?   In 1952, the American Psychiatric Association published the first edition of the *Diagnostic and Statistical Manual of Mental Disorders*, which describes mental-health disorders for children and adults. The number of disorders increased from 106 in 1952 to more than 300 in 2013, especially for childhood disorders.

The *DSM*'s ever-changing diagnoses and labels is an example of **medicalization**, a process that defines a nonmedical condition or behavior as an illness, disorder,

medicalization Defining a nonmedical condition or behavior as an illness, disorder, or disease that requires medical treatment.

or disease that requires medical treatment. For example, children with attention and behavior problems are now defined and treated with drugs for attention deficit hyperactivity disorder (ADHD). Since the 1990s, there's been a 900 percent increase in prescriptions for Ritalin, a drug for ADHD (Waters, 2011).

Many researchers and policy analysts are concerned that, because of the growth of medicalization, physicians and parents are increasingly overmedicating children. A study of 200,000 children ages 2 to 4 found that almost 2 percent were receiving stimulants (such as Ritalin), antidepressants (such as Prozac), or tranquilizers. About 4 percent of children ages 5 to 14 took Ritalin. By age 20, children might be taking a range of potent drugs that have been tested only on adults (Zito et al., 2003).

In 2002, psychiatrists prescribed antipsychotic drugs to children and adolescents at five times the rate they did in 1993. A third of the children—primarily white boys—were diagnosed as having "behavior disorders" and received new drugs that were usually given only to adults. Because they're largely untested, no one knows how the drugs will affect children in the long run (Olfson et al., 2006).

Some believe that the *DSM* is little more than an excellent doorstop because it medicalizes childhood behavior that, in the past, was deemed normal or simply disobedient (Carey, 2008). However, medicalization is lucrative for physicians, pharmacists, and particularly pharmaceutical corporations (Herzberg, 2009). It also benefits parents. For example, if children have been diagnosed with ADHD, frequent temper tantrums and irritability (Disruptive Mood Dysregulation Disorder, DMDD), or other *DSM* maladies, they're likely to be covered by insurance plans or receive special treatment, such as more attention from teachers and health specialists (Stetka, 2013).

ARE CHILDREN OVERSCHEDULED? Psychologist David Elkind (2007) has criticized children's hurried lives and scolded parents for pushing children to grow up too fast. Over the past two decades, he maintains, children have lost 12 hours of free time a week, including unstructured play at home and outside. Organized and more sedentary activities have replaced free play, Elkind says, and are less likely to enrich children's imagination, curiosity, creativity, and interaction with peers.

Others argue that not having enough free play time has been greatly exaggerated. Structured activities increase children's self-confidence and provide valuable interpersonal interactions. Only about 6 percent of American adolescents spend more than 20 hours a week in highly organized activities. In addition, some social scientists contend, organized activities are exciting and enjoyable; offer new skills (such as learning a sport); provide opportunities to interact with both peers and adults; and decrease the likelihood of engaging in unhealthy behaviors such as smoking, drinking, and using drugs (Mahoney et al., 2006).

Since you asked . . .
• Are children's lives too rushed?

Parenting Teenagers

Adolescence is a time of tremendous change. Teenagers are establishing their own identity and testing their autonomy as they mature and break away from parental supervision, a healthy process in human development (see Erikson's stages in *Table 12.1* on page 337).

CHANGES IN PARENT–CHILD RELATIONSHIPS A good parent–child relationship may shift suddenly during adolescence. As teenagers become more independent and more likely to confide in friends, parents may feel rejected and suspicious. The most difficult part of parenting adolescents, according to some mothers, is dealing with their changing moods and behavior: "She used to chatter incessantly on car rides; now . . . 'What's new in school today?' you ask. 'Nothing,' she answers" (Patner, 1990: C5). One mother dragged

Are American children overscheduled? Or have too much free play time?

Constraints   Should Parents Track Their Children?

2013 ("Chips off the Old Block," 2013; see also Brenoff, 2013).

Parents contend that such high-tech devices increase their children's safety, especially because kids will act more responsibly if they know they're being watched. Some teenagers don't mind the monitoring because it cuts down on annoying phone calls and text messages from their parents.

However, many teens and young adults complain that they feel like prisoners. "It's annoying," grumbles a 15-year-old who has been caught in a few places where he wasn't supposed to be: "It gives parents too much control." Some college students have simply left their GPS-enabled cell phones under their dorm room beds when they went off with friends ("High-Tech Gadgets . . .," 2005: B5).

Car accidents are the chief cause of death and disability among teenagers, who are killed at four times the rate of adults. There are many contributing factors, such as inexperience behind the wheel, being distracted by cell phones and text messages, and over-confidence in their skills, but three of the most common reasons are speed, intoxication, and driving with someone who's drunk (Lyon, 2009).

Increasingly, parents are using high-tech methods to track everything from where their children are driving to what they buy and whether they show up for classes. One gadget is a cell phone that transmits location data. Another device is a debit-like card used at school lunch counters. The car chip and the global positioning system (GPS), installed in a vehicle, monitor speed, distance, and driving habits.

The widespread use of smartphones has made parents' tracking their children easier than ever before. For example, the registered users of Life360, a free tracking app, rocketed from 1 million users in 2010 to nearly 25 million in early

STOP AND THINK . . .

- Do tracking devices keep teens and young adults safer? Or intrude on their privacy?
- Parents are accountable, even legally, for their teens' behavior. So should parents keep tabs on their children? Or should teens and young adults be allowed to learn from their mistakes, as their parents did?

Since you asked . . .

- Should parents demand more of their teens and not the other way around?

her 13-year-old son to a local hospital for a battery of tests: She was convinced that he had a hearing problem because he never seemed to respond to what she was saying (Shatzkin, 2004). As teens withdraw from the family, their parents try to keep in touch with them. Others take more drastic measures (see "Should Parents Track Their Children?").

For many years, people attributed such dramatic changes to "raging hormones." Scientists now believe that there's a link between a teen's baffling behavior and the fact that his or her brain may be changing far more than was thought previously. During adolescence, the brain matures at different rates. Areas involved in basic functions such as processing information from the senses and controlling physical movement mature first. The parts of the brain responsible for controlling impulses, avoiding risky behavior, and planning ahead—the hallmarks of adult behavior—are among the last to mature (National Institute of Mental Health, 2011).

In effect, then, "The teenage brain . . . is a turbocharged car with a set of brakes still under construction. It is primed to seek rewards and take risks," especially when adolescents are with friends (Monastersky, 2007: A16, A17). This may explain, in part, why adolescents have more accidents when there are other passengers, usually friends, in the car. In 2011, for example, of all teenage car crashes, 80 percent of those who died were passengers (Insurance Institute for Highway Safety, 2013; see also Copeland, 2013).

HELICOPTER AND PROBLEM PARENTS   Parental involvement is usually beneficial in a child's development, but "helicopter parents," who hover over their kids, are hyperinvolved, intrusive, and overcontrolling. Helicopter parenting can occur at any childhood or adult stage, but usually refers to parents of adolescents and young adults. Anecdotal examples include parents verbally attacking teachers about their adolescents' low grades, demanding that their child be moved to another class before the school year has even begun, completing difficult homework assignments, showing up in the guidance counselor's office with college applications that they have filled out for their children, and haggling with college professors over the student's grade on an exam or paper (Krache, 2008; Weintraub, 2010; Rochman, 2013).

Helicopter parenting diminishes teens' and young adults' ability to develop decision-making and problem-solving skills. However well-intentioned, helicopter parents increase their own stress and decrease their children's feelings of autonomy and competence. In turn, not believing in one's ability to successfully accomplish tasks and achieve goals on one's own leads to young adults' feeling anxious, depressed, and more dissatisfied with life (Schiffrin et al., 2013). Helicopter parenting also lowers the quality of parent–child communication because neither talks openly about their true feelings, and increases the young adult's sense of entitlement (e.g., "I deserve an extra break" or "I get annoyed by people who aren't interested in what I say or do") (Segrin et al., 2012).

Another widespread dilemma is what a report described as "problem parents"—those who by their actions or inactions increase their teenage children's risk of engaging in unhealthy behavior (see *Table 12.5*). The report concluded that "problem parents are a big part of why so many teens smoke, drink, get drunk and abuse illegal and prescription drugs" (National Center on Addiction and Substance Abuse, 2008: iii).

Simply telling teens to do or not to do something is much less effective than being a good role model. At any age, children pay closer attention to what parents do than what they preach: "Even fiercely independent teens are heavily influenced by their parents, so if you drink excessively or use drugs, don't be surprised if your teen follows suit." And, despite growing awareness about teen prescription drug addiction and the risk of overdose, most parents are convinced that *their* kids don't use drugs (Sack, 2013).

TABLE 12.5   **Are Parents Promoting Their Teens' Substance Abuse?**

According to the National Center on Addiction and Substance Abuse (2008), many parents don't monitor their 12- to 17-year-olds' behavior, which increases the likelihood of substance abuse. For example,

- 86 percent of parents said that their children are always at home by 10:00 P.M. on school nights (Monday through Thursday), but 46 percent of teens reported hanging out with their friends and not being at home by 10:00 P.M. on those nights.
- 76 percent of parents believed it's realistic to expect their teens not to smoke cigarettes; fewer than 66 percent felt the same way about their children's use of marijuana (which is now more common than smoking cigarettes).
- 50 percent of the prescription drugs that teenagers used to get high came from their parents' medicine cabinets.
- 25 percent of teens knew a parent of a classmate or friend who used marijuana; 10 percent said that a parent smoked marijuana with the teen's friends.

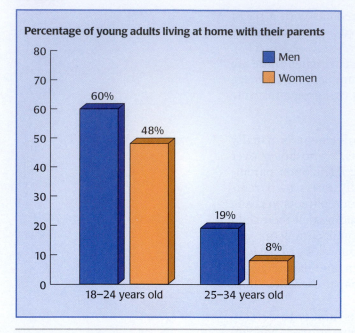

Percentage of young adults living at home with their parents

FIGURE 12.1 **Who Lives at Home?**
Source: Based on U.S. Census Bureau, Current Population Survey . . ., 2012, Table A2.

Many parents enjoy their teenagers but look forward to the end of child rearing. Often, however, children bounce back to the parental nest in young adulthood and later. According to one joke, "I childproofed my house, but they still get in."

Parenting in the Crowded Empty Nest

American poet Robert Frost wrote: "Home is the place where, when you have to go there, they have to take you in." Almost 22 million women and men ages 18 to 31 who live with their parents apparently agree (Fry, 2013).

RECENT TRENDS During the 1960s and 1970s, sociologists included the "empty nest" in describing the family life cycle (see Chapter 2). This is the stage in which parents, typically in their fifties, find they're alone at home after their children have married, gone to college, or found jobs and moved out.

Today young adults are living at home longer than in the past. The terms *boomerang children* and *boomerang generation* used to refer to young adults moving back in with their parents, but many people in their thirties, forties, and older—often with a spouse, girlfriend or boyfriend, and children in tow—are moving back home (Koss-Feder, 2009; see also Chapter 10).

Most young adults leave the parental nest by age 23, but the proportion of those ages 25 to 34 who are living with parents increased from 9 percent in 1960 to nearly 30 percent in 2011 (Fields and Casper, 2001; "More Young Adults . . .," 2011). Among young adults ages 18 to 34, men are more likely than women to live with their parents (see *Figure 12.1*).

Hosting an adult child who lives at home can cost between $8,000 to $18,000 a year, depending on how much parents are paying for extras such as travel and entertainment. About 26 percent of parents have taken on debt to pay for their adult children's expenses (Grind, 2013).

Some journalists have called boomerang children "adultolescents" because they're still "mooching off their parents" instead of living on their own, but this isn't solely an American phenomenon. The English call such young adults *kippers* ("kids in parents' pockets eroding retirement savings"). In Germany, they're *nesthockers* (literally translated as "nest squatters"), in Italy *bamboccioni* (grown babies who are still attached to mama's apron strings), and in Japan *freeter* (young adults who job hop and live at home) (van Dyk, 2005; Alini, 2007).

WHY ARE MANY ADULT CHILDREN LIVING AT HOME? Individual and macro factors intersect in explaining the delay in many Americans' transition to adulthood, especially living independently. On a micro level, one of my male students, in his late twenties, may be representative of other men his age who enjoy the comforts of their parents' home:

My mom loves my living with her. She enjoys cooking, cleaning my room, and just having me around. I don't pitch in for any of the expenses, but we get along great because she doesn't hassle me about my comings and goings. I have lots of freedom without worrying about bills (Author's files).

Women, too, move back with doting parents who support them financially and wait on them. A 32-year-old employed woman moved home with her parents because, among other things, her parents paid almost all of her credit card expenses. And when the daughter complained about being disturbed after she went to bed, dad ground his coffee beans at night instead of at 5 A.M., and

mom stopped doing laundry, including the daughter's, early in the morning or late at night when the daughter was sleeping (J. White, 2005).

Macro-level factors, especially the Great Recession, have been the major reasons that adult children live with their parents or moved back home. In 2011, 39 percent of young adults ages 18 to 34 either lived with their parents or moved back because of the economy. Nearly 78 percent of those ages 25 to 34 lived with their parents because they didn't have enough money to lead the kind of life they wanted (Parker, 2012).

Declining employment, financial insecurity, student loan debt, low wages, divorce, credit card debt, and going from job to job until they find work they enjoy have made it harder for young middle-class adults to maintain the lifestyles that their parents created. And the transition to independence gets tougher the lower a person's occupation and education (Qian, 2012; Parker, 2012; Fry, 2013).

Economic factors aren't the only reason for living at home. Almost one-third of today's parents, compared with 19 percent in 1993, say that children shouldn't be expected to be on their own financially until age 25 or later (Taylor et al., 2012). Among those ages 18 to 24, 87 percent live at home because parents "make it easy for me to stay" (Payne and Cobb, 2013).

Because of changing attitudes, the stigma traditionally linked to young adults living at home has faded. The phenomenon is widespread enough "to be considered socially acceptable rather than an indicator of the youth's personal failure" (Danziger, 2008: F8). In 2011, among those ages 25 to 34 who were living at home, 61 percent said they had friends or family members who had moved back in with their parents (Parker, 2012). The implication (and perhaps justification) of moving back home or not leaving is that "a lot of people are doing it."

© Mike Baldwin / Cornered

"Empty-nesters. They're hoping to sell before the flock tries to move back in."

Source: www.CartoonStock.com.

RELATIONSHIPS BETWEEN PARENTS AND BOOMERANG CHILDREN Some parents say that they tolerate but are unhappy that their adult children live under the same roof. There may be conflict about clothes, helping out, use of the family car, and the adult child's lifestyle. For example, "They walk past overflowing trash cans, leave their dirty dishes for someone else, keep their lights and other electricity-sucking devices on at all times, and respond to your suggestion that they rake leaves with [that] look" (Sollisch, 2012: 35).

Among young adults ages 19 to 22, 60 percent receive money from their parents. High- and low-income parents spend about 10 percent of their annual household income (almost $12,900 and $5,800, respectively) to help their adult children pay for bills, rent, tuition, and to buy a car (Wightman et al., 2012). Such financial support can sap parents' retirement savings.

Some college-educated fathers, especially, are angry about their children moving back home. This may be due, in part, to the fathers' high expectations for their children's success as well as the sacrifices the family made to pay for college tuition. Others, however, are quite willing to support adult children who have a low-paying job they "love," such as photography, instead of higher-paying jobs (with health benefits) that aren't as interesting (Shellenbarger, 2008: D1).

On the positive side, only 18 percent of 18- to 34-year-olds say that living at home or moving back has been bad for their relationship with their parents (see *Figure 12.2*). And, in a recent survey of parents who are 47 to 66 years old and whose adult children were living with them, 53 percent said that doing so was better than their children's struggling on their own

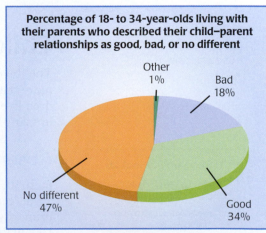

Percentage of 18- to 34-year-olds living with their parents who described their child–parent relationships as good, bad, or no different

Other 1%
Bad 18%
No different 47%
Good 34%

FIGURE 12.2 Boomerang Children and Family Dynamics
Source: Based on Parker, 2012.

(Huber, 2012/2013). Such data suggest, however, that large percentages of young adults and their parents would prefer severing the boomerang ties.

Parenting in Later Life

The number of multigenerational households that include parents, adult children age 25 or older, and grandchildren has spiked—from 11 percent in 1980 to 22 percent in 2010 (Parker, 2012). If adult children help pay for some of the household expenses, take over physically demanding chores such as mowing the lawn, and care for their aging parents who get sick or need assistance (e.g., driving to see a doctor), child–parent relationships generally improve. There are also strains, however, because adult children, their parents, or their grandparents may strongly disagree about child-rearing rules such as not jumping on furniture or doing chores (Fingerman et al., 2007; Koss-Feder, 2009).

A study of 14 European countries found that the adult children who left home in their early forties rather than their early twenties lived closer to their aging parents, maintained more frequent contact, and were as likely to provide as receive parental support. The support included the adult children helping with shopping and taking care of financial matters and the parents taking care of grandchildren (Leopold, 2012).

In the United States, the adult child–parent relationship has mixed outcomes. Adult children who receive parental financial and emotional support are happier than their counterparts who don't receive such support. However, parents often experience stress when their adult children are doing poorly and have to rely on their parents for financial and emotional support (Fingerman et al., 2012).

Because of the wars in Iraq and Afghanistan, many older American parents have been thrust into caregiving roles that they didn't expect. With more soldiers than ever surviving their war injuries, many recent veterans now depend on their parents—who are often in their fifties and sixties—for care because they're single or their spouses can't or won't care for them:

> *Across the nation, parents end up scrubbing burn wounds, suctioning tracheotomy tubes, and bathing their adult children. They assist with physical and occupational therapy. They fight for benefits. They deal with mental health crises and help children who have brain injuries to relearn skills. They drive back and forth to Veterans Affairs (VA) hospitals for outpatient appointments. In short, they put their own lives on hold (Yeoman, 2008: 62–63).*

MAKING CONNECTIONS

- Think about how your parents raised you or how you're raising your children. Do you think that mothers are too critical of fathers' parenting? Or are fathers too sensitive about mothers' comments?

- Do you think that parents should welcome their adult children (including grandchildren) with open arms? Or should they enjoy their empty nest and tell their adult children to move out and cope on their own?

12.7 Describe families' current child care arrangements.

Read on MySocLab

Document: Where's Papa?: Disappearing Dads Are Destroying Our Future

Child Care Arrangements

The Reverend Jesse Jackson reportedly said, "Your children need your presence more than your presents." Parental presence may be limited because many children live apart from their fathers, latchkey kids must fend for themselves, and, in many families, employed parents must rely on child care outside the family.

Absentee Fathers

In 2010, 27 percent of U.S. children lived apart from their fathers, up from only 11 percent in 1960 (Livingston and Parker, 2011). President Obama was raised primarily by his grandparents after his father abandoned the family. On Father's Day in 2009, he urged fathers to stay in their children's lives:

> *When fathers are absent, when they abandon their responsibility to their children, we know the damage that does to our families. I say this as someone who grew up without a father in my life. That's something that leaves a hole in a child's heart that governments can't fill (Cooper, 2009: 10).*

Among fathers who never completed high school, 40 percent live apart from their children compared with only 7 percent of fathers who graduated from college. Across racial-ethnic families, 21 percent of white fathers, 35 percent of Latino fathers, and 44 percent of black fathers don't live with their children. About 80 percent of black children can expect to spend at least part of their childhood living apart from their fathers (Jones, 2010; Livingston and Parker, 2011).

Father absence is due to many factors, including having babies during the teen years and not being able to provide for them financially, deserting unwed mothers, incarceration, physical or mental disabilities, drug abuse, divorce, and not paying child support (Fagan and Lee, 2011; Scott et al., 2012). Regardless of the reasons, absentee fathers increase their children's likelihood of economic and social deprivation.

ECONOMIC DEPRIVATION Nearly 47 percent of children headed by single mothers live below the poverty line compared with 13 percent of two-parent families (Children's Defense Fund, 2012). Many single-mother families were poor even before the father left, but his departure reduced a child's economic resources even further. Economic problems, in turn, affect a mother's ability to move into a neighborhood that has good schools and isn't ridden with drug dealers and gang activities, pay for child care, and provide access to enriching after-school and summer programs (Zhang and Fuller, 2012).

SOCIAL DEPRIVATION Absent fathers have a huge cost beyond their economic impact. Compared with two-parent homes, children of fatherless families have more behavior problems, do less well in school, have higher drug and alcohol usage rates, poorer physical and mental health, and are more likely to enter the juvenile justice system (Jones, 2010; see also Chapter 15).

Single mothers sometimes get financial and other support from "social fathers"—in other words, from grandfathers and other male relatives and from mothers' boyfriends who are like fathers to the children. Male relatives, especially, can enhance children's cognitive abilities by giving them books, reading to them, and spending time with them (Jayakody and Kalil, 2002; Smith, 2010). If social fathers leave, move away, or die, however, the children lose access to such resources.

 Watch on MySocLab

Video: Motherhood Manifesto: Clip 1

DEWK (dual-employed with kids) A family in which both parents are employed full time outside the home.

latchkey kids Children who return home after school and are alone until a parent or another adult arrives.

Latchkey Kids

Demographers sometimes refer to families in which both parents are employed full time as **DEWKs (dual-employed with kids)**. As the proportion of DEWK families has increased, so has the number of latchkey children.

There's nothing new about children being on their own at home. The phrase *latchkey children* originated in the early 1800s, when youngsters who were responsible for their own care wore the key to their home tied to a string around their necks. Today **latchkey kids** are children who return home after school and are alone until a parent or another adult arrives.

The number of latchkey kids has doubled since the 1970s. More than 4 million children ages 5 to 14 (11 percent of all children in this age group) care for themselves on a regular basis before or after school. As you might expect, the older children are, the more likely they are to be latchkey kids. For example, 13 percent of children in self-care are 5 to 11 years old, compared with 33 percent of 12- to 14-year-olds (Laughlin, 2013).

Both family structure and labor force participation affect children's self-care. Among children ages 5 to 14, for example, those living with a separated, divorced, or widowed mother are more likely to be in self-care (19 percent) than those living with a married mother (13 percent), or a never-married mother (7 percent).

Millions of latchkey kids return from school to an empty house. Most schools don't provide after-school care, and many parents—especially single mothers—can't afford expensive after-school programs.

Watch on MySocLab

Video: Motherhood
Manifesto: Clip 1

Children are most likely to be in self-care if parents are employed full time (Laughlin, 2013).

Most children enjoy being home alone, savoring the independence. Others are nervous about being by themselves, don't structure their time, don't do their homework, or invite friends over against house rules. Some researchers believe that most 6- to 9-year-olds aren't ready to care for themselves regularly, and certainly less able than older children to deal with household emergencies (Belle, 1999; Vandivere et al., 2003).

Who's Minding the Kids?

Child care has become an increasingly important part of American life and families. The demand for child care has risen because large numbers of mothers are in the labor force, a parent may be attending school, there are more single-parent households due to separation and divorce, and many parents want to provide their preschoolers with structured environments that enrich their development.

Watch on MySocLab

Video: Day Care

CHILD CARE PATTERNS AND CHARACTERISTICS When mothers are employed, the majority of children younger than age 5 receive care from nonrelatives, especially at day care centers, but fathers are an important source of care (see *Figure 12.3*). Fathers are more likely to provide care if they work evening and weekend shifts or if they're unemployed. Fathers in low-income families are also more likely than others to take care of their preschool children because child care costs are a large proportion of a poor family's budget—30 percent compared with 8 percent for other families (Laughlin, 2013).

Higher-income families are more likely to use child care arrangements, including day care centers, than are lower-income families. Nationally, the average cost of a day care center for children younger than age 5 is about $10,000 a year. The costs are higher for infants and for young children living in metropolitan areas (Urban Institute, 2008; Laughlin, 2013). In 37 states and the District of Columbia, the annual cost of child care for a preschooler is more than the annual tuition at a community college or a four-year public university (Children's Defense Fund, 2010).

Since you asked . . .

• How do child care centers affect young children?

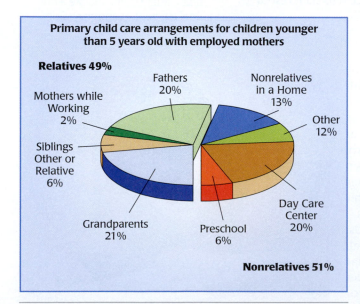

Primary child care arrangements for children younger than 5 years old with employed mothers

Relatives 49%

Mothers while Working 2%

Siblings Other or Relative 6%

Fathers 20%

Nonrelatives in a Home 13%

Other 12%

Day Care Center 20%

Grandparents 21%

Preschool 6%

Nonrelatives 51%

FIGURE 12.3 Who's Watching the Kids?
Note: "Other" includes kindergartens and multiple child care arrangements.
Source: Based on Laughlin, 2013, Table 3.

EFFECTS OF CHILD CARE ON CHILDREN AND PARENTS Those with conservative perspectives, especially, are critical of employed mothers who place their children in child care. They maintain that working mothers are responsible for juvenile delinquency, children's poor performance in school, childhood obesity, and a host of other maladies, including playground accidents (Eberstadt, 2004).

Such accusations increase mothers' feelings of guilt, but are they valid? No. A well-run child care center has positive effects on children's social and cognitive development. In high-quality day care, even children from low-income families outscore more advantaged children on IQ tests by the time they enter kindergarten. The higher the quality of child care in the first three years of life—among children from both poor and middle-income families—the greater the child's language abilities and school readiness skills such as counting and knowing the alphabet (NICHD, 2003; Loeb et al., 2005; Mollborn and Blalock, 2012).

The day care centers with the best results are small and have high staff-to-child ratios (see "How Can I Evaluate the Quality of Child Care?"). Because of continuous state budget cuts, many low-income families aren't eligible for child care programs, experience long waiting lists, and are subject to high co-payments that they can't afford. Even though it's the richest country in the world, the

ASK YOURSELF

How Can I Evaluate the Quality of Child Care?

Following are some questions that will help you evaluate the child care programs or providers you visit. Be sure, also, to talk to parents who are using or have used the facility or a private home.

1. ***What is the staff-to-child ratio?*** The best programs have enough staff members to give children plenty of attention. Suggested staff-to-child ratios are 1 to 3 for infants, 1 to 10 for 5- and 6-year-olds, and 1 to 12 for children older than age 6.

2. ***What is the staff turnover rate?*** If half the staff members leave every year, it probably means that they're paid extremely low wages or believe that the program isn't run well.

3. ***How do the staff and children look?*** If the children seem unhappy, have runny noses, and seem passive, and if the staff members seem distant or lackadaisical, look elsewhere.

4. ***How well equipped is the facility?*** There should be interesting indoor activities that give children a choice of projects, as well as ample playground space with swings, jungle gyms, and other exercise equipment. If there is no adjacent outdoor area, do the children go regularly to a park or playground? Is the facility clean and organized? Does it have a wide range of toys, books, materials, and activities?

5. ***What are the safety regulations and hygienic practices?*** Are children always accounted for when they arrive and leave? Are staff trained in first aid? What are the policies about children who take medications (for allergies, for example)?

6. ***Is the director of the center willing to have you talk to other parents who use the center?*** Better yet, does the center have video cameras so you can log on from work or home?

United States lags far behind other industrialized countries—such as Japan, France, Germany, and Sweden—where the government runs pre-school and child care centers or pays up to 90 percent of child care costs (Forry and Walker, 2006; see also Chapter 13).

Current Social Issues and Children's Well-Being

Government officials often proclaim that children are our most precious resources, tomorrow's leaders, and so on. Do public policies and parenting behavior contradict such noble sentiments? Let's look at the effects of electronic media on children, some of the risks that children face, and foster care.

The Impact of Electronic Media

Computer technology has revolutionized parenting. For better or worse, many of us—practically from birth to adulthood—spend much of our time staring at a screen.

BABIES, TODDLERS, AND PRESCHOOLERS Thousands of music, counting, and alphabet learning apps are now targeted at infants and toddlers (Kang and Tsukayama, 2012). Parents of toddlers "express proud wonderment at their offspring's ability to slide chubby fingers across the [iPhone] screen and pull up photographs and apps of their choice." The apps include "flash cards" to teach toddlers to read and spell and automated phone calls reminding them that it's time to "go potty" (Stout, 2010: ST1).

Some parents brag that their 1-, 2-, and 3-year-olds know their way around an iPhone or an iPad better than they do. One parent's 2-year-old had a Twitter account "practically at birth," and sent "baby tweets" (Wilson, 2010). (I, too, don't know what "baby tweets" are.)

A high-quality child care center can enhance a child's language, social, and pre-kindergarten skills.

12.8 Describe three contemporary issues that can affect a child's well-being.

Many parents are convinced that smartphones and apps are beneficial for preschoolers. In contrast, most pediatricians and educators say that such electronic devices aren't educational but passive amusements like television. Because the children are staring at screens, they don't interact with people around them, don't use language, and don't experience the wider world through exploration and play (Stout, 2010).

SCHOOL-AGE CHILDREN   In 2012, almost 8 million children age 12 and younger were on Facebook. Some of these kids' parents helped their children create a fake birth date to get access to Facebook because the parents feared their children's anger (Siegel, 2012).

A recent test of 400 popular smartphone and tablet apps aimed at children found that 80 percent of the apps didn't offer any information about their privacy policies. Of the 20 percent that contained any privacy-related disclosure, "many consisted of a link to a long, dense, and technical privacy policy that was filled with irrelevant information and would be difficult for most parents to read and understand" (Federal Trade Commission, 2012: 8). Of particular concern were the nearly 60 percent of children's apps that shared information about a user's mobile device and personal data (e.g., a user's name, e-mail address, friends list, geographic location) with other app developers and with third parties, particularly advertisers.

TEENS   Internet use among American teenagers has changed. Since 2006, 95 percent have been online, but 74 percent of adolescents ages 12 to 17 now access the Internet on cell phones, computer tablets, and other mobile devices (Madden et al., 2013). This means that many preteens and teens have more autonomy because they no longer have to share desktops and laptops with other family members.

For the vast majority of teens, social and other digital communications media are a daily part of life: 90 percent have used some form of social media, 87 percent text every day, and 75 percent have a profile on a social networking site, usually Facebook. A small number (5 percent) say that the Internet makes them feel more depressed and less outgoing, and 36 percent sometimes wish they could go back to a time when there was no Facebook. A majority (52 percent), however, believes that using social media has improved their relationships with friends, and 69 percent say that social networking has helped them get to know other students at their school better (Common Sense Media, 2012).

cyber-bullying Willful and repeated harm using computers, cell phones, or other electronic devices.

Advergaming, which combines online games with advertising, is growing rapidly. These sites attract millions of young children and provide marketers with an inexpensive way to sell products that keep children at the computer rather than physical activities, increasing children's obesity rates.

PARENTS   Many parents are wary of the electronic media's impact on their children. For example, 81 percent are concerned about how much information advertisers can learn about their child's online behavior, 72 percent are uneasy about how their teenagers interact online with people they don't know, and 69 percent worry that the online activity might have a negative effect on their children's reputation or future academic or employment possibilities. Despite such concerns, only 31 percent of parents have helped their children set up privacy settings for a social networking site (Madden et al., 2012).

Another source of parental concern is **cyber-bullying**, willful and repeated harm using computers, cell phones, or other electronic devices. Cyber-bullying among children begins before age 12, but is most common during the teen years. Approximately 32 percent of teens have experienced some type of online harassment (International Association of Chiefs of Police, 2012).

Parents often criticize their kids for spending too much time texting and surfing the Web, but they themselves may be the biggest technology abusers. For instance, 40 percent of parents admit that their mobile devices have distracted

In Beijing, the Chinese government defines youth (but not adult) Internet addiction as using the Web for six consecutive hours a day for three straight months. Internet addiction patients are required to stay at a treatment center for three months, isolated from the outside world, and without access to cell phones, computers, and other electronic media. The cost can total nearly $3,000—almost three months' salary for the average Chinese couple. Pictured here, young patients at an Internet addiction center follow a strict military routine (Jiang, 2009). There are no data, so far, on whether the patients change after "rehabilitation."

them from playing with their children, and 41 percent of teens report seeing their parents read or send an e-mail, or text, while driving "all the time" (AT&T, 2012; Gibbs, 2012). Young children have complained that they're tired of being pushed on the swing with one hand while Mom reads her email with the other hand, that a mother never looks up from her smartphone when picking her child up from school, and that parents are often so immersed in e-mail or texting that they give their youngsters little attention (Shute, 2011).

Since you asked . . .
- Should children limit their parents' use of electronic media?

Children at Risk

Life is improving for many American children. Compared with figures from 2000, today they're smoking and drinking alcohol less, graduating from high school in larger numbers, are less likely to die of motor vehicle injuries and to be exposed to secondhand smoke at home (Federal Interagency Forum . . ., 2009, 2013). There is also some bad news. For example,

- Approximately 36 percent of children and adolescents are overweight or obese, up from 6 percent in 1980 ("Childhood Obesity facts," 2013).

- Between 1991 and 2007, the number of incarcerated parents with children under age 18 increased by 79 percent (Glaze and Maruschak, 2010).

- About 67 percent of children (up from 59 percent in 2009) live in counties in which one or more air pollutants are above the allowable levels (Federal Interagency Forum . . ., 2012).

- Among all industrialized countries, the United States has the highest child poverty rates and the worst record in protecting children against gun violence (Children's Defense Fund, 2012).

If children are our most precious resource, we're squandering our assets (see "A Day in the Life of America's Children").

Foster Care

The obvious benefit of foster homes is that many children experience physical and emotional safety. Poverty, child abuse, and parental neglect are some of the major reasons for children's out-of-home placements, including care by relatives,

Choices   A Day in the Life of America's Children

The Children's Defense Fund (2010) reports a grim existence for many American children. Every day, for example,

2	mothers die in childbirth
4	children are killed by abuse or neglect
5	children or teens commit suicide
9	children or teens are killed by firearms
78	babies die before their first birthday
202	children are arrested for a violent crime
377	children are arrested for drug offenses
1,210	babies are born to unmarried teen mothers
1,240	public school students are corporally punished
2,222	high school students drop out
4,498	babies are born into poverty
18,493	public school students are suspended

STOP AND THINK . . .

- The United States ranks first in the world in defense and health expenditures, gross national product, and the number of billionaires. Why, then, are we first among all industrialized nations in the proportion of children living in poverty?
- Do you think that many of our children's problems are due to macro-level variables (such as the economy and political system)? To micro-level variables (such as parents' being irresponsible or uninvolved in their children's child rearing)? Or to other factors?

foster home An out-of-home placement in which adults raise children who aren't their own.

residential treatment facilities, and group homes. The most common out-of-home placement is the **foster home**, in which adults raise children who aren't their own.

Nationally, the number of U.S. children in foster care decreased by 30 percent between 2002 and 2011. In 2011, 410,000 children were in foster care at some point during the year; 104,000 were waiting to be adopted (Children's Bureau, 2012). In theory, foster homes are supposed to provide short-term care until children can be adopted or returned to their biological parents. In reality, many of the children wait up to five years to be adopted, go through multiple placements, and remain in foster care until late adolescence.

Estimates vary by city and state, but between 36 and 52 percent of older youth run away at least once, and nearly two-thirds do so multiple times. Unlike other runaways, youth who run away from foster care aren't trying to escape abuse or neglect, but want to be with family or friends, including girlfriends and boyfriends (Pergamit and Ernst, 2011).

Of the teenagers who "age out" of the foster care system when they turn 18 years old, about half don't complete high school, about a third are arrested, and almost as many are homeless. Only 38 percent of those working at age 18 are employed a year after leaving foster care, and among women, about half are pregnant within 12 to 18 months (Sittenfeld, 2011).

CONCLUSION

There have been numerous *changes* in child-rearing practices. Many fathers are now more involved in raising their children, but there are more at-risk children and a widespread need for high-quality day care. Social class, race, ethnicity, and other factors shape people's *choices*, but the most severe parenting *constraints* are due to political and economic conditions. The next chapter examines, specifically, families' economic situation.

On MySocLab

 **Study** and **Review** on MySocLab

REVIEW QUESTIONS

12.1. Describe parenthood's rewards and difficulties and compare idealized and realistic parenting roles.

1. What, specifically, are some of the benefits and costs of raising children?

2. How do mothers' and fathers' roles differ from those idealized by the mass media?

12.2. Compare three important child development theories.

3. How are Mead's, Piaget's, and Erikson's theories of child development similar? How do they differ?

12.3. Compare four parenting styles and describe the most effective discipline strategies.

4. Why do many parents experience problems in raising children? What are some of the common myths about child rearing?

5. How do authoritarian, permissive, authoritative, and uninvolved parenting styles differ? Which is the most effective?

6. Is physical punishment necessary and effective in disciplining children?

12.4. Compare parenting variations by race, ethnicity, and social class.

7. Which racial-ethnic groups are the most and least likely to spend time with their children? Why?

8. How, specifically, does social class affect children's outcomes?

12.5. Compare parenting in same-sex and opposite-sex couples.

9. How does a parent's sexual orientation affect children?

10. How are gay, lesbian, and heterosexual parenting similar? How do they differ?

12.6. Describe parenting across the life course.

11. What are some of the issues involved in parenting infants/babies, young children, and teenagers?

12. Why are many adult children still living with their parents or moving back home?

12.7. Describe families' current child care arrangements.

13. How do absentee fathers affect their children?

14. Particularly when mothers are employed, who's taking care of preschool children?

15. What kind of child care centers have the most positive effects on children?

12.8. Describe three contemporary issues that can affect a child's well-being.

16. How do electronic media affect children and parents?

17. Why are many children "at risk"?

18. What are some of the benefits and problems of foster care?

The Economy and Family Life

((•)) **Listen** to Chapter 13 on **MySocLab**

LEARNING OBJECTIVES

After you read and study this chapter you will be able to:

13.1 Explain how and why work in U.S. society has changed.

13.2 Explain five ways that the economy impacts families.

13.3 Compare the labor force participation of men and women.

13.4 Describe two ways that economic factors shape marital roles.

13.5 Describe three variations of two-income families.

13.6 Explain how and why workplace inequality affects families.

13.7 Describe four workplace policies that can benefit or disadvantage families.

- In 2012, the **U.S. median household income was $51,017:** $68,636 for Asians, $57,009 for whites, $39,005 for Latinos, and $33,321 for African Americans.

- In a recent Gallup poll, 2 percent of **Americans identified themselves** as upper class, 13 percent as upper-middle class, 42 percent as middle class, 31 percent as working class, and 10 percent as lower class. The remaining 2 percent didn't know or didn't answer.

- The **poverty rate of U.S. families rose** from 9.6 percent in 2000 to 13.1 percent in 2012

- In 1975, 34 percent of **mothers of children younger than age 3** were employed compared with 55 percent in 2012.

- About 51 percent of Americans say **it's best for young children if mothers don't work outside the home**.

- Out of 190 nations, the United States, Papua New Guinea, and Swaziland are **the only countries that have no national paid parental leave policy**.

Sources: Walsh, 2011; Dugan, 2012; DeNavas-Walt et al., 2013; "Happy Mother's Day . . .," 2013; Wang et al., 2013; *Women in the Labor Force . . .*, 2013.

Mark Cooper was the security manager for a *Fortune 500* company in Tempe, Arizona, overseeing a budget of $1.2 million and earning almost $70,000 a year. When the economy began to crash in late 2007, he lost his job and made $12 an hour cleaning an office building for a friend's janitorial company. Cooper was grateful for the job but said that he fought despair, discouragement, and depression every day (Luo, 2009). This example illustrates the close linkage between an individual's personal life and the **economy**—the social institution that determines how a society produces, distributes, and consumes goods and services. Let's begin with a brief look at why work is so important in our lives.

economy A social institution that determines how a society produces, distributes, and consumes goods and services.

Work in U.S. Society Today

13.1 Explain how and why work in U.S. society has changed.

Work is physical or mental activity that accomplishes or produces something, either goods or services. For most of us, money is a major motivator, but work provides other benefits as well. Generally, employment leads to better health, a sense of accomplishment and usefulness, and is a major source of many people's social identity. Work also provides a sense of stability, order, and a daily rhythm over the life course that we don't get from many other activities (Mirowsky and Ross, 2007). Thus, besides providing income, work has social meaning. What's especially striking is how much the economy and work have changed family lives since the 2007–2009 Great Recession.

work A physical or mental activity that accomplishes or produces something, either goods or services.

After 30 years at a factory in Ohio that made truck parts, Jeffrey Evans was earning more than $60,000 a year. When the plant shut down in 2008, Evans could find only sporadic construction work. He restarted at the bottom as a union pipe-fitting apprentice and made about $20,000 a year. "I lost everything I worked for all my life," he said (Eckholm, 2008: 14). Evans wasn't alone in feeling that he had lost everything he worked for all his life. There are many reasons for millions of Americans' recent downward slide; even those who lived modestly lost economic ground because of macro-level variables such as deindustrialization, globalization, offshoring, and weakened labor unions. The economic situation has improved, but more than half of the job gains since the recession have been in the restaurant and retail sectors, both of which pay low wages (Casselman, 2013; "Labor Day 2013. . .," 2013).

Read on MySocLab

Document: When Work Disappears

Deindustrialization, Globalization, Offshoring, and Labor Unions

deindustrialization A social and economic change resulting from the reduction of industrial activity, especially manufacturing.

DEINDUSTRIALIZATION Evans, like many others, is a casualty of **deindustrialization**, a process of social and economic change because of the reduction of industrial activity, especially manufacturing. Since 2000, 32 percent of U.S. manufacturing jobs have disappeared (Hargrove, 2011). In mid-2012, 304,000 manufacturing plants were operating in the United States, 27,000 fewer than at the end of 2007 (Philips, 2012).

One reason for this decline is that, beginning in the early 1960s, employers easily replaced workers with the lowest skill levels, usually those on assembly lines, with automation. Since then, employers have been spending more on machines than on people. According to a manager at a large company that manufactures plastic products, machines don't require interviews, drug tests, training, health care benefits, or pensions; they work 24 hours a day and don't complain about anything (Lee and Mather, 2008; Rampell, 2011).

globalization The growth and spread of investment, trade, production, communication, and new technology around the world.

GLOBALIZATION Deindustrialization accelerated because of **globalization**—the growth and spread of investment, trade, production, communication, and new technology around the world. One example of globalization is a motor vehicle that is assembled in the United States with practically all of its parts manufactured and produced in Germany, Japan, South Korea, or developing countries.

offshoring Sending work or jobs to another country to cut a company's costs at home (sometimes called *international outsourcing* and *offshore outsourcing*).

OFFSHORING **Offshoring** refers to sending work or jobs to another country to cut a company's costs at home. Sometimes called *international outsourcing* or *offshore outsourcing*, the transfer of manufacturing jobs overseas has been going on since at least the 1970s.

Between 2001 and 2011, U.S. companies moved more than 2.7 million jobs to China, 77 percent of them in manufacturing (Scott, 2012). Most of the offshored jobs go to India and China, but many have also moved to Canada, Hungary, Mexico, the Philippines, Poland, Russia, Egypt, Venezuela, Vietnam, and South Africa. Initially, most of the offshored jobs were blue-collar manufacturing jobs. Between 2000 and 2010, however, U.S. firms offshored 28 percent of high-level, well-paid information technology (IT) jobs, including those in accounting, computer science, and engineering (National Science Board, 2012). Companies can get accounting services from India for about $23,000 a year that would cost $70,000 in the United States. In Mexico, the average General Motors worker earns wages and benefits that cost less than $4 an hour compared with $55 an hour in the United States. Because of such large wage differences, American consumers can purchase products and services at low prices (Black, 2010; Coy, 2013; Guarino, 2013).

Since you asked . . .

- Would you pay 20 percent more for appliances, clothes, and other products if they were made in the United States?

labor unions Organized groups that seek to improve wages, benefits, and working conditions.

LABOR UNIONS Deindustrialization, globalization, and offshoring have affected **labor unions**, organized groups that seek to improve wages, benefits, and working conditions. Union membership has dropped sharply—from 35 percent of the workforce in the mid-1950s to 11 percent in 2012 (*Union Members—2012*, 2013). In the 1950s, 75 percent of Americans approved of labor unions, compared with only 52 percent in 2012 (Jones, 2012). Five states prohibit unionization, and in 2012, 24 states significantly restricted collective bargaining rights (Shah and Casselman, 2012).

This worker, age 49, moved in with his 73-year-old mother after losing his job at an automotive factory. He, like millions of other Americans, is a casualty of deindustrialization and globalization.

Opponents argue that unions have too much influence, that its members are overpaid, and that unions drain state resources because of the pension benefits and high salaries of public sector employees such as teachers, nurses, sanitation workers, and police. Critics also contend that unions have limited employers'

flexibility in hiring and firing decisions, and that ever-increasing labor and health care costs have forced employers to move their operations overseas to remain competitive (Rosenfeld, 2010; Greeley, 2011; Jones, 2011; Kohut, 2011; McKinnon, 2011; Schlesinger, 2011).

Proponents argue that unions are crucial for many workers and their families. Some maintain that states have experienced budget deficits because of the housing crisis and a recession that was due to Wall Street speculation and not overpaid public sector union members. Others point out that union members have made numerous concessions such as decreasing their wages and benefits. Most important, historically, unions have benefited almost all workers by insisting on paid holidays and vacations, greater workplace safety, overtime pay, and by challenging corporations that are becoming more dominant and powerful in both the economy and politics (Allegretto et al., 2011; Klein, 2011; Schlesinger, 2011; Welch, 2011; Gould and Shierholz, 2012).

Social Class, Wealth, and Income

Conventional wisdom says that money can't buy happiness, but a study of 155 countries, including the United States, concluded that the richer people are, the happier they are (Stevenson and Wolfers, 2013). Such findings refer to *social class*, groups of people who have a similar standing or rank based on wealth, income, education, power, prestige, and other valued resources.

Wealth is the money and economic assets that a person or family owns. It includes property (such as real estate), stocks and bonds, retirement and savings accounts, personal possessions (such as cars and jewelry), and income. **Income** is the amount of money a person receives, usually through wages or salaries, but it can also include rents, interest on savings accounts, dividends on stocks, or the proceeds from a business.

Measuring wealth and income differs depending on the variables and methodology, but most researchers agree on three points. First, U.S. wealth and income inequality is greater than in any other Western industrialized nation (Coy, 2013). Second, U.S. wealth and income inequality has risen since the 1960s (Mather, 2012). Third, the rich are getting richer, the middle class is shrinking, and the lower class has gotten poorer (Mishel et al., 2012).

THE RICH ARE GETTING RICHER U.S. wealth and income inequality is staggering. As *Figure 13.1* shows, the top 1 percent of Americans owns 35 percent of all wealth; the top 10 percent owns 76 percent of all wealth

Since you asked . . .
• Do we still need unions?

wealth Money and economic assets that a person or family owns.

income Amount of money a person receives, usually through wages or salaries.

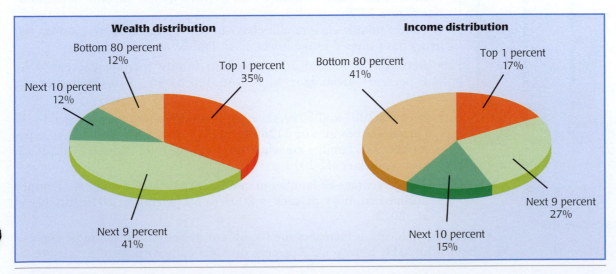

FIGURE 13.1 U.S. Wealth and Income Inequality
Source: Based on Wolff, 2012, Table 2.

compared with the bottom 80 percent of Americans owning only 12 percent of the wealth. Income inequality is less pronounced but also huge. The richest 1 percent of Americans have 17 percent of all income; the top 10 percent has 44 percent of all income compared with only 41 percent for the bottom 80 percent.

Regardless of how the economy is doing, the rich keep getting richer. Between 1983 and 2010, the number of U.S. households that had $10 million or more increased by 426 percent. In 2013, the United States had 442 billionaires, up from 413 in 2011, who comprised almost a third of the world's billionaires. These super-rich Americans averaged $4.3 billion per person and controlled almost $1.5 trillion of the nation's wealth. In 1962, the richest 1 percent of Americans had only 8 percent of the national income compared with 17 percent in 2010 ("Slowing Giant . . .," 2011; Wolff, 2012; Kroll and Dolan, 2013; Mac, 2013).

Some assets, such as stocks and bonds, are concentrated among a small share of households. In 2010, the wealthiest 5 percent owned 67 percent of all stock compared with the bottom 80 percent who owned only 8 percent of all stock (Mishel et al., 2012). When the stock market fluctuates, affluent households are less likely than those in the middle class to be affected by downturns.

THE MIDDLE CLASS IS SHRINKING A slight majority of Americans (51 percent) identify themselves as middle class, including 46 percent of those who make more than $100,000 a year, and 35 percent of those who earn under $30,000 a year (Taylor et al., 2012). The income range is so wide because self-reports are subjective, based on comparisons ("I'm not rich and not on welfare, so I must be middle class"), include current assets (e.g., homeownership, cars, and retirement income), and aspirations such as children going to college.

Instead of relying on self-reported social class, the U.S. Department of Commerce (2010) defines middle class for a two-parent-two-child family as having annual income between $51,000 to $123,000 and a median income of about $81,000. Exactly where the middle class begins and ends has no firm answer, but because over 87 percent of U.S. taxpayers make less than $100,000 a year on taxable income, earning more than this amount indicates that a family is *not* middle class (Pollack, 2012).

Since you asked . . .

• Who is middle class?

Definitions of middle class vary, but a number of recent studies show that the number of middle-class families has been decreasing and getting poorer. Between 1971 and 2011, for example, there was a sharp decline in the share of adults who lived in middle-income households (see *Figure 13.2*).

Some middle-class families have moved up the economic ladder, but many have slipped into a lower class. For example,

• Between 2000 and 2010, median family income decreased by 6 percent—from more than $66,000 to $62,300 (Mishel et al., 2012).

• Between 2007 and 2010, the median wealth of families plunged by 39 percent—from almost $126,400 to $77,300. This means that many middle-class families are where they were in 1992 (Bricker et al., 2012; Gottschalck et al., 2013).

• The percentage of families in middle-income levels who saved money declined from 61 percent in 2001 to 50 percent in 2010 (Bricker et al., 2012).

• A college education increases the likelihood of being in the middle class or higher. In 2011, however, 23 percent of Americans with a college degree or

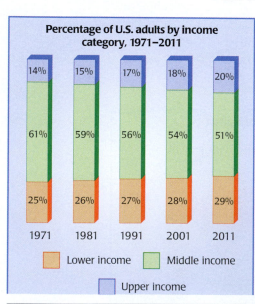

FIGURE 13.2 The Middle Class Has Been Shrinking
Source: Taylor et al., 2012, p. 11.

higher identified themselves as working or lower class, up from 18 percent in 2003 (Dugan, 2012).

Because of such data, social scientists have recently described the middle class as "collapsing," "squeezed," and as having lost a decade of any economic growth (Begala, 2012; Mishel et al., 2012; Wolff, 2012).

Many personal finance advisors blame Americans for being spendthrifts rather than savers (see for example Orman, 2008). Such criticism, although warranted in some cases, overlooks demographic and structural variables that affect families' financial lives. For example, most middle-class families—especially among African Americans and Latinos—depend on wages and salaries rather than inherited wealth that has been accumulated over time and passed on to the next generation. And, when there's a severe economic downturn, middle-class families may have to withdraw funds from their retirement accounts to pay for everyday expenses. The withdrawals deplete savings, decrease retirement security, and carry tax and other penalties that may be as high as one-third of the money withdrawn (Block and Petrecca, 2009).

WORKING AND LOWER CLASSES ARE BARELY SURVIVING In 2012, Mitt Romney, the Republican presidential nominee, created a national firestorm when he implied that 47 percent of Americans are "freeloaders" because they pay no income taxes. Romney was right about the "47 percent," but this figure includes 50 percent of families who don't owe income taxes because they're poor, 20 percent of older Americans whose Social Security income is too low to be taxed, 23 percent of affluent households that get tax breaks, and tax credits for employed low-income parents who are raising children. In fact, even the lowest 20 percent of U.S. earners pay 9 percent of their income for federal taxes (Gale and Marron, 2012; Grier, 2012).

In 2012, 31 percent of Americans described themselves as working class (about the same number as in 2001), but 10 percent described themselves as lower class, up from 3 percent in 2001 (Dugan, 2012). The lower class has grown (see *Figure 13.2*). As *Table 13.1* shows, the lower class, compared with middle and upper classes, have experienced more financial problems but are more likely to believe that hard work brings success.

A slowing economy affects all families, but why are so many families struggling more than did their parents and grandparents? "Some Reasons for the Rising U.S. Inequality" offers some explanations.

We've examined some macro-economic changes that affect American families. How do families cope with these changes on a daily basis?

TABLE 13.1 Social Class Differences in Everyday Life			
Percentage of Americans in each social class who say that they . . .			
	Lower Class	**Middle Class**	**Upper Class**
. . . are less financially secure than 10 years ago	63	42	24
. . . worry about not having enough income for retirement	58	32	18
. . . have had problems paying bills	64	29	13
. . . are frequently stressed	58	37	29
. . . believe that hard work brings success	45	29	27

Sources: Based on Morin and Motel, 2012; Taylor et al., 2012.

Constraints

Some Reasons for the Rising U.S. Inequality

Multiple factors have increased the inequality gap. Some social analysts contend that many Americans are in financial trouble because, over the past decades, we've shifted from a "culture of thrift" to a "culture of debt" (Brooks, 2008: 19). Others argue that our economic crisis is due, largely, to **corporate welfare**, an array of direct subsidies, tax breaks, and other favorable treatment that the government has created for businesses. For example,

- American taxpayers are paying $12.2 trillion for the federal government's bailing out of mismanaged financial institutions. The executives of the companies still receive multimillion-dollar annual salaries and benefits ("Adding up . . .," 2011; Mider and Green, 2012; Sparshott, 2013).

- Corporate income tax rates in the United States decreased from 53 percent in 1952 to 11 percent in 2010. In contrast, the tax burden of an average employee ranges from 33 percent to 41 percent (Anderson et al., 2011; Buffet, 2011).

- Some corporations pay no taxes at all. In 2010, General Electric—the nation's largest corporation—reported worldwide profits of $14.2 billion, received a federal tax benefit of $3.2 billion, paid its top CEO almost $12 million, and spent almost $42 million to lobby Congress for tax breaks (Anderson et al., 2011; Kocieniewski, 2011; Lublin, 2011; see also Niquette, 2011).

The Occupy Wall Street (OWS) movement began in mid-2011 in New York City's Wall Street financial district. The protestors' slogan, "We are the 99%," referred to the growing U.S. income inequality between the richest 1 percent and the rest of the population.

Why was the movement short-lived? Americans think that the richest 20 percent control about 59 percent of the wealth, but the real number is closer to 84 percent. Not understanding our nation's extreme wealth disparity helps explain why people aren't demanding greater economic equality (DeGraw, 2011; Norton and Ariely, 2011).

Second, 43 percent of Americans believe that the rich are more intelligent and hardworking than the average person (Parker, 2012). Such attitudes ignore the importance of inherited wealth, but reinforce the belief that hard work brings success.

Third, in both 1990 and 2012, 63 percent of Americans said that the country benefits from having a rich class of people (Newport, 2012; see also Trumbull, 2012). Such attitudes may be reflecting many Americans' hopes that they, too, will be wealthy someday, or many Americans don't see the connection between structural economic inequality and their own financial situation (Norton and Ariely, 2011).

STOP AND THINK . . .

- Some executive recipients of corporate welfare—such as Bill Gates, Warren Buffet, and businessman George Soros—have donated billions of dollars to improve education, health care, and human rights in the United States and other countries (Whelan, 2011). So, does corporate welfare benefit taxpayers?

- Do *you* believe that hard work brings success?

13.2 Explain five ways that the economy impacts families.

corporate welfare An array of direct subsidies, tax breaks, and other favorable treatment that the government has created for businesses.

How the Economy Affects Families

In 2013, 57 percent of Americans said that the economy was the most important issue facing the country, but down from 86 percent in 2009, which was the official end of the recession (Jones, 2013). Many Americans believe that the economy is improving, but millions of people have taken low-paying jobs and work nonstandard hours or part time. If these strategies fail, they find themselves among the unemployed, which, in turn, may lead to poverty and homelessness.

Low-Wage Jobs and Nonstandard Work Hours

One writer described the United States as "a nation of hamburger flippers" because of the explosion of low-wage jobs (Levine, 1994: E1). To survive, many family members also work nonstandard hours, at night, and on weekends.

LOW-WAGE JOBS   Only 30 percent of U.S. workers are satisfied with their pay (Saad, 2012). The federal minimum wage, which rose from $6.55 to $7.25 an hour in 2009, increased the wages of less than 4 percent of the workforce. Taking inflation into account, a worker earning a minimum wage today is worse off than one who made the base hourly wage of $1.60 in 1968. The current federal minimum wage is lower than that required by 19 states and the District of Columbia (Klein and Leiber, 2013).

Many small businesses are starting their workers at $10 an hour, but some of the wealthiest corporations contend that increasing the federal minimum wage would result in much higher consumer costs. If, however, the nation's largest low-wage employer, Wal-Mart, paid its 1.4 million U.S. workers $12 per hour and passed every penny of the costs to consumers, the average Wal-Mart customer would pay just 46 cents more per shopping trip, or about $12 a year (Jacobs et al., 2011; see also Benner and Jayaraman, 2012).

Except for registered nurses whose median annual salary is about $65,000, seven of the occupations expected to add the most jobs through 2020 are low paying, up to a maximum of about $24,000 a year. These occupations include home health aides and personal care aides who assist older and disabled people. Other fast-growing but low-paying jobs, from about $22,000 to $31,000 a year, include retail salespersons, general office clerks, and nurses' aides (Sommers and Franklin, 2012; Maher, 2013).

Almost 23 percent of America's poor are the **working poor**, people who spend at least 27 weeks a year in the labor force (working or looking for work) but whose wages fall below the official poverty level. Among married-couple families with children, more than 7 percent are the working poor (*A Profile of the Working Poor, 2010*, 2012).

NONSTANDARD WORK HOURS In many countries, workers are needed almost around the clock because business is being conducted somewhere almost every hour of the day, including weekends. Since 2004, 20 percent of all U.S. workers have had nonstandard schedules (working late at night, during the early morning hours, and on weekends) (Enchautegui, 2013). One-third of all two-income couples with children include at least one spouse who has nonstandard work hours (Presser and Ward, 2011).

Most reasons for nonstandard work hours (often called *shift work*) reflect the nature of the job. For example, police, firefighters, registered nurses, truck drivers, security guards, nurses' aides, hotel workers, and people who clean office buildings and hotels are needed day and night, and the demand for these workers is expected to increase in the future. Others work nonstandard hours because of personal preference (12 percent); because child care by a partner or relative is available only during those hours (16 percent); because the worker can't get a better job (8 percent); or because the job offers higher pay (7 percent) (McMenamin, 2007; Saenz, 2008).

Nonstandard work schedules can create problems because one or both parents spend less time with their children (especially on weekends and evenings) and provide less supervision and help with homework. The more nighttime hours that mothers work, the more likely they are to feel tired and anxious, and to spend less time in stimulating activities with their children such as playing games and reading books together. Some of the negative effects include children's developing fewer language skills, doing poorly in school (and being suspended), and being more depressed. Shift work can also increase the risk of divorce if couples don't spend time together or in family activities (Kalil et al., 2010; Gassman-Pines, 2011; Grzywacz et al., 2011; Enchautegui, 2013).

Nonstandard work schedules also have benefits. Because a parent works days or nights, there are few child care costs. Fathers can spend more time with their children and thus get to know them better. Shift-work parents of school-age children and adolescents can be at home when their children go to school or come home. Shift-work parents are also generally just as likely as those with day schedules to know

On average, housekeepers who work year-round and full time earn less than $21,000 a year. At many of the nation's fanciest hotels, maids and housekeepers are experiencing more arm, shoulder, and lower-back injuries. They now typically lift king-size mattresses (that weigh 115 pounds) up to 200 times a day, must bend to scrub dozens of large tubs and Jacuzzis every day, and have greater workloads because each room requires more tasks, such as changing more pillowcases, cleaning hair dryers, and washing coffeepots.

working poor People who spend at least 27 weeks in the labor force but whose wages fall below the official poverty level.

Since you asked . . .
- How do parents' nonstandard work hours affect children?

Heavy and tractor trailer drivers are in high demand, but the median pay is only $38,000 a year.

about their children's activities, even when adolescents become more independent (Perry-Jenkins et al., 2007; Davis et al., 2008; Presser and Ward, 2011).

Part-Time Workers

Of the almost 27 million part-timers (those who work less than 35 hours a week), 30 percent are involuntary because they can't find suitable full-time employment or employers have reduced their hours because of a business slowdown (BLS News Release, 2013). Part-time work, traditionally parceled out to lower-level hourly employees such as cashiers and administrative assistants, has spread to white-collar and professional sectors and now includes marketing directors, engineers, and financial officers (Davidson, 2011).

Employers save on costs, such as health insurance, vacations, and unemployment insurance, by hiring more (or all) part-time workers. The downside includes higher turnover and employees who are often less committed to turning out a better product or providing a better service. Although 20 percent of part-timers work at least two jobs to get by, many teeter near poverty (Davidson, 2011).

Unemployment

The U.S. unemployment rate surged between 2008 and 2010, but has dropped since then (see *Figure 13.3*). During the recent recession, the entire growth in jobs since 2001 was wiped out. Since 2010, unemployed workers have been jobless for longer periods, and a quick recovery is unlikely because the economy has fewer jobs than it did in 2001 (Shierholz, 2009).

The job losses have been so severe that the Bureau of Labor Statistics is now reporting *mass layoffs* that involve at least 50 workers from a single employer. During the first few months of 2013 alone, the nearly 2,500 mass layoffs left almost 225,000 workers jobless. The largest mass layoffs have been in construction, manufacturing, and wholesale and retail trade ("Mass Layoffs . . .," 2013).

Unemployment causes widespread economic hardship for all families, but it hits some groups and sectors harder than others. Recent job losses have been greatest among blacks and Latinos, government employees, people in construction and manufacturing industries, and those with less than a high school education. Blacks and Latinos are the most likely to experience long-term unemployment because there are fewer jobs in construction and manufacturing. Blacks and Latinos also receive low or no unemployment insurance payments: They often don't meet a state's eligibility rules due to low wages, don't know they can collect unemployment pay, or employers maintain that the workers aren't eligible for unemployment pay because they weren't laid off but quit (Acs and Martinez-Schiferl, 2012; Jacobe, 2012; Nichols and Simms, 2012; Gable, 2013; Shierholz, 2013).

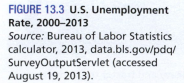

Since you asked . . .
- How accurate are official unemployment statistics?

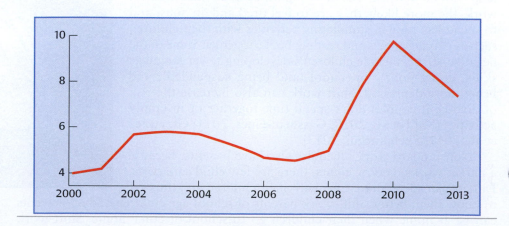

FIGURE 13.3 **U.S. Unemployment Rate, 2000–2013**
Source: Bureau of Labor Statistics calculator, 2013, data.bls.gov/pdq/SurveyOutputServlet (accessed August 19, 2013).

In good times and in bad, African American men have the highest unemployment rates. And, compared with their white counterparts, black workers are unemployed longer after their unemployment insurance benefits end. Pictured here are laid-off workers examining listings at a job fair.

DISCOURAGED WORKERS Sometimes called the "hidden unemployed," **discouraged workers** are available and want to work but have stopped searching for a job because they believe that job hunting is futile. In mid-2013, almost 1 million Americans had given up searching for jobs (BLS News Release, 2013).

Why do people give up? Discouraged workers include retirees who believe that they can't find work because of age discrimination, mothers who have been taking care of their children but can't find a suitable job after entering the job market, those who refuse to work for a minimum wage, and adults age 24 and younger who have dropped out of high school and don't have the necessary schooling or job experience that many employers seek (Davey and Leonhardt, 2003; Cohany, 2009).

Many employers say that a large number of jobs are going unfilled because companies can't find qualified workers (Jacobe, 2013). National data show that this "lack of skills" explanation doesn't jibe with the facts because there's a massive job shortage at all education levels. For example, the unemployment rates of people with at least a college degree are twice as high (8 percent) as they were in 2007 (4 percent). Thus, workers lack jobs, not skills (Shierholz, 2013).

UNDEREMPLOYED WORKERS Unemployment rates are also misleading because they ignore the **underemployed worker**—people who have part-time jobs but want full-time work or whose jobs are below their experience, skill, and education levels. In 2013, an estimated 18 percent of U.S. workers were underemployed compared with only 8 percent in 2007 (Mishel et al., 2012; Gallup, 2013).

Among the underemployed, almost 33 percent of those who graduated from college between 2006 and 2010 said that their postcollege job was below their education and skill level. Overall, racial and ethnic minorities are twice as likely as whites to be underemployed. Underemployed Americans are better off financially than the unemployed, but both groups experience similar levels of sadness, stress, anger, worry, and depression (Marlar, 2010; Godofsky et al., 2011; Mishel et al., 2012).

As this book goes to press, the official federal unemployment rate of 7.3 percent is misleading. If the definition included involuntary part-time workers as well as discouraged and underemployed workers, the unemployment rate would be closer to 24 percent (Economic Policy Institute, 2013; Williams, 2013). Because the gulf between the haves and have nots has widened and our economic problems continue, millions of Americans are poor. Before reading any further, take the quiz "How Much Do You Know about Poverty?"

discouraged worker A person who has stopped searching for a job because he or she believes that job hunting is futile.

underemployed worker A person who has a part-time job but would rather work full time or whose job is below his or her experience, skill, and educational level.

ASK YOURSELF

How Much Do You Know about Poverty?

True False

☐ ☐ **1.** The number of Americans living in poverty has decreased since 2000.

☐ ☐ **2.** Most Americans could get out of poverty if they worked harder.

☐ ☐ **3.** In absolute numbers, most poor people in the United States are white.

☐ ☐ **4.** According to the federal government, a family of four is poor if it earns less than $26,000 a year.

True False

☐ ☐ **5.** The U.S. child poverty rate is higher than in any other industrialized countries.

☐ ☐ **6.** Single fathers are as likely as single mothers to be poor.

☐ ☐ **7.** The poverty rate of people age 65 and older is lower than that of any other age group.

☐ ☐ **8.** Most poor people live in inner cities.

The answers are on page 376.

---

absolute poverty Not having enough money to afford the basic necessities of life.

relative poverty Not having enough money to maintain an average standard of living.

Since you asked . . .
- Who is poor?

poverty threshold The minimum income level that the federal government considers necessary for basic subsistence (also called a *poverty line*).

Watch on MySocLab

Video: Consequences of Poverty

Read on MySocLab

Document: The Poverty Clinic

Poverty

There are two ways to define poverty: absolute and relative. **Absolute poverty** is not having enough money to afford the basic necessities of life such as food, clothing, and shelter ("what I need"). **Relative poverty** is not having enough money to maintain an average standard of living ("what I want"). People who experience relative poverty may feel poor compared with a majority of others in society, but they have the basic necessities to survive.

THE POVERTY THRESHOLD The Official Poverty Measure (OPM) consists of a **poverty threshold** (also called a *poverty line*) that is the minimum income level that the federal government considers necessary for basic subsistence. To determine the poverty threshold, the Department of Agriculture (DOA) estimates the annual cost of food that meets minimum nutritional guidelines and then multiplies this figure by three to cover the minimum costs of clothing, housing, and other necessities. Anyone whose income is below this threshold is considered officially poor and is eligible for government assistance (such as food stamps).

The poverty threshold, which in 2012 was $23,492 for a family of four (two adults and two children), is adjusted every year to reflect cost-of-living increases. If a family makes a dollar more than the poverty line, then that family is not officially classified as poor and not eligible for public assistance. Many people in "deep poverty" live on considerably less than the poverty threshold. In 2012, for example, 44 percent of Americans earned less than half of the poverty threshold. That's about $11,650 a year for a family of four. In 2013, 24 percent of Americans weren't able to afford food that their families needed (Shaefer and Edin, 2012; Annual Statistical Supplement, 2013; Stokes, 2013).

Some believe that the official poverty line is too high. They argue, for example, that many people aren't as poor as they seem because the poverty threshold doesn't include the value of noncash benefits such as food stamps, medical services (such as Medicare and Medicaid), public housing subsidies, and unreported income (Eberstadt, 2009).

Others claim that the poverty line is too low because it doesn't include child care and job transportation costs or the cost-of-living expenses, particularly housing, that vary considerably across states, regions, and urban–rural areas. Some also argue that poverty estimates are too low because they exclude millions of Americans who live above the poverty threshold but rely on food banks, soup kitchens, and clothing thrift stores to survive (Fremstad, 2012).

To address such concerns, the federal government has been developing a Supplemental Poverty Measure (SPM) that augments, but doesn't replace, the OPM. The SPM takes into account expenses such as housing, utilities, and child care costs, as well as family resources such as food stamps and other in-kind state

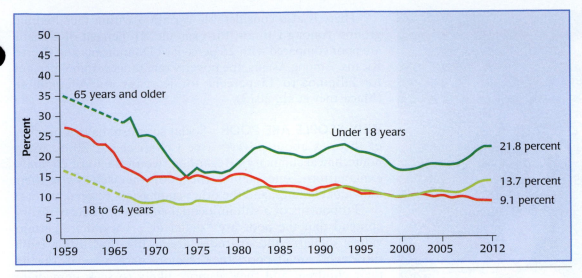

FIGURE 13.4 **U.S. Poverty Rates by Age, 1959–2012**
Note: Dotted lines indicate estimated data.
Source: DeNavas-Walt et al., 2013, Figure 5.

and federal subsidies. So far, the poverty rate is higher using the SPM, but various groups fare differently depending, for example, on a person's age and geographic location (Blank, 2011; Short, 2012).

In 2012 the official U.S. poverty rate was over 15 percent (46.5 million Americans), but poverty isn't random. Both historically and currently, the poor share some common characteristics that include age, gender, family structure, and race and ethnicity.

AGE In 2012 almost 22 percent of children under age 18 lived in poverty (up from a low of 16 percent in 2001), and 10 percent lived in deep poverty. Children were almost twice as likely as those aged 65 and older to be poor (see *Figure 13.4*). The poverty rate of older Americans is at an all-time low, and lower than that of any other age group, because government programs for the elderly, especially Medicare and Medicaid, have generally kept up with the rate of inflation. In contrast, many programs for children living in poverty have been reduced or eliminated since 1980. The poverty rate for young adults aged 25 to 34 living with parents was only 8 percent, but if poverty had been measured by personal income, 45 percent would have been officially poor (Mykyta and Macartney, 2012).

GENDER AND FAMILY STRUCTURE Women's poverty rates are slightly higher than those of men (16 percent and 14 percent, respectively), but family structure is an important factor. In 2012, 6 percent of married-couple families, 31 percent of female-headed families, and 16 percent of male-headed families lived in poverty (Gould, 2012; DeNavas-Walt et al., 2013).

Researcher Diana Pearce (1978) coined the term **feminization of poverty** to describe the likelihood that female heads of households will be poor. Because of increases in divorce, unmarried childbearing, and low-paying jobs, single-mother families are four to five times more likely to be poor than married-couple families who often have two wage earners (Mishel et al., 2012).

RACE AND ETHNICITY In absolute numbers, there are more poor whites (19 million) than poor Latinos (13.6 million), blacks (11 million), or Asians (2 million) (DeNavas-Walt et al., 2013). Proportionately, however, and as *Figure 13.5* shows, whites and Asian Americans are less likely to be poor than other racial-ethnic groups.

feminization of poverty The likelihood that female heads of households will be poor.

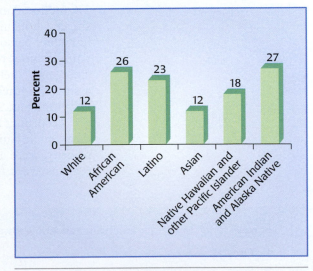

FIGURE 13.5 **Percentage of Americans Living in Poverty, by Race and Ethnicity, 2007–2011**
Source: Based on Macartney et al., 2013, p. 3.

Family poverty rates in the South and in many large metropolitan areas have increased (Redd et al., 2011). As poverty grows, so do the lines at local soup kitchens and food pantries.

There is also considerable variation within racial-ethnic groups. Among Latinos, for example, 16 percent of Cubans are poor compared with 26 percent of Dominicans and Puerto Ricans. Among Asians, the poverty rate ranges from 6 percent for Filipinos to 15 percent for Koreans and Vietnamese (Macartney et al., 2013).

WHY PEOPLE ARE POOR Social scientists have a number of theories about poverty (see Cellini et al., 2008, for a nontechnical summary). Regarding two of the most common explanations, one blames the poor themselves for their individual failings, and the other emphasizes societal factors.

Proponents of a still influential *culture of poverty* theory contend that the poor are "deficient": They share certain values, beliefs, and attitudes about life that differ from those who aren't poor; they're more permissive in raising their children; and they're more likely to seek immediate gratification instead of planning for the future (Lewis, 1966; Banfield, 1974). The assertion that these values are transmitted from generation to generation implies that the poor create their own problems through a self-perpetuating cycle of poverty ("like father, like son").

In contrast to blaming the poor, most sociologists maintain that macro-level factors create and sustain poverty. As you saw earlier, economic policies benefit corporations and already-wealthy individuals. Most of the poor aren't poor because they're lazy but because of economic conditions such as low wages, job loss, a lack of affordable housing, physical or mental disabilities, or an inability to afford health insurance, which in turn can result in acute health problems that interfere with employment. Regardless of individual characteristics, middle classes also get government assistance through programs for the disabled, veterans, college students, older people, and the unemployed (Appelbaum and Gebeloff, 2012; Kim et al., 2012; Mishel et al., 2012; Paletta and Porter, 2013).

Homelessness

One of the most devastating consequences of poverty is homelessness. Almost 1.6 million Americans spend at least one night in an emergency shelter or transitional housing program, a 2.2 percent increase from 2009. The number of homeless persons in families increased by 20 percent between 2007 and 2010. Families now represent a much larger share (35 percent) of all people who use emergency shelters than ever before. A majority of homeless families consist of a single mother with young children (U.S. Department of Housing and Urban Development, 2011).

According to an annual survey of the nation's 25 largest cities, in 2012, the three main causes of homelessness among families with children, in order of priority, were a lack of affordable housing, poverty, and unemployment. These reasons were followed by eviction, domestic violence, and low-paying jobs.

ANSWERS TO "How Much Do You Know about Poverty?"

1. False.
2. False.
3. True.
4. False.

5. True.
6. False.
7. True.
8. False.

All of the answers are based on the material in this chapter.

Because there aren't enough beds in emergency shelters, officials in 16 of the 25 cities surveyed had to turn away individuals and homeless families with children (United States Conference of Mayors, 2012).

Some analysts now differentiate between the *chronic homeless*—the longtime street residents who often suffer from mental illness, drug abuse, or alcoholism—and the *economic homeless*, the working and middle-class people who are the newly displaced from homes by layoffs, foreclosure, or other financial problems because of the recent economic recession. Homelessness is common in urban areas, but family homeless rates have jumped by 56 percent in suburbs and rural areas (Bazar, 2009; U.S. Department of Housing and Urban Development, 2011; see also Kneebone and Berube, 2013).

Such numbers are conservative because counting the entire homeless population is an ongoing problem. Not all homeless people seek assistance at shelters, soup kitchens, or regularly scheduled food vans (Smith et al., 2012). Government agencies can't calculate the "uncounted homeless" who live in automobiles and campgrounds, have makeshift housing (such as boxes in a city alley or under a bridge), stay with relatives for short periods, or crowd into a single motel room—often sharing it with another family—until everyone's money runs out.

We've seen that many families are struggling to survive. The situation would be much worse if women weren't employed.

MAKING CONNECTIONS

- In 2013, a Gallup poll asked Americans "What is the smallest amount of money a family of four needs to make each year to get by in your community?" The estimate, on average, was $58,000 (Saad, 2013). How would *you* answer this question for a family of two adults and two children? Why?

- What do you think can be done to reduce the number of homeless families? Or is it impossible to do anything at all?

Women's and Men's Participation in the Labor Force

In 2009, 54 percent of fathers with children under age 18 said the ideal situation for young children was to have a mother who didn't work outside the home. Just two years later, the number dropped to 37 percent (Parker and Wang, 2013). Such attitudes affect women's labor force participation, but men's employment rates have also changed.

13.3 Compare the labor force participation of men and women.

Read on MySocLab

Document: The Rhetoric and Reality of "Opting Out"

Changes in the Workforce

One of the most dramatic changes in the United States during the twentieth century was women's increasing participation in the labor force. Especially since 1980, men's employment rates have dropped and women's have climbed. By 2000, women made up almost half of the workforce (see *Table 13.2*).

The number of stay-at-home moms has plunged—from 60 percent in 1970 to 24 percent in 2012 (Hayghe, 1984; "Mother's Day . . .," 2013). There has been a corresponding increase in the numbers of employed mothers with young children. In 2012, 58 percent of mothers with children younger than age 6 were in the workforce, compared with 39 percent in 1975 (U.S. Department of Labor, 2008; "Happy Mother's Day . . .," 2013).

More than half of all U.S. mothers with a child younger than age 1 work, they work longer during a pregnancy, and they return to work more quickly. For example, 58 percent of women return to work within three months of childbirth, compared with 17 percent between 1961 and 1965 (Johnson, 2008; "Happy Mother's Day . . .," 2013).

Why More Women Work

Watch on MySocLab

Video: Women in the Workplace

Generally, women and men work outside the home for the same two basic reasons—supporting themselves and their dependents and personal satisfaction. The opportunity to succeed and be rewarded for competence enhances self-esteem,

TABLE 13.2	Women and Men in the Labor Force, 1890–2012		
	Percentage of Men and Women in the Labor Force		Women as Percentage of All Workers
Year	Men	Women	
1890	84	18	17
1900	86	20	18
1920	85	23	20
1940	83	28	25
1960	84	38	33
1980	78	52	42
2000	75	60	48
2012	70	58	47

Sources: Based on Bureau of Labor Statistics, 2013, and *Women in the Labor Force . . .*, 2013.

Since you asked . . .

● Why has men's labor force participation decreased?

which, in turn, increases overall well-being, especially for people who enjoy their jobs (Mirowsky and Ross, 2007).

You saw earlier that deindustrialization and offshoring have resulted in job losses, especially in male-dominated occupations such as manufacturing. Some observers also blame the recent recession on men's lower employment rate: "The construction, manufacturing, and, for a time, financial industries all shrank, leading ultimately to the loss of 7.5 million jobs, three out of four of them held by men" (Kolhatkar, 2012: 102).

However, more women than men were laid off during the recession, and, after the recession, men regained 19 percent of lost jobs while women regained only 6 percent (Mirabella, 2011). Note, also, that men's labor force participation has been decreasing steadily since 1960 (see *Table 13.2*). Among men ages 25 to 54, employment rates fell in the 1980s for those without a college degree, especially in white-collar jobs. Men have also been more likely than women to retire by age 65 because they have higher Social Security payments and well-paying pensions (Lee and Mather, 2008). Thus, men's declining labor force rates are due to both macro-level changes (such as deindustrialization and offshoring) and micro-level variables (such as inadequate education to qualify for middle income jobs).

Factors affecting the rise in women's employment rates are more complex. The vast majority of workers need a paycheck, but marital status affects women more than men. Wives married to men who work, who work more than 45 hours per week, and who have high earnings are more likely to exit the labor force than women, particularly mothers, who are separated, divorced, or never married (Mattingly and Smith, 2010; Shafer, 2011; Gibbs, 2012). "Variations in the Working Mother Role" examines motherhood and employment more closely.

Education also affects men and women differently. The large majority of fathers are employed regardless of their educational background, including 76 percent of those with no college education and 94 percent of those with postgraduate degrees. In contrast, the higher a woman's education, the more likely she is to work outside the home. For example, 48 percent of mothers with no high school diploma are employed compared with 66 percent of those with some college, 75 percent of those with a bachelor's degree, and 84 percent of those with a postgraduate degree (Saad, 2012). Compared with 8 percent of other mothers in the labor force, 19 percent of stay-at-home moms don't have a high school diploma ("Mother's Day . . .," 2013).

Watch on MySocLab

Video: Education and Financial Success

Changes | Variations in the Working Mother Role

Employed mothers reflect a variety of motivations. Here are four general categories (Moen, 1992: 42–44):

- *Captives* would prefer to be full-time homemakers. These mothers may be single parents who are sole breadwinners, wives of blue-collar workers whose incomes are insufficient to support the family, or middle-class wives who find two salaries necessary to maintain a desired standard of living. Captives remain in the labor force reluctantly.

- *Conflicteds* feel that their employment is harmful to their children.

They are likely to leave the workforce while their children are young, and many quit their jobs when their spouse secures better-paying work.

- *Copers* are women with young children who choose jobs with enough flexibility to accommodate family needs. As a result, they often settle for minimally demanding jobs that offer lower wages and fewer benefits, and in the long run they forgo promotions, seniority advantages, and pay increases.

- *Committeds* have both high occupational aspirations and

a strong commitment to marriage and family life. Even in two-income families, however, only a minority of mothers can afford good child care and are free to pursue careers.

STOP AND THINK . . .

- Do these categories also describe employed fathers?
- Do you think the mothers' level of education affects their motivations to work?

Women who have invested more time in their education have a greater commitment to their careers, can command higher salaries, and have more work experience than do women with fewer years of schooling. They have the resources to purchase child care services, especially if their spouses are also employed (Cotter et al., 2007; Percheski, 2008). Also, among employed mothers with a first birth, 66 percent of those with at least a bachelor's degree compared with 19 percent of those who haven't graduated from high school receive paid leave (i.e., maternity leave, sick leave, vacation) (Laughlin, 2011).

Being an employed or stay-at-home mom aren't the only options. There are other possibilities that reflect a couple's economic resources and personal choices.

MAKING CONNECTIONS

- "The greater a family's financial need, the more likely a woman is to be employed." Do you agree?
- Is a woman with a college degree "wasting" her education by being a full-time homemaker?

Marital Economic Roles

13.4 Describe two ways that economic factors shape marital roles.

In Chapter 5, we examined the traditional male breadwinner–female homemaker roles. There are two variations on the traditional division of labor within marriage: the two-person single career and the stay-at-home dad.

The Two-Person Single Career

In the **two-person single career**, a spouse participates in the other's career behind the scenes, without pay or direct recognition. The wives of many college professors, for example, support their husband's career by entertaining faculty and students, doing library research, helping write and edit journal articles or books, and grading exams.

College presidents and their spouses, too, often have a two-person single career. Whether the president is a man or a woman, the spouse spends considerable time in activities such as entertaining; organizing fund-raising events; attending campus events; meeting with faculty, students, and staff members; and often also running a household and raising their children (Oden, 2008; Wilson, 2008).

The best public example of the two-person single career is that of the first lady, who often enjoys considerable power. Nancy Reagan influenced her husband's staffing decisions, Barbara Bush criticized her husband's opponents,

two-person single career A spouse participates in the other's career behind the scenes without pay or direct recognition.

Hillary Rodham Clinton promoted her husband's domestic policies and defended him during his sex scandals, and Laura Bush endorsed improvements in teaching (Allgor, 2002). Michelle Obama, similarly, spends much of her time addressing groups and traveling abroad with her husband in support of the administration's domestic and foreign policies.

The military imposes numerous demands on family life that often require a two-person single career. Whether they live on military installations or in their own homes, the spouses of soldiers on active duty must often sacrifice their own interests to support the soldier's role (McFadyen et al., 2005). General David Petraeus's wife, Holly, said that their family moved 24 times in 37 years as he climbed the military ladder (Shapira, 2012). During long or frequent separations, Army spouses' and partners' psychological well-being improves if they have informal support networks such as friends, and access to formal support services such as financial assistance, health and mental health services, and recreation and fitness programs (Orthner and Rose, 2009).

Stay-at-Home Dads

Since you asked . . .

• Do stay-at-home dads parent differently than mothers?

Every year, the media feature and applaud stay-at-home dads, but their numbers are negligible. In 2012, 189,000 fathers cared for children younger than age 15 while their spouses worked outside the home. Among married couples, only about 3 percent of fathers are stay-at-home dads during a given year ("Father's Day . . ." 2013).

REASONS Being a stay-at-home dad is usually a temporary role that's due to unemployment or health problems. Others are retired or have remarried much younger women who are employed (Gutner, 2001). In 2012, 7 of the 18 women who were CEOs of Fortune 500 companies had a stay-at-home husband. Most of these men took early retirement from high-level executive positions, were wealthy, scaled back their careers, and hired nannies to assist them with child care (Morris, 2003; Hymowitz, 2012).

Sometimes male graduate students who are supported by their employed spouses take on a modified housekeeping role, doing household chores between classes and studying at the library. And, especially at well-financed private colleges and universities, some male faculty take advantage of generous one-year family leaves to care for their children while the mother works (Latessa, 2005).

BENEFITS AND COSTS Being a full-time dad is a mixed blessing. Some find child rearing a joy because they're more intimately involved with their kids: "I know my son's and daughter's friends. I know everything they like and dislike. I have the chance to be there to answer questions" (Barovick, 2002: B10).

Compared with mothers, at-home dads are more likely to let their children take more risks on the playground, to organize outdoor adventures, to instill problem-solving skills by letting young children figure things out for themselves, to use apps to manage household tasks such as grocery shopping, and to involve their kids in do-it-yourself projects. For example, a stay-at-home dad who was laid off decided to remodel the family's apartment to save money. He took his 2-year-old son "on a walking tour of Home Depot, where the toddler studied different kinds of hammers and learned how to use a tape measure" (Shellenbarger, 2013: D1).

On the other hand, some stay-at-home dads are concerned about losing their business skills and their professional place in line, and they feel unappreciated by their working spouses, who sometimes complain that the house is a mess. Even when stay-at-home dads say that it's one of the most rewarding experiences they've had, they often feel stigmatized and emasculated

Why do stay-at-home dads receive so much media attention?

by unemployment because much of their identity comes from being a good provider. Says an at-home dad who lost his job at a large investment bank, "I just can't shake the feeling that I'm out of step with the world" (Blomfield, 2009: 22).

In most families, parents don't have the choice of staying home with their children. Instead, both partners work either part time or full time, and sometimes both.

Two-Income Families

Two-income families are becoming more common. There are dual-earner and dual-career couples, commuter marriages, and marriages in which wives earn more than their husbands.

Dual-Earner and Dual-Career Families

When both spouses work full time, the median family income can be twice as high (see *Figure 13.6*). Two-income families include both dual-earner and dual-career couples.

HOW THEY DIFFER In **dual-earner couples** (also called *dual-income, two-earner, two-paycheck,* or *dual-worker* couples), both partners work outside the home. These couples make up 59 percent of all married-couple families. On average, wives in dual-earner couples increase their families' total income by 38 percent, up from 27 percent in 1970 ("Employment Characteristics . . .," 2013; *Women in the Labor Force . . .,* 2013).

Despite their two incomes, dual-earner families are seldom affluent. Only a small fraction has much **discretionary income**, money remaining after the costs of basic necessities such as food, rent, utilities, and transportation have been paid. Many dual-earner families are middle-aged people who are paying for their children's college education, saving for their own retirement, and sometimes helping low-income aging parents (Warren and Tyagi, 2003; see also Chapter 16).

In **dual-career couples**, both partners work in professional or managerial positions that require extensive training, a long-term commitment, and ongoing professional growth. The partners have a Ph.D. or a postgraduate degree in law,

13.5 Describe three variations of two-income families.

dual-earner couple Both partners work outside the home (also called *dual-income, two-earner, two-paycheck,* and *dual-worker* couples).

discretionary income Money remaining after the costs of basic necessities have been paid.

dual-career couple Both partners work in professional or managerial positions that require extensive training, a long-term commitment, and ongoing professional growth.

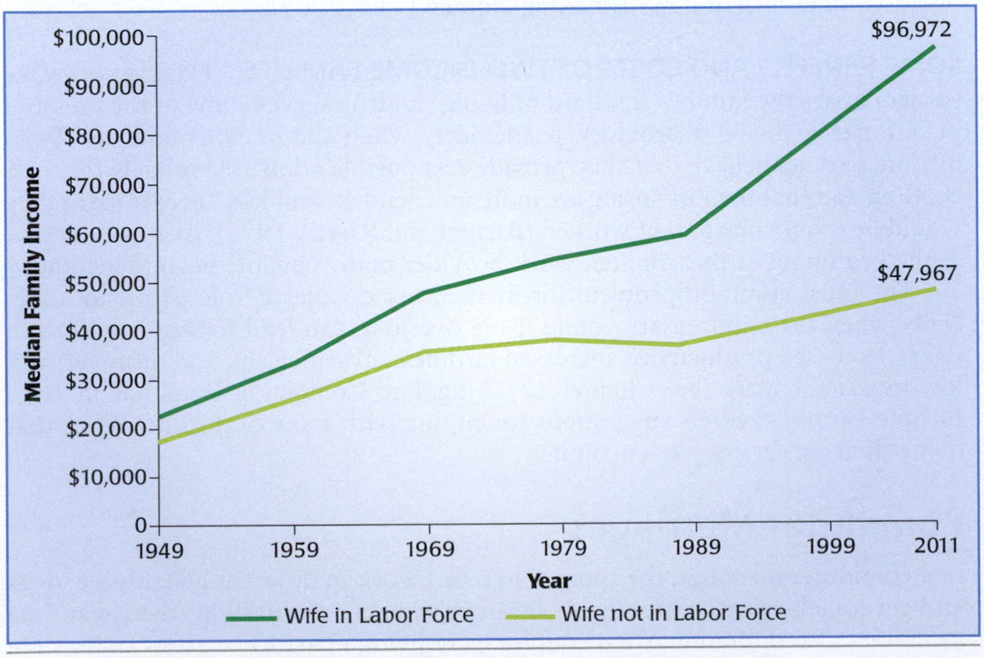

FIGURE 13.6 Median Family Income When Wives Work Full-Time, Year-Round, or Don't Work, 1949–2011
Source: U.S. Census Bureau, 2011. "Historical Income Tables—Families," Table F-13, www.census.gov (accessed August 20, 2013).

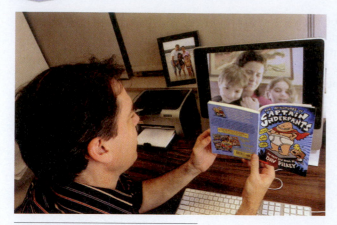

Many parents in commuter marriages stay in touch with their children via Skype. Here, a college professor who teaches in New Orleans reads to his children who live in Chicago with his wife.

medicine, or business. The better educated the couple, the more they earn, and the more hours they work. There are no national data on dual-career couples, but one survey found that among more than 9,000 full-time faculty at 13 U.S. research universities, 36 percent were dual-career academic couples (Schiebinger et al., 2008).

GENDER ROLES AND PARENTING   In a national survey, 72 percent of those born between 1977 and 1992, compared with 56 percent of adults age 65 and older, said that *both* spouses should have jobs *and* take care of the house and children (Wang and Taylor, 2011). Thus, many people are endorsing egalitarian gender roles regarding family and work responsibilities. Considerable research shows, however, that behavior hasn't caught up with attitudes because parenting is still gendered among many two-income couples.

Even though many dual-earner couples say that they believe in egalitarian roles, only 9 percent of the couples make similar domestic and employment contributions. Among 91 percent of the couples, the mothers have more responsibility for domestic tasks, especially child care (Hall and MacDermid, 2009). When there are conflicts between work and family responsibilities, mothers are more likely than fathers to hurt their careers by refusing out-of-town travel or working extra hours, to turn down promotions and interesting assignments, and to rearrange their work schedules (Maume, 2006).

A recent survey of dual-income couples found that when paid work, housework, and child care were considered, parents had almost equal "workloads"—59 hours for mothers and 58 hours for fathers each week. Fathers spent 26 percent more time than mothers in paid work, but mothers spent almost twice as much time as fathers on housework and child care (Parker and Wang, 2013).

Especially in professional and managerial jobs, the norm is a 60-hour week for both partners. The long work hours intensify gender inequality by reinforcing "separate spheres" at home and the workplace. That is, when the husband works long hours, his wife is more likely to quit because of child care responsibilities, but wives' long work hours don't affect men's employment status or child-rearing tasks. Even though most highly educated women are committed to their careers and work long hours, they're less likely than their male counterparts to advance in their jobs because cultural expectations and gender ideologies still endorse breadwinning men and homemaking women (Cha, 2009).

SOME BENEFITS AND COSTS OF TWO-INCOME FAMILIES   Having two wage earners raises the family's standard of living. It also relieves some of the pressure of one parent being a provider, particularly when she or he is laid off. Two-income parents believe that they provide responsible adult role models for their children and that their offspring are more independent and less "needy" than they would be if only one parent worked (Barnett and Rivers, 1996). Also, as you saw at the beginning of this chapter, work provides many benefits beyond income.

The most common problem for dual-earner couples is role overload, especially when the children are young. Role overload can lead to increased health risks; decreased productivity; increased tardiness, absenteeism, and turnover; and low morale at work (see Chapter 12). "Juggling Competing Demands in Two-Income Families" offers suggestions for coping with some of the difficulties that many dual earner couples encounter.

Commuter Marriages

In a **commuter marriage**, the spouses live and work in different geographic areas and get together intermittently, such as over weekends. In 2006 (the latest data available), 3.6 million married couples were living apart for reasons other than

commuter marriage Spouses live and work in different geographic areas and get together intermittently.

Applying What You've Learned   Juggling Competing Demands in Two-Income Families

As you read these suggestions for balancing work and family life, think about other strategies that have worked for you, your parents, or your friends.

- **Emphasize the positive.** Concentrate on the benefits you get from having a job: personal fulfillment, a higher standard of living, and providing more cultural and educational opportunities for your children.

- **Set priorities.** Because conflicts between family and job demands are inevitable, establish principles for resolving clashes. For example, parents might take turns staying home with sick children.

- **Compromise.** Striving for perfection in family and job responsibilities is unrealistic. Instead, aim for the best possible balance among your various activities, making compromises when necessary. For example, homes don't have to be immaculate.

- **Separate family and work roles.** Many mothers, especially, feel guilty while at work because they're not with their children. And when they're at home, they feel guilty about not working on office assignments. If you

must work at home, set time limits for the work and enjoy the rest of the time with your family.

- **Organize domestic duties.** Resolve domestic overload by dividing family work more equitably between adults and children. Many families find it useful to prepare a weekly or monthly job chart in which everyone's assignments are clearly written down. It's also useful to rotate assignments so that everyone gets to do both the "better" and the "worse" jobs.

- **Cultivate a sharing attitude.** Sit down with your partner periodically and discuss what you can do to help each other in your roles at home and at work. Most of us are happier when our spouses and partners provide a sounding board or offer encouragement.

- **Maintain a balance between responsibilities and recreation.** If you are both working to improve your standard of living, use some of your extra income to enjoy life. Otherwise, you'll have little energy left for activities that make life more enjoyable.

Sources: Based on Beck, 1988, and Crosby, 1991b.

---

marital discord. This represents almost 3 percent of all U.S. marriages, up from 2 percent in 2000. The numbers have probably increased because many couples are accepting jobs that require living apart, sometimes in another country, because of globalization (Kridel, 2009; Long Distance Relationships, 2013).

WHY THEY DO IT   There are several reasons for commuter marriages. First, and most important, when jobs are scarce, financial security is an important factor in launching a commuter marriage. Second, if one partner sees that relocation will have negative effects on her or his employment prospects, she or he may decide not to move. Third, if both partners have well-established careers in different cities, neither may be willing to make major job sacrifices after marriage. Fourth, a commuter marriage may avoid the stress of uprooting teenage children or aging parents.

SOME BENEFITS AND COSTS OF COMMUTER MARRIAGES   The major benefit of a commuter marriage is a paycheck, especially when higher-paying jobs are scarce. According to a partner at a large investment firm, "Eighteen months ago anyone searching for a new job would ask to be placed in their current location. Now they come in and say 'I am prepared to move,' even, if necessary, without the family" (Conlin, 2009: 1).

Long-distance couples believe that they can devote more attention to their work during the week and that they learn to appreciate and make the most of the time they have together. Each person is more independent and can take advantage of time alone to pursue hobbies or recreational interests that the other partner might not enjoy. As one commuter husband noted, "She can watch all the foreign movies she wants and eat sushi for lunch and dinner" (Justice, 1999: 12).

Commuter marriages also have disadvantages, including time constraints and extra costs. Frequent airplane flights and maintaining two residences can be expensive: "Two mortgages, property tax bills, electric bills, heating fuel bills, phone bills, garbage bills, grocery lists, driveways to plow, yards to maintain, and two houses to clean" (K. Smith, 2009: F15).

The commuting partner may also feel socially isolated, a situation that can lead to extramarital relationships on the part of either partner, or a divorce if

there has been previous marital conflict. The stay-at-home parent may resent the weekend parent, who shoulders little of the parenting responsibility. In other cases, the stay-at-home parent, who is usually the wife, sometimes doesn't look forward to the commuter's weekend visits because it means preparing more elaborate dinners and being stricter with the children (Cullen, 2007; Conlin, 2009).

Whether or not a two-income marriage involves long-distance commuting, women earn less than men, as you'll see later in this chapter. However, there's also an increasing number of families in which the wife earns more than her husband.

When Wives Earn More

In 2011, 28 percent of women earned more than their husbands, up from 18 percent in 1987. And, in 2011, the median family income was nearly $80,000 for couples in which the wife was the primary breadwinner, about $2,000 more than it was for couples in which the husband was the primary breadwinner (Bureau of Labor Statistics, 2012; Wang et al., 2013).

Between 1970 and 2011, marriage rates increased for the top 10 percent of female earners, but declined for the bottom 70 percent of female earners. From an economic perspective, then, many men benefit by marrying rather than being single. Also, the higher the wife's education, the greater her contribution to the household income (Fry and Cohn, 2010; Greenstone and Looney, 2012).

According to exchange and resource theories, the partner with the higher income typically has more power in a relationship (see Chapters 2 and 10). The data are mixed, however. In households where the husband brings in more income, buying decisions are made about equally, but if the wife earns more than her husband, she typically makes twice as many buying decisions as the man (Mundy, 2012). On the other hand, wives who earn more than their husbands do more, not less, housework than women who earn about the same amount as their husbands. Wives who outearn their husbands are deviating from cultural expectations that men should be the primary breadwinners. Wives may try to "neutralize" the deviance by increasing their housework time. Doing so reinforces domestic gender roles, doesn't threaten the husband's masculinity, doesn't invite jokes by family and friends about the man being "hen-pecked," and decreases the possibility of interpersonal conflict (Greenstein, 2000; Bittman et al., 2003; Tichenor, 2005; Schneider, 2011).

MAKING CONNECTIONS

- Do you think that two-income couples experience more benefits or more stresses than single-income couples? Why?

- If wives earn more than their husbands, should husbands do more of the housework and child care?

13.6 Explain how and why workplace inequality affects families.

Inequality in the Workplace

Worldwide, men are much more likely than women to be in the labor force, to work full time, and not to be underemployed (Marlar, 2011). In the United States, there are also striking differences between employed women and men. Let's begin by looking at income gaps between women and men and across racial-ethnic groups.

Women and Minorities in the Workplace

There are earning disparities across ethnic-racial groups, but the differences are especially striking by sex. As you examine *Figure 13.7*, note two general characteristics. First, earnings increase—across all racial-ethnic groups and for both sexes—as people go up the occupational ladder. For example, managers and professionals make considerably more than car mechanics and truck drivers. But, across *all* occupations, men have higher earnings than females of the same racial-ethnic group. At the bottom of the occupational ladder are African American women and Latinas, with the latter faring worse than any of the other groups. Thus, both sex *and* race-ethnicity affect earnings, and there's a gender pay gap across all racial-ethnic groups and occupations.

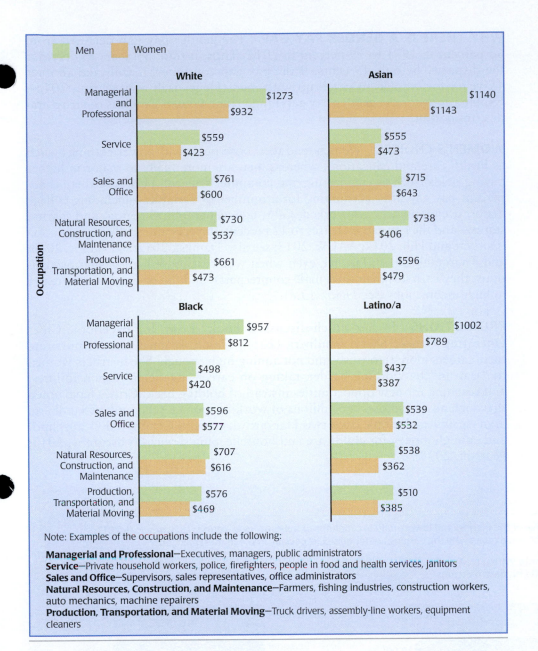

FIGURE 13.7 **Median Weekly Earnings of Full-Time Workers by Occupation, Sex, Race, and Ethnicity** *Source:* Based on Bureau of Labor Statistics, U.S. Department of Labor, *The Editor's Desk*, "Earnings and Employment by Occupation, Race, Ethnicity, and Sex, 2010," www.bls.gov/opub/ted/2011/ted_20110914.htm (accessed April 6, 2013*).

The Gender Pay Gap

In 2012, women who worked full time year-round had a median income of $36,088, compared with $45,500 for men. This means that women earned 79 cents for every dollar men earned. (In the same year, a woman with a college degree earned only slightly more per year than a man with an associate degree—$48,360 and $45,760, respectively) ("Usual Weekly Earnings . . ." 2013; *Women in the Labor Force . . .*, 2013). Stated differently, *the average woman must work almost four extra months every year to make the same wages as a man.*

The **gender pay gap** (sometimes called the *wage gap, pay gap,* or *gender wage gap*) is the overall income difference between women and men in the workplace. The pay gap varies—from 69 cents in Louisiana to 92 cents in California (U.S. Congress Joint Economic Committee, 2012). Over a lifetime, the average woman who works full time and year-round over four decades loses a significant amount of money because of the gender pay gap: $700,000 for high school graduates; $1.2 million for college graduates; and more than $2 million for women with a professional degree (such as business, medicine, or law). Lower wages and salaries reduce women's savings, purchasing power, quality of life, and result in smaller Social Security payments after retirement (Murphy and Graff, 2005; Soguel, 2009).

Watch on MySocLab

Video: Disparity in Earnings

gender pay gap The overall income difference between women and men in the workplace (also called the *wage gap, pay gap,* and *gender wage gap*).

Since you asked . . .
- Why, across all occupations, do women earn less than men?

WHY THERE IS A GENDER PAY GAP   The gender pay gap declined from 60 percent in 1971 to 79 percent in 2012. Thus, it took 35 years to decrease the disparity by only 19 cents. If the pay gap continues, it will take another 45 years for women to catch up with men (Hegewisch and Matite, 2013). Explanations for the gender pay gap range from women's choices to structural discrimination.

WOMEN'S CHOICES   Women tend to choose fields with lower earnings (such as health care and education), whereas men are more likely to major in higher paying fields (such as engineering and computer science). However, there is a 7 percent pay gap after accounting for a number of variables—including college major, occupation, hours worked, GPA, age, geographical region, and marital status—and the pay gap increases to 12 percent 10 years after college graduation (Corbett and Hill, 2012; AAUW, 2013; see also Damast, 2012/2013; Lips, 2013; and Tharenou, 2013). Further, even when women choose high-paying occupations, they earn less than their male counterparts, and the wage gaps are greater in high-income jobs (see *Figure 13.8*).

PROMOTIONS   In her much-discussed book, *Lean In*, Facebook Chief Operating Officer Sheryl Sandberg (2013) blames women for not pursuing their careers more rigorously and not aiming high enough. She instructs women to "lean in" by working harder, taking on career-advancing responsibilities, and reaching for new opportunities instead of holding back. Critics have noted that such advice ignores the millions of working women who, unlike Sandberg, aren't privileged, don't have two Harvard degrees, a wealthy CEO husband, and enough money for child care and housekeeping services (Luscombe, 2013; Pearson, 2013).

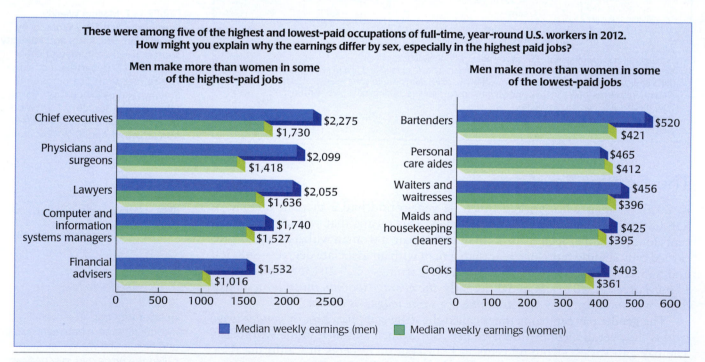

FIGURE 13.8 Women Earn Less Than Men Whether They're CEOs or Cooks

Note: Some of the differences between men's and women's median weekly earnings may seem small, but multiply each figure by 52 weeks. Thus, in annual earnings, male computer and information systems managers average more than $90,000 a year compared with $79,000 for females.

Source: Based on Labor Force Statistics from the Current Population Survey, 2013, Table 39, ìMedian Weekly Earnings of Full-Time Wage and Salary Workers by Detailed Occupation and Sex,î http://www.bls.gov/cps/cpsaat39.htm (accessed April 10, 2013).

Among 18- to 34-year-olds, 66 percent of women, compared with 59 percent of men, rate a high-paying career or profession as one of their life's top priorities (Patten and Parker, 2012). It's doubtful that these or other men or women would pass up a promotion. Instead of refusing promotions that require greater responsibility, women and men younger than age 29 are equally interested in jobs with greater responsibility, and there are few differences between mothers and women without children in this age group (Galinsky et al., 2009).

Many women hit a **glass ceiling**, attitudinal and organizational workplace obstacles that prevent women from advancing to leadership positions. Examples of obstacles include men's negative attitudes about women in the workplace (see Chapter 5), women's placement in staff positions that aren't on the career track to the top, a lack of mentoring, biased and damaging evaluations by male supervisors, and little or no access to highly visible committees or task forces (Barreto et al., 2009; Sandberg, 2013).

In contrast, many men who enter female-dominated occupations (such as nursing and teaching) receive higher wages and faster promotions, a phenomenon known as a **glass escalator**. In 2011, for example, men made up only 10 percent of all registered nurses, but the average female nurse earned $51,100, 16 percent less than the $60,700 that the average male nurse earned. Men on glass escalators tend to fare better even than men in male-dominated jobs; in female-dominated occupations, they easily move up to supervisory positions (Dewan and Gebeloff, 2012; Goudreau, 2012; Casselman, 2013).

THE MOTHERHOOD PENALTY   Many women's earnings suffer from a **motherhood penalty** (also called *motherhood wage penalty* or *mommy penalty*), a pay gap between women who are mothers and women who aren't mothers. On average, women without children make 90 cents to a man's dollar, mothers make 73 cents to a man's dollar, and single mothers make only 60 cents to a man's dollar (Rowe-Finkbeiner, 2012; Stevens, 2012).

A groundbreaking study of the motherhood penalty found that many employers believed that mothers, compared with nonmothers, are less committed to the workplace, less dependable, and less competent. Even though both groups had very similar résumés and work experience, the women who were mothers were offered $11,000 less in starting salaries than women who weren't mothers. Men were offered higher salaries than women, but fathers were offered $6,000 more than nonfathers, even though, again, both groups had similar résumés and work experience. The employers believed that fathers would be more dedicated to the job and needed a higher starting salary. In effect, then, parenthood penalizes employed mothers but tends to reward fathers (Correll et al., 2007; see also Glauber, 2007).

OCCUPATIONAL SEX SEGREGATION   Occupational sex segregation (sometimes called *occupational gender segregation*) is the process of channeling women and men into different types of jobs. Occupational sex segregation has decreased since the 1970s, but 40 percent of women are employed in traditionally female occupations (e.g., social work, teaching, nursing), and 44 percent of men work in traditionally male occupations (e.g., aerospace engineering, computer programming, firefighting) (AAUW, 2013).

Occupational sex segregation is a major factor behind the pay gap because female-dominated occupations pay lower wages (Hegewisch and Matite, 2013). In 2012, for example, among full-time employees, 98 percent of workers in construction, production, or transportation occupations were men; their annual median earnings were almost $39,000. Bank tellers—89 percent of whom are women—had annual median earnings of only $26,000 (Bureau of Labor Statistics, 2013). Many women and some men must also endure workplace abuses such as sexual harassment.

Are successful single workers experiencing workplace discrimination? Many maintain that they're expected to work longer hours than their co-workers who have spouses and children (Byrd, 2013).

glass ceiling Attitudinal and organizational workplace obstacles that prevent women from advancing to leadership positions.

glass escalator Men who enter female-dominated occupations and receive higher wages and faster promotions.

motherhood penalty Pay gap between women who are mothers and women who aren't mothers (also called a *motherhood wage penalty* and *mommy penalty*).

occupational sex segregation Channeling women and men into different types of jobs (also called *occupational gender segregation*).

Sexual Harassment

Before reading any further, take the "Do You Recognize Sexual Harassment?" quiz to see how attuned you are to this issue.

You certainly know by now that sexual harassment is illegal (see Chapter 5). In the workplace, sexual harassment is a display of power that is usually perpetrated by a boss and directed at a subordinate of the same or opposite sex. Because men dominate in positions of power, it's far more likely that a harasser will be a man than a woman. Some people claim that there's a fine line between sexual harassment, flirting, or simply giving a compliment. Wrong. If someone says, "Stop it,"

In 2004, a Burger King in St. Louis, Missouri, settled a sexual harassment lawsuit for a mere $400,000. The money was paid to seven high school female employees whose boss had subjected them to groping, vulgar sexual comments, and demands for sex.

ASK YOURSELF

Do You Recognize Sexual Harassment?

Is it sexual harassment if:

Yes No

1. An employee e-mails or texts sexual jokes to co-workers?

2. An employee continues to ask a co-worker to go out on dates despite repeated refusals?

3. Employees tell bawdy jokes to co-workers who enjoy them in nonworkplace settings?

4. Flirting occurs between mutually consenting individuals who are equal in power or authority?

5. Male and female co-workers repeatedly talk about their sexual affairs and relationships at the office?

6. A cashier in a restaurant greets each customer by calling him or her "honey" or "dearie"?

Yes No

7. A male supervisor tells a female employee, "You look very nice today"?

8. Employees put up pornographic material on company bulletin boards or in lockers?

9. Employees or supervisors make frequent comments to co-workers about sexually explicit material in the media (films, television, magazines)?

10. At the end of a staff meeting, a male manager says to two female secretaries, "Why don't you girls clean up this room?"

The answers are on page 392.

and the perpetrator doesn't stop, it's sexual harassment. Most people know—both instinctively and because of the other person's reaction—when sexual attentions are unwelcome.

Sexual harassment can be costly, both emotionally and financially. It constitutes wage discrimination because repeated incidents can cause the targets (who are usually women) to leave or lose their jobs and, consequently, forfeit potential raises and promotions. Victims of sexual harassment may also experience emotional and behavioral problems, including depression, that affect their families; changes in attitudes toward sexual relationships; irritability toward family members, friends, or co-workers; and alcohol and drug abuse (Rettner, 2011).

Families and Work Policies

How "family friendly" are workplace policies? In 2013, Yahoo!'s new CEO, Marissa Mayer, eliminated working from home. She also announced that she would take only two weeks of maternity leave. After the baby's birth, and having a nursery built next to her office, Mayer told an audience at *Fortune* magazine's Most Powerful Women dinner, "The baby's been way easier than everyone made it out to be" (Fuller, 2012). We'll address maternity leave shortly, but working mothers, particularly, criticized Mayer's dismissive attitude toward maternity leave and terminating working from home.

13.7 Describe four workplace policies that can benefit or disadvantage families.

Explore on MySocLab

Activity: Family vs. Job: Who Wins

Flextime

Flextime is a scheduling arrangement that permits employees to change their daily arrival and departure times. Some employers endorse flextime because it decreases tardiness resulting from arriving late due to seeing children off to school or leaving early because of being home when the kids leave school. Also, employees who work later shifts can accommodate more clients and customers, especially those in different time zones. However, women are less likely than men to have access to flextime because men are more likely to occupy higher-income and managerial positions that offer such options (Payne, 2013).

The more flexibility employees have, the higher their job satisfaction and the less likely they are to leave a company (Hill et al., 2010). Flexible work schedules reduce work–family conflicts that, in turn, decrease the likelihood of exhaustion, stress, depression, job turnover, absenteeism, and irritability with family members. Women, single parents, and those with high child care and housework workloads are especially likely to benefit from workplace flexibility, and at very little cost to an employer (Matos and Galinsky, 2011; Jang et al., 2012).

flextime Scheduling arrangement that permits employees to change their daily arrival and departure times.

telecommuting Working remotely through electronic linkups to a central office.

Telecommuting

Telecommuting, working remotely through electronic linkups to a central office, is a flexible option that allows parents to combine work and child rearing. According to some surveys, 80 to 86 percent of employees want the opportunity to work from home (Suddath, 2013).

Some policy analysts encourage employers to expand telecommuting. Doing so would cut a company's energy costs, reduce pollution because fewer people would be driving to work, decrease the pool of workers who experience transportation problems (especially in urban and rural areas), enhance productivity by reducing the number of trips to work, lower

"HOW FLEXIBLE ARE WE ON THE ISSUE OF FLEXTIME?"

Sales representatives, such as this mother, can often work from home, which enables them to interact with their children more frequently.

overhead costs by decreasing the amount of office space, and increase access to a larger pool of qualified workers (Cox, 2009; DeGray, 2012).

In 2010, 13.4 million people (almost 10 percent of U.S. workers) worked from home at least one day a week, up from 9.2 million (7 percent of U.S. workers) in 1997. The number of people in computer, engineering, and science jobs who worked exclusively or part time from home increased 69 percent between 2000 and 2010—from 252,000 to 432,000 workers. The median annual household income for employees who worked both at home and at the job site was higher ($96,000) than for those who worked exclusively at home ($74,000), or those who worked exclusively at the job site ($66,000), presumably because telecommuters tend to be highly educated (Mateyka et al., 2012; "Working at Home Is on the Rise," 2013). "Some Perks and Perils of Telecommuting" addresses some of the benefits and costs of working exclusively part time from home.

Pregnancy Discrimination

The Pregnancy Discrimination Act of 1978 makes it illegal for employers with more than 15 workers to fire, demote, or penalize a pregnant employee. Some state laws extend this protection to companies with as few as 4 employees. Despite such laws, the EEOC reports that charges of pregnancy discrimination have risen at least 33 percent in recent years. In 2011 alone, nearly 5,800 women filed complaints that they had been fired, demoted, or had some of their responsibilities taken away when their employers learned that the women were pregnant (U.S. Equal Employment Opportunity Commission, 2011). This is just the tip of the iceberg because only a fraction of women who encounter pregnancy discrimination ever take action: Many aren't aware of their rights and others don't have the resources to pursue lengthy lawsuits.

Changes | Some Perks and Perils of Telecommuting

On the *positive side* of telecommuting, workers can save almost $7,000 a year on gasoline costs, lunches, and an office wardrobe if they work from home for half of every workweek. Besides reducing the cost of child care, some report that working at home brings the family closer together: A parent is available when a child returns from school, and family members sometimes get involved in the telecommuter's work-related tasks.

Telecommuting can also boost productivity because it improves morale (for example, people have more control over their time and schedule). Workers waste less time (such as chatting with co-workers at the water cooler) and are less tired because they don't commute to and from a central office. People who work from home often put in more

hours because they don't have to cram everything into a 9 to 5 work schedule.

On the *negative side*, some telecommuters feel personally and professionally isolated and lonely. Employees who work remotely even part of the time risk getting smaller raises, worse performance evaluations, and fewer promotions than their co-workers at the office get because they have less "face time" (interaction with colleagues and supervisors at the same physical location). Consequently, they may work extra hours on nights or weekends. Also, 30 percent of supervisors believe that telecommuters may be "slacking off."

Telecommuting can also decrease the quality of family time. Some parents resent interruptions or distractions while they're working, or find that it's difficult to separate their family and business

lives. Noise from neighbors, children, pets, and appliances may also decrease productivity and create tension at home.

Sources: Hill et al., 2010; Price, 2011; DeGray, 2012; Elsbach and Cable, 2012; Suddath, 2013; Zimmerman, 2013.

STOP AND THINK . . .

- Between 63 and 66 percent of employers report increased productivity and fewer absences among telecommuters (Zimmerman, 2013). Why, then, isn't telecommuting more widespread?
- What are some of the ways that telecommuters—including those who work almost exclusively from home—can increase their face time?

Family and Medical Leave Policies

The Family and Medical Leave Act (FMLA) of 1993 allows eligible employees to take up to 12 weeks of *unpaid* annual leave, with continuation of health benefits, after the birth or adoption of a child, to care for a seriously sick family member, or to recover from their own illnesses. "A Tour of the Family and Medical Leave Act" provides a closer look at these rights.

BENEFITS OF THE FMLA The most obvious benefit of family leave policies is that employees don't have to lose their jobs because of sickness, childbirth, or parental leave. Also, most employees are guaranteed the same or equivalent job when they return. The Family and Medical Leave Act defines an "equivalent" position as one with the same pay, benefits, working conditions, and "substantially similar" duties and responsibilities. Most important, because the FMLA is the law, employees don't have to depend on the supervisor's good will for leave.

LIMITATIONS OF THE FMLA There are several problems with the Family and Medical Leave Act. First, the leave is unpaid. Second, the FMLA covers only major illnesses that typically require hospitalization. In most cases, children have frequent routine illnesses that last only a few days. Many working parents can't afford to take any unpaid leave because of the cost or the risk of being laid off (Phillips, 2004).

Third, about 40 percent of U.S. employees who work in companies with fewer than 50 employees aren't covered by the FMLA, and many who are covered

Since you asked . . .
• Does the FMLA reinforce traditional gender roles?

 Watch on MySocLab

Video: Government, Business, and Family Policy

Choices   A Tour of the Family and Medical Leave Act

Workers who know their rights under the Family and Medical Leave Act (FMLA) are more likely to take advantage of its benefits.

Who is covered? Any employee is eligible for 12 weeks of leave if she or he has worked at least 1,250 hours during a 12-month period—about the equivalent of 25 hours a week—at a company or work site that employs at least 50 people. However, the highest-paid 10 percent of employees aren't guaranteed a job on return if their absence causes "substantial and grievous economic injury" to the employer.

What are the purposes of leave? An employee may take family or medical leave for the birth or adoption of a child and to care for a newborn; to care for a spouse, child, or parent with a serious illness; or to recuperate from a serious illness that prevents the employee from working.

Who pays for the leave? The employee. A company may require or allow employees to apply paid vacation and sick leave to the

12 weeks of family leave, but it doesn't have to pay workers who take leave.

When should the employer be notified? In foreseeable cases, such as a birth, adoption, or planned medical treatment, 30 days' verbal or written notice is required. When that's impossible (for example, if a baby is born earlier than expected), the employer must be notified as soon as possible, generally within one or two business days. Employers can ask for medical proof that a leave is needed.

Must the leave be taken all at once? No. For example, the leave can be used to shorten the workweek when an employee wants to cut back after the birth of a child. Medical leave can also be taken piecemeal (to accommodate weekly appointments for chemotherapy treatments, for instance).

What if you believe that your rights have been violated? Any local or regional office of the U.S. Department of Labor's Wage

and Hour Division, Employment Standards Administration, will accept complaints, which must be filed within two years of the alleged violation. Private lawsuits must also be filed within two years of the violation.

According to a recent Supreme Court ruling (*Nevada Department of Human Resources v. Hibbs*), state employees can now sue agencies that violate the FMLA.

STOP AND THINK . . .

• The United States is the only industrialized country that doesn't provide paid parental leave. Should it do the same, even if it means increasing payroll taxes?

• Many U.S. employers now cover some paid maternity (but not paternity) leave under disability insurance. Why is pregnancy a "disability"? And why are men excluded from such "disability insurance"?

can't afford to take unpaid leave (Bernard, 2013). In addition, millions of workers in part-time, temporary positions (most of whom are women) are excluded from family leave policies.

Fourth, employees and employers may disagree about what constitutes "equivalent" jobs or "substantially similar" responsibilities. For example, does a person have an equivalent job if it involves driving an extra 30 minutes to an unfamiliar office at a less desirable location? Finally, the FMLA doesn't include elder care. About 79 percent of all companies say that they offer employees unpaid time off to care for aging parents without jeopardizing their jobs, but there are no guarantees (Bond et al., 2005).

STATES' FAMILY AND MEDICAL LEAVE POLICIES   Only 11 percent of private sector workers and 17 percent of public sector workers have access to paid family leave. Those who benefit are well-paid workers in managerial or professional occupations at companies with 100 or more employees (Houser and Vartanian, 2012). Some mothers stitch together paid leave (such as sick days and vacations) to cover childbirth and infant care for a few weeks or longer. The likelihood of doing so, however, is higher for women who are white, married, and have a college education. More than 83 percent of women with a high school diploma or less quit their jobs after a baby's birth (Laughlin, 2011).

Employees in California and New Jersey may take up to six weeks of leave that pays between 55 and 66 percent of the individual's average weekly earnings. The programs are financed entirely by short-term disability insurance and small payroll taxes that range from .06 to 1 percent. Hawaii, New York, and Rhode Island offer temporary disability insurance programs that cover some of the lost wages for leave during and immediately after pregnancy. Most companies don't incur any additional costs and save money because employee turnover drops (Houser and Vartanian, 2012).

COMPARISON WITH OTHER COUNTRIES   Out of 190 nations, 178 offer some form of paid maternity leave, and 54 guarantee paid leave for fathers. The United States, Papua New Guinea, and Swaziland are the only countries that have no national paid parental leave policy. Sweden has one of the most generous parental leave policies in the world—16 months of paid leave. The Netherlands, France, and Spain offer 16 weeks of maternity leave at full pay, Denmark provides 18 weeks at full pay, India provides 12 weeks at full pay, and Ireland offers 12 weeks at 80 percent of the worker's salary. Some countries—such as Belgium, Greece, France, Finland, Iceland, Israel, and Slovenia—provide between 4 weeks and 3 months of paid paternity leave at 80 to 100 percent of the worker's salary (Walsh, 2011; see also Weber, 2013).

ANSWERS TO "Do You Recognize Sexual Harassment?"

1. Yes, if repeated instances create an offensive and hostile work environment.
2. Yes.
3. No.
4. No.
5. No, if no one else is around and the talk is consensual. It could be sexual harassment if a passerby finds such talk offensive.
6. No, if the comments are directed at both sexes and aren't intentionally derogatory or degrading.
7. No.
8. Yes, this creates a hostile work environment.
9. Yes.
10. No, but it's a sexist comment.

CONCLUSION

Many families are struggling financially but have few *choices* such as working part time or full time. Macro-level economic *changes*, especially since 2008, have increased the number of women, mothers, and two-income couples in the labor force. Millions of families experience *constraints* that include unemployment, low wages, workplace inequality, and meager family leave policies. Many of the same economic forces also have an impact on family violence, a topic we examine in the next chapter.

On MySocLab

 **Study** and **Review** on MySocLab

---

REVIEW QUESTIONS

13.1. Explain how and why work in U.S. society has changed.

1. How have deindustrialization, globalization, offshoring, and unions affected workers and their families?

2. How, specifically, has the economy affected social class? And, in turn, how does social class affect families?

13.2. Explain five ways that the economy impacts families.

3. What's the difference between the working poor, discouraged workers, and underemployed workers?

4. Who is poor? And why?

13.3. Compare the labor force participation of men and women.

5. How and why has men's and women's labor force participation changed since the 1980s?

6. How does education affect women's and men's labor force participation?

13.4. Describe two ways that economic factors shape marital roles.

7. How does a two-person single career differ from a traditional male breadwinner–female homemaker marriage?

8. What are some of the benefits and costs of being a stay-at-home dad?

13.5. Describe three variations of two-income families.

9. What's the difference, if any, between dual-earner, dual-career, and commuter marriages?

10. What are some of the benefits and costs of two-income families?

13.6. Explain how and why workplace inequality affects families.

11. Why is there a gender pay gap? What are its outcomes?

12. How do the motherhood penalty and occupational sex segregation affect women's income?

13.7. Describe four workplace policies that can benefit or disadvantage families.

13. Do flextime and telecommuting differ? What are the benefits and costs of telecommuting for employers and workers?

14. What are the benefits and limitations of the Family and Medical Leave Act? How does the United States compare with other countries in paid parental leaves?

Domestic Violence and Other Family Health Issues

((⋅ **Listen** to Chapter 14 on **MySocLab**

LEARNING OBJECTIVES

After you read and study this chapter you will be able to:

14.1 Define and describe three types of intimate partner violence; explain why some women stay in abusive relationships; and discuss one-sided versus mutual partner violence.

14.2 Define, illustrate, and describe four types of child maltreatment and explain why adults abuse children.

14.3 Describe and illustrate sibling and adolescent abuse, as well as their prevalence, and outcomes of this type of abuse.

14.4 Define, illustrate, and describe elder mistreatment and explain why elder abuse occurs.

14.5 Describe the prevalence of violence in same-sex couples and in racial-ethnic groups, and explain why it occurs.

14.6 Compare five theoretical explanations of family abuse and violence.

14.7 Describe three lifestyle choices and their prevalence that affect families' health, and explain why family members experience depression and suicide.

14.8 Describe and illustrate two ways to combat domestic violence and other family health problems.

DATA DIGEST

- Between 1994 and 2011, child abuse decreased from 15.2 to 9.1 per 1,000 children; over a lifetime, **20 percent of U.S. children experience some form of maltreatment**.

- Nearly 33 percent of U.S. women and 10 percent of men **have experienced rape, physical violence, and/or stalking by an intimate partner**.

- Almost **35 percent of U.S. children live in violent households**.

- Every year, an estimated 8 to 10 percent of **Americans age 65 and older experience some form of elder mistreatment**.

- In 2011, **almost 23 million Americans age 12 or older (9 percent of the population) used illicit drugs** such as marijuana, cocaine, heroin, and hallucinogens; 71 percent of high school

students drank alcohol, and 45 percent smoked cigarettes.

- Between 1962 and 2010, the **percentage of obese American adults** rose from 13 to 36 percent.

Sources: Catalano, 2007; Black et al., 2011; "Child Maltreatment," 2012; Eaton et al., 2012; National Center on Elder Abuse, 2012; Ogden et al., 2012; Substance Abuse and Mental Health Services Administration, 2012; U.S. Department of Health and Human Services, 2012a.

Over a lifetime, we're much more likely to be assaulted or killed by a family member than a stranger (Truman and Planty, 2012). For example, almost 3-year-old Andrew died after his father, a computer systems engineer, took the unresponsive child to an emergency room. The toddler's ravaged body was covered with wounds, bruises, and lacerations, some of which had been sustained over a period of time. The boy's starvation was so advanced, his brain and heart had begun to shrink, and his muscles had atrophied so much that he couldn't walk. Andrew's room was splattered with his blood. His mother, a full-time homemaker with five other children, said that Andrew's injuries were caused by scratching himself and falling down the stairs (Barnhardt and Scharper, 2007; Madigan, 2009).

This chapter examines the different forms of domestic violence, other family-related health issues, and some prevention and intervention strategies. Let's begin with intimate partner violence, a serious problem that afflicts millions of Americans.

Intimate Partner Violence and Abuse

Intimate partner violence (IPV) is abuse that occurs between two people in a close relationship. The term *intimate partner* refers to current and former spouses, couples who live together, and current or former boyfriends or girlfriends. Chapter 8 examined dating violence; this chapter focuses primarily on other IPV couples. Some social scientists use the terms *intimate partner violence* and *domestic violence* interchangeably, whereas others use *intimate partner violence* to specifically address the people who are involved in a close personal relationship. I'll use *domestic violence* more frequently when we look at abuse that also includes children, siblings, and older family members.

Types of Intimate Partner Violence

Intimate partner violence ranges from a single episode to ongoing abuse. It includes three types of behavior:

- **Physical abuse** is threatening, trying to hurt, or hurting a partner by using physical force. Examples include throwing objects, pushing, grabbing, slapping, kicking, biting, hitting, beating, and choking.

14.1 Define and describe three types of intimate partner violence; explain why some women stay in abusive relationships; and discuss one-sided versus mutual partner violence.

intimate partner violence (IPV) Abuse between two people in a close relationship.

physical abuse Threatening, trying to hurt, or hurting a partner using physical force.

In intimate partner violence, women experience more chronic and injurious physical assaults than do men.

sexual abuse Threatening or forcing a partner to take part in a sex act when she or he doesn't consent.

emotional abuse Aggressive behavior that threatens, monitors, or controls a partner.

- **Sexual abuse** is threatening or forcing a partner to take part in a sex act when she or he doesn't consent. The most common examples are coercing a person to have sexual intercourse (the legal term is *rape*) or unwanted sexual activity (such as anal or oral sex).

- **Emotional abuse** is aggressive behavior that threatens, monitors, or controls a partner. Examples include name calling, intimidation, preventing a partner from seeing friends and family, and threatening his or her loved ones. Such psychological and verbal abuse are equally harmful because scorn, criticism, ridicule, or isolating a partner from family and friends can be emotionally crippling.

Often, intimate partner violence starts with emotional abuse that can escalate to physical or sexual violence. Several types of IPV can also occur together, as when a partner berates someone verbally while pummeling her or him. In measuring IPV rates, the Centers for Disease Control and Prevention (CDC) also include stalking and controlling a woman's reproduction (e.g., a man refuses to wear a condom or deliberately tries to get a woman pregnant when she doesn't want to do so) (Black et al., 2011; see also Chapters 6, 9, and 11).

Prevalence and Severity of Intimate Partner Violence

Intimate partner violence is pervasive in U.S. society. Nationwide, 36 percent of women and 29 percent of men say that they have been IPV victims at some time in their lives. In 2011, there were more than 1 million intimate partner victimizations, but this number is conservative. An estimated 42 percent of victims don't report IPV to the police because they're ashamed, believe that no one can help, or fear reprisal. Whether IPV is reported or not, it affects more than 12 million Americans each year, and that includes family members, employers, lawyers, and health care providers (Black et al., 2011; Truman and Planty, 2012).

From 1993 to 2010, the overall IPV rate in the United States declined for both women and men (see *Figure 14.1*). During this period, however, almost 86 percent of the victims were females.

Each year, IPV results in an estimated 1,200 deaths and 2 million injuries among women compared with 330 deaths and nearly 600,000 injuries among men (Catalano, 2007; Black and Breiding, 2008). When victims survive an assault, women are much more likely than men to report serious psychological

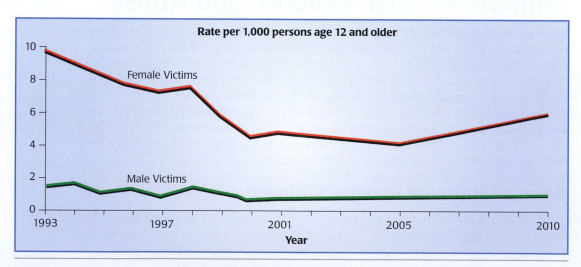

FIGURE 14.1 Intimate Partner Violence, by Sex, 1993–2010
Source: Based on Catalano, 2012, Appendix Table 1.

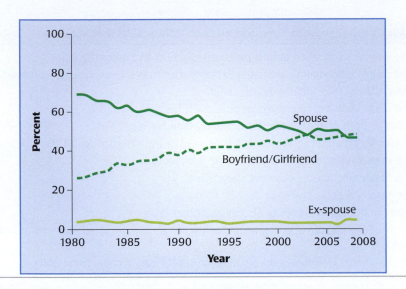

FIGURE 14.2 **Homicides of Intimate Partners, by Relationship of the Victim to Offender, 1980–2008** *Source:* Cooper and Smith, 2011, Figure 28.

distress (e.g., depression, nervousness, and feelings of hopelessness and worthlessness) and to attempt suicide. Women's poorer mental-health functioning is due to their greater likelihood of experiencing repeated abuse as well as both physical and sexual violence (Edwards et al., 2009; Black et al., 2011).

Women are also more likely than men to experience serious physical injuries because they're usually smaller than their partners and more likely to use their fists rather than weapons. Female intimate partners are more likely to be murdered with a firearm (53 percent) than all other means combined (Cooper and Smith, 2011). In 2008, the proportion of homicides committed by a spouse was nearly equal to the proportion committed by a boyfriend or girlfriend (see *Figure 14.2*). Of the 713 husband–wife murders in 2010, however, 85 percent of the victims were wives (Federal Bureau of Investigation, 2011).

The reason for the drop in marital homicides is unclear, but it might be due to a larger number of women in the workforce who have the finances to leave an abusive relationship. Also, many women have postponed marriage and parenthood, both of which decrease the likelihood of violence because the partners are older, more mature, and have better conflict-resolution skills (see Chapters 10, 12, and 13).

Some Characteristics of Abusive and Violent Households

Who batters? There's no "typical" batterer, but abusers share some common characteristics (see *Table 14.1*). Some are related to macro-level factors such as unemployment and poverty. Others are due to micro-level choices such as drug abuse. The more risk factors, the more likely that abuse and violence will occur, but IPV varies in terms of gender, age, race and ethnicity, and social class.

GENDER Women are much more likely than men to experience IPV over a lifetime, regardless of age, race or ethnicity, household income, and education level, but men are also victims (see *Table 14.2*). Over a lifetime, 14 percent of men and 24 percent of women have experienced *severe physical violence* by an intimate partner (e.g., hit with a fist or something hard, beaten, slammed against something, hurt by choking or suffocating, burned on purpose, or had a knife or gun used against them). Almost half of both sexes have experienced psychological abuse (e.g., name calling, insults, threats of physical harm, and controlling behavior), but men are less likely than women to experience multiple forms of violence that include physical violence, stalking, and rape (Black et al., 2011).

Men are also more likely than women to commit **familycide**, murdering one's spouse, ex-spouse, children, or other relatives before attempting or committing suicide. The men who slaughter their families are sometimes called *family*

Since you asked . . .

• Is there *one* major reason for intimate partner violence?

familycide Murdering one's spouse, ex-spouse, children, or other relatives before attempting or committing suicide.

TABLE 14.1 Risk Factors Associated with Intimate Partner Violence

- The woman's education or income level is higher than that of the man.
- The couple is cohabiting or separated rather than married, divorced, or widowed.
- The partners' race and/or ethnicity differ.
- The man is sadistic, aggressive, or obsessively jealous.
- Either or both partners were violent during their teenage years.
- One or both partners grew up seeing a parent or intimate partner hit the other.
- The man is unemployed and the woman is employed.
- The family's income is below the poverty line.
- The man is younger than age 35.
- Either or both partners abuse alcohol and other drugs.
- The man has assaulted someone outside the family or committed some other violent crime.
- The family is socially isolated from neighbors, relatives, and the community.

Sources: R. S. Thompson et al., 2006; Herrenkohl et al., 2007; Black and Breiding, 2008; Edwards et al., 2009; Wiersma et al., 2010; Berger et al., 2012; Catalano, 2012.

TABLE 14.2 Percentage of Americans Age 18 and Older Who Have Ever Experienced Intimate Partner Violence

	Women	Men
Total	26	12
Age		
18–24	24	18
25–34	30	21
35–44	30	18
45–54	31	16
55–64	27	13
65 and older	13	6
Race/Ethnicity		
White	27	16
Latino	21	16
Black	29	23
American Indian/Alaska Native	39	19
Asian	10	8
Multiracial	43	26
Annual Household Income		
Less than $15,000	36	21
$15,000–$24,999	29	20
$25,000–$34,999	31	16
$35,000–$49,999	27	16
$50,000 or higher	24	14

	Women	Men
Education		
Did not graduate from high school	28	16
High school graduate	25	16
Some college	32	19
College graduate	23	14

Note: This survey defined *intimate partner violence* as threatened, attempted, or completed physical or sexual violence or emotional abuse by a current or former intimate partner.
Source: Based on Black and Breiding, 2008, Table 1.

annihilators. Such crimes represent up to 2 percent of all homicides a year. Family annihilators are usually white, male, middle-aged, family breadwinners who are on the verge of a catastrophic economic loss or have been laid off; have never shown any signs of depression, anxiety, or hostility; behave normally; and have been plotting the murders of their wife and children sometimes for many months (Callahan, 2009).

AGE Intimate partner violence begins early in life. Among those who experienced rape, physical violence, and/or stalking by an intimate partner the first time, 22 percent of females and 15 percent of males were between 11 and 17 years old; 47 percent of females and 39 percent of males were between 18 and 24 years old (Black et al., 2011). Compared with all other age groups, females age 50 or older have the lowest IPV rates (Catalano, 2012). Lower IPV rates at later ages may be due to a victim's death. For example, homicide by a current or former intimate partner is the leading cause of death for women during pregnancy or within one year of giving birth (Cheng and Horon, 2010). In other cases, males might be incarcerated for a different crime or some females manage to leave an abusive relationship.

RACE AND ETHNICITY Across all racial-ethnic groups, women are more likely than men to be IPV victims over a lifetime. Multiracial and American Indian women report the highest abuse rates (43 percent and 39 percent, respectively), and Asian American women report the lowest (10 percent) (see *Table 14.2*). A national study that included stalking found that 46 percent of American Indian/Alaska Native and 54 percent of multiracial women have experienced IPV over a lifetime (Black et al., 2011).

It's unclear why multiracial women have the highest IPV rates. Explanations for the high IPV rates among American Indian/Alaska Native women include a combination of factors: "No place . . . is more dangerous than Alaska's isolated villages, where there are no roads in or out, and where people are further cut off by undependable telephone, electrical, and Internet service." At Indian Health Service hospitals, there are too few nurses trained to perform rape examinations, which are generally necessary to bring cases to trial; there isn't any discussion about IPV and alcohol abuse; and tribal police, often overwhelmed by crime at some reservations, discourage women from reporting and prosecuting IPV (Williams, 2012: A1).

SOCIAL CLASS Intimate partner violence cuts across all social classes, but is more common (or reported more often) in low-income families. Women living in households with annual incomes less than $7,500 a year are nearly seven times more likely to be victimized by an intimate partner than are women living in households with an annual income of at least $75,000 (Macomber, 2006).

Read on MySocLab

Document: Rape and the War Against Native Women

Former basketball star Dennis Rodman was arrested several times for intimate partner violence, once against his wife, and later against a girlfriend.

Social class itself doesn't "cause" IPV because, over a lifetime, perpetrators and victims include people from all income and education levels (Catalano, 2007; see also *Table 14.2*). However, socioeconomically disadvantaged women and men are more likely than others to have grown up in abusive households, to cohabit, to be unemployed, to live in poverty, and to have unintended pregnancies or more children than they can afford to raise—all of which increase the likelihood of IPV (Frias and Angel, 2005; O'Donnell et al., 2009; Jones et al., 2013).

Besides familycide, there are many other instances of IPV in middle-class families. For example, IPV is 2 to 4 times more common in police families than in the general population. The victims are particularly vulnerable because the abuser has a gun, knows the location of battered women's shelters, is rarely punished by his department, and knows how to manipulate the criminal justice system to avoid penalties (National Center for Women and Policing, 2009).

Women in high socioeconomic households also experience IPV. We often read about male Hollywood celebrities and National Football League players whose past and current girlfriends and wives accuse them of domestic violence (see, for example, Thompson and Barker, 2010; Wilson, 2012; Richter, 2013). *Behind Mansion Walls*, a popular television crime show, focuses on domestic violence among the rich and privileged.

In 2007, a women's shelter in Naples, Florida, added a new program, Women of Means, that specifically targets educated, professional, and/or affluent IPV victims. The program offers upscale services such as spas and beauty salons, and an array of attorneys, physicians, psychiatrists, dentists, and other professionals (Green, 2007). Whether wealthy women should get special treatment might be disputed, but the program shows that IPV isn't limited to low-income groups.

Marital Rape

marital rape A man forces his wife to have unwanted sexual intercourse (sometimes called *spousal rape* or *wife rape*).

Marital rape (sometimes called *spousal rape* or *wife rape*) is an abusive act in which a man forces his wife to have unwanted sexual intercourse. Marital rape has been a crime in all states since 1993. It's the most common type of rape in the United States, but some states define this assault as a lesser offense than stranger rape (Polisi, 2009).

An estimated 25 percent of women nationwide have been raped by their spouses, but very few report the crime. A traditional wife, believing that she has no choice but to perform her "wifely duty," may accept the situation as normal, especially if her husband doesn't use a weapon or threaten her with physical harm (Michael et al., 1994; Polisi, 2009).

When women report the crime, offenders are rarely prosecuted. It's almost impossible for a wife to prove that she's been raped if she doesn't have physical injuries, such as bruises or broken bones. Some husbands use physical force, but many rely on other forms of coercion such as threatening to leave or to cheat on a wife (Hines and Malley-Morrison, 2005).

The Cycle of Domestic Violence

battered-woman syndrome A woman who has experienced many years of physical abuse but feels unable to leave her partner.

Since 1978, state governors have granted clemency to several hundred women who were convicted of killing their abusers. The women were pardoned based on the defense of **battered-woman syndrome**, a condition that describes a woman who has experienced many years of physical abuse but feels unable to leave her partner. In a desperate effort to defend themselves, the women sometimes kill the abuser.

The battered-woman syndrome is controversial because, some argue, abused women have the option of leaving abusers instead of killing them. Others maintain that a well-known theory of the cycle of domestic violence supports the

Since you asked . . .
- Should women be pardoned for killing their abusers?

battered-woman syndrome defense (Walker, 1978, 2000). The cycle of domestic violence involves three phases.

PHASE ONE: THE TENSION-BUILDING PHASE   In the first phase of the cycle, when "minor" battering incidents occur, the woman tries to reduce her partner's anger by catering to him or staying out of his way. At the same time, the battered woman often believes that her partner's abuse is justified: "When he throws the dinner she prepared for him across the kitchen floor, she reasons that maybe she did overcook it, accidentally. As she cleans up his mess, she may think that he was a bit extreme in his reaction, but she is usually so grateful that it was a relatively minor incident that she resolves not to be angry with him" (Walker, 1978: 147). The victim hopes that the situation will change, but the tension typically escalates and leads to a battering incident.

PHASE TWO: THE ACUTE BATTERING INCIDENT   Abusers often have a Dr. Jekyll and Mr. Hyde personality in which the rational and gentle Dr. Jekyll changes, unpredictably, into an unreasonable and brutal Mr. Hyde. In this second phase, Mr. Hyde emerges, exploding in rage and beating or otherwise abusing his partner. Thus, the woman's feelings fluctuate: "I have two responses to Stu because I am responding to two different people, or two different parts of one person. There's the Stu who is very thoughtful and gentle and kind, and then there's the brutal and hostile Stu" (Strasser, 2004: 210).

Some women who have lived with abuse for a long time anticipate this phase and trigger the violent incident to get it over with. For example, a woman who wanted to go to a family party with her husband and sensed that an acute battering incident was about to occur deliberately provoked it during the week so that by the weekend her husband would be pleasant for the party (Walker, 1978).

PHASE THREE: CALM (THE "HONEYMOON PHASE")   Mr. Hyde becomes the kindly Dr. Jekyll in the third phase, begging the woman's forgiveness and promising that he will never beat her again: "He . . . will give up drinking, seeing other women, or whatever else affects his internal anxiety state. His sincerity is believable" (Walker, 1978: 152).

If the victim has been hospitalized because of her physical injuries, the man often deluges her with flowers, candy, cards, and gifts. He may also get his family members, relatives, and friends to build up the victim's guilt by telling her that

Explore on **MySocLab**

Activity: Violence over the Life Course

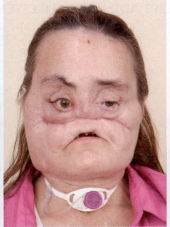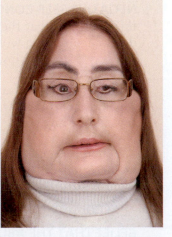

In 2004, Connie Culp's husband blasted her with a shotgun that left a hole where the middle of her face had been. He then turned the gun on himself, survived, and was sent to prison for seven years. In 2009, and after 30 operations, Culp became the fourth woman in the world to undergo a successful face transplant. The photos, from left to right, show her before the attempted murder, and before and after the face transplant.

a father shouldn't be separated from his children. Because many battered women hold traditional values about love and marriage, the wife convinces herself that *this* time he'll *really* change.

Because he's now loving and kind, the battered woman believes that the "good man," the one she loves, will honor his tearful promises to change. After a while, the calm and loving behavior gives way to battering incidents, and the cycle starts all over again, often including marital rape.

Why Do Women Stay?

Walker (2000) theorized that the cycle of violence often results in *learned helplessness:* The woman becomes depressed, loses her self-esteem, and feels incapable of seeking help or escaping the abusive relationship. It's not clear, however, whether women had these personality traits before they met the abusers, whether the traits are due to the abuse, or a combination of both (Rathus and O'Leary, 1997).

Still, the obvious question is: Why do these women stay? Despite the common tendency to think of abused women as passive punching bags, many resist or try to change the situation. Some of the strategies include hitting back; contacting local domestic violence shelters; calling the police; obtaining restraining/protection orders; disclosing their abusive experiences to family members, friends, neighbors, and/or co-workers; and terminating the relationship (Hamby and Bible, 2009).

Some women, like one of my students, find the courage to leave only when they suddenly realize that the abuse has spilled over to their children:

> John never laid a finger on our daughter, Sheri, but struck me in front of her. . . . One afternoon when I heard Sheri banging and yelling, I rushed to her room. . . . Sheri was hitting her doll and screaming four-letter words she often heard her father yell at me. She was just starting to talk, and that was what she was learning. That moment changed our lives forever. . . . I left John that night and never went back (Author's files).

The student left her husband because she had some resources—a good job at the Motor Vehicle Administration, a college degree, her own checking and savings accounts, and supportive family members who provided her and Sheri with temporary housing and emotional encouragement. Most abuse victims aren't that fortunate.

There is no single reason why some women don't leave violent relationships. Instead, there are multiple and overlapping explanations.

NEGATIVE SELF-CONCEPT AND LOW SELF-ESTEEM Most batterers convince their partners that they're worthless, stupid, and disgusting: "Behind a closed door, a man calls a woman a 'slut' and a 'whore.' He tells her that she is too fat, too sexy or too frumpy, that she is 'a poor excuse for a mother,' a worthless piece of dirt" (Goode et al., 1994: 24). And, according to a 33-year-old mother of two children: "He rarely says a kind word to me. The food is too cold or . . . too hot. The kids are too noisy. . . . I am too fat or too skinny. No matter what I do, he says it isn't any good. He tells me I am lucky he married me 'cause no one else would have me" (Gelles and Straus, 1988: 68).

Such tyranny is effective because in many cultures, including ours, many women's self-worth still hinges on having a man (see Chapters 7 and 8). Sometimes women are willing to pay any price to hold on to the relationship because they believe that no one else could love them.

BELIEF THAT THE ABUSER WILL CHANGE When I asked a woman I knew, her cheek still raw from her husband's beating, why she didn't leave, she said, "I'm still in love with him, and I know he's going to change as soon as he gets past these things that are troubling him." Thus, some women stay in violent relationships because they're seduced by the Cinderella fantasy. The woman believes

that, sooner or later, the abuser will change and she and Prince Charming will live happily ever after. Millions of women also stay in an abusive relationship because they hope to "rehabilitate" the man rather than break up the family (Sontag, 2002).

A college professor remained married to a batterer for 12 years because she believed that her husband would eventually change back to being a good man: "Before we married, my husband seemed to be the perfect man—kind, gentle, romantic, admiring of me and my academic successes." She clung to this illusion for over a decade even though the battering began three weeks after they married, when she learned that she was pregnant (Bates, 2005: C1).

ECONOMIC HARDSHIP AND HOMELESSNESS If abused women don't work outside the home or if they have few marketable skills, they see no way to survive economically if they leave the abuser. Many batterers keep their partners in economic chains. Nothing is in the woman's name—not checking or savings accounts, automobiles, or homes. Because most abusers isolate their victims from friends and relatives, the women have no one to turn to. Moreover, those who might give battered women a place to stay are afraid that they might endanger their own family. Without resources, some abused women who do leave become homeless (Browne, 1993; Choice and Lamke, 1997).

Abused women often have nowhere to go. Hundreds are turned away from shelters because of overcrowding and underfunding (Gonnerman, 2005). Thus, leaving a man or filing charges against him may push a woman and her children into poverty.

NEED FOR CHILD SUPPORT Many women believe that even an abusive partner is better than none. As one of my students, a former abused wife who eventually left her husband, once said in class, "This man brings in most of the family's income. Without him, you can't pay the rent, buy the groceries, or pay the electric bills. If he goes to jail, he'll probably lose his job. And then what will you and the kids do?"

SHAME OR GUILT Strong cultural factors may also keep a woman from leaving an abuser. In some Asian American communities, especially, there's strong pressure not to bring shame or disgrace on the family by exposing problems such as domestic violence. Immigrant women may be hesitant to report intimate partner violence because they fear deportation. Such fears are unfounded because nonimmigrant visas allow IPV victims to remain in the United States legally (American College of Obstetricians and Gynecologists, 2012).

BLAMING THEMSELVES Battered women often believe that, somehow, they brought the violence on themselves. Men who batter may be well-respected professional athletes, community leaders, or attorneys. The women start thinking that because the men have a good reputation, the abuse must be their fault (Parameswaran, 2003).

This is particularly likely if women have seen their mothers or grandmothers suffer similar treatment: "One woman whose bruises from her husband's beatings were clearly visible was told by her grandmother, 'You have to stop provoking him. You have two children, and the bottom line is you have nowhere to go. If he tells you to shut up, shut up!'" (Goode et al., 1994: 27).

Many people, including these Latina victims, have participated in rallies and demonstrations to end domestic violence.

Thus, an abusive tradition is passed on. Women believe that they're responsible for preventing male violence, and if they don't succeed, they must accept the consequences. Moreover, because some priests, ministers, and rabbis remind a woman that she's married "for better or for worse," religious

women may feel guilty and sinful for wanting to leave (R. K. Jones, 1993; Hines and Malley-Morrison, 2005).

FEAR Fear is a *major* reason for staying in an abusive relationship. Some men threaten to kill the woman, her relatives, and the children if she tries to escape. Several directors of battered women's shelters have told me that it's not unusual for husbands to track down their families from as far away as 1,000 miles and threaten violence to get them to return.

Even when judges issue protective orders, the orders are temporary, and the offenders can still assault their partners at home (even when the locks have been changed), workplaces, and public places such as parking lots. Because the man has been abusive before, threats of retaliation are real and many victims live in constant fear.

All these factors help explain why many women stay in abusive relationships: "Staying may mean abuse and violence, but leaving may mean death. A bureaucracy may promise safety, but cannot ensure it. For many battered women, this is a risk they cannot take" (Englander, 1997: 149–150).

Also, as some social scientists point out, leaving an abusive partner isn't as clear cut as it seems. It's often a long *process* that involves numerous changes, such as thinking about leaving, preparing to leave (e.g., trying to establish secret savings and checking accounts), taking action (such as speaking to a counselor), and trying to improve the relationship. In all of these stages, women may be ambivalent about preserving a father–child relationship that's not abusive, as well as having few available resources for themselves and their children (Khaw and Hardesty, 2009).

Intimate partner violence takes different forms, but the goal is always the same: control of the partner through fear and intimidation. "Some Warning Signs of Intimate Partner Abuse" provides examples of potential violence.

Applying What You've Learned

Some Warning Signs of Intimate Partner Abuse

There are numerous clues for potential IPV. How many of these red flags do you recognize in your or your friends' relationships?

- **Verbal abuse:** Constant criticism, ignoring what you say, mocking, name calling, yelling, and swearing.

- **Sexual abuse:** Forcing or demanding sexual acts that you don't want to perform.

- **Disrespect:** Interrupting, telling you what you should think and how you should feel, putting you down in front of other people, saying ugly things about your friends and family.

- **Isolation:** Trying to cut you off from family and friends, monitoring your phone calls, reading your e-mail or text messages, controlling where you go, taking your car keys and cell phone.

- **Emotional neglect:** Not expressing feelings, not giving compliments, not respecting your feelings and opinions.

- **Jealousy:** Very possessive, calling constantly or visiting unexpectedly, checking the mileage on your car, not wanting you to work because "you might meet someone."

- **Unrealistic expectations:** Expecting you to be the perfect mate and meet his/her every need.

- **Blaming others for problems:** It's *always* someone else's fault if something goes wrong.

- **Rigid gender roles:** Expecting you to serve, obey, and always stay home.

- **Extreme mood swings:** Switching from sweet to abusive and violent in minutes or being very kind one day and very vicious the next.

- **Cruelty to animals and children:** Killing or punishing pets brutally, expecting children to do things that are far beyond their ability or tease them until they cry.

- **Threats of violence:** Saying things such as "I'll break your neck" and then dismissing them with "I didn't really mean it" or "Everybody talks like that."

- **Destruction of property:** Destroying furniture, punching walls or doors, throwing things, breaking dishes or other household articles.

- **Self-destructive behavior:** Abusing drugs or alcohol, threatening self-harm or suicide, getting into fights with people, causing problems at work (such as telling off the boss).

Women Who Abuse Men

Sociologist Michael Johnson (2005, 2008) posits that there are two types of IPV. In *intimate terrorism*, the primary perpetrator is a male who uses multiple forms of abuse and escalates control to dominate his partner. In *situational couple violence*, both partners are perpetrators. They aren't necessarily seeking control, but the violence is a result of conflict that turns into disagreements that escalate to arguments, to verbal abuse, and, ultimately, to physical violence.

Sociologist Murray Straus (2011, 2013) argues, on the other hand, that women also engage in intimate terrorism because much partner violence is mutual. He points to over 200 studies which show that women are as likely as men to perpetrate nonsexual physical assaults. Straus maintains that victimization surveys (see *Figure 14.1* on page 396, *Table 14.2* on page 398, and related discussion) vastly underestimate violence by female partners. Because assaults by a male partner are much more likely to result in injury, women are more likely than men to report an attack to police and to researchers. Straus also challenges the contention that women engage in partner violence to defend themselves because several dozen studies have found that women initiate from 30 to 73 percent of violent incidents. In addition, male victims are less likely to call the police because the injury isn't severe, they fear arrest, or are embarrassed to report an assault (Felson and Paré, 2005).

Whether IPV is one-sided or mutual, it often spills over into violence against children. As many as 70 percent of court cases involve a co-occurrence of IPV and child abuse (Aycock and Starr, 2010).

MAKING CONNECTIONS

- Are learned helplessness and the battered-woman syndrome defense contradictory? That is, if a woman feels too beaten down to leave an abusive situation, why does she kill the batterer or hire someone else to do so?

- Look again at "Some Warning Signs of Intimate Partner Abuse." Do any of these characteristics describe your current relationship with an intimate partner? If so, what, if anything, are you doing about it?

Child Maltreatment

Abusing or killing one's children isn't a modern crime. Among the Puritans, men weren't the only offenders: In 1638, Dorothy Talbie "was hanged at Boston for murdering her own daughter, a child of 3 years old" (Demos, 1986: 79).

In 1946, after observing unexplained fractures in children he had seen over the years, pediatric radiologist John Caffey suggested that the children had been abused. And in what may have been the first formal paper on the subject, physician C. Henry Kempe (1962) and his colleagues published an article on the battered-child syndrome. Still, *child abuse* became a household term only in the 1980s.

14.2 Define, illustrate, and describe four types of child maltreatment and explain why adults abuse children.

 Read on MySocLab

Document: Injury, Gender, and Trouble

What Is Child Maltreatment?

Child maltreatment (often used interchangeably with *child abuse*) includes a broad range of behaviors that place a child at serious risk or result in serious harm. This term involves either harmful acts or failure to act responsibly by a biological parent, stepparent, foster parent, and adoptive parent. Other caregivers include clergy, coaches, teachers, and babysitters. The most common types of child maltreatment are physical and sexual abuse, neglect, and emotional abuse (Leeb et al., 2008).

child maltreatment A broad range of behaviors that place a child at serious risk or result in serious harm (often used interchangeably with *child abuse*).

Since you asked . . .

- Is physical abuse more harmful than emotional abuse?

PHYSICAL ABUSE *Physical abuse* is the use of force against a child that can or does cause bodily injury. It includes acts that range from those that don't leave a physical mark on the child to those that cause disability, disfigurement, or death. Examples include hitting, punching, beating, pushing, pulling, dragging, shaking, choking, scalding, and severe physical punishments.

SEXUAL ABUSE *Sexual abuse* is any situation that involves a child in a sexual act that provides the perpetrator sexual gratification or financial benefit. Examples include making a child watch sexual acts, fondling a child's genitals,

Oprah Winfrey is a successful media proprietor, talk show host, actress, and philanthropist. When she was 9 years old, Winfrey's 19-year-old cousin started to molest her sexually. At age 14, she gave birth to a premature baby who died shortly after birth. Winfrey says that she was too confused and afraid to report the abuse.

engaging a child in prostitution, committing statutory rape (having sexual intercourse with a minor), forcing a child to participate in sexual acts for pornography, and incest.

NEGLECT *Neglect* is failure to provide for a child's basic physical, emotional, medical, or educational needs. Examples include not talking to, playing with, or engaging in activities that nourish the child's cognitive development; being emotionally unresponsive; not seeking necessary medical attention; and allowing children to miss school without a good excuse.

EMOTIONAL ABUSE *Emotional abuse* (also called *psychological abuse*) is a caregiver's behavior that conveys to a child that she or he is flawed, worthless, unloved, or unwanted. Emotional abuse can be continual or triggered by a specific situation. Examples include constant criticism, put-downs, and sarcasm. Emotional abuse also includes *spurning* (rejecting the child verbally and nonverbally); *terrorizing* (threatening to hurt, kill, or abandon the child); *isolating* (denying the child opportunities to interact with peers or adults inside or outside the home); and *exploiting* or *corrupting* (being a poor role model and permitting or encouraging a child's antisocial behavior) (Hart et al., 2003).

Prevalence and Characteristics of Child Maltreatment

Child maltreatment rates in the United States have decreased since 2007 (see Data Digest), but many cases go undetected. According to local and state child protective services, for example, an estimated 9 percent of children were maltreated in 2010. In the same year, 53 percent of adults surveyed said that they had suffered physical, emotional, or sexual abuse during childhood (Bynum et al., 2010; U.S. Department of Health and Human Services, 2012a; except when noted otherwise, much of the material in this section is based on the latter report).

VICTIMS From birth to age 17, girls (51 percent) are slightly more likely than boys (49 percent) to be maltreated. The most common form of abuse is neglect (see *Figure 14.3*), but the most vulnerable children, those younger than 3 years old, account for 27 percent of all child victims. Except for sexual abuse, as you'll see shortly, children's victimization decreases with age.

Overall, 44 percent of all victims are white, 22 percent are black, and 22 percent are Hispanic. However, African American, American Indian/Alaska Native, and multiracial children have the highest victimization rates (see *Figure 14.4*). That is, child maltreatment percentages are highest among whites, but more prevalent among some minority groups than others.

PERPETRATORS AND FATALITIES More than 81 of the victims are maltreated by one or both parents, and in 37 percent of the cases, the abusers are mothers. An additional 7 percent of perpetrators are relatives or the parents' intimate partners, usually boyfriends.

Homicide is the leading cause of death among infants. Of the 1,570 children who died of abuse in 2011, almost 43 percent were younger than 1 year, and 82 percent were younger than 4 years. In effect, about five children die every day because of maltreatment.

About 78 percent of child deaths are caused by one or both of the child's parents, but 61 percent of all homicides involve just mothers, mothers and fathers,

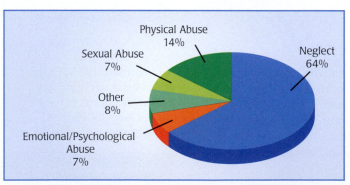

FIGURE 14.3 Types of Child Maltreatment, 2011
Note: "Neglect" includes medical neglect (almost 2 percent of these cases). "Other" includes categories that some states report, such as a parent's drug/alcohol abuse.
Source: Based on U.S. Department of Health and Human Services, 2012a, Table 3-8.

and boyfriends (see *Figure 14.5*). The first two months of an infant's life are usually the most deadly. A young mother may know little about parenting and be unable to cope with the constant crying of a normal infant. As one of my students said, "My daughter had colic and she cried all night long for three months. I thought I'd go crazy."

Many researchers maintain that official child homicide statistics are far too low. For example, studies in Colorado and North Carolina have estimated that as many as 50 to 60 percent of child deaths resulting from abuse or neglect are recorded as accidents. The underreporting is due to a number of factors, including inadequate training of people who investigate deaths, incorrect information on death certificates, parents' ability to conceal their children's deaths due to maltreatment, and infants' inadequate skeletal exams (Child Welfare Information Gateway, 2008; Perez-Rossello et al., 2010).

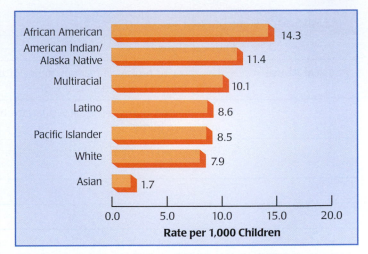

FIGURE 14.4 **Child Victimization Rates by Race and Ethnicity, 2011** *Source:* Based on U.S. Department of Health and Human Services, 2012a, Table 3-6.

Sexual Abuse and Incest

Children's sexual abuse by strangers gets a great deal of media publicity, but 90 percent of all these offenses are perpetrated by family members, friends of the family, and other persons children know (Gilgun, 2008). About 3 percent of infants and toddlers are sexually abused, but sexual abuse rises until a child is age 14 (see *Figure 14.6*), and 95 percent of the offenders are men. Across all cases, 10 percent are family members (usually fathers and brothers), and 64 percent are a family friend, a child's friend, or a caretaker (Finkelhor et al., 2008).

In 2009, the three sisters of "The 5 Browns," a popular musical group, alerted authorities that their father—a strict, college-educated Mormon—had sexually abused them between 1990 and 1998. Two years later, he pleaded guilty to felony sodomy charges. The group's manager described the father as "the sweetest, nicest guy you ever met in your life" (Tresniowski et al., 2011: 76). As this example illustrates, incest occurs across racial-ethnic groups, religious traditions, and social classes.

A man who sexually abuses his child or children usually starts doing so when the child is between 8 and 12 years old, although in some cases the child is still in diapers. The father may select only one child (usually the oldest daughter) as his victim, but it's common for several daughters to be victimized, either sequentially or simultaneously over the years. Incest offenders convince their daughters that the attacks are expressions of affection ("This is how daddies show their love"). Others intimidate their victims with promises of physical retaliation against the victim and other family members. They threaten that they'll be arrested or the family will break up if the incest is reported. Children remain silent out of fear and guilt because they believe that they're somehow responsible for the abuse (Allan, 2002; Wilson, 2006). The abusers' personality traits vary, but perpetrators share some common characteristics: "They tend to be highly entitled, self-centered, and manipulative men who use children to meet their own emotional needs. They are often controlling and view their daughters (or sons) as owned objects" (Bancroft, 2002: 245–246).

Incestuous relationships in childhood often lead to mistrust, fear of intimacy, and sexual dysfunctions in adulthood. *Table 14.3* summarizes some of the physical and behavioral signs that a child is being abused and needs protection.

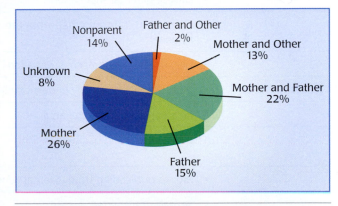

FIGURE 14.5 **Who Kills Children?** *Note:* Among nonparents, the largest number of perpetrators was relatives (3.2 percent), and a parent's girlfriend or boyfriend (3.4 percent). *Source:* Based on U.S. Department of Health and Human Services, 2012a, Exhibit 4-E.

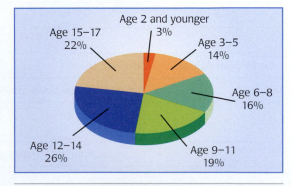

FIGURE 14.6 **Sexual Abuse by Child's Age, 2011** *Source:* Based on U.S. Department of Health and Human Services, 2012a, Exhibit 3-G.

TABLE 14.3 Signs of Child Abuse

	Physical Signs	Behavioral Signs
Physical Abuse	• Unexplained bruises (in various stages of healing), welts, human bite marks, bald spots	• Acts self-destructively
	• Unexplained burns, especially cigarette burns or immersion burns	• Is withdrawn and aggressive, displays behavioral extremes
	• Unexplained fractures, lacerations, or abrasions	• Arrives at school early or stays late, as if afraid to be at home
		• Is uncomfortable with physical contact
		• Displays chronic runaway behavior (adolescents)
		• Complains of soreness or moves uncomfortably
		• Wears inappropriate clothing to cover bruises
Physical Neglect	• Abandonment	• Is fatigued, listless, sleepy
	• Unattended medical needs	• Steals food, begs from classmates
	• Lack of parental supervision	• Reports that no caretaker is at home
	• Consistent hunger, inappropriate dress, poor hygiene	• Is frequently absent or tardy
	• Lice, distended stomach, emaciation	• Drops out of school (adolescents)
Sexual Abuse	• Torn, stained, or bloody underclothing	• Withdraws or is chronically depressed
	• Pain or itching in genital area	• Is excessively seductive
	• Difficulty walking or sitting	• Displays role reversal; overly concerned about siblings
	• Bruises or bleeding from external genitalia	• Displays lack of self-esteem
	• Sexually transmitted disease	• Experiences drastic weight gain or loss
	• Frequent urinary or yeast infections	• Displays hysteria or lack of emotional control
		• Has sudden school difficulties
		• Exhibits sex play or premature understanding of sex
		• Feels threatened by closeness, has problems with peers
		• Is promiscuous
		• Attempts suicide (especially adolescents)
Emotional Abuse	• Speech disorders	• Exhibits habit disorders (sucking, rocking)
	• Delayed physical development	• Is antisocial; responsible for destructive acts
	• Substance abuse	• Displays neurotic traits (sleep disorders, inhibition of play)
	• Ulcers, asthma, severe allergies	• Swings between passive and aggressive behaviors
		• Exhibits delinquent behavior (especially adolescents)
		• Exhibits developmental delay

Source: Based on American Humane Association, 2001, and Child Welfare Information Gateway, 2007.

Polyvictimization

Polyvictimization refers to experiencing multiple kinds of victimization such as physical abuse, sexual abuse, and IPV among adults. The victimization can be direct (parental emotional abuse) or indirect (witnessing family violence). About 49 percent of children age 17 and younger have experienced two or more types of victimization, both direct and indirect, and 8 percent have experienced seven or more types (Finkelhor et al., 2011).

A study of U.S. adults in five states found that 60 percent had suffered at least one "adversity" during childhood such as verbal, sexual, or physical abuse; parental absence due to divorce; witnessing domestic violence; and living with an alcoholic or someone who abused street or prescription drugs. Almost 9 percent reported three adverse experiences, 7 percent reported four such experiences, and 9 percent reported five or more. Among those who had experienced five or more adversities, the highest percentages were for respondents who didn't have a high school diploma and the victimizations occurred in all racial-ethnic groups (Bynum et al., 2010). Such studies help explain why many children who experience polyvictimization have multiple mental and physical problems in adulthood.

polyvictimization Experiencing multiple kinds of victimization.

Why Do Adults Abuse Children?

People tend to stereotype child abusers as mentally ill, but fewer than 10 percent are thought to be so (Goldman and Salus, 2003). Some of the reasons for child maltreatment are substance abuse, stress, poverty, partner violence, and divorce.

SUBSTANCE ABUSE   Children whose parents abuse alcohol and other drugs are three times more likely to be abused and almost five times more likely to be neglected. Substance-abusing parents usually have poor parenting skills: They typically don't give their children emotional support or monitor them (U.S. Department of Health and Human Services, 2009).

About 9 million children—almost 13 percent of all children in the United States—live in households where a parent or other adult uses, manufactures, or distributes illicit drugs. In 81 percent of the reported cases of child maltreatment, substance abuse is rated as either the worst or second worst problem in the home (U.S. Department of Justice, 2011). Here's how an 18-year-old described her first sexual abuse incident:

> When I was six, my mother's husband molested me. Then at age eight he raped me. I don't know why I didn't open my mouth, but I didn't. I thought my mom would know something was wrong with me, but she was on drugs with her man. He would beat on my mother and she would take it (Personal correspondence with Professor Raymond Crowell, Burlington County College, New Jersey).

STRESS   Stress also increases the likelihood of child maltreatment. As you saw earlier, IPV, unmarried teenage parenthood, and a colicky infant aggravate stress. In 2011, more than 11 percent of abused children had a mental disability, a visual or hearing impairment, a learning and/or behavioral problem, or a physical disability. Coping with a disability can increase parental stress and child abuse (U.S. Department of Health and Human Services, 2012a).

ECONOMIC CONDITIONS   Economic problems are especially likely to exacerbate child abuse. Social workers, child welfare agencies, and medical staff say that child abuse cases rose considerably in late 2008 when parents began to lose their jobs and homes (St. George and Dvorak, 2008; see also Lindo et al., 2013).

Keith Brown, patriarch of the hit classical music quintet "The 5 Browns," confessed to sexually abusing his three daughters when they were little.

Poverty is the single-best predictor of child maltreatment.

Poverty is the single-best predictor of child abuse and neglect. Most poor parents aren't abusers, but children from poor families are 22 times more likely than children from families with higher incomes to be abused or neglected. Poverty and child maltreatment often co-occur when parents experience problems such as substance abuse and domestic violence (Children's Defense Fund, 2005).

PARTNER VIOLENCE Child maltreatment is also more common in households in which the woman is abused. The greater the violence toward a partner, the greater the probability of child abuse, especially by a male. Women's victimization, fear of a partner, and exhaustion can also lead to child abuse. Because women who experience partner violence become depressed, their parenting becomes hostile and punitive. Mothers are also likely to adopt a male partner's violent behavior to control their own children. Guilt and shame can prevent abusive mothers from seeking help from family, friends, or social service agencies (Damant et al., 2010; Gustafsson and Cox, 2012).

DIVORCE The period just before and after divorce can increase the likelihood of child maltreatment because parental conflict and family tensions are high. For example, the custodial parent may be changing residences, working longer hours, and experiencing more turmoil. Parents who are already stressed may react abusively to infants who, affected by the parents' emotional state, become more irritable and harder to soothe. Often, children in divorcing families are caught in the middle of adult conflict and become victims of parental anger (see Chapter 15).

In 2006, for example, when a Maryland woman sought a protective order from her estranged husband, she told the judge that the husband had threatened to kill the children to punish her "by leaving her alone in the world." After a bitter divorce, the father got unsupervised visitation rights with the children. Two years later, he drowned the children—ages 2, 4, and 6—in a bathtub (Fuller and Gencer, 2008: A1).

A COMBINATION OF FACTORS Child maltreatment involves polyvictimization and other variables. In a study that interviewed 40 mothers jailed for killing their children, the women cited many interrelated problems that accumulated over the years. The most common reasons included growing up in a neglectful or violent home, not having mothers who were good child-rearing role models, experiencing abuse from a partner, poverty, early pregnancy, and substance abuse (Oberman and Meyer, 2008).

Even well-intentioned parents abuse their children when there are multiple risk factors. The risk factors include young parents who aren't prepared for the responsibilities of raising a child; overwhelmed single parents; families stressed by poverty, divorce, a child's disability, or unemployment; substance abuse; mental-health problems; and living in a dangerous neighborhood (Finkelhor et al., 2011; White and Lauritsen, 2012; Child Welfare Information Gateway, 2013).

How Abuse Affects Children

Whether abuse is physical, emotional, or sexual, children often suffer from a variety of physiological, social, and emotional problems, including headaches, bed-wetting, chronic constipation, difficulty communicating, learning disabilities, poor performance in school, and a variety of mental disorders. Children from violent families are often more aggressive than children from nonviolent families. Being abused or neglected as a child increases the likelihood of arrest as a juvenile by 59 percent, as an adult by 28 percent, and for a violent crime by 30 percent

(Widom and Maxfield, 2001; Currie and Tekin, 2006; Carrell and Hoekstra, 2009; see also Zimmerman and Pogarsky, 2011, and Hibbard et al., 2012).

Adolescents who experience maltreatment are more likely than their nonabused counterparts to engage in early sexual activity, have unintended pregnancies, suffer emotional and eating disorders, abuse alcohol and other drugs, and engage in delinquent behavior. In adulthood, abused children are twice as likely to be unemployed and in welfare programs. They're also more likely to be violent with their intimate partners (Ehrensaft et al., 2003; Zielinski, 2005; Conway and Hutson, 2008; Yun et al., 2011).

Witnessing domestic violence almost triples the likelihood of children having conduct disorders such as aggression, disobedience, and delinquency (Meltzer et al., 2009). However, many children aren't just passive observers of domestic abuse. According to a national study, half of the children yelled at the parents to stop the violence and 24 percent called the police for help (Hamby et al., 2011).

Childhood experiences of abuse and neglect are linked with serious life-long problems. For example, the victims are at least 5 times more likely to experience depression and 12 times more likely to attempt suicide. Physically abused adolescents are 12 times more likely to have alcohol and drug problems, and sexually abused adolescents are 21 times more likely to become substance abusers. As many as two-thirds of people in drug treatment programs report that they were abused as children (Putnam, 2006). Also, experiencing childhood physical abuse can negatively impact partner relationships: The victims have poor social skills that create difficulties in relating to a partner and are likely to get involved with people who mistreat them (Larsen et al., 2011).

MAKING CONNECTIONS

- Some people believe that emotional abuse—of both children and adults—is less harmful than physical abuse. Do you agree?
- When child neglect occurs in lower socioeconomic families or during economic downturns, who is to blame?

Hidden Victims: Siblings and Adolescents

14.3 Describe and illustrate sibling and adolescent abuse, their prevalence, and outcomes.

Violence between siblings and adolescent abuse are less visible, primarily because the authorities are rarely notified. Such abuse, however, can be just as harmful as other forms of domestic violence.

Sibling Abuse

Since you asked . . .
- Is hitting and teasing brothers and sisters a normal part of growing up?

Sibling conflict is so common that many parents dismiss it as normal. In fact, physical, emotional, and sexual abuse among siblings can leave lasting emotional scars. According to a recent national survey, sibling aggression (bullying, property damage, and physical fighting) increases children's depression, anxiety, and anger that last many years (Jenkins Tucker et al., 2013).

PHYSICAL AND EMOTIONAL ABUSE Almost all young children hit a sibling occasionally, but habitual attacks are more problematic. In 2009, almost 39 percent of children ages 2 to 17 had been physically assaulted by a sister or brother at least once. Among those ages 6 to 12, 72 percent had been physically assaulted. In 24 percent of all cases, the assaults were serious enough to call the police (Finkelhor et al., 2010).

Most sibling conflict doesn't involve weapons, but the clashes can be traumatic. Some of the most common forms of sibling abuse include the following (Wiehe and Herring, 1991):

- **Name calling and ridicule:** One woman is still bitter because her brothers called her "fatso" and "roly-poly" during most of her childhood. Another woman said, "My sister would get her friends to sing songs about how ugly I was" (p. 29).

Habitual sibling disputes often have long-term negative effects. Sibling relationships that are largely conflictual early in life are likely to remain so.

- **Degradation:** "The worst kind of emotional abuse I experienced was if I walked into a room, my brother would pretend he was throwing up at the sight of me. As I got older, he most often would pretend I wasn't there and would speak as if I didn't exist, even in front of my father and my mother" (p. 35).

- **Intimidation:** A woman in her forties still remembers (and resents) that her siblings would take her sister and her into the field to pick berries. "When we would hear dogs barking, they would tell us they were wild dogs, and then they'd run away and make us find our own way home. We were only five or six, and we didn't know our way home" (p. 37).

- **Torturing or killing a pet:** "My second-oldest brother shot my little dog that I loved dearly. It loved me—only me. I cried by its grave for several days. Twenty years passed before I could care for another dog" (p. 39).

- **Destroying personal possessions:** "My brother would cut out the eyes, ears, mouth, and fingers of my dolls and hand them to me" (p. 38).

Many children report that their parents rarely take physical or emotional abuse by siblings seriously: "'You must have done something to deserve it,' parents might say. My parents seemed to think it was cute when my brother ridiculed me. Everything was always a joke to them. They laughed at me. Usually their reply was for me to quit complaining—'You'll get over it'" (Wiehe and Herring, 1991: 22, 73).

Parents might escalate the violence by treating children differently or showing favoritism. They might describe one child as "the smart one" or "the lazy one." Such labeling discourages siblings' respect for one another and creates resentment. The preferred child might target a less-preferred sibling for maltreatment, especially when the parents aren't present (Updegraff et al., 2005).

Sibling aggression is more dangerous than many parents think. About 10 percent of all murders in families are **siblicides**, killing a brother or sister, and they account for more than 2 percent of all murders nationwide. The average age of siblicide victims is 33—during early and middle adulthood rather than during adolescence, as one might expect. Men are much more likely than women to be either offenders (88 percent) or victims (84 percent). The most common reason for siblicide is an argument between the perpetrator and the victim (Dawson and Langan, 1994; Fox and Zawitz, 2007).

Ignoring or intervening briefly in sibling violence doesn't teach children the skills they need for regulating their behavior throughout life. Children learn that aggression is acceptable not only between brothers and sisters but also later with their own spouses and children. Such perceptions increase the likelihood of bullying at school and aggressive behavior with friends and in dating relationships. Outside the home, peers, teachers, employers, and co-workers rarely tolerate impulsive and negative behavior because a group's stability and productivity require problem solving, anger management, negotiation, cooperation, and compromise (Simonelli et al., 2002; Smith and Ross, 2007; Kennedy and Kramer, 2008).

SEXUAL ABUSE Sexual abuse by a sibling is rarely an isolated incident. In most instances, the episodes continue over time. They are often accompanied by physical and emotional abuse and may escalate. According to one woman, "I can't remember exactly how the sexual abuse started but when I was smaller there was a lot of experimenting. My brother would do things to me like put his finger in my vagina. Then, as I got older, he would perform oral sex on me" (Wiehe, 1997: 72).

The perpetrators often threaten victims with violence: "I was about twelve years old. My brother told me if I didn't take my clothes off, he would take his baseball bat and hit me in the head and I would die. I knew he would do it because he had already put me in the hospital. Then he raped me" (Wiehe and Herring, 1991: 55). Most children say nothing to their parents about a sibling's sexual abuse either because they're afraid of reprisal or think that their parents won't believe them.

In most cases of sibling incest, older brothers molest younger sisters. Girls generally perceive themselves as less powerful than their brothers. Because of

siblicide Killing a brother or sister.

such gender-based power differences, an older brother and a younger sister are most at risk for sibling incest. As one woman explained,

> My brother was the hero of the family. He was the firstborn, and there was a great deal of importance placed on his being a male. My father tended to talk to him about the family business and ignore us girls. My mother would hang on every word my brother said. . . . If he ever messed up or did something wrong, my parents would soon forgive and forget. When I finally confronted them as a teenager about Shawn molesting me, at first they didn't believe me. Later, they suggested that I just get over it (Caffaro and Conn-Caffaro, 1998: 53).

Adolescent Abuse

The risks of family violence and child homicide decrease as children grow older, but many parents (or their intimate partners) abuse teenagers. As in early childhood, victimization during adolescence is the root of many problems later in life.

PREVALENCE OF ADOLESCENT ABUSE When adolescents fail to live up to their parents' expectations, parents sometimes use physical force—including spanking, hitting, and beating—to assert control (see Chapter 12). Of all child victims, 23 percent are ages 12 through 17. Within this age group, 56 percent have experienced neglect, 18 percent have been abused physically, and 16 percent have been sexually assaulted by a family member or an adult relative (U.S. Department of Health and Human Services, 2012a).

SOME CONSEQUENCES OF ADOLESCENT ABUSE Some teenagers strike back physically and verbally. Others rebel, run away from home, withdraw, use alcohol and other drugs, become involved in juvenile prostitution and pornography, or even commit suicide (Estes and Weiner, 2002).

Compared with nonvictims, abused adolescents are twice as likely to be victims of other violent crimes, domestic violence offenders, and substance abusers as adults. They're also almost three times more likely to commit serious property and violent crimes. Compared with 17 percent of nonvictim boys, 48 percent of boys who have been sexually assaulted engage in delinquent acts. About 20 percent of sexually assaulted girls become delinquent compared with 5 percent of their nonvictim counterparts (Kilpatrick et al., 2003; Wasserman et al., 2003; Herrenkohl et al., 2007).

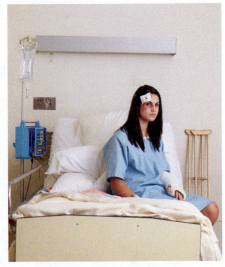

Some parents use physical force, including beating, to punish their adolescents.

Elder Mistreatment

Baby boomers are often called the **sandwich generation** because they must care not only for their own children but also for their aging parents (see Chapter 1). Most people in the sandwich generation are remarkably adept at meeting the needs of both the young and the old. Others mistreat their children, their elderly parents and relatives, or both.

What Is Elder Mistreatment?

Elder mistreatment, also called *elder abuse*, is a single or repeated act, or failing to do something, by a caregiver that results in harm or a risk of harm to an older person. Elder mistreatment includes the following:

- Physical abuse (e.g., hitting or slapping)
- Negligence (e.g., inadequate care)

14.4 Define, illustrate, and describe elder mistreatment and explain why elder abuse occurs.

sandwich generation Taking care of one's own children and aging parents.

elder mistreatment A single or repeated act, or failing to do something, by a caregiver that results in harm or a risk of harm to an older person (also called *elder abuse*).

Adult children, spouses, and cohabiting partners are the most likely to mistreat older people.

- Financial exploitation (e.g., stealing money or borrowing money and not repaying it)
- Psychological abuse (e.g., swearing at or blaming the elderly for one's own problems)
- Deprivation of basic necessities such as food and heat
- Isolation from friends and family
- Not administering needed medications

Police officers who are guest lecturers in my classes describe some horrific cases of elder abuse or neglect. Some old people die of starvation, and their bodies aren't discovered for a year or more. A 71-year-old woman was left in bed for so long that her bedsores became infested with maggots. A national study of people age 60 and older found that almost 12 percent had experienced at least one of the following types of mistreatment: emotional (4.6 percent), physical (1.6 percent), sexual (0.6 percent), financial (5.2 percent), and neglect (6 percent) (Acierno et al., 2010; see also Laumann et al., 2008).

Who Are the Victims?

Almost 83 percent of the victims of elder abuse are white; the average age is 76; 76 percent are women; 84 percent live in their own homes; 86 percent have a chronic disease or other health condition; 57 percent are married or cohabiting; 53 percent haven't graduated from high school; 50 percent suffer from dementia, Alzheimer's, or other mental illness; 46 percent feel socially isolated; and the average household income is less than $35,000 a year (Acierno et al., 2009; Jackson and Hafemeister, 2011).

Who Are the Abusers?

Most are adult children, spouses, other family members, or cohabiting partners (see *Table 14.4*). Less than a third are acquaintances, neighbors, or nonfamily service providers. The average age of the abuser is 45; 77 percent are white; 61 percent are males; 82 percent have a high school diploma or less; 50 percent abuse alcohol and/or other drugs; 46 percent have a criminal record; 42 percent are financially dependent on the elder; 37 percent live with the elder; 29 percent are chronically unemployed; and 25 percent have mental health problems (Jackson and Hafemeister, 2011).

Since you asked . . .

- Is elder mistreatment more common in nursing homes than elsewhere?

TABLE 14.4	Relationship of Perpetrators and Victims of Elder Mistreatment			
	Emotional Abuse	Physical Abuse	Sexual Abuse	Neglect
Spouse/Partner	25%	57%	40%	28%
Adult child/Grandchild	19%	10%	—	39%
Other relative	13%	9%	12%	7%
Acquaintance	25%	19%	40%	23%
Stranger	9%	3%	3%	—
Refused to answer	9%	2%	5%	3%

Source: Based on Acierno et al., 2009, Exhibits 2–5.

Why Do They Do It?

Why do family members mistreat the elderly? A number of micro and macro risk factors increase the likelihood of elder abuse and neglect (see Jackson and Hafemeister, 2013).

LIVING ARRANGEMENTS   A shared living situation is a major risk factor for elder mistreatment. Sharing a residence increases opportunities for contact, tensions that can't be decreased simply by leaving, and conflicts that arise in everyday situations (Bonnie and Wallace, 2003; Jackson and Hafemeister, 2011).

LOW SOCIAL SUPPORT   Elder abuse is more likely when family members don't have a strong social network of kin, friends, and neighbors. Care providers who don't have supportive networks to provide occasional relief from their caretaking activities experience strain and may become violent toward their elderly parents or relatives (Kilburn, 1996; Acierno et al., 2010).

ALCOHOL ABUSE   Alcohol use and abuse are common among offenders. Daily alcohol consumption is more than twice as likely among those who abuse elders as among those who do not (Reay and Browne, 2001; Bonnie and Wallace, 2003; Acierno et al., 2009).

IMPAIRMENT OF THE CAREGIVER OR THE CARE RECIPIENT   A 70-year-old "child" who cares for a 90-year-old parent—a situation that is common today—may be frail, ill, or mentally disabled and unaware that he or she is being abusive or neglectful. Older adults with cognitive impairment are abused at higher rates than older adults without such disabilities. Cognitive impairment may be due to dementia (deteriorated mental condition) after a stroke; frontotemporal dementia (FTD), a progressive deterioration of the brain's frontal lobe; or the onset of Alzheimer's disease (see Chapter 16). Some people with Alzheimer's might pinch, shove, bite, kick, or strike their caregivers. Caregivers who know little about debilitating diseases might hit back (Acierno et al., 2009; Jackson and Hafemeister, 2011; Heisler, 2012).

DEPENDENCE ON THE CAREGIVER   Elderly people who live with their children because they're too poor to live on their own may also suffer from incontinence, serious illness, or mental disabilities. They become physically as well as economically dependent on their caretakers. If the elderly are demanding, the caregivers may feel angry or resentful.

The dependency between the abuser and the victim is often mutual. Spouses, for example, may depend on each other for companionship. In the case of adult children and parents, the abuser may need the older person for money or housing, and the parent may need the abuser for help with chores or to alleviate loneliness. The adult child who is still dependent on an elderly parent for housing or finances might mistreat the parent to compensate for the lack or loss of power (Acierno et al., 2009; Jackson and Hafemeister, 2011).

FINANCIAL STRESS   Having to pay medical costs for an elderly relative may trigger abuse. Unlike low-income people, middle-class families aren't eligible for admission to public facilities. Few can pay for the in-home nursing care, high-quality nursing homes, and other services that upper-class families can afford. As a result, cramped quarters and high expenses increase the caregivers' stress. Adult children and relatives may also divert money for their own purposes, especially if they're experiencing hard times or are jobless (Acierno et al., 2009; Jackson and Hafemeister, 2011).

PERSONALITY   Sometimes personality characteristics of older people increase the risk of abuse. Chronic verbal aggression and hostility can spark physical and verbal maltreatment by a caretaking spouse, partner, or adult child (Comijs et al., 1998; Jackson and Hafemeister, 2011).

MAKING CONNECTIONS

- Think about your or your friends' current or past relationships with your/their brothers and sisters. Are/were the relationships abusive? Do/did the parents take sibling mistreatment seriously?
- Why do you think that most victims don't report elder mistreatment?

14.5

14.5 Describe the prevalence of violence in same-sex couples and racial-ethnic groups, and explain why it occurs.

Violence among Same-Sex Couples and Racial-Ethnic Groups

You've seen that many families experience conflict. Neither sexual orientation nor national origin deter abuse, violence, and neglect.

Same-Sex Couples

Same-sex couples are less likely than their opposite-sex counterparts to spank or physically punish their children (see Chapter 12). When growing up, however, lesbian women who described themselves as "butch" (being masculine in appearance and behavior) encountered more physical abuse and neglect than those who described themselves as "femme" (being feminine in appearance and behavior) (Lehavot et al., 2012).

What about adult life? A recent and first of its kind national survey found that lesbian women experienced more IPV than gay men. The rates were also higher for bisexual and heterosexual women than for bisexual and heterosexual men (see *Table 14.5*).

Over a lifetime, nearly 30 percent of lesbians, 50 percent of bisexual women, and 24 percent of heterosexual women experienced at least one form of severe physical violence by an intimate partner. In contrast, 16 percent of gay men and 14 percent of heterosexual men experienced similar severe physical violence by an intimate partner (the numbers of bisexual men were too small to report) (Walters et al., 2013).

It's not clear why heterosexuals have lower victimization rates than lesbians and gay men. It could be that many have experienced considerable humiliation, bullying, and rejection at school that increases the likelihood of violence in adulthood. Within same-sex relationships, homophobia can increase abusive behavior if a partner uses it as a psychological weapon by threatening to expose the relationship to parents or employers (Andersen and Witham, 2011; Ard and Makadon, 2011).

One study found that same-sex intimate partner violence was due to two related stressors: *internalized homophobia*, or having negative feelings about being lesbian or gay because of society's rejection of homosexuality, and *heterosexist discrimination*, or being treated unfairly because of one's homosexual orientation. The study concluded that both internalized homophobia and heterosexist discrimination increase the likelihood of lifetime IPV because lesbians and gay men who "harbor beliefs that they deserve the abuse" stay in abusive relationships (Balsam and Szymanski, 2005: 266).

Such research helps explain why same-sex IPV rates are high, but not why those of lesbians are higher than those of gay men. Perhaps men, regardless of sexual orientation, are more likely than women to underreport IPV. Also, the differences may be due to variables such as age, race, ethnicity, social class,

Since you asked . . .

- Is abuse more common among same-sex than opposite-sex couples?

 Watch on MySocLab

Video: Gay Violence

 Watch on MySocLab

Video: Lesbian Violence

TABLE 14.5	Lifetime Prevalence of Rape, Physical Violence, and/or Stalking by an Intimate Partner, by Sexual Orientation and Sex, 2010		
Women		**Men**	
Lesbian	44%	Gay	26%
Bisexual	61%	Bisexual	37%
Heterosexual	35%	Heterosexual	29%

Source: Based on Walters et al., 2013, Tables 3 and 4.

and the age at which lesbians and gay men experience abuse in childhood or adolescence—all factors that haven't been researched on a national level (Walters et al., 2013).

Racial-Ethnic Groups

Across all racial and ethnic groups, women have higher victimization rates than men, but women, too, are offenders (see *Figure 14.7*). Experiencing victimization varies by socioeconomic status, national origin, external stressors (such as discrimination), and other factors. Among Latinos, for example, there is a greater likelihood of mutual IPV when the cohabitors and married couples live in high-crime neighborhoods and if one or both partners abuse alcohol (Cunradi, 2009).

There are also variations among Asian American couples that reflect, among other variables, gender roles and employment status. For example, some men are more likely to be abusive if the wives violate traditional gender roles (e.g., they challenge the husband's decision making about household chores, child rearing, and finance). When wives earn as much or more than their husbands and, consequently, want to have more household decision-making power, some husbands—especially those who are older—may become abusive to reassert their control and authority (Chung et al., 2008).

A recent national study found that mutual IPV was higher among interracial and black couples than white couples, and higher among cohabitants than married couples. The researchers attributed the higher IPV rates among interracial couples to stressors such as cultural and communication differences, and negative attitudes toward the relationships by outsiders, friends, and family members. Black couples may not face the same obstacles as interracial couples, but they're more likely than white couples to encounter racial discrimination, unemployment, and few advancement opportunities—all of which increase stress and the likelihood of violence (Martin et al., 2013).

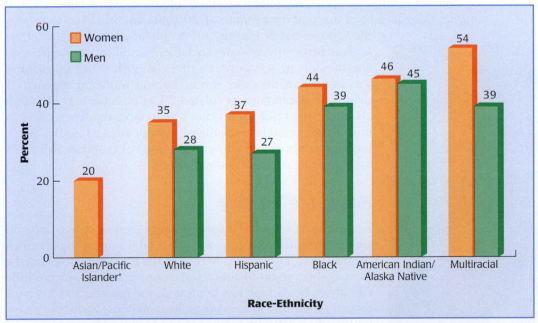

* Number of cases is too small to report an estimate

FIGURE 14.7 **Lifetime Prevalence of Rape, Physical Violence, and/or Stalking by an Intimate Partner, by Race/Ethnicity and Sex, 2010**
Source: Based on Black et al., 2011, Tables 4.3 and 4.4.

Since you asked . . .
- Is there one best explanation for intimate partner and family violence?

Explaining Family Abuse and Violence

Why are families abusive? There many competing explanations based on medical, political, psychological, and criminological models. Let's examine, briefly, five influential perspectives—feminist theories, social learning theory, resource theory, social exchange theory, and ecological systems theory. (You might want to refer to *Figure 2.1* on page 32 to refresh your memory of these perspectives.)

Feminist Theories

According to *feminist theories*, male aggression against women and children is common in patriarchal societies in which men have power, status, and privilege. Females, on the other hand, are marginalized and expected to accept male domination. Women's growing independence has resulted in some men using violence to reestablish their power in the relationship (Russell, 2011; Winstok, 2011).

Feminist scholars don't deny that women are violent, but they believe that women often resort to aggression to resist men's control and domination. Feminist perspectives maintain that women's physical violence is less likely to result in injuries than men's physical violence. In addition, when a couple's violence is mutual, women are more likely than men to comply with a partner's commands (Johnson, 2011; Anderson, 2013).

Social Learning Theory

According to *social learning theory*, we learn by observing the behavior of others. Some people try to avoid the behavior that they've experienced in the past. However, continuous exposure to abuse and violence during childhood increases the likelihood that a person will be both an assailant and a victim in adulthood (Busby et al., 2008; Cui et al., 2013).

When there's both physical and emotional abuse between adults in a household, children tend to model the behaviors and engage in sibling abuse instead of learning conflict resolution skills (Whiteman et al., 2011). A study of almost 1,300 couples who had been married an average of 20 years found that, over time, the spouses didn't become more similar on personality traits such as being affectionate, sociable, or ambitious. Aggression was the only personality trait that changed: When one spouse was aggressive, the other spouse became more aggressive over time. The researchers speculated, "It is possible that individuals might reinforce each other's aggressive tendencies due to hostile interpersonal exchanges" (Humbad et al., 2010: 828). It's not clear, however, why couples don't also imitate behaviors such as being sociable and ambitious.

Resource Theory

According to *resource theory*, because men usually command greater financial, educational, and social resources than women do, men have more power. Men with the fewest resources are the most likely to resort to abuse. For example, a man who has little education, holds a job low in prestige and income, and has poor communication skills may use violence to maintain his dominant position in a relationship or family. Many women can't assert themselves simply because they have even fewer resources than their partners (Babcock et al., 1993; Atkinson et al., 2005).

Besides an absence of resources, a decline of resources may also increase stress and provoke violence. If a man's contribution to earnings decreases relative to the wife's or if the man experiences spells of unemployment, the woman is more likely to experience abuse. The situation can be aggravated

Why does continuous exposure to parental conflict increase the likelihood of being either an offender or a victim of intimate partner violence or family abuse in adulthood?

by living in a disadvantaged neighborhood, having a large number of children, or the wife's refusal to work more hours outside the home (Fox et al., 2002).

Social Exchange Theory

According to *social exchange theory*, both assailants and victims tolerate or engage in violent behavior because they believe that the benefits outweigh the costs. You'll recall that many battered women stay in an abusive relationship for financial reasons. The rewards for perpetrators include release of anger and frustration and accumulation of power and control. They often spend little time in jail, and the abused women usually take them back (Sherman, 1992).

Violence also has costs. First, it's possible that the victim will hit back. For example, whether it's due to retaliation or other reasons, the proportion of parents killed by one of their children rose from 9.7 percent in 1980 to 13 percent in 2008 (Cooper and Smith, 2011). Second, a violent assault could lead to arrest or imprisonment and a loss of status among family and friends. Finally, the abuser may break up the family (Gelles and Cornell, 1990). However, if a patriarchal society condones male control of women and children, the costs will be minimal.

Ecological Systems Theory

Ecological systems theory explains domestic violence by analyzing the relationships between individuals and larger systems such as the economy, education, state agencies, and the community. For example, elder abuse is highest when there is a combination of micro and macro variables: Caregivers abuse drugs or have limited resources and experience stress, older people develop physical or mental disabilities, caregivers and the elderly are physically and socially isolated from a larger community, and there are few social service agencies that provide high-quality care (see Jackson and Hafemeister, 2013).

Moreover, cultural values—including television programs and movies—that demean, debase, and devalue women and children promote and reinforce abusive behavior. For example, even if hip-hop music, especially "gangsta rap," doesn't actually cause physical abuse against women, the lyrics are "often chillingly supportive of rape and violence" (Hill, 2005: 185; see also Chapter 5).

Using Several Theories

Researchers rarely rely on only one theory because the reasons for human behavior, including IPV and domestic violence, are complex. For example, resource theory suggests that men who have few assets are more likely to be violent toward their partners than are men with high incomes. Exchange theory posits that people stay in abusive relationships because the benefits outweigh the costs. Feminist theories contend that women's lower status in society encourages male aggression (Anderson, 2010). If we also consider personality variables and social exchange factors, explaining family violence becomes even more complex.

Other Family Health Issues

Family abuse is devastating, but other health-related issues can become crises. Lifestyle choices often result in sickness and death, but many families must also cope with depression and suicide.

Lifestyle Choices

The United States is among the wealthiest nations in the world, but it's far from the healthiest. Compared with 16 other high-income countries, the United States ranks last or near-last in nine key areas of health that include lung and heart

According to ecological systems theory, the reasons for a man beating up his girlfriend or wife may involve a combination of factors such as growing up in an abusive home, school problems, parents' poverty, and light penalties by the criminal justice system.

14.7 Describe three lifestyle choices and their prevalence that affect families' health, and explain why family members experience depression and suicide.

Should smoking be banned in all public places, including outside of office buildings?

Since you asked . . .

- Are Americans healthier than other people in high-income countries?

disease, homicide, and sexually transmitted diseases (Institute of Medicine, 2013). No single factor fully explains why Americans are now dying at younger ages than their counterparts in other high-income countries, but poorer health in the United States is due, largely, to lifestyle choices, particularly smoking, obesity, and substance abuse.

SMOKING   Worldwide and in the United States, tobacco use, primarily cigarette smoking, is the leading cause of preventable disease, disability, and death. In the United States, tobacco use is responsible for about 1 in 5 deaths annually, and, on average, smokers die 13 to 14 years earlier than nonsmokers. Smoking can cause cancer, heart disease, stroke, and lung diseases (including emphysema and bronchitis) and costs more than $193 billion each year in lost productivity and health care expenditures ("Smoking and Tobacco Use," 2012).

Cigarette smoking by adolescents and adults has decreased (see *Figure 14.8*), but is still high. Each day, more than 3,800 teenagers smoke their first cigarette, and more than 1,000 of them become daily cigarette smokers. The vast majority of Americans who smoke every day during adolescence become dependent on nicotine by young adulthood. Nearly all adults who smoke every day started smoking when they were 26 or younger (U.S. Department of Health and Human Services, 2012b).

Among high school students, the prevalence of having ever smoked cigarettes is slightly higher among males (46 percent) than females (43 percent), and higher among white and Hispanic than black students (44 percent, 49 percent, and 39 percent, respectively). Nationwide, more than 6 percent of high school students smoke more than a pack a day—8 percent of white students, 4 percent of Latino students, and 3 percent of black students (Eaton et al., 2012). Thus, white male students are the most likely to engage in this high-risk behavior.

Among adults, cigarette smoking has also decreased since 1965 (see *Figure 14.8*). Between 2000 and 2010, cigarette smoking among those ages 25 to 64 dropped from 26 percent to 22 percent, especially among those with a college degree or higher. During the same decade, there was no change in the smoking prevalence among adults 65 years and over (almost 10 percent), regardless of education level (National Center for Health Statistics, 2012). One might hypothesize that older Americans' cigarette smoking hasn't decreased because of nicotine addiction, relying on smoking to decrease stress, or having more discretionary income (see Chapter 13), but researchers don't know for sure.

Prevention is difficult because the tobacco industry spends almost $10 billion a year to market its products, half of all movies for children under 13 contain

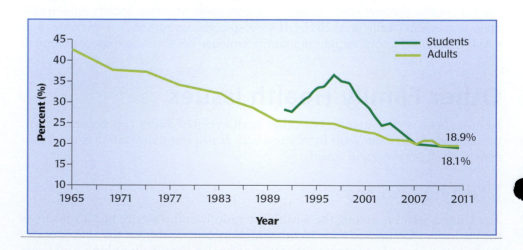

FIGURE 14.8 **Cigarette Smoking among U.S. High School Students and Adults, 1965–2011**
Source: Centers for Disease Control and Prevention, 2012.

scenes of tobacco use, half of the states continue to allow smoking in public places, and images and messages normalize tobacco use in magazines, on the Internet, and at retail stores frequented by youth. In 2011, states collected more than $25 billion from tobacco taxes and legal settlements, but spent only 2 percent of this money on tobacco prevention programs (U.S. Department of Health and Human Services, 2012b; see also Shadel et al., 2012).

OVERWEIGHT AND OBESITY   Obesity is the second top cause of disability and death. The most commonly used measure of weight status is body mass index, or BMI, which uses a simple calculation based on the ratio of a person's height and weight. For adults, a BMI between 25 and 29 is considered overweight, between 30 and 39 is obese, and extreme obesity is 40 or higher (Ogden and Carroll, 2010b).

Since the 1970s, the percentage of Americans who are overweight and obese has increased. Between 1971 and 2010, the prevalence of obesity among children ages 2 to 19 increased from 5 percent to 17 percent. In 1971, 15 percent of U.S. adults aged 20 and over were obese, and 1 percent were extremely obese. By 2010, 36 percent were obese, and 6 percent were extremely obese (Ogden and Carroll, 2010a, 2010b; Ogden et al., 2012; see also Brown, 2013).

In 1990, not a single state had an obesity rate above 15 percent. In 2012, all states had obesity rates above 20 percent, and 12 states had obesity rates equal to or greater than 30 percent. Since 1988, the prevalence of obesity has increased among adults at all income and education levels (Ogden et al., 2012). At the current rate, some medical researchers predict that 42 percent of American adults will be obese in 2030 (see *Figure 14.9*), and 25 percent of that group will be severely obese (Finkelstein et al., 2012).

Being overweight and obese increases a person's risk for heart disease, high blood pressure, strokes, diabetes, osteoporosis, and several types of cancer. Many people claim that being overweight is due to their genes. However, more than half of Americans admit to overeating and unhealthful eating, even though 91 percent say they have access to affordable fruits and vegetables in their communities (Cochrane, 2012). The 86 percent of full-time employees who are overweight have at least one chronic disease and high absenteeism rates, resulting in $153 billion in lost productivity every year (Witters and Angrawal, 2011).

Often, obesity is due to **binge eating**, consuming an unusually large amount of food and feeling that the eating is out of control. Binge eating is the most common eating disorder in the United States and affects about 4 percent of women and 2 percent of men. Most binge eaters are between the ages of 46 and 55 (Hudson et al., 2007; "Binge Eating Disorder," 2008).

Binge eaters report more health problems, stress, muscle and joint pain, headaches, menstrual problems, trouble sleeping, and suicidal thought than do people who aren't binge eaters. On the other hand, binge eating may trigger many of these problems. Some early-stage research suggests that genes may be involved in binge eating because it often occurs within families, but researchers don't know for sure ("Binge Eating Disorder," 2008).

Anorexia nervosa (usually abbreviated as *anorexia*) is a dangerous eating disorder. It's characterized by a fear of obesity, the conviction that one is fat, significant weight loss, and refusal to maintain weight within normal age and height limits. **Bulimia** is a cyclical pattern of eating binges followed by self-induced vomiting, fasting, excessive exercise, or using laxatives.

Study results vary, but at some point in their lives an estimated 4 percent of American women experience anorexia and another 7 percent are afflicted with bulimia. Ninety percent of anorexics and bulimics are females. Eating disorders

---

Since you asked . . .
- What's the difference between being overweight and obese?

binge eating Consuming an unusually large amount of food and feeling that the eating is out of control.

anorexia nervosa A dangerous eating disorder characterized by a fear of obesity.

bulimia A cyclical pattern of eating binges followed by self-induced vomiting, fasting, excessive exercise, or using laxatives.

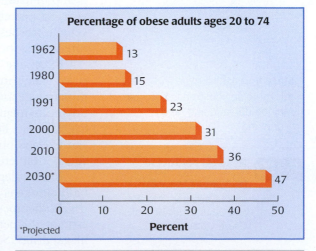

Percentage of obese adults ages 20 to 74

Year	Percent
1962	13
1980	15
1991	23
2000	31
2010	36
2030*	47

*Projected

FIGURE 14.9 **U.S. Adult Obesity Has Increased Since 1962**
Sources: Based on Ogden and Carroll, 2010b; Finkelstein et al., 2012; Ogden et al., 2012.

can affect people of all ages, but 86 percent report the onset of anorexia or bulimia before age 20 (Berkman et al., 2006; National Mental Health Association, 2006).

Anorexia may cause slowing of the heartbeat, loss of normal blood pressure, cardiac arrest, dehydration, skin abnormalities, hypothermia, lethargy, potassium deficiency, and kidney malfunction. With treatment, about half of anorexics get better, about 40 percent remain chronically ill, and 10 percent die of causes related to the disease (Fichter et al., 2006).

Bulimia's binge–purge cycle can cause fatigue, seizures, muscle cramps, an irregular heartbeat, and decreased bone density, which can lead to osteoporosis. Repeated vomiting can damage the esophagus and stomach, cause the salivary glands to swell, make the gums recede, and erode tooth enamel.

About half of the risk for developing anorexia might be due to a combination of a genetic predisposition and brain chemistry (Frank et al., 2005; Bulik et al., 2006). However, because eating disorders typically co-occur with other problems such as depression and sexual abuse, the relationship between genes and eating disorders is still indefinite.

SUBSTANCE ABUSE Use of some drugs—whether legal or illegal—can result in **substance abuse**, an overindulgence in and dependence on a drug or other chemical that harms an individual's physical and mental health. Excessive alcohol use is the third leading lifestyle-related cause of death in the nation. Approximately 80,000 Americans die each year because of excessive drinking, more than 1.6 million are hospitalized, and more than 4 million visit emergency rooms for alcohol-related problems ("Alcohol Use and Health," 2011; Kanny et al., 2012).

Excessive alcohol use includes *binge drinking*, having five or more drinks on the same occasion at least 1 day in the past 30 days, and *heavy drinking*, having five or more drinks on the same occasion 5 or more days in the past 30 days (Substance Abuse and Mental Health Services Administration, 2012: 31). Between 1993 and 2011, the prevalence of binge drinking increased from 14 to 17 percent, and the prevalence of heavy drinking increased from 3 to 6 percent ("Alcohol and Public Health," 2011; Substance Abuse and Mental Health Services Administration, 2012).

In 2011, 71 percent of high school students had drunk alcohol. Those ages 12 to 20 drink 11 percent of all alcohol consumed in the United States, and this group consumes more than 90 percent of its alcohol by binge drinking. Every year, 38 percent of young people under age 21 who are involved in fatal motor vehicle crashes are drunk (Crowe et al., 2012; Eaton et al., 2012; National Institute on Alcohol Abuse and Alcoholism, 2012).

Excessive alcohol use results in myriad immediate and long-term health risks. They include unintentional injuries, violence, risky sexual behaviors, miscarriage and stillbirth, physical and mental birth defects, alcohol poisoning, unemployment, psychiatric problems, heart disease, several types of cancer, and liver disease. For teenagers and young adults under age 25, alcohol consumption can irreversibly damage a part of the brain that involves memory, learning, and social interaction ("Alcohol Use and Health," 2011; Crowe et al., 2012).

Illicit (illegal) *drugs* include marijuana/hashish, cocaine and crack, heroin, hallucinogens (such as LSD and PCP), inhalants, and any prescription-type psychotherapeutic drug (such as stimulants and sedatives) used nonmedically. An estimated 9 percent of Americans (almost 23 million people) age 12 and older use illegal drugs (Substance Abuse and Mental Health Services Administration, 2012). Illicit drug use is more common among men (11 percent) than women (7 percent), most common among those ages 18 to 25 (21 percent), the unemployed (17 percent), those who haven't graduated from high school (17 percent), and least common among Asian Americans (4 percent) (Substance Abuse and Mental Health Services Administration, 2012; see also "Prescription Painkiller Overdoses," 2013, on the increasing number of women who are dying of overdoses).

In 2013, the prestigious and powerful American Medical Association (AMA), declared that obesity is a disease (Healy and Gorman, 2013). Does doing so increase all Americans' costs for health insurance? Physicians' greater likelihood of preventing and treating obesity? Peoples' not changing their behavior and lifestyles (such as overeating and not exercising) because they can now rely on expensive medical procedures and treatments?

substance abuse An overindulgence in and dependence on a drug or other chemical that harms an individual's physical and mental health.

Since you asked . . .
• Is there any difference between binge drinking and heavy drinking?

 Read on MySocLab

Document: Association is Not Causation: Alcohol and Other Drugs Do Not Cause Violence

Marijuana is the most commonly used illicit drug. Between 2007 and 2011, marijuana usage increased from almost 16 million to more than 18 million users (7 percent of the U.S. population). In 2011, 23 percent of high school students were using marijuana—up from 15 percent in 1991 (Eaton et al., 2012; Substance Abuse and Mental Health Services Administration, 2012).

In 2012, Colorado and Washington legalized marijuana. The District of Columbia and 15 states have legalized marijuana for medical reasons or plan to enact such laws in the future. About 2 percent of marijuana users are addicted, but most users smoke marijuana during periods of high stress, particularly unemployment (Van Gundy and Rebellon, 2010; Caulkins et al., 2012). A study of juvenile offenders in treatment programs found that those who abstained from all drugs, including alcohol and marijuana, for 12 months or longer were more likely to have jobs, better wages, and lower arrest rates than their counterparts who abstained for six or fewer months (Griffin et al., 2011).

Powerful prescription pain relievers such as Oxycontin and Vicodin are harder to get than in the past. In 2010, U.S. authorities and some states started cracking down on pain management centers where some doctors prescribed powerful narcotics and multiple refills without performing physical exams or requiring evidence of injury (Gwynne, 2011; Martin, 2013).

Prescription drug abuse has increased, however, partly because of the growth of illegitimate Internet pharmacies. In 2008, only 2 of the 365 websites that sold narcotic pain killers were certified. Of the remaining 363 sites, 85 percent didn't require a prescription, 15 percent required only that a prescription be faxed (making it possible for customers to forge prescriptions or use the same prescription multiple times), and there were no website controls to block the sale of drugs to adolescents (National Center on Addiction and Substance Abuse at Columbia University, 2008; Jena and Goldman, 2011).

Outside of the Internet, tighter restrictions on pain prescriptions have resulted in a surge of heroin use. Prescription pain pills containing narcotics sell for up to $80 for an 80 mg pill compared with $9 for a dose of heroin. Heroin has become so easy to get that, in many parts of the country, "dealers deliver to the suburbs and run specials to attract young, professional, upper-income customers." According to the substance abuse director at a North Carolina medical center, "Our heroin patients come from the five best neighborhoods" (Leger, 2013).

Illicit drugs have the same health risks as excessive alcohol use but can also have immediate life-threatening consequences, including death. In addition, illicit drug users, compared with non-users, have higher rates of mental illness, suicidal thought and behavior, major depressive episodes, and impair a person's ability to function at school, home, or work (Substance Abuse and Mental Health Services Administration, 2012).

Some researchers believe that marijuana users experience more difficulty with learning, schooling, and employment. Others maintain that such difficulties lead to marijuana use, and that marijuana is less addictive and lethal than excessive alcohol use or smoking.

Depression and Suicide

Two other serious problems that many families experience are depression and suicide. Both have negative consequences that can affect kin and friends throughout the life course.

DEPRESSION **Depression** is a mental disorder characterized by persistent sadness and loss of interest in everyday activities. Depression interferes with the ability to work, study, sleep, eat, and enjoy experiences that were formerly pleasurable (see *Table 14.6*). U.S. workers who have been diagnosed with depression miss an estimated 68 million days of work each year. The absenteeism costs employers $23 billion annually in lost productivity (Witters et al., 2013).

Over a lifetime, 14 percent of adolescents and 15 percent of adults experience at least one major depressive episode (one that lasts at least two weeks), but fewer than half ever seek treatment (Bostic and Miller, 2005). Depression is the single most common type of mental disorder reported by adolescents, and usually begins by age 14. Symptoms of depression are more common in girls (36 percent) than in

depression A mental disorder characterized by persistent sadness and loss of interest in everyday activities.

> ### TABLE 14.6 Some Symptoms of Depression
>
> - Persistent sadness, anxiety, or an "empty" feeling
> - Feelings of worthlessness, guilt, helplessness, hopelessness
> - Loss of interest or pleasure in usual hobbies and activities, including sex
> - Difficulty concentrating, remembering, making decisions
> - Fatigue and loss of energy
> - Restlessness, irritability
> - Changes in appetite and weight (weight loss or gain)
> - Disturbed sleep (insomnia or sleeping much of the time)
> - Suicidal thoughts or attempts
> - Persistent physical problems such as headaches, pain, and digestive disorders that don't respond to treatment

boys (22 percent), but some of the reasons are similar, such as hormonal changes, substance abuse, bullying (either as a victim or perpetrator), sexual or physical abuse, parental divorce, and a family history of mental disorders (Murphey et al., 2013).

During adulthood, and in all age groups, women are more likely than men to often feel depressed, but the prevalence of depression is highest among those aged 45 to 64 years (see *Figure 14.10*). There are a number of reasons for high depression rates in this age group: People face major life stresses such as divorce, losing a job, or the death of a loved one; menopausal women are going through hormonal changes; being part of the sandwich generation that's raising children, helping adult children, and caring for aging parents; and feeling sad about not having achieved one's "youthful dreams" (Weinstock, 2010: 120). As in the case of adolescents, many medical researchers believe that adults who have a genetic predisposition or family history of depression are more likely to be depressed, but it's not clear why the rates are higher for women and highest for both sexes at midlife.

SUICIDE Depression may lead to *suicide*, taking one's life. Here are some general facts about suicide:

- In 2010, more Americans died of suicide than in car accidents.
- More than 38,000 Americans killed themselves in 2010—an average of 105 each day.

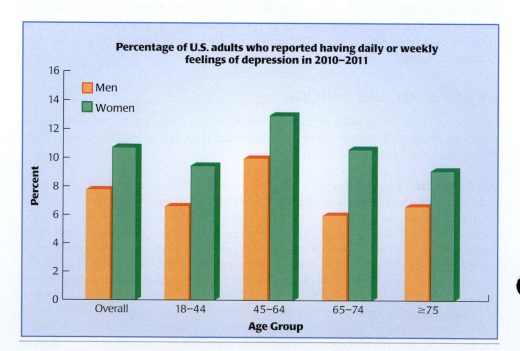

FIGURE 14.10 Women Are More Likely Than Men to Feel Depressed
Source: Clarke and Blackwell, 2013: 138.

- Males take their own lives at nearly four times the rate of females and represent 79 percent of all U.S. suicides.
- Suicide rates for males are highest among those age 75 and older, and highest for females ages 45 to 54.
- Suicide is the second leading cause of death among 25- to 34-year-olds and the third leading cause of death among 15- to 24-year-olds.
- In 2011, almost 13 percent of high school students planned how to commit suicide.
- Between 2002 and 2012, more U.S. soldiers, both active-duty and veterans, killed themselves than died in the Iraq and Afghanistan wars.
- In 2010, almost 9 million adults aged 18 and older (almost 4 percent of this population) seriously considered committing suicide (Center for Behavioral Health Statistics and Quality, 2012; Griffis, 2012; "Suicide," 2012; Dao and Lehren, 2013; Cloud, 2013; Sullivan et al., 2013).

From 1999 to 2010, the suicide rate among Americans ages 35 to 64 rose by nearly 30 percent—higher than other age groups. The most pronounced increases were among men in their fifties and women ages 60 to 64 (Sullivan et al., 2013). Across all age groups, suicide rates are "vastly underreported" (Parker-Pope, 2013: A1). Some of the reasons may include a family's guilt or shame and life insurance policies that don't pay out for deaths due to suicide.

Researchers are puzzled by the recent spike of suicides, especially among people in their fifties and sixties. They speculate that the upturn may be due to several reasons: The economic downturn that began in late 2007 and increased many families' turmoil; the widespread availability of opioid drugs such as Oxycontin that can be deadly if purposely consumed in large doses; men's reluctance to seek help when they're having problems; and women's inability to cope with the stresses of being members of a sandwich generation (Parker-Pope, 2013; Sullivan et al., 2013).

The reasons for suicide are complex, but taking one's life is associated with factors such as a family history of depression or other mental illness, substance abuse, physical illness, feeling alone, living with drug users, easy access to guns and poisons, bullying and other peer victimization among youth, sexual or physical abuse, and stress-related problems of active-duty and war veterans (Srabstein et al., 2008; Kaminski and Fang, 2009; Crowe et al., 2012; Thompson, 2012; Bandy et al., 2013). *Table 14.7* provides some of the symptoms of suicidal behavior.

MAKING CONNECTIONS

- Should a parent who suspects his or her child of substance abuse use a home drug-testing kit? Or would this create rebellion and more problems in the parent–child relationship?
- "The best way to help someone who's depressed is to try to cheer her or him up." Do you agree or disagree? Why?

TABLE 14.7 Some Common Warning Signs of Suicide
• Withdrawal from family or friends
• Verbal expression of suicidal thoughts or threats, even as a joke
• Major personality changes
• Changes in sleeping or eating habits
• Drug or alcohol abuse
• Difficulty concentrating
• Violent or rebellious outbursts
• Running away
• Recent suicide of a relative or friend
• Rejection by a boyfriend or girlfriend
• Unexplained, sudden drop in quality of schoolwork or athletic interests
• Giving or throwing away prized possessions
• Sudden lack of interest in friends or usual activities
• Extreme and sudden neglect of appearance
• Eating disorders (losing or gaining weight)

Combating Domestic Violence and Other Family Health Problems

Practically every research study and government report cited in this chapter recommends how to decrease a behavior, whether it's intimate partner violence, child mistreatment, substance abuse, or suicide. Two of the most effective strategies are prevention and intervention.

Prevention

Preventing domestic violence begins at home. How do you stop a 30-year-old man from beating his wife? "Talk to him when he's 12," writes a journalism professor, and as often as possible, about not abusing girls (Voss, 2003). The same could be said about talking to girls because, as you saw earlier, couple violence is often mutual. Family violence is one of the best predictors of IPV from childhood to old age. Domestic violence can be decreased by adults' solving conflict without being aggressive and teaching children that being a perpetrator, whether female or male, is equally unacceptable (Straus, 2009; Rhatigan et al., 2011).

Substance abuse problems, similarly, begin at home. For example,

Read on MySocLab

Document: Through a Sociological Lens: Social Structure and Family Violence

Since you asked . . .

- Is it *really* possible to reduce domestic violence and other family health problems?

- Children who learn about drugs and alcohol from their parents (rather than their friends) are up to 50 percent less likely to use alcohol or other drugs (Partnership at Drugfree.org, 2013).

- Adolescents are more likely to drink alcohol if their parents abuse alcohol (Crowe et al., 2012).

- Marijuana use among adolescents is much less prevalent (5 percent) among those whose parents "strongly disapprove" than among those (32 percent) whose parents say nothing (Substance Abuse and Mental Health Services Administration, 2012).

- Only 14 percent of teens say that their parents have discussed abusing prescription drugs; 20 percent of parents have given their teen a drug that wasn't prescribed for them; and 29 percent of parents believe that ADHD medication can improve their child's academic or testing performance, even if the teen doesn't have ADHD (MetLife Foundation and the Partnership at Drugfree.org, 2013).

- Despite test results, many parents deny that *their* teenagers are using illicit drugs; parents also lie about their own use and abuse of drugs such as cocaine, heroin, and narcotic pain pills (e.g., Vicodin and Oxycontin) (Delaney-Black et al., 2010).

Peers, siblings, schools, and the social media affect adolescents, but parents may unintentionally increase their children's substance abuse because they're poor role models and/or have permissive attitudes about alcohol and other drugs (Shih et al., 2010; see also Chapters 5 and 12).

Intervention

Thousands of U.S. programs and laws are designed to intervene in family crises. The Violence Against Women Act has been credited with lowering the rate of homicide for abused women by 65 percent since the law was passed in 1994 (AAUW, 2013). The Watchful Shepherd (www.watchful.org), a nonprofit organization founded in Pennsylvania, protects at-risk children with electronic devices that children can use to contact hospital emergency personnel when they feel threatened or fear abuse. An unexpected and positive outcome is use of the device by parents who fear that they're losing control and might hurt their child unless someone intervenes.

Many programs are ineffective because the staff is overworked, the agency is underfunded, or the police and judges don't enforce domestic violence laws. However, a number of interventions have been successful. For example,

- Abused women who obtain permanent (rather than temporary) court orders of protection are 80 percent less likely to be assaulted again.
- Counseling generally has little effect on a batterer's attitudes or behavior. Arrests, restraining orders, and intensive monitoring by police are far more effective.
- Kaiser Permanente, a national health maintenance organization, has launched a successful program that screens and treats domestic violence victims in emergency rooms and reports the abuse to police.
- Women who are treated for substance abuse during pregnancy are much more likely to have healthy babies than those who don't have prenatal care.
- Nurses and trained volunteers who visit low-income adolescent mothers and teach them parenting skills reduce the mothers' isolation and decrease child abuse by as much as 40 percent (Jackson et al., 2003; Vesely, 2005; Middlemiss and McGuigan, 2005; Paris and Dubus, 2005).

The U.S. Department of Justice and nonprofit organizations have published a number of reports that describe the most promising programs that coordinate domestic violence providers, child welfare agencies, law enforcement officers, and the judicial system (see, for example, Lowry and Trujillo, 2008, and Klein, 2009). A major problem is that Congress rarely passes laws to implement the recommendations of national task forces to combat family violence and substance abuse (see U.S. Department of Justice, 2012).

CONCLUSION

Millions of U.S. families are experiencing negative *changes*, such as family violence, and high drug use among middle school children and teenagers. As people become more informed about these and other problems, they have more *choices* in accessing supportive community resources and legal intervention agencies. These choices are sometimes eclipsed by a number of *constraints*. Laws aren't always enforced, our society still tolerates violence, and social service agencies are too understaffed and underfunded to deal with most problems. Many families must also navigate the choppy waters of separation, divorce, and living in a stepfamily, the topic of the next chapter.

On MySocLab — ✓ Study and Review on MySocLab

REVIEW QUESTIONS

14.1. Define and describe three types of intimate partner violence, explain why some women stay in abusive relationships, and discuss one-sided versus mutual partner violence.

1. How have U.S. IPV rates changed, by sex, since 1993?

2. How do abusive households differ in terms of gender, age, race, ethnicity, and social class?

3. Are women less abusive than men?

14.2. Define, illustrate, and describe four types of child maltreatment and explain why adults abuse children.

4. In child abuse, who are the victims and offenders? And what are some of the most important reasons for child abuse?

5. How does polyvictimization affect children?

6. How, specifically, does domestic violence affect children?

14.3. **Describe and illustrate sibling and adolescent abuse, as well as the prevalence and outcomes of this type of abuse.**

   7. Is sibling abuse normal? What are some of the consequences?

   8. How common is adolescent abuse? What are some of the consequences?

14.4. **Define, illustrate, and describe elder mistreatment and explain why elder abuse occurs.**

   9. Who, specifically, are the victims and perpetrators in elder abuse?

   10. What, specifically, are the reasons for elder mistreatment?

14.5. **Describe the prevalence of violence in same-sex couples and in racial-ethnic groups, and explain why it occurs.**

   11. How does same-sex and opposite-sex domestic violence differ? Why?

   12. Why do domestic violence rates vary across racial-ethnic families?

14.6. **Compare five theoretical explanations of family abuse and violence.**

   13. How do feminist, social learning, resource, social exchange, and ecological theories differ in their explanations of domestic violence?

   14. Why do researchers rarely rely on only one theory to explain IPV and domestic violence?

14.7. **Describe three lifestyle choices and their prevalence that affect families' health, and explain why family members experience depression and commit suicide.**

   15. In order of priority, and specifically, how do lifestyle choices affect many families' health?

   16. What are some of major reasons for depression and suicide?

14.8. **Describe and illustrate two ways to combat domestic violence and other family health problems.**

   17. Why are many parents poor role models in preventing domestic violence and their children's substance abuse?

   18. How effective are federal and state intervention policies and programs to reduce domestic violence?

Separation, Divorce, Remarriage, and Stepfamilies

CHAPTER 15

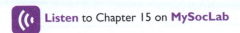

Listen to Chapter 15 on MySocLab

LEARNING OBJECTIVES
After you read and study this chapter you will be able to:

- 15.1 Describe the phases and outcomes of separation.
- 15.2 Describe the divorce process and explain why divorce rates have declined.
- 15.3 Explain the micro- and macro-level reasons for divorce.
- 15.4 Explain how and why divorce affects adults.
- 15.5 Explain how and why divorce affects children.
- 15.6 Describe the rate and process of remarriage, and explain how and why remarriages differ from first marriages.
- 15.7 Describe and explain the diversity and complexity of stepfamilies.
- 15.8 Describe and explain how stepfamilies differ from nuclear families.

- In 2013, 68 percent of Americans age 18 and older said that **divorce is morally acceptable**, up from 59 percent in 2001.

- On average, **first marriages that end in divorce last about eight years**.

- After a divorce, **82 percent of the custodial parents are mothers**. This proportion has been constant since 1994.

- The **median time between a divorce and a second marriage is about 4 years**.

- About 12 percent of men and women **have been married twice**, and 3 percent each **have been married three or more times**.

- Among U.S. adults, 42 **percent have at least one step relative**.

Sources: Grall, 2011; Kreider and Ellis, 2011b; Pew Social and Demographic Trends, 2011; Newport and Himelfarb, 2013.

S tatistically, two out of every five students reading this chapter probably come from divorced homes, and almost one in four grew up in a stepfamily. You'll see that divorces, remarriages, and stepfamilies are processes rather than single events, and all of these family structures have costs and benefits for adults and children. Let's begin by looking at separation, which usually precedes divorce.

15.1 Describe the phases and outcomes of separation.

separation Living apart before getting a divorce.

Separation: Process and Outcome

Separation can mean several things. It may be a temporary time-out during which the partners deliberate about continuing the marriage, and one person may move out of the home. Separation can also be a permanent arrangement if the couple's religious beliefs don't allow divorce. Or a couple may seek a legal separation—a temporary period of living apart that most states require before granting a divorce.

The Phases of Separation

Separation is usually a long and painful process that encompasses four phases: preseparation, early separation, midseparation, and late separation (Ahrons and Rodgers, 1987). Whether or not the partners go through all four stages, they often agonize for months or even years before making a final break.

PRESEPARATION During the *preseparation* phase, the couple experiences gradual emotional alienation. The financial costs of ending a marriage (especially one with children) are important considerations, but they're often less important than the emotional and psychological disadvantages of staying in an unhappy marriage (Hewitt, 2009). Couples often maintain a public pretense that nothing is wrong such as attending family and social functions together and holding hands in public.

During a separation, the spouses must perform housework and other tasks they might not have done during the marriage.

EARLY SEPARATION During the *early separation* phase, besides feeling ambivalent about leaving a marriage, the couple is plagued by many questions, both important and trivial: What should the partners tell their family and friends? Should the children's teachers be notified? Who gets the new car? What about the 60" plasma TV and the furniture? Couples must also confront economic issues such as paying bills and splitting old and new expenses.

MIDSEPARATION In the *midseparation* phase, the pressures of maintaining two households and meeting the children's emotional and physical needs mount, and stress intensifies. Because of such problems, as well as feeling guilty over breaking up the family, the couple may experience a "pseudo-reconciliation" and move back in together. The reunion rarely lasts. Soon the underlying problems that led to the separation in the first place surface again, conflicts reemerge, and the couple separates again (Blakeley, 2013).

LATE SEPARATION In the *late separation* phase, the partners must learn how to be singles again, such as now doing all the housework and home maintenance. Some friends may avoid both partners; others may take sides, which forces a separating couple to develop new individual friendships. Most important, partners must help their children deal with anxiety, anger, confusion, and sadness.

Some Outcomes of Marital Separation

Not all separations end in divorce. Sometimes people reconcile and try to give their marriage a second chance:

> After 25 years of marriage, my dad just moved out one day and lived in another state for almost three years. Then one day they reconciled and that was that. They never talk about it but . . . my parents recently celebrated their 31st wedding anniversary (Author's files).

SEPARATION AND RECONCILIATION According to a national study, approximately 10 percent of all married U.S. couples who have separated have gotten back together (Wineberg and McCarthy, 1993; see also Wineberg, 1996). In 10 percent of divorcing couples who had taken required parenting classes, both partners were interested in reconciliation, but there are no data on whether or not the couples reconciled (Doherty et al., 2011).

Since you asked . . .
• Do most couples reconcile after a separation?

SEPARATION WITHOUT DIVORCE Some people separate and even do the necessary paperwork, but never make the divorce official. In California, for example, 80 percent of divorcing people handled their own divorces to avoid high lawyer fees. About a third didn't finalize their divorces because they didn't realize that, after filing the papers in court, they must receive a decision from a judge. In effect, then, the couples are separated but not legally divorced (Garrison, 2007).

SEPARATION AND DIVORCE In most cases, separations end in **divorce**, the legal and formal dissolution of a marriage. The average time between separation and divorce is about 22 months (Payne and Gibbs, 2011).

divorce The legal and formal dissolution of a marriage.

Divorce: Process and Rates

Many marriages end in divorce after eight years (see Data Digest). Regardless of when it occurs, divorce is usually a painful process.

15.2 Describe the divorce process and explain why divorce rates have declined.

The Process of Divorce

Like separations, few divorces are spontaneous, spur-of-the-moment acts. Instead, many people go through a number of stages. One widely cited process is Bohannon's (1971) six "stations" of divorce: emotional, legal, economic, co-parental, community, and psychic.

Since you asked . . .
• Are divorces quick?

EMOTIONAL DIVORCE The *emotional divorce* begins before people take any legal steps. In the *beginning phase*, spouses feel disillusioned but hope that the marriage will improve. During the *middle phase*, their hurt or angry feelings

increase. The unhappier partner begins evaluating the rewards and costs of leaving the marriage. In the *end phase*, one of the partners stops caring and detaches emotionally from the other. Apathy and indifference replace loving, intimate feelings (Kersten, 1990; Hopper, 2001). Some couples postpone getting a divorce for at least five years, primarily because they worry about hurting their children (Montenegro, 2004), but most seek legal advice to end the marriage.

LEGAL DIVORCE   The *legal divorce* is the formal dissolution of a marriage. In part because divorce is an adversarial procedure during which each partner's attorney tries to maintain the upper hand, the process is rarely trouble free. Some issues may include **alimony** (sometimes called *spousal maintenance*), monetary payments by one ex-spouse to the other after a divorce. Other conflicts involve **child support**—monetary payments by the noncustodial parent to the custodial parent to help pay for child-rearing expenses. Because spouses often disagree on what's fair and equitable, they may use money to manipulate each other into making more concessions ("I'm willing to pay child support if you agree to sell the house and split the proceeds").

alimony Monetary payments by one ex-spouse to the other after a divorce (sometimes called *spousal maintenance*).

child support Monetary payments by the noncustodial parent to the custodial parent to help pay for child-rearing expenses.

ECONOMIC DIVORCE   During the *economic divorce*, the couple may argue about who should pay past debts, property taxes, and new expenses, such as braces for the children. Thus, conflict over financial issues may continue long after the legal questions have been settled. Couples may be involved in an economic divorce for several decades if their children are very young at the time of the divorce, if a parent violates the child support payment, or if an ex-spouse wants to change the original agreement about retirement funds and other assets.

CO-PARENTAL DIVORCE   The *co-parental divorce* involves agreements about legal responsibility for financial support of the children, their day-to-day care, and the rights of the custodial and noncustodial parents. Conflict may be short lived or long term, depending on how well the parents get along.

COMMUNITY DIVORCE   Partners also go through a *community divorce*, during which they inform friends, family, teachers, and others that they're no longer married. During this stage, relationships between grandparents and grandchildren often continue, but in-laws may sever ties. The partners may also make new friends, and typically start dating again.

PSYCHIC DIVORCE   In this final stage, the couple goes through a *psychic divorce* in which the partners separate from each other emotionally and establish separate lives. One or both spouses may undergo a process of mourning. Some people never complete this stage because they can't let go of their pain, anger, and resentment toward an ex-spouse, even after they remarry.

Not all couples go through all six of Bohannon's stations. Also, some couples may experience some stages, such as emotional and economic divorce, simultaneously. The important point is that divorce is a *process* that involves many people, not just the divorcing couple, and may take time to complete.

Sometimes people have divorce ceremonies, like this party, to celebrate the end of an unhappy marriage. Do you think that such ceremonies are tasteless? Or help people get closure on a divorce?

Divorce Rates

Marriages in the United States are lasting longer. In 2009, 55 percent of couples had been married for at least 15 years, 35 percent had reached their twenty-fifth anniversary, and 6 percent had been married 50 years or longer.

These percentages are several points higher than they were in 1996 (Kreider and Ellis, 2011b). One reason for marriages lasting longer is the drop in divorce rates.

DIVORCE RATES HAVE DECREASED Talk-show hosts and many journalists often proclaim that one in two U.S. marriages end in divorce. Such statements are misleading because they imply that in a given year, the people who marry are the same ones who get a divorce. In 2012, for example, 10 percent of Americans were divorced. Over a lifetime, between 43 percent and 46 percent of American marriages end in divorce (Schoen and Canudas-Romo, 2006; "America's Families and Living Arrangements," 2012).

Divorce rates rose steadily throughout the twentieth century (see *Figure 15.1*). They climbed during the 1960s and 1970s, plateaued, and started dropping in 1995. In effect, divorce rates are *lower* today than they were 30 years ago.

A major reason for the lower divorce rates is that many people are postponing marriage. In 2009, for example, about a third of women and men ages 25 to 29 had never been married (Kreider and Ellis, 2011b). Many cohabiting couples in trial marriages break up instead of getting married and then divorcing (Yin, 2007; see also Chapters 9 and 10). And as you'll see shortly, the more education people have, the more likely they are to stay married.

SAME-SEX DIVORCE We know little about same-sex divorce because U.S. laws allowing same-sex marriage are recent. In 2004, Massachusetts became the first state to legalize same-sex marriage, and other states followed, but some as recently as 2013 (see Chapters 9 and 10). A study of 11 states that have some form of legal partnership for same-sex couples found that just over 1 percent of the same-sex couples dissolved their unions each year, compared with almost 2 percent of opposite-sex married couples (Badgett and Herman, 2011; Bialik, 2013).

A study of same-sex divorce in Norway and Sweden, countries that have recognized same-sex marriages for some time, found several patterns. Compared with older couples, those who were young when they married were more likely to divorce. Lesbians were more than twice as likely to divorce as gay men (but the researchers don't explain why). The divorce rates of same-sex couples were higher than those of opposite-sex couples probably because, even in Norway and Sweden, same-sex couples get less support from the community and less encouragement from family and friends than heterosexual couples to make the marriage work (Andersson et al., 2006).

Since you asked . . .
- Why are U.S. divorce rates lower today than during the 1960s and 1970s?

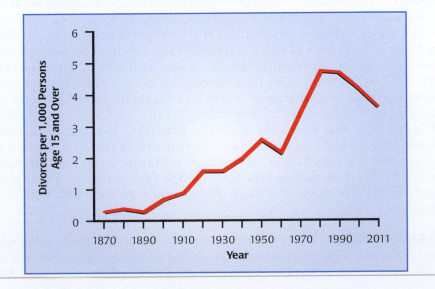

FIGURE 15.1 Divorce in the United States, 1870–2011
Sources: Based on Plateris, 1973; U.S. Census Bureau, 2008, Table 77; and "National Marriage and Divorce Rate Trends," 2013.

MAKING CONNECTIONS

- Based on your own or your friends' experiences, how well do Bohannon's six stations describe divorce? Would you add other stages, for example? Or believe that some are more important than others?

- According to one divorce attorney, even happily married couples should prepare for a divorce, especially financially. One example includes making regular deposits into a private account that a spouse won't notice (Fogle, 2006). Is such advice cynical? Or practical and realistic?

Many same-sex couples are also running into difficulties if they want to get a divorce in a state that doesn't recognize same-sex marriages. For example, a couple that marries in Massachusetts but moves to South Carolina, a state that forbids same-sex marriage, can't get a divorce in South Carolina. Some of the states, such as Maryland, that have recently recognized same-sex marriages haven't passed laws regarding same-sex divorces. In other states, such as Massachusetts, only a person who has lived there for a year can file for divorce. Moreover, because same-sex marriage is still a relatively new legal concept, same-sex divorces are more expensive than for heterosexual couples. Attorneys must spend more time unraveling issues such as when the gay partners' legal commitments began and who owns which assets (van Eeden-Moorefield et al., 2011; Siegel, 2012; Bialik, 2013; Williams, 2013). Thus, for both same-sex and opposite-sex couples, getting divorced is much more difficult than getting married.

15.3 Explain the micro- and macro-level reasons for divorce.

Why Do People Divorce?

Divorce rates vary in the United States and elsewhere because they're due to three interrelated reasons: macro or societal, demographic, and micro or interpersonal. As *Figure 15.2* shows, macro variables influence demographic variables, which, in turn, may lead to interpersonal problems that end a marriage.

Macro-Level Reasons for Divorce

Macro-level variables can increase or decrease divorce rates. Let's begin with the effect of divorce laws.

no-fault divorce Neither partner has to establish the guilt or wrongdoing of the other.

DIVORCE LAWS All states have **no-fault divorce** laws so that neither partner needs to establish guilt or wrongdoing on the part of the other. Before no-fault divorce laws, the partner who initiated the divorce had to prove that the other was to blame for the collapse of the marriage because of adultery, desertion, or physical and mental cruelty. Couples can now simply give "irreconcilable differences" or "incompatibility" as a valid reason for divorce. Also, the large number of attorneys and free legal clinics has made divorce more accessible and inexpensive.

ECONOMY The economy's impact on divorce is mixed. Some studies show that economic hardships (e.g., job loss, low income, home foreclosures) add to marital stress and increase the risk of divorce. On the other hand, economic hardship can reduce the occurrence of divorce: It may be too expensive to live separately, a spouse may lose health benefits, and the divorce itself may be expensive. During the 2007 to 2009 recession, for example, divorce rates fell, but rose when the economy began to recover, presumably because many people had postponed getting a divorce (Cohen, 2012; Chowdhury, 2013).

The economy also affects the quality of marriage. As more couples must work nonstandard and long hours, they experience more stress and tension and spend less time together. Fatigue, demanding child-rearing responsibilities, and job instability (such as moving from job to job or finding only part-time work) can increase the likelihood of divorce (Ahituv and Lerman, 2004; Kalil et al., 2010).

Listen on MySocLab

Audio: NPR: Military Combats High Divorce Rate

MILITARY SERVICE Military service can be a source of upward mobility when recruits learn new skills, earn promotions to higher ranks and higher pay, and take advantage of education benefits to earn college and graduate degrees. All of

these factors increase marital satisfaction and decrease the risk of divorce (Lundquist, 2006; Teachman and Tedrow, 2008).

Despite such benefits, military service—especially during the wars in Iraq and Afghanistan—is believed to have increased divorce rates because extended duty and deployment have been difficult on soldiers and their families. Divorce rates among male enlistees (but not officers) have gradually increased, but the rate among female soldiers has surged. By mid-2007, female soldiers in the U.S. Army were filing for divorce at a rate three times higher than that of their male counterparts. Civilian husbands often don't understand why their military wives have to work long hours—sometimes for months at a time and often on a moment's notice. Female soldiers married to servicemen often complain that their spouses are suspicious of the women's opportunities for infidelity and envious of their higher ranks (LaPlante, 2007). Such stresses can lead to disagreements and marital instability.

CULTURAL VALUES AND SOCIAL INTEGRATION Americans' acceptance of divorce has grown (see Data Digest). In 2013, a large majority of Americans (68 percent) said that divorce is more acceptable than gambling (64 percent), having a baby outside of marriage (60 percent), gay or lesbian relations (59 percent), or abortion (42 percent) (Newport and Himelfarb, 2013). In another national survey, 67 percent of Americans said that children are better off if their unhappy parents get a divorce rather than remain married (Taylor et al., 2007).

Some social scientists maintain that the greater acceptance of divorce is due to many Americans' emphasizing individual happiness over family commitments (Popenoe and Whitehead, 2009). Thousands of self-help books on how to get a divorce send the message that "divorce is okay," and television programs such as *Divorce Court* and many current sit-coms reinforce the idea that divorce is a normal and everyday occurrence.

Changes in cultural values and rising individualism have decreased **social integration**—the social bonds that people have with others and the community at large. Lower social integration increases divorce rates. Compared with 2000, for example, spouses are now less likely to interact and to spend time together and more likely to pursue interests and activities on their own rather than together. In addition, married people may value their privacy and prefer solitary activities—such as watching television or using social media—rather than interacting with spouses and children or socializing with friends (Amato et al., 2007).

TECHNOLOGY Technological advances have made divorce more accessible. Many people now go online to file for divorce to save money and time and to avoid the emotional clashes in lawyers' offices. Some online do-it-yourself divorces cost as little as $50 for all the necessary court forms and documents.

There are no national data, but some researchers suspect that online dating that leads to marriage may be especially likely to end in divorce. Many online daters are likely to act impulsively because they want to marry. They often don't know each other well, rush into marriage, and then discover that they have little in common or that one of the partners lied about his or her background (Gamerman, 2006; see, also, Chapter 8).

Macro-Level Reasons

- Divorce Laws
- Economy
- Military Service
- Cultural Values and Social Integration
- Technology

Demographic Variables

- Parental Divorce
- Age at Marriage
- Premarital Childbearing
- Cohabitation
- Gender
- Race and Ethnicity
- Social Class
- Religion

Micro-Level Reasons

- Extramarital Affairs
- Domestic Violence
- Substance Abuse
- Conflict over Money
- Lack of Communication
- Annoying Personality Characteristics and Habits
- Not Being at Home Enough
- Growing Apart

DIVORCE

FIGURE 15.2 What Affects Divorce Rates?

social integration The social bonds that people have with others and the community at large.

To combat the high divorce rates among active-duty soldiers and officers, the military offers numerous weekend retreats and marriage education classes. Pictured here, a family enjoys Christmas presents, an activity sponsored by the Army National Guard in Eugene, Oregon. The organization offers families many other services, including marital counseling.

Demographic Variables and Divorce

Demographic variables also help explain why some couples are prone to divorce. Let's begin with having divorced parents.

PARENTAL DIVORCE If the parents of one or both partners in a marriage were divorced when their children were young, the children themselves are more likely to divorce after they marry. Children of divorced parents are often less willing than those whose parents haven't divorced to tolerate unhappy marriages. Many children of divorced parents also have trouble making the kind of commitment that's necessary for marital success, presumably because they don't have role models who persevere despite problems (Glenn, 2005; Wolfinger, 2005).

AGE AT MARRIAGE The younger the partners are when they marry, the more likely they are to divorce. Early marriage—especially before age 18—is one of the strongest predictors of divorce. After 10 years of marriage, for example, 48 percent of first marriages of women younger than age 18 dissolved, compared with 24 percent of first marriages of women who were at least age 25 at the time of the marriage (Kurdek, 1993; Bramlett and Mosher, 2002).

Those who delay marriage until their twenties are usually more mature than teens and better able to handle the challenges of married life. Moreover, teen marriages are often hastened by a premarital pregnancy, another high-risk factor that increases the likelihood of divorce. However, marrying during one's mid-twenties (or later) doesn't guarantee a happy marriage if one "settles" for a spouse due to a shrinking marriage market (Glenn et al., 2010; see also Chapter 8).

PREMARITAL CHILDBEARING Women who conceive or give birth to a child before marriage have higher divorce rates than women who conceive or have a child after marriage. Divorce is especially likely among adolescent parents, who generally lack the education or income to maintain a stable family life (Garfinkel et al., 1994; Teachman, 2002).

COHABITATION Couples who live together have a higher chance of divorce if they marry, but the risk of divorce is highest among those who engage in serial cohabitation by living with different partners over time. Cohabitants

tend to be more accepting of divorce, less committed to marriage, and have fewer skills in coping with marital problems (Lichter and Qian, 2008; Popenoe and Whitehead, 2009; Tach and Halpern-Meekin, 2012). However, as you saw in Chapter 9, a marital commitment prior to cohabitation (e.g., engagement, definite plans for marriage) decreases the likelihood of negative interaction and divorce. Some recent research also shows that, among the cohabitants who marry, divorce rates vary depending on the people's attitudes and marital expectations as well as their race, ethnicity, and socioeconomic status (Stanley et al., 2010; Copen et al., 2012; Manning and Cohen, 2012).

GENDER Women are twice as likely as men to initiate a divorce, primarily because of husbands' not being responsive to relationship problems (Montenegro, 2004; Amato et al., 2007). Across all age groups, women in unhappy marriages are more likely to get a divorce if they can support themselves. However, holding joint assets such as savings and stock decreases many unhappy wives' likelihood of seeking a divorce because they expect that they'll have a lower standard of living after a divorce. In terms of exchange theory, joint assets "can actually restrict the choices of women vis-à-vis divorce" (Dew, 2009: 29).

RACE AND ETHNICITY One of the most consistent research findings is that, in terms of population size and marriage rates, blacks are more likely to divorce than are people in any other racial-ethnic group. Asian women have the lowest divorce rates (see *Figure 15.3*). These differences persist at all income, age, educational, and occupational levels (Saluter, 1994; Elliott and Simmons, 2011; Kreider and Ellis, 2011b; Kim, 2012).

Race and ethnicity don't "cause" divorce. Rather, divorce is more prevalent among African Americans because of a combination of macro, demographic, and micro factors that include the following: Higher rates of teenage premarital pregnancy; young age at marriage; presence of children from previous relationships; serial cohabitation; and poverty, financial strain, and male unemployment. Low Asian American divorce rates also reflect a combination of variables. Recent immigrants, for example, are likely to endorse traditional values that encourage staying married, even if there's domestic violence. Moreover, nonmarital birthrates for Asian American women are low—another factor that decreases the risk of divorce (Willie and Reddick, 2003; Costigan et al., 2004; Montenegro, 2004; Amato, 2010).

SOCIAL CLASS In general, divorce rates are lowest among those with a college degree, highest for those with some college (a two-year program or an incomplete four-year program), whereas those with a high school education or less have divorce rates that fall between the other two groups (Isen and Stevenson, 2010; Gibbs and Payne, 2011). In 2009, for example, among divorced women age 25 and older, 16 percent had a college degree, compared with 26 percent of high school graduates and 39 percent with some college (Elliott and Simmons, 2011).

Do people with college degrees have lower divorce rates because they're smarter? No. Rather, obtaining a college degree postpones marriage, with the result that college graduates are often more mature and able to deal with personal crises when they marry. They have higher incomes and better health care, both of which reduce financial stress. Also, some of the characteristics required for completing college (such as persistence, dependability, and responsibility) also increase the likelihood of having a stable marriage (Glenn, 2005; Isen and Stevenson, 2010).

Education is closely related to income, another predictor of the likelihood of divorce. In 2009, for example, 57 percent of women with a household income less than $50,000 were divorced, compared with 23 percent

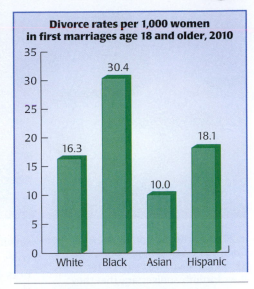

FIGURE 15.3 Divorce among Racial-Ethnic Groups
Source: Gibbs and Payne, 2011, Figure 2.

Since you asked . . .

- Why do college graduates have lower divorce rates than those with less education?

In 2010, former vice president Al Gore, age 62, and Tipper Gore, age 61, announced, two weeks after their fortieth anniversary, that they were getting a divorce. The Gores said they just "grew apart," according to an email they sent family and friends (Jayson, 2010: 7D).

of those with a household income of $75,000 and over (Elliott and Simmons, 2011). People with higher and lower incomes hold similar values toward marriage, have similar standards for choosing a marriage partner, and experience similar relationship problems. Economic problems are more common among lower-income couples, however, increasing the likelihood of stress, arguments, and divorce (Trail and Karney, 2012).

RELIGION Strong religious beliefs and behavior can either strengthen or weaken a marriage. Compared with their less religious counterparts, the risk of divorce is much lower among couples that are religiously homogamous (e.g., belong to the same faith or denomination), attend the same religious services regularly, and have similar gender ideologies about women's and men's roles at home. On the other hand, the likelihood of divorce is high if the partners belong to different faiths, if one spouse attends services more often than the other, and if one partner is theologically more conservative (e.g., the Bible is always right). Such spousal differences fuel arguments about traditional versus egalitarian gender roles at home, time or money devoted to the congregation, and pressuring a partner to convert or attend services more frequently (Amato et al., 2007; Vaaler et al., 2009).

Micro-Level Reasons for Divorce

People grow apart for many reasons. Some of the most common micro-level reasons for getting a divorce are the following:

- People often have *unrealistic expectations* about marriage that are fueled by television shows and movies that always have a happy ending (see Chapters 1, 5, and 10).

- A study of newlyweds found that 19 percent of the women and 14 percent of the men who had *pre-marital doubts* were divorced four years later (Lavner et al., 2012).

- *Financial problems and disagreements* are a stronger predictor of divorce than arguments about issues such as household tasks, spending time together, sex, or in-law relationships (Dew et al., 2012; Souter, 2013).

- A national study of ex-spouses found that 42 percent of women and 9 percent of men said that *verbal, physical, or emotional abuse* was "the most significant reason for divorce" (Glenn, 2005; see also Chapter 14).

- *Extramarital affairs* are one of the top reasons for divorce. The cheater is almost always repentant, but infidelity crumbles a relationship (Glenn, 2005; Olver, 2013).

- *Communication problems* (e.g., chronic complaining, criticizing, yelling, withdrawing, blaming) and the inability to resolve conflict lead to marital dissatisfaction and divorce. A strong predictor of divorce is negative interaction *before* the couple marries (Gottman, 1994; Birditt et al., 2010; see also Chapter 10).

- *Substance abuse* often leads to divorce because the user focuses on obtaining and consuming a drug and neglects the marriage and family (McWade, 2013; Olver, 2013).

- Continuous disagreements about *how to raise and discipline children* can increase marital dissatisfaction and trigger a divorce (Hetherington and Kelly, 2002; Montenegro, 2004).

The divorce rate among those age 50 and older has risen from fewer than 10 percent of all divorces in 1990 to more than 25 percent in 2009 (Brown and Lin, 2012; Lin and Brown, 2012). Why? People may decide to leave a long-term

unhappy marriage; they want to have a more satisfying life because they realize that disability and death are approaching. In other cases, as people change, so do their priorities, and couples grow apart (Ross, 2011; Stevens, 2012; Olver, 2013). For example, a wife may decide that she wants to pursue a college degree whereas a husband is determined to devote much of his time to his religious congregation.

MAKING CONNECTIONS

- Think about the people you know who have had a divorce. Were the reasons macro, demographic, micro, or a combination?
- What would you add to the list of micro-level reasons for divorce?

How Divorce Affects Adults

Divorce affects the ex-spouses' physical, emotional, psychological, and economic well-being. Parents must also deal with child-custody and child-support arrangements.

15.4 Explain how and why divorce affects adults.

Physical, Emotional, and Psychological Effects

Divorced people are generally worse off than married people. They report more health problems, greater social isolation, more stress, less social support, and more depression (Waite et al., 2002; Amato et al., 2007).

Explore on **MySocLab**

Activity: The Difficulty of Divorce

PHYSICAL WELL-BEING   Generally, there's a negative association between divorce and health. In 2011, for example, 70 percent of divorced Americans compared with 78 percent of those who were married reported health problems such as obesity, frequent sickness or colds, flu, and headaches. Also, 60 percent of those divorced, compared with 66 percent of those who were married, said that they smoked, didn't exercise weekly, and didn't eat healthy food (Brown and Jones, 2012).

A study that examined national data from 1972 to 2003 found that the self-rated health of divorced people worsened over the 31 years compared with that of married people, and more so for women than men. The researchers concluded that "getting married increases one's risk for eventual marital dissolution, and marital dissolution seems to be worse for self-rated health now than at any point in the past three decades" (Liu and Umberson, 2008: 252).

Among those older than age 50, divorced men and women suffer a greater decline in physical health than do married people. Those who spent more years divorced reported about 20 percent more chronic health problems such as heart disease, diabetes, and cancer, as well as mobility problems such as difficulty climbing stairs. Thus, getting and being divorced "may damage health" (Hughes and Waite, 2009: 356; see also Zhang and Hayward, 2006).

Such studies don't imply or conclude that divorce "causes" health problems. Instead, poor health, especially poor mental health, can decrease marital satisfaction, increasing the likelihood of a separation or divorce (Hughes and Waite, 2009). Also, worse health after a divorce may be due to the process of divorce that creates or magnifies emotional and psychological problems.

EMOTIONAL AND PSYCHOLOGICAL WELL-BEING   You saw earlier that the psychic divorce may continue for many years. Even when both partners know that their marriage can't be salvaged, they may be ambivalent about getting a divorce. They may fluctuate between a sense of loss and a feeling of freedom; they may have periods of depression punctuated with spurts of happiness. "Do You Know Someone with Divorce Hangover?" examines some of the adjustments that newly divorced people face.

More married people (81 percent) than those divorced (73 percent) report good emotional health (Brown and Jones, 2012). Divorce often brings an initial decline in social support networks because people lose contact with in-laws, married friends, and neighbors when one or both partners change residences. Other stressors include fathers' lower contact with their children and mothers' child care problems and lower family income (Amato and Hoffman, 2010; Kamp Dush, 2013).

Applying What You've Learned

Do You Know Someone with Divorce Hangover?

After a divorce, one or both ex-spouses may suffer from "divorce hangover" (Walther, 1991; Everett and Everett, 1994). In each of the following statements, fill in the blanks with the name of someone you know who has just gone through a divorce. Understanding some of these divorce hangover symptoms can help overcome divorce-related stress.

- **Sarcasm** When someone mentions the ex-spouse, _____ is sarcastic or takes potshots at the former partner. The sarcasm may be focused on the marriage in particular or unsupported generalizations such as "All men leave the minute their wives turn 40."

- **Using the children** _____ tries to convince the children that the divorce was entirely the other person's fault and may grill the children for information about the other parent.

- **Lashing out** _____ may try to assert control (such as blowing up at a friend who invites the ex-spouse to a party or other social gathering).

- **Paralysis** _____ can't seem to get back on track by going back to school, getting a new job, or finding new friends. Sometimes it's even hard for _____ to get up in the morning and go to work, clean the house, or return phone calls.

- **Holding on** The ex-spouse's photograph is still sits on _____'s wall, and his or her clothing or other possessions are in view, keeping the ex-spouse's presence alive in _____'s daily life.

- **Throwing out everything** _____ may throw away things of value—even jewelry, art, or expensive collections—that are reminders of the ex-spouse.

- **Blaming and finding fault** _____ maintains that everything that went wrong in the marriage or the divorce was someone else's fault: the ex-spouse, family, friends, kids, boss, and so on.

- **Excessive guilt** _____ feels guilty about the divorce, regardless of which partner left the other. _____ buys the children whatever they want and gives in to the children's or ex-spouse's demands, however unreasonable they may be.

- **Dependency** To fill the void left by the ex-spouse, _____ leans heavily on other people, particularly new romantic involvements.

The degree of emotional and psychological distress varies. When people leave an unhappy marriage characterized by a long period of conflict, hostility, and violence, they experience much less depression and stress than those who were simply dissatisfied. Psychological well-being problems are greatest for parents with young children. Divorce has fewer negative psychological consequences for adults without young children (Kalmijn and Monden, 2006; Williams and Dunne-Bryant, 2006; Amato and Hohmann-Marriott, 2007).

Adult children's divorce also affects their parents' well-being. If parents, particularly mothers, strongly support the institution of marriage, they may experience depressive feelings, such as sadness and tension, when their adult children separate or divorce. In contrast to parents who have more liberal attitudes about marriage, those with traditional views may feel shame and failure for not having raised their children "in the right way." These feelings, in turn, may decrease parental happiness when their children divorce (Kalmijn and De Graaf, 2012).

Economic Effects

Divorce often results in economic setbacks. The couple's wealth decreases, alimony is divisive, and women usually fare worse financially than men after divorce.

Listen on MySocLab

Audio: NPR: Fathers Become Vocal on Parents' Rights

WEALTH Marriage generally builds wealth; divorce depletes it. On average, among people ages 41 to 49, a couple's wealth increases about 16 percent for each year of marriage. In contrast, divorced couples lose about 77 percent of their shared wealth within five years of the divorce (Zagorsky, 2005). Married couples accumulate more wealth than single people for many reasons: They maintain one household, save more money, invest more of their income, and may work harder and seek promotions to pay for their children's education. Divorce reverses all these benefits. Ex-spouses often have two mortgages or rents, two sets of household expenses, and they rarely pool their assets to pay for their children's educational costs.

ALIMONY Annually, an estimated 420,000 Americans receive alimony either permanently or for a specific number of years. Traditionally, men paid spousal support because they were sole or higher earners, but this is changing. Nationally, 47 percent of divorce lawyers say that more women are paying alimony because they outearn their former spouses (Reaney, 2012; Luscombe, 2013).

In 28 states and the District of Columbia, "marital fault" is still a relevant factor in awarding alimony. Because alimony laws vary across states and judges have a great deal of discretion, "the amount and duration of alimony often varies wildly" (Luscombe, 2013: 47). As a result, alimony increases the ex-spouses' bitterness and stress.

In about a dozen states, a growing movement, often spearheaded by employed second wives, is pushing to abolish lifetime alimony. The second wives maintain that many ex-wives are capable of supporting themselves, they don't have children, stay-at-home moms no longer have children living in the home, or the first wives are cohabiting with someone who supports them financially. Others argue that cutting off alimony, particularly for women with little work experience, would thrust them into poverty (Alcindor, 2012; Campo-Flores, 2013; Luscombe, 2013).

GENDER In 2009, recently divorced women were twice as likely as recently divorced men to be in poverty (22 percent and 11 percent, respectively). Approximately 27 percent of the women, compared with 17 percent of the men, had less than $25,000 in annual household income, and the women, despite high labor participation rates, were more likely than men to be receiving public assistance (Elliott and Simmons, 2011).

A major reason for women's financial strain is that, in 82 percent of all divorce cases, the children live with the mother (Grall, 2011). Nationally, about 5 percent of divorced mothers improve their economic situation by marrying successful men, finding high-paying jobs, or both. Most, however, have financial problems, even after moving in with parents or siblings, because they lack marketable skills for well-paying jobs and receive little, if any, alimony or child support or public assistance (Ananat and Michaels, 2008). As one accountant observed, "The man usually walks out with the most valuable asset, earning ability, while the woman walks out with the biggest cash drain, the kids and house" (Gutner, 2000: 106).

The Second Wives Club is a growing reform movement in at least 12 states. The members believe that their spouses' ex-wives should be able to support themselves after a decade or more of alimony, especially when there are no children in the home.

Child Custody

Children often are caught in the middle of custody battles:

> **Mark, age eight:** *"I don't think either one of them should get me. All they ever do is fight and yell at each other. I'd rather live with my grandma."*
>
> **Robin, age seven:** *"Mom wants me to live with her and Dad wants me to live with him. But I want to live with both of them. Why do I have to choose? I just want us to be happy again"* (Everett and Everett, 1994: 84–85).

Custody is a court-mandated ruling regarding which divorced parent will have the primary responsibility for the children's upbringing. Children live with a custodial parent but see the noncustodial parent according to specific visitation schedules. In some cases, fathers get child custody by default: The biological mother doesn't want to raise the children, child protective agencies seek the father's involvement, or a child wants to live with the father.

TYPES OF CUSTODY There are three types of custody: sole, split, and joint. In **sole custody**, one parent is responsible for raising the child; the other parent has specified visitation rights. Parents may negotiate informally over issues such as schedules or holidays. If they disagree, the legal custodian has the right to make the final decisions.

In **split custody**, the children are divided between the parents either by sex (the mother gets the daughters and the father gets the sons) or by choice (the children are allowed to choose the parent with whom they want to live). In **joint custody**,

custody A court-mandated ruling regarding which divorced parent will have the primary responsibility for the children's upbringing.

sole custody One parent is responsible for raising the child; the other parent has specified visitation rights.

split custody The children are divided between the parents either by sex or the children's choice.

joint custody Children divide their time between their parents, who share decisions about the children's upbringing (sometimes called *dual residence custody*).

Fathers 4 Justice, a social movement that began in Great Britain, has become popular in the United States. The fathers, both unmarried and divorced, demand more contact with their children.

sometimes called *dual residence custody*, the children divide their time between their parents, who share decisions about the children's upbringing.

There are two types of joint custody. In *joint legal custody*, both parents share decision making on issues such as the child's education, health care, and religious training. In *joint physical custody*, the court specifies how much time children will spend in each parent's home.

Because joint legal *and* physical custody is rare, many noncustodial fathers are pushing for *co-parenting*, divorced parents' sharing legal and physical custody more equally. Co-parenting doesn't mean that divorced parents must interact face to face, but it does involve communication between parents about child rearing (Markham et al., 2007; Amato and Hoffman, 2010).

Co-parenting isn't a legal type of custody, but more states are requiring parents to file a co-parenting plan as part of the divorce process (Segal et al., 2009). Co-parenting is most effective when parents communicate with each other about discipline, if the father is responsible (such as picking children up from school on time), if fathers share child-related expenses even when there's no court-ordered child support, if both parents share information about the children, and if parents don't control or limit the children's e-mail and text messages with parents (Ganong et al., 2012; Markham and Coleman, 2012).

Child Support

When couples separate or divorce, child support is usually a critical issue. Let's begin by looking at who pays and gets child support.

WHO PAYS AND GETS CHILD SUPPORT?   In 2009, almost 14 million parents had custody of 22 million children while the other parent lived somewhere else (nonresident parent). Of all these custodial parents, a majority (51 percent) had some type of legal court agreement for child support. The top reasons for not seeking a legal award were having informal agreements, each parent providing what she or he could for support, and believing that the noncustodial parent couldn't afford to pay anything (Grall, 2011).

As *Figure 15.4* shows, a parent is most likely to receive the full amount of court-ordered child-support payments if she or he has at least a college degree, has divorced (rather than breaking up outside of marriage), is age 40 or older, and works full-time year-round. The custodial parents who are the least likely to receive child support are never married black mothers who are younger than age 30, don't have a high school diploma, and depend on public assistance (Grall, 2011). Thus, those with greater resources, such as a college degree, are able to collect more financial support. They may have ex-husbands (and sometimes ex-wives) who can provide more support or are more aggressive in pursuing enforcement.

Approximately 30 percent of custodial parents receive less child support than they're supposed to, and 30 percent receive none. On average, mothers receive about $3,700 a year, and fathers receive $3,100 a year. Even when parents (most of whom are mothers) receive the full court-ordered support, the average amount is less than $6,000 a year, and about one-third that amount if the father has a high school diploma or less, is poor, or unemployed (Grall, 2011). The payments are small, but they lifted a million adults and children from poverty in 2008 (Sorensen, 2010).

Some noncustodial parents provide noncash support. About 56 percent of custodial parents, typically mothers, receive birthday, holiday, or other gifts; clothes or diapers for the children (40 percent); food and groceries (28 percent); medical assistance other than health insurance (18 percent); or partial or full payments for

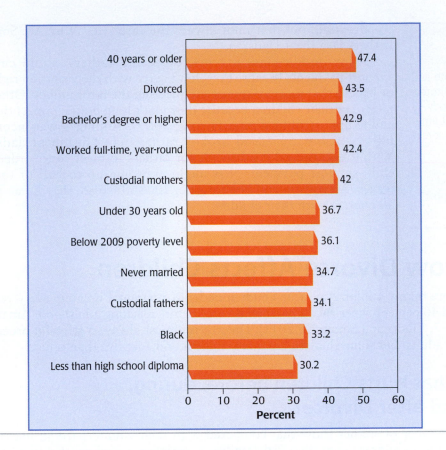

FIGURE 15.4 **Percent of Custodial Parents Who Received Full Child-Support Payments, 2009** *Source:* Grall, 2011, Figure 5.

child care or summer camp (10 percent) (Grall, 2011). Noncash support declines, however, if the mother has a child with a new partner (Meyer and Cancian, 2012).

CHILD SUPPORT AND VISITATION In 2011, 83 percent of mothers who received child support also had visitation arrangements with the child's father (Grall, 2011). Child support usually increases when it involves

Choices   Why Are Some Fathers Deadbeat Dads?

Most noncustodial fathers say they love their kids but may evade child support orders. These nonpaying fathers generally fall into one or more of the following categories (Nuta, 1986):

- The *irresponsible parent*, representing the greatest number of child-support dodgers, simply doesn't take his parental duties seriously. He may expect others to take care of his family ("Welfare will pay" or "Her family has more money than I do"), or he thinks that taking care of himself is more important than providing for his children. The irresponsible parent often includes noncustodial fathers with psychological and drug abuse problems

who don't seek employment or can't keep a job (Dion et al., 1997).

- The *overextended parent* is overburdened with financial obligations ("I can't afford it"). Anxious to get out of a marriage as soon as possible, he may agree to pay more support than he can afford. He may remarry and, unable to support two families, not provide for the children of his first marriage (Manning et al., 2003).
- The *parent in pain* may feel shut out of the family and distance himself physically or emotionally from his children. He may even rationalize his distancing ("She turned the kids against me"). Other

fathers are angry if they believe that their visitation rights are unfair.

- The *vengeful parent* uses child support as a form of control. He may use nonpayment to change a visitation agreement or to punish his wife for initiating the divorce ("She's getting what she deserves").

STOP AND THINK . . .

- Do you think that any or all of these fathers have legitimate reasons for not paying child support?
- Why do you think we hear almost nothing about "deadbeat moms"?

MAKING CONNECTIONS

- Judges have vast discretion in divorce proceedings, which vary from state to state and from case to case. The American Law Institute has proposed that courts grant child custody to parents in proportion to the amount of time they spent caring for a child before the divorce. Do you agree with this proposal?

- Among low-income households, should noncustodial parents have visitation rights even if they can't (or don't) pay child support? Why or why not?

15.5 Explain how and why divorce affects children.

Since you asked . . .

- Should parents stay together for the sake of the kids?

Watch on **MySocLab**

Video: Divorce and Adolescence

co-parenting, but that's not always the case (see "Why Are Some Fathers Deadbeat Dads?").

Many middle-class parents, especially fathers, avoid child support payments because they don't agree with the visitation rights or believe that their ex-spouse is squeezing them for money. Others rarely see their children because they work long hours to meet their child-support obligations (Huang, 2009). Among lower-income fathers, many are "dead broke" rather than "deadbeat dads." With low earnings, it's difficult for fathers to meet court-ordered child-support payments that might consume up to half of their wages (Martinson and Nightingale, 2008). Instead, they break off all contact with their children.

How Divorce Affects Children

More than 1 million American children undergo a parental breakup every year, and 40 percent experience a parental divorce before reaching adulthood (Amato, 2007; Elliott and Simmons, 2011). Divorce is almost always a stressful process for adults, but some children are more resilient and adaptive than others.

What Hurts Children before, during, and after Divorce?

A number of studies show that compared with their counterparts in married families, children from divorced families experience a variety of difficulties, including lower academic achievement, behavioral problems, a lower self-concept, and some long-term health problems (Furstenberg and Kiernan, 2001; Osborne and McLanahan, 2007; Cavanagh and Huston, 2008; Amato et al., 2011; Kim, 2011; Parcel et al., 2012).

Some negative effects of divorce are short term, but others last longer. Why do some children adjust to their parents' divorce better than others? Let's begin by looking at pre-divorce difficulties.

PARENTAL PROBLEMS BEFORE A DIVORCE   Typically, divorce crystallizes rather than creates long-standing family problems. That is, partners who divorce are likely to have poor parenting skills, high levels of marital conflict, or suffer from persistent economic stress well before a separation or divorce occurs (Furstenberg and Teitler, 1994; Doyle and Markiewicz, 2005; Lansford, 2009).

Children in these pre-divorce families have more internalizing problems (e.g., feeling sad, lonely), more externalizing problems (e.g., being impulsive, quick-tempered), and poor social skills (e.g., not getting along with peers). These difficulties increase the likelihood of poor academic progress at least three years before the divorce (Sun, 2001; Potter, 2010). Children can also experience several years of lower test scores in school and more disciplinary problems even if their parents initiate divorce proceedings but then change their minds (Hoekstra, 2006).

ONGOING PARENTAL CONFLICT AND HOSTILITY   Often it's not the divorce itself but parental attitudes during and after the divorce that affect children's behavior. The end of a highly conflicted marriage typically improves children's well-being. Freed from anxiety, stress, and depression, their mental health improves and their antisocial behavior decreases. In fact, children with parents in high-conflict marriages fare worse as adults than

"Your father loves me very much, in his own way, and I love your father very much, in my own way, and that's why we're getting a divorce."

those from families in which the high-conflict marriage ends in divorce. The latter are less likely to feel caught in the middle when their parents argue and feel pressure to take sides, and to experience less stress when feuding parents finally break up (Amato and Afifi, 2006; Yu et al., 2010).

Some researchers maintain that divorces that dissolve low-conflict marriages may have negative effects on children. The divorce is unexpected, unwelcome, and a source of turmoil and instability in children's lives. Because nearly two-thirds of divorces end low-conflict marriages, some scholars question whether these marriages should be ended (Amato, 2003; Strohschein, 2005; Glenn and Sylvester, 2006).

Much depends on the quality of the low-conflict marriage, however. Parents who stay in unhappy marriages "for the sake of the kids" may be distant, depressed, or abuse alcohol. In retrospect, 40 percent of young adults who grew up in intact homes believed their families might have been better off if the parents had broken up. The children felt guilty or responsible for what the unhappy parent (usually the mother) might have sacrificed or gone through on their behalf (Gerson, 2010).

QUALITY OF PARENTING   Children's adjustment to divorce depends, to a great extent, on the quality of parenting after the marriage ends. As one of my students remarked in class, "It wasn't my parents' divorce that left the most painful scars. It was their inability to be effective parents afterward." After a divorce, cooperative parenting benefits children's well-being when both parents communicate regularly, maintain similar rules in both households, and support each other's authority. The children have fewer behavior problems than those with feuding parents and closer relationships with their nonresidential parents (the great majority of whom are fathers) (Ahrons, 2011; Amato et al., 2011).

Twenty years after their parents' divorce, 62 percent of children said that their relationship with their noncustodial father had improved or remained stable over time. Thus, it's not custody itself that affects the quality of the relationship but a combination of pre- and post-divorce factors, especially continued conflict between the parents, a father's low involvement with his children after a divorce, and a father's quick remarriage (Kelly and Emery, 2003; Ahrons, 2004).

ECONOMIC HARDSHIP   A divorce may reduce parental conflict, but the financial problems usually increase, especially for mothers. The mother's income usually drops by about a third after the divorce. Men's income typically increases, with estimates ranging from 8 to 41 percent. Men's income increases for a number of reasons: not having physical custody of the children, not complying with child-support orders, having higher-paying jobs than their ex-wives do, and often taking some of the family's wealth—such as stocks and bonds—with them after the divorce (Sun and Li, 2002; Barber and Demo, 2006; Sayer, 2006).

In the first two years following divorce, family income falls 30 percent for white children and 53 percent for African American children. A major reason for this difference is that white mothers receive 10 times as much child support as do black women. The long-term economic costs of divorce are especially pronounced for black women because they're less likely to remarry and more likely to divorce after a remarriage (Page and Stevens, 2005).

The chances of experiencing negative economic outcomes double if, by age 18, adolescents undergo multiple parental transitions such as many romantic relationships, cohabiting, remarrying, or getting a divorce after a remarriage (Sun and Li, 2008). In effect, then, greater stability after their parents' divorce increases children's financial well-being in adulthood.

INTERRELATED AND CUMULATIVE EFFECTS OF DIVORCE   Divorce usually decreases children's well-being both initially and over the life course. For children, parental income loss, residential changes, and school relocation may be more harmful than the divorce itself. Children lose a stable environment, emotional and economic security, and ready access to both parents. Such stressful transitions

Noncustodial fathers who co-parent can maintain close relationships with their children by seeing them as often as possible, setting rules, discussing problems, and providing guidance.

may undermine self-confidence and create difficulties in forming and maintaining satisfying intimate relationships later in life (Amato and Hoffman, 2010; Coontz, 2010; Neuman, 2013).

Children who grow up in a divorced family are up to twice as likely to end their own marriages. Although debated, this *divorce cycle* or *intergenerational transmission of divorce* posits that children model their parents' conflictual relationships, and experience adverse consequences after a parent's divorce (Wolfinger, 2005, 2011; Li and Wu, 2008). When grandparents divorce, for example, the second generation experiences lower educational attainment and problematic relationships: "These outcomes in turn become the causes of similar problems in the third generation" (Amato and Cheadle, 2005: 204).

What Helps Children before, during, and after Divorce?

According to many researchers and family clinicians, parents can lessen some of a divorce's negative effects in many ways:

- They can reassure the children that both parents will continue to love and care for them, emphasizing that they'll remain actively involved with them and that the children should always feel free to love both parents.

- They should talk about their own feelings to encourage open communication between parents and children. Parents can discuss their unhappiness and even their anger, but they should *never* blame the other parent because doing so forces the children to take sides.

- They should emphasize that the children aren't responsible for problems between their parents, pointing out that each adult is divorcing the other partner but not the children. They should also reassure the children that they'll continue to see their cousins, grandparents, and other relatives on both sides of the family.

- They should maintain an ongoing relationship with the children, be consistent in setting and following household rules, and never complain about financial problems, particularly child support.

- They should encourage their children to talk about their feelings and experiences freely and openly with significant people in their lives such as grandparents, teachers, coaches, and clergy (Barber, 1994; Harvey and Fine, 2004; Denham, 2013; Pescosolido, 2013).

Research has consistently shown that the difficulties that children and adults who go through a divorce experience can be reduced if co-parents are civil and cooperative and work together to improve their children's well-being. Even 20 years after the divorce, according to one study, when the children are grown and have children of their own, what they want most is for their parents to just get along: "There were those special family occasions, such as graduations, weddings, and grandchildren's birthdays, that most of the grown children wanted to share with *both* of their parents" (Ahrons, 2006: 59, emphasis added).

Some Positive Outcomes of Divorce for Children and Adults

The biggest benefit of divorce is that it decreases the amount of stress that children undergo in a high-conflict, quarrelsome home in which adults yell, scream, throw things, or poison the atmosphere with emotional or physical abuse. Generally,

children and young adults fare well if the ex-spouses maintain good communication with their children and each other, if the children are comfortable staying in both parents' homes, if they can spend a lot of time with their nonresident parent, and if a parent's relocation doesn't disrupt the children's everyday life (Fabricius, 2003; Warshak, 2003).

Noncustodial fathers may spend more time with their children than they did before the divorce. Also, noncustodial fathers' and their children's ties improve when adolescents and young adults—especially those with few educational or occupational resources—feel that they can count on their fathers for financial support and advice regarding issues such as an unwanted pregnancy or marriage at a young age (Scott et al., 2007). The major positive outcome for adults is ending a high-conflict marriage. Those who leave a violent or abusive marriage are physically and mentally stronger and, consequently, more able to establish a healthier relationship with their children (Yu et al., 2010).

Both sexes cite gains two years after a divorce, but women are more likely to do so than men. Women are especially likely to say that they enjoy their new-found freedom, developing their own self-identity, and not having to answer to a domineering husband. Divorced men also report benefits such as spending more money on themselves or their hobbies, being better off financially (especially if they don't support their ex-wives or children), having more leisure time, and dating numerous people (Montenegro, 2004; Friedman and Martin, 2011).

Even with high divorce rates, most people aren't disillusioned about marriage. Many remarry, some more than once, and the resulting family relationships can be intricate. We'll look at remarriage and stepfamilies separately, but the two family forms often overlap because many remarriages include children.

Since you asked . . .
- Should more unhappy couples get a divorce?

MAKING CONNECTIONS

- Should it be harder to get a divorce if parents have children under age 18? Why or why not?
- Do you think that the United States should have renewable 2-year marriage licenses?

Remarriage: Rates, Process, and Characteristics

15.6 Describe the rate and process of remarriage, and explain how and why remarriages differ from first marriages.

Many people start dating again even before a divorce is legally final. Courtship is usually brief because half of all women and men who remarry after a divorce from their first marriages do so within four years (Kreider and Ellis, 2011b). In other cases, cohabitation replaces dating, both in the short run and long term.

Half of all remarriages begin with cohabitation. In fact, living together is more common after a divorce than before a first marriage (Xu et al., 2006). Cohabitation can hasten matrimony because most adults court for only brief periods before plunging into a remarriage. Living together can also delay remarriage. If cohabitants move from one relationship to another over a number of years, it may take a long time to select a marriage partner. Or if one or both people are reluctant to marry, cohabitation may lead to a long-term relationship that includes children from a past marriage and those born to the cohabiting couple (Ganong et al., 2006; Xu et al., 2006).

How Common Is Remarriage?

In 2010, only 29 percent of divorced adults said they would like to marry again. Among widowed men and women, only 8 percent wanted to remarry. Among all divorced and widowed, 54 percent of women compared with 31 percent of men said that they did *not* want another trip down the aisle (Pew Research Center, 2010; Cohn, 2013).

Many Americans don't plan to remarry, but remarriage is common. In 2009, people in a second marriage accounted for 12 percent of all married people, and those who were married three or more times accounted for another 3 percent

Dating and cohabitation after a divorce or widowhood, including among midlife people, provide couples with companionship.

(Kreider and Ellis, 2011b). The U.S. remarriage rate is the highest in the world, the median time between a divorce and a second marriage is short (see Data Digest), and millions of Americans have married three or more times. As a result, remarriage has spawned a huge industry of services, magazines, and books. For example, a popular magazine, *Bride Again*, targets "encore brides" who marry more than once.

Like divorce, remarriage is a process rather than a one-time act. And, like divorce, remarriage involves a series of stages.

Remarriage as a Process

The remarriage process may involve a series of steps similar to the six stations of divorce that you read about earlier (Goetting, 1982). As with divorce, the stages of remarriage aren't necessarily sequential, and not every couple goes through all of them or with the same intensity. If partners can deal successfully with each stage, however, they're more likely to emerge with a new identity as a couple.

The *emotional remarriage* stage is often a slow process. Besides the physical attraction, a divorced person has to establish a commitment to and trust in a new partner. Remarriages are also emotionally intricate because roles aren't clear. For example, what are a spouse's responsibilities to new in-laws?

In the *psychic remarriage* stage, people's identity changes from that of a single individual to that of a couple. For many men, a shift in marital status doesn't require an extreme change in personal identity. For a traditional woman, the remarriage represents recovery of a valued identity as a wife. A nontraditional woman, on the other hand, may worry about the loss of her highly valued independence.

During the *community remarriage* stage, people often sever close personal ties that they established after a divorce and lose valuable friendships. Remarried couples may move to another community, which requires meeting new neighbors, going to a different place of worship, and changing the children's schools.

The *parental remarriage* stage involves developing relationships between a partner and the children of the new spouse. Especially when one or both partners have children from previous marriages, there may be little time to cultivate workable and comfortable marital relationships and to cement a husband-wife bond. Instead, adults must deal with the difficulties of assuming both marital and parental roles simultaneously.

In the *economic remarriage* stage, the couple reestablishes a marital household as an economic unit. There may be friction about the distribution of resources. In the case of parents who remarry when their children are young, for example, who's responsible for the children's expenses, especially college costs—only the biological parents? Or the stepparents who played an important role in raising the children and encouraging them to go to college?

Because the legal system doesn't specify remarriage responsibilities, people must deal with new issues during the *legal remarriage* stage. For example, a remarriage raises questions such as which wife deserves a man's life and accident insurance, medical coverage, retirement benefits, pension payments, and property—the former wife, who played a major role in building up the estate, or the current wife? Even when stepchildren are mentioned in a will, many state inheritance laws don't recognize stepchildren as legitimate heirs. Stepchildren may have to go to court and battle biological children even when a stepparent has left the estate or other assets to a stepchild.

Some Characteristics of Remarried Couples

First marriages and remarriages differ in many ways. Variables such as age, gender, race-ethnicity, and social class are interrelated in understanding remarriage characteristics and rates.

AGE AND GENDER Being single after a divorce doesn't last long. Half of Americans who remarry after divorcing from their first marriage do so within about four years; the average age of a first remarriage is 33 for women and 36 for men (Kreider and Ellis, 2011b). As *Figure 15.5* shows, remarriage rates are lower for those age 49 and younger. In contrast, about one in five men and women ages 50 to 69 have married twice. At age 60 and older, men are more likely than women to have been married three or more times.

The women who are most likely to remarry are those who married at a young age the first time, have low education levels, few marketable skills, and want children. They're especially attractive to older divorced or widowed men who want a traditional wife. Remarriage is less common among college-educated women: They postpone marriage, have lower divorce rates, and are less likely than their less-educated counterparts to rely on men for economic resources (Isen and Stevenson, 2010).

Generally, the older a woman is, the harder it is for her to remarry. In each age group, because men tend to choose women who are younger and women tend to choose men who are older, the pool of eligible (and acceptable) marriage partners expands for men but shrinks for women (see Chapters 7 and 8). Another reason for women's lower remarriage rates, especially at age 60 and older (see *Figure 15.5*), is that they want more freedom, whereas older men often remarry to have a caregiver in their old age (Sweeney, 2010).

GENDER AND RACE-ETHNICITY White Americans have the highest remarriage rates and Asian Americans the lowest, including getting married three or more times. Within racial-ethnic groups, women and men have fairly similar remarriage rates (see *Figure 15.6*).

There are several interwoven reasons for the variation in remarriage rates across racial-ethnic groups. First, and as you saw in Chapters 9 and 10, African Americans have the lowest marriage rates, which means that remarriage is less likely. Second, blacks also have the highest cohabitation rates. People with the

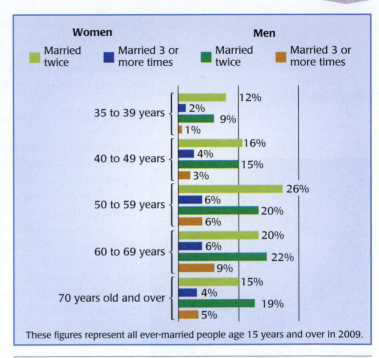

These figures represent all ever-married people age 15 years and over in 2009.

FIGURE 15.5 Percentage of Americans Who Have Remarried, Age 35 and Older, by Sex
Source: Based on Kreider and Ellis, 2011b, Table 6.

Since you asked . . .
• Why do white Americans have the highest remarriage rates?

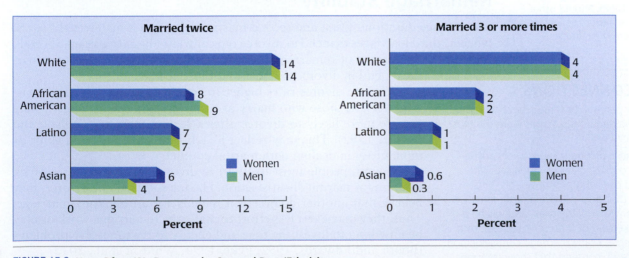

FIGURE 15.6 How Often We Remarry, by Sex and Race/Ethnicity
Note: These figures represent the percentage of Americans age 15 and older in 2009.
Source: Based on data in U.S. Census Bureau, Survey of Income and Program Participation (SIPP), 2008 Panel, Wave 2 Topical Module, Table 1, 2011, http://www.census.gov/hhes/socdemo/marriage/data/sipp/2009/tables.html (accessed June 30, 2013).

highest cohabitation rates are the most likely to delay marriage or not marry at all, which affects remarriage rates (Wu and Schimmele, 2005). Third, Latinos and Asian Americans, especially recent immigrants, encourage marriage and discourage cohabitation and divorce (see Chapter 4). Thus, cultural values decrease the likelihood of remarrying.

SOCIAL CLASS   In general, the least-educated men and the most-educated women are the least likely to remarry. Low-SES women can improve their financial situation if they marry a man who's employed, but low-SES men gain no economic benefits from remarriage because their eligible partners are usually unemployed. College-educated women may have few incentives to remarry because they're often economically independent (Shafer and James, 2013).

In the marriage market, men tend to be worth more than women of the same age because they're usually financially better off. Divorced women, on the other hand, often have severe financial problems. For many women, then, the surest way to avoid or escape poverty is to remarry. Thus, young, less-educated, low-income divorcees are more likely to remarry than are divorced women who are older, highly educated, and financially independent (Folk et al., 1992; Wu, 1994; Ganong and Coleman, 1994).

Remarriage Satisfaction

An old song tells us that "love is better the second time around," but the data on remarital satisfaction are mixed. People in first marriages report greater satisfaction than do remarried spouses, but the differences are small. Especially if the remarried parents have a stable relationship and the mother feels that the children's lives are going well, remarried mothers benefit psychologically from remarriage and are happier than divorced mothers (Demo and Acock, 1996; Whitton et al., 2013).

Some researchers report that remarried spouses are more likely than those in first marriages to be critical, angry, and irritable. Especially during the first few years of remarriage, stress could reflect the same poor communication and problem-solving skills that led to a previous divorce. Remarriages may also suffer from increased stress due to the behavior problems of adolescent stepchildren (Bray and Kelly, 1999; Coleman et al., 2002).

Remarriage Stability

The average duration of first and second marriages is approximately eight years, whereas third marriages that end in divorce typically last about five years. Overall, 60 percent of remarriages, compared with 45 percent of first marriages, end in divorce (Kreider and Ellis, 2011b).

Why are divorce rates higher for remarriages than for first marriages? First, those who marry as teenagers and remarry at a young age are more likely to divorce after a second marriage (Wilson and Clarke, 1992). This may reflect a lack of problem-solving skills or immaturity in dealing with marital conflict.

Second, people most likely to re-divorce see divorce as a quick solution for marital dissatisfaction. Having survived one divorce, they believe that another divorce is a remedy for an unhappy marriage. Thus, they may exert less effort to make the remarriage work or may be unwilling to invest the time and energy to try to resolve problems (Booth and Edwards, 1992; Pyke, 1994; Whitton et al., 2013).

Third, women who have a child between marriages are more likely to divorce. Such *intermarital birth* may require a newly married couple to cope with an infant rather than devote time to their relationship (Wineberg, 1991).

Since you asked . . .
- Why do many remarried couples divorce?

Actor/director Will Smith married his second wife, actress Jada Pinkett Smith, in 1997. When asked about the secret to their success because lasting marriages in Hollywood are rare, Smith said that he and Jada had decided that divorce just wasn't an option: "We're like listen, we're going to be together one way or the other, so we might as well try to be happy" (Dyball, 2008). Should other remarried couples adopt the Smiths' philosophy? Or are the Smiths unrealistic?

MAKING CONNECTIONS
- If you, your parents, or friends have remarried, which of the remarriage stages were the most problematic? Why?
- Many financial planners and lawyers advise remarried couples to set up three separate savings and checking accounts—his, hers, and theirs. Doing so will avoid arguments over different spending styles, and will help partners take care of themselves in case of a second divorce. Many marriage counselors, on the other hand, contend that separate funds show a lack of trust and can spark marital problems (Palmer, 2007). With which side do you agree? Why?

Finally, remarried couples must deal with more boundary maintenance issues than people in first marriages. For example, those in remarriages often have to insulate themselves against interference from ex-spouses and ex–in-laws. Remarried couples must also devote more effort to establishing boundaries with new family members and new relatives, especially if one of the partners is a custodial parent (Browning, 1994).

The Diversity and Complexity of Stepfamilies

15.7 Describe and explain the diversity and complexity of stepfamilies.

Stepfamilies come in many shapes and sizes. We'll look at various types of stepfamilies first, consider the unique challenges of gay and lesbian families, and then examine some of the ways that stepfamilies differ from nuclear families. Let's begin with what a stepfamily is.

What Is a Stepfamily?

A **stepfamily** is a household in which two adults who are biological or adoptive parents (heterosexual, gay, or lesbian) with a child from a previous relationship marry or cohabit. As in the case of defining *family* (see Chapter 1), not everyone may agree with this definition because it includes cohabitants. Nevertheless, this definition is more inclusive. It encompasses nontraditional stepfamilies because "concepts of and research about stepfamilies too often reflect the experiences of white, middle-class, heterosexual couples" (Stewart, 2007: 209).

Sometimes journalists and social scientists use terms such as *reconstituted family* and *binuclear family* interchangeably with *stepfamily*. However, *reconstituted* and *binuclear* are awkward and confusing terms that are rarely used by family sociologists (Ganong and Coleman, 2004). Some researchers use *blended family* interchangeably with *stepfamily*, but the leaders of some stepfamily organizations disagree. For example, according to Margorie Engel (2000), a past president of the Stepfamily Association of America, stepfamilies don't "blend." Instead, there are more parents, children have divided loyalties, and stepfamilies must develop new and unfamiliar roles for all their members, both adults and children.

stepfamily A household in which two adults who are biological or adoptive parents (heterosexual, gay, or lesbian) with a child from a previous relationship marry or cohabit.

Since you asked . . .
- Are the terms *stepfamily* and *blended family* interchangeable?

Types of Stepfamilies

When a couple forms a stepfamily, new family networks emerge. These new networks are often traced through a *genogram*, a diagram of the biological relationships among family members. The genogram in *Figure 15.7* shows some of the complexity of family systems that are created when a divorced couple remarries.

Although they vary in parent–child relationships, there are three basic types of stepfamilies:

- In a **mother–stepfather family**, all the children are biological children of the mother and stepchildren of the father.
- In a **father–stepmother family**, all the children are biological children of the father and stepchildren of the mother.
- In a **joint stepfamily**, at least one child is the biological child of both parents, at least one child is the biological child of only one parent and the stepchild of the other parent, and no other type of child is present.

Stepfamilies can be even more complicated. In a *complex stepfamily*, both adults have children from previous marriages. And in *joint step–adoptive families* and in *joint biological–step–adoptive families*, at least one child is a biological child of one parent and a stepchild of the other parent, and one or both parents

mother–stepfather family All the children are biological children of the mother and stepchildren of the father.

father–stepmother family All the children are biological children of the father and stepchildren of the mother.

joint stepfamily At least one child is the biological child of both parents, at least one child is the biological child of only one parent and the stepchild of the other parent, and no other type of child is present.

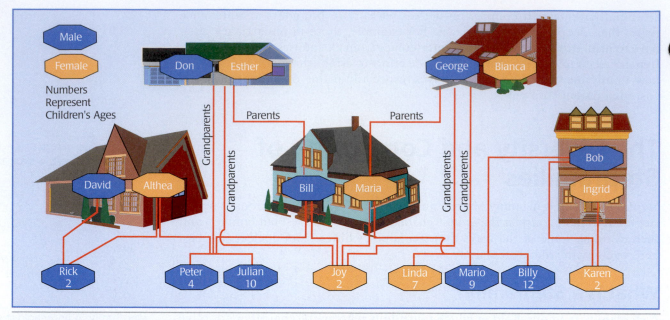

FIGURE 15.7 Stepfamily Networks
Each set of parents of our target couple, Bill and Maria, are grandparents to at least two sets of children. For example, Maria's parents are the grandparents of her children with her former husband, Bob (Billy, Mario, and Linda) and of her child with Bill (Joy). Depending on the closeness of the relationship Bill maintains with his former wife, Althea, however, Maria's parents might play a grandparental role to Peter and Julian as well as to Bill and Althea's boys.
Source: Based on Everett and Everett, 1994, p. 132.

stepsibling Brothers or sisters who share a biological or adoptive parent and a stepparent.

half sibling Brothers or sisters who share only one biological or adoptive parent.

 Read on MySocLab

Document: Stepfamilies in the United States: A Reconsideration

have adopted at least one child. Nor does the term *complex stepfamily* take account of the relationships between cohabitants, one or both of whom may have been married and have children from previous unions.

Stepfamilies can be fairly simple, composed of only a biological parent and his or her children and a stepparent. They can also be intricate. Children may suddenly find themselves with **stepsiblings**—brothers or sisters who share a biological or adoptive parent and a stepparent. Others are **half siblings**—brothers or sisters who share only one biological or adoptive parent. Children may also gain stepgrandparents, stepaunts, and a host of other steprelatives.

Some Demographic Characteristics of Stepfamilies

About 42 percent of American adults have at least one steprelative—a stepparent, a step or half sibling, or a stepchild. However, stepfamilies have some distinct demographic patterns that vary by age, race-ethnicity, and social class. For example,

- Among adults under age 30, 52 percent have at least one steprelative compared with only 34 percent of those age 65 and older.
- A higher share of blacks (60 percent) than Latinos (46 percent) or whites (39 percent) have stepfamily members. Also, black men (24 percent) are much more likely than white (15 percent) or Latino men (7 percent) to have stepchildren.
- Only 33 percent of college graduates have at least one steprelative compared with 46 percent of those without a college degree. About 36 percent of those with annual incomes of $75,000 or higher have at least one stepfamily member compared with 50 percent of those with annual incomes of less than $30,000 (Pew Research Social & Demographic Trends, 2011).

These variations reflect changing attitudes and family structures. Young adults are much more likely than their older counterparts to have grown up in divorced families or with unmarried parents; black marriage rates have dropped since the

1960s; and college graduates are likely to postpone marriage and have lower divorce rates (see Chapters 4, 9, 10, and 11). All of these factors help explain why some groups are more likely than others to have stepfamilies.

Gay and Lesbian Stepfamilies

Gay and lesbian stepfamilies are similar to opposite-sex stepfamilies and encounter many of the same problems, such as disciplining children and providing them with the necessary resources to be happy and healthy (Stewart, 2007). The usual difficulties often are aggravated, however, by lesbian and gay stepfamilies' *triple stigmatization*. First, they're often denounced because many people view homosexuality as immoral. Second, gay and lesbian stepfamilies are often still seen as deficient compared with nuclear families because they don't have adult role models of both sexes. Third, because only a handful of states allow same-sex marriage, couples may not get custody of children who were born during an opposite-sex marriage (Berger, 2000; see also Chapters 7, 11, and 12).

It's important for stepfamilies to make sure that all the children receive love and attention. If signs of jealousy appear, both parents should listen to the children's concerns and work to resolve them.

Despite such obstacles, gay stepfamilies are resilient and as diverse as heterosexual stepfamilies. Research on stepfamilies headed by same-sex partners is almost nonexistent (Amato, 2010; Sweeney, 2010). However, a study of lesbian stepfamilies found three distinct stepparent roles (Wright, 1998):

- In the *co-parent family*, the nonbiological mother is a supporter of and helper and consultant to the biological mother, an active parent of the children, and a dedicated and committed family member.

- The *stepmother family* parallels heterosexual stepmother families. That is, the lesbian stepmother performs most of the traditional mothering tasks, but the biological mother (like the biological father in heterosexual families) retains most of the decision-making power.

- In the *co-mother family*, both mothers have equal rights and responsibilities in everyday decisions and child-rearing tasks.

How Stepfamilies and Nuclear Families Differ

Stepfamilies may look like nuclear families because they're composed of adults and children living in the same household. However, stepparenting is more difficult for a number of reasons that range from the structure of stepfamilies to the ambiguous roles of stepfamily members.

Since you asked . . .

- What are the some of the biggest problems that stepfamilies face?

1. *The structure of stepfamilies is complex.* Stepfamilies create new roles: stepparents, stepsiblings, half siblings, and stepgrandparents. This structure doesn't make stepfamilies better or worse than nuclear families; they're just different.

2. *A stepfamily must cope with unique tasks.* The stepparent may struggle to overcome rejection because the children may still be grieving their parents' divorce, or the stepparent may disagree with the biological parent about discipline and household rules (Hetherington and Kelly, 2002).

   One of the most common tasks is redefining and renegotiating family boundaries. This may include making "visiting" children feel welcome and working out "turf" problems:

   Consider the stepfamily in which the husband's three children rejoined the household every 3–4 days for a few days' time. The house was small, and the mother's three children who lived in the household

had to shift where they slept, where they put their clothes, and where they could go to relax or to be alone to accommodate the extra family members . . . the continual chaos created tension and instability for everyone (Visher and Visher, 1993: 241).

In such situations, it's difficult to develop clear and consistent rules about property rights and private spaces for each family member.

3. **Stepfamilies often experience more stress and conflict.** A major source of tension is the adjustment that family members must make all at once rather than gradually, as in a nuclear family. Stress may come from several sources: More people make more demands, parents may differ on how to discipline children, one partner may feel excluded from the relationship between her or his spouse and the spouse's biological children, or there may not be enough resources to meet the larger family's needs (Whitsett and Land, 1992).

4. **Stepfamily integration typically takes years rather than months.** As "The Stepfamily Cycle" shows, it may take as long as eight years for

---

Changes | The Stepfamily Cycle

In a well-known study, family clinician Patricia Papernow (1993: 70–231) divides the process of becoming a stepfamily into three major stages. The early stage is characterized by fantasies, confusion, and slowly getting to know the other family members; in the middle stage, the family begins to restructure; and in the late stage the family achieves its own identity.

The Early Stages: Getting Started without Getting Stuck

Stage 1: Fantasy

Most remarrying couples start out with the fantasy that they'll love the children of the person they love and be loved by them, and that they'll be welcomed into a ready-made family (Hetherington and Kelly, 2002).

Children in new stepfamilies also have fantasies that involve a mixture of hope and fear. Some children still hope that their biological parents will be reunited. Or they may fear losing or hurting one of their own parents if they come to love a stepparent.

Stage 2: Immersion

Chaos and confusion often characterize this stage. Biological parents, children, and stepparents may see problems differently. Stepparents may feel left out of the biological parent–child unit and may experience jealousy and resentment.

Biological parents are often caught in the middle. Some exhaust themselves trying to meet everyone's needs and make the stepfamily work; others ignore the difficulties. The children may feel lost or rejected. Some respond with angry outbursts; others withdraw.

Stage 3: Awareness

Members of the stepfamily get to know each other. Stepparents can learn about the children's likes and dislikes, their friends, and their memories without trying to influence the children. Children should be encouraged to look at the positive aspects of the stepfamily, such as the parents' love.

The Middle Stages: Restructuring the Family

Stage 4: Mobilization

Many stepfamilies fall apart at this critical stage. The stepparent's task is to identify a few essential strategies for change (such as holding family meetings to deal with difficult issues).

The biological parent's task is to voice the needs of her or his children and ex-spouse while supporting and addressing the stepparent's concerns. Children should voice their own needs to ease the pressures created by their conflicting loyalties.

Stage 5: Action

In this stage, the stepfamily can begin to make some joint decisions about the family. The stepparent begins to play a

more active role in the family, and the biological parent doesn't feel the need to be all things to all people.

The Later Stages: Solidifying the Stepfamily

Stage 6: Contact

Family members begin to interact more easily in this stage. There's less withdrawal and more recognition of one another's efforts. The stepparent has a firm relationship with the partner and has begun to forge a more intimate, authentic relationship with at least some of the stepchildren.

Stage 7: Resolution

Relationships begin to feel comfortable. The stepparent role is well defined and solid. Stepparents become mentors to some of their stepchildren. Other stepparent–stepchild relationships have achieved a mutually suitable distance. In this stage, the stepfamily finally has a sense of its own identity.

STOP AND THINK . . .

- Do you think that the stepfamily cycle differs for women and men, both as adults and children? Why or why not?

- Why do you think that many stepfamilies don't get beyond Stage 4?

a couple to consolidate their family and to work as a team. And if the remarried couple has a baby or there are unexpected problems such as unemployment or a death in the family, the process may take even longer.

5. *Important relationships may be cut off or end abruptly, and others spring up overnight.* As you saw earlier, many noncustodial fathers have no contact with their children after a divorce. Moreover, siblings who are sometimes split between parents in custody agreements may rarely see one another. Children are especially distressed if a parent's wedding announcement comes as a surprise. According to both researchers and family clinicians, the new partner and the children should get to know one another over the course of a year or two: They should go on vacations and have meals together, and just hang around the house getting to know one another (Bray and Kelly, 1998; Knox and Leggett, 1998).

6. *There are continuous transitions and adjustments rather than stability.* In a stepfamily, the people living in a household can change continuously. The boundaries between who is a member of a stepfamily are sometimes blurry. For example, is the new spouse of a child's noncustodial parent a part of the child's family? If a child has parents who are remarried or living together, it may be difficult to juggle individual needs, family traditions, and emotional ties between as many as four families.

7. *Stepfamilies are less cohesive than nuclear or single-parent households.* Stepchildren often feel closer to biological parents than to stepparents. Children may feel alienated if their noncustodial parents don't visit or contact them or because of "unfair" economic support, as when only certain children in a stepfamily are supported during college. They may also resent unequal gifts and inheritances by stepgrandparents (Stewart, 2010).

8. *Stepfamilies have less flexibility in their everyday behavior.* Varying custody and residential arrangements require different daily or weekly routines. Moreover, within the household, the expected ways in which a family operates may not apply. For example, what happens when it's Amy's day to stay at Mom's house, but over at Dad's they're going to play miniature golf?

   The need for flexibility may decrease over time, but situations often arise (such as weddings, births, deaths, and holidays) that may require unusual solutions and arrangements. For example, should a noncustodial father who rarely visits his children pay for his daughter's wedding, or should her stepfather do so? And who should walk down the aisle at her wedding? One or both of them?

9. *Stepfamily members often have unrealistic expectations.* Stepfamilies often compare themselves with nuclear families and have idealized expectations. There's no reason why stepfamily members—aside from newly remarried adults—should automatically feel any sort of familial relationship or affection. It's physically and emotionally impossible for a stepfamily to mirror a nuclear family; there are too many players and too many new relationships. As you saw in "The Stepfamily Cycle," stepfamilies must forge their own rules and identities.

10. *There's no shared family history.* The stepfamily is a group of individuals who must develop meaningful, shared experiences. To do so, they must learn one another's verbal and nonverbal communication patterns and learn to interact differently. New stepfamily members sometimes feel as

Children in stepfamilies often feel divided loyalties among their noncustodial biological father, with whom they spend time periodically, their biological mother, and their stepfather.

if they're in an alien environment. For example, mealtimes and the meals themselves may be different from those they were used to in the past.

One way to ease some of the strangeness is to mesh rituals. In one remarried family, when a major holiday was approaching, family members were asked to suggest favorite foods. By preparing and serving these dishes, the new family honored some of the traditions of the previous families (Imber-Black and Roberts, 1993).

11. *There may be loyalty conflicts.* Accusations of liking one parent more than another often arise in all families, but loyalty conflicts are intensified in stepfamilies. For example, suppose that a child in the stepfamily feels closer to the noncustodial parent or to a parent's new spouse than to the biological and custodial parent or that parent's new spouse. Should these relationships be nurtured despite the resentment of the custodial parent or stepparent?

12. *Stepfamily roles are often ambiguous.* A positive aspect of role ambiguity is that it provides freedom of choice because an adult can play a variety of roles with children and other adults. For example, a stepparent who is willing to be a friend to the children, rather than a strict parent, can serve as a mediator when there's conflict between the children and the biological custodial parent. However, ambiguity creates problems because people don't always know what's expected of them or what to expect from others. For instance, a partner may want a spouse to be supportive when he or she disciplines the children.

MAKING CONNECTIONS

- Did you or someone you know grow up in a stepfamily? Review the list of 12 characteristics of stepfamilies just presented. Which ones were the most difficult for you or someone you know?

- What are some advantages and disadvantages of growing up in a stepfamily compared with a nuclear family?

15.8 Describe and explain how stepfamilies differ from nuclear families.

 Read on MySocLab

Document: Transitions in Parental Repartnering after Divorce

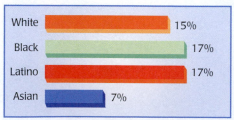

FIGURE 15.8 Percentage of Children Living in Stepfamilies
Note: According to the most recent available data, in 1996, 21 percent of American Indian/Alaska Native children lived in stepfamilies.
Source: Based on Kreider and Ellis, 2011a, Table 6.

Living in a Stepfamily

When adults have problems, so do children. If adults are resilient and adjust, so do children. What, more specifically, are the ways that stepfamilies affect children?

Parenting in Stepfamilies

Almost 16 percent of American children younger than age 18 live in a stepfamily (Kreider and Ellis, 2011a). Asian American children are the least likely to do so (see *Figure 15.8*), probably because Asian women have the lowest nonmarital birth rates and divorce rates (see Chapters 5 and 11).

Most stepfamilies face a number of issues when they attempt to merge two households. They include naming, sexual boundaries, legal issues, and distributing economic and emotional resources.

NAMING The English language has fairly clear terms for relationships in biological families, such as *father, mother, brother,* and *daughter.* Suppose, however, that stepchildren want to call their stepfather "Dad." The biological children may feel threatened and annoyed if they don't accept their stepsiblings as "really" family. One of my friends admits that she feels pangs of anger and envy when her son calls his stepmother "Mom."

One stepmother was uncomfortable having her three young stepchildren call her by her first name (as her husband does) because it seemed impersonal and disrespectful. She came up with a name that worked—"Smom." "Even my husband's ex-wife calls me that. Sometimes, the kids have variations, like 'Smommy' or 'Smama.' I'm happy, they're happy" (Ann Landers, 2000: C11).

The name children call a stepfather—whether he's married to or cohabiting with their mother—has special meaning for men. Hearing oneself called "Dad," as opposed to one's first name or "Stepdad," is a sign of acceptance and belonging. Many stepfathers still remember first hearing "Daddy" or "Dad" as a thrilling and momentous occasion because the use of kinship terms goes hand in hand with a feeling of genuine fatherhood (Marsiglio and Hinojosa, 2006).

SEXUAL BOUNDARIES Our laws forbid sexual relations between siblings and between parents and children in biological families. However, there are rarely any legal restrictions on sexual relations between stepfamily members, either between stepchildren or between a stepparent and a stepchild. As a result, stepsiblings may drift into romantic relationships that can damage family relationships. Estimates of the extent of child abuse in stepfamilies vary, but researchers agree that children are at greater risk for both physical and sexual abuse if they live in a household with an adult who isn't their biological parent. When sexual abuse occurs, the perpetrator is typically a male, and often a stepfather (Ganong and Coleman, 2004; Reading, 2006; see also Chapter 14).

LEGAL ISSUES Financial matters are more complicated in stepfamilies than in first marriages. Unless there's a prenuptial agreement that allows a new spouse to waive his or her rights to a share of an estate, children from a previous marriage may be disinherited even though this wasn't the parent's intention. Some biological children may resent their inheritance being divided with stepsiblings. In other cases, adult children feel devastated when an aging dad has a new wife and changes his will, leaving most of the deceased mother's jewelry and other personal belongings to his stepchildren (Cohn, 2005; see also *Appendix F* on premarital and nonmarital agreements).

Legal experts advise setting up a trust fund to safeguard the biological children's or grandchildren's inheritance. Trusts allow parents to transmit gifts and inheritances to whomever they choose while they're alive or after their death. In addition, to minimize family friction, attorneys advise partners to discuss their estate plans with their biological and stepchildren (Ebeling, 2007).

DISTRIBUTING ECONOMIC RESOURCES The children of remarried fathers typically are at a financial disadvantage if the children live with their custodial mother. The stepchildren living with their remarried father may receive more support, such as loans, gifts, and health coverage. Loss of economic support can impoverish biological children and create hostility.

In a stepfamily, the partners must decide whether to pool their resources and how to do so. They may experience stress and resentment if there are financial obligations to a former family (such as child-support awards, mortgage payments, or outstanding debts). Disagreements may range from seemingly petty issues, such as how much should be spent on birthday presents for relatives, to drastically different attitudes about whether money should be saved or spent.

Because men typically have more economic resources than women, stepfathers may have more decision-making power in the new family. Sometimes men use money to control their wives' and stepchildren's behavior ("If you don't shape up, you can pay for your own car insurance next time"). This kind of manipulation creates hostility.

Involving both custodial and visiting (nonresidential) children in stepfamily activities can make the visiting children feel more welcome and a part of the family.

DISTRIBUTING EMOTIONAL RESOURCES Resources such as time, space, and affection must also be distributed equitably so that all the family's members are content with the new living arrangements. Mothers sometimes are angry about

spending much of their time and energy on live-in stepchildren but receiving few rewards: "My husband's kids don't see me as their mother . . . because I really don't count. I can do things for the kids and my husband gets the credit, not me. I resent them at those moments, and I resent him" (Vissing, 2002: 193–194). Custodial mothers can strengthen ties between their children and stepfathers by encouraging them to spend time together. As one mother said, "I'd send them off to the movies or to a park. They had to form a relationship without me intervening" (Wolcott, 2000: 16).

Stepparent–Stepchild Relationships

Stepparent–stepchild relationships vary considerably because stepfamilies are more diverse than biological families. Four of the important issues are gender roles, stepchild–stepparent relationship development, discipline and closeness, and intergenerational relationships.

GENDER ROLES Relationships with stepchildren are often more difficult for stepmothers than stepfathers. If the stepmother is at home more than her husband, she may be expected to be more actively involved in domestic duties, including raising the stepchildren. Noncustodial mothers and stepmothers typically play a more important role than noncustodial fathers and stepfathers in shaping family dynamics. Women are usually the *kinkeepers* who arrange visits between family members, remember birthday and holiday greetings and gifts, and give children affection and emotional support. They're also influential *gatekeepers* when they encourage relationships between noncustodial parents and biological children or cut off contact (Schmeeckle, 2007; Ganong et al., 2011).

STEPCHILD–STEPPARENT RELATIONSHIP DEVELOPMENT Stepchildren are less likely to experience conflict if the stepparent raised them from infancy or early childhood, if the children liked the stepparent from the beginning because of mutual interests and spending time together on activities that the children liked, and if the stepparent (usually a stepfather) brought material goods that the family couldn't afford previously (e.g., allowances, vacations, better houses and neighborhoods). Also, children living with a custodial mother have a better relationship with a stepfather if he marries rather than lives with the mother (King, 2009; Ganong et al., 2011).

DISCIPLINE AND CLOSENESS Especially between stepfathers and adolescent stepchildren, children generally dislike being disciplined by stepparents until they form strong bonds (Ganong et al., 2011). Teenagers complain, "He's not my father! I don't have to listen to him!" Stepfathers often resent not being obeyed, both because they consider themselves authority figures and they're working hard to support the family. Mothers often feel caught in the middle. They love their husbands, but may feel guilty for having married someone the children don't like, or they may complain about the stepfather's disciplinary methods (Hetherington and Stanley-Hagan, 2002).

When parents form strong relationships with the children of a new partner, they may feel that they're betraying their biological children. Similarly, children may feel guilty if they find themselves liking a stepparent better than a biological parent because the stepparent is more fun, more understanding, or easier to get along with (Papernow, 1993; Ganong et al., 2011).

Friendship may be the best way to enhance steprelationships. If stepparents go slowly in approaching stepchildren, especially adolescents, they have a better chance of establishing discipline or setting rules. Some stepparents act as *quasi-kin*, a role midway between that of parent and friend. That is, they assume some of the functions of parents but let the biological parents make final decisions about their children (Coleman et al., 2001).

Taking a quasi-kin role is easier with nonresidential (visiting) children than with custodial children and with older children than with younger children. This role is also more common among stepfathers than among stepmothers, who are often responsible for everyday monitoring and discipline.

Remarried partners sometimes have a child, hoping that the new addition will cement stepfamily bonds. The birth of a half sibling can promote a sense of family solidarity. If, however, stepparents shift all of their focus to the baby, they may become less involved with preadolescent children who also need their attention (Stewart, 2005; Ganong et al., 2011).

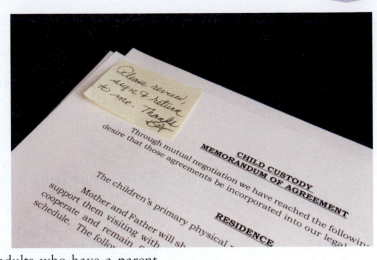

INTERGENERATIONAL RELATIONSHIPS Among adults who have a parent and stepparent, 85 percent would feel obligated to help out their biological parents compared with 56 percent who feel the same way about a stepparent (Pew Research Social & Demographic Trends, 2011). However, older divorced fathers (with an average age of 65) who cohabit or remarry and have new biological children or stepchildren have less contact with their adult children from a previous marriage and are less likely to provide them with financial support (Noël-Miller, 2013). One implication is that, in intergenerational relationships, children feel more obligated to help out their biological parents than do biological fathers, who have remarried, to help out their children.

Ties across generations, especially with grandparents and step-grandparents, can be close and loving or disruptive and intrusive. After a divorce or remarriage, grandparents can provide an important sense of continuity for children at a time when many other things are changing. Even if children aren't as attached to their new stepgrandparents as they are to their biological grandparents, they may resent new stepgrandparents who seem to neglect or reject them (e.g., the biological grandkids get more Christmas gifts than the stepgrandchildren) (Everett and Everett, 1994). Such behavior decreases contact and closeness between stepgrandparents and stepgrandchildren (Spitze et al., 1994; see also Chapter 16).

How Stepfamilies Affect Children

Are stepfamilies beneficial or harmful to children? Among other factors, the results vary according to the family's social class and degree of parental conflict.

HOW CHILDREN FARE The data are mixed, but, overall, studies show that children in stepfamilies don't fare as well as children in biological families. They tend to have more problems academically, such as lower grades, scores on achievement tests, school attendance, and high school graduation rates. Even if the family's economic resources increase after a remarriage, alternating residences during the school year raises a child's risk of dropping out of school or having problems with school authorities (Bogenscheider, 1997; Pong, 1997; Tillman, 2007; see also Menning et al., 2007).

How children fare depends greatly on the relationships among children, their custodial and noncustodial parents, and their stepparents. Close relationships with stepfathers, noncustodial fathers, and noncustodial mothers are associated with better adolescent outcomes, such as decreasing the likelihood of externalizing behavior (e.g., delinquency, violence, alcohol and drug use, and having nonmarital births) and internalizing behavior (e.g., depression, a negative outlook on life, and low self-esteem). Noncustodial fathers who are involved with their children have a stronger relationship with their children in adulthood than those who lose contact. Also, stepfathers and noncustodial fathers who are cooperative rather than competitive in their relationships with children increase the children's

well-being (Aquilino, 2006; Ganong et al., 2006; King, 2006, 2007; Marsiglio and Hinojosa, 2007; Sweeney, 2010). Thus, as in married and divorced families, children benefit when adults get along (see Chapter 12).

THEORETICAL EXPLANATIONS OF THE EFFECTS OF STEPFAMILIES ON CHILDREN There are about a dozen theoretical explanations of the effects of stepfamilies on children. Four of the most common are family stress theories, risk and resilience theories, social capital models, and the cumulative effects hypothesis.

Family stress theories say that living in a stepfamily creates numerous difficulties for children and other family members. The stressful events include possibly moving to another home or neighborhood (and therefore a new school), adapting to a variety of steprelatives after a parent's remarriage, following different rules and schedules, experiencing ongoing hostility between divorced parents, and economic problems that decrease marital quality (Stewart, 2007; Shapiro and Stewart, 2011; Schramm and Adler-Baeder, 2012). These and other factors contribute to the children's greater likelihood of externalizing and internalizing problem behaviors.

Risk and resilience theories maintain that the effects of remarriage on children involve both costs (risks) and benefits (resources that increase resilience). Remarriage can lift many single mothers out of poverty. If children have a good relationship with a stepfather and a noncustodial father, they experience about the same number of problems as children from nuclear families. In addition, supportive schools and peers decrease the likelihood of adjustment problems. Children are less resilient, however, if the ex-spouses' "anger and acrimony undermine the happiness, health, and adjustment of family members" (Hetherington and Stanley-Hagan, 2000: 177; see also White and Gilbreth, 2001; Rodgers and Rose, 2002).

According to *social capital theories*, children in stepfamily households have more problems than children in nuclear families because the stepparents often invest less time and energy in raising their children. Children thrive when their social capital includes parents who are involved in school activities and homework and who value learning, and when there's minimal tension between the adults (Pong, 1997; Kim et al., 1999). In many stepfamilies, however, children's social capital decreases because of poor parenting, a custodial parent's or stepparent's gatekeeping, and conflict between adults.

In the *cumulative effects hypothesis*, children whose parents have had several partners over time display more internalizing and externalizing problems than children who lived with a parent who had remarried only once. Thus, children who undergo multiple transitions experience more emotional and behavioral difficulties because the problems snowball (Kurdek and Fine, 1993; Cherlin, 2009).

MAKING CONNECTIONS

- Should stepparents be parents, friends, quasi-kin, or some combination of these roles?
- What kinds of traditions, rituals, and celebrations might stepfamilies implement to build a new identity for both stepchildren and stepparents?

Some Characteristics of Successful Stepfamilies

Six characteristics are common to stepfamilies in which children and adults experience warm interpersonal relations and satisfaction. Some of these characteristics, as you might expect, are the opposite of the problems we examined earlier.

Since you asked . . .
- What can stepparents do to have happier families?

- Successful stepfamilies *develop realistic expectations.* They've rejected the myth of instant love because they realize that trying to force friendship or love simply doesn't work. In addition, they don't try to replicate the biological family because they accept the fact that the stepfamily is "under construction." Teenagers who are beginning to rebel against authority are

particularly sensitive to adult supervision. As one teenager in a stepfamily put it, "Two parents are more than enough. I don't need another one telling me what to do" (Visher and Visher, 1993: 245).

- Adults in successful stepfamilies *let children mourn their losses* because they're sensitive to children's sadness and depression after their parents' divorce. The stepparents also accept the children's expressions of fear, confusion, and anger, neither punishing them nor interpreting their reactions as rejection.

- The adults in well-functioning stepfamilies *forge a strong couple relationship.* Doing so provides stability because it reduces the children's anxiety about another parental breakup. It also gives children a model of a couple who can work together effectively as a team and solve problems rationally (Kheshgi-Genovese and Genovese, 1997).

- Except when young children are present, the *stepparent takes on a disciplinary role gradually.* As one of my students stated, "My stepfather wasn't ever in my face, which was good, because I would've been mad if he had tried to discipline me." The biological parent should be the disciplinarian while the stepparent supports his or her rules. In successful stepfamilies, adults realize that relations between a stepparent and step-children can vary: The stepparent may be a parent to some of the children, a companion to others, or just a good friend to all. And even if there are no warm interpersonal ties, it's enough that family members are tolerant and respectful of one another.

- Successful *stepfamilies develop their own rituals.* They recognize that there's more than one way to do the laundry, bake a turkey, or celebrate a birthday. Successful stepfamilies may combine previous ways of sharing household tasks or develop new schedules for the things they do together on the weekends. The most important criteria are flexibility and cooperation.

- Well-functioning stepfamilies *work out arrangements between the children's households.* Adults don't have to like one another to get along during family events such as children's birthdays, holidays, graduations, and weddings. The most successful stepfamilies have two sets of parents but one set of rules. They collaborate at school functions, parent–teacher meetings, and after-school activities. For example, if each child has a list in his or her backpack, both sets of parents can check off items (such as homework, musical instruments, and gym shorts) when the children move back and forth from house to house.

Communication is critical in successful stepfamilies. If adult relationships are strained, relying on e-mail or texting can "take the 'feelings' out of communication. You can simply put the facts down, and you don't have to talk to the person" (Cohn, 2003: 13; see also Braithwaithe et al., 2006; Brimhall et al., 2008; Saint-Jacques et al., 2011). In contrast, face-to-face interaction is crucial in stepchild–stepparent communication.

CONCLUSION

Greater acceptance of divorce in the late twentieth and early twenty-first centuries created *changes* in family structures. A large segment of the adult population remarries or cohabits and forms stepfamilies in which children and adults must adapt and live together. People have more *choices* in leaving an unhappy marriage, and can establish a satisfying family life through remarriage and stepfamilies. Choices also bring *constraints*: Divorcing parents and their children often experience emotional pain and economic problems, and stepfamilies must deal with difficulties in establishing a new household. These changing family structures affect families in later life, the topic of the next chapter.

On MySocLab

✓ **Study** and **Review** on MySocLab

REVIEW QUESTIONS

15.1. Describe the phases and outcomes of separation.

1. How does separation differ from the early to the late phase?

2. How common is reconciliation? Why don't many people finalize their separations?

15.2. Describe the divorce process and explain why divorce rates have declined.

3. Why is divorce a process rather than a quick event?

4. Why are divorce rates lower today than they were during the 1960s and 1970s?

15.3. Explain the micro- and macro-level reasons for divorce.

5. How do micro- and macro-level reasons for divorce differ?

6. What, specifically, are the demographic variables that help explain divorce rates?

15.4. Explain how and why divorce affects adults.

7. Among adults, what are the physical, emotional, psychological, and economic effects of divorce?

8. What are the different types of child custody? Who pays and gets child support?

15.5. Explain how and why divorce affects children.

9. What, specifically, helps and hurts children before, during, and after a divorce?

10. What are some of the positive outcomes of divorce for children and adults?

15.6. Describe the rate and process of remarriage, and explain how and why remarriages differ from first marriages.

11. Why is remarriage a process? Why are divorce rates higher after a remarriage than after a first marriage?

12. How and why do remarriage rates vary by age, gender, race-ethnicity, and social class?

15.7. Describe and explain the diversity and complexity of stepfamilies.

13. What, specifically, are the types of stepfamilies?

14. How and why are stepfamilies more complex than nuclear families?

15.8. Describe and explain how stepfamilies differ from nuclear families.

15. What, specifically, are the issues that stepfamilies encounter?

16. Do stepfamilies help or hurt children? What are the characteristics of successful stepfamilies?

Families in Later Life

((ᴄ Listen to Chapter 16 on MySocLab

DATA DIGEST

- The **average U.S. life expectancy** was 47 in 1900, 68 in 1950, and almost 79 in 2010 (81 years for women and 76.2 years for men).

- The **percentage of the U.S. population age 65 and older has been increasing steadily:** 4 percent in 1900, 5 percent in 1920, 7 percent in 1940, 9 percent in 1960, and 13.3 percent in 2011. It's expected to grow to 17 percent by 2020.

- The **percentage of racial and ethnic minorities age 65 and older** in the U.S. population will increase from 20 percent in 2010 to 42 percent by 2050.

- The number of **children living with a grandparent** increased from 6.1 million in 2006 to 7.1 million in 2012.

- The **average annual health care costs** for each Medicare recipient age 65 and older increased

from $9,850 in 1992 to $15,709 in 2008.

- By 2015, worldwide and for the first time in history, **people age 65 and older will outnumber children younger than age 5**.

Sources: "Grandparents Day 2008 . . .," 2008; U.S. Census Bureau, 2008; Kinsella and He, 2009; Administration on Aging, 2012; Federal Interagency Forum on Aging-Related Statistics, 2012; National Center for Health Statistics, 2013; "National Grandparents Day . . .," 2013.

At age 100, Astrid works 40 hours a week in her son's insurance agency, handling the books and double-checking calculations. She's also an avid reader and knitter—and not easy patterns, she points out. "We all have aches and pains," Astrid says, "but I don't have time to think about them" (Hobson, 2010: 36).

Are people like Astrid typical of most older Americans? Probably not, but as we continue into the twenty-first century, more older people are vigorous and productive. Before you read any further, take the "Ask Yourself" quiz to see how much you already know about our aging population.

16.1 Describe how and explain why U.S. life expectancy and the older population are changing.

Watch on **MySocLab**

Video: The Longevity Revolution

Our Aging Society

One of my friends, age 53, was shocked and insulted when he ordered a meal at a fast-food restaurant, and the worker called out "One senior meal!" The *Baltimore Sun* (2012) recently reported on the death of an "elderly" man in a house fire. He was age 62.

When Is "Old"?

Researchers often use the terms *elderly*, *aged*, and *older people* interchangeably, but what images come to mind when you hear the word *old?* My mother once remarked, "It's very strange. When I look in the mirror, I see an old woman, but I don't recognize her. I know I'm 85, but I feel at least 30 years younger." She knew her health was failing, yet my mother's identity, like that of many older people, came from within, despite her chronological age.

"Old" is a social construction. In societies where people rarely live past age 50 because of diseases, 40 is old. In industrialized societies, where the average person lives to at least age 75, 40 is considered young. Our perception and definition of old also depends on our age. In a national survey, for example, Americans ages 18 to 29 said that 60 is old; those ages 50 to 64 said that 72 is old (Taylor, Morin, et al., 2009).

Regardless of how we feel, society usually defines *old* in chronological age. In the United States, people are typically deemed old at age 65, 66, or 67 because they can retire and become eligible for Medicare and full Social Security benefits.

Gerontologists—scientists who study the biological, psychological, and social aspects of aging—emphasize that older people shouldn't be lumped into one group. Instead, there are significant differences between the **young-old** (65 to 74 years old), the **old-old** (75 to 84 years old), and the **oldest-old** (85 years and older) in their ability to live independently and to work, and in their health needs.

Life Expectancy

Life expectancy is the average number of years a person can expect to live. For example, American children born in 2010 have a life expectancy of almost 79 years compared with 47 years in 1900 and 71 years in 1970 (National Center for Health Statistics, 2013). However, life expectancy varies by sex, social class, and race-ethnicity.

VARIATIONS BY SEX, RACE-ETHNICITY, AND SOCIAL CLASS Historically and currently, women live longer than men, and a life expectancy sex gap is expected to narrow only slightly by 2050 (Vincent and Velkoff, 2010). Across the three largest racial-ethnic groups, women have higher life expectancy rates than men, and Latinos have the longest lifespans (see *Figure 16.1*). Women begin to outnumber men at about age 35, but the gender gap widens considerably at age 70 (He et al., 2005; National Center for Health Statistics, 2013).

Between 2003 and 2008, the life expectancy gap between whites and blacks narrowed by about two years partly because the health of blacks improved and, for both groups, fewer deaths were due to heart disease, cancer, and HIV/AIDS. The primary reason for the smaller gap, however, was a surge of white deaths (for both sexes) from overdoses of powerful prescription medications such as Oxycontin and Vicodin and accidental poisoning due to illicit drugs (e.g., opium, heroin, cocaine) (Harper et al., 2012; "Prescription Painkiller Overdoses," 2013).

The higher rates of cigarette smoking, heavy drinking, gun use, employment in hazardous occupations, and risk taking in recreation and driving are responsible for many males' higher death rates. The deaths are usually due to lung cancer, accidents, suicide, and homicide. The gender gap has narrowed, however. Since the 1990s, there's been an increase in women's smoking, use of alcohol and other drugs, obesity (which increases the risk of hypertension and heart disease), and stresses related to multiple roles such as employment and caring for children and older family members (Yin, 2007; "Catching Up," 2013).

Across almost all racial-ethnic groups and regardless of sex, higher socioeconomic levels increase life expectancy. Generally, people with a college degree

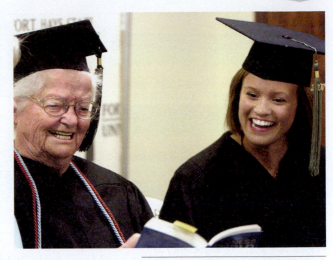

In 2007, Nola Ochs, age 95, and her 21-year-old granddaughter, Alexandra, were in the same graduating class at Fort Hays State University in Kansas. Ochs plugged along over 35 years by taking correspondence courses and finally finishing at the university. When she was handed her degree, the crowd gave her a standing ovation, breaking a rule against applauding until the names of all 2,176 graduates had been read.

gerontologist A scientist who studies the biological, psychological, and social aspects of aging.

young-old People between ages 65 and 74.

old-old People between ages 75 and 84.

oldest-old People age 85 and older.

life expectancy The average number of years a person can expect to live.

 Explore on MySocLab

Activity: The Graying of America

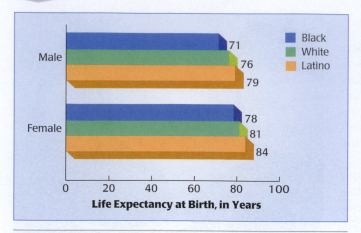

FIGURE 16.1 U.S. Life Expectancy at Birth, by Sex and Race-Ethnicity, 2010 *Note:* Recent data for other groups aren't available. In 2006, however, Asian American women had the highest life expectancy (85.8 years) in the United States (Office of Minority Health, 2012). *Source:* Based on National Center for Health Statistics, 2013, Table 18.

Since you asked . . .

- How does a longer life expectancy affect U.S. society?

centenarian A person who is 100 years old or older.

old-age dependency ratio The number of working-age adults ages 18 to 64 for every person age 65 and older who's not in the labor force (sometimes called the *elderly support ratio*).

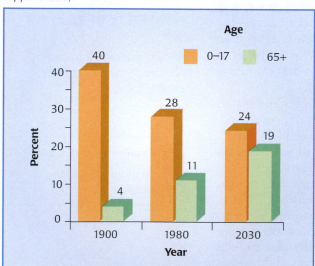

FIGURE 16.2 The Young and the Old in the United States, 1900 to 2030 *Source:* Based on U.S. Senate Special Committee on Aging et al., 1991: 9, and Vincent and Velkoff, 2010, Table A-1.

and higher are more likely to be employed, avoid financial hardship, and have employment-related health insurance. They're also more likely to exercise, not smoke, drink alcohol in moderation, and maintain a healthy body weight compared with less educated adults. An exception is Latinos, who have among the lowest education levels and household incomes but the highest life expectancy rates (see *Figure 16.1*).

Researchers hypothesize that Latinos have longer life spans both because only the healthiest migrate to the United States and because many foreign-born Latinos return to their country of origin when they fall ill. Also, U.S.-born Latinos, compared with whites, are less likely to smoke and more likely to have strong social support networks that provide assistance when people get sick (Miech et al., 2011; Olshansky et al., 2012; Montez and Zajacova, 2013; Pollard and Scommegna, 2013; see also Chapters 4 and 13).

UNITED STATES LAGS IN LIFE EXPECTANCY Despite our record high life expectancy, it's lower than 16 other industrialized countries' longevity rates, and the gap has been widening since the 1990s. Researchers attribute Americans' shorter lives to factors such as high obesity and diabetes rates, car crashes, heart and lung disease, homicides, alcohol and other drug abuse, and high infant mortality rates (Institute of Medicine, 2013).

A Growing Older Population

The older population has been increasing steadily since 1900 (see Data Digest). A "graying America" has several important implications for our society, especially a shrinking younger population, and, consequently, an expanding old-age dependency ratio.

OUR SHRINKING YOUNGER POPULATION Whereas the number of older Americans is booming, the proportion of younger people is decreasing. By 2030, there will be only a slightly higher number of younger than older people (see *Figure 16.2*). As a result, many adult children will care for aging parents, and many young children will have not only great-grandparents but also great-great-grandparents.

One of the fastest-growing groups is the oldest-old, a population that increased from 100,000 in 1900 to almost 6 million in 2010. In 2010, almost 53,400 Americans were **centenarians**—people age 100 or older, and 80 percent of the centenarians were women. Centenarians are much rarer in the United States than in France or Japan, but this population increased 66 percent between 1980 and 2010 compared with a 36 percent increase for the general population (Vincent and Velkoff, 2010; Meyer, 2012). As the number of older people increases, so does the old-age dependency ratio.

OUR GROWING OLD-AGE DEPENDENCY RATIO The **old-age dependency ratio** (sometimes called the *elderly support ratio*) is the number of working-age adults ages 18 to 64 for every person age 65 and older who's not in the labor force. In effect, this ratio shows the burden of the working-age population to support those age 65 and older who aren't employed.

As *Figure 16.3* shows, the old-age dependency ratio has increased considerably since 1900. By 2030, only 3 working-age people will be supporting each unemployed older person compared with 14 workers per older person in

1900. Thus, many people will have to pay much higher federal and state taxes to support our graying population.

High rates of young immigrants have stabilized the old-age dependency ratio, but they, too, age. Low-skilled workers with low-paying jobs are the least likely to seek early treatment for chronic illnesses, but they'll require medical care as they age (Population Reference Bureau, 2008).

Growing Racial and Ethnic Diversity

As America's older population grows larger, it's also becoming more racially and ethnically diverse. By 2050, as *Figure 16.4* shows, older white Americans will comprise only 58 percent of this population, down from 80 percent in 2010. In contrast, the older population among all racial and ethnic groups will grow. By 2050, older Latinos are projected to be larger in number than the older black population.

An important contributor to the declining share of older whites is that our immigration rates are the highest in the world (see Chapter 4). Also, because some racial-ethnic groups, especially Latinos, immigrated when they were young; have had higher birthrates than whites, blacks, and Asians; and have higher life expectancies than others, their children will increase the share of the older population by 2050 (Jacobsen et al., 2011; Bloom and Lorsch, 2012).

Across all racial-ethnic groups, living longer has created millions of **later-life families**—families that are beyond the child-rearing years who have launched their children, or child-free families that are beginning to plan for retirement. As later-life families age, they experience a variety of physical and social changes.

Health and Ageism

We often hear that "age is just a number." The implication is that people's attitude, personality, behavior, and other characteristics are more important than their biological age. Is this really true? Let's look first at physical and mental health and then at societal stereotypes about older people.

Physical Health

In 2011, almost 41 percent of Americans age 65 and older reported being in very good or excellent health, and 67 percent of those age 85 and older said that their health was good (Federal Interagency Forum on Aging-Related Statistics, 2012; Kramarow, 2013). Some older people are healthier than others, of course, but physical decline is normal and inevitable as we age. A gradual process of physical deterioration begins during one's late thirties, affecting all of the body's systems:

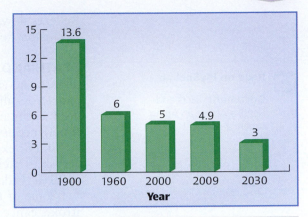

FIGURE 16.3 U.S. Old-Age Dependency Ratio, 1900 to 2030
Source: Based on Jacobsen et al., 2011, Figure 10.

 Explore on MySocLab

Activity: What Do Older Families Look Like?

later-life family A family that is beyond the child-rearing years and has launched the children or a child-free family beginning to plan for retirement.

16.2 Describe how and explain why physical and mental health and ageism affect older people.

Watch on MySocLab

Video: Physical Challenges of Living Longer

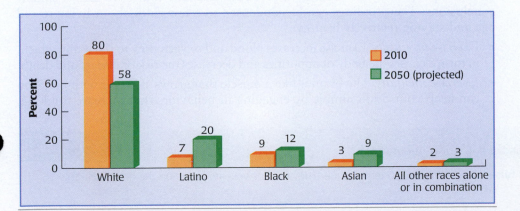

FIGURE 16.4 U.S. Population Age 65 and Older, by Race and Ethnicity, 2010 and 2050
Note: "All other races alone or in combination" includes American Indian and Alaska Native alone; Native Hawaiian and Other Pacific Islander alone; and all people who reported two or more races.
Source: Federal Interagency Forum on Aging-Related Statistics, 2012, p. 4.

Reflexes slow, hearing and eyesight dim, and stamina and muscle strength decrease. No matter how well tuned we keep our bodies, the parts eventually wear down.

Read on MySocLab

Document: Facts and Fictions About an Aging America

DEATH AND PHYSICAL DISABILITY   Among Americans age 65 and over, heart disease and cancer are the top two leading causes of death for women and men and across all racial-ethnic groups. Death rates for heart disease and stroke have declined by more than 50 percent since 1981, but millions of older Americans experience *chronic diseases*, long-term illnesses that are increasing and are rarely cured. For example, the prevalence of diabetes for persons age 65 and over, and across all racial-ethnic groups, increased from 13 percent in 1998 to 21 percent in 2010 (Federal Interagency Forum on Aging-Related Statistics, 2012).

Some of the most common and costly chronic diseases (e.g., heart disease, stroke, cancer, diabetes) can be prevented or delayed. Chronic health conditions vary by sex and race-ethnicity. In 2010, women had higher levels of asthma, arthritis, and hypertension, whereas men had higher levels of heart disease, cancer, and diabetes. Compared with whites, blacks have higher levels of hypertension, and both blacks and Latinos have higher levels of diabetes (Federal Interagency Forum on Aging-Related Statistics, 2012).

Chronic diseases increase the likelihood of having a physical disability that prevents people from carrying out daily tasks such as shopping and cooking meals (we'll examine the different types of physical disabilities shortly). Disability rates among older Americans declined during the 1980s and 1990s, but have recently increased, especially among baby boomers and those 10 years younger than baby boomers. The higher disability rates might be reflecting a greater awareness of health conditions and better diagnoses by physicians, but data show that baby boomers are more likely than the previous generation to be obese, have diabetes, or high blood pressure (Scommegna, 2013).

The reasons for older people's physical decline, disability, and death mirror those of life expectancy. That is, the higher a person's education and income, the better her or his health. Because, generally, whites have more resources than racial-ethnic groups, they're more likely to live longer, be healthier in old age, and pay for assistance when they experience chronic health problems and disabilities (Kramarow, 2013; Mendes, 2013; Pollard and Scommegna, 2013).

Some gerontologists believe that living a long life depends on a number of variables: About 50 percent is based on lifestyle, 30 percent on genes, and 20 percent on other factors, especially social class (Schneider, 2002). We can't change our genes or often our social class, but we can live longer and better by changing our lifestyles.

The people of Sardinia, Italy, and Okinawa, Japan, have the largest percentage of centenarians in the world. The centenarians credit their long life to a healthy diet and staying active, such as the older Okinawan women practicing their local dance pictured here.

Since you asked. . .

• Is poor health in later life inevitable?

HOW TO LIVE LONGER AND BETTER   A number of medical researchers have followed people's health from their seventies and later and have drawn similar conclusions. Their findings can be condensed to a few rules about living to old age and staying relatively healthy:

• *Exercise physically.* Exercise increases blood and oxygen flow to the brain, which, in turn, cleanses the body of impurities and decreases the risk of disease and death.

• *Exercise mentally.* The brain is like a muscle that grows stronger with use. You can keep your brain nimble by engaging in behaviors that increase thinking,

ANSWERS TO "How Much Do You Know about Aging?"

Odd-numbered statements are **false**; even-numbered statements are **true**. The answers are based on the material in this chapter.

such as playing board games, musical instruments, and "cognitive" computer games that require quick decisions.

- *Lose weight and don't smoke.* Smoking and obesity are linked to diabetes, heart disease, some cancers, and arthritis, among other diseases.

- *Watch what you eat.* Eating a diet that includes fruit, vegetables, whole grains, and nuts while avoiding food that contains saturated fats is healthy at any age. Well before we reach age 65, fat concentrates around vital organs and increases the risk of disease.

- *Control your blood pressure and avoid diabetes.* High blood pressure increases the likelihood of stroke, heart attack, and kidney failure. Diabetes, which affects every organ in the body, can cause blindness and kidney and heart failure.

- *Establish strong social networks.* Social relationships lower blood pressure (which decreases the risk of stroke) and reduces stress, anxiety, and depression (Tucker et al., 2005; Manini et al., 2006; Hall, 2008; Yates et al., 2008; Reddy, 2013).

Mental Health

Two of the most common mental health problems among older people are depression and dementia. Depression is easier to diagnose and more treatable than dementia, but both have a negative impact on individuals and their families.

DEPRESSION   *Depression* is a mental disorder (see Chapter 14) that affects 14 percent of Americans age 65 and older. As people age, depression increases—from 12 percent for people ages 70 to 74 to 18 percent for those age 85 and older (Federal Interagency Forum on Aging-Related Statistics, 2012).

Scientists believe that depression is due to a combination of genetic, personal history, and environmental factors. Older people who weather multiple stressful life experiences or crises (such as divorce, losing a job, or ongoing health and financial problems) are more likely to develop depression. Medical illnesses such as a stroke, a heart attack, cancer, Parkinson's disease, and hormonal disorders can lead to depression because of the body's physical changes. Depression can also be a side effect of some medications (Strock, 2002; Caspi et al., 2003).

dementia The loss of mental abilities that most commonly occurs late in life.

Alzheimer's disease A progressive, degenerative disorder that attacks the brain and impairs memory, thinking, and behavior.

DEMENTIA   **Dementia** is the loss of mental abilities that most commonly occurs late in life. Nearly 15 percent of Americans age 71 or older (almost 4 million people) have dementia. By 2040, the number is expected to balloon to 9.1 million. The health care for each person with dementia costs about $56,000 a year, more than treating heart disease and cancer (Hurd et al., 2013).

The incidence of dementia among people age 65 and older is lower among those who are better educated. Researchers believe that people who are better educated are more likely to control their blood pressure and cholesterol, both of which decrease the likelihood of mini-strokes and other vascular damage that increases the likelihood of dementia (see Kolata, 2013).

The most debilitating form of dementia is **Alzheimer's disease**, a progressive, degenerative disorder that attacks the brain and impairs memory, thinking, and behavior. In 2013, an estimated 5.2 million Americans of all ages, and 11 percent of those age 65 and older, had Alzheimer's: 4 percent were under age 65, 13 percent were 65 to 74, 44 percent were 75 to 84, and 38 percent were 85 or older. According to some estimates, because Americans are living longer, the number of people with Alzheimer's will reach 7.1 million in 2025 (a 40 percent increase) and to 16 million in 2050 (Alzheimer's Association, 2013; Hebert et al., 2013).

Many baby boomers, believing that they can slow down the aging process, join health spas and gyms to exercise regularly.

Among people age 65 and older, Alzheimer's is "only" the fifth leading cause of death. The disease has generated much research because the patients live an average of 10 years after the illness is diagnosed, and the emotional and financial costs for family members can be devastating. According to some estimates, by 2050, Alzheimer's care will cost more than $1 trillion annually (McDermott, 2007; Hebert et al., 2013).

No one knows the cause of Alzheimer's, but medical researchers have linked it to genes that cause a dense deposit of protein and debris called "plaque," along with twisted protein "tangles" that kill the brain's nerve cells. Alzheimer's spreads quickly, destroying more and more brain cells as it progresses. After two years, the disease engulfs almost the entire brain in some patients (Reilly, 2000; Thompson et al., 2003).

Alzheimer's is incurable and fatal, but there are several promising experimental drugs (among dozens that are being tested) that seem to slow down the progression of the disease, decrease memory loss, and might prevent the buildup of plaque that destroys the brain's nerve cells (Park, 2010).

All of us experience memory slips such as misplacing car keys or cell phones, forgetting someone's name, or being unable to recall the name of a movie we saw a few weeks ago. The symptoms of Alzheimer's are much more severe (see "Ten Warning Signs of Alzheimer's Disease"). A number of studies report that regular exercise throughout life and avoiding obesity, especially during middle age, may prevent or at least delay the onset of dementia and even the forgetfulness often associated with normal aging (Whitmer et al., 2005; Simon et al., 2006; Wang et al., 2006; Baldauf, 2010).

Ageism and Stereotypes

Anti-aging beauty products and services flood stores and Internet sites. Anti-aging websites routinely tell visitors that "anyone who desires a more youthful appearance can have one" or that "aging is a treatable condition that can be slowed or reversed" (Calasanti, 2007: 342).

Applying What You've Learned
Ten Warning Signs of Alzheimer's Disease

The Alzheimer's Association (www.alz.org) provides a list of symptoms that warrant medical evaluation. Have you seen any of these symptoms in family members or friends?

1. **Memory loss:** Although it's normal to forget names or telephone numbers, people with dementia forget such things more often and don't remember them later (for example, "I never made that doctor's appointment").

2. **Difficulty performing familiar tasks:** Not knowing the steps involved in preparing a meal, using a household appliance, or participating in a lifelong hobby.

3. **Problems with language:** Forgetting simple words. If someone with Alzheimer's can't find his or her toothbrush, for example, the person may ask for "that thing for my mouth."

4. **Disorientation to time and place:** Becoming lost on her or his own street, forgetting where he or she is and how he or she got there, and not knowing how to get back home.

5. **Poor or decreased judgment:** Dressing regardless of the weather, such as wearing several sweaters on a hot day or very little clothing in cold weather. Showing poor judgment about money, such as giving away large amounts of money to telemarketers or paying for home repairs or products one doesn't need.

6. **Problems with abstract thinking:** In balancing a checkbook, for example, someone with Alzheimer's could forget completely what the numbers are and what should be done with them.

7. **Misplacing things:** Putting things in unusual places, such as an iron in the freezer or a wristwatch in the sugar bowl.

8. **Changes in mood or behavior:** Showing rapid mood swings—from calm to tears or anger—for no apparent reason.

9. **Changes in personality:** Becoming extremely confused, suspicious, fearful, or suddenly very dependent on a family member.

10. **Loss of initiative:** Becoming very passive, such as sitting in front of the television for hours, sleeping much of the time, or not wanting to engage in usual activities.

Do anti-aging products work? No. Recently, for example, the Food and Drug Administration warned Avon Products to stop claiming that some of their anti-wrinkle skin creams stimulate cells or "tighten the connections between the skin's layers" (Dooren, 2012: B2). According to scientists, there's no known way to stop, slow, or reverse human aging. Nonetheless, we spend billions of dollars every year on "anti-aging quackery, hucksterism, and snake oil" that promises a fountain of youth (Perls, 2004: B682; see also Olshansky et al., 2004a, 2004b; and Weintraub, 2010).

AGEISM   In his classic book *Why Survive? Being Old in America*, physician Robert Butler (1975) coined the term **ageism** to refer to discrimination against people on the basis of age, particularly against older people. Among other things, Butler pointed out the persistence of the "myth of senility"—the notion that if old people show forgetfulness, confusion, and inattention, they're senile.

If a 16-year-old boy can't remember why he went to the refrigerator, we say he's "off in the clouds" or in love; if his 79-year-old grandfather forgets why he went to the refrigerator, we're likely to call him senile. Our language is full of ageist words and phrases that stereotype and generally disparage older people— for example, *biddy, old bat, old bag, old fart, old fogey, old goat, dirty old man, geezer,* and *over the hill* (Palmore, 1999). Older people are especially annoyed by ageist language that they believe devalues and demeans them. "Don't 'Sweetie,' 'Dear,' and 'Young Lady' Me!" examines some of this belittling language.

STEREOTYPES   When you turn on the TV, what kinds of images of older people do you see? Probably those complaining about their health, such as bladder problems, dentures, diabetes, and other diseases. Children as young as 5 years old often have stereotypes of older people and see them as incompetent (Kwong See and Rasmussen, 2003). Young adults also stereotype older people. For example, a national survey found that 63 percent of those ages 18 to 29 said that most older people experience memory loss, but only 25 percent of people age 65 and older sometimes do so (Taylor, Morin, et al., 2009).

ageism Discrimination against people on the basis of age, particularly against older people.

Constraints

Don't "Sweetie," "Dear," and "Young Lady" Me!

A woman in her late 70s went to one of the huge do-it-yourself home improvement stores to buy a replacement part for her toilet tank. She stopped at the front desk to find out where to find the part. "The thirtysomething clerk looked at me and then made an announcement over the loudspeaker, 'Will someone from plumbing please escort this young lady to aisle 14?'" When the woman realized that the clerk meant her when he referred to "this young lady," she became furious at his "condescending description" (Immel, 2006: 18).

She's not alone in experiencing such condescension. Many older people, especially women, say that it rankles them when store clerks, waiters, and others address them as "dear," "sweetie," or "young lady." "People

think they're being nice," says an 83-year-old woman, "but when I hear 'dear,' it raises my hackles" (Leland, 2008: A1).

A 68-year-old police psychologist fumed when people called her "young lady," which she described as "mocking and disingenuous." To discourage such belittlement, she says that she often sprinkles her conversation with profanities when she's among people who don't know her: "That makes them think this is someone to be reckoned with. A little sharpness seems to help" (Leland, 2008: A1; see also Dickinson, 2011).

Journalists who write about retirement and aging are in a quandary about how to refer to those in their midlife and later years because they realize that the words they use help define

and shape attitudes in both positive and negative ways. The top choice seems to be *older*, followed by *seniors. Boomers* is fine, but not *baby boomers* because this generation is no longer babies (Gardner, 2007: 15).

STOP AND THINK . . .

- Do you agree or disagree with older people who are offended by being addressed or referred to as "dear," or "young lady"? Or are they being too sensitive?
- Is there anything older people can do to counteract the words and phrases that they find demeaning?
- How do *you* think we should refer to old people?

The Zimmers may be the world's oldest rock band. In 2009, the British group, composed of about 40 people, had a 92-year-old lead singer and a combined age of more than 3,000 years.

Since you asked . . .

- Do most people become nastier as they age?

MAKING CONNECTIONS

- Scientists can now predict Alzheimer's disease with about 80 percent accuracy (Roe et al., 2013). Would you want to be tested? Why or why not?

- Do you sometimes get impatient or mutter under your breath when older people fumble to pay for purchases in checkout lines or drive more slowly than you do?

16.3 Explain why work patterns and retirement income vary for older persons.

 Read on MySocLab

Document: Facts and Fictions About an Aging America

Since you asked . . .

- Why are many older Americans working longer?

A common stereotype is that older people are stuck in the past and have outdated interests and skills. In 2012, however, 69 percent of Americans age 65 and older owned a cell phone, 53 percent used the Internet or email, and, in 2013, 43 percent used social networking sites such as Facebook (Zickuhr and Madden, 2012; Brenner and Smith, 2013; see also File, 2013). A major reason for older people not being online is the cost of computers and monthly fees for high-speed Internet connections rather than disinterest or fear of new technologies (Morales, 2009).

AGING AND PERSONALITY One of the most common stereotypes is that people become crankier as they age. In reality, most people's personalities are fairly stable throughout life (Belsky, 1988). If you're grumpy or unpleasant at 75 years old, you were probably grumpy and unpleasant at ages 15, 35, and 55. Work, marriage, and other life experiences affect people, but generally those who are hostile, anxious, or self-centered in their twenties are likely to be hostile, anxious, or self-centered in old age.

Even if personalities are fairly stable over the life course, behavior can change. For example, and contrary to the popular notion that people become more stubborn as they age, seniors are usually more flexible than younger people. Older people are more likely to avoid confrontation and to be patient and less critical when there are interpersonal problems. In many stressful situations, older adults are more likely than young and midlife adults to do nothing rather than to argue or yell (Birditt et al., 2005; Birditt and Fingerman, 2005; Dawson, 2011). When older people "suddenly" seem stubborn and defiant, they may simply be shedding some long-term inhibitions:

One of the greatest thrills of being a woman of 70 is having the luxury to be open about what I really think. When I was younger, I was so afraid of hurting people or worried about what they would think of me that I . . . kept my mouth shut. Now when I don't like something, I speak up. . . . Age has made me more truthful . . . and I feel better about myself now than I have at any other time in life (Belsky, 1988: 65–66).

As people age, their family roles change. Retirement is a major transition for most older adults, but whether or not they reenter the labor force depends on many factors, especially social class and health.

Work and Retirement

Many young Americans ages 18 to 29 are optimistic about *retirement*, the exit from the paid labor force: 37 percent expect to retire before age 65, and 66 percent say they'll live comfortably in retirement (Brown, 2013a; 2013b). In contrast, 62 percent of people ages 45 to 60 plan to delay retirement, up from 42 percent in 2010. In the general population, 85 percent of Americans worry about their retirement, and almost 50 percent of workers have little or no confidence that they'll have enough money to retire comfortably (Helman et al., 2013; Oakley and Kenneally, 2013; Weber, 2013). Because of such concerns, many Americans are working longer than they had expected or planned.

Working past Age 65

Anthropologist Margaret Mead once said, "Sooner or later I'm going to die, but I'm not going to retire." True to her word, Mead authored and co-authored several books before she died at age 77. Like Mead, many people work until they die.

Many Americans stop working at age 65. In 2013, 7 percent did so by choice, but 47 percent found themselves retiring earlier than planned due to health problems and disabilities, company layoffs, having to care for a spouse or other family member, or work-related reasons such as changes in the skills required in their jobs (Helman et al., 2013).

Whether by choice or necessity, many older Americans are postponing retirement. In 2013, almost 18 percent of people age 65 and older were working—up from 11 percent in 1985 and 14 percent in 2000 (Kromer and Howard, 2013; Bureau of Labor Statistics Economic News Release, 2013). You saw in Chapter 13 that the poverty rate for Americans age 65 and older has dropped steadily and is now lower than that for any other age group, including children. Why, then, are so many older Americans working either full time or part time well past age 65? Some of the reasons include the following:

- **Social Security**, a public retirement pension system administered by the federal government, provides income to more than 90 percent of older Americans, but the benefits depend on how long people have been in the labor force and how much they've earned. Because Social Security replaces only about 42 percent of the average older person's preretirement income, many must continue to work (Munnell and Soto, 2005).

- The retirement age for full Social Security benefits increased from 65 to 66 for people born between 1943 and 1954, and has risen to age 67 for those born after 1959. As a result, Americans must work longer to receive full retirement benefits (Mermin et al., 2008a).

- The Great Recession (see Chapter 13) destroyed 40 percent of Americans' personal wealth. Since then, many older people have been unemployed; their health-care costs and debt have surged; interest rates on savings have plummeted; they've dipped into their retirement savings to pay for everyday expenses; and of the pre-retirement workers who consulted professional financial advisors, only 27 percent followed the advice about investments (Brandon, 2013; Fletcher, 2013; Helman et al., 2013).

- **Medicare**, created in 1965, is a federal health insurance program for people age 65 and older that provides almost universal health coverage. However, the higher one's retirement income, the higher the monthly premiums. Also, Medicare doesn't cover dental and eye care, long-term care, and coverage of prescription drugs is minimal. This means that low- and middle-income retirees must pay these costs themselves or postpone retirement (Lei, 2009).

- Since the early 1990s, many companies (especially in the steel, airline, and auto industries) have reduced or eliminated their employee pension plans. As a result, many older people plan to continue working indefinitely (Mermin et al., 2008a; Helman et al., 2013; "Who Pays the Bill?" 2013).

Social Security A public retirement pension system administered by the federal government.

Medicare A federal health insurance program for people age 65 and older that provides almost universal health coverage.

Variations in Retirement Income

In 2011, households headed by persons age 65 and older had a median income of almost $48,600 (Administration on Aging, 2012). However, there are large variations by gender, race and ethnicity, marital status, and social class.

GENDER   In every age group, older women have a lower median income than men. For women age 65 and older, the median income in 2011 was $15,362 compared with $27,707 for men in the same age group. In the same year, almost twice as many older women (11 percent) as men (6 percent) lived below the poverty level (Administration on Aging, 2012; see also Gould and Cooper, 2013).

Some employers hire older workers because they're perceived as being more reliable, having a stronger work ethic, and more engaged in the work than younger people. Other employers believe that they're wasting their money by training older people.

There are many interrelated reasons for women's lower income during the retirement years. Compared with men, for example, women

- Earned less, even in comparable jobs (see Chapters 5 and 13)
- Spent less time in the labor force or never entered because of child-rearing responsibilities
- Didn't contribute at a high enough level to take advantage of the company match, which is typically 50 cents for every dollar up to 6 percent
- Invested more conservatively and started saving later
- Didn't make enough investments because 90 percent were unsure about how to manage their finances
- Withdrew funds before retirement
- Cashed out retirement savings rather than rolling them into other investments when changing jobs (Fleck, 2007; "Women Live Longer But . . .," 2008; Rix, 2013).

On average, women are likely to live from 6 to 14 years longer than men. As a result, they're more likely than men to run out of financial resources in late life (Yin, 2008).

RACE–ETHNICITY   Regardless of the age group, older whites and Asian Americans have higher median incomes than do African Americans and Latinos (see *Figure 16.5*). Older blacks and Latinos fare less well for a combination of reasons such as lower educational levels, low-paying jobs, less employment experience, and job-related discrimination (see Chapters 4 and 13).

Among racial-ethnic groups, later life income varies considerably across subgroups. For example, a study of six Asian American groups age 65 and older found that the income of Japanese Americans was the highest, and very similar to that of older whites, whereas the poorest were older Korean and Vietnamese Americans. The researcher attributed the differences to factors such as educational attainment, household size, and recent immigration. Thus, older Japanese Americans had the highest income because they had high education levels, small households (which result in fewer expenses and more savings), and had lived in the United States for at least six generations (Sharpe, 2008).

MARITAL STATUS   Married couples have almost twice the median income of single men and more than twice that of single women. This difference characterizes every age group. Even at age 75 and older, when many people have depleted most of their savings, married couples have an annual income of almost $41,076, compared with $23,211 for single men and $17,217 for single women (U.S. Census Bureau, Current Population Survey, 2012 Annual . . ., 2012.

Divorced or separated older women are the most vulnerable because they have lower incomes and fewer economic resources. Getting and staying married builds household wealth whereas divorce depletes it. As a result, middle-aged women who postpone marriage, cohabit, or divorce have significantly less income and wealth after age 65 (Addo and Lichter, 2013).

Widows age 65 and older fare better than divorced or married women primarily because they usually receive spousal and survivor benefits, can cash in one or more of a late husband's life insurance policies, and inherit other holdings such as a home—the biggest middle-class asset—as well as cars, jewelry, and

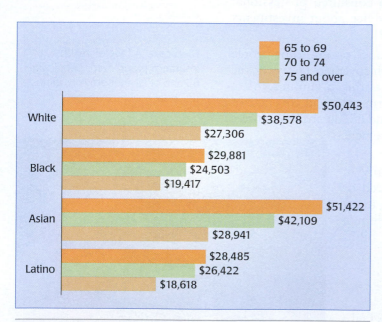

FIGURE 16.5 Median Income of Older Americans by Age and Race-Ethnicity, 2011

Source: Based on U.S. Census Bureau, Current Population Survey. 2012. Annual Social and Economic Supplement, detailed tables, Table HINC-02, www.census.gov/hhes/www/cpstables (accessed July 12, 2013).

other property. In contrast, divorced women, especially if they don't get the house or a favorable legal settlement, are generally cut off from their ex-husband's assets (Favreault, 2005; Yin, 2008).

SOCIAL CLASS   Social class is probably the most important factor in retirement income because it has a big effect on people's physical and emotional well-being. Regardless of age, gender, race and ethnicity, and marital status, older people in higher socioeconomic levels typically live longer and healthier lives than do those from low socioeconomic levels because they have more wealth (see Chapter 13).

People in higher social classes have more income during retirement for a number of interrelated reasons: They have (1) higher Social Security income because they had higher lifetime earnings, (2) more savings, (3) more property (including homes with paid-off mortgages), (4) higher investments in employer-sponsored retirement programs (such as a 401[k]), (5) employment pensions, and (6) they or their spouses still work in high-paying professional jobs. In contrast, lower-income people, those without college degrees, and most minority groups have little wealth and depend on Social Security for their retirement income (Mermin et al., 2008b; Jones, 2013; Linn, 2013).

Retirement is an important role transition. Well before retirement, however, many adults take on another important role—that of grandparent.

Grandparenting

In many ways, grandparents are the glue that keeps a family close. They typically represent stability in family relationships and a continuity of family rituals and values. Grandparents often help their adult children with parenting (such as babysitting) and provide support during emergencies or crises, including illness and divorce (see Szinovacz, 1998, and Smith and Drew, 2002, for summaries of grandparenting across racial-ethnic groups).

Grandparenting Styles

Grandparents usually take great pleasure in their grandchildren. The new role of grandparent often invigorates their lives and provides them with new experiences. There are a number of different grandparenting styles, however. Some of the most common are remote or detached, companionate and supportive, involved and influential, advisory and authoritative, and cultural transmitter.

REMOTE OR DETACHED   In the *remote* or *detached* relationship, the grandparents and grandchildren live far apart and see each other infrequently, maintaining a largely ritualistic, symbolic relationship. For example, some grandparents see their grandchildren only on holidays or special occasions. In other cases, grandparents are remote or detached because they're experiencing health problems. The relationships may be cordial but uninvolved and fleeting (Thompson and Walker, 1991; Davies and Williams, 2002).

Grandparents may be close to one grandchild but detached from others. Sometimes grandparents see a particular grandchild as "special" because of the child's personality, accomplishments, or respect for his or her grandparents. Not surprisingly, then, grandparents sometimes spend more time with some grandchildren than with others (Smith and Drew, 2002; Mueller and Elder, 2003).

COMPANIONATE AND SUPPORTIVE   The *companionate and supportive* style of grandparenting is the most common pattern. Supportive grandparents see their grandchildren often, frequently do things with them, and offer them

MAKING CONNECTIONS

- Many women drop out of the labor force to raise children or to care for sick or aging relatives. Doing so decreases their Social Security benefits later in life. Should the government compensate these women when they reach age 65?

- When do *you* plan to retire? How much retirement planning have you done? Do you have enough wealth to retire at age 65, 66, 67, or earlier? If you've already retired, is your income adequate?

16.4   Compare grandparenting styles and describe grandparent-grandchild relationships.

Since you asked . . .

- How do grandparents affect their grandchildren?

emotional and instrumental support (such as giving them money), but they don't seek authority in the grandchild's life. These grandparents are typically on the maternal side of the family, are younger, and have more income than other grandparents, but they avoid getting involved in parental child-rearing decisions (Mueller and Elder, 2003).

Grandparent–grandchild bonds are especially close, even when a grandchild becomes an adult, if a parent has a good relationship with his or her own parents. Also, mothers are more likely than fathers to influence grandparent–grandchild relations with either side of the family. Thus, mothers play a key kin-keeping role in encouraging or discouraging grandparent–grandchild ties (Monserud, 2008).

INVOLVED AND INFLUENTIAL   In the *involved and influential* grandparenting style, grandparents play an active role in their grandchildren's lives. They may be spontaneous and playful, but they also exert substantial authority over their grandchildren, imposing definite—and sometimes tough—rules. African American grandmothers, especially, say that they're concerned with teaching their grandchildren the value of education, providing emotional support, and involving them in the extended family and community activities (Gibson, 2005).

Compared with past generations, many of today's grandfathers are more involved in their grandchildren's daily activities. According to a director of a child care center, for example, "We used to see grandfathers only at special events or in emergencies. Now, every day, grandfathers drive carpools, carry backpacks, and chat with teachers." Grandfathers are particularly influential in single-mother households. When grandfathers are involved, children (especially boys) have fewer social problems, are more self-confident, and do better academically (Zaslow, 2006: D1).

ADVISORY AND AUTHORITATIVE   In the fourth type of grandparenting, *advisory and authoritative*, the grandparent serves as an advisor, a "reservoir of family wisdom" (Neugarten and Weinstein, 1964). The grandfather, who may be the family patriarch, may also act as a financial provider, and the grandmother often plays a crucial advisory role in the grandchildren's lives.

School-age children whose parents suffer from physical or mental illnesses are at relatively high risk for a number of difficulties such as depression, misbehavior, substance abuse, and learning difficulties. Grandparents who have strong emotional ties with their grandchildren and are their confidantes reduce the likelihood of such problems when parents experience mental health problems, poverty, or stress (Silverstein and Ruiz, 2006).

Even when parents have healthy parenting skills, many adolescents turn to their grandparents for advice or understanding. According to a 17-year-old boy, "With my grandpa we discuss usually technical problems. But sometimes some other problems, too. He told me how to refuse to drink alcohol with other boys." A 16-year-old girl said that she and her grandmother go for walks and added, "I can tell her about everything" (Tyszkowa, 1993: 136). Sometimes the roles reverse, with teenage grandchildren helping their grandparents with errands or chores.

CULTURAL TRANSMITTERS   Advisory grandparenting often overlaps with a fifth role, in which grandparents are *cultural transmitters* of values and norms. In American Indian families, for example, grandmothers often teach their grandchildren domestic chores, responsibility, and discipline that reflect tribal tradition. Grandfathers may transmit knowledge of tribal history and cultural practices through storytelling (Woods, 1996; see also Chapter 4).

Many recent Asian immigrants live in extended families and are more likely to do so than any other group, including Latinos. In such co-residence, grandparents

This grandmother illustrates which one or more of the grandparenting styles?

are often "historians" who transmit values and cultural traditions to their grandchildren even if there are language barriers. Chinese American grandparents, for example, help develop their grandchildren's ethnic identity by teaching them Chinese, passing on traditional practices and customs during holidays, and reinforcing cultural values such as respecting parents and other adults (Tam and Detzner, 1998; Tan, 2004).

Grandparents as Surrogate Parents

A grandparent is sometimes a *surrogate* because she, he, or they provide regular care or raise the grandchildren. Three of the most common types of surrogate grandparents are custodial, living-with, and day-care grandparents (Jendrek, 1994).

CUSTODIAL GRANDPARENTS *Custodial* grandparents have a legal relationship with their grandchildren through adoption and guardianship. In many cases, however, grandparents become the primary caregivers informally because of the parents' drug abuse, teen pregnancy, divorce, unemployment, mental illness, child neglect or abandonment, and the death or incarceration of parents.

Whether custody is legal or informal, in 2012, almost 1.5 million children were being raised by grandparents with no parent living in the home, down from more than 1.8 million in 2009 (Kreider and Ellis, 2011a; U.S. Census Bureau, Current Population Survey, 2012; see also Ellis, 2013). Of the nearly 1.5 million children being raised entirely by grandparents, many are white (see *Figure 16.6*).

For custodial grandparents, parenting a second time around is rewarding because they love their grandchildren. According to a 64-year-old grandmother, for example, "My husband and I love our grandson deeply; we can't imagine our lives without him" (Weiss, 2013: R6). On the other hand, compared with their non–caregiving peers, custodial grandparents are more likely to be poor; have more health, emotional, and financial problems; experience increased marital difficulties; and return to work to support grandchildren (Smith and Hancock, 2010; Baker and Mutchler, 2010; Scommegna and Mossaad, 2011).

Grandchildren who were raised solely by grandparents love them and are grateful that they didn't grow up in a foster home. On the other hand, they report much conflict because of a generation gap regarding strict rules about clothes, dating, household chores, and leisure activities. Children raised by grandparents also have lower educational attainment than those raised by parents because of the grandparents' limited economic resources and less academic monitoring (Dolbin-MacNab and Keiley, 2009; Monserud and Elder, 2011; Scommegna, 2012).

Older custodial grandparents also worry about the long-term care of a child. According to an African American grandfather, "I won't live long enough to see her grow up because she [the grandchild] is still a baby. My wife might be around, but I probably won't be living to help her out. It worries me" (Bullock, 2005: 50).

LIVING-WITH GRANDPARENTS *Living-with* grandparents typically have the grandchild in their own home or, less often, live in the home of a grandchild's parents. Living-with grandparents take on child-rearing responsibilities either because their children haven't yet moved out of the house or because teenage or adult parents can't afford to live on their own with their young children. These living arrangements have increased the number of **multigenerational households**, homes in which three or more generations live together. Such households represent almost 6 percent of all American family households (Lofquist, 2012).

In 2012, 10 percent (7.1 million) children lived with a grandparent—up from 5 percent in 1990—and the majority of these children lived in the grandparent's

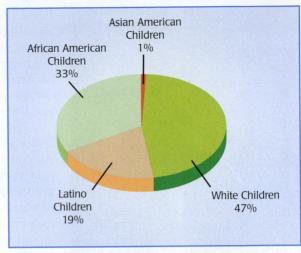

FIGURE 16.6 Grandparents Raising Grandchildren, 2012
Source: Based on data in U.S. Census Bureau, Current Population Survey, 2012. Annual Social and Economic Supplement, "Families and Living Arrangements," http://www.census.gov/hhes/families/data/cps2012.html, Table C4 (accessed July 10, 2013).

multigenerational household A home in which three or more generations live together.

 Watch on MySocLab

Video: ABC Primetime: Grandmothers Raising Grandchildren

When Michael Jackson died in 2009, a judge named his mother, Katherine Jackson, then age 79 (pictured here with two of her grandchildren), as the permanent guardian of his three children, at that time ages 7 to 12. Do you think that old-old grandparents (those between ages 75 and 84) should be given custody of their grandchildren?

home (Ellis, 2013; "National Grandparents Day . . .," 2013). Multigenerational households vary by race and ethnicity. White children (7 percent) are less likely than Asian (15 percent), black (14 percent), and Latino children (13 percent) to live with a grandparent and parent. However, only 25 percent of Asian children live in a grandparent's (as opposed to a parent's) home compared with 60 percent of Latino children, 71 percent of white children, and 76 percent of black children (Ellis, 2013).

The high percentage of Asian children living in multigenerational households but in a parent's home reflects both culture and social class. As you saw in Chapters 4 and 13, many Asian American adults believe that they should care for their aging parents, and grandparents teach grandchildren cultural values and traditions. Compared with the general population, Asian Americans have higher educational levels that, in turn, mean that adults don't have to rely on their parents for financial assistance, including housing.

The data on the effects of multigenerational households are mixed. Grandparents who live with their adult children and grandchildren may provide crucial economic support. On the other hand, if the multigenerational household is struggling with finances, if the grandmother is also raising her own children, if the grandmother resents her daughter becoming pregnant at a young age and not being able to raise the child herself, and if there's mother–grandmother conflict, grandparents experience emotional problems, including less happiness, and more stress, worry, and anger (Barnett et al., 2012; Pilkauskas, 2012; Deaton and Stone, 2013).

DAY-CARE GRANDPARENTS Because of the high cost of day care (see Chapter 13), *day-care grandparents* assume responsibility for the physical care of their grandchildren, usually a daughter's children, until the parents come home from work. Day-care grandparents help their adult children save money by not having to pay for child care costs. They also provide other benefits such as cooking meals for their grandchildren, caring for them when they are sick, and allowing parents to work late or travel on weekends to advance their careers (McGuire, 2011).

A national study of children ages 2 and 3 found that those cared for by a grandparent while the parent was working had half the injuries that required medical attention than children in other settings. Even when compared with organized day care or care by the mother or relatives, having a grandmother watch the child decreased a child's injuries (Bishai et al., 2008).

Many grandmothers enjoy caring for their grandchildren, but they often combine caregiving with careers and express emotions ranging from joy and satisfaction to fatigue and resentment. As one grandmother said, "It's very sad that after a lifetime of working full time, grandparents should have a second full-time job of caring for their grandchildren unpaid. . . . Something's wrong here" (Gardner, 2002: 16).

Grandparents' Divorce

Traditionally, divorce meant that a grandparent would have to establish new relationships with the ex-spouse or stepparent. More recently, family ties have shifted because grandparents themselves are getting a divorce.

The overall U.S. divorce rate has decreased since 1990 (see Chapter 15). For adults ages 50 and older, however, the divorce rate has more than doubled—from 10 percent in 1990 to 25 percent in 2009, an all-time high for this age group, and the rate is expected to rise (Brown and Lin, 2012; Lin and Brown, 2012). Because divorce rates among older people are increasing, many grandchildren will experience their grandparents' breakup.

When grandparents split up, both they and their grandchildren may suffer. Grandparents who divorce don't have as much contact with their grandkids, feel less close to them, and consider the role of grandparent less important in their lives. Divorced grandfathers, especially, have less contact with their grandchildren either because the grandmothers no longer encourage the grandfathers' involvement with their grandchildren or because the adult child–father relationship (that may have been fragile) dwindles after a divorce. Grandchildren may also have less contact with their divorced grandparents if the parents argue about which parent, stepparent, or other older relative to support financially after a divorce (Barnett et al., 2010; Doyle et al., 2010; Taylor, 2012).

Sibling Relationships in Later Life

Parent–child and sibling relations are usually complex because they often involve **intergenerational ambivalence**, contradictions that arise both from kinship roles and personal emotions. For example, our society's gendered division of domestic work obligates women to care for aging parents and in-laws. In such caregiving situations, a daughter or daughter-in-law may feel close to her aging parents or in-laws but may also resent their critical or demanding behavior (Willson et al., 2003; see also Chapter 5).

About 80 percent of older people have siblings. Because brother–sister relationships usually last longer than any other family ties, siblings can be important sources of companionship and emotional support.

According to medical sociologist Deborah Gold (1989, 1990), sibling relationships in later life generally fall into five groups, the last two of which are negative:

- *Intimate siblings* are close and consider each other to be best friends and close confidants. They help each other no matter what and are in frequent contact.

- *Congenial siblings* feel close and see each other as good friends, but they feel closer to a spouse or an adult child. They contact each other weekly or monthly but give help only when it doesn't conflict with their obligations to their spouse or children.

- *Loyal siblings* are available because of family bonds rather than affection or closeness. Disagreements don't erode the siblings' ties because they believe that family ties are important whether or not family members like each other.

- *Apathetic siblings* are indifferent, rarely think about each other, and have little contact with each other.

- *Hostile siblings* are angry and resentful and have had negative ties for a long time. They spend considerable time demeaning each other and arguing about the past, inheritances, and so on.

Sibling relationships can change over time, especially during family crises. Over the years, for instance, a number of my students in their forties and fifties said that their sibling relationships changed from apathetic to warm when a parent, grandparent, or great-grandparent became ill and needed ongoing care. In other cases, divorce and widowhood often bring indifferent siblings closer together (Russo, 2013).

Whether or not they have children and grandchildren, aging couples can enjoy many years together because of our greater life expectancy. Sooner or later, however, family members must cope with another important life course event—the death of a loved one.

MAKING CONNECTIONS

- What are/were the grandparenting styles in your family? Do/did they differ depending on the grandparent's age and gender, for example?

- Should older grandparents not divorce to maintain close ties with their adult children and grandchildren?

16.5 Describe sibling relationships in later life.

intergenerational ambivalence Contradictions that arise both from kinship roles and personal emotions.

Since you asked . . .
- Do siblings become closer or more distant as they age?

This out-of-town sister participated in a surprise 65th birthday party for her "little brother." She and her daughter compiled a photo album of his childhood and presented him with a traditional Lithuanian sash (saying "Congratulations!") that celebrates important events during the life course.

16.6 Describe how people deal with dying, death, and bereavement.

Watch on **MySocLab**

Video: Planning for the End of Life

dying trajectory The speed with which a person dies.

Dying, Death, and Bereavement

In 1900, when the average U.S. life expectancy was 49 years, death was a normal part of everyday life at all life stages—from infancy to adulthood. Today, most deaths are among the old-old and the oldest-old, and dying usually occurs in institutional settings (such as hospitals, hospices, and nursing homes) rather than at home (Federal Interagency Forum on Aging-Related Statistics, 2012).

Experiencing Death and Dying

How we experience death depends on whether we're medical personnel treating the patient, relatives or friends of the patient, or the patient himself or herself. Each may have a different perspective on death and dying.

HEALTH CARE PROFESSIONALS   A **dying trajectory** is the speed with which a person dies. In a *lingering trajectory*—for example, death from a terminal illness such as cancer—medical personnel do everything possible to treat the patient, but ultimately custodial care predominates. In contrast, the *quick trajectory* is an acute crisis caused by cardiac arrest or a serious accident. Staff members typically work feverishly to preserve the patient's life and well-being, sometimes successfully.

When an older person suffers from a terminal illness such as advanced cancer, health care professionals expect the patient to have a lingering death. Overworked hospital staff, especially, may respond to the patient's requests more slowly, place the patient in more remote wards, or even bathe and feed him or her less frequently. Family members, in contrast, typically expect their older relatives to be treated as painstakingly as any other patient (Atchley and Barusch, 2004).

PATIENTS, FAMILIES, AND FRIENDS   Among the several perspectives on the dying process, probably the best known is that of psychiatrist Elisabeth Kübler-Ross (1969). Based on work with 200 primarily middle-aged cancer patients, Kübler-Ross proposed five stages of dying: (1) *denial* ("The doctors must be wrong"), (2) *anger* ("Why me?"), (3) *bargaining* ("If you let me live longer, God, I promise to be a better person"), (4) *depression* ("There's no point in seeing family members or friends"), and (5) *acceptance* ("I might as well get my financial records in order").

Many have criticized this stage-based theory. Some contend that not everyone experiences the stages or in the same order. Others point out that the stages don't apply to older people because they've been thinking about the possibility of death for many years. Rather than deny death, the oldest-old, especially, may welcome it. Many have seen their spouses and friends die over the years, and they often view death as an end to chronic pain, social isolation, dependency, and loneliness.

Thus, the oldest-old may not experience Kübler-Ross's stages because they've been undergoing a "social death" over many years (Retsinas, 1988).

The Kübler-Ross stages also ignore the feeling of relief that many family members experience after a loved one dies. For example, "there are those who suffered from chronic physical illness, the cancer that kept recurring, and the Alzheimer's victims who had died inside years earlier when they stopped recognizing family members." Thus, the death of a loved one can end the prolonged agony that family members have endured (Elison, 2007: 18).

Many people are personalizing their funerals. Here, mourners are treated to ice cream at the graveside of a man who had driven an ice cream truck for many years.

hospice A place for the care of terminally ill patients.

Hospice Care for the Dying

A **hospice** is a place for the care of terminally ill patients, usually when death is imminent (generally a prognosis of six or fewer months to live). Hospice care is available in a variety of settings: patients' homes, hospitals, nursing homes, or other inpatient facilities.

Ideally, physicians, nurses, social workers, and clergy associated with a hospice work as a team to meet the physical, emotional, and spiritual needs of the patient and his or her family. Hospices provide pain control, give dying people full and accurate information about their condition, and help family members and friends deal with their sorrow.

In reality, hospice care—which Medicare and Medicaid (a federal government program for the poor) cover—is often unused, in part because of cultural and language barriers. For example, a comprehensive study of California—the most ethnically diverse state in America—found that 4 percent of Asian Americans, 6 percent of blacks, and 15 percent of Latinos, compared with 74 percent of whites, died at hospices. Some of the reasons for the differences were due to racial-ethnic groups' beliefs that people should die at home rather than an institutional setting, such as a hospice. There were also structural obstacles. Especially among many Latinos and Asian Americans, older immigrants weren't eligible for federal and state health care benefits, the terminally ill patients and their family members had problems communicating with hospice staff because of language barriers, or they found that staff members provided a low quality of care (Crawley and Singer, 2007).

The Right to Die with Dignity

Older men, especially those age 75 and older, have the highest suicide rates (see *Table 16.1*). This is especially true for white males age 65 and older, who commit suicide at almost triple the national rate (National Center for Health Statistics, 2013). It's not clear why suicide rates for older white men are so high and increase after age 65. Some reasons may include social isolation, loneliness, a feeling of uselessness, financial hardship, multiple losses of loved ones, and chronic illness and pain. White men, especially those from higher socioeconomic levels, may also fear becoming a burden to others and losing their control and dignity as their mental and physical capabilities diminish (DeSpelder and Strickland, 2005; see also Chapter 14).

Some maintain that older men's suicide rates would decrease if people had the legal right to die with dignity on their own terms. Both historically and currently, one of the most controversial issues has involved end-of-life decisions. Oregon legalized physician-assisted

"His last words were: Tell Martha to pay the doctors first."

TABLE 16.1	U.S. Suicide Rates, by Age and Sex, 2010	
Suicide deaths per 100,000 population		
Age Group	**Male**	**Female**
15–24	12	4
25–34	23	5
35–44	25	8
45–54	30	9
55–64	28	8
65–74	24	5
75–84	32	4
85 and older	47	3
All ages	20	5

Source: Based on National Center for Health Statistics, 2013, Table 35.

Choices | Should Physician-Assisted Suicide Be Legal in Every State?

How do Americans feel about physician-assisted suicide? It depends on how the question is worded. According to a recent Gallup poll, 51 percent of Americans agreed that doctors should be allowed to "assist the patient to commit suicide," but 70 percent said that doctors should be allowed to "end the patient's life by some painless means." Thus, not using the word *suicide* gets much more support even though the patient's outcome is the same (Saad, 2013).

Theoretically, Americans can decide on their end-of-life care through a **living will**, a legal document that specifies the medical treatments a person would like to receive if incapacitated. A **durable power of attorney for health care (DPAHC)**, similarly, permits a person appointed by the patient to make end-of-life decisions.

In reality, there are several problems with living wills and DPAHCs. First, fewer than one-third of Americans ages 18 to 64 have a DPAHC. As a result, older married couples often make end-of-life decisions according to their own rather than their partner's wishes (Moorman and Inoue, 2013).

Second, people from higher socioeconomic classes are much more likely than those from lower socioeconomic classes to prepare living wills and DPAHCs (Carr, 2012). Thus, even death reflects social class.

Third, and across social classes, whites are more likely than blacks and Latinos to prepare living wills and DPAHCs. The limited use of such documents has been linked to blacks' and Latinos' belief that family should make decisions about end-of-life care and that legal directives aren't necessary because "God alone determines the timing and nature of death" (Pollard and Scommegna, 2013: 7).

Fourth, legal documents don't guarantee compliance. Physicians and hospitals may refuse to honor living wills if their policies support prolonging life at any cost, if family members contest the living will, or if there's any question about the patient's mental competence when the will was drawn up.

Fifth, even in the few states that have passed PAS legislation, physicians, nurses, and pharmacists aren't legally obligated to assist a patient

who requests to die (Gershman, 2013).

Moreover, at least 67 percent of cardiac arrests occur at home or in a public place. Family members may know that the afflicted person has signed a do-not-resuscitate (DNR) order, but the patient is usually resuscitated because family members can't produce the paperwork (Grudzen et al., 2009). Some patients recover, but many, even though their brains aren't functioning, may be connected to feeding tubes for many years.

STOP AND THINK . . .

- What's your position on PAS? Why?
- Among those age 65 and older, 35 percent have never talked to their children about end-of-life medical decisions (Parker, 2009). Have you discussed such issues with your parents, grandparents, or aging relatives? Why or why not?

---

living will A legal document that specifies the medical treatments a person would like to receive if incapacitated.

durable power of attorney for health care (DPAHC) A legal document that permits a person appointed by the patient to make end-of-life decisions.

bereavement The process of recovery after the death of someone we felt close to.

grief The emotional response to loss.

suicide (PAS) in 1998 but strictly prohibits lethal injections or euthanasia (sometimes called *mercy killing*). Modeling Oregon's Death with Dignity law, Montana, Vermont, and the state of Washington legalized PAS (sometimes called *physician-aid-in-dying*) between 2008 and 2013.

The Oregon law allows mentally competent adults who declare their intentions in writing and have been diagnosed as terminally ill independently by two physicians to take a doctor-prescribed lethal drug themselves, orally, after a waiting period of 15 days. Opponents of the Death with Dignity law predicted massive PAS deaths. Between 1998 and 2013, however, only 1,050 patients have received lethal prescriptions (Bendavid, 2013). "Should Physician-Assisted Suicide Be Legal in Every State?" examines this issue further.

Coping with Death

Bereavement is the process of recovery after the death of someone we felt close to. Grief and mourning are two common manifestations of bereavement.

GRIEF AND MOURNING   **Grief** is the emotional response to loss. It usually involves a variety and combination of feelings such as sadness, longing, bewilderment, anguish, self-pity, anger, guilt, and loneliness, as well as relief.

The grieving process may last a few months or continue throughout one's lifetime. However long it lasts, grieving usually encompasses physical, behavioral, and emotional responses. In terms of behavior, bereaved people may talk incessantly about the deceased and the circumstances of the death. Others may

talk about everything except their loss because it's too painful to do so (DeSpelder and Strickland, 2005).

Mourning is the customary outward expression of grief. Mourning ranges from normal grief to pathological melancholy that may lead to physical illness or depression. Whether it's the death of a child, a parent, or a grandparent, most people don't "recover" and finish mourning. Instead, they adapt and change, such as donating the dead person's clothes to a charity and establishing new relationships (Silverman, 2000).

Coping with death varies across cultural and racial-ethnic groups. Many U.S. ethnic groups maintain traditional ceremonies that reinforce family ties and religious practices (see "Death and Funeral Traditions among Racial-Ethnic Families").

PHASES OF GRIEF There are phases of grief (Hooyman and Kiyak, 2002). People respond *initially* with shock, numbness, and disbelief. After one of my uncles died, for example, my aging aunt refused to get rid of any of his clothes because "he might need them when he comes back." The grieving person may be unable to sleep, lose interest in food, and not answer phone calls or even read sympathy cards because of an all-encompassing sorrow.

In the *intermediate stage* of grief, people often idealize loved ones who have died and may even actively search for them. A widow may see her husband's face in a crowd. Recent widows or widowers may also feel guilty, regretting every lapse: "Why wasn't I more understanding?" "Why did we argue that morning?" Survivors may also become angry, blowing up at children and friends over little things in a seemingly irrational way.

The *final stage* of grief, recovery and reorganization, may not occur for several years, although many people begin to adjust after about six months. In later life, grieving is often more complex than it is for younger people because an

mourning The customary outward expression of grief.

Since you asked . . .
- How does grieving change over time?

Cross-Cultural and Multicultural Families — Death and Funeral Rituals among Racial-Ethnic Families

There are cultural, religious, and ethnic differences in how families cope with death. The variations include rituals, the appropriate length of mourning, celebrating anniversary events, and beliefs about the afterlife. For example, many African American families give the deceased a "good send-off" that includes buying the best casket the family can afford and a funeral with stirring songs and eulogies.

In many Middle Eastern families, Muslims usually mourn the death of a loved one for at least one year. They organize big gatherings of relatives and friends on the third day, the fortieth day, and one year after the death of a loved one.

Despite their heterogeneity, for Mexican American and other Latino families, funeral rites strengthen family values and ties in several ways:

- There's a common belief that it's more important to attend a funeral than almost any other family event. During the funeral,

the family and the community offer emotional and spiritual support.

- Socialization to death begins at a young age. Children attend wakes and funerals regularly and participate in memorial masses and family gatherings after the funeral.

- Many Mexican Americans cope with death through ritualistic acts such as a rosary, a mass, a graveside service, and the annual observance of All Souls' Day on November 2, which is more commonly known as the Day of the Dead (Día de los Difunios).

Recently, many cemeteries and mortuaries—whose directors are usually white—have adapted services to immigrant customs. Some funeral homes have removable pews so that Hindu and Buddhist mourners can sit on the floor. Funeral homes may also provide incense sticks and have common rooms where mourners can gather to snack and chat when funerals span several days.

Deceased Muslims are often propped on one shoulder inside their coffins so they face Mecca. Some funeral homes supply white shrouds, Egyptian spray perfume, and a particular soap that Muslims use to wash and dress the dead. Managers of funeral homes also make sure that women employees are working on days when female Muslims are washed in case an employee has to enter the preparation room.

Sources: Sharifzadeh, 1997; Willis, 1997; Murray, 2000; Martinez, 2001; Brulliard, 2006.

STOP AND THINK . . .
- How do some of these rituals differ from those of your family? How are they similar?
- Talk to some of the international students on your campus or in class. How do their families cope with death? What kinds of rituals do they practice? And why?

older person may experience, over a few years, the deaths of many people who were important to him or her.

DURATION AND INTENSITY OF GRIEF   Death affects older people differently than it does younger people. A national study of couples age 65 and older found that up to 22 percent of spouses died within a year of being widowed. These "widower effects" (when a spouse dies shortly after being widowed) may reflect changes in the survivor's behavior, such as sleeping less, using sleep medications more often, consuming more alcohol, and losing weight. Even daily routines such as getting around, meal preparation, and household tasks may become more difficult both physically and emotionally (Christakis and Allison, 2006; Pienta and Franks, 2006; Utz, 2006).

For the most part, however, older bereaved people are very resilient. For example, almost half accept the death of a spouse as part of life and take great comfort in their memories. About 10 percent are relieved at the death of a partner because they had been trapped in a bad marriage or had provided stressful caregiving for a number of years. About 16 percent experience chronic grief lasting more than 18 months, but 24 percent show an improvement in psychological well-being within a year or so after a partner's death (Mancini et al., 2006).

The duration and intensity of a person's grief depend on a number of factors, including the quality of the lost relationship, the age of the deceased person, whether the death was sudden or anticipated, and the quality of care the dying person received at the end of his or her life (Carr et al., 2006). Many families now turn to the Internet to express their grief. Their websites feature video montages of the deceased, webcasts of funeral or memorial services, audio messages prepared by the terminally ill for distribution after death, and a space to leave condolences or to share memories of the deceased (Harris, 2007).

MAKING CONNECTIONS

- Most people use euphemisms (such as *passed, passed on, passed away, expired, left us*) instead of *died*. Why? Do such euphemisms help us cope with death? Or do they imply that death isn't a normal part of life?

- Do you think that Internet sites about a dead family member are a good idea? Or do you think that grieving should be a private rather than a public matter? Why?

- Hallmark is now producing "sympathy" cards to send people who know they're dying ("The American Way of Death," 2013). Would you send such a card?

16.7   Compare widowhood for women and men.

Being Widowed in Later Life

A spouse's death is one of the most distressing of all life events; it often means not just the loss of a life companion but the end of a way of life. Friendships may change or even end because many close relationships during marriage were based on being a couple. Some ties, such as relationships with in-laws, may weaken or erode. Widowed persons may also forge new relationships through dating, cohabitation, and remarriage.

There Are More Widowed Women than Men

In 2012, men age 65 and older were much more likely to be married than older women—72 percent and 45 percent, respectively. Women were also three times more likely than men to be widowed, and more likely than men to be divorced or separated (see *Figure 16.7*). In the same year, there were over four times as many widows (almost 9 million) as widowers (2.1 million) (Administration on Aging, 2012). Even among the oldest-old (age 85 and older), only 36 percent of men, compared with 73 percent of women, were widowed ("America's Families and Living Arrangements," 2012).

There are five major reasons for the gender differences in widowhood. First, women tend to live longer than men (see Data Digest), which increases their likelihood of being widowed. Second, a wife typically is three or four years younger than her husband, which also increases the likelihood that she will survive him. Third, at age 65 and older, there are 77 males for every 100 females ("U.S. Census Bureau Projections . . .," 2012). This means that the marriage market (see Chapter 8) for older males is better than for their female counterparts. Fourth,

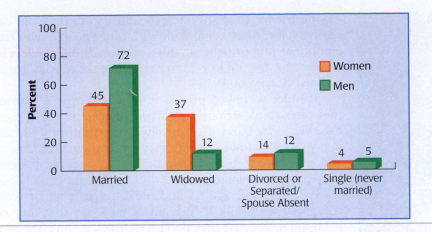

FIGURE 16.7 Marital Status of Americans Age 65 and Older, 2012
Source: Administration on Aging, 2012, Figure.

among women and men age 50 and older, 63 percent of men, compared with only 22 percent of women, want to date someone who's much younger. And the older a man is, the more likely that he wants to date a much younger woman (Akitunde, 2013). Finally, widowers age 65 and older are eight times more likely than women to remarry. Especially if they have the resources to attract a new mate, and given the large pool of eligible women (those who are younger, widowed, divorced, or never married) and the shortage of men, it's easier for older men than older women to remarry (Lin and Brown, 2012; see also Chapter 15).

Facing Widowhood

Some recently widowed older people have depressive symptoms such as insomnia, loss of appetite, and dissatisfaction with themselves. As you saw earlier, however, many usually recover within a year or so, especially if they no longer experience the stress of caring for a dying spouse or partner.

If they're healthy and financially self-sufficient, most older Americans, including the widowed, value their independence and prefer to live alone rather than move in with their children. Others may feel isolated, especially when children or relatives live at a distance or rarely visit. Some also relocate and move in with adult children to help care for grandchildren, forming a multigenerational household.

How does widowhood affect a family's relationships? A national study found that much depends on a late-life widowed parent's personality. The adult children of widowed mothers who were highly extroverted (e.g., high spirited), had a wide range of intellectual interests, were emotionally stable, and self-reliant had a poorer relationship than those whose widowed mothers were needy, depressed, and dependent. Perhaps, according to the researchers, the adult children resented the widowed mothers' "lack of appropriate grief" (Pai and Ha, 2012).

Another national study examined the social networks of people age 65 and older at 6 and 18 months after a spouse's death. Initially, the widowed person had considerable support from adult children and relatives, who provided instrumental help (such as making funeral arrangements and help with relocating) and emotional support (such as listening and making the widowed person feel loved and cared for). Eighteen months later, however, friends played a more important role as confidants, people with whom the widowed person shared private feelings and concerns (Ha, 2008). Thus, social networks and support change over time as a person adjusts to being widowed.

Forging New Relationships

Some widows and many widowers begin to date within a few years of a mate's death. Many family members may disapprove, but companionship is the most important reason for dating. Like younger people, older people enjoy

Since you asked . . .
• How soon should widowed people begin dating after a partner's death?

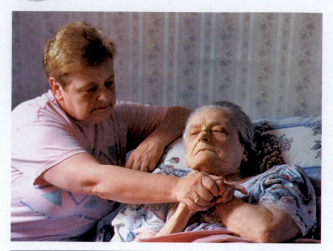

As life expectancy increases, many middle-aged adults find themselves caring for their aging parents. Most of the care is provided in the children's or the older person's home rather than in institutions such as nursing homes.

16.8 Describe family caregiving in later life and explain how and why caregiving styles differ.

caregiver A person, paid or unpaid, who attends to the needs of someone who is old, sick, or disabled.

((• Listen on MySocLab

Audio: NPR: Raising Children, Caring for Parents

having friends to share interests and whom they can call in emergencies. After being widowed, older people who receive emotional support from family and friends may be less likely to want to date or to remarry than are those who are more isolated (Carr, 2004).

If older widowed people form a romantic relationship, they often think seriously about whether to just date, move in together, or remarry. As you saw earlier and in Chapter 15, many older widowed people may increase their income taxes and reduce or lose an ex-spouse's Social Security benefits or pension if they remarry.

Among those age 65 and older, 34 percent of women, compared with only 14 percent of men, say that they enjoy being single because they don't have to clean up after another person. Also, 17 percent of women in this age group, compared with 7 percent of men, like having a bed to themselves (PR Newswire, 2013). Many widows aren't eager to provide caregiving to an older second or third husband because they've already done so. All of these issues can discourage remarriage, especially for older women. Nevertheless, caregivers are vital in providing emotional and physical help as we age.

Family Caregiving in Later Life

The *sandwich generation* is composed of midlife men and women who care for aging parents, are raising a child under age 18, or supporting a grown child; 71 percent who do so are ages 40 to 59 (Parker and Patten, 2013; see also Chapters 1 and 13). A **caregiver** is a person, paid or unpaid, who attends to the needs of someone who is old, sick, or disabled. Nationally, 39 percent of Americans are family caregivers; 16 percent provide care for one or more family members age 65 and older (Bureau of Labor Statistics American Time Use Survey, 2013; Fox et al., 2013).

Who Are the Recipients and Caregivers?

The older we get, the more likely we are to give and receive help. Most people age 65 and older develop disabilities as they age and eventually require assistance with basic everyday tasks. And, as you might expect, the older people are, the more help they need.

RECIPIENTS   Among people age 65 and older, 41 percent (about 17 million Americans) need help because they have one or more physical, mental, emotional, or memory problems. The difficulties interfere with the activities of daily living (ADLs) or with instrumental activities of daily living (IADLs) (Interagency Forum on Aging-Related Statistics, 2012).

ADL limitations include dressing, walking across a room, bathing or showering, eating (such as cutting up food), getting in or out of bed, and using the toilet (including getting up or down). Problems in IADL include preparing meals, shopping for groceries, making phone calls, taking medications, and managing money (such as paying bills and keeping track of expenses). The larger the number of ADL and IADL disabilities, the greater the reliance on caregivers.

Physical functioning problems increase as people age, but more older women (49 percent) than men (35 percent) have ADL and IADL disabilities. For those age 85 and older, 53 percent of women compared with 40 percent of men have at least one physical limitation that requires caregiving (Interagency Forum on Aging-Related Statistics, 2012).

CAREGIVERS The average U.S. caregiver is a 49-year-old woman who works outside the home and spends nearly 20 hours per week providing unpaid care to a parent, usually her mother, for nearly five years. About 67 percent of family caregivers are female, and the average age of the care recipient is 77 (Feinberg al., 2011). *Table 16.2* offers a demographic profile of eldercare providers.

Across all racial and ethnic groups, the majority of caregivers are women—wives, daughters, daughters-in-law, and female neighbors and friends (Johnson and Wiener, 2006; National Alliance for Caregiving/AARP, 2009; Fox and Brenner, 2012). Among those who work full time or part time, women (20 percent) are slightly more likely than men (16 percent) to be caregivers of family members or relatives age 65 and older (Cynkar and Mendes, 2011).

According to some scholars, these gender differences reflect broad cultural norms that assign caretaking tasks to women, who are believed to be naturally more nurturing than men and who are expected to provide more care for children and aging parents (see Chapter 5). Women may also be more likely than men to help older family members because women develop informal support networks (friends, neighbors) that they can count on when needed (Kahn et al., 2011).

Others maintain that the gender gap reflects structural factors such as employment. That is, women provide more caregiving to older adults because they're less likely than men to have well-paid, demanding, or satisfying jobs. As a result, men in high-income jobs are more likely to purchase help rather than take advantage of the Family and Medical Leave Act, which doesn't provide paid leave (Sarkisian and Gerstel, 2004; Neal and Hammer, 2007; see also Chapter 13).

Caregiving Styles

Families help their older members in various ways—financially, physically, and emotionally—but adult children provide most of the assistance. Because many of us grow up with brothers and sisters, how do siblings share the care? Matthews and Rosner (1988) found five primary types of caregiving for aging parents, some more cooperative than others.

ROUTINE HELP *Routine help* is the backbone of caring for older parents. The adult child incorporates assistance into his or her ongoing activities and is regularly available. Routine involvement may include a wide range of activities: household chores, checking in with the person, providing outings, running errands, managing finances, and visiting.

BACKUPS In a second style, siblings serve as *backups*. One person gives routine care to an aging parent, but a brother or sister may step in when needed. For example, one sister explained, "I do what my sisters tell me to do." She responded

Since you asked . . .
- Why are women usually the caregivers for older family members?

Read on MySocLab

Document: Women and Men in the Caregiving Role

TABLE 16.2 Who Provides Care for Older Family Members?
• 67 percent are women
• 54 percent are age 50 or older; 30 percent are age 65 or older
• 76 percent are white
• 59 percent are married
• 53 percent have less than a college degree
• 56 percent have an annual household income of $50,000 or more
• 61 percent work full time or part time
• 70 percent live in suburbs or rural areas

Note: The care recipients are age 50 or older.
Source: Based on National Alliance for Caregiving/AARP, 2009: 45-47, and Fox et al., 2013.

Some caregivers are monitoring older family members from afar. The technology includes video conferencing systems and webcams positioned throughout the house that track movement and notify caregivers if there are any deviations from a routine that might indicate an accident or illness.

to her sisters' requests but didn't initiate involvement. In other cases, a sibling may contact a "favorite child" when a parent refuses to do something that the routine caregiver thinks is necessary (such as taking medicine every day, regardless of its cost).

CIRCUMSCRIBED The *circumscribed* style is limited but predictable and agreed on among the siblings. For example, one respondent said of her brother, "He gives a routine, once-a-week call" that a parent eagerly awaited. The brother wasn't expected to increase his caregiving participation, however.

Siblings who adopt this style can be counted on to help, but they have made clear that there are limits to their availability. For example, in one family, a son who was a physician gave medical advice but wasn't expected to assume any other responsibility.

SPORADIC In contrast to the first three types of caregiving, the *sporadic* style describes adult children who provide services to parents at their own convenience. As one daughter said, "My brother comes when he feels like it to take Mother out on Sunday, but it's not a scheduled thing." Some siblings don't mind this behavior, but others resent brothers and sisters who avoid the most demanding tasks:

> [My sister and I] were always very close, and we're not now. . . . She calls, big deal: that's very different from spending three to four hours a day. . . . She does not wheel my mother to the doctor, she does not carry her to the car, she does not oversee the help (Abel, 1991: 154).

DISASSOCIATED In *disassociation*, sisters and brothers know that they can't count on a sibling at all. Siblings use geographic distance, employment, and other family responsibilities as excuses for not assuming caregiving responsibilities. Such justifications, however, may increase resentment among those who provide care (Ingersoll-Dayton et al., 2003).

Unequal caregiving burdens can create distance between siblings ("He never helps" or "I want to help but she rejects all my offers"). On the other hand, sisters and brothers sometimes overcome ancient grudges as they band together for their parents' sake. They might make mutual decisions about an aging parent's living in a retirement community, share information about a parent's health, and work out visiting schedules for siblings who are geographically scattered (Russo, 2010).

Caregiving Satisfactions and Strains

Exchange theory suggests that caregivers experience both costs and benefits. The costs of caring for older family members sometimes outweigh the benefits, especially for women in a sandwich generation with full-time jobs, but caregiving can also be fulfilling.

CAREGIVING SATISFACTION Some people enjoy caregiving, believing that family relationships can be renewed or strengthened by helping older family members. They see caregiving as a labor of love because of strong affection that has always existed in the family. For others, caregiving provides a feeling of being useful and needed. As one daughter said, "For me, that's what life's all about!" (Guberman et al., 1992: 611; see also Saldana and Dassori, 1999).

Satisfaction varies. Adult caregivers report more positive than negative experiences when the care recipient has few problem behaviors (e.g., hiding belongings, swearing, being angry), reciprocates (e.g., gives money, is emotionally supportive), if other caregivers help out, if family members are appreciative, and if the recipients aren't totally dependent on the caregivers (Lin et al., 2012).

CAREGIVING STRAINS Caregiving also creates stress and strain. Older people usually need support at a time when their children's lives are complicated and demanding. Families are often unprepared for the problems involved in caring for an older person. Sandwiched caregivers frequently experience a lower quality of life because daily routines are disrupted and parent–adult child conflict may increase. Parents who are mentally impaired, can't perform basic daily self-care tasks, or engage in disruptive behavior are the most difficult to care for (Dilworth-Anderson et al., 1999; Rubin and White-Means, 2009).

The most common difficulties include always feeling rushed, social isolation, exhaustion, spending an average of more than 10 percent of one's annual income on caregiving expenses, and missing work, which, in turn, decreases pay, retirement savings, and Social Security income. Moreover, employed caregivers of older family members who are chronically ill experience increased physical and psychological problems such as high blood pressure, weight gain or loss, sleep problems, continuous anxiety, and depression (Feinberg et al., 2011; Mendes, 2011; Witters, 2011; Fox et al., 2013; Parker and Patten, 2013).

Competition for Scarce Resources

When Congress passed the Social Security Act in 1935, life expectancy was just below 62 years, compared with almost 79 today. In the years ahead, the increasing numbers of older Americans will put a significant strain on the nation's health care services and retirement income programs. What are some of the financial costs of our aging society? And are there any solutions?

Some Financial Costs of an Aging Society

Many Americans are living longer, but, as you saw earlier, they're not always healthier. Between 1990 and 2010, for example, the amount of time that people age 65 and older spent with chronic disability rose from 9 to 10 years (Murray et al., 2013). A year's difference may not seem like much, but the medical costs are significant when multiplied by almost 40 million Americans age 65 and older.

The size of the U.S. older population (13 percent) is about half that of the child population age 18 and younger (26 percent). However, the federal government spends 31 percent on the elderly, primarily through Social Security and Medicare, compared with 10 percent on children (Isaacs et al., 2012). The older people get, the higher the medical costs. For example,

- Chronically ill patients, comprising only 5 percent of the population, are responsible for almost 50 percent of all U.S. health care spending (Schoenman and Chockley, 2011).

- In 2008, the average annual health care costs for Medicare recipients age 85 and over were almost $24,000 compared with $12,000 for those ages 65 to 74 (Federal Interagency Forum on Aging-Related Statistics, 2012).

- The top U.S. medical centers spend anywhere from $30,000 to almost $94,000 a year per patient in his or her last two years of life, and all of the costs are covered by Medicare or Medicaid (Wennberg et al., 2008).

- Medical care for patients in the last year of life accounts for more than one-quarter of annual Medicare expenditures (Carr, 2012).

- A study of 1.8 million Medicare recipients who died in 2008 found that one-third had surgery in the last year of life. Nearly 1 in 5 had surgery in the last month of life, and nearly 1 in 10 had surgery in the last week of life. Among those undergoing end-of-life surgery, almost 60 percent were age 80 and older (Kwok et al., 2011).

- It costs $93,000 per patient to treat advanced prostate cancer; the treatment prolongs life by an average of four months (Beil, 2012).

16.9 Explain why there's a competition for resources in caring for our graying population.

Since you asked . . .
- How much should we pay for one more month of life?

The financial costs of our aging society are expected to increase in the future. By 2020, health care expenses, which are rising every year, will consume $1 of every $5 in the economy (Centers for Medicare & Medicaid Services, 2012).

By 2030, half of the boomers will have arthritis, four times more hip replacements, and eight times more knee replacements; 33 percent will be obese (which results in numerous health problems); and 20 percent will have diabetes, which, like obesity, generates considerable health costs. However, because boomers have higher educational levels than previous generations, they're likely to demand more and more expensive health care services (American Hospital Association, 2007).

A major reason why older people have relatively generous health care coverage is that they're one of the largest and politically best organized groups in the nation. They vote in large numbers, follow issues carefully, and usually come to congressional hearings well prepared to defend their positions. An especially influential group is the AARP. It has at least a half million volunteers and one of the country's most influential lobbying groups in Congress that support politicians from both parties. It takes AARP little time to mobilize its members and flood lawmakers with hundreds of thousands of letters and e-mail messages when there's a threat of cutting Medicare or Social Security (Donnelly, 2007; K. Johnson, 2011).

According to some analysts, younger generations can't count on federally financed health care and retirement benefits in the future. Medicare funds are supposed to last until 2026, and Social Security through 2033 (The Board of Trustees . . ., 2013), but there are no guarantees.

Despite rising health care costs, 69 percent of Americans want to live to age 79 through 100—about 11 years longer than the current average U.S. life expectancy of almost 79 years (see Data Digest). Moreover, 38 percent want medical treatments that would allow them to live to at least 120 years (Lugo et al., 2013; see also Lipka and Stencel, 2013).

Are There Any Solutions?

One question is whether the oldest-old already get too much treatment. Some people believe that we waste precious resources by providing care for dying elderly people to prolong their lives by a few weeks or months. Many of these patients spend most of their time in intensive-care units, connected to feeding tubes and oxygen tanks. Because physicians and family members know that such end-of-life treatments are fruitless, should the funds be redirected to children's health care and other programs that improve schools and decrease domestic violence?

There's no easy fix for our increasing health care costs for older Americans, but one solution might be to redefine old age. If, for example, the definition of old age and the time of mandatory retirement were pushed up to age 70 or later, many productive older Americans could continue to work and contribute to Social Security. As a result, the burden of supporting an aging population wouldn't fall wholly on those employed.

Analysts have suggested other ways to curb health care costs: Reform immigration laws to allow more people to work legally and pay taxes; require higher-income people to pay a larger share of the Medicare costs; standardize health care costs nationally; decrease fraud and waste; and closely monitor doctors' and other medical professionals' unnecessary treatments and deliberately inflating their bills (Schulte et al., 2012; Trumbull, 2013). Providing people, especially boomers, with incentives for healthier behaviors—including reducing smoking and obesity—would also lower health care costs in the future.

MAKING CONNECTIONS

- Would you undergo medical treatments to increase your life span to 120 years? Why or why not?
- Do you think that much longer life spans would help the economy because people could work longer? Or strain the country's health care resources?

CONCLUSION

As this chapter shows, some major *changes* include an aging and diverse population, a growth of multigenerational households, and more years of grandparenting. Because of increased life expectancy, many of us will have more *choices* in how to spend our later years. On the other hand, we will also face *constraints* such as caring for aging family members, coping with our own disabilities, and managing ever-increasing health costs.

On MySocLab

 Study and **Review** on MySocLab

REVIEW QUESTIONS

16.1. Describe how and explain why U.S. life expectancy and the older population are changing.

   1. How does U.S. life expectancy vary by sex, race-ethnicity, and social class? Why?

   2. Why has the old-age dependency ratio increased? And what are its effects?

   3. How is America's older population becoming more racially and ethnically diverse? Why?

16.2. Describe how and explain why physical and mental health and ageism affect older people.

   4. What are the most common reasons for death and physical disability among older Americans?

   5. How do depression, dementia, and Alzheimer's disease differ?

   6. How are ageism and stereotypes interconnected?

16.3. Explain why work patterns and retirement income vary for older people.

   7. Why are many older people still working?

   8. How, specifically, does retirement income differ by gender, race-ethnicity, marital status, and social class? Why?

16.4. Compare grandparenting styles and describe grandparent-grandchild relationships.

   9. What are the five grandparenting styles?

   10. How do custodial, living-with, and day-care grandparents differ in their relationships with their grandchildren?

16.5. Describe sibling relationships in later life.

   11. What are the five most common sibling relationships in later life?

16.6. Describe how people deal with dying, death, and bereavement.

   12. What are the Kübler-Ross stages of dying? Why have scholars criticized her perspective?

   13. Why is physician-assisted suicide controversial?

   14. How do bereavement, grief, and mourning differ?

16.7. Compare widowhood for women and men.

   15. Why are there more widowed women than men?

   16. How, specifically, does widowhood affect older Americans? Why?

16.8. Describe family caregiving in later life and explain how and why caregiving styles differ.

   17. In later life, who are the caregiving recipients? And who are the caregivers?

   18. What, specifically, are the five caregiving styles?

   19. What, specifically, are some of the caregiving satisfactions and strains?

16.9. Explain why there's a competition for resources in caring for our graying population.

   20. What are the financial costs of our aging society?

   21. Are there any solutions in lowering the health care costs of older Americans?

Glossary

A

abortion The expulsion of an embryo or fetus from the uterus.

absolute poverty Not having enough money to afford the basic necessities of life.

acculturation Adapting to the language, values, beliefs, roles, and other characteristics of the host culture.

acquaintance rape Unwanted and forced sexual intercourse of a person who knows or is familiar with the rapist.

acquired immunodeficiency syndrome (AIDS) A degenerative disease that attacks the body's immune system and makes it unable to fight a number of diseases.

adoption Taking a child into one's family through legal means and raising her or him as one's own.

agape Love that is altruistic and self-sacrificing and is directed toward all humankind.

ageism Discrimination against people on the basis of age, particularly against older people.

alimony Monetary payments by one ex-spouse to the other after a divorce (sometimes called *spousal maintenance*).

Alzheimer's disease A progressive, degenerative disorder that attacks the brain and impairs memory, thinking, and behavior.

amniocentesis A procedure in which fluid is withdrawn from a woman's abdomen and analyzed for abnormalities in the fetus.

anorexia nervosa A dangerous eating disorder that is characterized by a fear of obesity.

arranged marriage Parents or relatives choose the children's marriage partners.

artificial insemination (AI) A medical procedure in which semen is introduced artificially into the vagina or uterus during ovulation (sometimes called *donor insemination*, or DI).

asexual Lacking any interest in or desire for sex.

assimilation Conformity of ethnic group members to the dominant group's culture.

assisted reproductive technology (ART) A general term that includes all treatments and procedures that involve handling eggs and sperm to establish a pregnancy.

attachment theory Proposes that infants need to develop a relationship with at least one primary caregiver, usually the mother, for normal social and emotional development.

authoritarian style Parenting that is demanding, controlling, rigid, and punitive.

authoritative style Parenting that is demanding but also supportive and responsive.

autoeroticism Arousal of sexual feeling without an external stimulus.

B

baby boomers People born between 1946 and 1964.

battered-woman syndrome A woman who has experienced many years of physical abuse but feels unable to leave her partner.

bereavement The process of recovery after the death of someone we felt close to.

bigamy Marrying a second person while a first marriage is still legal.

binge eating Consuming an unusually large amount of food and feeling that the eating is out of control.

bisexual A person who is sexually attracted to people of both sexes.

boomerang generation Young adults who move back into their parents' homes after living independently for a while.

bride price The required payment by the groom's family to the bride's family.

bulimia A cyclical pattern of eating binges followed by self-induced vomiting, fasting, excessive exercise, or using laxatives.

C

caregiver A person, paid or unpaid, who attends to the needs of someone who is old, sick, or disabled.

centenarian A person who is 100 years old or older.

child maltreatment A broad range of behaviors that place a child at serious risk or result in serious harm (often used interchangeably with *child abuse*).

child support Monetary payments by the noncustodial parent to the custodial parent to help pay for child-rearing expenses.

chlamydia A sexually transmitted bacterial infection.

chorionic villi sampling (CVS) A prenatal test to determine abnormalities in the fetus.

clinical research The study of individuals or small groups of people who seek help from mental health professionals or other social scientists.

closed adoption The records of the adoption are kept sealed, the birth parent is not involved in the adoptee's life, and the child has no contact with the biological parents or little, if any, information about them.

cognitive development theory Posits that children acquire female or male values on their own by thinking, reasoning, and interpreting information in their environment.

cohabitation A living arrangement in which two unrelated people are unmarried but live together and are in a sexual relationship.

common-law marriage A nonceremonial relationship that people establish by living together.

commuter marriage Spouses live and work in different geographic areas and get together intermittently.

companionate family A type of family built on mutual affection, sexual attraction, compatibility, and personal happiness between husband and wife.

companionate love Love that is characterized by feelings of togetherness, tenderness, deep affection, and supporting each other over time.

conflict-habituated marriage The partners fight both verbally and physically but don't believe that fighting is a good reason for divorce.

conflict theory Examines how groups disagree, struggle for power, and compete for scarce resources such as wealth and power.

content analysis A data-collection method that systematically examines some form of communication.

contraception The prevention of pregnancy by behavioral, mechanical, or chemical means.

corporate welfare An array of direct subsidies, tax breaks, and other favorable treatment that the government has created for businesses.

cult of domesticity An ideology that glorified women's domestic roles.

cunnilingus Oral stimulation of a woman's genitals.

custody A court-mandated ruling regarding which divorced parent will have the primary responsibility for the children's upbringing.

cyber-bullying Willful and repeated harm using computers, cell phones, or other electronic devices.

D

date rape Unwanted, forced sexual intercourse in a dating situation.

dating The process of meeting people socially for possible mate selection.

dating cohabitation A living arrangement in which a couple who spends a great deal of time together eventually decides to move in together.

deindustrialization A social and economic change resulting from the reduction of industrial activity, especially manufacturing.

dementia The loss of mental abilities that most commonly occurs late in life.

depression A mental disorder characterized by persistent sadness and loss of interest in everyday activities.

developmental tasks Specific role expectations and responsibilities that must be fulfilled as people move through the family life cycle.

devitalized marriage The partners were initially in love, one or both may now be unhappy but are committed to staying married.

DEWK (dual-employed with kids) A family in which both parents are employed full time outside the home.

discouraged worker A person who has stopped searching for a job because he or she believes that job hunting is futile.

discretionary income Money remaining after the costs of basic necessities have been paid.

discrimination An *act* that treats people unequally or unfairly.

divorce The legal and formal dissolution of a marriage.

dominant group Physically or culturally distinctive group that has the most economic and political power, the greatest privileges, and the highest social status.

dowry The money, goods, or property a woman brings to a marriage.

dual-earner couple Both partners work outside the home (also called *dual-income, two-income, two-earner,* and *dual-worker* couples).

durable power of attorney for health care (DPAHC) A legal document that permits a person appointed by the patient to make end-of-life decisions.

dying trajectory The speed with which a person dies.

E

ecological theory Examines how a family influences and is influenced by its environment.

economy A social institution that determines how a society produces, distributes, and consumes goods and services.

egalitarian family system Both partners share power and authority about equally.

egg freezing A procedure that allows women to store their eggs for future use.

elder mistreatment A single or repeated act, or failing to do something, by a caregiver that results in harm or a risk of harm to an older person (also called *elder abuse*).

emotional abuse Aggressive behavior that threatens, monitors, or controls a partner.

endogamy A cultural practice that requires marrying within one's group (often used interchangeably with *homogamy*).

endometriosis A condition in which tissue spreads outside the womb and attaches itself to other pelvic organs.

engagement The formalization of a couple's decision to marry.

equity theory Proposes that an intimate relationship is satisfying and stable if both partners see it as equitable and mutually beneficial.

eros Love based on beauty and physical attractiveness.

ethnic group People who identify with a common national origin or cultural heritage.

evaluation research The process of determining whether a social intervention has produced the intended result (also known as *program evaluation*).

exogamy A cultural practice that requires marrying outside one's group (often used interchangeably with *heterogamy*).

experiment A carefully controlled artificial situation that allows researchers to manipulate variables and measure the effects.

expressive role The supportive and nurturing role of the wife or mother who sustains the family unit.

extended family A family that consists of parents and children as well as other kin, such as uncles and aunts, nieces and nephews, cousins, and grandparents.

F

familism A cultural belief that family relationships take precedence over the concerns of individual family members.

family An intimate group of two or more people who (1) live together in a committed relationship, (2) care for one another and any children, and (3) share activities and close emotional ties.

family development theory Examines the changes that families experience over the lifespan.

family life cycle The transitions that a family makes as it moves through a series of stages or events.

family of orientation The family into which a person is born or adopted.

family policy The measures that governments take to improve the well-being of families.

family of procreation The family a person forms by marrying and having or adopting children.

family systems theory Views the family as a functioning unit that solves problems, makes decisions, and achieves collective goals.

familycide Murdering one's spouse, ex-spouse, children, or other relatives before attempting or committing suicide.

father–stepmother family All the children are biological children of the father and stepchildren of the mother.

fellatio Oral stimulation of a man's penis.

female infanticide The intentional killing of baby girls because of a preference for sons.

feminist theories Examine social, economic, and political inequality between women and men in society.

feminization of poverty The likelihood that female heads of households will be poor.

fertility drugs Medications that stimulate the ovaries to produce eggs.

fertility rate The number of live children born per year per 1,000 women ages 15 to 44.

fetal alcohol spectrum disorders (FASD) A range of permanent birth defects caused by a mother's use of alcohol during pregnancy.

fictive kin A family in which nonrelatives are accepted as part of a family.

field research Data are collected by systematically observing people in their natural surroundings.

filter theory Posits that people sift eligible mates according to specific criteria and thus reduce the pool of potential partners to a small number of candidates.

flextime Scheduling arrangement that permits employees to change their daily arrival and departure times.

foster home An out-of-home placement in which adults raise children who aren't their own.

G

gender The learned attitudes and behaviors that characterize women and men.

gender identity An individual's perception of himself or herself as masculine or feminine.

gender ideology Attitudes regarding the appropriate roles, rights, and responsibilities of women and men in society.

gender pay gap The overall income difference between women and men in the workplace (also called the *wage gap, pay gap,* and *gender wage gap*).

gender roles The characteristics, attitudes, feelings, and behaviors that society expects of males and females.

gender script How society says someone is supposed to act because of her or his sex.

gender stereotype Expectations about how people will look, act, think, and feel based on their sex.

generalized other People who don't have close ties to a child but who influence the child's internalization of society's norms and values.

genetic engineering A set of technologies that can change the makeup of cells by manipulating genetic material to make an organism better in some way.

gerontologist A scientist who studies the biological, psychological, and social aspects of aging.

glass ceiling Attitudinal and organizational workplace obstacles that prevent women from advancing to leadership positions.

glass escalator Men who enter female-dominated occupations and receive higher wages and faster promotions.

globalization The growth and spread of investment, trade, production, communication, and new technology around the world.

grief The emotional response to loss.

H

half sibling Brothers or sisters who share only one biological or adoptive parent.

heterogamy Dating or marrying someone with social characteristics that differ from your own (sometimes called *exogamy*).

heterosexism The belief that heterosexuality is superior to and more natural than homosexuality.

heterosexual A person who is sexually attracted to people of the opposite sex.

homogamy Dating or marrying someone with similar social characteristics (sometimes called *endogamy*).

homophobia A fear and hatred of homosexuality.

homosexual A person who is sexually attracted to people of the same sex.

hormones Chemical substances secreted into the bloodstream by endocrine glands.

hospice A place for the care of terminally ill patients.

human immunodeficiency virus (HIV) The virus that causes AIDS.

hypergamy Marrying up to a higher social class.

hypogamy Marrying down in social class.

I

identity bargaining The process of partners negotiating adjustments to their new married roles.

in vitro fertilization (IVF) The surgical removal of eggs from a woman's ovaries, fertilizing them in a petri dish with sperm from her husband or another donor, and transferring the embryos into the woman's uterus.

incest taboo Cultural norms and laws that forbid sexual intercourse between close blood relatives, such as brother and sister, father and daughter, or mother and son.

income Amount of money a person receives, usually through wages or salaries.

infant mortality rate The number of babies under age 1 who die per 1,000 live births in a given year.

infertility The inability to conceive a baby.

instrumental role The breadwinner role of the father or husband who provides food and shelter for the family.

intergenerational ambivalence Contradictions that arise both from kinship roles and personal emotions.

intersexuals People whose medical classification at birth isn't clearly male or female.

intimate partner violence (IPV) Abuse between two people in a close relationship.

J

joint custody Children divide their time between their parents, who share decisions about the children's upbringing (sometimes called *dual residence custody*).

joint stepfamily At least one child is the biological child of both parents, at least one child is the biological child of only one parent and the stepchild of the other parent, and no other type of child is present.

K

kinship system A network of people who are related by marriage, blood, or adoption.

L

labor unions Organized groups that seek to improve wages, benefits, and working conditions.

latchkey kids Children who return home after school and are alone until a parent or another adult arrives.

latent functions Purposes and activities that are unintended, unrecognized, and not immediately obvious.

later-life family A family that is beyond the child-rearing years and has launched the children or a child-free family beginning to plan for retirement.

life expectancy The average number of years a person can expect to live.

living will A legal document that specifies the medical treatments a person would like to receive if incapacitated.

ludus Love that is carefree and casual, "fun and games."

M

machismo A concept of masculinity that stresses attributes such as dominance, assertiveness, pride, and sexual prowess.

macro-level perspective A social science perspective that focuses on large-scale patterns and processes that characterize society as a whole.

mania Love that is obsessive, jealous, and possessive.

manifest functions Purposes and activities that are intended, recognized, and clearly evident.

marital burnout The gradual deterioration of love and ultimate loss of an emotional attachment between partners.

marital rape A man forces his wife to have unwanted sexual intercourse (sometimes called *spousal rape* or *wife rape*).

marital roles The specific ways that married people define their behavior and structure their time.

marriage A socially approved mating relationship.

marriage market A process in which prospective spouses compare the assets and liabilities of eligible partners and choose the best available mate.

marriage squeeze A sex imbalance in the ratio of available unmarried women and men.

masturbation Sexual self-pleasuring that involves some form of direct physical stimulation.

maternal gatekeeping A mother's behavior that encourages or discourages a father's involvement in family matters.

matriarchal family system The oldest females control cultural, political, and economic resources.

matrilineal Children trace their family descent through their mother's line, and property is passed on to female heirs.

matrilocal residence pattern Newly married couples live with the wife's family.

medicalization Defining a nonmedical condition or behavior as an illness, disorder, or disease that requires medical treatment.

Medicare A federal health insurance program for people age 65 and older that provides almost universal health coverage.

micro-level perspective A social science perspective that focuses on people's social interaction patterns in specific settings.

minority group People who may be treated differently or unequally because of their physical or cultural characteristics, such as gender, sexual orientation, religion, or skin color.

miscegenation Marriage or sexual relations between a man and a woman of different races.

monogamy One person is married exclusively to another person.

motherhood penalty Pay gap between women who are mothers and women who aren't mothers (also called a *motherhood wage penalty* and *mommy penalty*).

mother–stepfather family All the children are biological children of the mother and stepchildren of the father.

mourning The customary outward expression of grief.

multigenerational household A home in which three or more generations live together.

N

neolocal residence pattern Newly married couples set up their own residence.

no-fault divorce Neither partner has to establish the guilt or wrongdoing of the other.

nonprobability sample There is little or no attempt to get a representative cross-section of a population.

norm A culturally defined rule for behavior.

nuclear family A family made up of a wife, a husband, and their biological or adopted children.

O

occupational sex segregation Channeling women and men into different types of jobs (also called *occupational gender segregation*).

offshoring Sending work or jobs to another country to cut a company's costs at home (sometimes called *international outsourcing* and *offshore outsourcing*).

old-age dependency ratio The number of working-age adults ages 18 to 64 for every person age 65 and older who's not in the labor force (sometimes called the *elderly support ratio*).

oldest-old People age 85 and older.

old-old People between ages 75 and 84.

open adoption The practice of sharing information and maintaining contact between biological and adoptive parents throughout the child's life.

P

parenting style A general approach to interacting with and disciplining children.

passive-congenial marriage The partners have little emotional investment in the marriage and few expectations of each other.

patriarchal family system The oldest males control cultural, political, and economic resources.

patrilineal Children trace their family descent through their father's line, and property is passed on to male heirs.

patrilocal residence pattern Newly married couples live with the husband's family.

peer group People who are similar in age, social status, and interests.

pelvic inflammatory disease (PID) An infection of the uterus that spreads to the fallopian tubes, ovaries, and surrounding tissues.

permissive style Parenting that is usually warm, responsive, and indulgent, but not demanding.

physical abuse Threatening, trying, or hurting a partner using physical force.

pluralism Maintaining aspects of immigrants' original cultures while living peacefully with the host culture.

polygamy A woman or man has two or more spouses.

polyvictimization Experiencing multiple kinds of victimization.

popular culture Beliefs, practices, activities, and products that are widely shared among a population in everyday life.

population Any well-defined group of people (or things) that researchers want to know something about.

postpartum depression (PPD) A serious illness that can occur up to a year after childbirth.

poverty threshold The minimum income level that the federal government considers necessary for basic subsistence (also called a *poverty line*).

power The ability to impose one's will on others.

pragma Love that is rational and based on practical considerations, such as compatibility and perceived benefits.

preimplantation genetic diagnosis (PGD) A procedure that enables physicians to identify genetic diseases in the embryo before implantation.

prejudice An *attitude* that prejudges people, usually in a negative way.

premarital cohabitation A living arrangement in which a couple tests its relationship before getting married.

primary group A small group of people who are characterized by close, long-lasting, intimate, and face-to-face interaction.

probability sample Each person (or thing) has an equal chance of being chosen because the selection is random.

propinquity Geographic closeness.

Q

qualitative research A data-collection process that examines and interprets nonnumerical material.

quantitative research A data-collection process that focuses on a numerical analysis of people's responses or specific characteristics.

R

racial-ethnic group People with distinctive racial and cultural characteristics.

racial group People who share physical characteristics, such as skin color, that

members of a society consider socially important.

racial socialization Parents teach their children to negotiate race-related barriers and experiences in a racially stratified society and to take pride in their ancestry.

racism Beliefs that one's own racial group is inherently superior to others.

relative poverty Not having enough money to maintain an average standard of living.

role The obligations and expectations attached to a particular status or position in society.

role conflict The frustrations and uncertainties a person experiences when the expectations of two or more roles are incompatible.

role model A person we admire and whose behavior we imitate.

role overload Feeling overwhelmed by multiple commitments.

role strain Conflicts that someone feels *within* a role.

S

same-sex marriage A legally recognized marriage between two people of the same biological sex (also called *gay marriage*).

sample A group of people (or things) that are representative of the population that researchers want to study.

sandwich generation Taking care of one's own children and aging parents.

secondary analysis An examination of data that have been collected by someone else.

secondary group A temporary collection of people who are characterized by formal, impersonal, and short-term relationships and work together to achieve common tasks or activities.

self-disclosure Open communication in which one person offers his or her honest thoughts and feelings to another person in the hope that truly open communication will follow.

semi-open adoption There is communication between the adoptive parents, birth parents, and adopted children, but through a third party (sometimes called *mediated adoption*).

separation Living apart before getting a divorce.

serial cohabitation Living with different sexual partners over time.

serial monogamy Individuals marry several people, but one at a time.

sex The biological characteristics with which we are born and that determine whether we are male or female.

sex ratio The proportion of men to women in a country or group.

sexism An attitude or behavior that discriminates against one sex, usually females, based on the assumed superiority of the other sex.

sexual abuse Threatening or forcing a partner to take part in a sex act when she or he doesn't consent.

sexual identity Awareness of ourselves as male or female and the ways that we express sexual values, attitudes, feelings, and beliefs.

sexual orientation A preference for sexual partners of the same sex, the opposite sex, both sexes, or neither sex.

sexual response A physiological reaction to sexual stimulation.

sexual script Specifies the formal or informal norms for acceptable or unacceptable sexual activity.

sexually transmitted diseases (STDs) Observable symptoms that occur after a sexually transmitted infection.

sexually transmitted infections (STIs) Illnesses transmitted through sexual activity.

siblicide Killing a brother or sister.

significant others People in our primary groups who play an important role in our socialization.

social class A group of people who have a similar standing or rank based on wealth, education, power, prestige, and other valued resources.

social exchange theory Proposes that people seek through their interactions to maximize their rewards and minimize their costs.

social integration The social bonds that people have with others and the community at large.

social learning theory Posits that people learn attitudes, beliefs, and behaviors through social interaction.

Social Security A public retirement pension system administered by the federal government.

socialization The process of acquiring the language, accumulated knowledge, attitudes, beliefs, and values of one's society and culture and learning the social and interpersonal skills needed to function effectively in society.

sociobiology The study of how biology affects social behavior.

socioeconomic status (SES) An overall ranking of a person's position in society based on income, education, and occupation.

sole custody One parent is responsible for raising the child; the other parent has specified visitation rights.

split custody The children are divided between the parents either by sex or the children's choice.

stepfamily A household in which two adults who are biological or adoptive parents (heterosexual, gay, or lesbian) with a child from a previous relationship marry or cohabit.

stepsibling Brothers or sisters who share a biological or adoptive parent and a stepparent.

storge Love that is slow-burning, peaceful, and affectionate.

structural functional theory Examines how a society's interdependent parts work together to ensure its survival (often shortened to *functionalism*).

substance abuse An overindulgence in and dependence on a drug or other chemical

that harms an individual's physical and mental health.

substitute marriage A long-term commitment between two people who don't plan to marry.

surrogacy An arrangement in which a woman carries and delivers a child for another person or couple.

surveys Data-collection methods that systematically collect information from respondents through questionnaires or interviews.

symbolic interaction theory Examines the everyday behavior of individuals.

T

telecommuting Working remotely through electronic linkups to a central office.

theory A set of statements that explains why a particular phenomenon occurs.

total fertility rate (TFR) The average number of children born to a woman during her lifetime.

total marriage The partners participate in each other's lives at all levels and have little tension or unresolved hostility.

transgender people A term that encompasses transsexuals, intersexuals, and transvestites.

transsexuals People who are born with one biological sex but choose to live their life as another sex.

transvestites People who cross-dress at times but don't necessarily consider themselves a member of the opposite sex.

trial marriage An arrangement in which people live together to find out what marriage might be like.

two-person single career A spouse participates in the other's career behind the scenes without pay or direct recognition.

U

underemployed worker A person who has a part-time job but would rather work full time or whose job is below his or her experience, skill, and educational level.

unintended pregnancy A pregnancy that is either *mistimed* (occurs sooner than desired) or unwanted.

uninvolved style Parenting that is neither supportive nor demanding because parents are indifferent.

V

validation Showing respect for a person who has a different opinion or point of view.

vital marriage The partners have a close relationship, resolve conflicts quickly through compromise, and often make sacrifices for each other.

W

wealth Money and economic assets that a person or family owns.

work A physical or mental activity that accomplishes or produces something, either goods or services.

working poor People who spend at least 27 weeks in the labor force but whose wages fall below the official poverty level.

Y

young-old People between ages 65 and 74.

References

The references that are new to this edition are printed in blue.

A

A profile of the working poor, 2010. 2012. Bureau of Labor Statistics, March.

AARP. 2012. To be a bride again at 100. *AARP Bulletin*, February 22, 4.

AAUW. 2013. The simple truth about the gender pay gap.

AAUW. 2013. Violence Against Women Act finally reauthorized. *Outlook* (Spring/Summer): 6.

ABDULRAHIM, R. 2008. A match-making tradition with an up-to-date twist. *Los Angeles Times*, December 26.

ABEL, E. R. 1991. *Who cares for the elderly? Public policy and the experience of adult daughters.* Philadelphia: Temple University Press.

ABMA, J. C., G. M. MARTINEZ, AND C. E. COPEN. 2010. Teenagers in the United States: Sexual activity, contraceptive use, and childbearing, National Survey of Family Growth 2006–2008. *Vital Health Statistics* 23 (30): 1–57.

ABORTION VIEWS BY RELIGIOUS AFFILIATION. 2009. January 15.

ABRAHAMS, G., AND S. AHLBRAND. 2002. *Boy v. girl? How gender shapes who we are, what we want, and how we get along.* Minneapolis: Free Spirit.

ABUDABBEH, N. 1996. ARAB FAMILIES. In *Ethnicity and family therapy*, 2nd ed., eds. M. McGoldrick, J. Giordano, and J. K. Pearce, 333–46. New York: Guilford.

ACADEMY OF MEDICAL ROYAL COLLEGES. 2011. Induced abortion and mental health: A systematic review of the mental health outcomes of induced abortion, including their prevalence and associated factors. National Collaborating Centre for Mental Health, December.

ACEVEDO, B. P., AND A. ARON. 2009. Does a long-term relationship kill romantic love? *Review of General Psychology* 13 (March): 59–65.

ACIERNO, R., M. HERNANDEZ, A. B. AMSTADTER, H. S. RESNICK, K. STEVE, W. MUZZY, AND D. G. KILPATRICK. 2010. Prevalence and correlates of emotional, physical, sexual, and financial abuse and potential neglect in the United States: The national elder mistreatment study. *American Journal of Public Health* 100 (February): 292–97.

ACIERNO, R., M. HERNANDEZ-TEJADA, W. MUZZY, AND K. STEVE. 2009. National elder mistreatment study. National Criminal Justice Reference Service, March.

ACKERMAN, D. 1994. *A natural history of love.* New York: Random House.

ACS, G., AND M. MARTINEZ-SCHIFERL. 2012. Identifying those at greater risk of long-term unemployment. Urban Institute Unemployment and Recovery Project, June.

ACUNA, R. 1988. *Occupied America: A history of Chicanos*, 3rd ed. New York: Harper & Row.

ADAMS, B. 1980. *The family.* Chicago: Rand McNally.

ADAMS, B. N. 2004. Families and family study in international perspective. *Journal of Marriage and Family* 66 (December): 1076–88.

ADAMS, B. N., AND R. A. SYDIE. 2001. *Sociological theory.* Thousand Oaks, CA: Pine Forge Press.

ADAMS, J. S. 2012. Federal judge forwards racially charged email about Obama. *Great Falls Tribune*, March 1.

ADAMSON, P. 2012. Measuring child poverty: New league tables of child poverty in the world's rich countries. UNICEF, Report Card 10, May.

Adding up the government's total bailout tab. 2011. *New York Times*, July 24.

ADDO, F. R., AND D. T. LICHTER. 2013. Marriage, marital history, and black-white wealth differentials among older women. *Journal of Marriage and Family* 75 (April): 342–62.

ADIMORA, A., AND V. SCHOENBACH. 2005. Social context, sexual networks, and racial disparities in rates of sexually transmitted infections. *Journal of Infectious Diseases* 191, S115–S122.

ADLER, S. M. 2003. Asian-American families. In *International encyclopedia of marriage and family*, 2nd ed., Vol. 2, ed. J. J. Ponzetti, Jr., 82–91. New York: Macmillan.

ADMINISTRATION ON AGING. 2012. A profile of older Americans: 2012.

AFIFI, T. O., N. P. MOTA, P. DASIEWICZ, H. L. MACMILLAN, AND J. SAREEN. 2012. Physical punishment and mental disorders: Results from a nationally representative US sample. *Pediatrics* 130 (August): 184–92.

AHITUV, A., AND R. LERMAN. 2004. Job turnover, wage rates, and marital stability: How are they related? The Urban Institute, November.

AHRONS, C. 2004. *We're still family.* New York: HarperCollins.

AHRONS, C. R. 2006. Family ties after divorce: Long-term implications for children. *Family Process* 46 (March): 53–65.

AHRONS, C. R. 2011. Commentary on "Reconsidering the 'good divorce.'" *Family Relations* 60 (December): 528–32.

AHRONS, C. R., AND R. H. RODGERS. 1987. *Divorced families: A multidisciplinary developmental view.* New York: Norton.

AINSWORTH, M., ET AL. 1978. *Patterns of attachment: A psychological study of the strange situation.* Hillsdale, NJ: Erlbaum.

AIZENMAN, N. C. 2005. In Afghanistan, new misgivings about an old but risky practice. *Washington Post*, April 17, A16.

AJROUCH, K. 1999. Family and ethnic identity in an Arab-American community. In *Arabs in America: Building a new future*, ed. M. W. Suleiman, 129–39. Philadelphia: Temple University Press.

AKERS, A. Y., E. B. SCHWARZ, S. BORRERO, AND G. CORBIE-SMITH. 2010. Family discussions about contraception and family planning: A qualitative exploration of black parent and adolescent perspectives. *Perspectives on Sexual and Reproductive Health* 42 (September): 160–67.

AKERS, A. Y., M. A. GOLD, T. COYNE-BEASLEY, AND G. CORBIE-SMITH. 2012. A qualitative study of rural black adolescents' perspectives on primary STD prevention strategies. *Perspectives on Sexual and Reproductive Health* 44 (June): 92–99.

AKITUNDE, A. 2013. Single baby boomers love dating and their freedom (study). *Huffington Post*, February 13.

ALBAS, D., and C. ALBAS. 1987. The pulley alternative for the wheel theory of the development of love. *International Journal of Comparative Sociology* 28 (3–4): 223–27.

ALBERT, B., S. BROWN, AND C. M. FLANNIGAN, EDS. 2003. 14 and younger: The sexual behavior of young adolescents. The National Campaign to Prevent Teen Pregnancy.

ALCINDOR, Y. 2012. Should alimony laws be changed? *USA Today*, January 5.

ALCOHOL AND PUBLIC HEALTH. 2011. Centers for Disease Control and Prevention, October 28.

ALCOHOL USE AND HEALTH. 2011. Centers for Disease Control and Prevention, October 28.

ALFORD, J. R., P. K. HATEMI, J. R. HIBBING, N. G. MARTIN, AND L. J. EAVES. 2011. The politics of mate choice. *Journal of Politics* 73 (April): 362–79.

ALI, L. 2008. Having kids makes you happy. *Newsweek*, July 7/July 14, 62–63.

ALINI, E. 2007. In Italy, hard to get the kids to move out. *Christian Science Monitor*, November 15, 7.

AL-JADDA, S. 2006. Seeking love, American Muslim style. *Christian Science Monitor*, February 14, 9.

AL-JASSEM, D. 2011. Women in polygamous marriages suffering psychological torture. March 8, ArabNews.

ALLAN, J. 2002. *Because I love you: The silent shadow of child sexual abuse.* Charlottesville, VA: Virginia Foundation for the Humanities Press.

ALLEGRETTO, S. A., K. JACOBS, AND L. LUCIA. 2011. The wrong target: Public sector unions and state budget deficits. UC Berkeley Labor Center, October.

ALLEN, J. 2012. Partners' main source of happiness around the globe: Poll. Reuters, February 14.

ALLEN, K. R., E. H. HUSSER, D. J. STONE, AND C. E. JORDAL. 2008. Agency and error in young adults' stories of sexual decision making. *Family Relations* 57 (October): 517–29.

ALLEN, R. E. S., AND J. L. WILES. 2013. How older people position their late-life childlessness: A qualitative study. *Journal of Marriage and Family* 75 (February): 206–20.

ALLEN, S. M., AND A. J. HAWKINS. 1999. Maternal gatekeeping: Mothers' beliefs and behaviors that inhibit greater father involvement in family work. *Journal of Marriage and the Family* 61 (February): 199–212.

ALLGOR, C. 2002. *Parlor politics: In which the ladies of Washington help build a city and a government.* Charlottesville: University of Virginia Press.

ALSEVER, J. 2007. In the computer dating game, room for a coach. *New York Times*, March 11, 5.

ALTON, B. G. 2001. You think being a dad is a good deal? *Business Week*, April 2, 20.

ALTONJI, J. G., S. CATTAN, AND I. WARE. 2010. Identifying sibling influence on teenage substance use. National Bureau of Economic Research, October.

ALTSTEIN, H. 2006. For adoption, leave race out of the discussion. *Baltimore Sun*, January 25, 15A.

ALVAREZ, L. 2006. (Name her) is a liar and a cheat. *New York Times* (February 16): E1–E2.

ALVEAR, M. 2003. The annual rite: Dumbing down love. *Christian Science Monitor*, February 14, 11.

ALZHEIMER'S ASSOCIATION. 2013. 2013 Alzheimer's disease facts and figures.

AMATO, P. 2004. The future of marriage. In *Vision 2004: What is the future of marriage?* eds., Paul Amato and N. Gonzalez, 99–101. Minneapolis, MN: National Council on Family Relations.

AMATO, P. R. 2003. Reconciling divergent perspectives: Judith Wallerstein, quantitative family research, and children of divorce. *Family Relations* 52 (October): 332–339.

AMATO, P. R. 2007. Divorce and the well-being of adults and children. *Family Focus* 52 (December): F3–F4, F18.

AMATO, P. R. 2010. Research on divorce: Continuing trends and new developments. *Journal of Marriage and Family* 72 (June): 650–66.

AMATO, P. R., A. BOOTH, D. R. JOHNSON, AND S. J. ROGERS. 2007. *Alone together: How marriage in America is changing.* Cambridge, MA: Harvard University Press.

AMATO, P. R., AND B. HOFFMAN. 2010. Divorce and the well-being of adults and children. *Family Focus*, Winter, F11–F13.

AMATO, P. R., AND B. HOHMANN-MARRIOTT. 2007. A comparison of high- and low-distress marriages that end in divorce. *Journal of Marriage and Family* 69 (August): 621–38.

AMATO, P. R., J. B. KANE, AND S. JAMES. 2011. Reconsidering the "good divorce." *Family Relations* 60 (December): 511–24.

AMATO, P. R., AND J. CHEADLE. 2005. The long reach of divorce: Divorce and child well-being across three generations. *Journal of Marriage and Family* 67 (February): 191–206.

AMATO, P. R., AND T. D. AFIFI. 2006. Feeling caught between parents: Adult children's relations with parents and subjective well-being. *Journal of Marriage and Family* 68 (February): 222–35.

AMBERT, A.-M. 2001. *The effect of children on parents*, 2nd ed. New York: Haworth.

AMBROSE, E. 2010. All you need is love . . . and a healthy credit report. *Baltimore Sun*, February 14, 18.

AMBROSE, E. 2010. Some good financial reasons for getting married. *Baltimore Sun*, December 19, 1, 3.

AMERICAN ACADEMY OF PEDIATRICS. 1998. Guidance for effective discipline. *Pediatrics* 101 (April): 723–728.

AMERICAN ACADEMY OF PEDIATRICS. 2001. Children, adolescents, and television. *Pediatrics* 107 (February): 423–26.

AMERICAN ACADEMY OF PEDIATRICS. 2012. Policy statement: Emergency contraception. *Pediatrics* 130 (December 1): 1174–82.

AMERICAN COLLEGE OF OBSTETRICIANS AND GYNECOLOGISTS. 2012. Intimate partner violence. *Obstetrics & Gynecology* 119 (February): 412–17.

AMERICAN COUNCIL ON EDUCATION. 2010. *Minorities in higher education: Twenty-fourth status report 2010.*

AMERICAN HOSPITAL ASSOCIATION. 2007. When I'm 64: How boomers will change health care.

AMERICAN HUMANE ASSOCIATION. 2001. Answers to common questions about child abuse and neglect.

AMERICAN INDIAN AND ALASKA NATIVE HERITAGE MONTH: NOVEMBER 2012. 2012. U.S. Census Bureau News, CB12-FF.22, October 25.

AMERICAN KENNEL CLUB. 2006. AKC survey finds dog owners looking for canine qualities in human partners. January 30.

AMERICAN LAW INSTITUTE. 2002. *Principles of the law of family dissolution: Analysis and recommendations.* New York: Matthew Bender & Company.

AMERICAN PSYCHOLOGICAL ASSOCIATION. 2011. Answers to your questions: About transgender people, gender identity, and gender expression.

AMERICAN RHETORIC ONLINE SPEECH BANK. 2004. Bill Cosby—address at the NAACP on the 50th anniversary of *Brown v. Board of Education.* May 17.

AMERICAN SOCIETY FOR AESTHETIC PLASTIC SURGERY. 2012. Cosmetic surgery national data bank statistics.

AMERICAN SOCIOLOGICAL ASSOCIATION. 1999. *Code of ethics and policies and procedures of the ASA committee on professional ethics.*

AMERICAN WAY OF DEATH, THE. 2013. *The Economist*, June 29, 30.

AMERICA'S FAMILIES AND LIVING ARRANGEMENTS. 2012. U.S. Census Bureau, Detailed tables.

AN, R., AND R. STURM. 2012. School and residential neighborhood food environment and diet among California youth. *American Journal of Preventive Medicine* 42 (February): 129–35.

ANANAT, E. O., AND G. MICHAELS. 2008. The effect of marital breakup on the income distribution of women and children. *Journal of Human Resources* 43 (3), 611–29.

ANDERSEN, M., AND D. H. WITHAM. 2011. *Thinking about women*, 9th ed. Upper Saddle River, NJ: Pearson.

ANDERSON, C. A., et al. 2003. The influence of media violence on youth. *Psychological Science in the Public Interest* 4 (December): 81–110.

ANDERSON, E. 1999. *Code of the street: Decency, violence, and the moral life of the inner city.* New York: Norton.

ANDERSON, J. Q., AND L. RAINIE. 2010. The future of social relations. Pew Research Center, July 2.

ANDERSON, K. L. 2010. Conflict, power, and violence in families. *Journal of Marriage and Family* 72 (June): 726–42.

ANDERSON, K. L. 2013. Why do we fail to ask "why" about gender and intimate partner violence? *Journal of Marriage and Family* 75 (April): 314–18.

ANDERSON, S., C. COLLINS, S. KLINGER, AND S. PIZZIGATI. 2011. Executive excess 2011: The massive CEO rewards for tax dodging. Institute for Policy Studies, August 31.

ANDERSSON, G., T. NOACK, A. SEIERSTAD, AND H. WEEDON-FEKJAER. 2006. The demographics of same-sex marriages in Norway and Sweden. *Demography* 43 (February): 79–98.

ANN LANDERS. 2000. *Washington Post*, May 9, C11.

ANNUAL STATISTICAL SUPPLEMENT. 2013. Appendix C: Poverty data.

ANOREXIA NERVOSA AND RELATED EATING DISORDERS, INC. 2006. Statistics: How many people have eating disorders? January 16.

ANTONUCCI, T. C., H. AKIYAMA, AND A. MERLINE. 2001. Dynamics of social relationships in midlife. In *Handbook of midlife development*, ed. M. E. Lachman, 571–98. New York: Wiley.

APPELBAUM, B., AND R. GEBELOFF. 2012. Even critics of safety net increasingly depend on it. *New York Times*, February 11.

APTER, T. 2009. *What do you want from me?: Learning to get along with in-laws.* New York: W. W. Norton.

AQUILINO, W. S. 2006. The non-custodial father-child relationship from adolescence into young adulthood. *Journal of Marriage and Family* 68 (November): 929–46.

ARAB AMERICAN INSTITUTE FOUNDATION. 2012a. Demographics. Washington, DC.

ARAB AMERICAN INSTITUTE FOUNDATION. 2012b. Quick facts about Arab Americans. Washington, DC.

ARD, K. L., AND H. J. MAKADON. 2011. Addressing intimate partner violence in lesbian, gay, and transgender patients. *Journal of General Internal Medicine* 26 (August): 930–33.

Are high house prices hurting women more than men? 2013. *The Economist*, July 13, 39–40.

ARENDELL, T. 1997. A social constructionist approach to parenting. In *Contemporary parenting: Challenges and issues*, ed. T. Arendell, 1–44. Thousand Oaks, CA: Sage.

ARIÈS, P. 1962. *Centuries of childhood.* New York: Vintage.

ARMARIO, C. 2005. More Muslims find online dating a good match. *Christian Science Monitor*, January 19, 16.

ARMSTRONG, E. 2004a. Gay marriages unite, and divide, families. *Christian Science Monitor*, May 20, 4–5.

ARMSTRONG, E. 2004b. Should she pop the question? *Christian Science Monitor* (February 13): 1, 11.

ARMSTRONG, E. A., L. HAMILTON, AND P. ENGLAND. 2010. Is hooking up bad for young women? *Contexts* 9 (Summer): 23–27.

ARMSTRONG, E. A., P. ENGLAND, and A. C. K. FOGARTY. 2012. Accounting for women's orgasm and sexual enjoyment in college hookups and relationships. *American Sociological Review* 77 (June): 435–62.

ARONSON, E. 1995. *The social animal*, 7th ed. New York: W. H. Freeman.

ASHBURN, E. 2007. A race to rescue native tongues. *Chronicle of Higher Education*, September 28, B15.

ASHBURN, E. 2007. A race to rescue native tongues. *Chronicle of Higher Education*, September 28, B15.

ASI, M., AND D. BEAULIEU. 2013. Arab households in the United States: 2006–2010. American Community Survey Briefs, U.S. Census Bureau, May.

ASIAN/PACIFIC AMERICAN HERITAGE MONTH: MAY 2013. 2013. U.S. Census Bureau News, CB13-FF.09, March 27.

ASIANS FASTEST-GROWING RACE OR ETHNIC GROUP IN 2012, Census Bureau reports. 2013. Newsroom, June 13.

ASK AMY. 2008. Ring on finger isn't the kind she wants. *Baltimore Sun*, January 18, 6C.

ASSOCIATED PRESS. 2010. 2010 Census, extreme edition: Remote housing requires creative transportation. Published in *Washington Post*, March 23, B3.

ASTHMA IN THE U.S. 2011. Centers for Disease Control and Prevention, May.

ASWAD, B. C. 1997. Arab American families. In *Families in cultural context: Strengths and challenges in diversity*, ed. M. K. DeGenova, 213–47. Mountain View, CA: Mayfield.

ASWAD, B. C. 1999. Attitudes of Arab immigrants toward welfare. In *Arabs in America: Building a new future*, ed. M. W. Suleiman, 177–91. Philadelphia: Temple University Press.

AT&T. 2012. 3% of teens say they text & drive; 77% say adults warn against risks, but text & drive "all the time." May 14.

ATCHLEY, R. C., AND A. S. BARUSCH. 2004. *Social forces and aging: An introduction to social gerontology*, 10th ed. Belmont, CA: Wadsworth.

ATKINSON, M. P., T. N. GREENSTEIN, AND M. M. LANG. 2005. For women, breadwinning can be dangerous: Gendered resource theory and wife abuse. *Journal of Marriage and Family* 67 (December): 1137–48.

AUD, S., W. HUSSAR, F. JOHNSON, G. KENA, E. ROTH, E. MANNING, X. WANG, AND J. ZHANG. 2012. *The condition of education 2012*. U.S. Department of Education, National Center for Education Statistics, Washington DC.

AUMANN, K., E. GALINSKY, AND K. MATOS. 2011. The new male mystique. Families and Work Institute.

AUNOLA, K., AND J.-E. NURMI. 2005. The role of parenting styles in children's problem behavior. *Child Development* 76 (November/December): 1144–59.

AUSTER, C. J., AND C. S. MANSBACH. 2012. The gender marketing of toys: An analysis of color and type of toy on the Disney store website. *Sex Roles* 67 (October): 375–88.

AUSTRALIAN PASSPORTS NOW OFFER "M" FOR MALE, "F" FOR FEMALE OR "X." 2011. *Baltimore Sun*, September 18, 24.

Authorities crack down on rogue pain clinics. 2010. National Public Radio, July 15.

AVELLAR, S., AND P. SMOCK. 2005. The economic consequences of the dissolution of cohabiting unions. *Journal of Marriage and Family* 67 (May): 315–27.

AYCOCK, S., AND Z. R. W. STARR. 2010. Balancing the risk and safety needs of domestic violence victims. CASA for Children, October.

B

BABBIE, E. 2013. *Social research counts.* Belmont, CA: Wadsworth.

BABCOCK, J. C., J. WALTZ, N. S. JACOBSON, AND J. M. GOTTMAN. 1993. Power and violence: The relation between communication patterns, power discrepancies, and domestic violence. *Journal of Consulting and Clinical Psychology* 61 (1): 40–50.

BACA ZINN, M. 2000. Feminism and family studies for a new century. *Annals of the American Academy of Political and Social Science* 571 (September): 42–56.

BACA ZINN, M., AND A. Y. H. POK. 2002. Tradition and transition in Mexican-origin families. In *Minority families in the United States: A multicultural perspective*, 3rd ed., ed. R. L. Taylor, 79–100. Upper Saddle River, NJ: Prentice Hall.

BACHMAN, J. G., K. N. WADSWORTH, P. M. O'MALLEY, L. D. JOHNSTON, AND J. E. SCHULENBERG. 1997. *Smoking, drinking, and drug use in young adulthood: The impacts of new freedoms and new responsibilities.* Hillsdale, NJ: Erlbaum.

BACK, M. D., S. C. SCHMUKLE, AND B. EGLOFF. 2010. Why are narcissists so charming at first sight? Decoding the narcissism-popularity link at zero acquaintance. *Journal of Personality & Social Psychology* 98 (January): 132–45.

BADGETT, M. V. L., AND J. L. HERMAN. 2011. Patterns of relationship recognition by same-sex couples in the United States. The Williams Institute, November.

BADINTER, E. 2012. *The conflict: How modern motherhood undermines the status of women.* New York: Metropolitan Books.

BAHRAMPOUR, T. 2012. Immigrants lead record tumble in U.S. birthrate. *Baltimore Sun*, December 2, 25.

BAILEY, B. 1988. *From front porch to back seat: Courtship in twentieth-century America.* Baltimore: Johns Hopkins University Press.

BAILEY, W., M. YOUNG, C. KNICKERBOCKER, AND T. DOAN. 2002. A cautionary tale about conducting research on abstinence education: How do state abstinence coordinators define "sexual activity"? *American Journal of Health Education* 33 (September/October): 290–96.

BAKER, C. R., AND S. M. STITH. 2008. Factors predicting dating violence perpetration among male and female college students. *Journal of Aggression, Maltreatment & Trauma* 17 (September): 227–44.

BAKER, L. A., AND J. E. MUTCHLER. 2010. Poverty and material hardship in grandparent-headed households. *Journal of Marriage and Family* 72 (August): 947–62.

BALDAUF, S. 2010. Afraid you'll get Alzheimer's? How to lower the odds. *U.S. News & World Report*, February 10, 48–49.

BALDAUF, S. 2010. In Africa, new heat on gays. *Christian Science Monitor*, December 13, 12.

BALSAM, K. F., AND D. M. SZYMANSKI. 2005. Relationship quality and domestic violence in women's same-sex relationships: The role of minority stress. *Psychology of Women Quarterly* 29 (September): 258–69.

Baltimore Sun. 2012. Elderly man dies in fire at single-family home. December 9, 5.

BANCROFT, L. 2002. *Why does he do that? Inside the minds of angry and controlling men.* New York: Berkley Trade.

BANDURA, A., AND R. H. WALTERS. 1963. *Social learning and personality development.* New York: Holt, Rinehart & Winston.

BANDY, T. 2012. What works for male children and adolescents: Lessons from experimental evaluations of programs and interventions. Child Trends Research Brief, August.

BANDY, T., M. TERZIAN, AND K. A. MOORE. 2013. Measuring associations between symptoms of depression and suicide in adolescence and unhealthy romantic relationships in young adulthood. Child Trends, Research Brief, April 11.

BANERJEE, A., E. DUFLO, M. GHATAK, AND J. LAFORTUNE. 2009. Marry for what: Caste and mate selection in modern India. National Bureau of Economic Research, Working Paper 14958.

BANERJEE, N. 2006. Clergywomen find hard path to bigger pulpit. *New York Times*, August 26, A1, A12.

BANFIELD, EDWARD C. 1974. *The unheavenly city revisited.* Boston: Little, Brown.

BANNER, L. W. 1984. *Women in modern America: A brief history*, 2nd ed. New York: Harcourt Brace Jovanovich.

BARASH, D. P. 2002. Evolution, males, and violence. *Chronicle of Higher Education*, May 24, B7–B9.

BARASH, D. P. 2012. The evolutionary mystery of homosexuality. *Chronicle Review*, November 21, B4–B5.

BARBER, B. K. 1994. Cultural, family, and personal contexts of parent-adolescent conflict. *Journal of Marriage and the Family* 56 (May): 375–86.

BARBER, B. L., AND D. H. DEMO. 2006. The kids are alright (at least, most of them): Links between divorce and dissolution and child well-being. In *Handbook of divorce and relationship dissolution*, eds. M. A. Fine and J. H. Harvey, 289–311. Mahwah, NJ: Lawrence Erlbaum.

BARKIN, S., B. SCHEINDLIN, E. H. IP, I. RICHARDSON, AND S. FINCH. 2007. Determinants of parental discipline practices: A national sample from primary care practices. *Clinical Pediatrics* 46 (January): 64–69.

BARNES, C. 2006. China's "kingdom of women." *Slate*, November 17.

BARNES, G. M., A. S. REIFMAN, M. P. FARRELL, AND B. A. DINTCHEFF. 2000. The effects of parenting on the development of adolescent alcohol misuse: A six-wave latent growth model. *Journal of Marriage and the Family* 62 (February): 175–86.

BARNES, R. 2011. Limits on video games rejected. *Washington Post*, June 28, A1.

BARNETT, M. A., L. V. SCARAMELLA, T. K. NEPPL, L. ONTAI, AND R. D. CONGER. 2010. Intergenerational relationship quality, gender, and grandparent involvement. *Family Relations* 59 (February): 28–44.

BARNETT, M. A., W. R. MILLS-KOONCE, H. GUSTAFSSON, AND M. COX. 2012. Mother-grandmother conflict, negative parenting, and young children's social development in multigenerational families. *Family Relations* 61 (December): 864–77.

BARNETT, R. C., AND C. RIVERS. 1996. *She works, he works: How two-income families are happy, healthy, and thriving.* Cambridge, MA: Harvard University Press.

BARNETT, R. C., A. STEPTOE, AND K. C. GAREIS. 2005. Marital-role quality and stress-related psychobiological indicators. *Annals of Behavioral Medicine* 30: 1 (36–43).

BARNHARDT, L., AND J. SCHARPER. 2007. Dead tot bruised, underfed, police say. *Baltimore Sun*, December 29, 1A, 9A.

BAROT, S. 2012. Governmental coercion in reproductive decision making: See it both ways. *Guttmacher Policy Review* 15 (Fall): 7–12.

BAROVICK, H. 2002. Domestic dads. *Time*, August 15, B4–B10.

BARRET-DUCROCQ, F. 1991. *Love in the time of Victoria: Sexuality, class and gender in nineteenth-century London.* New York: Verso.

BARRETO, M., M. K. RYAN, AND M. T. SCHMITT, EDS. 2009. *The glass ceiling in the 21st century: Understanding barriers to gender equality.* Washington, DC: American Psychological Association.

BARRINGER, H. R., R. W. GARDNER, AND M. J. LEVIN. 1993. *Asians and Pacific Islanders in the United States.* New York: Russell Sage Foundation.

BARTLETT, T. 2007. "I suffer not a woman to teach." *Chronicle of Higher Education*, April 13, A10–A12.

BASKEN, P. 2011. U. of Pennsylvania professor accuses colleagues of slanted research. *Chronicle of Higher Education*, July 12.

BATALOVA, J. 2011. Asian immigrants in the United States. Migration Information Source, May 24.

BATES, M. 2005. Tenured and battered. *Chronicle of Higher Education*, September 9, C1–C4.

BATTAN, M. 1992. *Sexual strategies.* New York: Putnam.

BAUM, K., S. CATALANO, AND M. RAND. 2009. Stalking victimization in the United States. U.S. Department of Justice, Bureau of Justice Statistics, January, NCJ 224527.

BAUM, S., AND K. PAYEA. 2011. Trends in student aid 2011. College Board Advocacy & Policy Center.

BAUMEISTER, R. F., AND K. D. VOHS. 2004. Sexual economics: Sex as female resource for social exchange in heterosexual interactions. *Personality and Social Psychology Review* 8 (4): 339–63.

BAUMEISTER, R. F., AND S. R. WOTMAN. 1992. *Breaking hearts: The two sides of unrequited love.* New York: Guilford.

BAUMRIND, D. 1968. Authoritarian versus authoritative parental control. *Adolescence* 3, 255–72.

BAUMRIND, D. 1989. Rearing competent children. In *Child development today and tomorrow*, ed. W. Damon, 349–78. San Francisco: Jossey-Bass.

BAUMRIND, D. 1991. The influence of parenting styles on adolescent competence and substance use. *Journal of Early Adolescence* 11 (February): 56–95.

BAZAR, E. 2009. Economic casualties pile into tent cities. *USA Today*, May 5.

BAZELON, E. 2009. 2 kids + 0 husbands = family. *New York Times Magazine*, February 1, 30.

BEADLE, A. P. 2012. Teen pregnancies highest in states with abstinence-only policies. ThinkProgress, April 10.

BEARAK, B. 2006. The bride price. *New York Times Magazine*, July 9, 45–49.

BECK, A. T. 1988. *Love is never enough: How couples can overcome misunderstandings, resolve conflicts, and solve relationship problems through cognitive therapy*. New York: Harper & Row.

BECK, M. 2012. Boys starting puberty much sooner. *Wall Street Journal*, October 20, A3.

BECKLES, G. L., AND B. I. TRUMAN. 2011. Education and income—United States, 2005 and 2009. *MMWR* 60 (Suppl, January 14): 13–18.

BEEDE, D., T. JULIAN, D. LANGDON, G. MCKITTRICK, B. KHAN, AND M. DOMS. 2011. Women in STEM: A gender gap to innovation. Economics and Statistics Administration, Issue Brief #04-11, August.

BEGALA, P. 2012. Middle class, R.I.P. *Newsweek*, June 25, 22.

BEGLEY, S. 2009. Ignoring the evidence. Why do psychologists reject science? *Newsweek*, October 12, 30.

BEHNKE, A. O., S. M. MACDERMID, S. L. COLTRANE, R. D. PARKE, AND K. F. WIDAMAN. 2008. Family cohesion in the lives of Mexican American and European American parents. *Journal of Marriage and Family* 70 (November): 1045–59.

BEIL, L. 2012. How much would you pay for three more months of life? *Newsweek*, September 3, 40–44.

BELL, K., M. A. TERZIAN, AND K. A. MOORE. 2012. What works for female children and adolescents: Lessons from experimental evaluations of programs and interventions. Child Trends Research Brief, August.

BELLAH, R. N., R. MADSEN, W. M. SULLIVAN, A. SWIDLER, AND S. M. TIPTON. 1985. *Habits of the heart: Individualism and commitment in American life*. Berkeley: University of California Press.

BELLE, D. 1999. *The after-school lives of children: Alone and with others while parents work*. Mahwah, NJ: Erlbaum.

BELLUCK, P. 2010. As H.I.V. babies come of age, problems linger. *New York Times*, November 5, A1.

BELLUCK, P. 2013. Pregnancy centers gain influence in anti-abortion arena. *New York Times*, January 5, A1.

BELSKY, J. K. 1988. *Here tomorrow: Making the most of life after fifty*. Baltimore: Johns Hopkins University Press.

BENASSI, M. A. 1985. Effects of romantic love on perception of strangers' physical attractiveness. *Psychological Reports* 56 (April): 355–58.

BENDAVID, N. 2013. For Belgium's tormented souls, euthanasia-made-easy beckons. *Wall Street Journal*, June 15–16, A1, A12.

BENNER, C., AND S. JAYARAMAN. 2012. A dime a day: The impact of the Miller/Harkin minimum wage proposal on the price of food. The Food Labor Research Center at the University of California, Berkeley, and the Food Chain Workers Alliance & the Restaurant Opportunities Centers, October 24.

BENNETT, J. 2009. Tales of a modern diva. *Newsweek*, April 6, 42–43.

BENNETT, J., AND J. ELLISON. 2010. "I don't": The case against marriage. *Newsweek*, June 21, 42–45.

BENNETT, R. L., ET AL. 2002. Genetic counseling and screening of consanguineous couples and their offspring: Recommendations of the National Society of Genetic Counselors. *Journal of Genetic Counseling* 11 (April): 97–119.

BENNETTS, L. 2008. The truth about American marriage. *Parade Magazine*, September 21, 4–5.

BENOKRAITIS, N. V., AND J. R. FEAGIN. 1995. *Modern sexism: Blatant, subtle, and covert discrimination*, 2nd ed. Upper Saddle River, NJ: Prentice Hall.

BENOKRAITIS, N. V., ED. 2000. *Feuds about families: Conservative, centrist, liberal, and feminist perspectives*. Upper Saddle River, NJ: Prentice Hall.

BERDAN, S. N. 2012. The world has changed. *New York Times*, January 30.

BERGER, A., E. WILDSMITH, J. MANLOVE, AND N. STEWARD-STRENG. 2012. Relationship violence among young adult couples. Child Trends Research Brief, June.

BERGER, A., J. MANLOVE, E. WILDSMITH, K. PETERSON, AND L. GUZMAN. 2012. What young adults know—and don't know—about women's fertility patterns: Implications for reducing unintended pregnancies. Child Trends, September.

BERGER, E. M. 2008. Postnups. *Forbes Life Executive Woman*, Spring, 54–55.

BERGER, R. 2000. Gay stepfamilies: A triple-stigmatized group. *Families in Society* 81 (5): 504–16.

BERGMAN, P. M. 1969. *The chronological history of the Negro in America*. New York: Harper & Row.

BERK, B. R. 1993. The dating game. *Good House-keeping* (September.): 192, 220–21.

BERKMAN, N. D., ET AL. 2006. Management of eating disorders. Evidence Report/Technology Assessment No. 135. Rockville, MD: Agency for Healthcare Research and Quality.

BERLIN, I. 1998. *Many thousands gone: The first two centuries of slavery in North America*. Cambridge, MA: Belknap Press of Harvard University.

BERMUDEZ, E. 2008. Central American immigrants adopt Mexican ways in U.S. *Los Angeles Times*, November 3.

BERNARD, T. S. 2008. The key to wedded bliss? Money matters. *New York Times*, September 10, SPG-5.

BERNARD, T. S. 2013. In paid family leave, U.S. trails most of the globe. *New York Times*, February 22, B1.

BERNHARD, L. A. 1995. Sexuality in women's lives. In *Women's health care: A comprehensive handbook*, eds. C. I. Fogel and N. F. Woods, 475–95. Thousand Oaks, CA: Sage.

BERNIER, J. C., AND D. H. SIEGEL. 1994. Attention-deficit hyperactivity disorder: A family and ecological systems perspective. *Families in Society: The Journal of Contemporary Human Services* (March): 142–50.

BERNSTEIN, D. E. 2011. Overt vs. covert. *New York Times*, May 22.

BERNSTEIN, E. 2013. Small acts, big love. *Wall Street Journal*, February 12, D1, D4.

BERSAMIN, M. M., D. A. FISHER, S. WALKER, D. L. HILL, AND J. W. GRUBE. 2007. Defining virginity and abstinence: Adolescents interpretations of sexual behaviors. *Journal of Adolescent Health* 41 (August): 182–88.

BERSCHEID, E., K. DION, E. WALSTER, AND G. W. WALSTER. 1982. Physical attractiveness and dating choice: A test of the matching hypothesis. *Journal of Experimental Social Psychology* 1, 173–89.

BHATTACHARYA, S. 2003. Obesity breaks up sperm DNA.

BIALIK, C. 2013. For gays, breaking up is hard to do—Or measure. *Wall Street Journal*, May 4–5, A2.

BIANCHI, S. M., AND M. A. MILKIE. 2010. Work and family research in the first decade of the 21st century. *Journal of Marriage and Family* 72 (June): 705–25.

BIBLARZ, T. J., AND E. SAVCI. 2010. Lesbian, gay, bisexual, and transgender families. *Journal of Marriage and Family* 72 (June): 480–97.

BIEHLE, S. N., AND K. D. MICKELSON. 2012. First-time parents' expectations about the division of childcare and play. *Journal of Family Psychology* 36 (1): 36–45.

BINGE EATING DISORDER. 2008. National Institute of Diabetes and Digestive and Kidney Diseases. June.

BIRDITT, K. S., AND K. L. FINGERMAN. 2005. Do we get better at picking our battles? Age group differences in descriptions of behavioral reactions to interpersonal tensions. *Journals of Gerontology: Psychological Sciences and Social Sciences* 60 (May): P121–P128.

BIRDITT, K. S., E. BROWN, T. L. ORBUCH, AND J. M MCILVANE. 2010. Marital conflict behaviors and implications for divorce over 16 years. *Journal of Marriage and Family* 72 (October): 1188–1204.

BIRDITT, K. S., K. L. FINGERMAN, AND D. M. ALMEIDA. 2005. Age differences in exposure and reactions to interpersonal tensions: A daily diary study. *Psychology and Aging* 20 (June): 330–40.

BIRDITT, K. S., L. M. MILLER, K. L. FINGERMAN, AND E. S. LEFKOWITZ. 2009. Tensions in the parent and adult child relationship: Links to solidarity and ambivalence. *Psychology and Aging* 24 (June): 287–95.

BIRNS, B. 1999. Attachment theory revisited: Challenging conceptual and methodological sacred cows. *Feminism & Psychology* 9 (February): 10–21.

BIRO, F. M., et al. 2010. Pubertal assessment method and baseline characteristics in a mixed longitudinal study of girls. *Pediatrics* 126 (September): e583–e590.

BISHAI, D., ET AL. 2008. Risk factors for unintentional injuries in children: Are grandparents protective? *Pediatrics* 122 (November): e980–e987.

BISSON, M. A., AND T. R. LEVINE. 2009. Negotiating a friends with benefits relationship. *Archives of Sexual Behavior* 38 (February): 66–73.

BITTMAN, M., P. ENGLAND, N. FOLBRE, L. C. SAYER, AND G. MATHESON. 2003. When does gender trump money? Bargaining and time in household work. *American Journal of Sociology* 109 (July): 186–214.

BLACK, M. C., AND M. J. BREIDING. 2008. Adverse health conditions and health risk behaviors associated with intimate partner violence—United States, 2005. *MMWR Weekly*, 57 (February 8): 113–17.

BLACK, M. C., K. C. BASILE, M. J. BREIDING, S. G. SMITH, M. L. WALTERS, M. T. MERRICK, J. CHEN, AND M. R. STEVENS. 2011. *The national intimate partner and sexual violence survey (NISVS): 2010 summary report*. National Center for Injury Prevention and Control, Centers for Disease Control and Prevention.

BLACK, T. 2010. More car jobs shift to Mexico. *Bloomberg Businessweek*, June 28–July 4, 10–11.

Blakeley, K. 2013. 7 things you should consider before getting back together with your ex. *Huffington Post*, March 8.

Blank, R. M. 2011. The supplemental poverty measure: A new tool for understanding U.S. poverty. *Pathways* (Fall): 11–14.

Blau, P. M. 1986. *Exchange and power in social life*, rev. ed. New Brunswick, NJ: Transaction.

Block, S., and L. Petrecca. 2009. For many minorities, saving isn't so easy. *USA Today*, July 6.

Blomfield, J. 2009. Branded with the "Scarlet U." *Newsweek*, March 23, 22.

Bloom, D. E., and J. W. Lorsch. 2012. Viewing U.S. economic prospects through a demographic lens. *The Reporter* 44 (December): 12–17.

Bloomberg News. In China's dating scene, women get pickier. 2012. *Bloomburg Businessweek*, June 18–24, 12, 14–15.

BLS News Release. 2013. The employment situation—April 2013. Bureau of Labor Statistics, May 3.

Bluestein, G. 2005. 78-year-old accused of killing ex-flame. *Washington Post*, June 25, A2.

Bluestone, C., and C. S. Tamis-Le Monda. 1999. Correlates of parenting styles in predominantly working- and middle-class African American mothers. *Journal of Marriage and the Family* 61 (November): 881–93.

Blumenstyk, G. 2009. Company says research it sponsored at Pitt and Hopkins was fraudulent. *Chronicle of Higher Education*, September 4.

Blumstein, P. W. 1975. Identity bargaining and self-conception. *Social Forces* 53 (3): 476–85.

Board of Trustees, The. 2013. *The 2013 annual report of the board of trustees of the federal old-age and survivors insurance and federal disability insurance trust funds.*

Bobroff-Hajal, A. 2006. Why cousin marriages matter in Iraq. *Christian Science Monitor*, December 26, 9.

Bodnar, J. 1985. *The transplanted: A history of immigrants in urban America*. Bloomington: Indiana University Press.

Bogenschneider, K. 1996. An ecological risk/protective theory for building prevention programs, policies, and community capacity to support youth. *Family Relations* 45 (April): 127–38.

Bogenschneider, K. 1997. Parental involvement in adolescent schooling: A proximal process with transcontextual validity. *Journal of Marriage and the Family* 59 (August): 718–33.

Bogenschneider, K., and T. J. Corbett. 2010. Family policy: Becoming a field of inquiry and subfield of social policy. *Journal of Marriage and Family* 72 (June): 783–803.

Bogle, K. A. 2008. *Hooking up: Sex, dating, and relationships on campus*. New York: New York University Press.

Bohannon, P. 1971. *Divorce and after*. New York: Doubleday.

Bolton, E. 2012. Fighting the birth control backlash. AAUW *Outlook*, Spring/Summer, 20–21.

Bond, J. T., Ellen G., Stacy S. Kim, and E. Brownfield. 2005. 2005 National study of employers. Families and Work Institute.

Bonilla-Silva, E. 2009. *Racism without racists: Color-blind racism and the persistence of racial inequality in the United States*, 2nd ed. Boulder, CO: Rowman & Littlefield.

Bonnie, R. J., and R. B. Wallace, eds. 2003. *Elder mistreatment: Abuse, neglect, and exploitation in an aging America*. Washington, DC: The National Academies Press.

Boodman, S. G. 1992. Questions about a popular prenatal test. *Washington Post Health Supplement*, November 3, 10–13.

Boonstra, H. D. 2009. Advocates call for a new approach after the era of "abstinence-only" sex education. *Guttmacher Policy Review* 12 (Winter): 6–11.

Boonstra, H. D. 2012. Progressive *and* pragmatic: The national sexuality education standards for U.S. public schools. *Guttmacher Policy Review* 15 (Spring): 2–7.

Boonstra, H. D., R. B. Gold, C. L. Richards, and L. B. Finer. 2006. Abortion in women's lives. Guttmacher Institute.

Boorstein, M. 2011. Church for single Mormons in Crystal City comes with pressure to marry. *Washington Post*, May 28.

Booth, A., and J. N. Edwards. 1992. Starting over: Why remarriages are more unstable. *Journal of Family Issues* 13 (June): 179–94.

Boren, C. 2010. Tiger Woods' ex-wife Elin Nordegren: "I've been through hell." *Washington Post*, August 25.

Borgerhoff Mulder, M. 2009. Serial monogamy as polygyny or polyandry? Marriage in the Tanzanian Pimbwe. *Human Nature* 20 (Summer): 130–50.

Borland, D. M. 1975. An alternative model of the wheel theory. *Family Coordinator* 24 (July): 289–92.

Bornstein, M. H. 2002. Parenting infants. In *Handbook of parenting*, 2nd ed., Vol. 1: Children and parenting, ed. M. H. Bornstein, 3–43. Mahwah, NJ: Erlbaum.

Bos, H., N. Goldberg, L. van Gelderen, and N. Gartrell. 2012. Adolescents of the U.S. National Longitudinal Lesbian Family Study: Male role models, gender role traits, and psychological adjustment. *Gender & Society* 26 (August): 603–38.

Bosman, J. 2010. Lusty tales and hot sales: Romance e-books thrive. *New York Times*, December 8, A1.

Bostic, J. Q., and M. C. Miller. 2005. When should you worry? *Newsweek*, April 25, 60.

Bowe, J. 2010. *Us: Americans talk about love*. London: Faber & Faber.

Bowlby, J. 1969. *Attachment and loss*, Vol. 1: Attachment. New York: Basic Books.

Bowlby, J. 1984. *Attachment and loss*, Vol. 1, 2nd ed. Harmondsworth, UK: Penguin.

Bradshaw, C., A. S. Kahn, and B. K. Saville. 2010. To hook up or date: Which gender benefits? *Sex Roles* 62 (May): 661–69.

Brady, D., and C. Palmeri. 2007. The pet economy. *Business Week*, August 6, 45–54.

Braithwaite, D. O., P. Schrodt, and L. A. Baxter. 2006. Understudied and misunderstood: Communication in stepfamily relationships. In *Widening the family circle: New research on family communication*, eds. K. Floyd and M. T. Moorman, 153–170. Thousand Oaks, CA: Sage.

Bramlett, M. D., and W. D. Mosher. 2002. Cohabitation, marriage, divorce, and remarriage in the United States. Centers for Disease Control and Prevention, Vital and Health Statistics.

Brander, B. 2004. *Love that works: The art and science of giving*. West Conshohocken, PA: Templeton Foundation Press.

Brandon, E. 2013. Why more Americans are working past age 65. *U.S. News & World Report*, February 11.

Braund, K. E. H. 1990. Guardians of tradition and handmaidens to change: Women's roles in Creek economic and social life during the eighteenth century. *American Indian Quarterly* 14 (Summer): 239–58.

Bravin, J. 2013. Historic win for gay marriage. *Wall Street Journal*, June 27, A1, A4.

Bray, J. H., and J. Kelly. 1998. *Stepfamilies: Love, marriage, and parenting in the first decade*. New York: Broadway.

Brehm, S. S. 1992. *Intimate relationships*, 2nd ed. New York: McGraw-Hill.

Brehm, S. S., R. S. Miller, D. Perlman, and S. M. Campbell. 2002. *Intimate relationships*, 3rd ed. Boston, MA: McGraw-Hill.

Brenner, J., and A. Smith. 2013. 72% of online adults are social networking site users. Pew Research Center, August 8.

Brenoff, A. 2013. How I spy on my kids online. *Huffington Post*, March 22.

Brett, K., W. Barfield, and C. Williams. 2008. Prevalence of self-reported postpartum depressive symptoms—17 states, 2004–2005. *MMWR Weekly* 57 (April 11): 361–66.

Bricker, J., A. B. Kennickell, K. B. Moore, and J. Sabelhaus. 2012. Changes in U.S. family finances from 2007 to 2010: Evidence from the survey of consumer finances. *Federal Reserve Bulletin* 98 (June): 1–80.

Bringing up baby. 1999. *Public Perspective* 10 (October/November): 19.

Brink, S. 2007. This is your brain on love. *Los Angeles Times*, July 30.

Brittingham, A., and G. P. de la Cruz. 2005. We the people of Arab ancestry in the United States. Census 2000 Special Reports, CENSR-21, March.

Brizendine, L. 2006. *The female brain*. New York: Morgan Road Books.

Broadwater, L. 2012. Wells Fargo settles bias suit for $175M. *Baltimore Sun*, July 13, 1, 11.

Broderick, C. B. 1988. To arrive where we started: The field of family studies in the 1930s. *Journal of Marriage and the Family* 50 (August): 569–84.

Broderick, C. B. 1993. *Understanding family process: Basics of family systems theory*. Thousand Oaks, CA: Sage.

Brody, G. H., S. Dorsey, R. Forehand, and L. Armistead. 2002. Unique and protective contributions of parenting and classroom processes to the adjustment of African American children living in single-parent families. *Child Development* 63 (January–February): 274–86.

Bronfenbrenner, U. 1979. *The ecology of human development: Experiments by nature and design*. Cambridge, MA: Harvard University Press.

Bronfenbrenner, U. 1986. Ecology of the family as a context for human development: Research perspectives. *Developmental Psychology* 22: 723–42.

Bronner, E. 2012. Adultery, an ancient crime that remains on many books. *New York Times*, November 15, A12.

Bronte-Tinkew, J., M. E. Scott, and A. Horowitz. 2009. Male pregnancy intendedness and children's mental proficiency and attachment security during toddlerhood. *Journal of Marriage and Family* 71 (November): 1001–1025.

Brooks, D. 2008. The culture of debt. *New York Times*, July 22, 19.

Brotherson, S. E., and W. C. Duncan. 2004. Rebinding the ties that bind: Government efforts to preserve and promote marriage. *Family Relations* 53 (October): 459–68.

Brown, A. 2013. Snapshot: U.S. obesity rate ticking up. Gallup, June 21.

Brown, A. 2013a. Americans more optimistic about a comfortable retirement. Gallup, May 30.

Brown, A. 2013b. In U.S., average retirement age up to 61. Gallup, May 15.

BROWN, A., AND J. M. JONES. 2012. Separation, divorce linked to sharply lower wellbeing. *Gallup*, April 20.

BROWN, E., T. L. ORBUCH, AND J. A. BAUERMEISTER. 2008. Religiosity and marital stability among black American and white American couples. *Family Relations* 57 (April): 172–85.

BROWN, J. D., J. R. STEELE, AND K. WALSH-CHILDERS, EDS. 2002. *Sexual teens, sexual media: Investigating media's influence on adolescent sexuality*. Mahwah, NJ: Lawrence Erlbaum.

BROWN, P. L. 2012. This prom has everything, except for boys. *New York Times*, May 2, A13.

BROWN, P. M. 1995. *The death of intimacy: Barriers to meaningful interpersonal relationships*. New York: Haworth.

BROWN, S. L. 2004. Family structure and child well-being: The significance of parental cohabitation. *Journal of Marriage and Family* 66 (May): 351–67.

BROWN, S. L., AND I-F. LIN. 2012. The gray divorce revolution: Rising divorce among middle-aged and older adults, 1990–2009. National Center for Family & Marriage Research, March.

BROWN, S. L., AND W. D. MANNING. 2011. Counting couples, counting families. National Center for Family & Marriage Research.

BROWN, S. L., J. R. BULANDA, AND G. R. LEE. 2012. Transitions into and out of cohabitation in later life. *Journal of Marriage and Family* 74 (August): 774–93.

BROWNE, A. 1993. Family violence and homelessness: The relevance of trauma histories in the lives of homeless women. *American Journal of Orthopsychiatry* 63 (July): 370–84.

BROWNING, S. W. 1994. Treating stepfamilies: Alternatives of traditional family therapy. In *Stepparenting: Issues in theory, research, and practice*, eds. K. Pasley and M. Ihinger-Tallman, 175–98. Westport, CT: Greenwood.

BRULLIARD, K. 2006. Last rites, tailored to immigrant customs. *Washington Post*, April 24, A1.

BRULLIARD, K. 2009. Which Mrs. Zuma will be South Africa's first lady? *Washington Post*, May 9.

BRYANT, C. M., K. A. W. WICKRAMA, J. BOLLAND, B. M. BRYANT, C. E. CUTRONA, and E. E. STANIK. 2010. Race matters, even in marriage: Identifying factors linked to marital outcomes for African Americans. *Journal of Family Theory & Review* 2 (September): 157–74.

BUFFET, W. 2011. Stop coddling the super-rich. *New York Times*, August 14, B21.

BUHI, E. R., E. M. DALEY, A. OBERNE, S. A. SMITH, T. SCHNEIDER, AND H. J. FUHRMANN. 2010. Quality and accuracy of sexual health information Web sites visited by young people. *Journal of Adolescent Health* 47 (August): 206–08.

BUHLE, M., T. MURPHY, AND J. GERHARD. 2008. *Women and the making of America*, vol. 2. Upper Saddle River, NJ: Prentice Hall.

BULIK, C. M., ET AL. 2006. Prevalence, heritability, and prospective risk factors for anorexia nervosa. *Archive of General Psychiatry* 63 (March): 305–12.

BULLOCK, K. 2005. Grandfathers and the impact of raising grandchildren. *Journal of Sociology and Social Welfare* 32 (March): 43–59.

BUREAU OF LABOR STATISTICS. 2012. Wives who earn more than their husbands, 1987–2011. November 20.

BUREAU OF LABOR STATISTICS. 2013. Labor force statistics from the Current Population Survey, Table 2, household data.

BUREAU OF LABOR STATISTICS AMERICAN TIME USE SURVEY. 2013. American time use survey—2012 results. June 20.

BUREAU OF LABOR STATISTICS ECONOMIC NEWS RELEASE. 2013. Employment situation, July 5.

BUREAU OF LABOR STATISTICS NEWS. 2011. American time-use survey—2010 results. Bureau of Labor Statistics, June 22.

BURGESS, E. W., AND H. J. LOCKE. 1945. *The family: From institution to companionship*. New York: American Book Company.

BURGESS, E. W., H. J. LOCKE, AND M. M. THOMES. 1963. *The family from institution to companionship*. New York: American Book Co.

BURKHART, J. A. 2011. The birth police—Rights of pregnant women and their families. Women's Media Center, April 5.

BURLESON, B. R., AND W. H. DENTON. 1997. The relationships between communication skill and marital satisfaction: Some moderating effects. *Journal of Marriage and the Family* 59 (November): 884–902.

BURR, W. R. 1995. Using theories in family science. In *Research and theory in family science*, eds. R. D. Day, K. R. Gilbert, B. H. Settles, and W. R. Burr, 73–90. Pacific Grove, CA: Brooks/Cole.

BURT, S. A., M. B. DONNELLAN, M. N. HUMBAD, B. M. HICKS, M. McGUE, AND W. G. IACONO. 2010. Does marriage inhibit antisocial behavior? An examination of selection vs. causation via a longitudinal twin design. *Archives of General Psychiatry* 67 (December): 1309–15.

BURTON, L. 2007. Childhood adultification in economically disadvantaged families: A conceptual model. *Family Relations* 56 (October): 329–45.

BURTON, L. M., AND C. B. STACK. 1993. Conscripting kin: Reflections on family, generation, and culture. In *Family, self, and society: Toward a new agenda for family research*, eds. P. A. Cowan, D. Field, D. A. Hansen, A. Skolnick, and G. E. Swanson, 115–42. Hillsdale, NJ: Erlbaum.

BURTON, L. M., D. BONILLA-SILVA, V. RAY, R. BUCKELEW, AND E. H. FREEMAN. 2010. Critical race theories, colorism, and the decade's research on families of color. *Journal of Marriage and Family* 72 (June): 440–59.

BUSBY, D., M. BRANDT, C. GARDNER, AND N. TANIGUCHI. 2005. The family of origin parachute model: Landing safely in adult romantic relationships. *Family Relations* 54 (April): 254–64.

BUSBY, D. M., T. B. HOLMAN, AND E. WALKER. 2008. Pathways to relationship aggression between adult partners. *Family Relations* 57 (January): 72–83.

BUSHMAN, B. J., R. F. BAUMEISTER, S. THOMAES, E. RYU, S. BEGEER, AND S. G. WEST. 2009. Looking again, and harder, for a link between low self-esteem and aggression. *Journal of Personality* 77 (April): 570–78.

BUSS, D. M. 2000. *The dangerous passion: Why jealousy is as necessary as love and sex*. New York: Free Press.

BUSS, D. M., AND D. P. SCHMITT. 1993. Sexual strategies theory: An evolutionary perspective on human mating. *Psychological Review* 100 (April): 204–32.

BUSS, D. M., R. J. LARSEN, AND D. WESTEN. 1996. Commentary: Sex differences in jealousy: Not gone, not forgotten, and not explained by alternative hypotheses. *Psychological Science* 7 (November): 373–75.

BUSSEY, K., AND A. BANDURA. 1992. Self-regulatory mechanisms governing gender development. *Child Development* 63 (October): 1236–50.

BYERS, E. S., AND H. A. SEARS. 2012. Mothers who do and do not intend to discuss sexual health with their young adolescents. *Family Relations* 61 (December): 851–63.

BYNUM, L., et al. 2010. Adverse childhood experiences reported by adults—Five states, 2009. *Morbidity and Mortality Weekly Report* 59 (49): 1609–13.

BYRD, A. 2013. The single girl's second shift. *Marie Claire*, July, 87–89.

BYRON, E. 2012. A truce in the chore wars. *Wall Street Journal*, December 5, D1–D2.

C

CACIOPPO, J. T., ET AL. 2002. Loneliness and health: Potential mechanisms. *Psychosomatic Medicine* 64 (May/June): 407–17.

CAFFARO, J. V., AND A. CONN-CAFFARO. 1998. *Sibling abuse trauma: Assessment and intervention strategies for children, families, and adults*. New York: Haworth.

CAHILL, S., M. BOTZER, AND G. CHEUNG. 2007. Black, Latino, Asian same-sex couples have most to gain, lose from marriage fight. *Peacework* 34.

CALASANTI, T. 2007. Bodacious Berry, potency wood and the aging monster: Gender and age relations in anti-aging ads. *Social Forces* 86 (September): 335–55.

CALDWELL, M. A., AND L. A. PEPLAU. 1990. The balance of power in lesbian relationships. In *Perspectives on the family: History, class, and feminism*, ed., C. Carlton, 204–15. Belmont, CA: Wadsworth.

CALLAHAN, M. 2009. The rise of "familycide:" What's behind the shocking trend. *Washington Post*, April 26, 23.

CALLAWAY, E. 2012. Fathers bequeath more mutations as they age. *Nature* 488 (August 23): 439.

CALLIS, R. R., AND L. B. CAVANAUGH. 2009. Census Bureau reports on residential vacancies and homeownership. U.S. Census Bureau News, CB09-57, April 27.

CALVERT, S. 2006. South Africans defend the price of tying the knot. *Baltimore Sun*, July 24, 1A, 10A.

CAMARILLO, A. 1979. *Chicanos in a changing society: From Mexican pueblos to American barrios in Santa Barbara and southern California, 1848–1930*. Cambridge, MA: Harvard University Press.

CAMP DUSH, C. M. 2013. Marital and cohabitation dissolution and parental depressive symptoms in fragile families. *Journal of Marriage and Family* 75 (February): 91–109.

CAMPO-FLORES, A. 2013. New checks on alimony pay. *Wall Street Journal*, April 17, A3.

CANCIAN, F. M. 1990. The feminization of love. In *Perspectives on the family: History, class, and feminism*, ed. C. Carlson, 171–85. Belmont, CA: Wadsworth.

CAPLAN, J. 2005. Metrosexual matrimony. *Time*, October 3, 67.

CARD, D., AND L. GIULIANO. 2011. Peer effects and multiple equilibria in the risky behavior of friends. National Bureau of Economic Research, May.

CAREY, B. 2004. Long after Kinsey, only the brave study sex. *New York Times*, November 9, F1.

CAREY, B. 2005. Experts dispute Bush on gay-adoption issue. *New York Times*, January 29, A16.

CAREY, B. 2008. Psychiatrists revise the book of human troubles. *New York Times*, December 18, 1.

CARLSON, K. S., AND P. F. GJERDE. 2009. Preschool personality antecedents of narcissism in adolescence and young adulthood: A 20-year longitudinal study. *Journal of Research in Personality* 43 (August): 570–78.

CARLSON, M., S. MC LANAHAN, AND P. ENGLAND. 2004. Union formation in fragile families. *Demography* 41 (May): 237–61.

CARMALT, J. H., J. CAWLEY, K. JOYNER, AND J. SOBAL. 2008. Body weight and matching with a physically attractive romantic partner. *Journal of Marriage and Family* 70 (December): 1287–96.

CARMON, I. 2011. Why does everything seem to be going wrong for women's progress? AlterNet, December 21.

CARNAGEY, N. L., AND CRAIG A. ANDERSON. 2005. The effects of reward and punishment in violent video games on aggressive affect, cognition, and behavior. *Psychological Science* 16 (November): 882–89.

CARNEY, S. 2010. Cash on delivery. *Mother Jones*, March/April, 69–73.

CARNOY, M., AND D. CARNOY. 1997. *Fathers of a certain age: The joys and problems of middle-aged fatherhood*. Minneapolis, MN: Fairview Press.

CARPENTER, C. 2008. "Tough love" pervades self-help books. *Christian Science Monitor*, February 7, 17.

CARPENTER, D., T. FULLER, AND L. ROBERTS. 2013. Wikileaks and Iraq body count: The sum of parts may not add up to the whole. A comparison of two tallies of Iraqi civilian deaths. *Prehospital and Disaster Medicine* 28 (June): 223–29.

CARPENTER, S. 2008. No recession for online dating sites. *Los Angeles Times*, December 28, www.latimes.com (accessed December 29, 2008).

CARR, D. 2004. The desire to date and remarry among older widows and widowers. *Journal of Marriage and Family* 66 (November): 1051–68.

CARR, D. 2010. Cheating hearts. *Contexts* 9 (Summer): 58–60.

CARR, D. 2012. The social stratification of older adults' preparations for end-of-life health care. *Journal of Health and Social Behavior* 53 (3): 297–312.

CARR, D., C. B. WORTMAN, AND K. WOLFF. 2006. How older Americans die today: Implications for surviving spouses. In *Spousal bereavement in late life*, eds. D. Carr, R. M. Nesse, and C. B. Wortman, 49–78. New York: Springer.

CARRASQUILLO, H. 2002. The Puerto Rican family. In *Minority families in the United States: A multicultural perspective*, 3rd ed., ed. R. L. Taylor, 101–13. Upper Saddle River, NJ: Prentice Hall.

CARRELL, S. E., AND M. L. HOEKSTRA. 2009. Domino effect. *Education Next*, Summer, 59–63.

CARRELL, S. E., M. HOEKSTRA, AND J. E. WEST. 2010. Is poor fitness contagious? Evidence from randomly assigned friends. National Bureau of Economic Research, November.

CARTER, M., D. HENRY-MOSS, L. HOCK-LONG, A. BERGDALL, AND K. ANDES. 2010. Heterosexual anal sex experiences among Puerto Rican and black young adults. *Perspectives on Sexual and Reproductive Health* 42 (December): 267–74.

CARTER, S., AND J. SOKOL. 1993. *He's scared, she's scared: Understanding the hidden fears that sabotage your relationships*. New York: Delacorte.

CASLER, L. 1974. *Is marriage necessary?* New York: Human Sciences Press.

CASPI, A., ET AL. 2003. Influence of life stress on depression: Moderation by a polymorphism in the 5-HTT gene. *Science* 301 (July 18): 386–89.

CASSELMAN, B. 2013. Low wages blur job picture. *Wall Street Journal*, August 3–4, A1–A2.

CASSELMAN, B. 2013. Male nurses earn more. *Wall Street Journal*, February 26, A2.

CATALANO, S. 2007. Intimate partner violence in the United States. Bureau of Justice Statistics.

CATALANO, S. 2012. Intimate partner violence 1993–2010. Bureau of Justice Statistics, November.

CATALANO, S. 2012. Stalking victims in the United States—Revised. Bureau of Justice Statistics, September.

CATALYST. 2013. Women CEOs of the Fortune 1000. May 8.

CATCHING UP. 2013. *The Economist*, January 12, 67–68.

CATE, R. M., AND S. A. LLOYD. 1992. *Courtship*. Thousand Oaks, CA: Sage.

CAULKINS, J. P., A. HAWKEN, B. KILMER, AND M. A. R. KLEIMAN. 2012. Important facts about marijuana legalization. RAND, July 13.

CAVAN, R. S., AND K. H. RANCK. 1938. *The family and the Depression: A study of one hundred Chicago families*. Chicago: University of Chicago Press.

CAVANAGH, S. E., AND A. C. HUSTON. 2008. The timing of family instability and children's social development. *Journal of Marriage and Family* 70 (December): 1258–69.

CAVANAGH, S. E., S. R. CRISSEY, AND R. K. RALEY. 2008. Family structure history and adolescent romance. *Journal of Marriage and Family* 70 (August): 698–714.

CDC FACT SHEET. 2011. 10 ways STDs impact women differently from men. Centers for Disease Control and Prevention, April.

CDC FACT SHEET. 2013. Incidence, prevalence, and cost of sexually transmitted infections in the United States. Centers for Disease Control and Prevention, February.

CDC NATIONAL PREVENTION INFORMATION NETWORK. 2012. STDs today. Centers for Disease Control Prevention, October 16.

CDC VITAL SIGNS TOWN HALL TELECONFERENCE. 2012. Binge drinking transcript. Centers for Disease Control, January 17.

CECH, E., B. RUBINEAU, S. SILBEY, AND C. SERON. 2011. Professional role confidence and gendered persistence in engineering. *American Sociological Review* 70 (October): 641–69.

CELLINI, S. R., S. MCKERNAN, AND C. RATCLIFFE. 2008. The dynamics of poverty in the United States: A review of data, methods, and findings. *Journal of Policy Analysis and Management* 27 (Summer): 577–605.

2010 census mail participation rate map. 2010. U.S. Census Bureau, 2010.

CENSUS BUREAU RELEASES ESTIMATES OF SAME-SEX MARRIED COUPLES. 2011. September 27.

CENTER FOR AMERICAN WOMEN AND POLITICS. 2013. Women in elective office 2013.

CENTER FOR BEHAVIORAL HEALTH STATISTICS AND QUALITY. 2012. 8.6 million adults had suicidal thoughts in past year. *Data Spotlight*, Substance Abuse and Mental Health Services Administration, September.

CENTERS FOR DISEASE CONTROL AND PREVENTION, AMERICAN SOCIETY FOR REPRODUCTIVE MEDICINE, SOCIETY FOR ASSISTED REPRODUCTIVE TECHNOLOGY. 2012. *2010 Assisted reproductive technology fertility clinic success rates report*. Atlanta, GA: U.S. Department of Health and Human Services.

CENTERS FOR DISEASE CONTROL AND PREVENTION. 2010. Diagnoses of HIV infection and AIDS in the United States and dependent areas, 2010. *HIV Surveillance Report*, vol. 22.

CENTERS FOR DISEASE CONTROL AND PREVENTION. 2012. Trends in current cigarette smoking among high school students and adults, United States, 1965–2011. December 7.

CENTERS FOR DISEASE CONTROL AND PREVENTION. 2012. Understanding teen dating violence.

CENTERS FOR DISEASE CONTROL AND PREVENTION. 2012a. HIV in the United States: At a glance. July.

CENTERS FOR DISEASE CONTROL AND PREVENTION. 2012b. *Sexually transmitted disease surveillance 2011*. Atlanta, GA: U.S. Department of Health and Human Services.

CENTERS FOR MEDICARE & MEDICAID SERVICES. 2012. National health expenditure projections: 2010–2020. April 11.

CENTRAL INTELLIGENCE AGENCY. 2012. *The world factbook: Sex ratio*.

CENTRAL STATISTICS ORGANIZATION AND UNICEF. 2012. Afghanistan multiple indicator cluster survey 2010–2011. Final Report. Kabul.

CESI DEBT SOLUTIONS. 2010. National survey reveals truth about marriage and credit cards. July.

CHA, Y. 2009. Reinforcing the "separate spheres" arrangement: The effect of spousal overwork on the employment of men and women in dual-earner households. *American Sociological Review*, forthcoming.

CHADWICK MARTIN BAILEY. 2013. The evolution of dating: Match.com and Chadwick Martin Bailey behavioral studies uncover a fundamental shift. April 20.

CHAFE, W. H. 1972. *The American woman: Her changing social, economic, and political roles, 1920–1970*. New York: Oxford University Press.

CHAMBERS, A. L., AND A. KRAVITZ. 2011. Understanding the disproportionately low marriage rate among African Americans: An amalgam of sociological and psychological constraints. *Family Relations* 60 (December): 648–60.

CHAMBERS, V. 2003. *Having it all? Black women and success*. New York: Doubleday.

CHAN, S. 1997. Families with Asian roots. In *Developing cross-cultural competence: A guide for working with children and families*, 2nd ed., eds. E. W. Lynch and M. J. Hanson, 251–353. Baltimore: Paul H. Brookes.

CHAN, S. 1999. Families with Asian roots. In *Developing cross-cultural competence: A guide for working with children and their families*, 2nd ed., eds. E. W. Lynch and M. J. Hanson, 251–344. Baltimore: Paul H. Brookes.

CHANDRA, A., G. A. MARTINEZ, W. D. MOSHER, J.C. ABMA, AND J. JONES. 2005. Fertility, family planning, and reproductive health of U.S. women: Data from the 2002 national survey of family growth. *Vital and Health Statistics* (Series 23, No. 25). Hyattsville, MD: National Center for Health Statistics.

CHANDRA, A., W. D. MOSHER, AND C. COPEN. 2011. Sexual behavior, sexual attraction, and sexual identity in the United States: Data from the 2006–2008 National Survey of Family Growth. *National Health Statistics Reports*, no. 36, March 3.

CHAO, R., AND V. TSENG. 2002. Parenting of Asians. In *Handbook of parenting*, 2nd ed., Vol. 4: Social conditions and applied parenting, ed. M. H. Bornstein, 59–93. Mahwah, NJ: Erlbaum.

CHARLES, K. K., E. HURST, AND A. KILLEWALD. 2011. Marital sorting and parental wealth. National Bureau of Economic Research, January.

CHARLES, M. 2011. What gender is science? *Contexts* 10 (Spring): 22–28.

CHARLES, S. T., AND L. L. CARSTENSEN. 2002. Marriage in old age. In *Inside the American couple: New thinking/new challenges*, eds. M. Yalom and L. L. Carstensen, 236–54. Berkeley: University of California Press.

CHARLES, V. E., C. B. POLIS, S. K. SRIDHARA, AND R. W. BLUM. 2008. Abortion and long-term mental health outcomes: A systematic review of the evidence. *Contraception* 78 (December): 436–50.

CHEAH, C. S. L., C. Y. Y. LEUNG, M. TAHSEEN, AND D. SCHULTZ. 2009. Authoritative parenting among immigrant Chinese mothers of preschoolers. *Journal of Family Psychology* 23 (June): 311–20.

CHELALA, C. 2002. World violence against women a great unspoken pandemic. *Philadelphia Inquirer*, November 4.

CHEN, J., AND D. T. TAKEUCHI. 2011. Intermarriage, ethnic identity, and perceived social standing among Asian women in the United States. *Journal of Marriage and Family* 73 (August): 876–88.

CHEN, Z.-Y., AND H. B. KAPLAN. 2001. Intergenerational transmission of constructive parenting. *Journal of Marriage and Family* 63 (February): 17–31.

CHENG, D., AND I. L. HORON. 2010. Intimate-partner homicide among pregnant and postpartum women. *Obstetrics & Gynecology* 115 (June): 1181–86.

CHENG, Y. A., AND N. S. LANDALE. 2010. Adolescent overweight, social relationships and the transition to first sex: Gender and racial variations. *Perspectives on Sexual and Reproductive Health* 43 (March): 6–15.

CHERLIN, A. J. 2009. *The marriage-go-round: The state of marriage and the family in America today*. New York: Alfred A. Knopf.

CHERLIN, A. J. 2010. Demographic trends in the United States: A review of research in the 2000s. *Journal of Marriage and Family* 72 (June): 403–19.

CHESHIRE, T. C. 2001. Cultural transmission in urban American Indian families. *American Behavioral Scientist* 44 (May): 1528–35.

CHESHIRE. T. 2006. American Indian families: Strength and answers from our past. In *Families in global and multicultural perspective*, 2nd ed., eds. B. B. Ingoldsby and S. D. Smith, 315–27. Thousand Oaks, CA: Sage.

CHESLER, P. 2006. The failure of feminism. *Chronicle of Higher Education*, February 26, B12.

CHESLEY, N., AND B. FOX. 2012. E-mail's use and perceived effect on family relationship quality: Variations by gender and race/ethnicity. *Sociological Focus* 45 (1): 63–84.

CHESNEY-LIND, M., AND L. PASKO. 2004. *The female offender: Girls, women, and crime*, 2nd ed. Thousand Oaks, CA: Sage.

CHILD MALTREATMENT. 2012. Centers for Disease Control and Prevention.

CHILD TRENDS DATA BANK. 2012. Attitudes toward spanking: Indicators on children and youth. October.

CHILD TRENDS DATA BANK. 2012. Dating. May.

CHILD TRENDS DATA BANK. 2012. Parental expectations for their children's academic attainment: Indicators on children and youth. July.

CHILD WELFARE INFORMATION GATEWAY. 2007. Recognizing child abuse and neglect: Signs and symptoms.

CHILD WELFARE INFORMATION GATEWAY. 2008. Child abuse neglect fatalities: Statistics and interventions. March.

CHILD WELFARE INFORMATION GATEWAY. 2009. Foster care statistics. U.S. Department of Health and Human Services, Administration for Children and Families. February.

CHILD WELFARE INFORMATION GATEWAY. 2013. Preventing child maltreatment and promoting well-being: A network for action.

Childhood Obesity Facts. 2013. Centers for Disease Control and Prevention, February 19.

CHILDREN'S BUREAU. 2012. Trends in foster care and adoption—FY 2002–FY 2011. U.S. Department of Health and Human Services, Administration on Children, Youth, and Families.

CHILDREN'S DEFENSE FUND. 2005. *State of America's children 2005*. Washington, DC: Children's Defense Fund.

CHILDREN'S DEFENSE FUND. 2010. *State of America's children*. Washington, DC.

CHILDREN'S DEFENSE FUND. 2012. *State of America's children handbook*. Washington, DC.

CHIN, E. 2001. *Purchasing power: Black kids and American consumer culture*. Minneapolis: University of Minnesota Press.

Chips off the Old Block. 2013. *The Economist*, January 12, 53–54.

CHMIELEWSKI, D. C., AND C. ELLER. 2010. Disney restyles "Rapunzel" to appeal to boys. *Los Angeles Times*, March 9.

CHO, W., AND S. E. CROSS. 1995. Taiwanese love styles and their association with self-esteem and relationship quality. *Genetic, Social, and General Psychology Monographs* 121: 283–309.

CHOICE, P., AND L. K. LAMKE. 1997. A conceptual approach to understanding abused women's stay/leave decisions. *Journal of Family Issues* 18 (May): 290–314.

CHOWDHURY, A. 2013. 'Til recession do us part: Booms, busts and divorce in the United States. *Applied Economics Letters* 20 (3): 255–261.

CHRIQUI, E. 2013. Make my Valentine's Day jewelry conflict-free. *Huffington Post*, February 8.

CHRISLER, A., AND K. A. MOORE. 2012. What works for disadvantaged and adolescent parent programs: Lessons from experimental evaluations of social programs and interventions for children. Child Trends Fact Sheet, August.

CHRISTAKIS, E. 2012. The overwhelming maleness of mass homicide. *Time*, July 24.

CHRISTAKIS, N. A., AND J. H. FOWLER. 2007. The spread of obesity in a large social network over 32 years. *New England Journal of Medicine* 357 (July 26): 370–79.

CHRISTAKIS, N. A., AND P. D. ALLISON. 2006. Mortality after the hospitalization of a spouse. *New England Journal of Medicine* 354 (February 16): 719–30.

CHRISTIAN, L., S. KEETER, K. PURCELL, AND A. SMITH. 2010. Assessing the cell phone challenge to survey research in 2010. Pew Research Center, May 20.

CHRISTIANSEN, S. 2009. The changing culture of Japanese fatherhood. *Family Focus* 54 (Spring): F12, F14.

CHRISTIE-MIZELL, C. A., E. M. PRYOR, AND E. R. B. GROSSMAN. 2008. Child depressive symptoms, spanking, and emotional support: Differences between African American and European American youth. *Family Relations* 57 (July): 335–50.

CHRISTINA, G. 2011. Puritan pundits should chill out—Here are 5 reasons I'm happy I've had lots of casual sex. *AlterNet*, August 28.

CHRISTINA, G. 2011. Wealthy, handsome, strong, packing endless hard-ons: The impossible ideals men are expected to meet. Independent Media Institute, June 20.

CHRISTOPHER, F. S. 2001. *To dance the dance: A symbolic interactional exploration of premarital sexuality*. Mahwah, NJ: Erlbaum.

CHRISTOPHER, F. S., AND T. S. KISLER. 2004. Sexual aggression in romantic relationships. In *The handbook of sexuality in close relationships*, eds. J. Harvey, A. Wenzel, and S. Sprecher, 287–409. Mahwah, NJ: Lawrence Erlbaum.

CHU, H. 2006. Wombs for rent, cheap. *Los Angeles Times*, April 19, A1.

CHU, K. 2013. China factories try karaoke, speed dating to keep workers. *Wall Street Journal*, May 3, B1.

CHU, K., AND E. RAMSTAD. 2012. Asian women fight barriers. *Wall Street Journal*, July 2, B4.

CHUA, A. 2011. *Battle hymn of the tiger mother*. New York: Penguin Press.

CHUNG, E. K., L. MATHEW, A. C. ROTHKOPF, I. T. ELO, J. C. COYNE, AND J. F. CULHANE. 2009. Parenting attitudes and infant spanking: The influence of childhood experiences. *Pediatrics* 124 (August): e278–e286.

CHUNG, G. H., M. B. TUCKER, AND D. TAKEUCHI. 2008. Wives' relative income production and household male dominance: Examining violence among Asian American enduring couples. *Family Relations* 57 (April): 227–38.

CIA World Factbook. 2012. Country comparison: Infant mortality rate.

CIA World Factbook. 2012. Literacy. October 4.

CIA World Factbook. 2013. Country comparison: Total fertility rate.

CLARK, A. 2008. Tribes strive to save native tongues. *Christian Science Monitor*, May 23, 2.

CLARK, C. L., P. R. SHAVER, AND M. F. ABRAHAMS. 1999. Strategic behaviors in romantic relationship initiation. *Personality and Social Psychology Bulletin* 25: 707–20.

CLARK, J. M. 1999. *Doing the work of love: Men & commitment in same-sex couples*. Harriman, TN: Men's Studies Press.

CLARK, M. 2011. Shocking Congo rape statistics obscure key points: Husbands rape more than soldiers, rebels do. *Christian Science Monitor*, May 12.

CLARKE, J. N. 2010. The domestication of health care: Health advice to Canadian Mothers 1993–2008 in *Today's Parent*. *Family Relations* 59 (April): 170–79.

CLARKE, T. C., AND D. BLACKWELL. 2013. Quickstats. *Morbidity and Mortality Weekly Report* 62 (7): 38.

CLARK-FLORY, T. 2012. How risky is oral sex? *Salon*, August 19.

CLEARFIELD, M. W., AND N. M. NELSON. 2006. Sex differences in mothers' speech and play behavior with 6-, 9-, and 14-month-old infants. *Sex Roles* 54 (January): 127–37.

CLEMENT, S. 2011. Workplace harassment drawing wide concern. *Washington Post*, November 16.

CLIFTON, D. 2012. Most women in Afghanistan justify domestic violence. Population Reference Bureau, September.

CLIFTON, D., AND A. FROST. 2011. The world's women and girls: 2011 data sheet. Population Reference Bureau.

CLIFTON, D., AND C. FELDMAN-JACOBS. 2011. 2011 international day of zero tolerance to female genital mutilation/cutting. Population Reference Bureau, February.

CLOKE, B. 2012. Why do men have such trouble with intimacy? AlterNet, August 7.

CLOUD, D. S. 2013. On base, suicide a team fight. *Baltimore Sun*, April 14, 21.

CLOUD, D. S. 2013. Pentagon adds benefits for same-sex couples. *Baltimore Sun*, February 12, 6.

CLUNIS, D. M., AND G. D. GREEN. 2000. *Lesbian couples: A guide to creating healthy relationships*. Seattle: Seal.

COATES, T-N. 2008. This is how we lost to the white man. *Atlantic Monthly*, May.

COBB, M. 2012. *Single: Arguments for the uncoupled*. New York: New York University Press.

COCHRANE, M. 2012. Fewer Americans report healthy eating habits in 2011. Gallup, April 11.

COHAN, C. I., AND S. KLEINBAUM. 2002. Toward a greater understanding of the cohabitation effect: Premarital cohabitation and marital communication. *Journal of Marriage and Family* 64 (February): 180–92.

COHANY, S. 2009. Ranks of discouraged workers and others marginally attached to the labor force rise during recession. Issues in Labor Statistics, U.S. Bureau of Labor Statistics, April.

COHEN, D. L. 2013. A pricier path to parenthood. *Baltimore Sun*, April 21, 2.

COHEN, J. 2013. Gay marriage support hits new high in Post-ABC poll. *Washington Post*, March 18.

COHEN, N. 2011. Define gender gap? Look up Wikipedia's contributor list. *New York Times*, January 31, A1.

COHEN, P. N. 2012. Recession and divorce in the United States: Economic conditions and the odds of divorce, 2008–2010. Maryland Population Research Center, April.

COHEN, S. A. 2008. Abortion and women of color: The bigger picture. *Guttmacher Policy Review* 11 (Summer): 2–5, 12.

COHN, D. 2011. India census offers three gender options. Pew Research Center, February 7.

COHN, D. 2013. Love and marriage. Pew Research Center, February 13.

COHN, D., J. S. PASSEL, W. WANG, AND G. LIVINGSTON. 2011. Barely half of U.S. adults are married—A record low. Pew Research Center, December 14.

COHN, L. 2003. One child, four parents. *Christian Science Monitor*, February 19, 11–13.

COHN, L. 2005. Remarriage after retirement. *Christian Science Monitor*, June 8, 11–12.

COLAPINTO, J. 1997. The true story of John/Joan. *Rolling Stone*, December 11, 54–73, 92–97.

COLAPINTO, J. 2001. *As nature made him: The boy who was raised as a girl*. New York: Harper Perennial.

COLAPINTO, J. 2004. What were the real reasons behind David Reimer's suicide? *Slate*, June 3.

COLE, M. G., AND N. DENDUKURI. 2003. Risk factors for depression among elderly community subjects: A systematic review and meta-analysis. *American Journal of Psychiatry* 160 (June): 1147–56.

COLEMAN, M., AND L. NICKLEBERRY. 2009. An evaluation of the remarriage and stepfamily self-help literature. *Family Relations* 58 (December): 549–61.

COLEMAN, M., L. H. GANONG, AND S. WEAVER. 2001. Relationship maintenance and enhancement in remarried families. In *Close romantic relationships: Maintenance and enhancement*, eds. J. H. Harvey and A. Wenzel, 255–76. Mahwah, NJ: Erlbaum.

COLEMAN, M., L. H. GANONG, AND M. FINE. 2002. Reinvestigating remarriage: Another decade of progress. In *Understanding families into the new millennium: A decade in review*, ed. R. M. Milardo, 507–26. Minneapolis: National Council on Family Relations.

COLEMAN, T. F. 2007. Single women take large share of homebuyer market. Unmarried America, April 30.

COLL, STEVE. 2008. *The Bin Ladens: An Arabian family in the American century*. New York: Penguin.

COLLIER, J. 1947. *The Indians of the Americas*. New York: Norton.

COLLINS, C. 2005. N.H. adoptees gain access to records. *Christian Science Monitor*, Januaary 13, 11–12.

COLLINS, J., AND F. LIDZ. 2013. The gay athlete. *Sports Illustrated*, May 6, 34–41.

COLLISON, M. N.-K. 1993. A sure-fire winner is to tell her you love her; women fall for it all the time. In *Women's studies: Thinking women*, eds. J. Wetzel, M. L. Espenlaub, M. A. Hagen, A. B. McElhiney, and C. B. Williams, 228–30. Dubuque, IA: Kendall/Hunt.

COMIJS, H. C., A. M. POT, H. H. SMIT, AND C. JONKER. 1998. Elder abuse in the community: Prevalence and consequences. *Journal of the American Geriatrics Society* 46 (7): 885–88.

COMMON SENSE MEDIA. 2012. Social media, social life: How teens view their digital lives. Summer.

CONFER, J. C., AND M. D. CLOUD. 2011. Sex differences in response to imagining a partner's heterosexual or homosexual affair. *Personality and Individual Differences* 50 (January): 129–34.

CONGRESSIONAL HEARING EXPLORES HIGH SUICIDE RATES AMONG AMERICAN INDIAN YOUTH. 2009. Kaiser Family Foundation, March 3.

CONKLIN, K. 2012. Standards, standoffs, and the hidden curriculum: A summary report on sexuality education controversies, 2011–2012. SIECUS.

CONLIN, J. 2009. Living apart for the paycheck. *New York Times*, January 2, 1.

ConsumerReports.org. 2009. 6 top reasons for not having sex, February.

CONWAY, T., AND R. Q. HUTSON. 2008. Healthy marriage and the legacy of child maltreatment: A child welfare perspective. CLASP Policy Brief, May, 1–13.

COOK, B., AND Y. KIM. 2012. *The American college president 2012*. Washington, DC: American Council on Education.

COOLEY, C. H. 1909/1983. *Social organization: A study of the larger mind*. New Brunswick, NJ: Transaction Books.

COONTZ, S. 1992. *The way we never were: American families and the nostalgia trap*. New York: Basic Books.

COONTZ, S. 2005. *Marriage, a history: How love conquered marriage*. New York: Penguin.

COONTZ, S. 2010. Divorce and dissolution: Recognizing reality. *Family Focus*, Winter, F3–F5.

COOPER, A., AND E. L. SMITH. 2011. Homicide trends in the United States, 1980–2008: Annual rates for 2009 and 2010. Bureau of Justice Statistics, November.

COOPER, H. 2009. President delivers exhortation to fathers. *New York Times*, June 20, 10.

COOPERMAN, A. 2010. Ask the expert. Pew Research Center, December 29.

COPELAND, L. 2013. Rash of fatal teen wrecks puts focus on parents. *USA Today*, March 15.

COPEN, C. E., A. CHANDRA, AND G. MARTINEZ. 2012. Prevalence and timing of oral sex with opposite-sex partners among females and males aged 15–24: United States, 2007–2010. *National Health Statistics Reports*, August16.

COPEN, C. E., K. DANIELS, AND W. D. MOSHER. 2013. First premarital cohabitation in the United States: 2006–2010 National Survey of Family Growth. *National Health Statistics Reports*, Number 64, April 4.

COPEN, C. E., K. DANIELS, J. VESPA, AND W. D. MOSHER. 2012. First marriages in the United States: Data from the 2006–2010 National Survey of Family Growth, *National Health Statistics Reports*, Number 49, March 22.

COPLAN, J. H. 2008. Reconcilable differences. *Working Wealth*, Winter, 16–21

CORBETT, C., AND C. HILL. 2012. Graduating to a pay gap: The earnings of women and men one year after college graduation. AAUW, October.

COSBY, B., AND A. F. POUSSAINT. 2007. *Come on people: On the path from victims to victors*. Nashville, TN: Thomas Nelson.

COSE, E. 2005. Does Cosby help? *Newsweek*, January 3, 66–69.

COSTIGAN, C. L., D. P. DORIS, AND T. F. SU. 2004. Marital relationships among immigrant Chinese couples. In *Vision 2004: What is the future of marriage?* eds. P. Amato and N. Gonzalez, 41–44. Minneapolis, MN: National Council on Family Relations.

COTT, N. F. 1976. Eighteenth century family and social life revealed in Massachusetts divorce records. *Journal of Social History* 10 (Fall): 20–43.

COTT, N. F. 1977. *The bonds of womanhood*. New Haven, CT: Yale University Press.

COTT, N. F., AND E. H. PLECK, EDS. 1979. *A heritage of her own: Toward a new social history of American women*. New York: Simon & Schuster.

COTTEN, S. R. 1999. Marital status and mental health revisited: Examining the importance of risk factors and resources. *Family Relations* 48 (July): 225–33.

COTTER, D., P. ENGLAND, AND J. HERMSEN. 2007. Trends in mothers' employment and which mothers stay home. Council on Contemporary Families, May 10.

COUGHLIN, P., AND J. C. WADE. 2012. Masculinity ideology, income disparity, and romantic relationship quality among men with higher earning female partners. *Sex Roles* 67 (September): 311–22.

COVEL, S. 2003. Cheating hearts. *American Demographics* 25 (June): 16.

COWAN, C. P., AND P. A. COWAN. 2000. *When partners become parents: The big life change for couples*. Mahwah, NJ: Erlbaum.

COWAN, P. A., C. P. COWAN, M. K. PRUETT, AND K. PRUETT. 2009. Six barriers to father involvement and suggestions for overcoming them. *Family Focus* 54 (Spring): F1, F2, F4.

COX, R. R. JR., B. BURR, A. J. BLOW, AND J. R. PARRA CARDONA. 2011. Latino adolescent substance use in the United States: Using the bioecodevelopmental model as an organizing framework for research and practice. *Journal of Family Theory & Review* 3 (June): 96–123.

COX, W. 2009. Executive summary: Improving quality of life through telecommuting. Information Technology & Innovation Foundation, January.

COY, P. 2013. The gap between rich and poor widens. *Bloomberg Businessweek*, October 15–21, 80.

COY, P. 2013. What happened to work? *Bloomberg Businessweek*, May 13–19, 10–11.

CRANDELL, S. 2005. Oh, baby. *AARP Magazine*, September/October, 108–18.

CRAWFORD, D. W., R. M. HOUTS, T. L. HUSTON, AND L. J. GEORGE. 2002. Compatibility, leisure, and satisfaction in marital relationships. *Journal of Marriage and Family* 64 (May): 433–49.

CRAWLEY, L., AND M. K. SINGER. 2007. Racial, cultural, and ethnic factors affecting the

quality of end-of-life care in California: Findings and recommendations. California HealthCare Foundation, March.

CREA, T. M., AND R. P. BARTH. 2009. Patterns and predictors of adoption openness and contact: 14 years postadoption. *Family Relations* 58 (December): 607–20.

CRISPELL, D. 1992. Myths of the 1950s. *American Demographics* (August): 38–43.

CRITTENDEN, D. 1999. *What our mothers didn't tell us: Why happiness eludes the modern woman.* New York: Simon & Schuster.

CROSBY, A. E., L. ORTEGA, AND M. R. Stevens. 2011. Suicides—United States, 1999–2007. *MMWR* 60 (Suppl, January 14): 56–59.

CROSBY, F. J. 1991a. *Illusion and disillusion: The self in love and marriage,* 5th ed. Belmont, CA: Wadsworth.

CROSBY, F. J. 1991b. *Juggling: The unexpected advantages of balancing career and home for women and their families.* New York: Free Press.

CROSNOE, R., AND A. KALIL. 2010. Educational progress and parenting among Mexican immigrant mothers of young children. *Journal of Marriage and Family* 72 (August): 976–990.

CROSNOE, R., AND G. H. ELDER. 2002. Adolescent twins and emotional distress: The interrelated influence of nonshared environment and social structure. *Child Development* 73 (November/December): 1761–74.

CROSS, T. L. 1998. Understanding family resiliency from a relational world view. In *Resiliency in Native American and immigrant families,* eds. H. I. McCubbin, E. A. Thompson, A. I. Thompson, and J. E. Fromer, 143–57. Thousand Oaks, CA: Sage.

CROUSE, K. 2007. Fatherhood puts game in perspective. *New York Times,* November 2, 1.

CROWE, A. H., T. G. MULLINS, K. A. COBB, AND N. C. LOWE. 2012. Effects and consequences of underage drinking. *Juvenile Justice Bulletin,* Office of Juvenile Justice and Delinquency Prevention, September.

CROWE, E. 2010. Measuring what matters: A stronger accountability model for teacher education. Center for American Progress, July.

CROWELL, J. A., AND E. WATERS. 1994. Bowlby's theory grown up: The role of attachment in adult love relationships. *Psychological Inquiry* 5 (1): 31–34.

CRUZ, J. 2013. Marriage: More than a century of change. National Center for Family & Marriage Research.

CUBER, J., AND P. HAROFF. 1965. *Sex and the significant Americans.* Baltimore: Penguin.

CUI, M., M. GORDON, K. UENO, AND F. D. FINCHAM. 2013. The continuation of intimate partner violence from adolescence to young adulthood. *Journal of Marriage and Family* 75 (April): 300–13.

CULLEN, L. T. 2007. Till work do us part. *Time,* October 8, 63–64.

CULLEN, L. T., AND C. MASTERS. 2008. We just clicked. *Time,* January 28, 86–89.

CUNNINGHAM, J. D., AND J. K. ANTILL. 1995. Current trends in nonmarital cohabitation: In search of the POSSLQ. In *Under-studied relationships: Off the beaten track,* eds. J. T. Wood and S. Duck, 148–72. Thousand Oaks, CA: Sage.

CUNNINGHAM, M., AND A. THORNTON. 2005. The influence of union transitions on white adults' attitudes toward cohabitation. *Journal of Marriage and Family* 67 (August): 710–20.

CUNRADI, C. B. 2009. Intimate partner violence among Hispanic men and women: The role of drinking, neighborhood disorder, and acculturation-related disorders. *Violence and Victims* 24 (January): 83–97.

CURRIE, J., AND E. TEKIN. 2006. Does child abuse cause crime? Cambridge, MA: National Bureau of Economic Research, Working Paper 12171.

CUTRONA, C. E. 1996. *Social support in couples: Marriage as a resource in times of stress.* Thousand Oaks. CA: Sage.

CYNKAR, P., AND E. MENDES. 2011. More than one in six American workers also act as caregivers. Gallup, July 26.

D

D'ONOFRIO, B. M., AND B. B. LAHEY. 2010. Biosocial influences on the family: A decade review. *Journal of Marriage and Family* 72 (June): 762–82.

DADIGAN, M. 2011. What makes a tribe? *Christian Science Monitor,* August 15 & 22, 30–31.

DAGHER, V. 2013. Adopting? Prepared to be surprised. *Wall Street Journal,* February 25, R9.

Daily Mail Reporter. 2011. The world's biggest family: The man with 39 wives, 94 children and 33 grandchildren. February 19.

DALLA, R. L., AND W. C. GAMBLE. 1997. Exploring factors related to parenting competence among Navajo teenage mothers: Dual techniques of inquiry. *Family Relations* 46 (April): 113–21.

DAMANT, D., S. LAPIERRE, C. LEBOSSE, S. THIBAULT, G. LESSARD, L. HAMELIN-BRABANT, C. LAVERGNE, AND A. FORTIN. 2010. Women's abuse of their children in the context on domestic violence: Reflection from women's accounts. *Child and Family Social Work* 15 (February): 12–21.

DAMAST, A. 2012/2013. She works hard for less money. *Bloomberg Businessweek,* December 24–January 6, 31–32.

DANG, D. T. 2008. Be wary in doing online survey. *Baltimore Sun,* June 10, 1D, 5D.

DANIEL, J., AND A. MCCANN. 2013. Fighting *Roe v. Wade. Bloomberg Businessweek,* January 21–27, 56–57.

DANIELS, K., J. JONES, AND J. ABMA. 2013b. Use of emergency contraception among women aged 15–44: United States, 2006–2010. NCHS Data Brief, No. 112, February.

DANIELS, K., W. D. MOSHER, AND J. JONES. 2013a. Contraceptive methods women have ever used: United States, 1982–2010. *National Health Statistics Reports,* Number 62, February 14.

DANIS, F. S., AND K. A. ANDERSON. 2008. An underserved population and untapped resource: A preliminary study of collegiate sorority response to dating violence. *Journal of Aggression, Maltreatment & Trauma* 17 (3): 336–51.

DANZIGER, S. 2008. The price of independence: The economics of early adulthood. *Family Focus* 53 (March): F7–F8.

DAO, J. 2011. After combat, the unexpected perils of coming home. *New York Times,* May 29, A1.

DAO, J., AND A. W. LEHREN. 2013. Baffling rise in suicides plagues the U.S. military. *New York Times,* May 16, A1.

DAUM, M. 2009. Moms in their 60s—oh, baby! *Los Angeles Times,* July 23.

DAUM, M. 2009. The age of friendaholism. *Los Angeles Times,* March 7.

2006 Dating Trends Survey. 2006. He says/ she says: The real scoop on dating. America Online.

DAVÉ, S., I. PETERSEN, L. SHERR, AND I. NAZARETH. 2010. Incidence of maternal and paternal depression in primary care: A cohort study using a primary care database. *Archives of Pediatrics and Adolescent Medicine* 164 (November): 1038–44.

DAVEY, M., AND D. LEONHARDT. 2003. Jobless and hopeless, many quit the labor force. *New York Times,* April 27.

DAVIDSON, P. 2011. Season of part-time jobs kicks off with holidays. *USA Today,* November 25–27, A1–A2.

DAVIES, C., AND D. WILLIAMS. 2002. *The grandparent study 2002 report.* AARP.

DAVIS, K. D., W. B. GOODMAN, A. E. PIRRETTI, AND D. M. ALMEIDA. 2008. Nonstandard work schedules, perceived family well-being, and daily stressors. *Journal of Marriage and Family* 70 (November): 991–1003.

DAVIS, K. E. 1985. Near and dear: Friendship and love compared. *Psychology Today* 19: 22–30.

DAVIS, P. W. 1996. Threats of corporal punishment as verbal aggression: A naturalistic study. *Child Abuse & Neglect* 20 (4): 289–304.

DAWSON, E. 2011. Baltimore research benefits people 50+. *AARP Bulletin,* July–August, 44.

DAWSON, J. M., AND P. A. LANGAN. 1994. *Murder in families.* Washington, DC: Bureau of Justice Statistics.

DAY, R. D. 1995. Family-systems theory. In *Research and theory in family science,* eds. R. D. Day, K. R. Gilbert, B. H. Settles, and W. R. Burr, 91–101. Pacific Grove, CA: Brooks/Cole.

DAY, R. D., AND A. ACOCK. 2013. Marital well-being and religiousness as mediated by relational virtue and equality. *Journal of Marriage and Family* 75 (February): 164–177.

DE LA CANCELA, V. 1994. "Coolin": The psychosocial communication of African and Latino men. In *African American males: A critical link in the African American family,* ed. D. J. Jones, 33–44. New Brunswick, NJ: Transaction.

De ROSA, C. J., et al. 2010. Sexual intercourse and oral sex among public middle school students: Prevalence and correlates. *Perspectives on Sexual and Reproductive Health* 42 (September): 197–205.

DEARDOFF, J., J. M. TSCHANN, E. FLORES, AND E. J. OZER. 2010. Sexual values and risky sexual behaviors among Latino youths. *Perspectives on Sexual and Reproductive Health* 42 (March): 23–32.

Death penalty for 10 for "honor killings" in India; they killed couple who wed within clan. 2011. *Washington Post,* June 9.

DEATON, A. S. 2009. Aging, religion, and health. National Bureau of Economic Research, August.

DEATON, A., AND A. A. STONE. 2013. Grandpa and the snapper: The wellbeing of the elderly who live with children. National Bureau of Economic Research, June.

DEBIAGGI, S. D. 2002. *Changing gender roles: Brazilian immigrant families in the U.S.* New York: LFB Scholarly Publishing.

DEE, T. S. 2006. The why chromosome. *Education Next* No. 4 (Fall): 69–75.

DEGLER, C. 1981. *At odds: Women and the family in America from the Revolution to the present.* New York: Oxford University Press.

DEGLER, C. N. 1983. The emergence of the modern American family. In *The American family in social-historical perspective,* 3rd ed., ed. M. Gordon, 61–79. New York: St. Martin's.

DEGRAW, D. 2011. Americans don't realize just how badly we're getting screwed by the top 0.1 percent hoarding the country's wealth. AlterNet, August 14.

DeGray, B. 2012. The perks and perils of telecommuting. *Washington Post*, May 5.

Delaney-Black, V., L. M. Chiodo, J. H. Hannigan, M. K. Grenwald, J. Janisse, G. Patterson, M. A. Huestis, J. Ager, and R. J. Sokol. 2010. Just say "I don't": Lack of concordance between teen report and biological measures of drug use. *Pediatrics* 126 (November): 887–93.

delCastillo, R. G. 1984. *La familia: Chicano families in the urban Southwest, 1848 to the present*. Notre Dame, IN: University of Notre Dame Press.

DeLeire, T., and A. Kalil. 2005. How do cohabiting couples with children spend their money? *Journal of Marriage and Family* 67 (May): 286–95.

DeLong, D. 2011. Beloved wife day: Hug your wife at 8:09! Japanapalooza, January 31.

DeMaris, A. 2001. The influence of intimate violence on transitions out of cohabitation. *Journal of Marriage and Family* 63 (February): 235–46.

DeMaris, A., and W. MacDonald. 1993. Premarital cohabitation and marital instability: A test of the unconventionality hypothesis. *Journal of Marriage and the Family* 55 (May): 399–407.

Demo, D. H., and A. C. Acock. 1996. Singlehood, marriage, and remarriage. *Journal of Family Issues* 17 (May): 388–407.

Demos, J. 1970. *A little commonwealth: Family life in Plymouth colony*. New York: Oxford University Press.

Demos, J. 1986. *Past, present, and personal: The family and the life course in American history*. New York: Oxford University Press.

DeMunck, V. C. 1998. Lust, love, and arranged marriages in Sri Lanka. In *Romantic love and sexual behavior: Perspectives from the social sciences*, ed. V. C. de Munck, 295–300. Westport, CT: Praeger.

DeNavas-Walt, C., B. D. Proctor, and J. C. Smith. 2012. *Income, poverty, and health insurance coverage in the United States: 2011*. U.S. Census Bureau, Current Population Reports, P60-243. Washington, DC: U.S. Government Printing Office.

DeNavas-Walt, C., B. D. Proctor, and J. C. Smith. 2013. *Income, poverty, and health insurance coverage in the United States: 2012*. U.S. Census Bureau, Current Population Reports, P60-245, September.

Denham, E. 2013. Keeping kids out of the middle. *Huffington Post*, February 22.

Denizet-Lewis, B. 2004. Friends, friends with benefits and the benefits of the local mall. *New York Times*, May 30, F30.

Denny, C. H., J. Tsai, R. L. Floyd, and P. P. Green. 2009. Alcohol use among pregnant and nonpregnant women of childbearing age—United States, 1991–2005. *MMWR Weekly* 58 (May 22): 529–32.

DePaulo, B. 2006. *Single out: How singles are stereotyped, stigmatized, and ignored, and still live happily ever after*. New York: St. Martin's Griffin.

DePaulo, B. 2012. Are you single at heart? *Psychology Today*, January/February, 54–55.

Deprez, E. E. 2013a. Chipping away at *Roe v. Wade*. *Bloomberg Businessweek*, April 22–28, 26–27.

Deprez, E. E. 2013b. For abortion pills, you must "see" your doctor. *Bloomberg Businessweek*, February 18–24, 25–26.

Deresiewicz, W. 2009. Faux friendship. *The Chronicle Review*, December 11, B6–B10.

Derlega, V. J., S. Metts, S. Petronio, and S. T. Margulis. 1993. *Self-disclosure*. Thousand Oaks, CA: Sage.

Desai, S. D., D. Chugh, and A. P. Brief. 2012. Marriage structure and resistance to the gender revolution in the workplace. Social Science Research Network.

Designer Babies. 2012. *Christian Science Monitor Weekly*, June 25, 33.

DeSilver, D. 2013. 5 fast facts about moms. Pew Research Center, May 10.

DeSimone, J. S. 2010a. Binge drinking and risky sex among college students. National Bureau of Economic Research, April.

DeSimone, J. S. 2010b. Binge drinking and sex in high school. National Bureau of Economic Research, June.

DeSpelder, L. A., and A. L. Strickland. 2005. *The last dance: Encountering death and dying*, 7th ed. New York: Mc-Graw Hill.

DeSteno, D., M. Y. Bartlett, J. Braverman, and P. Salovey. 2002. Sex differences in jealousy: Evolutionary mechanism or artifact of measurement? *Journal of Personality and Social Psychology* 83 (November): 1103–16.

Dew, J. 2008. Debt change and marital satisfaction change in recently married couples. *Family Relations* 57 (January): 60–71.

Dew, J. 2009. The gendered meaning of assets for divorce. *Journal of Family and Economic Issues* 30 (March): 20–31.

Dew, J., and W. B. Wilcox. 2011. If momma ain't happy: Explaining declines in marital satisfaction among new mothers. *Journal of Marriage and Family* 73 (February): 1–12.

Dew, J., S. Britt, and S. Huston. 2012. Examining the relationship between financial issues and divorce. *Family Relations* 61 (October): 615–28.

Dewan, S., and R. Gebeloff. 2012. More men enter fields dominated by women. *New York Times*, May 21, A1.

Diamond, M., and K. Sigmundson. 1997. Sex reassignment at birth: Long-term review and clinical implications. *Archives of Pediatrics & Adolescent Medicine* 15 (March): 298–304.

Dickinson, A. 2010. Ask Amy. *Baltimore Sun*, March 4, 5.

Dickinson, A. 2011. Ask Amy. *Baltimore Sun*, February 14, 7.

Dickinson, A. 2011. Dear Amy. *Baltimore Sun*, March 29, 7.

Diduch, M. 2012. Advance warning. *Psychology Today*, July/August, 14.

Diener, M. L., S. C. Mangelsdorf, J. L. McHale, and C. A. Frosch. 2002. Infants' behavioral strategies for emotion regulation with fathers and mothers: Associations with emotional expressions and attachment quality. *Infancy* 3 (May): 153–74.

Dilman, I. 1998. *Love: Its forms, dimensions, and paradoxes*. New York: St. Martin's.

Dilworth-Anderson, P., L. M. Burton, and W. L. Turner. 1993. The importance of values in the study of culturally diverse families. *Family Relations* 42 (July): 238–42.

Dilworth-Anderson, P., S. W. Williams, and T. Cooper. 1999. The contexts of experiencing emotional distress among family caregivers to elderly African Americans. *Family Relations* 48 (October): 391–96.

Dion, M. R., S. L. Braver, S. A. Wolchik, and I. N. Sandler. 1997. Alcohol abuse and psychopathic deviance in noncustodial parents as predictors of child-support payment and visitation. *American Journal of Orthopsychiatry* 67 (January): 70–79.

Diversity Inc. 2008. Fortune 500 black, Latino, Asian CEOs. July 22.

Dixit, J. 2009. You're driving me crazy! *Psychology Today*, March/April, www.psychologytoday.com (accessed April 27, 2009).

Do, D. D. 1999. *The Vietnamese Americans*. Westport, CT: Greenwood.

Dodson, L., and W. Luttrell. 2011. Families facing untenable choices. *Contexts* 10 (Winter): 38–42.

Doherty, R. W., E. Hatfield, K. Thompson, and P. Choo. 1994. Cultural and ethnic influences on love and attachment. *Personal Relationships* 1: 391–98.

Doherty, W. J., B. J. Willoughby, and B. Peterson. 2011. Interest in marital reconciliation among divorcing parents. *Family Court Review* 49 (April): 313–21.

Dokoupil, T. 2009. Men will be men. *Newsweek*, March 12, 50.

Dokoupil, T. 2011. The coffee shop baby. *Newsweek*, October 10 & 17, 44–47.

Dolbin-MacNab, M. L., and M. K. Keiley. 2009. Navigating interdependence: How adolescents raised solely by grandparents experience their family relationships. *Family Relations* 58 (April): 162–75.

Donnelly, D. A., and E. O. Burgess. 2008. The decision to remain in an involuntarily celibate relationship. *Journal of Marriage and Family* 70 (May): 519–35.

Donnelly, S. B. 2007. Growing younger. *Time*, January, A13–A14.

Dooren, J. C. 2012. FDA warns Avon on wrinkle claims. *Wall Street Journal*, October 17, B2.

Dooren, J. C. 2013. FDA lowers age for emergency contraceptive to 15. *Wall Street Journal*, May 1, A6.

Doss, B. D., G. K. Rhoades, S. M. Stanley, and H. J. Markman. 2009. The effect of the transition to parenthood on relationship quality: An 8-year prospective study. *Journal of Personality and Social Psychology* 96 (March): 601–19.

Double Bind. 2012. *The Economist*, December 15, 31.

Douglas, J. D., and F. C. Atwell. 1988. *Love, intimacy, and sex*. Beverly Hills, CA: Sage.

Downs, E., and S. L. Smith. 2010. Keeping abreast of hypersexuality: A video game character content analysis. *Sex Roles* 62 (June): 721–33.

Doyle, A. B., and D. Markiewicz. 2005. Parenting, marital conflict, and adjustment from early- to mid-adolescence: Mediated by adolescent attachment style? *Journal of Youth and Adolescence* 34 (April): 97–110.

Doyle, M., C. O'Dywer, and V. Timonen. 2010. "How can you just cut off a whole side of the family and say move on?" The reshaping of paternal grandparent–grandchild relationships following divorce or separation in the middle generation. *Family Relations* 59 (December): 587–98.

Doyle, R. P. 2012. Books challenged or banned in 2010–2011. American Library Association.

Drexler, P. 2012. The new face of infidelity. *Wall Street Journal*, October 21, C3.

Dubberley, E. 2007. *I'd rather be single than settle: Satisfied solitude and how to achieve it*. London: Vision Press.

Duck, S. 1998. *Human relationships*, 3rd ed. Thousand Oaks, CA: Sage.

Dugan, A. 2012. Americans most likely to say they belong to the middle class. Gallup, November 30.

Duncan, M. 2011. It takes a village to fix up a child. *Baltimore Sun*, February 18, 4.

Dunleavey, M. P. 2010. Take the lid off secret spending. *Money*, December, 48.

Durrant, J., and R. Ensom. 2012. Physical punishment of children: Lessons from 20 years of research. *Canadian Medical Association Journal* 4 (12): 1373–77.

Dush, C., M. Kamp, and P. R. Amato. 2005. Consequences of relationship status and

quality for subjective well-being. *Journal of Social and Personal Relationships* 22 (October): 607–27.

DUSTER, T. 2005. Race and reification in science. *Science* 307 (February 18): 1050–51.

DUVALL, E. M. 1957. *Family development.* Philadelphia: Lippincott.

DYBALL, R. 2008. Will Smith: "Divorce is not an option." May 27.

DYE, J. L., AND T. D. JOHNSON. 2007. A child's day: 2003 (selected indicators of child well-being). Current Population Reports, P70-109. Washington, DC: U.S. Census Bureau.

DYSON, M. E. 2005. *Is Bill Cosby right? Or has the middle class lost its mind?* New York: Basic Civitas Books.

E

EARLE, A. M. 1899. *Child life in colonial days.* New York: Macmillan.

EAST, P. L., AND T. S. WEISNER. 2009. Mexican American adolescents' family caregiving: Selection effects and longitudinal associations with adjustments. *Family Relations* 58 (December): 562–77.

EATON, A. A., AND S. M. ROSE. 2012. Scripts for actual first date and hanging-out encounters among young heterosexual Hispanic adults. *Sex Roles* 67 (September): 285–99.

EATON, A. A., AND S. ROSE. 2011. Has dating become more egalitarian? A 35 year review using *Sex Roles. Sex Roles* 64 (June): 843–62.

EATON, D. K., ET AL. 2008. Youth risk behavior surveillance—United States, 2007. *MMWR* 57, June 5, No. SS-4.

EATON, D. K., ET AL. 2012. Youth risk behavior surveillance—United States, 2011. *Morbidity and Mortality Weekly Report* 61 (June 8): 1–162.

EBELING, A. 2007. The second match. *Forbes*, November 12, 86–89.

EBERSTADT, M. 2004. *Home-alone America: The hidden toll of day care, behavioral drugs, and other parent substitutes.* New York: Penguin.

EBERSTADT, N. 2009. Poor statistics. *Forbes*, March 2, 26.

EBLING, R., AND R. W. LEVENSON. 2003. Who are the marital experts? *Journal of Marriage and Family* 65 (February): 130–42.

ECKHOLM, E. 2008. Blue-collar jobs disappear, taking families' way of life along. *New York Times*, January 16, 14.

ECKLAND, B. K. 1968. Theories of mate selection. *Eugenics Quarterly* 15 (1): 71–84.

ECONOMIC POLICY INSTITUTE. 2013. A more comprehensive measure of slack in the labor market. *The state of working America*, March 8.

EDIN, K., AND L. LEIN. 1997. *Making ends meet: How single mothers survive welfare and low-wage work.* New York: Russell Sage Foundation.

EDIN, K., AND M. KEFALAS. 2005. Unmarried with children. *Contexts* 4 (Spring): 16–22.

EDMONSTON, B. 1999. The 2000 census challenge. *Population Reference Bureau* 1 (February): 1.

EDWARDS, V. J., M. C. BLACK, S. DHINGRA, L. McKNIGHT-ELLY, AND G. S. PERRY. 2009. Physical and sexual intimate partner violence and reported serious psychological distress in the 2007 BRFSS. *International Journal of Public Health* 54 (June): 37–42.

EGGEBEEN, D. J. 2005. Cohabitation and exchanges of support. *Social Forces* 83 (May): 1097–1110.

EHRENREICH, B. 2009. *Bright-sided: How the relentless promotion of positive thinking has undermined America.* New York: Metropolitan Books.

EHRENSAFT, M. K., ET AL. 2003. Intergenerational transmission of partner violence: A 20-year prospective study. *Journal of Consulting and Clinical Psychology* 71 (August): 741–53.

EISENBERG, M. E., L. H. BEARINGER, R. E. SIEVING, C. SWAIN, AND M. D. RESNICK. 2004. Parents' beliefs about condoms and oral contraceptives: Are they medically accurate? *Perspectives on Sexual and Reproductive Health* 36 (March/April): 50–57.

EISENBERG, N., ET AL., 2005. Relations among positive parenting, children's effortful control, and externalizing problems: A three-wave longitudinal study. *Child Development* 76 (September/October): 1055–71.

ELIOT, L. 2012. *Pink brain, blue brain: How small differences grow into troublesome gaps—And what we can do about it.* Oxford, England: Oneworld Publications.

ELISON, J. 2007. The stage of grief no one admits to: Relief. *Newsweek*, January 29, 18.

ELKIND, D. 2007. *The power of play: Learning what comes naturally.* New York: De Capo Press.

ELLINGWOOD, K. 2009. Kissing ban sparks a Mexican revolution. *Baltimore Sun*, February 15, 16.

ELLIOTT, D. B., AND T. SIMMONS. 2011. Marital events of Americans: 2009. American Community Survey Reports, ACS-13, August, U.S. Census Bureau.

ELLIOTT, S. 2012. *Not my kid: What parents believe about the sex lives of their teenagers.* New York: New York University Press.

ELLIS, A. 1963. *The origins and the development of the incest taboo.* New York: Lyle Stuart.

ELLIS, L., P. E. GAY, AND E. PAIGE. 2001. Daily hassles and pleasures across the lifespan. Paper presented at the Annual American Psychological Association meetings, San Francisco.

ELLIS, R. 2013. Changes in coresidence of grandparents and grandchildren. *Family Focus*, Summer, F13, F15, F17.

ELLISON, C. G., A. M. BURDETTE, AND W. B. WILCOX. 2010. The couple that prays together: Race and ethnicity, religion, and relationship quality. *Journal of Marriage and Family* 72 (August): 963–75.

ELSBACH, K., AND D. CABLE. 2012. Why showing your face at work matters. *MIT Sloan Management Review* 53 (Summer): 10–12.

Employment characteristics of families, 2012. 2013. Bureau of Labor Statistics, *The Editor's Desk*, April 30.

ENCHAUTEGUI, M. E. 2013. Nonstandard work schedules and the well-being of low-income families. Urban Institute, July.

ENGEL, M. 2000. Stepfamilies are not blended. Stepfamily Association of America.

ENGLAND, P., AND R. J. THOMAS. 2009. The decline of the date and the rise of the college hook up. In *Family in transition*, 15th ed., eds. A. S. Skolnick and J. H. Skolnick, 141–52. Boston: Pearson Higher Education.

ENGLAND, P., E. F. SHAFER, AND A. C. K. FOGARTY. 2007. Hooking up and forming romantic relationships on today's college campuses. Unpublished paper.

ENGLANDER, E. K. 1997. *Understanding violence.* Hillsdale, NJ: Erlbaum.

ENNIS, S. R., M. RIOS-VARGAS, AND N. G. ALBERT. 2011. The Hispanic population: 2010. 2010 Census Briefs, May.

EPSTEIN, G. A. 2005. Matchmaking is just a walk in park. *Baltimore Sun* (August 3): 1A, 11A.

EPSTEIN, R. 2008. Same-sex marriage is too limiting. *Los Angeles Times*, December 4, 2008.

EPSTEIN, R. 2010. How science can help you fall in love. *Scientific American Mind*, January/February, 26–33.

EQUALITY MAINE. 2013. Marriage, civil union, and domestic partnerships: A comparison.

ERICKSON, R. J. 1993. Reconceptualizing family work: The effect of emotion work on perceptions of marital quality. *Journal of Marriage and the Family* 55 (November): 888–900.

ERIKSON, E. 1963. *Childhood and society.* New York: Norton.

ESPELAGE, D. L. 2011. Research meeting on longitudinal data on teen dating violence. Commissioned paper for National Institute of Justice.

ESPIRITU, Y. L. 1995. *Filipino American lives.* Philadelphia: Temple University Press.

ESPOSITO, J. L., AND D. MOGAHED. 2007. *Who speaks for Islam? What a billion Muslims really think.* New York: Gallup Press.

ESSED, P., AND D. T. GOLDBERG, EDS. 2002. *Race critical theories: Text and context.* Malden, MA: Blackwell Publishers.

ESTES, R. J., AND N. A. WEINER. 2002. The commercial sexual exploitation of children in the U.S., Canada, and Mexico. University of Pennsylvania, School of Social Work.

EVAN B. DONALDSON ADOPTION INSTITUTE. 2008. Finding families for African American children: The role of race & law in adoption from foster care. May.

EVANS, M. D. R., J. KELLEY, J. SIKORA, AND D. J. TREIMAN. 2010. Family scholarly culture and educational success: Books and schooling in 27 nations. *Research in Social Stratification and Mobility* 28 (June): 171–79.

EVERETT, C., AND S. V. EVERETT. 1994. *Healthy divorce.* San Francisco: Jossey-Bass.

EXNER-CORTENS, D. J. ECKENRODE, AND E. ROTHMAN. 2013. Longitudinal associations between teen dating violence victimization and adverse health outcomes. *Pediatrics* 131 (January): 71–78.

EXPERT GROUP ON COMMISSIONING NHS INFERTILITY PROVISION. 2009. Regulated fertility services: A commissioning aid. Department of Health, June.

F

FABRICIUS, W. V. 2003. Listening to children of divorce: New findings that diverge from Wallerstein, Lewis, and Blakeslee. *Family Relations* 52 (October): 385–96.

FAGAN, J., AND M. BARNETT. 2003. The relationship between maternal gatekeeping, paternal competence, mothers' attitudes about the father role, and father involvement. *Journal of Family Issues* 24 (November): 1020–43.

FAGAN, J., AND Y. LEE. 2011. Do coparenting and social support have a greater effect on adolescent fathers than adult fathers? *Family Relations* 60 (July): 247–58.

FAGAN, J., M. F. SCHMITZ, AND J. J. LLOYD. 2007. The relationship between adolescent and young fathers' capital and marital plans of couples expecting a baby. *Family Relations* 56 (July): 231–43.

FAGUNDES, C. P. 2011. Implicit negative evaluations about ex-partner predict break-up adjustment: The brighter side of dark cognitions. *Cognition and Emotion* 25 (January): 164–73.

FAIOLA, A. 2010. Kate Middleton's "commoner" status stirs up Britons' old class divide. *Washington Post*, December 19.

FALBA, T. A., AND J. L. SINDELAR. 2008. Spousal concordance in health behavior change. *Health Services Research* 43 (February): 96–116.

FARAGHER, J. M. 1986. *Sugar Creek: Life on the Illinois prairie.* New Haven, CT: Yale University Press.

FARBER, B. 1972. *Guardians of virtue: Salem families in 1800.* New York: Basic Books.

FARHI, P. 2012. Adam Lanza, and others who committed mass shootings, were white males. *Washington Post,* December 20.

FARR, R. H., S. L. FORSSELL, AND C. J. PATTERSON. 2010. Gay, lesbian and heterosexual adoptive parents: Couple and relationship issues. *Journal of GLBT Family Studies* 6 (April): 199–213.

FARRELL, D. M. 1997. Jealousy and desire. In *Love analyzed,* ed. Roger E. Lamb, 165–88. Boulder, CO: Westview.

FARRELL, E. F., AND E. HOOVER. 2005. Getting schooled in student life. *Chronicle of Higher Education,* July 29, A36.

FARRIS, C., T. A. TREAT, R. J. VIKEN, AND R. M. MCFALL. 2008. Perceptual mechanisms that characterize gender differences in decoding women's sexual intent. *Psychological Science* 19 (April): 348–54.

FASS, A. 2004. The dating game. *Forbes* (July 5): 137, 139.

Father's day: June 16, 2013. 2013. U.S. Census Bureau News, CB13-FF.13, April 18.

FAUSSETT, R. 2011. Alabama sets new standard. *Baltimore Sun,* June 10, 6.

FAVREAULT, M. M. 2005. Women and Social Security. The Urban Institute, December.

FEDERAL BUREAU OF INVESTIGATION. 2011. *Crime in the United States, 2010.*

FEDERAL BUREAU OF INVESTIGATION. 2012. FBI releases 2011 hate crime statistics. December 10.

FEDERAL INTERAGENCY FORUM ON AGING-RELATED STATISTICS. 2012. *Older Americans 2012: Key indicators of well-being.* June.

FEDERAL INTERAGENCY FORUM ON CHILD AND FAMILY STATISTICS. 2009. *America's children: Key national indicators of well-being, 2009.* Washington, DC: U.S. Government Printing Office.

FEDERAL INTERAGENCY FORUM ON CHILD AND FAMILY STATISTICS. 2012. *America's children in brief: Key indicators of well-being.* Washington, DC: U.S. Government Printing Office.

FEDERAL INTERAGENCY FORUM ON CHILD AND FAMILY STATISTICS. 2013. *America's children in brief: Key indicators of well-being.* Washington, DC: U.S. Government Printing Office.

FEDERAL TRADE COMMISSION. 2012. Mobile apps for kids: Disclosures still not making the grade. December.

FEENEY, J., AND P. NOLLER. 1996. *Adult attachment.* Thousand Oaks, CA: Sage.

FEHR, B. 1999. Laypeople's conceptions of commitment. *Journal of Personality and Social Psychology* 76 (January): 90–103.

FEINBERG, L., S. C. REINHARD, A. HOUSER, AND R. CHOULA. 2011. Valuing the invaluable: 2011 update, the growing contributions and costs of family caregiving. AARP Public Policy Institute.

FEINGOLD, A. 1988. Matching for attractiveness in romantic partners and same-sex friends: A meta-analysis and theoretical critique. *Psychological Bulletin* 104 (September): 226–35.

FELDMAN, H. 1931. *Racial factors in American industry.* New York: Harper & Row.

FELICIANO, C., R. LEE, AND B. ROBNETT. 2011. Racial boundaries among Latinos: Evidence from Internet daters' racial preferences. *Social Problems* 58 (May): 189–212.

FELSON, R. B., AND P.-P. PARÉ. 2005. The reporting of domestic violence and sexual assault by nonstrangers to the police. *Journal of Marriage and Family* 67 (August): 597–610.

FERNANDEZ, S. 2005. Getting to know you. *Washington Post* (May 30): C1.

FERREE, M. M. 2010. Filling the glass: Gender perspectives on families. *Journal of Marriage and Family* 72 (June): 420–39.

FESTINOER, T. 2002. After adoption: Dissolution or permanence. *Child Welfare* 81: 515–33.

FETSCH, R. J., R. K. YANG, AND M. J. PETTIT. 2008. The RETHINK parenting and anger management program: A follow-up validation study. *Family Relations* 57 (December): 543–52.

FETTO, J. 2003. Love stinks. *American Demographics* 25 (February): 10–11.

FEW, A. L., AND K. H. ROSEN. 2005. Victims of chronic dating violence: How women's vulnerabilities link to their decisions to stay. *Family Relations* 54 (April): 265–79.

FICHTER, M. M., N. QUADFLIEG, AND S. HEDLUND. 2006. Twelve-year course and outcome predictors of anorexia nervosa. *International Journal of Eating Disorders* 39 (March): 87–100.

FIELD, A. E., ET AL. 2005. Exposure to the mass media, body shape concerns, and use of supplements to improve weight and shape among male and female adolescents. *Pediatrics* 116 (August): 214–20.

FIELDS, J. 2004. America's families and living arrangements: 2003. Current Population Reports, P20–553. Washington, DC: U.S. Census Bureau.

FIELDS, J., AND L. M. CASPER. 2001. America's families and living arrangements: 2000. U.S. Census Bureau, Current Population Reports, P20–537.

FILE, T. 2013. Computer and Internet use in the United States. U.S. Census Bureau, Population Characteristics, May.

FINCHAM, F. D., AND S. R. BEACH. 2010. Marriage in the new millennium: A decade in review. *Journal of Marriage and Family* 72 (June): 630–49.

FINER, L. B., AND J. M. PHILBIN. 2013. Sexual initiation, contraceptive use, and pregnancy among young adolescents. *Pediatrics* 31 (May): 886–91.

FINER, L. B., AND K. KOST. 2011. Unintended pregnancy rates at the state level. *Perspectives on Sexual and Reproductive Health* 43 (2): 78–87.

FINER, L. B., AND M. R. ZOLNA. 2011. Unintended pregnancy in the United States: Incidence and disparities, 2006. *Contraception* 84 (November): 478–85.

FINER, L. B., J. JERMAN, AND M. L. KAVANAUGH. 2012. Changes in use of long-acting contraceptive methods in the United States, 2007–2009. *Fertility and Sterility* 98 (October): 893–97.

FINER, L. B., L. F. FROHWIRTH, L. A. DAUPHINEE, S. SINGH, AND A. M. MOORE. 2005. Reasons U.S. women have abortions: Quantitative and qualitative perspectives. *Perspectives on Sexual and Reproductive Health* 37 (September): 110–18.

FINGERMAN, K. L., E. L. HAY, C. M. CAMP DUSH, D. E. CICHY, AND S. HOSTERMAN. 2007. Parents' and offspring's perception of change in continuity when parents transition to old age. *Advances in Life Course Research* 12 (June): 275–306.

FINGERMAN, K. L., Y-P CHENG, E. D. WESSELMANN, S. ZARIT, F. FURSTENBERG, AND K. S. BIRDITT. 2012. Helicopter parents and landing pad kids: Intense parental support of grown children. *Journal of Marriage and Family* 74 (August): 880–96.

FINK, D. 1992. *Agrarian women: Wives and mothers in rural Nebraska, 1880–1940.* Chapel Hill: University of North Carolina Press.

FINKEL, E. J., P. W. EASTWICK, B. R. KARNEY, H. T. REIS, AND S. SPRECHER. 2012. Online dating: A critical analysis from the perspective of psychological science. *Psychological Science in the Public Interest* 13 (January): 3–66.

FINKELHOR, D., H. HAMMER, AND A. J.SEDLAK. 2008. Sexually assaulted children: National estimates and characteristics. U.S. Department of Justice, Office of Justice Programs, August.

FINKELHOR, D., H. TURNER, R. ORMROD, AND S. L. HAMBY. 2010. Trends in childhood violence and abuse exposure. March.

FINKELHOR, D., H. TURNER, S. HAMBY, AND R. ORMROD. 2011. Polyvictimization: Children's exposure to multiple types of violence, crime, and abuse. *Juvenile Justice Bulletin,* Office of Juvenile Justice and Delinquency Prevention, October.

FINKELSTEIN, E. A., O. A. KHAVJOU, H. THOMPSON, J. G. TROGDON, L. PAN, B. SHERRY, AND W. DIETZ. 2012. Obesity and severe obesity forecasts through 2030. *American Journal of Preventive Medicine* 42 (June): 563–70.

FISHER, H. 2004. *Why we love: The nature and chemistry of romantic love.* New York: Henry Holt.

FISHER, H. 2008. Of lost love and old bones. *Chronicle of Higher Education,* June 6, B5.

FISHER, H. E., L. L. BROWN, A. ARON, G. STRONG, AND D. MASHEK. 2010. Reward, addiction, and emotion regulation systems associated with rejection in love. *Journal of Neurophysiology* 104 (May): 51–60.

FISHER, L. 2005. New gloss on motherhood, but few changes. Women's e-news, February 18.

FITZPATRICK, J., E. A. SHARP, AND A. REIFMAN. 2009. Midlife singles' willingness to date partners with heterogeneous characteristics. *Family Relations* 58 (February): 121–33.

FLECK, C. 2007. Two steps forward, one step back. *AARP Bulletin,* October, 24.

FLEISHMAN, J. 2010. An unwilling Afghan bride's defiance leads to death. *Los Angeles Times,* March 25.

FLEMING, C. B., H. R. WHITE, AND R. F. CATALANO. 2010. Romantic relationships and substance use in early adulthood: An examination of the influences of relationship type, partner substance use, and relationship quality. *Journal of Health and Social Behavior* 51 (2): 153–67.

FLETCHER, G. 2002. *The new science of intimate relationships.* Malden, MA: Blackwell.

FLETCHER, M. A. 2013. Fiscal trouble ahead for most future retirees. *Washington Post,* February 16.

FLORES, G., AND J. BROTANEK. 2005. The healthy immigrant effect: A greater understanding might help us improve the health of all children. *Archives of Pediatrics & Adolescent Medicine* 159 (3): 295–97.

FOLAN, K. L. 2010. *Don't bring home a white boy: And other notions that keep black women from dating out.* New York: Gallery Press.

FOLK, K. F., J. W. GRAHAM, AND A. H. BELLER. 1992. Child support and remarriage: Implications for the economic well-being of children. *Journal of Family Issues* 13, 142–57.

FOMBY, P., AND A. ESTACION. 2011. Cohabitation and children's externalizing behavior in low-income Latino families. *Journal*

of Marriage and Family 73 (February): 46–66.

FONG, M. 2009. It's cold cash, not cold feet, motivating runaway brides in China. *Wall Street Journal*, June 5, A1.

FONG, T. P. 2002. *The contemporary Asian American experience: Beyond the model minority*, 2nd ed. Upper Saddle River, NJ: Prentice Hall.

FORD, A. 2011. *The soulmate secret: Manifest the love of your life with the law of attraction*. New York: HarperOne.

FORD, P. 2009. Foreign men lose appeal. *Christian Science Monitor*, April 19, 5.

FORERO, J. 2011. Birth plummets in Brazil. *Washington Post*, December 29.

"For richer or poorer." 2005. *Mother Jones* 30 (January/February): 24–25.

FORRY, N. D., AND S. K. WALKER. 2006. *Public policy, child care, and families in the United States*. National Council on Family Relations, Family Focus on Families and Public Policy, March, F5–F6.

FORSYTH, J. 2011. Leader of polygamist sect given life term. *Baltimore Sun*, August 10, 8.

FORWARD, S. 2002. *Obsessive love: When it hurts too much to let go*. New York: Bantam.

FOST, D. 1996. Child-free with an attitude. *American Demographics* 18 (April): 15–16.

FOSTER, D. G., H. GOULD, J. TAYLOR, AND T. A. WEITZ. 2012. Attitudes and decision making among women seeking abortions at one U.S. clinic. *Perspectives on Sexual and Reproductive Health* 44 (June): 117–124.

FOX, G. L., AND V. M. MURRY. 2001. Gender and families: Feminist perspectives and family research. In *Understanding families into the new millennium: A decade of review*, ed. R. M. Milardo, 379–91. Lawrence, KS: National Council on Family Relations.

FOX, G. L., M. L. BENSON, A. A. DE MARIS, AND J. VAN WYK. 2002. Economic distress and intimate violence: Testing family stress and resources theories. *Journal of Marriage and Family* 64 (August): 793–807.

FOX, J. A., AND M. W. ZAWITZ. 2007. Homicide trends in the United States. Bureau of Justice Statistics.

FOX, S. 2011. The social life of health information, 2011. Pew Research Center, May 12.

FOX, S., AND J. BRENNER. 2012. Family caregivers turn to Internet for information and guidance. Pew Research Center, July 12.

FOX, S., M. DUGGAN, AND K. PURCELL. 2013. Family caregivers are wired for health. Pew Research Center, June 20.

FRANK, G. K., ET AL. 2005. Increased dopamine D2/D3 receptor binding after recovery from anorexia nervosa measured by positron emission tomography and [11^{C}] raclopride. *Biological Psychiatry* 58 (December): 908–12.

FRANTZ, O., AND N. BRAND. 2012. What about the men? Why our gender system sucks for men, too. The Good Men Project, July 11.

FRAZIER, E. F. 1939. *The Negro family in the United States*. Chicago: University of Chicago Press.

FRECH, A., AND K. WILLIAMS. 2007. Depression and the psychological benefits of entering marriage. *Journal of Health and Social Behavior* 48 (June): 149–63.

FREDRICKSON, B. 2013. *Love 2.0: How our supreme emotion affects everything we feel, think, do, and become*. New York: Penguin Books.

FREESE, J. 2008. Genetics and the social science explanation of individual outcomes. *American Journal of Sociology* 114 (Suppl.): S1–S35.

FREITAS, D. 2008. *Sex and the soul: Juggling sexuality, spirituality, romance, and religion on America's college campuses*. New York: Oxford University Press.

FREMSTAD, S. 2012. The poverty rate is higher than the federal government says it is. Center for Economic and Policy Research, September 21.

FRIEDAN, B. 1963. *The feminine mystique*. New York: Norton.

FRIEDEN, T. R. 2011. Forward. *MMWR* 60 (Suppl, January 14): 1–2.

FRIEDMAN, H. S. 2012. US infant mortality rate higher than other wealthy countries. *Huffington Post*, June 25.

FRIEDMAN, H. S., AND L. R. MARTIN. 2011. *The longevity project: Surprising discoveries for health and long life from the landmark eight-decade study*. New York: Hudson Street Press.

FRIEDMAN, L. F. 2011. Intelligent intercourse. *Psychology Today*, July/August, 41–42.

FRIEDMAN, M. 2011. How do I love thee? Let me tweet the ways. *Time*, March 28, 62, 65.

FRIEDMAN, R. A. 2009. Postpartum depression strikes fathers, too. *New York Times*, December 8, D6.

FROMM, E. 1956. *The art of loving*. New York: Bantam.

FROST, J. J., AND L. D. LINDBERG. 2013. Reasons for using contraception: Perspectives of US women seeking care at specialized family planning clinics. *Contraception* 87 (April): 465–72.

FROST, J. J., L. D. LINDBERG, AND L. B. FINER. 2012. Young adults' contraceptive knowledge, norms, and attitudes: Associations with risk of unintended pregnancy. *Perspectives on Sexual and Reproductive Health* 44 (June): 107–16.

FRY, R. 2012. No reversal in decline of marriage. Pew Research Center, November 20.

FRY, R. 2013. A rising share of young adults live in their parents' home. Pew Research Center, August 1.

FRY, R. 2013. Young adults after the recession: Fewer homes, fewer cars, less debt. Pew Research Center, February 21.

FRY, R., AND D. COHN. 2010. New economics of marriage: The rise of wives. Pew Research Center, January 19.

FRY, R., AND D. COHN. 2011. Living together: The economics of cohabitation. Pew Research Center, June 27.

FRYAR, C. D., R. HIRSCH, K. S. PORTER, B. KOTTIRI, D. J. BRODY, AND T. LOUIS. 2007. Drug use and sexual behaviors reported by adults: United States, 1999–2002. Advance Data from Vital and Health STATISTICS, no. 384. Hyattsville, MD: National Center for Health Statistics.

FRYER, R. G. JR., D. PAGER, AND J. L. SPENKUCH. 2011. Racial disparities in job finding and offered wages. National Bureau of Economic Research, September.

FUCHS, D. 2003. In Spain's lonely country side, a Cupid crusade. *Christian Science Monitor*, June 10, 1, 14.

FULIGNI, A. J., AND H. YOSHIKAWA. 2003. Socioeconomic resources, parenting, and child development among immigrant families. In *Socioeconomic status, parenting, and child development*, eds. M. H. Bornstein and R. H. Bradley, 107–24. Mahwah, NJ: Lawrence Erlbaum.

FULLER, B. 2012. Yahoo CEO Marissa Mayer: Please don't minimize being a working mom. Huffington Post, November 28.

FULLER, N., AND A. GENCER. 2008. Father admits he drowned kids. *Baltimore Sun*, April 1, 1A, 4A.

FURSTENBERG, F. F., AND K. E. KIERNAN. 2001. Delayed parental divorce: How much do children benefit? *Journal of Marriage and Family* 63 (May): 446–57.

FURSTENBERG, F. F., JR., AND J. O. TEITLER. 1994. Reconsidering the effects of marital disruption: What happens to children of divorce in early adulthood? *Journal of Family Issues* 15 (June): 173–90.

FUTRIS, T. G., AND S. J. SCHOPPE-SULLIVAN. 2007. Mothers' perceptions of barriers, parenting alliance, and adolescent fathers' engagement with children. *Family Relations* 56 (July): 258–69.

G

GABLE, M. 2013. Ongoing joblessness: A national catastrophe for African American and Latino workers. Economic Policy Institute, May 29.

GADOUA, S. P. 2008. *Contemplating divorce: A step-by-step guide to deciding whether to stay or go*. Oakland, CA: New Harbinger Publications.

GAERTNER, B. M., T. L. SPINRAD, N. EISENBERG, AND K. A. GREVING. 2007. Parental child-drearing attitudes as correlates of father involvement during infancy. *Journal of Marriage and Family* 69 (November): 962–76.

GAGER, C. T., AND L. SANCHEZ. 2003. Two as one?: Couples' perceptions of time spent together, marital quality, and the risk of divorce. *Journal of Family Issues* 24 (January): 21–50.

GAGER, C. T., AND S. T. YABIKU. 2010. Who has the time? The relationship between household labor time and sexual frequency. *Journal of Family Issues* 31 (February): 135–63.

GAGNON, J. 2011. The lonely hearts club. *Bloomburg Businessweek*, January 24–30, 107.

GAILEY, J. A. 2012. Fat shame to fat pride: Fat women's sexual and dating experiences. *Fat Studies* 1 (1): 114–127.

GALE, W., AND D. MARRON. 2012. What's the truth about the 47 percent? *Washington Post*, September 12.

GALINSKY, E., K. AUMANN, AND J. T.BOND. 2009. Times are changing: Gender and generation at work and at home. Families and Work Institute.

GALLUP HISTORICAL TRENDS. 2013. Marriage. Gallup.

GALLUP, G., JR., AND T. NEWPORT. 1990. Virtually all adults want children, but many of the reasons are intangible. *Gallup Poll Monthly* (June): 8–22.

GALLUP. 2013. U.S. employment (weekly). Gallup.

GALVIN, K. M., AND B. J. BROMMEL. 2000. *Family communication: Cohesion and change*, 5th ed. New York: Addison-Wesley-Longman.

GAMACHE, D. 1990. Domination and control: The social context of dating violence. In *Dating violence: Young women in danger*, ed. B. Levy, 69–118. Seattle: Seal.

GAMERMAN, E. 2006. Dating Web sites now trying to prevent divorce. *Wall Street Journal*, April 3, (accessed April 5, 2006).

GANEVA, T. 2012. Is your sex life really private? The truth about online dating sites. AlterNet, March 6.

GANONG, L. H., AND M. COLEMAN. 1994. *Remarried family relationships*. Thousand Oaks, CA: Sage.

GANONG, L., M. COLEMAN, AND J. HANS. 2006. Divorce as prelude to stepfamily living and the consequences of redivorce. In *Handbook of divorce and relationship dissolution*,

eds. M. A. Fine and J. H. Harvey, 409–34. Mahwah, NJ: Lawrence Erlbaum.

GANONG, L. H., AND M. COLEMAN. 2004. *Stepfamily relationships: Development, dynamics, and interventions.* New York: Kluwer Academic/Plenum Publishers.

GANONG, L. H., M. COLEMAN, AND T. JAMISON. 2011. Patterns of stepchild–stepparent relationship development. *Journal of Marriage and Family* 73 (April): 396–413.

GANONG, L. H., M. COLEMAN, R. FEISTMAN, T. JAMISON, AND M. S. MARKHAM. 2012. Communication technology and postdivorce coparenting. *Family Relations* 61 (July): 397–409.

GARBARINO, J. 2006. *See Jane hit: Why girls are growing more violent and what can be done about it.* New York: Penguin.

GARCÍA, A. M. 2002. *The Mexican Americans.* Westport, CT: Greenwood Press.

GARCÍA, C. Y. 1998. Temporal course of the basic components of love throughout relationships. *Psychology in Spain* 2(1): 76–86.

GARCIA, M. T. 1980. La familia: The Mexican immigrant family, 1900–1930. In *Work, family, sex roles, language*, eds. M. Barrera, A. Camarillo, and F. Hernandez, 117–40. Berkeley, CA: Tonatiua-Quinto Sol International.

GARDNER, M. 2002. Grandmothers weigh in on providing child care. *Christian Science Monitor*, August 14, 16.

GARDNER, M. 2007. Whatever you do, don't say "elderly." *Christian Science Monitor*, August 8, 15.

GARFINKEL, I., S. S. MC LANAHAN, AND P. K. ROBINS, EDS. 1994. *Child support and child well-being.* Washington, DC: Urban Institute.

GARIETY, B. S., AND S. SHAFFER. 2007. Wage differentials associated with working at home. *Monthly Labor Review* 130 (March): 61–67.

GARRISON, J. 2007. Do-it-yourself doesn't always sever ties. *Los Angeles Times*, January 1.

GARRISON, M. M., AND D. A. CHRISTAKIS. 2005. A teacher in the living room? Educational media for babies, toddlers and preschoolers. Kaiser Family Foundation, December.

GARTRELL, N., H. M. W. BOS, H. PEYSER, A. DECK, AND C. RODAS. 2012. Adolescents with lesbian mothers describe their own lives. *Journal of Homosexuality* 59 (9): 1211–29.

GASSMAN-PINES, A. 2011. Low-income mothers' nighttime and weekend work: Daily associations with child behavior, mother-child interactions, and mood. *Family Relations* 60 (February): 15–29.

GATES, G. J. 2011. Family formation and raising children among same-sex couples. National Council on Family Relations, *Family Focus*, Winter, F1–F4.

GATES, G. J. 2011a. How many people are lesbian, gay, bisexual, and transgender? Williams Institute, April.

GATES, G. J. 2011b. Gay people count, so why not count them correctly? *Washington Post*, April 7.

GATES, G. J. 2013. LGBT parenting in the United States. The Williams Institute University of California School of Law, February.

GATES, G. J., AND F. NEWPORT. 2012. Special report: 3–4% of U.S. adults identify as LGBT. Gallup, October 18.

GATES, G. J., AND J. OST. 2004. *The gay & lesbian atlas.* Washington, DC: The Urban Institute Press.

GAUNT, R. 2006. Couple similarity and marital dissatisfaction: Are similar spouses happier? *Journal of Personality* 74 (October): 1401–20.

GAVIN, L., ET AL. 2013. Self-reported hypertension and use of antihypertensive medication among adults—United States, 2005–2009. *Morbidity and Mortality Weekly Report* 62 (April 5): 248–255.

GAY AND LESBIAN ALLIANCE AGAINST DEFAMATION. 2012. 2011: Where are we on TV?

GAY AND Lesbian Rights. 2012. Gallup, November.

GEER, J. H., AND G. M. MANGUNO-MIRE. 1996. Gender differences in cognitive processes in sexuality. *Annual Review of Sex Research* 7: 90–124.

GELLES, R. J., AND C. P. CORNELL. 1990. *Intimate violence in families*, 2nd ed. Thousand Oaks, CA: Sage.

GELLES, R. J., AND M. A. STRAUS. 1988. *Intimate violence.* New York: Simon & Schuster.

GENOVESE, E. D. 1981. Husbands and fathers, wives and mothers, during slavery. In *Family life in America: 1620–2000*, eds. M. Albin and D. Cavallo, 237–51. St. James, NY: Revisionary Press.

GERSHMAN, J. 2013. Lawmakers in Vermont approve assisted suicide. *Wall Street Journal*, May 15, A7.

GERSHOFF, E. T. 2002. Corporal punishment by parents and associated child behaviors and experiences: A meta-analytic and theoretical review. *Psychological Bulletin* 128 (July): 539–79.

GERSON, K. 2010. *The unfinished revolution: Coming of age in a new era of gender, work, and family.* New York: Oxford University Press.

GERSTEL, N., AND N. SARKISIAN. 2006. Marriage: The good, the bad, and the greedy. *Contexts* 5 (Fall): 16–21.

GETTLEMAN, J. 2011. For Somali women, pain of being a spoil of war. *New York Times*, December 28, A1.

GIBBS, L. 2012. Women's employment rate, 2010. National Center for Family and Marriage Research, December 20.

GIBBS, L., AND K. K. PAYNE. 2011. First divorce rate, 2010. (FP-11-09). National Center for Family & Marriage Research.

GIBBS, N. 2007. Abortion in America: 1 woman at a time. *Time*, February 26, 23–31.

GIBBS, N. 2012. Your life is fully mobile. *Time*, August 27, 32–39.

GIBSON, C. L., AND H. V. MILLER. 2010. Crime and victimization among Hispanic adolescents: A multilevel longitudinal study of acculturation and segmented assimilation. U.S. Department of Justice, November.

GIBSON, M. 2012. Celebrities offering scientific "facts"? Just say no. Time Newsfeed, January 3.

GIBSON, P. A. 2005. Intergenerational parenting from the perspective of African American grandmothers. *Family Relations* 54 (April): 280–97.

GIBSON-DAVIS, C. M., K. MAGNUSON, L. A. GENNETIAN, AND G. J. DUNCAN. 2005. Employment and the risk of domestic abuse among low-income women. *Journal of Marriage and Family* 67 (December): 1149–68.

GILES, L. C., G. F. V. GLONEK, M. A. LUSZCZ, AND G. R. ANDREWS. 2005. Effect of social networks on 10-year survival in very old Australians: The Australian longitudinal study of aging. *Journal of Epidemiology and Community Health* 59 (May): 574–79.

GILGOFF, D. 2004. The rise of the gay family. *U.S. News & World Report*, May 24, 40–45.

GILGUN, J. F. 2008. Child sexual abuse: One of the most neglected social problems of our time. *Family Focus* 53 (December): F5–F7.

GILGUN, J. F. 2012. Enduring themes of qualitative family research. *Journal of Family Theory & Review* 4 (June): 80–95.

GILLES, K., AND C. FELDMAN-JACOBS. 2012. When technology and tradition collide: From gender bias to sex selection. Population Reference Bureau, September.

GILLIS, J. R. 1996. *A world of their own making: Myth, ritual, and the quest for family values.* New York: Basic Books.

GILLIS, J. R. 2004. Marriages of the mind. *Journal of Marriage and Family* 66 (November): 988–91.

GILLMORE, M. R. ET AL. 2002. Teen sexual behavior: Applicability of the theory of reasoned action. *Journal of Marriage and Family* 64 (November): 885–97.

GINTY, M. M. 2011. Cyberstalking turns Web technologies into weapons. Women's eNews, May 2.

GIORDANO, P. C., M. A. LONGMORE, AND W. D. MANNING. 2006. Gender and the meanings of adolescent romantic relationships: A focus on boys. *American Sociological Review* 71 (April): 260–87.

GLASS, S. 2002. *Not "just friends": Protect your relationship from infidelity and heal the trauma of betrayal.* New York: Free Press.

GLASS, S. P., AND J. C. STAEHELI. 2004. *Not "just friends": Rebuilding trust and recovering your sanity after infidelity.* New York: Free Press.

GLAUBER, R. 2007. Marriage and the motherhood wage penalty among African Americans, Hispanics, and whites. *Journal of Marriage and Family* 69 (November): 951–61.

GLAUBER, R., AND K. L. GOZJOLKO. 2011. Do traditional fathers always work more? Gender ideology, race, and parenthood. *Journal of Marriage and Family* 72 (October): 1133–48.

GLAZE, L. E., AND L. M. MARUSCHAK. 2010. Parents in prison and their minor children. Bureau of Justice Statistics Special Report, revised March 30.

GLENN, E. N., AND S. G. H. YAP. 2002. Chinese American families. In *Minority families in the United States: A multicultural perspective*, 3rd ed., ed. R. L. Taylor, 134–63. Upper Saddle River, NJ: Prentice Hall.

GLENN, N. 2005. With this ring . . . : A national survey on marriage in America. National Fatherhood Initiative.

GLENN, N. D. 1991. Quantitative research on marital quality in the 1980s. In *Contemporary families: Looking forward, looking back*, ed. A. Booth, 28–41. Minneapolis: National Council on Family Relations.

GLENN, N. D. 2002. A plea for greater concern about the quality of marital matching. In *Revitalizing the institution of marriage in the twenty-first century*, eds. L. D. Wardle and D. O. Coolidge, 45–58. Westport, CT: Praeger.

GLENN, N. D., J. UECKER, AND R. W. B. LOVE, Jr. 2010. Later first marriage and marital success. *Social Science Research* 39 (September): 787–800.

GLENN, N., AND T. SYLVESTER. 2006. The denial: Downplaying the consequences of family structure for children. Institute for American Values.

GLYNN, L. M., N. CHRISTENFELD, AND W. GERIN 2002. The role of rumination in recovery from reactivity: Cardiovascular consequences of emotional states. *Psychosomatic Medicine* 64 (September/October): 714–26.

GOBLE, P., C. L. MARTIN, L. D. HANISH, AND R. A. FABES. 2012. Children's gender-typed

activity choices across preschool social contexts. *Sex Roles* 67 (October): 435–51.

GODDARD, H. W. 1994. *Principles of parenting.* Auburn, AL: Auburn University, Department of Family and Child Development.

GODFREY, S., C. L. RICHMAN, AND T. N. WITHERS. 2000. Reliability and validity of a new scale to measure prejudice: The GRISMS. *Current Psychology* 19 (March): 1046–1310.

GODOFSKY, J., C. ZUKIN, AND C. VAN HORN. 2011. Unfulfilled expectations: Recent college graduates struggle in a troubled economy. Work Trends, May.

GOETTING, A. 1982. The six stations of remarriage: Developmental tasks of remarriage after divorce. *Family Relations* 31 (April): 231–22.

GOFFMAN, E. 1959. *The presentation of self in everyday life.* New York: Doubleday Anchor Books.

GOFFMAN, E. 1963. *Stigma: Notes on the management of spoiled identity.* Upper Saddle River, NJ: Prentice Hall.

GOFFMAN, E. 1969. *Strategic interaction.* Philadelphia: University of Pennsylvania Press.

GOLD, D. T. 1989. Sibling relationships in old age: A typology. *International Journal on Aging and Human Development* 28 (1): 37–51.

GOLD, D. T. 1990. Late-life sibling relationships: Does race affect typological distribution? *The Gerontologist* 30 (December): 741–48.

GOLD, R. B., AND E. NASH. 2012. Troubling trend: More states hostile to abortion rights as middle ground shrinks. *Guttmacher Policy Review* 15 (Winter): 14–19.

GOLDBERG, A. E., AND A. SAYER. 2006. Lesbian couples' relationship quality across the transition to parenthood. *Journal of Marriage and Family* 68 (February): 87–100.

GOLDBERG, A. E., AND K. A. KUVALANKA. 2012. Marriage (in)equality: The perspectives of adolescents and emerging adults with lesbian, gay, and bisexual parents. *Journal of Marriage and Family* 74 (February): 34–52.

GOLDBERG, A. E., J. B. DOWNING, AND A. M. MOYER. 2012. Why parenthood, and why now? Gay men's motivations for pursuing parenthood. *Family Relations* 61 (February): 157–74.

GOLDIN, C., AND M, SHIM. 2004. Making a name: Women's surnames at marriage and beyond. *Journal of Economic Perspectives* 18 (Spring): 143–60.

GOLOMBOK, S., AND F. TASKER. 1996. Do parents influence the sexual orientation of their children? Findings from a longitudinal study of lesbian families. *Developmental Psychology* 32 (1): 3–11.

GONNERMAN, J. 2005. The unforgiven. *Mother Jones,* July/August, 38–43.

GONZAGA, G. C., B. CAMPOS, AND T. BRADBURY. 2007. Similarity, convergence, and relationship satisfaction in dating and married couples. *Journal of Personality and Social Psychology* 93 (July): 24–48.

GONZÁLEZ, R. 1996. *Muy macho: Latino men confront their manhood.* New York: Anchor.

GONZALEZ-BARRERA, A., AND M. H. LOPEZ. 2013. A demographic portrait of Mexican-origin Hispanics in the United States. Pew Hispanic Center, May 1.

GOO, S. K. 2012. Facebook: A profile of its "friends." Pew Research Center, May 16.

GOODALE, G. 2013. Behind a looming baby bust. *Christian Science Monitor,* February 4, 21–23.

GOODE, E. 1990. *Deviant behavior,* 3rd ed. Upper Saddle River, NJ: Prentice Hall.

GOODE, E., ET AL. 1994. Till death do them part? *U.S. News & World Report,* July 4, 24–28.

GOODE, W. J. 1963. *World revolution and family patterns.* New York: Free Press.

GOODING, G. E., AND R. M. KREIDER. 2010. Women's marital naming choices in a nationally representative sample. *Journal of Family Issues* 31 (5): 681–701.

GOODMAN, E. 2008. What we demand of a political wife. *Baltimore Sun,* March 14, 21A.

GOODMAN, W. B., A. C. CROUTER, S. T. LANZA, AND M. J. CR0. 2008. Paternal work characteristics and father-infant interactions in low-income, rural families. *Journal of Marriage and Family* 70 (August): 640–53.

GOODWIN, J. 2010. IVF, fertility drugs might boost autism risk. *U.S. News,* May 19.

GOODWIN, J. 2010. Many girls now begin puberty at age 7, 8. *U.S. News & World Report,* August 9.

GOODWIN, R., AND C. FINDLAY. 1997. "We were just fated together." Chinese love and the concept of yuan in England and Hong Kong. *Personal Relationships* 4: 85–92.

GOOTMAN, E. 2012. So eager for grandchildren, they're paying the egg-freezing clinic. *New York Times,* May 14, A1.

GORCHOFF, S. M., O. P. JOHN, AND R. HELSON. 2008. Contextualizing change in marital satisfaction during middle age: An 18-year longitudinal study. *Psychological Science* 19 (November): 1194–1200.

GORDON, L. H. 1993. Intimacy: The art of working out your relationships. *Psychology Today* 26 (September/October): 40–43, 79–82.

GOSE, B. 1994. Spending time on the reservation. *Chronicle of Higher Education,* August 10, A30–A31.

GOTTLIEB, L. 2010. *Marry him: The case for settling for Mr. Good Enough.* New York: Dutton.

GOTTMAN, J. M. 1982. Emotional responsiveness in marital conversations. *Journal of Communication* 32, 108–20.

GOTTMAN, J. M. 1994. *What predicts divorce? The relationships between marital processes and marital outcome.* Hillsdale, NJ: Erlbaum.

GOTTMAN, J. M., AND J. DE CLAIRE. 2001. *The relationship cure: A five-step guide for building better connections with family, friends, and lovers.* New York: Crown.

GOTTSCHALCK, A., M. VORNOVYTSKY, AND A. SMITH. 2013. Household wealth in the U.S.: 2000 to 2011. U.S. Census Bureau, March 21.

GOUDREAU, J. 2012. A new obstacle for professional women: The glass escalator. *Forbes,* May 21.

GOULD, E. 2012. Two in five female-headed families with children live in poverty. Economic Policy Institute, November 14.

GOULD, E., AND D. COOPER. 2013. Financial security of elderly Americans at risk. EPI Briefing Paper, Economic Policy Institute, June 6.

GOULD, E., AND H. SHIERHOLZ. 2012. Average worker in "right-to-work" state earns $1500 less each year. Economic Policy Institute, December 13.

GRABE, S., L. M. WARD, AND J. S. HYDE. 2008. The role of the media in body image concerns among women: A meta-analysis of experimental and correlational studies. *Psychological Bulletin* 134 (May): 460–76.

GRACIA, E., AND J. HERRERO. 2008. Is it considered violence? The acceptability of physical punishment of children in Europe. *Journal of Marriage and Family* 70 (February): 210–17.

GRAHAM, L. O. 1996. *Member of the club: Reflections on life in a racially polarized world.* New York: HarperCollins.

GRALL, T. S. 2011. Custodial mothers and fathers and their child support: 2009. U.S. Census Bureau, Current Population Reports, December.

GRANDPARENTS DAY 2008: Sept 7. 2008. U.S. Census Bureau Newsroom, Facts for Feature, July 7, 2008.

GRANT, J. M., L. A. MOTTET, J. TANIS, J. HARRISON, J. L. HERMAN, AND M. KEISLING. 2011. Injustice at every turn: A report of the national transgender discrimination survey. Washington, DC: National Center for Transgender Equality and National Gay and Lesbian Task Force.

GRAVES, J. L., JR. 2001. *The emperor's new clothes: Biological theories of race at the millennium.* New Brunswick, NJ: Rutgers University Press.

GRAY, M. R., AND L. STEINBERG. 1999. Unpacking authoritative parenting: Reassessing a multidimensional construct. *Journal of Marriage and the Family* 61 (August): 574–87.

GRAY, P. S., J. B. WILLIAMSON, D. R. KARP, AND J. R. DALPHIN. 2007. *The research imagination: An introduction to qualitative and quantitative methods.* New York: Cambridge University Press.

GREELEY, B. 2011. The union, jacked. *Bloomberg Businessweek,* February 28–March 6, 8–9.

GREEN, J. 2011. The silencing of sexual harassment. *Bloomberg Businessweek,* November 21–27, 27–28.

GREEN, J. 2012. The boardroom's still the boys' room. *Bloomberg Businessweek,* October 29–November 4, 25–26.

GREEN, M. T. 2007. Florida shelter offers hope to women of means. Jewish Women International, June.

GREEN, P. 2007. Whose bed is it anyway? *Baltimore Sun,* March 11, D1, D6.

GREENBERG, I. 2006. After a century, public polygamy is re-emerging in Tajikistan. *New York Times,* November 13, A10.

GREENBERG, J., AND M. RUHLEN. 1992. Linguistic origins of Native Americans. *Scientific American* 267: 94.

GREENSTEIN, T. N. 2000. Economic dependence, gender, and the division of labor in the home: A replication and extension. *Journal of Marriage and the Family* 62 (May): 322–35.

GREENSTEIN, T. N. 2006. *Methods of family research,* 2nd ed. Thousand Oaks, CA: Sage.

GREENSTONE, M., AND A. LOONEY. 2012. The marriage gap: The impact of economic and technological change on marriage rates. Brookings Institution, February 3.

GREIDER, L. 2000. How not to be a monster-in-law. *Modern Maturity* (March/April): 57–59.

GREIDER, L. 2004. Unmarried together. *AARP Bulletin,* October, 14–16.

GRIECO, E. M., AND E. N. TREVELYAN. 2010. Place of birth of the foreign-born population: 2009. U.S. Census Bureau, American Community Survey Briefs, October.

GRIECO, E. M., Y. D. ACOSTA, G. P. DE LA CRUZ, C. GAMBINO, T. GRYN, L. J. LARSEN, E. N. TREVELYAN, AND N. P. WALTERS. 2012. The foreign-born population in the United States: 2010. May.

GRIER, P. 2012. Briefing: Who are the "47 percent"? *Christian Science Monitor,* October 1, 12.

GRIFFIN, B. A., R. RAMCHAND, M. O. EDELEN, D. F. MCCAFFREY, AND A. R. MORRAL. 2011. Associations between abstinence in adolescence and economic and educational

outcomes seven years later among high-risk youth. *Drug and Alcohol Dependence* 113 (2-3): 118–124.

GRIFFIS, M., ED. 2012. Casualties in Iraq. Anti-War.com, February 11.

GRIND, K. 2013. Mother, can you spare a room? *Wall Street Journal*, May 4–5, B1, B10.

GRISKEVICIUS, V., J. M. TYBUR, J. M. ACKERMAN, A. W. DELTON, T. E. ROBERTSON, AND A. E. WHITE. 2012. The financial consequences of too many men: Sex ratio effects on saving, borrowing, and spending. *Journal of Personality and Social Psychology* 102 (1): 69–80.

GRISWOLD, R. L. 1993. *Fatherhood in America: A history*. New York: Basic Books.

GROMOSKE, A. N., AND K. MAGUIRE-JACK. 2012. Transactional and cascading relations between early spanking and children's social-emotional development. *Journal of Marriage and Family* 74 (October): 1054–68.

GROSE, T. K. 2008. When "I do" is an order, not a choice. *U.S. News & World Report*, May 26/June 2, 13.

GROTEVANT, H. D. 2001. Adoptive families: Longitudinal outcomes for adolescents. Report to the William T. Grant Foundation. http://fsos.che.umn.edu (accessed August 17, 2003).

GROVES, E. R. 1928. *The marriage crisis*. New York: Longmans, Green.

GRUDZEN, C. R., W. J. KOENIG, J. R. HOFFMAN, J. BOSCARDIN, K. A. LORENZ, AND S. M. ASCH. 2009. Potential impact of a verbal prehospital DNR policy. *Prehospital Emergency Care* 13 (2): 166–72.

GRUNWALD, M. 2012. One nation on welfare: Living your life on the dole. *Time*, September 17, 28–37.

GRZYWACZ, J. G., S. S. DANIEL, J. TUCKER, J. WALLS, AND E. LERKES. 2011. Nonstandard work schedules and developmentally generative parenting practices: An application of propensity score techniques. *Family Relations* 60 (February): 45–59.

GUARINO, M. 2013. Auto jobs are back, too, but at lower wages. *Christian Science Monitor*, May 13, 22–23.

GUBERMAN, N., P. MAHEU, AND C. MAILLE. 1992. Women as family caregivers: Why do they care? *The Gerontologist* 32 (5): 607–17.

GUEST, J. 1988. *The mythic family*. Minneapolis: Milkweed.

GUILAMO-RAMOS, V., J. JACCARD, P. DITTUS, A. BOURIS, B. GONZALEZ, E. CASILLAS, AND S. BANSPACH. 2011. A comparative study of interventions for delaying the initiation of sexual intercourse among Latino and black youth. *Perspectives on Sexual and Reproductive Health* 43 (December): 247–54.

GUILMOTO, C. Z. 2007. Sex-ratio imbalance in Asia: Trends, consequences and policy responses. In *Sex-ratio imbalance in Asia: Trends, consequences and policy responses. Executive Summary, Regional Analysis*, 1–12. United Nations Population Fund.

GUNDERSON, E. A., G. RAMIREZ, S. C. LEVINE, AND S. L. BEILOCK. 2012. The role of parents and teachers in the development of gender-related math attitudes. *Sex Roles* 66 (August): 153–66.

GUSTAFSSON, H. C., AND M. J. COX. 2012. Relations among intimate partner violence, maternal depressive symptoms, and maternal parenting behaviors. *Journal of Marriage and Family* 74 (October): 1005–20.

GUTMAN, H. 1976. *The black family in slavery and freedom, 1750–1925*. New York: Pantheon.

GUTMAN, H. G. 1983. Persistent myths about the Afro-American family. In *The American family in socio-historical perspective*, 3rd ed., ed. M. Gordon, 459–81. New York: St. Martin's.

GUTNER, T. 2000. Getting your fair share in a divorce. *Business Week*, May 29, 250.

GUTNER, T. 2001. Househusbands unite! *Business Week*, January 22, 106.

GUTTMACHER INSTITUTE. 2005. An overview of abortion in the United States. 2005. Physicians for Reproductive Choice and Health and the Guttmacher Institute, June.

GUTTMACHER INSTITUTE. 2008. Facts on induced abortion in the United States. July.

GUTTMACHER INSTITUTE. 2011. Facts on induced abortion in the United States. August.

GUTTMACHER INSTITUTE. 2012. Facts on American teens' sexual and reproductive health. August.

GUTTMACHER INSTITUTE. 2012. Facts on unintended pregnancy in the United States. January.

GUTTMACHER INSTITUTE. 2013. U.S. women who have abortions. Infographics.

GUZZO, K. B., AND H. LEE. 2008. Couple relationship status and patterns in early parenting practices. *Journal of Marriage and Family* 70 (February): 44–61.

GWYNNE, K. 2011. Drug company profiteering, pill mills and thousands of addicts: How Oxycontin has spread through America. Alternet, June 20.

H

HA, J-H. 2008. Changes in support from confidants, children, and friends following widowhood. *Journal of Marriage and Family* 70 (April): 306–18.

HACKER, A. 2003. *Mismatch: The growing gulf between women and men*. New York: Scribner.

Half of young children in the U.S. are read to at least once a day, Census Bureau reports. 2011. Newsroom, August 11.

HALL, J. A., AND M. CANTERBERRY. 2011. Sexism and assertive courtship strategies. *Sex Roles* 65 (December): 840–53.

HALL, K. S., C. MOREAU, AND J. TRUSSELL. 2012. Associations between sexual and reproductive health communication and health service use among U.S. adolescent women. *Perspectives on Sexual and Reproductive Health* 44 (March): 6–12.

HALL, S. S., AND S. M. MACDERMID. 2009. A typology of dual earner marriages based on work and family arrangements. *Journal of Family and Economic Issues* 30 (September): 215–25.

HALL, W. J. 2008. Centenarians: Metaphor becomes reality. *Archives of Internal Medicine* 168 (February 11): 262–63.

HALPERIN, D. M. 2012. How to be gay. *Chronicle Review*, September 7, B13–B17.

HALPERN-MEEKIN, S., W. D. MANNING, P. C. GIORDANO, AND M. A. LONGMORE. 2013. Relationship churning, physical violence, and verbal abuse in young adult relationships. *Journal of Marriage and Family* 75 (February): 2–12.

HAMBURG, M., AND K. HILL. 2012. *Commitment*. Kennebunkport, ME: Cider Mill Press.

HAMBY, S., AND A. BIBLE. 2009. Battered women's protective strategies. Applied Research Forum: National Online Resource Center on Violence Against Women, July.

HAMBY, S., D. FINKELHOR, H. TURNER, AND R. ORMROD. 2011. Children's exposure to intimate partner violence and other family violence. *Juvenile Justice Bulletin*, Office of Juvenile Justice and Delinquency Prevention, October.

HAMILTON, B. E., AND P. D. SUTTON. 2012. Recent trends in births and fertility rates through June 2012. CDC National Center for Health Statistics, December.

HAMILTON, B. E., AND S. J. VENTURA. 2012. Birth rates for U.S. teenagers reach historic lows for all age and ethnic groups. NCHS Data Brief, No. 89, April.

HAMILTON, B. E., J. A MARTIN, AND S. J. VENTURA. 2009. Births: Preliminary data for 2007. *National Vital Statistics Reports*, vol. 57, no 12. Hyattsville, MD: National Center for Health Statistics.

HAMILTON, B. E., J. A. MARTIN, AND S. J. VENTURA. 2012. Births: Preliminary data for 2011. *National Vital Statistics Reports* 61 (5): 1–19.

HAMMOND, R. J., AND B. BEARNSON. 2003. *The marriages and families activities workbook*. Belmont, CA: Wadsworth.

HAMPTON, K. N., L. S. GOULET, L. RAINIE, AND K. PURCELL. 2011. Social networking sites and our lives. Pew Internet & American Life Project, June 16.

HANDLER, J. 2009. I won't roll the biological dice. *Newsweek*, April 27, 16.

HANES, S. 2004. Mail-order bride wins damage award. *Baltimore Sun* (November 19): 1A, 4a.

HANES, S. 2010. In an affair's wake. *Christian Science Monitor*, February 14, 26–29.

HANES, S. 2011. Pretty in pink? *Christian Science Monitor*, September 26, 26–31.

HANES, S. 2012. Bikini onesie: Really? *Christian Science Monitor*, July 5.

HANNA, S. L. 2003. *Person to person: Positive relationships don't just happen*, 4th ed. Upper Saddle River, NJ: Prentice Hall.

HANS, J. D., M. GILLEN, AND K. AKANDE. 2010. Sex redefined: The reclassification of oral-genital contact. *Perspectives on Sexual and Reproductive Health* 42 (June): 74–78.

HANSEN, M. E., AND D. POLLACK. 2007. Transracial adoption of black children: An economic analysis. *Bepress Legal Series*, Working Paper 1942, January 17.

Happy Mother's Day from BLS: Working Mothers in 2012. Bureau of Labor Statistics, *The Editor's Desk*, May 10.

HAQ, H. 2011. How marriage is faring. *Christian Science Monitor*, February 14, 21.

HARARI, S. E., AND M. A. VINOVSKIS. 1993. Adolescent sexuality, pregnancy, and childbearing in the past. In *The politics of pregnancy: Adolescent sexuality and public policy*, eds. A. Lawson and D. I. Rhode, 23–45. New Haven, CT: Yale University Press.

HAREVEN, T. K. 1984. Themes in the historical development of the family. In *Review of child development research*, Vol. 7: The family, ed. R. D. Parke, 137–78. Chicago: University of Chicago Press.

HARGROVE, T. 2011. Disappearing jobs illustrate U.S. manufacturing revolution. Knox News, November 13.

HARLEY, W. F., JR. 2002. *Buyers, renters & freeloaders: Turning revolving-door romance into lasting love*. Grand Rapids, MI: Fleming H. Revell.

HARPER, S., D. RUSHANI, AND J. S. KAUFMAN. 2012. Trends in the black-white life expectancy gap, 2003–2008. *JAMA* 307 (June 6): 2257–59.

HARRIS, G. 2013. India's new focus on rape shows only the surface of women's perils. *New York Times*, January 12.

HARRIS, L. 1996. The hidden world of dating violence. *Parade Magazine*, September 22, 4–6.

HARRIS, M. 1994. *Down from the pedestal: Moving beyond idealized images of womanhood*. New York: Doubleday.

HARRIS, M. 2007. Families turn to Internet to grieve. *Baltimore Sun*, February 23, 1A, 6A.

HARRIS, T. 2003. Mind work: How a Ph.D. affects black women. *Chronicle of Higher Education*, April 11, B14–B15.

HARRISON, A. T., L. GAVIN, AND P. A. HASTINGS. 2012. Prepregnancy contraceptive use among teens with unintended pregnancies resulting in live births—Pregnancy risk assessment monitoring system (PRAMS), 2004–2008. *Morbidity and Mortality Weekly Report* 61 (January 20): 26–29.

HART, S. N., M. R. BRASSARD, N. J. BINGGELI, AND H. A. DAVIDSON. 2003. Psychological maltreatment. In *International encyclopedia of marriage and family*, 2nd ed., Vol. 1, ed. J. J. Ponzetti, Jr., 221–27. New York: Macmillan.

HARTILI, L. 2001. Vow or never. *Christian Science Monitor*, July 18, 15–17.

HARVEY, J. H., AND A. L. WEBER, 2002. *Odyssey of the heart: Close relationships in the 21st century*, 2nd ed. Mahwah, NJ: Erlbaum.

HARVEY, J. H., AND M. A. FINE. 2004. *Children of divorce: Stories of loss and growth*. Mahwah, NJ: Lawrence Erlbaum.

HARWOOD, R., B. LEYENDECKER, V. CARLSON, M. ASENCIO, AND A. MILLER. 2002. Parenting among Latino Families in the U.S. In *Handbook of parenting*, 2nd ed., Vol. 4: Social conditions and applied parenting, ed. M. H. Bornstein, 21–46. Mahwah, NJ: Erlbaum.

HASLETT, A. 2004. *George Washington's rules of civility*. New York: Akashic Books.

HATFIELD, E. 1983. What do women and men want from love and sex? In *Changing boundaries: Gender roles and sexual behavior*, eds. E. R. Allgeier and N. B. McCormick, 106–34. Mountain View, CA: Mayfield.

HAUB, C., AND T. KANEDA. 2012. 2012 world population data sheet. Washington, DC: Population Reference Bureau, wall poster.

HAUSMANN, R., L. D. TYSON, AND S. ZAHIDI. 2012. The global gender gap report 2012. World Economic Forum.

HAYANI, I. 1999. Arabs in Canada: Assimilation or integration? In *Arabs in America: Building a new future*, ed. M. W. Suleiman, 284–303. Philadelphia: Temple University Press.

HAYASHI, G. M., AND B. R. STRICKLAND. 1998. Longterm effects of parental divorce on love relationships: Divorce as attachment disruption. *Journal of Social & Personal Relationships* 15 (February): 23–38.

HAYFORD, S. R., AND K. B. GUZZO. 2013. Racial and ethnic variation in unmarried young adults' motivation to avoid pregnancy. *Perspectives on Sexual and Reproductive Health* 45 (March): 41–51.

HAYGHE, H. 1984. Working mothers reach record number in 1984. *Monthly Labor Review* 107 (December): 31–34.

HAYS, S. 1998. The fallacious assumptions and unrealistic prescriptions of attachment theory: A comment on parents' socioemotional investment in children. *Journal of Marriage and the Family* 60 (August): 782–95.

HAZAN, C., AND P. R. SHAVER. 1987. Conceptualizing romantic love as an attachment process. *Journal of Personality and Social Psychology* 52: 511–24.

HE, W., M. SENGUPIA, V. A. VELKOFF, AND K. A. DE BARROS. 2005. 65+ in the United States: 2005. U.S. Census Bureau, Current Population Reports, P23–209. Washington, DC: U.S. Government Printing Office.

HEALY, J. 2011. In Afghanistan, rage at young lovers. *New York Times*, July 31, A1.

HEALY, M. 2003. Fertility's new frontier. *Los Angeles Times*, July 21, F1.

HEALY, M., AND A. GORMAN. 2013. AMA votes to declare obesity now a disease. *Baltimore Sun*, June 19, 11.

HEBERT, L. E., J. WEUVE, P. A. SCHERR, AND D. A. EVANS. 2013. Alzheimer disease in the United States (2010–2050) estimated using the 2010 census. *Neurology* 80 (19): 1778–83.

HEGEWISCH, A., AND M. MATITE. 2013. The gender wage gap by occupation. Institute for Women's Policy Research, April.

HEIMAN, J. R., J. S. LONG, S. N. SMITH, W. A. FISHER, M. S. SAND, AND R. C. ROSEN. 2011. Sexual satisfaction and relationship happiness in midlife and older couples in five countries. *Archives of Sexual Behavior* 40 (4): 741–53.

HEISLER, C. 2012. Elder abuse. Office for Victims of Crime Training and Technical Assistance Center.

HELLIWELL, J. F., AND H. HUANG. 2013. Comparing the happiness effects of real and on-line friends. National Bureau of Economic Research, January.

HELM, B. 2008. Online polls: How good are they? *Business Week*, June 16, 86.

HELMAN, R., M. GREENWALD, N. ADAMS, C. COPELAND, AND J. VANDERHEI. 2013. The 2013 retirement confidence survey: Perceived savings needs outpace reality for many. Employee Benefit Research Institute, March, No. 384.

HELMS, H. M., A. J. SUPPLE, AND C. M. PROULX. 2011. Mexican-origin couples in the early years of parenthood: Marital well-being in ecological context. *Journal of Family Theory & Review* 3 (June): 67–95.

HENDRICK, C., AND S. HENDRICK. 1992a. *Liking, loving, and relating*, 2nd ed. Monterey, CA: Brooks/Cole.

HENDRICK, S., AND C. HENDRICK. 1992b. *Romantic love*. Thousand Oaks, CA: Sage.

HERBENICK, D., M. REECE, V. SCHICK, S. A. SANDERS, B. DODGE, AND J. D. FORTENBERRY. 2010a. An event-level analysis of the sexual characteristics and composition among adults ages 18 to 59: Results from a national probability sample in the United States. *Journal of Sexual Medicine* 7, Supplement 5 (October): 346–61.

HERBENICK, D., M. REECE, V. SCHICK, S. A. SANDERS, B. DODGE, AND J. D. FORTENBERRY. 2010b. Sexual behavior in the United States: Results from a national probability sample of men and women ages 14–94. *Journal of Sexual Medicine* 7, Supplement 5 (October): 255–265.

HERBENICK, D., M. REECE, V. SCHICK, S. A. SANDERS, B. DODGE, AND J. D. FORTENBERRY. 2010c. Sexual behaviors, relationships, and perceived health status among adult women in the United States: Results from a national probability sample. *Journal of Sexual Medicine* 7, Supplement 5 (October): 277–90.

HERMAN-GIDDENS, M. E., ET AL. 2012. Secondary sexual characteristics in boys: Data from the pediatric research in office settings network. *Pediatrics* 130 (November): e1058–e1068.

HERNANDEZ, D. J. 2011. Double jeopardy: How third-grade reading skills and poverty influence high school education. Annie E. Casey Foundation.

HERRENKOHL, T. I., R. KOSTERMAN, W. A. MASON, AND J. DAVID. 2007. Youth violence trajectories and proximal characteristics of intimate partner violence. *Violence and Victims* 22 (July): 259–74.

HERRING, D. J. 2007. The Multiethnic Placement Act: Threat to foster child safety and wellbeing. University of Pittsburgh School of Law Working Paper Series, Paper 51.

HERRMANN, A. 2003. Children of divorce in no rush to repeat error. Chicago Sun Times, June 10.

HERTZ, R. 2006. *Single by chance, mothers by choice: How women are choosing parenthood without marriage and creating the new American family*. New York: Oxford University Press.

HERVISH, A., AND C. FELDMAN-JACOBS. 2011. Who speaks for me? Ending child marriage. Population Reference Bureau, April.

HERZBERG, D. 2009. *Happy pills in America: From Miltown to Prozac*. Baltimore, MD: Johns Hopkins University Press.

HESKETH, T., L. LU, AND Z. W. XING. 2011. The consequences of son preference and sex-selective abortion in China and other Asian countries. *Canadian Medical Association Journal* 183 (12): 1374–77.

HETHERINGTON, E. M., AND J. KELLY. 2002. *For better or for worse: Divorce reconsidered*. New York: W. W. Norton.

HETHERINGTON, E. M., AND M. M. STANLEY-HAGAN. 2000. Diversity among stepfamilies. In *Handbook of family diversity*, eds. D. H. Demo, K. R. Allen, and M. A. Fine, 173–96. New York: Oxford University Press.

HETHERINGTON, E. M., AND M. M. STANLEY-HAGAN. 2002. Parenting in divorced and remarried families. In *Handbook of parenting*, 2nd ed., Vol. 3: Being and becoming a parent, ed. M. H. Bornstein, 287–315. Mahwah, NJ: Erlbaum.

HETHERINGTON, E. M., R. D. PARKE, AND V. O. LOCKE. 2006. *Child psychology: A contemporary viewpoint*, 6th ed. Boston: McGraw-Hill.

HEWITT, B. 2009. Which spouse initiates marital separation when there are children involved? *Journal of Marriage and Family* 71 (May): 362–72.

HIBBARD, R., J. BARLOW, AND H. MACMILLAN. 2012. Psychological maltreatment. American Academy of Pediatrics.

HIGGINS, J. A., R. A. POPKIN, AND J. S. SANTELLI. 2012. Pregnancy ambivalence and contraceptive use among young adults in the United States. *Perspectives on Sexual and Reproductive Health* 44 (December): 236–43.

High-tech gadgets help parents keep track of what their kids are doing. 2005. *Baltimore Sun*, September 5, B2.

HILL, C., C. CORBETT, AND A. ST. ROSE. 2010. Why so few? Women in science, technology, engineering, and mathematics. American Association of University Women.

HILL, E. J., J. J. ERICKSON, AND E. K. HOLMES. 2010. Workplace flexibility, work hours, and work-life conflict: Finding an extra day or two. *Journal of Family Psychology* 24 (3): 349–58.

HILL, S. A. 2005. *Black intimacies: A gender perspective on families and relationships*. Walnut Creek, CA: AltaMira Press.

HILLAKER, B. D., H. E. BROPHY-HERB, F. A. VILLARRUEL, AND B. E. HH0. 2008. The contributions of parenting to social competencies and positive values in middle school youth: Positive family communication, maintaining standards, and supportive family relationships. *Family Relations* 57 (December): 591–601.

HIMMELSTEIN, K. E. W., AND H. BRÜCKNER. 2011. Criminal-justice and school sanctions against nonheterosexual youth: A national longitudinal study. *Pediatrics* 127 (January): 49–57.

HINES, D. A., AND K. MALLEY-MORRISON. 2005. *Family violence in the United States: Defining, understanding, and combating abuse*. Thousand Oaks, CA: Sage.

HING, J. 2011. 5 ways Alabama's new anti-immigrant law is even worse than Arizona's SB 1070. AlterNet, June 24.

HISPANIC HERITAGE MONTH 2012: Sept. 15–Oct. 15. 2012. U.S. Census Bureau News, CB12-FF.19, August 6.

HOBBS, F., AND N. STOOPS 2002. Demographic trends in the 20th century. U.S. Census Bureau, 2000 Special Reports, Series CENSR-4.

HOBSON, K. 2004. The biological clock on ice. U.S. News & World Report, September 27, 62-63.

HOBSON, K. 2010. Sailing past 90 with lots left to do. U.S. News & World Report, February 10, 32–37.

HOEFER, M., N. RYTINA, AND B. C. BAKER. 2011. Estimates of the unauthorized immigrant population residing in the United States: January 2010. Office of Immigration Statistics, Homeland Security, Population Estimates, February.

HOEFFEL, E. M., S. RASTOGI, M. O. KIM, AND H. SHAHID. 2012. The Asian population: 2010. 2010 Census Briefs, U.S. Census Bureau, March.

HOEKSTRA, M. L. 2006. "Just kidding, dear": Using dismissed divorce cases to identify the effect of parental divorce on student performance. University of Pittsburgh, Department of Economics. Unpublished paper.

HOFFERTH, S. L. 2005. Secondary data analysis in family research. Journal of Marriage and Family 67 (November): 891–907.

HOJAT, M., R. SHAPURIAN, D. FOROUGHI, H. NAYERAHMADI, M. FARZANEH, M. SHAFIEYAN, AND M. PARSI. 2000. Gender differences in traditional attitudes toward marriage and the family: An empirical study of Iranian immigrants in the United States. Journal of Family Issues 21 (May): 419–34.

HOLDEN, G. W. 2011. Stress, not race. New York Times, August 14.

HOLLIST, C. S., AND R. B. MILLER. 2005. Perceptions of attachment style and marital quality in midlife marriage. Family Relations 54 (January): 46–57.

HOLMAN, T. B., AND W. R. BURR. 1980. Beyond the beyond: The growth of family theories in the 1970s. Journal of Marriage and the Family 42 (November): 729–41.

HOLMAN, T. B., J. H. LARSON, AND S. L. HARMER. 1994. The development and predictive validity of a new premarital assessment instrument: The preparation for marriage questionnaire. Family Relations 43 (January): 46–52.

HOLSON, L. M. 2011. Who's on the family tree? Now it's complicated. New York Times, July 5, A1.

HOLSON, L. M. 2012. "What were you thinking?" For couples, new source of online friction. New York Times, April 26, E1.

HOLT, T., L. GREENE, AND J. DAVIS. 2003. National survey of adolescents and young adults: Sexual health knowledge, attitudes and experiences. The Henry Kaiser Family Foundation.

HOMANS, G. 1974. Social behavior: Its elementary forms, rev. ed. New York: Harcourt Brace Jovanovich.

HONEY, M. 1984. Creating Rosie the Riveter: Class, gender, and propaganda. Amherst: University of Massachusetts Press.

HOOYMAN, N. R., AND H. A. KIYAK. 2002. Social gerontology: A multidisciplinary perspective, 6th ed. Boston, MA: Allyn & Bacon.

HOPPER, J. 2001. The symbolic origins of conflict in divorce. Journal of Marriage and Family 63 (May): 430–45.

HOPPMANN, C. A., D. GERSTORF, AND A. HIBBERT. 2011. Spousal associations between functional limitation and depressive symptom trajectories: Longitudinal findings from the study of asset and health dynamics among the oldest old (AHEAD). Health Psychology 30 (2): 153–62.

HORWITZ, A. V., AND J. C. WAKEFIELD. 2006. The epidemic in mental illness: Clinical fact or survey artifact? Contexts 5 (Winter): 19–23.

HORWITZ, A. V., H. R. WHITE, AND S. HOWELL-WHITE. 1996. Becoming married and mental health: A longitudinal study of a cohort of young adults. Journal of Marriage and the Family 58 (November): 895–907.

HOSSAIN, Z. 2001. Division of household labor and family functioning in off-reservation Navajo Indian families. Family Relations 50 (July), 255–61.

HOUSEKNECHT, S. K., AND S. K. LEWIS. 2005. Explaining teen childbearing and cohabitation: Community embeddedness and primary ties. Family Relations 54 (December): 607–20.

HOUSER, L., AND T. P. VARTANIAN. 2012. Pay matters: The positive economic impacts of paid family leave for families, businesses and the public. Rutgers Center for Women and Work, January.

How queer is that? 2010. Newsweek, June 7, 56.

HOYERT, D. L., AND J. XU. 2012. Deaths: Preliminary data for 2011. National Vital Statistics Reports 61 (6), October 10.

HUANG, C-C. 2009. Mothers' reports of nonresident fathers' involvement with their children: Revisiting the relationship between child support payment and visitation. Family Relations 58 (February): 54–64.

HUBER, R. 2012/2013. Are kids too close to their parents? AARP Magazine, December/January, 62–65.

HUDAK, M. A. 1993. Gender schema theory revisited: Men's stereotypes of American women. Sex Roles 28 (5/6): 279–92.

HUDSON, J. I., E. HIRIPI, H. G. POPE JR., AND R. C. KESSLER. 2007. The prevalence and correlates of eating disorders in the national comorbidity survey replication. Biological Psychiatry 61 (February): 348–58.

HUGHES, M. E., AND L. J. WAITE. 2009. Marital biography and health at mid-life. Journal of Health and Social Behavior 50 (September): 344–58.

HULL, K. E., A. MEIER, AND T. ORTYL. 2010. The changing landscape of love and marriage. Contexts 9 (Spring): 32–37.

HUMAN RIGHTS CAMPAIGN. 2012. Growing up LGBT in America.

HUMBAD, M. N., M. B. DONNELLAN, W. G. IACONO, M. MCGUE, AND S. A. BURT. 2010. Is spousal similarity for personality a matter of convergence or selection? Personality and Individual Differences 49 (November): 827–30.

HUNT, J. 1991. Ten reasons not to hit your kids. In Breaking down the wall of silence: The liberating experience of facing painful trust, ed. A. Miller, 168–71. Meridian, NY: Dutton.

HUNT, J. 2010. Why do women leave science and engineering? National Bureau of Economic Research, March.

HUPKA, R. B. 1991. The motive for the arousal of romantic jealousy: Its cultural origin. In The psychology of jealousy and envy, ed. P. Salovey, 252–70. New York: Guilford.

HUPPKE, R. W. 2012. Working women learn to swim with sharks. Baltimore Sun, September 20, 2.

HURD, M. D., P. MARTORELL, A. DELAVANDE, K. J. MULLEN, AND K. M. LANGA. 2013. Monetary costs of dementia in the United States. New England Journal of Medicine 368 (April 14): 1326–34.

HURH, W. M. 1998. The Korean Americans. Westport, CT: Greenwood.

HUTTER, M. 1998. The changing family, 3rd ed. Boston: Allyn & Bacon.

HWANG, A. C., A. KOYAMA, D. TAYLOR, J. T. HENDERSON, AND S. MILLER. 2005. Advanced practice clinicians' interest in providing medical abortion: Results of a California survey. Perspectives on Sexual and Reproductive Health 37 (June): 92–97.

HWANG, S.-S., R. SAENZ, AND B. F. AGUIRRE. 1994. Structural and individual determinants of outmarriage among Chinese-, Filipino-, and Japanese-Americans in California. Sociological Inquiry 64 (November): 396–414.

HYDE, J. S. 2005. The gender similarities hypothesis. American Psychologist 60 (September): 581–92.

HYDE, J. S. 2006. Gender similarities still rule. American Psychologist 61 (September): 641–42.

HYMOWITZ, C. 2012. The rise of the CEO mom has created a new kind of trophy husband. Bloomberg Businessweek, January 9–January 15, 54–59.

I

IDAHO Committee. 2012. The international day against homophobia and transphobia: Annual report 2012.

I-Fairy robot weds Tokyo couple in tinny voice. USA Today, May 17.

IGNATIUS, D. 2013. Newfound status for Saudi women. Washington Post, January 18.

IKRAMULLAH, E., M. BARRY, J. MANLOVE, AND K. A. MOORE. 2011. Facts at a glance: A fact sheet reporting national, state, and city trends in teen childbearing. Child Trends, April.

ILKKARACAN, P., AND S. JOLLY. 2007. Gender and sexuality: Overview report. BRIDGE, January.

IMBER-BLACK, E., AND J. ROBERTS. 1993. Family change: Don't cancel holidays! Psychology Today 26 (March/April): 62, 64, 92–93.

IMMEL, M. B. 2008. I'm old—and I'm just fine with that. Newsweek, July 31, 18.

India explores ways to curb prodigious food waste and extravagant wedding parties. 2011. Washington Post, July 21.

INDIAN HEALTH SERVICE. 2006. Facts on Indian health disparities. January.

INGERSOLL-DAYTON, B., M. B. NEAL, J.-H. HA, AND L. B. HAMMER. 2003. Redressing inequity in parent care among siblings. Journal of Marriage and Family 65 (February): 201–12.

INGOLDSBY, B. B., S. R. SMITH, AND J. E. MILLER. 2004. Exploring family theories. Los Angeles, CA: Roxbury Publishing.

INSTITUTE FOR WOMEN'S LEADERSHIP. 2011. Women heads of state. Women's Leadership fact sheet, May.

INSTITUTE OF MEDICINE. 2013. U.S. health in international perspective: Shorter lives, poorer health. Report Brief, January.

INSURANCE INSTITUTE FOR HIGHWAY SAFETY. 2013. Fatality facts 2011: Teenagers.

INTERNATIONAL ASSOCIATION OF CHIEFS OF POLICE. 2012. Law enforcement and cyberbullying fact sheet. Bureau of Justice Assistance, November.

INTERNICOLA, D. 2010. Nearly-weds part on, and on. Baltimore Sun, July 26, 15.

INTER-PARLIAMENTARY UNION. 2011. Women in parliaments: World classification.

IRAQ BODY COUNT. 2013. Documented civilian deaths from violence.

ISAACS, J., K. TORAN, H. HAHN, K. FORTUNY, AND C. E. STEUERLE. 2012. Kids' share 2012:

Report on federal expenditures on children through 2011. Urban Institute.

ISEN, A., AND B. STEVENSON. 2010. Women's education and family behavior: Trends in marriage, divorce, and fertility. National Bureau of Economic Research, February.

ISHII-KUNTZ, M., 2004. Asian American families: Diverse history, contemporary trends, and the future. In *Handbook of contemporary families: Considering the past, contemplating the future*, eds. M. Coleman and L. H. Ganong, 369–84. Thousand Oaks, CA: Sage.

IT'S JUST LUNCH. 2006. January 5.

ITO, A., AND M. YUI. 2010. Bureaucrats play matchmaker in Japan. *Bloomburg Businessweek*, August 30–September 5, 11–12.

J

JACKSON, S. L., AND T. L. HAFEMEISTER. 2011. Financial abuse of elderly people vs. other forms of elder abuse: Assessing their dynamics, risk factors, and society's response. National Criminal Justice Reference Service, February.

JACKSON, S. L., AND T. L. HAFEMEISTER. 2013. Understanding elder abuse: New directions for developing theories of elder abuse occurring in domestic settings. National Institute of Justice, June.

JACKSON, S., L. FEDER, D. R. FORDE, R. C. DAVIS, C. D. MAXWELL, AND B. G. TAYLOR. 2003. *Batterer intervention programs: Where do we go from here?* Washington, DC: U.S. Department of Justice.

JACOBE, D. 2012. Federal government jobs disappearing at a rapid pace. Gallup, January 14.

JACOBE, D. 2013. U.S. small businesses struggle to find qualified employees. Gallup, February 15.

JACOBS, C. 2012. My life in a binder. Women's Media Center, October 24.

JACOBS, K., D. GRAHAM-SQUIRE, AND S. LUCE. 2011. Living wage policies and big-box retail: How a higher wage standard would impact Walmart workers and shoppers. Center for Labor Research and Education, April.

JACOBSEN, L. A., M. KENT, M. LEE, AND M. MATHER. 2011. America's aging population. *Population Bulletin* 66 (February): 1–16.

JACOBSEN, L. A., M. MATHER, AND G. DUPUIS. 2012. Household change in the United States. *Population Bulletin* 67 (September): 1–12.

JACOBY, S. 2005. Sex in America. *AARP* (July/August): 57–62, 114.

JAIMES, M. A., WITH T. HALSEY. 1992. American Indian women: At the center of indigenous resistance in contemporary North America. In *The state of Native America: Genocide, colonization, and resistance*, ed. M. A. Jaimes, 311–44. Boston: South End.

JAKUBOWSKI, S. F., E. P. MILNE, H. BRUNNER, AND R. B. MILLER. 2004. A review of empirically supported marital enrichment programs. *Family Relations* 53 (October): 528–36.

JAMES, S. 2012. How I escaped. *Newsweek*, March 12, 19.

JAMES, S. D. 2013. Why men don't teach elementary school. March 25.

JAMISON, T. B., AND L. GANONG. 2011. "We're not living together:" Stayover relationships among college-educated emerging adults. *Journal of Social and Personal Relationships* 28 (November): 536–57.

JANG, S. J., A. ZIPPAY, AND R. PARK. 2012. Family roles as moderators of the relationship between schedule flexibility and stress. *Journal of Marriage and Family* 74 (August): 897–912.

JANKOWIAK, W. R., AND E. P. FISCHER. 1992. A cross-cultural perspective on romantic love. *Ethnology* 31 (April): 149–55.

JANMOHAMED, S. Z. 2010. *Love in a headscarf.* Boston: Beacon Press.

JANOFSKY, M. 2003. Young brides stir new outcry on Utah polygamy. *New York Times*, February 28, 1.

JAYAKODY, R., AND A. KALIL. 2002. Social fathering in low-income, African American families with preschool children. *Journal of Marriage and Family* 64 (May): 504–16.

JAYAKODY, R., AND N. CABRERA. 2002. What are the choices for low-income families? Cohabitation, marriage, and remaining single. In *Just living together: Implications of cohabitation on families, children, and social policy*, eds. A. Booth and A. C. Crouter, 85–96. Mahwah, NJ: Erlbaum.

JAYAKUMAR, A. 2012. Mobile dating apps grow in popularity. *Washington Post*, August 18.

JAYSON, S. 2009. I want you to get married. *Chicago Sun-Times*, February 24.

JAYSON, S. 2010. The Gores put focus on late-stage divorces. *USA Today*, June 3, 7D.

JAYSON, S. 2012. Dating sites—for all ages—focus on keeping it real. *USA Today*, December 3.

JEFFRIES, W. L. IV. 2011. The number of recent sex partners among bisexual men in the United States. *Perspectives on Sexual and Reproductive Health* 43 (September): 151–57.

JELLESMA, F. C., AND A. J. J. M. VINGERHOETS. 2012. Crying in middle childhood: A report on gender differences. *Sex Roles* 67 (October): 412–21.

JENA, A. B., AND D. P. GOLDMAN. 2011. Growing Internet use may help explain the rise in prescription drug abuse in the United States. *Health Affairs* 6 (June): 1192–99.

JENDREK, M. P. 1994. Grandparents who parent their grandchildren: Circumstances and decisions. *The Gerontologist* 34 (2): 206–16.

JENKINS TUCKER, C., D. FINKELHOR, H. TURNER, AND A. SHATTUCK. 2013. Association of sibling aggression with child and adolescent mental health. *Pediatrics* 132 (July 1): 79–84.

JERNIGAN, D. 2010. Alcohol marketing and youth: Why it's a problem and what you can do. Center for Alcohol Marketing and Youth, December 14.

JIAN, M. 2013. China's brutal one-child policy. *New York Times*, May 22, A27.

JIANG, C. 2011. Why more Chinese singles are looking for love online. *Time*, April 25.

JIANG, J. 2009. Postcard: Beijing. *Time*, March 2, 7.

JOHN, D., AND B. A. SHELTON. 1997. The production of gender among black and white women and men: The case of household labor. *Sex Roles* 36 (February): 171–93.

JOHN, R. 1988. The Native American family. In *Ethnic families in America: Patterns and variations*, 3rd ed., eds. C. H. Mindel, R. W. Habenstein, and R. Wright, Jr., 325–66. New York: Elsevier.

JOHNSON, C. Y. 2010. Author on leave after Harvard inquiry. *Boston Globe*, August 10.

JOHNSON, E. M., AND T. L. HUSTON. 1998. The perils of love, or why wives adapt to husbands during the transition to parenthood. *Journal of Marriage and the Family* 60 (February): 195–204.

JOHNSON, K. 2011. Between young and old, a political collision. *New York Times*, June 4, A10.

JOHNSON, K. M., AND D. R. JOHNSON. 2009. Partnered decisions? U.S. couples and medical help-seeking for infertility. *Family Relations* 58 (October): 431–44.

JOHNSON, L., AND J. LLOYD. 2004. *Sentenced to everyday life: Feminism and the housewife.* New York: Berg.

JOHNSON, M. P. 2005. Domestic violence: It's not about gender—or is it? *Journal of Marriage and Family* 67 (December): 1126–30.

JOHNSON, M. P. 2008. *A typology of domestic violence: Intimate terrorism, violent resistance, and situational couple violence.* Boston, MA: Northeastern University Press.

JOHNSON, M. P. 2011. Gender and types of intimate partner violence: A response to an anti-feminist literature review. *Aggression and Violent Behavior* 16 (July–August): 289–86.

JOHNSON, R. 1985. Stirring the oatmeal. In *Challenge of the heart: Love, sex, and intimacy in changing times*, ed. J. Welwood. Boston: Shambhala.

JOHNSON, R. W. AND J. M. WIENER. 2006. A profile of frail older Americans and their caregivers. The Urban Institute, February.

JOHNSON, S. 2011. Study details causes of high maternal death rates. Women's e-news, April 26.

JOHNSON, T. D. 2008. *Maternity leave employment patterns of first-time mothers: 1961–2003.* Current Population Report, P70-113. Washington, DC: U.S. Census Bureau.

JONES, A., AND S. SCHECHTER. 1992. *When love goes wrong: What to do when you can't do anything right.* New York: HarperCollins.

JONES, H. W., JR. 2007. Iatrogenic multiple births: A 2003 checkup. *Fertility and Sterility* 87 (March): 453–55.

JONES, J. 1985. *Labor of love, labor of sorrow: Black women, work and the family from slavery to the present.* New York: Basic Books.

JONES, J. 2011. Approval of labor unions holds near its low, at 52%. Gallup, August 31.

JONES, J. 2013. Same-sex marriage support solidifies above 50% in U.S. Gallup, May 13.

JONES, J. M. 2006. Ideal age for marriage: 25 for women and 27 for men. Gallup News Service, June 22.

JONES, J. M. 2012. In U.S., labor union approval steady at 52%. Gallup, August 31.

JONES, J. M. 2012. Most in U.S. say gay/lesbian bias is a serious problem. Gallup, December 6.

JONES, J. M. 2013. Fewer mention economic issues as top problem. Gallup, March 14.

JONES, J. M. 2013. Pensions are top income source for wealthier U.S. retirees. Gallup, May 21.

JONES, J. T. JR. 2010. Driving away dads. *Baltimore Sun*, June 17, 19.

JONES, M. 2003. The mystery of my eggs. *New York Times*, March 16, 44.

JONES, N. A., AND J. BULLOCK. 2012. The two or more races population: 2010. 2010 Census Briefs, September.

JONES, R. K. 1993. Female victim perceptions of the causes of male spouse abuse. *Sociological Inquiry* 63 (August): 351–61.

JONES, R. K., A. M. MOORE, AND L. F. FROHWIRTH. 2011. Perceptions of male knowledge and support among U.S. women obtaining abortions. *Women's Health Issues* 21 (March–April): 117–23.

JONES, R. K., AND A. E. BIDDLECOM. 2011a. Exposure to and views of information about sexual abstinence among older teens. *American Journal of Sexuality Education* 6 (4): 381–95.

JONES, R. K., AND A. E. BIDDLECOM. 2011b. Is the Internet filling the sexual health information gap for teens? An exploratory study. *Journal of Health Communication* 16 (January): 112–23.

Jones, R. K., and A. E. Biddlecom. 2011c. The more things change . . . : The relative importance of the Internet as a source of contraceptive information for teens. *Sexuality Research and Social Policy* 8 (March): 27–37.

Jones, R. K., and J. Dreweke. 2011. Countering conventional wisdom: New evidence on religion and contraceptive use. Guttmacher Institute, April.

Jones, R. K., and K. Kooistra. 2011. Abortion incidence and access to services in the United States, 2008. *Perspectives on Sexual and Reproductive Health* 43 (1): 41–50.

Jones, R. K., and M. L. Kavanaugh. 2011. Changes in abortion rates between 2000 and 2008 and lifetime incidence of abortion. *Obstetrics & Gynecology* 117 (June): 1358–66.

Jones, R. K., L. B. Finer, and S. Singh. 2010. Characteristics of U.S. abortion patients, 2008. Guttmacher Institute.

Jones, R. K., L. Frohwirth, and A. M. Moore. 2013. More than poverty: Disruptive events among women having abortions in the USA. *Journal of Family Planning and Reproductive Health Care* 39 (January): 36–43.

Jones, R. K., M. R. S. Zolna, S. K. Henshaw, and L. B. Finer. 2008. Abortion in the United States: Incidence and access to services, 2005. *Perspectives on Sexual and Reproductive Health* 40 (March): 6–16.

Jones, W. H., and M. P. Burdette. 1994. Betrayal in relationships. In *Perspectives on close relationships*, eds. A. L. Weber and J. H. Harvey, 243–62. Boston: Allyn & Bacon.

Jordan, M. 2012. Heartland draws Hispanics to help revive small towns. *Wall Street Journal*, November 9, A1, A10.

Jordan, M. 2012. Recession big factor as birth-rate falls. *Wall Street Journal*, November 30, A2.

Jordan, M., and M. Peters. 2013. Tight market for farmhands. *Wall Street Journal*, February 20, A3.

Joseph, S. ed. 1999. *Intimate selving in Arab families: Gender, self, and identity.* New York: Syracuse University Press.

Josselson, R. 1992. *The space between us: Exploring the dimensions of human relationships.* San Francisco: Jossey-Bass.

Justice, G. 1999. We're happily married and living apart. *Newsweek*, October 18, 12.

K

Kahn, J. R., B. S. McGill, and S. M. Bianchi. 2011. Help to family and friends: Are there gender differences at older ages? *Journal of Marriage and Family* 73 (February): 77–92.

Kaiser Family Foundation. 2008. Sexual health of adolescents and young adults in the United States. September.

Kaiser Family Foundation. 2011. Health care spending in the United States and selected OECD countries. April.

Kalata, J. 2006. *Looking at act II of women's lives: Thriving & striving from 45 on.* AARP Foundation, April.

Kalil, A., K. M. Ziol-Guest, and J. L. Epstein. 2010. Nonstandard work and marital instability: Evidence from the National Longitudinal Survey of Youth. *Journal of Marriage and Family* 72 (October): 1289–1300.

Källén, B., O. Finnström, A. Lindam, E. Nilsson, K-G. Nygren, and P. O. Olausson. 2010. Cancer risk in children and young adults conceived by in vitro fertilization. *Pediatrics* 126 (August 1): 270–76.

Kalmijn, M. 1998. Intermarriage and homogamy: Causes, patterns, trends. *Annual Review of Sociology* 24: 395–421.

Kalmijn, M., and C. W. S. Monden. 2006. Are the negative effects of divorce on well-being dependent on marital quality? *Journal of Marriage and Family* 68 (December): 1197–213.

Kalmijn, M., and P. M. De Graaf. 2012. Life course changes of children and well-being of parents. *Journal of Marriage and Family*, 74 (April): 269–80.

Kambayashi, T. 2008. Japanese men shout the oft-unsaid: "I love you." *Christian Science Monitor*, February 13, 1, 11.

Kaminski, J. W., and X. Fang. 2009. Victimization by peers and adolescent suicide in three US samples. *Journal of Pediatrics* 155 (November): 683–88.

Kamp Dush, C. M., M. G. Taylor, and R. A. Kroeger. 2008. Marital happiness and psychological well-being across the life course. *Family Relations* 57 (April): 211–26.

Kan. Case highlights legal issues for sperm donors. 2013. *USA Today*, January 4.

Kang, C., and H. Tsukayama. 2012. Toys R Us markets a tablet for the youngest users. *Washington Post*, September 10.

Kanny, D., Y. Liu, and R. D. Brewer. 2011. Binge drinking—United States, 2009. *MMWR* 60 (Suppl, January 14): 101–04.

Kanny, D., Y. Liu, R. D. Brewer, W. S. Garvin, and L. Balluz. 2012. Vital signs: Binge drinking prevalence, frequency, and intensity among adults—United States, 2010. *MMWR* 61 (January 13): 14–19.

Kantrowitz, M. 2011. The distribution of grants and scholarships by race. September 2.

Kapp, D. 2013. Can new building toys for girls improve math and science skills? *Wall Street Journal*, April 17, D1, D3.

Karraker, A., and J. DeLamater. 2013. Past-year sexual inactivity among older married persons and their partners. *Journal of Marriage and Family* 75 (February): 142–63.

Karraker, M. W. 2008. *Global families.* Boston: Pearson Education.

Kashef, Z. 2003. The fetal position. *Mother Jones* (January/February): 18–19.

Kass, L. R. 1997. The end of courtship. *The Public Interest* 126 (Winter): 39–63.

Kaufman, G., and E. Bernhardt. 2012. His and her job: What matters most for fertility plans and actual childbearing? *Family Relations* 61 (October): 686–97.

Kaufmann, J-C. 2008. *The single woman and the fairytale prince.* Malden, MA: Polity Press.

Kavanaugh, M. L., J. Jerman, K. Ethier, and S. Moskosky. 2013. Meeting the contraceptive needs of teens and young adults: Youth-friendly and long-acting reversible contraceptive services in U.S. family planning facilities. *Journal of Adolescent Health* 52 (March): 284–92.

Kawamoto, W. T., and R. P. Viramontez Anguino. 2006. Asian and Latino immigrant families. In *Families in global and multicultural perspective*, 2nd ed., eds. B. B. Ingoldsby and S. D. Smith, 209–30. Thousand Oaks, CA: Sage.

Kawamoto, W. T., and T. C. Cheshire. 2004. A "seven-generation" approach to American Indian families. In *Handbook of contemporary families: Considering the past, contemplating the future*, eds. M. Coleman and L. H. Ganong, 385–93. Thousand Oaks, CA: Sage.

Kay, B. 2011. Wedding prep 101. *Christian Science Monitor*, October 17, 7.

Kaye, K., K. Suellentrop, and C. Sloup. 2009. The fog zone: How misperceptions, magical thinking, and ambivalence put young adults at risk for unplanned pregnancy. The National Campaign to Prevent Teen and Unplanned Pregnancy.

Kayser, K. 1993. *When love dies: The process of marital dissatisfaction.* New York: Guilford.

Keenan, N. L., and K. A. Rosendorf. 2011. Prevalence of hypertension and controlled hypertension—United States, 2005–2008. *MMWR* 60 (Suppl, January 14): 94–97.

Keeter, S. 2009. New tricks for old—and new—dogs: Challenges and opportunities facing communications research. Pew Research Center Publications, March 3.

Keeter, S. 2010. Ask the expert. Pew Research Center, December 29.

Keizer, R., P. A. Dykstra, and A. R. Poortman. 2010. Life outcomes of childless men and fathers. *European Sociological Review* 26 (1): 1–15.

Kelly, G. F. 1994. *Sexuality today: The human perspective*, 4th ed. Guilford, CT: Dushkin.

Kelly, J. B., and R. E. Emery. 2003. Children's adjustment following divorce: Risk and resilience perspectives. *Family Relations* 52 (October): 352–62.

Kempe, C. H., F. N. Silverman, B. F. Steele, W. Droegmuller, and H. K. Silver. 1962. The battered-child syndrome. *Journal of the American Medical Association* 181 (July): 17–24.

Kempner, J., C. S. Perlis, and J. F. Merz. 2005. Ethics: Forbidden knowledge. *Science* 307 (February 11): 854.

Kendall, B., and J. A. Favole. 2013. Social Security rules defy same-sex verdict. *Wall Street Journal*, June 28, A7.

Kendall, D. 2002. *The power of good deeds: Privileged women and the social reproduction of the upper class.* Lanham, MD. Rowman & Littlefield.

Kenen, R. H. 1993. *Reproductive hazards in the workplace: Mending jobs, managing pregnancies.* New York: Haworth.

Kennedy, A., K. Lavail, G. Nowak, M. Basket, and S. Landry. 2011. Confidence about vaccines in the United States: Understanding parents' perceptions. *Health Affairs* 30 (June): 1151–59.

Kennedy, D. E., and L. Kramer. 2008. Improving emotion regulation and sibling relationship quality: The More Fun with Sisters and Brothers program. *Family Relations* 57 (December): 567–78.

Kennedy, R. 2002. *Nigger: The strange career of a troublesome word.* New York: Pantheon.

Kennedy, T. L. M., A. Smith, A. T. Wells, and B. Wellman. 2008. Networked families. Pew Internet & American Life Project, October 19.

Kenrick, D. 2013. I love being a guy. *Psychology Today*, January/February, 45–48.

Kenrick, D. T., G. E. Groth, M. R. Trost, and E. K. Sadalla. 1993. Integrating evolutionary and social exchange perspectives on relationships: Effects of gender, self-appraisal, and involvement level on mate selection criteria. *Journal of Personality and Social Psychology* 64 (6): 951–69.

Kent, M. M., and M. Mather. 2002. What drives U.S. population growth? *Population Bulletin* 57 (December): 1–40. Washington, DC: Population Reference Bureau.

Kerckhoff, A. C., and K. E. Davis. 1962. Value consensus and need complementarity in mate selection. *American Sociological Review* 27 (June): 295–303.

Kern, S. 1992. *The culture of love: Victorians to moderns.* Cambridge, MA: Harvard University Press.

Kershaw, S. 2003. Saudi Arabia awakes to the perils of inbreeding. *New York Times*, May 1, A3.

KERSTEN, K. K. 1990. The process of marital disaffection: Interventions at various stages. *Family Relations* 39 (July): 257–65.

KETTNER, P. M., R. M. MORONEY, AND L. L. MARTIN. 1999. *Designing and managing programs: An effectiveness-based approach*, 2nd ed. Thousand Oaks, CA: Sage.

KHAW, L. B. L., AND J. L. HARDESTY. 2009. Leaving an abusive partner: Exploring boundary ambiguity using the stages of change model. *Journal of Family Theory & Review* 1(March): 38–53.

KHAZAN, O. 2012. Russia has company in limiting foreign adoptions. *Baltimore Sun,* December 20, 18.

KHESHGI-GENOVESE, Z., AND T. A. GENOVESE. 1997. Developing the spousal relationship within stepfamilies. *Families in Society: The Journal of Contemporary Human Services* 78 (May/June): 255–64.

KIECOLT-GLASER, J. K., AND T. L. NEWTON. 2001. Marriage and health: His and hers. *Psychological Bulletin* 127 (July): 472–503.

KIECOLT-GLASER, J. K., T. J. LOVING, J. R. STOWELL, W. B. MALARKEY, S. LEMESHOW, S. L. DICKINSON, AND R. GLASER. 2005. Hostile marital interactions, proinflammatory cytokine production, and wound healing. *Archives of General Psychiatry* 62 (December): 1377–84.

KIEFER, H. M. 2005. U.S. weddings: "Something borrowed" usually money. Gallup Organization, June 28.

KILBURN, J. C., JR. 1996. Network effects in care-giver to care-recipient violence: A study of care-givers to those diagnosed with Alzheimer's disease. *Journal of Elder Abuse & Neglect* 8 (1): 69–80.

KILLOREN, S. E., K. A. UPDEGRAFF, F. S. CHRISTOPHER, AND A. J. UMAÑA-TAYLOR. 2011. Mothers, fathers, peers, and adolescents' sexual intentions. *Journal of Marriage and Family* 73 (February): 209–20.

KILPATRICK, D. G., B. E. SAUNDERS, AND D. W. SMITH. 2003. *Youth victimization: Prevalence and implications.* Washington, DC: U.S. Department of Justice.

KIM, H. S. 2011. Consequences of parental divorce for child development. *American Sociological Review* 76 (June): 487–511.

KIM, J. 2012. Educational differences in marital dissolution: Comparison of white and African American women. *Family Relations* 61 (December): 811–24.

KIM, J. E., E. M. HETHERINGTON, AND D. ROSS. 1999. Associations among family relationships, antisocial peers, and adolescents' externalizing behaviors. *Child Development* 70 (September/October): 1209–30.

KIM, J., S. K. IRVING, AND T. A. LOVELESS. 2012. Dynamics of economic well-being: Participation in government programs, 2004 to 2007 and 2009. Who gets assistance? U.S. Census Bureau. Current Population Reports, July.

KIM, Y. M. 2011. Minorities in higher education. American Council on Education.

KIMPORT, K., K. FOSTER, AND T. A.WEITZ. 2011. Social sources of women's emotional difficulty after abortion: Lessons from women's abortion narratives. *Perspectives on Sexual and Reproductive Health* 43 (June): 103–09.

KING, M., AND A. BARTLETT. 2006. What same sex civil partnerships may mean for health. *Journal of Epidemiology and Community Health* 60 (March): 188–91.

KING, V. 2006. The antecedents and consequences of adolescents' relationships with stepfathers and nonresident fathers. *Journal of Marriage and Family* 68 (November): 910–28.

KING, V. 2007. When children have two mothers: Relationships with nonresident mothers, stepmothers, and fathers. *Journal of Marriage and Family* 69 (December): 1178–93.

KING, V. 2009. Stepfamily formation: Implications for adolescent ties to mothers, nonresident fathers, and stepfathers. *Journal of Marriage and Family* 71 (November): 954–68.

KING, V., AND M. E. SCOTT. 2005. A comparison of cohabiting relationships among older and younger adults. *Journal of Marriage and Family* 67 (May): 271–85.

KING, W. 1996. "Suffer with them till death": Slave women and their children in nineteenth-century America. In *More than chattel: Black women and slavery in the Americas*, eds. D. B. Caspar and D. C. Hine, 147–68. Bloomington: Indiana University Press.

KINSELLA, K., AND W. HE. 2009. *An aging world: 2008.* Washington, DC: U.S. Government Printing Office.

KINSEY INSTITUTE. 2011. Continuum of human sexuality.

KINSEY, A. C., W. B. POMEROY, AND C. E. MARTIN. 1948. *Sexual behavior in the human male.* Philadelphia: Saunders.

KINSEY, A. C., W. B. POMEROY, C. E. MARTIN, AND P. H. GEBHARD. 1953. *Sexual behavior in the human female.* Philadelphia: Saunders.

KIRBY, D. B. 2008. The impact of abstinence and comprehensive sex and STD/HIV education programs on adolescent sexual behavior. *Sexuality Research & Social Policy* 5 (September): 18–27.

KIRK, D. 2013. An adoption spat widens: Behind South Korea's dispute with US couple. *Christian Science Monitor,* February 4, 16–17.

KISSMAN, K., AND J. A. ALLEN. 1993. *Single-parent families.* Beverly Hills, CA: Sage.

KIVISTO, P., AND W. NG. 2004. *Americans all: Race and ethnic relations in historical, structural, and comparative perspectives*, 2nd ed. Los Angeles, CA: Roxbury.

KLEIN, A. R. 2009. Practical implications of current domestic violence research: For law enforcement, prosecutors, and judges. NIJ Special Report, June.

KLEIN, E. 2011. Do we still need unions? Yes: Why they're worth fighting for. *Newsweek,* March 7, 18.

KLEIN, K. 2006. Parents, wake up! Your kid is annoying. *Los Angeles Times,* January 3, B11.

KLEIN, K. E., AND N. LEIBER. 2013. $9 an hour doesn't sound so bad. *Bloomberg Businessweek,* February 25–March 3, 46–48.

KLEIN, M. 2012. 8 paranoid sex myths spread by America's anti-sex crusaders (debunked by science). *Huffington Post,* April 30.

KLINENBERG, E. 2012. *Going solo: The extraordinary rise and surprising appeal of living alone.* New York: Penguin Books.

KLINGAMAN, M. 2008. His brother's keeper. *Baltimore Sun,* March 9, 1, 8.

KLOFSTAD, C. A., R. MCDERMOTT, AND P. K. HATEMI. 2012. Do bedroom eyes wear political glasses? The role of politics in human mate attraction. *Evolution and Human Behavior* 33 (March): 100–08.

KLUGER, J. 2013. Too old to be a dad? *Time,* April 22, 36–43.

KNAPP, M. L., AND J. A. HALL. 1992. *Nonverbal communication in human interaction*, 3rd ed. New York: Holt, Rinehard & Winston.

KNEEBONE, E., AND A. BERUBE. 2013. Cul-de-sac poverty. *New York Times,* May 20.

KNICKMEYER, E. 2007. For young Libyans, old-style marriage is a dream too far. *Washington Post,* November 14, A13.

KNIGHT, G. P., C. BERKEL, A. J. UMAÑA-TAYLOR, N. A. GONZALES, I. ETTEKAL, M. JACONIS, AND B. M. BOYD. 2011. The familial socialization of culturally related values in Mexican American families. *Journal of Marriage and Family* 73 (October): 913–25.

KNOX, D., WITH K. LEGGETT. 1998. *The divorced dad's survival book: How to stay connected with your kids.* New York: Insight.

KNOX, N. 2006. Dream house, sans spouse: More women buy homes. *USA Today,* February 14.

KNUDSON-MARTIN, C. 2012. Attachment in adult relationships: A feminist perspective. *Journal of Family Theory & Review* 4 (December): 299–305.

KOCHHAR, R. 2005. Survey of Mexican migrants: The economic transition to America. Pew Hispanic Center, December 6.

KOCHHAR, R. 2007. 1995–2005: Foreign-born Latinos make progress on wages. Pew Hispanic Center, August 21.

KOCIENIEWSKI, D. 2011. G.E.'s strategies let it avoid taxes altogether. *New York Times,* March 24, A1.

KOHLBERG, L. 1969. Stage and sequence: The cognitive-developmental approach to socialization. In *Handbook of socialization theory and research*, ed. D. A. Goslin, 347–480. Chicago: Rand McNally.

KOHLER, P. K., L. E. MANHART, AND W. E. LAFFERTY. 2008. Abstinence-only and comprehensive sex education and the initiation of sexual activity and teen pregnancy. *Journal of Adolescent Health* 42 (April): 344–51.

KOHUT, A. 2011. Labor unions seen as good for workers, not U.S. competitiveness. Pew Research Center, February 17.

KOHUT, A., C. DOHERTY, M. DIMOCK, AND S. KEETER. 2011. Beyond red vs. blue political typology. Pew Research Center, May 4.

KOHUT, A., R. WIKE, J. M. HOROWITZ, AND E. CARRIERE-KRETSCHMER. 2010. Gender equality universally embraced, but inequalities acknowledged. Pew Research Center, July 1.

KOLATA, G. 2013. Dementia rate is found to drop sharply, as forecast. *New York Times,* July 17, A8.

KOLHATKAR, S. 2012. Emasculation nation. *Bloomberg Businessweek,* September 17–September 23, 102–03.

KOLHATKAR, S. 2012. The mother of all traps. *Bloomberg Businessweek,* April 30–May 6, 82–83.

KOMANDO, K. 2012. Preventing online infidelity. *USA Today,* March 29.

KONIGSBERG, R. D. 2011. Chore wars. *Time,* August 8, 45–49.

KOROPECKYJ-COX, T., AND G. PENDELL. 2007. The gender gap in attitudes about childlessness in the United States. *Journal of Marriage and Family* 69 (November): 899–915.

KOSMIN, B. A., AND A. KEYSAR. 2009. *American religious identification survey [ARIS 2008].* Summary Report, March.

KOSOVA, W., AND P. WINGERT. 2009. Crazy talk. *Newsweek,* June 8, 54–62.

KOSS-FEDER, L. 2009. Bunking in with mom and dad. *Time,* March 2, 45–46.

KOWAL, A. K., AND L. BLINN-PIKE. 2004. Sibling influences on adolescents' attitudes toward safe sex practices. *Family Relations* 53 (July): 377–84.

Kowitt, B., and R. Arora. 2011. The 50 most powerful women. *Fortune*, October 17, 125–131.

Krache, D. 2008. How to ground a "helicopter parent." CNN, August 19.

Kramarow, E. A. 2013. QuickStats: Percentage of adults aged ≥ 65 years who reported excellent or very good health, by selected race/ethnicity and poverty status—National Health Interview Survey, 2009–2011. *Morbidity and Mortality Weekly Report 62* (21): 431.

Kratchick, J. L., T. S. Zimmerman, S. A. Haddock, and J. H. Banning. 2005. Best-selling books advising parents about gender: A feminist analysis. *Family Relations 54* (January): 84–100.

Kreager, D. A., and J. Staff. 2009. The sexual double standard and adolescent peer acceptance. *Social Psychology Quarterly 72* (June): 143–164.

Kreeger, K. Y. 2002a. Sex-based differences continue to mount. *The Scientist 16* (February 18).

Kreeger, K. Y. 2002b. X and Y chromosomes concern more than reproduction. *The Scientist 16* (February 4).

Kreider, R. 2010. Increase in opposite cohabiting couples from 2009 to 2010 in the Annual and Social Economic Supplement (ASEC) to the Current Population Survey.

Kreider, R. M., and D. B. Elliott. 2009. America's families and living arrangements: 2007. U.S. Census Bureau, Current Population Reports, P20-561, September.

Kreider, R. M., and R. Ellis. 2011a. Living arrangements of children: 2009. U.S. Census Bureau, Current Population Reports, June.

Kreider, R. M., and R. Ellis. 2011b. Number, timing, and duration of marriages and divorces: 2009. U.S. Census Bureau, Current Population Reports, P70-125, May.

Kridel, K. 2009. Going the distance for love. *Los Angeles Times*, March 9.

Kridel, K. 2012. Infertility can be a man's issue, too. *Baltimore Sun*, May 24, 7.

Kristof, N. D. 2011. A rite of torture for girls. *New York Times*, May 12, A29.

Krokoff, L. J. 1987. The correlates of negative affect in marriage: An exploratory study of gender differences. *Journal of Family Issues 8* (March): 111–35.

Kroll, L., and K. A. Dolan. 2013. Forbes billionaires. *Forbes*, March 25, 85–90.

Kromer, B., and D. Howard. 2013. Labor force participation and work status of people 65 years and older. U.S. Census Bureau, American Community Survey Briefs, January.

Kuai, A. 2011. Coming out in China: The true cost of being gay in Beijing. *Time*, July 13.

Kübler-Ross, E. 1969. *On death and dying*. New York: Macmillan.

Kulczycki, A., and A. P. Lobo. 2001. Deepening the melting pot: Arab-Americans at the turn of the century. *Middle East Journal 3* (Summer): 459–73.

Kulczycki, A., and A. P. Lobo. 2002. Patterns, determinants, and implications of intermarriage among Arab Americans. *Journal of Marriage and Family 64* (February): 202–10.

Kunkel, D., K. Eyal, K. Finnerty, E. Biely, and E. Donnerstein. 2005. Sex on TV. Kaiser Family Foundation.

Kurdek, L. A. 1993. Predicting marital dissolution: A 5-year prospective longitudinal study of newlywed couples. *Journal of Personality and Social Psychology 64* (2): 221–42.

Kurdek, L. A. 1994. Areas of conflict for gay, lesbian, and heterosexual couples: What couples argue about influences relationship satisfaction. *Journal of Marriage and the Family 56* (November): 923–24.

Kurdek, L. A. 1998. Relationship outcomes and their predictors: Longitudinal evidence from heterosexual married, gay cohabiting, and lesbian cohabiting couples. *Journal of Marriage and the Family 60* (August): 553–68.

Kurdek, L. A. 2006. Differences between partners from heterosexual, gay, and lesbian cohabiting couples. *Journal of Marriage and Family 68* (May): 509–28.

Kurdek, L. A. 2007. The allocation of household labor by partners in gay and lesbian couples. *Journal of Family Issues 28* (January): 132–48.

Kurdek, L. A., and M. A. Fine. 1993. The relation between family structure and young adolescents' appraisals of family climate and parenting behavior. *Journal of Family Issues 14*: 279–90.

Kurland, S. P. 2004. *Everlasting love*. Baltimore, MD: Noble House.

Kutner, L., and C. Olson. 2008. *Grand theft childhood*. New York: Simon & Schuster.

Kwok, A. C., et al. 2011. The intensity and variation of surgical care at the end of life: A retrospective cohort study. *The Lancet*, October 6.

Kwong See, S. T., and C. Rasmussen. 2003. An early start to age stereotyping: Children's beliefs about an older experimenter. Cited in *University of Alberta News*.

L

Lab42. 2011. The relationship status update. November 4.

Labor Day 2013: Sept. 2. 2013. U.S. Census Bureau News, CB13-FF.20, July 23.

Ladly, M. D. 2012. Defying parents, some Pakistani women risk all to marry whom they choose. *New York Times*, September 9, A6.

LaFrance, M., M. A. Hecht, and E. L. Paluck. 2003. The contingent smile: A meta analysis of sex differences in smiling. *Psychological Bulletin 129* (March): 305–35.

LaFraniere, S., and L. Goodstein. 2007. Anglicans rebuke U.S. branch on blessing same-sex unions. *New York Times*, February 20, A1, A11.

Laird, J. 1993. Lesbian and gay families. In *Normal family processes*, 2nd ed., ed. F. Walsh, 282–330. New York: Guilford.

Lakoff, R. T. 1990. *Talking power: The politics of language*. New York: Basic Books.

Lakshmanan, I. A. R. 1997. Marriage? Think logic, not love. *Baltimore Sun*, September 22, 2A.

Lam, C. B., S. M. McHale, and A. C. Crouter. 2012. The division of household labor: Longitudinal changes and within-couple variation. *Journal of Marriage and Family 74* (October): 944–52.

Landale, N. S., and S. E. Tolnay. 1991. Group differences in economic opportunity and the timing of marriage. *American Sociological Review 56* (February): 33–45.

Landry, D. J., L. D. Lindberg, A. Gemmill, H. Boonstra, and L. B. Finer. 2011. Review of the role of faith- and community-based organizations in providing comprehensive sexuality education. *American Journal of Sexuality Education 6* (1): 75–103.

Langer, G., C. Arnedt, and D. Sussman. 2004. Primetime Live poll: American sex survey. ABC News.

Lansford, J. E. 2009. Parental divorce and children's adjustment. *Perspectives on Psychological Science 4* (2): 140–52.

Lansford, J. E., L. B. Wager, J. E. Bates, G. S. Pettit, and K. A. Dodge. 2012. Forms of spanking and children's externalizing behaviors. *Family Relations 61* (April): 224–36.

Lantz, H. R. 1976. *Marital incompatibility and social change in early America*. Beverly Hills, CA: Sage.

Lapierre, M. A., J. T. Piotrowski, and D. L. Linebarger. 2012. Background television in the homes of US children. *Pediatrics 130* (Supplement, June 1): e1373–e1630.

LaPlante, M. D. 2007. Military divorce rates on the rise. Scripps News, December 24.

Larimer, M. E., A. R. Lydum, and A. P. Turner. 1999. Male and female recipients of unwanted sexual contact in a college student sample: Prevalence rates, alcohol use, and depression symptoms. *Sex Roles 40* (February): 295–308.

Larmer, B. 2013. The price of marriage in China. *New York Times*, March 3, BU1ff.

LaRossa, R. ed. 1984. *Family case studies: A sociological perspective*. New York: Free Press.

LaRossa, R., and D. C. Retizes. 1993. Symbolic interactionism and family studies. In *Sourcebook of family theories and methods: A contextual approach*, eds. P. G. Boss, W. J. Doherty, R. LaRossa, W. R. Schumm, and S. K. Steinmetz, 135–63. New York: Plenum.

Larsen, C. D., J. G. Sandberg, J. M. Harper, and R. Bean. 2011. The effects of childhood abuse on relationship quality: Gender differences and clinical implications. *Family Relations 60* (October): 435–45.

Larzelere, R. E., and D. Baumrind. 2010. Are spanking injunctions scientifically supported? *Law and Contemporary Problems 73* (Spring): 57–87.

Lasch, C. 1977. *Haven in a heartless world: The family besieged*. New York: Basic Books.

Laslett, P. 1971. *The world we have lost*, 2nd ed. Reading, MA: Addison-Wesley.

Lasswell, T. E., and M. E. Lasswell. 1976. I love you but I'm not in love with you. *Journal of Marriage and Family Counseling 2* (July): 211–24.

Last, J. V. 2013. America's baby bust. *Wall Street Journal*, February 2–3, C1–C2.

Latessa, D. 2005. From financial aid to fatherhood. *Chronicle of Higher Education*, October 21, C3.

Lau, C. Q. 2012. The stability of same-sex cohabitation, different-sex cohabitation, and marriage. *Journal of Marriage and Family 74* (October): 973–88.

Laudadio, M. 2013. Elton John's family album. *People*, February 11, 110–12.

Lauerman, J. 2013. Colleges slow to investigate assaults. *Baltimore Sun*, June 20, 10.

Laughlin, L. 2011. Maternity leave and employment patterns of first-time mothers: 1961–2008. U.S. Census Bureau, Current Population Reports, October.

Laughlin, L. 2013. Who's minding the kids? Child care arrangements: Spring 2011. U.S. Census Bureau, Household Economic Studies, P70-135, April.

Laumann, E. O., S. A. Leitsch, and L. J. Waite. 2008. Elder mistreatment in the United States: Prevalence estimates from a nationally representative study. *Journal of Gerontology: Social Sciences 63B* (4): S248–S254.

Lavner, J. A., and T. N. Bradbury. 2012. Why do even satisfied newlyweds eventually go on to divorce? *Journal of Family Psychology 26* (1): 1–10.

Lavner, J. A., B. R. Karney, and T. N. Bradbury. 2012. Do cold feet warn of trouble ahead? Premarital uncertainty and four-year marital outcomes. *Journal of Family Psychology 46* (December): 1012–17.

LAWLESS, J. L., AND R. L. FOX. 2005. *It takes a candidate: Why women don't run for office.* New York: Cambridge University Press.

LAWRANCE, K., AND E. S. BYERS. 1995. Sexual satisfaction in long-term heterosexual relationships: The interpersonal exchange model of social satisfaction. *Personal Relationships* 2: 267–85.

Laws affecting reproductive health and rights: 2012 state policy review. 2012. Guttmacher Institute.

LAYTON, L., AND D. EGGEN. 2011. Industries lobby against voluntary nutrition guidelines for food marketed to kids. *Washington Post*, July 9.

LEAPER, C. 2002. Parenting girls and boys. In *Handbook of parenting*, 2nd ed., Vol. 1, ed. M. H. Bornstein, 189–215. Mahwah, NJ: Erlbaum.

LEAPER, C., AND M. M. AYRES. 2007. A meta-analytic review of gender variations in adults' language use: Talkativeness, affiliative speech, and assertive speech. *Personality and Social Psychology Review* 11 (November): 328–63.

LEDERER, W. J., AND D. D. JACKSON. 1968. *The mirages of marriage.* New York: Norton.

LEDGER, K. 2009. Sociology and the gene. *Contexts* 8 (Summer): 16–20.

LEE, J. A. 1973. *The colors of love.* Upper Saddle River, NJ: Prentice Hall.

LEE, J. A. 1974. The styles of loving. *Psychology Today* (October): 46–51.

LEE, M. A., AND M. MATHER. 2008. U.S. labor force trends. *Population Bulletin* 63 (June): 1–17.

LEE, S. M., AND B. EDMONSTON. 2005. New marriages, new families: U.S. racial and Hispanic intermarriage. *Population Bulletin* 60 (June): 1–40.

LEEB, R. T., L. PAULOZZI, C. MELANSON, T. SIMON, AND I. ARIAS. 2008. Child maltreatment surveillance: Uniform definitions for public health and recommended data elements, Version 1.0. Centers for Disease Control and Prevention, National Center for Injury Prevention and Control, January.

LEGER, D. L. 2013. OxyContin a gateway to heroin for upper-income addicts. *USA Today*, April 25.

LEGO FRIENDS. 2012. Building playsets for girls. Squidoo.

LEHAVOT, K., Y. MOLINA, AND J. M. SIMONI. 2012. Childhood trauma, adult sexual assault, and adult gender expressions among lesbian and bisexual women. *Sex Roles* 67 (September): 272–84.

LEHMILLER, J. J., AND C. R. AGNEW. 2007. Perceived marginalization and the prediction of romantic relationship stability. *Journal of Marriage and Family* 69 (November): 1036–49.

LEI, S. 2009. It's not easy being gray: The new rules of retirement. Urban Institute, February, no. 25.

LEITENBERG, H., M. J. DETZER, AND D. SREBNIK. 1993. Gender differences in masturbation and the relation of masturbation experience in preadolescence and/or early adolescence to sexual behavior and sexual adjustment in young adulthood. *Journal of Social Behavior* 22 (April): 87–98.

LELAND, J. 2008. In "sweetie" and "dear," a hurt for the elderly. *New York Times*, October 7, A1.

LEMIEUX, R., AND J. L. HALE. 2002. Cross-sectional analysis of intimacy, passion, and commitment: Testing the assumptions of the triangular theory of love. *Psychological Reports* 90 (June): 1009–14.

LEONARD, K. I. 1997. *The South Asian Americans.* Westport, CT: Greenwood.

LEOPOLD, T. 2012. The legacy of leaving home: Long-term effects of coresidence on parent–child relationships. *Journal of Marriage and Family* 74 (June): 399–412.

LESLIE, L. A., J. R. SMITH, AND K. M. HRAPCZYNSKI. 2013. Racial socialization in transracial adoptive families: Does it help adolescents deal with discrimination stress? *Family Relations* 62 (February): 72–81.

LEVARO, L. G. 2009. Living together or living apart together: New choices for old lovers. National Council on Family Relations newsletter, *Family Focus* (Summer): F9.

LEVAY, S. 2011. *Gay, straight, and the reason why: The science of sexual orientation.* New York: Oxford University Press.

LEVESQUE, R. J. R. 1993. The romantic experience of adolescents in satisfying love relationships. *Journal of Youth and Adolescence* 11 (3): 219–50.

LEVIN, D. E., AND J. KILBOURNE. 2009. *So sexy so soon: The new sexualized childhood and what parents can do to protect their kids.* New York: Ballantine Books.

LEVINE, M. V. 1994. A nation of hamburger flippers? *Baltimore Sun*, July 31, 1E, 4E.

LEVY, J. A. 1994. Sex and sexuality in later life stages. In *Sexuality across the life course*, ed. A. S. Rossi, 287–309. Chicago: University of Chicago Press.

LEWIS, M. 1997. *Altering fate: Why the past does not predict the future.* New York: Guilford.

LEWIS, O. 1966. The culture of poverty. *Scientific American* 115 (October): 19–25.

LI, D-K. ET AL. 2011. Urine bisphenol-A (BPA) level in relation to semen quality. *Fertility and Sterility* 95 (February): 625–30.

LI, J-C. A., AND L. L. WU. 2008. No trend in the intergenerational transmission of divorce. *Demography* 45 (November): 875–83.

LI, Y.-F., B. LANGHOLZ, M. T. SALAM, AND F. D. GILLILAND. 2005. Maternal and grandmaternal smoking patterns are associated with early childhood asthma. *Chest* 127 (April): 1232–41.

LICHTER, D. T., AND Z. QIAN. 2008. Serial cohabitation and the marital life course. *Journal of Marriage and Family* 70 (November): 861–78.

LICHTER, D. T., D. R. GRAEFE, AND J. B. BROWN. 2003. Is marriage a panacea? Union formation among economically disadvantaged unwed mothers. *Social Problems* 50 (February): 60–86.

LICK, S. F. 2013. I'm childless—But I have something many women don't. *Huffington Post*, February 26.

LIEBER, R. 2010. What love joins together, debt can put asunder. *New York Times*, September 7.

LIEBER, R. 2011. When love outgrows gifts on Valentine's day. *New York Times*, February 12, B1.

LIKE A VIRGIN? 2006. *Today Online*, January 11.

LIN, I-F., AND S. L. BROWN. 2012. Unmarried boomers confront old age: A national portrait. *The Gerontologist* 52 (2): 153–65.

LIN, I-F., H. R. FEE, AND H-S. WU. 2012. Negative and positive caregiving experiences: A closer look at the intersection of gender and relationship. *Family Relations* 61 (April): 343–58.

LIN, M. H., V. S. Y. KWAN, A. CHEUNG, AND S. T. FISKE. 2005. Stereotype content model explains prejudice for an envied outgroup: Scale of anti-Asian American stereotypes. *Personality and Social Psychology Bulletin* 31 (January): 34–47.

LINCOLN, K. D., L. M. CHATTERS, AND R. J. TAYLOR. 2005. Social support, traumatic events, and depressive symptoms among African Americans. *Journal of Marriage and Family* 67 (August): 754–66.

LINDAU, S. T., L. P. SCHUMM, E. O. LAUMANN, W. LEVINSON, C. A. O'MUIRCHEARTAIGH, AND L. J. WAITE. 2007. A study of sexuality and health among older adults in the United States. *New England Journal of Medicine* 357 (August 23): 762–74.

LINDBERG, L. D., R. JONES, AND J. S. SANTELLI. 2008. Non-coital sexual activities among adolescents. *Journal of Adolescent Health* 42 (February): 44–45.

LINDO, J. M., J. SCHALLER, AND B. HANSEN. 2013. Economic conditions and child abuse. National Bureau of Economic Research, April.

LINDSEY, E. W., P. R. CREMEENS, AND Y. M. CALDERA. 2010. Gender differences in mother-toddler and father-toddler verbal initiations and responses during a caregiving and play context. *Sex Roles* 63 (September): 399–411.

LINDSEY, L. L. 2005. *Gender roles: A sociological perspective*, 4th ed. Upper Saddle River, NJ: Prentice Hall.

LINN, A. 2013. Plan on working past age 65? You'll have company. January 31.

LINO, M. 2013. Expenditures on children by families, 2012. U.S. Department of Agriculture, Center for Nutrition Policy and Promotion.

LIPKA, M., AND S. STENCEL. 2013. Racial and ethnic groups view "radical life extension" differently. Pew Research Center, August 8.

LIPKA, S. 2008. The case for Mr. Not-Quite-Right. *The Atlantic Journal*, February 19.

LIPKA, S. 2011. Colleges court gay students with e-mail and dance parties. *Chronicle of Higher Education*, May 6, A11–A12.

LIPS, H. M. 2013. Acknowledging discrimination as a key to the gender pay gap. *Sex Roles* 68 (February): 223–30.

LIU, H., AND D. J. UMBERSON. 2008. The times they are a changin': Marital status and health differentials from 1972 to 2003. *Journal of Health and Social Behavior* 49 (September): 239–53.

LIVINGSTON, G. 2011. In a down economy, fewer births. Pew Research Center, October 12.

LIVINGSTON, G., AND D. COHN. 2010. Childlessness up among all women: Down among women with advanced degrees. Pew Research Center, June 25.

LIVINGSTON, G., AND D. COHN. 2010. The new demography of American motherhood. Pew Research Center, August 19.

LIVINGSTON, G., AND D. COHN. 2012. U.S. birth rate falls to a record low; decline is greatest among immigrants. Pew Research Center, November 29.

LIVINGSTON, G., AND D. COHN. 2013. Record share of new mothers are college educated. Pew Research Center, May 10.

LIVINGSTON, G., AND K. PARKER. 2011. A tale of two fathers: More are active, but more are absent. Pew Social & Demographic Trends, June 15.

LIVINGSTON, J. N., AND J. L. MCADOO. 2007. The roles of African American fathers in the socialization of their children. In *Black families*, 4th ed., ed. H. P. McAdoo, 219–37. Thousand Oaks, CA: Sage.

LIZ CLAIBORNE INC. 2008. Tween and teen dating violence and abuse study. February.

LLANA, S. M. 2007. Why Guatemala is roiling over its adoption boom. *Christian Science Monitor*, September 12, 1, 4.

Llana, S. M. 2012. Home again in Mexico. *Christian Science Monitor*, April 9, 26–28, 30–31.

LLOYD, E. A. 2005. *The case of the female orgasm: Bias in the science of evolution.* Cambridge, MA: Harvard University Press.

LLOYD, S. A. 1991. The dark side of courtship: Violence and sexual exploitation. *Family Relations* 40 (January): 14–20.

LODGE, A. C., AND D. UMBERSON. 2012. All shook up: Sexuality of mid- to later life married couples. *Journal of Marriage and Family* 74 (June): 428–443.

LOEB, S., M. BRIDGE, D. BASSOK, B. FULLER, AND R. RUMBERGER. 2005. How much is too much? The influence of preschool centers on children's social and cognitive development. December, NBER Working paper No. W11812.

LOFQUIST, D. 2012. Multigenerational households: 2009–2011. U.S. Census Bureau, American Community Survey Briefs, October.

LOFQUIST, D. 2012. Same-sex couples' consistency in reports of marital status. U.S. Census Bureau.

LOFQUIST, D., T. LUGAILA, M. O'CONNELL, AND S. FELIZ. 2012. Households and families: 2010. April.

LOGAN, J. E., S. G. SMITH, AND M. R. STEVENS. 2011. Homicides—United States, 1999–2007. *MMWR* 60 (Suppl, January 14): 67–70.

LOIKO, S. L. 2012. Putin makes U.S. adoptions of Russian orphans unlawful. *Baltimore Sun*, December 29, 10.

Long Distance Relationships. 2013. FAQs about long distance relationships.

LONGMORE, M. A., A. L. ENG, P. C. GIORDANO, AND W. D. MANNING. 2009. Parenting and adolescents' sexual initiation. *Journal of Marriage and Family* 71 (November): 969–82.

LOPEZ, M. H., AND G. VELASCO. 2011. Childhood poverty among Hispanics sets record, leads nation: The toll of the Great Recession. Pew Hispanic Center, September 28.

LÓPEZ, R. A. 1999. Las comadres as a social support system. *Affilia* 14 (Spring): 24–41.

LORBER, J. 2005. *Gender inequality: Feminist theories and politics*, 3rd ed. Los Angeles, CA: Roxbury.

LORBER, J., AND L. J. MOORE. 2007. *Gendered bodies: Feminist perspectives*. Los Angeles: Roxbury.

LOWRY, S. M., AND O. TRUJILLO. 2008. Cross-system dialogue: An effective strategy to promote communication between the domestic violence community, child welfare system, and the courts. National Council of Juvenile and Family Court Judges.

LUBLIN, J. S. 2011. CEO pay in 2010 jumped 11%. *Wall Street Journal*, May 6.

LUCAS, R. E., A. E. CLARK, Y. GEORGELLIS, AND E. DIENER. 2003. Reexamining adaptation and the set point model of happiness: Reactions to changes in marital status. *Journal of Personality and Social Psychology* 84 (March): 527–39.

LUCAS, S. R. 2008. *Theorizing discrimination in an era of contested prejudice*. Philadelphia, PA: Temple University Press.

LUGO, L., A. COOPERMAN, AND C. FUNK. 2013. Living to 120 and beyond: Americans' views on aging, medical advances and radical life extension. Pew Research Center, August 6.

LUHAR, M. 2013. Being a daughter of an arranged marriage. AlterNet, May 13.

LUKEMEYER, A., M. K. MEYERS, AND T. SMEEDING. 2000. Expensive children in poor families: Out-of-pocket expenditures for the care of disabled and chronically ill children in welfare families. *Journal of Marriage and the Family* 62 (May): 399–415.

LUNDQUIST, J. 2006. The black-white gap in marital dissolution among young adults: What can a counterfactual scenario tell us? *Social Problems* 3 (August): 421–41.

LUO, M. 2009. Forced from executive pay to hourly wage. *New York Times*, March 1, 1.

LUO, S., AND E. C. KLOHNEN. 2005. Assortative mating and marital quality in newlyweds: A couple-centered approach. *Journal of Personality and Social Psychology* 88 (February): 304–26.

LUSCOMBE, B. 2010. Finding Mom on Facebook. *Time*, August 16, 45–46.

LUSCOMBE, B. 2013. Confidence woman. *Time*, March 18, 34–42.

LUSCOMBE, B. 2013. The end of alimony. *Time*, May 27, 44–49.

LYNCH, F. R. 2007. Saving my cat: Why no price was too high. *Newsweek*, July 30, 14.

LYNN, D. B. 1969. *Parental and sex role identification: A theoretical formulation*. Berkeley, CA: McCutchen.

LYON, L. 2009. Helping teens steer clear of trouble. *U.S. News & World Report*, February, 40–43.

LYONS, L. 2004. How many teens are cool with cohabitation? The Gallup Organization, April 13.

LYTTON, H., AND L. GALLAGHER. 2002. Parenting twins and the genetics of parenting. In *Handbook of parenting*, 2nd ed., Vol. 1: Children and parenting, ed. M. H. Bornstein, 227–53. Mahwah, NJ: Erlbaum.

M

MAC, R. 2013. The trillionaire. *Forbes*, March 25, 69–76.

MACARTNEY, S., A. BISHAW, AND K. FONTENOT. 2013. Poverty rates for selected detailed race and Hispanic groups by state and place: 2007–2011. U.S. Census Bureau, American Community Survey Briefs, February.

MACCOBY, E. E. 1990. Gender and relationships: A developmental account. *American Psychologist* 45 (4): 513–20.

MACDONALD, L. J. 2010. *How to help your spouse heal from your affair: A compact manual for the unfaithful*. Gig Harbor, WA: Healing Counsel Press.

MACHAMER, A. M., AND E. GRUBER. 1998. Secondary school, family, and educational risk: Comparing American Indian adolescents and their peers. *Journal of Educational Research* 91 (July/August): 357–69.

MACOMBER, J. 2006. An overview of selected data on children in vulnerable families. Urban Institute and Child Trends, August 10.

MACUNOVICH, D. J. 2002. Using economics to explain U.S. fertility trends. *Population Bulletin* 57 (December): 8–9. Washington, DC: Population Reference Bureau.

MADDEN, M., A. LENHART, M. DUGGAN, S. CORTESI, AND U. GASSER. 2013. Teens and technology 2013. Pew Internet & American Life Project, March 13.

MADDEN, M., S. CORTESI, U. GASSER, A. LENHART, AND M. DUGGAN. 2012. Parents, teens, and online privacy. Pew Internet & American Life Project, November 14.

MADERA, J. H., M. R. HEBL, AND R. C. MARTIN. 2009. Gender and letters of recommendation for academia: Agentic and communal differences. *Journal of Applied Psychology* 94 (November): 1591–99.

MADIGAN, N. 2003. Suspect's wife is said to cite polygamy plan. *New York Times*.

MADIGAN, N. 2009. Couple guilty in tot's death. *Baltimore Sun*, February 22, 1, 8.

MADKOUR, A. S., T. FARHAT, C. T. HALPERN, S. N. GABHAINN, AND E. GODEAU. 2012. Parents' support and knowledge of their daughters' lives, and females' early sexual initiation in nine European countries. *Perspectives on Sexual and Reproductive Health* 44 (September): 167–75.

MAGNIER, M. 2006. Sri Lanka still wed to system. *Los Angeles Times* (January 23): A1.

MAGNIER, M., AND P. RAMASWAMY. 2009. Indian extremist group targets Valentine's Day. *Los Angeles Times*, February 14.

MAHER, K. 2013. Unions target home workers. *Wall Street Journal*, June 20, A3.

MAHONEY, J. L., A. L. HARRIS, AND J. S. ECCLES. 2006. Organized activity participation, positive youth development, and the over-scheduling hypothesis. *Social Policy Report* 20 (4): 3–32.

MAHONEY, M. 2002. The economic rights and responsibilities of unmarried cohabitants. In *Just living together: Implications of cohabitation on families, children, and social policy*, eds. A. Booth and A. C. Crouter, 247–54. Mahwah, NJ: Erlbaum.

MAIER, T. 1998. *Dr. Spock: An American life*. New York: Harcourt Brace.

MAITRA, P. 2004. Effect of socioeconomic characteristics on age at marriage and total fertility in Nepal. *Journal of Health, Population, and Nutrition* 22 (March): 84–96.

MAJOR, B., M. APPELBAUM, L. BECKMAN, M. A. DUTTON, N. F. RUSSO, AND C. WEST. 2008. Report of the APA task force on mental health and abortion. August 13, American Psychological Association.

MANCINI, A. D., D. L. PRESSMAN, AND G. A. BONANNO. 2006. Clinical interventions with the bereaved: What clinicians and counselors can learn from the changing lives of older couples study. In *Spousal bereavement in late life*, eds. D. Carr, R. M. Nesse, and C. B. Wortman, 255–78. New York: Springer.

MANDARA, J., AND C. L. PIKES. 2008. Guilt trips and love withdrawal: Does mothers' use of psychological control predict depressive symptoms among African American adolescents? *Family Relations* 57 (December): 602–12.

MANINI, T. M., ET AL. 2006. Daily activity energy expenditure and mortality among older adults. *Journal of the American Medical Association* 296 (July 12): 171–79.

MANLOVE, J., C. LOGAN, K. A. MOORE, AND E. IKRAMULLAH. 2008. Pathways from family religiosity to adolescent sexual activity and contraceptive use. *Perspectives on Sexual and Reproductive Health* 40 (June): 105–17.

MANLOVE, J., N. STEWART-STRENG, K. PETERSON, M. SCOTT, AND E. WILDSMITH. 2013. Racial and ethnic differences in the transition to a teenage birth in the United States. *Perspectives on Sexual and Reproductive Health* 45 (June): 89–100.

MANNING, C. 1970. *The immigrant woman and her job*. New York: Ayer.

MANNING, W. D., AND J. A. COHEN. 2012. Premarital cohabitation and marital dissolution: An examination of recent marriages. *Journal of Marriage and Family* 74 (April): 377–87.

MANNING, W. D., AND K. A. LAMB. 2003. Adolescent well-being in cohabiting, married, and single-parent families. *Journal of Marriage and Family* 65 (December): 876–93.

MANNING, W. D., AND P. J. SMOCK. 2005. Measuring and modeling cohabitation: New perspectives from qualitative data. *Journal of Marriage and Family* 67 (November): 989–1002.

MANNING, W. D., J. A. COHEN, AND P. J. SMOCK. 2011. The role of romantic partners, family, and peer networks in dating couples' views about cohabitation. *Journal of Adolescent Research* 26 (January): 115–49.

MANSFIELD, H. C. 2004. On the consensual campus. *Doublethink* (Winter): 24.

MARANO, H. E. 2012. From promise to promiscuity. *Psychology Today*, July/August, 61–69.

MARCELL, A. V., E. ALLAN, E. A. CLAY, C. WATSON, and F. L. SONENSTEIN. 2013. Effectiveness of a brief curriculum to promote condom and health care use among out-of-school young adult males. *Perspectives on Sexual and Reproductive Health* 45 (1): 33–40.

MARCUS, A. D. 2003. Guys, your clock is ticking, too: Doctors now say male fertility falls as early as age 35; the case for banking your sperm. *Wall Street Journal*, April 1, D1.

MARDER, D. 2002. For $9,600, women taught how to find a mate. *Knight Ridder News Service*, January 13.

MARIN, P., AND B. BROWN. 2008. The school environment and adolescent well-being: Beyond academics. Child Trends Research Brief, November.

MARKETDATA ENTERPRISES. 2004. Self-improvement market grows 50% since 2000: Personal coaching and infomercials soar.

MARKHAM, M. S., AND M. COLEMAN. 2012. The good, the bad, and the ugly: Divorced mothers' experiences with coparenting. *Family Relations* 61 (October): 586–600.

MARKHAM, M. S., L. H. GANONG, AND M. COLEMAN. 2007. Coparental identity and mothers' cooperation in coparental relationships. *Family Relations* 56 (October): 369–77.

MARLAR, J. 2010. The emotional cost of underemployment. Gallup, March 9.

MARLAR, J. 2011. World's women less likely to have good jobs. Gallup, June 23.

MARQUARDT, E., D. BLANKENHORN, R. I. LERMAN, L. MALONE-COLÓN, AND W. B. WILCOX. 2012. The President's marriage agenda for the forgotten sixty percent. *The state of our unions*. Charlottesville, VA: National Marriage Project and Institute for American Values.

MARSHALL, M. J. 2002. *Why spanking doesn't work: Stopping this bad habit and getting the upper hand on effective discipline*. Springville, Utah: Bonneville Books.

MARSIGLIO, W., AND R. HINOJOSA. 2006. Stepfathers and the family dance. In *Couples, kids, and family life*, eds. J. F. Gubrium and J. A. Holstein, 178–96. New York: Oxford University Press.

MARSIGLIO, W., AND R. HINOJOSA. 2007. Managing the multifather family: Stepfathers as father allies. *Journal of Marriage and Family* 69 (August): 845–62.

MARTIN, A. 1993. *The lesbian and gay parenting handbook: Creating and raising our families*. New York: HarperPerennial.

MARTIN, B. A., M. CUI, K. UENO, AND F. D. FINCHAM. 2013. Intimate partner violence in interracial and monoracial couples. *Family Relations* 62 (February): 202–11.

MARTIN, J. A., B. E. HAMILTON, S. J. VENTURA, M. J. K. OSTERMAN, AND T. J. MATHEWS. 2013. Births: Final data for 2011. *National Vital Statistics Reports* 62 (1), June 28.

MARTIN, J. A., B. E. HAMILTON, S. J. VENTURA, M. J. K. OSTERMAN, E. C. WILSON, AND T. J. MATHEWS. 2012. Births: Final data for 2010. *National Vital Statistics Reports* 61 (1), August 28.

MARTIN, J. D. 2010. Sexual harassment in Egypt: Why men blame women. *Christian Science Monitor*, August 18.

MARTIN, K. A., AND K. LUKE. 2010. Gender differences in the ABC's of the birds and the bees: What mothers teach young children about sexuality and reproduction. *Sex Roles* 62 (February): 278–91.

MARTIN, M. A. 2008. The intergenerational correlation in weight: How genetic resemblance reveals the social role of families.

American Journal of Sociology 114 (Suppl.): S67–S105.

MARTIN, P., AND E. MIDGLEY. 2010. Immigration in America 2010. *Population Bulletin Update*, June, pp. 1–6.

MARTIN, T. W. 2013. New Georgia law aims to control "pill mills." *Wall Street Journal*, May 3, A6.

MARTINEZ, E. A. 2001. Death: A family event for Mexican Americans. *Family Focus*, National Council on Family Relations, December, F4.

MARTINEZ G., C. E. COPEN, AND J. C. ABMA. 2011. Teenagers in the United States: Sexual activity, contraceptive use, and childbearing, 2006–2010 National Survey of Family Growth. *Vital and Health Statistics*, 2011, Series 23, No. 31. October.

MARTINEZ, G., J. ABMA, AND C. COPEN. 2010. Educating teenagers about sex in the United States. Centers for Disease Control and Prevention, NCHS Data Brief, No. 44, September.

MARTINEZ, G., K. DANIELS, AND A. CHANDRA. 2012. Fertility of men and women aged 15–44 years in the United States: National Survey of Family Growth, 2006–2010. *National Health Statistics Reports*, Number 51, April 12.

MARTINEZ, R. O. 2011. *Latinos in the Midwest*. East Lansing: Michigan State University Press.

MARTINS, N., D. C. WILLIAMS, K. HARRISON, AND R. A. RATAN. 2009. A content analysis of female body imagery in video games. *Sex Roles* 61 (December): 824–36.

MARTINSON, K., AND D. NIGHTINGALE. 2008. Ten key findings from responsible fatherhood initiatives. Urban Institute, February.

MARTY, R. 2012. Brownback signs law that allows pharmacists to guess if women are having an abortion, refuse them service. AlterNet, May 15.

MASCI, D. 2008a. Two perspectives on gay marriage. The Pew Forum on Religion & Public Life, April 24.

MASCI, D. 2008b. A stable majority: Most Americans still oppose same-sex marriage. Pew Forum on Religion and Public Life, April 1.

MASCI, D. 2013. The new legal battlefield over abortion. Pew Research Center, July 31.

MASCI, D., E. SCIUPAC, AND M. LIPKA. 2013. Gay marriage around the world. Pew Forum on Religion & Public Life, February 8.

MASIS, J. 2011. A wife is not a free maid. *Christian Science Monitor*, April 11, 6.

MASS LAYOFFS—FEBRUARY 2013. 2013. Bureau of Labor Statistics, February.

MASTERS, N. T., B. A. BEADNELL, D. M. MORRISON, M. J. HOPPE, AND M. R. GILLMORE. 2008. The opposite of sex? Adolescents' thoughts about abstinence and sex, and their sexual behavior. *Perspectives on Sexual and Reproductive Health* 40 (June): 87–93.

MASTERS, W. H., V. E. JOHNSON, AND R. C. KOLODNY. 1992. *Human sexuality*, 4th ed. New York: HarperCollins.

MATEYKA, P. J., M. A. RAPINO, AND L. C. LANDIVAR. 2012. Home-based workers in the United States: 2010. U.S. Census Bureau, Current Population Reports, October.

MATHER, M. 2012. Fact sheet: The decline in U.S. fertility. Population Reference Bureau, July.

MATHER, M. 2012. Income inequality rises across the United States. Population Reference Bureau. September.

MATHER, M., AND D. LAVERY. 2010. In U.S. proportion married at lowest recorded levels. Population Reference Bureau.

MATHES, V. S. 1981. A new look at the role of women in Indian society. In *The American

Indian: Past and present*, 2nd ed., ed. R. L. Nichols, 27–33. New York: Wiley.

MATHIAS, B. 1992. Yes, Va. (Md. & D.C.), there are happy marriages. *Washington Post*, September 22, B5.

MATOS, K., AND E. GALINSKY. 2011. Workplace flexibility in the United States: A status report. Families and Work Institute.

MATTES, J. 1994. *Single mothers by choice*. New York: Times Books.

MATTHAEI, J. A. 1982. *An economic history of women in America: Women's work, the sexual division of labor, and the development of capitalism*. New York: Schocken.

MATTHEWS, S. H., AND T. T. ROSNER. 1988. Shared filial responsibility: The family as the primary caregiver. *Journal of Marriage and the Family* 50 (February): 185–95.

MATTINGLY, M. J., AND K. E. SMITH. 2010. Changes in wives' employment when husbands stop working: A recession-prosperity comparison. *Family Relations* 59 (October): 343–57.

MAUME, DAVID J. 2006. Gender differences in restricting work efforts because of family responsibilities. *Journal of Marriage and Family* 68 (November): 859–69.

MAUSHART, S. 2002. *Wifework: What marriage really means for women*. New York: Bloomsbury.

MAY, E. T. 1995. *Barren in the promised land: Childless Americans and the pursuit of happiness*. New York: Basic Books.

MAY, P. A. 1999. The epidemiology of alcohol abuse among American Indians: The mythical and real properties. In *Contemporary Native American cultural issues*, ed. D. Champagne, 227–44. Walnut Creek, CA: AltaMira.

MAYER, C. E. 1999. For a generation in denial, a fountain of youth products. *Washington Post*, May 6, A1, A16.

MAYO, Y. 1997. Machismo, fatherhood, and the Latino family: Understanding the concept. *Journal of Multicultural Social Work* 5 (1/2): 49–61.

McADOO, H. P. 2002. African American parenting. In *Handbook of parenting*, 2nd ed., Vol. 4: Social conditions and applied parenting, ed. M. H. Bornstein, 47–58. Mahwah, NJ: Erlbaum.

McADOO, J. L. 1986. Black fathers' relationships with their preschool children and the children's development of ethnic identity. In *Men in families*, eds. R. A. Lewis and R. E. Salt, 159–68. Thousand Oaks, CA: Sage.

McCABE, J., K. L. BREWSTER, AND K. H. TILLMAN. 2011. Patterns and correlates of same-sex sexual activity among U.S. teenagers and young adults. *Perspectives on Sexual and Reproductive Health* 43 (September): 15–21.

McCANN, A. 2013. Etc. Romance. *Bloomberg Businessweek*, March 4–10, 72–73.

McCARTHY, B., AND T. CASEY. 2008. Love, sex, and crime: Adolescent romantic relationships and offending. *American Sociological Review* 73 (December): 944–69.

McCARTHY, E. 2009. Small lies about height or weight are frequently on online dating site profiles. *Washington Post*, December 20, E10.

McCAULEY, M., AND P. CHENOWITH. 2011. Measles—United States, January–May 20, 2011. *Morbidity and Mortality Weekly*, May 27.

McCLAIN, L. R. 2011. Better parents, more stable partners: Union transitions among cohabiting parents. *Journal of Marriage and Family* 73 (October): 889–901.

McCORMACK, K. 2011. The feminization of the college degree? Women's Media Center, May 31.

McDermott, T. 2007. Scientists can't get their minds around Alzheimer's. *Los Angeles Times*, December 27.

McDonald, K. A. 1999. Studies of women's health produce a wealth of knowledge on the biology of gender differences. *Chronicle of Higher Education*, June 25, A19, A22.

McElhaney, K. B., J. Antonishak, and J. P. Allen. 2008. "They like me, they like me not": Popularity and adolescents' perceptions of acceptance predicting social functioning over time. *Child Development* 79 (May/June): 720–31.

McElvaine, R. S. 1993. *The great depression: America, 1929–1941.* New York: Times Books.

McFadyen, J. M., J. L. Kerpelman, and F. Adler-Baeder. 2005. Examining the impact of workplace supports: Work-family fit and satisfaction in the U.S. military. *Family Relations* 54 (January): 131–44.

McGirk, T. 2011. Big love in Abbottabad: How Osama bin Laden kept three wives under one roof. *Time*, May 12.

McGoldrick, M., M. Heiman, and B. Carter. 1993. The changing family life cycle: A perspective on normalcy. In *Normal family processes*, 2nd ed., ed. F. Walsh, 405–43. New York: Guilford.

McGonagle, K. A., R. C. Kessler, and I. H. Gotlib. 1993. The effects of marital disagreement style, frequency, and outcome on marital disruption. *Journal of Social and Personal Relationships*, 10 (August): 385–404.

McGrath, E. 2002. The power of love. *Psychology Today*, December 1.

McGregor, J. 2011. Anne Mulcahy on women in the boardroom. *Washington Post*, October 6.

McGuire, K. 2011. Grandparents come to rescue. *Baltimore Sun*, June 11, 8.

McHale, S. M., K. A. Updegraff, and S. D. Whiteman. 2012. Sibling relationships and influences in childhood and adolescence. *Journal of Marriage and Family* 74 (October): 913–30.

McIntosh, P. 1995. White privilege and male privilege: A personal account of coming to see correspondences through work in women's studies. In *Race, class, and gender: An anthology*, 2nd ed., eds. M. L. Andersen and P. H. Collins, 76–87. Belmont, CA: Wadsworth.

McKernan, S-M., C. Ratcliffe, M. Simms, and S. Zhang. 2012. Do financial support and inheritance contribute to the racial wealth gap? Urban Institute, September.

McKinnon, M. 2011. Do we still need unions? No: Let's end a privileged class. *Newsweek*, March 7, 19.

McLeod, J. D., and S. Knight. 2010. The association of socioemotional problems with early sexual initiation. *Perspectives on Sexual and Reproductive Health* 42 (June): 93–101.

McMenamin, T. M. 2007. A time to work: Recent trends in shift work and flexible schedules. *Monthly Labor Review* 130 (December): 3–14.

McNeeley, C., and R. Crosnoe. 2008. Social status, peer influence, and weight gain in adolescence. *Archives of Pediatrics & Adolescent Medicine* 162 (January): 91–92.

McNulty, J. K., L. A. Neff, and B. R. Karney. 2008. Beyond initial attraction: Physical attractiveness in newlywed marriage. *Journal of Family Psychology* 22 (February): 135–43.

McPharlin, P. 1946. *Love and courtship in America.* New York: Hastings House.

McPherson, M., L. Smith-Lovin, and M. Brashears. 2008. The ties that bind are fraying. *Contexts* 7 (Summer): 32–36.

McQuillan, J., A. L. Greil, K. M. Shreffler, P. A. Winch-Hill, K. C. Gentzler, and J. D. Hathcoat. 2012. Does the reason matter? Variations in childlessness concerns among U.S. women. *Journal of Marriage and Family* 74 (October): 1166–81.

McQuillan, J.A. L. Grei l, L. White, and M. Casey Jacob. 2003. Frustrated fertility: Infertility and psychological distress among women. *Journal of Marriage and Family* 65 (November): 1007–18.

McRae, S. 1999. Cohabitation or marriage? Cohabitation. In *The sociology of the family*, ed. G. Allan, 172–90. Malden, MA: Blackwell.

McWade, M. 2013. Insurmountable marital problems that lead to divorce. *Huffington Post*, February 20.

McWhirter, C., and G. Fields. 2012. Communities struggle to break a grim cycle of killing. *Wall Street Journal*, August 18.

Mead, G. H. 1934. *Mind, self, and society.* Chicago: University of Chicago Press.

Mead, G. H. 1938. *The philosophy of the act.* Chicago: University of Chicago Press.

Mead, G. H. 1964. *On social psychology.* Chicago: University of Chicago Press.

Mead, M. 1935. *Sex and temperament in three primitive societies.* New York: Morrow.

Mehl, M. R., S. Vazire, N. Ramírez-Esparza, R. B. Slatcher, and J. W. Pennebaker. 2007. Are women really more talkative than men? *Science* 317 (July): 82.

Mellott, L. M., Z. Qian, and D. T. Lichter. 2005. Like mother, like daughter? The international transmission of union formation patterns. Paper presented at the annual meeting of the American Sociological Association, Philadelphia, August.

Meltzer, H., L. Doos, P. Vostanis, T. Ford, and R. Goodman. 2009. The mental health of children who witness domestic violence. *Child and Family Social Work* 14 (November): 491–501.

Meltzer, N., Ed. 1964. *In their own words: A history of the American Negro, 1619–1865.* New York: Crowell.

Mendes, E. 2011. Most caregivers look after elderly parent; invest a lot of time. Gallup, July 28.

Mendes, E. 2013. Americans favor giving illegal immigrants a chance to stay. Gallup, April 12.

Mendes, E. 2013. Preventable chronic conditions plague Medicaid population. Gallup, April 4.

Mendes, E., L. Saad, and K. McGeeney. 2012. Stay-at-home moms report more depression, sadness, anger. Gallup, May 18.

Menning, C., M. Holtzman, and C. Kapinus. 2007. Stepfather involvement and adolescents' disposition toward having sex. *Perspectives on Sexual and Reproductive Health* 39 (June): 82–89.

Mermin, G. B. T., R. W. Johnson, and E. J. Toder. 2008a. Will employers want aging boomers? The Urban Institute, July.

Mermin, G. B. T., S. R. Zedlewski, and D. J. Toohey. 2008b. Diversity in retirement wealth accumulation. The Urban Institute, December.

Messmer, R., L. D. Miller, and C. M. Yu. 2012. The relationship between parent–infant bed sharing and marital satisfaction for mothers of infants. *Family Relations* 61 (December): 798–810.

Meston, C. M., and D. M. Buss. 2007. Why humans have sex. *Archives of Sexual Behavior* 36 (August): 477–507.

Meteyer, K. B., and M. Perry-Jenkins. 2009. Dyadic parenting and children's externalizing symptoms. *Family Relations* 58 (July): 289–302.

MetLife Foundation and the Partnership at Drugfree.org. 2013. 2012 partnership attitude tracking study. April.

Metts, S. 1994. Relational transgressions. In *The dark side of interpersonal communication*, eds. W. R. Cupach and B. H. Spitzberg, 217–39 Hillsdale, NJ: Erlbaum.

Meyer, C. L., and M. Oberman. 2001. *Mothers who kill their children: Understanding the acts of moms from Susan Smith to the "prom mom."* New York: New York University Press.

Meyer, D. R., and M. Cancian. 2012. "I'm not supporting his kids": Nonresident fathers' contributions given mothers' new fertility. *Journal of Marriage and Family* 74 (February): 132–51.

Meyer, J. 2012. Centenarians: 2010. U.S. Census Bureau, 2010 Census Special Reports, December.

Miall, C. 1986. The stigma of involuntary childlessness. *Social Problems* 33 (April): 268–82.

Michael, R. T., J. H. Gagnon, E. O. Laumann, and G. Kolata. 1994. *Sex in America: A definitive study.* Boston: Little, Brown.

Middlemiss, W., and W. McGuigan. 2005. Ethnicity and adolescent mothers' benefit from participation in home-visitation services. *Family Relations* 54 (April): 212–24.

Mider, Z. R., and J. Green. 2012. Heads or tails, some CEOs win the pay game. *Bloomberg Businessweek*, October 8–14, 23–24.

Miech, R., F. Pampel, J. Kim, and R. G. Rogers. 2011. The enduring association between education and mortality: The role of widening and narrowing disparities. *American Sociological Review* 76 (December): 913–34.

Miell, D., and R. Croghan. 1996. Examining the wider context of social relationships. In *Social interaction and personal relationships*, eds. D. Miell and R. Dallos, 267–318. Thousand Oaks, CA: Sage.

Mikulincer, M., and P. R. Shaver. 2012. Adult attachment orientations and relationship processes. *Journal of Family Theory & Review* 4 (December): 259–74.

Milan, L. 2012. Characteristics of doctoral scientists and engineers in the United States: 2008. National Science Foundation, December.

Milbourn, T. 2006. Taking refuge. January 2.

Miles, I. J., B. C. Le, C. Wejnert, A. Oster, E. DiNenno, and G. Paz-Bailey. 2013. HIV infection among heterosexuals at increased risk—United States, 2010. *Morbidity and Mortality Weekly Report*, 62 (10): 183–87.

Milkman, R. 1976. Women's work and the economic crisis: Some lessons from the Great Depression. *Review of Radical Political Economics* 8 (Spring): 73–97.

Miller, B. C. 1986. *Family research methods.* Beverly Hills, CA: Sage.

Miller, C. 2011. Mobile social media: Networking, dating & virtual goods 2011–2016. Juniper Research, November.

Miller, D. P., J. Waldfogel, and W-J. Han. 2012. Family meals and child academic and behavioral outcomes. *Child Development*, early online version, August 7.

Miller, D. W. 2001. DARE Reinvents itself—With help from its social-scientist critics. *Chronicle of Higher Education*, October 16, A12–A14.

Miller, K. 2005. *Communication theories.* New York: McGraw Hill.

MILLMAN, J. 2012a. Many apples, few pickers. *Wall Street Journal*, October 10, A3.

MILLMAN, J. 2012b. Tribes clash over gambling. *Wall Street Journal*, November 10–11, A3.

MILLNER, D., AND N. CHILES. 1999. *What brothers think, what sistahs know: The real deal on love and relationships*. New York: Morrow.

MIN, P. G. 2002. Korean American families. In *Minority families in the United States: A multicultural perspective*, 3rd ed., ed. R. L. Taylor, 193–211. Upper Saddle River, NJ: Prentice Hall.

MIN, P. G., AND C. KIM. 2009. Patterns of intermarriages and cross-generational in-marriages among native-born Asian Americans. *International Migration Review* 43 (Fall): 447–70.

MINIÑO, A. M. 2011. Death in the United States, 2009. NCHS Data Brief, July.

MINTZ, S., AND S. KELLOGG. 1988. *Domestic revolution: A social history of American family life*. New York: Free Press.

MIRABELLA, L. 2011. Hiring inequity. *Baltimore Sun*, March 20, 1, 18.

MIRANDE, A. 1985. *The Chicano experience: An alternative perspective*. Notre Dame, IN: University of Notre Dame Press.

MIROWSKY, J. 2005. Age at first birth, health, and mortality. *Journal of Health and Social Behavior* 46 (March): 32–50.

MIROWSKY, J., AND C. E. ROSS. 2007. Creative work and health. *Journal of Health and Social Behavior* 48 (December): 385–403.

MISHEL, L., J. BIVENS, E. GOULD, AND H. SHIERHOLZ. 2012. *The state of working America*, 12th ed. Ithaca, NY: Cornell University Press.

MITCHELI, B. A., AND E. M. GEE. 1996. "Boomerang kids" and midlife parental marital satisfaction. *Family Relations* 45 (October): 442–48.

MITCHELL, A. A. 2002. Infertility treatment: More risks and challenges. *New England Journal of Medicine* 346 (March 7): 769–70.

MODO, I. V. O. 2005. Nigerian families. In *Handbook of world families*, eds. B. N. Adams and J. Trost, 25–46. Thousand Oaks, CA: Sage.

MOEN, P. 1992. *Women's two roles: A contemporary dilemma*. Westport, CT: Auburn House.

MOHR, J. 1981. The great upsurge of abortion, 1840–1880. In *Family life in America: 1620–2000*, eds. M. Albin and D. Cavallo, 119–30. St. James, NY: Revisionary Press.

MOLIN, A. 2012. In Sweden, playtime goes gender-neutral for holidays. *Wall Street Journal*, November 29, D1–D2.

MOLINARI, L. S. 2010. True marital romance is a gas. *Washington Post*, January 24, C3.

MOLLBORN, S., AND C. BLALOCK. 2012. Consequences of teen parents' child-care arrangements for mothers and children. *Journal of Marriage and Family* 74 (August): 846–65.

MONASTERSKY, R. 2007. Who's minding the teenage brain? *Chronicle of Higher Education*, January 12, A14–A17.

MONEA, E., AND A. THOMAS. 2011. Unintended pregnancy and taxpayer spending. *Perspectives on Sexual and Reproductive Health* 43 (June): 88–93.

MONEY, J., AND A. A. EHRHARDT. 1972. *Man & woman, boy & girl*. Baltimore: Johns Hopkins University Press.

MONIN, J. K., AND M. S. CLARK. 2011. Why do men *benefit* more from marriage than do women? Thinking more broadly about interpersonal processes that occur within *and* outside of marriage. *Sex Roles* 65 (5/6): 320–26.

MONSERUD, M. A. 2008. Intergenerational relationships and affectual solidarity between grandparents and young adults. *Journal of Marriage and Family* 70 (February): 182–95.

MONSERUD, M. A., AND G. H. ELDER, JR. 2011. Household structure and children's educational attainment: A perspective on coresidence with grandparents. *Journal of Marriage and Family* 73 (October): 981–1000.

MONTENEGRO, X. P. 2004. *Divorce experience: A study of divorce at midlife and beyond*. Washington, DC: AARP.

MONTEZ, J. K., AND A. ZAJACOVA. 2013. Explaining the widening education gap in mortality among U.S. white women. *Journal of Health and Social Behavior* 54 (June): 165–81.

MONTGOMERY, M. J., AND G. T. SORELL. 1997. Differences in love attitudes across family life stages. *Family Relations* 46 (January): 55–61.

MOORE, A. M., L. FROHWIRTH, AND E. MILLER. 2010. Male reproductive control of women who have experienced intimate partner violence in the United States. *Social Science & Medicine* 70 (June): 1737–44.

MOORE, D. M. 2005. Lobster and love? Think again. Gallup poll, February 1.

MOORE, J. 2013. AIDS: How South Africa is beating the epidemic. *Christian Science Monitor Weekly*, June 24, 26–32.

MOORE, J., AND H. PACHON. 1985. *Hispanics in the United States*. Upper Saddle River, NJ: Prentice Hall.

MOORE, K. A., A. KINGHORN, AND T. BANDY. 2011. Parental relationship quality and child outcomes across subgroups. Child Trends Research Brief, April.

MOORE, K. A., ET AL. 2006. Depression among moms: Prevalence, predictors, and acting out among third grade children. Child Trends Research Brief, March.

MOORE, M. R., AND P. L. CHASE-LANSDALE. 2001. Sexual intercourse and pregnancy among African American girls in high-poverty neighborhoods: The role of family and perceived community environment. *Journal of Marriage and Family* 63 (November): 1146–57.

MOORE, R. L. 1998. Love and limerence with Chinese characteristics: Student romance in the PRC. In *Romantic love and sexual behavior: Perspectives from the social sciences*, ed. V. C. deMunck. 251–88. Westport, CT: Praeger.

MOORMAN, S. M., AND M. INOUE. 2013. Predicting a partner's end-of-life preferences, or substituting one's own. *Journal of Marriage and Family* 75 (June): 734–45.

MORALES, L. 2009. Nearly half of Americans are frequent Internet users. Gallup News Service, January 2.

MORALES, L. 2011. U.S. adults estimate that 25% of Americans are gay or lesbian. Gallup, May 27.

More young adults are living in their parents' home, Census Bureau finds. 2011. U.S. Census Bureau Newsroom, November 3.

MORELLO, C. 2010. An unexpected result for some census takers: The wrath of irate Americans. *Washington Post*, June 20, A4.

MORGAN, C. 2012. Top 5 plastic surgeries men get: The pressure to be physically perfect now for men, too. AlterNet, May 10.

MORGAN, P. D. 1998. *Slave counterpoint: Black culture in the eighteenth-century Chesapeake & lowcountry*. Chapel Hill: University of North Carolina Press.

MORGAN, W. L. 1939. *The family meets the depression: A study of a group of highly selected families*. Westport, CT: Greenwood.

MORIN, M., AND G. MOHAN. 2013. Judge ends age limit on Plan B. *Baltimore Sun*, April 6, 6.

MORIN, R. 2011. The public renders a split verdict on changes in family structure. Pew Research Center, February 16.

MORIN, R., AND S. MOTEL. 2012. A third of Americans now say they are in the lower classes. Pew Research Center, September 10.

MORR SEREWICZ, M. C. 2008. Toward a triangular theory of the communication and relationships of in-laws: Theoretical proposal and social relations analysis of relational satisfaction and private disclosure in in-law triads. *Journal of Family Communication* 8 (October): 264–92.

MORRIS, M. 2003. Love in a hurry. *Baltimore Sun*, January 12, 1N, 4N.

MOSHER, W. D., AND W. F. PRATT. 1991. Fecundity and infertility in the United States: Incidence and trends. *Fertility and Sterility* 56 (August): 192–93.

MOSS-RACUSIN, C. A., J. F. DOVIDIO, V. L. BRESCOLL, M. J. GRAHAM, AND J. HANDELSMAN. 2012. Science faculty's subtle gender biases favor male students. *Proceedings of the National Academy of Science* 109 (October 9): 16474–79.

MOSTAGHIM, R., AND E. ALPERT. 2012. Iran mulls websites to fix "marriage crisis." *Baltimore Sun*, September 30, 22.

Mother's day: May 12, 2013. 2013. U.S. Census Bureau News, CB13-FF.11, April 3.

Movement Advancement Project, Family Equality Council, and Center for American Progress. 2012. Finding children forever homes: LGBT foster and adoptive families. June.

MOWRER, E. R. 1972. War and family solidarity and stability. In *The American family in World War II*, ed. R. A. Abrams, 100–106. New York: Arno and New York Times.

MOYNIHAN, D. P., ED. 1970. *Toward a national urban policy*. New York: Basic Books.

MUEHLENHARD, C. L., AND Z. D. PETERSON. 2011. Distinguishing between *sex* and *gender*: History, current conceptualizations, and implications. *Sex Roles* 64 (June): 791–803.

MUELLER, M. M., AND G. H. ELDER, JR. 2003. Family contingencies across the generations: Grandparent–grandchild relationships in holistic perspective. *Journal of Marriage and Family* 65 (May): 404–17.

MUELLER, T. E., L. E. GAVIN, AND A. KULKARNI. 2008. The association between sex education and youth's engagement in sexual intercourse, age at first intercourse, and birth control use at first sex. *Journal of Adolescent Health* 42 (January): 89–96.

MUKHOPADHYAY, S. 2011. *Outdated: Why dating is ruining your life*. Berkeley, CA: Seal Press.

MULAC, A. 1998. The gender-linked language effect: Do language differences really make a difference? In *Sex differences and similarities in communication: Critical essays and empirical investigations of sex and gender in interaction*, eds. D. J. Canary and K. Dindia, 127–53. Mahwah, NJ: Lawrence Erlbaum Associates.

MULFORD, C., AND P. C. GIORDANO. 2008. Teen dating violence: A closer look at adolescent romantic relationships. *NIJ Journal*, No. 261 (October): 34–40.

MULLEN, N. 2009. Problem of female genital mutilation growing in the EU. *Irish Medical Times*, April 3.

MUMME, D. L., AND A. FERNALD. 2003. The infant as onlooker: Learning from emotional reactions observed in a television scenario. *Child Development* 74 (January/February): 221–37.

Mundy, L. 2012. Women, money and power. *Time*, March 26, 30–34.

Munk-Olsen, T., T. M. Laursen, C. B. Pedersen, Ø. Lidegaard, and P. B. Mortensen. 2011. Induced first-trimester abortion and risk of mental disorder. *New England Journal of Medicine* 364 (January 27): 332–39.

Munk-Olsen, T., T. M. Laursen, C. B. Pederson, O. Mors, and P. B. Mortensen. 2006. New parents and mental disorders: A population-based register study. *JAMA* 296 (December 6): 2582–89.

Munnell, A. H., and M. Soto. 2005. How much pre-retirement income does Social Security replace? Center for Retirement Research, Boston College, November, no. 36.

Murphey, D., M. Barry, and B. Vaughn. 2013. Mental health disorders. Child Trends, January.

Murphy, D. 2011. Global trends you may have missed. *Christian Science Monitor*, January 3, 12.

Murphy, E., and E. J. Graff. 2005. *Getting even: Why women don't get paid like men— and what to do about it*. New York: Simon & Schuster.

Murray, C. I. 2000. Coping with death, dying, and grief in families. In *Families & change: Coping with stressful events and transitions*, 2nd ed., eds. P. C. McKenry and S. J. Price, 120–53. Thousand Oaks, CA: Sage.

Murray, C. J. et al., 2013. The state of US health, 1990–2010: Burden of diseases, injuries, and risk factors. *JAMA* 310 (July 10): E1–E18.

Murray, J. E. 2000. Marital protection and marital selection: Evidence from a historical-prospective sample of American men. *Demography* 37 (November): 511–21.

Murray, S. L., D. W. Griffin, J. L. Derrick, B. Harris, M. Aloni, and S. Leder. 2011. Tempting fate or inviting happiness? Unrealistic idealization prevents the decline of marital satisfaction. *Psychological Science* 22 (May): 619–26.

Murstein, B. I. 1974. *Love, sex, and marriage through the ages*. New York: Springer.

Musick, K., and L. Bumpass. 2012. Reexamining the case for marriage: Union formation and changes in well-being. *Journal of Marriage and Family* 74 (February): 1–18.

Mutzabaugh, B. 2011. Reports: Thai airline recruits "third-sex" attendants. *USA Today*, January 29.

Mykyta, L., and S. Macartney. 2012. Sharing a household: Household composition and economic well-being: 2007–2010. U.S. Census Bureau, Current Population Reports, June.

N

Naimi, T. S., et al. 2008. Alcohol-attributable deaths and years of potential life lost among American Indians and Alaska Natives— United States, 2001–2005. *MMWR Weekly* 57 (August 29): 938–41.

Najib, A., J. P. Lorberbaum, S. Kose, D. E. Bohning, and M. S. George. 2004. Regional brain activity in women grieving a romantic relationship breakup. *American Journal of Psychiatry* 161 (December): 2245–56.

Nalavany, B. A., L. M. Glidden, and S. D. Ryan. 2009. Parental satisfaction in the adoption of children with learning disorders: The role of behavior problems. *Family Relations* 58 (December): 621–33.

Narayan, A. 2013. In India, arranged marriages hit the Web. *Bloomberg Businessweek*, April 8–14, 18–19.

Nass, G. D., R. W. Libby, and M. P. Fisher. 1981. *Sexual choices: An introduction to human sexuality*. Belmont, CA: Wadsworth.

Nathan, R. 2005. *My freshman year: What a professor learned by becoming a student*. Ithaca, NY: Cornell University Press.

National Abortion Federation. 2006. Crisis pregnancy centers: An affront to choice. Washington, DC.

National Adoption Information Clearinghouse. 2002. Pros and cons of each type of adoption for the involved parties. U.S. Department of Health & Human Services.

National Adoption Information Clearinghouse. 2006. Openness in adoption: A bulletin for professionals. U.S. Department of Health and Human Services.

National Alliance for Caregiving/AARP. 2009. Caregiving in the U.S.: A focused look at those caring for someone age 50 or older. November.

National Campaign to Prevent Teen and Unplanned Pregnancy, The. 2010. 88% of unmarried young adults have had sex.

National Center for Health Statistics. 2011. *Health, United States, 2010: With special feature on death and dying*. Hyattsville, MD.

National Center for Health Statistics. 2012. *Health, United States, 2011: With special feature on socioeconomic status and health*. Hyattsville, MD.

National Center for Health Statistics. 2013. *Health, United States, 2012: With special feature on emergency care*.

National Center for Women and Policing. 2009. Police family violence fact sheet.

National Center on Addiction and Substance Abuse. 2008. National survey of American attitudes on substance abuse XIII: Teens and parents. August.

National Center on Addiction and Substance Abuse at Columbia University. 2008. "You've got drugs!" V: Prescription drug pushers on the Internet. A CASA White Paper, July.

National Center on Elder Abuse. 2012. Statistics/Data. February.

National Conference of State Legislatures. 2012. State laws regarding marriages between first cousins.

National Conference of state legislatures. 2013. Common-law marriage. State laws limiting marriage to opposite-sex couples. June 26.

National Endowment for Financial Education. 2011. Three in 10 Americans admit to financial deception with partners. January 13.

National Grandparents Day 2013: Sept. 8. 2013. U.S. Census Bureau Newsroom, Facts for Features, July 8, 2013.

National Institute of Mental Health. 2011. The teen brain: Still under construction.

National Institute on Alcohol Abuse and Alcoholism. 2012. National Institutes of Health, March.

National Institute on Drug Abuse. 2011. Club drugs (GHB, Ketamine, and Rohypnol). June.

National Institutes of Health. 2006. *Women of color health data book: Adolescents to seniors*.

National marriage and divorce rate trends. 2013. Centers for Disease Control and Prevention.

National Mental Health Association. 2006. Eating disorders.

National Organization on Fetal Alcohol Syndrome. 2012. FASD: What everyone should know.

National Retail Federation. 2013. Cautious consumers keep cupid at bay this year, according to NRF. January 31.

National Science Board. 2012. *Science and engineering indicators 2012*. Arlington, VA: National Science Foundation.

Nauck, B., and D. Klaus. 2005. Families in Turkey. In *Handbook of world families*, eds. B. N. Adams and J. Trost, 364–388. Thousand Oaks, CA: Sage.

Neal, M. B., and L. B. Hammer. 2007. *Working couples caring for children and aging parents*. Mahwah, NJ: Lawrence Erlbaum.

Nelson, C. M. 2013. Poll finds broad immigration support. *Wall Street Journal*. April 11, A4.

Nelson, M. K. 2011. *Parenting out of control: Anxious parents in uncertain times*. New York: New York University Press.

Nelson, S. K., K. Kushlev, T. English, E. W. Dunn, and S. Lyubomirsky. 2013. In defense of parenthood: Children are associated with more joy than misery. *Psychological Science* 24 (1): 3–10.

Nesteruk, O., and A. Gramescu. 2012. Dating and mate selection among young adults from immigrant families. *Marriage & Family Review* 48 (January): 40–58.

Neugarten, B. L., and K. K. Weinstein. 1964. The changing American grandparents. *Journal of Marriage and the Family* 26 (May): 199–204.

Neumann, M. G. 2013. The long way home for adults who were children of divorce. *Huffington Post*, March 25.

Newark-French, C. 2011. Mobile dating apps: The second (lady) killer app category. The Flurry Blog, August 2.

Newport, F. 2009. Extramarital affairs, like Sanford's, morally taboo. Gallup, June 25.

Newport, F. 2011. Americans prefer boys to girls, just as they did in 1941. Gallup, June 23.

Newport, F. 2011. Americans still prefer male bosses; many have no preference. Gallup, September 8.

Newport, F. 2012. Americans like having a rich class, as they did 22 years ago. Gallup, May 11.

Newport, F. 2012. Religion big factor for Americans against same-sex marriage. Gallup, December 5.

Newport, F. 2013. In U.S., 87% approve of black-white marriage, vs. 4% in 1958. Gallup, July 25.

Newport, F., and I. Himelfarb. 2013. In U.S., record-high say gay, lesbian relations morally OK. Gallup, May 20.

Newton-Small, J. 2012. Frozen assets. *Time*, April 16, 49–52.

NICHD Early Child Care Research Network. 2003. Does amount of time in child care predict socioemotional adjustment? *Child Development* 74 (July/August): 976–1005.

Nichols, A., and M. Simms. 2012. Racial and ethnic differences in receipt of unemployment insurance benefits during the great recession. Urban Institute Unemployment and Recovery Project, June.

Niquette, M. 2011. State vs. state in the war for jobs. *Bloomberg Businessweek*, May 9– May 15, 29–30.

Nissinen, S. 2000. *The conscious bride: Women unveil their true feelings about getting hitched*. Oakland, CA: New Harbinger.

Noël-Miller, C. M. 2013. Repartnering following divorce: Implications for older fathers' relations with their adult children. *Journal of Marriage and Family* 75 (June): 697–712.

Noguchi, Y. 2005. Life and romance in 160 characters or less. *Washington Post* (December 29): A1.

Nolan, K. 2011. Gold losing shine in wedding rings. *Christian Science Monitor*, April 25, 22.

Noller, P. 1984. *Nonverbal communication and marital interaction*. New York: Pergamon.

NOLLER, P., AND M. A. FITZPATRICK. 1993. *Communication in family relationships.* Upper Saddle River, NJ: Prentice Hall.

NOMAGUCHI, K. M., P. C. GIORDANO, W. D. MANNING, AND M. A. LONGMORE. 2011. Adolescents' gender mistrust: Variations and implications for the quality of romantic relationships. *Journal of Marriage and Family* 73 (October): 1032–47.

NORDLAND, R. 2010. In bold display, Taliban order stoning deaths. *New York Times,* August 16, A1.

NORRIS, T., P. L. VINES, AND E. M. HOEFFEL. 2012. The American Indian and Alaska Native Population: 2010. 2010 Census Briefs, January.

NORTON, M. I., AND D. ARIELY. 2011. Building a better America—One wealth quintile at a time. *Perspectives on Psychological Science* 6 (1): 9–12.

NORTON, M. I., AND S. R. SOMMERS. 2011. Whites see racism as a zero-sum game that they are now losing. *Perspectives on Psychological Science* 6 (3): 215–18.

NOSSITER, A. 2011. Hinting at an end to a curb on polygamy, interim Libyan leader stirs anger. *New York Times,* October 30, A6.

NOWINSKI, J. 1993. *Hungry hearts: On men, intimacy, self-esteem, and addiction.* New York: Lexington.

NUTA, V. R. 1986. Emotional aspects of child support enforcement. *Family Relations* 35 (January): 177–82.

NYE, F. I., AND F. M. BERARDO, EDS. 1981. *Emerging conceptual frameworks in family analysis.* New York: Praeger.

NYHOLT, D. R., ET AL. 2012. Genome-wide association meta-analysis identifies new endometriosis risk loci. *Nature Genetics* 44 (December): 1355–59.

O

O'SULLIVAN, L. F., M. M. CHENG, K. M. HARRIS, AND J. BROOKS-GUNN. 2007. I wanna hold your hand: The progression of social, romantic and sexual events in adolescent relationships. *Perspectives on Sexual and Reproductive Health* 39 (November/December): 100–107.

OAKLEY, D., AND K. KENNEALLY. 2013. Pensions and retirement security 2013: A roadmap for policy makers. National Institute on Retirement Security, February.

OBER, A. J., ET AL. 2011. The relative role of perceived partner risks in promoting condom use in a three-city sample of high-risk, low-income women. *AIDS Behavior* 15 (7): 1347–58.

OBERMAN, M., AND C. L. MEYER. 2008. *When mothers kill: Interviews from prison.* New York: New York University Press.

OCAMPO, V. W., G. A. SHELLEY, AND L. H. JAYCOX. 2007. Latino teens talk about help seeking and help giving in relation to dating violence. *Violence Against Women* 13 (February): 172–89.

OCOBOCK, A. 2013. The power and limits of marriage: Married gay men's family relationships. *Journal of Marriage and Family* 75 (February): 191–205.

ODEN, T. J. 2008. The first gentleman. *Chronicle of Higher Education,* March 21, C2–C3.

OFFICE OF MINORITY HEALTH. 2012. Asian American/Pacific Islander profile. U.S. Department of Health & Human Services, September 17.

OFFICE OF THE DEPUTY CHIEF OF STAFF FOR INTELLIGENCE. 2006. Arab cultural awareness: 58 factsheets. January.

OFFICE ON WOMEN'S HEALTH. 2011. Emergency contraception (emergency birth control).

U.S. Department of Health and Human Services, November 21.

OGDEN, C. L., AND M. D. CARROLL. 2010a. Prevalence of obesity among children and adolescents: United States, trends 1963–1965 through 2007–2008. National Center for Health Statistics, June.

OGDEN, C. L., AND M. D. CARROLL. 2010b. Prevalence of overweight, obesity, and extreme obesity among adults: United States, trends 1960–1962 through 2007–2008. National Center for Health Statistics, June.

OGDEN, C. L., M. D. CARROLL, B. K. KIT, AND K. M. FLEGAL. 2012. Prevalence of obesity in the United States, 2009–2010. NCHS Data Brief No. 82, January.

OGILVIE, J. P. 2012. Is sharing a bed with baby healthful or risky? *Baltimore Sun,* April 5, 3.

OJEDA, L., R. ROSALES, AND G. E. GOOD. 2008. Socioeconomic status and cultural predictors of male role attitudes among Mexican American men: ¿Son más machos? *Psychology of Men & Masculinity* 9 (no. 3): 133–38.

OJITO, M. 2009. Doctors in Cuba start over in the U.S. *New York Times,* August 4, D1.

OLDER Americans month: May 2013. 2013. U.S. Census Bureau News, March 7.

OLEN, H., AND K. BLAKELEY. 2009. My turn, your turn. *Forbes Woman,* April 22, 55–57.

OLFSON, M., C. BLANCO, L. LIU, C. MORENO, AND G. LAJE. 2006. *Archives of General Psychiatry* 63 (June): 679–85.

OLIVER, M. L., AND T. M. SHAPIRO. 2001. Wealth and racial stratification. In *America becoming: Racial trends and their consequences,* Vol. 2, eds. N. J. Smelser, W. J. Wilson, and F. Mitchell, 222–51. Washington, DC: National Academy Press.

OLSHANSKY, S. J., ET AL. 2012. Differences in life expectancy due to race and educational differences are widening, and many may not catch up. *Health Affairs* 31 (August): 1803–13.

OLSHANSKY, S. J., L. HAYFLICK, AND T. T. PERLS. 2004a. Anti-aging medicine: the hype and the reality—part I. *Journal of Gerontology: Biological Sciences* 59A (6): 513–14.

OLSHANSKY, S. J., L. HAYFLICK, AND T. T. PERLS. 2004b. Anti-aging medicine: the hype and the reality—part II. *Journal of Gerontology: Biological Sciences* 59A (7): 649–51.

OLSHEN, E., K. H. MCVEIGH, R. A. WUNSCH-HITZIG, AND V. I. RICKERT. 2007. Dating violence, sexual assault, and suicide attempts among urban teenagers. *Archives of Pediatrics & Adolescent Medicine* 161 (June): 539–45.

OLSON, D. H., AND A. K. OLSON. 2000. *Empowering couples: Building on your strengths.* Minneapolis: Life Innovations.

OLSON, D. H., AND A. OLSON-SIGG. 2002. Overview of cohabitation research: For use with PREPARECC. Life Innovations.

OLSON, I. R., AND C. MARSHUETZ. 2005. Facial attractiveness is appraised in a glance. *Emotion* 5 (December): 498–502.

OLSON, J. R. 2010. Choosing effective youth-focused prevention strategies: A practical guide for applied family professionals. *Family Relations* 59 (April): 207–20.

OLSON, T. B. 2010. The conservative case for gay marriage. *Newsweek,* January 18, 48–53.

OLVER, K. 2013. Divorce causes: 5 marriage mistakes that lead to divorce. *Huffington Post,* March 7.

ONISHI, N. 2007. Betrothed at first sight: A Korean-Vietnamese courtship. *New York Times,* February 22, A1, A12.

OOMS, T. 2002. Strengthening couples and marriage in low-income communities. In *Revitalizing the institution of marriage for the twenty-first century,* eds. A. J. Hawkins, L. D. Wardle, and D. O. Coolidge, 79–100. Westport, CT: Praeger.

OOMS, T., S. BOUCHET, AND M. PARKE. 2004. Beyond marriage licenses: Efforts in states to strengthen marriage and two-parent families. Center for Law and Social Policy.

OPDYKE, J. D. 2010. Questions to ask after "I will" but before "I do." *Wall Street Journal,* February 14.

OPPENHEIMER, M. 2012. "Purity balls" get attention, but might not be all they claim. *New York Times,* July 2, A7.

ORBUCH, T., J. BAUERMEISTER, E. BROWN, AND B. MCKINLEY. 2013. Early family ties and marital stability over 16 years: The context of race and gender. *Family Relations* 62 (April): 255–68.

ORDOÑEZ, J. 2007. Tying the financial knot. *Newsweek,* April 9, 46–48.

ORENSTEIN, P. 2000. *Flux: Women on sex, work, kids, love, and life in a half-changed world.* New York: Doubleday.

ORENSTEIN, P. 2011. Should the world of toys be gender-free? *New York Times,* December 30, A23.

ORMAN, S. 2008. *Suze Orman's 2009 action plan.* New York: Spiegel & Grau.

ORNISH, D. 2005. Love is real medicine. *Newsweek,* October 3, 56.

ORNSTEIN, C., AND T. WEBER. 2011. Medical schools plug holes in conflict-of-interest policies. ProPublica, May 19.

OROPESA, R. S., AND N. S. LANDALE. 2004. The future of marriage and Hispanics. *Journal of Marriage and Family* 66 (November): 901–20.

ORR, K., AND M. STOUT. 2007. Harlequin romance report 2007: The romance revolution.

ORRENIUS, P. M., and M. ZAVODNY. 2009. Do immigrants work in riskier jobs? *Demography* 46 (August): 535–51.

ORTHNER, D. K., AND R. ROSE. 2009. Work separation demands and spouse psychological well-being. *Family Relations* 58 (October): 392–403.

OSBORNE, C., AND S. MCLANAHAN. 2007. Partnership instability and child well-being. *Journal of Marriage and Family* 69 (November): 1065–83.

OSBORNE, C., W. D. MANNING, AND P. J. SMOCK. 2007. Married and cohabiting parents' relationship stability: A focus on race and ethnicity. *Journal of Marriage and Family* 69 (December): 1345–66.

OUTCALT, T. 1998. *Before you say "I do:" Important questions for couples to ask before marriage.* New York: Perigee.

OWEN, D. J., A. M. S. SLEP, AND R. E. HEYMAN. 2012. The effect of praise, positive nonverbal response, reprimand, and negative nonverbal response on child compliance: A systematic review. *Clinical Child and Family Psychology Review* 15 (December): 364–85.

P

PAGE, C. 2008. Another alpha male caught behaving badly: Why do they do it? *Baltimore Sun,* March 18, 15A.

PAGE, M. E., AND A. H. STEVENS. 2005. Understanding racial differences in the economic costs of growing up in a single-parent family. *Demography* 42 (February): 75–90.

PAI, M., AND J-H. HA. 2012. Impact of widowhood on parent–child relations: Does parents' personality matter? *Journal of Marriage and Family* 74 (June): 494–509.

PAIK, I. 2007. Getting a job: Is there a mother-hood penalty? *American Journal of Sociology* 112 (March): 1297–338.

PAIK, A. 2010. The contexts of sexual involvement and concurrent sexual partnerships. *Perspectives on Sexual and Reproductive Health* 42 (March): 33–42.

PAINTER, J. N., ET AL. 2011. Genome-wide association study identifies a locus at 7p15.2 associated with endometriosis. *Nature Genetics* 43 (January): 51–54.

Pakistan Taliban shoot girl activist. 2012. *Wall Street Journal*, October 10, A13.

PALETTA, D., AND C. PORTER. 2013. Use of food stamps swells even as economy improves. *Wall Street Journal*, March 28, 1, A12.

PALEY, A. R. 2008. For Kurdish girls, a painful ancient ritual. *Washington Post*, December 29, A9.

PALMER, K. 2007. Accountability: His and hers. *U.S. News & World Report*, October 8, 51–53.

PALMER, K. 2008. Keeping money unmarried. *U.S. News & World Report*, April 16, 58–59.

PALMORE, E. B. 1999. *Ageism: Negative and positive*. New York: Springer.

PAPERNOW, P. L. 1993. *Becoming a step family: Patterns of development in remarried families*. San Francisco: Jossey-Bass.

PAPP, L. M., E. M. CUMMINGS, AND M. C. GOEKE-MOREY. 2009. For richer, for poorer: Money as a topic of marital conflict in the home. *Family Relations* 58 (February): 91–103.

PARAMESWARAN, L. 2003. Battered wives often recant or assume blame. Women's E-News, August 2.

PARCEL, T. L., L. A. CAMPBELL, AND W. ZHONG. 2012. Children's behavior problems in the United States and Great Britain. *Journal of Health and Social Behavior* 53 (June): 165–82.

PARIS, R., AND N. DUBUS. 2005. Staying connected while nurturing an infant: A challenge of new motherhood. *Family Relations* 54 (January): 72–83.

PARK, A. 2010. Alzheimer's unlocked. *Time*, October 25, 53–59.

PARK, R. L. 2003. The seven warning signs of bogus science. *Chronicle of Higher Education*, January 31, B20.

PARK, S. 2011. Korean multiculturalism and the marriage squeeze. *Contexts* 10 (Summer): 64–65.

PARKE, R. D. 1996. *Fatherhood*. Cambridge, MA: Harvard University Press.

PARKER, K. 2009. Coping with end-of-life decisions. Pew Research Center, August 20.

PARKER, K. 2012. The boomerang generation: Feeling OK about living with mom and dad. Pew Social & Demographic Trends, March 15.

PARKER, K. 2012. Yes, the rich are different. Pew Research Center, August 27.

PARKER, K., AND E. PATTEN. 2013. The sandwich generation: Rising financial burdens for middle-aged Americans. Pew Research Center, January 30.

PARKER, K., AND W. WANG. 2013. Modern parenthood: Roles of moms and dads converge as they balance work and family. Pew Social & Demographic Trends, March 14.

PARKER, S. 1996. Full brother-sister marriage in Roman Egypt: Another look. *Cultural Anthropology* 11 (August): 362–76.

PARKER-POPE, T. 2009. What are friends for? A longer life. *New York Times*, April 21, 1.

PARKER-POPE, T. 2013. Suicide rates rise sharply in U.S. *New York Times*, May 2, A1.

PARRAMORE, L. 2012. How job insecurity if messing up your love life. AlterNet, July 31.

PARSONS, T., AND R. F. BALES. 1955. *Family, socialization and interaction process*. Glencoe, IL: Free Press.

PARTINGTON, S. N., D. L. STEBER, K. A. BLAIR, AND R. A. CISLER. 2009. Second births to teenage mothers: Risk factors for low birth weight and preterm birth. *Perspectives on Sexual and Reproductive Health* 41 (June): 101–9.

Partnership at Drugfree.org. 2013. Parents have more influence over their child than friends, music, TV, the Internet and celebrities.

PASCOE, C. J. 2007. *Dude, you're a fag: Masculinity and sexuality in high school*. Berkeley: University of California Press.

PASSEL, J. S., AND D. COHN. 2011. Unauthorized immigrant population: National and state trends, 2010. Pew Hispanic Center, February 1.

PASSEL, J. S., D. COHN, AND M. H. LOPEZ. 2011. Census 2010: 50 million Latinos; Hispanics account for more than half of nation's growth in past decade. Pew Hispanic Center, March 24.

PASSEL, J. S., G. LIVINGSTON, AND D. COHN. 2012. Explaining why minority births now outnumber white births. Pew Research Center, May 17.

PASSEL, J. S., W. WANG, AND P. TAYLOR. 2010. Marrying out: One-in-seven new U.S. marriages is interracial or interethnic. Pew Research Center, June 15.

PASTOR, M., J. SCOGGINS, J. TRAN, AND R. ORTIZ. 2010. The economic benefits of immigrant authorization in California. Center for the Study of Immigrant Integration, January.

PATNER, M. M. 1990. Between mothers and daughters: Pain and difficulty go with the territory. *Washington Post*, November 8, C5.

PATTEN, E., AND K. PARKER. 2012. A gender reversal on career aspirations. Pew Research Center, March 19.

PATTERSON, C. J. 2002. Lesbian and gay parenthood. In *Handbook of parenting*, 2nd ed., Vol. 3: Being and becoming a parent, ed. M. H. Bornstein, 317–38. Mahwah, NJ: Erlbaum.

PATTERSON, J., AND P. KIM. 1991. *The day America told the truth: What people really believe about everything that really matters*. Upper Saddle River, NJ: Prentice Hall.

PATZ, A. 2000. Will your marriage last? *Psychology Today* 33 (January/February): 58–63.

PAUL, P. 2001. Childless by choice. *American Demographics* 23 (November): 45–50.

PAUL, P. 2002. Make room for granddaddy. *American Demographics* 24 (April): 41–45.

PAUL, P. 2010. By her support, does she earn his infidelity? *New York Times*, September 24, ST8.

PAULOZZI, L. J. 2011. Drug-induced deaths—United States, 2003–2007. *MMWR* 60 (Suppl, January 14): 60–61.

PAULSON, J. F., AND S. D. BAZEMORE. 2010. Prenatal and postpartum depression in fathers and its association with maternal depression. *JAMA* 303 (19): 1961–69.

PAYNE, B. M. 2012. Occupy Valentine's day: Celebrate love, not commerce. AlterNet, February 13.

PAYNE, C. 2013. Moms are primary breadwinners in 40% of U.S. households. *USA Today*, May 29.

PAYNE, K. K., AND J. COPP. 2013. Young adults in the parental home and the Great Recession. National Center for Family & Marriage Research.

PAYNE, K. K., AND L. GIBBS. 2011. Marital duration at divorce, 2010. (FP-11-13). National Center for Family & Marriage Research.

PAZOL, K., A. A. CREANGA, S. B. ZANE, K. D. BURLEY, AND D. J. JAMIESON. 2012. Abortion surveillance—United States, 2009. *MMWR* 61 (8): 1–44.

PEARCE, D. 1978. The feminization of poverty: Women, work, and welfare. *Urban and Social Change Review* 11: 28–36.

PEARSON, A. 2013. Waiting for superwoman. *Bloomberg Businessweek*, March 11–March 17, 6–7.

PEAVY, L., AND U. SMITH. 1994. *Women in waiting in the westward movement: Life on the home frontier*. Norman: University of Oklahoma Press.

PEELE, S., WITH A. BRODSKY. 1976. *Love and addiction*. New York: New American Library.

PEIPERT, J. F., T. MADDEN, J. E. ALLSWORTH, AND G. M. SECURA. 2012. Preventing unintended pregnancies by providing no-cost contraception. *Obstetrics & Gynecology* 120 (December): 1291–97.

PELLERIN, L. A. 2005. Applying Baumrind's parenting typology to high schools: Toward a middle-range theory of authoritative socialization. *Social Science Research* 34 (June): 282–303.

PENHA-LOPES, V. 1995. "Make room for daddy": Patterns of family involvement among contemporary African American men. In *American families: Issues in race and ethnicity*, ed. C. K. Jacobson, 179–99. New York: Garland.

PEPLAU, L. A., R. C. VENIEGAS, AND S. M. CAMPBELL. 1996. Gay and lesbian relationships. In *The lives of lesbians, gays, AND bisexuals: Children to adults*, eds. R. C. Savin-Williams and K. M. Cohen, 250–73. New York: Harcourt Brace.

PERCHESKI, C. 2008. Opting out? Cohort differences in professional women's employment rates from 1960 to 2005. *American Sociological Review* 73 (November): 497–517.

PÉREZ, L. 2002. Cuban American families. In *Minority families in the United States: A multicultural perspective*, 3rd ed., ed. R. L. Taylor, 114–30. Upper Saddle River, NJ: Prentice Hall.

PEREZ-ROSSELLO, J. M., S. A. CONNOLLY, A. W. NEWTON, K. H. ZOU, AND P. K. KLEINMAN. 2010. Whole-body MRI in suspected infant abuse. *American Journal of Roentgenology* 195 (September): 744–50.

PERGAMIT, M. R., AND M. ERNST. 2011. Running away from foster care: Youths' knowledge and access of services. April 9.

PERLS, T. T. 2004. Anti-aging quackery: Human growth hormone and tricks of the trade—more dangerous than ever. *Journals of Gerontology: Biological and Medical Sciences* 59 (July): B682–B691.

PERLSTEIN, L. 2005. A user's guide to middle school romance. *Washington Post Magazine*, February 13, 20–23, 33.

PERRIN, E. C. 2002. Technical report: Coparent or second-parent adoption by same-sex parents. *Pediatrics* 109 (February): 341–44.

PERRIN, E. C., AND B. S. SIEGEL. 2013. Promoting the well-being of children whose parents are gay or lesbian. *Pediatrics* 131 (4): e1374–e1383.

PERRIN, P. B., ET AL. 2011. Aligning Mars and Venus: The social construction and instability of gender differences in romantic relationships. *Sex Roles* 64 (May): 613–28.

PERRY, S. W. 2004. American Indians and crime. U.S. Department of Justice, Bureau of Justice Statistics, December.

PERRY-JENKINS, M., A. E. GOLDBERG, C. P. PIERCE, AND A. G. SAYER. 2007. Shift work, role overload, and the transition to parenthood. *Journal of Marriage and Family* 69 (February): 123–38.

Perry-Jenkins, M., and A. Claxton. 2011. The transition to parenthood and the reasons "Momma ain't happy." *Journal of Marriage and Family* 73 (February): 23–28.

Pescosolido, A. 2013. 5 tips for co-parenting after divorce. *Huffington Post*, May 16.

Pessar, P. R. 1995. *A visa for a dream: Dominicans in the United States*. Boston: Allyn & Bacon.

Peter, T. A. 2012. Mistreatment of Afghan women caused by far more than Taliban. *Christian Science Monitor*, January 31.

Peterman, A., T. Palermo, and C. Bredenkamp. 2011. Estimates and determinants of sexual violence against women in the Democratic Republic of Congo. *American Journal of Public Health* 101 (June): 1060–67.

Petersen, A. 2012. Smarter ways to discipline kids. *Wall Street Journal*, December 26, D1, D3.

Peterson, B. D., C. R. Newton, K. H. Rosen, and R. S. Schulman. 2006. Coping processes of couples experiencing infertility. *Family Relations* 55 (April): 227–39.

Peterson, J. L., J. J. Card, M. B. Eisen, and B. Sherman-Williams. 1994. Evaluating teenage pregnancy prevention and other social programs: Ten stages of program assessment. *Family Planning Perspectives* 26 (May): 116–20, 131.

Peterson, K. S. 2002. Having it all, except children. *USA Today*, April 7, 2D.

Petside. 2010. Who's the better listener, your husband or your dog? April 27.

Pew Center on the States. 2009. One in 31: The long reach of American corrections. March.

Pew Forum on Religion & Public Life. 2008. U.S. religious landscape survey: Religious beliefs and practices: Diverse and politically relevant. June.

Pew Forum on Religion & Public Life. 2008a. An overview of the same-sex marriage debate. April 1.

Pew Forum on Religion & Public Life. 2008b. U.S. religious landscape survey. February.

Pew Hispanic Center. 2004. Assimilation and language. March.

Pew Hispanic Center. 2013. A nation of immigrants: A portrait of the 40 million, including 11 million unauthorized. January 29.

Pew Research Center for the People & the Press. 2012. Assessing the representativeness of public opinion surveys. Pew Research Center, May 15.

Pew Research Center. 2010. The decline of marriage and rise of new families. November 18.

Pew Research Center. 2012a. Gay marriage.

Pew Research Center. 2012b. Only one true love.

Pew Research Social & Demographic Trends. 2011. A portrait of stepfamilies. January 13.

Pewewardy, C. 1998. Fluff and feathers: Treatment of American Indians in the literature and the classroom. *Equity & Excellence in Education* 31 (April): 69–76.

Philips, M. 2012. Manufacturing: A rebound, not a renaissance. *Bloomberg Businessweek*, December 17–December 23, 9–10.

Phillips, J. A., and M. M. Sweeney. 2005. Premarital cohabitation and marital disruption among white, black, and Mexican American women. *Journal of Marriage and Family* 67 (May): 296–314.

Phillips, K. R. 2004. Getting time off: Access to leave among working parents. The Urban Institute, April 22.

Phinney, J. S., B. Horenczyk, K. Liebkind, and P. Vedder. 2001. Ethnic identity, immigration, and well-being: An interactional perspective. *Journal of Social Issues* 57: 493–510.

Piaget, J. 1932. *The moral judgment of the child*. New York: Harcourt, Brace.

Piaget, J. 1954. *The construction of reality in the child*. New York: Basic Books.

Piaget, J. 1960. *The child's conception of the world*. London: Routledge.

Pickert, K. 2010. When the adopted can't adapt. *Time*, June 28, 34–39.

Pickert, K. 2013. What choice? *Time*, January 14, 38–46.

Pienta, A. M., and M. M. Franks. 2006. A closer look at health and widowhood: Do health behaviors change after loss of a spouse? In *Spousal bereavement in late life*, eds. D. Carr, R. M. Nesse, and C. B. Wortman, 117–142. New York: Springer.

Pilkauskas, N. V. 2012. Three-generation family households: Differences by family structure at birth. *Journal of Marriage and Family* 74 (October): 931–43.

Piore, A. 2007. The dog wears Prada. *Christian Science Monitor*, February 21, 20.

Piorkowski, G. K. 1994. *Too close for comfort: Exploring the risks of intimacy*. New York: Plenum.

Pittman, F. 1990. *Private lies: Infidelity and the betrayal of intimacy*. New York: W.W. Norton.

Pittman, F. 1999. *Grow up! How taking responsibility can make you a happy adult*. New York: Golden Books.

Pittz, W. 2005. Closing the gap: Solutions to race-based health disparities. Applied Research Center & Northwest Federation of Community Organizations, June.

Plan B contraceptive approved for all ages. 2013. *Baltimore Sun*, June 21, 10.

Planned Parenthood Federation of America Inc. 2013. What is the abortion pill?

Plateris, A. A. 1973. *100 years of marriage and divorce statistics: 1867–1967*. Rockville, MD: National Center for Health Statistics.

Platt, S. F. 2006. *Letters from the front lines: Iraq and Afghanistan*. Point Roberts, WA: Granville Island Publishing.

Polgreen, L. 2010. One bride for 2 brothers: A custom fades in India. *New York Times*, July 16, A4.

Polis, C. B., and L. S. Zabin. 2012. Missed conceptions or misconceptions: Perceived infertility among unmarried young adults in the United States. *Perspectives on Sexual and Reproductive Health* 44 (March): 30–38.

Polisi, C. J. 2009. Spousal rape laws continue to evolve. Women's eNews, July 1.

Pollack, E. 2012. Households making between $250K and $1M a year are not "middle class." Economic Policy Institute, June 13.

Pollard, K. 2011. The gender gap in college enrollment and graduation. Population Reference Bureau, April.

Pollard, K., and P. Scommegna. 2013. The health and life expectancy of older blacks and Hispanics in the United States. *Today's Research on Aging*, No. 28, June, 1–8.

Pong, S.-L. 1997. Family structure, school context, and eighth grade math and reading achievement. *Journal of Marriage and the Family* 59 (August): 734–46.

Pong, S.-L. Hao, and E. Gardner. 2005. The roles of parenting styles and social capital in the school performance of immigrant Asian and Hispanic adolescents. *Social Science Quarterly* 86 (December): 928–50.

Pool, B., and C. Bousada. 2007. Fooling nature, and the fertility doctor. *Los Angeles Times*, January 30.

Popenoe, D. 1996. *Life without father: Compelling new evidence that fatherhood and marriage are indispensable for the good of children and society*. New York: Free Press.

Popenoe, D., and B. D. Whitehead. 2002. *Should we live together? What young adults need to know about cohabitation before marriage: A comprehensive review of recent research*, 2nd ed. New Brunswick, NJ: The National Marriage Project, Rutgers University.

Popenoe, D., and B. D. Whitehead. 2006. The state of our unions 2006: The social health of marriage in America. The National Marriage Project.

Popenoe, D., and B. D. Whitehead. 2009. The state of our unions 2008: The social health of marriage in America. The National Marriage Project, Rutgers University.

Population Reference Bureau. 2008. Interview with Ron Lee on what are the financial implications of aging in the United States. November 6.

Porter, N., and Y. Sano. 2009. Father involvement in Japanese families. *Family Focus* 54 (Spring): F13, F15.

Portes, A. 2012. Stalled immigration reform. *Contexts* 11 (Summer): 16–18.

Poston, D. L. Jr., E. Conde, and B. DeSalvo. 2011. China's unbalanced sex ratio at birth, millions of excess bachelors and societal implications. *Vulnerable Children and Youth Studies* 6 (December): 314–20.

Potter, D. 2010. Psychological well-being and the relationship between divorce and children's academic achievement. *Journal of Marriage and Family* 72 (August): 933–46.

Powell, B., C. Bolzendahl, C. Geist, and L. C. Steelman. 2010. *Counted out: Same-sex relations and Americans' definitions of family*. New York: Russell Sage Foundation.

Powell, E. 1991. *Talking back to sexual pressure*. Minneapolis: CompCare.

Powers, C. H. 2004. *Making sense of social theory: A practical introduction*. Lanham, MD: Rowman & Littlefield.

PR Newswire. 2013. Single baby boomers hip to the dating scene. February 13.

Prescription painkiller overdoses. 2013. CDC *Vital Signs*, July.

Presser, H. B., and B. W. Ward. 2011. Nonstandard work schedules over the life course: A first look. *Monthly Labor Review* 134 (July): 3–16.

Price, J. A. 1981. North American Indian families. In *Ethnic families in America: Patterns and variations*, 2nd ed., eds. C. H. Mindel and R. W. Habenstein, 245–68. New York: Elsevier.

Price, M. 2011. Take a pay cut to telecommute? *Christian Science Monitor*, July 25, 22.

Prior, M. 2009. The immensely inflated news audience: Assessing bias in self-reported news exposure. *Public Opinion Quarterly* 73 (Spring): 130–43.

Project on Government Oversight. 2010. Letter to NIH on ghostwriting academics. November 29.

Prothrow-Stith, D., and H. R. Spivak. 2005. *Sugar and spice and no longer nice: How can we stop girls' violence?* San Francisco, CA: Jossey-Bass.

Proulx, C. M., C. Buehler, and H. Helms. 2009. Moderators of the link between marital hostility and change in spouses' depressive symptoms. *Journal of Family Psychology* 23 (4): 540–50.

Pryor, J. H., S. Hurtado, L. DeAngelo, L. P. Blake, and S. Tran. 2010. *The American freshman: National norms fall 2010*. Los Angeles: Higher Education Research Institute, UCLA.

Pryor, J. H., S. Hurtado, V. B. Saenz, J. L. Santos, and W. S. Korn. 2007. *The American freshman: Forty year trends*. Los

Angeles: Higher Education Research Institute, UCLA.

PULITZER CENTER. 2012. China's bachelor village.

PURCELL, P., AND D. B. WHITMAN. 2006. Topics in aging: Income of Americans age 65 and older, 1969 to 2004. CRS Report for Congress.

PUTNAM, F. W. 2006. The impact of trauma on child development. *Juvenile and Family Court Journal* 57 (Winter): 1–11.

PYKE, K. D. 1994. Women's employment as a gift or burden? Marital power across marriage, divorce, and remarriage. *Gender and Society* 8 (March): 73–91.

Q

QIAN, Z. 2012. During the Great Recession, more young adults lived with parents. Census Brief prepared for Project US2010, August.

QIAN, Z., AND D. T. LICHTER. 2011. Changing patterns of interracial marriage in a multicultural society. *Journal of Marriage and Family* 73 (October): 1054–84.

QIAN, Z., D. T. LICHTER, L. M. MELLOTT. 2005. Out-of-wedlock childbearing, marital prospects and mate selection. *Social Forces* 84 (September): 473–91.

QUEEN, S. A., R. W. HABENSTEIN, AND J. S. QUADAGNO. 1985. *The family in various cultures*, 5th ed. New York: Harper & Row.

R

RACKIN, H., AND C. M. GIBSON-DAVIS. 2012. The role of pre- and postconception relationships for first-time parents. *Journal of Marriage and Family* 74 (June): 389–98.

RADNOFSKY, L., AND A. JONES. 2013. Support grows for *Roe v. Wade. Wall Street Journal*, January 22, A2.

RADWIN, D. 2009. High response rates don't ensure survey accuracy. *Chronicle Review*, October 9, B8–B9.

RALEY, R. K., AND E. WILDSMITH. 2004. Cohabitation and children's family instability. *Journal of Marriage and Family* 66 (February): 210–19.

RAMACHANDRAN, N. 2005. The parent trap: Boomerang kids. *U.S. News & World Report*, December 12, 64.

RAMCHANDANI, P., A. STEIN, J. EVANS, AND T. G. O'CONNOR. 2005. Paternal depression in the postnatal period and child development: A prospective population study. *The Lancet*, 365 (9478): 2201–05.

RAMPELL, C. 2011. Companies spend on equipment, not workers. *New York Times*, June 10, A1.

RANDLES, J. 2009. Parenting in poverty and the politics of commitment: Promoting marriage for poor families through relationship education. Institute for the Study of Social Change, December 2.

RANK, M. R. 2011. Rethinking American poverty. *Contexts* 10 (Spring): 16–21.

RASHAD, M. 2012. Saudi women take over lingerie shops. *Baltimore Sun*, January 12, 12.

RATHUS, J. H., AND K. D. O'LEARY. 1997. Spouse-specific dependency scale: Scale development. *Journal of Family Violence* 12 (June): 159–68.

RATTRAY, S. 2010. 2010 toy sales. June 23.

READ, J. G. 2004. Family, religion, and work among Arab American women. *Journal of Marriage and Family* 66 (November): 1042–50.

READING, R. 2006. Child deaths resulting from inflicted injuries: Household risk factors and perpetrator characteristics. *Child: Care, Health & Development* 32 (March): 253.

REANEY, P. 2012. Lawyers say more women are on hook for alimony, child support. *Baltimore Sun*, May 13, 14.

REARDON-ANDERSON, J., M. STAGNER, J. E. MACOMBER, AND J. MURRAY. 2005. Systematic review of the impact of marriage and relationship programs. Urban Institute, February 11.

REAY, A. M., AND K. D. BROWNE. 2001. Risk factors for caregivers who physically abuse or neglect their elderly dependents. *Aging and Mental Health* 5 (1): 56–62.

REDD, Z., T. S. KARVER, D. MURPHEY, K. A. MOORE, AND D. KNEWSTUB. 2011. Two generations in poverty: Status and trends among parents and children in the United States, 2000–2010. Child Trends Research Brief, November.

REDDY, S. 2013. When computer games may keep the brain nimble. *Wall Street Journal*, May 14, D1, D2.

REECE, M., D. HERBENICK, V. SCHICK, S. A. SANDERS, B. DODGE, AND J. D. FORTENBERRY. 2010. Sexual behaviors, relationships, and perceived health among adult men in the United States: Results from a national probability sample. *Journal of Sexual Medicine* 7, Supplement 5 (October): 291–304.

REEFHUIS, J., M. A. HONEIN, L. A. SCHIEVE, A. CORREA, C. A. HOBBS, AND S. A. RASMUSSEN. 2009. Assisted reproductive technology and major structural birth defects in the United States. *Human Reproduction* 24 (February): 360–66.

REFKI, D., A. ESHETE, AND S. HAJIANI. 2012. Women in federal and state-level judgeships. Center for Women in Government & Civil Society, Summer.

REGAN, P. 2003. *The mating game: A primer on love, sex, and marriage.* Thousand Oaks, CA: Sage.

REGAN, P. C., AND E. BERSCHEID. 1999. *Lust; What we know about human sexual desire.* Thousand Oaks, CA: Sage.

REGNERUS, M. D. 2007. *Forbidden fruit: Sex & religion in the lives of American teenagers.* New York: Oxford University Press.

REGNERUS, M., AND J. UECKER. 2011. *Premarital sex in America: How young Americans meet, mate, and think about marrying.* New York: Oxford University Press.

REICH, D., ET AL. 2012. Reconstructing Native American population history. *Nature* 488 (August 16): 370–74.

REID, J. 1993. Those fabulous '50s. *Utne Reader* 55 (January): 18–19.

REILLY, P. R. 2000. *Abraham Lincoln's DNA and other adventures in genetics.* New York: Cold Spring Harbor Laboratory.

REINER, W. G., AND J. P. GEARHART. 2004. Discordant sexual identity in some genetic males with cloacal exstrophy assigned to female sex at birth. *New England Journal of Medicine* 350 (January 22): 333–41.

REINHOLD, S. 2010. Reassessing the link between premarital cohabitation and marital instability. *Demography* 47 (August): 719–33.

REISS, I. 1960. Toward a sociology of the heterosexual love relationship. *Marriage and Family Living* 22 (May): 139–45.

REISS, I. L. 1971. *The family system in America.* New York: Holt, Rinehart & Winston.

REISS, I. L., AND G. R. LEE. 1988. *Family systems in America*, 4th ed. New York: Holt, Rinehart & Winston.

RENN, J. A., AND S. L. CALVERT. 1993. The relation between gender schemas and adults' recall of stereotyped and counterstereotyped televised information. *Sex Roles* 28 (7/8): 449–59.

REPAK, T. A. 1995. *Waiting on Washington: Central American workers in the nation's capital.* Philadelphia: Temple University Press.

RETHERFORD, D., AND N. OGAWA. 2006. Japan's baby bust: Causes, implications, and policy responses. In *The baby bust: Who will do the work? Who will pay the taxes?* ed. F. R. Harris, 5–47. Lanham, MD: Rowman & Littlefield.

RETSINAS, J. 1988. A theoretical reassessment of the applicability of Kübler-Ross's stages of dying. *Death Studies* 12 (3): 207–16.

RETTNER, R. 2011. 6 ways sexual harassment damages women's health. Live Science, November 9.

REVELL, J. 2011. Getting married? Get a prenup. *Fortune*, July 4, 42.

REYNOLDS, S. S. 2007. Book review: *Leap! What will we do with the rest of our lives?* Los Angeles Times, April 6.

RHATIGAN, D. L., C. STEWART, AND T. M. MOORE. 2011. Effects of gender and confrontation on attributions of female-perpetrated intimate partner violence. *Sex Roles* 64 (June): 875–87.

RHEINGOLD, H. L. 1969. The social and socializing infant. In *Handbook of socialization theory and research*, ed. D. A. Goslin, 779–90. Chicago: Rand McNally.

RICCIARDELLI, R., K. A. CLOW, AND P. WHITE. 2010. Investigating hegemonic masculinity: Portrayals of masculinity in men's lifestyle magazines. *Sex Roles* 63 (March): 64–78.

RICHARDS, S. E. 2012. We need to talk about our eggs. *New York Times*, October 23, A23.

RICHARDSON, J. 2012. Deporting the hand that feeds us: How anti-immigrant laws are causing a farm labor shortage. Alternet, July 12.

RICHARDSON-BOUIE, D. 2003. Ethnic variation/ethnicity. In *International encyclopedia of marriage and family*, 2nd ed., Vol. 2, ed. J. J. Ponzetti, Jr., 525–30. New York: Macmillan.

RICHMOND, M., AND F. KRAUSE-JACKSON. 2011. In South Sudan, brides cost plenty—in cows. *Bloomburg Businessweek*, August 8–14, 13–14.

RICHTER, G. 2013. Former, current NFL players speak out against domestic violence. March 23, Newsmax, March 23.

RICK, S. I., D. A. SMALL, AND E. J. FINKEL. 2011. Fatal (fiscal) attraction: Spendthrifts and tightwads in marriage. *Journal of Marketing Research* 48 (April): 228–37.

RIDEOUT, V. J., U. G. FOEHR, AND D. F. ROBERTS. 2010. Generation M²: Media in the lives of 8- to 18-year-olds. Kaiser Family Foundation, January.

RIEGER, G., M. CHIVERS, AND M. J. BAILEY. 2005. Sexual arousal patterns of bisexual men. *Psychological Science* 16 (August): 579–84.

RIINA, E. M., AND M. E. FEINBERG. 2012. Involvement in childrearing and mothers' and fathers' adjustment. *Family Relations* 61 (December): 836–50.

RIVERS, C. 2001. Study: Young people seeking soul mates to marry. Women's E-News, June 20.

RIVERS, C. 2010. "Marry him?" More bad advice for the lovelorn. Women's eNews, February 26.

RIX, S. 2013. More and more it's an older woman's world—of work. *Huffington Post*, February 11.

RIZOS, E. C., E. E. NTZANI, E. BIKA, M. S. KOSTAPANOS, AND M. S. ELISAF. 2012. Association between Omega-e fatty acid supplementation and risk of major cardiovascular disease events: A systematic review and meta-analysis. *JAMA* 308 (September 12): 1024–33.

ROAN, S. 2005. Breasts, redefined. *Los Angeles Times*, June 13, F1.

ROBERTS, D. 2012. China's cutest, scarcest resource. *Bloomberg Businessweek*, April 23–29, 11–12.

ROBERTS, D. F., L. HENRIKSEN, AND U. G. FOEHR. 2009. Adolescence, adolescents, and media. In *Handbook of adolescent psychology*, 3rd ed., eds. R. M. Lerner and L. Steinberg, 314–44. New York: Wiley.

ROBEY, E. B., D. J. CANARY, AND C. S. BURGGRAF. 1998. Conversational maintenance behaviors of husbands and wives: An observational analysis. In *Sex differences and similarities in communication: Critical essays and empirical investigations of sex and gender in interaction*, eds. D. J. Canary and K. Dindia, 373–92. Mahwah, NJ: Lawrence Erlbaum Associates.

ROBINSON, B. 2008. The disruption of marital e-harmony: Distinguishing mail-order brides from online dating in evaluating "good faith marriage." *Loyola Public Interest Law Reporter* 13 (Summer): 252–70.

ROBNETT, B., AND C. FELICIANO. 2011. Patterns of racial-ethnic exclusion by Internet daters. *Social Forces* 89 (March): 807–28.

ROCCA, C. H., AND C. C. HARPER. 2012. Do racial and ethnic differences in contraceptive attitudes and knowledge explain disparities in method use? *Perspectives on Sexual and Reproductive Health* 44 (September): 150–58.

ROCCA, C. H., C. C. HARPER, AND T. R. RAINEBENNETT. 2013. Young women's perceptions of the benefits of childbearing: Associations with contraceptive use and pregnancy. *Perspectives on Sexual and Reproductive Health* 45 (March): 23–32.

ROCHMAN, B. 2009. The ethics of octuplets. *Time*, February 16, 43–44.

ROCHMAN, B. 2012. The end of an epidemic? *Time*, February 6, 16.

ROCHMAN, B. 2013. Hover no more: Helicopter parents may breed depression and incompetence in children. *Time*, February 22.

RODBERG, G. 1999. Woman and man at Yale.

RODGERS, K. B., AND H. A. ROSE. 2002. Risk and resiliency factors among adolescents who experience marital transitions. *Journal of Marriage and Family* 64 (November): 1024–37.

Roe *v*. Wade at 40: Most oppose overturning abortion decision; Millennials far less aware of historic ruling. 2013. Pew Research Center, January 16.

ROE, C. M., ET AL. 2013. Amyloid imaging and CSF biomarkers in predicting cognitive impairment up to 7.5 years later. *Neurology* 80 (19): 1784–91.

ROHNER, R. P., AND R. A. VENEZIANO. 2001. The importance of father love: History and contemporary evidence. *Review of General Psychology* 5 (4): 382–405.

ROLLINS, A., AND A. G. HUNTER. 2013. Racial socialization of biracial youth: Maternal messages and approaches to address discrimination. *Family Relations* 62 (February): 140–53.

ROMANCE WRITERS AMERICA. 2012. Romance literature statistics.

ROMANO, A., AND A. SAMUELS. 2012. Is Obama making it worse? *Newsweek*, April 6, 40–45.

RONEN, S. 2010. Grinding on the dance floor: Gendered scripts and sexualized dancing at college parties. *Gender & Society* 24 (June): 355–77.

ROSCHELLE, A. R., M. I. TORO -MORN, AND E. FACIO. 2005. Families in Cuba: From colonialism to revolution. In *Handbook of world families*, eds. B. N. Adams and J. Trost, 414–39. Thousand Oaks, CA: Sage.

ROSE, S., AND I. H. FRIEZE. 1993. Young singles' contemporary dating scripts. *Sex Roles* 28 (May): 499–509.

ROSEMOND, J. 2000. *Raising a nonviolent child*. Kansas City, MI: Andrews McMeel Publishing.

ROSEN, B. C. 1982. *The industrial connection: Achievement and the family in developing societies*. New York: Aldine.

ROSEN, K. H., AND S. M. STITH. 1993. Intervention strategies for treating women in violent dating relationships. *Family Relations* 42 (October): 427–33.

ROSENBAUM, J. E. 2009. Patient teenagers? A comparison of the sexual behavior of virginity pledgers and matched nonpledgers. *Pediatrics* 123 (May): e110–e120.

ROSENBERG, A. 2011. Marriage with a twist. *Psychology Today*, July/August, 65–71.

ROSENBERG, J. 1993. Just the two of us. In *Reinventing love: Six women talk about lust, sex, and romance*, eds. L. Abraham, L. Green, M. Krance, J. Rosenberg, J. Somerville, and C. Stoner, 301–7. New York: Plume.

ROSENBLATT, P. C. 1994. *Metaphors of family systems theory: Toward new constructions*. New York: Guilford.

ROSENBLOOM S. 2010. New online-date detectives can unmask Mr. or Ms. Wrong. *New York Times*, December 18, A1.

ROSENBLOOM, S. 2011. Second love at first click. *New York Times*, October 6, E1.

ROSENFELD, J. 2010. Little labor: How union decline is changing the American landscape. *Pathways*, Summer, 3–6.

ROSENFELD, M. J. 2002. Measures of assimilation in the marriage market: Mexican Americans 1970–1990. *Journal of Marriage and Family* 64 (February): 152–62.

ROSENZWEIG, P. M. 1992. *Married and alone: The way back*. New York: Plenum.

ROSIN, H. 2010. The end of men. *The Atlantic*, July/August.

ROSIN, H. 2012. Boys on the side. *The Atlantic*, September.

ROSS, T. 2011. Fewer couples think an affair is a reason to divorce. *Telegraph*, August 31.

ROTHENBERG, P. S. 2008. *White privilege: Essential readings on the other side of racism*. New York: Worth.

ROTHMAN, B. K. 1984. *Hands and hearts: A history of courtship in America*. New York: Basic Books.

ROTHMAN, E. K. 1983. Sex and self-control: Middle-class courtship in America, 1770–1870. In *The American family in social-historical perspective*, 3rd ed., ed. M. Gordon, 393–410. New York: St. Martin's.

ROTHMAN, S. M. 1978. *Women's proper place: A history of changing ideals and practices, 1870 to the present*. New York: Basic Books.

ROUG, L. 2005. The time seems ripe to tie the knot in Iraq. *Los Angeles Times*, June 12, A1.

ROWE, M. L., AND S. GOLDIN-MEADOW. 2009. Differences in early gesture explain SES disparities in child vocabulary size at school entry. *Science* 323 (February 13): 951–953.

ROWE-FINKBEINER, K. 2004. *The f-word: Feminism in jeopardy, women, politics, and the future*. Emeryville, CA: Seal Press.

ROWE-FINKBEINER, K. 2012. It's not a "mommy war," it's a war on moms. MomsRising, April 14.

ROWLAND, L. 2011. Top 20 toys for Christmas 2011. Kidspot.

RUBIN, A. J. 2012. For punishment of elder's misdeeds, Afghan girl pays the price. *New York Times*, February 17, A1.

RUBIN, L. B. 1985. *Just friends: The role of friendship in our lives*. New York: Harper & Row.

RUBIN, R. M., AND S. I. WHITE-MEANS. 2009. Informal caregiving: Dilemmas of sandwiched caregivers. *Journal of Family and Economic Issues* 30 (September): 252–67.

RUBIN, S. 2013. Gain weight or get off runway. *Christian Science Monitor Weekly*, January 21, 16.

RUGGIERO, J. A. 2010. When adoption isn't easy. *Newsweek*, April 26, 14.

RUSSELL, D. E. H. 2011. "Femicide"—The power of a name. Women's Media Center, October 5.

RUSSO, F. 2002. That old feeling. *Time*, February 13, G1–G3.

RUSSO, F. 2010. Who takes care of mom? *Time*, February 1, 43–44

RUSSO, F. 2013. The science of siblings. *Parade Magazine*. June 23, 9–16.

RUTHERFORD, M. B. 2009. Children's autonomy and responsibility: An analysis of child-drearing advice. *Qualitative Sociology* 32 (December): 337–53.

RUTTER, V., AND P. SCHWARTZ. 2012. *The gender of sexuality: Exploring sexual possibilities*, 2nd ed. Lanham, MD: Rowman & Littlefield.

RYAN, M. P. 1983. *Womanhood in America: From colonial times to the present*, 3rd ed. New York: Franklin Watts.

S

S. Korea orders lights out to boost birthrate. 2010. *The Independent*, January 24.

SAAD, L. 2004. Romance to break out nationwide this weekend. Gallup Organization, February 13.

SAAD, L. 2008. Americans evenly divided on morality of homosexuality. Gallup, June 18.

SAAD, L. 2011. Americans' preference for smaller families edges higher. Gallup, June 30.

SAAD, L. 2012. In U.S., half of women prefer a job outside the home. Gallup, September 7.

SAAD, L. 2012. Stay-at-home moms in U.S. lean independent, lower-income. Gallup, April 19.

SAAD, L. 2012. U.S. workers least happy with their work stress and pay. Gallup, November 12.

SAAD, L. 2013. Americans say family of four needs nearly $60K to "get by." Gallup, May 17.

SAAD, L. 2013. Gov't budget, healthcare join economy as top U.S. concerns. Gallup, March 26.

SAAD, L. 2013. Majority of Americans still support *Roe v. Wade* decision. Gallup, January 22.

SAAD, L. 2013. U.S. support for euthanasia hinges on how it's described. Gallup, May 29.

SABATELLI, R. M., AND S. BARTLE -HARING. 2003. Family-of-origin experiences and adjustment in married couples. *Journal of Marriage and Family* 65 (February): 159–69.

SACK, D. 2013. 5 things parents do that may encourage teen substance abuse. *Huffington Post*, March 4.

SAFILIOS-ROTHSCHILD, C. 1977. *Love, sex, and sex roles*. Upper Saddle River, NJ: Prentice Hall.

SAGIRI, Y. 2001. *United National Indian Tribal Youth, Inc.* Washington, DC: U.S. Department of Justice.

SAINT-JACQUES, M-J, C. ROBITAILLE, E. GODBOUT, C. PARENT, S. DRAPEAU, AND M-H GAGNE. 2011. The processes distinguishing stable from unstable stepfamily couples: A qualitative analysis. *Family Relations* 60 (December): 545–61.

SALDANA, D. H., AND A. M. DASSORI. 1999. When is caregiving a burden? Listening to Mexican American women. *Hispanic Journal of Behavioral Sciences* 21 (August): 283–301.

SALUTER, A. F. 1994. Marital status and living arrangements: March 1993. U.S. Census

Bureau, *Current Population Reports*, Series P20–478. Washington, DC: U.S. Government Printing Office.

Salvy, S-J., K. de la Haye, J. C. Bowker, and R. C. J. Hermans. 2012. Influence of peers and friends on children's and adolescents' eating and activity behaviors. *Physiology & Behavior* 106 (June): 369–78.

Samek, D. R., and M. A. Rueter. 2011. Associations between family communication patterns, sibling closeness, and adoptive status. *Journal of Marriage and Family* 73 (October): 1015–31.

Sampson, R. 2002. Acquaintance rape of college students. U.S. Department of Justice, Office of Community Oriented Policing Services, Guide No. 17.

Samuels, G. M. 2009. "Being raised by white people": Navigating racial difference among adopted multiracial adults. *Journal of Marriage and Family* 71 (February): 80–94.

Samuels, L. 2008. Stay in the closet, or else. *Newsweek*, September 8, 8.

Sanchez-Way, R., and S. Johnson. 2000. Cultural practices in American Indian prevention programs. *Juvenile Justice* 7 (December): 20–30.

Sandberg, S. 2013. Why I want women to lean in. *Time*, March 18, 44–45.

Sanders, S. A., M. Reece, D. Herbenick, V. Schick, B. Dodge, and J. D. Fortenberry. 2010. Condom use during most recent vaginal intercourse event among a probability sample of adults in the United States. *Journal of Sexual Medicine* 7, Supplement 5 (October): 266–76.

Sandler, L. 2013. None is enough. *Time*, August 12, 38–45.

Sang-Hun, C. 2007a. Traditional Korean marriage meets match on the Internet. *New York Times*, June 6, 13.

Sang-Hun, C. 2007b. Where boys were kings, a shift toward baby girls. *New York Times*, December 23, 1.

Santana, W. 2008. Vietnam women marry foreigners to escape poverty. *Los Angeles Times*, August 23.

Sappenfield, M. 2007. In India, a public kiss is *not* just a kiss. *Christian Science Monitor*, April 30, 1, 10.

Sarch, A. 1993. Making the connection: Single women's use of the telephone in dating relationships with men. *Journal of Communications* 43 (Spring): 128–44.

Sarkisian, N., and N. Gerstel. 2004. Explaining the gender gap in help to parents: The importance of employment. *Journal of Marriage and Family* 66 (May): 431–51.

Sarkisian, N., M. Gerena, and N. Gerstel. 2007. Extended family integration among Euro and Mexican Americans: Ethnicity, gender, and class. *Journal of Marriage and Family* 68 (February): 40–54.

Sarmiento, S. T. 2002. *Making ends meet: Income-generating strategies among Mexican immigrants*. New York: LFB Scholarly Publishing.

Sassler, S. 2004. The process of entering into cohabiting unions. *Journal of Marriage and Family* 66 (May): 491–505.

Sassler, S., and A. J. Miller. 2011. Class differences in cohabitation processes. *Family Relations* 60 (April): 163–177.

Sassler, S., F. R. Addo, and D. T. Lichter. 2012. The tempo of sexual activity and later relationship quality. *Journal of Marriage and Family* 74 (August): 708–25.

Saudi Arabia and its women. 2011. *New York Times*, September 27.

Saudi king announces new rights for women. 2011. *Baltimore Sun*, September 26, 8.

Saul, S. 2009. 21st century babies—Building a baby, with few ground rules. *New York Times*, December 13, A1.

Saul, S. 2009. Birth of octuplets puts focus on fertility clinics. *New York Times*, February 11, 1.

Saulny, S. 2011. Counting by race can throw off some numbers. *New York Times*, February 10, A1.

Save the Children. 2013. State of the world's mothers—Surviving the first day. May.

Sayer, L. C. 2006. Economic aspects of divorce and relationship dissolution. In *Handbook of divorce and relationship dissolution*, eds. M. A. Fine and J. H. Harvey, 385–406. Mahwah, NJ: Lawrence Erlbaum.

Scelfo, J. 2007. Come back, Mr. Chips. *Newsweek*, September 17, 44.

Schecter, S., and A. Ganely. 1995. *Domestic violence: A national curriculum for family preservation practitioners*. San Francisco: Family Violence Prevention Fund.

Schefft, J. 2007. *Better single than sorry: A no-regrets guide to loving yourself and never settling*. New York: HarperCollins.

Schick, V., D. Herbenick, M. Reece, S. A. Sanders, B. Dodge, and J. D. Fortenberry. 2010. Sexual behaviors, condom use, and sexual health of Americans over 50: Implications for sexual health promotion for older adults. *Journal of Sexual Medicine* 7, Supplement 5 (October): 315–29.

Schiebinger, L., A. D. Henderson, and S. K. Gilmartin. 2008. Dual-career academic couples: What universities need to know. Michelle R. Clayman Institute for Gender Research.

Schiesel, S. 2011. Supreme Court has ruled; now games have a duty. *New York Times*, July 29, C1.

Schiffrin, H. H., M. Liss, H. Miles-McLean, K. A. Geary, M. J. Erchull, and T. Tashner. 2013. Helping or hovering? The effects of helicopter parenting on college students' well-being. *Journal of Child and Family Studies*, published online, February 9, Springer, DOI 10.1007/s10826-013-9716-322.

Schindler, M. 2009. Failed relationships attributed to 60 percent of Army-wide suicides. The Military Wire, March 6, blog.seattlepi.com/militarywire (accessed April 26, 2009).

Schlesinger, R. 2011. Two takes: Collective bargaining rights for public sector unions? *U.S. News Weekly*, February 25, 15–16.

Schmeeckle, M. 2007. Gender dynamics in stepfamilies: Adult stepchildren's views. *Journal of Marriage and Family* 69 (February): 174–89.

Schmeer, K. K. 2011. The child health disadvantage of parental cohabitation. *Journal of Marriage and Family* 73 (February): 181–193.

Schmitt, D. P., and D. M. Buss. 2001. Interpersonal relations and group processes: Human mate poaching—tactics and temptations for infiltrating existing mateships. *Journal of Personality and Social Psychology* 80 (June): 894–917.

Schnall, M. 2012. Exclusive: Letting girls be girls—A global campaign. Women's Media Center, January 24.

Schnarch, D. 2011. "Mind-mapping:" How we manipulate the people we love. AlterNet, December 7.

Schneider, D. 2011. Market earnings and household work: New tests of gender performance theory. *Journal of Marriage and Family* 73 (August): 845–60.

Schneider, J. 2002. 100 and counting. *U.S. News & World Report*, June 3, 86.

Schneiderman, I., O. Zagoory-sharon, J. F. Leckman, and R. Feldman. 2012.

Oxytocin during the initial stages of romantic attachment: Relations to couples' interactive reciprocity. *Psychoneuroendocrinology* 37 (August): 1277–85.

Schnittker, J. 2008. Happiness and success: Genes, families, and the psychological effects of socioeconomic position and social support. *American Journal of Sociology* 114 (Suppl.): S233–S259.

Schoen, R., and V. Canudas-Romo. 2006. Timing effects on divorce: 20th century experience in the United States. *Journal of Marriage and Family* 68 (August): 749–58.

Schoenborn, C. A. 2004. *Marital status and health: United States, 1999–2002. Advance data from vital and health statistics*. Hyatsville, MD: National Center for Health Statistics.

Schoenman, J. A., and N. Chockley. 2011. Understanding U.S. health care spending. NIHCM Foundation Data Brief, July.

Schoppe-Sullivan, S. 2010. Maternal gatekeeping: Listening for the "creeaak." National Council on Family Relations Report, Winter, F24–F26.

Schramm, D. G., and F. Adler-Baeder. 2012. Marital quality for men and women in stepfamilies: Examining the role of economic pressure, common stressors, and stepfamily-specific stressors. *Journal of Family Issues* 33 (10): 1373–97.

Schulte, F., J. Eaton, and D. Donald. 2012. Doctors, others billing Medicare at higher rates. *Washington Post*, September 15.

Schwartz, D. J., V. Phares, S. Tantleff-Dunn, and J. K. Thompson. 1999. Devin body image, psychological functioning, and parental feedback regarding physical appearance. *International Journal of Eating Disorders* 25: 339–43.

Schwartz, E. 2007. A host of trouble. *U.S. News & World Report*, October 8, 47–49.

Schwartz, M. J. 2000. *Born in bondage: Growing up enslaved in the antebellum South*. Cambridge, MA: Harvard University Press.

Schwartz, P. 2006. *Finding your perfect match*. New York: Penguin.

Schwartz, P. 2010. Love American style. *AARP Magazine*, January/February, 40–41.

Schwartzberg, J. 2009. Slouching toward fatherhood. *Newsweek*, April 15, 17.

Schweiger, W. K., and M. O'brien. 2005. Special needs adoption: An ecological systems approach. *Family Relations* 54 (October): 512–22.

Schwyzer, H. 2011. How our sick culture makes girls think they have to be gorgeous to be loved. AlterNet, April 12.

Scommegna, P. 2012. More U.S. children raised by grandparents. Population Reference Bureau, March.

Scommegna, P. 2012. The pill, sterilization, and condoms top list of U.S. birth control choices. Population Reference Bureau, March.

Scommegna, P. 2013. Aging U.S. baby boomers face more disability. Population Reference Bureau, March.

Scommegna, P., and N. Mossaad. 2011. The health and well-being of grandparents caring for grandchildren. Population Reference Bureau, December.

Scott, B. 2011. Dinner dates: The top 10 dos and don'ts. *Huffington Post*, February 21.

Scott, D., and B. Wishy, eds. 1982. *America's families: A documentary history*. New York: Harper & Row.

Scott, M. E., A. Booth, V. King, and D. R. Johnson. 2007. Postdivorce father-adolescent closeness. *Journal of Marriage and Family* 69 (August): 1194–209.

Scott, M. E., E. Wildsmith, K. Welti, S. Ryan, E. Schelar, and N. R. Steward-Streng. 2011. Risky adolescent sexual behaviors and reproductive health in young adulthood. *Perspectives on Sexual and Reproductive Health* 43 (June): 110–18.

Scott, M. E., N. R. Steward-Streng, J. Manlove, and K. A. Moore. 2012. The characteristics and circumstances of teen fathers: At the birth of their first child and beyond. Child Trends Research Brief, June.

Scott, R. E. 2012. The China toll: Growing U.S. trade deficit with China cost more than 2.7 million jobs between 2001 and 2011, with job losses in every state. Economic Policy Institute Briefing Paper, August 23.

Sears, W., M. Sears, R. Sears, and J. Sears. 2005. *The baby sleep book: The complete guide to a good night's rest for the whole family.* New York: Little, Brown.

Secor-Turner, M., B. McMorris, R. Sieving, and L. H. Bearinger. 2013. Life experiences of instability and sexual risk behaviors among high-risk adolescent females. *Perspectives on Sexual and Reproductive Health* 45 (June): 101–07.

Secret to wedded bliss. 2005.

Seeman, T. E., B. H. Singer, C. D. Ryff, G. D. Love, and L. Levy-Storms. 2002. Social relationships, gender, and allostatic load across two age cohorts. *Psychosomatic Medicine* 64 (May/June) 395–406.

Segal, J. 1989. 10 myths about child development. *Parents* (July): 81–84, 87.

Segal, J., G. Kemp, J. Jaffe, and D. Russell. 2009. Raising kids with your ex: Co-parenting after a separation or divorce.

Segrin, C., A. Woszidlo, M. Givertz, A. Bauer, and M. T. Murphy. 2012. The association between overparenting, parent-child communication, and entitlement and adaptive traits in adult children. *Family Relations* 61 (April): 237–52.

Seligson, H. 2010. Think women are naturally bad with finances? Maybe this will change your mind. *Washington Post,* November 14, 2010.

Seligson, H. 2011. Jilted in the U.S., a new site finds love in India. *New York Times,* February 20, BU1.

Seltzer, J. A. 2004. Cohabitation and family change. In *Handbook of contemporary families: Considering the past contemplating the future,* eds. M. Coleman and L. H. Ganong, 57–78. Thousand Oaks, CA: Sage.

Seltzer, S. 2012. Skinny Minnie? Our culture's bizarre obsession with stick-thin women. AlterNet, October 16.

Seltzer, S. 2012. The 5 most offensive sexist and homophobic moves by conservatives: This month alone! AlterNet, May 17.

Semuels, A. 2006. You can date now, meet later. *Los Angeles Times,* October 12.

Semuels, A. 2008a. Gay marriage may be a gift to California's economy. *Los Angeles Times,* June 2.

Semuels, A. 2008b. R U ready to txt for D8s? Don't LOL. *Los Angeles Times,* October 31.

Shackelford, T. K., A. T. Goetz, D. M. Buss, H. A. Euler, and S. Hoier. 2005. When we hurt the ones we love: Predicting violence against women from men's mate retention. *Personal Relationships* 12 (December): 447–63.

Shadel, W. G., S. Martino, C. M. Setodji, A. M. Haviland, B. A. Primack, and D. M. Scharf. 2012. Motives for smoking in movies affect future smoking risk in middle school students. *Drug and Alcohol Dependence* 123 (June): 66–71.

Shaefer, H. L., and K. Edin. 2012. Extreme poverty in the United States, 1996 to 2011. National Poverty Center, February.

Shafer, E. F. 2011. Wives' relative wages, husbands' paid work hours, and wives' labor-force exit. *Journal of Marriage and Family* 73 (February): 250–63.

Shafer, K., and S. L. James. 2013. Gender and socioeconomic status differences in first and second marriage formation. *Journal of Marriage and Family* 75 (June): 544–64.

Shah, N., and B. Casselman. 2012. "Right-to-work" economics. *Wall Street Journal,* December 15–16, A3.

Shakir, E. 1997. *Bint Arab: Arab and Arab American women in the United States.* Westport, CT: Praeger.

Shamoo, A. E., and B. Bricker. 2011. The threat of bad science. *Baltimore Sun,* January 11, 13.

Shanahan, M. J., S. Bauldry, and J. Freeman. 2010. Beyond Mendel's ghost. *Contexts* 3 (Fall): 34–39.

Shapira, I. 2010. For infertile couples, Facebook is a minefield. *Washington Post,* October 25, B1.

Shapira, I. 2012. Gen. Petraeus's affair tarnishes seemingly idyllic marriage. *Washington Post,* September 10.

Shapiro, D. N., and A. J. Stewart. 2011. Parenting stress, perceived child regard, and depressive symptoms among stepmothers and biological mothers. *Family Relations* 60 (December): 533–44.

Shapiro, J. R., and A. M. Williams. 2012. The role of stereotype threats in undermining girls' and women's performance and interest in STEM fields. *Sex Roles* 66 (February): 175–83.

Shapiro, L. 1990. Guns and dolls. *Newsweek,* May 28, 57–65.

Sharifzadeh, V.-S. 1997. Families with Middle Eastern roots. In *Developing cross-cultural competence: A guide for working with children and families,* eds. E. W. Lynch and M. J. Hanson, 441–82. Baltimore: Paul H. Brookes.

Sharp, E. A., D. SoRelle-Miner, J. M. Bermudez, and M. Walker. 2008. "The glass ceiling is kind of a bummer": Women's reflections on a gender development course. *Family Relations* 57 (October): 530–41.

Sharpe, D. L. 2008. Economic status of older Asians in the United States. *Journal of Family and Economic Issues* 29 (December): 570–83.

Shatil, B. 2010. Fathering in Japan: Men risk it all by going home. *Baltimore Sun,* July 3, 6.

Shattuck, R. M., and R. M. Kreider. 2013. Social and economic characteristics of currently unmarried women with a recent birth: 2011. United States Census Bureau, American Community Survey Reports, May.

Shatzkin, K. 2004. Meeting of the minds. *Baltimore Sun,* June 6, 1N, 4N.

Shatzkin, K. 2005. A twist in healthful benefits of marriage. *Baltimore Sun,* November 4, 1D-2D.

Shaver, P., C. Hazan, and D. Bradshaw. 1988. Love as attachment. In *The psychology of love,* eds. R. J. Sternberg and M. L. Barnes, 68–99. New Haven, CT: Yale University Press.

Shea, J. A., and G. R. Adams. 1984. Correlates of romantic attachment: A path analysis study. *Journal of Youth and Adolescence* 13 (1): 27–44.

Shell, A. 2011. Legal gay marriage doesn't end money headaches. *USA Today,* July 21.

Shellenbarger, S. 2008. When 20-somethings move back home, it isn't all bad. *Wall Street Journal,* May 21, D1.

Shellenbarger, S. 2009. Housework pays off between the sheets. *Wall Street Journal,* October 21.

Shellenbarger, S. 2013. At-home dads make parenting more of a "guy" thing. *Wall Street Journal,* January 23, D1.

Sheng, X. 2005. Chinese families. In *Handbook of world families,* eds. B. N. Adams and Jan Trost, 99–128. Thousand Oaks, CA: Sage.

Shepherd, J. E. 2011. Alabama Latinos flee immigration law, leaving insufficient workforce for Tuscaloosa tornado cleanup. AlterNet, June 30.

Sheppard, K. 2013a. Keeping choice alive. *Mother Jones,* January/February, 42–45.

Sheppard, K. 2013b. Scientific misconceptions: The junk science behind anti-abortion advocates' wildest claims. *Mother Jones,* January/February, 14.

Sherman, L. 1992. *Policing domestic violence: Experiment and dilemmas.* New York: Free Press.

Shevell, T., et al., 2005. Assisted reproductive technology and pregnancy outcome. *Obstetrics & Gynecology* 106 (November): 1039–45.

Shierholz, H. 2009. Nine years of job growth wiped out. Economic Policy Institute, July 2.

Shierholz, H. 2010. The effects of citizenship on family income and poverty. Economic Policy Institute, February 24.

Shierholz, H. 2013. Workers don't lack skills, they lack work. Economic Policy Institute, January 16.

Shih, R., J. Miles, J. Tucker, A. Zhou, and E. D'Amico. 2010. Racial/ethnic differences in adolescent substance use: Mediation by individual, family and school factors. *Journal on Alcohol and Drugs* 71 (September): 640–51.

Shilo, G., and R. Savaya. 2011. Effects of family and friend support on LGB youths' mental health and sexual orientation milestones. *Family Relations* 60 (July): 318–30.

Short, K. 2012. The research supplemental poverty measure: 2011. U.S. Census Bureau, Current Population Reports, November.

Shute, N. 2011. Parents, not kids, are the biggest abusers of technology. *U.S. News & World Report,* February 9.

Siecus. 2011. A portrait of sexuality education and abstinence-only-until-marriage programs in the states: An overview fiscal year 2010 edition.

Siegel, A. F. 2012. Same-sex divorce a legal tangle. *Baltimore Sun,* March 18, 1, 13.

Siegel, D. H. 2012. Growing up in open adoption: Young adults' perspectives. *Families in Society* 93 (2): 133–40.

Siegel, L. 2012. The kids aren't alright: The perils of parenting in the digital age. *Newsweek,* October 15, 18–20.

Siegel, R., D. Naishadham, and A. Jemal. 2012. Cancer statistics for Hispanics/Latinos, 2012. *CA: A Cancer Journal for Clinicians* 62 (September/October): 283–98.

Signorella, M. L., and J. E. Cooper. 2011. Relationship suggestions from self-help books: Gender stereotyping, preferences, and context effects. *Sex Roles* 65 (September): 371–82.

Silver-Greenberg, J. 2012. Perfect 10? Never mind that. Ask her for her credit score. *New York Times,* December 25, A1.

Silverman, I. 2006. *I married my mother-in-law.* New York: Riverland.

Silverman, J. G., A. Raj, L. A. Mucci, and J. E. Hathaway. 2001. Dating violence against adolescent girls and associated substance use, unhealthy weight control, sexual risk behavior, pregnancy, and suicidality. *JAMA* 286 (August 1): 572–79.

SILVERMAN, J. G., H. L. McCAULEY, M. R. DECKER, E. MILLER, E. REED, AND A. RAJ. 2011. Coercive forms of sexual risk and associated violence perpetrated by male partners of female adolescents. *Perspectives on Sexual and Reproductive Health* 43 (March): 60–65.

SILVERMAN, P. R. 2000. *Never too young to know: Death in children's lives*. New York: Oxford University Press.

SILVERMAN, R. E. 2003. Provisions boost rights of couples living together. *Wall Street Journal*, March 5, D1.

SILVERSTEIN, M., AND S. RUIZ. 2006. Breaking the chain: How grandparents moderate the transmission of maternal depression to their grandchildren. *Family Relations* 55 (December): 601–12.

SIMON, G. E., ET AL. 2006. Association between obesity and psychiatric disorders in the U.S. adult population. *Archives of General Psychiatry* 63 (July): 824–30.

SIMON, J. P. 1996. Lebanese families. In *Ethnicity and family therapy*, 2nd ed., eds. M. McGoldrick, J. Giordano, and J. K. Pearce, 364–75. New York: Guilford.

SIMON, R. W. 2008. The joys of parenthood, reconsidered. *Contexts* 7 (Spring): 40–45.

SIMON, R. W., AND A. E. BARRETT. 2010. Nonmarital romantic relationships and mental health in early adulthood: Does the association differ for women and men? *Journal of Health and Social Behavior* 51 (June): 168–82.

SIMON, R. W., AND L. E. NATH. 2004. Gender and emotion in the United States: Do men and women differ in self-reports of feelings and expressive behavior? *American Journal of Sociology* 109 (March): 1137–76.

SIMON, S. 2005. Parents cast fight as sexual vs. religious tolerance. *Los Angeles Times*, October 20, A14.

SIMONELLI, C. J., T. MULLIS, A. N. ELLIOTT, AND T. W. PIERCE. 2002. Abuse by siblings and subsequent experiences of violence within the dating relationship. *Journal of Interpersonal Violence* 17 (February): 103–21.

SIMPSON, J. A., W. A. COLLINS, S. TRAN, AND K. C. HAYDON. 2007. Attachment and the experience and expression of emotions in romantic relationships: A developmental perspective. *Journal of Personality and Social Psychology* 92 (February): 355–67.

SINGH, J. P. 2005. The contemporary Indian family. In *Handbook of world families*, eds. B. N. Adams and J. Trost, 129–66. Thousand Oaks, CA: Sage.

SITTENFELD, C. 2011. Foster care: Extreme edition. *Time*, January 10, 50–54.

SIWOLOP, S. 2002. In Web's divorce industry, bad (and good) advice. *New York Times*.

SKOLNICK, A. 1991. *Embattled paradise: The American family in an age of uncertainty*. New York: Basic Books.

SLACKMAN, M. 2008. Generation faithful. *New York Times*, May 12, A1.

SLACKMAN, M. 2008. Stifled, Egypt's young turn to Islamic fervor. *New York Times*, Feb. 17, 1.

SLADE, E. P., AND L. S. WISSOW. 2004. Spanking in early childhood and later behavior problems: A prospective study of infants and toddlers. *Pediatrics* 113 (May): 1321–30.

SLATER, D. 2013. Darwin was wrong about dating. *New York Times*, January 13, SR1.

SLEVIN, P. 2009. Antiabortion efforts move to the state level. *Washington Post*, June 8, A1.

Slowing giant: U.S. loses some of its lead. 2011. *Forbes*, March 28, 108–09.

SMILER, A. P., AND R. F. PLANTE. 2013. Let's talk about sex on campus. *Chronicle of Higher Education*, May 24, A33–A34.

SMITH, A. 2011. 35% of American adults own a smartphone. Pew Research Center, August 11.

SMITH, A. A. 2010. Standing in the "GAP": The kinship care role of the invisible black grandfather. In *The myth of the missing black father*, eds., R. L. Coles and C. Green, 170–91. New York: Columbia University Press.

SMITH, A. S., C. HOLMBERG, AND M. JONES-PUTHOFF. 2012. The emergency and transitional shelter population: 2012. U.S. Census Bureau. 2010 Census Special Reports, September.

SMITH, G. C., AND G. R. HANCOCK. 2010. Custodial grandmother–grandfather dyads: Pathways among marital distress, grandparent dysphoria, parenting practice, and grandchild adjustment. *Family Relations* 59 (February): 45–59.

SMITH, J., AND H. ROSS. 2007. Training parents to mediate sibling disputes affects children's negotiation and conflict understanding. *Child Development* 78 (May): 790–805.

SMITH, K. 2009. Nohabitation: A less than ideal situation. National Council on Family Relations newsletter, *Family Focus* (Summer): F15–F16.

SMITH, L. H., AND J. FORD. 2010. History of forced sex and recent sexual risk indicators among young adult males. *Perspectives on Sexual and Reproductive Health* 42 (June): 87–92.

SMITH, P. K., AND L. M. DREW. 2002. Grandparenthood. In *Handbook of parenting*, 2nd ed., Vol. 3: Being and becoming a parent, ed. M. H. Bornstein, 141–72. Mahwah, NJ: Erlbaum.

SMITH, S. L., AND M. CHOUEITI. 2011. Gender inequality in cinematic content? A look at females on screen and behind the camera in top-grossing 2008 films. Annenberg School for Communication & Journalism, University of Southern California. April 22.

SMITH, S. L., K. M. PIEPER, A. GRANADOS, AND M. CHOUEITI. 2010. Assessing gender-related portrayals in top-grossing G-rated films. *Sex Roles* 62 (June): 774–86.

SMITH, T. W. 1994. Can money buy you love? *Public Perspective* 5 (January/February): 33–34.

SMOCK, P. J., AND F. R. GREENLAND. 2010. Diversity in pathways to parenthood: Patterns, implications, and emerging research directions. *Journal of Marriage and Family* 72 (June): 576–93.

SMOCK, P. J., W. D. MANNING, AND M. PORTER. 2005. "Everything's there except money": How money shapes decisions to marry among cohabitors. *Journal of Marriage and Family* 67 (August): 680–96.

Smoking and tobacco use. 2012. Centers for Disease Control and Prevention, January 24.

SMOLAK, L., M. P. LEVINE, AND F SCHERMER. 1999. Parental input and weight concerns among elementary school children. *International Journal of Eating Disorders* 25: 263–71.

SNIPP, C. M. 1996. A demographic comeback for American Indians? *Population Today* 24 (November): 4–5.

SNIPP, C. M. 2002. American Indians: Clues to the future of other racial groups. In *The new race question: How the census counts multiracial individuals*, eds. J. Perlmann and M. C. Waters, 189–214. New York: Russell Sage Foundation.

SNYDER, T. D., AND S. A. DILLOW. 2012. *Digest of education statistics 2011*. National Center for Education Statistics, June.

SOGUEL, D. 2009. Wage gap study arrives in time for Equal Pay Day. Women's eNews, April 28.

SOLLISCH, J. 2012. Boomerang parenting. *Christian Science Monitor*, May 14, 35–36.

SOLOMON, R. C. 2002. Reasons for love. *Journal for the Theory of Social Behaviour* 32 (March): 1–28.

SOLOT, D., AND M. MILLER. 2002. *Unmarried to each other: The essential guide to living together as an unmarried couple*. New York: Marlowe & Company.

SOMMERS, D., AND J. C. FRANKLIN. 2012. Overview of projections to 2020. *Monthly Labor Review* 135 (January): 3–20.

SONFIELD, A., K. KOST, R. B. GOLD, AND L. B. FINER. 2011. The public costs of births resulting from unintended pregnancies: National and state-level estimates. *Perspectives on Sexual and Reproductive Health* 43 (June): 94–102.

SONTAG, D. 2002. Fierce entanglements. *New York Times Magazine*, November 17, 52.

SORENSEN, E. 2010. Child support plays an increasingly important role for poor custodial families. Urban Institute, December.

SORIANO, C. G. 2006. "Bored" by her kids, she's getting it full-bore. *USA Today*, July 31, www.usatoday.com(accessed August 3, 2006).

SOUTER, E. 2013. Marriage problems: Real women share their relationship issues. *Huffington Post*, August 5.

SOUTH, S. C., AND R. F. KRUEGER. 2013. Marital satisfaction and physical health: Evidence for an orchid effect. *Psychological Science* 24 (January): 1–6.

SPARSHOTT, J. 2013. TARP firms' pay unchecked. *Wall Street Journal*, January 29, C3.

SPENCER, R. F., AND J. D. JENNINGS. 1977. *The Native Americans: Ethnology and backgrounds of the North American Indians*. New York: Harper & Row.

SPIEKER, S. J., N. C. LARSON, AND L. GILCHRIST. 1999. Developmental trajectories of disruptive behavior problems in preschool children of adolescent mothers. *Child Development* 70 (March): 443–58.

SPITZE, G., J. R. LOGAN, G. DEANE, AND S. ZERGER. 1994. Adult children's divorce and intergenerational relationships. *Journal of Marriage and the Family* 56 (May): 279–93.

SPRECHER, S. 1999. "I love you more today than yesterday": Romantic partners' perceptions of changes in love and related affect over time. *Journal of Personality and Social Psychology* 76 (January): 46–53.

SPRECHER, S. 2001. Equity and social exchange in dating couples: Associations with satisfaction, commitment, and stability. *Journal of Marriage and Family* 63 (August): 509–613.

SPRECHER, S., AND K. McKINNEY. 1993. *Sexuality*. Thousand Oaks, CA: Sage.

SPRIGG, P. 2011. Marriage's public purpose. *Baltimore Sun*, February 2, 27.

Spurious science triumphs as U.S. court upholds South Dakota "suicide advisory" law. 2012. Guttmacher Institute, July 27.

SQUIER, D. A., AND J. S. QUADAGNO. 1988. The Italian American family. In *Ethnic families in America: Patterns and variations*, 3rd ed., eds. C. J. Mindel, R. W. Habenstein, and R. Wright, Jr., 109–37. New York: Elsevier.

SRABSTEIN, J., B. L. LEVENTHAL, AND J. MERRICK. 2008. Bullying: A global public health risk. *International Journal of Adolescent Medicine and Health* 20 (2): 99–100.

SRINIVASAN, P., AND G. R. LEE. 2004. The dowry system in northern India: Women's attitudes and social change. *Journal of Marriage and Family* 66 (December): 1108–17.

ST. GEORGE, D. 2010. Text messages become a growing weapon in dating violence. *Washington Post*, June 21, B2.

St. George, D., and P. Dvorak. 2008. Child neglect cases multiply as economic woes spread. *Washington Post*, December 29, B1.

Stacey, J. 2003. Gay and lesbian families: Queer like us. In *All our families: New policies for a new century*, 2nd ed., eds. M. A. Mason, A. Skolnick, and S. D. Sugarman, 144–69. New York: Oxford University Press.

Stanik, C., R. Kurzban, and P. Ellsworth. 2010. Rejection hurts: The effect of being dumped on subsequent mating efforts. *Evolutionary Psychology* 8 (4): 682–94.

Stanley, A. 2012. On Indian TV, "I do" means to honor and obey the mother-in-law. *New York Times*, December 26, A1.

Stanley, S. M. 2007. Assessing couple and marital relationships: Beyond form and toward a deeper knowledge of function. In *Handbook of measurement issues in family research*, eds. L. M. Casper and S. L. Hoffereth, 85–100. Mahwah, NJ: Lawrence Erlbaum & Associates.

Stanley, S. M., and G. K. Rhoades. 2009. "Sliding vs. deciding": Understanding a mystery. National Council on Family Relations newsletter, *Family Focus* (Summer): F1–F4.

Stanley, S. M., and G. Smalley. 2005. *The power of commitment: A guide to active, lifelong love*. San Francisco, CA: Jossey-Bass.

Stanley, S. M., G. A. Rhoades, P. R. Amato, H. J. Markman, and C. A. Johnson. 2010. The timing of cohabitation and engagement: Impact on first and second marriages. *Journal of Marriage and Family* 72 (August): 906–18.

Stannard, D. E. 1979. Changes in the American family: Fiction and reality. In *Changing images of the family*, eds. V. Tufte and B. Myerhoff, 83–98. New Haven, CT: Yale University Press.

Staples, R. 1988. The black American family. In *Ethnic families in America: Patterns and variations*, 3rd ed., eds. C. H. Mindel, R. W. Habenstein, and R. Wright, Jr., 303–24. New York: Elsevier.

Starr, A. 2001. Shotgun weddings by Uncle Sam? *Business Week*, June 4, 68.

Starr, C. R., and G. M. Ferguson. 2012. Sexy dolls, sexy grade-schoolers? Media & maternal influences on young girls' self-sexualization. *Sex Roles* 67 (October): 463–76.

State-level assault on abortion rights continues in first half of 2013. Guttmacher Institute, July 8.

Statistic Brain. 2012. Online dating statistics. June 20.

Statistic Brain. 2012. Television watching statistics. February 7.

Steil, J. M. 1997. *Marital equality: Its relationship to the well-being of husbands and wives*. Thousand Oaks, CA: Sage.

Stein, P. J., ed. 1981. *Single life: Unmarried adults in social context*. New York: St. Martin's.

Steinberg, J. R., and L. B. Finer. 2011. Examining the association of abortion history and current mental health: A reanalysis of the National Comorbidity Survey using a common-risk-factors model. *Social Science & Medicine* 72 (1): 72–82.

Sternberg, R. J. 1986. A triangular theory of love. *Psychological Review* 93 (2): 119–35.

Sternberg, R. J. 1988. *The triangle of love*. New York: Basic Books.

Stetka, B. S. 2013. Disruptive Mood Dysregulation Disorder (DMDD). Medscape Psychiatry, May 21.

Steve Jobs: Adopted child who never met his biological father. *Telegraph*, October 6.

Stevens, A. 2012. Join me: Get mad about Mom-Dad pay gap. Women's e-News, May 1.

Stevens, H. 2012. Love lessons from the boomers. *Chicago Tribune*, October 3.

Stevenson, B., and J. Wolfers. 2013. Subjective well-being and income: Is there any evidence of satiation? *American Economic Review, Papers and Proceedings* 103 (May): 598–604.

Stewart, S. D. 2005. How the birth of a child affects involvement with stepchildren. *Journal of Marriage and Family* 67 (May): 461–73.

Stewart, S. D. 2007. *Brave new stepfamilies: Diverse paths toward stepfamily living*. Thousand Oaks, CA: Sage.

Stewart, S. D. 2010. Children with nonresident parents: Living arrangements, visitation, and child support. *Journal of Marriage and Family* 72 (October): 1078–91.

Stillars, A. L. 1991. Behavioral observation. In *Studying interpersonal interaction*, eds. B. M. Montgomery and S. Duck, 197–218. New York: Guilford.

Stinnett, N., and J. De Frain. 1985. *Secrets of strong families*. Boston: Little, Brown.

Stockel, H. H. 1991. *Women of the Apache nation*. Reno: University of Nevada Press.

Stokes, B. 2013. U.S. stands out as a rich country where a growing minority say they can't afford food. Pew Research Center, May 24.

Stombler, M. 2009. In the hot seat. *Chronicle of Higher Education*, May 1, A31, A33.

Stout, H. 2005. Family matters: Singles therapy. *Wall Street Journal* (April 28): D1.

Stout, H. 2010. Toddlers' favorite toy: The iPhone. *New York Times*, October 15, ST1.

Strasburger, v. c., et al. 2006. Children, adolescents, and advertising. *Pediatrics* 118 (December): 2563–69.

Strasser, J. 2004. *Black eye: Escaping a marriage, writing a life*. Madison: University of Wisconsin Press.

Stratton, J. L. 1981. *Pioneer women: Voices from the Kansas frontier*. New York: Simon & Schuster.

Straus, M. 2007. Do we need a law to prohibit spanking? *Family Focus* 52 (June): F7, F19.

Straus, M. 2008. Ending spanking can make a major contribution to preventing physical abuse. *Family Focus* 53 (December): F14–F16.

Straus, M. A. 2009. Gender symmetry in partner violence: Evidence and implications for prevention and treatment. In *Preventing partner violence: Research and evidence-based intervention strategies*. Eds. D. J. Whitaker and J. R. Lutzker, 245–71. Washington, DC: American Psychological Association.

Straus, M. A. 2010. Ending spanking can make a major contribution to preventing physical abuse. *Family Focus* 55.3 (Winter): F35–F36, F40.

Straus, M. A. 2011. Gender symmetry and mutuality in preparation of clinical-level partner violence: Empirical evidence and implications for prevention and treatment. *Aggression and Violent Behavior*, 16 (July–August): 279–88.

Straus, M. A. 2013. Addressing violence by female partners is vital to prevent or stop violence against women: Evidence from the multisite batterer intervention evaluation. *Violence Against Women* (in press).

Straus, M. A., and C. J. Field. 2003. Psychological aggression by American parents: National data on prevalence, chronicity, and severity. *Journal of Marriage and Family* 65 (November): 795–808.

Straus, M. A., and J. H. Stewart. 1999. Corporal punishment by American parents: National data on prevalence, chronicity, severity, and duration, in relation to child and family characteristics. *Clinical Child and Family Psychology Review* 2 (June): 55–70.

Strock, M. 2002. Depression. National Institutes of Mental Health.

Stroebe, M., M. van Son, W. Stroebe, R. Kleber, H. Schut, and J. van den Bout. 2000. On the classification and diagnosis of pathological grief. *Clinical Psychology Review* 20 (January): 57–75.

Strohschein, L. 2005. Parental divorce and child mental health trajectories. *Journal of Marriage and Family* 67 (December): 1286–1300.

Stutzer, A., and B. S. Frey. 2006. Does marriage make people happy, or do happy people get married? *Journal of Socio-Economics* 35 (April): 326–47.

Su, J. H. 2012. Pregnancy intentions and parents' psychological well-being. *Journal of Marriage and Family* 74 (October): 1182–96.

Substance Abuse and Mental Health Services Administration. 2006. *Results from the 2005 national survey on drug use and health: National findings*. Rockville, MD: Office of Applied Studies, NSDUH Series H-30, DHHS Publication No. SMA 06-4194.

Substance Abuse and Mental Health Services Administration. 2012. Results from the 2011 national survey on drug use and health: Summary of national findings. NSDUH Series H-44, HHS Publication (SMA) 12-4713.

Sudarkasa, N. 2007. African American female-headed households: Some neglected dimensions. In *Black families*, 4th ed., ed. H. P. McAdoo, 172–83. Thousand Oaks, CA: Sage.

Suddath, C. 2013. Navigating love at the office. *Bloomberg Businessweek*, March 18–24, 70.

Suddath, C. 2013. Work-from-home truths, half-truths, and myths. *Bloomberg Businessweek*, March 4–March 10, 75.

Sugg, D. K. 2000. Subtle signs of heart disease in women are often missed. *Baltimore Sun*, January 25, 1A, 13A.

Suicide. 2010. Centers for Disease Control, Summer.

Suicide. 2012. National Center for Injury Prevention and Control.

Sullivan, A., ed. 1997. *Same-sex marriage, pro and con: A reader*. New York: Vintage.

Sullivan, E. M., J. L. Annest, F. Luo, T. R. Simon, and L. L. Dahlberg. 2013. Suicide among adults aged 35–64 years—United States, 1999–2010. *Morbidity and Mortality Weekly Report* 62 (17): 321–24.

Sullivan, J. 2006. The Cupid index. *Christian Science Monitor* (February 14): 20.

Sullivan, M. 2009. How to end the war over sex ed. *Time*, March 30, 40–43.

Sulzberger, A. G. 2011. Hispanics reviving faded towns on the Plains. *New York Times*, November 13, A1.

Sulzberger, A. G. 2011. Wichita doctor takes up fight for abortions. *New York Times*, July 10, A1.

Sun, Y. 2001. Family environment and adolescents' well-being before and after parents' marital disruption: A longitudinal analysis. *Journal of Marriage and Family* 63 (August): 697–713.

Sun, Y., and Y. Li. 2002. Children's well-being during parents' marital disruption process: A pooled time-series analysis. *Journal of Marriage and Family* 64 (May): 472–88.

Sun, Y., and Y. Li. 2008. Stable postdivorce family structures during late adolescence and socioeconomic consequences in adulthood. *Journal of Marriage and Family* 70 (February): 129–43.

Sunderam, S., et al. 2009. Assisted reproductive technology surveillance—United States, 2006. *MMWR* 58 (June 12): 1–25.

Sundie, J. M., D. T. Kenrick, V. Griskevicius, J. M. Tybur, K. D. Vohs, and D. J. Beal. 2011. Peacocks, Porsches, and Thorstein

Veblen: Conspicuous consumption as a sexual signaling system. *Journal of Personality and Social Psychology* 100 (April): 664–80.

SUTPHIN, S. T. 2010. Social exchange theory and the division of household labor in same-sex couples. *Marriage and Family Review* 46 (3): 191–206.

SUTTON, C. T., AND M. A. Broken Nose. 1996. American Indian families: An overview. In *Ethnicity and family therapy*, 2nd ed., eds. M. McGoldrick, J. Giordano, and J. K. Pearce, 31–54. New York: Guilford.

SUTTON, P. D., B. E. HAMILTON, AND T. J. MATHEWS. 2011. Recent decline in births in the United States, 2007–2009. NCHS Data Brief, No. 60, March.

SVOBODA, E. 2011. The thoroughly modern guide to breakups. *Psychology Today*, January/February, 64–69.

SWANBROW, D. 2007. Time, money, and who does the laundry. University of Michigan, Institute for Social Research, January.

SWARNS, R. L. 2012. Male couples face pressure to fill cradles. *New York Times*, September 10, A1.

SWEENEY, M. M. 2010. Remarriage and stepfamilies: Strategic sites for family scholarship in the 21st century. *Journal of Marriage and Family* 72 (June): 667–84.

SWEET, E. 2012. Date rape revisited. Women's Media Center, February 12.

SZINOVACZ, M. E., ED. 1998. *Handbook on grandparenthood*. Westport, CT: Greenwood.

SZUCHMAN, P., AND J. ANDERSON. 2012. It's not you, it's the dishes (originally published as *Spousonomics): How to minimize conflict and maximize happiness in your relationship*. New York: Random House.

T

TACH, L., AND S. HALPERN-MEEKIN. 2009. How does premarital cohabitation affect trajectories of marital quality? *Journal of Marriage and Family* 71 (May): 298–317.

TACH, M., AND S. HALPERN-MEEKIN. 2012. Marital quality and divorce decisions: How do premarital cohabitation and nonmarital childbearing matter? *Family Relations* 61 (October): 571–85.

TAFFEL, R. 2012. The decline and fall of parental authority. AlterNet, February 22.

TAIT, R. 2012. Alarm as hundreds of children under age of 10 married in Iran. *Telegraph*, August 26.

TALBOT, L. 2007. *Singular existence: Because it's better to be alone than wish you were!* New York: Citadel Press.

TAM, V. C.-W., AND D. F. DETZNER. 1998. Grandparents as a family resource in Chinese-American families: Perceptions of the middle generation. In *Resiliency in Native American and immigrant families*, eds. H. I. McCubbin, E. A. Thompson, A. I. Thompson, and J. E. Fromer, 243–64. Thousand Oaks, CA: Sage.

TANNEN, D. 1990. *You just don't understand: Women and men in conversation*. New York: Ballantine.

TANUR, J. M. 1994. The trustworthiness of survey research. *Chronicle of Higher Education*, May 25, B1–B3.

TAVERNISE, S. 2011. Married couples are no longer a majority, census finds. *New York Times*, May 26, A22.

TAVERNISE, S. 2013. The health toll of immigration. *New York Times*, May 19, A1.

TAVRIS, C. 1992. *The mismeasure of woman*. New York: Simon & Schuster.

TAYLOR, C. 2012. Divorces double the trouble. *Baltimore Sun*, November 25, 3.

TAYLOR, C. A., J. A. MANGANELLO, S. J. LEE, AND J. C. RICE. 2010. Mothers' spanking of 3-year-old children and subsequent risk of children's aggressive behavior. *Pediatrics* 125 (5): 1057–65.

TAYLOR, K. H. 2011. Stayover relationships redefine young adult commitment. MSNBC, July 29.

TAYLOR, P., AND M. H. LOPEZ. 2011. The Mexican-American boom: Births overtake immigration. Pew Hispanic Center, July 14.

TAYLOR, P., C. FUNK, AND A. CLARK. 2007. As marriage and parenthood drift apart, public is concerned about social impact. Pew Research Center, July 1.

TAYLOR, P., C. FUNK, AND P. CRAIGHILL. 2006. A barometer of modern morals: Sex, drugs, and the 1040. Pew Research Center, March 28, http://pewresearch.org (accessed May 20, 2009).

TAYLOR, P., ET AL. 2012. The lost decade of the middle class: Fewer, poorer, gloomier. Pew Research Center, August 22.

TAYLOR, P., ET AL. 2012. The rise of Asian Americans. Pew Research Center, July 12.

TAYLOR, P., ET AL. 2013. A survey of LGBT Americans: Attitudes, experiences and values in changing times. Pew Research Center, June 13.

TAYLOR, P., K. PARKER, R. KOCHHAR, R. FRY, AND C. FUNK. 2012. Young, underemployed and optimistic: Coming of age, slowly, in a tough economy. Pew Research Center, February 9.

TAYLOR, P., M. H. LOPEZ, J. H. MARTINEZ, AND G. VELASCO. 2012. When labels don't fit: Hispanics and their views of identity. Pew Hispanic Center, April 4.

TAYLOR, P., R. MORIN, K. PARKER, AND D. COHN. 2009. Growing old in America: Expectations vs. reality. Pew Research Center, June 29.

TAYLOR, P., R. MORIN, K. PARKER, D. COHN, AND W. WANG. 2009. Growing old in America: Expectations vs. reality. Pew Research Center, June 29.

TAYLOR, S. C. 2003. *Brown skin: Dr. Susan Taylor's prescription for flawless skin, hair, and nails*. New York: HarperCollins.

TAYLOR, Z. E., D. LARSEN-RIFE, R. D. CONGER, AND K. F. WIDAMAN. 2012. Familism, interpersonal conflict, and parenting in Mexican-origin families: A cultural-contextual framework. *Journal of Marriage and Family* 74 (April): 312–27.

TEACHMAN, J. D. 2002. Childhood living arrangements and the intergenerational transmission of divorce. *Journal of Marriage and Family* 64 (August): 717–29.

TEACHMAN, J. D. 2003. Premarital sex, premarital cohabitation, and the risk of subsequent marital dissolution among women. *Journal of Marriage and Family* 65 (May): 444–55.

TEACHMAN, J. D., AND L. TEDROW. 2008. Divorce, race, and military service: More than equal pay and equal opportunity. *Journal of Marriage and Family* 70 (November): 1030–44.

TEITLER, J. O., D. DAS, L. KRUSE, AND N. E. REICHMAN. 2012. Prenatal care and subsequent birth intervals. *Perspectives on Sexual and Reproductive Health* 44 (March): 13–21.

TELLEEN, S., S. MAHER, AND R. C. PESCE. 2003. Building community connections for youth to reduce violence. *Psychology in the Schools* 40 (September): 549–63.

TERANISHI, R. 2011. Asian Americans and Pacific Islanders: Facts, not fiction—Setting the record straight. CARE and College Board.

TERZIEFF, J. 2006. New law puts brakes on international bride brokers. Women's e-news, March 8.

THARENOU, P. 2013. The work of feminists is not yet done: The gender pay gap—A stubborn anachronism. *Sex Roles* 68 (February): 198–206.

THEE, M. 2007. Cellphones challenge poll sampling. *New York Times*, December 7, 29.

THERNSTROM, M. 2005. The new arranged marriage. *New York Times Magazine*, February 13, 35–41, 72–78.

THOMAS, J. 2009. Virginity pledgers are just as likely to matched nonpledgers to report premarital intercourse. *Perspectives on Sexual and Reproductive Health* 41 (March): 63.

THOMAS, W. I., AND F. ZNANIECKI. 1927. *The Polish peasant in Europe and America*, vol. 2. New York: Knopf. (Originally published 1918 by the University of Chicago Press.)

THOMPSON, A. 2010. 16, Pregnant . . . and famous: Teen moms are newest stars. *USA Today*, November 23.

THOMPSON, A. E., AND L. F. O'SULLIVAN. 2012. Gender differences in associations of sexual and romantic stimuli: Do young men really prefer sex over romance? *Archives of Sexual Behavior* 41 (August): 949–57.

THOMPSON, A., AND O. BARKER. 2010. For Mel Gibson, scandal puts him in a harsh light again. *USA Today*, July 13.

THOMPSON, K. M., AND F. YOKOTA. 2004. Violence, sex, and profanity in films: Correlation of movie ratings with content. *Medscape General Medicine* 6 (3): 1–19.

THOMPSON, L., AND A. J. WALKER. 1991. Gender in families. In *Contemporary families: Looking forward, looking back*, ed. A. Booth, 76–102. Minneapolis: National Council on Family Relations.

THOMPSON, M. 2012. The insidious enemy. *Time*, July 23, 22–31.

THOMPSON, P. M., ET AL. 2003. Dynamics of gray matter loss in Alzheimer's disease. *Journal of Neuroscience* 23 (February 1): 994–1005.

THOMPSON, R. S., ET AL. 2006. Intimate partner violence: Prevalence, types, and chronicity in adult women. *American Journal of Preventive Medicine* 30 (June): 447–57.

THORNTON, A. 2001. The developmental paradigm, reading history sideways, and family change. *Demography* 38 (November): 449–65.

TICHENOR, V. J. 2005. *Earning more and getting less: Why successful wives can't buy equality*. New Brunswick, NJ: Rutgers University Press.

TILLMAN, K. H. 2007. Family structure pathways and academic disadvantage among adolescents in stepfamilies. *Sociological Inquiry* 77 (August): 383–424.

TILSLEY, A. 2010. New policies accommodate transgender students. *Chronicle of Higher Education*, July 2, A19–A20.

Time. 2009. Verbatim. November 2, 8.

TIMMER, S. G., AND T. L. ORBUCH. 2001. The links between premarital parenthood, meanings of marriage, and marital outcomes. *Family Relations* 50 (April): 178–85.

TJADEN, P., AND N. THOENNES. 2006. *Extent, nature, and consequences of rape victimization: Findings from the National Violence against Women Survey*. Washington, DC: U.S. Department of Justice, Office of Justice Programs.

TOHID, O. 2003. Pakistanis abroad trick daughters into marriage. *Christian Science Monitor*, May 15, 1, 7.

TOPPING, A. 2011. "Slutwalking" phenomenon comes to UK with demonstrations in four cities. *The Guardian*, May 9.

TOPPO, G. 2008. In-laws in White House may add new meaning to domestic policy. *USA Today*, December 4.

Toro-Morn, M. I. 1998. The family and work experiences of Puerto Rican women migrants in Chicago. In *Resiliency in Native American and immigrant families*, eds. H. I. McCubbin, E. A. Thompson, A. I. Thompson, and J. E. Fromer, 277–94. Thousand Oaks, CA: Sage.

Toth, J. F., and X. Xu. 2002, Fathers' child-rearing involvement in African American, Latino, and white families. In *Contemporary ethnic families in the United States: Characteristics, variations, and dynamics*, ed. N. V. Benokraitis, 130–40. Upper Saddle River, NJ: Prentice Hall.

Towner, B. 2009. 50 and still a doll. *AARP Bulletin* (March): 35.

Trail, T. E., and B. R. Karney. 2012. What's (not) wrong with low-income marriages. *Journal of Marriage and Family* 74 (June): 413–27.

Trenholm, C., B. Devaney, K. Fortson, M. Clark, L. Quay, and J. Wheeler. 2008. Impacts of abstinence education on teen sexual activity, risk of pregnancy, and risk of sexually transmitted diseases. *Journal of Policy Analysis and Management* 27 (March): 255–76.

Tresniowski, A., H. Breuer, C. Free, and A. J. Vicens. 2011. A family shattered. *People*, March 21, 74–78.

Trost, J., and I. Levin. 2005. Scandinavian families. In *Handbook of world families*, eds. Bert N. Adams and Jan Trost, 347–63. Thousand Oaks, CA: Sage.

Trotter, R. J. 1986. Failing to find the father-infant bond. *Psychology Today* (February): 18.

Truman, J. L., and M. Planty. 2012. Criminal victimization, 2011. Bureau of Justice Statistics, October.

Trumbull, D. A., and D. Ravenel. 1999. Spare the rod? New research challenges spanking critic. Family Policy, Family Research Council, January 22.

Trumbull, M. 2012. What the wealth gap means. *Christian Science Monitor*, February 20, 16–18.

Trumbull, M. 2013. Can Medicare costs be tamed? *Christian Science Monitor*, April 8, 21–23.

Truong, L. 2010. 5 reasons to skip the diamond engagement ring. *U.S. News & World Report*, August 10.

Trustlaw. 2011. The world's five most dangerous countries for women. Women's Rights Homepage, June 17.

Tsai, J. L., D. E. Przymus, and J. L. Best. 2002. Toward an understanding of Asian American interracial marriage and dating. In *Inside the American couple: New thinking/new challenges*, eds. M. Yalom and L. L. Carstensen, 189–210. Berkeley: University of California Press.

Tsapelas, I., A. Aron, and T. Orbuch. 2009. Marital boredom now predicts less satisfaction 9 years later. *Psychological Science* 20 (5): 543–45.

Tucker, C. 2007. Lingering sexism impedes women's path to highest level of power. *Baltimore Sun*, January 8, A9.

Tucker, K. L., J. Hallfrisch, N. Qiao, D. Muller, R. Andres, and J. L. Fleg. 2005. The combination of high fruit and vegetable and low saturated fat intakes is more protective against mortality in aging men than is either alone: The Baltimore longitudinal study of aging. *Journal of Nutrition* 135 (March): 556–61.

Tucker, R. K. 1992. Men's and women's ranking of thirteen acts of romance. *Psychological Reports* 71: 640–42.

Tulumello, J. S. 2012. Behind those polls: A peek inside the machinery of polling.

Christian Science Monitor, July 9 & 16, 27–32.

Turkle, S. 2011. *Alone together: Why we expect more from technology and less from each other*. New York: Basic Books.

Tuttle, W. M., Jr. 1993. *Daddy's gone to war: The Second World War in the lives of America's children*. New York: Oxford University Press.

Twenge, J. M., and W. K. Campbell. 2009. *The narcissism epidemic: Living in an age of entitlement*. New York: Free Press.

Twenge, J., and W. Campbell. 2003. "Isn't it fun to get the respect that we're going to deserve?" Narcissism, social rejection, and aggression. *Personality and Social Psychology Bulletin* 29 (2): 261–72.

Two-thirds of democrats now support gay marriage: Obama endorsement has limited impact. 2012. Pew Research Center, July 31.

Tyszkowa, M. 1993. Adolescents' relationships with grandparents: Characteristics and developmental transformations. In *Adolescence and its social worlds*, eds. S. Jackson and H. Rodriguez-Tomé, 121–43. East Sussex, UK: Erlbaum.

Tzeng, O. C. S. 1993. *Measurement of love and intimate relations: Theories, scales, and applications for love development, maintenance, and dissolution*. Westport, CT: Praeger.

U

U.S. House of Representatives. 2006. False and misleading health information provided by federally funded pregnancy resource centers. Committee on Government Reform—Minority Staff, Special Investigations Division, July.

U.S. Bureau of Labor Statistics News. 2005. Time-use survey—First results announced by BLS. Bureau of Labor Statistics, January 12.

U.S. Bureau of Labor Statistics, American Time Use Survey. 2012. Charts by topic: Household activities, care of household children. November 16.

U.S. Bureau of Labor Statistics, American Time Use Survey. 2013. American Time Use Survey—2012 results. USDL-13-1178, June 20.

U.S. Census Bureau News. 2008. Unmarried and single Americans week Sept. 21–27, 2008. U.S. Census Bureau.

U.S. Census Bureau News. 2012. Unmarried and single Americans week Sept. 16–22, July 31.

U.S. Census Bureau Newsroom. 2012. Most children younger than age 1 are minorities, Census Bureau reports. May 17.

U.S. Census Bureau Newsroom. 2012. U.S. Census Bureau projections show a slower growing, older, more diverse nation a half century from now. December 12.

U.S. Census Bureau Public Information Office. 2013. Census Bureau reports "delayer boom" as more educated women have children later. January 24.

U.S. Census Bureau, Current Population Survey, 2009. March and Annual Social and Economic Supplements, 2008 and earlier, January, Table MS-2.

U.S. Census Bureau, Current Population Survey, 2012 Annual Social and Economic Supplement. 2012. Families and Living Arrangements, Tables A1 and C3, November.

U.S. Census Bureau, Current Population Survey, 2012 Annual Social and Economic Supplement. 2012. Family status and household relationship of people 15 years and

over, by marital status, age, and sex: 2012, Table A2.

U.S. Census Bureau, Current Population Survey. 2012. 2012 Annual Social and Economic Supplement. November.

U.S. Census Bureau. 2002. *Statistical abstract of the United States: 2002*. Washington, DC: U.S. Government Printing Office.

U.S. Census Bureau. 2008. *Statistical abstract of the United States 2009* (128th edition). Washington, DC: U.S. Government Printing Office.

U.S. Census Bureau. 2011. Same-sex couple households: American community survey brief.

U.S. Census Bureau. 2012. *Statistical Abstract of the United States: 2012*, 131st ed. Washington, DC: Government Printing Office.

U.S. Census Bureau. 2013. America's foreign-born in the last 50 years. March 4.

U.S. Congress Joint Economic Committee. 2012. Mother's day report: Paycheck fairness helps families, not just women. Joint Economic Committee, May 9.

U.S. Department of Commerce. 1993. We the American foreign born. U.S. Bureau of the Census. Washington, DC: U.S. Government Printing Office.

U.S. Department of Commerce. 2010. Middle class in America. Economics and Statistics Administration, January.

U.S. Department of Health and Human Services. 2009. *Protecting children in families affected by substance use disorders*. Washington, DC: U.S. Government Printing Office.

U.S. Department of Health and Human Services. 2012a. Child maltreatment 2011. Administration for Children and Families, December.

U.S. Department of Health and Human Services. 2012b. *Preventing tobacco use among youth and young adults: A report of the Surgeon General*. Atlanta, GA: National Center for Chronic Disease Prevention and Health promotion, Office on Smoking and Health.

U.S. Department of Housing and Urban Development. 2011. The 2010 annual homeless assessment report to Congress. Office of Community Planning and Development, June 14.

U.S. Department of Justice. 2011. U.S. attorney announces drug endangered children task force. May 31.

U.S. Department of Justice. 2012. Report of the attorney general's national task force on children exposed to violence. December.

U.S. Department of Labor. 2008. *Women in the labor force: A databook*. Washington, DC: U.S. Government Printing Office.

U.S. Department of State. 2013. Intercountry adoption. Bureau of Consular Affairs,

U.S. Equal Employment Opportunity Commission. 2011a. Pregnancy discrimination charges, EEOC & FEPAs combined: FY 1997–FY 2011.

U.S. Equal Employment Opportunity Commission. 2011b. Sexual harassment charges, EEOC & FEPAs combined: FY 1997–FY2011.

U.S. Senate Special Committee on Aging, American Association of Retired Persons, Federal Council on the Aging, and U.S. Administration on Aging. 1991. Aging America: Trends and projections, 1991. Washington, DC: Department of Health and Human Services.

Umberson, D., K. Williams, D. A. Powers, H. Liu, and B. Needham. 2005. Stress in childhood and adulthood: Effects on marital

quality over time. *Journal of Marriage and Family* 67 (December): 1332–47.

UMBERSON, D., T. PUDROVSKA, AND C. RECZEK. 2010. Parenthood, childlessness, and well-being: A life course perspective. *Journal of Marriage and Family* 72 (June): 612–29.

UNION MEMBERS—2012. 2013. Bureau of Labor Statistics, January 23.

UNITED NATIONS CHILDREN'S FUND. 2011. The state of the world's children 2011.

UNITED NATIONS POPULATION FUND. 2012. Sex imbalances at birth: Current trends, consequences and policy implications.

UNITED STATES CONFERENCE OF MAYORS. 2012. Hunger and homelessness survey. December.

Unmarried and single Americans week: Sept. 15–21, 2013. 2013. U.S. Census Bureau News, July 30.

Unmarried and single Americans week: Sept. 16–22, 2012. 2012. U.S. Census Bureau News, July 31.

UPCHURCH, D. M., L. A. LILLARD, AND C. W. A. PANIS. 2001. The impact of non-marital child-bearing on subsequent marital formation and dissolution. In *Out of wedlock: Causes and consequences of nonmarital fertility*, eds. L. L. Wu and B. Wolfe, 344–80. New York: Russell Sage Foundation.

UPDEGRAFF, K. A., S. M. THAYER, S. D. WHITEMAN, D. J. DENNING, AND S. M. MC HALE. 2005. Relational aggression in adolescents' sibling relationships: Links to sibling and parent–adolescent relationship quality. *Family Relations* 54 (July): 373–85.

URBAN INSTITUTE. 2008. Child care. June 4.

Usual weekly earnings of wage and salary workers, fourth quarter 2012. 2013. Bureau of Labor Statistics, January 18.

UTZ, R. L. 2006. Economic and practical adjustments to late life spousal loss. In *Spousal bereavement in late life*, eds. D. Carr, R. M. Nesse, and C. B. Wortman, 167–92. New York: Springer.

V

VAALER, M. L., C. G. ELLISON, AND D. A. POWERS. 2009. Religious influences on the risk of marital dissolution. *Journal of Marriage and Family* 71 (November): 917–34.

VACCARINO, V., ET AL. 2002. Sex differences in hospital mortality after coronary artery bypass surgery: Evidence for a higher mortality in younger women. *Circulation* 105 (February 18): 1176–81.

VAKILI, B., ET AL. 2002. Sex-based differences in early mortality of patients undergoing angioplasty for first acute myocardial infarction. *Circulation* 104 (December 18): 3034–38.

VALENTI, J. 2012. *Why have kids? A new mom explores the truth about parenting and happiness.* New York: Houghton Mifflin Harcourt.

VALLOTTON, C., AND C. AYOUB. 2011. Use your words: The role of language in the development of toddlers' self-regulation. *Early Childhood Research Quarterly* 26 (2): 169–81.

VAN CAMPEN, K. S., AND A. J. ROMERO. 2012. How are self-efficacy and family involvement associated with less sexual risk taking among ethnic minority adolescents? *Family Relations* 61 (October): 548–58.

VAN DYK, D. 2005. Parlez-vous twixter? *Time*, January 24, 49.

VAN EEDEN-MOOREFIELD, B., C. R. MARTELL, M. WILLIAMS, AND M. PRESTON. 2011. Same-sex relationships and dissolution: The connection between heteronormativity and homonormativity. *Family Relations* 60 (December): 562–71.

VAN GELDER, M. M. H. J., J. REEFHUIS, A. M. HERRON, M. L. WILLIAMS, AND N. ROELEVELD. 2011. Reproductive health characteristics of marijuana and cocaine users: Results from the 2002 National Survey of Family Growth. *Perspectives on Sexual and Reproductive Health* 43 (September): 164–72.

VAN GELDEREN, L., H. M. W. BOS, N. GARTRELL, J. M. A. HERMANNS, AND E. C. PERRIN. 2012a. Quality of life of adolescents raised from birth by lesbian mothers: The U.S. National Longitudinal Lesbian Family Study. *Journal of Developmental & Behavioral Pediatrics* 33 (January): 17–23.

VAN GELDEREN, L., N. GARTRELL, H. M. W. BOS, F. B. VAN ROOIJ, AND J. M. A. HERMANNS. 2012b. Stigmatization associated with growing up in a lesbian-parented family: What do adolescents experience and how do they deal with it? *Children and Youth Services Review* 34 (May): 999–1006.

VAN GUNDY K., AND C. J. REBELLON. 2010. A life-course perspective on the "gateway hypothesis." *Journal of Health and Social Behavior* 51 (September): 244–59.

VAN HOOF, H. B., AND M. J. VERBEETEN. 2005. Wine is for drinking, water is for washing: Student opinions about international exchange programs. *Journal of Studies in International Education* 9 (Spring): 42–61.

VAN HOOK, J., AND C. E. ALTMAN. 2012. Competitive food sales in schools and childhood obesity: A longitudinal study *Sociology of Education* 85 (January): 23–39.

VANAUSDALE, D., AND J. R. FEAGIN. 2001. *The first R: How children learn race and racism.* Lanham, MD: Rowman & Littlefield.

VANDERKAM, L. 2010. What else could that ring buy? *USA Today*, February 10, 13A.

VANDEWATER, E. A., V. J. RIDEOUT. A. WARTELLA, X. HUANG, J. H. LEE, AND M. SHIM. 2007. Digital childhood: Electronic media and technology use among infants, toddlers, and preschoolers. *Pediatrics* 119 (May): e1006–e1015.

VANDIVERE, S., K. MALM, AND L. RADEL. 2009. *Adoption USA: A chartbook based on the 2007 national survey of adoptive parents.* Washington, DC: U.S. Department of Health and Human Services, Office of the Assistant Secretary for Planning and Evaluation.

VANDIVERE, S., K. TOUT, J. CAPIZZANO, AND M. ZASLOW. 2003. Left unsupervised: A look at the most vulnerable children. Washington, DC: Child Trends.

VARADARAJAN, T. 2012. China wants land: Russia needs babies. *Newsweek*, December 24, 9.

VARGA, C. M., C. B. GEE, AND G. MUNRO. 2011. The effects of sample characteristics and experience with infidelity on romantic jealousy. *Sex Roles* 65 (December): 854–66.

VENKATESH, S. 2008. *Gang leader for a day: A rogue sociologist takes to the streets.* New York: Penguin Press.

VENTURA, S. J., J. A. MARTIN, S. C. CURTIN, T. J. MATHEWS, AND M. M. PARK. 2000. Births: final data for 1998. *National Vital Statistics Reports* 48, March 28, Centers for Disease Control and Prevention.

VENTURA, S. J., S. C. CURTIN, J. C. ABMA, AND S. K. HENSHAW. 2012. Estimated pregnancy rates and rates of pregnancy outcomes for the United States, 1990–2008. *National Vital Statistics Reports* 60 (7), June 20.

VEROFF, J., E. DOUVAN, AND S. HATCHETT. 1995. *Marital instability: A social and behavioral study of the early years.* Westport, CT: Praeger.

VESELY, R. 2005. Hospital program identifies more domestic violence. Women's e-news, June 13.

VINCENT, G. K., AND V. A. VELKOFF. 2010. The next four decades: The older population in the United States: 2010 to 2050. Current Population Reports, Population estimates and projections, May.

VIORST, J. 2003. *Grown-up marriage.* New York: Free Press.

VISHER, E. B., AND J. S. VISHER. 1993. Remarriage families and stepparenting. In *Normal family processes*, 2nd ed., ed. F. Walsh, 235–53. New York: Guilford.

VISSING, Y. 2002. *Women without children: Nurturing lives.* New Brunswick, NJ: Rutgers University Press.

VITELLO, P. 2006. The trouble when Jane becomes Jack. *New York Times* (August 20): H1, H6.

VOLZ, M. 2012. $3.4 billion Indian land royalty settlement upheld. *Salon*, May 22.

VOSS, K. W. 2003. New anti-violence campaigns aim at boys, young men. Women's E-News, February 28.

VOTRUBA-DRZAL, E. 2003. Income changes and cognitive stimulation in young children's home learning environments. *Journal of Marriage and Family* 65 (May): 341–55.

VUCHINICH, S. 1987. Starting and stopping spontaneous family conflicts. *Journal of Marriage and the Family* 49 (August): 591–601.

W

WADE, C., AND S. CIRESE. 1991. *Human sexuality*, 2nd ed. New York: Harcourt Brace Jovanovich.

WAITE, L. J., AND K. JOYNER. 2001. Emotional satisfaction and physical pleasure in sexual unions: Time horizon, sexual behavior, and sexual exclusivity. *Journal of Marriage and Family* 63 (February): 247–64.

WAITE, L. J., D. BROWNING, W. J. DOHERTY, M. GALLAGHER, Y. LUO, AND S. M. STANLEY. 2002. Does divorce make people happy? Findings from a study of unhappy marriages. Institute for American Values.

WAKSCHLAG, L. S., B. L. LEVENTHAL, D. S. PINE, K. E. PICKETT, AND A. S. CARTER. 2006. Elucidating early mechanisms of developmental psychopathology: The case of prenatal smoking and disruptive behavior. *Child Development* 77 (July/August): 893–906.

WALD, M. L. 2012. Woman becomes first openly gay general. *New York Times*, August 13, A8.

WALKER, A. K. 2012. For infertility, frozen eggs. *Baltimore Sun*, December 9, 1, 21.

WALKER, L. 1978. Treatment alternatives for battered women. In *The victimization of women*, eds. J. R. Chapman and M. Gates, 143–74. Beverly Hills, CA: Sage.

WALKER, L. E. A. 2000. *The battered woman syndrome*, 2nd ed. New York: Springer.

WALLER, W. 1937. The rating and dating complex. *American Sociological Review* 2 (October): 727–34.

WALLIS, C. 2011. Performing gender: A content analysis of gender display in music videos. *Sex Roles* 64 (February): 160–72.

WALLS, M. 2011. High court strikes down Calif. law on violent video games. *Education Week*, June 27.

WALSH, A. 1991. *The science of love: Understanding love and its effects on mind and body.* Buffalo, NY: Prometheus.

WALSH, F., ED. 1993. *Normal family processes*, 2nd ed. New York: Guilford.

WALSH, J. 2011. Failing its families: Lack of paid leave and work-family supports in the US. Human Rights Watch.

WALSTER, E., E. BERSCHEID, AND G. W. WALSTER. 1973. New directions in equity research.

Journal of Personality and Social Psychology 25 (2): 151–76.

WALTERS, M. L., J. CHEN, AND M. J. BREIDING. 2013. The national intimate partner and sexual violence survey (NISVS): 2010 findings on victimization by sexual orientation. National Center for Injury Prevention and Control, Centers for Disease Control and Prevention, Atlanta (GA), January.

WALTHER, A. N. 1991. *Divorce hangover*. New York: Pocket Books.

WANG, L., E. B. LARSON, J. D. BOWEN, AND G. VAN BELLE. 2006. Performance-based physical function and future dementia in older people. *Archives of Internal Medicine* 166 (May 22): 1115–20.

WANG, S. S. 2013. The decline in male fertility. *Wall Street Journal*, July 16, D1, D3.

WANG, W. 2012. The rise of intermarriage: Rates, characteristics vary by race and gender. Pew Research Center, February 16.

WANG, W., AND P. TAYLOR. 2011. For millennials, parenthood trumps marriage. Pew Research Center, March 9.

WANG, W., K. PARKER, AND P. TAYLOR. 2013. Breadwinner moms. Pew Research Center, May 29.

WANIC, R., AND J. KULIK. 2011. Toward an understanding of gender differences in the impact of marital conflict on health. *Sex Roles* 65 (5/6): 297–312.

Want ad proves a woman's work is never done. 1997. Ann Landers column. *Baltimore Sun*, September 20, 3D.

WARNER, J. 2005. *Perfect madness: Motherhood in the age of anxiety*. New York: Riverhead Books.

WARNER, W. L., AND P. S. LUNT. 1941. *The social life of a modern community*. New Haven, CT: Yale University Press.

WARREN, E., AND A. W. TYAGI. 2003. *The two income trap: Why middle-class mothers & fathers are going broke*. New York: Basic Books.

WARREN, J. T., S. M. HARVEY, AND J. T. HENDERSON. 2010. Do depression and low self-esteem follow abortion among adolescents? Evidence from a national study. *Perspectives on Sexual and Reproductive Health* 42 (December): 230–35.

WARREN, J. T., S. M. HARVEY, AND M. L. BOVBJERG. 2011. Characteristics related to effective contraceptive use among a sample of nonurban Latinos. *Perspectives on Sexual and Reproductive Health* 43 (December): 255–62.

WARREN, K. R. 2012. NIH statement on international FASD awareness day. National Institutes of Health, September 5.

WARSHAK, R. A. 2003. Payoffs and pitfalls of listening to children. *Family Relations* 52 (October): 373–84.

Washington Post. 2012. *Washington Post*-Kaiser Family Foundation poll. January 22.

WASSERMAN, G. A., ET AL. 2003. *Risk and protective factors of child delinquency*. Washington, DC: U.S. Department of Justice.

WATERS, R. 2011. Are psychiatrists inventing mental illness to feed Americans more pills? AlterNet, December 27.

WATKINS, M. L., S. A. RASMUSSEN, M. A. HONEIN, L. D. BOTTO, AND C. A. MOORE. 2003. Maternal obesity and risk for birth defects. *Pediatrics* 111 (May): 1152–58.

WATKINS, T. H. 1993. *The great depression: America in the 1930s*. New York: Little, Brown.

WATSON INSTITUTE FOR INTERNATIONAL STUDIES. 2013. The costs of war since 2001: Iraq, Afghanistan, and Pakistan. March.

WATTERS, E. 2003. *Urban tribes: A generation redefines friendship, family and commitment*. New York: Bloomsbury.

WAX, E. 2008a. Can love conquer caste? *Washington Post*, November 22, A1.

WAX, E. 2008b. In thriving India, wedding sleuths find their niche. *Washington Post*, Feb. 23, A1.

WAYNE, T. 2011. Matchmaker, catch me a Czech. *Bloomburg Businessweek*, January 10–11, 69–71.

WEATHERFORD, D. 1986. *Foreign and female: Immigrant women in America, 1840–1930*. New York: Schocken.

WEAVER, J. 2007. Lust, love & loyalty. msnbc.com, April 16.

WEBBER, R. 2012. Are you with the right mate? *Psychology Today*, January/February, 58–65.

WEBER, L. 2013. Americans rip up retirement plans. *Wall Street Journal*, February 1, B1.

WEBER, L. 2013. Why dads don't take paternity leave. *Wall Street Journal*, June 13, B1, B7.

WEBLEY, K. 2013. The baby deficit. *Time*, January 21, 32–39.

Wedding report. 2013. Cost of wedding.

WEDEN, M. M., AND J. N. V. MILES. 2012. Intergenerational relationships between the smoking patterns of a population-representative sample of US mothers and the smoking trajectories of their children. *American Journal of Public Health* 102 (April): 723–31.

WEINHOLD, B. 2012. A steep learning curve: Decoding epigenetic influences on behavior and mental health. *Environmental Health Perspectives* 120 (October): A396–A401.

WEINSTOCK, C. P. 2010. Depression at midlife. *Woman's Day*, November 1, 111–114, 119–121.

WEINTRAUB, A. 2010. Break that hovering habit early. *U.S. News & World Report*, September, 42–43.

WEINTRAUB, A. 2010. *Selling the fountain of youth: How the anti-aging industry made a disease out of getting old—And made billions*. New York: Basic Books.

WEIR, F. 2002. East meets West on love's risky cyberhighway. *Christian Science Monitor*, June 11, 1, 7.

WEISE, E. 2012. Fish oil supplements don't prevent heart attacks, study says. *USA Today*, September 11.

WEISS, C. H. 1998. *Evaluation research: Methods for assessing program effectiveness*, 2nd ed. Upper Saddle River, NJ: Prentice Hall.

WEISS, L. P. 2013. When retirement calls you to be a parent—Again. *Wall Street Journal*, May 20, R6.

WELCH, D. 2011. For the UAW, a bargaining dilemma. *Bloomberg Businessweek*, September 19–25, 23–24.

WELTER, B. 1966. The cult of true womanhood: 1820–1860. *American Quarterly* 18 (2): 151–74.

WELTI, K., E. WILDSMITH, AND J. MANLOVE. 2011. Trends and recent estimates: Contraceptive use among U.S. teens and young adults. Child Trends Research Brief, August.

WENNBERG, J. E., E. S. FISHER, D. C. GOODMAN, AND J. S. SKINNER. 2008. *Tracing the care of patients with severe chronic illness/The Dartmouth Institute for Health Policy and Clinical Practice*.

WEST, B. A., AND R. B. NAUMANN. 2011. Motor vehicle-related deaths—United States, 2003–2007. *MMWR* 60 (Suppl, January 14): 52–55.

WHEELER, L. 1998. Excavation reveals slaves as entrepreneurs. *Washington Post*, October 13, B3.

WHEELER, L. A., K. A. UPDEGRAFF, AND S. M. THAYER. 2010. Conflict resolution in Mexican-origin couples: Culture, gender, and marital quality. *Journal of Marriage and Family* 72 (August): 991–1005.

WHELAN, D. 2011. In one pocket, out the other. *Forbes*, June 6, 30, 32.

WHISMAN, M. A., AND D. K. SNYDER. 2007. Sexual infidelity in a national survey of American women: Differences in prevalence and correlates as a function of method of assessment. *Journal of Family Psychology* 21 (June): 147–54.

WHISMAN, M. A., K. C. GORDON, AND Y. CHATAV. 2007. Predicting sexual infidelity in a population-based sample of married individuals. *Journal of Family Psychology* 21 (June): 320–24.

WHITE, J. 2005. Four-star general relieved of duty. *Washington Post* (August 10), A1.

WHITE, J. W., AND D. M. KLEIN. 2002. *Family theories*, 2nd ed. Thousand Oaks, CA: Sage.

WHITE, L., AND J. G. GILBRETH. 2001. When children have two fathers: Effects of relationships with stepfathers and noncustodial fathers on adolescent outcomes. *Journal of Marriage and Family* 63 (February): 155–67.

WHITE, M. P., AND P. DOLAN. 2009. Accounting for the richness of daily activities. *Psychological Science* 20 (August): 1000–08.

WHITE, N., AND J. L. LAURITSEN. 2012. Violent crime against youth: 1994–2010. Bureau of Justice Statistics, December.

WHITE, R. R. 2011. Measuring up: How our culture's obsession with porn-sized penises hurts men. AlterNet, June 22.

WHITE, T. 2008. Seniors reach digital age. *Baltimore Sun*, March 14, 1B, 10B.

WHITEFORD, L. M., AND L. GONZALEZ. 1995. Stigma: The hidden burden of infertility. *Social Science and Medicine* 40 (January): 27–36.

WHITEHEAD, B. D. 1996. The decline of marriage as the social basis of childrearing. In *Promises to keep: Decline and renewal of marriage in America*, eds. D. Popenoe, J. B. Elshtain, and D. Blankenhorn, 3–14. Lanham, MD: Rowman & Littlefield.

WHITEHEAD, B. D., AND D. POPENOE. 2008. Life without children: The social retreat from children and how it is changing America. The National Marriage Project, Rutgers University.

WHITEMAN, S. D., S. M. MCHALE, and A. C. CROUTER. 2007. Longitudinal changes in marital relationships: The role of offspring's pubertal development. *Journal of Marriage and Family* 69 (November): 1005–20.

WHITEMAN, S. D., S. M. MCHALE, AND A. SOLI. 2011. Theoretical perspectives on sibling relationships. *Journal of Family Theory & Review* 3 (June): 124–39.

WHITMAN, S., J. ORSI, AND M. HURLBERT. 2012. The racial disparity in breast cancer mortality in the 25 largest cities in the United States. *Cancer Epidemiology* 36 (April): e147–e141.

WHITMER, R. A., ERICA P. GUNDERSON, E. BARRETT-CONNOR, C. P. QUESENBERRY, JR., AND K. YAFFE. 2005. Obesity in middle age and future risk of dementia: A 27 year longitudinal population based study. *British Medical Journal* 330 (June 11): 1360–65.

WHITMORE, S. K., ET AL. 2012. Vital signs: HIV infection, testing, and risk behaviors among youths—United States. *Morbidity and Mortality Weekly Report* 61 (November 30): 971–76.

WHITSETT, D., AND H. LAND, 1992. The development of a role strain index for stepparents. Families in Society: *The Journal*

of *Contemporary Human Services* 73 (January): 14–22.

Whitton, S. W., S. M. Stanley, H. J. Markman, and C. A. Johnson. 2013. Attitudes toward divorce, commitment, and divorce proneness in first marriages and remarriages. *Journal of Marriage and Family* 75 (April): 276–87.

Who pays the bill? 2013. *The Economist*, July 27, 24–26.

Whyte, M. K. 1990. *Dating, mating, and marriage*. New York: Aldine de Gruyter.

Wickrama, K. A. S., C. W. O'Neal, and F. O. Lorenz. 2013. Marital functioning from middle to later years: A life course-stress process framework. *Journal of Family Theory & Review* 5 (March): 15–34.

Wickrama, K. A. S., F. O. Lorenz, R. D. Conger, and G. H. Elder, Jr. 1997. Marital quality and physical illness: A latent growth curve analysis. *Journal of Marriage and the Family* 59 (February): 143–55.

Widom, C. S., and M. G. Maxfield. 2001. *An update on the "cycle of violence."* Washington, DC: U.S. Department of Justice.

Wiehe, V. R. 1997. *Sibling abuse: Hidden physical, emotional, and sexual trauma*, 2nd ed. Thousand Oaks, CA: Sage.

Wiehe, V. R., with T. Herring. 1991. *Perilous rivalry: When siblings become abusive*. Lexington, MA: Lexington.

Wiersma, J. D., H. H. Cleveland, V. Herrera, and J. L. Fischer. 2010. Intimate partner violence in adult dating, cohabiting, and married drinking partnerships. *Journal of Marriage and Family* 72 (April): 360–74.

Wightman, P., R. Schoeni, and K. Robinson. 2012. Familial financial assistance to young adults. Paper prepared for the annual meetings of the Population Association of America, May 3.

Wiik, K. A., R. Keizer, and T. Lappegård. 2012. Relationship quality in marital and cohabiting unions across Europe. *Journal of Marriage and Family* 74 (June): 389–98.

Wilcox, W. B. 2002. Sacred vows, public purposes: Religion, the marriage movement and marriage policy. The Pew Forum on Religion and Public Life.

Wilcox, W. B., and E. Marquardt. 2010. The state of our unions, marriage in America 2010: When marriage disappears—The new middle America. Institute for American Values.

Wilcox, W. B., and E. Marquardt. 2011. The state of our unions, marriage in America 2011: When baby makes three. Institute for American Values.

Wildsmith, E., E. Schelar, K. Peterson, and J. Manlove. 2010. Sexually transmitted diseases among young adults: Prevalence, perceived risk, and risk-taking behaviors. Child Trends Research Brief, May.

Wildsmith, E., K. B. Guzzo, and S. R. Hayford. 2010. Repeat unintended, unwanted and seriously mistimed childbearing in the United States. *Perspectives on Sexual and Reproductive Health* 42 (March): 14–22.

Williams, G. 2013. For gay couples, divorce equality needed. *Baltimore Sun*, July 14, 3.

Williams, J. 2013. Alternate unemployment charts. Shadow Government Statistics, March 8.

Williams, K., A. Frech, and D. L. Carlson. 2010. Marital status and mental health. In *A handbook for the study of mental health*, T. L. Scheid and T. N. Brown, eds., 306–20. Cambridge, UK: Cambridge University Press.

Williams, K., and A. Dunne-Bryant. 2006. Divorce and adult psychological well-being: Clarifying the role of gender and child age. *Journal of Marriage and Family* 68 (December): 1178–96.

Williams, N. 1990. *The Mexican American family: Tradition and change*. New York: General Hall.

Williams, R. A. ed. 2007. *Eliminating healthcare disparities in America: Beyond the IOM report*. Totowa, NJ: Humana.

Williams, T. 2011. Tackling infant mortality rates among blacks. *New York Times*, October 14, A10.

Williams, T. 2012. For Native American women, scourge of rape, rare justice. *New York Times*, May 23, A1.

Williams, T., and T. Maher. 2009. Iraq's newly open gays face scorn and murder. *New York Times*, April 8.

Williams, W. H., and S. T. Ceci. 2012. When scientists choose motherhood. *American Scientist* 100 (March/April).

Willie, C. V., and R. J. Reddick. 2003. *A new look at black families*, 5th ed. Walnut Creek, CA: AltaMira.

Willis, S. L., and J. D. Reid, eds. 1999. *Life in the middle: Psychological and social development in middle age*. San Diego, CA: Academic Press.

Willis, W. 1997. Families with African American roots. In *Developing cross-cultural competence: A guide for working with children and families*, eds. E. W. Lynch and M. J. Hanson, 165–202. Baltimore: Paul H. Brookes.

Willson, A. E., K. M. Shuey, and G. H. Elder, Jr. 2003. Ambivalence in the relationship of adult children to aging parents and in-laws. *Journal of Marriage and Family* 65 (November): 1055–1072.

Wilmot, W. W., and J. L. Hocker. 2007. *Interpersonal conflict*, 7th ed. Boston: McGraw-Hill.

Wilson, A. 2012. Suggs' girlfriend claimed abuse. *Baltimore Sun*, December 8, 2.

Wilson, B. F., and S. C. Clarke. 1992. Remarriages: A demographic profile. *Journal of Family Issues* 13 (June): 123–41.

Wilson, E. K., B. T. Dalberth, and H. P. Koo. 2010b. "We're the heroes!": Fathers' perspectives on their role in protecting their preteenage children from sexual risk. *Perspectives on Sexual and Reproductive Health* 42 (June): 117–24.

Wilson, C. 2010. Parents worry about toddlers' tiny fingers itching for iPhones. *USA Today*, November 8.

Wilson, E. K., B. T. Dalberth, H. P. Koo, and J. C. Gard. 2010a. Parents' perspectives on talking to preteenage children about sex. *Perspectives on Sexual and Reproductive Health* 42 (March): 56–63.

Wilson, J. Q. 2002. *The marriage problem: How our culture has weakened families*. New York: HarperCollins.

Wilson, M. 2012. CEO and pregnant; Yahoo! But wait a minute. . . . WeNews, July 19.

Wilson, R. 2008. 2 colleges, 2 presidents, one marriage. *Chronicle of Higher Education*, February 22, A1, A8.

Wilson, R. F. 2006. Sexually predatory parents and the children in their care: Remove the threat, not the child. In *Handbook on children, culture, and violence*, eds. N. E. Dowd, D. G. Singer, and R. F. Wilson, 39–58. Thousand Oaks, CA: Sage.

Wilson, S. 2002. The health capital of families: An investigation of the inter-spousal correlation in health status. *Social Science & Medicine* 55 (October): 1157–72.

Wilson, S. M., L. W. Ngige, and L. J. Trollinger. 2003. Connecting generations: Kamba and Maasai paths to marriage in Kenya. In *Mate selection across cultures*, eds. R. R. Hamon and B. B. Ingoldsby, 95–118. Thousand Oaks, CA: Sage.

Winch, G. 2011. The antidote to anger and frustration: The power of emotional validation. *Psychology Today*, June 18.

Winch, R. F. 1958. *Mate selection: A study of complementary needs*. New York: Harper & Row.

Wineberg, H. 1991. Intermarital fertility and dissolution of the second marriage. *Social Science Quarterly* 75 (January): 62–65.

Wineberg, H. 1996. The prevalence and characteristics of blacks having a successful marital reconciliation. *Journal of Divorce & Remarriage* 25 (1/2): 75–86.

Wineberg, H., and J. Mc Carthy. 1993. Separation and reconciliation in American marriages. *Journal of Divorce & Remarriage* 20: 21–42.

Wingert, P. 2008. Wanted: A bundle of joy. *Newsweek*, October 13, 12.

Winseman, A. L. 2004. Women in the clergy: Perception and reality. Gallup, March 30.

Winstok, Z. 2011. The paradigmatic cleavage on gender differences in partner violence perpetration and victimization. *Aggression and Violent Behavior* 16 (July–August): 303–11.

Winton, C. A. 1995. *Frameworks for studying families*. Guilford, CT: Dushkin.

Witt, G. E. 1998. Vote early and often. *American Demographics* 20 (December): 23.

Witt, M. G., and W. Wood. 2010. Self-regulation of gendered behavior in everyday life. *Sex Roles* 62 (May): 635–46.

Witte, S. S., N. El-Bassel, L. Gilbert, E. Wu, and M. Chang. 2010. Lack of awareness of partner STD risk among heterosexual couples. *Perspectives on Sexual and Reproductive Health* 42 (March): 49–55.

Witters, D. 2011. Caregiving costs U.S. economy $25.2 billion in lost productivity. Gallup, July 27.

Witters, D., and S. Agrawal. 2011. Unhealthy U.S. workers' absenteeism costs $153 billion. Gallup, October 17.

Witters, D., S. Agrawal, and D. Liu. 2013. Depression costs U.S. workplaces $23 billion in absenteeism. Gallup, July 24.

Wittstein, I. S. et al. 2005. Neurohumoral features of myocardial stunning due to sudden emotional stress. *New England Journal of Medicine* 352 (February 10): 539–48.

Wizemann, T. M., and M. L. Pardue, eds. 2001. *Exploring the biological contributions to human health: Does sex matter?* Washington, DC: National Academy Press.

Wolcott, J. 2000. Finding Mrs. Right (and all the little Rights). *Christian Science Monitor*, February 23, 15–17.

Wolcott, J. 2004. Is dating dated on college campuses? *Christian Science Monitor* (March 2): 11, 14.

Wolff, E. N. 2012. The asset price meltdown and the wealth of the middle class. National Bureau of Economic Research, Working Paper 18559, November.

Wolfinger, N. H. 2005. *Understanding the divorce cycle: The children of divorce in their own marriages*. New York: Cambridge University Press.

Wolfinger, N. H. 2011. More evidence for trends in the intergenerational transmission of divorce: A completed cohort approach using data from the General Social Survey. *Demography* 48 (May): 581–92.

Wolfradt, J. J., S. Hempel, and J. N. V. Miles. 2003. Perceived parenting styles, depersonalization, anxiety and coping behavior in adolescents. *Personality and Individual Differences* 34 (February): 521–32.

Wolgin, P. E., and A. M. Kelley. 2011. Your state can't afford it: The fiscal impact of states' anti-immigrant legislation. Center for American Progress, July.

Women in the labor force: A databook. 2013. February, Report 1040.

Women live longer but aren't saving enough for it. *Baltimore Sun*, July 10, 6C.

WONDERGEM, T. R., AND M. FRIEDLMEIER. 2012. Gender and ethnic differences in smiling: A yearbook photographs analysis from kindergarten through 12th grade. *Sex Roles* 67 (October): 403–11.

WOOD, H. M., B. J. TROCK, AND J. P. GEARHART. 2003. In vitro fertilization and the cloacal–bladder exstrophy–epispadias complex: Is there an association? *Journal of Urology* 169 (April): 1512–15.

WOOD, J. T. 2011. *Gendered lives: Communication, gender, and culture*, 9th ed. Boston: Wadsworth.

WOOD, J. V., W. Q. E. PERUNOVIC, AND J. W. LEE. 2009. Positive self-statements: Power for some, peril for others. *Psychological Science* 20 (July): 860–66.

WOOD, R. G., Q. MOORE, A. CLARKWEST, A. KILLEWALD, AND S. MONAHAN. 2012. The long-term effects of building strong families: A relationship skills education program for unmarried parents, executive summary. U.S. Department of Health and Human Services, November.

WOODS, R. D. 1996. Grandmother roles: A cross cultural view. *Journal of Instructional Psychology* 23 (December): 286–92.

Working at home is on the rise. 2013. U.S. Census Bureau, March 5.

WORLD HEALTH ORGANIZATION. 2005. WHO multi-country study on women's health and domestic violence against women: Summary report of initial results on prevalence, health outcomes and women's responses. Geneva: World Health Organization.

WORLD HEALTH ORGANIZATION. 2012. HIV/AIDS. Global Health Observatory.

WRIGHT, C. N., A. HOLLOWAY, AND M. E. ROLOFF. 2007. The dark side of self-monitoring: How high self-monitors view their romantic relationships. *Communication Reports* 20 (October): 101–14.

WRIGHT, D. B. 2009. Ten statisticians and their impacts for psychologists. *Perspectives on Psychological Science* 6 (November): 587–97.

WRIGHT, J. 1997. Motherhood's gray area. *Washington Post*, July 29, E5.

WRIGHT, J. M. 1998. *Lesbian step families: An ethnography of love*. New York: Haworth.

WRIGHT, M. O., D. L. NORTON, AND J. A. MATUSEK. 2010. Predicting verbal coercion following sexual refusal during a hookup: Diverging gender patterns. *Sex Roles* 62 (May): 647–60.

WRITER'S ALMANAC. 2010. Trends: A short history of dating services. September 29

WTULICH, J. 1986. *Writing home: Immigrants in Brazil and the United States, 1890–1891*. Boulder, CO: East European Monographs.

WU, L. L. 1996. Effects of family instability, income, and income instability on the risk of a premarital birth. *American Sociological Review* 61 (June): 386–406.

WU, L. L., AND E. THOMSON. 2001. Race difference in family experience and early sexual initiation: Dynamic models of family structure and family change. *Journal of Marriage and Family* 63 (August): 682–96.

WU, Z. 1994. Remarriage in Canada: A social exchange perspective. *Journal of Divorce & Remarriage* 21 (3/4): 191–224.

WU, Z., AND C. M. SCHIMMELE. 2005. Repartnering after first union disruption. *Journal of Marriage and Family* 67 (February): 27–36.

X

X Factor, The. 2011. *Fortune*, October 17, S1–S3.

XIE, Y., J. RAYMO, K. GOYETTE, AND A. THORNTON. 2003. Economic potential and entry into marriage and cohabitation. *Demography* 40 (May): 351–67.

XU, X., C. D. HUDSPETH, AND S. ESTES. 1997. The effects of husbands' involvement in child rearing activities and participation in household labor on marital quality: A racial comparison. *Journal of Gender, Culture, and Health* 2(3): 171–93.

XU, X., CLARK, D. HUDSPETH., AND J. P. BARTKOWSKI. 2006. The role of cohabitation in remarriage. *Journal of Marriage and Family* 68 (May): 261–74.

Y

YABIKU, S. T., AND C. T. GAGER. 2009. Sexual frequency and the stability of marital and cohabiting unions. *Journal of Marriage and Family* 71 (November): 983–1000.

YANCEY, K. 2011. Bad economy? A good time for a steamy affair. *USA Today*, September 10.

YATES, L. B., L. DJOUSSÉ, T. KURTH, J. E. BURING, AND M. GAZIANO. 2008. Exceptional longevity in men. *Archives of Internal Medicine* 168 (February 11): 284–90.

YEH, H., F. O. LORENZ, K. A. S. WICKRAMA, AND G. ELDER. 2006. Relationships among sexual satisfaction, marital quality, and marital instability at midlife. *Journal of Family Psychology* 20 (June): 329–43.

YELLOWBIRD, M., AND C. M. SNIPP. 2002. American Indian families. In *Minority families in the United States: A multicultural perspective*, 3rd ed., ed. R. L. Taylor, 227–49. Upper Saddle River, NJ: Prentice Hall.

YEMMA, J. 2010. What we see when we see race. *Christian Science Monitor*, September 20, 5–6.

YEOMAN, B. 2008. When wounded vets come home. *AARP Magazine*, July/August, 60–64, 82–83.

YIN, S. 2007. Gender disparities in health and mortality. Population Reference Bureau, November.

YIN, S. 2008. How older women can shield themselves from poverty. Population Reference Bureau, March.

YOON, I.-J. 1997. *On my own: Korean businesses and race relations in America*. Chicago: University of Chicago Press.

YOUNG, J. R. 2011. Programmed for love. *Chronicle of Higher Education*, January 21, B6–B11.

YOUNG, K. 2001. *Tangled in the Web: Understanding cybersex from fantasy to addiction*. Bloomington, IN: 1st Books Library.

YOUNG, L. 2009. Love: Neuroscience reveals all. *Nature* 457 (January 8): 148.

YOUNT, K., AND L. LI. 2010. Domestic violence against married women in Egypt. *Sex Roles* 63 (September): 332–37.

YU, R. 2007. Indian-Americans book years of success. *USA Today*, April 18, 1B–2B.

YU, T., G. S. PETTIT, J. E. LANSFORD, K. A. DODGE, AND J. E. BATES. 2010. The interactive effects of marital conflict and divorce on parent–adult children's relationships. *Journal of Marriage and Family* 72 (April): 282–92.

YUN, H., J. D. BALL, AND H. LIM. 2011. Disentangling the relationship between child maltreatment and violent delinquency: Using a nationally representative sample. *Journal of Interpersonal Violence* 26 (January): 88–110.

Z

ZAFIROVSKI, M. 2005. Social exchange theory under scrutiny: A positive critique of its economic-behaviorist formulations. *Electronic Journal of Sociology*.

ZAGORSKY, J. L. 2005. Marriage and divorce's impact on wealth. *Journal of Sociology* 41 (December): 406–24.

ZAIDI, A. U., AND M. SHURAYDI. 2002. Perceptions of arranged marriages by young Pakistani Muslim women living in a Western society. *Journal of Comparative Family Studies* 33 (Autumn): 495–514.

ZAREMBO, A. 2009. DNA can reveal ancestors' lies and secrets. *Los Angeles Times*, January 18.

ZASLOW, J. 2006. Mr. moms grow up: A new generation of granddads is helping raise the kids. *Wall Street Journal*, June 8, D1.

ZEZIMA, K. 2010. For many, "washroom" seems to be just a name. *New York Times*, September 13, A14.

ZHANG, S., AND T. FULLER. 2012. Neighborhood disorder and paternal involvement of nonresident and resident fathers. *Family Relations* 61 (July): 501–13.

ZHANG, Y., T. L. DIXON, AND K. CONRAD. 2010. Female body image as a function of themes in rap music videos: A content analysis. *Sex Roles* 62 (June): 787–97.

ZHANG, Z., AND M. HAYWARD. 2006. Gender, the marital life course, and cardiovascular diseases in late midlife. *Journal of Marriage and Family* 68 (August): 639–57.

ZHOU, H., Y. LI, B. ZHANG, AND M. ZENG. 2012. The relationship between narcissism and friendship qualities in adolescents: Gender as a moderator. *Sex Roles* 67 (October): 452–62.

ZHU, W. X., AND T. HESKETH. 2009. China's excess males, sex selective abortion, and one child polity: Analysis of data from 2005 national intercensus survey. *British Medical Journal* online, April 9.

ZICKUHR, K., AND M. MADDEN. 2012. Older adults and Internet use. Pew Internet & American Life Project, June 6.

ZIELINSKI, D. S. 2005. Long-term socioeconomic impact of child abuse and neglect: Implications for public policy. Center for Child and Family Policy.

ZIMMERMAN, E. 2013. Rise of the telecommuting class. *Christian Science Monitor Weekly*, April 22 & 29, 27–31.

ZIMMERMAN, F. J., D. A. CHRISTAKIS, AND A. N. MELTZOFF. 2007. Associations between media viewing and language development in children under age 2 years. *Journal of Pediatrics* 151 (October): 364–68.

ZIMMERMAN, G. M., AND G. POGARSKY. 2011. The consequences of parental underestimation and overestimation of youth exposure to violence. *Journal of Marriage and Family* 73 (February): 194–208.

ZITO, J. M. ET AL. 2003. Psychotropic practice patterns for youth. *Archives of Pediatrics & Adolescent Medicine* 157 (January): 17–25.

ZOLNA, M., AND L. LINDBERG. 2012. Unintended pregnancy: Incidence and outcomes among young adult unmarried women in the United States, 2001 and 2008. Guttmacher Institute, April.

ZOROYA, G. 2005. Letters home from Iraq. *USA Today*, October 25.

ZUEHLKE, E. 2009. Immigrants work in riskier and more dangerous jobs in the United States. Population Reference Bureau, November.

ZURBRIGGEN, E. L., AND A. M. SHERMAN. 2010. Race and gender in the 2008 U.S. presidential election: A content analysis of editorial cartoons. *Analyses of Social Issues and Public Policy* 10 (December): 223–247.

ZURBRIGGEN, E. L., ET AL. 2007. *Report of the APA task force on the sexualization of girls*. Washington, DC: American Psychological Association.

Photo Credits

Name Index